# The Quarterly Journal Of The Geological Society Of London, Volume 64...

Geological Society of London

# THE

# QUARTERLY JOURNAL

OF THE

# GEOLOGICAL SOCIETY OF LONDON.

EDITED BY

## THE ASSISTANT-SECRETARY OF THE GEOLOGICAL SOCIETY.

---

Quod si cui mortalium cordi et curæ sit non tantum inventis hærere, atque iis uti, sed ad ulteriora penetrare; atque non disputando adversarium, sed opere naturam vincere; denique non belle et probabiliter opinari, sed certo et ostensive scire; tales, tanquam veri scientiarum filii, nobis (si videbitur) se adjungant.—*Novum Organum, Præfatio.*

---

## VOLUME THE SIXTY-FOURTH.

## 1908.

LONDON:

LONGMANS, GREEN, AND CO.

PARIS: CHARLES KLINCKSIECK, 11 RUE DE LILLE.

SOLD ALSO AT THE APARTMENTS OF THE SOCIETY.

MDCCCCVIII.

# List
### OF THE
## *OFFICERS*
### OF THE
# GEOLOGICAL SOCIETY OF LONDON.

Elected February 21st, 1908.

## President.

Prof. William Johnson Sollas, LL.D., Sc.D., F.R.S.

## Vice-Presidents.

Frederick William Rudler, I.S.O.

Aubrey Strahan, Sc.D., F.R.S.

J. J. Harris Teall, M.A., D.Sc., F.R.S.

Arthur Smith Woodward, LL.D., F.R.S.

## Secretaries.

Prof. William Whitehead Watts, Sc.D., M.Sc., F.R.S.

Prof. Edmund Johnston Garwood, M.A.

## Foreign Secretary.

Sir Archibald Geikie, K.C.B., D.C.L., LL.D., Sc.D., Pres.R.S.

## Treasurer.

Horace Woollaston Monckton, Treas.L.S.

## COUNCIL.

Prof. Samuel Herbert Cox, F.C.S., A.R.S.M.

Prof. Edmund Johnston Garwood, M.A.

Sir Archibald Geikie, K.C.B., D.C.L., LL.D., Sc.D., Pres.R.S.

Alfred Harker, M.A., F.R.S.

Wilfrid H. Hudleston, M.A., F.R.S., F.L.S.

Finlay Lorimer Kitchin, M.A., Ph.D.

George William Lamplugh, F.R.S.

Richard Lydekker, B.A., F.R.S.

Principal Henry Alexander Miers, M.A., F.R.S.

Horace Woollaston Monckton, Treas.L.S.

Richard Dixon Oldham.

Prof. Sidney Hugh Reynolds, M.A.

Frederick William Rudler, I.S.O.

Prof. William Johnson Sollas, LL.D., Sc.D., F.R.S.

Leonard James Spencer. M.A.

Aubrey Strahan, Sc.D., F.R.S.

Charles Fox Strangways.

J. J. Harris Teall, M.A., D.Sc., F.R.S.

Richard Hill Tiddeman, M.A.

Prof. William Whitehead Watts, Sc.D., M.Sc., F.R.S.

Henry Woods, M.A.

Arthur Smith Woodward, LL.D., F.R.S., F.L.S.

George William Young.

## Assistant-Secretary, Clerk, Librarian, and Curator.

L. L. Belinfante, M.Sc.

## Assistants in Office, Library, and Museum.

W. Rupert Jones.     Clyde H. Black.

A. S. H. Dutneall.

## STANDING PUBLICATION COMMITTEE.

Prof. W. J. Sollas, *President*.

Prof. W. W. Watts.
Prof. E. J. Garwood. } *Secretaries.*

Prof. S. H. Cox.

Sir Archibald Geikie.

Dr. F. L. Kitchin.

Mr. G. W. Lamplugh.

Mr. R. Lydekker.

Principal H. A. Miers.

Mr. H. W. Monckton.

Mr. L. J. Spencer.

Dr. A. Strahan.

Dr. J. J. H. Teall.

Mr. H. Woods.

Dr. A. S. Woodward.

# TABLE OF CONTENTS.

Page

ADAMS, Prof. FRANK DAWSON. On the Structure and Relations of the Laurentian System in Eastern Canada (Plates XI–XIII) 127

BARROW, GEORGE. The High-Level Platforms of Bodmin Moor and their Relation to the Deposits of Stream-Tin and Wolfram (Plates XLV & XLVI) .................................. 384

BASEDOW, H. (& J. D. ILIFFE). On a Formation known as 'Glacial Beds of Cambrian Age' in South Australia ................ 260

BONNEY, Prof. T. G. On Antigorite and the Val Antigorio, with Notes on other Serpentines containing that Mineral ....... 152

BRYDONE, REGINALD MARR. On the Subdivisions of the Chalk of Trimingham, Norfolk (Plates XLVII & XLVIII) ........ 401

BUCKMAN, S. S. Brachiopod Homœomorphy: 'Spirifer glaber' .. 27

BURY, H. Notes on the River Wey (Plates XXXVI & XXXVII) 318

CLAYDEN, Principal ARTHUR WILLIAM. On the Occurrence of Foot-prints in the Lower Sandstones of the Exeter District (Plate LI) 496

DALTON, LEONARD V. Notes on the Geology of Burma (Plates LIV–LVII) .................................. .......... 604

DEWEY, HENRY (& C. REID). The Origin of the Pillow-Lava near Port Isaac in Cornwall (Plates XXVII & XXVIII) ........ 264

ELSDEN, JAMES VINCENT. The St. David's-Head 'Rock Series', Pembrokeshire (Plates XXIX–XXXII) .................... 273

EVANS, the late Sir JOHN. Some Recent Discoveries of Palæolithic Implements ...................................... 1

GREEN, JOHN FREDERICK NORMAN. The Geological Structure of the St. David's Area, Pembrokeshire (Plate XLIV)......... 363

GROOM, Dr. THEODORE (& P. LAKE). The Bala and Llandovery Rocks of Glyn Ceiriog, North Wales (Plate LIII) .......... 546

*a* 2

Page

HILL, WILLIAM. On a Deep Channel of Drift at Hitchin (Hertfordshire) .............................................. 8

HOWCHIN, the Rev. WALTER. Glacial Beds of Cambrian Age in South Australia (Plates XIX–XXVI) ................... 234

ILIFFE, J. D. (& H. BASEDOW). On a Formation known as ' Glacial Beds of Cambrian Age ' in South Australia ................ 260

LAKE, PHILIP (& Dr. T. T. GROOM). The Bala and Llandovery Rocks of Glyn Ceiriog, North Wales (Plate LIII) ......... 546

LEEDS, E. THURLOW. On *Metriorhynchus brachyrhynchus* (Deslong.) from the Oxford Clay near Peterborough (Plates XL & XLI).. 345

LESLIE, THOMAS NICHOLAS (& Prof. A. C. SEWARD). Permo-Carboniferous Plants from Vereeniging, Transvaal (Plates IX & X)................................................. 109

MATLEY, Dr. CHARLES ALFRED (& Dr. A. VAUGHAN). The Carboniferous Rocks at Loughshinny (County Dublin), with an Account of the Faunal Succession and Correlation (Plates XLIX & L)................................................. 413

PARKINSON, JOHN. A Note on the Petrology and Physiography of Western Liberia, West Coast of Africa (Plate XXXV) ...... 313

REED, FREDERICK RICHARD COWPER (& Prof. S. H. REYNOLDS). On the Fossiliferous Rocks of the Southern Half of the Tortworth Inlier........................................... 512

REID, CLEMENT (& H. DEWEY). The Origin of the Pillow-Lava near Port Isaac in Cornwall (Plates XXVII & XXVIII) .... 264

REYNOLDS, Prof. SIDNEY HUGH. The Basic Intrusion of Bartestree, near Hereford (Plate LII) ......................... 501

—— (& F. R. C. REED). On the Fossiliferous Silurian Rocks of the Southern Half of the Tortworth Inlier.................. 512

SEWARD, Prof. ALBERT CHARLES. On a Collection of Fossil Plants from South Africa (Plates II–VIII) .................... 83

—— (& T. N. LESLIE). Permo-Carboniferous Plants from Vereeniging, Transvaal (Plates IX & X) ................. 109

SIBLY, Dr. THOMAS FRANKLIN. The Faunal Succession in the Carboniferous Limestone (Upper Avonian) of the Midland Area [North Derbyshire and North Staffordshire] (Plate I) .. 34

SORBY, the late Dr. HENRY CLIFTON. On the Application of Quantitative Methods to the Study of the Structure and History of Rocks (Plates XIV–XVIII) .................... 171

SPICER, the Rev. E. C. Solution-Valleys in the Glyme Area, Oxfordshire (Plates XXXVIII & XXXIX) ................ 335

Page

THOMSON, JAMES ALLAN. The Hornblendic Rocks of Glendalough and Greystones (County Wicklow) ...................... 475

VAUGHAN, Dr. ARTHUR (& Dr. C. A. MATLEY). The Carboniferous Rocks at Loughshinny (County Dublin), with an Account of the Faunal Succession and Correlation (Plates XLIX & L) .. 413

WOODWARD, Dr. ARTHUR SMITH. On some Fossil Fishes discovered by Prof. Ennes de Souza in the Cretaceous Formation at Ilhéos (State of Bahia), Brazil (Plates XLII & XLIII) .... 358

WRIGHT, Prof. GEORGE FREDERICK. Chronology of the Glacial Epoch in North America ............................... 149

WRIGHT, WILLIAM BOURKE. The Two Earth-Movements of Colonsay (Plates XXXIII & XXXIV) .................... 297

YOUNG, Dr. ALFRED PRENTICE. On the Stratigraphy and Structure of the Tarnthal Mass (Tyrol) ........................ 596

## PROCEEDINGS.

Proceedings of the Meetings ........................... i, cxxvi
Annual Report ...................................... ix
Lists of Donors to the Library ........................ xiv
List of Foreign Members ............................. xxvi
List of Foreign Correspondents ....................... xxvii
List of Wollaston Medallists ......................... xxviii
List of Murchison Medallists ......................... xxx
List of Lyell Medallists ............................. xxxii
List of Bigsby Medallists ............................. xxxiv
List of Prestwich Medallists ......................... xxxiv
Applications of the Barlow-Jameson Fund .............. xxxv
Awards of the Daniel-Pidgeon Fund ................... xxxv, cxxix
Financial Report .................................... xxxvi
Award of the Medals and Proceeds of Funds............. xliii
Anniversary Address of the President .................. 1
Special General Meetings .................... cxxvii, cxxxi, cxxxii

# LIST OF THE FOSSILS DESCRIBED AND FIGURED

## IN THIS VOLUME.

| Name of Species. | Formation. | Locality. | Page |
|---|---|---|---|
| **EQUISETALES.** | | | |
| *Schizoneura africana*, fig. 2 ... | Beaufort Series. | Roggeveld (Fish River) ......... | 89 |
| —— *Carrerei*, pl. ii, fig. 1 ... | Molteno Beds... | Dordrecht (S.A.) | 85–86 |
| —— sp. *a*, pl. iii, figs. 1 & 2 . | Burghersdorp Beds ......... | Burghersdorp... | 86 |
| —— sp. *β*, fig. 1 .............. | Stormberg Beds. | Basutoland ...... | 86–87 |
| **FILICALES.** | | | |
| *Callipteridium*, sp., pl. ix, fig. 3 & text-fig. 7 .............. | Permo-Carboniferous ......... | Vereeniging ... | 118 |
| *Cladophlebis (Todites) Rœserli*, pl. viii .................. | Molteno Beds ... | Indwe River ... | 98 |
| *Danœopsis Hughesi*, pl. vi & fig. 5 .................. | Burghersdorp Beds ......... | Lady Frere ...... | 95–97 |
| *Gangamopteris cyclopteroides*, pl. x, fig. 3 .............. | | | 117–18 |
| *Glossopteris angustifolia* ...... | | | 116 |
| —— var. *tæniopteroides*, nov., pl. ix, fig. 2 & text-figs. 2-3 .............. | Permo-Carboniferous ..... ... | Vereeniging ... | 113–16 |
| —— *Browniana*, figs. 4 & 5... | | | 117 |
| —— *indica* .................. | | | 116–17 |
| —— sp. cf. *retifera*, fig. 6 ... | | | 117 |
| *Odontopteris Browni*, sp. nov., pl. vii .................. | Burghersdorp Beds ......... | Aliwal North ... | 97–98 |
| *Tæniopteris Carruthersi*, fig. 6. | Molteno & Burghersdorp Beds ......... | Indwe River, etc. ............ | 98–99 |
| *Thinnfeldia odontopteroides*, pl. iv, fig. 1, pl. v, fig. 1, & text-figs. 3-4 .................. | Molteno Beds... | Vaalbank, etc. ... | 92–94 |

| Name of Species. | Formation. | Locality. | Page |
|---|---|---|---|

### FILICALES (*continued*).

| | | | |
|---|---|---|---|
| *Thinnfeldia sphenopteroides,* sp. nov., pl. iv, fig. 2 & pl. v, fig. 2 | Molteno & Burghersdorp Beds | Konings-Kroon, etc. | 94-95 |
| —— sp., pl. ii, figs. 2 & 3 | Molteno Beds | Maudesley | 95 |

### LYCOPODIACEÆ.

| | | | |
|---|---|---|---|
| *Lepidodendron Pedroanum,* pl. ix, fig. 1 | Permo-Carboniferous | Vereeniging | 120 |
| —— *vereenigingense,* sp. nov., pl. x, figs. 1-2, & text-fig. 8. | | | 119-20 |
| *Sigillaria Brardi* | | | 118 |

### GINKGOALES.

| | | | |
|---|---|---|---|
| *Baiera moltenensis,* sp. nov., pl. ii, fig. 4 | Molteno Beds | Dordrecht (S.A.) | 99-100 |

### CONIFERALES (?)

| | | | |
|---|---|---|---|
| *Conites,* sp., fig. 11 | Permo-Carboniferous | Vereeniging | 122 |
| *Stigmatodendron dubium,* sp. nov., pl. iii, fig. 3 | Burghersdorp Beds | Aliwal North | 100–101 |
| *Strobilites laxus,* sp. nov., pl. v, fig. 3 & text-fig. 7 | | | 101–102 |

### CYCADOPHYTA.

| | | | |
|---|---|---|---|
| *Pterophyllum* sp. cf. *Tietzii,* pl. ii, fig. 5 | Burghersdorp Beds | Kraai River Bridge | 103 |
| —— sp., pl. ii, fig. 6 | Molteno Beds | Konings-Kroon. | 104 |

### CORDAITEÆ.

| | | | |
|---|---|---|---|
| *Cordaites Hislopi,* figs. 9 & 10. | Permo-Carboniferous | Vereeniging | 120-22 |

### FORAMINIFERA.

| | | | |
|---|---|---|---|
| *Nummulites Beaumonti* (?) | Eocene | Kyetubok | 633 |
| *Operculina canalifera* | | Minbu district | 633 |
| —— *Hardiei* | | Magyisan | 633 |

### MADREPORARIA APOROSA.

| | | | |
|---|---|---|---|
| *Cyathaxonia rushiana,* pl. xlix, fig. 9 | Cyathaxonia-Beds | Loughshinny district | 460 |

| Name of Species. | Formation. | Locality. | Page |
|---|---|---|---|

### MADREPORARIA RUGOSA.

| Name of Species. | Formation. | Locality. | Page |
|---|---|---|---|
| *Carcinophyllum curkeenense,* sp. nov., pl. xlix, fig. 5 ...... | *Dihunophyllum-* Limestone ... | Loughshinny district ...... | 464 |
| —— (Lonsdaloid), pl. xlix, fig. 12 ...... | *Posidonomya-* Beds ......... | | 464 |
| *Clisiophyllum* aff. *M'Coyanum,* pl. i, fig. 4 ...... | Avonian ......... | Darleybridge ... | 73–74 |
| Clisiophyllid (new genus), fig. 16 ...... | Holmpatrick Limestone, etc. | Loughshinny district ...... | 464–65 |
| *Cyathophyllum regium* ......... | | Midland area ... | 70 |
| *Densiphyllum rushianum,* sp. nov. ...... | | Loughshinny district ...... | 459–60 |
| *Dihunophyllum derbiense,* sp. nov., pl. i, fig. 1......... | Avonian ......... | Monsal Dale ... | 75 |
| —— *matlockense,* sp. nov., pl. i, fig. 2 ...... | | Wensley ......... | 74–75 |
| —— aff. *Muirheadi,* pl. xlix, figs. 4 *a* & 4 *b* ...... | *Dihunophyllum-* Limestone ... | Loughshinny district ...... | 463 |
| *Diphyphyllum subibicinum,* pl. xlix, fig. 7 ...... | Holmpatrick Limestone ... | | 461 |
| *Koninckophyllum proprium,* sp. nov., pl. i, fig. 3 ......... | Avonian ......... | Wensley ......... | 70–71 |
| —— sp. ...... | | Midland area ... | 71–72 |
| —— sp., pl. xlix, fig. 14 ...... | *Posidonomya-* Beds ......... | | 461 |
| *Lithostrotion* cf. *offine,* pl. xlix, fig. 10 ......... | Avonian ......... | Loughshinny district ...... | 462 |
| —— *irregulare* (Diphy-phylloid variant) ...... | | | 462 |
| *Lithostrotion-*like Clisio-phyllid, pl. xlix, figs. 1 & 2. | *Megastoma-* Beds, etc. .... | | 462–63 |
| *Lonsdalia duplicata,* pl. i, fig. 5 ...... | Avonian ......... | Monsal Dale ... | 72–73 |
| *Zaphrentis Enniskilleni,* pl. xlix, fig. 13 ...... | *Posidonomya-* Beds ......... | Loughshinny district ...... | 456–57 |
| —— *Omaliusi,* var. *ambigua,* pl. xlix, figs. 6 *a* & 6 *b* ...... | Lane Limestone. | | 457–58 |
| —— —— —— mut. σ, pl. xlix, fig. 8 ...... | *Cyatharonia-* Beds ......... | | 458 |
| —— (Densiphylloid), pl. xlix. fig. 2 ...... | *Dihunophyllum-* Limestone ... | | 459 |

### MADREPORARIA PERFORATA.

| Name of Species. | Formation. | Locality. | Page |
|---|---|---|---|
| *Actinacis Nætlingi,* sp. nov., pl. liv, fig. 1 ...... | Miocene ......... | Toungu (Burma) ...... | 622 |
| *Beaumontia* aff. *Egertoni* ...... | | Midland area ... | 70 |
| *Michelinia glomerata* ......... | | | 69 |
| —— *megastoma* ......... | Avonian ......... | Loughshinny district ...... | 455 |
| —— *tenuisepta,* fig. 15 ...... | | | 455–56 |
| —— —— var. *favositoides,* nov., pl. xlix, fig. 11 ......... | | | 456 |

| Name of Species. | Formation. | Locality. | Page |
|---|---|---|---|

BRACHIOPODA.

| Name of Species. | Formation. | Locality. | Page |
|---|---|---|---|
| *Actinoconchus (?)* pl. l, fig. 10 | Upper *Posidono-mya*-Beds ... | Loughshinny district ...... | 470 |
| *Athyris* cf. *planosulcata*, pl. l, fig. 6 .................. | Lower *Posidono-mya*-Beds ... | | 469–70 |
| *Chonetes compressa*, nom. nov., pl. i, figs. 7 *a*–7 *b*, & text-fig. 6 .................. | Avonian ........ | Wirksworth ... | 78–79 |
| —— *crassistria* ............. | | Midland Area... | 78 |
| —— cf. *hardrensis* ........... | | | 78 |
| *Martinia glabra*, mut. P, pl. l, fig. 8 .................. | Upper *Posidono-mya*-Beds ... | Loughshinny district ...... | 468 |
| —— *ovaliglabra*, sp. nov., pl. l, fig. 5 .................. | Lower *Posidono-mya*-Beds ... | | 468–69 |
| *Productus concinnus*............ | Avonian ........ | Midland Area... | 76 |
| —— *Martini* .................. | | | 76 |
| —— *proboscideus*, pl. l, fig. 1 | Lower *Posidono-mya*-Beds ... | Loughshinny district ...... | 466 |
| —— *setosus*, var. *tissingtonensis* nov., pl. i, figs. 6 *a* & 6 *b* .................. | Avonian ........ | Tissington ...... | 77 |
| —— *striatus*, pl. l, fig. 2...... | Lower *Posidono-mya*-Beds ... | | 466–67 |
| —— sp. nov. .................. | | | 467 |
| *Reticularia lineata* ............ | Dibunophyllum-Limestone, etc. ............ | | 469 |
| *Schizophoria resupinata*, pl. l, fig. 7 .................. | Middle *Posidono-nomya*-Beds ... | Loughshinny district ...... | 470 |
| *Spirifer bisulcatus* var., pl. l, figs. 3 *a* & 3 *b* ............. | Lower *Posidono-mya*-Beds ... | | 467 |
| —— cf. *convolutus*, pl. l, fig. 4 .................. | Middle *Posido-nomya*-Beds.. | | 468 |
| *Spiriferina insculpta*, pl. l, fig. 9 .................. | Upper *Posidono-mya*-Beds ... | | 468 |

LAMELLIBRANCHIATA.

| Name of Species. | Formation. | Locality. | Page |
|---|---|---|---|
| *Alectryonia Newtoni*, sp. nov., pl. liv, fig. 4 .................. | Eocene ........ | Subagyidan...... | 635–36 |
| *Arca manensis*, sp. nov., pl. liv, figs. 5 & 6 ............. | | Magyisan ...... | 634–35 |
| *Batissa kodoungensis*, pl. lvi, figs. 1 & 2 .................. | Miocene ........ | Sawmyo ......... | 624 |
| *Cardita protovariegata*, pl. liv, fig. 8 .................. | | | 625 |
| *Cardium ambiguum*............ | Eocene ........ | Minbu district... | 636 |
| *Corbula harpa* .................. | | Magyisan ...... | 637 |
| *Jouannetia protocumingi*, sp. nov., pl. liv, fig. 7 ......... | Miocene ........ | Toungu ......... | 626 |
| *Lucina globulosa*, pl. lv, fig. 1 | | Padoukbin ...... | 625 |
| *Nucula Alcocki*.................. | | Mindegyi ...... | 623 |
| *Ostrea yomaensis*, sp. nov., pl. liv, figs. 2 & 3............ | Eocene ........ | Thabyemyoung. | 635 |
| *Tellina* sp. .................. | Miocene ........ | Sawmyo ......... | 625–26 |
| *Venus granosa* .................. | Eocene ........ | Myegya ......... | 637 |

| Name of Species. | Formation. | Locality. | Page |
|---|---|---|---|
| **GASTEROPODA.** | | | |
| *Busycon canaliculatum*, pl. lv, fig. 2 ............... | Miocene ......... | Sawmyo ......... | 631 |
| *Cantharus Martinianus*, pl. lv, figs. 6 & 7 ............ | | Mindegyi ...... | 630–31 |
| *Cassidea acanthina*, sp. nov., pl. lvii, fig. 1 ............... | | Lanywa ......... | 629 |
| *Cerithium (?)*, sp., pl. liv, fig. 9 ............... | Eocene ......... | Magyisan ...... | 638–39 |
| *Conus scalaris* ............ ...... | | Ngalaingyoung . | 632 |
| *Cypræa Everwijni (?)*, pl. lvii, figs. 5 & 6 ............ | | Toungu ......... | 628 |
| —— *(Cyprædia) elegans*, pl. lvii, figs. 7 & 8 ............... | Miocene ......... | Sawmyo ......... | 629 |
| *Distorsio cancellinus*, pl. lv, fig. 4 ............... | | Padoukbin ...... | 629–30 |
| *Dolium* sp., pl. lv, fig. 3 ...... | | Magyisan ...... | 639 |
| *Fusus* sp. ............... | | Subagyidan ... | 639–40 |
| *Natica (Ampullina) grossa*, var. *oblonga*, pl. lvi, figs. 3 & 4 ............... | Eocene ......... | Minbu district . | 637–38 |
| —— (——) *ponderosa* ...... | | Kyetubok ...... | 638 |
| —— (——) *spherica (?)* ... | | Magyisan ...... | 637 |
| —— *(Globularia) gibberosa*, pl. lvii, figs. 2 & 3 ......... | Miocene ......... | Sawmyo ...... ... | 627–28 |
| *Oliva* sp. ......... ...... | Eocene ......... | Kyetubok ...... | 640 |
| *Pleurotoma Stoppanii (?)* ... | | Magyisan ...... | 641 |
| *Sigaretus javanus* ............ | | Toungu ......... | 627 |
| *Terebra* sp. ............... | Miocene ......... | Mindegyi....... | 632 |
| *Turritella acuticarinata*, pl. lvii, fig. 9 ............... | | Banbyin ......... | 628 |
| —— sp. 3 ............... | Eocene ......... | Burma ......... | 638 |
| *Voluta (!) birmanica*, sp. nov., pl. lvii, fig. 10 ...... | Miocene ......... | Banbyin ......... | 632 |
| —— *D'Archiaci*, sp. nov., pl. lv, fig. 5 ............ | Eocene ......... | Subagyidan ... | 640 |
| —— *pernodosa*, sp. nov., pl. lvii, fig. 4 ............... | | | 640 |
| **GANOIDEI.** | | | |
| *Lepidotus Souzai*, sp. nov., pl. xliii, figs. 1 & 2 ......... | Lower Cretaceous ... | Ilhéos (Bahia).. | 359–60 |
| *Mauronia minor*, sp. nov., pl. xlii, figs. 1–3 ............ | | | 358–59 |
| **TELEOSTEI.** | | | |
| *Scombroclupea scutata*, sp. nov., pl. xliii, figs. 3 & 4... | Lower Cretaceous ... | Ilhéos (Bahia).. | 360–61 |
| **CROCODILIA.** | | | |
| *Metriorhynchus brachyrhynchus*, pls. xl & xli ............ | Oxford Clay ... | Peterborough ... | 345–56 |

# EXPLANATION OF THE PLATES.

**PLATE**                                                 **PAGE**

I     AVONIAN CORALS & BRACHIOPODS FROM THE MIDLAND AREA, to illustrate Dr. T. F. Sibly's paper on the Faunal Succession in the Carboniferous Limestone of that area ..................................    34

II–VIII     *SCHIZONEURA, PTEROPHYLLUM*, etc.; *SCHIZONEURA* & *STIGMATODENDRON*; *THINNFELDIA*; *THINNFELDIA* & *STROBILITES*; *DANÆOPSIS HUGHESI*; *ODONTOPTERIS BROWNI*, sp. nov.; and *CLADOPHLEBIS* (*TODITES*) *RŒSSERTI*, to illustrate Prof. A. C. Seward's paper on Fossil Plants from South Africa ......................    83

IX–X     *LEPIDODENDRON, GLOSSOPTERIS,* & *CALLIPTERIDIUM* (?); and *LEPIDODENDRON* & *GANGAMOPTERIS*, to illustrate Prof. A. C. Seward's & Mr. T. N. Leslie's paper on Permo-Carboniferous Plants from Vereeniging ...........................    109

XI–XIII     AMPHIBOLITE INVADED BY GRANITE OF THE METHUEN BATHYLITH; 'FEATHER-AMPHIBOLITE'; and GEOLOGICAL MAP OF PORTIONS OF HASTINGS, HALIBURTON, & PETERBOROUGH COUNTIES (PROVINCE OF ONTARIO), to illustrate Prof. F. D. Adams's paper on the Structure and Relations of the Laurentian System in Eastern Canada ............    127

XIV–XVIII     GREEN SLATE, LANGDALE, SHOWING THE BREAKING-UP OF A SEMI-LIQUID DEPOSIT; SIMILAR SLATE, SHOWING RIPPLE-DRIFT, WITH GENTLE CURRENT & RAPID DEPOSITION; SIMILAR SLATE, WITH MORE CURRENT & SLOWER DEPOSITION; MICROSCOPE-SECTIONS OF OOLITE FROM GRANTHAM & OF CORALLINE OOLITE FROM SCARBOROUGH; AND MICROSCOPE-SECTIONS OF WENLOCK LIMESTONE FROM EASTHOPE & CARBONIFEROUS LIMESTONE FROM BRISTOL; to illustrate the late Dr. H. C. Sorby's paper on the Application of Quantitative Methods to the Study of the Structure and History of Rocks ...........................    171

PLATE                                                                                              PAGE

XIX-XXVI {
POLISHED AND ICE-SCRATCHED BOULDER FROM THE
CAMBRIAN TILL OF PETERSBURG (SOUTH AUS-
TRALIA); GORGE OF THE RIVER STURT IN CAMBRIAN
TILL; VIEWS OF CAMBRIAN TILL IN THE STURT-
RIVER GORGE, ONE INCLUDING A BIG SUBANGULAR
BOULDER OF QUARTZITE WITH TRANSVERSE FRAC-
TURES; VIEWS OF CHARACTERISTIC CAMBRIAN TILL
IN WATERFALL CREEK, BAROOTA, FLINDERS
RANGES, ONE INCLUDING A BIG ANGULAR ERRATIC
OF QUARTZITE; and SECTION IN BLACKWOOD
RAILWAY-CUTTING: to illustrate the Rev. W.
Howchin's paper on Glacial Beds of Cambrian
Age in South Australia ............................ } 234

XXVII &
XXVIII {
PILLOW-LAVA OF PENTIRE (CORNWALL); and THE
SAME, SHOWING CENTRAL CAVITY OF A PILLOW, to
illustrate Mr. C. Reid's & Mr. H. Dewey's paper
on the Origin of the Pillow-Lava near Port
Isaac in Cornwall ............ .................... } 264

XXIX-XXXII {
MICROSCOPE-SECTIONS OF IGNEOUS ROCKS FROM
ST. DAVID'S HEAD, to illustrate Mr. J. V.
Elsden's paper on the St. David's-Head 'Rock
Series' (Pembrokeshire) ............................ } 273

XXXIII &
XXXIV {
CLEAVAGE PRODUCED BY THE SECOND EARTH-MOVE-
MENT IN THE NORTH-EAST OF COLONSAY; and
MICROSCOPE-SECTIONS OF PHYLLITES FROM THAT
ISLAND, to illustrate Mr. W. B. Wright's paper
on the Two Earth-Movements of Colonsay ...... } 297

XXXV {
SKETCH-MAP OF PART OF WESTERN LIBERIA, to
illustrate Mr. J. Parkinson's paper on the
Petrology & Physiography of that region......... } 313

XXXVI &
XXXVII {
MAP SHOWING THE SIX SECTIONS OF THE RIVER WEY
WHICH LIE WITHIN THE WEALDEN AREA; and
MAP OF THE ALTON DISTRICT, to illustrate
Mr. H. Bury's paper on the River Wey ......... } 318

XXXVIII
&
XXXIX {
BROOK VALLEY ENTERING GLYME VALLEY & MOUTH
OF DRY VALLEY ENTERING THE FORMER; THE
GLYME, WITH SOAKAGE-BOWL AT THE DORN JUNC-
TION (WOOTTON), & THE GLYME VALLEY, FLOODED,
to illustrate the Rev. E. C. Spicer's paper on
Solution-Valleys in the Glyme Area (Oxford-
shire) ............................................ } 335

XL & XLI {
UPPER AND PALATAL ASPECTS OF SKULLS OF METRIO-
RHYNCHUS BRACHYRHYNCHUS, FROM THE OXFORD
CLAY, NEAR PETERBOROUGH, to illustrate Mr. E.
T. Leeds's paper on that fossil .................... } 345

XLII & XLIII {
MAWSONIA MINOR, sp. nov : and LEPIDOTUS
SOUZAI, sp. nov. & SCOMBROCLUPEA SCUTATA, sp.
nov., to illustrate Dr. A. S. Woodward's paper
on Fossil Fishes from the Cretaceous Formation
of Ilhéos (Bahia) ................................ } 358

PLATE                                                               PAGE

XLIV { GEOLOGICAL MAP OF THE ST. DAVID'S AREA (PEM-
       BROKESHIRE), to illustrate Mr. J. F. N. Green's
       paper on the Geological Structure of that area...    363

XLV & XLVI { WOLFRAM-DEPOSIT, BUTTERN HILL; and old
             STREAM-WORKINGS IN HIGH-LEVEL WASH, to illus-
             trate Mr. G. Barrow's paper on the High-Level    384
             Platforms of Bodmin Moor & their Relation to
             the Deposits of Stream-Tin & Wolfram .........

XLVII & XLVIII { PLANS OF BLOCKS A, B, & C OF THE CHALK EXPOSED
                 ON THE SHORE AT TRIMINGHAM (NORFOLK), to
                 illustrate Mr. R. M. Brydone's paper on the    401
                 Subdivisions of that formation ..............

XLIX & L { AVONIAN CORALS FROM THE RUSH-SKERRIES SECTION;
           and BRACHIOPODS FROM LOUGHSHINNY (COUNTY
           DUBLIN), to illustrate Dr. A. C. Matley's & Dr. A.    413
           Vaughan's paper on the Carboniferous Rocks at
           Loughshinny .......................................

LI { PART OF SLAB E, to illustrate Principal A. W.
     Clayden's paper on the Occurrence of Footprints          490
     in the Lower Sandstones of the Exeter District .

LII { MICROSCOPE-SECTIONS OF IGNEOUS & ALTERED ROCKS
      FROM BARTESTREE (HEREFORDSHIRE), to illustrate
      Prof. S. H. Reynolds's paper on the Basic              501
      Intrusion at that locality............................

LIII { GEOLOGICAL MAP OF THE NEIGHBOURHOOD OF GLYN
       CEIRIOG (NORTH WALES), to illustrate Dr. T.
       Groom's & Mr. P. Lake's paper on the Bala &          546
       Llandovery Rocks of that area ....................

LIV-LVII { TERTIARY FOSSILS FROM BURMA, to illustrate Mr. L.
           V. Dalton's paper on the Geology of that country }  604

CORRIGENDUM.

Page 111, lines 6-7 from the top, *for* 'Lower Carboniferous,' *read* 'late Carboniferous.'

# PROCESS-BLOCKS AND OTHER ILLUSTRATIVE FIGURES,

## BESIDES THOSE IN THE PLATES.

| Fig. | | Page |
|---|---|---|
| 1. | [Flint-implement from Gaddesden Row, Hemel Hempstead.] . | 2 |
| 2. | [Flint-implement from Ellingham's Pit, Leverstock Green, Hemel Hempstead.] | 4 |
| 1. | Map of the Hitchin Valley | 9 |
| 2. | Section across the Hitchin and Stevenage Gap | 10 |
| 3. | Section through the Langley-Ippolitts Valley | 14 |
| 4. | Section through the Hitchin Valley | 16 |
| 1. | Sketch-map showing the outcrop of the Carboniferous Limestone in the Midland Area | 35 |
| 2. | Vertical section of the typical Carboniferous - Limestone sequence in that area | 39 |
| 3. | Section from Litton Tunnel to Miller's-Dale lime-works | 40 |
| 4. | Diagrammatic section of Newton-Grange cutting | 60 |
| 5. | Section in a quarry near Old Mill, east of Youlgreave | 62 |
| 6. | Median longitudinal section of *Chonetes compressa* | 78 |
| 1. | *Schizoneura* sp. β | 87 |
| 2. | *Schizoneura africana*, Feistmantel | 89 |
| 3. | Pinnules of *Thinnfeldia odontopteroides* and *Ptilozamites* | 91 |
| 4. | *Thinnfeldia odontopteroides* | 93 |
| 5. | *Danæopsis Hughesi*, Feistmantel | 96 |
| 6. | *Tæniopteris Carruthersi*, Ten. Woods | 99 |
| 7. | *Strobilites laxus*, sp. nov. | 103 |

FIG. PAGE

1. General section at Vereeniging ...... 110

2 & 3. *Glossopteris angustifolia* var. *tæniopteroides*, nov. ...... 114

4 & 5. *Glossopteris Browniana* ...... 116

6. *Glossopteris* sp. cf. *Gl. retifera*, Feistm ...... 117

7. *Callipteridium* sp ...... 118

8. *Lepidodendron vereenigingense*, sp. nov. ...... 119

9 & 10. *Cordaites Hislopi* ...... 121

11. *Conites* sp. ...... 122

1. Sketch-map, showing the position of the Haliburton and Bancroft areas in relation to the Laurentian Highlands, etc. 128

2. Fragments of amphibolite in granite, pulled out into bands or streaks by the movement of the granite, near Barry's Bay (Ontario) ...... 134

3. Limestone with lit-par-lit injections of granite, Maxwell's Crossing, township of Glamorgan (Ontario) ...... 140

— Sketch-map of the Val-Antigorio district ...... 154

— Tooth-like structure penetrating, by removal, a fossil shell and the surrounding limestone ...... 225

1. Diagrammatic section of the Lower Cambrian beds, from the River Torrens to Gulf St. Vincent ...... 236

2. Ice-scratched boulder from the Cambrian till, Black Rock, near Orroroo ...... 242

3. Grooved and striated boulder, with fragments of indurated till attached thereto, from the Cambrian glacial beds, Pekina Hill, near Orroroo ...... 243

4. Fragments broken from a big polished and striated boulder in the Cambrian till, Appila Gorge ...... 244

5. Ice-scratched boulder, in place, in the Cambrian till, Petersburg Ranges (South Australia) ...... 245

6. Quartzite-boulder from the Cambrian till of Petersburg (South Australia) ...... 246

7. Sketch-section across the glacial beds of the Onkaparinga Valley ...... 249

8. Sketch-section of the glacial beds in the valley of the River Sturt ...... 250

9. Weathered face of Cambrian till in the Sturt-River Valley ... 252

10. Sketch-section of the glacial beds in the Appila Gorge ...... 254

FIG.                                                        PAGE

11. Diagrammatic section of the glacial beds in a west-and-east-
    direction, from Port Germein to Mount Grainger ........... 256

12. Diagrammatic section of the glacial beds in a south-and-north
    direction, from the Yunta ranges to Oopina ................. 257

1. Geological sketch-map of the St. David's-Head area ........... 274

2. Diagram illustrating the chemical relations of the various
   types of the St. David's Head 'rock-series' .................... 291

1. Sketch-map of the stratigraphy of Colonsay and Oronsay ...... 298

2. Diagram illustrating the general increase in the second [earth-]
   movement [in Colonsay] from west to east ..................... 301

3. Section on the coast, north of Port-na-Cuilce ..................... 302

4. Section on the shore, south-east of Eilean Dubh and north of
   Port-na-Cuilce ............................................... 303

5. Margin of lamprophyre in phyllite, on the coast north of
   Kiloran Bay ................................................. 303

6. Lamprophyre-dyke on the shore, north of Port-an-Obain ...... 304

7. Sketch-map of the Kiloran syenite-intrusion ................... 305

8. Margin of an east-and-west vogesite-dyke north of Port-na-
   Cuilce ...................................................... 307

9. Sketch-map showing the strike and dip of the axial planes of the
   secondary folds and of the strain-slip cleavage in Colonsay
   and Oronsay ................................................. 310

— Map showing the relation of the Wey to the Blackwater ...... 320

— Sketch-map of the Wootton region [Oxfordshire] ............. 336

1. Restoration of the hinder portion of the palatal aspect of
   Metriorhynchus brachyrhynchus ............................... 352

2. Sections of the nasal canals of Metriorhynchus brachyrhynchus. 354

1. Map of the Porth-clais area ................................... 378

2. Cambrian conglomerate involved in a basic intrusion, west of
   Carn-arwig, Ramsey Sound .................................... 381

1. Wolfram-deposit in high-level wash, Buttern Hill, north-west
   of Altarnun (Cornwall) ....................................... 388

2. Stream-tin workings in Kenton Marsh, north-west of Buttern
   Hill (Cornwall) .............................................. 392

1. Plan showing the positions on the shore of the areas of Chalk
   at Trimingham ............................................... 402

2. Section presented by the North Bluff (Trimingham) in 1904 ... 407

Fig.                                                                PAGE

1. Map of the outcrops of Carboniferous Limestone, etc. along the coast in the neighbourhood of Loughshinny ...................... 414

2. Horizontal section through the *Cyathaxonia*-Beds, from Brook's End to Roaring Well Bay ......................................... 415

3. Parallel vertical sections of the *Cyathaxonia*-Beds exposed on the south side and at the south-eastern corner of Drumanagh Headland ............................................................ 416

4. Section in the cliff at the north-western corner of Roaring Well Bay, showing the decalcification of the *Cyathaxonia*-Beds ... 417

5. Decalcified *Cyathaxonia*-Beds in the cliff, Roaring Well Bay... 418

6. Horizontal section, from the south side of Drumanagh Headland to Loughshinny village, near the Coastguard Station. 420-21

7. Vertical section of the beds exposed between the fault on the east side of Drumanagh Headland and Loughshinny Bay ... 422

8. South-western corner of Loughshinny Bay : junction of the *Posidonomya*-Limestones with the Loughshinny Black Shales. 423

9. Loughshinny Bay : fold in the *Posidonomya*-Limestones, showing the passage from a normal anticline into an overfold ......... 425

10. Folded *Posidonomya*-Limestones, Loughshinny ................... 425

11. 'Augen'-like cracks filled with calcite, in the *Posidonomya*-Limestones, Loughshinny Bay................. ................. 426

12. Horizontal section along the coast, from Loughshinny Harbour to the Lane Limestone ................................................ 427

13. Horizontal section, north of the angular fault, along the coast in the townlands of Lane and Holmpatrick .............. 429

14. Lane Conglomerate ...................................................... 430

15. *Michelinia tenuisepta* (Phillips): enlarged view of the calices, from the *Cyathaxonia*-Beds of Rush ............................... 456

16. A new genus of Olisiophyllid ......................................... 465

1. Hornblende-peridotite from Glendalough ........................... 477

2 & 3. Amphibolite from Glendalough ................................ 480, 481

4. Actinolite-rock from Glendalough .................................... 483

5. Clinozoisite-vein in amphibolite from Glendalough .............. 484

6-8. The ' mixed rock,' Glendalough .......................... 487, 488, 489

9. Biotite-muscovite-garnet hornfels at the contact with peridotite, Glendalough ............................................................ 492

— Diagram of the Bartestree Quarry ..................................... 504

FIG.                                                        PAGE

1. Geological map of the Tortworth Inlier and the immediate neighbourhood ............................................................... 513

2. View of part of Cullimore's Quarry, Charfield Green ........... 515

3. Geological sketch-map of the neighbourhood of Daniel's Wood and Middlemill ..................................................... 518

4. Plan of trenches dug on the hill-slope south of Little Daniel's Wood ........................................................................ 529

5. Section from Eastwood to Charfield Green ......................... 532

6. Section from near Woodford to Tortworth Rectory............... 532

1. Section from Pont-y-meibion to Pont Bell ......................... 552

2. Section of the southernmost crag on the banks of the Morda, south of Llechrhydau ................................................. 556

3. Slate-fragments in the grits of the Teirw Beds, at the quarries on the right bank of the Ceiriog at Pandy .................... 557

4. Diagrammatic section south of Tan-y-graig ...................... 560

5. Sketch of the western end of the ash-block shown in the previous figure ........................................................... 561

6 & 7. Microscopic sections of the Craig-y-Pandy Ash ................. 562

8. Columnar jointing in the Craig-y-Pandy Ash at Cae Deicws... 563

9. Section at the top of the Craig-y-Pandy Ash, in the China-clay Quarry ....................................................................... 565

10. Diagram illustrating the variation in thickness of the Glyn Grit.............................................................................. 576

11. Section shown by excavation in Nant Llafar....................... 576

12-15. [Figures illustrating some of the effects of thrusting on faults]............................................................... 581, 582

16. Section along the Cae-mawr Fault .................................... 586

1. Sketch-map of the Tarnthaler Köpfe ................................. 596

2. Section [through the Tarnthaler Köfel and the Hairnspitze]... 597

3. Section [through the Röckner, etc.] .................................. 597

4. Section from Knappenkuchel to the Nederer summit ........... 599

1. Sketch-map of the Padoukbin district ............................... 607

2. Sketch-map illustrating Expedition B [Burma] .................... 610

3. Sketch-map illustrating Expedition D [Burma] .................... 614

# *ANNUAL GENERAL MEETING,*

February 21st, 1908.

Sir ARCHIBALD GEIKIE, K.C.B., D.C.L., LL.D., Sc.D., Sec.R.S.,
President, in the Chair.

## REPORT OF THE COUNCIL FOR 1907.

THE flourishing condition of the Society was marked in the past year by a further increase in the Number of Fellows. In 1907 the Fellows elected numbered 74 (as compared with 54 in 1906), and 58 of these paid their Admission-Fees before the end of the year. Moreover, 16 Fellows who had been elected in the previous year paid their Admission-Fees in 1907, making the total Accession of new Fellows within the twelve months under review amount to 74.

Setting against this number a loss of 47 Fellows (27 by death, 9 by resignation, and 11 by removal from the List, under Bye-Laws, Sect. VI, Art. 5), it will be noted that there is an increase in the Number of Fellows of 27 (as compared with an increase of 12 in 1906, and a decrease of 12 in 1905).

The total Number of Fellows is thus increased to 1278, made up as follows :—Compounders, 266 (7 less than in 1906); Contributing Fellows, 981 (35 more than in 1906, and 55 more than in 1905); and Non-Contributing Fellows, 31 (1 less than in 1906).

Turning now to the Lists of Foreign Members and Foreign Correspondents, we have to deplore the loss of two illustrious Foreign Members, Prof. Marcel Bertrand and Dr. Edmund Mojsisovics; and also the loss of one Foreign Correspondent, Prof. Carl Klein. Moreover, at the end of 1906, there had remained one vacancy in the List of Foreign Correspondents. These vacancies were, in part, filled by the transfer of Dr. E. E. A. Tietze and Prof. A. Issel from the List of Foreign Correspondents to that of Foreign Members; and by the election of Baron G. J. de Geer and Prof. A. Baltzer as Foreign Correspondents. At the end of 1907 there were still 2 vacancies in the List of Foreign Correspondents.

With regard to the Income and Expenditure of the Society during the year 1907, the figures set forth in detail in the Balance-Sheet may be summarized as follows :—

The actual Receipts, excluding the Balance of £216 1s. 7d. brought forward from the previous year, amounted to £3100 17s. 10d., being £34 19s. 10d. more than the estimated Income.

On the other hand, the total Expenditure during the same year amounted to £3148 2s. 0d., being £164 16s. 0d. less than the estimated Expenditure for the year, and £47 4s. 2d. more than the actual Receipts, the year closing with a Balance in hand of £168 17s. 5d.

'The History of the Geological Society,' prepared by Mr. H. B. Woodward, was issued during the latter part of the summer. The volume has met with general acceptance, both on the part of the Fellows and on that of the public, its intrinsic interest being increased by the excellent portraits which accompany it and by the careful way in which it has been edited and printed. The Council believe that the Fellows will heartily agree with them in placing on record the indebtedness of the Society to Mr. H. B. Woodward, the author and editor; to Prof. E. J. Garwood, who supervised the preparation of the illustrations; and to Mr. R. S. Herries, who was responsible for the section connected with the Charter and Bye-Laws, for their ungrudging expenditure of time and labour in connexion with the ' History.

The Centenary of the Society was celebrated on September 26th, 27th, and 28th. Its remarkable success was largely due to the attendance of an unprecedented number of geologists from all parts of the world. The Society is much indebted to the kindness of several other Learned Societies and to many individuals, for acts of hospitality which gave very much help in the entertainment of its guests. It is proposed to publish, in a style uniform with that of the Quarterly Journal, a Centenary Record which will include, besides a general account of the Proceedings, the Centennial Address delivered by the President and the addresses of congratulation received from kindred Societies and public bodies in this country and abroad.

The Council have to announce the completion of Vol. LXIII and the commencement of Vol. LXIV of the Society's Quarterly Journal.

Certain particulars in regard to Mr. C. Davies Sherborn's admirably-compiled Card-Catalogue of the Library are set forth in the appended Report from the Library-and-Museum Committee.

The fifth Award from the Daniel-Pidgeon Trust-Fund was made, on May 15th, 1907, to Miss I. L. Slater, B.A., Newnham College, Cambridge, who proposed to investigate the Lower Palæozoic rocks in the neighbourhood of Llandeilo.

The following Awards of Medals and Funds have also been made by the Council :—

The Wollaston Medal is awarded to Prof. Paul von Groth, For.Memb.G.S., of Munich, in recognition of the value of his ' researches concerning the mineral structure of the Earth,' and more particularly of the services which he has rendered to the science of Crystallography.

The Murchison Medal, together with a Sum of Ten Guineas from the Murchison Geological Fund, is awarded to Prof. Albert Charles Seward, F.R.S., in recognition of the services rendered by him in the advancement of Geological Science by means of his studies in Palæobotany.

The Lyell Medal, together with a Sum of Twenty-Five Pounds from the Lyell Geological Fund, is awarded to Mr. Richard Dixon Oldham, 'as a mark of honorary distinction, and as an expression on the part of the Council that he has deserved well of the Science,' especially by his researches on the Geology of India, and on the phenomena and origin of Earthquakes.

The Balance of the Proceeds of the Wollaston Donation-Fund is awarded to Mr. Herbert Henry Thomas, M.A., in recognition of his work on the Composition of Sedimentary Rocks and on the Palæozoic Series of South Wales, and to encourage him in further work.

The Balance of the Proceeds of the Murchison Geological Fund is awarded to Miss Ethel Gertrude Skeat, D.Sc., in acknowledgment of her researches among the Glacial and Lower Palæozoic deposits, and to encourage her in further work.

A moiety of the Balance of the Proceeds of the Lyell Geological Fund is awarded to Mr. Harold J. Osborne White, in recognition of his researches among the Cretaceous and Pleistocene deposits of Berkshire and Oxfordshire, and as an encouragement to further work.

A second moiety of the Balance of the Proceeds of the Lyell Geological Fund is awarded to Mr. Thomas Franklin Sibly, B.Sc., in recognition of his work on the zonal divisions of the Carboniferous Limestone, and to stimulate him to further research.

In response to an appeal issued jointly by the National Trust for Places of Historic Interest or Natural Beauty, the Wiltshire Archæological & Natural History Society, and the Marlborough-College Natural History Society, the Council have contributed from the Barlow-Jameson Fund a Sum of Twenty Pounds, towards the amount which is being raised to secure the preservation of the Sarsen-Stones on the Marlborough Downs, known as 'The Grey Wethers.'

---

REPORT OF THE LIBRARY-AND-MUSEUM COMMITTEE FOR 1907.

The Committee have pleasure in reporting that the Additions made to the Library during the year under review have more than maintained, both in number and in importance, the standard of previous years.

During the past twelve months the Library has received by Donation 267 Volumes of separately-published Works, 402 Pamphlets, 49 Detached Parts of Works, 304 Volumes and 30 Detached Parts of Serial Publications, and 25 Volumes of Newspapers.

The total Number of Accessions to the Library by Donation is thus found to amount to 596 Volumes, 402 Pamphlets, and 79 Detached Parts. Moreover, 204 Sheets of Geological Maps were presented to the Library, including 10 Folios of the 'Geologic Atlas of the United States'; 149 Sheets received from the Geological Survey of England & Wales and 34 Sheets from the Geological Survey of Scotland (the majority in both cases being on the 6-inch scale); 5 Sheets from the Geological Survey of Japan; 4 Sheets from the Geological Survey of Sweden; 3 Sheets from that of Hungary, as also a mineral-occurrence map of that kingdom presented by the Ministry of Finance; and 8 Sheets of the Geological Map of Nova Scotia, from the Canadian Geological Survey. Dr. F. Oswald presented his Geological Map of Armenia; Mr. J. P. Howley presented his Geological Map of Newfoundland; Mr. W. A. E. Ussher presented his Geological Map of Devon (from the 'Victoria History of the Counties of England'); and Mr. Norton Griffith his mineral-occurrence map of a portion of the Semipalatinsk Territory (Siberia).

Among the Books and Pamphlets mentioned in the foregoing paragraph, especial attention may be directed to the following works:—Prof. A. Lacroix's 'Éruption du Vésuve en Avril 1906'; Prof. J. P. Iddings's 'Rock-Minerals, their Chemical & Physical Characters, etc.': Vol. II, Part I, of the new Edition of Prof. H. Rosenbusch's 'Mikroskopische Physiographie der Mineralien & Gesteine'; the second edition of Prof. R. Beck's 'Lehre von der Erzlagerstätten'; Prof. J. J. Stevenson's 'Carboniferous of the Appalachian Basin'; Prof. A. Fritsch's 'Problematica silurica' and 'Miscellanea palæontologica'; 'A Journey through England & Scotland to the Hebrides in 1784,' by E. Faujas de St. Fond, edited with Notes & a Memoir of the Author by Sir Archibald Geikie; Mr. A. P. Low's Report on the Dominion Government Expedition to Hudson Bay and the Arctic Islands; Mr. H. B. Woodward's new edition of Stanford's Geological Atlas of Great Britain & Ireland; Prof. R. Zeiller's work on the Coal-Measure & Permian Flora of Blanzy & Le Creusot; Dr. L. Waagen's work on the Lamellibranchs of the *Pachycardia*-Tuffs of the Seiser Alm; Prof. J. Perner's description of the Silurian Gasteropoda of Bohemia (Vol. IV of the continuation of Barrande's 'Système silurien'); Dr. Bailey Willis's & Mr. Eliot Blackwelder's 'Research in China' (Publication No. 54 of the Carnegie Institution of Washington); Dr. R. F. Scharff's 'European Animals: their Geological History & Geographical Distribution'; Part I of Prof. Haug's 'Traité de Géologie'; Vol. I (Geology) of the Natural History of the National Antarctic Expedition; Sir Boverton Redwood's 'Petroleum & its Products'; Mr. A. J. Jukes-Browne's 'Hills & Valleys of Torquay'; the Geological-Survey Memoirs on the Structure of the North-West Highlands of Scotland, on the Land's End, Newquay, Falmouth & Truro, Wellington & Chard, Hungerford & Newbury; also those on the Leicestershire & South Derbyshire Coalfield; on the Oil-Shales of the Lothians; on Gower & the Swansea District, on the Limerick District, and on Islay. Moreover, many valuable publications, too numerous to particularize in this place, were received from the Geological Surveys of India, the Cape of Good Hope, the Transvaal, Egypt, Denmark, Finland, Switzerland, Rumania, New York, Maryland, Vermont, the United States, and São Paulo. Prof. H. de Dorlodot presented 28 reprints of his papers from various publications.

The Books and Maps, enumerated above, were the gift of 138 Government Departments and other Public Bodies; of 184 Societies and Editors of Periodicals; and of 225 Personal Donors.

The Purchases, made on the recommendation of the standing Library Committee, included 24 Volumes and 4 Detached Parts of separately-published Works; 31 Volumes and 9 Parts of Works published serially; and 12 Sheets of Geological Maps.

The Expenditure incurred in connexion with the Library during the Year 1907 was as follows:—

|  | £ | s. | d. |
|---|---|---|---|
| Books, Periodicals, etc. purchased.......... | 64 | 17 | 6 |
| Binding of Books and Mounting of Maps.... | 89 | 8 | 2 |
|  | £154 | 5 | 8 |

With regard to the Card-Catalogue of the Library, Mr. C. D. Sherborn reports as follows:—

'The editing of the Card-Catalogue has now reached the letter L. Progress was interrupted in the autumn for two months (as must yearly happen in future) by the preparation, checking, and sorting-in of the 7500 cards furnished by the Annual List of Geological Literature received by the Society during 1906. This was all incorporated by October. It is hoped that early in 1909 the present material, *plus* that in the 1907 List (to be issued about June 1908) will be in order, and the literature previous to 1894 will then be regularly taken in hand as originally planned, till the Card-Catalogue in the Library of the Geological Society of London will eventually provide a complete reference-index to all geological, mineralogical, palæozoological, and palæobotanical literature since 1800. Mr. Alec Field has, during the past year, collected together, had bound, and catalogued all the unbound authors' copies, etc. (some 400 volumes), and the cards have been indexed and incorporated in the Card-Catalogue.'

### Museum.

For the purpose of study and comparison, the Society's Collections were visited on 27 occasions during the year, the contents of 87 drawers being thus examined. The permission of the Council having been duly obtained, about 155 specimens were lent during 1907 to various investigators.

No expenditure has been incurred in connexion with the Museum during the past year.

A most valuable collection of specimens from the Cambrian Glacial Deposits of South Australia has been presented by the Rev. Walter Howchin, F.G.S., Lecturer in Geology in the University of Adelaide.

The appended Lists contain the Names of Government Departments, Public Bodies, Societies, Editors, and Personal Donors, from whom Donations to the Library have been received during the year under review :—

## I. Government Departments and other Public Bodies.

Alabama.—Geological Survey, Montgomery (Ala.).
American Museum of Natural History. New York.
Argentina.—Ministerio de Agricultura, Buenos Aires.
Australia (S.), etc. *See* South Australia, *etc.*
Austria.—Kaiserlich-Königliche Geologische Reichsanstalt. Vienna.
Bavaria.—Königliches Bayerisches Oberbergamt. Munich.
Belgium.—Académie Royale des Sciences, des Lettres & Beaux-Arts de Belgique. Brussels.
——. Musée Royal d'Histoire Naturelle. Brussels.
Bergen.—Bergens Museum.
Berlin.—Königliche Preussische Akademie der Wissenschaften.
Birmingham, University of.
Bohemia.—Naturwissenschaftliche Landesdurchforschung. Prague.
——. Royal Museum of Natural History. Prague.
Bristol.—Public Library.
British Columbia.—Department of Mines, Victoria.
British Guiana.—Department of Mines, Georgetown.
British South Africa Company. London.
Buenos Aires.—Museo Nacional de Buenos Aires.
California, University of. Berkeley (Cal.).
Cambridge (Mass.).—Museum of Comparative Zoology, Harvard College.
Canada.—Geological & Natural History Survey. Ottawa.
——, High Commissioner for. London.
Cape Colony.—Department of Agriculture : Geological Commission. Cape Town.
——. South African Museum. Cape Town.
Chicago.—'Field' Museum of Natural History.
——. John Crerar Library.
Connecticut State Library.—Geological & Natural History Survey. Hartford (Conn.).
Córdoba (Argentine Republic).—Academía Nacional de Ciencias.
Cracow.—Académie des Sciences. (Akademie Umiejetnosci.)
Denmark.—Commission for Ledelsen af de Geologiske og Geographiske Undersögelser i Grönland. Copenhagen.
——. Geologisk Undersögelse. Copenhagen.
——. Kongelige Danske Videnskabernes Selskab. Copenhagen.
Dublin.—Royal Irish Academy.
Egypt.—Survey Department. Cairo.
Finland.—Finlands Geologiska Undersökning. Helsingfors.
France.—Ministère des Travaux Publics. Paris.
——. Muséum d'Histoire Naturelle. Paris.
Georgia.—Geological Survey. Atlanta (Ga.).
Germany.—Kaiserliche Leopoldinisch-Carolinische Deutsche Akademie der Naturforscher. Halle an der Saale.
Great Britain.—Army Medical Department. London.
——. British Museum (Natural History). London.
——. Colonial Office. London.
——. Geological Survey. London.
——. Home Office. London.
——. India Office. London.
Hesse.—Geologische Landesanstalt. Darmstadt.
Holland.—Departement van Kolonien. The Hague.
Hull.—Municipal Museum.
Hungary.—Königliche Ungarische Geologische Anstalt (Magyar Földtani Tarsulat). Budapest.
——. Royal Hungarian Ministry of Finances. Budapest.
India.—Department of Mines. Calcutta.

India.—Geological Survey. Calcutta.
——. Indian Museum. Calcutta.
——. Surveyor-General's Office. Calcutta.
Iowa Geological Survey. Des Moines (Iowa).
Ireland.—Department of Agriculture & Technical Instruction. Dublin.
Italy.—Reale Comitato Geologico. Rome.
Japan.—Earthquake-Investigation Committee. Tokio.
——. Geological Survey. Tokio.
Jassy, University of.
Kansas.—University Geological Survey. Lawrence (Kan.).
Kentucky Geological Survey. Lexington (Ky.).
Kingston (Canada).—Queen's College.
La Plata.—Museo de La Plata.
London.—City of London College.
——. Imperial Institute.
——. Royal College of Surgeons.
——. University College.
Lund Museum. (Copenhagen.)
Madrid.—Real Academía de Ciencias exactas, fisicas y naturales. Madrid.
Magdeburg.—Museum für Natur- und Heimatkunde.
Melbourne (Victoria).—National Museum.
Mexico.—Instituto Geológico. Mexico City.
Michigan College of Mines. Houghton (Mich.).
Milan.—Reale Istituto Lombardo di Scienze & Lettere.
Missouri.—Bureau of Geology & Mines. Jefferson City (Mo.).
Munich.—Königliche Bayerische Akademie der Wissenschaften.
Mysore Geological Department. Bangalore.
Nancy.—Académie de Stanislas.
Naples.—Accademia delle Scienze.
Natal.—Department of Mines. Pietermaritzburg.
——. Geological Survey. Pietermaritzburg.
——. Government Museum. Pietermaritzburg.
Newcastle-upon-Tyne.—Armstrong College.
New Jersey.—Geological Survey. Trentham (N.J.).
New South Wales, Agent-General for. London.
——. Department of Mines & Agriculture. Sydney (N.S.W.).
——. Geological Survey. Sydney (N.S.W.).
New York State Museum. Albany (N.Y.).
New Zealand.—Department of Mines. Wellington (N.Z.).
——. Geological Survey. Wellington (N.Z.).
Nova Scotia.—Department of Mines. Halifax (N.S.).
Ohio Geological Survey. Columbus (Ohio).
Padua.—Reale Accademia di Scienze, Lettere & Arti.
Paris.—Académie des Sciences.
Perak Government. Taiping.
Peru.—Ministerio de Fomento. Lima.
Pisa, Royal University of.
Portugal.—Commissão dos Trabalhos Geologicos. Lisbon.
Prussia.—Ministerium für Handel & Gewerbe. Berlin.
——. Königliche Preussische Geologische Landesanstalt. Berlin.
Queensland, Agent-General for. London.
——. Department of Mines. Brisbane.
——. Geological Survey. Brisbane.
Redruth School of Mines.
Rhodesia.—Chamber of Mines. Bulawayo.
Rhodesian Museum. Bulawayo.
Rio de Janeiro.—Museu Nacional.
Rome.—Reale Accademia dei Lincei.
Rumania.—Geological Institute. Bukharest.
Russia.—Comité Géologique. St. Petersburg.
——. Section Géologique du Cabinet de S.M. l'Empereur. St. Petersburg.
São Paulo.—Commissão Geographica e Geologica do Estado de São Paulo. São Paulo.
South Australia, Agent-General for. London.
——. Geological Survey. Adelaide.
Spain.—Comision del Mapa Geológico. Madrid.
Stockholm.—Kongliga Svenska Vetenskaps Akademi.
Sweden.—Sveriges Geologiska Undersökning. Stockholm.

Switzerland.—Geologische Kommission der Schweiz.  Berne.
Tasmania.—Secretary for Mines.  Hobart.
Tokio.—Imperial University.
——.  College of Science.
Transvaal.—Geological Survey.  Pretoria.
——.  Mines Department.  Pretoria.
Turin.—Reale Accademia delle Scienze.
United States.—Department of Agriculture.  Washington (D.C.).
——.  Geological Survey.  Washington (D.C.).
——.  National Museum.  Washington (D.C.).
Upsala, University of.
Vermont Geological Survey.  Montpelier (Vt.).
Victoria (Austral.).—Geological Survey.  Melbourne.
——.  Agent-General for.  London.
——.  Department of Mines.  Melbourne.
Vienna.—Kaiserliche Akademie der Wissenschaften.
Washington (D.C.).—Smithsonian Institution.
Western Australia, Agent-General for.  London.
——.  Department of Mines.  Perth (W.A.).
——.  Geological Survey.  Perth (W.A.).
Wisconsin.—Geological & Natural History Survey.  Madison (Wisc.).

## II. Societies and Editors.

Acireale.—Accademia di Scienze, Lettere & Arti.
Adelaide.—Royal Society of South Australia.
Agram.—Societas Historico-Naturalis Croatica.
Alnwick.—Berwickshire Naturalists' Club.
Basel.—Naturforschende Gesellschaft.
Bath.—Natural History & Antiquarian Field-Club.
Belgrade.—Servian Geological Society.
Bergen.—'Naturen.'
Berlin.—Deutsche Geologische Gesellschaft.
——.  Gesellschaft Naturforschender Freunde.
——.  'Zeitschrift für Praktische Geologie.'
Berne.—Schweizerische Naturforschende Gesellschaft.
Bishop Auckland.—Wearside Naturalists' Field-Club.
Bombay Branch of the Royal Asiatic Society.
Bordeaux.—Société Linnéenne.
Boston (Mass.).—American Academy of Arts & Sciences.
——.  Boston Society of Natural History.
Bristol Naturalists' Society.
Brooklyn (N.Y.) Institute of Arts & Sciences.
Brunswick.—Verein für Naturwissenschaft zu Braunschweig.
Brussels.—Société Belge de Géologie, de Paléontologie & d'Hydrologie.
Budapest.—Földtani Közlöny.
Buenos Aires.—Sociedad Científica Argentina.
Buffalo (N.Y.) Society of Natural Sciences.
Bulawayo.—Rhodesian Scientific Association.
Caen.—Société Linnéenne de Normandie.
Calcutta.—Asiatic Society of Bengal.
——.  'Indian Engineering.'
Cambridge Philosophical Society.
Cape Town.—South African Association or the Advancement of Science.
——.  South African Philosophical Society.
Cardiff.—South Wales Institute of Engineers.
Chambéry.—Société d'Histoire Naturelle de Savoie.
Cheltenham Natural Science Society.
Chicago.—'Journal of Geology.'
Christiania.—Norsk Geologisk Forening.
——.  'Nyt Magazin for Naturvidenskaberne.'
Colombo.—Ceylon Branch of the Royal Asiatic Society.
Colorado Springs.—'Colorado College Studies.'
Copenhagen.—Dansk Geologisk Forening.
Croydon Natural History & Scientific Society.

Denver.—Colorado Scientific Society.
Dijon.—Académie des Sciences, Arts & Belles Lettres.
Dorpat (Jurjew).—Naturforschende Gesellschaft.
Douglas.—Isle of Man Natural History and Antiquarian Society.
Dresden.—Naturwissenschaftliche Gesellschaft.
———. Verein für Erdkunde.
Edinburgh Geological Society.
———. Royal Physical Society.
———. Royal Scottish Geographical Society.
———. Royal Society.
Ekaterinburg.—Société Ouralienne d'Amateurs des Sciences Naturelles.
Frankfurt am Main.—Senckenbergische Naturforschende Gesellschaft.
Freiburg im Breisgau.—Naturforschende Gesellschaft.
Geneva.—Société de Physique & d'Histoire Naturelle.
Giessen.—Oberhessische Gesellschaft für Natur- & Heilkunde.
Glasgow.—Geological Society.
Gloucester.—Cotteswold Naturalists' Field-Club.
Gratz.—Naturwissenschaftlicher Verein für Steiermark.
Haarlem.—Société Hollandaise des Sciences.
Halifax (N.S.).—Nova Scotian Institute of Science.
Hamilton (Canada) Scientific Association.
Hanau.—Wetterauische Gesellschaft für Gesammte Naturkunde.
Havre.—Société Géologique de Normandie.
Helsingfors.—Société Géographique de Finlande.
Hereford.—Woolhope Naturalists' Field-Club.
Hermannstadt.—Siebenbürgischer Verein für Naturwissenschaft.
Hertford.—Hertfordshire Natural History Society.
Hull Geological Society.
Indianapolis (Ind.).—Indiana Academy of Science.
Johannesburg.—Geological Society of South Africa.
Kiev.—Société des Naturalistes.
Lancaster (Pa.).—'Economic Geology.'
Lausanne.—Société Vaudoise des Sciences Naturelles.
Lawrence (Kan.).—'Kansas University Bulletin.'
Leeds Geological Association.
———. Philosophical & Literary Society.
———. Yorkshire Geological Society.
Leicester Literary & Philosophical Society.
Leipzig.—'Zeitschrift für Krystallographie & Mineralogie.'
Liége.—Société Géologique de Belgique.
———. Société Royale des Sciences.
Lille.—Société Géologique du Nord.
Lima.—'Revista de Ciencias.'
Lisbon.—Sociedade de Geographia.
———. Société Portugaise des Sciences Naturelles.
Liverpool Geological Society.
———. Literary & Philosophical Society.
London.—'The Athenæum.'
———. British Association for the Advancement of Science.
———. British Association of Waterworks Engineers (now The Association of Water-Engineers).
———. Chemical Society.
———. 'The Chemical News.'
———. 'The Colliery Guardian.'
———. 'The Geological Magazine.'
———. Geologists' Association.
———. Institution of Civil Engineers.
———. Institution of Mining & Metallurgy.
———. Iron & Steel Institute.
———. 'Knowledge.'
———. Linnean Society.
———. 'The London, Edinburgh, & Dublin Philosophical Magazine.'
———. Mineralogical Society.
———. 'The Mining Journal.'
———. 'Nature.'
———. Palæontographical Society.
———. 'The Quarry.'
———. Ray Society.

London.—'Records of the London & West-Country Chamber of Mines.'
——.  Royal Agricultural Society.
——.  Royal Astronomical Society.
——.  Royal Geographical Society.
——.  Royal Institution.
——.  Royal Meteorological Society.
——.  Royal Microscopical Society.
——.  Royal Photographic Society.
——.  Royal Society.
——.  Royal Society of Arts.
——.  Society of Biblical Archæology.
——.  'The South-Eastern Naturalist' (S.E. Union of Scientific Societies).
——.  Victoria Institute.
——.  'Water.'
——.  Zoological Society.
Manchester Geological & Mining Society.
——.  Literary & Philosophical Society.
Melbourne (Victoria).—Australasian Institute of Mining Engineers.
——.  Royal Society of Victoria.
——.  'The Victorian Naturalist.'
Mexico.—Sociedad Científica 'Antonio Alzate.'
Moscow.—Société Impériale des Naturalistes.
New Haven (Conn.).—'The American Journal of Science.'
New York.—Academy of Sciences.
——.  American Institute of Mining Engineers.
——.  'Science.'
Newcastle-upon-Tyne.—Institution of Mining Engineers.
——.  North-of-England Institute of Mining & Mechanical Engineers.
——.  University-of-Durham Philosophical Society.
Northampton.—Northamptonshire Natural History Society.
Nürnberg.—Naturhistorische Gesellschaft.
Oporto.—Academia Polytecnica.  [Coimbra.]
Ottawa.—Royal Society of Canada.
Paisley.—Philosophical Institution.
Paris.—Commission Française des Glaciers.
——.  Société Française de Minéralogie.
——.  Société Géologique de France.
——.  'Spelunca.'
Penzance.—Royal Geological Society of Cornwall.
Perth.—Perthshire Society of Natural Science.
Philadelphia.—Academy of Natural Sciences.
——.  American Philosophical Society.
Pisa.—Società Toscana di Scienze Naturali.
Plymouth.—Devonshire Association for the Advancement of Science.
Rennes.—Société Scientifique & Médicale de l'Ouest.
Rochester( N.Y.).—Academy of Science.
——.  Geological Society of America.
Rome.—Società Geologica Italiana.
Rugby School Natural History Society.
Santiago de Chile.—Sociedad Nacional de Minería.
——.  Société Scientifique du Chili.
São Paulo (Brazil).—Sociedade Scientifica.
Scranton (Pa.).—'Mines & Minerals.'
St. John (N.B.).—Natural History Society of New Brunswick.
St. Petersburg.—Russische Kaiserliche Mineralogische Gesellschaft.
Stockholm.—Geologiska Förening.
Stratford.—Essex Field-Club.
Stuttgart.—'Centralblatt für Mineralogie, Geologie & Paläontologie.'
——.  'Neues Jahrbuch für Mineralogie, Geologie & Paläontologie.'
——.  Oberrheinischer Geologischer Verein.
——.  Verein für Vaterländische Naturkunde in Württemberg.
——.  'Zeitschrift für Naturwissenschaften.'
Sydney (N.S.W.).—Linnean Society of New South Wales.
——.  Royal Society of New South Wales.
Toronto.—Canadian Institute.
Toulouse.—Société d'Histoire Naturelle.
Truro.—Royal Institution of Cornwall.

Vienna.—'Beiträge zur Paläontologie & Geologie Œsterreich-Ungarns & des Orients.'
——. 'Berg- & Hüttenmännisches Jahrbuch.'
——. Kaiserlich-Königliche Zoologisch-Botanische Gesellschaft.
Washington (D.C.).—Academy of Sciences.
——. Biological Society.
——. Philosophical Society.
Wellington (N.Z.).—New Zealand Institute.
Wiesbaden.—Nassauischer Verein für Naturkunde.
York.—Yorkshire Philosophical Society.

## III. PERSONAL DONORS.

Abbott, G.
Adams, F. D.
Allen, H. A.
Ameghino, F.
Ampferer, O.
Anderson, R.
Anderson, W.
Andersson, J. G.
Arber, E. A. N.
Arnold-Bemrose, H. H.

Ball, J.
Bardarson, G. G.
Barlow, A. E.
Barrow, G.
Bascom, Miss F.
Bauerman, H.
Beck, R.
Bevan, J. O.
Biddlecombe, A.
Blake, W. P.
Bodman, C.
Bonney, T. G.
Borredon, C. G.
Borromeo, Conte G.
Branner, J. C.
Breton, L.
Broeck, E. van den.
Brögger, W. C.
Brown, H. Y. L.
Brown, J. C.
Burr, M.
Buxtorf, A.

Cadell, H. M.
Campbell, W.
Carey, A. E.
Cayeux, L.
Chapman, F.
Chavannes, J. D. A.
Cheesman, T. F.
Clarke, J. M.
Cole, G. A. J.
Conwentz, H.
Cook, T.
Coomáraswámy, A. K.
Corstorphine, G. S.
Cossmann, M.
Courty, G.
Credner, H.

Crick, G. C.
Crisp, Sir F.
Cumings, E. R.
Cummings, C. E.
Currie, J.

Daly, R. A.
Darton, W. N.
Davidson, A. A.
Davies, J.
Davis, W. M.
Davison, C.
Dawkins, W. B.
Derby, O. A.
Dollfus, G. F.
Dorlodot, H. de.
Douglas, N.

Elgee, F.
Elles, Miss G. L.
Ells, R. W.
Elsden, J. V.
Evans, Sir John.
Evans, J. W.

Fearnsides, W. G.
Fisher, Rev. O.
Flett, J. S.
Ford, W. E.
Fox, H.
Fox, W. S.
Fritsch, A.

Gagel, C.
Garwood, E. J.
Geikie, Sir Archibald.
Gelissard de Marignac, J. C.
Gilbert, G. K.
Greenwell, A.
Gregory, J. W.
Griffith, N.
Grubenmann, U.

Handlirsch, A.
Harder, E. C.
Harmer, F. W.
Harrington, B. J.
Harrison, W. J.
Hatch, F. H.

Haug, E.
Henriquez, H.
Hill, J. B.
Hinden, F.
Hobbs, W. H.
Holland, P.
Holmberg, O.
Holmes, T. V.
Holmes, W. H.
Hopkinson, J.
Hovey, E. O.
Howley, J. P.
Hutton, Mrs. F. W.

Iddings, J. P.

Jamieson, G. S.
Johnson, D. W.
Johnson, J. P.
Johnston, R. M.
Johnston-Lavis, H. J.
Jukes-Browne, A. J.

Kiedel, H.
Kirsopp, jun., J.
Kitson, A. E.
Knight, C. W.
Kœnen, A. von.

Lacroix, A.
Lambe, L. M.
Lamplugh, G. W.
Larcombe, C. O. G.
Lemière, L.
Leslie, T. N.
Leuche, K.
Lewis, F. J.
Liversidge, A.
Lomas, J.
Louderback, G. D.

MacAlister, D. A.
McKellar, P.
Maclaren, J. M.
Maitland, A. G.
Mandy, J. T.
Manson, M.
Marr, J. E.
Marshall, P.
Martin, E. A

Masche, E.
Mason, O. T.
Mawson, D.
Mellor, E. T.
Mennell, F. P.
Merrill, G. P.
Meunier, S.
Miller, W. G.
Millett, F. W.
Molyneux, A. J. C.
Monckton, H. W.
Morozewicz, J.
Mountmorres, Viscount.
Mourlon, M.

Nacken, R.
Nares, Sir George.
Nathorst, A. G.
Newton, R. B.
Niethammer, G.
Nopcsa, jun., Baron F.

Oswald, F.
Ouin, J. T.

Pachundaki, D. E.
Pavlov, A. P.
Penck, A.
Perkins, G. H.
Portis, A.
Preiswerk, H.

Quilliam, W. H.

Rastall, R. H.
Reade, T. M.
Renier, A.
Ricciardi, L.
Roberti, I. L. A.
Rogers, A. W.

Sacco, F.
Salinas, E.
Salter, A. E.
Sauvage, E.
Sawyer, A. R.
Schardt, H.
Schmidt, C.
Schuchert, C.
Schwartz, E. H. L.
Scrivenor, J. B.
See, T. J. J.
Seward, A. C.
Sheppard, T.
Sherborn, C. D.
Shrubsole, W. H.
Smith, B.
Smith, E. A.
Spencer, J. W. W.
Stahl, A. F.
Stanley, W. F.
Steinmann, G.
Stevenson, J. J.
Stirrup, M.

Termier, P.
Thiéry, P.

Thompson, B.
Tobler, A.
Törnquist, S. L.
Twelvetrees, W. H.
Tyrrell, J. B.

Upham, W.
Ussher, W. A. E.

Van der Wiele, C.
Vaughan, T. W.
Vetters, H.
Vogdes, A. W.
Voit, F. W.
Vredenburg, E. W.

Waagen, L.
Wahl, W.
Warren, S. H.
Washington, H. S.
Whitaker, W.
Wieland, G. R.
Wilckens, O.
Wilkins, O.
Willcox, O. W.
Willis, B.
Woods, H.
Woodward, H. B.
Woolacott, D.
Wollemann, A.

Zeiller, R.

COMPARATIVE STATEMENT OF THE NUMBER OF THE SOCIETY AT THE
CLOSE OF THE YEARS 1906 AND 1907.

|  | Dec. 31st, 1906. |  | Dec. 31st, 1907. |
|---|---|---|---|
| Compounders . . . . . . . . . . . . | 273 | . . . . . . | 266 |
| Contributing Fellows . . . . . . | 946 | . . . . . . | 981 |
| Non-Contributing Fellows . . | 32 | . . . . . . | 31 |
|  | 1251 |  | 1278 |
| Foreign Members . . . . . . . . | 40 | . . . . . . | 40 |
| Foreign Correspondents . . . . | 39 | . . . . . . | 38 |
|  | 1330 |  | 1356 |

*Comparative Statement, explanatory of the Alterations in the Number of Fellows, Foreign Members, and Foreign Correspondents at the close of the years 1906 and 1907.*

| | | |
|---|---|---|
| Number of Compounders, Contributing and Non-Contributing Fellows, December 31st, 1906 .. } | | 1251 |
| *Add* Fellows elected during the former year and paid in 1907 ........................} | | 16 |
| *Add* Fellows elected and paid in 1907 ........ | | 58 |
| | | 1325 |
| *Deduct* Compounders deceased................ | 8 | |
| Contributing Fellows deceased .......... | 18 | |
| Non-Contributing Fellow deceased ...... | 1 | |
| Contributing Fellows resigned .......... | 9 | |
| Contributing Fellows removed .......... | 11 | |
| | — | 47 |
| | | 1278 |
| Number of Foreign Members and Foreign Correspondents, December 31st, 1906 ......... } | 79 | |
| *Deduct* Foreign Members deceased ........ | 2 | |
| Foreign Correspondent deceased .... | 1 | |
| Foreign Correspondents elected Foreign Members ..........} | 2 | |
| | — 5 | |
| | 74 | |
| *Add* Foreign Members elected .......... | 2 | |
| Foreign Correspondents elected .... | 2 | |
| | — 4 | |
| | | — 78 |
| | | 1356 |

## DECEASED FELLOWS.

### Compounders (8).

Allendale, Lord.
Hector, Sir James.
Hughes, T. H.
Jones, T.

Kitchener, A. B.
Routh, Dr. S. J.
Stirrup, M.
Walker, J. F.

### Resident and other Contributing Fellows (18).

Baron, Rev. R.
Booth, J.
Dennant, J.
Doyle, P.
Ellis, W. R.
Gale, Dr. J.
Griesbach, C. L.
Hodson, G.
Kennedy, Prof. G. T.

Middleton, Rev. G.
Power, E. D.
Propert, Dr. W. P.
Robinson, Rev. W.
Savage, W. A.
Slater, R.
White, J. F.
Williams, H. W.
Wynne, A. B.

### Non-contributing Fellow (1).

Greg, R. P.

### DECEASED FOREIGN MEMBERS (2).

Bertrand, Prof. M.    |    Mojsísovics, Dr. E.

### DECEASED FOREIGN CORRESPONDENT (1).

Klein, Prof. J. F. C.

---

### FELLOWS RESIGNED (9).

Ballard, G. H.
Barclay, E. F.
Bowdler, Capt. B. W.
Callaway, Dr. C.
Kitchingman, D.

Singh, Lala Kishen.
Taylor, W.
Tucker, W. T.
Weldon, H.

---

FELLOWS REMOVED (11).

Barlow, S. C.
Bonwick, E. W.
Curry, W. T.
Harrop, W. N.
Higgs, M. S.
Kemper-Voss, E.

Pinfold, Rev. J. T.
Price, Rev. E. D.
Smedley, H. E. H.
Storey, T. E.
Vincent, Major W. S.

*The following Personages were elected Foreign Members during the year 1907:—*

Tietze, Hofrath Dr. Emil Ernst August, of Vienna.
Issel, Commendatore Prof. Arturo, of Genoa.

*The following Personages were elected Foreign Correspondents during the year 1907:—*

Prof. Baron Gerard Jakob de Geer, of Stockholm.
Prof. Armin Baltzer, of Berne.

After the Reports had been read, it was resolved:—

That they be received and entered on the Minutes of the Meeting, and that such parts of them as the Council shall think fit be printed and circulated among the Fellows.

It was afterwards resolved:—

That the thanks of the Society be given to Sir Archibald Geikie, retiring from the office of President.

That the thanks of the Society be given to Dr. J. E. Marr, retiring from the office of Vice-President.

That the thanks of the Society be given to Sir John Evans, retiring from the office of Foreign Secretary.

That the thanks of the Society be given to Mr. H. H. Arnold-Bemrose, Sir John Evans, Prof. Charles Lapworth, Dr. J. E. Marr, and Mr. H. B. Woodward, retiring from the Council.

———

After the Balloting-Glasses had been closed, and the Lists examined by the Scrutineers, the following gentlemen were declared to have been duly elected as the Officers and Council for the ensuing year :—

## OFFICERS AND COUNCIL.—1908.

### *PRESIDENT.*

Prof. William Johnson Sollas, Sc.D., LL.D., F.R.S.

### *VICE-PRESIDENTS.*

Frederick William Rudler, I.S.O.
Aubrey Strahan, Sc.D., F.R.S.
J. J. Harris Teall, M.A., D.Sc., F.R.S.
Arthur Smith Woodward, LL.D., F.R.S., F.L.S.

### *SECRETARIES.*

Prof. William Whitehead Watts, M.A., M.Sc., F.R.S.
Prof. Edmund Johnstone Garwood, M.A.

### *FOREIGN SECRETARY.*

Sir Archibald Geikie, K.C.B., D.C.L., LL.D., Sc.D., Sec.R.S.

### *TREASURER.*

Horace Woollaston Monckton, Treas.L.S.

---

### *COUNCIL.*

Prof. Samuel Herbert Cox, F.C.S., Assoc.R.S.M.
Prof. Edmund Johnstone Garwood, M.A.
Sir Archibald Geikie, K.C.B., D.C.L., LL.D., Sc.D., Sec.R.S.
Alfred Harker, M.A., F.R.S.
Wilfrid Hudleston Hudleston, M.A., F.R.S., F.L.S.
Finlay Lorimer Kitchin, M.A., Ph.D.
George William Lamplugh, F.R.S.
Richard Lydekker, B.A., F.R.S.
Prof. Henry Alexander Miers, M.A., F.R.S.
Horace Woollaston Monckton, Treas.L.S.
Richard Dixon Oldham.

Prof. Sidney Hugh Reynolds, M.A.
Frederick William Rudler, I.S.O.
Prof. William Johnson Sollas, Sc.D., LL.D., F.R.S.
Leonard James Spencer, M.A.
Aubrey Strahan, Sc.D., F.R.S.
Charles Fox Strangways.
J. J. Harris Teall, M.A., D.Sc., F.R.S.
Richard Hill Tiddeman, M.A.
Prof. William Whitehead Watts, M.A., M.Sc., F.R.S.
Henry Woods, M.A.
Arthur Smith Woodward, LL.D., F.R.S., F.L.S.
George William Young.

LIST OF

# THE FOREIGN MEMBERS

OF THE GEOLOGICAL SOCIETY OF LONDON, in 1907.

Date of
Election.
1874.  Prof. Albert Jean Gaudry, *Paris.*
1877.  Prof. Eduard Suess, *Vienna.*
1880.  Geheimrath Prof. Ferdinand Zirkel, *Leipzig.*
1884.  Commendatore Prof. Giovanni Capellini, *Bologna.*
1885.  Prof. Jules Gosselet, *Lille.*
1886.  Prof. Gustav Tschermak, *Vienna.*
1890.  Geheimrath Prof. Heinrich Rosenbusch, *Heidelberg.*
1891.  Prof. Charles Barrois, *Lille.*
1893.  Prof. Waldemar Christofer Brœgger, *Christiania.*
1893.  M. Auguste Michel-Lévy, *Paris.*
1893.  Prof. Alfred Gabriel Nathorst, *Stockholm.*
1894.  Prof. George J. Brush, *New Haven, Conn.* (*U.S.A.*).
1894.  Prof. Edward Salisbury Dana, *New Haven, Conn.* (*U.S.A.*).
1895.  Prof. Grove Karl Gilbert, *Washington, D.C.* (*U.S.A.*).
1895.  Dr. Friedrich Schmidt, *St. Petersburg.*
1896.  Prof. Albert Heim, *Zürich.*
1897.  M. Édouard Dupont, *Brussels.*
1897.  Dr. Anton Fritsch, *Prague.*
1897.  Prof. Albert de Lapparent, *Paris.*   (*Deceased.*)
1897.  Dr. Hans Reusch, *Christiania.*
1898.  Geheimrath Prof. Hermann Credner, *Leipzig.*
1898.  Dr. Charles Doolittle Walcott, *Washington, D.C.* (*U.S.A.*).
1899.  Senhor Joaquim Felipe Nery Delgado, *Lisbon.*
1899.  Prof. Emanuel Kayser, *Marburg.*
1899.  M. Ernest Van den Broeck, *Brussels.*
1899.  Dr. Charles Abiathar White, *Washington, D.C.* (*U.S.A.*).
1900.  M. Gustave F. Dollfus, *Paris.*
1900.  Prof. Paul von Groth, *Munich.*
1900.  Dr. Sven Leonhard Tœrnquist, *Lund.*
1901.  M. Alexander Petrovich Karpinsky, *St. Petersburg.*
1901.  Prof. Alfred Lacroix, *Paris.*
1903.  Prof. Albrecht Penck, *Berlin.*
1903.  Prof. Anton Koch, *Budapest.*
1904.  Prof. Joseph Paxson Iddings, *Chicago* (*U.S.A.*).
1904.  Prof. Henry Fairfield Osborn, *New York* (*U.S.A.*).
1905.  Prof. Louis Dollo, *Brussels.*
1905.  Prof. August Rothpletz, *Munich.*
1906.  Prof. Count Hermann zu Solms-Laubach, *Strasburg.*
1907.  Hofrath Dr. Emil Ernst August Tietze, *Vienna.*
1907.  Commendatore Prof. Arturo Issel, *Genoa.*

## LIST OF

# THE FOREIGN CORRESPONDENTS

## OF THE GEOLOGICAL SOCIETY OF LONDON, in 1907.

Date of
Election.

1874. Prof. Igino Cocchi, *Florence.*

1879. Dr. H. Émile Sauvage, *Boulogne-sur-Mer.*

1889. Dr. Rogier Diederik Marius Verbeek, *The Hague.*

1890. Geheimer Bergrath Prof. Adolph von Kœnen, *Göttingen.*

1892. Prof. Johann Lehmann, *Kiel.*

1893. Prof. Aléxis P. Pavlow, *Moscow.*

1893. M. Ed. Rigaux, *Boulogne-sur-Mer.*

1894. M. Perceval de Loriol-Lefort, *Campagne Frontenex, near Geneva.*

1894. Dr. Francisco P. Moreno, *La Plata.*

1894. Prof. J. H. L. Vogt, *Christiania.*

1895. Prof. Constantin de Kroustchoff, *St. Petersburg.*

1896. Prof. Johannes Walther, *Halle an der Saale.*

1897. M. Emmanuel de Margerie, *Paris.*

1898. Dr. Marcellin Boule, *Paris.*

1898. Dr. W. H. Dall, *Washington, D.C. (U.S.A.).*

1899. Dr. Gerhard Holm, *Stockholm.*

1899. Prof. Theodor Liebisch, *Göttingen.*

1899. Prof. Franz Lœwinson-Lessing, *St. Petersburg.*

1899. M. Michel F. Mourlon, *Brussels.*

1899. Prof. Gregorio Stefanescu, *Bucharest.*

1899. Prof. René Zeiller, *Paris.*

1900. Prof. Ernst Koken, *Tübingen.*

1900. Prof. Federico Sacco, *Turin.*

1901. Prof. Friedrich Johann Becke, *Vienna.*

1902. Prof. Thomas Chrowder Chamberlin, *Chicago, Ill. (U.S.A.).*

1902. Dr. Thorvaldr Thoroddsen, *Copenhagen.*

1902. Prof. Samuel Wendell Williston, *Chicago, Ill. (U.S.A.).*

1904. Dr. William Bullock Clark, *Baltimore (U.S.A.).*

1904. Dr. Erich Dagobert von Drygalski, *Charlottenburg.*

1904. Prof. Giuseppe de Lorenzo, *Naples.*

1904. The Hon. Frank Springer, *Burlington, Iowa (U.S.A.).*

1904. Dr. Henry S. Washington, *Locust, N.J. (U.S.A.).*

1905. Prof. Bundjirô Kôtô, *Tokyo.*

1906. Prof. John M. Clarke, *Albany, N.Y. (U.S.A.).*

1906. Prof. William Morris Davis, *Cambridge, Mass. (U.S.A.).*

1906. Dr. Jakob Johannes Sederholm, *Helsingfors.*

1907. Prof. Baron Gerard Jakob de Geer, *Stockholm.*

1907. Prof. Armin Baltzer, *Berne.*

---

# AWARDS OF THE WOLLASTON MEDAL
## UNDER THE CONDITIONS OF THE 'DONATION-FUND'
### ESTABLISHED BY
## WILLIAM HYDE WOLLASTON, M.D., F.R.S., F.G.S., ETC.

'To promote researches concerning the mineral structure of the Earth, and to enable the Council of the Geological Society to reward those individuals of any country by whom such researches may hereafter be made,'—'such individual not being a Member of the Council.'

1831. Mr. William Smith.
1835. Dr. Gideon A. Mantell.
1836. M. Louis Agassiz.
1837. { Capt. T. P. Cautley. / Dr. Hugh Falconer.
1838. Sir Richard Owen.
1839. Prof. C. G. Ehrenberg.
1840. Prof. A. H. Dumont.
1841. M. Adolphe T. Brongniart.
1842. Baron Leopold von Buch.
1843. { M. Élie de Beaumont. / M. P. A. Dufrénoy.
1844. The Rev. W. D. Conybeare.
1845. Prof. John Phillips.
1846. Mr. William Lonsdale.
1847. Dr. Ami Boué.
1848. The Very Rev. W. Buckland.
1849. Sir Joseph Prestwich.
1850. Mr. William Hopkins.
1851. The Rev. Prof. A. Sedgwick.
1852. Dr. W. H. Fitton.
1853. { M. le Vicomte A. d'Archiac. / M. E. de Verneuil.
1854. Sir Richard Griffith.
1855. Sir Henry De la Beche.
1856. Sir William Logan.
1857. M. Joachim Barrande.
1858. { Herr Hermann von Meyer. / Prof. James Hall.
1859. Mr. Charles Darwin.
1860. Mr. Searles V. Wood.
1861. Prof. Dr. H. G. Bronn.
1862. Mr. R. A. C. Godwin-Austen.
1863. Prof. Gustav Bischof.
1864. Sir Roderick Murchison.
1865. Dr. Thomas Davidson.
1866. Sir Charles Lyell.
1867. Mr. G. Poulett Scrope.
1868. Prof. Carl F. Naumann.
1869. Dr. Henry C. Sorby.
1870. Prof. G. P. Deshayes.

1871. Sir Andrew Ramsay.
1872. Prof. James D. Dana.
1873. Sir P. de M. Grey Egerton.
1874. Prof. Oswald Heer.
1875. Prof. L. G. de Koninck.
1876. Prof. Thomas H. Huxley.
1877. Mr. Robert Mallet.
1878. Dr. Thomas Wright.
1879. Prof. Bernhard Studer.
1880. Prof. Auguste Daubrée.
1881. Prof. P. Martin Duncan.
1882. Dr. Franz Ritter von Hauer.
1883. Dr. William Thomas Blanford.
1884. Prof. Albert Jean Gaudry.
1885. Mr. George Busk.
1886. Prof. A. L. O. Des Cloizeaux.
1887. Mr. John Whitaker Hulke.
1888. Mr. Henry B. Medlicott.
1889. Prof. Thomas George Bonney.
1890. Prof. W. C. Williamson.
1891. Prof. John Wesley Judd.
1892. Baron Ferdinand von Richthofen.
1893. Prof. Nevil Story Maskelyne.
1894. Prof. Karl Alfred von Zittel.
1895. Sir Archibald Geikie.
1896. Prof. Eduard Suess.
1897. Mr. Wilfrid H. Hudleston.
1898. Prof. Ferdinand Zirkel.
1899. Prof. Charles Lapworth.
1900. Prof. Grove Karl Gilbert.
1901. Prof. Charles Barrois.
1902. Dr. Friedrich Schmidt.
1903. Prof. Heinrich Rosenbusch.
1904. Prof. Albert Heim.
1905. Dr. J. J. Harris Teall.
1906. Dr. Henry Woodward.
1907. Prof. William Johnson Sollas.
1908. Prof. Paul von Groth.

# AWARDS

## OF THE

## BALANCE OF THE PROCEEDS OF THE WOLLASTON 'DONATION-FUND.'

1831. Mr. William Smith.
1833. Mr. William Lonsdale.
1834. M. Louis Agassiz.
1835. Dr. Gideon A. Mantell.
1836. Prof. G. P. Deshayes.
1838. Sir Richard Owen.
1839. Prof. C. G. Ehrenberg.
1840. Mr. J. De Carle Sowerby.
1841. Prof. Edward Forbes.
1842. Prof. John Morris.
1843. Prof. John Morris.
1844. Mr. William Lonsdale.
1845. Mr. Geddes Bain.
1846. Mr. William Lonsdale.
1847. M. Alcide d'Orbigny.
1848. { Cape-of-Good-Hope Fossils. / M. Alcide d'Orbigny.
1849. Mr. William Lonsdale.
1850. Prof. John Morris.
1851. M. Joachim Barrande.
1852. Prof. John Morris.
1853. Prof. L. G. de Koninck.
1854. Dr. Samuel P. Woodward.
1855. Drs. G. and F. Sandberger.
1856. Prof. G. P. Deshayes.
1857. Dr. Samuel P. Woodward.
1858. Prof. James Hall.
1859. Mr. Charles Peach.
1860. { Prof. T. Rupert Jones. / Mr. W. K. Parker.
1861. Prof. Auguste Daubrée.
1862. Prof. Oswald Heer.
1863. Prof. Ferdinand Senft.
1864. Prof. G. P. Deshayes.
1865. Mr. J. W. Salter.
1866. Dr. Henry Woodward.
1867. Mr. W. H. Baily.
1868. M. J. Bosquet.
1869. Mr. William Carruthers.
1870. M. Marie Rouault.

1871. Mr. Robert Etheridge.
1872. Dr. James Croll.
1873. Prof. John Wesley Judd.
1874. Dr. Henri Nyst.
1875. Prof. Louis C. Miall.
1876. Prof. Giuseppe Seguenza.
1877. Mr. Robert Etheridge, Jun.
1878. Prof. William Johnson Sollas.
1879. Mr. Samuel Allport.
1880. Mr. Thomas Davies.
1881. Dr. Ramsay Heatley Traquair.
1882. Dr. George Jennings Hinde.
1883. Prof. John Milne.
1884. Mr. Edwin Tulley Newton.
1885. Dr. Charles Callaway.
1886. Mr. J. Starkie Gardner.
1887. Dr. Benjamin Neeve Peach.
1888. Dr. John Horne.
1889. Dr. Arthur Smith Woodward.
1890. Mr. William A. E. Ussher.
1891. Mr. Richard Lydekker.
1892. Mr. Orville Adelbert Derby.
1893. Mr. John George Goodchild.
1894. Dr. Aubrey Strahan.
1895. Prof. William W. Watts.
1896. Mr. Alfred Harker.
1897. Dr. Francis Arthur Bather.
1898. Prof. Edmund J. Garwood.
1899. Prof. John B. Harrison.
1900. Dr. George Thurland Prior.
1901. Mr. Arthur Walton Rowe.
1902. Mr. Leonard James Spence
1903. Mr. L. L. Belinfante.
1904. Miss Ethel M. R. Wood.
1905. Dr. H. H. Arnold-Bemrose.
1906. Dr. Finlay Lorimer Kitchin.
1907. Dr. Arthur Vaughan.
1908. Mr. Herbert Henry Thomas.

# AWARDS OF THE MURCHISON MEDAL

UNDER THE CONDITIONS OF THE

### 'MURCHISON GEOLOGICAL FUND,'

ESTABLISHED UNDER THE WILL OF THE LATE

#### SIR RODERICK IMPEY MURCHISON, Bart., F.R.S., F.G.S.

'To be applied in every consecutive year, in such manner as the Council of the Society may deem most useful in advancing Geological Science, whether by granting sums of money to travellers in pursuit of knowledge, to authors of memoirs, or to persons actually employed in any enquiries bearing upon the science of Geology, or in rewarding any such travellers, authors, or other persons, and the Medal to be given to some person to whom such Council shall grant any sum of money or recompense in respect of Geological Science.'

1873. Mr. William Davies.
1874. Dr. J. J. Bigsby.
1875. Mr. W. J. Henwood.
1876. Mr. Alfred R. C. Selwyn.
1877. The Rev. W. B. Clarke.
1878. Prof. Hanns Bruno Geinitz.
1879. Sir Frederick M'Coy.
1880. Mr. Robert Etheridge.
1881. Sir Archibald Geikie.
1882. Prof. Jules Gosselet.
1883. Prof. H. R. Gœppert.
1884. Dr. Henry Woodward.
1885. Dr. Ferdinand von Rœmer.
1886. Mr. William Whitaker.
1887. The Rev. Peter B. Brodie.
1888. Prof. J. S. Newberry.
1889. Prof. James Geikie.
1890. Prof. Edward Hull.
1891. Prof. Waldemar C. Brœgger.

1892. Prof. A. H. Green.
1893. The Rev. Osmond Fisher.
1894. Mr. William T. Aveline.
1895. Prof. Gustaf Lindström.
1896. Mr. T. Mellard Reade.
1897. Mr. Horace B. Woodward.
1898. Mr. Thomas F. Jamieson.
1899. { Dr. Benjamin N. Peach. Dr. John Horne.
1900. Baron A. E. Nordenskiœld.
1901. Mr. A. J. Jukes-Browne.
1902. Mr. Frederic W. Harmer.
1903. Dr. Charles Callaway.
1904. Prof. George A. Lebour.
1905. Mr. Edward John Dunn.
1906. Mr. Charles T. Clough.
1907. Mr. Alfred Harker.
1908. Prof. Albert Charles Seward.

AWARDS

OF THE

BALANCE OF THE PROCEEDS OF THE

'MURCHISON GEOLOGICAL FUND.'

1873. Prof. Oswald Heer.
1874. Mr. Alfred Bell.
1874. Prof. Ralph Tate.
1875. Prof. H. Govier Seeley.
1876. Dr. James Croll.
1877. The Rev. John F. Blake.
1878. Prof. Charles Lapworth.
1879. Mr. James Walker Kirkby.
1880. Mr. Robert Etheridge.
1881. Mr. Frank Rutley.
1882. Prof. Thomas Rupert Jones.
1883. Dr. John Young.
1884. Mr. Martin Simpson.
1885. Mr. Horace B. Woodward.
1886. Mr. Clement Reid.
1887. Dr. Robert Kidston.
1888. Mr. Edward Wilson.
1889. Prof. Grenville A. J. Cole.
1890. Mr. Edward B. Wethered.

1891. The Rev. Richard Baron.
1892. Mr. Beeby Thompson.
1893. Mr. Griffith John Williams.
1894. Mr. George Barrow.
1895. Prof. Albert Charles Seward.
1896. Mr. Philip Lake.
1897. Mr. Sydney S. Buckman.
1898. Miss Jane Donald.
1899. Mr. James Bennie.
1900. Mr. A. Vaughan Jennings.
1901. Mr. Thomas S. Hall.
1902. Mr. Thomas H. Holland.
1903. Mrs. Elizabeth Gray.
1904. Dr. Arthur Hutchinson.
1905. Mr. Herbert Lister Bowman.
1906. Dr. Herbert Lapworth.
1907. Dr. Felix Oswald.
1908. Miss Ethel Gertrude Skeat.

# AWARDS OF THE LYELL MEDAL

### UNDER THE CONDITIONS OF THE

## 'LYELL GEOLOGICAL FUND,'

### ESTABLISHED UNDER THE WILL AND CODICIL OF THE LATE

### SIR CHARLES LYELL, Bart., F.R.S., F.G.S.

The Medal 'to be cast in bronze and to be given annually' (or from time to time) 'as a mark of honorary distinction and as an expression on the part of the governing body of the Society that the Medallist (who may be of any country or either sex) has deserved well of the Science,'—'not less than one third of the annual interest [of the fund] to accompany the Medal, the remaining interest to be given in one or more portions, at the discretion of the Council, for the encouragement of Geology or of any of the allied sciences by which they shall consider Geology to have been most materially advanced, either for travelling expenses or for a memoir or paper published, or in progress, and without reference to the sex or nationality of the author, or the language in which any such memoir or paper may be written.'

There is a further provision for suspending the award for one year, and in such case for the awarding of a Medal to 'each of two persons who have been jointly engaged in the same exploration in the same country, or perhaps on allied subjects in different countries, the proportion of interest always not being less to each Medal than one third of the annual interest.'

1876. Prof. John Morris.
1877. Sir James Hector.
1878. Mr. George Busk.
1879. Prof. Edmond Hébert.
1880. Sir John Evans.
1881. Sir J. William Dawson.
1882. Dr. J. Lycett.
1883. Dr. W. B. Carpenter.
1884. Dr. Joseph Leidy.
1885. Prof. H. Govier Seeley.
1886. Mr. William Pengelly.
1887. Mr. Samuel Allport.
1888. Prof. Henry A. Nicholson.
1889. Prof. W. Boyd Dawkins.
1890. Prof. Thomas Rupert Jones.
1891. Prof. T. McKenny Hughes.
1892. Mr. George H. Morton.

1893. Mr. Edwin Tulley Newton.
1894. Prof. John Milne.
1895. The Rev. John F. Blake.
1896. Dr. Arthur Smith Woodward.
1897. Dr. George Jennings Hinde.
1898. Prof. Wilhelm Waagen.
1899. Lt.-Gen. C. A. McMahon.
1900. Dr. John Edward Marr.
1901. Dr. Ramsay Heatley Traquair.
1902. { Prof. Anton Fritsch. / Mr. Richard Lydekker. }
1903. Mr. Frederick William Rudler.
1904. Prof. Alfred Gabriel Nathorst.
1905. Dr. Hans Reusch.
1906. Prof. Frank Dawson Adams.
1907. Dr. Joseph F. Whiteaves.
1908. Mr. Richard Dixon Oldham.

# AWARDS

### OF THE

## BALANCE OF THE PROCEEDS OF THE
## 'LYELL GEOLOGICAL FUND.'

1876. Prof. John Morris.
1877. Mr. William Pengelly.
1878. Prof. Wilhelm Waagen.
1879. Prof. Henry A. Nicholson.
1879. Dr. Henry Woodward.
1880. Prof. F. A. von Quenstedt.
1881. Prof. Anton Fritsch.
1881. Mr. G. R. Vine.
1882. The Rev. Norman Glass.
1882. Prof. Charles Lapworth.
1883. Mr. P. H. Carpenter.
1883. M. Ed. Rigaux.
1884. Prof. Charles Lapworth.
1885. Mr. Alfred J. Jukes-Browne.
1886. Mr. David Mackintosh.
1887. The Rev. Osmond Fisher.
1888. Dr. Arthur H. Foord.
1888. Mr. Thomas Roberts.
1889. Dr. Louis Dollo.
1890. Mr. Charles Davies Sherborn.
1891. Dr. C. I. Forsyth Major.
1891. Mr. George W. Lamplugh.
1892. Prof. John Walter Gregory.
1892. Mr. Edwin A. Walford.
1893. Miss Catherine A. Raisin.
1893. Mr. Alfred N. Leeds.
1894. Mr. William Hill.

1895. Prof. Percy Fry Kendall.
1895. Mr. Benjamin Harrison.
1896. Dr. William F. Hume.
1896. Dr. Charles W. Andrews.
1897. Mr. W. J. Lewis Abbott.
1897. Mr. Joseph Lomas.
1898. Mr. William H. Shrubsole.
1898. Mr. Henry Woods.
1899. Mr. Frederick Chapman.
1899. Mr. John Ward.
1900. Miss Gertrude L. Elles.
1901. Dr. John William Evans.
1901. Mr. Alexander McHenry.
1902. Dr. Wheelton Hind.
1903. Mr. Sydney S. Buckman.
1903. Mr. George Edward Dibley.
1904. Dr. Charles Alfred Matley.
1904. Prof. Sidney Hugh Reynolds.
1905. Mr. E. A. Newell Arber.
1905. Mr. Walcot Gibson.
1906. Mr. William G. Fearnsides.
1906. Mr. Richard H. Solly.
1907. Mr. T. Crosbee Cantrill.
1907. Mr. Thomas Sheppard.
1908. Mr. H. J. Osborne White.
1908. Mr. Thomas Franklin Sibly.

# AWARDS OF THE BIGSBY MEDAL,

### FOUNDED BY THE LATE

### Dr. J. J. BIGSBY, F.R.S., F.G.S.

To be awarded biennially 'as an acknowledgment of eminent services in any department of Geology, irrespective of the receiver's country; but he must not be older than 45 years at his last birthday, thus probably not too old for further work, and not too young to have done much.'

1877. Prof. Othniel Charles Marsh.
1879. Prof. Edward Drinker Cope.
1881. Prof. Charles Barrois.
1883. Dr. Henry Hicks.
1885. Prof. Alphonse Renard.
1887. Prof. Charles Lapworth.
1889. Dr. J. J. Harris Teall.
1891. Dr. George Mercer Dawson.

1893. Prof. William Johnson Sollas.
1895. Mr. Charles D. Walcott.
1897. Mr. Clement Reid.
1899. Prof. T. W. E. David.
1901. Mr. George W. Lamplugh.
1903. Dr. Henry M. Ami.
1905. Prof. John Walter Gregory.
1907. Dr. Arthur W. Rogers.

# AWARDS OF THE PRESTWICH MEDAL,

### ESTABLISHED UNDER THE WILL OF THE LATE

### SIR JOSEPH PRESTWICH, F.R.S., F.G.S.

'To apply the accumulated annual proceeds ... at the end of every three years, in providing a Gold Medal of the value of Twenty Pounds, which, with the remainder of the proceeds, is to be awarded ... to the person or persons, either male or female, and either resident in England or abroad, who shall have done well for the advancement of the science of Geology; or, from time to time to accumulate the annual proceeds for a period not exceeding six years, and apply the said accumulated annual proceeds to some object of special research bearing on Stratigraphical or Physical Geology, to be carried out by one single individual or by a Committee; or, failing these objects, to accumulate the annual proceeds for either three or six years, and devote such proceeds to such special purposes as may be decided.'

1903. John Lubbock, Baron Avebury.
1906. Mr. William Whitaker.

## AWARDS OF THE PROCEEDS OF THE BARLOW-JAMESON FUND,

### ESTABLISHED UNDER THE WILL OF THE LATE

### DR. H. C. BARLOW, F.G.S.

'The perpetual interest to be applied every two or three years, as may be approved by the Council, to or for the advancement of Geological Science.'

1879. Purchase of Microscope.

1881. Purchase of Microscope-Lamps.

1882. Baron C. von Ettingshausen.

1884. Dr. James Croll.

1884. Prof. Leo Lesquereux.

1886. Dr. H. J. Johnston-Lavis.

1888. Museum.

1890. Mr. W. Jerome Harrison.

1892. Prof. Charles Mayer-Eymar.

1893. Purchase of Scientific Instruments for Capt. F. E. Younghusband.

1894. Dr. Charles Davison.

1896. Mr. Joseph Wright.

1896. Mr. John Storrie.

1898. Mr. Edward Greenly.

1900. Mr. George C. Crick.

1900. Dr. Theodore T. Groom.

1902. Mr. William M. Hutchings.

1904. Mr. Hugh J. Ll. Beadnell.

1906. Mr. Henry C. Beasley.

1908. Donation to secure the preservation of 'The Grey Wethers,' Marlborough Downs.

---

## AWARDS OF THE PROCEEDS

### OF THE

### 'DANIEL-PIDGEON FUND,'

### FOUNDED BY MRS. PIDGEON, IN ACCORDANCE WITH THE WILL OF THE LATE

### DANIEL PIDGEON, F.G.S.

'An annual grant derivable from the interest on the Fund, to be used at the discretion of the Council, in whatever way may in their opinion best promote Geological Original Research, their Grantees being in all cases not more than twenty-eight years of age.'

1903. Prof. Ernest Willington Skeats.

1904. Mr. Linsdall Richardson.

1905. Mr. Thomas Vipond Barker.

1906. Miss Helen Drew.

1907. Miss Ida L. Slater.

1908. Mr. James Archibald Douglas.

*Estimates for*

## INCOME EXPECTED.

| | £ | s. | d. | £ | s. | d. |
|---|---|---|---|---|---|---|
| Compositions ........................................ | | | | 140 | 0 | 0 |
| Due for Arrears of Admission-Fees .......... | 94 | 10 | 0 | | | |
| Admission-Fees, 1908 ...................... | 264 | 12 | 0 | | | |
| | | | | 359 | 2 | 0 |
| Arrears of Annual Contributions ............ | 140 | 0 | 0 | | | |
| Annual Contributions, 1908, from Resident and Non-Resident Fellows ..................... | 1780 | 0 | 0 | | | |
| Annual Contributions in advance ............ | 55 | 0 | 0 | | | |
| | | | | 1975 | 0 | 0 |
| Sale of the Quarterly Journal, including Longmans' Account ......................... | | ...... | | 160 | 0 | 0 |
| Sale of the 'History of the Geological Society'. | | ...... | | 30 | 0 | 0 |
| Sale of Transactions, General Index, Library-Catalogue, Museum-Catalogue, Hutton's 'Theory of the Earth' vol. iii, Hochstetter's 'New Zealand,' and List of Fellows ........ | | ...... | | 6 | 0 | 0 |
| Miscellaneous Receipts........................ | | ...... | | 8 | 0 | 0 |
| Interest on Deposit-Account ................ | | ...... | | 20 | 0 | 0 |
| Dividends on £2500 India 3 per cent. Stock .. | 75 | 0 | 0 | | | |
| Dividends on £300 London, Brighton, & South Coast Railway 5 per cent. Consolidated Preference-Stock ......................... | 15 | 0 | 0 | | | |
| Dividends on £2250 London & North-Western Railway 4 per cent. Preference-Stock ...... | 90 | 0 | 0 | | | |
| Dividends on £2800 London & South-Western Railway 4 per cent. Preference-Stock ...... | 112 | 0 | 0 | | | |
| Dividends on £2072 Midland Railway 2½ per cent. Perpetual Preference-Stock .......... | 51 | 16 | 0 | | | |
| Dividends on £267 6s. 7d. Natal 3 per cent. Stock. | 8 | 0 | 0 | | | |
| | | | | 351 | 16 | 0 |
| | | | | 3049 | 18 | 0 |
| Estimated excess of Expenditure over Income .......... | | | | 129 | 0 | 0 |
| | | | | £3178 | 18 | 0 |

*the Year 1908.*

## EXPENDITURE ESTIMATED.

|  | £ | s. | d. | £ | s. | d. |
|---|---|---|---|---|---|---|
| House-Expenditure: | | | | | | |
| Taxes ................................................... | | 15 | 0 | | | |
| Fire-Insurance ...................................... | 15 | 0 | 0 | | | |
| Electric Lighting and Maintenance ............ | 50 | 0 | 0 | | | |
| Gas ..................................................... | 18 | 0 | 0 | | | |
| Fuel .................................................... | 35 | 0 | 0 | | | |
| Furniture and Repairs............................. | 30 | 0 | 0 | | | |
| House-Repairs and Maintenance ............... | 45 | 0 | 0 | | | |
| Annual Cleaning .................................... | 15 | 0 | 0 | | | |
| Tea at Meetings .................................... | 20 | 0 | 0 | | | |
| Washing and Sundry Expenses ................. | 35 | 0 | 0 | | | |
| | | | | 263 | 15 | 0 |
| Salaries and Wages, etc.: | | | | | | |
| Assistant-Secretary ............................... | 350 | 0 | 0 | | | |
| „      half Premium Life-Insurance... | 10 | 15 | 0 | | | |
| Assistant-Librarian ................................ | 150 | 0 | 0 | | | |
| Assistant-Clerk..................................... | 150 | 0 | 0 | | | |
| Junior Assistant .................................... | 85 | 0 | 0 | | | |
| House-Porter and Upper Housemaid ......... | 95 | 0 | 0 | | | |
| Under Housemaid .................................. | 48 | 18 | 0 | | | |
| Charwoman and Occasional Assistance......... | 10 | 0 | 0 | | | |
| Accountants' Fee ................................... | 10 | 10 | 0 | | | |
| | | | | 910 | 3 | 0 |
| Office-Expenditure: | | | | | | |
| Stationery ............................................ | 35 | 0 | 0 | | | |
| Miscellaneous Printing, etc. ..................... | 50 | 0 | 0 | | | |
| Postages and Sundry Expenses ................. | 90 | 0 | 0 | | | |
| | | | | 175 | 0 | 0 |
| Library (Books and Binding)........................ | | | | 220 | 0 | 0 |
| Library-Catalogue: | | | | | | |
| Cards .................................................. | 15 | 0 | 0 | | | |
| Compilation ......................................... | 50 | 0 | 0 | | | |
| | | | | 65 | 0 | 0 |
| Publications: | | | | | | |
| Quarterly Journal, including Commission on | | | | | | |
| Sale, and Centenary Volume* ...............| 1100 | 0 | 0 | | | |
| Postage on Journal, Addressing, etc............ | 90 | 0 | 0 | | | |
| Record of Geological Literature ............... | 120 | 0 | 0 | | | |
| List of Fellows .................................... | 35 | 0 | 0 | | | |
| Abstracts, including Postage ..................... | 100 | 0 | 0 | | | |
| 'History of the Geological Society' (Reprint)*. | 100 | 0 | 0 | | | |
| | | | | 1545 | 0 | 0 |

\* These items are in the nature of Capital Expenditure,
    or are not likely to recur.

£3178  18  0

HORACE W. MONCKTON, *Treasurer.*

*January 24th, 1908.*

*Income and Expenditure during the*

RECEIPTS.

| | £ | s. | d. | £ | s. | d. |
|---|---|---|---|---|---|---|
| To Balance in the hands of the Bankers at January 1st, 1907 | 214 | 10 | 3 | | | |
| „ Balance in the hands of the Clerk at January 1st, 1907 | 1 | 11 | 4 | | | |
| | | | | 216 | 1 | 7 |
| „ Composition | | | | 35 | 0 | 0 |
| „ Admission-Fees: | | | | | | |
| Arrears | 100 | 16 | 0 | | | |
| Current | 352 | 16 | 0 | | | |
| | | | | 453 | 12 | 0 |
| „ Arrears of Annual Contributions | 109 | 4 | 0 | | | |
| „ Annual Contributions for 1907 :— | | | | | | |
| Resident Fellows | 1789 | 2 | 0 | | | |
| Non-Resident Fellows | 4 | 14 | 6 | | | |
| „ Annual Contributions in advance | 67 | 4 | 0 | | | |
| | | | | 1970 | 4 | 6 |
| „ Publications : | | | | | | |
| Sale of Quarterly Journal * : | | | | | | |
| „ Vols. i to lxii | 116 | 18 | 10 | | | |
| „ Vol. lxiii | 49 | 8 | 7 | | | |
| | | | | 166 | 7 | 5 |
| „ 'History of the Geological Society'. | | | | 70 | 13 | 0 |
| „ General Index (Quarterly Journal). | 1 | 2 | 6 | | | |
| „ Abstracts | | 2 | 6 | | | |
| „ Record of Geological Literature | 6 | 17 | 0 | | | |
| „ List of Fellows | | 12 | 0 | | | |
| „ Transactions | | 10 | 0 | | | |
| „ Hutton's 'Theory of the Earth,' vol. iii | | 11 | 3 | | | |
| „ Hochstetter's 'New Zealand' | | 4 | 6 | | | |
| „ Museum-Catalogue | | 2 | 9 | | | |
| „ Ormerod's Index | | 11 | 6 | | | |
| | | | | 10 | 14 | 0 |
| „ Miscellaneous Receipts | | | | 8 | 7 | 6 |
| „ Repayment of Income-Tax (1 year) | | | | 17 | 11 | 9 |
| „ Interest on Deposit-Account | | | | 23 | 1 | 2 |
| „ Murchison & Lyell Trust-Fund, repayment of balance of advance for Cost of Medals | | | | 11 | 2 | 0 |
| „ Dividends (less Income-Tax):— | | | | | | |
| £2500 India 3 per cent. Stock | 71 | 5 | 0 | | | |
| £300 London, Brighton, & South Coast Railway 5 per cent. Consolidated Preference-Stock | 14 | 5 | 0 | | | |
| £2250 London & North-Western Railway 4 per cent. Preference-Stock | 85 | 10 | 0 | | | |
| £2800 London & South-Western Railway 4 per cent. Preference-Stock | 106 | 8 | 0 | | | |
| £2072 Midland Railway 2½ per cent. Perpetual Preference-Stock | 49 | 4 | 2 | | | |
| £267 6s. 7d. Natal 3 per cent. Stock | 7 | 12 | 4 | | | |
| | | | | 334 | 4 | 6 |

*Year ended December 31st, 1907.*

### PAYMENTS.

| | £ | s. | d. | £ | s. | d. |
|---|---|---|---|---|---|---|
| By House-Expenditure: | | | | | | |
| Taxes | | 15 | 0 | | | |
| Fire and other Insurance | 16 | 1 | 6 | | | |
| Electric Lighting and Maintenance | 46 | 16 | 0 | | | |
| Gas | 19 | 2 | 1 | | | |
| Fuel | 39 | 11 | 6 | | | |
| Furniture and Repairs | 43 | 1 | 8 | | | |
| House-Repairs and Maintenance | 16 | 10 | 11 | | | |
| Annual Cleaning | 15 | 5 | 6 | | | |
| Tea at Meetings | 17 | 8 | 1 | | | |
| Washing and Sundry Expenses | 36 | 17 | 0 | | | |
| | | | | 251 | 9 | 3 |
| ,, Salaries and Wages : | | | | | | |
| Assistant-Secretary | 350 | 0 | 0 | | | |
| ,, half Premium Life-Insurance | 10 | 15 | 0 | | | |
| Assistant-Librarian | 150 | 0 | 0 | | | |
| Assistant-Clerk | 150 | 0 | 0 | | | |
| Junior Assistant | 82 | 3 | 0 | | | |
| House-Porter and Upper Housemaid | 103 | 15 | 6 | | | |
| Under Housemaid | 37 | 14 | 0 | | | |
| Charwoman and Occasional Assistance | 8 | 16 | 0 | | | |
| Accountants' Fee | 10 | 10 | 0 | | | |
| | | | | 903 | 13 | 6 |
| ,, Office-Expenditure : | | | | | | |
| Stationery | 26 | 14 | 10 | | | |
| Miscellaneous Printing | 92 | 6 | 3 | | | |
| Postages and Sundry Expenses | 77 | 15 | 0 | | | |
| | | | | 196 | 16 | 1 |
| ,, Library (Books and Binding) | | | | 154 | 5 | 8 |
| ,, Library-Catalogue : | | | | | | |
| Cards | 11 | 2 | 5 | | | |
| Compilation | 51 | 1 | 0 | | | |
| | | | | 62 | 3 | 5 |
| ,, Publications : | | | | | | |
| Quarterly Journal, Vols. i-lxii, Commission on Sale thereof | 10 | 5 | 8 | | | |
| Quarterly Journal, Vol. lxiii, Commission on Sale thereof | 3 | 1 | 6 | | | |
| Paper, Printing, and Illustrations | 737 | 10 | 8 | | | |
| Postage on Journal, Addressing, etc. | 94 | 5 | 3 | | | |
| Record of Geological Literature | 116 | 7 | 6 | | | |
| List of Fellows | 35 | 12 | 6 | | | |
| Abstracts, including Postage | 100 | 4 | 7 | | | |
| | | | | 1097 | 7 | 8 |
| 'History of the Geological Society' | | | | 311 | 8 | 5 |
| ,, Centenary Fund Expenses | 759 | 17 | 0 | | | |
| *Less* Hospitality Fund £412 19 0 | | | | | | |
| Other Receipts, as audited. 176 0 0 | | | | | | |
| | 588 | 19 | 0 | | | |
| | | | | 170 | 18 | 0 |
| ,, Balance in the hands of the Bankers at December 31st, 1907 | 155 | 4 | 4 | | | |
| ,, Balance in the hands of the Clerk at December 31st, 1907 | 13 | 13 | 1 | | | |
| | | | | 168 | 17 | 5 |

We have compared this Statement with
the Books and Accounts presented to us,
and find them to agree.

A. E. SALTER,  } *Auditors.*  £3316 19 5
R. H. TIDDEMAN,

HORACE W. MONCKTON, *Treasurer.*

## Statement of Trust-Funds : December 31st, 1907.

### 'WOLLASTON DONATION-FUND.' TRUST-ACCOUNT.

| RECEIPTS. | £ | s. | d. | PAYMENTS. | £ | s. | d. |
|---|---|---|---|---|---|---|---|
| To Balance at the Bankers' at January 1st, 1907 | 32 | 3 | 10 | By Cost of Medal | 10 | 10 | 0 |
| ,, Dividends (less Income-Tax) on the Fund invested in £1073 Hampshire County 3 per cent. Stock | 30 | 11 | 6 | ,, Award from the Balance of the Fund | 21 | 13 | 10 |
| ,, Repayment of Income-Tax (1 year) | 1 | 12 | 4 | ,, Balance at the Bankers' at December 31st, 1907 | 32 | 3 | 10 |
| | £64 | 7 | 8 | | £64 | 7 | 8 |

### 'MURCHISON GEOLOGICAL FUND.' TRUST-ACCOUNT.

| RECEIPTS. | £ | s. | d. | PAYMENTS. | £ | s. | d. |
|---|---|---|---|---|---|---|---|
| To Balance at the Bankers' at January 1st, 1907 | 21 | 0 | 2 | By Cost of Medals | 4 | 19 | 0 |
| ,, Dividends (less Income-Tax) on the Fund invested in £1334 London & North-Western Railway 3 per cent. Debenture-Stock | 38 | 0 | 4 | ,, Award to the Medallist | 10 | 10 | 0 |
| ,, Repayment of Income-Tax (1 year) | 2 | 0 | 0 | ,, Award from the Balance of the Fund | 28 | 13 | 4 |
| | | | | ,, Balance at the Bankers' at December 31st, 1907 | 16 | 18 | 2 |
| | £61 | 0 | 6 | | £61 | 0 | 6 |

### 'LYELL GEOLOGICAL FUND.' TRUST-ACCOUNT.

| RECEIPTS. | £ | s. | d. | PAYMENTS. | £ | s. | d. |
|---|---|---|---|---|---|---|---|
| To Balance at the Bankers' at January 1st, 1907 | 53 | 12 | 10 | By Cost of Medals | 6 | 3 | 0 |
| ,, Dividends (less Income-Tax) on the Fund invested in £2010 1s. 0d. Metropolitan 3½ per cent. Stock | 66 | 16 | 8 | ,, Award to the Medallist | 25 | 0 | 0 |
| ,, Repayment of Income-Tax (1 year) | 3 | 10 | 4 | ,, First Award from the Balance of the Fund | 22 | 3 | 0 |
| | | | | ,, Second Award from the Balance of the Fund | 22 | 3 | 0 |
| | | | | ,, Balance at the Bankers' at December 31st, 1907 | 48 | 10 | 10 |
| | £123 | 19 | 10 | | £123 | 19 | 10 |

### 'BARLOW-JAMESON FUND.' TRUST-ACCOUNT.

| RECEIPTS. | £ | s. | d. | PAYMENTS. | £ | s. | d. |
|---|---|---|---|---|---|---|---|
| To Balance at the Bankers' at January 1st, 1907 | 19 | 5 | 1 | By Grant (Preservation of 'The Grey Wethers') | 20 | 0 | 0 |
| ,, Dividends (less Income-Tax) on the Fund invested in £468 Great Northern Railway 3 per cent. Debenture-Stock | 13 | 6 | 10 | ,, Balance at the Bankers' at December 31st, 1907 | 13 | 5 | 11 |
| ,, Repayment of Income-Tax (1 year) | | 14 | 0 | | | | |
| | £33 | 5 | 11 | | £33 | 5 | 11 |

## 'DIGBY FUND.' TRUST-ACCOUNT.

| RECEIPTS. | £ | s. | d. | PAYMENTS. | £ | s. | d. |
|---|---|---|---|---|---|---|---|
| To Balance at the Bankers' at January 1st, 1907 ......... | 9 | 12 | 2 | By Medal ........................ | 12 | 12 | 0 |
| " Dividends (less Income-Tax) on the Fund invested in £210 Cardiff 3 per cent. Stock .............. | 5 | 19 | 8 | " Balance at the Bankers' at December 31st, 1907 ..... | 3 | 6 | 2 |
| " Repayment of Income-Tax (1 year) .............. | | 6 | 4 | | | | |
| | £15 | 18 | 2 | | £15 | 18 | 2 |

## 'GEOLOGICAL RELIEF-FUND.' TRUST-ACCOUNT.

| RECEIPTS. | £ | s. | d. | PAYMENTS. | £ | s. | d. |
|---|---|---|---|---|---|---|---|
| To Balance at the Bankers' at January 1st, 1907 ......... | 31 | 5 | 5 | By Grant ........................ | 2 | 2 | 0 |
| " Dividends (less Income-Tax) on the Fund invested in £139 3s. 7d. India 3 per cent. Stock .............. | 3 | 19 | 4 | " Balance at the Bankers' at December 31st, 1907 ..... | 33 | 6 | 11 |
| " Repayment of Income-Tax (1 year) .............. | | 4 | 2 | | | | |
| | £35 | 8 | 11 | | £35 | 8 | 11 |

## 'PRESTWICH TRUST-FUND.' TRUST-ACCOUNT.

| RECEIPTS. | £ | s. | d. | PAYMENTS. | £ | s. | d. |
|---|---|---|---|---|---|---|---|
| To Balance at the Bankers' at January 1st, 1907 ......... | 1 | 10 | 0 | By Balance at the Bankers' at December 31st, 1907 ..... | 22 | 9 | 9 |
| " Dividends (less Income-Tax) on the Fund invested in £700 India 3 per cent. Stock .............. | 19 | 19 | 0 | | | | |
| " Repayment of Income-Tax (1 year) .............. | 1 | 0 | 9 | | | | |
| | £22 | 9 | 9 | | £22 | 9 | 9 |

## 'DANIEL-PIDGEON FUND.' TRUST-ACCOUNT.

*Statement relating to the Society's Property :*
*December 31st, 1907.*

|  | £ | s. | d. | £ | s. | d. |
|---|---|---|---|---|---|---|
| Balance in the Bankers' hands, December 31st, 1907 : |  |  |  |  |  |  |
|     On Current Account ............................. | 155 | 4 | 4 |  |  |  |
| Balance in the Clerk's hands, December 31st, 1907 | 13 | 13 | 1 |  |  |  |
|  |  |  |  | 168 | 17 | 5 |
| Due from Messrs. Longmans & Co., on account of Quarterly Journal, Vol. LXIII, etc. ........ | ...... |  |  | 60 | 18 | 4 |
| Arrears of Admission-Fees ................... | 94 | 10 | 0 |  |  |  |
| Arrears of Annual Contributions .............. | 231 | 2 | 0 |  |  |  |
|  |  |  |  | 325 | 12 | 0 |
|  |  |  |  | £555 | 7 | 9 |

Funded Property, at cost price :—

|  | £ | s. | d. | £ | s. | d. |
|---|---|---|---|---|---|---|
| £2500 India 3 per cent. Stock ............ | 2623 | 19 | 0 |  |  |  |
| £300 London, Brighton, & South Coast Railway 5 per cent. Consolidated Preference-Stock .............................. | 502 | 15 | 3 |  |  |  |
| £2250 London & North-Western Railway 4 per cent. Preference-Stock ............ | 2898 | 10 | 6 |  |  |  |
| £2800 London & South-Western Railway 4 per cent. Preference-Stock ............ | 3607 | 7 | 6 |  |  |  |
| £2072 Midland Railway 2¼ per cent. Perpetual Preference-Stock ................ | 1850 | 19 | 6 |  |  |  |
| £267 6s. 7d. Natal 3 per cent. Stock........ | 250 | 0 | 0 |  |  |  |
|  |  |  |  | 11,733 | 11 | 9 |

[*N.B.—The above amount does not include the value of the Collections, Library,
Furniture, and Stock of unsold Publications. The value of the Funded Property
of the Society at the prices ruling at the close of business on December 31st, 1907,
amounted to £10,417 19s. 2d.*]

HORACE W. MONCKTON, *Treasurer.*

*January 24th, 1908.*

### AWARD OF THE WOLLASTON MEDAL.

In handing the Wollaston Medal, awarded to Prof. PAUL VON GROTH, F.M.G.S., to Mr. F. W. RUDLER, I.S.O., for transmission to the recipient, the PRESIDENT addressed him as follows :—

Mr. RUDLER,—

The Council of the Geological Society has this year assigned its highest distinction, the Wollaston Medal, to Prof. Paul von Groth in recognition of the value of his lifelong services in the investigation of 'the mineral structure of the Earth.' His original researches have placed him among the leaders of mineralogy and crystallography in our day; and his right to that eminent position has been greatly enhanced by the genius which he has shown in the teaching of his subject, by the organization of his laboratory for advanced training, by the admirable arrangement and execution of his text-books, and by the zeal and success with which for thirty years he has edited and published his now indispensable 'Zeitschrift für Krystallographie & Mineralogie.' His laboratory has become the Mecca of modern mineralogy, to which pilgrims repair from all parts of the world to learn the methods of the great Master at Munich. His remarkable personal charm has endeared him to all who have come into close contact with him, and who discover that he is at once one of the most retiring and yet most popular of scientific men.

It is to myself a peculiar pleasure that I should be privileged on the present occasion to transmit the award of the Council to so old a personal friend of my own. He will, I am sure, regard the Medal with special interest, since it bears the name and the effigy of one of the foremost of English mineralogists, whose reflecting goniometer was doubtless a familiar instrument in Prof. von Groth's hands from his student-days onwards. In asking you to receive it for him, I would wish you to convey with it an expression of the cordial wishes of the Society for his prolonged health and activity. We earnestly trust that he will not only be able to complete the gigantic task of his 'Chemische Krystallographie,' but continue for many years thereafter to reap the fruits of his labour by witnessing the quickened advance of the science to which he has so unremittingly devoted his strenuous life.

*d* 2

Mr. RUDLER, in reply, read the following message received from the recipient :—

Mr. PRESIDENT,—

I regret that official duties at Munich prevent me from coming to London to receive the Wollaston Medal, and from thanking in person the Council of the Geological Society for the great honour conferred upon me.

As my researches in Physical and Chemical Crystallography have not been very closely related to Geology, while my Mineralo-geological work on the mineral-deposits of the Alps, the rocks of the Vosges, etc., has been of itself too unimportant to have afforded a reason for the gift to me of the highest distinction that the Geological Society of London has to bestow, I am compelled to regard the award of the Medal as intended to be a recognition of my work, during many years, as a teacher of Mineralogy and Crystallography to pupils who were, many of them, Geological students.

I rejoice to be able to say that from no country have better pupils come to my laboratory and lectures than from England itself, and that it has been a great happiness to continue with such pupils the work which Prof. Miller founded at Cambridge with his introduction of Rational Indices, and which my highly-esteemed friend Prof. Maskelyne did so much to encourage at Oxford by his lectures on Crystalline Symmetry.

In this sense, as a fellow-worker in the scientific training of the junior mineralogists of England, I have pleasure in accepting, with the most hearty thanks, the distinction conferred upon me, and hope to be permitted to give like help to other pupils from the same country in the more immediate future.

---

## AWARD OF THE MURCHISON MEDAL.

The PRESIDENT then presented the Murchison Medal to Prof. ALBERT CHARLES SEWARD, F.R.S., addressing him in the following words :—

Professor SEWARD,—

The Murchison Medal is awarded by the Council to you as a mark of appreciation of the services you have rendered to geological science by the skill, zeal, and success with which you have for many years pursued the study of fossil plants.   Your researches have embraced a wide botanical range and an extended series of geological formations, while the materials on which you have worked have come to you from many different and distant regions of the globe.   Your studies of the Wealden flora have enabled you to present an ampler and more vivid picture of the vegetation of later Mesozoic time than was before obtainable.   Your discussions of the *Glossopteris*-flora and of the European and Eastern Mesozoic floras have been full of suggestion to geologists.   It is only by trained and persistent students who, like yourself, have an intimate knowledge of living forms, that the structure and genetic relations of the plants and animals of past time can be satisfactorily elucidated.   We wish you many long years of active life, and we confidently expect that, from the Chair of Botany in Cambridge, you will continue to advance the study of Palæobotany, and will in this way sustain and extend the reputation of the great Cambridge geological school.

Prof. SEWARD replied as follows:—

Mr. PRESIDENT,—

I desire to express my sincere thanks to the Council of the Society for selecting me as the recipient of the Murchison Medal: the news of the award came to me as one of the pleasantest surprises that I have ever had.   A student is not supposed to look forward to material rewards for what little he is able to contribute towards the advancement of Natural Knowledge; but, when a reward comes, it awakens feelings no less pleasurable than those of a school-boy receiving his first prize.   I little thought, Sir, when I first became acquainted with your name nearly thirty years ago, that I should ever have the pleasure and privilege of receiving a Medal from your hands.   As I have been for some years, officially at least, a botanist, the high compliment paid to me by the Society is the more appreciated.   This is, perhaps, one of the very few occasions when it is pardonable to speak of oneself.   The first stimulus I received which made me respond to the attraction of Geology, was supplied by some University Extension Lectures delivered by my oldest geological friend, Dr. Marr.   A few years later I began to read Botany at the suggestion of Prof. McKenny Hughes, a suggestion for which I have every reason to be grateful; but it was the fascination of Geology which caused me to diverge from the path originally marked out for me, and to give my allegiance to Natural Science.

On looking through the list of Murchison Medallists I was reminded that last year the award was made to Mr. Harker; though I have often regretted that Palæontology did not secure his affection, I am proud to appear next him in so honourable a list. In my under-graduate-days Harker was one of my best friends, whose generous help I am not likely to forget. I rejoice also to find myself in the company of Prof. Gœppert and Prof. Rœmer in the list of Medallists. It was once my privilege to spend some weeks in examining the classic collections of Gœppert in the University of Breslau, where the hospitality of the late Ferdinand Rœmer taught me that differences in age and nationality count for little among those whose lives are devoted to the common cause of Science. Prof. Geinitz, another Murchison medallist, received me in Dresden twenty years ago with a friendliness which made a lasting impression. The name of Prof. Newberry reminds me of another friendly senior, who once gave me more pleasure than he imagined by inviting me to luncheon at his London hotel.

To follow such men as I have named is not merely an honour, but a strong incentive to do my utmost to render myself less unworthy of being permanently associated with them in the records of the Society.

## AWARD OF THE LYELL MEDAL.

In handing the Lyell Medal, awarded to Mr. RICHARD DIXON OLDHAM, F.G.S., to Mr. G. W. LAMPLUGH, F.R.S., for transmission to the recipient, the PRESIDENT addressed him as follows :—

Mr. LAMPLUGH,—

In asking you to transmit to Mr. Oldham the Lyell Medal, which has been awarded to him, I would wish you to express to him the appreciation of the Council of the value of the work which he has done in the advancement of Geology. During his long connexion with the Geological Survey of India, he was able to add much to our knowledge of the geological structure of that great dependency. At the same time he was always alive to the bearing of his observations on the wider problems of our science. Besides his ordinary official duties, he from time to time has undertaken special subjects of enquiry. Of these, probably the most important was his careful investigation of the effects of the great Indian Earthquake of June 12th, 1897. Since he retired from his Indian appointment he has continued to take part in the discussion of seismic phenomena, and he has written some noteworthy papers dealing more particularly with the relations of the subject to the internal constitution of the globe. I greatly regret his absence to-day from illness.

It would have been to me no small satisfaction that it should have fallen to me to present this Medal, for one of the pleasant memories of my life is that I counted his father among my friends. As the worthy son of a distinguished sire, he has carried on the family-tradition. Will you tell him that the Society trusts that, as he is now once more resident in this country, we may often see him at our Meetings, and that for many years to come we may be favoured with communications from him on the geological questions in which we are all interested?

Mr. LAMPLUGH, in reply, said :—

Mr. PRESIDENT,—

In the unavoidable absence of Mr. Oldham, I will ask your permission to read the following letter, explaining the circumstances, which I received from him this morning :—

' If you are not, like me, laid up with a mild attack of the universal influenza, I should be very much obliged if you would represent me to-morrow, accept the Medal, and express on my behalf my gratitude for the favour which the Council has accorded me. The grant is the more gratifying, as, since I have been free to follow my own inclinations, these have led me to a branch of our science which had almost ceased to be regarded as Geology, but finds its proper place in the "Principles" of the founder of the Medal which I ask you to accept on my behalf.'

————

AWARD OF THE WOLLASTON DONATION-FUND.

In presenting the Balance of the Proceeds of the Wollaston Donation-Fund to Mr. HERBERT HENRY THOMAS, M.A., the PRESIDENT addressed him in the following words :—

Mr. THOMAS,—

The Balance of the Proceeds of the Wollaston Donation-Fund has been by the Council awarded to you, in recognition of the value of your investigations into the composition of sedimentary rocks and also of the work done by you in the Palæozoic series of South Wales. The Society hopes that you may be encouraged to continue your interesting enquiries into the derivation of the finer sediment in ancient stratified formations—a subject which has hitherto been comparatively little studied, but from the pursuit of which much light may be expected to be thrown on the geographical conditions of former geological periods.

### AWARD OF THE MURCHISON GEOLOGICAL FUND.

The PRESIDENT then presented the Balance of the Proceeds of the Murchison Geological Fund to Miss ETHEL GERTRUDE SKEAT, D.Sc., addressing her as follows:—

Miss SKEAT,—

The Council has this year awarded to you the Balance of the Proceeds of the Murchison Geological Fund as a mark of appreciation of your geological work, especially among the Glacial deposits of Denmark and the Lower Palæozoic rocks of Wales. It is with much gratification that we hail in you another woman who is worthily placed on the roll of those who have gained our awards. We trust that you may be able to devote many active and happy years to the further prosecution of the studies in which you have shown such conspicuous success.

### AWARDS FROM THE LYELL GEOLOGICAL FUND.

In presenting a moiety of the Balance of the Proceeds of the Lyell Geological Fund to Mr. HAROLD J. OSBORNE WHITE, F.G.S., the President addressed him in the following words:—

Mr. OSBORNE WHITE,—

A moiety of the Balance of the Proceeds of the Lyell Geological Fund has been awarded to you by the Council, in acknowledgment of the service which you have rendered to Geology by your researches among the Cretaceous and Pleistocene deposits of Berkshire and Oxfordshire. Your detailed investigation of the zones of the Upper

Chalk has brought to light some interesting indications of flexures and of a considerable erosion of the Chalk before the deposition of the Reading Beds; while your papers on the Plateau- and Valley-Gravels in the western part of the London Basin have important bearings on the history of the rivers of that region and on the origin of the present configuration of the ground. We hope that you may be encouraged to continue and extend these observations.

The PRESIDENT then handed the other moiety of the Balance of the Proceeds of the Lyell Geological Fund, awarded to Mr. THOMAS FRANKLIN SIBLY, B.Sc., to Prof. E. J. GARWOOD, M.A., for transmission to the recipient, addressing him as follows:—

Professor GARWOOD,—

A second moiety of the Balance of the Proceeds of the Lyell Geological Fund has been assigned to Mr. Sibly, on whose behalf I would ask you to receive it, as a mark of the Council's appreciation of the zeal and ability with which he has applied the method of zonal classification to the Carboniferous Limestone of various districts in England. There still remain many tracts of the British Isles in which that portion of the Palæozoic series has never yet been worked out in detail. We shall be glad if he will be encouraged to enter some of them, and thus to continue the work which he has already so successfully pursued.

# THE ANNIVERSARY ADDRESS OF THE PRESIDENT.

## Sir Archibald Geikie, K.C.B., D.C.L., LL.D., Sc.D., Sec.R.S.

The losses sustained by the Society this year through death have been heavy, alike as regards the number and the distinction of the deceased. We have to mourn the departure of two of our Foreign Members, one of our Foreign Correspondents, and upwards of thirty of our ordinary Fellows, including some who have done good service in the cause of Geology and in the furtherance of the work of the Society.

By the death of Marcel Bertrand the Society has lost one of its most eminent Foreign Members. His father, Joseph Bertrand, distinguished as a mathematician, was for many years the Perpetual Secretary of the Academy of Sciences of Paris, and enjoyed, besides, the rare distinction of being elected as one of the forty members of the French Academy. Our lamented colleague was born on February 2nd, 1847. Coming of such parentage, he naturally took to a scientific career. At the age of twenty he entered the École Polytechnique, and passed as Ingénieur Ordinaire des Mines in 1872. Five years later he was attached to the service of the Geological Survey of France; and in 1886, when thirty-nine years of age, he became Ingénieur-en-chef des Mines and Professor of Geology at the School of Mines in Paris, while still retaining his connection with the Survey.

His first official field-work was carried on in the Jura, where he spent eight strenuous years, entirely completing by himself four sheets of the detailed geological map of France and revising part of a fifth. The Jurassic rocks of the region which he surveyed had never before been closely studied. It was, therefore, his first task to master the true order of succession of the formations, and to apply to them the system of zonal classification which had been employed with so much success elsewhere. Starting from the work done by M. Choffat in Portugal, he traced the lithological and palæontological changes of the strata as they advance southwards, and he was able to note the passage of the northern into the Mediterranean Jurassic province. He showed that the reef-building corals of the period retired gradually from the Paris Basin to the Alpine sea, round which they built long chains of reefs.

It was in the course of these early years in the field that Bertrand was led into that special tectonic domain where he achieved his fame and did most signal service to the cause of geological science. The Jura Mountains had long been classic ground, on account of the striking examples which they present of simple anticlinal and synclinal folding. This structure is most conspicuously displayed in the higher or Swiss portion of the chain. But Bertrand found that, as the folded strata extend into French territory, their folds become complicated with faults. As he contemplated this marked difference of structure, which he was convinced must be a part of the general process of mountain-making, he asked himself whether the fold and the fault should be looked upon as features independent of each other, marking different movements and arising from distinct causes. The longer he pondered over this question, the more fundamental it became in his eyes. To quote his own words :—

'The idea of making a fault a subject of study and not an object to be merely determined has been the most important step in the course of my methods of observation. If I have obtained some new results it is to this that I owe it.'[1]

He not only recognized the normal relations between plication and fracture, but on the margin of the Jura chain, around Besançon and Salins, he discovered the existence of nearly horizontal faults whereby the older had been driven over the younger formations. These displacements were indeed of small magnitude, but it was the first time that they had been observed in France, and they must always possess an historic interest for the influence which they had in directing Bertrand along the path that led to his later generalizations.[2]

The next stage in the evolution of his ideas regarding the character and origin of mountain-structure was gained as the result of an attentive study of Prof. Heim's description of the Glarus, and a comparison of the published sections of that mountain with those which Prof. Gosselet and others had given of the Franco-Belgian coal-field. In 1884 he communicated a paper on this subject to the Geological Society of France, wherein he affirmed that, in place of Prof. Heim's ' double fold,' there stretches from

[1] 'Notice sur les Travaux Scientifiques de M. Marcel Bertrand' 1894, being a statement of his work prepared by himself for the information of the Academy of Sciences when he was a candidate for election into that body. In preparing the present Obituary Notice I am much indebted to this interesting autobiographical tract, a copy of which has been kindly lent to me by my friend M. Emmanuel de Margerie.

[2] His account of this discovery was published as far back as 1881, in the Bull. Soc. Géol. France, ser. 3, vol. x, p. 114.

the Glarus away to the far Alps of Savoy one great continuous overlapping sheet (nappe de recouvrement) of older rocks, which has been pushed, as an immense canopy, over the younger formations, and has since been so deeply worn away by denudation that in parts of its extent it has been reduced to mere scattered fragments.[1]

In the year 1884 Bertrand was selected as one of the French mission which, under the directorship of Fouqué, was sent to report on the great earthquake in Andalusia. Together with M. Kilian, he there studied the Secondary and Tertiary formations of the provinces of Granada and Malaga. While still engaged in the mapping of the French Jura, he had also assigned to him the survey of some parts of Provence, especially the districts of Toulon and Marseilles, and a portion of the districts represented on the Aix and Draguignan sheets of the detailed map. It had been generally taken for granted that this region of Southern France is one of comparatively simple geological structure. But Bertrand, whose eye was now trained to detect evidence of abnormal disturbance, soon discovered that Provence, despite its likeness to an ordinary plain, is in reality, as regards the disposition of its rocks, a portion of the Alpine Chain, and forms a connecting-link between the Alps and the Pyrenees. He found that its folds are horizontal (plis couchés), and that, although reduplicated upon themselves, the strata retain or have regained a horizontal position. In the formation of such plications, where the Trias, resting upon Cretaceous beds, had been shifted for a distance of more than 6 kilometres, horizontal displacements had played the chief part. In making known what he regarded as the true structure of the ground, he boldly asserted that how difficult soever it might be to conceive of vast flat folds of sedimentary strata moving bodily over younger formations, as if they had rolled onward like flows of basalt, yet theoretical difficulties could not stand against the evidence of observed facts.[2]

Besides these leading elements of structure, he detected in Provence other features which he eventually recognized on a more gigantic scale in the Alps. He was led also from these tectonic studies to return once more to the consideration of the Franco-Belgian Coal-field. He convinced himself that the structure of what has been called 'the great fault' of that region had been misinterpreted, that all the phenomena there displayed point to a

[1] Bull. Soc. Géol. France. ser. 3, vol. xii (1884) p. 318.
[2] *Ibid.* vol. xv (1887) p. 667.

vast movement (charriage) of the rocks, and that the Coal-Measures would be found to extend underneath for several kilometres to the south of their recognized limit.

It was to the study of the Chain of the French Alps that he devoted most of the last years of his field-work. The death of Charles Lory in 1890 had left a serious gap in the ranks of the French geologists who were charged with the difficult task of unravelling the complicated structure of these mountains. Marcel Bertrand was accordingly selected as the fittest man to be placed at the head of the band of observers who were to continue the work of the Grenoble professor. He threw himself with great ardour into this congenial task, and from time to time published interesting reports of his progress. His theoretical opinions regarding tectonic problems were always stated with great lucidity, and his conclusions were given with a definiteness which indicated the confidence that he felt in his methods of observation. It is indeed impossible not to admire the singular breadth of view with which he discussed these problems, even where one may be inclined to hesitate in accepting some of the explanations which he offered. There must, however, be general agreement with the justice of his affirmation that ' the part played by horizontal displacements is one of the fundamental features in the geology of the Alps.'

In the year 1890 the Academy of Sciences proposed as the subject of the Vaillant prize, ' A study of the compressions which have affected the terrestrial crust, and the rôle of horizontal displacements.' Only one memoir was presented. It bore the motto, ' E pur si muove,' and was found to have come from the accomplished Professor of Geology at the École des Mines. It was so excellent that the prize was unanimously awarded to him, and the essay would then have been printed in the ' Mémoires des Savants Étrangers,' had not the author requested and obtained permission to reclaim his manuscript, in order that he might revise and improve it before publication. But the revision was never made. Year after year passed, each too crowded with fresh original work to allow him leisure enough to give to his essay that completeness which he desired. Only a few unimportant alterations have been made by him on the manuscript. Since his death some of his friends and members of his family have resolved that this essay, of which the brilliance was recognized at the time of its reception, should at last be published in the precise state in which its author left it. As a picture of the condition of the whole problem of mountain-structure at the time at which it was written, it will possess great historical value, and its appearance in the 'Mémoires de l'Académie' will be welcomed by the geologists of every country. It is being edited by its author's devoted friend M. Emmanuel de Margerie, and Prof. Termier has contributed a genial and appreciative preface.

Geologists in this country will remember that in 1892 Bertrand paid a visit to the North-West of Scotland for the purpose of examining, under the guidance of the officers of the Geological Survey, the tectonic structure of that region, which afforded so many parallels to the phenomena observed by him in France, and that he published an interesting account of what he saw in Sutherland and Ross.[1] In the following year he prepared a paper on the connection of the Coal-Measure basins of the North of France and the North of England.[2] He was elected a Foreign Correspondent of this Society in 1893, and a Foreign Member in 1899.

The last years of this brilliant worker were years of sadness and gloom. The sudden tragic death of a daughter deeply affected him, and he gradually sank into a state of increasingly feeble health, from which at last death released him on February 13th, 1907.

Marcel Bertrand's gentle and kindly nature and the great charm of his manner made him a delightful companion and a valued friend. His enthusiasm for his subject and his remarkable power of lucid exposition gained for him the respect and regard of his colleagues on the Survey and of his devoted pupils in the School of Mines. His originality and breadth of view, his grasp of the problems with which he had to grapple, and the new light which he threw on the fascinating questions of mountain-building placed him in the forefront of the geologists of his day. We mourn in him the loss of one of the masters of tectonic geology, who has left the mark of his genius deeply impressed on the history of that department of our science.

Another distinguished geologist and devoted student of the Alps has been removed from our ranks by the death of JOHANN AUGUST EDMUND MOJSISOVICS, Edler von Mojsvàr. Belonging to an old Hungarian family, he was born on October 18th, 1839, in Vienna, where his father was an eminent medical man. After passing

---

[1] 'Les Montagnes de l'Écosse' Revue Générale des Sciences Pures & Appliquées, Dec. 15th, 1892; and Geol. Mag. 1893, p. 118.

[2] Ann. des Mines, ser. 9, vol. iii (1893) p. 5 & vol. v (1894) p. 569. An abridged reprint of this essay appeared in the Trans. Fed. Inst. Mining Engin. vol. v (1892–93) p. 106.

through the Schottengymnasium in the Austrian capital, he studied jurisprudence, and took the degree of Doctor of Laws at the University of Graz in 1864. But he was not destined to follow the legal profession. While a student he showed a keen of love of the mountains, and he succeeded in rousing a similar enthusiasm among a number of his associates at the University, with whom he formed a brotherhood of Alpine climbers. Out of this society, of which he was the inspiring soul, there eventually grew the ' Deutscher & Österreichischer Alpenverein,' which was founded in 1873. He took an active part in the earlier progress of this Verein, editing the publications and stimulating the work, so that he came to be acknowledged as one of the leading alpinists of his country. This close personal contact with the mountains ultimately shaped his whole future career. It led him to take note of the rock-features which appeal alike to the eye and to the imagination, and induced him to seek an explanation of the meaning of these features, and thus to add geological studies to his legal training. It may readily be believed that his bent towards our science could not but be encouraged and strengthened by the persuasive eloquence of Prof. Suess, under whom he studied and with whom he made excursions into the Eastern Alps. It is, at least, certain that geology proved to have more attraction for him than the law. Before long he had made such progress in geological pursuits that he was able to qualify himself for the position of Privatdozent in the Vienna University, which he obtained in 1871. In that capacity he continued for some years to lecture on stratigraphy, the geology of the Alps and the Austrian Empire, and conducted geological excursions.

Having now resolved to give up his life to the study of his beloved mountains, he offered himself, and on February 18th, 1865, was accepted, as a volunteer on the staff of the Austrian Geological Survey. He proved to be so efficient a worker that in the course of two or three years he was taken into the regular service of the establishment, and remained there for thirty-three years. By the end of December 1870 he had become a Bergrath and one of the chief geologists, and in the summer of 1879 he rose to the rank of Oberbergrath. In 1892, on the appointment of Stache to the directorate in succession to Stur, Mojsisovics was made Vice-Director. In 1900, the state of his health having compelled him to give up active field-work, he retired from official life, with the title of Hofrath in recognition of his long and distinguished services.

He had been elected a Foreign Correspondent of the Geological Society as far back as 1884, and became a Foreign Member in 1893.

In the spring of 1871 he happily married Miss Charlotte Vœlker, daughter of a banker in London, who survives him. His retirement from the Survey did not mean a cessation of work on his part. It probably lengthened his life by several years, and enabled him to continue the literary tasks on which he had been engaged, and to take the same effective part which he had done for many years in the earthquake-investigations of the Vienna Academy. In summer he escaped from the distractions of the Austrian capital to his country-home at Mallnitz, one of the loveliest spots on the southern slopes of the Hohe Tauern. While he was staying there in the autumn of last year, a cancerous growth developed itself in his tongue and throat. The malignant disease made rapid progress, in spite of all that medical skill and wifely devotion could do to arrest it. He bore with heroic patience the tortures which he suffered, until they were ended by his death on October 2nd, 1907.

The special department of geology to which Mojsisovics gave up his energies was the study of the Trias of the Eastern Alps. The Salzkammergut had claimed his early affection, and it was there that the idea shaped itself in his mind to devote himself to the investigation of its rocks. Perhaps the autumn-excursions in that delightful region which he took with Prof. Suess as far back as 1866 may have, in some measure, determined his resolution. Certainly it was the rocks of the Salzkammergut that first fascinated him, and to which he constantly returned all through his life. He there realised that, in spite of the admirable work already done by Franz von Hauer, Dionys Stur, Ferdinand von Richthofen, and others, a wide field remained to be explored which might demand the labour of a lifetime.

One of the most fortunate circumstances in the career of our lamented associate was that circumstances allowed him to concentrate his energies on this one subject and this one region. With the exception of the year 1879, when, with Tietze and Bittner, he was sent to make a geological reconnaissance of the provinces of Bosnia and Herzegovina, which Austria had shortly before undertaken to occupy, he continued to work at the Trias of the Eastern Alps. Again and again, year after year, he climbed the rugged slopes of these mountains, striving to make sure of the order and to trace the distribution and variations of the strata, and collecting

from them the abundant fossils with which he enriched the museum
in Vienna. He was at once a stratigrapher and a palæontologist.
His constant aim was not only to place the successive formations
in their true chronological order, to follow their lithological
changes from district to district, and to connect these details with the
ancient geographical conditions of the Alpine region, but above all
to ascertain the facies of each fossiliferous group of strata so as to
obtain a palæontological basis for their stratigraphical subdivisions,
and at the same time such evidence of the progressive evolution of
the organic forms as might be preserved among the deposits. Oppel
and Quenstedt had shown how a system of zonal classification by
means of fossils could be worked out among the Jurassic formations;
and Mojsisovics sought to apply a similar principle to the enormously
developed and abundantly fossiliferous Trias of the Salzkammergut
and surrounding districts. When he began this work no one had
divined that the structure of the Alps is so largely determined by
horizontal displacements as it has since been ascertained to be, that
in an apparently continuous and unbroken series of flat stratified
formations the sequence may be deceptive, and that the oldest parts
of the section may really lie at the top. It is possible that he may
here and there have been misled by this delusive structure. We
know that at various times he changed his views as to the true
stratigraphical position of some members of the Trias.

Mojsisovics was the author of many papers on his favourite
subject, the larger portion of which appeared in the various publications of the Austrian Geological Survey. They began in 1862
with a contribution on the age of the Hierlatz-Schichten, and hardly
a year elapsed from that time up to the end of his life without
some contributions from his pen. In these numerous writings
the story of his progress in the exploration and description of the
Alpine Trias is revealed. But probably his most generally appreciated and best-known memoir is that which he published in 1879 as
an independent work, with the title of ' Die Dolomitriffe von Südtirol
& Venetien.' This volume, with its large geological map and its
discussion of the geological and biological problems of the Alpine
Trias, marks a notable epoch in the literature of Alpine geology,
and has had much influence on the subsequent progress of the
subject of which it treats.

It is probable, however, that our departed friend will take
higher rank as a palæontologist than as a stratigraphical geologist.
Here again he concentrated his efforts on one limited domain, of

which he made himself the acknowledged master. The remarkable and abundant assemblage of cephalopods in the Trias of the Eastern Alps furnished him with an attractive and ample field for the exercise of his singularly acute eye for delicacies of form and structure. His researches among these organisms brought him Triassic material from all quarters for comparison and determination. Thus from the Geological Survey of India he received the large assemblage of cephalopods collected from the Upper Triassic groups of the Himalayas, which he named and described. From the Arctic Regions, from Spain and the Mediterranean basin, from Astrakhan, from Japan, from New Caledonia, and other regions, Triassic cephalopods found their way to him, and enabled him to form those suggestive pictures which he presented of the distribution of land and sea and the zoological provinces of Triassic time over the globe.

Mojsisovics took an active interest in earthquake-research, and for many years was the leading member of the Seismological Commission of the Vienna Academy, by which a network of stations was planted over Austria for the purpose of registering earthquake-disturbances. He was a frequent attendant at the meetings of the International Geological Congress, where he was welcomed by geologists from all regions of the globe, and where his assistance was always readily given towards the preparation of the great International Geological Map of Europe. His helpfulness to science will long outlive him, for he has by his will left to the Vienna Academy the greater part of his estate of more than a million of crowns, to be applied, after the decease of his widow, for the furtherance of scientific studies.[1]

Dr. JOHANN FRIEDRICH CARL KLEIN had for the last forty years been an accomplished and constant contributor to the literature of descriptive mineralogy. He had also studied the crystallography of various artificial compounds. His 'Mineralogische Mittheilungen' have long been a conspicuous feature in the 'Neues Jahrbuch.' His eminence in his own subject was recognized by his being appointed Professor of Mineralogy in the University of Berlin, and by his being

[1] In preparing this sketch of my lamented friend I have been much indebted to two necrologies of him—one by Prof. Diener of the Vienna University ('Beiträge zur Paläontologie & Geologie Österreich-Ungarns & des Orients' vol. xx, 1907, p. 272), and one by Dr. Tietze, Director of the K.-k. Geologische Reichsanstalt (Verhandl. Geol. Reichsanst. 1907, No. 14).

created a Geheimer Bergrath. He was elected a Foreign Correspondent of this Society in 1903.

In Sir RICHARD STRACHEY, G.C.S.I., who was born in 1817, the
Society has lost almost its oldest and certainly one of its most
distinguished Fellows. His connection with geology dates back to
a time before most of us were born, and he has been a Fellow of
the Society since 1851. He belonged to a family which for some
generations has been closely associated with administrative work
in India, and it was there that he also laid the foundations of the
great scientific reputation which he ultimately attained. Trained
as a military engineer, he in 1836 entered the Bombay Engineers
in the Service of the East India Company, and was soon engaged
in the construction of irrigation-canals. These peaceful operations,
however, were occasionally interrupted by outbreaks of war, and
the engineer-officers were called off into active service against the
insurgent tribes. In this way Strachey took part in the first Sikh
war, had his horse shot under him at the battle of Aliwal, and was
present at the action of Sobraon. Promoted to a brevet-majority
for his services in the field, he returned to irrigation and other
engineering works. Eventually, however, he was compelled by
frequent attacks of fever to betake himself to the hill-station of
Naini Tal, where he had opportunities of devoting himself to
scientific investigation, especially in regard to botany, geology, and
physical geography. It was during this time that he made his
expeditions across the passes into Tibet, and ascertained the existence of the Kumaon glaciers. He then likewise made important
discoveries in regard to the presence of Palæozoic, Mesozoic, and
Kainozoic formations along the line of these passes. His observations were communicated to this Society in 1851, in a paper on the
'Geology of Part of the Himalaya Mountains & Tibet,'[1] with a
sketch-map and sections of the country that he had traversed.
Three years later he sent in a paper on the 'Physical Geology
of the Himalaya,' of which an abstract was published in the tenth
volume of the 'Quarterly Journal' (1854) p. 249.

These scientific expeditions restored his health and strength, so
that he was able to resume for a short time irrigation-work in
Bundelkhund. But he was soon called to enter on the administrative duties which proved to be the main feature of his career and to
become of such lasting benefit to India. His first appointment was

---

[1] Quart. Journ. Geol. Soc. vol. vii, p. 292.

that of the Under-Secretaryship to Government in the Public Works Department, from which he was transferred in 1857 to be Secretary to Sir John Peter Grant in the Government of the Central Provinces. He afterwards became Consulting Engineer for Railways, and acted as Secretary of Public Works in the North-West Provinces. In 1866 he was made Inspector-General of Irrigation, but in three years thereafter he returned to his former office of Secretary for Public Works. In this commanding position he was enabled greatly to further progress in India, not only by fostering the construction of irrigation-works and of railways, but in influencing the general administration of the country. He retired from India in 1871, and received the thanks of the Indian Government for his valuable services.

But, though he returned to England, he continued for many years to take an active share in the administration of our Indian Empire. He was appointed a member of the Council of India, and in that capacity was able to bring his ripe experience and wide knowledge of Indian conditions to the assistance of his colleagues. In 1877 he was sent once more to India with reference to arrangements for the purchase of the East India Railway, and he was then put at the head of the first Famine Commission, and for a time acted as Finance Minister. When he came back to this country in 1879 he was reappointed to the Council of India, and held the position for ten years, when he resigned it in order to accept the Chairmanship of the East India Railway. At the head of this important organization he had the opportunity of displaying his remarkable powers of administration and his engineering skill. Under his chairmanship the railway was largely increased in mileage and became the most prosperous trunk-line in the world. He continued to hold this office, combined with the Chairmanship of the Bengal-Assam Railway, until the beginning of last year, when his increasing deafness caused him to resign these appointments.

In the midst of all this official and professional work General Strachey continued to find time for scientific pursuits. It was to meteorology that he more especially devoted himself in his later years. While in India he had recognized the great practical value of meteorological investigation in regard to prognostications of drought and prospective famine. But he saw that this investigation must be based on strictly scientific lines, and on these lines he laid the foundations of the meteorology of India. He was thus easily led to interest himself in the prosecution of meteorological enquiries in this country when he once more became resident here, and it was a fitting recognition of his eminence in this branch of science that in 1883 he was appointed Chairman of the Meteorological Council, an office which he continued to hold up to the reorganization of the institution in 1905. He served repeatedly on the Council of the Royal Society, and was selected as a member of most of its Committees that deal with physical science in any form.

Sir Richard married in 1859 a Highland lady, daughter of his old chief Sir John Peter Grant, and had five sons and five daughters. Advancing years had latterly confined him for the most part to his home in Hampstead, where he died on the morning of the 12th of February, 1908, in the 91st year of his age.

Sir JAMES HECTOR, son of Alexander Hector, Writer to the Signet, was born in Edinburgh in 1834. He studied medicine at the Edinburgh University, and took the degree of M.D. in 1856. Through the teaching of Edward Forbes, his interest had been aroused in subjects of natural history, and especially in geology; and in 1857 he was chosen, through the influence of Sir Roderick Murchison, as surgeon, geologist, and naturalist to accompany the Government Exploring Expedition, under Captain John Palliser, to parts of British North America, from Lakes Superior and Winnipeg to Vancouver Island. On that journey he made important ethnological and geographical observations, discovered the pass by which the Canadian Pacific Railway now crosses the Rocky Mountains, and afterwards brought before this Society an important paper on the geology of the region he had examined. In 1861, by Murchison's recommendation, he was appointed geologist to the Provincial Government of Otago, New Zealand, and thenceforth devoted his energies to that colony. He became Director of the Geological Survey of New Zealand in 1865, and held the post until 1903. Subsequently he was appointed Director also of the New Zealand Institute and of the Colonial Museum at Wellington; and at the time of his death he was Chancellor of the New Zealand University. He was elected a Fellow of the Royal Society in 1866, and was created K.C.M.G. in 1887. As a geologist, his principal works include Reports on the Coal-Deposits, on the Geology of Otago and other parts of New Zealand, and a geological sketch-map of the Islands, accompanied in 1886 by 'Outlines of New Zealand Geology.' The volcanic phenomena and thermal springs, the fossil birds and reptiles, the recent zoology and botany, and the meteorology of New Zealand likewise engaged his attention. He was awarded the Lyell Medal by the Council of the Geological

Society in 1877, of which Society he had been elected a Fellow in the year 1861.  His death took place in November 1907.

ARTHUR BEAVOR WYNNE was born in October 1835.  In his early years he was for a time Assistant in the General Valuation Office of Ireland under Sir Richard Griffith, but in the spring of 1855 he received from the Director of the Geological Survey, Sir Henry De la Beche, a nomination as Assistant Geologist on the Irish Geological Survey.  In conjunction with Jukes, Du Noyer, and Kinahan he mapped large tracts of Counties Tipperary, Waterford, and Cork. In 1862, two years after he had been elected into this Society, he was appointed to the Indian Geological Survey, then in charge of Dr. Thomas Oldham, and he remained in that service for twenty-one years.  In his Indian career he was first employed in the Bombay Presidency, and published two memoirs on the geology of Bombay Island.  He was next transferred to Kutch, on the geology of which he published a memoir.  Thereafter he moved into the Punjab, and for the rest of his service was engaged in the elucidation of the geology of the Salt Range.  His three memoirs, supplemented by Prof. Waagen's descriptions of the fossils collected during the progress of the Survey, remain the standard work on the geology of that interesting and complicated ground.  At various times during his connection with the Indian Survey he was obliged, on account of bad health, to take prolonged periods of furlough.  At last, in April 1883, he found it necessary to resign his appointment.  Having settled in Ireland, he was once more appointed on the staff of the Irish Geological Survey, as resident officer in Dublin, charged with the general conduct of the office and official correspondence.  In consequence of a reorganization of this Survey in 1890, he was retired from the service. After that time he resided chiefly in Switzerland.  In 1889 he became President of the Royal Geological Society of Ireland, and filled this position during the last session of the existence of that Society.  He died in December 1906.  Mr. Wynne was a talented artist.  He contributed to the Survey Memoirs excellent sketches illustrative of the geology and scenery of various parts of Ireland. He exhibited at the Royal Hibernian Academy and elsewhere his charming water-colour sketches of scenery, which were always popular.[1]

[1] For this obituary, notes have been supplied by Mr. H. B. Woodward and Mr. T. H. D. La Touche.

By the death of CARL LUDOLF GRIESBACH another former member of the Indian Geological Survey has been removed from our membership. He came of an old Hanoverian family. His grandfather settled in England in the reign of George III., and his father remained a British subject. He himself was born in Vienna on December 11th, 1847, and was educated at the University there. Having shown an aptitude for geological pursuits, he for a time obtained employment on the Austrian Geological Survey. In 1869–70 he was engaged on a German scientific expedition to Portuguese East Africa. Before leaving that region he had collected materials for an account of the geology of Natal, which was read before this Society in December 1870. Therein he published (1871)[1] a geological map of the Colony, together with figures and descriptions of some new mollusca from the Izinhluzabalungu deposits of Cretaceous age. In 1878 he was appointed an Assistant Superintendent on the Geological Survey of India; he became Director in 1894, and retired in 1903. During his service in India he was employed in 1886 on the Afghan Boundary Commission, and was created a Companion of the Order of the Indian Empire in recognition of his services. His most important work was his ' Memoir on the Geology of the Central Himalayas,' published by the Indian Geological Survey in 1891. He was elected a Fellow of this Society in 1874.[2]

THEODORE W. H. HUGHES, a third retired member of the Indian Geological Survey, has also been removed from our midst. He was educated at the Royal School of Mines (1859–62), of which he became an Associate. Joining the Geological Survey of India in 1862, at the age of 19, he was first employed for six years in surveying the smaller coal-fields of Bengal and Chota Nagpur; and he prepared memoirs on a number of them, so that he became a recognized authority on the Gondwana coal-bearing rocks of India. During the next ten years he was employed in enquiries in regard to coal and iron in various parts of the country. It was as the result of his investigations that an extensive colliery in South Rewah was discovered and opened up. So valuable had his experience become in reference to mineral fields that his services were

[1] Quart. Journ. Geol. Soc. vol. xvii, p. 53.
[2] A list of his papers was published in Geol. Mag. 1903, p. 288; see also *ibid.* 1907, p. 240.

lent for the purpose of exploring the mineral resources of the Nizam's territories and the tin-bearing deposits of Burma. In the course of his scientific explorations he had always been a keen sportsman, and is said to have shot more than a hundred tigers during his Indian career. But at the beginning of 1893 he met with a shooting accident, receiving a charge of shot in the face, by which he lost the sight of both eyes. He was consequently obliged to retire from the public service in October 1894, to the great regret of his colleagues. He had contributed in his time twenty-six papers to the Records and nine Memoirs to the publications of the Indian Survey. He became a Fellow of this Society in 1865.[1]

The Rev. RICHARD BARON, F.L.S., born at Kendal in 1847, spent most of his life in the service of the London Missionary Society. From 1872 onward till last year he was engaged at Antananarivo in Madagascar. In the intervals of his missionary labours he found time for the indulgence of his tastes as an enthusiastic naturalist, especially in the departments of botany and geology. The results of his geological observations were communicated to this Society in 1889 in a paper entitled 'Notes on the Geology of Madagascar,' accompanied by a geological map of the northern part of the island. The fossils he had collected, described and figured by Mr. R. Bullen Newton, with aid from Prof. T. R. Jones and others, consisted of Eocene, Cretaceous, and Jurassic invertebrata, 'forming nearly the first series of Malagasy fossils that have ever reached this country.' Dr. F. H. Hatch discussed the older crystalline and volcanic rocks. A further communication from Mr. Baron was brought before us in November 1894, together with an additional series of fossils, which were again described by Mr. R. B. Newton, who took the opportunity to append a list of all the recognized fossils from Madagascar. Mr. Baron was elected into this Society in 1889; and three years later, in acknowledgment of his geological work, which had been carried on amid many discouragements, the Council awarded to him the proceeds of the Murchison Geological Fund. He died at Morecambe, while on a visit to this country, on December 12th, 1907.

Dr. BERNARD J. HARRINGTON, who died on November 29th, 1907, was born in Canada on August 5th, 1848, and was educated at

[1] From notes supplied by Mr. T. H. D. La Touche.

McGill University, Montreal, where he graduated B.A. with first-class honours in Natural Science and gained the Logan gold medal. He afterwards attended Yale College and took the degree of Ph.D. with honours. In 1871 he was appointed Lecturer on Chemistry at McGill University. In the following year he succeeded T. Sterry Hunt as chemist and mineralogist to the Geological Survey of Canada and retained the appointment until 1878, when he decided to give his whole attention to the teaching work at the McGill University. There he became Professor, not only of Chemistry but also of Mining, and lectured on mineralogy and metallurgy. Marrying the eldest daughter of Sir William Dawson, the Principal of the University, he was in close touch with all the geological activity of the Dominion. He wrote numerous reports and papers on the rocks and minerals of Canada, giving analyses of coals, iron-ores, and other mineral substances. He was author also of the ' Life of Sir William E. Logan,' published in 1883. In the course of his career he was President of the Natural History Society of Montreal, of the Chemical and Physical Section of the Royal Society of Canada, and Vice-President of the Chemical Section of the British Association during the meeting held at Toronto. He was elected into our Society in 1883.

Dr. EDWARD JOHN ROUTH, F.R.S., who was born at Quebec, in Canada, on January 20th, 1831, became distinguished as a mathe-matician and physicist, and also as the most famous of Cambridge tutors. After studying at University College School under De Morgan he entered Peterhouse, Cambridge, in 1851, continuing his studies under Todhunter and afterwards under William Hopkins, a former President of this Society. In 1854 he graduated as Senior Wrangler, and was elected a Fellow of Peterhouse. He then took up the profession of teaching or ' coaching,' and exercised it with unprecedented success. During a period of thirty-one years, from 1857 to 1888, he helped nearly seven hundred pupils through the Mathematical Tripos, five hundred of them becoming Wranglers and twenty-seven Senior Wranglers. He published many papers on mathematical subjects, and likewise treatises on statics and dynamics. He was elected a Fellow of the Geological Society in 1864. He died at Cambridge on June 7th, 1907.

By the death of MARK STIRRUP the geological circle of Manchester has lost one of its most active and enthusiastic members. From the cotton-trade in which he had been engaged in Manchester he retired some thirty years ago, and he devoted himself thereafter to the pursuit of science. For over forty years he took a keen interest in all the scientific societies centred in that city. He became a Fellow of our Society in 1876. Joining the Manchester Geological Society in 1880, he held the office of its Honorary Secretary for about ten years, and in 1896–97 was elected its President. In recognition of his services he was in 1904 made an Honorary Member. He contributed many papers to that Society's Trans-actions, amongst which may be mentioned one on the Glacial Geology of Llandudno (1883). He likewise took an active part in the proceedings of the Manchester Field-Naturalists' & Archæo-logical Society and the Literary & Philosophical Society. He identified himself with every fresh development of geological science, more particularly taking interest in the application of the microscope to geology and biology. He became a Member of the British Association in 1867, and was a regular attendant at its meetings. As a member of the Association Française pour l'Avance-ment des Sciences, his fluency in the French language made him an effective representative of his own country. In the pursuit of his scientific enquiries he travelled much on the Continent, more particularly in Italy, where he was generally taken for a French-man. He lived out his life to the end, dying on June 10th, 1907, in the 76th year of his age. He has left the whole of his property to the University of Manchester, for the advancement of scientific knowledge in his own city.[1]

WENTWORTH BLACKETT BEAUMONT, BARON ALLENDALE, of Allendale and Hexham, the son of Thomas Wentworth Beaumont, was born on April 11th, 1829, and was educated at Harrow and Trinity College, Cambridge. He succeeded to extensive lead-mines in North-umberland and Durham on the death of his father in 1848. He became a Fellow of our Society in 1851. He was M.P. for South Northumberland from 1852 to 1885, and for the Tyneside division of the county from 1886 to 1892. He was raised to the peerage in 1906. His famous lead-mines known as the 'W. B. Lead-mines,' from the initials of William Blackett, a former owner, yielded metal of high quality, but were considered in 1845 to be nearly exhausted. At that date he appointed as chief agent Thomas Sopwith, who, in

[1] This notice has been supplied by Mr. B. Hobson.

that capacity, resided for twelve years at Allenheads, and introduced great improvements both in Allendale and Weardale, which he was enabled to do through the enlightened policy of the owner of the mines, who was ever anxious to promote the education, recreation, and general welfare of the mine-workers.[1]

JOHN FRANCIS WALKER was born at York on November 25th, 1839. He began the study of geology and chemistry at the age of 18, when he went to the Royal Agricultural College at Cirencester, whence in 1863 he proceeded with an open scholarship in Natural Science to Sidney Sussex College, Cambridge. Three years later he was bracketed first in the Natural Science Tripos, and took his degree in the following year. It was in the same year (1867) that he was elected into the Geological Society. For a time he continued in residence at Cambridge, superintending the laboratory-teaching of his college, until he went to Germany for the purpose of enlarging his chemical training. Though he qualified as a barrister he never went into the actual practice of the law. His tastes were now so thoroughly linked with scientific studies, that in 1878 he returned to Cambridge and remained as Natural Science Lecturer there until 1882. After his marriage and a second sojourn in Germany at the University of Bonn, he returned to his native city, where he spent the rest of his life.

During his second residence at Cambridge, though he devoted himself mainly to the teaching of chemistry, his great delight was to gather the geological students round him, to aid them in their collections with encouragement and gifts, to help them with advice and stimulus, and to extend to them the privilege of his friendship. Most of the geological students of that date at the University owe him a debt which, though difficult to express in words, will always keep his memory green among them.

His earliest geological efforts were given to the investigation of the fauna of the Lower Cretaceous phosphatic deposits of Cambridge-shire and Bedfordshire, and more particularly to the brachiopoda. From these days (1866–1868) onward his chief occupation was the collecting of Mesozoic brachiopoda from all parts of the world, for purposes of comparison and study. He thus became one of the most accomplished palæontologists in that department of the science. He published little, but his rich collections and his ample store of knowledge were always at the service of other workers. These

[1] This notice has been supplied by Mr. H. B. Woodward.

collections of brachiopoda, wherein all the specimens had been laboriously cleaned, measured, and sorted into their proper specific relations, have most generously been presented by his executors to the Natural History Museum, South Kensington.    Mr. Walker became a Fellow of Sidney Sussex College in 1889, but having ample means of his own he would not accept the emoluments attached to the Fellowship.    He married in 1882 Miss Alice Cracknell, of Knowle House, Ealing.    He was an admirable example of the cultured, leisured, non-professional man of science, so much more frequently met with in this country than anywhere else, who has time and means to devote to the subject which he loves, with no ambition to shine before the world, but ever ready to place himself at the service of those who share his tastes and his enthusiasm. He died after a short illness on May 23rd, 1907.[1]

ROBERT LAW, of Fenny Royd Hall, Hipperholme, near Halifax, who became a Fellow of this Society in 1886, was an enthusiastic worker on the geology and archæology of the borders of Yorkshire and Lancashire.    Born at Walsden, north of Rochdale, on June 21st, 1840, he entered business at an early age in a large cotton-mill in Lancashire, and was enabled to retire about 18 years ago.    When he was a lad, the rocks and fossils of the country around his home attracted his attention, and he pursued the study with such avidity that he was able in due course to act as geological teacher under the Science & Art Department, in many technical schools in the district.    By his lectures and excursions he stirred up much local interest.    A frequent attendant at meetings of the British Association, he occasionally communicated to that body, as well as to the Geological Societies of Manchester and Yorkshire, the results of his researches.    Among his papers may be mentioned those written conjointly with James Horsfall, on the discovery of fossils in a basement Carboniferous conglomerate at Moughton Fell, near Settle; and on the occurrence of tiny flint-implements near Rochdale and Todmorden.    Mr. Law died on December 29th, 1907.

EDWARD POWER, who was elected a Fellow of this Society in 1892, was much interested in the progress of geology, and may be looked upon as a patron of the science.    He purchased the geological collection of the late W. C. Lucy, of Gloucester, and presented it to the Natural History Museum at South Kensington.

[1] For the details of this notice I am indebted to Mr. G. W. Lamplugh; the second paragraph has been furnished by Prof. W. W. Watts.

Percy Leonard Addison, Assoc.M.Inst.C.E., was born at
Glasgow on December 25th, 1855, and died at Bigrigg, Cumberland,
on November 14th, 1906.   He was Assistant Resident Engineer on
the Lancashire and Yorkshire Railway from 1874 to 1878, and
subsequently Assistant Engineer on the Eastern Bengal Railway.
From 1883 to 1891 he superintended the mines of Messrs. D. &
J. Ainsworth, at Cleator in Cumberland.   He became a Fellow of
this Society in 1888, and in 1890 contributed a description of the
Cleator Iron Company's barytes and umber-mines and refining-
mills to the Proceedings of the Institution of Civil Engineers.

## THE PUBLISHED WORK OF THE GEOLOGICAL SOCIETY OF LONDON DURING THE FIRST CENTURY OF THE SOCIETY'S EXISTENCE.

In the Address which I had the honour of presenting at the
Centenary Celebration of the Society last September, I gave a
sketch of the state of geological science at the end of the eighteenth
and the beginning of the nineteenth century.   I then endeavoured
to show amidst what diverse currents of theoretical opinion,
leading to prolonged and acrimonious controversy, the Geological
Society took its rise.   I now propose to resume the continuation of
this subject and to trace, as far as may be possible within the
limits of an Anniversary Discourse, the main features of the work
done by this Society, from which such influence has sprung as,
during the first hundred years of its existence, the Society may
have been able to exert upon the progress of our science.   Obviously
by far the largest share of this influence must be ascribed, rather
to the independent labours of the more active and eminent Fellows
of the Society than to any corporate action of the Society itself.
When we look back upon the long roll of our membership, with its
crowded procession of illustrious names, we must admit that the
renown which these names have won in the literature of science
has in large measure arisen from writings that were neither
communicated to nor published by the Society.   Though such men
as Macculloch and Buckland, Sedgwick and Murchison, Lyell and
De la Beche, Darwin and Owen, were loyal and helpful members of
our association, their fame rests mainly on what they gave to the
world in other publications than ours.   Nevertheless, the well-
known connection of such men with the Geological Society was
unquestionably at the time a source of strength to our body, and

their renown may be considered as still forming part of the distinction which in the course of years the Society has gained. Hence, in trying to appraise the influence of the Society on the early development and progress of geology, we ought not to gauge it solely by the bulk and quality of the publications which the Society itself has issued. We should also take into account the prestige which the Society acquired, from having among its Presidents and other office-bearers and among its unofficial members men who had gained world-wide celebrity from the works which they had published elsewhere.

Into this wide field of independent publication, however, I do not mean to enter. I wish to confine my remarks to a rapid review of the more salient features of the general mass of contributions to geology which have appeared in the Society's own publications during the century of which we have lately celebrated the close. Obviously such a review will not supply a complete picture of the contemporaneous progress of the science even in this country, but it will at least include an indication of not a few of the more marked phases and steps in that progress.

Born at a time of keen conflict between two rival schools of thought, the Geological Society could hardly fail to be affected by the controversy that was then being waged outside its walls, both in this country and on the Continent. Our founders, indeed, started with the laudable desire to collect and examine the facts of Nature, rather than to discuss any theoretical explanations of them. As Lyell has recorded,

'The reaction provoked by the intemperance of the conflicting parties produced a tendency to extreme caution. Speculative views were discountenanced, and through fear of exposing themselves to the suspicion of a bias towards the dogmas of a party, some geologists became anxious to entertain no opinion whatever on the causes of the phenomena, and were inclined to scepticism even where the conclusions deducible from observed facts scarcely admitted of reasonable doubt.' [1]

---

[1] 'Principles of Geology' 10th edit. (1867) p. 85. Greenough, the first President of the Society, was the living embodiment of this excessive dislike of speculation, and not improbably the influence of his example perpetuated it after his time. As an illustration of the position which he took up, the following passage may be cited from his Presidential Address for 1834, wherein he opposed the modern doctrine of the elevation of land :—'A heated central nucleus is a mere invention of fancy, traceable, I believe, to no other source than the hope of obtaining a good argument from the multiplication of bad ones. To the Huttonian and every other geological sectary who relies on this postulate, I say, be cautious: "*incedis per ignes dolosos*".' (Proc. Geol. Soc. vol. ii, p. 61.)

But in spite of their resolve not to commit themselves to any theory of the earth, it was almost inevitable that the early members of the Geological Society, who were for the most part mineralogists, should incline towards the doctrines of Werner, wherein mineralogical considerations played so important a part. Some of them, indeed, had actually studied under Werner himself at Freiberg, and would naturally adopt his system of classification and his terminology, and apply them to the rocks of Britain. Hence the papers that appeared in the three earliest volumes of our Transactions were in large measure framed on the Wernerian model. That this should have been the case with those of J. F. Berger was to be expected, for that observer had been a pupil of the great Freiberg professor, and, when employed for some years by a few members of the Society to describe the geology of different parts of our islands, he naturally used the language which he had learnt from his master. Yet even he, when he came to apply the Wernerian classification to the rocks of Devon and Cornwall, found himself puzzled to decide whether the serpentine of that district should be assigned to the 'older' or 'younger formation' of Werner; and he even ventured to assert his independence so far as to regard the distinction between the two to be so vague as to lead to a suspicion that 'the terms were designedly obscure, in order to avoid being more explicit in the definition.' But, like a true disciple of the Neptunist school, he could see no evidence that the Cornish granite had been injected into the grauwacke. On the contrary, he thought that it may have been 'softened by the grauwacke acting upon it as a solvent, so far as to permit pieces of that rock to amalgamate with it.'[1]

On the whole, however, the reticence of the early contributors to the Society's publications in the assertion of theoretical opinions is a marked characteristic of their papers. Thus, when Arthur Aikin presented his account of the Wrekin and the Coal-field of Shropshire, he adopted the Wernerian grouping of the formations, but he was careful to guard himself by stating that, although the greenstone of Steeraway Hill may have been the active agent in tilting the limestone there, he was yet 'by no means prepared to affirm that this fluidity was that of igneous fusion.'[2] Again, when Dr. Kidd described the mineralogy of St. Davids, he announced his conviction that the rocks of that district are 'all of chemical and

[1] Trans. Geol. Soc. ser. 1, vol. i (1811) pp. 137, 147 note.
[2] Ibid. p. 207. The same writer, some years later, when describing a bed of 'trap' in a Staffordshire colliery, would not decide as to the aqueous or igneous origin of the rock, ibid. vol. iii (1816) p. 251.

contemporaneous origin.' But at the same time, 'conceiving it would be improper, on the present occasion, to enter into the particulars or on the defence' of this opinion, he thinks it more 'respectful to the Society to be silent on those points.'[1]  J. J. Conybeare, too, while declaring that he could find no confirmation of Plutonist views among the rocks of Cornwall, did not go further than to say that he was 'strongly tempted to regard the elvans as of contemporaneous formation with the schistose rock which they traverse.'[2]

The followers of Hutton within the Society do not seem to have been always able to restrain the ardour of their belief with the same success as their opponents. And, as their cause was manifestly gaining ground in the country, they became more outspoken in the expression of their convictions. One of their number, Leonard Horner (whom some of us well remember in his latest years), avoiding theory, grouped the rocks of the Malvern Hills in 'the primitive class of the Wernerian system,' but he could not refrain, at the same time, from expressing his opinion that the rocks of that district 'exhibit appearances very inconsistent with the Wernerian system of geognosy' and from declaring that, in his judgment, 'the Huttonian theory offers a more satisfactory explanation of these phenomena than any other with which we are yet acquainted.' The conclusion of his paper contains the following passage :—

'As I have related the facts I observed, independently of any theory, if they are at all valuable in the geological history of this country, their value will remain undiminished, whether the speculations I have entered into are just or fallacious. If the geologist strictly guards against the influence of theory in his observations of nature and faithfully records what he has seen, there is no danger of his checking the progress of science, however much he may indulge in the speculative views of his subject.'[3]

A few years after the reading of Horner's paper, John Macculloch, in one of his earliest communications to the Society, threw down the gauntlet to the Neptunists by bringing forward what he claimed to be a crucial proof of the truth of Hutton's explanation of the origin of 'trap' or 'whinstone.' The case cited by him was that of

[1] Trans. ser. 1, vol. ii (1814) p. 93.

[2] *Ibid.* vol. iv (1817) p. 403.

[3] *Ibid.* vol. i (1811) p. 321. The danger, however, may have been more real than Horner supposed. It is not every mind that is gifted with the power of keeping its observing faculty entirely unbiassed by the hypothetical explanations which suggest themselves in the course of a research.

Stirling Castle, which, though not more remarkable or instructive than those in the neighbourhood of Edinburgh wherewith Hutton and Playfair had made geologists familiar, gave him the opportunity to affirm that

'no hypothesis is competent to explain geological phenomena at large, which does not admit of the forcible displacement of the strata which accompany them [the trap-rocks], and on which the marks of violence are so evidently impressed.'[1]

In subsequently presenting to the Society a collection of rock-specimens from a large portion of Scotland, he accompanied it with some miscellaneous remarks, in which he began by objecting to Werner's scheme of rock-classification, that it takes for granted the very matter to be proved.[2]

In the summer of the year 1813 Conybeare and Buckland made their tour together along the coasts of Antrim and Derry, and obtained the material for the preparation of their classic essay on the geology of that part of Ireland. Among their observations they confirmed the Huttonian explanation which Playfair had given of the reputed fossiliferous basalt of Portrush, so long and so loudly claimed by the Neptunists as a proof of the aqueous origin of basalts in general.[3]

Among the signs afforded in the pages of the Society's publications that a strong reaction was setting in against the dominant Wernerian doctrines as to the history of the earth's crust, reference may here be made to the excellent and memorable paper by James Parkinson on the strata in the neighbourhood of London, wherein he recognized the broken and displaced condition of the stratified formations of this country, and regarded this condition as proof of the operation of 'some prodigious and mysterious power.'[4]

But, though steadily losing ground, Neptunism could still be heard from time to time within the walls of the Society, and yet more outside of them, for it continued to be stoutly maintained by Jameson at Edinburgh. It is interesting in this connection to remember that when, after his election to the Woodwardian Professorship in the year 1818, Sedgwick began to study geology, it was from the Wernerian side that he entered upon it. His earliest papers, worthy of a staunch disciple of the school of Freiberg, were not

---

[1] Trans. ser. 1, vol. ii (1814) p. 308.
[2] Ibid. p. 390.
[3] Ibid. vol. iii (1816) p. 13.
[4] Ibid. vol. i (1811) p. 336.

communicated, however, to our Society, but to the Cambridge Philosophical Society, which he had recently helped to found. By the time he brought his contributions to the Geological Society he had abandoned the Neptunist faith. In later life he used playfully to refer to these early days in his career before he had 'learned to shake off the Wernerian nonsense he had been taught;' when he was 'eaten up with the Wernerian notions—ready to sacrifice his senses to that creed—a Wernerian slave,' and when, as he admitted, he 'was troubled with water on the brain,' until 'light and heat had completely dissipated it.'[1]

Twenty years after the foundation of our Society, on February 15th, 1828, Fitton, in the first annual Presidential Address which has been preserved, could speak of 'the complete subsidence or almost oblivion of the Wernerian and Neptunist hypotheses,' and 'the universal adoption of a modified volcanic theory.' 'Whatever be the fate of the Huttonian theory in general,' he remarks, 'it must be admitted that many of its leading propositions have been confirmed in a manner which the inventor could not have foreseen.' I cannot perhaps more fittingly close this brief account of what appears in the Society's records regarding the famous Neptunist and Vulcanist controversy than by quoting from the same address Fitton's eloquent and genial tribute to the memory of Playfair (Proc. vol. i, 1834, pp. 55, 56):—

'The geological writings of that distinguished man,' he remarks, 'have had, indirectly, an effect in accelerating the progress of our subject, the benefit of which we experience at this moment, and probably shall long continue to feel. He clothed our subject with the dignity of an eloquence most happily adapted to philosophic inquiry; and redeemed the geologist from association with that class of naturalists who lose sight of general laws, and are occupied incessantly with details,—placing him, where he ought to stand, beside the mathematician, the astronomer, and the chemist, and permanently raising our science into an elevated department of inductive inquiry. His mild and tolerant character threw an assuaging influence upon the waves of a controversy, which in his time considerations, entirely foreign to science, had exasperated into unusual violence; and if, fortunately, there is no longer any trace of this asperity, the change must, in a great degree, be ascribed to the tone of Mr. Playfair's writings, enforced by the manly and consistent tenour of his blameless life.'

In order to keep our survey of the work of the Geological Society within some reasonable compass, the subject may conveniently be

---

[1] 'Life & Letters of Adam Sedgwick' by J. W. Clarke & T. McKenny Hughes, vol. i (1890) pp. 251, 284.

divided into sections, in each of which it may be more or less practicable to follow the chronological order, and to trace the gradual development of particular lines of research. I propose therefore to arrange my remarks under the following heads :—1st, British Geology ; 2nd, Foreign Geology ; 3rd, Petrography ; 4th, Palæontology ; and 5th, Physiography. These subdivisions do not embrace the whole of the wide range of the Society's work, but they may suffice to enable us to form a fairly adequate conception of what the general nature and amount of that work have been.

## I. British Geology.

It was natural and proper that the Society should devote its attention mainly to the study of the geology of the British Islands, and that a considerable part of the bulk of its publications should consist of detailed descriptions of the characters, distribution, and local variations of the geological formations of which these islands are built up. This feature, which appeared from the beginning of the Society's career, remains a dominant characteristic down to the present day. There are not many districts of the country regarding which no information will be met with in our Transactions, Proceedings, or Quarterly Journal, while of many places the earliest or fullest account is to be found in these publications. As a compendium of original contributions to British Geology the Society's volumes must always remain a standard work of reference. Inasmuch as geology was young when the Society was born, many of the early papers, though dealing only with local observations, have come to possess an historic interest in the literature of our science, more particularly when they gave the first descriptions of definite groups of strata, and afforded stratigraphical types which could be applied to the elucidation of the geological succession in other countries. To some of these now classic memoirs I shall refer in the sequel.

Without attempting to enumerate more than a small proportion of the total number of papers on British Geology which the Society has published, I may select for special mention such as will best serve to illustrate the character of this part of the Society's activity, and for the sake of clearness and brevity I will group my references in stratigraphical order.

Should any geological student wish to trace the story of the investigation of the pre-Cambrian rocks of these islands, he must, in the first place, turn to the publications of the Geological Society.

Some important contributions to the subject have, indeed, appeared elsewhere, but the main part of the original papers in which the successive steps in the enquiry have been taken is to be found in our volumes. To some of the early numbers of the Transactions Macculloch communicated a long series of his observations among the crystalline rocks of the Scottish Highlands, and gave the first clear account of· their mineralogical characters and their distribution.[1] He recognized the existence of an ancient gneiss, overlain unconformably by a thick mass of red sandstone, which he believed to pass upwards into various kinds of schists. Some years later his observations were confirmed by Sedgwick & Murchison,[2] who, however, went astray in regarding as Old Red Sandstone what he had correctly 'ranked in the class of primary rocks.' For nearly thirty years thereafter, the Archæan rocks of the North of Scotland remained without further exploration until in 1854 the discovery, by Charles Peach, of fossils in the limestone of Durness aroused keen interest. Murchison and Nicol began the renewed study of the geology of that district, and published the results of their labours in the Society's Quarterly Journal. These two able observers in the end arrived at different conclusions as to the sequence of the rocks. We are all familiar with the later contributions to the discussion of the problem, and nearly all those who took part in it are happily still with us. The main question in dispute has been satisfactorily solved, and it is a matter of gratification to us that some of the more important steps that led to this satisfactory ending have been chronicled in the pages of the Quarterly Journal. But the rocks of the Scottish Highlands still offer many questions which remain undetermined. In particular, the true stratigraphical relations of the Dalradian or Eastern (Moine) Schists present difficulties which may continue for a long time to tax the combined efforts of the field-geologist and the petrographer. A few interesting and suggestive papers, however, which have been published by the Society, have thrown some light on parts of the subject. I would especially refer to the communications of Messrs. Barrow,[3] Horne & Greenly,[4] J. B. Hill,[5] and Cunningham-Craig.[6]

---

[1] Trans. ser. 1, vols. ii, iii, iv, & ser. 2, vol. i.

[2] *Ibid.* ser. 2, vol. iii (1829) pp. 21, 125.

[3] Quart. Journ. Geol. Soc. vol. xlix (1893) p. 330. This publication is hereinafter cited by the abbreviation Q. J.

[4] Q. J. lii (1896) 633.

[5] Q. J. lv (1899) 470.        [6] Q. J. lx (1904) 10.

The gradual recoguition of detached areas of pre-Cambrian rocks, which rise up from amidst the Palæozoic and Mesozoic formations of England and Wales, has been recorded in successive volumes of our Quarterly Journal. The papers on this part of the subject began with the memorable contribution of Holl on the Malvern Hills, which appeared in 1864.[1] Prof. Bonney and the Rev. E. Hill subsequently described the interesting core of Charnwood Forest, with its remarkable volcanic series.[2] Dr. Callaway made known other pre-Cambrian masses of various ages in the Malvern Hills, Shropshire, and Anglesey.[3] Unfortunately, these various inliers of the most ancient parts of the framework of the country are so extensively buried under much younger sedimentary accumulations that their relations to each other, and their stratigraphical position in the pre-Cambrian series of rocks, are still unknown. Is it too much to hope that some petrographical method may yet be devised which may help to clear away these obscurities, and that a future number of the Quarterly Journal may earn the distinction of making the discovery known to the world?

The subdivisions and sequence of the older Palæozoic rocks of Britain were first worked out by two of the most illustrious Fellows of this Society, but the record of their observations and conclusions is only partially preserved in its publications. The story of their labours, which resulted in laying the foundations of the Palæozoic geology of the whole globe, has, in large measure, to be gleaned from various outside sources. Sedgwick, indeed, contributed to the Transactions, Proceedings, and early volumes of the Quarterly Journal a number of important papers on the rocks of the Lake District and of North Wales, which reveal some of the stages in the progress of his researches. But he never completed a connected narrative of what he had done in the field, and the historian who would follow the footsteps of the Woodwardian Professor, and do justice to his large and luminous views regarding the older formations of this country, must trace them through many scattered papers in various journals. Murchison was less communicative of his progress to the Geological Society. He reserved the account of his labours for the chapters of his great 'Silurian System.'

[1] Q. J. xx, 413 & xxi (1865) 72.

[2] Q. J. xxxiii (1877) 754; xxxiv (1878) 199; xxxvi (1880) 337; xlvii (1891) 78.

[3] Q. J. xxxv (1879) 643; xxxvi (1880) 536; xxxvii (1881) 210; xxxviii (1882) 119; xl (1884) 567.

Since the pioneer-work of these two illustrious men, the Cambrian and Silurian rocks of the British Isles have been sedulously studied by many enthusiastic and competent observers, and their palæontology has been developed in far greater detail than the founders of the two systems ever dreamt of. In particular the system of zonal subdivision, originally employed in the elucidation of the Jurassic formations, has been applied with much success to our most ancient fossiliferous deposits, which have now been classified on a biological basis, in such manner as to become more than ever types for the investigation of the older Palæozoic rocks of other countries. The Geological Society may point with justifiable pride to the large proportion which it has published of the results of the stratigraphical and palæontological investigation of the older Palæozoic rocks of the British Isles.

In Wales the Cambrian and Silurian rocks were studied by Salter and Hicks, who have been followed, in ever-increasing minuteness of detail, by a long succession of observers, including Messrs. Marr,[1] W. Keeping,[2] Lake,[3] Groom,[4] Cowper Reed,[5] Reynolds,[6] D. C. Evans,[7] C. Lloyd Morgan,[8] and H. Lapworth.[9]

Our knowledge of the Lower and Upper Silurian rocks of the Lake District has been enlarged and improved by the papers of the late Prof. Nicholson and Dr. Marr,[10] which were communicated to the Society. The Silurian Uplands of the South of Scotland, which so long refused to reveal their internal structure, have had their secret extracted from them by Prof. Lapworth, whose papers on the subject in the Quarterly Journal[11] have been the stimulus and guide for all subsequent correlations of the stratigraphical subdivisions of that region with the corresponding formations elsewhere at home and abroad. In the far North-West of Scotland the pioneer work of Charles Peach, Murchison, and Salter among the Durness Limestones has been ably extended and completed by the Geological

---

[1] Q. J. xxxiv (1878) 871 & xli (1885) 476.

[2] Q. J. xxxvii (1881) 141.

[3] Q. J. xlix (1893) 426; li (1895) 9; lii (1896) 511.

[4] Q. J. xlix (1893) 426, & vols. lv, lvi, lvii, & lviii (1899-1902).

[5] Q. J. li (1895) 149.

[6] Q. J. lii (1896) 511 & lvii (1901) 267.

[7] Q. J. lxii (1906) 597.

[8] Q. J. lvii (1901) 267.

[9] Q. J. lvi (1900) 67.

[10] Q. J. xliv (1888) 654 & xlvii (1891) 500.

[11] Q. J. xxxiv (1878) 240 & xxxviii (1882) 537.

Survey. The papers published by the Society from Dr. B. N. Peach and Dr. Horne have made known the existence of the *Olenellus*-fauna in these fossiliferous strata, thus definitely placing them in the Cambrian System and demonstrating the pre-Cambrian age of the Torridon Sandstone.[1] The Lower and Upper Silurian rocks of Ireland have in recent years had much fresh light thrown upon them by the papers of Mr. Gardiner and Prof. Reynolds published in our Quarterly Journal.[2]

Here let me remark parenthetically that a distinctive feature in the succession of authors whose papers have been published by the Society during the last twenty years is to be seen in the advent of women as original observers and writers of geological papers. That women could take a keen interest in our science, and could do much for its advancement, had been long ago made evident by the career of Mary Anning, by the collections and writings of Etheldred Benett, and by the well-known letter wherein Mrs. Graham gave so graphic a description of the geological effects of the great Chile earthquake of 1822, printed in our Transactions and quoted by Lyell. But for many long years our printed records contained no communications from the other sex. In the year 1887, however, owing to some general impulse, of which it would be interesting to trace the causes, women began to send in to the Society papers descriptive of their observations, which have found a place in the Quarterly Journal. The number of this fair company of contributors has steadily increased, and their papers have not only been published by us, but the authors have in more than one instance been deemed worthy recipients of the honour of our Awards. The subjects of these papers are, in some cases, petrographical, involving the microscopic study of thin rock-slices; but for the most part they treat of fossils, either from the stratigraphical or from the palæontological side. The subdivision of the older Palæozoic rocks into life-zones has especially appealed to these authors, and valuable papers on the subject have been contributed by them. I need only refer here to those of Misses Crosfield & Skeat,[3] Elles,[4] Wood,[5] and Slater.[6]

---

[1] Q. J. xlviii (1892) 227 & l (1894) 661.

[2] Q. J. lii (1896) 587; liii (1897) 520; liv (1898) 135; lviii (1902) 226.

[3] Q. J. lii (1896) 523.

[4] Q. J. lii (1896) 273; liii (1897) 186; liv (1898) 463; lvi (1900) 370; lxii (1906) 195.

[5] Q. J. lii (1896) 273 & lvi (1900) 415.    [6] Q. J. lxii (1906) 195.

The history of the investigation of the later Palæozoic rocks of the British Isles may likewise be in no small measure gleaned from the publications of our Society, where some of the most important chapters of that history were for the first time recorded. Perhaps no more interesting episode in the progress of geological discovery can be quoted than that of the establishment of the Devonian System, when, from a region of extreme stratigraphical complexity, a new system was added to the geological record not only of this country but of the world. We are all familiar with the details of this episode, how after various errors and misconceptions, Sedgwick & Murchison were guided by the genius of William Lonsdale to the true solution of their problem, and how, provided with the key which Lonsdale supplied to them, they were enabled to relegate to its proper place in the series of fossiliferous formations a large part of the old 'grauwacke' of the South-West of England, and ultimately of wide tracts on the Continent of Europe. It was one of the earliest and greatest achievements gained by the comparative study of organic remains, demonstrating, as had never been done so strikingly before, the value of fossils in the investigation of the stratigraphical succession of rocks. Well might Sedgwick and Murchison declare that 'this is undoubtedly the greatest change which has ever been attempted at one time in the classification of British rocks.' Though these authors fully acknowledge their indebtedness to Lonsdale, the share of that great palæontological master in this important reformation of geological nomenclature is perhaps less generally appreciated than it should be. His modest account of the successive steps by which he was led to conclude that the South Devon limestones 'would prove to be of the age of the Old Red Sandstone' is a fascinating narrative in the literature of geology. The Society may count as not the least of its distinctions that its publications were the channel through which this remarkable series of observations and generalizations was laid before the world.[1]

The Society has published various other communications on the Devonian groups of the South-West of England. Valuable papers by Godwin-Austen appeared in the later volumes of the Transactions

---

[1] The paper by Sedgwick & Murchison 'On the Physical Structure of Devonshire, & on the Subdivisions & Geological Relations of the Older Stratified Deposits' is contained in the fifth volume of the second series of the Transactions (1840) pp. 633-703, and Lonsdale's 'Notes on the Age of the Limestones of South Devonshire' follow on pp. 721-38.

and in the Proceedings. To a much more recent date belong the communications of Jukes, which at the time aroused so much discussion as to give rise to what has been called 'the Devonian question.' His first paper on the subject was printed in the Quarterly Journal of 1866. A second communication, refused by the Society, was printed privately by the author. His main contention was that, with the exception of the sandstones and grits of Pickwell Down and the North Foreland, which he grouped with the Old Red Sandstone, the Devonian rocks are the equivalent in time of the Carboniferous Slate and Limestone of the South of Ireland. A view so opposed to the established and orthodox opinion could hardly be allowed to go without reply. At Murchison's request Etheridge went down into Devonshire, spent some time there in traversing the various sections, and as the result of his labours presented to the Society the elaborate memoir which appeared in the 23rd volume of the Quarterly Journal. He therein maintained the distinctive palæontological value of the Devonian fossils, and the controversy was thereafter allowed to die out. Later volumes of the Journal have contained papers on Devonian subjects by T. M. Hall,[1] Champernowne,[2] Hicks,[3] Ussher,[4] and other writers, but it can hardly be said that the peculiarly complicated structure of the south-western counties and the detailed stratigraphical relations of the different rock-groups of that region have even yet been wholly unravelled.

The Carboniferous System of this country, as was to be expected in the case of rocks so full of interest and so well developed here, has been the subject of many communications to the Society. Although each may have had its value in adding more or less to the general knowledge of the subject, they do not include in their number any one of such original and cardinal importance in general geology as the great Devonian paper to which reference has just been made.[5] In the early decades of last century the origin of coal was still a matter of dispute. It was by no means universally

[1] Q. J. xxiii (1867) 371.

[2] Q. J. xxxv (1879) 67, 532; xl (1884) 497; xlv (1889) 369.

[3] Q. J. lii (1896) 254 & liii (1897) 438.

[4] Q. J. xxxv (1879) 532 & xlvi (1890) 487.

[5] The general characters and distribution of the Carboniferous System were so excellently depicted in the classic 'Outlines' of Conybeare & Phillips that it seems surprising that the sketch of the subject given by these authors was not sooner followed up by a detailed study of the several formations and districts which they described.

admitted that this substance was formed from ancient vegetation, and even by those who connected it with the abundant plant-remains in the associated strata, it was commonly looked upon as so much drifted vegetation which was washed off the land and buried under sand and mud on the neighbouring sea-floor.  The reiterated devastations of successive seasons were supposed to have produced the repetition and alternation of coal-seams with the sandstones and shales among which they are intercalated.  Towards the solution of this interesting question one of the first steps was obviously the careful study of the structure and relations of all the coal-bearing strata.  The first observer who made this detailed examination was a Fellow of this Society, W. E. Logan, who found that in the South Wales coal-field the seams of coal rest upon an underclay through which *Stigmaria*-roots freely branch, and which, in his opinion, represents the soil whereon the vegetation actually grew that has been changed into coal.  Although this observation might not be applicable to every coal-field or to every seam in any single coal-field, its importance was at once recognized, and it has influenced all the subsequent discussion of the subject.[1]

Of the numerous papers on the stratigraphy of the Carboniferous formations which have been printed in our publications, the earliest and by no means the least valuable was N. J. Winch's description of these rocks as developed in Northumberland and Durham, which was read to the Society in 1814, and is contained in the fourth volume of the Transactions.  Availing himself of the copious information supplied by mining records, the author was enabled to present the first detailed account of the successive subdivisions of one of our great mineral-fields.  Another early and valuable memoir was that by Buckland & Conybeare on the south-western coal-district of England, which was published in the Transactions for 1824.  The Coalbrookdale coal-field was the subject of Prestwich's well-known essay, which was printed in the fifth volume of the second series of the Transactions (1840).  In more recent years the detailed study of our coal-fields has been, for the most part, undertaken by the Geological Survey, and the results have been given in a series of official memoirs.  But a few papers of considerable interest and importance have appeared in our Quarterly Journal.  I may particularly refer to Mr. Cantrill's account of the coal-field of Wyre Forest, wherein he strongly supported the view, which had been

---

[1] The paper in which it was recorded appeared in the sixth volume of the second series of Transactions, published in 1841.

already expressed, that much of the so-called 'Permian' rocks
should be regarded as really reddened Coal-measures with *Spirorbis*-
limestone.[1]  Mr. Walcot Gibson also, in a later communication,
drew a similar conclusion in regard to the district of Staffordshire,
Denbighshire, and Nottinghamshire.[2]

Although the Carboniferous flora and fauna of these islands have
long been the subject of careful study, it is not many years since
the principle of stratigraphical subdivision into life-zones was
applied to them.  Dr. Kidston has in this country led the way
in the zonal treatment of the plants.  The late J. W. Kirkby,
Dr. Marr, Prof. Garwood, Dr. Wheelton Hind, and others have
done good service in making similar use of the invertebrate fauna.
It is singular, however, that in the case of a thick calcareous
formation, so crowded with organisms as our Carboniferous
Limestone, such slow progress should have been made in determining the vertical range of the fossils and turning them to use
as indications of stratigraphical position and sequence.  After the
good preliminary work by the late G. H. Morton in Flintshire
and Denbighshire, the most important step in this direction has
recently been taken by Dr. Arthur Vaughan in his paper on 'The
Palæontological Sequence in the Carboniferous Limestone of the
Bristol Area,' which was read to the Society in the summer of
1904.[3]  The biological succession observed by him has also been
applied by Mr. Sibly to the Mendip area and Derbyshire,[4] and we
may hope that it will be found to be likewise available in the thick
Mountain-Limestone Series of Ireland, where a beginning has been
made by Dr. Matley,[5] and among the marine bands in the corresponding group of strata in Scotland.

Of all the papers which the Society has published dealing with
the Carboniferous rocks of this country, none seems to me so instinct
with scientific genius as that by Godwin-Austen, 'On the possible
Extension of the Coal-Measures beneath the South-Eastern Part of
England.'  It was read on May 30th, 1855, and appeared in the
twelfth volume of the Quarterly Journal.  For its wide and detailed
acquaintance with the facts observable on the two sides of the
Channel, its careful and logical presentation of the evidence, and
its cautious yet convincing indication of the conclusions to be
drawn, it must ever rank as one of the masterpieces of English

[1] Q. J. li (1895) 528.   [2] Q. J. lvii (1901) 251.   [3] Q. J. lxi (1905) 181.
[4] Q. J. lxi (1905) 548; lxii (1906) 324; lxiv (1908) 34.
[5] Q. J. lxii (1906) 275.

geological literature. The sagacity of its reasoning has in recent years been triumphantly demonstrated by the deep borings in Kent, which have brought to light the actual existence of Coal-Measures beneath the Secondary formations of the south-eastern counties.

For many years after the foundation of the Geological Society, that portion of the stratified rocks of this country which lies between the top of the Coal-Measures and the bottom of the Lias was regarded as a single connected series of deposits, generally known as the New Red Sandstone, in contradistinction to the mass of red sandstones beneath the Carboniferous System. The first and most masterly essay on these rocks was Sedgwick's great memoir on the Magnesian Limestone, which fills nearly ninety pages of the third volume of the second series of the Transactions, issued in 1835. In this remarkable paper the distribution was described of the various subdivisions of the series, which the author had traced with great personal labour over a large extent of country, and their general sequence was for the first time worked out in detail. A parallelism was then established between them and their equivalent groups on the Continent, and thus a basis and a starting-point were fixed for all subsequent research in this department of British Geology. Some years later, after the term 'Permian' had been introduced by Murchison as one of the results of his Russian travels, the so-called 'New Red Sandstone' of England was divided into two portions: the lower being named Permian and assigned to the top of the Palæozoic Systems; while the upper took the German title of Trias, and was regarded as the lowest member of the Mesozoic series of formations.[1] The line of division between the strata thus separated from each other is in this country often indefinable, and some geologists have been disinclined to recognize its existence. But the trend of the palæontological evidence in its favour was eventually allowed to prevail. The papers of J. W. Kirkby which appeared in the Quarterly Journal from 1857 onward, and his monograph published by the Palæontographical Society, had much influence in procuring the admission of the Permian as a

---

[1] This re-arrangement in the classification of the geological record was not made without calling forth protests, and Murchison & De Verneuil, after their first communication of the results of their journeys in Russia to the Society in the spring of 1841 (Proc. vol. iii, p. 398), had to return to the subject three years later and vindicate the claims of their Permian System to recognition as part of the Palæozoic series of formations (Proc. vol. iv, p. 327).

distinct member of the stratigraphical series in this country, in
spite of the acknowledged practical difficulty in satisfactorily
defining its boundaries.    That large areas were classed as Permian
which should have been kept in the Coal-Measures is now generally
acknowledged.

A novel idea was presented to the Society in 1855 when A.
C. Ramsay read his paper on the breccias of Shropshire and
Worcestershire, which he claimed as evidence of the existence of
glaciers and icebergs in the Permian Period.    It was, so far as I
know, the first published suggestion that the climate of any portion
of Palæozoic time in our latitudes could have been cold enough to
admit of glacial action.    Although the proposition did not meet
with universal acceptance, it had the effect, like other original ideas
of its gifted author, of stimulating enquiry, and thus preparing the
way for the reception of other evidence of Palæozoic glaciation from
widely separated parts of the world.[1]    At a later date, Ramsay
returned to the subject of the geographical and climatological
conditions under which the red sedimentary deposits of the country
were accumulated, and communicated to the Society two papers, one
on the Triassic and the other on the Palæozoic red sandstones, which
were printed in the 27th volume of our Quarterly Journal (1871).
He there insisted that all these formations indicate deposition in
lakes or inland seas during continental conditions of geography.

The great series of Secondary formations, so admirably developed
in England, and filling so prominent a place in the history of
geological science from the use made of them by William Smith,
have naturally engrossed a large share of the attention of English
geologists.    Not a district in which they are well displayed has
escaped examination and, in most cases, detailed description.    The
various sections in which they are best exposed have been measured
in minute detail, their local variations in character and in thickness
have been traced across the country, their enclosed organic remains,

---

[1] Reference may be most conveniently made here to papers published by the
Society, bearing on old glacial periods.  W. T. Blanford discussed the evidence
for glacial conditions in India during the Palæozoic era, Q. J. xlii (1886) 249.
Prof. T. W. Edgeworth David has furnished much information regarding
similar evidence found in the Carboniferous or Permo-Carboniferous rocks of
Australia, Q. J. xliii (1887) 190 & lii (1896) 289.  Dr. A. Strahan has described
glacial phenomena of Palæozoic age in the Varanger Fjord, Q. J. liii (1897)
137.  Mr. E. T. Mellor has contributed a paper on the glacial or Dwyka
Conglomerate of the Transvaal, Q. J. lxi (1905) 679.

sedulously collected by thousands of observers, have been accurately
determined and amply described, while their life-zones have been
defined with greater precision than those of any other part of the
Geological Record in these islands, save perhaps the Upper Chalk.
It is needless to say that a large proportion of the numerous papers
which present the results of all this manifold and enthusiastic labour
in the field and in the cabinet has been laid before the Society and
has been printed in our publications.   It is, of course, impracticable
to particularize on the present occasion even the more important
of these papers.   I can only refer to a few of those which stand
out as landmarks in the progress of the science.   One of the
earliest of them was the valuable memoir by Lonsdale, read to the
Society in 1829, in which he gave a detailed account of the Jurassic
series in the Bath district.[1]   Somewhat later came the great monograph of Fitton, bearing the title of 'Observations on some of the
Strata between the Chalk & the Oxford Oolite in the South-East
of England.'   This remarkable production fills 285 pages of the
fourth volume of the second series of Transactions, and is probably
the longest single paper ever published by the Society.   But its
high merit amply justified the space allotted to it.   Its exhaustive
examination of the stratigraphy, distribution, and palæontology of
the various groups of strata to which it relates has guided all
subsequent research in this section of English geology.   Its literary
excellence, hardly less conspicuous than its scientific merit, is
marked by that logical precision, conciseness, and grace of diction
which distinguished all its author's writings.   Fitton's essay has
long since taken its place among the geological classics of this
country.

Of much younger date are the monographs which, embodying
the general results obtained by previous observers, together with
much fresh material, have successively appeared in the Quarterly
Journal.   A most material service is rendered to the advancement
of geology through the preparation of such monographs by those
who are themselves acknowledged masters of the subject of which
they treat.   The important paper by Mr. Hudleston & the late
Prof. Blake on the Corallian Rocks of England, which we published in 1877, may be taken as the type of this kind of essay.
To the same class belong Prof. Blake's papers on the Kimeridge
Clay (1875), on the Portland Rocks (1880), and on the correlation
of the Upper Jurassic Rocks of England and the Continent (1881);

[1] Trans. ser. 2, vol. iii, pp. 241-76.

likewise Mr. F. G. H. Price's contribution on the Gault of Folkestone (1874). More recently we are indebted to Mr. S. S. Buckman for a succession of papers on the Inferior Oolite (Bajocian) and to Mr. L. Richardson for others on the Rhætic Beds, Lias, and Inferior Oolite, which supplement the earlier observations of Thomas Wright and Charles Moore. The application of the method of classification by palæontological zones permits of much greater minuteness of detail than was formerly practicable in the treatment of these strata.

The Liassic and Cretaceous groups of the North-East of Ireland, first worked out in detail by Ralph Tate, were described by him in papers which appeared in the Quarterly Journal between 1864 and 1867, while a more minute study of the Cretaceous rocks of that district was communicated to us in 1897 by Dr. W. Fraser Hume. The Jurassic rocks of Scotland, first noted by Macculloch and afterwards in more detail by Sedgwick and Murchison, began to be brought into closer correlation with their English equivalents in 1851, when Edward Forbes detected estuarine beds of the age of the Oxford Clay in the north of Skye,[1] and when, in 1858, Thomas Wright, from a collection of fossils submitted to him, recognized the presence of Lower and Middle Lias in the district of Southern Skye.[2] In later years this work was continued and extended by Bryce and Tate (1873).[3] But for the first connected account of the distribution and subdivisions of the whole Secondary Series of Scotland we are indebted to Prof. Judd, whose series of papers on the subject was communicated to the Society between 1873 and 1878.[4]

The work of Hébert, who applied to the Chalk of the South-East of England the zonal classification which he had worked out in the North of France, was taken up and extended in this country by our esteemed Foreign Member Prof. Barrois, whose masterly essay, 'Recherches sur le Terrain Crétacé Supérieur de l'Angleterre & de l'Irlande,' published in 1876, has influenced all the subsequent investigation of the Cretaceous formations of this country. In recent years we have seen the same zonal principle carried into still further detail by Dr. A. W. Rowe, who, employing among other fossils the species and 'group-forms' of the genus *Micraster*, has been able to show that the recognized zones of the White Chalk are capable of still more detailed yet serviceable subdivision. His suggestive series of papers have been communicated to the Geologists'

[1] Q. J. vii, 104.    [2] Q. J. xiv, 24.
[3] Q. J. xxix, 317-51.    [4] Q. J. xxix, xxx, xxxiv.

Association, and we may congratulate our younger sister Society on the distinction which they have conferred on successive volumes of her Proceedings.

As the Geological Society has its seat in London, it was natural and fitting that the Tertiary deposits of the London Basin should be made the subject of constant study on the part of the Fellows resident in or near the capital. As far back as the year 1816, Buckland, amidst his excursions into so many parts of the geological domain, gave his attention to the Plastic Clay near Reading and compared it with its equivalents in France.[1] But among all the early pioneers in the Tertiary geology of this country the foremost place must be assigned to Thomas Webster, whose essay ' On the Freshwater Formations of the Isle of Wight, with some Observations on the Strata over the Chalk in the South-East Part of England,' is contained in the second volume of the Transactions (1814) p. 161. Referring to the then recent work of Cuvier and Brongniart on the Paris Basin, and stating that his object was to describe a similar series of formations in this country, he produced a singularly able memoir in which the stratigraphy of the formations was worked out, together with their organic remains.    Long years afterwards Edward Forbes, who had the art to lend an added interest to every subject which he handled, returned with Bristow to the study of these Isle-of-Wight Tertiary strata and gave to the Society his memorable paper on the ' Fluvio-Marine Tertiaries of the Isle of Wight' (1853), with a new reading of the stratigraphy.[2]    It is interesting to remember that two of Lyell's earliest papers were devoted to the Plastic Clay of Dorset and to the freshwater strata of Hordwell Cliff, Hampshire, to which attention had previously been called by Webster.[3]    Many years later, when successive editions of his ' Principles' and ' Elements' had made his classification of the Tertiary formations widely known, he communicated to the Society (1852) his long and detailed paper on the Tertiary strata of Belgium and French Flanders.[4]

But among the names of those who have enriched geological science and increased the reputation of our Quarterly Journal by their contributions to Tertiary geology, that of our late revered colleague and esteemed friend Joseph Prestwich stands pre-eminent. As far back as 1846[5] he began a series of papers on the older

---

[1] Trans. ser. 1, vol. iv, p. 277.            [2] Q. J. ix. 259.
[3] *Ibid.* ser. 2, vol. ii, pp. 279, 287.        [4] Q. J. viii, 277.
[5] In the second volume of the Quarterly Journal.

Tertiary formations, which culminated in the admirable detailed Memoirs on the correlation of the Lower Tertiary series of England with that of France.[1]   Having worked out these older members of the Tertiary formations, he afterwards devoted himself with no less enthusiasm to the elucidation of the newer groups, and communicated to the Society a series of papers on the Crag of Norfolk and Suffolk.[2]   To him chiefly, in early association with Hugh Falconer and with our accomplished associate Sir John Evans, we owe the recognition of the significance of the discoveries of Boucher de Perthes in the implement-bearing gravels of the Somme valley, and the initiation of the researches which established the antiquity of the human race in this island.   Prestwich was ever loyal to the Geological Society.   Nearly all his scientific papers were presented to it, and were printed in its publications.

Probably no one now living has acquired such an intimate acquaintance with the Eocene deposits of the London Basin as our friend Mr. Whitaker, but the results of his long years of observation have been chiefly consigned, as was proper, to the Memoirs of the Geological Survey.   To two other members of the staff of the Survey, Mr. Clement Reid and Mr. E. T. Newton, we are largely indebted for their contributions to the Pliocene geology of this country; but, in their case also, their writings have chiefly appeared as official memoirs.   Our Pliocene deposits, and their relations to those of Holland and Belgium, have been lately discussed in a series of papers by Mr. F. W. Harmer.[3]   The Tertiary volcanic series of the West of Scotland and the North of Ireland has been the subject of many communications to the Society.   The sequence of eruptions and the petrography of the rocks have been discussed by Prof. Judd and Mr. Harker, while the interesting terrestrial flora contained in the intercalated leaf-beds has been dealt with by Mr. J. Starkie Gardner.

Hardly any portion of the contributions of our Society to the literature of geology has surpassed in interest and importance that which relates to the history of the Glacial Period.   It was the appearance of a group of papers in the third volume of our Proceedings that started the modern development of this branch of the science along the path which it has since so successfully followed.   Nearly a century ago Sir James Hall first called

[1] Q. J. xi (1855) 206 & xiii (1857) 89.
[2] Q. J. xxvii (1871) 115, 325, 452.
[3] Q. J. lii (1896) 748; liv (1898) 308; & lvi (1900) 705.

attention to the smoothed and striated rock-surfaces now known as roches moutonnées. After a study of them as displayed in Scotland, he came to the conclusion that they can only have been produced by sudden and violent débâcles which, set in motion by gigantic earthquakes and laden with mud and stones, swept from the ocean across the face of the country.[1] This opinion, or some modification of it, continued to prevail for some thirty years. Among those who, towards the end of that time, supported it was the able mathematician William Hopkins. In a paper which he communicated to the Society in 1842, 'On the Elevation & Denudation of the District of the Lakes of Cumberland & Westmoreland,' he delivered an emphatic judgment against any glacial theory, whether of glaciers or icebergs. He looked upon the boulders scattered over the district as proofs of dispersal by waves caused by sudden upheaval of the sea-bottom, and he thought that this explanation completely removed the difficulties of the subject.[2] A few years of further consideration, however, led this convulsionist to revise his confidently expressed conviction, and the change of view to which the accumulating evidence brought him illustrates the general transformation of opinion which was then in progress throughout the country, as the result of the publication of the group of papers above mentioned.

At the beginning of last century Playfair, with that philosophic insight which so distinguished him, pointed out that the most powerful agency in nature for the transport of large masses of rock is that of glaciers.[3] But the indication which he thus supplied was long lost sight of amid the strife of contending schools. Nobody dreamt that glaciers could ever have existed in these islands, or that, if they did exist among our mountains, they could ever have crept down across the plains and hills of the lowlands, carrying thither the débris of the higher grounds. That the climate around

[1] 'On the Revolutions of the Earth's Surface' Trans. Roy. Soc. Edin. vol. vii (1812–14) p. 139. It should be remembered, however, that in the same year Col. Imrie, in his paper on the Campsie Hills (Mem. Werner. Soc. vol. ii, p. 35) had noticed the dressed surfaces of the trap-rocks of that district, and looked on them as evidence of the general movement of a current from the west.

[2] Only an abstract of this paper appeared at the time in the Proceedings (vol. iii, p. 757), but it was afterwards printed in full in vol. iv of the Quarterly Journal (1848). It may be remembered that a similar explanation of the erratics of the Jura and the southern slope of the Alps was published many years earlier by Scrope in his 'Considerations on Volcanoes' 1825, p. 217.

[3] 'Illustrations of the Huttonian Theory' 1802, § 349.

Britain, however, was once much colder than it is now, was proved
on palæontological evidence by James Smith, of Jordanhill, who
ascertained that some of the species of shells found in the raised
sea-bottoms of the Clyde Basin no longer live in the adjacent seas,
but are northern forms, still flourishing in boreal and arctic waters.
The importance of this discovery, which was communicated to the
Geological Society in April 1839,[1] was not immediately appreciated.

The significance of the presence of northern shells in some of
our younger deposits only began to be recognized after the papers
and debates which marked the opening of the Geological Society's
session in November 1840.   Stimulated by the Alpine glacier-work
of Venetz and Charpentier, which had been so admirably followed
up and extended by Agassiz, Buckland had gone to Switzerland,
and under the guidance of the great Swiss palæontologist, had been
convinced, by the cogency of the evidence brought before him, that
the Alpine glaciers had once stretched for many miles beyond their
present terminations, had polished and striated the rocks over
which they moved, and had transported huge blocks of stone across
the great plain of Switzerland from the sides of the Central Alps
to the slopes of the Jura.   As the Swiss phenomena appeared to
him to have the closest resemblance to those with which he was
familiar in this country,[2] he induced Agassiz to come to England
in the summer of 1840 and make a prolonged excursion with him
in the northern counties, over a large portion of Scotland, and
through parts of Ireland.   The results of this tour were communicated to the Society at two successive meetings in the following
month of November.[3]   The two travellers then boldly announced
their belief that not only had glaciers filled the valleys of our
mountain-groups, but that they had spread far over the plains,
bearing with them, and leaving behind as they melted, the boulders
still found strewn in abundance over so large an area of this country.

[1] Proc. vol. iii, p. 118.

[2] He had examined them in Scotland in 1811 and again in 1824, and had
adopted the usual belief that they marked the passage of diluvial waves across
the country. He, for a time, looked upon them as proofs of the action of
Noah's Flood.

[3] Proc. vol. iii (1841): L. Agassiz 'On Glaciers & the Evidence of their
having once Existed in Scotland, Ireland, & England' p. 327; W. Buckland,
'On the Evidence of Glaciers in Scotland & the North of England' pp. 332,
345, 579. An abstract of the debates which followed the reading of these
papers will be found in 'The History of the Geological Society of London,' by
H. B. Woodward (1907) pp. 138, 143.

These novel and startling views in British geology met with a cool reception from the general body of geologists here. They were violently opposed and sarcastically ridiculed at the Society's Meetings when they were communicated, and for some years they met with but little acceptance. Nevertheless, they undoubtedly quickened the general interest in the subject, and set a number of geologists hunting for traces of glaciers among the higher hills of the British Isles. Lyell found a fine group of well-preserved moraines nestling in the recesses of the Forfarshire hills, not far from his paternal estate.[1] James David Forbes, who had made himself familiar with the Swiss glaciers and published in 1843 his classic volume on 'Travels through the Alps,' brought to light the striking glaciation of the Cuillin Hills of Skye.[2] Charles Maclaren found traces of glaciers among the glens of Argyllshire,[3] and Charles Darwin called attention to those which have been left in the mountain-group of North Wales.[4]

But even the geologists who were ready to admit the former presence of glaciers among the hills of Britain could not, for the most part, persuade themselves to accept Agassiz's contention that vast sheets of ice once spread over the low grounds of these islands. They had, however, to account somehow for the dispersion of the erratic blocks, and they preferred to do so by supposing that the land was partly submerged in a sea over which icebergs carried and dropped the boulders. They even applied the same solution to the case of Switzerland. It seemed to them more credible that not only the British Isles, but the centre of the European Continent, should have been first submerged for many hundreds of feet under an icy sea and then re-elevated, than that land-ice could ever have been massive enough, not merely to form vast glaciers among the valleys of the Alps, but to advance from the mountains across the plains, carrying a vast burden of stones and soil.[5]

---

[1] His account of them was communicated to the Society and appears in the same volume of the Proceedings with the papers of Agassiz and Buckland, p. 337.

[2] Edin. New Phil. Journ. vol. xl (1845-46) p. 76.

[3] *Ibid.* p. 125.

[4] Phil. Mag. vol. xxi (1842) p. 180.

[5] It will be remembered that, among others, Lyell once held this view of European submergence. It was expressed in the first and subsequent editions of his 'Elements of Geology' (1838) p. 136, but he afterwards abandoned it in face of the accumulating evidence against it. See the 6th edition of the same work (1865) p. 142.

The printed records of the Geological Society, among their other interesting chronicles, show how long and how obstinately some erroneous beliefs have been held and defended even by the scientific leaders of their day. For many years after the visit of Agassiz and after the recognition of moraines and glacier-borne boulders in many parts of this country, the old notion still had strenuous advocates that the drift and erratic blocks could not be satisfactorily accounted for without the help of sudden upheavals of the sea-bottom, whereby vast waves were generated which swept across the land with destructive vehemence. Some geologists of note held this view, and yet also admitted the contemporaneous agency of floating ice. Thus, in 1846, Murchison, after a journey in Scandinavia, communicated to the Geological Society a paper in which, while admitting the co-operation of icebergs in the distribution of the northern erratics, as he had already done in his ' Russia & the Ural Mountains,' he still stoutly maintained that the transport of the drift and the great erosion of the rocky surface of the country had been effected by ' powerful currents or waves of translation caused by sudden heaves of the Scandinavian continent' (Q. J. vol. ii, p. 349).

This convulsionist creed received strong support from two Cambridge mathematicians. In 1847 Whewell gave to the Society a paper bearing the title ' On the Wave of Translation in connection with the Northern Drift.'[1] In this communication he stated that he looked upon the drift as ' an irresistible proof of paroxysmal action,' and he proceeded to offer a mathematical demonstration of the truth of this belief. Assuming a mass of water 4500 cubic miles in dimension to be suddenly upraised to the extent of a tenth of a mile, or a mass of sea 45,000 square miles in area and a tenth of a mile in depth to be raised through a tenth of a mile, he reasoned (*op. cit.* p. 231) that

' if we suppose a sea-bottom 450 miles long by 100 miles broad, which is $\frac{1}{10}$ of a mile below the surface of the water, to be raised to the surface by paroxysmal action, we shall have the force which we require for the distribution of the northern drift, on the numerical assumptions which have been made.'

Hopkins returned to the subject in 1851, when he read to the Society a paper ' On the Granitic Blocks of the South Highlands of Scotland.' By this time he had come to realize in some degree the strength of the proofs in favour of the view that glaciers and floating ice had been concerned in the transport

[1] Q. J. iii, 227.

of the boulder-drift. Yet he still clung to the notion that during the time of submergence

'currents produced by repeated elevatory movements not only swept away new sedimentary deposits, but also still more deeply excavated the pre-existing valleys.' (Q. J. vol. viii (1852) p. 20.)

In spite, however, of these efforts to support it, the paroxysmal explanation of the northern drift was slowly but surely being exploded in this country by the progress of more extended and detailed study of the drift and dressed rocks, though it continued to maintain its sway on the Continent. When English geologists dropped it as a possible aid in the interpretation of the striated rock-surfaces and the boulder-drift, they fell back, not on the explanation offered by Agassiz, but on submergence and icebergs. The hypothesis of floating ice, with or without the aid of sub-terranean paroxysms, continued for nearly twenty years after Agassiz's visit to be the generally accepted method of accounting for the facts. Yet during those lean years of progress in this part of British geology a few able observers, notably Robert Chambers among them, advocated the claims of land-ice to attentive con-sideration. Their appeal to the evidence of the polished and grooved rock-surfaces, to the divergence of the striæ from the central uplands, and to the radiation of the boulders from these centres of dispersion met with little heed, until about the year 1860 a marked revival of interest in the subject set in. Some new and active investigators, following the example of Chambers, began to study the phenomena in more detail than had been done before. They ascertained beyond all question that the dressed rock-surfaces must have been produced by some agent that not merely rubbed them down, but moulded itself upon their uneven surfaces, and, diverging on every side from the higher grounds, moved steadily across the surrounding lowlands regardless of their minor topo-graphical features. It was found that the erratic blocks followed the same lines of radiation. The whole of the appearances seemed to be inexplicable by the capricious movements of bergs and floes variously driven by winds and currents. These floating masses of ice might conceivably grate along submerged rocks, but could never descend into each hollow and mount over each protuberance of the roches moutonnées. The only theory which would explain all the facts was recognized to be that proposed by Agassiz twenty years before, that not merely local glaciers occupied the valleys among our mountains, but that these mountains, like those of Greenland, were in large measure buried under a continuous mantle of ice which moved outward in all directions towards the sea. Some of the earlier papers which helped forward the adoption of this explanation of the phenomena were published in our Quarterly Journal ; those of A. C. Ramsay [1] and T. F. Jamieson [2] were specially effective.

While we may reflect with no little pleasure that the Geological Society can claim to have had a conspicuous share in starting the active study of the glaciation of Britain, not less satisfaction may be derived from the part taken by the Society in the great subsequent development of the subject. The growth of Pleistocene literature during the latter half of last century has been one of the most remarkable features in the modern advancement of geology, and a large portion of this literature, including some of its best parts, has been given to the world in the volumes of the Quarterly Journal. Thus, in looking through these volumes, the geologist will find that the march of the ice-sheet over the Shetland Isles has been followed by Dr. Peach & Dr. Horne,[3] and over the Outer Hebrides by Prof. James Geikie.[4] The later stages of the Ice-Age in Northern Scotland have been traced by Mr. Jamieson. The relics of some of the last glaciers in the Southern Uplands have been described by the late Prof. John Young.[5] The glaciation of the Eden Valley and the west part of Yorkshire has been explored by the late J. G. Goodchild [6] ; that of the Lake District by the late J. C. Ward [7] and D. Mackintosh.[8] Mr. Mellard Reade has furnished papers on the Drift of the north-western counties and of the Vale of Clwyd,[9] while Mr. Tiddeman has given an account of the traces left by the ice-sheet from Yorkshire through North Lancashire into Westmorland.[10] Dr. Strahan has discussed the glaciation of South Lancashire and the Welsh border [11]; Dr. Dwerryhouse that of Teesdale, Weardale, and the Tyne Valley.[12] Prof. Kendall has drawn a suggestive picture

[1] Q. J. xv (1859) 200 & xviii (1862) 185.

[2] Q. J. xviii (1862) 164 ; xix (1863) 235 ; xxi (1865) 161 ; xxii (1866) 261 ; xxx (1874) 317.

[3] Q. J. xxxv (1879) 778 & xxxvi (1880) 648.

[4] Q. J. xxix (1873) 532 & xxxiii (1877) 819.

[5] Q. J. xx (1864) 452.

[6] Q. J. xxxi (1875) 55.

[7] Q. J. xxix (1873) 422 ; xxx (1874) 96 ; xxxi (1875) 152.

[8] Q. J. xxx (1874) 174, 711.

[9] Q. J. xxx (1874) 27 ; xxxix (1883) 83 ; liii (1897) 341.

[10] Q. J. xxviii (1872) 471.          [11] Q. J. xlii (1886) 369.

[12] Q. J. lviii (1902) 572.

of the margin of the northern ice-sheet where it ponded back the drainage of the Cleveland Hills.[1]  Mr. Lamplugh has studied the Boulder-Clays of the coast by Bridlington and Flamborough Head.[2] Mr. Jukes-Browne has given us descriptions of the Drift of Lincolnshire.  In East Anglia the Drifts were studied in earlier years by Joshua Trimmer, and subsequently in more detail by Searles V. Wood, Jun., by W. H. Penning,[3] by Mr. F. W. Harmer,[4] and others; while on our extreme southern shores the peculiar glacial phenomena there presented, which were described many years ago by Godwin-Austen,[5] have been further elucidated by Mr. Clement Reid.[6]  Thus there are comparatively few of the glaciated portions of the country of which investigations have not been recorded in the Society's publications.

The valley-gravels and later post-Glacial deposits of our islands have likewise found a place in our Journal.  Among the papers dealing with this part of the geological record, those of Prestwich are specially noteworthy.  The bone-caves of England and their organic contents have been the subject of various communications to the Society.  The papers of Prof. Boyd Dawkins[7] and the Rev. Magens Mello[8] are well-known, likewise those by Hicks and De Rance on the Cae-Gwyn Cavern.[9]  The interesting ossiferous fissures near Ightham have been fully described by Mr. J. W. L. Abbott & Mr. E. T. Newton,[10] while within the last few years fresh examples of bone-caves have been brought to light by Mr. H. N. Davies from the Cheddar limestone,[11] and by Dr. H. H. Arnold-Bemrose & Mr. E. T. Newton from that of Derbyshire.[12]

## II. Foreign Geology.

From the outset of its career the Geological Society has not confined its attention to the rocks of this country, but has welcomed and published communications on the geology of all quarters of the globe.  In the early decades of the last century the growing spirit of travel induced many of our countrymen who had geological

[1] Q. J. lviii (1902) 471.          [2] Q. J. xl (1884) 312 & xlvii (1891) 384.
[3] Q. J. xxxii (1876) 191.          [4] Q. J. xxiii (1867) 87 & xxxiii (1877) 74.
[5] Q. J. vi & vii (1850-51).        [6] Q. J. xliii (1887) 364 & xlviii (1892) 344.
[7] Q. J. xviii, xix, xxxii, xxxiii, lix (1862-63, 1876-77, 1903).
[8] Q. J. xxxi, xxxii, xxxiii, xxxv (1875-79).
[9] Q. J. xlii (1886) 3 & xliv (1888) 561.          [10] Q. J. l (1894) 171.
[11] Q. J. lx (1904) 335.          [12] Q. J. lxi (1905) 43.

proclivities to make journeys in foreign lands and bring home notes of their observations, and not infrequently collections of specimens. In those days the number of learned societies to which such notes could appropriately be presented was much more limited than it is now; the periodical press was still in its infancy, and the more ambitious or successful travellers were generally disposed, then as now, to give their narratives to the world in the form of independent works. The Transactions of the Geological Society opened a new and convenient channel for the publication of scientific notes of foreign travel, and the Quarterly Journal has since been equally available for similar communications. The progress of time, however, has effected considerable changes in the facilities for making known the results of scientific journeys. The number has much increased of societies publishing papers, not only in our own land but among all the civilized nations of the globe. National geological surveys have been established in most countries, and the geology of these countries is now largely in the hands of native officials, by whom it is worked out in systematic detail. The little-known areas of the earth's surface which offer a field for the enterprising geologist who can only afford time for rapid traverses of new country are growing every year fewer and smaller. It is natural, therefore, that important papers on foreign geology should tend to become less frequent, and that the Geological Society should more rarely receive communications respecting the geology of regions which have the benefit of possessing native or local observers, as well as a sufficiency of scientific journals. Such communications, it is felt, are in general more appropriately published in the countries to which they refer, although the Society still gladly receives such papers on foreign geology as have not merely a local significance, but bear in an interesting or novel manner on the principles of the science.

In the early days of the Geological Society, the face of the earth presented many untrodden fields to the geologist. And even the regions that had often been traversed and described had received such diverse interpretations from the antagonistic schools of doctrine that their true structure and geological history were in dispute. These well-known tracts were apt to become battle-fields for the triumph of theoretical opinions, rather than training-grounds for the establishment of truth. The twelve volumes of our Transactions, covering the years from 1807 to 1856, furnish interesting evidence of the kind of journeys which the founders and early members of the Society took abroad, and of the nature of the observations which they deemed worthy of permanent record. Among these contributions some have taken a notable place in the history of the growth of geology. As a rule, like those on the geology of our own country, they exemplify the guiding principle on which the Society was established, that hypothesis and theory should as far as possible be discountenanced, and that attention should mainly be given to the ascertainment and registration of the actual facts of nature. From the Continent of Europe there came the memoir of Strangways on Russia,[1] which so usefully opened a way for the subsequent work of Murchison, De Verneuil, and Keyserling. Scrope sent his observations on the Ponza Isles and the volcanic district of Naples.[2] Buckland and De la Beche supplied papers on the rocks of the Riviera coast.[3] Lyell described what he had seen among the Cretaceous and Tertiary strata of the Danish islands of Seeland and Möen.[4] Leonard Horner communicated the account which his sojourn at Bonn enabled him to prepare of that district of Rhineland.[5]

But perhaps the most memorable papers on foreign geology which appeared in the Transactions were the joint contributions of Sedgwick & Murchison. The great monograph which contained the results of their explorations in the Eastern Alps was a bold pioneering attempt to unravel the complicated structure of that mountain-chain.[6] Still more epoch-making was their memoir 'On the Distribution & Classification of the Older or Palæozoic Deposits of the North of Germany & Belgium, & their Comparison with Formations of the same Age in the British Isles.'[7] The Devonian System, which the two authors had successfully established in this country, was recognized and traced by them over a large part of Central Europe. They were able to detect the Continental equivalents of the English subdivisions, and thus to place, in its true stratigraphical position, a large portion of the ancient and still undefined domain of the Grauwacke. The progress of research since their day has, of course, greatly extended and improved their work; but the broader features of the Devonian System in the region over which they were traced by these two leaders remain essentially the same, and the name 'Devonian' has become a familiar term in the geological nomenclature of all parts of the world.

[1] Trans. ser. 2, vol. i, p. 1.
[2] Ibid. vol. ii, pp. 195, 337.
[3] Ibid. vol. iii, pp. 171, 187.
[4] Ibid. vol. v, p. 243.
[5] Ibid. vol. iv, p. 433.
[6] Ibid. vol. iii, pp. 301-420.
[7] Ibid. vol. vi, p. 221.

As might be expected from the political connections of this country with the East, papers on Asiatic geology find a place in most of the volumes of the Transactions, chiefly with reference to India. They include Cautley's notes on the structure and fossils of the Sewalik Hills,[1] C. W. Grant's map of Cutch,[2] Malcolmson's description of the basaltic region of India,[3] and likewise the interesting series of communications from H. E. Strickland[4] and W. J. Hamilton on Asia Minor.[5]

South African geology takes up most of the last volume of the Transactions, where the papers of A. G. Bain on the Karroo formation brought to notice the remarkable organic remains of that deposit, and where the Report by Owen on its bidental reptiles first made known this new type of organisms. Some of the other fossils were described by Sir Joseph Hooker and Sir Philip Egerton.

The other side of the Atlantic is represented in the early series of the Society's publications by several papers on the West Indian Islands, including De la Beche's excellent description of the geology of Jamaica,[6] Nelson's interesting and oft-quoted paper on the Bermudas,[7] and Nugent's account of the pitch-lake of Trinidad, of the soufrière of Montserrat and of Antigua.[8] From Canada came the first communication sent by Bigsby to the Society, descriptive of the geology of the Lake-Huron district[9]; also Bayfield's notes on the northern coast of Labrador.[10]

An interesting feature in the communications on foreign geology made to the Society in its younger days is to be seen in the preliminary reports furnished by Fellows regarding their journeys and observations abroad. The Transactions, and after them the Quarterly Journal, supplied a convenient means of recording discoveries or new facts of general interest. Early publicity was not always secured in these publications, for complaints used to be heard of the slowness with which the Society's printed records made their appearance. There can, I think, be little doubt that a spirit of loyalty to the Society prevailed among its members, which prompted them to offer it at least the first-fruits of their labours, without waiting until the whole results of their observations could be elaborated into independent volumes which they could present to the library. As examples of this spirit, reference may be made to the numerous communications

---

[1] Trans. ser. 2, vol. v, p. 267.    [2] Ibid. p. 289.    [3] Ibid. p. 537.
[4] Ibid. pp. 385, 393, 403.    [5] Ibid. p. 583 & vol. vi, pp. 1–40.
[6] Ibid. vol. ii, p. 143.    [7] Ibid. vol. v, p. 103.
[8] Ibid. ser. 1, vol. i, pp. 63, 185 & vol. v, p. 459.
[9] Ibid. ser. 2, vol. i, p. 175.    [10] Ibid. vol. v, p. 89.

sent by Lyell in the course of his first journeys in North America which are printed in the third and fourth volumes of the Proceedings and the first volume of the Quarterly Journal. Another instance was that of Murchison & De Verneuil, when, in the spring of 1841, they gave to the Society the first account of the general results of their traverses of the northern and central governments of Russia during the previous summer.

By the time that the more regular and frequent publication of the Society's papers was secured by the establishment of the Quarterly Journal, other geological societies had made their appearance in this country and abroad. The Geological Survey of the United Kingdom had been set on foot, largely through the influence of Fellows of this Society, and had given to other lands an example of national recognition of the need for the accurate determination and mapping of the rocks of a country. A change in the number and character of the communications on foreign geology now began to be perceptible. The regions described became more and more restricted to our own colonies and dependencies, and to tracts of the earth's surface that had been little visited and of which the geology was still unknown. This change, however, was so gradual that for some years the Journal continued to receive papers conceived, both as to subject and as to treatment, in the earlier style of the Transactions. Thus Murchison filled more than 150 pages of the fifth volume with an account of the geological structure of the Alps, Apennines, and Carpathian Mountains, his more particular object being to prove a transition from Secondary into Tertiary formations, and to show the development of Eocene deposits in Southern Europe. No part of the European continent has bulked so largely in our publications as the Chain of the Alps. But papers of the type of Murchison's on that region are no longer presented to us. Such rapid sketches of wide areas of complicated ground have given place to records of much more detailed observations of particular lines of section or special rocks of the chain. Yet in these later and more localized communications questions of extreme interest and importance in regard to the history of the Alps and to general problems in geology may be discussed. I need only refer, in this connection, to the long series of papers by Prof. Bonney on the crystalline rocks of these mountains.

The geology of our Colonies must necessarily now come less frequently before us, seeing that most of these Colonies have their own scientific journals in which the labours of their resident geologists may be recorded. But, in turning over the volumes of the Quarterly Journal, we see how frequent and valuable have been the Colonial communications in past years. The Canadian contributions have been especially numerous and important. Bigsby continued to supply notices of the geology of Canada and the United States for some twenty years after the Journal was started. The papers of Sir William Dawson, which for more than fifty years he continued to present for publication by the Society, range over a wide field of the geology of the Dominion. Especially valuable were his contributions to our knowledge of the flora of the Devonian and Carboniferous Periods in North America. His discovery of land-shells, myriapods, and reptiles in the heart of erect Coal-Measure trees supplied a vivid picture of the conditions in which these strata were accumulated. Though the progress of investigation has not confirmed his view of the organic nature of the famous *Eozoon*, his discussions on the most ancient crystalline rocks of Canada are full of suggestiveness. Another early Canadian contributor to the Quarterly Journal was Richard Brown, whose descriptions of the erect fossil trees and other features in the Cape Breton coal-field appeared in successive years from 1847 to 1850.

The geology of New Zealand has been illustrated in our Journal by communications from Julius von Haast, James Hector, and F. W. Hutton, all of whom have now passed away. But younger men are rising to carry on the geological exploration of that Dominion, and we quite recently published a good paper by Prof. P. Marshall on the geology of Dunedin.

African geology has been often the subject of communications to the Society since the time of Bain's memoirs already referred to. In the earlier volumes of the Quarterly Journal it was chiefly with Egypt that the papers were concerned. But the opening-up of the Dark Continent, and the extension of our colonies and protectorates over its surface, have led to much exploration and to the rapid increase of our knowledge of large areas of territory. In the southern portion of the continent, as well as in the north, geological surveys have been organized, whereby more detailed information is being continually made available. Among the pioneering papers regarding East and South Africa which the Society has published, reference may be made to Prof. Gregory's series of communications on Mount Kenya and Ruwenzori,[1] Mr. Walcot Gibson's memoir[2] and

[1] Q. J. l (1894) 515 & lvi (1900) 205, 223.
[2] Q. J. xlviii (1892) 404.

that of Dr. Hatch [1] on the geology of the Transvaal, Mr. Molyneux's geological account of Southern Rhodesia,[2] and Mr. Lamplugh's paper on the Zambesi Basin.[3]   The intimate relations of Great Britain with Egypt, and the establishment of a geological survey in that country under British direction, have brought us some interesting communications from Capt. Lyons on the Libyan and Nubian Deserts,[4] and an excellent paper by Mr. H. J. L. Beadnell on the Eocene and Cretaceous systems in the Nile Valley.[5]

The geology of many parts of Asia has been described for the first time in the pages of the Quarterly Journal.   The institution of the Geological Survey of India having provided a staff of trained observers and ample facilities for publication, it is not now necessary or desirable that at least local descriptive papers should any longer be sent to us from that great dependency.   But we can look back on not a few important memoirs which have come thence to our Journal.   Thus the papers of S. Hislop, from their beginning in 1854 to his death in 1864, contain information of more than merely local significance.   They include, for example, the earliest description of the shells, insects, and cyprids which indicate that the lavas of the vast Indian volcanic plateau were poured out on the land, and not under the sea.   The geology of portions of the Himalayas and of Tibet was elucidated as far back as 1851 by the late Sir Richard Strachey, while nine years later further light was thrown upon the rocks of that vast mountain-chain and of those of Cashmere by Col. Godwin-Austen, who is happily still with us.

During the progress of a Demarcation-Commission on the Turco-Persian frontier from 1849 to 1852, a large amount of information, obtained by W. K. Loftus, was communicated by him in a long and valuable paper which appeared in the Quarterly Journal in 1855. Another important contribution was made by our late lamented colleague W. T. Blanford in 1873, in which he described the valleys and deserts of Central Persia.[6]   The same volume in which that paper was printed contains also Frederick Drew's suggestive account of the alluvial deposits of the Upper Indus.   The results of Dr. Blanford's long years of work in Indian geology were properly reserved for the official publications of the Survey to which he belonged, but the Geological Society was privileged to enjoy the benefit of his ripe knowledge of the subject.   The work of his

[1] Q. J. liv (1898) 73.      [2] Q. J. lix (1899) 266.
[3] Q. J. lxiii (1907) 162.   [4] Q. J. l (1894) 531 & liii (1897) 360.
[5] Q. J. lxi (1905) 667.     [6] Q. J. xxix, 493.

colleague H. B. Medlicott was in like manner loyally given to the Indian service, but he communicated to the Society one paper, for the writing of which his long Indian experience specially qualified him—a comparison of the structure of the Alps and Himalayas.[1]

The West Indies have provided material for numerous communications to the Society, from the time of those that were published in the Transactions down to the present day. Specially deserving of mention are those of Mr. Jukes-Browne and Prof. J. B. Harrison on Barbados and Trinidad,[2] of P. Martin Duncan on the fossil corals of the West Indies,[3] and of Prof. Gregory on the palæontology and physical geology of the region.[4] The most recent accounts received by us of the geology of this archipelago are the notices of a number of the islands supplied by Prof. J. W. Spencer.[5]

Perhaps the most notable paper on South American geology published by the Society is that by David Forbes, which appeared in the Quarterly Journal for 1861. It gave an account of the geology of Bolivia and Southern Peru, with a map of the region and sections across the Andes, showing the fresh contributions which he had made to our knowledge. Charles Darwin's important observations on South America were published elsewhere, but he communicated to the Society his well-known paper on the Falkland Islands, which appeared in the volume of the Quarterly Journal for 1846.[6] The same volume contains his account of the fine dust which falls on vessels in the Atlantic Ocean.

Various papers connected with the geology of the Arctic regions have from time to time appeared in our Journal. Of especial consequence are those descriptive of fossils brought home by explorers, for they have thrown light on the extension of Palæozoic, Mesozoic, and Tertiary formations into high latitudes. Some of the most valuable of these communications have been made within the last ten years, particularly those by Dr. Teall, Mr. E. T. Newton, and

---

[1] Q. J. xxiv (1868) 34.

[2] Q. J. xlvii (1891) 197 ; xlviii (1892) 170 ; lv (1899) 177.

[3] Q. J. xix, xx, xxi, xxiv, xxix (1863-65, 1868, 1873).

[4] Q. J. li (1895) 255.

[5] Q. J. lvii & lviii (1901-02).

[6] The latest geologist who has visited these islands, Dr. J. G. Andersson, now Director of the Geological Survey of Sweden, confirms the excellence of Darwin's account of their geology. He has named after the great naturalist the large 'stone-river' which Darwin described, and has furnished a map and panorama of this remarkable feature. See 'Schwedische Süd-Polar-Expedition, 1901-1903' vol. iii, pt. 2 (1907).

*A*

Dr. Kœttlitz on the rocks and fossils of Franz Josef Land.[1] Some interesting additions to our acquaintance with the glacial phenomena of the Far North have been made by Col. Feilden,[2] Prof. Garwood, and Prof. Gregory.[3]

Lastly, as regards the information which we receive on foreign geology, I would refer to the notices from time to time communicated to the Society by different Government Departments, as received from officers in the Army, Navy, and Diplomatic or Consular Service. Many new and interesting facts have thus been brought to our knowledge, and through our Quarterly Journal have been made known to the world at large. As an example of such communications I may cite the notes and specimens submitted by the late Hydrographer, Admiral Sir William Wharton, from Clipperton Atoll in the North Pacific Ocean, which enabled Dr. Teall to describe the remarkable phosphatization of a trachyte underlying a deposit of guano.[4]

## III. Petrography.

For many centuries before the Geological Society was founded the science of Mineralogy had flourished as an important and popular branch of natural knowledge. It was held to embrace the whole mineral kingdom, but in practice its cultivators devoted their attention chiefly to those parts of the terrestrial crust which appear in the form of simple minerals. Collectors might add to their cabinets beautiful or singular examples of rocks, concretions, organic remains, or other mineral substances, but these were generally gathered together rather as curiosities than as objects having a history worthy of patient study. Naturally, therefore, when at last attention was awakened to the many interesting questions suggested by the various materials that compose the earth's crust, those who occupied themselves with such subjects were chiefly mineralogists. The various sciences which have since grown up in the course of the investigation of that crust—geology, petrography, and palæontology—had not yet taken shape, but all lay in embryo within the time-honoured domain of Mineralogy.[5]

[1] Q. J. liii (1897) 477 & liv (1898) 620, 646.   [2] Q. J. lii (1896) 52, 721.
[3] Q. J. liv (1898) 197 & lv (1899) 681.   [4] Q. J. liv (1898) 230.
[5] As an interesting survival of this period, reference may be made to the present constitution of the Academy of Sciences in the Institute of France, which was founded in 1795. Mineralogy still holds its place there as the title of one of the eleven sections into which the Academy is divided. But it includes the cognate sciences, though these are not named, and almost all its members are now geologists.

The first volume of the Transactions of the Geological Society bears witness to the mineralogical bent of our founders. Not only do almost all the papers deal with the mineralogical rather than the palæontological aspect of rocks, but they include some which are entirely devoted to the description of simple minerals. It is curious to note the rapid disappearance of such papers from the Society's publications. There can be no doubt that this disappearance was the sign of a gradual and widespread change in the general attitude of the scientific mind in this country towards the study of the mineral kingdom.[1] The uprise of geology and the absorbing interest of its problems regarding the history of our planet and the succession of plants and animals which have lived on its surface, gradually drew attention away from the study of minerals and of rocks considered as mineral masses. Mineralogy, in the modern sense of the term, ceased to be prominent as one of the departments of science which the Society cultivated, while the investigation of rocks likewise fell into neglect. Probably in no country where geology was actively cultivated did the petrographical branch of the science drop so far behind as it did here. We have only to look at the English text-books of the time to perceive how little regard was paid to the mineralogical and chemical composition of rocks, or to their genetic relations to each other as part of the evolution of the earth's crust. Now and then an attempt was made to remedy this deficiency. Thus Macculloch published in 1821 his 'Classification of Rocks'; but it failed to awaken an abiding interest in the subject. Ten years later, De la Beche, who, more than any other English geologist of his time, realized the importance of the study of rocks, published his excellent 'Geological Manual,' in which he treated the 'unstratified rocks,' chiefly from the chemical side, as fully as his space and the available knowledge of the day would permit. Still more valuable were his suggestive

---

[1] The condition of the petrographical side of the science, fifteen years after the rise of the Geological Society, may be judged from the classic 'Outlines' of Conybeare & Phillips, published in 1822. It is true that this volume deals almost entirely with the stratified fossiliferous formations of the country, the eruptive masses as a whole being reserved for the second part of the work, which unfortunately was never written. But the igneous rocks associated with the Carboniferous System were discussed. In taking a general view of this part of their subject, the authors confess that ' it is to be regretted that little attention has been paid by our English geologists, with the exception of Dr. Macculloch, to the precise determination of the mineralogical characters of these rocks ' (p. 439).

pages on this subject, in his little volume of 'Researches in
Theoretical Geology,' published in 1834. But his efforts also
failed to arouse general recognition of the true value of a branch
of geology which had ceased to be actively cultivated in this
country. In contrast to this neglect, the study of minerals and
rocks, under the prolonged impulse that had been given by Werner,
was pursued in Germany with persistent energy, and produced many
papers and treatises.

But even on the Continent further progress in the investigation
of this branch of geology was seriously retarded by the difficulty
in determining the actual mineral composition of the large series
of rocks which have too close a texture to allow their individual
mineral constituents to be recognized, either with the naked eye or
with a lens. Extensive use had, indeed, been made of chemical
analysis, although it then lacked the delicate refinement to which
it has since been carried. The general chemical composition of
rocks had been fairly well ascertained. Nevertheless, although it
might often be possible to infer with some confidence from chemical
analysis what separate minerals have been aggregated together in
the formation of a particular rock, no means had yet been discovered
of actually determining the presence and proportions of the mineral
ingredients in fine-grained masses.

In the early years of last century, indeed, Cordier had described
a method of crushing down such rocks, washing and separating
the grains of their powder, and examining these grains under
the microscope.[1] By this process it was possible to ascertain the
mineral constitution of some rocks, and to study the characters of
their individual minerals. But, as these minerals were detached
from each other and from their matrix, and were often opaque,
comparatively little light could be obtained on the intimate structure
of the rocks composed of them. It may, therefore, be affirmed that,
up to the middle of the nineteenth century, no means had been
devised for determining with precise accuracy the various microscopic elements of rocks, the order in which these elements solidified,
and the conditions in which their solidification took place.

But from that time onward a great revolution was accomplished
in the methods of rock-analysis. Petrography was so completely
transformed as to be ushered, with widened capabilities and freshened
interest, into a new career of rapid development. From being a

[1] Ann. de Chimie & Physique, vol. iii (1830) p. 285. Cordier's paper was
read to the Academy of Sciences in 1815.

subordinate and comparatively neglected branch of geology, it may now claim the dignity of an almost independent science. In contemplating this revolution—undoubtedly the most momentous of the last fifty years in any department of geological science—we of the Geological Society of London may be pardoned if, with a feeling of pride, we remember that it was started and received its earliest impulse within our walls at the hands of one of our Fellows who is happily still with us, and still in his old age communicates the results of his continued researches.[1] No pages in the volumes of our Quarterly Journal have been so fecund as those which announced to the world the advent of this new era in the investigation of the materials of the crust of the earth. In the eight years which followed 1850 Mr. Henry Clifton Sorby communicated to the Society a series of papers,[2] in which he showed how by adopting the method of preparing thin transparent slices of mineral substances, a process which had been devised before the year 1831 by William Nicol,[3] of Edinburgh, the minutest structures of rocks could be revealed and examined. He began by describing the constitution of the Calcareous Grit of Yorkshire and various limestones. Gaining courage with experience, he realized the endless capabilities of this method of petrographical analysis, and soon boldly attacked various metamorphic and igneous rocks. He showed how it was now possible to investigate with precision the mineral constitution of rocks, to determine their microscopic structure, to ascertain the probable conditions and depths at which they consolidated, and to trace the subsequent changes which they have undergone.

This epoch-marking demonstration of the fruitfulness of the application of the microscope to the elucidation of the composition and genesis of rocks was published in the Quarterly Journal for 1858. Its appearance might have been supposed certain at

[1] As these pages are passing through the press the news has reached me that our veteran colleague has passed away. Though confined to bed, he had retained his mental faculties unimpaired. Only a fortnight before his death I received a letter from him in his own clear handwriting, in which he enquired after the disposition of specimens which he had studied half a century ago.

[2] Q. J. vii, 1 ; ix, 344; x, 328 ; xii, 137 ; xiv, 453. See also his Presidential Addresses in vols. xxxv & xxxvi (1879-80).

[3] Nicol's invention consisted in polishing thin pieces of stone, fixing them on glass with Canada balsam, and reducing them in thickness until they became transparent. It was applied by him to the elucidation of the structure of fossil wood, and the first account of it was prepared by him for Henry Witham's ' History of Fossil Vegetables,' published in 1831.

once to awaken the geologists of this country from their long petrographical lethargy. But some nine years seem to have passed away before a single one of them showed by any published paper that he realized the capabilities of the method of research which had now been placed in his hands. In 1867 a paper by David Forbes on 'The Microscope in Geology' was, I think, the first public evidence that the seed sown by Dr. Sorby was beginning to germinate here.[1] That seed fell on more responsive soil in Germany, where several geologists began to avail themselves of the new method.[2] But it was the energy and enthusiasm of Prof. Zirkel which launched that method into active prosecution on the Continent. From the time of his earliest account of it to the Vienna Academy in 1863, he continued year after year to publish papers and separate volumes, dealing with different parts of the subject. These works, with their wealth of new material, and the originality of the conclusions which they established, led the way in the reconstitution of petrography. Prof. Rosenbusch followed with a fuller development of microscopic optics and a brilliant exposition of the whole subject. By these two great leaders, and by the enthusiastic disciples whom they have gathered round them, Germany has been placed in the forefront of the nations in which this study is pursued.

About a quarter of a century, however, passed away after Dr. Sorby's first indication of the significance of the new method of research, before his example began to be followed in earnest in this country. In 1874 the late Samuel Allport gave to the Geological Society his now classic paper on British Carboniferous Dolerites,[3]

---

[1] Popular Science Review, vol. vi (October 1867) p. 355. It was about the same time that I added a microscope and thin rock-sections to my geological outfit for field-work. In the course of my mapping of the various igneous rocks of Ayrshire for the Geological Survey I had slices prepared from them, of which I availed myself to aid the determinations made in the field. When, in the summer of 1868, Prof. Zirkel paid me a visit at Largs, I was able to show him a series of microscopic slides of the dykes and lavas in the Carboniferous formations of that district: see Zirkel, Zeitschr. Deutsch. Geol. Gesellsch. vol. xxiii (1871) p. 27.

[2] In particular Oschatz, at the meeting of the German Geological Society on January 7th, 1852, referred to the value of the method of preparing thin slices of minerals and inorganic substances, and gave examples of some of the preparations which he had made. On April 5th, 1854, he described further studies of the microscopic structure of rocks, and pointed out the importance of this mode of examination as controlling deductions made from chemical analysis. (Op. cit. vol. iv, p. 13 & vol. vi, p. 261.)

[3] Q. J. vol. xxx, p. 529.

which contained the first account of the employment of the microscope for the elucidation of the structure of a group of English igneous rocks, and in which the essential identity of structure and composition between ancient and modern lavas was maintained. He followed up this memoir with others of great value, wherein he described the characters of ancient devitrified pitchstones and perlites,[1] and traced the nature of the metamorphism that has been induced around the granite of Land's End.[2] John Arthur Phillips now entered the gradually increasing ranks of British modern petrographers, and from 1875 till 1882 continued to contribute to the Quarterly Journal a series of excellent papers, containing the results of his chemical and microscopic analyses of the igneous rocks of the south-western counties and of North Wales.[3] From these crystalline masses he turned to the investigation of clastic materials. His essays on grits and sandstones[4] and on the red sands of the Arabian Desert[5] gave promise of how much he might have accomplished in the study of sedimentary formations had his health and life been prolonged.

Among the other observers who now appeared in quick succession as exponents of the new petrography in its application to the rocks of this country, J. Clifton Ward and Frank Rutley may be mentioned as having both begun their communications on the subject to the Geological Society in 1875. Prof. Bonney, about the same time, started the long succession of his petrographical papers which for so many years have appeared in the Quarterly Journal. Ranging over a great variety of rocks, not only of the British Isles, but from many other parts of the world, his papers rise from mere mineralogical details into broader questions of the origin or age of rocks and of mountain-structure. Those which deal with the Alps, based as they are, not only on repeated personal examination of the ground, but on the careful study of microscopic preparations of the rocks of the chain, will always remain as a monument of his unwearied enthusiasm in the cause of our science. He has not only been himself a prolific author, but he has inspired a school of followers who have done signal service in raising petrography from its former neglected condition amongst us to the important position which it now holds in this country. It would be invidious to single out from these still living and active followers any for special notice

---

[1] Q. J. xxxiii (1877) 449.     [2] Q. J. xxxii (1876) 407.
[3] Q. J. xxxi, 319; xxxiii, 423; xxxiv, 471; xxxv, 490; xxxvi, 1.
[4] Q. J. xxxvii (1881) 6.     [5] Q. J. xxxviii (1882) 110.

here; but I feel sure that the Society will permit me to name one who may be regarded as the type and leader among them, and who has long since gained our esteem and our admiration.    Dr. Teall from the time when, in 1884, he contributed his paper on the dykes in the North of England has continually enriched the petrographical literature of this country.    His separate volume on 'British Petrography,' published in 1888, which will long remain the standard treatise on the subject, probably did more than any other work to gain from foreign geologists an appreciation of the high place to which the study of rocks has at last attained in the country of Sorby.    Not by any means the least important feature in the Society's Quarterly Journal for the last twenty years has been the number and excellence of the petrographical papers.    The names of Profs. Judd, Cole, and Watts, of Mr. Harker, the late General McMahon, Dr. Arnold-Bemrose, Miss Raisin, and others will always be associated with the great petrographical revival of the nineteenth century in Britain.

Naturally this renewed interest in the study of the rocks of the country has been mainly directed to the crystalline masses.    Our volcanic rocks of all ages from the pre-Cambrian to the Tertiary series have been diligently studied, and our knowledge of them now stands in amazing contrast to our ignorance thirty years ago.    The schists and other metamorphic rocks have likewise been made the subjects of prolonged examination, and have had a flood of new light thrown upon their origin and history, though they still bristle with difficulties.    But the sedimentary formations, offering perhaps less obvious attraction, have remained comparatively neglected.    Yet it was with calcareous grits, limestones, and marls that Dr. Sorby began the series of expositions with which he tried to awaken his brother-geologists to the value of the microscope as an adjunct to other instruments of geological research.    It was to sedimentary rocks, too, that he devoted the two suggestive addresses which he gave to the Society during his Presidency in 1879 and 1880.    In spite of his example, however, we have had but few communications on this branch of petrography.    I have already referred to the papers by J. A. Phillips.    Mr. Wethered has given us a series of descriptions of Silurian, Devonian, and Jurassic limestones.    Dr. Teall also, in his Presidential address in 1902, dealt with the petrography of the sedimentary rocks.    Mr. Thomas has discussed the mineralogical constitution of the finer material of the Bunter pebble-beds in the West of England.    But there can be no doubt that much still remains to be done before our knowledge of the sedimentary rocks is brought up-to a level with that of the igneous and metamorphic masses. A steady application of modern methods of research in this investigation should be encouraged by the reflection that, in determining the mineral composition and source of ancient sediments, we may provide materials for the solution of deeply interesting questions regarding the geographical conditions of different geological periods, the nature of the rocks constituting the land, the direction and force of marine currents, the varying rates at which sediment was laid down, the internal changes which the consolidated detritus has since undergone, and probably other points connected with sedimentation, of which we at present may have no inkling. When the recently received paper from Dr. Sorby dealing with this subject, which was read on the 6th of last month, is printed, my earnest hope is that it will stimulate vigorous efforts to follow his methods, to carry out further the experiments which he has initiated, and thus to give to the petrography of the sedimentary rocks a greater share of the attractiveness and interest which have so long been monopolized by the igneous masses.

## IV. Palæontology.

The publications of the Geological Society contain interesting evidence of the gradual development of Palæontology during the nineteenth century. In the first series of the Transactions scarcely any papers are to be found dealing with fossils at all, though the last volume includes a paper by De la Beche & Conybeare on *Ichthyosaurus* and *Plesiosaurus*, which marked the rise of a new interest in organic remains. In the second series this awakened appreciation is seen to be rapidly gaining ground. The first volume of that series includes papers on the Liassic reptiles by Conybeare, and on *Megalosaurus* by Buckland. In the second volume the number of palæontological contributions is much increased in number and range of subject, for it includes accounts of fossil plants, as well as invertebrates and vertebrates. The fifth volume is still more markedly palæontological. In it Sir Philip Egerton's first paper appears, likewise the earliest of the long series of memoirs contributed by Owen. The sixth volume is full of communications from Owen on the new organisms that were brought to him—marsupials from the Stonesfield Slate; bird, tortoise, and lizard from the Chalk; vertebrates from the Eocene series of the Isle of Wight; *Hyracotherium*, *Lithornis*, and *Palæophis* from the London Clay;

likewise descriptions of *Zeuglodon*, *Glyptodon*, and *Labyrinthodon*. The seventh and last volume is especially memorable for Owen's memoirs on the Theriomorphs from the Karroo formation of South Africa.

When the Quarterly Journal replaced the Transactions, the luxurious quarto plates, so dear to the souls of palæontologists, necessarily gave way to a less attractive form of illustration. But the advance of palæontology by the Society was not perceptibly checked in consequence of the change. Egerton continued for nearly thirty years to furnish his contributions on fossil fishes. Owen likewise maintained an almost uninterrupted supply of papers on vertebrate palæontology, up to within five years of the end of his long and strenuous life. Few volumes of the Quarterly Journal appeared without communications from him. His capacity for work seemed to increase with age. From 1874, when he was 70 years of age, he never failed each year to send at least one paper, sometimes as many as three, until in 1887, when he had reached his eighty-third year, failing strength brought the long and splendid series to a close. Among the claims which our Society has on the respect of the scientific world, surely not the least is that it was honoured by being the channel through which so much of the labour of the greatest comparative anatomist of his time was given to the world.

Although Mantell's palæontological work chiefly appeared in independent publications, the first eight volumes of the Quarterly Journal contain a number of his papers and in particular his description of *Telerpeton elginense*, which is now a landmark in the history of investigation among British Triassic rocks. Huxley's earliest communication was made to the Society in 1856, and for more than thirty years thereafter he communicated palæontological papers of the greatest value, besides giving three memorable Presidential addresses. His studies in comparative anatomy took a wide range over the invertebrate and vertebrate divisions of the animal kingdom. His papers in the Quarterly Journal deal with Upper Silurian crustacea, the Devonian ostracoderms, the Carboniferous labyrinthodonts, the Triassic and Liassic reptiles. From the individual specimens he passed on to skilful and pregnant generalizations as to the evidence yielded by the organisms towards the history of evolution. All that he wrote was marked by the strength and suggestiveness of an acute and original mind, and by the felicity of expression which comes from wide literary culture.

Among those no longer living whom the Society holds in high regard for their palæontological contributions we number Hugh Falconer, whose papers on the species of *Mastodon* and Elephant appeared in the Quarterly Journal; J. W. Hulke, so complete a master of the structure of the saurian organisms found in Kimeridge and Wealden formations; J. W. Salter, one of the most brilliant and versatile of all the contributors to British palæontology; Thomas Davidson, the acknowledged chief of brachiopodists; P. Martin Duncan, whose labours on fossil corals and echinoids enabled him to offer suggestive generalizations as to former geographical changes; Robert Etheridge, specially distinguished for his intimate knowledge of Mesozoic fossils; Thomas Wright, whose work among the invertebrata of the Jurassic formations was fitly recognized by the award to him of the Wollaston Medal; and H. A. Nicholson, whose papers on graptolites and other forms placed him high among the students of Palæozoic fossils.

Although death has removed from us many of our most illustrious colleagues in all departments of Palæontology, we are still able to count in our membership a strong phalanx of palæontologists. The structure of extinct vertebrates has been ably discussed by Prof. Seeley in the valuable series of papers which he has communicated to the Society since 1863. Mr. E. T. Newton has given us some interesting papers on fossil fishes and on the mammalia of the newer Pliocene deposits of this country. Dr. Smith Woodward and Dr. Traquair have made themselves masters of fossil Ichthyology. Dr. C. W. Andrews has given us a discussion of the Plesiosaurian skull. Mr. Lydekker, who began his contributions in 1885, has enriched the Quarterly Journal with a large number of papers dealing with Mesozoic reptiles and higher vertebrates from later formations. Dr. Henry Woodward has long been at the head of those whose special labours lie among extinct crustacea; and Prof. Rupert Jones is equally acknowledged to be our highest authority on ostracods and foraminifera.

The inevitable specialization which now attends the development of every branch of our science has led many palæontologists to confine their researches not only to definite and restricted groups of fossils, but to those from a special and limited stratigraphical range. The Mesozoic madreporaria have been looked after by R. F. Tomes; the polyzoa from the Palæozoic rocks by G. W. Shrubsole and G. R. Vine; those from Mesozoic formations by Mr. E. A. Walford and Mr. Vine; those from the North of Italy and other foreign regions by Mr. A. W. Waters. Mesozoic ammonites have long been in the charge of Mr. S. S. Buckman, who has recently also taken over the brachiopods. Fossil crinoids have been well described by Prof. J. W. Gregory and Dr. F. A. Bather. Dr. G. J. Hinde is our chief authority on radiolaria and sponge-spicules. Dr. Wheelton Hind has devoted himself more particularly to the Carboniferous bivalves; and Mr. H. Woods has contributed an exhaustive account of the mollusca of the Chalk Rock.

The Society has been fortunate in counting among its Associates enthusiastic palæontologists devoted to the study of fossil plants. In earlier years the veteran Sir Joseph Hooker, and also Sir Charles Bunbury, contributed papers on this subject. In later days the progress of fossil botany was aided by E. W. Binney and Mr. W. Carruthers. Dr. R. Kidston is now at the head of those who in this country study the structure and range of Carboniferous plants. The value of Prof. Seward's contributions to the Quarterly Journal on Mesozoic plants, as well as of his other writings on Palæo-botany, has been fitly recognized this year by the award to him of the Murchison Medal. Mr. Arber has recently described the plants of the Upper Culm-Measures of Devon and Cornwall.

I have already alluded to the excellent work done by women among fossils, particularly in tracing out palæontological zones among the Palæozoic formations. But some of these workers devote themselves to the study of the zoological characters and relations of the organisms. Thus we have received and published papers on the Carboniferous gasteropods by Miss Donald (Mrs. Longstaff); on graptolites, especially in their zonal relations, by Miss Elles and Miss Wood (Mrs. Shakespear); and on some of the fossils in the Oxford Museum by Miss Sollas and Miss Healey.

## V. Physiography.

The Geological Society having started on its career with the resolution of gathering facts rather than framing theories to account for them, has adhered to this resolution with remarkable constancy. No one can peruse the extended series of the Society's publications without noticing how small is the proportion of the theoretical element in them. For a long time, indeed, anything in the shape of a new theory, though the reading of it might be tolerated at an evening meeting (perhaps for the pleasure and excitement of pulling it to pieces in discussion), was almost certain to be declined for publication.[1]    The practice was so far beneficial in that it excluded crude speculation, and kept the attention of geologists fixed on the accumulation of facts which might afterwards become the basis of sound generalizations.    But it is now no longer rigidly followed.    We receive and print communications which would have been unanimously rejected a generation ago.

One branch of enquiry in our science lies so temptingly open even to beginners, and so seductively fosters speculation that our founders and their successors would have stood on a still higher philosophical level than we can claim for them, had they altogether debarred themselves from entering upon it.    I refer to the origin and history of the present features of the surface of the land, or what has been termed 'physiographical geology.'    The vaguest and most erroneous opinions were long prevalent on this subject.    It was never considered as a whole, nor were its several parts ever worked out in detail, with the view of trying to ascertain their relations to each other in the general evolution of the topography of the land.    In the early stages of geology such a methodized treatment of the subject was obviously impossible ; and even now, with all the light which the progress of investigation has introduced, physiography, while it still remains one of the most attractive, continues at the same time to be one of the most delusive branches of our science.    It will readily be believed that the publications of the Society contain few speculative papers on this subject, but they do include some of historic interest and importance to which I may briefly allude.

Charles Darwin, who took so wide and philosophical a survey of the whole domain of geological enquiry, enriched our publications with a few physiographical memoirs, which have a special interest from the way in which they illustrate, on the one hand, the remarkable breadth of his generalizations, and, on the other, the extreme minuteness of his observations as well as the extraordinary patience with which he conducted them.    The first outline of his memorable theory of vast movements of the ocean-floor, based on a study of coral-reefs, was read to the Society on May 31st, 1837.[2]

[1] My old friend and colleague A. C. Ramsay told me that his paper on the glacial origin of lakes was regarded as so speculative that, but for his being President of the Society at the time, it would certainly have been refused a place in the Quarterly Journal.

[2] Proc. vol. ii, p. 552.    The full title of this paper is ' On certain Areas of Elevation & Subsidence in the Pacific & Indian Oceans, as deduced from the Study of Coral Formations.'

This essay and the expansion of it in his subsequently published volume, even if all the later criticism of it should be sustained, must still be regarded as having formed, at the time when it was promulgated, perhaps the most momentous generalization that had ever been made, from actual observations, regarding the possible movements of the ocean-bed.  In the same year he presented another paper to the Society 'On the Connexion of certain Volcanic Phenomena in South America, & on the Formation of Mountain-Chains & Volcanoes as the Effects of the same Power by which Continents are Elevated.'[1]  In his journeys he had been much impressed with the evidence of extensive uprise on the South American coast, and although he connected this elevatory movement with the volcanic energy so abundantly manifested in the same region, he cautiously refrained from confident deductions, concluding with the following sentence:—

'The furthest generalisation which the consideration of the volcanic phenomena described in this paper appears to lead to, is, that the configuration of the fluid surface of the earth's nucleus is subject to some change—its cause completely unknown ; its action slow, intermittent, but irresistible.'

While dealing with the traces of stupendous movements of the terrestrial crust, Darwin was at the same time engaged upon some of the minuter aspects of geological change.  He was watching with scrupulous patience, on some of his pastures in Kent, the action of earthworms in bringing up the finer particles of soil to the surface.[2]  No one had previously thought it worth while to reckon this apparently insignificant action among the geological operations concerned in altering the surface of the land; and yet Darwin was able to show, by measurement and computation, how appreciable the alteration may be in the course of years. The early studies in this subject which he communicated to the Society were resumed by him forty years afterwards, when his fame as a naturalist had become world-wide, and his essay of 1840 in our Transactions was expanded by him into his volume 'The Formation of Vegetable Mould through the Action of Worms' (1881).

One of the most obvious questions suggested by an examination of the surface of the land is the origin of the valleys by which that surface is diversified.  Hutton and Playfair had maintained

[1] Trans. ser. 2, vol. v (1840) p. 601.
[2] 'On the Formation of Mould' *ibid*. p. 505.

that these topographical features are the result of the erosive work
of the streams that flow in them.   But this view, lacking as it did
the favourite paroxysmal relish which so gratified the taste of our
fathers, was generally looked upon as merely one of the speculative
vagaries of the Huttonian school.   It was therefore, for the most
part, rejected in favour of some indefinite conception of a combination of underground movements with the excavating power of
great débâcles of water rushing over the land.   In the first paper
on this subject published by the Society, Buckland, in discussing
the valleys of Dorset and Devon, attributed their formation to the
erosive action of ' a violent and transient inundation.'[1]   A few
years later he contributed a further paper ' On the Formation of
Valleys by the Elevation of the Strata that Enclose them.'[2]   The
argument from the nice adjustment of the valleys to the drainage-
system of a country, which Playfair had so eloquently urged, made
no impression on those who in this country discussed the subject
for many years after his time.   One of the earliest English
geologists who realized its force was Scrope, who in this, as in
many other branches of geological enquiry, was much in advance
of his contemporaries.   We find him remarking, as far back as
1825, that a convincing proof

' of the slowness of the process by which many very considerable river-valleys
were excavated is their sinuosity.  This character can only be accounted for by
a lent and gradual abrasion, and where this exists it is idle to talk of sudden
catastrophes, debacles, or deluges, as having been the excavating forces.'[3]

This accurate observer was, moreover, the first geologist to lay
before English readers a detailed demonstration, from actual
concrete examples, that deep and wide valleys have been hollowed
out of the surface of the land by the long-continued erosion of
running water.   Following the earlier investigations of Desmarest,
his luminous exposition and admirable sketches showed how
the valleys of Auvergne have been cut out of a series of
freshwater marls and of successive lava-sheets which lie at
different levels and belong to different periods of eruption.[4]

[1] Trans. ser. 2, vol. i, p. 95: read April 1822.
[2] *Ibid.* vol. ii (1829) p. 119.
[3] ' Considerations on Volcanoes' 1825, p. 215.
[4] In his ' Geology & Extinct Volcanoes of Central France,' of which the
first edition was published in 1826 and the second in 1858.  I have elsewhere
called attention to the singular oblivion which fell on the work of Desmarest,
who was really the first to maintain that the valleys of Auvergne were carved
out by the streams which still flow in them (' Founders of Geology' 2nd ed.

So convincing an argument ought to have settled the question, and to have started an investigation of the valley-systems of this country, which, however, was not begun until forty years later. Scrope's testimony had indeed the effect of sending Lyell and Murchison in company to Auvergne, with his volume in their hands. So impressed were these observers with the cogency of the evidence there conspicuously presented, that one of the first things they did, after the opening of the next session of the Geological Society, was to read a conjoint paper ' On the Excavation of Valleys as Illustrated by the Volcanic Rocks of Central France.' [1]   But the impression then produced on their minds did not permanently convert either of them to a belief in the paramount influence of subaërial denudation in the formation of valleys.   Scrope, on the other hand, followed up his observations in Auvergne by extending them into other parts of the Continent, where he obtained fresh confirmation of his views.   In the spring of 1830 he laid before our Society another excellent contribution to the subject, in the form of a paper ' On the Gradual Excavation of the Valleys in which the Meuse, the Moselle, & some Other Rivers Flow.' [2]

There seems to have been an invincible repugnance to admit that what seems to be so feeble an agent as running water could of itself be sufficient to carve deep and wide valleys out of solid, undisturbed rock.   Hence, even when denudation was admitted as a more or less important factor in the process, there was a general conviction that it must have been largely aided by underground movements; that valleys must at least have been initially determined by lines of fault; and thus that the action of any superficial agencies must always have been guided and controlled by the structure of the terrestrial crust.   This prevalent opinion was expressed by Hopkins, in his well-known paper ' On the Geological Structure of the Wealden District.' [3]   He believed that the area of the

---

1905, pp. 159, 247).  Commenting on the paper by Lyell & Murchison, above cited, Fitton, in his Presidental Address for 1829, remarks in a footnote that Playfair seems to have been unaware of the existence of the ' Essai ' by Montlosier, who had been cited as the original propounder of the subaërial erosion of the Auvergne valleys.  But Fitton himself does not appear to have been acquainted with the still earlier writings of Desmare t, which were certainly known to Montlosier.

[1] Proc. vol. i, p. 89.   The paper was read on Dec. 5th & 16th, 1828.

[2] *Ibid.* p. 170.

[3] Trans. ser. 2, vol. vii, p. 1.   Although read to the Society in 1841, this paper was not published until 1845.

Weald was suddenly upheaved, and that as a consequence of this disturbance a series of longitudinal folds was formed, with transverse fissures at right angles to them. He looked upon the transverse valleys as marking the lines of the faults by which they had been determined. Subsequent detailed examination of the ground has failed to reveal these theoretical faults, and though perhaps traces of some of them may ultimately be detected, there can hardly be any doubt that, as a whole, the valleys have been carved out independently of any dislocations. Hopkins's explanation of the topography of the Weald was based on a detailed mathematical discussion of the action of the underground forces by which the elevation of the great Wealden anticline was supposed to have been effected. But, in spite of its imposing mathematical basis, the data which it assumed did not agree with the actual facts as since ascertained, and its resulting conclusions were not less erroneous than other speculations on the subject.[1]

It was not until the summer of 1862 that in this country the subject of the origin of valleys was taken up in serious earnest, and worked out on the ground in definite reference to a group of actual rivers. On the 18th of June in that year J. B. Jukes read to the Society his memorable essay ' On the Mode of Formation of some of the River-Valleys in the South of Ireland.' I can well remember the vivid impression made on my own mind by the appearance of this paper in the Quarterly Journal. It threw a flood of fresh light on the whole question, suggested new ways of approaching the subject, and confirmed views which one had long been tentatively adopting. There can, I think, be no doubt that it was this essay that started the vigorous study of the origins of landscape, which has been so characteristic a feature in the geological activity of the last forty years. Here, again, is a conspicuous instance of the impulse given to the development of geological research by papers published by this Society.

It would lead me far beyond the limits which I have traced for myself in this Address to attempt to give here any sketch of the subsequent progress of the enquiries initiated by Jukes. A large part of the considerable mass of literature which has been devoted to the subject has been published in various forms outside of this

---

[1] It may be mentioned here that the natural presumption, that the transverse valleys by which the surrounding Chalk-escarpments of the Wealden area were breached had their lines determined by faults, was held long before. See. for instance, Scrope, ' Considerations on Volcanoes' 1825, p. 214.

Society. But to some of the contributions which have appeared
in our Journal a brief allusion may be made. One of the earliest
and most important of these was the conjoint memoir by Topley
& Le Neve Foster 'On the Superficial Deposits of the Medway
Valley, & Remarks on the Denudation of the Weald.'[1] This
essay greatly cleared the ground, by showing how little relation
there may be between the lines of valleys and the positions of
faults, how fatal are the objections to the theory of marine erosion
as applied to the valleys of the South-East of England, and how
convincingly all the accumulated evidence points to long-continued
subaërial denudation by rain and rivers. Ramsay had, shortly
before, published similar conclusions in his 'Physical Geology &
Geography of Great Britain,'[2] but he did not communicate any
paper on the subject to the Society until February 1872, when
he read one on 'The River-Courses of England & Wales.' In
perusing this suggestive essay we can note the broadening of
the author's views on the whole subject, and the growth of
his vivid realization of the fact that before the history of the
present valley-system of a country can be interpreted, a prolonged
investigation is necessary, not only into the geological structure
of the ground as it is now to be seen, but also into the evidence of
the extent to which the surface of the land was once covered with
material that has since been removed by denudation. His later
papers communicated to the Society contain further applications
of the same methods of enquiry.[3] If some of their data were
perhaps too indefinite and uncertain to warrant even the tentative
outlines of physiographical restoration which he based upon them,
the papers were at least eminently suggestive and did good service
by fostering an interest in the subject, even where they may not
have greatly advanced its development.

Of all Ramsay's contributions to this branch of geological
research, that which attracted most notice at the time, and has
given rise to the largest amount of discussion since, was his
famous paper on the glacial origin of lakes.[4] As the subject is

[1] Q. J. vol. xxi (1865) p. 443.
[2] The first edition of this work appeared in 1863, the second in 1864.
[3] 'Physical History of the Rhine Valley' Q. J. vol. xxx (1874) p. 81; 'How
Anglesey became an Island' ibid. vol. xxxii (1876) p. 116; 'Physical History
of the River Dee' ibid. p. 219.
[4] Q. J. vol. xviii (1862) p. 185. The glacial origin of lakes by the accumulation of moraines or other forms of drift had been previously noted: see,
for example, T. Codrington, Q. J. vol. xvi (1860) p. 345.

still one of controversy, I refrain from further reference to it, save to express my own conviction that Ramsay's memoir, which appeared in our Quarterly Journal nearly half a century ago, was one of the boldest and most original essays on a physiographical subject that has been written in our day and, within definable limits, furnishes a satisfactory solution of one of the most puzzling features in the topography of northern latitudes.

The interest in physiographical questions has greatly increased since the publication of Ramsay's papers. But the recent literature of the subject is to be sought mainly outside of the publications of the Society. Among the papers which have been printed in our Quarterly Journal, I may refer to that of Mr. Clement Reid, 'On the Origin of Dry Valleys &' of Coombe-Rock,'[1] in which the ingenious suggestion is made, that if during the Glacial Period the surface of a tract of porous Chalk were frozen for some distance downward, so as to prevent the ready descent of superficial water, considerable erosion might take place each summer during the rapid melting of snow, and that in this way valleys in the Chalk, which are now quite dry, might have been eroded.

I have already referred to the contributions of the late Dr. Blanford and Mr. Drew on topographical features resulting from the manner in which detrital materials are spread over low grounds by the streams that descend from the mountains of Persia and the Upper Indus. In this connection I would call attention to the very able paper 'On the Estuaries of the Severn & its Tributaries,'[2] by Prof. Sollas, who has entered as an independent observer into almost every department of geology, and has left on each the impress of his brilliant and original genius. In this essay he discussed the nature, origin, and distribution of the tidal sediment of these rivers, and the extremely slow manner in which alluvial flats are formed.

In concluding this outline of the Geological Society's labours during the past hundred years, I wish to allude to one characteristic feature of our history which ought not to be omitted from such a review. The loyalty of the Fellows to the Society, which has shown itself in so many ways, has been testified by a few of the most eminent of their number, not only in their lifetime, but by legacies, which continue, after their death, to enable the Society to encourage research, and to confer distinction on those

[1] Q. J. vol. xliii (1887) p. 364.    [2] Q. J. vol. xxxix (1883) p. 611.

by whom research is most successfully pursued. To one of the earliest and most illustrious of our Fellows, William Hyde Wollaston, we are in this way indebted for the Donation Fund which bears his name, and which for the last seventy-six years has been employed in awarding annually the Society's oldest and highest prize, the Wollaston Medal, to a long succession of geological leaders, foreign as well as native. The roll of those on whom this distinction has been conferred, beginning with William Smith in 1831, includes many of the most prominent names in the history of modern geology. The same Donation Fund has provided the means of assisting and encouraging many diligent workers, whose papers have appeared in the Quarterly Journal and elsewhere. Roderick Impey Murchison, Charles Lyell, Joseph Prestwich, and John J. Bigsby have left provision for the allocation of similar awards, and have thus greatly increased the opportunities of the Society to mark its appreciation of solid work in the service of our favourite science, and to connect its awards with the memory of these illustrious masters. By the late Daniel Pidgeon and H. C. Barlow funds have been left which have proved of much use in aiding investigation and in furthering the work of the Society. In my own opinion, we now possess as many medals and awards as the Council can satisfactorily adjudicate year after year. The pious donors of the future would more directly benefit the Society by bequeathing funds, the interest of which could be employed for the general purposes of the Society. It would not be difficult to secure that each such fund should perpetuate the name of the testator; while, if the Council were left with liberty to use the money in the way that would best promote the cause of geology and the progress of the Society, much which is at present impossible for lack of means might then be accomplished.

This Address has reached a greater length than I intended when its preparation was begun. A still longer narrative, however, would have been required to present anything like a complete sketch of what the Geological Society has done for the advancement of our favourite science by the publication of the papers which have been read before it. The theme is worthy of much ampler treatment than has been possible within the limits of an Anniversary discourse. Yet I would fain hope that, imperfect as it is, the outline which I have now traced to you may serve the purpose which I had in view. Our memories are short and our time for reading the literature of the past is sometimes scanty enough ; so that, in the hurry and bustle of the active scientific work of our own day, we are apt to lose sight of what has been achieved by our predecessors. It is well, however, that we should realize how much has been done by them to prepare the paths along which we have ourselves been able to advance. More especially is a retrospect of this kind incumbent upon the members of such a corporate body as that whose Anniversary we celebrate to-day. The Geological Society, after a hundred years of strenuous service, has gained an honourable place among the scientific institutions of the world. We are all proud to belong to it. Our pride, however, should spring not merely from a consciousness of the reputation which the Society holds in the outer world, but also from our own personal knowledge of the grounds upon which that reputation has been gained. We owe it as a duty to the Society and to ourselves, from time to time to peruse the writings of those who have gone before us, and this not with regard only to branches of investigation which we may have made specially our own. Such an association with the works of the early masters of our science cannot but increase our loyalty and affection for the Society which they founded and fostered.

A more intimate acquaintance with the writings of our predecessors than is usually thought to be sufficient for all modern purposes may be urged on further grounds. It will lead us to a better appreciation of the successive phases through which our science has passed in its progress to its present position, and will thus broaden our own outlook over the domain of knowledge which has now been conquered. We may find, every here and there, germinal ideas which have remained unnoticed, but which may indicate fresh lines of enquiry, to be pursued in the clearer light of modern research. We may even now and then discover that observations, which we fondly believed had been first made by ourselves, were noted and published ere we were born, or that generalizations, of which we were disposed to claim the authorship, were really suggested by others. The increase of greater facilities for the speedy dissemination of new facts and discoveries has in our time fostered a tendency towards premature publication. Haste to secure priority, which was unknown in the leisurely days of our forefathers, has grown apace in recent years. The hurried preparation of papers is apt to beget careless composition, and though, in our case, a watchful Assistant Secretary may be trusted to correct mistakes in grammar, we cannot expect him to remedy incurable defects of style.    Moreover, the growth of minuter observation and specialization has engendered an excessive love of details, which, although essential to be noted in the course of an investigation, may not be necessary in the presentation of its results.    We are naturally attached to particulars which it has cost us much time and labour to obtain, and we are sometimes tempted to forget that they may, nevertheless, have little general interest or importance, and when introduced too copiously into a paper, may so overload it as to make it wearisome and unreadable, and to obscure such really valuable points as we desire to make known.    A good paper should not consist mainly of rough laboratory-notes, or of the jottings of a field-notebook.

As a means of awakening us to the existence and increase of these regrettable modern tendencies, and perhaps in some degree as a corrective of them, I would urge that the papers which record the early stages of a science deserve attentive reading.    In no case, perhaps, is such reading more beneficial than in our own. In perusing the volumes of the Society's Transactions we find ourselves amidst an atmosphere of quiet and leisurely work, undisturbed by the signs of any race for priority or any hurry for notice.    We are sensible of a general compactness of arrangement and elegance of style, which betoken culture.    We see, too, that the Society was as deliberate in the publication of papers as the authors were in the preparation of them, several years sometimes elapsing between the reading of a paper and its issue in printed form.    A return to these bygone ways is of course impossible, and even if it were possible, it would not always be desirable.    Science, like every other branch of human progress, marches with swifter strides than it did when our Society was young.    We could not now forego our quarterly publication of the papers that have been read at our meetings.    We should not wish to delay the appearance of any good paper until the results contained in it had been forestalled elsewhere.

In conclusion, let me say that I have long been of opinion that the Fellows of the Society who contribute papers do not always realize to the full their responsibility in so doing.    It ought never to be forgotten that we are trustees of the good repute of the Society, and are bound to hand it down unimpaired to the generations that succeed us. Each of our number, by the quality of the papers which he sends in, has it in his power to raise or to lower the Society's prestige. It behoves us, therefore, each to do his utmost to make his contributions, alike in matter and in style, worthy of inclusion in the long series of publications wherein are enshrined so many of the masterpieces of our founders and predecessors.

With these parting counsels, which I offer with all deference, but with a sincere conviction that they are not unnecessary, I have now to resign the Chair in which your kind suffrages placed me two years ago. These years form an eventful period in the history of the Society, closing as they do the first century of its existence, and opening the commencement of the second. Most fervently do I hope that the new era on which we have entered will be at least as prosperous, useful, and distinguished as that of which we have celebrated the conclusion. We cannot look far into the future, but I am sure you will agree with me in believing that we could not start on our fresh career under better auspices than under the guidance of the distinguished successor of Buckland, of Phillips, of Prestwich, and of Green in the University of Oxford. Prof. Sollas brings to the discharge of the duties of President a scientific reputation which is world-wide, and an experience of the conduct of the Society's affairs which can only be gained by service on the Council. His range of acquirement, which we have all watched with wonder and admiration, will enable him to discuss with knowledge and insight every conceivable subject which may be brought before the Society. In his capable hands, therefore, the interests of the Society are well secured. In vacating my office in his favour let me thank you all once more for the distinguished and rare honour of a second election to this Presidency, an honour which I have most deeply appreciated, and likewise for the patience, courtesy, and consideration which, in the discharge of my duties, I have uniformly received from the Officers, the Council, and the general body of the Fellows.

March 4th, 1908.

Prof. W. J. SOLLAS, LL.D., Sc.D., F.R.S., President,
in the Chair.

David Bowen, 129 Inverness Place, Roath Park, Cardiff; and Daniel James Mahony, B.Sc., Geological Survey of Victoria, Mines Department, Melbourne (Victoria), were elected Fellows of the Society.

The List of Donations to the Library was read.

The following communications were read :—

1. 'On *Metriorhynchus brachyrhynchus*, Deslong., from the Oxford Clay near Peterborough.' By E. Thurlow Leeds, B.A. (Communicated by Dr. Henry Woodward, F.R.S., F.G.S.)

2. 'The High-Level Platforms of Bodmin Moor, and their Relation to the Deposits of Stream-Tin and Wolfram.' By George Barrow, F.G.S. (Communicated by permission of the Director of H.M. Geological Survey.)

The following specimens were exhibited :—

Specimens of *Metriorhynchus brachyrhynchus*, Deslong., from the Oxford Clay, near Peterborough, exhibited on behalf of E. Thurlow Leeds, B.A., in illustration of his paper.

Skull of a Teleosaurian (*Metriorhynchus*) and remains of a Ganoid Fish (*Hypsocormus*), obtained by the National Museum of Argentina from the Jurassic of Neuquen (Northern Patagonia), exhibited by Dr. A. Smith Woodward, F.R.S., F.L.S., V.P.G.S.

Specimen of surface-deposit, after the finer mud and peat has been washed out and the larger lumps removed by a fork, from Bodmin Moor; and wolframite from the Buttern-Hill deposit, in 'head,' Cornwall, exhibited by George Barrow, F.G.S., in illustration of his paper.

March 18th, 1908.

Prof. W. J. SOLLAS, LL.D., Sc.D., F.R.S., President,
in the Chair.

Charles Hawker Dinham, B.A., Magdalen College, Oxford; Isaac Thomas Hawkins, Assoc.M.Inst.C.E., Lagos (Southern Nigeria), and Royal Societies' Club, 63 St. James's Street, S.W.; Frederick Willoughby Penny, 3 Winchester Road, South Hampstead, N.W.; and Mark Arthur Wolff, F.C.S., c/o Banco Anglo-Sud-Americano, Antofagasta (Chile), were elected Fellows of the Society.

The List of Donations to the Library was read.

The following communications were read :—

1. 'The Carboniferous Rocks at Loughshinny (County Dublin), with an Account of the Faunal Succession and Correlation.' By Charles Alfred Matley, D.Sc., F.G.S., and Arthur Vaughan, B.A., D.Sc., F.G.S.

2. 'A Note on the Petrology and Physiography of Western Liberia (West Coast of Africa).' By John Parkinson, M.A., F.G.S.

The following specimens and lantern-slides were exhibited :—

Specimens of Carboniferous corals, brachiopods, etc., and lantern-slides, exhibited by Dr. C. A. Matley, F.G.S., and Dr. A. Vaughan, B.A., F.G.S., in illustration of their paper.

Rock-specimens, microscope-sections, and lantern-slides, exhibited by J. Parkinson, M.A., F.G.S., in illustration of his paper.

----

April 1st, 1908.

Prof. W. J. SOLLAS, LL.D., Sc.D., F.R.S., President,
in the Chair.

William H. C. Geikie, Mining Engineer, c/o The Borneo Company, Kuching, Sarawak ; Granville Poole, B.Sc., Tollington House, Amblecote, Stourbridge; and Alfred A. Roberts, Ph.D., Regent House, Regent Street, W., were elected Fellows of the Society.

The List of Donations to the Library was read.

The PRESIDENT announced that the Council had adopted the following resolution :—

'The Council of the Geological Society has heard with much regret of the death of Dr. HENRY CLIFTON SORBY, who served on the Council for many years, and occupied the Presidential Chair during the Sessions 1878-80. The Council desires to place on record its high appreciation of the invaluable services rendered by Dr. Sorby to the Society and to the Science of Geology.'

----

A SPECIAL GENERAL MEETING was held at 7.45 P.M., before the Ordinary Meeting, for the purpose of considering and voting upon the following motion, proposed by Mr. E. A. Martin, and seconded by Mr. W. H. Shrubsole :—

'That the Council be requested to take the necessary steps, at an early date, in order to allow of the admission of women to full Fellowship of the Geological Society of London.'

After discussion, the following amendment proposed by Dr. A. Smith Woodward, and seconded by Mr. H. A. Allen, was voted upon, and passed by 43 to 34 :

'That it is desirable that women should be admitted as Fellows of the Society, assuming that this can be done under the present Charter.'

The foregoing amendment having then been declared a substantive motion, the following amendment to it was proposed by Mr. H. B. Woodward, and seconded by Mr. O. T. Jones :

'That a poll of all the Fellows of the Society resident in the United Kingdom be taken, to ascertain whether a majority is in favour of admitting women to the Society, and, if so, whether as Fellows or as Associates.'

This was agreed to by 54 to 24, and was declared a substantive motion by show of hands.

An Associate is defined in the proposed New Section of the Bye-Laws, submitted to the Special General Meeting held on May 15th, 1907, see Quart. Journ. Geol. Soc. vol. lxiii, Proc. p. lxxiii.

---

April 15th, 1908.

Dr. J. J. Harris Teall, M.A., F.R.S., Vice-President, in the Chair.

The List of Donations to the Library was read.

The following communications were read :—

1. 'The Geological Structure of the St. David's Area (Pembrokeshire).' By John Frederick Norman Green, B.A., F.G.S.

2. 'Notes on the Geology of Burma.' By Leonard V. Dalton, B.Sc., F.R.G.S. (Communicated by Dr. A. Smith Woodward, F.R.S., F.L.S., V.P.G.S.)

The following specimens, etc. and maps were exhibited :—

Rock-specimens, sections, and lantern-slides, exhibited by J. F. N. Green, B.A., F.G.S., in illustration of his paper.
Maps, presented by the Director of H.M. Geological Survey :—Special 1-inch Oxford Sheet, 1908 ; Sheet 125, n.s., Derby (Drift), colour-printed, and Sheet 295, n.s., Taunton (Drift), colour-printed, 1908 ; also 6-inch maps—Edinburghshire, n.s., Sheet 12 S.E. (Solid & Drift) 1907, and Haddingtonshire, n.s., Sheet 4 S.W. (Drift) and 4 S.E. (Solid & Drift) 1907.

---

May 6th, 1908.

Prof. W. J. SOLLAS, LL.D., Sc.D., F.R.S., President,
in the Chair.

Reginald W. Brock, Director of the Geological Survey of Canada
& Deputy Minister of Mines, Ottawa; Harold Brodrick, M.A.,
7 Aughton Road, Birkdale (Lancashire); Walter Hunter, M.Inst.C.E.,
M.I.M.E., 2 Chartfield Avenue, Putney Hill, S.W.; and Henry
Hurd Swinnerton, D.Sc., F.Z.S., Lecturer in Geology & Zoology,
University College, Nottingham, were elected Fellows; and
Prof. Hans Schardt, Veytaux, near Montreux (Switzerland), was
elected a Foreign Correspondent of the Society.

The List of Donations to the Library was read.

The following communications were read :—

1. 'Solution-Valleys in the Glyme Area of Oxfordshire.' By the
Rev. E. C. Spicer, M.A., F.G.S.

2. 'On the Stratigraphy & Structure of the Tarnthal Mass
(Tyrol).' By Dr. Alfred Prentice Young, F.G.S.; with a 'Note on
Two Cephalopods, collected by Dr. A. P. Young on the Tarnthal
Köpfe (Tyrol).' By George C. Crick, Assoc. R.S.M., F.G.S.

The following specimens and lantern-slides were exhibited :—

Lantern-slides, etc. exhibited by the Rev. E. C. Spicer, M.A.,
F.G.S., in illustration of his paper.
Specimens of rocks and fossils exhibited by Dr. A. P. Young,
F.G.S., in illustration of his paper.
Flint-implements from Frant (Sussex), exhibited by E. A. Martin,
F.G.S.
Specimens of weathering from Pentreath (Anglesey), exhibited by
J. H. Woodhead, F.G.S.

————

May 20th, 1908.

Prof. W. J. SOLLAS, LL.D., Sc.D., F.R.S., President,
in the Chair.

The List of Donations to the Library was read.

The PRESIDENT announced that the Daniel-Pidgeon Fund for
1908 had been awarded to JAMES ARCHIBALD DOUGLAS, B.A., F.G.S.,
who proposes to investigate the zonal succession of the Lower
Carboniferous Rocks of Western Ireland.

The PRESIDENT read out the Result of the Poll, taken to ascertain the opinion of the Fellows resident in the United Kingdom as to the Admission of Women to the Society, as follows :— .

Papers sent out ........................ 870
Answers received  ...................... 477

### ANALYSIS OF REPLIES.

(1) Are you in favour of the Admission of Women to the Geological Society of London ?

Yes ................................. 342
No .................................. 133
Not specified ...................... 2
                                      —— 477

(2) Are you in favour of the Admission of Women as Fellows, or as Associates only ?  The 342 in favour of Admission voted :—

As Fellows ............................. 248
As Associates .......................... 84
Not specified .......................... 10
                                          —— 342

(3) If there should not be a majority of those voting in favour of Women Fellows, are you in favour of their Admission as Associates ?

Yes ................................. 304
No .................................. 35
Not specified ...................... 3
                                      —— 342

Add votes of those against Admission of
    Women at all .............. ... ........     133
And those who are neutral ...........      2
                                          —— 477

(4) The foregoing analysis shows that there were :

In favour of the Admission of } 248
Women as Fellows ........ }

Against the Admission of } 217   { 133 against the Admission of Women
Women as Fellows ........ }         {      at all.
                            ——       { 84 in favour of the Admission of
Majority in favour of the }            {     Women as Associates only.
Admission of Women as } 31
Fellows .................. }

The following communications were read :—

1. 'On some Fossil Fishes discovered by Prof. Ennes de Souza. in the Cretaceous Formation at Ilhéos, State of Bahia (Brazil). By Arthur Smith Woodward, LL.D., F.R.S., F.L.S., V.P.G.S.

2. 'The Bala and Llandovery Rocks of Glyn Ceiriog (North Wales).'  By Dr. Theodore Groom, M.A., F.G.S., and Philip Lake, M.A., F.G.S.

The following specimens, etc. were exhibited :—

Fish-remains from Lower Cretaceous shale at Ilhéos, State of Bahia (Brazil), exhibited by Dr. A. Smith Woodward, F.R.S., F.L.S., V.P.G.S., in illustration of his paper.

Specimens and microscope-sections of Bala and Llandovery

rocks, exhibited by Dr. Theodore Groom, M.A., F.G.S., & Philip Lake, M.A., F.G.S., in illustration of their paper.

Five cartoons representing restorations of Vesuvius at different times during its growth, exhibited by Dr. H. J. Johnston-Lavis, M.A., F.G.S.

---

### June 3rd, 1908.

Prof. W. J. SOLLAS, LL.D., Sc.D., F.R.S., President,
in the Chair.

Ernest Dickson, 99 Bloomfield Gardens, Bath, and 37 Endell Street, London, W.C.; and Basil Francis Newall Macrorie, Geologist to the Burma Oil Company, P.O. Box 181, Rangoon (Burma), were elected Fellows of the Society.

The list of Donations to the Library was read.

The Names of certain Fellows of the Society were read out for the first time, in conformity with the Bye-Laws, Sect. VI, Art. 5, in consequence of the Non-Payment of the Arrears of their Contributions.

The PRESIDENT announced that the Council had passed the following resolutions :—

'The Council of the Geological Society desires to express the profound regret with which it has heard of the death of Sir John Evans, K.C.B., F.R.S. Sir John Evans served the Society for many years in the Council, occupied the Presidential Chair from 1874 to 1876 (being the Senior President living), and subsequently discharged the duties of Foreign Secretary for twelve years. Geological Science has gained much from the researches of Sir John Evans, and the place which he has occupied in the Society and the Council will be hard to fill.'

'The Council also desire to express its regret at the loss of Prof. Albert de Lapparent, who had been a Foreign Correspondent and Member of the Society since 1887, and who, as recently as last year, attended the celebration of the Society's Centenary and contributed no little to the proceedings on that occasion.'

The PRESIDENT announced that, in accordance with a requisition 'signed by five or more Fellows' of the Society (Bye-Laws, Sect. XI, Art. 4), a Special General Meeting would be held at the Society's Apartments, on Wednesday, June 17th, 1908, at 7.45 P.M., in order to consider the following resolution, which would be proposed by Dr. J. Malcolm Maclaren and seconded by Mr. A. Gibb Maitland :—

'That Fellows non-resident in the United Kingdom be invited to express an opinion concerning the Admission of Women to Fellowship or Associateship of the Geological Society of London.'

The following communication was read :—

'On the Fossiliferous Rocks of the Southern Half of the Tortworth Inlier.' By Frederick Richard Cowper Reed, M.A., F.G.S., and Prof. Sidney Hugh Reynolds, M.A., F.G.S.

The following specimens, lantern-slides, and maps were exhibited :—

Rock-specimens and lantern-slides, exhibited by F. R. C. Reed, M.A., F.G.S., & Prof. S. H. Reynolds, M.A., F.G.S., in illustration of their paper.

Four sheets of the Geological-Survey Map of Cape Colony, on the scale of 1 : 238,000, by A. W. Rogers & A. L. Du Toit, presented by the Director of that Survey.

———

## June 17th, 1908.

### Prof. W. J. Sollas, LL.D., Sc.D., F.R.S., President, in the Chair.

The List of Donations to the Library was read.

The Names of certain Fellows of the Society were read out for the second time, in conformity with the Bye-Laws, Sect. VI, Art. 5, in consequence of the Non-Payment of the Arrears of their Contributions.

The following communications were read :—

1. 'The Hornblendic Rocks of Glendalough and Greystones (County Wicklow).'  By James Allan Thomson, B.A., B.Sc., F.G.S.

2. 'On the Occurrence of Footprints in the Lower Sandstones of the Exeter District.'  By Principal Arthur William Clayden, M.A., F.G.S.

3. 'The Basic Intrusion of Bartestree, near Hereford.'  By Prof. Sidney Hugh Reynolds, M.A., F.G.S.

The following specimens, etc. were exhibited :—

Rock-specimens, microscope-sections, and lantern-slides, exhibited by J. A. Thomson, B.A., B.Sc., F.G.S., in illustration of his paper.

Photographs, exhibited by Principal A. W. Clayden, M.A., F.G.S., in illustration of his paper.

Rocks, microscope-sections, photographs, and lantern-slides, exhibited by Prof. S. H. Reynolds, M.A., F.G.S., in illustration of his paper.

Recent siliceous encrustations on slate and a microscope-section of the sinter from Rigg-Head Quarry, near Grange (Borrowdale), exhibited by John Postlethwaite, F.G.S.

———

A Special General Meeting was held before the Ordinary Meeting on Wednesday, June 17th, at 7.45 P.M., in order to consider the Resolution, proposed by Dr. J. Malcolm Maclaren and seconded by Mr. A. Gibb Maitland, as announced on June 3rd (see p. cxxxi) This Resolution was passed by 30 votes to 11.

# PROCEEDINGS

OF THE

# GEOLOGICAL SOCIETY OF LONDON.

SESSION 1907-1908.

November 6th, 1907.

Sir ARCHIBALD GEIKIE, K.C.B., D.C.L., Sc.D., Sec.R.S., President, in the Chair.

Archibald Allan Clifford Dickson, Rejoulie P.O., *via* Nawadah, E.I. Ry., Gaya District, Bengal (India); Baron Maurice de Komorowicz, 26 Schlüterstrasse, Charlottenburg IV, Berlin; James Stephen Neil, F.C.I.S., General Hospital, Wolverhampton; and Robert Speight, M.A., M.Sc., Lecturer in Geology at Canterbury College, Christchurch (New Zealand), were elected Fellows; and Dr. Emil Ernst August Tietze, Director of the K. k. Geologische Reichsanstalt, Vienna, was elected a Foreign Member of the Society.

The List of Donations to the Library was read.

The following communications were read:—

1. 'On a Collection of Fossil Plants from South Africa.' By Prof. Albert Charles Seward, M.A., F.R.S., F.L.S., F.G.S.

2. 'Permo-Carboniferous Plants from Vereeniging (South Africa).' By Prof. Albert Charles Seward, M.A., F.R.S., F.L.S., F.G.S., and Thomas Nicholas Leslie, F.G.S.

3. 'On the Structure and Relations of the Laurentian System of Canada.' By Prof. Frank Dawson Adams, M.A.Sc., Ph.D., F.G.S.

ii  PROCEEDINGS OF THE GEOLOGICAL SOCIETY.    [Feb. 1908,

The following maps were exhibited:—

Geological Survey of England and Wales: 1-inch maps, n. s., Sheets 230, 247, 267, and 351 & 358, 1907, presented by the Director of H.M. Geological Survey.

Geological Map of Newfoundland, by J. P. Howley, Director of the Geological Survey of Newfoundland: 1 inch = 6·9 miles—1907. presented by the Author.

Geological Commission of the Cape of Good Hope: Geological Map, Sheet 45, $\frac{1}{233,000}$, by A. L. Du Toit—1907, presented by the Director of that Commission.

Geological Commission of Portugal: Hypsometric Map, $\frac{1}{500,000}$, 1907, presented by the Director of that Commission.

Geological Map of Armenia, by F. Oswald: 1 inch = 16 miles—1907, presented by the Author.

Map of the Goldfields & Mines in the Ustkamenogorsk and Zaisansk Districts of the Semipalatinsk Territory (Siberia), by Norton Griffith: 1 inch = 3·3 miles—1907, presented by the Author.

———

At 8 P.M. on Wednesday, November 13th, 1907, the actual anniversary of the foundation of the Society in 1807, the Fellows met informally, to the number of about 100, at the Society's Rooms in Burlington House, where the various Addresses presented on September 26th were on view.

———

November 20th, 1907.

Sir Archibald Geikie, K.C.B., D.C.L., Sc.D., Sec.R.S., President, in the Chair.

David Burns, C.E., Vallum View, Burgh Road, Carlisle; Henry Bury, M.A., F.L.S., late Fellow of Trinity College, Cambridge, Mayfield House, Farnham (Surrey); and Edward Wilson Dixon, M.Inst.C.E., Wimborne, Kent Road, Harrogate (Yorkshire), were elected Fellows of the Society.

The List of Donations to the Library was read.

The following communications were read:—

1. 'Glacial Beds of Cambrian Age in South Australia.' By the Rev. Walter Howchin, F.G.S., Lecturer in the University of Adelaide.

2. 'On a Formation known as "Glacial Beds of Cambrian Age" in South Australia.' By H. Basedow and J. D. Iliffe. (Communicated by Dr. J. Malcolm Maclaren, F.G.S.)

The following specimens, lantern-slides, etc. were exhibited:—

Specimens from the glacial Cambrian beds in South Australia, and lantern-slides, exhibited by the Rev. W. Howchin, F.G.S., in illustration of his paper.

Lantern-slides and photographs exhibited by Dr. J. M. Maclaren, F.G.S., in illustration of the paper by Messrs. H. Basedow & J. D. Iliffe.

Specimens of rocks from the supposed glacial beds in the Griquatown Series of Cape Colony, exhibited by A. W. Rogers, M.A., F.G.S.

A coal-pebble from the conglomerate-bed resting directly upon the Nanaimo Seam at Nanaimo, Vancouver Island (B.C.), exhibited by Dr. H. S. Poole, F.G.S.

---

## December 4th, 1907.

Sir ARCHIBALD GEIKIE, K.C.B., D.C.L., Sc.D., Sec.R.S., President, in the Chair.

Tom Esmond Geoffrey Bailey, B.A. (Cantab.), Mineralogical Survey of British Central Africa, Imperial Institute, South Kensington, S.W.; Walter Barratt, Armsyde, Padstow (Cornwall); John F. Browne, Newdigate Colliery, Bedworth, Nuneaton; Dr. Whitman Cross, United States Geological Survey, Washington (D.C.), U.S.A.; Ernest Henry Davison, The Hollies, Sandbach (Cheshire); Alfred Eastwood, B.Sc., Assoc.R.C.S., 50 Clovelly Road, Southampton; Lawrence Wright Edwards, Bradley House, Bradley, Bilston (Staffordshire): William H. Goodchild, Assoc.R.S.M., A.I.M.M., Elmwood Lodge, Long Lane, Finchley (Middlesex); William Hay, Vernon House, Shirebrook, near Mansfield; Joseph Kelly, Assoc.R.S.M., Moate (Co. Westmeath); Dr. George Frederick Kunz, M.A., Hon. Curator of Gems in the American Museum of Natural History, 401 Fifth Avenue, New York City (U.S.A.); Charles Oswald George Larcombe, Geological Survey of New South Wales, Sydney (N.S.W.); Peter Macnair, Curator of the Natural History Collection in the Kelvingrove Museum, Glasgow, N.B.; William Maurice, M.Inst.C.E., Hucknall Torkard (Nottinghamshire); Lewis Mitchell, Assoc.M.Inst.C.E., 26 Chorley New Road, Bolton; Lewis Moysey, B.A., M.B., B.C. (Cantab.), St. Moritz, Ilkeston Road, Nottingham; James O'Connell, The Limes, Whitstable (Kent); William Henry Abdullah Quilliam Bey, B.A., LL.D., Fern Bank, Fairfield Crescent, Liverpool; Walter Maxwell Henderson Scott, Assoc.R.S.M., York House, Blenkarne Road, Wandsworth Common, S.W.; and Flower Thomas Spackman, Craigside, Bath Road, Worcester, were elected Fellows of the Society.

The List of Donations to the Library was read.

The following communications were read :—

1. 'The Faunal Succession in the Carboniferous Limestone (Upper Avonian) of the Midland Area (North Derbyshire and North Staffordshire).' By Thomas Franklin Sibly, B.Sc., F.G.S.

2. 'Brachiopod Homœomorphy : "*Spirifer glaber*".' By S. S. Buckman, F.G.S.

The following specimens and maps were exhibited : —

Specimens of *Reticularia* showing dental plates and median septum, and *Martinia glabra*, exhibited by Prof. E. J. Garwood, M.A., Sec.G.S.

Forty-two specimens of *Spirifer*, exhibited on behalf of H.M. Geological Survey.

Sheets Nos. 123, 134, 137, & 140 of the Swedish Geological-Survey Map, $\frac{1}{50,000}$, 1907, presented by the Director of that Survey.

Three Sheets of the Hungarian Geological-Survey Map, $\frac{1}{75,000}$, 1905, presented by the Director of that Survey.

———

December 18th, 1907.

Sir Archibald Geikie, K.C.B., D.C.L., Sc.D., Sec.R.S., President, in the Chair.

Thomas Samuel Parrott, 173 Exploration-Buildings, Johannesburg (Transvaal) ; Edwin Hall Pascoe, M.A.(Cantab.), B.Sc.(Lond.), Assistant-Superintendent of the Geological Survey of India, 27 Chowringhee, Calcutta (India) ; and Robert Knox Paton, The Evançon Gold-Mining Co., Verrès, Val d' Aosta (Italy), were elected Fellows ; Commendatore Arturo Issel, Professor of Geology in the University of Genoa, Via Brignole de Ferrari, No. 16, Genoa, was elected a Foreign Member ; and Dr. Armin Baltzer, Professor of Geology in the University of Berne, and Prof. Baron Gerard Jakob de Geer, Stockholm, were elected Foreign Correspondents of the Society.

The List of Donations to the Library was read.

The following communications were read :—

1. 'Some Recent Discoveries of Palæolithic Implements.' By Sir John Evans, K.C.B., D.C.L., LL.D., F.R.S., F.S.A., F.G.S.

2. 'On a Deep Channel of Drift at Hitchin (Hertfordshire).' By William Hill, F.G.S.

The following specimens and maps were exhibited :—

A series of flint-implements from the Palæolithic deposits of Bedfordshire and Hertfordshire, exhibited by Sir John Evans, K.C.B., D.C.L., LL.D., F.R.S., F.S.A., F.G.S., in illustration of his paper.

Specimens of glaciated jet and a portion of a tusk from the Boulder-Drift of East Yorkshire, exhibited on behalf of P. M. Crosthwaite, M.Inst.C.E., by H. B. Woodward, F.R.S., F.G.S.

Rock-specimen and (?) fossil from the Upper Greensand near Mintern Magna (Dorset), exhibited on behalf of E. A. Ffooks, by H. B. Woodward, F.R.S., F.G.S.

Palæolithic ' anvil-stone '(?) from Ruscombe (Berkshire), 170 feet above sea-level, exhibited by Ll. Treacher, F.G.S.

Viscid flow-structure in bottle-glass, produced accidentally by hydrofluoric acid, exhibited by H. Bauerman, F.G.S.

Geological Survey of Ireland :—1-inch map—Sheet 8, Ballycastle, new edition, 1907, presented by that Department.

Map showing the Occurrence of Metals, Coal, Salt, & other Minerals in Hungary, on the scale of $\frac{1}{900,000}$, by J. Bœckh & A. Gesell, 1898, presented by the Royal Hungarian Minister of Finance.

Five sheets of the Geological-Survey Map of Japan, on the scale of $\frac{1}{20,000}$, presented by the Director of that Survey.

Map of the New Rand Goldfield (Orange River Colony), on the scale of 17·04 miles to the inch, by A. R. Sawyer, 1907, presented by the Author.

---

## January 8th, 1908.

Sir Archibald Geikie, K.C.B., D.C.L., Sc.D., Sec.R.S., President, in the Chair.

Austin J. R. Atkin, Mining Engineer, Steynsdorp, Transvaal (South Africa), and G. C. Cossar, B.A. (Oxon.), East Craigs, Corstorphine (Midlothian), were elected Fellows ; and Dr. Feodor Černyshev, of St. Petersburg, was elected a Foreign Correspondent of the Society.

The following Fellows, nominated by the Council, were elected Auditors of the Society's Accounts for the preceding year :—Richard Hill Tiddeman, M.A., and Alfred Edward Salter, D.Sc.

The List of Donations to the Library was read.

The following communications were read :—

1. 'Chronology of the Glacial Epoch in North America.' By Prof. George Frederick Wright, F.G.S.A. (Communicated by Prof. E. J. Garwood, M.A., Sec.G.S.)

2. 'On the Application of Quantitative Methods to the Study of the Structure and History of Rocks.' By Henry Clifton Sorby, LL.D., F.R.S., F.L.S., F.G.S.

The following lantern-slides and maps were exhibited :—

Lantern-slides, exhibited on behalf of Prof. G. F. Wright, F.G.S.A., in illustration of his paper.

Lantern-slides, exhibited by Dr. H. C. Sorby, F.R.S., F.L.S., F.G.S., in illustration of his paper.

Geologic Atlas of the United States : Folios 141 & 142, 1906 ; 143-150, 1907, presented by the Director of the United States Geological Survey.

———

## January 22nd, 1908.

Sir ARCHIBALD GEIKIE, K.C.B., D.C.L., Sc.D., Sec.R.S., President, in the Chair.

The List of Donations to the Library was read.

The following communications were read :—

1. 'The Origin of the Pillow-Lava near Port Isaac in Cornwall.' By Clement Reid, F.R.S., F.L.S., F.G.S., and Henry Dewey, F.G.S. (Communicated by permission of the Director of H.M. Geological Survey.)

2. 'On the Subdivision of the Chalk at Trimmingham (Norfolk).' By Reginald Marr Brydone, F.G.S.

The following specimens, lantern-slides, and maps were exhibited : -

Specimens of pillow-lava from Port Isaac (Cornwall), and lantern-slides, exhibited by C. Reid, F.R.S., F.L.S., F.G.S., and H. Dewey, F.G.S., in illustration of their paper.

Specimens and lantern-slides exhibited by R. M. Brydone, F.G.S., in illustration of his paper.

Geological Survey of England and Wales : twelve sheets of the 6-inch maps of South Wales, presented by the Director of H.M. Geological Survey.

Geological Survey of the Transvaal : Sheet No. 1—Pretoria, 1 inch = $2\frac{1}{2}$ miles, presented by the Director of that Survey.

———

February 5th, 1908.

Sir ARCHIBALD GEIKIE, K.C.B., D.C.L., Sc.D., Sec.R.S., President,
in the Chair.

John Frederick Norman Green, 15 Bramshill Gardens, Dartmouth
Park, N.W.; Harold S. Harger, 42 Cullinan Buildings, Johannes-
burg (Transvaal); George H. Cory Wright, LL.B., 88 Hardturm
Strasse, Zürich (Switzerland); and William Wright, 9 Endlesham
Road, Nightingale Lane, S.W., were elected Fellows of the Society.

The List of Donations to the Library was read.

The following communications were read :—

1. 'On Antigorite and the Val Antigorio, with Notes on other
Serpentines containing that Mineral.' By Prof. T. G. Bonney,
Sc.D., LL.D., F.R.S., F.G.S.

2. 'The St. David's-Head "Rock-Series" (Pembrokeshire).' By
James Vincent Elsden, B.Sc., F.G.S.

The following specimens and maps were exhibited :—

Rock-specimens and microscope-sections, exhibited by Prof. T. G.
Bonney, Sc.D., F.R.S., F.G.S., in illustration of his paper.

Photographs, rock-specimens, and lantern-slides, exhibited by
J. V. Elsden, B.Sc., F.G.S., in illustration of his paper.

Two hundred and eight Sheets of the $\frac{1}{40,000}$ Geological Map of
the Belgian Geological Survey, presented by the Director of that
Survey, M. M. F. Mourlon, F.C.G.S.

February 19th, 1908.

Sir ARCHIBALD GEIKIE, K.C.B., D.C.L., Sc.D., Sec.R.S., President,
in the Chair.

Alfred William Gustave Bleeck, M.E., Ph.D. (Munich), 5 Rainey
Park, Ballygunge, Calcutta (India); Alexander Östrand Brown, B.A.,
Assoc.R.S.M., Minas Peña del Hierro, por Rio Tinto, Huelva
(Spain); Henry Charles Drake, 6 Leo Street, Hull; Robert Marcus
Gunn, M.A., M.B., F.R.C.S., 54 Queen Anne Street, Cavendish
Square, W.; William H. Marston, B.Sc., 63 Stanmore Road,
Edgbaston, Birmingham; and Basil Schön, M.A., Seafield-Park
Engineering College, Fareham (Hampshire), were elected Fellows
of the Society.

The List of Donations to the Library was read.

The following communications were read :—

1. 'The Two Earth-Movements of Colonsay.' By William Bourke Wright, B.A., F.G.S. (Communicated by permission of the Director of H.M. Geological Survey.)

2. 'Notes on the River Wey.' By Henry Bury, M.A., F.L.S., F.G.S.

The following lantern-slides and maps were exhibited :—

Lantern-slides, exhibited by W. B. Wright, B.A., F.G.S., in illustration of his paper.

Geological Survey of England and Wales: 1-inch maps, n. s., Sheets 348 and 353 (colour-printed), 1907, presented by the Director of H.M. Geological Survey.

Geological Survey of Canada: geological map of a group of townships adjoining Lake Timiskaming (Quebec), on the scale of 2 miles to the inch, 1906, presented by the Director of that Survey.

K. k. Geologische Reichsanstalt: $\frac{1}{75,000}$ geological map—S.W. Group, Sheets 6, 13, 18, 93, and 94; N.W. Group, Sheet 85, 1907, presented by the Director of that Institution.

THE

# QUARTERLY JOURNAL

OF

# THE GEOLOGICAL SOCIETY OF LONDON.

## Vol. LXIV.

1. *Some Recent Discoveries of Palæolithic Implements.* By Sir John Evans, K.C.B., D.C.L., LL.D., F.R.S., F.S.A., F.G.S. (Read December 18th, 1907.)

By the kind courtesy of Mr. Worthington G. Smith, F.L.S., of Dunstable, I am enabled to call attention to some recent discoveries of palæolithic implements on the southern borders of Bedfordshire and in the north-western part of Hertfordshire.

Mr. Worthington Smith's remarkable discoveries of implements and of a palæolithic floor at Caddington, not very far from Dunstable, are well known and have been fully recorded in his excellent and profusely-illustrated book 'Man, the Primeval Savage,' published in 1894—a summary of which I gave in the second edition of my 'Ancient Stone-Implements,' which appeared in 1897.

The original surface of the ground at some of the Caddington brick-fields was as much as 550 to 590 feet above the Ordnance-datum[1]; but at Kensworth,[2] about 2 miles to the west of Caddington, Mr. Smith found a palæolithic implement upon the surface at an elevation of 760 feet. Quite recently an excellent ovate implement ($5 \times 3\frac{5}{8}$ inches), black and lustrous, was found by a Dunstable school-boy at the surface on Blow Downs at an elevation of 600 feet. The exact position is slightly to the south of 'Little John's Wood,' as shown on the 6-inch Ordnance-Survey Map of Bedfordshire. It is far from any existing stream, and the ground slopes away from the direction of the Ver.

[1] 'Nature' vol. xl (1889) p. 151.
[2] 'Man, the Primeval Savage' 1894, p. 65.

From Whipsnade Heath, about $2\frac{1}{2}$ miles to the south of Dunstable, Mr. Smith has obtained a good ovate implement ($3\frac{7}{8} \times 2\frac{5}{8}$ inches), ochreous, from brown clay, a thin water-laid material resting upon Red Clay-with-Flints. The elevation is 651 feet above O.D., at least 210 feet above the Ver, assuming it to rise at Markyate

Fig. 1.

Street, as it now very rarely does. I may incidentally mention that I have known that stream to have its source $5\frac{1}{2}$ miles higher up its valley in one year than it had in another.

The discoveries that I have hitherto been recording were made in Bedfordshire, but I now turn to some others which have been made in Hertfordshire.

At the north-western end of Gaddesden Row in the parish of Great Gaddesden, and at a short distance south of the Baptist Chapel, is a brick-field of little area but of considerable depth. The surface of the ground is about 544 feet above O.D. and the spot is on what may be called 'table-land,' between the valleys of the Ver and of the Gade, being barely $2\frac{1}{2}$ miles from the bed of the former stream and barely $1\frac{1}{4}$ miles from that of the latter. It is about 184 feet above the course of the Gade, and about 144 feet above that of the Ver.

The sides of the pit exhibit vertical sections of a deposit of brown brick-earth, from 15 to 20 feet thick, in which occur three or four layers of rough and more or less angular flints. A considerable number of palæolithic implements have been found in this brick-earth, mostly at a depth of about 10 feet, or towards the base of the deposit. They are, as a rule, of ovate form, from $3\frac{1}{4}$ to 5 inches in length and from $2\frac{3}{8}$ to $3\frac{1}{2}$ inches in width. Most of them are obtained of a more or less deep ochreous colour, but one beautifully-finished specimen is of an ivory-white (see fig. 1, p. 2).

Another new locality is a brick-field about a mile and a half to the north-east of the town of Hemel Hempstead. It is known as Ellingham's Pit, Leverstock Green, and is situate north-east of the 'Saracen's Head' public-house, at an elevation of about 460 feet above Ordnance-datum and about 170 feet above the level of the Gade. The greater part of the brick-making material is of Eocene origin, but above this deposit is a dark-brown argillaceous Drift, in places 12 or more feet thick, in others measuring not more than a few inches. It sometimes occurs in pot-holes only, and in some parts of the pit is absent.

Mr. Worthington Smith has obtained at least six well-formed implements from the dark-brown Drift at this locality. They are of ovate form, from $3\frac{3}{4}$ to 5 inches long and from $2\frac{1}{4}$ to $3\frac{1}{4}$ inches broad. The majority have a slightly-ochreous patina, though one somewhat unsymmetrical but carefully-finished implement is of an ivory-white (see fig. 2, p. 4).

In my 'Ancient Stone-Implements' [1] I have recorded the finding by myself of two palæolithic implements in the neighbourhood of Bedmond, from 2 to $2\frac{1}{4}$ miles south-east of Ellingham's Pit, which not improbably were originally connected with similar deposits.

It seems by no means impossible that the implement from the neighbourhood of Dunstable, which I have engraved as fig. 17 in 'Ancient Stone-Implements,' 2nd ed. (1897) p. 72, may after all be palæolithic, and not neolithic.

The drifts which cap the hills in the north-western part of Hertfordshire are of a remarkable character, and seem to consist of patches of very variable origin. A great part of the material is

[1] 2nd ed. (1897) pp. 596-97.

Fig. 2.

derived from clay-deposits of Eocene age, but little remaniés. In some of the Leverstock-Green pits these deposits are still in their original position.[1] In excavations in connexion with my new house, 'Britwell,' on the borders of Berkhamsted Common, I have found masses of bright ochreous clay and of Red Clay-with-Flints, reposing on a much-eroded surface of Chalk. With the flints in these deposits, some of which were of a mixed nature, a number of large quartzite-pebbles (derived presumably from Glacial beds) occurred. There was, moreover, found a slab of 'Hertfordshire' Lower Tertiary conglomerate (puddingstone), about 24 inches by 14 in superficies and about 5 inches thick, one side of which, to the extent of about 10 inches by 3, has been ground smooth, apparently by glacial action.

In discussing the question of the occurrence of palæolithic implements at such high levels above the neighbouring valleys, it would be wrong not to mention the discoveries of Mr. Benjamin Harrison, of Ightham, who in Kent has obtained more or less isolated implements at elevations of 760 and 770 feet above Ordnance-datum, and a considerable number of them near Ash at an elevation of over 500 feet.

It seems to me probable, having all the conditions of the case in view, that it is safest not to invoke river-action for the formation of the high-level deposits, which extend over a wide area and are in the main argillaceous, and not gravelly or sandy in character; but to adopt Mr. Worthington Smith's view that in early times lakes or marshes existed on these implementiferous spots, the borders of which were inhabited by Palæolithic Man. The evidence which he has brought forward as to the implements having been, in some of the Caddington pits, manufactured on the spot, most fully corroborates this view. Moreover, in many places the Drift-deposits are so impervious to water that at the present day numerous ponds exist on their surface, some of which rarely, if ever, become absolutely dry.

I will only add that I have unfortunately not been able personally to visit all the localities that I have mentioned, but in compiling this short paper I have been much indebted to Mr. Worthington Smith for information given to me by him, whose authority on the subject of Early Man is beyond all question. Through his kindness I was able at the reading of this paper to exhibit a series of specimens, two of which are figured.

### DISCUSSION.

Mr. DALE said that he had obtained, from the valleys of the Test and Itchen in Hampshire, implements similar to those exhibited

---

[1] In Mr. Whitaker's 'Geology of London' Mem. Geol. Surv. vol. i (1889) p. 208, is the following passage:—'At Wood-Lane End kiln, more than a mile east of Hemel Hempstead, it would seem that masses of the mottled clay of the Reading Beds are included in the brick-earth, or that there are pipes of the former.'

at the highest levels above the existing rivers. They were absolutely un-waterworn, and he had always regarded them as representing the latest stage of the palæolithic epoch—some, indeed, had almost a neolithic facies. He considered that they were made on the spot. With regard to the reference to Mr. Benjamin Harrison's discoveries on the high levels of Kent, he understood that these were rough implements and considered by some to represent even an earlier epoch than the palæolithic; whereas the highly-finished tools now shown must be regarded more as of the time when the palæolithic epoch was passing away.

Mr. CLEMENT REID also thought that palæolithic implements at high levels did not necessarily indicate fluviatile action, but had in many cases been dropped where they were now found. He went further, suggesting that some of the fine-grained clays and loams in which the implements often occurred might have been dust-deposits. Undoubted æolian loess with *Succinea oblonga* formed a considerable sheet as near as Sangatte, where it contained 'seams' of palæolithic implements.

Mr. H. B. WOODWARD referred to the high-level Drift described by the Author as made up largely of Eocene débris, and recalled attention to the Drift at Croxley Green, near Rickmansworth. There an interesting discovery of palæolithic implements had been made known by Sir John Evans. The specimens occurred at the base of gravelly deposits, which contained masses of clay and grey-wethers derived from the Reading Beds. The deposits were grouped as Glacial on the Geological-Survey map, and they appeared to the speaker to be of torrential character, due perhaps to the melting of ice during the Glacial Epoch.

Mr. N. F. ROBARTS thought that there was no connexion between Mr. Benjamin Harrison's eolithic implements and those described in the paper, merely because they were found at about the same elevation: those described were found in brick-earth, while Mr. Harrison's occurred in an altogether different deposit.

Dr. A. E. SALTER remarked that he understood the Author to refer to palæolithic implements which had been found on the surface at high levels on the Kentish Plateau and near Ightham by Mr. Benjamin Harrison and the late Mr. Stopes, and not, as the previous speaker stated, to eoliths found in the same localities. The speaker was not aware of any palæoliths having been found in stratified gravel at a greater height than about 150 feet above the present river-courses.

Mr. O. A. SHRUBSOLE said that it was singular that the specimens exhibited were all of the same form, having a sharp cutting-edge all round. This must be regarded as the highest development of the palæolithic type. The chipping also reminded one of neolithic work: this was consistent with a comparatively-late date.

Mr. HAZZLEDINE WARREN said that he could not agree with the last speaker in throwing doubt upon the palæolithic age of the implements exhibited, although there was little question that they belonged to a somewhat late stage of that period. He was particularly pleased that the Author did not consider these hill-drifts to have been formed by river-action.  The speaker had examined a clay-drift on the summit of the ridge of Chalk Downs in the Isle of Wight, which likewise could not be explained in this manner.  This contained palæolithic implements, some of which were of a similar type to those shown on the table.  This deposit was an unctuous clay with angular flints, and it appeared to have been formed by surface-drifting and rain-wash, rather than by the æolian action suggested by Mr. Clement Reid.

Mr. Ll. TREACHER remarked on the similarity in shape of the implements exhibited to some found in the valley-gravels at Farn-ham (Surrey), in association with pointed forms of the ordinary river-drift type.  He hesitated, however, to suggest that they were of the same age, as, judging from his experience as a collector, the shape-peculiarity of a palæolithic implement was characteristic of locality rather than of age.

Mr. H. BURY ventured to question Mr. C. Reid's deduction that sharpness of edge in palæoliths was opposed to the theory of river-action; and he produced an implement from Farnham, found in a pocket of clay in the midst of a bed of gravel of undoubted fluviatile origin.  This gravel was not at plateau-level, but quite low down the slope of the Wey Valley, where wind-blown beds were improbable, yet the edges of the implement were as sharp as possible.

Mr. A. S. KENNARD said that, judged by their facies, the age of the implements was late palæolithic.  They were obviously much later than the implements from the 100-foot terrace of the Thames, and could not be correlated with those from the middle-terrace brick-earths.  They greatly resembled the series that had been obtained from the site of rock-shelters at Ightham by Mr. Benjamin Harrison, the only difference being one of size.

Mr. W. WHITAKER said that he was glad to hear so many speakers object to mere height being taken as an index of antiquity; it was relative height only, in regard to the bottom of a valley, that should be taken.  Nevertheless, he had seen height above the sea brought forward as pointing to the great age of eoliths; but now they knew that well-made palæoliths occurred at much the same level.  He was sometimes in doubt as to whether gravels coloured as of Glacial age were really so: it was often, in doubtful cases, a matter of expediency as to what colour should be given to a gravel on the Survey-Map.  In the midst of a district of Glacial Drift it was clearly safer to colour a doubtful gravel as of that age, than to introduce another subdivision.

One of the chief points of the paper was the suggestion of a lacustrine origin for the brick-earths of the Chalk-plateau.  These deposits were difficult to explain, and, although he had known them for nearly 50 years, he had never felt confident as to any view of their origin.  It should be remembered that they were sometimes bedded, and even finely so.

Every one must be pleased to have this evidence of the vitality of the Author and of his zeal for the Society.

2. *On a* DEEP CHANNEL *of* DRIFT *at* HITCHIN (HERTFORDSHIRE).
By WILLIAM HILL, F.G.S.   (Read December 18th, 1907.)

CONTENTS.

|  |  | Page |
|---|---|---|
| I. | Introduction | 8 |
| II. | Physical Features of the Hitchin and Stevenage Gap | 9 |
| III. | Evidence of the Deep Channel in the Drift | 13 |
| IV. | Materials filling the Hitchin and Stevenage Gap | 19 |
| V. | Summary | 21 |

## I. INTRODUCTION.

DEEP channels filled with Drift occurring in Scotland and in the North of England have long been noticed by geologists,[1] and more recently the existence of similar buried valleys has been discovered in the East of England.   In 1890 Mr. W. Whitaker[2] drew attention to a deep channel of Drift in the valley of the Cam; and in 1898 Dr. A. Irving recorded a great depth of Drift in the valley of the Stort.[3]

It has long been known that a considerable thickness of Drift covers the Chalk immediately to the south of Hitchin, wells and road-cuttings indicating that deposits of sand, gravel, or Boulder-Clay were at least 60 feet thick in certain localities; a boring at Messrs. Lucas & Co.'s brewery at Hitchin in the year 1831[4] was carried to a depth of 466 feet, passing through 3 feet of soil and 77 feet of sand.   But the Chalk is so frequently seen that an exceptional thickness of Drift was unsuspected.

During the last few years five borings have been made in the neighbourhood of Hitchin, all of which have disclosed a greater thickness of Drift than was expected.   They happen to have been made in a line running about north and south nearly at right angles to the outcrop of the Chalk, the southernmost being 3 miles south of Hitchin, and the northernmost 4 miles north of the town.   The object of this paper is to record these borings, which, with other evidence, seem to point to the existence of a deep and narrow channel of Drift, the length of which (as at present ascertained) is about 7 miles, although probably it extends farther.

[1] Sir A. Geikie, 'On the Phenomena of the Glacial Drift of Scotland' Trans. Geol. Soc. Glasgow, vol. i, pt. ii (1863) pp. 49–66; J. Croll, 'Two River-Channels buried under Drift' Trans. Edin. Geol. Soc. vol. i (1869–70) pp. 330–45; T. M. Reade, 'The Buried Valley of the Mersey' Proc. Liverpool Geol. Soc. vol. ii (1873–74) Sess. xiv, p. 42.
[2] 'On a Deep Channel of Drift in the Valley of the Cam, Essex' Quart. Journ. Geol. Soc. vol. xlvi, p. 333; see also the same author's 'Water-Supply of Suffolk' Mem. Geol. Surv. 1906, p. 3 *et passim*.
[3] Proc. Geol. Assoc. vol. xv, p. 224.
[4] 'The Geology of the London Basin' Mem. Geol. Surv. vol. iv (1872) p. 453.

## II. PHYSICAL FEATURES OF THE HITCHIN AND STEVENAGE GAP.

Approached from the north-west, Hitchin will be seen to be in a bay-like indentation of the Chalk-escarpment. The north-eastern extremity of this indentation is marked by a projecting spur called

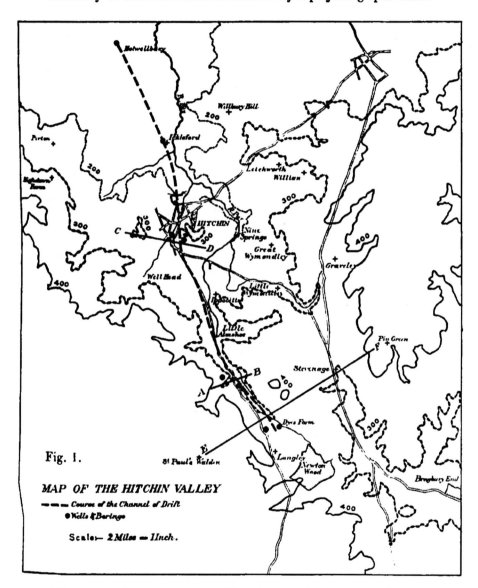

Fig. 1.

*MAP OF THE HITCHIN VALLEY*

— • — • Course of the Channel of Drift
● Wells & Borings

Scale:— 2 Miles = 1 Inch.

Wilbury Hill, the crest of which rises to 284 feet above the sea; but, sloping gently upwards, the ground reaches a height of over 300 feet half a mile to the south-east. The south-western extremity is marked by the bolder headland of Highdown, which rises rapidly from the Gault-plain to over 450 feet above Ordnance-datum, the distance between the two headlands being rather more than 4½ miles.

Referring to a contoured map, it will be seen that from the headlands above mentioned the 300-foot contour-line (if for the moment the sinuosities of lateral valleys are disregarded) takes roughly the form of a V, reaching back in a south-easterly direction into the Chalk-escarpment, and its apex, somewhat drawn out, nearly touches Langley, 4 miles south of Hitchin. Along the western side of the V is a Chalk-ridge indented by lateral valleys, rising to 400 and sometimes 500 feet above sea-level, within half a mile of the 300-foot contour. This ridge, which may be regarded as a buttress of the Chiltern Hills, continues for 2 miles to the southward, its slopes gradually passing into those of the Lea Valley. On the eastern side the ground, though rising considerably above 300 feet, does not, with the exception of two knolls near the apex of the V, attain a height of 400 feet for some 2 miles eastward.

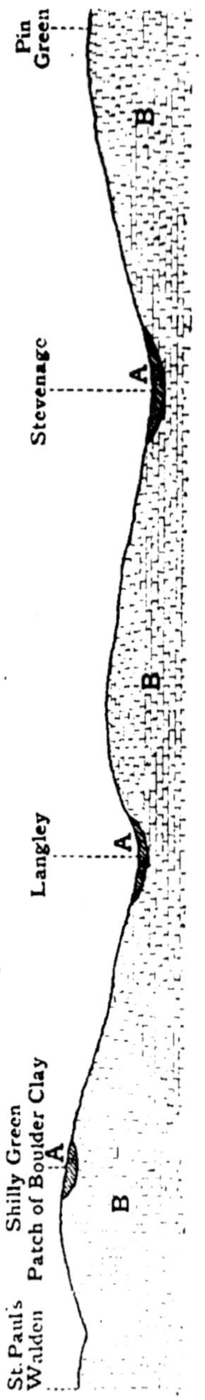

This V-shaped valley is, in fact, only part of a wider depression or gap in the escarpment of the Chalk, a feature which has been called the Hitchin and Stevenage Gap. The width of this gap, from the 400-foot contour-line near Langley to the same contour-line east of Stevenage, is about 2 miles; and it is occupied by the heads of two valleys, the one drawing towards the north, the other towards the south, but overlapping one another by a space of a mile or more.

The western of these two valleys runs from Newton Wood east of Langley by Ippollitts and Hitchin into the Ouse; the eastern rising at Stevenage opens southwards into that of the River Beane, which is a tributary of the Thames. The actual watershed between the heads of the two valleys is a sinuous line running from the north of Stevenage by Symonds Green and Norton Green to the ridge between Langley and Knebworth. On this line there are two cols, or low divides between the

Fig. 2.—*Section across the Hitchin and Stevenage Gap, along the line EF in the map, fig. 1 (p. 9).*

[A = Drift. B = Chalk. Scales : horizontal, 3 inches = 1 mile ; vertical, 1 inch = 500 feet.]

heads of valleys—one at the northern end of Stevenage, where the ground is only 315 feet above the sea; and one south of Norton Green, where the divide between the two systems is only about 305 feet above Ordnance-datum.

It has long been known that this gap is largely filled with Drift-deposits which are partly at any rate of Glacial age, and the surface-area of these deposits is shown on the Geological-Survey Map. Some of these Drifts near Hitchin were briefly described in a report of an excursion to that place in 1896; and Dr. A. E. Salter then pointed out their position at the

'northern entrance of one of the few gaps which penetrate the Chalk hills to the north and north-west of London.'[1]

No one, however, has yet given a complete account of them, so that the depth to which they extend is at present unknown, and the relations of the existing surface-features to those of the pre-Glacial contours could only be a matter of speculation. Until some information was obtained with regard to the varying depth of the Chalk-floor upon which the Drifts rest, it was impossible to say whether the ancient (buried) valley extended northwards from Langley and Stevenage, or southwards to some point outside the present Chalk-escarpment.

The western flank of the valley just defined is almost entirely bare Chalk down to, sometimes below, the 300-foot contour-line; but the highest ground on the summit of the escarpment is covered with Clay-with-Flints. Along the summit occur, near the edge of the slope, five patches of Boulder-Clay, all of insignificant dimensions, but sufficient to lead to the belief that the high ground as well as the low was once covered by that material.

The lower slopes of the eastern flank are also bare Chalk, but from Wilbury Hill, south-eastwards as far as Little Wymondley, on the plateau of the Middle Chalk, is a large area of Boulder-Clay which descends in some places below the 300-foot contour-line. The area of this clay is broken at Letchworth by a narrow outcrop of Chalk 250 feet above Ordnance-datum; at Willian, by a tongue of gravel[2] half a mile wide; and again by alluvium at Little Wymondley, where the Purwell valley turns to the eastward: but on the other side of this valley nearer Stevenage, it seems to be continued by a small patch. Besides the tongue of gravel at Willian, several other areas of gravel occur lying on the slopes just below the edges of the Boulder-Clay.

All the country enclosed within the angle of the V, with the exception of two knolls, to be mentioned hereafter, is below the 300-foot contour. The country between the headlands already mentioned north of Hitchin, is fairly level and is about 200 feet above the sea, with the exception of a shallow and narrow channel cut by the rivers Purwell and Hiz. It is here covered with Boulder-Clay; but nearer Hitchin gravel and sand take its place on

[1] Proc. Geol. Assoc. vol. xiv (1895-96) p. 415.
[2] Wells show that this tongue of gravel is about 60 feet thick.

the surface. South of Hitchin the ground rises and becomes more uneven, the natural drainage having cut valleys which run in sinuous courses far back into the escarpment. These valleys are bordered by ridges rising in some instances to 290 feet above sea-level. Most of these ridges appear to be mounds of sand and gravel (possibly with a core of Chalk), but some are bosses or discontinuous ridges of the bare Chalk cropping out through the mantle of sand and gravel which masks a pre-existing contour of the Chalk-escarpment. From the ground between the headlands to the gap, there is, however, a gradual ascent from 200 to 320 feet.

The present drainage of the district remains to be noticed. Again referring to the 300-foot contour-line, it will be seen that on its eastern limb is a deep indentation which carries back the escarpment to within half a mile of Stevenage, from which point it makes a bold curve to the eastward to Graveley. This is the valley of the Purwell, as indicated on the maps of the Ordnance Survey. Though the water takes a well-defined but a sinuous course, the first 3 miles of the valley-way must be considered as only a temporary water-course flowing in the winter or during wet weather, for in the summer months it is not infrequently dry. No spring occurs in the valley until it has passed under the Great Northern Railway at Nine Springs, near Hitchin, where a great deal of water comes to the surface.

Separated from the Purwell by a well-marked ridge, which can be followed in almost a straight line down the V nearly to Hitchin, and dividing it almost in its centre, is another line of drainage. This commences at the water-parting within the Gap. In wet weather a considerable body of water draining from the ridge intervening between the two waterways, and also from the main ridge lying to the westward, descends in a north-westerly direction along a narrow well-marked channel, and is lost in a swallow-hole about 2 miles distant from the divide within the Gap. A mile lower down the valley, at Ippollitts, some of this water is probably seen again in the springs that rise in swampy land, which together form a constantly-running rivulet known as Ippollitts Brook. This brook, taking first a northward direction for three-quarters of a mile, turns to the east, and seems to have cut through the ridge separating the two waterways. Joining the Purwell at Nine Springs, the two flow together as the Purwell northwards towards the Ouse basin.

The channel of Drift now to be described follows this line of drainage to the point where the Ippollitts Brook changes its direction, its course then seeming to be north-westward straight out between the Headlands.

Another drainage-line is that of the River Hiz. This takes its rise in a strong spring known as Well Head, a mile and a half west of the town. The water increased by minor springs along its course flows nearly parallel with the escarpment, that is, in a north-north-easterly direction, for 2 miles, when its water joins that of the Purwell at Grove Mill. Thence the combined water, now called the River Hiz, flows northwards into the valley of the Ivel and so into the Ouse. The waters of the Hiz are still further augmented by the Orton, which rises about a mile south-east of High Down. Like the Hiz, its waters take a north-easterly direction till it joins that river after a course of 2 miles.

### III. Evidence of the Deep Channel in the Drift.

Beginning near the water-parting of the Hitchin and Stevenage Gap and proceeding north-westwards, the first evidence of a deep channel in the Drift is found in the Langley-Ippollitts Valley at Langley Bottom. Here, near the base of the western slope, at a height of 326 feet O.D., are two wells both of which touch the Chalk. They are on opposite sides of the main road to London, that on the eastern side being slightly deeper than that on the western. The occupier of the house on the eastern side has lived there for 30 years, and has seen his well cleared out and deepened. He tells me that his well passes through 75 feet of sand and gravel before reaching Chalk, the depth being about 80 feet.

Chalk comes to the surface in the fields about 300 yards west of the well, and there are numerous chalk-pits in the locality. To the east the surface shows gravel and sand.

About 650 yards due east of the last well, at a corresponding point on the other side of the valley, but actually in the floor of it, and close to the water-course of the valley-drainage, is Dye's Farm, 302 feet O.D. The well here, once shallow, was deepened about three years ago. Mr. John Shilcock, the agent of the estate, kindly furnishes me with the following details :—

|                                                            | Feet. |
| ---------------------------------------------------------- | ----- |
| Original depth of the well—soil, red loam                  | 24    |
| Deepening.                                                 |       |
| Sand and ballast (gravel)                                  | 18    |
| Blue clay with chalk-lumps                                 | 22    |
| Boring.                                                    |       |
| Blue clay with chalk-lumps                                 | 14    |
| Chalk —plenty of water as soon as it was touched           | 2     |
|                                                            | 80    |

The material from the well was still to be seen in May 1907. The clay at the bottom of the well and in the boring was the blue Boulder-Clay with Chalk-pebbles in it. Bare Chalk occurs in the fields about 250 yards up the eastern flank of the valley, and there are chalk-pits along the ridge.

Three-quarters of a mile to the north-west a boring was made by Mr. W. Jackson, of Hill End, in a meadow immediately to the east of the London road, and about 200 yards from it. I estimate that the mouth of the boring was just under 300 feet O.D., and was almost in the valley-bottom. The boring was made by Messrs.

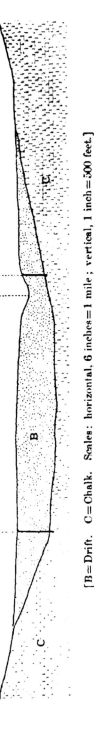

Fig. 3.—*Section through the Langley-Ippolits Valley, along the line AB in the map, fig. 1 (p. 9).*

[B = Drift.  C = Chalk.  Scales: horizontal, 6 inches = 1 mile; vertical, 1 inch = 300 feet.]

Cheeld, of Chesham (Bucks). It was carried down 100 feet to blowing-sand which choked the bore-hole, and although some water occurred the boring was abandoned. Messrs. Cheeld say :

'We started with fine gravel, which became sand as we got down. At 83 feet there was 18 inches of clay, and between that and 100 feet there were several layers of this material.'

Another boring was made by the Hitchin Joint Hospital Board, in order to obtain water for a new Isolation Hospital which it was proposed to build. The site of the boring was rather high on the western slope, about 300 yards west of the London road, almost exactly opposite the third milestone from Hitchin, and one-third of a mile north-west of the last-described boring. The level of the site was some 318 feet above O.D. Chalk is exposed about 300 yards west of the boring and about 800 yards east of it. The work was placed in the hands of Messrs. Le Grand & Sutcliff, whose account is as follows :—

| | Thickness. | Depth in feet. |
|---|---|---|
| Clay and flints ............ | 76 | |
| Brown loamy sand ...... | 9 | 85 |
| Blue clay and flints ...... | 29 | 114 |
| Brown blowing-sand ... | 19 | 133 |
| Sand and gravel ......... | 21 | 154 |
| Coloured clay ............ | 5 | 159 |
| Rubbly chalk and flints... | 13 | 172 |
| Chalk and flints ...... ... | 28 | 200 |

The blowing-sand at 133 feet was probably the same bed as that encountered by Messrs. Cheeld a little higher up the valley; a thickness of 159 feet of Drift was here pierced before Chalk was reached.

So far the evidence of the channel has been in the Langley-Ippollitts Valley: hills of bare Chalk rise in gentle slopes on each side, and on the maps of the Geological Survey

(Drift series) there is a narrow width of sand and gravel along its bottom. Between the last boring and the next the features of the valley alter, and deserve special notice. Proceeding down it towards Hitchin, the highest ridge of the Chalk-escarpment on the left trends rapidly to the west, and the ground descends to the lower level of the Middle-Chalk plain.

The western flank of the valley of the Ippollitts Brook now ceases to be bare Chalk, and a gradually-widening spread of gravel and loam, which well-sections show to be at least 50 to 60 feet thick, comes in. This, forming a broad and fairly-level plateau nearly a mile wide, thins away westwards, and the Chalk again appears at the surface as a low ridge nowhere below 260 feet O.D., which runs in a north-westerly direction from the escarpment to Charlton, and forms the watershed between the valleys of the Ippollitts Brook and the Hiz. At Charlton, however, this ridge, like that which separates the Purwell stream from the Ippollitts Brook, is breached by the Hiz; and, although the natural features are complicated by a lateral valley of the Hiz drainage-system, the ridge can nevertheless be followed on the other side of the valley of the Hiz, where it rises to a well-marked knoll at Fox Holes or Mount Pleasant, a little over 300 feet above the level of the sea.

On the eastern side, except for a narrow lateral valley at Little Almshoe, the ground rises immediately in a well-marked acclivity nearly to 300 feet O.D.; and although this is covered in places with a very considerable thickness of Drift, a Chalk-ridge can be followed to a little north of Ippollitts. Here the ground sinks where the ridge is breached by the Ippollitts Brook, but, rapidly rising again, the Chalk can be followed to Highbury, where it rises as a knoll just over 300 feet above Ordnance-datum.

Here, then, we seem to have evidence of the gradual widening of an old valley in the Chalk-escarpment, its confines being outlined by ridges of Chalk to the east and to the west, while its embouchure on to the Lower-Chalk plain from that of the Middle Chalk is marked by prominent headlands rising to 300 feet above the present sea-level. It will be seen in the sequel that the deep channel in the Drift runs between them. The whole of this old valley is now filled in with Drift of great thickness; and there seems to be good reason for thinking that it once nearly filled up the space between the two headlands, with perhaps a saddle or low col between them. By this the drainage-system of the Hiz probably made its way, cutting the deep trench which it now occupies obliquely to the direction of the old buried valley.

At the present time the southern side of the Hiz valley is steep, rising from 200 to 300 feet O.D. Between the ridge which marks the old valley on the west and the headland on the east there is no sign of Chalk, and the hill which overlooks Hitchin from this direction is a mass of Drift banked against the eastern knoll. On the northern bank of the Hiz the ground rises sharply also; the first part is gravel and sand, but there then occurs a platform of bare Chalk

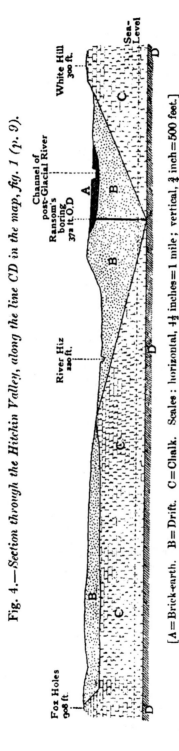

Fig. 4.—*Section through the Hitchin Valley, along the line CD in the map, fig. 1 (p. 9).*

[A = Brick-earth.   B = Drift.   C = Chalk.   Scales : horizontal, 1⅔ inches = 1 mile ; vertical, ¾ inch = 500 feet.]

from 200 to 300 yards wide some 30 feet above the river-bed. Beyond that the ground again rises to the westernmost knoll at Fox Holes. All this rising ground seems to be a mass of Drift banked against the Chalk. Mr. Tindal Lucas, of Fox Holes, in digging a well for water, pierced 100 feet of Boulder-Clay and gravel without reaching water or Chalk, although that rock is exposed close by. He tried again some 25 or 30 yards nearer the outcrop, and then found the Chalk close to the surface.

The next boring was made a little way down the south-eastern slope of a hill of Drift on the south side of the Hiz. It was made in the brickyard of Mr. Theodore Ransom, in order to obtain a better water-supply. The site was some 200 yards east of the London road on the outskirts of Hitchin, and about 2½ miles in a direct line north-west from the boring of the Hitchin Joint Hospital Board. It will be seen that it began at the bottom of an existing well, where the surface is 272 feet above O.D. That a considerable thickness of Drift would have to be pierced here was fairly obvious, but there seemed little doubt that Chalk would be reached, for it can be seen at the surface about 500 yards eastward, while on the western side Chalk is about 1000 yards distant. Messrs. Le Grand & Sutcliff made the boring, of which Mr. Ransom has kindly sent me the following details :—

|  | Thickness. | Depth in feet. |
|---|---|---|
| Existing dug well (mostly brick-earth) ............ | 64 |  |
| Loamy ballast ......................................... | 3 | 67 |
| Live blue sand ....................................... | 20 | 87 |
| Sandy clay and stones ................................ | 3 | 90 |
| Sandy ballast ......................................... | 36½ | 126½ |
| Sandy clay ............................................ | 3 | 129½ |
| Clay, stones, and small pieces of chalk ............ | 6½ | 136 |
| Stiff clay ............................................ | 5 | 141 |
| Sandy clay and sand .................................. | 7 | 148 |
| Sand ................................................. | 16 | 164 |
| Stiff clay and stones (some lignite, 169 to 177 feet). | 32 | 196 |
| Clayey sand .......................................... | 10 | 206 |
| Clay and stones ...................................... | 4 | 210 |
| Very hard sand ....................................... | 7 | 217 |
| Live sand ............................................ | 29½ | 246½ |
| Sand and stones ...................................... | 26½ | 273 |
| Stony clay ........................................... | 21½ | 294½ |
| Blowing sand ......................................... | 4 | 298½ |
| Stony clay ........................................... | 14½ | 313 |
| Clayey sand, stones, and small pieces of chalk ... | 4 | 317 |
| Blue sandy clay ...................................... | 15 | 332 |
| Sandy clay and stones ................................ | 8 | 340 |
| Gault ................................................ | 5 | 345 |

Here it will be seen that 340 feet of Drift was encountered, and the Chalk was absent altogether. I was fortunately present when the auger brought up Gault, a stiff dark-blue clay: in my judgment, it was not the top of the Gault. At Arlesey the upper 20 feet or so is paler in colour than that lower down, and I think that the Gault touched in this boring was below the upper and paler part of it. Nothing like Cambridge Greensand was passed through, and I examined very carefully the material which had been brought up by the auger.

Another boring here deserves attention. The great thickness of Drift encountered at Mr. Ransom's brickyard led me to consider a boring made at Messrs. Lucas & Co.'s brewery in Hitchin in the year 1831, the details of which are given in the 'Geology of the London Basin.'[1] After having passed through 80 feet of surface-soil and sand, 149 feet of white and grey marl was pierced before reaching the Gault. It will be noticed that Mr. Whitaker questions the identity of this white marl with the Chalk. The mouth of this boring was about 220 feet above O.D., and it must have been commenced just below the Melbourn Rock. As there is not more than 170 feet of Lower Chalk in this locality, Gault should have been reached at that depth at least; but it was not touched until 229 feet, which puts the base of the Chalk 60 feet lower than it should be and gives it a thickness of some 225 feet. It will be seen that the surface of the Gault was at nearly the same height above sea-level in both borings. I am inclined to think, and I believe that Mr. Whitaker agrees with me, that much of the white and grey marl mentioned in this boring may be Drift.

[1] Mem. Geol. Surv. vol. iv (1872) p. 453.

I may here mention another well in Hitchin. It was situated at the northern end of the town, three-quarters of a mile north-north-west of Mr. Ransom's boring. It was dug so long ago that the details are lost; indeed, the well itself was filled in a few years back. The tenant of the cottage is, however, alive and recollects the circumstances, which are also corroborated by Mr. Frederic Seebohm, of The Hermitage, Hitchin. The well (bench-mark on cottage, 209 O.D.) was sunk about 90 feet in blue clay; but, as an insufficient supply of water was obtained, boring was resorted to. The bore was carried down in blue clay for about the same depth as the well, that is, about 90 feet more—and still no water was obtained. The blue Boulder-Clay with chalk-pebbles certainly occurs 250 yards to the south-east at the gas-works; some 25 or 30 feet was proved there, immediately below the surface, when a new gas-holder was constructed. A fairly-strong spring is thrown out by the Chalk 800 yards to the north-east, and it seems certain that if that rock had been reached water would have been found.

The next boring was made at Ickleford Rectory, nearly 2 miles north-west of Mr. Ransom's boring on the hill. Ickleford is just within the arms of the indentation of the escarpment; the country is but little over 200 feet above sea-level, and may be described as flat, save for the slight depressions along lines of local drainage: as a whole, it descends very gently to the plain of the Gault. On each side, the flanks of the main escarpment consist of bare Chalk and rise in gradual slopes. All along the valley-bottom, here more than a mile and a half in width, all features of the Chalk are obscured by spreads of gravel and Boulder-Clay. On the eastern side, the Hiz has made for itself a shallow valley less than 200 feet above the sea. The site of the boring is in the rectory-garden, 180 feet above O.D., and in the valley of the Hiz. Bare Chalk occurs 350 yards to the eastward; on the west there is no outcrop of it for a mile. The account kindly sent to me by Messrs. Le Grand & Sutcliff is as follows :—

| | Thickness. | Depth in feet. |
|---|---|---|
| Top-soil—mould | 2 | |
| Clay and stones | 15 | 17 |
| Sand and gravel | 12 | 29 |
| Sand and thin veins of clay | 10 | 39 |
| Sandy clay | 11 | 50 |
| Boulder-Clay, with pieces of chalk-flint, etc.; thin layer of flints at 75 feet, with water. | 66 | 116 |
| Boulder-Clay, with grains of chalk diminishing in number | 30 | 146 |

I have seen the sample from 146 feet; I am not quite satisfied that it is Gault, but it may be. It is a somewhat sandy clay, although the sand may have come down the bore-hole and mixed with it. I did not know of the boring until it was completed and the material had been removed. Nothing like Cambridge Greensand was detected.

The last boring was made at Holwell Bury for Mr. Kenneth. Its site was about a quarter of a mile west of the main road to Bedford, 180 feet above sea-level, and nearly 2 miles directly north of that at Ickleford. It is well outside the indentation of the escarpment, and is just south of the point where the Gault should come to the surface; but the position of the outcrop is quite obscured by a thick deposit of Boulder-Clay. Chalk-Marl is seen half a mile to the south-west and nearly a mile away to the east. Between these two borings a curious elongate boss of the Lower Chalk rises to the surface. Mr. Kenneth kindly sent me the following particulars :—

|  | Thickness. | Depth in feet. |
|---|---|---|
| Surface-soil and Boulder-Clay : water at 95 feet. | 98 | 98 |
| Shingle | 4 | 102 |
| Sand | 19 | 121 |
| Sandy clay | 12 | 133 |
| Gault bored | 205 | 338 |

The water-bearing strata at 95 feet seem to me to be the same as these passed through in the Ickleford boring at 75 feet, the water in both cases being strongly impregnated with iron. This bed appears to have a considerable lateral extension; cottages close to the Bedford road, as also the wells at Ramerick Farm, all take their water from it.

### IV. Materials filling the Hitchin and Stevenage Gap.

North or south of Hitchin but little information is to be obtained of the nature of the superficial deposits which fill up the inequalities of the old Chalk-surface of the Hitchin Valley below the 300-foot contour-line; but around the town are many gravel-pits where good sections of the Drift can be seen.

Wherever exposed, the Drift as a whole seems to consist chiefly of flints and chalk-pebbles, with which is mixed a heterogeneous assemblage of rocks from the northward. Usually these materials are distinctly stratified, but they vary in degrees of coarseness; and beds containing, besides flints and chalk, big boulders of Jurassic débris, sandstone, limestone, and ironstone, pebbles of quartz, quartzite, and red chalk, all more or less rolled, alternate with layers of finer gravel or quartz-sand, the latter sometimes showing current-bedding. The high dip and the frequently contorted aspect of the bedding seem to indicate that these gravels were laid down by water under 'tumultuous' conditions. Boulder-Clay occurs closely associated with the gravels, and between beds of gravel intervene not infrequently layers of blue or grey clay containing ice-scratched stones. But there does not seem to be any regular order of superposition, either in the gravels themselves or in their relation to the Boulder-Clay.

I may now give a brief description of the more interesting sections of Drift to be seen near Hitchin.

At the gravel-pit belonging to Messrs. Logsdon & Jackson,

immediately south-west of the Union Workhouse, about 25 feet of Drift is exposed. This pit is in a mass of Drift banked against the western Chalk-knoll; it forms a ridge extending for some little distance towards the north, which gradually descends to the Lower-Chalk plain. The material seen here consists chiefly of subangular and rounded flints with a large proportion of chalk-pebbles, together with Jurassic and Carboniferous limestones, ironstone, pebbles of quartz and quartzite, and red chalk. In some parts the stratification is even and regular, in others the bedding is contorted, and the strata dip at a high angle in more than one direction. From a thin bed of blue clay I picked out a chalk-pebble showing striations which were obviously due to ice-action.

Near the Vicarage (235 feet O.D.) a recently-opened pit yields the following section :—

|  | *Thickness in feet.* |
|---|---|
| Gravelly soil | 3 |
| Chalky Boulder-Clay | 4 |
| Pale-grey clay | 2¼ |
| Pale-brown sandy silt, with discontinuous layers of fine chalky gravel | 3½ |
| Sandy gravel seen for about | 12 |

The clay which follows the Boulder-Clay is quite free from stones and is much like Gault; moreover, it contains many whitish concretions similar to those in the upper part of the Gault at Arlesey. The gravel, as usual, consists of rolled and subangular flints and chalk, with a varied assemblage of other rocks, many gryphæas, belemnites, etc. This section is quite close to the platform of Chalk mentioned on p. 15, and the beds dip at a high angle towards it, to the west. Bare Chalk occurs 100 yards to the north, and about 250 yards to the south-west. There are many gravel-pits on the high ground to the south and east of the town, all of which are in the Drift banked against the eastern knoll. At Highbury (300 feet O.D.) is a shallow pit from which a clayey gravel has been dug. This gravel contains big blocks of limestone and sandstone, large and small chalk-flints and chalk-pebbles. The depth to which the gravel is dug is governed by what appears to be Boulder-Clay.

Cleaner gravel is to be seen in a pit belonging to Mr. Theodore Ransom, about 300 yards south of the last. [This also was shallow, but a thickness of 25 feet of gravel was exposed here in January 1908.]

A few hundred yards still farther south, Messrs. Logsdon & Jackson work another pit. This shows a face of nearly 30 feet, and the section of the northern part of it seen in June 1907 was as follows :—

|  | *Thickness in feet.* |
|---|---|
| Gravelly soil | 3½ |
| Sharp sandy gravel, chiefly small flints and chalk-stones... | 4 |
| Sandy loam, with seams of chalky gravel | 3 |
| Quartz-sand with much fine chalk, small flints, and chalk-pebbles | 2¼ |
| Coarse gravel, in well-marked layers divided by seams of loam or sharp sand, seen for about | 15 |

The coarse gravel contains a large quantity of Jurassic débris, much of which occurs in rounded boulders, many as big as a man's head. These are of soft material, and are picked out and cast aside by the workmen. Up to the present the bottom of this gravel has not been reached.

At Mr. Theodore Ransom's lime-works at Hitchin Railway-station, Boulder-Clay, from which ice-scratched blocks of limestone and sandstone of very considerable size have been obtained, is seen overlying the Chalk. At Gravelly Hill, near Great Wymondley, the material consists of Jurassic débris, limestone, sandstone, quartz, and quartzite-pebbles, etc. Several pits at the Folly, Hitchin, expose gravels of similar nature. Overlying these, and covered by a considerable thickness of brick-earth, is the old river-bed described by Mr. C. Reid.[1]

Recent excavations for building purposes have shown that Boulder-Clay with ice-scratched stones occurs in patches all along the highest parts of the Highbury Ridge.

A gravel of different character occurs on Wilbury Hill. In an old gravel-pit on the summit of the hill, a thickness of about 8 feet of it is shown, overlain by about 7 feet of pale-brown calcareous loam. This gravel consists almost entirely of smallish angular and subangular flints and many well-rounded chalk-pebbles. Besides these, it contains pebbles of quartz and quartzite, rolled fragments of a pinkish or red rock (not red chalk), none of which exceed $1\frac{1}{2}$ inches in length, and also many small pieces of ironstone. The Jurassic débris seen in the pits near Hitchin, with fossiliferous limestones, gryphæas, and belemnites, is absent. About a third of a mile to the north-east, the same gravel has been extensively dug by the 'Garden City' authorities, some of the sections showing 12 to 14 feet of it. It is here much seamed by layers of quartz-sand containing also a good deal of fine chalk: these layers show current-bedding. Still farther on, the gravel seems to pass laterally into a sharp quartz-sand with a few chalk-stones. The sand is closely associated with Boulder-Clay, although the actual relation of the one to the other has not yet been disclosed. There is good reason for believing, however, that the sand and the gravel are overlain by the clay, for the 3 or 4 feet of soil overlying the gravel contains large pebbles of sandstone, limestone, etc. ; and in the pit where the sand is dug, masses of Boulder-Clay full of large weathered and rounded fragments of Melbourn Rock have been encountered near the surface. It is curious that the outcrop of the Melbourn Rock occurs within 200 or 300 yards. It seems probable that these gravels of Wilbury Hill are older than any part of the Drift seen at Hitchin.

## V. SUMMARY.

From the evidence adduced in the foregoing pages there seems little reason to doubt that a channel of considerable depth, now filled with Drift, occupies the centre of an old valley in the Chalk-

[1] Proc. Roy. Soc. vol. lxi (1897) p. 40; see also Proc. Geol. Assoc. vol. xiv (1895–96) p. 415.

escarpment, which we may call the Hitchin Valley. Like the valley in which it occurs, the channel takes a north-north-westerly direction from what is known as the Hitchin and Stevenage Gap, out into the plain beyond the escarpment, from point to point a distance of 7 or 8 miles. For the first 3 miles it appears to be contained within narrow limits, persistent ridges of Chalk occurring on each side, and it might almost be compared with a Chalk combe. At Hitchin, after passing between two well-marked knolls, its confines become less clear, and there seems to be some evidence of broadening as it emerges on to the Lower-Chalk plain and leaves the higher ground of the main Chalk-escarpment.

The greatest depth to which the channel has been proved is at Mr. Ransom's boring 68 feet below sea-level. If we may take the well and boring in the northern outskirts of Hitchin as approximately correct, its bottom here is 24 feet above sea-level, at Ickleford it is 29 feet, and at Holwell Bury 34 feet above it. The boring of the Hitchin Joint Hospital Board, 3 miles south of Hitchin, reaches Chalk 159 feet above sea-level ; yet I feel sure that this is not the centre of the channel, but on the western side of it. And the fact that the borings may not be coincident with the centre may account for the differences of depth at Ickleford and Holwell. The channel cannot be due to any faulting of the Chalk, for the outcrops of the Totternhoe Stone, the Melbourn Rock, and of the Chalk-Rock, all occupy their normal positions on each side of it ; the erosive action of running water seems to be the most reasonable explanation of its formation.

If the channel be due to the effects of running water, the question naturally arises as to which way the current flowed. Are we dealing with the effects of a 'consequent' stream formed during the first great uplift of the Chalk, with its water flowing southwards, or with the effects of a 'subsequent' stream due to the gradual wearing-back of the Cretaceous rocks with a current flowing northwards?

If it flowed southwards, unless we conceive local earth-movements of which there is no indication, the floor of the channel between Dye's Farm and Langley Bottom, a distance of 650 yards, must be at least as much below sea-level as at Mr. Ransom's boring, and there would be a thickness of some 380 feet of Drift between the two points—not perhaps impossible, though hardly probable.

The course of the channel to the southward of this is determined by ridges of Chalk which rise to the east and to the west, up to the 300-foot contour-line, and the only place where it could pass is at Bragbury End, 3¼ miles east-south-east of Langley. Here bare Chalk is seen on both sides of the valley of the Beane, very little below the 300-foot contour-line, the space between the bare Chalk-ridges being about 450 yards.

Almost in the centre of this space is the house of Mr. Berger, and I am informed by Mr. Milne, agent for the Earl of Lytton, that in a well dug here a few years back, Chalk was reached within 50 feet of the surface. I think that this conclusively proves that the channel did not extend much farther south than Langley, and that any water which may have found its way into it flowed towards the north.

It seems, on the whole, more probable that the floor of the buried valley sloped northwards below the Drifts which now occupy the Hitchin and Stevenage Gap, and we should expect to find the valley continuing northwards into and below that of the Ouse.

With regard to the age of the channel, it must be older than the Chalky Boulder-Clay which still partly fills it as far south as Langley, which may have blocked it to the southward and have given rise to the features now presented in the drainage on the northern slope of the escarpment.

It will be noticed that silty clay was met with at the bottom of Mr. Ransom's, the Ickleford, and Holwell-Bury borings, the colour of which is similar to that of the rocks over which the channel passes. This might be taken as evidence of the gradual silting-up of the river-bed due to the slow sinking of the land at the advent of the Chalky Boulder-Clay, the second phase of the Glacial Epoch.

If the channel was formed before Glacial times, the main features of the escarpment must have then existed, and, although the Boulder-Clay may have spread over the country as a mantle in varying degrees of thickness, those features were not obscured, and the courses of the streams formed subsequently must have already been outlined.[1] Torrential rains following the Glacial Epoch might have swept away the lighter parts of the Boulder-Clay, and converted the remainder into the gravel which now fills up the inequalities of the old Chalk-surface and now lies between the knolls at Hitchin.

Though this explanation may in part account for the accumulation of gravel in the Hitchin Valley, it is not wholly satisfactory. The spread of the Boulder-Clay, which contains large blocks of ice-scratched limestone on the summit of the eastern knoll, its presence on the western knoll, and its occurrence interstratified among gravels of lower elevations, show, I think, that ice must have played no unimportant part in damming-up the old Chalk-valley at Hitchin. Whether this ice was in the form of a glacier moving down from the northward, or whether it was bay-ice formed during the last phase of the Glacial Epoch, must remain an open question. Granting that the main features of the escarpment were in existence before the time of the Chalky Boulder-Clay, the position is one in which, on the gradual emergence of land from the sea at the conclusion of the Glacial Epoch, bay-ice might accumulate; and, catching the ground at the rise of the Middle-Chalk plain, it might remain there and form with the débris which it carried an effective dam in the pre-existing valley. It seems clear also that the drainage-lines of the upper part of the Hitchin Valley have been turned towards the east by the mass of Drift which lies immediately to the south-east of Hitchin Town. There yet remain traces of a past

[1] A. J. Jukes-Browne, 'Stratigraphical Geology' 1902, pp. 571-72.

Glacial stream,[1] which may have been the precursor and originator of the valley now occupied by the Purwell and Ippollitts Brook.

The present drainage of the Hiz, before it is joined by the Purwell, seems to be fully accounted for by the probable configuration of the escarpment in early pre-Glacial days, the water making its way by a saddle or col between the two knolls, and having since then deepened its channel.

A glance at the Drift-Map published by the Geological Survey would perhaps suggest the possibility of another channel buried under the broad area of Boulder-Clay and gravel which lies immediately south of Stevenage and extends to the north as far as Letchworth and Wilbury Hill. But a narrow space of bare Chalk at an elevation of 240 feet O.D., connecting large areas east and west of it, precludes the occurrence of a channel farther north than Letchworth.

Few wells of any depth occur between this point and Stevenage. At Little Wymondley, however, Mr. Courtenay, in sinking one for his water-supply, encountered 80 feet of Drift, 35 feet of which immediately overlying the Chalk was blue Boulder-Clay. Although I have been unable to find other evidence, deep clay- and gravel-pits show that there is a very considerable thickness of Drift north and south of Stevenage.

Again referring to the Drift-Map, it will be noticed that a stream of gravel turns eastwards from the narrow valley in which the channel described in these pages occurs, and passing through Ippollitts and Titmore Green joins the larger spread just north of Stevenage. Three or four wells in the centre of this stream touch the Chalk 70 to 80 feet from the surface, so that a ridge of this rock must continue here about 200 feet above sea-level. Although there is no evidence on the Stevenage side of the Gap, I am inclined to think that an old channel formed by a drainage-system which once flowed into that of the Thames is buried here beneath the gravels and Boulder-Clay. If such be the case, its only course must be through the narrow passage at Bragbury End.

### DISCUSSION.

Mr. CLEMENT REID said that he had just visited the area in company with the Author, and had been impressed with the size and importance of the buried valley. It was probably pre-Glacial: but none of these Drift-filled channels had as yet yielded anything closely resembling marsh-deposits or alluvium, nor had they yielded fossils. The lowest beds, just above the solid rock, deserved close examination.

As an alternative hypothesis, he suggested that the valley might be sub-Glacial, not pre-Glacial, the drainage flowing southward towards the Thames, instead of northward towards the Ouse. The

[1] Proc. Roy. Soc. vol. lxi (1897) p. 40; and Proc. Geol. Assoc. vol. xiv (1895–96) p. 415.

locality was not far from the edge of the great ice-sheet, where the ice thinned rapidly southwards. The water underneath the ice, if unable to escape northwards, would escape southwards, flowing uphill towards the thin edge of the ice. Water in a sub-Glacial stream did not descend in the same direction as its containing channel; it resembled a tidal scour which could cut out long channels or basins, with closed ends, in the sea-bed.

Mr. G. BARROW drew attention to the general resemblance of the phenomena described, and the conformation of the ground, to that seen in the Cleveland area of North-East Yorkshire. The able explanation of the Glacial phenomena of that area, which had been published by Prof. P. F. Kendall, seemed quite applicable to the Hitchin district; and the deep Drift-filled hollow connecting the low-lying area on the north of the town with the valley-system on the south, might easily have been a gorge-like gash, cut through the watershed by a stream flowing along the edge of a mass of melting ice lying in the great hollow north of Hitchin.

Mr. R. H. TIDDEMAN mentioned that, when he was mapping the ground about 40 years ago, there was a brick-field section of Glacial Drifts at Stevenage, and he was struck by the Northern character of the boulders and more especially by the occurrence among them of Carboniferous Limestone.

Dr. A. E. SALTER was much interested in the detailed account given by the Author of these puzzling deposits in the neighbourhood of the Hitchin and Stevenage Gap. In and to the south of the Gap the gravels could be shown to belong to a 'Drift Series' in which the higher members had a much simpler composition than those below, and appeared to have been deposited by an old stream draining the Midlands at a time when the Chalk-escarpment was much farther north. The deposits described by the Author were of later date, and belonged to an obsequent stream draining northwards. The northward deepening of the channel excluded the possibility of its being of Glacial origin; and the fact that it was in places below sea-level pointed to the extreme probability of earth-movements of a regional character having taken place, which caused the old valley to be filled in by débris. There was no necessity and, so far as he could see, no evidence to invoke the aid of a great ice-sheet in the Midlands to explain the phenomena observed by the Author.

Mr. G. W. YOUNG dwelt on the similarity between the features of the district described in the paper and certain features studied by him along the North Downs. He did not perceive the necessity of invoking the presence of Glacial streams to account for the phenomena, which could be sufficiently explained by long-continued solution of the Chalk.

Mr. H. B. WOODWARD remarked that, in a boring at Glemsford, north-west of Sudbury, described by Mr. Whitaker, 470 feet of Drift had been encountered, when Chalk had been expected within about 40 feet of the surface. In this case the base of the Drift was 348 feet below Ordnance-datum. The data brought forward by the Author would be of great service in the study of the old channels filled with Drift in East Anglia. He added that, in the coarse gravelly Drift at High Down, north of Hitchin, there were pebbles or rolled lumps of Chalky Boulder-Clay.

Mr. A. S. KENNARD expressed the opinion that, if this deep channel were part of a river-system, then this system must have extended over the East of England, and that where it entered the sea the channel must have been at least 200 feet below the present sea-level; but nowhere round the coast was there any evidence of so deep a channel. Moreover, all the buried channels in the East and South-East of England were obviously much later than the Glacial Epoch. In his opinion, it would probably be found that earth-movements had much to do with the present position of the channel.

The AUTHOR said that he could reply but little to the remarks of Mr. Reid, but thought that it was unnecessary to imagine water running up hill in order to account for the erosion of the Hitchin Valley. He believed that the valley now filled with Drift existed in pre-Glacial times with its drainage flowing to the north; but he thought it possible that, when the valley was dammed up in Glacial times, water might have found its way southwards through the Stevenage Gap. If ice had played no part in the filling-up of the valley, how were the ice-scratched stones on the hills south and south-east of Hitchin to be accounted for? He believed that the drainage of the old valley was connected with a system which followed the course of the Ouse, but which like the Hitchin Valley was now filled with Drift; and he drew attention to the fact that borings between Biggleswade and Sandy yielded evidence of a great thickness of Drift in the Ouse Valley. That old river-courses now filled with Drift or Boulder-Clay existed below the present sea-level was shown in the case of the Humber.

3. BRACHIOPOD HOMŒOMORPHY : ' *SPIRIFER GLABER.*'
By S. S. BUCKMAN, F.G.S.  (Read December 4th, 1907.)

IT is easy, but it is very dangerous, to group together under one name a series of shells of similar appearance, especially when they are in the smooth catagenetic stage; because this smooth stage may have been attained by the loss of different distinctive features, pointing to polygenetic origins.  An instructive case in this respect is found in the series of forms called *Spirifer glaber.*

As *Spirifera glabra,* Davidson [1] figured a series of shells which do not all agree in being smooth; for, though most of them are smooth, some are radially costate.  And they do not agree in shape: some have a pronounced mesial fold, others hardly any; some are very transverse, others are narrow.  Then in his synonymy he combined under this name many species of other authors : *Sp. obtusus, Sp. oblatus,* Sowerby, *Sp. linguifera, Sp. symmetrica, Sp. decora,* Phillips, *Sp. lævigatus,* von Buch.

Of late years this *glaber*-series of the Carboniferous, and certain smooth Spiriferids of the Devonian, have been ranged in M‘Coy's genus *Martinia.*

A somewhat similar series of Spiriferids is grouped under *Reticularia,* M‘Coy : their distinguishing character is a reticulate surface.  Davidson makes the principal species *Spirifera lineata* (Martin), and ranges under it *Terebratula (?) imbricata,* Sowerby, *Spirifera elliptica* and *Sp. mesoloba,* Phillips, *Reticularia reticulata* and *Martinia stringocephaloides,* M‘Coy.

In *Reticularia* the ornament is in the catagenetic stage, decreasing in intensity; so that partially or wholly smooth *Reticulariæ* are to be expected.

There is good evidence that several of the forms ranged under *Spirifera glabra* are *Reticulariæ,* more or less smooth.  Thus the *Sp. obtusus,* Sowerby, is a *Reticularia.*  Examination of the type-specimen shows faint but distinct traces of a reticulate youth developing into a smooth adult; and in the broken beak may be seen the dental plates.  *Sp. obtusus* is allied to *Sp. elliptica,* Phillips; but perhaps it is a smooth development of *R. reticulata,* M‘Coy : at any rate, it must be removed from the *glaber*-series and be classed as *Reticularia obtusa.*

Accelerated development along the same line should produce a wholly smooth shell, and the only evidence that it was a *Reticularia* would be the possession of dental plates.  There are such smooth forms called *Sp. glaber,* which show dental plates; they are like the fossil depicted by Davidson in his pl. xii, fig. 1 : in shape and degree of mesial fold they look just like reduced editions of *R. obtusa.*  It may be that this species is the one named by Brown

---

[1] ' Monogr. Carb. Brachiop.' (Palæont. Soc. 1858–63) pls. xi & xii.  Other references to Davidson are to the same work.

*Spirifer lata*[1]: he cites as synonym ' Phillips, *Sp. glabra*, pl. x, fig. 12.' At any rate, these forms with dental plates are not *Sp. glabra*; they belong to *Reticularia*, and may be referred to, at present, as *R. lata (?)*.

In his pl. xi, figs. 3 & 4, Davidson depicts a thin, very transverse shell; and he remarks (p. 62) that de Koninck suggests the name *Sp. glaberrimus* for this form. It is well to adopt this suggestion, taking fig. 3 as the type. Of this thin, transverse form there are specimens in the British Museum (Natural History) from Kildare. Of these, B 20857, a rather large example, shows strong dental plates; B 20859, a small specimen, has a broken beak, exposing the dental plates in section; in B 20858 the presence of the plates is not certain, on account of test, but there is a suggestion of reticulation. In another specimen, the largest registered under ' *Spirifer glaber*, No. 43400,' the dental plates are well shown.

On this evidence *Sp. glaberrimus* must be removed from the *glaber*-series, and must be classed as a *Reticularia*: it is closely allied to *R. elliptica* (Phill.); its likeness in shape to that species suggested that it was a *Reticularia* before the fact of the dental plates was noted.

In other forms ranged under *Sp. glabra* quite a different ancestry is evident. Davidson depicts (pl. xii, figs. 3–5) forms with faint radial ribbing. The likeness of *Sp. linguifera*, Phillips (Davidson, pl. xii, fig. 4) to *Sp. ovalis* (Dav. pl. ix, fig. 20) forces the suggestion that the former is the smooth development of the latter.

On similar grounds of likeness in shape it seems possible to suggest that *Sp. glabra* (Dav. pl. xi, fig. 1) is the much-accelerated smooth form of *Sp. eximius*, de Koninck (Dav. pl. x, fig. 12), and that *Sp. oblatus* (Dav. pl. xi, fig. 8) is the smooth form of *Sp. pinguis* (Dav. pl. x, fig. 6). Then *Sp. glabra* (Dav. pl. xii, fig. 3) looks as if it were the young form of pl. xi, fig. 2, well enough preserved to show faint radial ribbing: in that case, the form in pl. xi, fig. 2, looks like a smooth development of ' *Sp. subrotundatus*' (Dav. pl. x, fig. 10).

The type of *Sp. decora*, Phill., shows traces of faint radial costation; but it is not easy to suggest the costate ancestor in this case: *Sp. planata* (Dav. pl. vii, figs. 25–36) and *Sp. Reedii* (Dav. pl. v, figs. 40–48) look something like what one would expect such a form to be.

If the various costate forms, *Sp. pinguis, Sp. ovalis*, etc., are kept under distinct names as distinct species, it follows that if the smooth forms be their derivatives, those smooth forms must be kept under distinct names: they cannot be grouped together as *Sp. glaber*. Further, the forms derived from reticulate ancestors must be separated not only specifically but generically from those derived from radially-costate ancestors.

Thus the British forms called *Spirifer glaber* are a very heterogeneous series. It may be doubted whether foreign species so

---

[1] ' Illustr. Foss. Conch.' 1844, p. 112 & pl. li, fig. 24.

named are correctly identified. Certainly the large smooth *Spirifer* from the Permo-Carboniferous of Australia, which passes by this name, has no connexion with any British species; it is the smooth development of *Spirifer subradiatus*, Sowerby.

The use of the generic name *Martinia* for various smooth Spiriferids of the Devonian and Carboniferous becomes wholly unjustifiable. *Martinia* thus used does not mark a genetic series, as it ought; but it simply denotes a stage of catagenetic development at which several different stocks of Spirifers arrive. On the other hand, *Reticularia* does seem to indicate a fairly homogeneous series, which shows various phases of decline of reticulation until partial, or even complete, smoothness is attained. It is possible, however, that there are two series now combined under *Reticularia*—one with an extended area, of which *R. elliptica* is the best representative; the other with a very short area, *R. imbricata*. Possibly there are further structural differences to be found in these two series. The first would be the true *Reticularia*.

The distribution of the forms called '*Spirifer glaber*' into the various genetic series of which they are presumed to be the catagenetic developments involves the following consideration of some of the generic names which have been given to Spirifers. The allocation of species to these genera must in some cases be regarded as requiring confirmation—in the shape of evidence of structural details.

### Genus SPIRIFER, Sowerby.

(Type: *Anomites striatus*, Martin)

The *striatus*-type of the Aperturati, Hall & Clarke.

Wide, with extended hinge-line; fine ribs medianly and laterally; short dental plates.

British species:—*A. striatus*[1]; *Spirifer attenuatus*; *Sp. clathratus*; *Sp. semicircularis*; ? *Sp. princeps*.

American species:—*Sp. condor*, d'Orbigny; *Sp. cameratus*, Morton (Hall & Clarke).

Indian species:—*Sp. moosakhailensis*, Davidson.

NOTE.—*Sp. princeps*, M'Coy, *Sp. tornacensis*, de Koninck, *Sp. cinctus*, Keyserling, seem to form a group together, distinct from the *striatus*-series and having somewhat the appearance externally of *Choristites*; but de Koninck says that *Sp. cinctus* does not possess the strong dental plates of *Sp. mosquensis*.

### Genus FUSELLA, M'Coy.

(Type, as indicated by the name: *Spirifera fusiformis*, Phillips)

Wide; extended hinge-line; ribs coarse laterally, tending to be deficient medianly.

The type is in the smooth stage when nearly all ribs have been lost.

British species:—*Sp. trigonalis*; *Sp. grandicostata*; *Sp. ornitho-*

---

[1] The species left without authors' names are those taken from Davidson's monograph on the British Carboniferous Brachiopoda; that they correctly interpret the original authors is not implied.

*rhyncha*; *Sp. triangularis*; *Sp. rhomboidea*; *Sp. subconvoluta*, de Kon.; *Sp. convoluta*; *Sp. fusiformis*.

Foreign species :—*Sp. vespertilio*, Sow.; *Sp. avicula*. Sow.; *Sp. Strangwayi*, Vern.

### Genus CHORISTITES, Fischer.

(Type: *Choristites mosquensis*, Fischer)

Narrow; short hinge-line; fine ribs medially and laterally. Large dental plates.

British species :—*Ch. mosquensis*; *Sp. humerosa*.

Foreign species :—*Sp. Grimesi*, Hall; *Ch. mosquensis*, Fischer; *Ch. Sowerbyi*, Fischer.

### Genus TRIGONOTRETA, Kœnig.

(Type: *Trigonotreta Stokesi*, Kœnig)

Coarsely costate Spiriferids.

The Australian form called '*Spirifer glaber*' may be the catagenetic development of this genus—at least, it is the smooth development of a coarsely costate form; and it has dental plates.

### Genus BRACHYTHYRIS, M'Coy.

(Type, as figured by M'Coy: *Spirifera ovalis*, Phillips)

Narrow; tumid; hinge-line shorter than breadth of shell; ribs broad and flat on sides, deficient or wanting on fold. (? Dental plates small or absent.)

Completely smooth forms are developed.

British species :—*Sp. ovalis*; *Sp. linguifera*; *Sp. rhomboidalis* *Sp. pinguis*; *Sp. oblatus*.

*Sp. Beani*, Brown, and *Sp. bisulcatus*, Sow., probably belong here.

### Genus MARTINIA, M'Coy.

The type of this genus requires discussion. M'Coy evidently, from using Martin's name, intended Martin's species *Anomites glaber* to be the type; yet he depicted[1] a broad form, which he and others considered to be *Spirifer glaber*. But this broad form is probably a smooth *Reticularia*; and to take this as the type would destroy M'Coy's intention. The case may therefore be regarded as one in which there are two genosyntypes—*Anomites glaber*, Martin, indicated by the name, and *Spirifer glaber*, auctt. *non* Martin = ? *Sp. latus*, Brown, indicated by the figure. From these selection may be made; and *Anomites glaber* becomes the genolectotype. Then it may be said :—

(Type—genolectotype: *Anomites glaber*, Martin)

A series of shells which in costate and levigate stages are only

---

[1] 'Synopsis Char. Carb. Limest. Foss. Ireland' 1844, fig. 18, p. 128.

distinguished from *Brachythyris* by being broader and flatter. No dental plates.[1]

British species :—*Sp. eximius*, de Kon.; ‘*Sp. subrotundatus*’; *Anomites glaber*.

### Genus RETICULARIA, M‘Coy.

(Type: *Reticularia reticulata*, M‘Coy)

Spiriferids with reticulate surface—the final forms become nearly or quite smooth. Distinct dental plates.

British species :—*Sp. imbricatus*; *Reticularia reticulata*; *Anomites lineatus*; *Sp. mesoloba*; *Martinia stringocephaloides*; *Sp. elliptica*,[2] Phill.; *Sp. glaberrimus*, de Kon. in Dav.; *Sp. glaber*, auctt. = ? *Sp. latus*, Brown; *Sp. glaber*, Phill.[3] *non* Martin.

The various species of smooth Spirifers mentioned at the beginning of this article as being grouped under the name *Sp. glaber* have now been distributed into three genetic series. There are two exceptions, *Sp. symmetrica* and *Sp. decora*. The first, which differs from *Sp. oblatus* in deficiency of mesial fold, may perhaps be assigned to *Brachythyris*; but *Sp. decora* does not appear to fit in anywhere. The types of these two species do not seem to possess any dental plates.

NOTE.—Some, perhaps all, of the British Silurian species of *Spirifer* would be correctly classed under the genus *Delthyris*, Dalman.

### APPENDIX.

### Revised Explanations of Davidson’s pls. xi & xii, ‘Monogr. Carb. Brach.’ (Palæont. Soc.).[4]

#### Plate xi.

Fig. 1. *Martinia* sp.
2. *Martinia glabra*, Martin sp.
3. *Reticularia glaberrima*, de Koninck sp. Type.
4. *Reticularia glaberrima*, young form.
5. *Brachythyris* sp., cf. pl. xii, fig. 9.

Fig. 6. *Brachythyris symmetrica*, Phillips sp.
7. *Martinia glabra*, Martin sp.
Figs. 8, 9. *Brachythyris oblata*, Sowerby sp.
Fig. 10. *Reticularia mesoloba*, Phillips sp.

---

[1] Absence of dental plates is said to be a distinction of *Martinia*, that is, the *glaber*-series; and this character does apply to many smooth forms. But forms with and without dental plates have been called ‘*Spirifer glaber*.’ It is part of the object of this paper to call attention to the necessity of examining all these smooth forms, especially casts, to see which have and which have not these plates.

So with the costate forms, where dental plates are given as a generic character: it has not been possible to verify their presence or size in regard to all the species attributed to such a genus; and figures too often fail to give the information.

[2] The type (British Museum, Natural History, B 266) shows in the broken beak strong dental plates.

[3] ‘Geol. Yorks.’ pt. ii (1836) p. 219 & pl. x, fig. 10. The original specimen shows dental plates.

[4] Subject to what may be discovered by handling the original specimens, now dispersed in many collections.

Plate xii.

Fig. 1. *Reticularia lata (?)* Brown sp.
2. *Brachythyris* sp.
3. *Martinia glabra*, Martin sp.
Figs. 4, 5. *Brachythyris linguifera*, Phillips sp.
6, 7. *Brachythyris rhomboidalis*, M'Coy sp.
Fig. 8. *Brachythyris* sp. = pl. xii, fig. 2.
9. *Brachythyris* sp. = ? pl. xi, fig. 5.

Fig. 10. *Brachythyris oblata (?)* Sowerby sp.
Figs. 11, 12. *Brachythyris (?) decora*, Phillips sp.
13, 14. *Ambocœlia Urei*, Fleming sp.
15, 16. *Reticularia stringocephaloides*, M'Coy sp.

### DISCUSSION.

Dr. IVOR THOMAS congratulated the Author upon a paper which was especially interesting from a philosophic standpoint. The co-operation of the field-geologists would probably be required, in order to substantiate satisfactorily many of the points brought forward. Hall & Clarke divided the *Glabrati*-section of Spirifers into the two groups : (a) *Aseptati* (= *Martinia*, M'Coy) containing shells in which dental plates and septa are wanting, and (b) *Septati* in which the shells contain well-developed dental plates or septa. The latter comprised the two groups *Martiniopsis*, Waagen, from the *Productus*-Limestone of India, and *Mentzelia*, Quenstedt. It would be interesting to know the relationship between *Martiniopsis* and the forms of ' *Martinia* ' which contained dental plates.

Dr. F. A. BATHER remembered the difficulty that he had found in comparing the supposed *Martinia glabra* of Australia with the European species, and he welcomed the Author's explanation of its origin. This was another illustration of the difference of the Australian Carboniferous fauna from the European, although at first the two were supposed to contain many species in common. It was unfortunate that the Author had not had time to expound more fully those methods of correlating the various stages of phylogeny, ontogeny, and morphogeny, in which he took the lead, at least in this country. In other countries such methods were working a revolution in systematic palæontology, and in time they would do so here also.

The AUTHOR expressed his thanks for the kindly reception accorded to his paper. In reply to Dr. Thomas, who had mentioned the genera *Mentzelia* and *Martiniopsis*, he said that there were many glabrous Spiriferids the relationship of which it would be interesting to work out; and it seemed likely that they would prove to be the expressions of the smooth catagenetic stage of varied ribbed or spinous stocks.

### POSTSCRIPT TO THE DISCUSSION.

[The reference made by Dr. Ivor Thomas in the discussion to *Martiniopsis* suggests to the Author that a possible reticulate ancestor of such a glabrous form may be looked for in certain small reticulate Spiriferids of the British Carboniferous which have a very short hinge-line (referred to above, p. 29) and very small areas. Since the reading of the paper the Author has found a note that he had made with regard to the genus *Squamularia*, Gemmellaro, a genus fully discussed by Dr. Girty.[1]  *Squamularia* comprises reticulate Spiriferids which have neither dental nor septal plates; and, according to Girty, many of the Upper Carboniferous species of India and America referred to *Reticularia* are really *Squamulariæ*. Prof. Garwood writes (*in litt.*, Dec. 5th, 1907) that he has a British *Spirifer lineatus* without dental plates.  If so, it is perhaps a *Squamularia*; and it seems as if, not only between *Martinia* and *Reticularia*, but among the supposed *Reticulariæ* themselves, there is a most complicated homœomorphy, only to be understood by accurate observation of the internal characters.  What the Author regarded as *Sp. lineatus* has dental plates.—*S. S. B., December 11th, 1907.*]

[1] 'Carb. Form. & Faunas of Colorado' U.S. Geol. Surv. Prof. Paper 16 (1903) p. 387.

4. *The* FAUNAL SUCCESSION *in the* CARBONIFEROUS LIMESTONE (UPPER AVONIAN) *of the* MIDLAND AREA (NORTH DERBYSHIRE *and* NORTH STAFFORDSHIRE). By THOMAS FRANKLIN SIBLY, B.Sc., F.G.S. (Read December 4th, 1907.)

[PLATE I—FOSSILS.]

CONTENTS.

|  |  | Page |
|---|---|---|
| I. | Introduction | 34 |
| II. | The Typical Sequence of the Midland Area | 37 |
| III. | The Faunal Succession | 42 |
|  | (1) *Dibunophyllum* θ-Subzone. |  |
|  | (2) *Lonsdalia*-Subzone. |  |
|  |     Variation of the Faunal Facies of the *Lonsdalia*-Subzone. |  |
|  | (3) *Cyathaxonia*-Subzone. |  |
| IV. | Description of certain Sections of the *Lonsdalia*-Subzone: Variation of the Lithological Facies | 53 |
| V. | Description of certain Sections of the *Cyathaxonia*-Subzone: Relation of the *Cyathaxonia*-Subzone to the Pendleside Series | 57 |
| VI. | Local Unconformity between the Carboniferous Limestone and the Pendleside Series | 63 |
| VII. | Comparison of the Faunal Succession in the Midland Area with that in other Areas | 64 |
| VIII. | Summary of Conclusions | 68 |
| IX. | Description of certain Corals and Brachiopods from the Midland Area | 69 |

I. INTRODUCTION.

THE area of Avonian rocks with which this paper deals, and which I term the Midland Area, includes the large, irregularly-shaped periclinal mass of Carboniferous Limestone, forming the southern termination of the Pennine anticline, south of the Peak, and comprises also a few small inliers adjacent to this main outcrop. (See map, fig. 1, p. 35.) The main part of this area is included in Derbyshire, but a small, south-western portion lies in Staffordshire.

In the Geological-Survey Memoir on North Derbyshire, the Carboniferous-Limestone succession of this area, as shown by the extensive section between Buxton and Monsal Dale, is briefly described [1]; details of a few other sections are given [2]; and the nature of the junction between the Carboniferous Limestone and the overlying shales, as seen at various points, is discussed.[3] An account of the elementary tectonics of the area, and of the general features of the Carboniferous Limestone, is contained in a paper by Mr. H. H. Arnold-Bemrose, entitled 'A Sketch of the Geology of the Lower Carboniferous Rocks of Derbyshire,' published in the

---

[1] 'Geology of the Carboniferous Limestone, &c., of North Derbyshire' Mem. Geol. Surv. 2nd ed. (1887) pp. 18–21 & pl. ii.

[2] *Ibid.* pp. 21–24.        [3] *Ibid.* pp. 26–33.

Proceedings of the Geologists' Association, vol. xvi (1899–1900)
p. 165.  Details of a few sections in the area are given in papers
by Mr. Arnold-Bemrose and by Dr. Wheelton Hind, published in

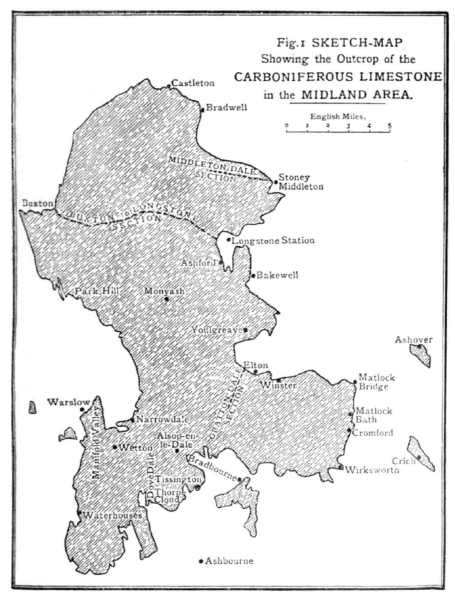

Fig. 1 SKETCH-MAP
Showing the Outcrop of the
CARBONIFEROUS LIMESTONE
in the MIDLAND AREA.

the Quarterly Journal of the Geological Society and elsewhere:
I refer to these in the course of the present paper.

The tectonic structure of this area has not yet been adequately
investigated.  However, the detailed mapping of the igneous rocks

associated with the Carboniferous Limestone, by Mr. Arnold-
Bemrose, whose results are embodied in a recent paper,[1] has laid
the foundations for such an investigation ; and, moreover, the
structure of the south-eastern portion of the area is now being
worked out by Mr. C. B. Wedd, of H.M. Geological Survey, in the
course of the re-survey of the East Derbyshire coalfield.

No systematic attempt to zone the Carboniferous Limestone of
the Midland area was made until Mr. C. B. Wedd commenced his
examination of the Matlock district, an investigation which is now
approaching completion. In the 'Summary of Progress of the
Geological Survey' for 1904, pp. 8 & 9, Mr. Wedd gave a preliminary account of the faunal sequence in the Matlock district, and in
the same publication for 1905, p. 14, he stated that

'The corals and brachiopods show that the bulk of the limestone of the district,
at least down to the second toadstone, belongs to the Upper *Dibunophyllum*-
Zone ($D_2$) of Dr. Vaughan's classification.'

My own work in this area, carried out in 1906 & 1907, during
the tenure of an 1851-Exhibition Science-Research Scholarship,
has had for its object the investigation of the faunal succession
in the Carboniferous Limestone throughout the area. The account
here presented deals mainly, therefore, with the palæontological
features of that formation ; but a few important tectonic features
which came under my notice are described, and I have also attempted
a brief description of those striking lithological changes which take
place, between different parts of the area, in certain portions of the
sequence.

The base of the Carboniferous Limestone is not visible in the
Midland area, and the whole of the series exposed constitutes a
greatly-expanded development of the uppermost zone of the typical
Avonian succession of the South-Western Province, namely, the
*Dibunophyllum*-Zone. In this Midland development three subzones
can be distinguished : these are as follows, in descending order :—

$D_3$ = Subzone of *Cyathaxonia rushiana*.
$D_2$ = Subzone of *Lonsdalia floriformis*.
$D_1$ = Subzone of *Dibunophyllum θ*.

The scheme of the present paper is as follows. The section along
the line of the Midland Railway, between Longstone and Buxton,
being the most extensive in the area, is selected as typical, and
is described in some detail. The general faunal succession in the
Midland area is then described, and the fauna[2] of each subzone
analysed in detail. In this connexion, the marked variation of
faunal facies exhibited by the *Lonsdalia*-subzone is discussed.
Certain important sections of the *Lonsdalia*-subzone are next

[1] 'The Toadstones of Derbyshire: their Field-Relations & Petrography'
Quart. Journ. Geol. Soc. vol. lxiii (1907) p. 241.
[2] Throughout this paper attention is confined entirely to the corals and
brachiopods, in interpreting the faunal succession. These two groups alone are
sufficiently abundant to be reliable in zoning.

described briefly, and the changes of lithological facies in that subzone discussed. The *Cyathaxonia*-subzone is then traced, in its varying development, throughout certain parts of the area, and the relation of this highest subdivision of the Avonian to the overlying Pendleside Shales is exemplified. A local unconformity between the Carboniferous Limestone and the Pendleside Shales is described in a separate section. After a comparison of the succession in the Midlands with that in other areas, and a summary of conclusions, the paper concludes with the description of certain corals and brachiopods.

## II. The Typical Sequence of the Midland Area.

### Section along the course of the Midland Railway between Longstone and Buxton.

This is by far the most extensive sequence exposed in the area. The cuttings on the railway, together with numerous quarries and other exposures adjoining the line, afford a nearly-continuous section, which extends over more than 8 miles, in a roughly east-and-west direction, through the dales. The succession is described and illustrated in the Geological-Survey Memoir,[1] pp. 18–21, fig. 2 & pl. ii.

At the eastern end of the section a cutting west of Longstone Station shows the uppermost beds of the Carboniferous Limestone, dipping eastwards to pass conformably under the Pendleside Shales. Westwards from this point, as far as Pig-Tor Tunnel, a distance of about 6½ miles, successively lower parts of the Carboniferous Limestone are seen. Throughout this distance the beds have a very gentle easterly dip, interrupted here and there by slight undulations. The base of the Carboniferous Limestone is not seen, for at Pig-Tor Tunnel the anticlinal axis is reached, and the westerly dip which there sets· in persists to the end of the section. At the western end, on the railway near Buxton, a considerable thickness of the upper beds of the Carboniferous Limestone has been faulted out, and the junction of the lower beds with the Pendleside Shales is obscured.

In a section so extensive as this one, and with slightly-inclined and undulating beds, estimations of vertical thickness are necessarily open to considerable error. In the accompanying table (p. 38) my own reading of the sequence is given, together with that of the Geological-Survey Memoir. The difference between the two estimates of total thickness is comparatively small, and lies within the probable error of determination. With reference to these two estimates, we may conclude that the total thickness of Carboniferous Limestone exposed in this section, exclusive of the intercalated toadstones, approximates to 1500 feet.

In one or two important points, my own reading of the section differs from that which is set forth in the Geological-Survey Memoir.

[1] 'Geology of the Carboniferous Limestone, &c., of North Derbyshire' 2nd ed. 1887.

## THE TYPICAL CARBONIFEROUS-LIMESTONE SEQUENCE OF THE MIDLAND AREA.

**Section along the course of the Midland Railway between Longstone and Buxton.**

Avonian (DIBUNOPHYLLUM-Zone).

CYATHAXONIA-Subzone (D₃). [including at least 70 feet of (b)].

LONSDALIA-Subzone (D₂).

DIBUNOPHYLLUM θ-Subzone (D₁).

Feet.

(a) Limestones and black shales; limestone predominating in the lower part, shales in the upper part. To top of section ............

(b) Limestones; thinly bedded and dark-coloured or black throughout the greater part, with thin shaly partings in places; showing throughout almost their whole extent a development of nodular and lenticular chert ............ about 450

(c) Thickly-bedded whitish limestones ........ 120

Horizon of Upper Toadstone.

(d) Thickly-bedded white limestones; with 20 to 30 feet of thinly-bedded, dark limestones at the top ............ 160

Horizon of Lower Toadstone.

(e) Limestones; the upper 400 or 450 feet consisting entirely of massive, white or light-grey limestone; the lower part containing much limestone which is less thickly bedded, with dark-grey or black beds frequently developed. To base of section ............ 800 to 850

800 to 850

1530 to 1580

**Reading of the same section given in the Geological-Survey Memoir.[1]**

Yoredale Rocks (Lower Group) = (a).

Mountain Limestone = (b) to (e).

Feet.

1. Thinly-bedded limestone, somewhat earthy, with layers and nodules of chert, and thin shale-partings in the lower beds ............ 250

2. Thickly-bedded limestone ............ 50

3. Thinly-bedded limestone with chert ... 90

4. Toadstone.

5. Massive white limestone, Miller's-Dale rock, with perhaps a bed of toadstone in the middle ............ at least 320

6. Toadstone.

7. Very thickly-bedded white limestone, Chee-Tor rock ............ 500 to 600

8. Limestones, more or less concretionary, with shale-partings ............ 150

9. Limestones, some thickly and some thinly bedded; to base of section ... 100

1460 to 1560

[1] 'The Carboniferous Limestone, &c., of North Derbyshire.' 2nd ed. (1887) p. 18.

Fig. 2.—*Vertical section of the typical Carboniferous-Limestone sequence in the Midland area.*

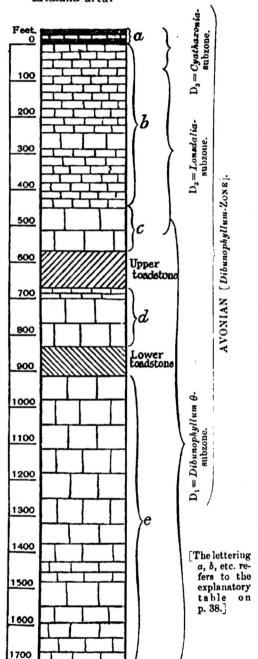

[The lettering *a, b,* etc. refers to the explanatory table on p. 38.]

My estimate of the thickness of the cherty-limestone series is 450 feet, as opposed to 390 feet given in the Memoir. Some 400 feet of this series can be directly measured, upwards from the base, in the hill over Cressbrook Tunnel, and there we do not reach the uppermost beds. Further, the horizon of the upper toadstone is incorrectly given in the Geological-Survey Memoir, the error being due to an inaccurate reading of the stratigraphical relations of the cherty limestones and this toadstone. My conclusions on this point,[1] and the evidence on which they are based, may be stated as follows. At the western end of Litton Tunnel, cherty limestones are seen to rest conformably upon massive white limestones (see explanatory section, fig. 3, p. 40). Westward from the tunnel a slight undulation carries the massive limestones below the level of the

[1] Mr. H. H. Arnold-Bemrose, with whom I had the pleasure of examining the ground, agreed with me in the conclusions here stated, and he has summarized them in his recent paper on 'The Toadstones of Derbyshire' Quart. Journ. Geol. Soc. vol. lxiii (1907) p. 244.

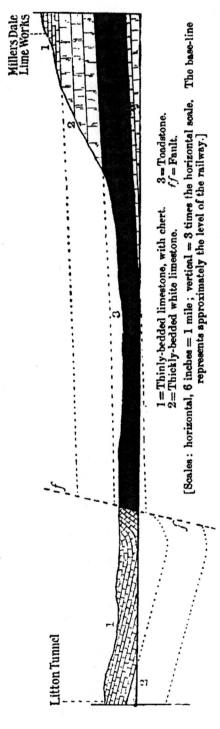

Fig. 3.—*Section from Litton Tunnel to Miller's-Dale Lime-Works, illustrating the faulted juxtaposition of cherty limestones and toadstones, seen in a railway-cutting-west of Litton Tunnel.*

1 = Thinly-bedded limestone, with chert.   3 = Toadstone.
2 = Thickly-bedded white limestone.        ff = Fault.

[Scales: horizontal, 6 inches = 1 mile; vertical = 3 times the horizontal scale. The base-line represents approximately the level of the railway.]

railway. In a cutting 400 yards from the tunnel the cherty beds are horizontal, but about 200 yards farther westward they suddenly rear up, with an easterly dip of about 30°, and abut against a mass of toadstone. According to the Geological-Survey Memoir (p. 19), the cherty beds here rest in undisturbed sequence on the toadstone (which is the upper lava-flow of the section), the absence of the latter at Litton Tunnel and elsewhere being attributed to a very rapid thinning-out of the lava-flow. The junction is, however, obviously a faulted one. Moreover, the toadstone can be followed westwards along the railway, and in a large quarry (Miller's-Dale Lime-Works), south of the line, massive white limestones, with a thickness of about 120 feet, are found to overlie it. These massive white limestones are themselves succeeded by thinly-bedded cherty limestones.

My conclusions are, therefore, as follows:— The upper toadstone is, in normal sequence, separated from the cherty-limestone series by about 120 feet of massive white limestones. A fault, with a downthrow to the east of about 200 feet, has brought these massive white limestones down to the level of the railway at Litton Tunnel, and has thrown the lowest beds of the cherty-limestone series into juxtaposition with the lower part of the toadstone, in the cutting west of Litton Tunnel.

The whole of the Carboniferous Limestone exposed in this section is included in the *Dibunophyllum*-Zone, in which the three following subzones are recognizable :—

The *Cyathaxonia*-subzone ($D_3$) includes the limestone-and-shale series which constitutes a passage into the overlying Pendleside Shales, and at least 70 feet of the cherty-limestone series.

The *Lonsdalia*-subzone ($D_2$) includes the remainder of the cherty-limestone series.

The *Dibunophyllum* $\theta$-subzone ($D_1$) includes the whole of the series below the upper toadstone, down to the base of the section. [The massive limestones, about 120 feet thick, which lie between the upper toadstone and the cherty limestone, are relatively unfossiliferous, and are not definitely assigned either to $D_2$ or to $D_1$.]

The nature of the exposures at various horizons may be briefly noted.

$D_3$.—The beds of this subzone are well exposed in the railway-cutting immediately east of Headstone Tunnel, west of Longstone Station.

$D_2$.—The highest levels exposed in $D_2$ are seen on the slopes of Monsal Dale, both immediately above the western mouth of Headstone Tunnel, and in White Cliff and other adjacent exposures on the north side of the dale. The main part of the cherty-limestone series is exposed in the cuttings between Headstone Tunnel and Cressbrook Tunnel ; also at certain points on the northern side of Monsal Dale ; and in several exposures on the hill over Cressbrook Tunnel. The base of the series is seen at the western end of Cressbrook Tunnel and at both ends of Litton Tunnel. The cuttings immediately west of Litton Tunnel expose limestones very near the base of the cherty series ; but the fault which has been already mentioned soon comes in, and thence onwards to Miller's-Dale Station the cuttings lie in the upper toadstone and the massive limestone underlying it ($D_1$). The lowest beds of the cherty series are again exposed on the slopes above the large quarry (Miller's-Dale Lime-Works) south of the railway. The quarry itself exposes the massive white limestones, immediately overlying the upper toadstone, which may belong either to $D_2$ or to $D_1$.

Excellent supplementary exposures of the *Lonsdalia*-subzone are afforded by the cliffs and rock-masses at ' Hob's House,' on the east side of Monsal Dale, a short distance south of the railway-viaduct.

$D_1$.—The following are the best exposures of the limestones between the two toadstones :—(1) A disused quarry on the south side of the railway, below Miller's-Dale Lime-Works. The base of the upper toadstone and the fossiliferous uppermost beds of $D_1$ are here exposed. (2) The large quarries, north of the railway, west of Miller's-Dale Station. The base of the upper toadstone is again exposed and the underlying limestones are well seen. (3) The cutting at the eastern entrance to Chee-Tor Tunnel. The lower toadstone and the limestones overlying it are here exposed.

The massive white limestones which underlie the lower toadstone form the magnificent precipice of Chee Tor. The uppermost beds of this series are poorly exposed on the hill over Chee-Tor Tunnel, while the lower beds are exposed in cuttings west of that tunnel.

Farther westward, on the Buxton branch of the railway, lower beds, comprising much dark-grey or black limestone, less thickly bedded, are seen in the cuttings. Topleypike Quarry affords a good exposure of these beds.

The lowest beds seen are exposed in cuttings between Topleypike Quarry and Pig-Tor Tunnel. These are grey limestones, thickly or thinly bedded. The exposures are separated by considerable gaps. The beds undulate to within a short distance of the tunnel, where a persistent westerly dip sets in.

A large quarry, opened up on the north side of the Manchester branch of the railway, shows a fine, if somewhat inaccessible, section of a considerable thickness of limestones which lie below the white limestones of Chee Tor.

The duplicate section of this subzone, afforded by the cuttings and adjacent quarries between Pig-Tor Tunnel and Buxton, in the western limb of the anticline, does not present any features of special interest. The section extends up to the limestones immediately overlying the lower toadstone. The thick series of massive white limestones, underlying this toadstone, is exposed in the Ashwood-Dale quarries and in the cuttings farther west. At Ashwood-Dale Tunnel the lower toadstone is seen : west of this point the limestones are considerably disturbed, and the end of the section is soon reached.

### III. The Faunal Succession.

#### *Dibunophyllum*-Zone.

$D_1 =$ Subzone of *Dibunophyllum* $\theta$.

Faunal list:—

Corals :

Syringopora cf. *distans*, Fischer.
Syringopora cf. *geniculata*, Phil.
Syringopora cf. *reticulata*, Goldf.
Alveolites *septosa* (Flem.) and var. *depressa* (Flem.).
Lithostrotion aff. *irregulare* (Phil.).
Lithostrotion *junceum* (Flem.).
Lithostrotion *Martini*, Ed. & H.

(?) Petalaxis *Portlocki*, Ed. & H.
Diphyphyllum, including *D. lateseptatum*, M'Coy, and Cyathophylloid forms.
Cyathophyllum aff. *Murchisoni* (?) Ed. & H.
Dibunophyllum (cf. *D.* $\theta$, Vaughan).
Carcinophyllum aff. $\theta$, Vaughan.

Brachiopods:

*Athyris* cf. *expansa* (Phil.).
*Martinia glabra* (Mart.).
*Cyrtina septosa* (Phil.).
*Orthothetes* cf. *crenistria* (Phil.).
*Productus* aff. *corrugatus*, M'Coy.
*Productus corrugato-hemisphericus.*
*Productus hemisphericus*, Sow.

*Productus* aff. *giganteus* (Mart.).
*Productus* aff. *pustulosus*, Phil.
*Productus punctatus* (Mart.).
*Productus* aff. *concinnus*, Sow.
Papilionaceous *Chonetes.*
*Daviesiella* aff. *comoides* (Sow.).

This subzone includes all that part of the limestone series which underlies the upper toadstone, in the typical section, and its total thickness is estimated at 950 to 1000 feet. Considered as a whole, the subzone is poorly fossiliferous ; but the uppermost beds contain corals in considerable abundance. The lowest beds, about 150 feet in thickness, have not yielded any corals. They contain, however, *Productus* aff. *giganteus* and *Daviesiella* aff. *comoides*, brachiopods which occur throughout the subzone, and they have not yielded any distinctive fossils. I therefore include them in the *Dibunophyllum* θ-subzone.

Faunal characters (excluding the lowest beds referred to above):—

*Dibunophylla* of a simple type occur rarely throughout the main part, and commonly at one or two levels near the top of the subzone.

*Diphyphyllum lateseptatum* is common in the uppermost beds. *Lithostrotion junceum*, *Syringopora* cf. *distans*, and *S.* cf. *geniculata* are abundant at the same level, but uncommon at lower horizons. *Lithostrotion Martini* occurs sparingly throughout the main part of the subzone and more commonly in the upper beds.

*Cyathophyllum* aff. *Murchisoni* (?) and *Alveolites* are somewhat rare in occurrence. A single specimen of *Carcinophyllum* aff. θ has been recorded.

*Productus* aff. *giganteus* occurs throughout, but is never very abundant. The specimens do not attain any great size, and show no such extraordinary variation as is exhibited in the succeeding subzone. The typical form of *Productus giganteus* has not been recorded in this subzone.

*Daviesiella* aff. *comoides*, in a form closely similar to that which characterizes $D_1$ in the South-Western Province, occurs very commonly at certain levels.

All the other brachiopods and corals included in the faunal list are of rare occurrence.

Few sections in the area, other than the typical section, afford any vertically-extensive exposure of this subzone: and the foregoing account of faunal characters is based almost entirely on the observations made in the examination of the typical section. The large quarries at Peak Forest and Doveholes, north of Buxton, show fine exposures of the massive white limestones which form a part of the subzone, but I have not examined these sections in detail. Among other sections of D₁, that given by the Grin Works, near Buxton, may be specially noted. The beds there exposed are massive white limestones, which probably represent the 'Chee-Tor beds,' that is, the beds under the lower toadstone of the typical section. The common occurrence of *Cyrtina septosa*, in association with abundant specimens of *Daviesiella comoides* and *Alveolites septosa*, merits especial mention.

Note on the probable horizon of the *Productus-humerosus* beds of Caldon Low.—The limestones extensively quarried on Caldon Low, south of Waterhouses, at the south-western extremity of the area, contain *Productus humerosus*, Sow., a remarkable species which has not been recorded in any other part of the area. The series of beds exposed in the Caldon-Low quarries consists mainly of very massive, white or light-grey limestones, and is, as a whole, poorly fossiliferous. In addition to *Productus humerosus*, the only brachiopods that I have recorded are *Daviesiella* aff. *comoides*, which is abundant in certain beds of grey limestone, and *Orthothetes* cf. *crenistria*; and the only coral found is *Syringopora* sp. (?). On account of the extensive faulting in this locality, I have not succeeded, in the course of a brief investigation, in obtaining any stratigraphical proof of the horizon of this series of beds. Lithologically, however, the series resembles the upper part of D₁, as seen in the typical section and in many other parts of the area; while the abundance of *Daviesiella* aff. *comoides* in certain beds and the apparent absence of any fossils characteristic of a higher horizon than D₁ support the reference of the series to this subzone.

## D₂ = Subzone of *Lonsdalia floriformis*.

Faunal list :—

Corals :

Zaphrentids of several types, including *Zaphrentis* aff. *Enniskilleni*, Ed. & H.
*Cyathaxonia rushiana*, Vaughan.
*Michelinia glomerata*, M'Coy.
*Syringopora* cf. *distans*, Fischer.
*Syringopora* cf. *geniculata*, Phil.
*Syringopora* cf. *reticulata*, Goldf.
*Alveolites septosa* (Flem.) & var. *depressa* (Flem.).
*Campophyllum derbiense*, Vaughan (MS.).
*Campophyllum* aff. *caninoides*, Sibly.
*Cyathophyllum* aff. *Murchisoni* (!), Ed. & H.
*Cyathophyllum regium*, Phil.
*Diphyphyllum*, including *D. lateseptatum*, M'Coy; and Cyathophylloid forms, such as *Cyathophyllum parricida*, M'Coy.
*Lithostrotion junceum* (Flem.).

*Lithostrotion irregulare* (Phil.) & mut. towards *L. Martini*, Ed. & H.
*Lithostrotion Martini*, Ed. & H.
*Lithostrotion* aff. *Portlocki* (Bronn), Ed. & H.
*Lithostrotion* aff. *M'Coyanum*, Ed. & H.
*Lithostrotion Flemingi*, M'Coy.
*Koninckophyllum proprium*, sp. nov.
*Lonsdalia duplicata* (Mart.).
*Lonsdalia floriformis* (Flem.).
Simple Clisiophyllids of numerous types, including *Clisiophyllum* aff. *M'Coyanum*, Thoms.; *Dibunophyllum*, represented by *D. matlockense*, sp. nov., *D. derbiense*, sp. nov., and other forms; *Histiophyllum, Rhodophyllum*, and *Cymatiophyllum*; and *Cyclophyllum* aff. *pachyendothecum*, Thoms.

Brachiopods:

*Dielasma hastata* (Sow.).
*Seminula ambigua* (Sow.).
*Athyris* cf. *expansa* (Phil.).
*Athyris* cf. *glabristria* (Phil).
*Athyris planosulcata* (Phil.).
*Athyris* cf. *lamellosa* (L'Éveillé).
*Martinia glabra* (Mart.).
*Martinia lineata* (Mart.).
*Martinia ovalis* (Phil.).
*Spirifer bisulcatus*, Sow.
*Spirifer* aff. *grandicostatus*, M'Coy.
*Spirifer duplicicosta*, Phil.
*Spirifer integricosta*, Phil.
*Spirifer pinguis*, Sow.
*Spirifer planicosta* (M'Coy).
*Spirifer striatus* (Mart.).
*Syringothyris cuspidata* (Mart.).
*Camarophoria crumena* (Mart.).
*Pugnax acuminatus* (Mart.).
*Pugnax pugnus* (Mart.).
*Leptæna analoga* (Phil.).
*Orthothetes* cf. *crenistria* (Phil.).
*Rhipidomella* aff. *Michelini* (L'Éveillé).
*Schizophoria resupinata* (Mart.).
*Productus corrugatus*, M'Coy.

*Productus corrugato-hemisphericus.*
*Productus hemisphericus*, Sow.
*Productus giganteus* (Mart.).
*Productus longispinus*, Sow.
*Productus* aff. *lobatus*, Sow.
*Productus* aff. *setosus*, Phil.
*Productus concinnus*, Sow.
*Productus Martini*, Sow.
*Productus semireticulatus* (Mart.).
*Productus costatus*, Sow.
*Productus muricatus*, Phil.
*Productus scabriculus* (Mart.).
*Productus pustulosus*, Phil.
*Productus fimbriatus*, Sow.
*Productus punctato-fimbriatus*, including *Pr. elegans*, M'Coy.
*Productus punctatus* (Mart.).
*Productus aculeatus* (Mart.).
*Productus spinulosus*, Sow.
*Productus mesolobus*, Phil.
*Productus plicatilis*, Sow.
*Chonetes* cf. *crassistria* (M'Coy), Vaughan.
*Chonetes compressa*, nom. nov.
*Daviesiella* aff. *comoides* (Sow).

Diagnosis:—

The extent of this subzone in the typical section is defined by the range of *Lonsdalia*. *Lonsdalia floriformis* ranges throughout, but *L. duplicata* has been found to occur only in the upper beds. Characteristic features of the subzonal fauna, in its typical development, are as follows:—The occurrence of *Lonsdalia floriformis* and *Cyathophyllum regium*. The abundance of *Lithostrotion junceum* and of a *Lithostrotion* intermediate in characters between *L. irregulare* and *L. Martini*. The common occurrence of *Lithostrotion Martini* and *L.* aff. *Portlocki*, associated with *L.* aff. *M'Coyanum*. The great variety of the simple Clisiophyllids, certain groups of which frequently attain extreme abundance. An enormous abundance of *Productus giganteus* and variants, and the very common occurrence of *Productus concinnus*, *Pr. Martini*, and *Pr. semireticulatus*, in association with *Productus punctatus*, *Pr. scabriculus*, *Spirifer bisulcatus*, *Sp. planicosta*, and *Martinia glabra*.

Analysis of Faunal Characters:—

Corals:

*Lonsdalia floriformis*, although generally distributed, is not often abundant. *L. duplicata* occurs locally in the upper beds.
*Cyathophyllum regium* is common. Simple *Cyathophylla*, having a widely-conical form and a partly-tabulate central

area, occur sparingly.   Cylindrical forms, doubtfully referred to *Cyathophyllum Murchisoni*, are very rare.

*Campophyllum derbiense* is generally distributed, though rarely of common occurrence.   Caninoid forms of *Campophyllum*, allied to *C. caninoides*, are locally common.

*Lithostrotion junceum* and *L. Martini* are abundant, especially the former.   Typical specimens of *Lithostrotion irregulare* are comparatively rare, but a slightly-bigger *Lithostrotion*, intermediate in characters between *L. irregulare* and *L. Martini*, occurs very commonly.   *Lithostrotion* aff. *Portlocki* occurs generally, and is locally abundant.   *L.* aff. *M'Coyanum* is not infrequent.   *L. Flemingi* is very localized in distribution, but sometimes occurs commonly.

*Diphyphyllum lateseptatum* and closely-related forms are of frequent occurrence.

*Koninckophyllum* is comparatively uncommon.

*Dibunophyllum* occurs commonly in this subzone, though rarely attaining a marked abundance.   A common type is *Dibunophyllum matlockense*.   *D. derbiense* is a rare species.   Small, conical forms, which bear considerable structural resemblance to *Dibunophyllum* φ, Vaughan, occur locally.

Clisiophyllids belonging to the generic groups *Histiophyllum*, *Rhodophyllum*, and *Cymatiophyllum*, and exhibiting great variety, occur in profusion in several localities.

*Cyclophyllum* aff. *pachyendothecum* is characteristic, but distinctly uncommon.   *Clisiophyllum* aff. *M'Coyanum* is of rare occurrence.

*Alveolites* is often abundant.   *Syringopora* cf. *distans* and *S.* cf. *reticulata* are both abundant forms.   *Syringopora* cf. *geniculata* is occasionally common.

*Michelinia glomerata* is of local occurrence only.   Zaphrentids occur somewhat rarely in the uppermost part of the subzone.   *Cyathaxonia rushiana* is extremely rare.

Brachiopods:

Several varieties of *Spirifer bisulcatus* are represented.   The species ranges throughout, and is frequently abundant.   Variants of *Sp. bisulcatus*, which in shape and in the nature of their ribbing closely approach *Sp. grandicostatus*, occur rarely.

*Spirifer planicosta* is frequently common, and locally attains marked abundance.

*Martinia glabra* occurs abundantly; but *M. lineata* and *M. ovalis* are distinctly rare.

*Orthothetes* cf. *crenistria* is widely distributed, though not often abundant.

*Schizophoria resupinata* is generally rare, but locally it occurs in some abundance.   *Rhipidomella* aff. *Michelini* is very rare.

*Productus giganteus* occurs in great abundance throughout this subzone, and a considerable variety of forms are represented.   The typical form, very large and thick-shelled, with highly-irregular fine ribbing and a longitudinally-wrinkled shell, occurs abundantly. Comparatively-small forms, with slightly-differentiated wings and strong well-spaced ribs (= *Productus edelburyensis*, Phil.), are extremely common. Small transverse forms, closely approximating to *Pr. latissimus*, Sow., are not infrequent.

*Productus corrugatus* is rare, but a large form of *Pr. corrugato-hemisphericus* is locally common. Typical specimens of *Pr. hemisphericus* occur very rarely.

Big specimens of *Productus semireticulatus*, exhibiting many varieties of form, are generally common, and locally very abundant. *Pr. costatus* is rather rare.

*Productus concinnus* and *Pr. Martini* always occur, and are locally abundant.

*Productus scabriculus* is generally rare, but in certain localities typical specimens are abundant. *Pr. punctatus* always occurs, though it is never very common.

*Productus longispinus* and its allies, including *Pr.* aff. *lobatus* and *Pr.* aff. *setosus*, range throughout the greater part of the subzone, and are common locally.

*Chonetes compressa*, a well-defined papilionaceous type, is characteristic of this subzone, and, while usually uncommon, attains great abundance in some localities.

All the other brachiopods recorded in the list are either rare or very localized in occurrence.

### Variation of the Faunal Facies of the *Lonsdalia*-subzone.

In the foregoing account the faunal lists include all those corals and brachiopods that I have recorded in the *Lonsdalia*-subzone of the Midland area, exclusive of those species which are confined to the 'brachiopod-beds' (see below); while the analysis of faunal characters also deals with the subzone in its normal development. The term 'normal development' is here employed to define that generally-prevalent facies of the subzone in which the coral-fauna and the brachiopod-fauna are about equally predominant, as opposed to the abnormal, localized facies of the subzone (the 'brachiopod-beds'), in which an enriched brachiopod-fauna predominates almost to the exclusion of the coral-fauna.

A study of the faunal facies of this subzone in the Midland area reveals the following outstanding features :—(1) The distinctness of a localized brachiopod-facies, apparently confined to the western part of the area, from the generally-prevalent coral-and-brachiopod facies. (2) A subsidiary change of facies, within the latter, typical development.

We will first consider that change of facies which is found within the 'normal development' itself, proceeding afterwards to a discussion of the 'brachiopod-beds.' This change is shown by a marked difference between the faunal assemblage in the eastern part of the area and that in the south-western [1] part. To some extent, the observed differences may perhaps be apparent rather than real, because sections of $D_2$ are numerous in the eastern, but fewer and far less extensive in the south-western district. This factor could not, however, account for all the observed discrepancies.

The relation between the eastern and the south-western facies may be summarized as follows :—

In the eastern district, the coral-fauna includes *Lonsdalia flori-formis*, *Lithostrotion junceum*, *Alveolites septosa*, and Clisiophyllids belonging to the 'genera' *Histiophyllum*, *Rhodophyllum*, and *Cymatiophyllum*. None of these corals have been recorded in the south-western district. On the other hand, *Dibunophyllum matlock-ense* and other corals, including *Cyathophyllum regium*, *Lithostrotion Martini*, and *Campophyllum derbiense*, are common to both districts, and in both the brachiopod-fauna is essentially identical.

The accompanying table illustrates the difference between the two facies. The typical section (Monsal Dale and Miller's Dale) illustrates the eastern facies, and the Waterhouses section exemplifies the south-western facies. Only the most predominant and characteristic corals and brachiopods of the typical, eastern fauna are selected for illustration.

|  | Waterhouses. | Monsal Dale and Miller's Dale. |
|---|---|---|
| *Alveolites septosa* ..................... | ...... | * |
| *Cyathophyllum regium* ............ | * | * |
| *Lithostrotion junceum* ............... | ...... | * |
| *Lithostrotion Martini* ............... | * | * |
| *Lonsdalia floriformis* ............... | ...... | * |
| *Dibunophyllum matlockense* ...... | * | * |
| *Histiophyllum, Rhodophyllum, & Cymatiophyllum* ............... .. | ...... | * |
| *Spirifer bisulcatus* ................... | * | * |
| *Spirifer planicosta* ................... | * | * |
| *Productus giganteus* ................... | * | * |
| *Productus semireticulatus* ......... | * | * |
| *Productus concinnus* ............... | * | * |
| *Productus punctatus* ............... | * | * |
| *Martinia glabra* ................... | * | * |

The abnormal localized facies of this subzone represented by the 'brachiopod-beds' may now be considered.

The richly-fossiliferous brachiopod-limestones of certain localities

---

[1] In the north-western part of the area, where the *Lonsdalia*-subzone has been lost in places through faulting, good sections of the subzone do not exist.

in the Midland area of Carboniferous Limestone have long been famous for the beautiful specimens which they have yielded. The chief localities of these beds are as follows, taken in order from north to south :—Treak Cliff, west of Castleton ; Park Hill, north of Longnor ; Narrowdale, north of Wetton ; and Thorpe Cloud, at the mouth of Dove Dale. The first-named of these lies at the northern extremity, and the last-named on the southern margin, of the limestone-area : all of them lie within the western part of the area. As a rule, these 'brachiopod-beds' form part of a thick series of white limestones, the structural relations of which are obscure ; and I am not aware of any instance in which their horizon can be demonstrated by elementary stratigraphical reasoning. Nevertheless, the following evidence appears to me to fix their horizon with some certainty :—

(i) The 'brachiopod-beds', which are very rich in species and individuals, contain in abundance, not only certain species of brachiopods which are rare in the normal *Lonsdalia*-subzone of the area, but also certain other species which I have not recorded in the normal *Lonsdalia*-subzone. But all those species of brachiopods that are found in the normal *Lonsdalia*-subzone occur, at one or more localities, in the 'brachiopod-beds'.

(ii) Although corals are generally rare in the 'brachiopod-beds', I have found, in these beds at Park Hill, *Lithostrotion Martini* in abundance, associated with *L. Flemingi, Campophyllum derbiense,* and a large species of *Carcinophyllum*—an assemblage of corals which would indicate $D_2$.

This evidence indicates, with tolerable certainty, that the 'brachiopod-beds' form an abnormal phase, which locally replaces the normal *Lonsdalia*-subzone. In support of this conclusion, arrived at by considering the faunal assemblage of the beds, we have the following important negative evidence:—The normal *Lonsdalia*-subzone is apparently never developed in the immediate neighbourhood of the 'brachiopod-beds'.

As examples of $D_2$ brachiopods which attain a greater abundance in the 'brachiopod-beds', the following may be mentioned :— *Dielasma hastata, Martinia lineata, M. ovalis, Spirifer duplicicosta, Pugnax acuminatus, P. pugnus, Schizophoria resupinata, Productus longispinus, Pr. fimbriatus,* and *Pr. Martini.*

The 'brachiopod-beds', which are confined to the western part of the area, indicate the localized prevalence of conditions especially favourable to brachiopod-life, and at the same time, apparently, unfavourable to coral-life. It would appear that these conditions prevailed, to some extent, over an area considerably larger than that actually covered by the 'brachiopod-beds'. For example, throughout Dove Dale, and in the neighbourhood of Alstonfield and Wetton, that is, in the vicinity of the 'brachiopod-beds' of Thorpe Cloud and Narrowdale, there appears to be an extensive development of $D_2$, possessing a typical brachiopod-fauna, but an impoverished coral-fauna. Moreover, the influence of these conditions seems evident in the fact, that even where the *Lonsdalia*-subzone of the western part of the area presents its most nearly typical development, the coral-fauna is considerably less rich than in that really-typical facies which is coextensive with the eastern half of the area. That is to say, the difference between an eastern and a south-western facies of $D_2$, which has already been pointed out, may probably be attributed to the influence of those conditions which determined the presence of the 'brachiopod-beds' in the western part of the area.

To sum up, it may be stated that the *Lonsdalia*-subzone of the Midland area exhibits two very distinct facies, which are as follows :—

(i) A coral-and-brachiopod facies, in which the coral-fauna and the brachiopod-fauna are equally predominant. This, which is most typically developed in the eastern part of the area, is by far the more extensive facies, and is to be regarded as typical.

(ii) A clearly-developed, yet localized brachiopod-facies, found only in the western part of the area. Here the coral-fauna is very feebly developed, but the brachiopod-fauna, while retaining all the essential features of the typical development, is considerably enriched.

It is possible that the 'brachiopod-beds', while mainly representing $D_2$, encroach on the succeeding subzone. That is to say, the typical *Cyathaxonia*-subzone is perhaps locally replaced, in part at least, by a portion of the 'brachiopod-beds'. In the absence of stratigraphical evidence, I am unable to form a definite opinion on this question.

### $D_3$ = Subzone of *Cyathaxonia rushiana*.

Faunal list :—

Corals :

*Cladochonus bacillarius* (M'Coy).
*Cladochonus crassus* (M'Coy).
Zaphrentids of numerous types, including *Zaphrentis Enniskilleni*, Ed. & H.; Densiphyllids; and forms of *Amplexi-Zaphrentis*, Vaughan.
*Cyathaxonia costata*, M'Coy.
*Cyathaxonia rushiana*, Vaughan.
*Syringopora* cf. *distans*, Fischer.
*Favosites parasitica* (Phil.).
*Beaumontia* aff. *Egertoni*, Ed. & H.

*Michelinia glomerata*, M'Coy.
*Campophyllum* aff. *derbiense*, Vaughan (MS.).
*Cyathophyllum regium*, Phil.
*Lithostrotion junceum* (Flem.).
Koninckophylloid *Lithostrotion*.
*Koninckophyllum* spp.
*Dibunophyllum* sp.
*Clisiophyllum* aff. *curkesnense* (?), Vaughan.
*Cyclophyllum* sp.

Brachiopods:

*Orbiculoidea nitida* (Phil.).
*Seminula ambigua* (Sow.).
*Seminula globularis* (Phil.).
*Athyris* cf. *expansa* (Phil.).
*Athyris planosulcata* (Phil.).
*Martinia glabra* (Mart.).
*Martinia lineata* (Mart.).
*Spirifer bisulcatus*, Sow.
*Spirifer grandicostatus*, M'Coy.
*Spirifer planicosta* (M'Coy).
*Syringothyris* aff. *laminosa* (M'Coy).
*Syringothyris subconica* (Mart.).
*Spiriferina octoplicata*, Sow.
*Orthothetes* cf. *crenistria* (Phil.).
*Rhipidomella* aff. *Michelini* (L'Eveillé).
*Schizophoria resupinata* (Mart.).
*Camarotœchia* (?) aff. *flexistria* (Phil.).
*Productus corrugatus*, M'Coy.
*Productus* aff. *hemisphericus*, Sow.
*Productus giganteus* (Mart.).
*Productus latissimus*, Sow.
*Productus striatus* (Fischer).

*Productus undatus*, Defrance.
*Productus longispinus*, Sow.
*Productus* aff. *lobatus*, Sow.
*Productus* aff. *setosus*, Phil., & var. *tissingtonensis*, nov.
*Productus concinnus*, Sow.
*Productus Martini*, Sow.
*Productus semireticulatus* (Mart.).
*Productus costatus*, Sow.
*Productus scabriculus* (Mart.).
*Productus pustulosus*, Phil.
*Productus* sp. (cf. *Pr. ovalis*, Phil.).
*Productus fimbriatus*, Sow.
*Productus punctato-fimbriatus.*
*Productus punctatus* (Mart.).
*Productus spinulosus*, Sow.
*Chonetes* cf. *hardrensis*, Phil.
*Chonetes crassistria* (M'Coy).
*Chonetes* cf. *crassistria* (M'Coy), Vaughan.
Papilionaceous *Chonetes*.

This subzone comprises the uppermost part of the Carboniferous Limestone, above the *Lonsdalia*-subzone, and includes also the series of alternating shales and limestones which constitutes a passage into the overlying Pendleside Series, wherever such transition-beds are developed. The varying development of the subzone, and its relation to the nature of the junction between the Carboniferous Limestone and the Pendleside Series, are discussed in a separate section (pp. 57–63).

Diagnosis:—

The coral-fauna is essentially distinct from that of the *Lonsdalia*-subzone. *Lonsdalia floriformis* is absent [1]; *Dibunophyllum* and *Cyathophyllum regium* are extremely rare; and the Clisiophyllids generally are poorly represented. *Lithostrotion* is uncommon, *L. Martini*, *L. irregulare*, and *L.* aff. *Portlocki* being absent. In its typical development, the subzone is characterized by the abundance of *Cyathaxonia*, associated with abundant Zaphrentids of varied types.

The brachiopod-fauna does not differ in many essentials from that of the *Lonsdalia*-subzone, although a few uncommon forms— for example *Syringothyris subconica* and *Spiriferina octoplicata*— are characteristic.

[1] *Lonsdalia duplicata*, which is common only in the uppermost part of $D_2$, probably ranges into this subzone. Mr. O. B. Wedd informs me that, in a section near Wirksworth, he has recently found *L. duplicata* to occur abundantly a few feet below the horizon of a typical $D_3$ fauna.

Analysis of faunal characters:—

Corals:

*Cyathaxonia rushiana* and *C. costata* are both widely distributed, and the former especially occurs in considerable abundance locally. These two species are not, however, often found in association.

The Zaphrentids, which occur in abundance, exhibit great variety, and include several new forms.[1] *Zaphrentis Enniskilleni* is common; Densiphylloid types, including *Densiphyllum charlestonense*, Thoms., occur abundantly; and types of *Amplexi-Zaphrentis*, Vaughan,[2] are abundant.

*Beaumontia* aff. *Egertoni* is very localized in occurrence, but when present it is abundant. *Cladochonus* is locally abundant.

All the other corals mentioned in the faunal list are of rare occurrence.

Brachiopods:

*Seminula ambigua* and *S. globularis* are common locally. *Martinia glabra* is frequently abundant.

*Spirifer bisulcatus* is abundant. Variants of that form towards *Sp. grandicostatus* occur locally, and typical specimens of the latter species are occasional.

*Syringothyris subconica* is characteristic, but very rare. *S.* aff. *laminosa*, identical with the form figured by Davidson, 'Monogr. Brit. Foss. Brachiop.' (Palæont. Soc.) vol. ii (1858–63) pl. vii, figs. 21 & 22, occurs very rarely. Typical specimens of *Spiriferina octoplicata* occur.

*Orthothetes* cf. *crenistria* is not uncommon.

*Camarotœchia (?)* aff. *flexistria* occurs rarely. Numerous crushed specimens, of a Rhynchonellid which I refer doubtfully to this species, occur in the shales of this subzone in certain localities.

*Productus giganteus* occurs in abundance, and all the varieties found in $D_2$ are represented. *Pr. latissimus* is rare. *Pr. striatus* generally occurs, and is abundant locally.

*Productus concinnus* and *Pr. Martini* always occur. The former is often exceedingly abundant. Large forms of *Pr. semireticulatus* are locally abundant.

Typical specimens of *Productus costatus* and *Pr. scabriculus* are not uncommon. The typical form of *Pr. longispinus* attains its maximum in this subzone, and is locally very common. *Pr.* aff. *setosus* occurs, and a characteristic variant, *Pr. tissingtonensis*, is locally common.

*Productus punctatus* is common. *Pr. pustulosus* is rare; but an allied form, with very numerous, small spine-bases and indistinct concentric banding (compare *Pr. ovalis*, Phil.), is locally common.

[1] No description of the Zaphrentids is given in the present paper, for it would be unprofitable to attempt the description of any new forms until I have completed a thorough examination of the very large number of specimens which I have collected.

[2] Quart. Journ. Geol. Soc. vol. lxii (1906) pp. 315–16 & pl. xxix, fig. 7.

*Chonetes* cf. *hardrensis* occurs commonly in the shales of this subzone.

All the other brachiopods recorded in the faunal list are rare.

Other groups:

Ostracods occur commonly in the shales and limestones in the upper beds of the subzone.

Polyzoa,[1] which include species of *Polypora*, *Penniretepora*, and *Rhabdomeson*, are highly abundant locally.

The lamellibranchs and cephalopods, occurring in the passage-beds included in this subzone, and representing the first appearance of the fauna of the Pendleside Series, are recorded in the subsequent descriptions of certain sections of the subzone (pp. 57–63).

## IV. DESCRIPTION OF CERTAIN SECTIONS OF THE *LONSDALIA*-SUBZONE: VARIATION OF THE LITHOLOGICAL FACIES.

Without attempting a detailed account of the very numerous good exposures of the *Lonsdalia*-subzone which are to be found within the area, I may briefly describe certain of the more extensive sections of that subzone. This description will serve to exemplify the changes in the lithological facies of the subzone which occur within the area.

### (A) Sections in the Eastern Part of the Area.

#### (i) The typical section.

In the typical section, already described (pp. 37–42), $D_2$ is seen only in the eastern limb of the anticline, being faulted out on the western side. The subzone here exhibits a remarkable lithological facies. A series of cherty limestones, about 450 feet thick, here forms the lower part of $D_3$ and the whole of $D_2$, the latter subzone comprising not much less than 400 feet of beds. This cherty series consists very largely of dark-grey or black limestones, as a rule thinly bedded, and often compact in texture, with black shaly partings frequently developed. Beds of lighter colour occur, however, and in the lower part of $D_2$ a conspicuous development of massive white limestones forms a break in the cherty series. The chert is abundantly developed, and, in addition to forming nodular and lenticular masses of no great size, frequently occurs in large ramifying masses, and in well-defined bands of considerable horizontal extent.

This section shows a much greater development of the cherty series than is found elsewhere in the eastern part of the area, as the following details of certain sections will show.

---

[1] Mr. W. D. Lang, M.A., F.G.S., very kindly determined my specimens of Polyzoa.

(ii) Sections north of the typical section.

### (a) The Bradwell-Dale section, extending south-wards from Bradwell.

This section, which is confined to $D_2$, shows from 150 to 200 feet of that subzone. The limestones are very variable in character, consisting largely of light-grey or white beds, often oolitic, and including also dark-grey or blue bands. Chert is strongly developed at various levels throughout the section, but there is no development of compact black limestones similar to those of the typical section.

### (b) The Middleton-Dale section, extending west-wards from Stoney Middleton.

The cliff-sections and numerous quarries in Middleton Dale show, at a rough estimate, rather over 300 feet of Carboniferous Lime-stone. The highest beds exposed, which are thinly-bedded black limestones with abundant chert, include the uppermost part of $D_2$, and probably also the lower part of $D_3$; 50 or 60 feet of these are seen. Below these beds, the limestones contain a typical $D_2$ fauna, down to within a short distance of the base of the section. The series below the black cherty beds consists of white, grey, or light-brown limestones, thickly and thinly bedded, very variable in texture. Chert is largely developed at various levels, down to within about 70 feet of the base of the section.

(iii) Sections south of the typical section.

### (a) The Gratton-Dale section, near Elton.

Next to the typical section this is, probably, the most extensive in the area. The exposure is, however, by no means continuous, and the estimate of the thickness of the beds, given below, can only be considered as an approximation. The following is the sequence, given in descending order :—

*Thickness in feet.*

(1) Limestones to top of section.
    The uppermost beds consist partly of thinly-bedded, grey-blue limestones without chert ; partly of hard, black, compact lime-stones, with abundant chert and thin partings of shale. The beds are dolomitized in places.
    The main series consists of limestones, variably white or grey in colour, without chert, but with occasional black beds. Many beds are highly crinoidal .................. ...........................  250

(2) Lava ................................................................................   70

(3) Grey limestones ...................................... ......................  290

(4) Yellowish-brown, dolomitic limestones.....................................  630

(5) Dark-grey limestones, to base of section ...................................   —

                                                          1240

The uppermost beds represent a.high level in $D_2$, and the whole of the series, down to the lava (2), clearly belongs to this subzone.[1] The series underlying the lava presumably represents $D_1$, but, in the failure to record any characteristic fossils of that subzone, I have not obtained any palæontological evidence to prove this. Fossils are rare in the grey limestones (3), and in the dolomitic series the fossils, if originally present, have been largely obliterated, casts of crinoid-ossicles alone having been detected.

### (b) The Matlock district.

Numerous sections of $D_2$, more or less extensive, are to be found in the area adjacent to Matlock, but I have not examined them in detail.   The Carboniferous Limestone of this district is being investigated by Mr. C. B. Wedd, of H.M. Geological Survey, who has already given a preliminary account of the succession.[2]   For the present purpose, of comparison with the lithological sequence in other parts of the area, the following brief description of the succession in this district will suffice.   The thinly-bedded, blue or dark-grey limestones with chert, which constitute the uppermost division of the Carboniferous Limestone, have an average thickness of about 50 feet, and include only a small part of $D_2$.   Locally, indeed, where the cherty limestones are reduced in thickness, they are all included in $D_3$, and the whole of $D_2$ consists of white or light-grey limestones without chert.

### (c) The Wirksworth quarry-sections.

At Wirksworth, the Middlepeak Quarries and adjacent quarries lying farther south show over 200 feet of $D_2$.   The highest beds seen are thinly-bedded, dark-grey and blue, cherty limestones, about 30 feet thick, exposed in Dale Quarry.   The underlying series, which is free from chert, comprises limestones of varying lithological character.   Light-grey or white limestones, oolitic in parts and forming massive beds, predominate; but dark-grey or black limestones, with occasional shaly partings, occur at more than one level.   The best section is afforded by Stoneycroft Quarry, immediately adjacent to the Middlepeak Quarries.

### (B) Sections in the South-Western Part of the Area.

In the south-western part of the area, extensive and readily-accessible sections of $D_2$ are very few in number.[3]

---

[1] Mr. Arnold-Bemrose considers the lava of this section to be the lower lava of the Matlock area; see Quart. Journ. Geol. Soc. vol. lxiii (1907) p. 258. If we regard the horizon of this lava as the base of $D_2$, the Gratton-Dale section agrees with the sequence in the Matlock district, where, as Mr. C. B. Wedd informs me, the lower lava represents approximately the base of $D_2$.

[2] 'Summary of Progress of the Geological Survey for 1904' 1905, pp. 8 & 9.

[3] Dove Dale and its immediate neighbourhood afford excellent sections; but the stratigraphy of the district is not easy of interpretation, and a profitable description of the sections would require much more careful investigation of the ground than I have had time to make.

## (i) The Waterhouses section.

At Waterhouses, the quarries on each side of the valley, together with small railway-cuttings on the south side, give an excellent series of exposures. On account of the discontinuity of the exposure and the variable dip of the beds, I have not been able to estimate the vertical extent of the section; but it is certain that the series exposed includes a very large part of $D_2$. The limestones are of varied character, including some thinly-bedded dark-grey bands, with black shale-partings, but there is no considerable development of chert in any part of the section.

## (ii) The Manifold Valley.

In the Manifold Valley, a few miles north of Waterhouses, cuttings on the light railway between Grindon and Ecton Stations expose a much-folded and faulted series of thinly-bedded, dark-grey or blue limestones with strong chert. These beds belong to $D_2$. The cherty series evidently attains a great thickness, but no estimation is possible.

The foregoing notes illustrate the fact that considerable variations in the lithological character of the limestones composing the *Lonsdalia*-subzone occur, in passing from point to point in the area. Undoubtedly, the most striking feature is the variable development of cherty limestones. The greatest measurable development of the cherty series is found in the typical section, in the eastern part of the area, in which practically the whole of $D_2$ consists of strongly-cherty limestones. It is quite possible, however, that in the Manifold Valley, in the south-western part of the area, the cherty limestones attain as great a thickness. Outside these two localities of maximum development, the cherty series generally plays a much less important part in $D_2$. In the eastern part of the area, where the nature of the exposures enables us to estimate the vertical extent of the cherty series with some approach to accuracy, it is found that the decrease in the downward extent of the chert is more pronounced in a southerly direction from the typical section than in a northerly direction.

It is a noteworthy fact that, whatever its vertical extent, the chert-facies, once firmly established, usually persists to the top of the Carboniferous Limestone without considerable interruption. Further, an abundant development of chert, though sometimes found in massive light-coloured limestones, is in most cases confined either to thinly-bedded blue limestones, or to thinly-bedded dark-grey or black limestones of compact texture. I do not know of any instance in which the peculiar compact black limestones, such as those of the Ashford ' Black-Marble Quarry ',[1] are developed without an abundant accompaniment of chert.

[1] The black limestones of Ashford, well-known as being used for ornamental purposes, occur in $D_3$, but limestones of precisely-similar lithological character are developed in $D_2$, in the typical section and elsewhere.

So far as I am aware, no extensive development of chert occurs anywhere below D$_2$. By its restriction to D$_2$ and D$_3$, therefore, the presence of an extensive series of cherty beds constitutes a feature of stratigraphical value. Beyond this, however, the presence of chert cannot be said to have any significance as an indication of horizon, except within very limited areas.

The changes of lithological facies which take place in various portions of the sequence, and especially in this subzone, will probably be found, in the light of further investigation, to be of importance in their relation to faunal facies. In this connexion it may be mentioned here that the abnormal faunal facies of the *Lonsdalia*-subzone presented by the 'brachiopod-beds' (see above, p. 49) is associated with a distinctive lithological facies: namely, a conspicuous development of pure, white limestones.

V. DESCRIPTION OF CERTAIN SECTIONS OF THE *CYATHAXONIA*-SUBZONE: RELATION OF THE *CYATHAXONIA*-SUBZONE TO THE PENDLESIDE SERIES.

The *Cyathaxonia*-subzone varies considerably in different parts of the area, both as regards its thickness and as regards the abundance of its fauna. Where the subzone attains a considerable thickness, the fauna is, as a rule, proportionately well developed. It has already been stated that this subzone includes the highest beds of the Carboniferous Limestone, succeeding the *Lonsdalia*-subzone, and also the passage-beds between the Carboniferous Limestone and the Pendleside Shales, wherever such passage-beds are developed. I have not discovered any section in the Midland area that exhibits a complete sequence, from the uppermost part of the Carboniferous Limestone, through a well-developed series of passage-beds, up into the Pendleside Shales. Numerous good sections of D$_3$ are to be found, but the majority of these are confined either to the topmost beds of the Limestone, or to the passage-beds between the latter and the true Pendleside Shales; and such exposures of an unfaulted junction of the Carboniferous Limestone and the Pendleside Series as do exist, occur in localities where the change from one division to the other is sharp.

In order to give some idea of the varying development of the subzone and its relation to the Pendleside Series, I append the following notes on the more important sections examined by me. Among the sections here described, the most instructive are those of Longstone, Matlock Bath and Cromford, Tissington, Newton Grange, and Manor Farm near Wetton.

### (A) Sections in the Eastern Part of the Area.

#### (i) Longstone.

In the typical section, the railway-cutting immediately east of Headstone Tunnel, west of Longstone Station, gives an excellent exposure of $D_3$. Thinly-bedded limestones with strong chert are here conformably succeeded by a series of alternating limestones and black shales, with some hard calcareous bands in the latter. Shales become predominant in the uppermost part of the section, but corals and brachiopods typical of $D_3$ occur throughout, and the true Pendleside Series is not reached. Detailed measurements of this section are given in the Geological-Survey Memoir.[1]

## (ii) Ashford.

$D_3$ has a thick development at Ashford, 1 mile south of the Longstone section. In the 'Black-Marble Quarry' at this village, thinly-bedded black limestones, with shaly partings and abundant chert, contain a rich $D_3$ fauna. At least 150 feet of limestones must overlie these beds. The junction with the Pendleside Shales is not exposed in the vicinity.

## (iii) Matlock Bridge.

In Cawdor Quarry, Matlock Bridge, the thinly-bedded cherty limestones contain a typical $D_3$ fauna. The cherty series is here probably not more than 30 feet thick, being thinner than in other parts of the Matlock district. The junction of the cherty limestones with the Pendleside Shales is not seen.

## (iv) Matlock Bath and Cromford.

In the railway-cutting south of Matlock-Bath Station, at the entrance to Willersley Tunnel, the Pendleside Shales are seen resting conformably on the cherty limestones. The uppermost beds of the latter contain a $D_3$ fauna, but the subzone is not well-developed. The junction is here very sharp, with no development of passage-beds.

At the southern end of the same tunnel, at Cromford Station, a small exposure shows a more gradual passage into the Pendleside Shales. The $D_1$ fauna is well represented in the limestone-and-shale series at the base of the section. In the upper part of the section, the black shales contain *Posidonomya membranacea (?)*.[2]

## (B) Sections in the Southern Part of the Area.

The *Cyathaxonia*-subzone probably attains its maximum development in the southern part of the area. Certainly, the finest

---

[1] 'Geology of the Carboniferous Limestone, &c., of North Derbyshire' 2nd ed. (1887) p. 19 ('section showing the junction of the Yoredale Beds and the Mountain Limestone at the east end of Monsal Dale Tunnel').

[2] These two sections are briefly described in the 'Summary of Progress of the Geological Survey for 1904' 1905. pp. 9 & 10, where the following additional fossils are recorded from the shales at Cromford Station :—*Posidoniella, Pterinopecten papyraceus,* and *Glyphioceras Phillipsi.*

sections of passage-beds belonging to this subzone are to be found in that district. The most extensive exposures are those afforded by the cuttings on the Ashbourne & Buxton branch of the London & North-Western Railway, between Tissington and Alsop-en-le-Dale Stations. The geology of these cuttings has been admirably described by Mr. H. H. Arnold-Bemrose, in whose papers[1] detailed measurements of all the sections will be found.

### (i) Sections on the railway between Tissington and Alsop-en-le-Dale.

#### (a) Tissington cutting.[2]

In this section, a series of alternating limestones and shales, about 100 feet thick, overlies the bedded tuff; but the true Pendleside Shales are not reached. Both lithologically and palæontologically this series constitutes a splendid development of passage-beds. Thin bands of limestone, often argillaceous, and generally cherty, alternate with thick and thin beds of black shale; and massive beds of shelly, crinoidal limestone are occasionally intercalated. The limestones in this series contain an abundant and typical $D_2$ fauna of corals and brachiopods; while the shales contain lamellibranchs, including *Pterinopecten papyraceus*, *Posidonomya Becheri*, and *Posidoniella lævis*. A bed of black shale, only a few feet above the base of the series, contains *Pterinopecten papyraceus* in abundance.

#### (b) Highway-Close Barn cutting and Crake-Low cutting.[3]

The sections in Highway-Close Barn cutting and in the northern part of Crake-Low cutting show parts of the series exposed in Tissington cutting. A comparison of these two sections illustrates the rapid variation in the development of shale at this horizon. In Crake-Low cutting the series overlying the tuff contains no appreciable amount of shale, but in Highway-Close Barn cutting, nearer Tissington, black shales are strongly developed at the same level.

#### (c) Newton-Grange cutting.

In Newton-Grange cutting the section exposes an anticline, and a comparison of the succession in the eastern and western limbs of

---

[1] 'Geology of the Ashbourne & Buxton Branch of the London & North-Western Railway: Part I. Ashbourne to Crake Low' Quart. Journ. Geol. Soc. vol. lv (1899) p. 224; and 'Part II. Crake Low to Parsley Hay' *ibid.* vol. lix (1903) p. 337. In the present partly-overgrown state of the embankments, the structure of some sections, where the beds are greatly contorted, is by no means easy to interpret; and I have found the descriptions given in these papers to be of great assistance in my investigations.

[2] H. H. Arnold-Bemrose, Quart. Journ. Geol. Soc. vol. lv (1899) pp. 226–29 & pls. xvii–xviii. This section was independently described by Dr. Wheelton Hind, Trans. North Staffs. Field Club, vol. xxxii (1897–98) pp. 114–16 & pl.

[3] H. H. Arnold-Bemrose, Quart. Journ. Geol. Soc. vol. lv (1899) pp. 229–30 & pls. xvii–xviii.

the fold respectively brings out features of considerable interest. Detailed measurements of the beds in both limbs of the anticline have been recorded by Mr. H. H. Arnold-Bemrose, from whose description [1] the thicknesses given in the following account have been taken.

In the eastern limb of the fold the descending sequence is as follows :—

|  | | Thickness in feet. |
|---|---|---|
| (4) Shales and thin limestones ........................... about | 17 |
| (3) Tuff ....................................................................... | 6 |
| (2) Shales and thin limestones ...................................... | 26 |
| (1) Thinly-bedded limestones, compact in texture, with chert ; shale-partings in the upper portion ... about | 100 |

That part of the section which comprised (2), (3), & (4) is now over-grown, but the whole series of cherty limestones (1) is excellently displayed.   As a whole, the cherty-limestone series is poorly fossiliferous ; but certain beds contain fossils commonly, and yield corals and brachiopods characteristic of $D_2$.

The fold is clearly dissected, and individual beds may be traced from one limb to another.   In the western limb the descending sequence is as follows :—

|  | | Thickness in feet. |
|---|---|---|
| (2) Grey, crinoidal, limestones without chert : to top of section ................................................................. | 47 |
| (1) Thinly-bedded, compact limestones with chert ............ | 60 |

The crinoidal limestones (2) clearly represent the upper portion of the cherty limestones of the eastern limb.   They are highly crinoidal throughout most of their thickness, and contain brachiopods

Fig. 4.—*Diagrammatic section of Newton-Grange cutting.*

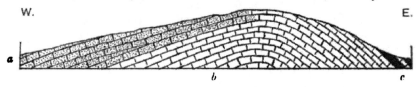

a = Compact limestone, with chert and shaly partings.   b = Crinoidal limestone, without chert.   c = Black shale.

[Length of section = about 200 yards.]

in great abundance.   In the lower part they have a conspicuous, wedge-like bedding, the beds thickening westwards.   At the top of the cutting the gradual change from blue, compact, unfossiliferous limestone with chert into light-grey, highly-crinoidal limestone without chert, may be seen to occur within individual beds as these are followed from east to west.   This change of lithological

--------

[1] Quart. Journ. Geol. Soc. vol. lix (1903) p. 339.

character, with a very localized development of highly-fossiliferous deposits, on a given horizon, constitutes a remarkable feature. Fig. 4 (p. 60) illustrates the section just described.

If the tuff occurring in this section is an attenuated portion of the thick tuff seen in Tissington cutting, the *Cyathaxonia*-subzone attains, in this neighbourhood, a thickness of well over 200 feet. About 100 feet of the subzone are represented above the tuff in Tissington cutting, while a thickness of about 125 feet is seen underneath the tuff in Newton-Grange cutting.

## (ii) Bradbourne.

In the Bradbourne inlier, immediately south of the main mass of limestone and 2 miles east of Tissington, numerous small exposures indicate a considerable development of $D_3$, with an abundant fauna. A quarry north of Bank House, at the eastern end of Bradbourne village, shows a good section of the thin limestones, with shale-partings, included in the subzone.

## (C) Sections in the South-Western Part of the Area.

### (i) Waterhouses.

In the extreme south-west of the area, exposures showing a highly-fossiliferous development of $D_3$ are afforded by two small quarries in the fields north of Waterhouses. These quarries lie respectively north-east and north-west of Field House. The beds consist of limestones with occasional shale-bands, chert being developed in the limestones.

### (ii) Warslow.

On the western margin of the area, about 5 miles north of Waterhouses, three adjacent quarries lying to the east of the village of Warslow afford an extensive exposure of the upper part of the Carboniferous Limestone. The vertical extent of this section is over 300 feet, and the greater part, at least, must be assigned to the *Cyathaxonia*-subzone, but an upward sequence into the Pendleside Series is not seen. The beds exposed consist mainly of dark, thinly-bedded, cherty limestones.

Farther east, in the Manifold Valley, near Hulme End, cuttings on the light railway expose a series of thinly-bedded, cherty limestones with interbedded shales, belonging to $D_3$. The beds are considerably folded, and no great vertical thickness is seen.

### (iii) Manor Farm, near Wetton.

East of the Manifold Valley, about $1\frac{1}{2}$ miles south-east of Warslow, and nearly 1 mile north of Wetton, a very interesting little section shows the uppermost beds of the Carboniferous Limestone and the lowest beds of the Pendleside Series in conformable

Black shale
(Pendleside Series).

Grey limestones
with strong chert
(Carboniferous
Limestone :
*Lonsdalia*-subzone).

*a*

*b*

H. H. Arnold-Bemrose photogr.

sequence. The section lies beside a stream, in a field immediately east of Manor Farm. The exposures are separated by gaps, but the beds throughout the section maintain a nearly-uniform dip, and there seems to be no doubt as to the undisturbed nature of the sequence.

The lowest beds of the Pendleside Series consist of hard black limestones, with interbedded black shales containing hard calcareous bands. Fossils, which are fairly common, include *Posidonomya Becheri*, *Posidoniella minor*, *P. lævis*, *Aviculopecten Losseni*, *Glyphioceras striatum*, and *Nomismoceras rotiforme*. No considerable development of passage-beds occurs, for a bed of black crinoidal limestone, crammed with brachiopods, is exposed a few yards from the lowest exposure of Pendleside Shales, and below this level no shale is found in the limestone-series. Underlying the black crinoidal limestones is a series of compact, greyish limestones, slightly cherty, and relatively unfossiliferous, but yielding corals typical of the *Cyathaxonia*-subzone.

## VI. LOCAL UNCONFORMITY BETWEEN THE CARBONIFEROUS LIMESTONE AND THE PENDLESIDE SERIES.

Throughout the Midland area generally, wherever the succession has not been broken by faulting, the absence of a physical break between the Carboniferous Limestone and the Pendleside Shales is clearly evident. Of considerable interest, therefore, is the proof of a local unconformity between the two divisions, furnished by a section in the eastern part of the area.[1]

This section is found in a quarry near Old Mill, beside the Bakewell-and-Winster road, rather more than a mile east of Youlgreave. Fig. 5 (p. 62) is reproduced from a photograph of the section, taken by Mr. H. H. Arnold-Bemrose, who kindly made a special visit to the quarry for the purpose. The black shales of the Pendleside Series, containing *Posidoniella lævis*, are here seen to rest with unconformity on the limestones of the *Lonsdalia*-subzone. The shales, which show no sign of disturbance, rest evenly upon a surface formed by the truncated edges of the limestone-beds.

This section affords evidence of local earth-movement and erosion, contemporaneous with the deposition, in other parts of the area, of the uppermost beds of the Carboniferous Limestone or the lowest beds of the Pendleside Series. The limestones in the section represent a high level in the *Lonsdalia*-subzone. The absence of the *Cyathaxonia*-Beds may be due, either to their removal by denudation during early Pendleside-time, or to the locality having formed land during *Cyathaxonia*-time.

[1] Previous to the commencement of my work in the Midland area, Mr. C. B. Wedd had discovered and investigated a somewhat similar example of local unconformity at Darleybridge, a few miles distant from the section here described. His description is not yet published. (But see the Discussion on the present paper, p. 81.)

In addition to the main disturbance which determined this unconformity, minor movements during the formation of the Upper *Lonsdalia*-beds are suggested by the peculiar nature of the bedding in the lower part of the section. In one part of the sequence, the truncated edges of a series of limestone-beds form a surface upon which another series of beds, less steeply inclined, rests. This is shown, although not very clearly, in the lower part of the photograph (fig. 5, p. 62): the beds have been quarried back to a large joint-face, and the bedding-planes are consequently inconspicuous; but the direction of the bedding in each series is approximately indicated by the trend of the chert-bands. This phenomenon seems to indicate contemporaneous elevation and erosion, causing local unconformity; though it is possible that the discordance of the two sets of beds may be due to local thrusting. Dr. Wheelton Hind & Mr. J. T. Stobbs have described [1] a similar phenomenon in the upper beds of the Carboniferous Limestone, seen in Waenbrodlas Quarry, Halkyn Mountain (Flintshire).

### VII. Comparison of the Faunal Succession in the Midland Area with that in other Areas.

### (A) Correlation of the Carboniferous Limestone of the Midland Area with the *Dibunophylium*-Zone of the South-Western Province. [2]

#### $D_1$ = Subzone of *Dibunophyllum* $\theta$.

This subzone may be correlated with the Lower *Dibunophyllum*-Zone ($D_1$) of the South-Western Province, the correlation being based on the following characters common to the two developments:—

    (1) The occurrence of *Dibunophylla* of simple type.
    (2) The common occurrence of *Daviesiella* aff. *comoides.*
    (3) The absence of *Cyathophyllum regium*, *Lonsdalia*, and specialized Clisiophyllids.

$D_1$ of the Midland area is much less richly fossiliferous than the corresponding subzone of the South-Western Province. Corals such as *Cyathophyllum Murchisoni* and *Carcinophyllum* $\theta$, characteristically abundant in the South-Western sequence, are absent or very rare in the Midlands. *Productus hemisphericus* abounds in $D_1$ of the South-Western Province, but is distinctly uncommon in $D_1$ of the Midland area.

[1] Geol. Mag. n. s. dec. v, vol. iii (1906) p. 396 & pl. xxii.
[2] On the Carboniferous Limestone of the South-Western Province, see A. Vaughan, 'The Palæontological Sequence in the Carboniferous Limestone of the Bristol Area' Quart. Journ. Geol. Soc. vol. lxi (1905) pp. 181 *et seqq.*; and 'The Carboniferous Limestone Series (Avonian) of the Avon Gorge' Proc. Bristol Nat. Soc. ser. 4, vol. i, pt. ii (1906) pp. 74 *et seqq.* Also T. F. Sibly, 'On the Carboniferous Limestone (Avonian) of the Mendip Area (Somerset)' Quart. Journ. Geol. Soc. vol. lxii (1906) pp. 324 *et seqq.*

### $D_2$ = Subzone of *Lonsdalia floriformis*.

Comparing the faunal assemblage of this subzone with that of the Upper *Dibunophyllum*-Zone ($D_2$) of the South-Western Province, the following important points of agreement are evident :—

(1) The occurrence of *Lonsdalia floriformis*, *Cyathophyllum regium*, *Lithostrotion Portlocki*, and *Dibunophylla* of a more specialized type than those found in $D_1$.

(2) Although the brachiopod-fauna of $D_2$ in the Midland area is considerably richer than that of $D_2$ in the South-Western Province. yet it includes, with very few exceptions, all the species and varieties found in the latter development.

The chief points in which the coral-fauna of $D_2$ in the Midland area differs from that of $D_2$ in the South-Western Province are as follows :—

(1) Clisiophyllids belonging to the 'genera' *Histiophyllum*, *Rhodophyllum*, and *Cymatiophyllum* occur in abundance. No similar forms have been found in the South-Western Province.

(2) *Lithostrotion junceum* is abundant, and *L. Martini* occurs in considerable variety and abundance. The typical form of *Lithostrotion irregulare* is uncommon, but a *Lithostrotion* which I regard as intermediate between that species and *L. Martini* is characteristically common. In the South-Western Province, the abundance of *L. irregulare* characterizes $D_2$, but *L. Martini* is comparatively uncommon, and *L. junceum* is rare.

(3) *Syringopora* cf. *reticulata* is common. This form does not occur in $D_2$ in the South-Western Province.

The distinctive features of the brachiopod-fauna of $D_2$ in the Midland area, as compared with $D_2$ in the South-Western Province, may be summarized as follows :—

*Productus giganteus* and its variants occur in great abundance. *Pr. semireticulatus*, *Pr. concinnus*, and *Pr. Martini* are abundant. Punctate, scabriculate, and costate *Producti* are of frequent occurrence. *Productus longispinus* and its allies occur not uncommonly. *Spirifer bisulcatus* and *Martinia glabra* are abundant, and *Spirifer planicosta* occurs commonly. *Schizophoria resupinata* always occurs.

This statement makes the difference between the brachiopod-fauna of the Midland area and that of the South-Western Province appear very great. It is important, therefore, to note that nearly all the brachiopods here mentioned have been recorded, though rarely, in $D_2$ of the South-Western Province; and that certain species, for example *Productus concinnus* and *Martinia glabra*, are locally abundant in the South-Western Province. Moreover, in comparing the two developments, it is important to appreciate the impoverishing influence of the conditions which prevailed during Upper *Seminula*-time in the South-Western

Province, on the brachiopod-fauna of the *Dibunophyllum*-Zone in that Province.[1]

It must be noted that the brachiopod-fauna of $D_2$ in the Midland area, here contrasted with that of the South-Western Province, occurs in association with the typical $D_2$ coral-fauna, in the typical facies of the subzone. The locally-developed 'brachiopod-bed'[2] facies of this subzone in the Midland area, in which the coral-fauna is very poor, has no representation in the South-Western Province.

### $D_3$ = Subzone of *Cyathaxonia rushiana*.

This subzone is unrepresented in the South-Western Province, except by the uppermost beds of the Avonian at Oystermouth (Gower), in which *Amplexi-Zaphrentis* and *Zaphrentis* aff. *Enniskilleni* are abundant.[3] Since the *Cyathaxonia*-subzone of the Midland area directly succeeds beds which can be correlated with the Upper *Dibunophyllum*-Zone of the South-Western Province, it constitutes a horizon at least as high as the top of the typical Avonian sequence. The occurrence of *Productus scabriculus* and *Pr. costatus* would at first suggest an accurate correlation with Horizon $\epsilon$ of the South-Western Province, but it is found that both these species range throughout the greater part of $D_2$, as well as $D_3$, in the Midland area. In the typical succession of the South-Western Province, Horizon $\epsilon$ and the lower part of the Millstone Grit may be taken as representing the *Cyathaxonia*-subzone of the Midland sequence.

### (B) Comparison of the Succession in the Midland Area with that in North Wales.

The faunal succession in the Midland area bears a close resemblance to that in North Wales, recently described by Dr. Wheelton Hind & Mr. J. T. Stobbs,[4] and the similarity of these two developments is of considerable interest. Those writers have demonstrated that the basement-conglomerate of the Carboniferous Series in North Wales is of Upper Avonian age, and that no part of the Avonian, lower than the uppermost portion of the *Seminula*-Zone, is represented in that area. I have found no evidence of any horizon lower than the *Dibunophyllum*-Zone, in the Midland area; and the limestones immediately overlying the basement-conglomerate in certain parts of the North-Wales area, which contain *Seminula ficoides* and *Daviesiella llangollensis*, must be regarded as of lower horizon than any beds seen in the typical section of the

[1] See A. Vaughan, Quart. Journ. Geol. Soc. vol. lxii (1906) p. 302, footnote.
[2] See above, p. 49.
[3] A. Vaughan, Quart. Journ. Geol. Soc. vol. lxii (1906) p. 302.
[4] 'The Carboniferous Succession below the Coal-Measures in North Shropshire, Denbighshire, & Flintshire' Geol. Mag. n. s. dec. 5, vol. iii (1906) pp. 385–400, 445–59, & 496–507.

Midland area. It is unfortunate that the base of the Carboniferous Limestone is not exposed in the Midland area; for, in view of the relative geographical position of the Midland and North-Wales areas, and the general similarity of their facies, there is some reason to expect that the base of the Carboniferous Limestone occurs at approximately the same horizon in both areas. A knowledge of the horizon of the base of the Carboniferous Limestone in the Midland area would afford valuable evidence in an important branch of Carboniferous physiography.

The relation between the faunal succession in the two areas may be summarized as follows :—$D_1$ of North Wales presents a more normal character, compared with the South-Western Province, than $D_1$ of the Midland area. This is exemplified by the abundance of *Cyathophyllum Murchisoni* and *Productus hemisphericus* in the North-Wales development.

It is in the characters of the faunal assemblage of $D_2$ that the two areas are most closely linked. Both areas exhibit a characteristic $D_2$ coral-fauna, and the differences are unimportant, as compared with the points of identity; while the North-Wales area possesses a rich brachiopod-fauna, practically identical with that of the Midland area.

In the development of $D_3$ there is a considerable difference between the two areas. The Midland succession includes a well-developed *Cyathaxonia*-subzone, which possesses a coral-fauna essentially distinct from that of the *Lonsdalia*-subzone, *Cyathaxonia* and various Zaphrentids being abundant, while *Lonsdalia floriformis* is absent. The *Cyathaxonia*-fauna attains a fine development in the passage-beds between the Carboniferous Limestone and the Pendleside Shales, and the subzone often includes a considerable thickness of the uppermost beds of the Carboniferous Limestone proper. In the North-Wales succession, on the other hand, while the $D_3$ coral-fauna is partly developed in the uppermost portion of $D_2$, associated with *Lonsdalia* and other characteristic $D_2$ corals; and, while *Cyathaxonia* and *Amplexi-Zaphrentis* do occur in passage-beds at the top of the Carboniferous Limestone, there is no development of a distinct *Cyathaxonia*-subzone at all nearly equal to that of the Midland area.

On the whole evidence, it may be concluded that the Carboniferous Limestone of the Midland area and that of North Wales belong to one Province, distinct from the South-Western Province. The *Dibunophyllum*-Zone of this Midland Province differs from that of the South-Western Province in the richness of its brachiopod-fauna, and the Midland Province is further distinguished by the development of a *Cyathaxonia*-subzone at the top of the *Dibuno-phyllum*-Zone. This *Cyathaxonia*-subzone has its typical development in Derbyshire and North Staffordshire, and is less clearly developed in North Wales.

(C) Comparison of the *Cyathaxonia*-subzone of the Midland area with the *Cyathaxonia*-Beds of the Rush sequence, Co. Dublin.

The close similarity between the faunas of the *Cyathaxonia*-Beds of the Midland succession and the Rush sequence, respectively, will be apparent, on comparing my faunal lists (pp. 50 & 51) with those tabulated [1] by Dr. A. Vaughan in his account of the Rush beds. A few specially-noticeable differences may be mentioned. *Cyathaxonia contorta*, which occurs at Rush, is replaced in the Midlands by *C. costata*. *Beaumontia*, which is locally abundant in the Midland area, is not recorded from Rush. The brachiopod-fauna of the Midland series, while agreeing with that of the Rush beds in its main essentials, is considerably more varied.

## VIII. SUMMARY OF CONCLUSIONS.

(1) The base of the Carboniferous Limestone is not exposed in the Midland area. The most extensive section in the area, namely, that along the course of the Midland Railway between Longstone and Buxton, shows a thickness of about 1500 feet of Carboniferous Limestone. All the beds seen in this section are included in the *Dibunophyllum*-Zone, which may be correlated, broadly, with the *Dibunophyllum*-Zone of the South-Western Province.

(2) Three subzonal divisions are distinguished in the Midland sequence. These, in descending order, are as follows:—

$D_3$ = Subzone of *Cyathaxonia rushiana*. Represented in the typical succession of the South-Western Province by Horizon $\epsilon$ and the lower part of the Millstone Grit.

$D_2$ = Subzone of *Lonsdalia floriformis*. Correlated with the Upper *Dibunophyllum*-Zone ($D_2$) of the South-Western Province.

$D_1$ = Subzone of *Dibunophyllum* θ. Correlated with the Lower *Dibunophyllum*-Zone ($D_1$) of the South-Western Province.

(3) An abnormal development of the *Lonsdalia*-subzone, consisting of richly-fossiliferous brachiopod-beds, in which the typical coral-fauna has very little representation, forms a conspicuous local feature in various parts of the western half of the area.

(4) The passage-beds between the Carboniferous Limestone and the Pendleside Shales are included in the *Cyathaxonia*-subzone. Locally, these passage-beds attain a thick development.

(5) A local unconformity between the Carboniferous Limestone and the Pendleside Series, indicating contemporaneous elevation and erosion, occurs in the eastern part of the area.

(6) A close general similarity exists between the *Dibunophyllum*-Zone of the Midland area and that of North Wales. These

[1] Quart. Journ. Geol. Soc. vol. lxii (1906) pp. 297-99 & 301.

two areas should be regarded as constituting a Midland Province.

(7) A comparison of the *Dibunophyllum*-Zone of the Midland and South-Western Provinces, respectively, brings out the following more important differences:—

(a) The brachiopod-fauna of the *Lonsdalia*-subzone of the Midland Province is considerably richer than that of the equivalent part of the South-Western sequence.

(b) The *Cyathaxonia*-subzone of the Midland Province, which attains a maximum development in Derbyshire and North Staffordshire, is practically undeveloped in the South-Western Province.

In conclusion, I would express my thanks to those geologists who have assisted me during the course of my investigations.

I am indebted to Prof. Charles Lapworth for his valuable advice and continual encouragement; to Mr. H. H. Arnold-Bemrose, with whom I have had the pleasure of examining some parts of the area, for generously placing his thorough knowledge of the district at my service; to Dr. Wheelton Hind for some assistance in the field, and for kindly identifying the lamellibranchs and cephalopods collected by me in the Pendleside Beds; and to Mr. C. B. Wedd, not only for valuable information and for some assistance in the field, but also for helpful criticism during the later stages of my work.

My thanks are due to the Director of H.M. Geological Survey, for kindly permitting me to examine the collections of fossils recently obtained from the Midland area by the Officers of the Survey.

The excellent photographs (reproduced in Pl. I) illustrating the palæontological part of this paper are the work of Mr. J. W. Tutcher, to whom I offer my sincere thanks.

## IX. DESCRIPTION OF CERTAIN CORALS AND BRACHIOPODS FROM THE MIDLAND AREA.

### (A) CORALS.

### Michelinia.

MICHELINIA GLOMERATA, M'Coy.

Described & figured in ' Brit. Palæoz. Foss.' 1855, p. 80 & pl. iii B, fig. 14.

The specimens which I include here are characterized as follows:—The corallites are never specially elongated. The tabulæ are convex upwards; a few of them are continuous across a corallite, but the great majority, which are not so continuous, form large vesicles.

This form occurs somewhat uncommonly in the upper part of $D_2$ and in $D_3$.

The tabular structure of *Michelinia glomerata* is much less finely vesicular than in the Lower Avonian species of *Michelinia*, namely, *M.* cf. *favosa* and *M.* cf. *megastoma*. In the simplification of its tabulæ, *Michelinia glomerata* approaches *Beaumontia*, which characterizes the uppermost part of the Avonian, that is, $D_1$.

## Section Beaumontia.

BEAUMONTIA aff. EGERTONI, Edwards & Haime.

A coral which occurs in D$_3$, and is locally abundant, agrees precisely with *Beaumontia Egertoni*, as described and figured in ' Monogr. Brit. Foss. Corals ' (Palæont. Soc.) pt. iii (1852) p. 160 & pl. xlv, fig. 1. This form is a typical representative of the *Beaumontia*-section (genus *Michelinia*). The corallum forms a large, elongate mass, and the corallites are narrow and elongated. The tabulæ, which are either flat, or very slightly convex or concave, nearly all stretch completely across a corallite.

## Cyathophyllum.

CYATHOPHYLLUM REGIUM, Phil.

See A. Vaughan, Proc. Bristol Nat. Soc. ser. 3, vol. x (1903) pp. 114–15, & Quart. Journ. Geol. Soc. vol. lxi (1905) pp. 275–76.

This species is widely distributed, and often abundant, in D$_2$; it persists into D$_3$, but is there extremely rare.

Specimens from Derbyshire have been figured by M'Coy, ' Brit. Pal. Foss.' 1855, pl. iii A, figs. 7, 7 a, & pl. iii B, fig. 1 (*Astræa carbonaria*). All the Midland specimens which I include in *Cyathophyllum regium* are compound forms.

Specimens of *Cyathophyllum regium* from the Midland area exhibit considerable individual variation in the structure of the central area, as seen in vertical section. The replacement of tabulæ by a vaulted arrangement of fine vesicles is never so complete as in specimens from the South-Western Province. In the majority of Midland specimens, the narrow central space shows a regular development of very closely-packed, flat, subvesicular tabulæ; but in some specimens this structure is partly replaced by a vaulted arrangement of vesicles. Certain specimens possess an unusually-strong development of flattened tabulæ. These forms, however, agree with the typical vesicular form of *Cyathophyllum regium* in all other characters, and cannot be regarded as anything but a local variety; they do not occur in association with the more typical vesicular forms.

## Koninckophyllum.

KONINCKOPHYLLUM PROPRIUM, sp. nov.    (Pl. I, fig. 3.)

Habit of growth: simple.    Form: elongate-conical.

The calyx shows a broad central area, occupied by the tabulæ, and only very partially radiated by the septa. The columella projects as a small, central ridge.

A horizontal section shows a stout, simple columella. The columella is surrounded by one or more oval rings, produced by the intersection of the plane of section with one or more of the centrally-elevated tabulæ.

The primary septa are slightly thickened in the medial area,

thinner and slightly flexuous in the external area. Their inner
ends fall short of the columella by a considerable distance. The
broad external area, which is rather closely vesicular, is radiated
both by the primary septa, which extend to the outer wall, and by
a secondary series of septa. The latter extend from the outer wall
inwards almost, or quite, to the inner wall, which is defined by the
closer approximation of the innermost rows of dissepiments. The
septal fossula is generally inconspicuous.

In a median vertical section, the columella forms a strong,
continuous median line. The broad central area is occupied by subvesicular tabulæ which are distinctly elevated centrally. The tabulæ
bend downwards at their outer ends, and merge into large vesicles
which constitute a narrow medial area. The external area is broad,
and formed by very small vesicles, arranged in outwardly ascending
rows.

Dimensions.—The type-specimen is about 2·5 centimetres in
diameter at the calyx, and about 5·5 cm. in length.

Horizon.—*Koninckophyllum proprium* occurs in $D_2$ in the
Midland area.

Discussion.—Typical representatives of the genus *Koninckophyllum* [1] bear considerable resemblance to *Lithostrotion*. In
addition to their usually simple habit of growth, they are distinguished from the latter genus by (1) the more rudimentary
development of the primary septa, which are only very slightly
produced over the broad tabulæ; and (2) the greater development
of the external, vesicular zone.

*Koninckophyllum proprium* exhibits all the essential characters
of a typical *Koninckophyllum*. It differs from *Koninckophyllum
magnificum*, Thoms. & Nich.,[2] the genotype, in the following
respects :—(1) Its smaller size. (2) The nature of the external
area, as seen in horizontal section : in *Koninckophyllum proprium*
the external area is filled with more or less rectangular dissepiments;
in *K. magnificum* the vesicular structure of the external area is
much closer, and to a large extent highly irregular, so that the
septa can only be traced with difficulty. (3) The wider spacing of
the tabulæ, which are less markedly subvesicular. (4) The stouter
nature of the columella.

KONINCKOPHYLLUM sp.

A *Koninckophyllum*, occurring in $D_3$ in the Midland area, exhibits,
in horizontal section, thin spidery septa, an external area not very
closely vesicular and not strongly demarcated, and a very small
columella. This is, apparently, a distinctive form; but the imperfect

[1] For an accurate description of the genus *Koninckophyllum*, see J. Thomson
& H. A. Nicholson (the authors of the genus) in Ann. & Mag. Nat. Hist. ser. 4,
vol. xvii (1876) pp. 297–300.
[2] Figured in Ann. & Mag. Nat. Hist. ser. 4, vol. xvii (1876) pl. xii, figs. 2
& 2 a ; and in Proc. Phil. Soc. Glasgow, vol. xiv (1882-83) pl. xi, figs. 1 & 1 a.

nature of my specimens does not justify the creation of a new species. This form is closely similar to *Koninckophyllum* sp., figured by James Thomson in Proc. Phil. Soc. Glasgow, vol. xiv (1882-83) pl. xi, figs. 5 & 6.

### Lonsdalia.

LONSDALIA DUPLICATA (Martin).    (Pl. I, fig. 5.)

Habit of growth and form.—Compound, dendroid, the corallites being cylindrical, very unequal in diameter, and loosely aggregated.

Epitheca.—Thick, concentrically rugose, and distinctly costate.

In a horizontal section of a corallite:—The central area is generally loose and rather irregular in structure, the radial lamellæ being few in number and often incompletely developed. The mesial plate is usually well-developed.

The primary septa, which extend inwards to the boundary of the central area, are thickened and very prominent within the inner wall. They usually terminate a very short distance outside the inner wall, and very rarely reach the outer wall. Secondary septa are, as a rule, either absent or of very rudimentary development. The inner wall, produced by a thickening of the dissepiments, is very conspicuous.

The external area, radiated by the septa and containing dissepiments, is extremely narrow and inconstant. The broad peripheral area, composed of very large vesicles, has a width approximately equal to half the radius of the corallite.

Discussion.—William Martin's original description and figure[1] of *Lonsdalia duplicata* furnish no details of the internal structure of the coral; and although M'Coy[2] gave a detailed description of the species, based on Derbyshire specimens, his description is not accompanied by a figure. Specimens collected by me in the Midland area agree in external form with the original specimen of *Lonsdalia duplicata*, as represented in Martin's work, and also agree completely with M'Coy's description of the species. I have, therefore, thought it advisable to redescribe the species, at the same time figuring a typical specimen.

The coral figured as *Lonsdalia duplicata* by Thomson & Nicholson,[3] is in fact widely different from that species, as shown by the following characters of a horizontal section:—(1) A sharply-bounded central area, in which radial lamellæ are generally numerous and regular. (2) Thin, flexuous primary septa, and a regularly-developed secondary series. (3) A comparatively-wide external area, radiated by the septa; and a poorly-defined inner wall. (4) A peripheral area composed of comparatively-small vesicles.

Horizon.—*Lonsdalia duplicata* occurs in the upper part of $D_2$

[1] 'Petrificata Derbiensia' 1809, pl. xxx.
[2] 'Brit. Pal. Foss.' 1855, p. 105.
[3] Ann. & Mag. Nat. Hist. ser. 4, vol. xvii (1876) pl. xvi, figs. 2 & 2 a.

in the Midland area.  It is locally abundant in the uppermost beds of that subzone, and probably ranges into $D_3$.

Comparison with other Species.—*Lonsdalia floriformis* (Flem.) differs from *L. duplicata* in its usually massive habit of growth, and also in the following structural details, as seen in a horizontal section :—

(1) The central area is, as a rule, finely reticulate in structure, with numerous radial lamellæ, and is sharply bounded.
(2) The primary septa are not so strongly thickened ; and a secondary series is usually well developed.
(3) The inner wall is less strongly thickened, and the external area, radiated by the septa, is broader and more constant.
(4) The vesicles of the peripheral area are usually smaller.

*Lonsdalia rugosa*, M'Coy, resembles *L. duplicata* in its dendroid habit of growth, but is widely different [1] in internal structure.  As seen in a horizontal section, no purely-vesicular peripheral area is developed ; all the septa extend to the outer wall ; and the external dissepimental area is very broad.

### The simple Clisiophyllids.

The following descriptions do not include any account of those very interesting corals, belonging chiefly to the genera *Histiophyllum*, *Rhodophyllum*, and *Cymatiophyllum*, which I have found to occur in great abundance in the *Lonsdalia*-subzone of the Midland area.  I had originally intended to include a description of these forms in the present paper ; and with that intention, I had sections cut of a large number of specimens.  These corals, however, exhibit such remarkable variation that a satisfactory description of their relationships will involve prolonged study, and must be of considerable length.  I have decided, therefore, to defer the description of them ; but I hope soon to describe and figure the important Midland types in a separate communication, supplementary to the present paper.

### Clisiophyllum, Dana (*pars*) ; Thoms. & Nich.[2]

CLISIOPHYLLUM aff. M'COYANUM, Thomson.    (Pl. I, fig. 4.)

Description.—The form is elongate-conical.

In a horizontal section :—The large, subcircular, central area is finely reticulate in structure, numerous thin radial lamellæ, which are distinctly curved spirally, being united by closely-set tabular intersections.  The strong mesial plate falls considerably short of the circumference of the area on either side.

[1] The inclusion of ' *Lonsdalia* ' *rugosa* in the same genus with *L. floriformis* and *L. duplicata* is open to great objection.  The absence of a peripheral purely-vesicular area, the strong development of the external dissepimental area, and the complete (or nearly complete) bisection of the central area by the mesial plate, are essential characters of M'Coy's species, which, taken together, call for its generic separation from *Lonsdalia floriformis* and *L. duplicata*.
[2] For a full description of the genus *Clisiophyllum*, and an explanation of the terms employed in describing the Clisiophyllids, see J. Thomson & H. A. Nicholson, Ann. & Mag. Nat. Hist. ser. 4, vol. xvii (1876) pp. 451–57.

The closely-set primary septa are thickened in the medial area, thin and flexuous in the external area, and extend to the outer wall. Their inner ends are attached to the mesh of the central area. The secondary septa, which are regularly developed, are thin and flexuous in the external area; their thickened ends project a short distance inwards from the inner wall. The septal fossula is conspicuous.

The external area, radiated by both series of septa, is filled with rectangular dissepiments; and the inner wall is defined by a thickening of the innermost dissepiments.

Discussion.—This coral, which occurs somewhat rarely in the upper part of $D_2$ in the Midland area, is essentially identical with *Clisiophyllum M'Coyanum*, Thomson, as described and figured in Proc. Phil. Soc. Glasgow, vol. xiii (1880–82) p. 526 & pl. v, figs. 4–4 *b*. In Thomson's figures, however, the central area is more closely reticulate than in the Midland specimens.

### Dibunophyllum, Thoms. & Nich.[1]

DIBUNOPHYLLUM MATLOCKENSE, sp. nov.    (Pl. I, fig. 2.)

Description.—The form is elongate-conical.

In a horizontal section:—The central area is completely, or nearly completely, bisected by a strong mesial plate. The mesial plate, which is of practically-uniform thickness throughout its length, always extends to the circumference of the area on the fossular side, but sometimes falls short of the circumference, by a short distance, on the opposite side. In some sections, the mesial plate is seen to be produced into the fossula, and to become attached to the primary septum occupying the fossula; while in some other sections it bends round at the end, and becomes attached to one of the septa bounding the fossula. The radial lines, representing the cut edges of the vertical lamellæ, are well-spaced, strong, and fairly straight.

The primary septa are appreciably thickened in the medial area, thin and flexuous in the external area, and extend to the outer wall. Thin secondary septa are generally well-developed in the external area, but they rarely reach the inner wall, and never extend inside it. The septal fossula is always conspicuous.

The external area, of moderate width, is uniformly and rather closely vesicular. An irregular thickening of the dissepiments round the inner margin of the external area gives rise to a poorly-defined inner wall.

Horizon.—This species occurs in the *Lonsdalia*-subzone of the Midland area, and is there the predominant *Dibunophyllum*.

Variation.—The forms which I include in *Dibunophyllum matlockense* show marked individual variation as regards the development of a secondary series of septa, and the number of radial lamellæ in the central area. The figured type has secondary septa

---

[1] This genus is fully described by Thomson & Nicholson, Ann. & Mag. Nat. Hist. ser. 4, vol. xvii (1876) pp. 457–59.

well-developed, and shows comparatively few radial lamellæ in the central area.

Comparison with the typical *Dibunophylla* of the South-Western Province.—As compared with *Dibunophyllum* θ,[1] *D. matlockense* possesses a larger, more clearly-bounded central area, a more specialized septal system, and a rather more clearly-differentiated external area.

*Dibunophyllum* ψ,[2] which is more widely conical in form than *D. matlockense*, further differs from the Midland species in the following characters, as seen in horizontal section:—The central area is more strongly bounded, and the vertical lamellæ, which are more numerous, are usually curved; while the mesial plate, which is markedly thickened in the centre of the area, almost invariably falls short of the circumference of the area, on the antifossular side, by a considerable distance. The external area is relatively broader, and is more closely vesicular, and the inner wall is strongly defined. The septa not infrequently stop short of the outer wall.

DIBUNOPHYLLUM DERBIENSE, sp. nov.   (Pl. I, fig. 1.)

Description.—The form is elongate-conical and large, some specimens attaining a diameter of 2 inches.

In a horizontal section :—The central area appears to be completely bisected by a flexuous mesial plate, which is thickened centrally, and continued into the septal fossula as a thin lamella. The radial lines, representing the cut edges of the vertical lamellæ, are irregularly and unequally developed.

The primary septa, which are closely set (there are 72 of them in the figured section, which is about 2 inches in diameter), are appreciably thickened in the medial area. They taper outwards in the external area, but extend to the outer wall, and are for the most part straight throughout their length. The rudimentary secondary septa have a very inconstant development. The septal fossula is clearly marked.

The broad external area, approximately equal in width to half the radius of the coral, is closely vesicular, the dissepiments being irregularly and very closely packed near its inner boundary. A well-defined inner wall is formed by the thickening of the innermost rows of dissepiments.

In the medial area, rectangular dissepiments, representing the cut edges of the outward prolongations of the tabulæ, are numerous.

*Dibunophyllum derbiense* is a highly-distinctive form, differing widely from any previously-described species with which I am acquainted. It occurs rarely in the *Lonsdalia*-subzone of the Midland area.

[1] A. Vaughan, Quart. Journ. Geol. Soc. vol. lxi (1905) p. 283 & pl. xxiv, fig. 1.
[2] *Id. ibid.* p. 284 & pl. xxiv, figs. 2 & 2 *a*.

## (B) BRACHIOPODS.

### Productus.

PRODUCTUS CONCINNUS, Sow., and PR. MARTINI, Sow.

Both these species occur abundantly in D₂ and D₃ in the Midland area. I have examined Sowerby's type-specimens,[1] and numerous specimens collected by myself in the Midlands, and the relationship of the two species appears to me to be as follows.

Typical examples of *Productus concinnus* and *Pr. Martini*, which agree in the nature of their ribbing and in the development of spines on the flanks of the convex valve, differ in the following respects :—In *Productus Martini*, the convex valve is non-sulcate ; the skirt-like, frontal portion of the valve is greatly developed ; semireticulation is generally inconspicuous ; and the intersection of the two valves is approximately square-shaped. In *Productus concinnus*, which is a smaller shell, the convex valve is sulcate ; the skirt-like, frontal portion of the valve is less extensive ; semi-reticulation is strong on the wings, and sometimes extends over the body of the valve ; and the intersection of the two valves is slightly transverse.

Typical examples of these two species are readily distinguished, and such specimens occur quite commonly ; but intermediate forms, which may be referred indifferently either to one species or to the other, are equally common. The most frequently-occurring of these intermediate types has the greatly-developed 'skirt' of *Productus Martini*, with the sulcate form and marked semireticulation of *Pr. concinnus*, and shows a valve-intersection which is sometimes square and sometimes transverse. This intermediate type occurs most commonly in D₂. The typical form of *Productus Martini* attains its maximum in the localized D₂ 'brachiopod-beds,' while the typical *Pr. concinnus* has its maximum in D₃.

### Gens of *Productus longispinus*, Sow.

*Producti* belonging to this group range throughout almost the whole vertical extent of D₂, and occur very commonly in D₃, in the Midland area. Many forms are represented.

Specimens closely similar to the typical form of *Productus longispinus* (Sowerby, 'Min. Conch.' vol. i, 1812, pl. lxviii, fig. 1 ; & Davidson, 'Monogr. Brit. Foss. Brachiop.' Palæont. Soc. vol. ii, 1858–63, pl. xxxv, fig. 5) occur in D₂, and more commonly in D₃.

A form which closely resembles *Productus lobatus*, Sow. ('Min.

[1] Now preserved in the British Museum (Natural History), South Kensington. The types of *Productus concinnus*, figured in Sowerby's 'Min. Conch.' vol. iv (1823) pl. cccxviii, fig. 1, were obtained from Derbyshire. The locality of the type of *Productus Martini* (*ibid.* pl. cccxvii, fig. 2) is not definitely stated ; but Sowerby mentions that the species is 'not uncommon in the Derbyshire Limestone'; and the specimen was probably obtained from the Midland area, where identical specimens occur in many localities.

Conch.' vol. iv, 1823, pl. cccxviii, figs. 2-6) occurs commonly in $D_2$ in certain localities, and less frequently in $D_3$.

A small, very globose shell, identical with that figured by Davidson, 'Monogr. Brit. Foss. Brachiop.' (Palæont. Soc.) vol. ii (1858-63) pl. xxxv, figs. 19 & 19 a, is of rare occurrence in $D_2$ and $D_3$.

The specimens which I refer to *Productus setosus*, Phil., exhibit the following distinctive characters, compared with *Pr. longispinus*. The shell usually is considerably larger, and the ribbing is much coarser : in the more typical specimens, the ribs increase very little by bifurcation : the convex valve exhibits a sharp, mesial, frontal elevation, which is generally ornamented like the remainder of the shell. [Compare Phillips, 'Geol. Yorks.' vol. ii (1836) pl. viii, fig. 17 ; & Davidson, ' Monogr. Brit. Foss. Brachiop. (Palæont. Soc.) vol. ii (1858-63) pl. xxxv, fig. 16.]

PRODUCTUS SETOSUS, Phil., var. TISSINGTONENSIS, nov. (Pl. I, figs. 6 a & 6 b.)

Description.—The form approximates to that of a typical *Productus longispinus*, but the wings (which are rarely preserved) are somewhat more extended.

Convex valve.—The flattened, rostral portion of the valve is covered with coarse, rounded, radial ribs, gradually increasing in thickness towards the margin ; semireticulation is strong and regular. The flank-ribs show a fairly-regular increase in width towards the margin, with a little irregular thickening. On the frontal portion of the valve, the ribs show a highly-irregular behaviour (Pl. I, fig. 6 b). Some remain of practically uniform thickness; others die out altogether; while others again become greatly broadened and often bifurcate. A sharp mesial fold, originating in the fusion of two or more ribs, starts some distance from the margin, and rapidly increases in prominence towards the margin : it may be either smooth or faintly ribbed. Two specially-strong ribs are frequently developed, bordering the flanks, one on each side of the mesial fold. One or two spines project from each wing, and a few strong spines are developed on the flanks and on the frontal portion of the valve. Two specially-prominent spines are frequently present, one on each of the thickened ribs bordering the flanks.

Discussion. — *Productus setosus* var. *tissingtonensis* is completely distinguished from the typical form of *Pr. setosus* by the remarkable irregular nature of its ornament. The variety *tissingtonensis* occurs in $D_3$, and is especially common in that subzone at Tissington, near Ashbourne. In virtue of its external ornament, this variety may be regarded as indicating the convergence of *Productus setosus* with the more highly-ornate forms of *Pr. costatus*, Sow., the latter also being especially characteristic of $D_3$.

## Chonetes.

### CHONETES cf. HARDRENSIS, Phil.

Specimens which are locally abundant in the shales of the *Cyathaxonia*-subzone have a small, somewhat rectangular form, with slight convexity, and are ornamented with very fine ribs, increasing in number by forking. The hinge-line of an average specimen measures 10 millimetres.

### CHONETES CRASSISTRIA (M'Coy).

Small, convex, alate shells, with coarse, simple ribs, occur rarely in $D_3$. These resemble very closely the Derbyshire specimen described and figured by M'Coy in 'Brit. Pal. Foss.' 1855, p. 454 & pl. iii H, fig. 5, as *Leptæna (Chonetes) crassistria*, but are smaller than M'Coy's figured specimen.

### CHONETES cf. CRASSISTRIA (M'Coy), Vaughan.

I am unable to distinguish certain specimens, which are found rarely in $D_2$ and $D_3$, from the form, described and figured by Dr. A. Vaughan in Quart. Journ. Geol. Soc. vol. lxi (1905) p. 294 & pl. xxvi, fig. 2, which abounds in the *Cleistopora*-Zone of the South-Western Province.

### CHONETES COMPRESSA, nom. nov.    (Pl. I, figs. 7 a & 7 b.)

Description.—The form is semicircular, the hinge-line forming the widest part of the shell. Both valves are almost completely flat, the pedicle-valve being very slightly convex and the brachial valve very slightly concave. The shell is thin. Each valve possesses a well-developed area, that of the pedicle-valve being considerably the larger, and being divided by a wide-angled delthyrium, which is partly closed by a pseudo-deltidium. A row of spines project from the cardinal edge of the pedicle-valve.

Fig. 6.—*Median longitudinal section of* Chonetes compressa *(natural size).*

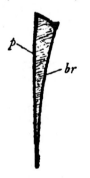

[ *p* = pedicle-valve ; *br* = brachial valve.]

The external surface of the valves is covered with fine, thread-like, slightly-flexuous, radiating ribs, which increase in number towards the margin by bifurcation and by the intercalation of fresh ribs. The ribs exhibit small spine-apertures at intervals; and the fairly-regular arrangement of these spine-apertures gives a characteristic appearance to the shell. In the under layer of the shell, the pits in the radial furrows are small and closely packed.

Dimensions.—The hinge-line of an average specimen measures about 6 centimetres. Large specimens attain a width of 8 or 9 centimetres.

Horizon.—*Chonetes compressa* occurs in the *Lonsdalia*-subzone of the Midland area, and is apparently confined to that subzone. Locally, it attains great abundance.

Discussion.—The characters of flattened form, large size, and fine ribbing, possessed by *Chonetes compressa*, would generally determine its reference to *Ch. papilionacea* (Phil.).

Since the holotype [1] of *Ch. papilionacea* is an imperfect specimen, exhibiting only a part of the interior of the brachial valve, with small attached fragments of the marginal part of the pedicle-valve, the species is actually very insufficiently known. All large, flattened, finely-ribbed Carboniferous *Chonetes* have been, however, generally referred to *Ch. papilionacea* (Phil.), consequent upon Davidson's [2] recognition of that species. Until the nomenclature of the group has been adequately revised, some such unsatisfactory method is unavoidable; and the plan of employing the term ' papilionaceous *Chonetes* ' to connote members of the group seems advisable, in that it emphasizes the unsatisfactory state of their nomenclature.

The application of a distinctive name to the form here described and figured seems to me to be both justifiable and expedient. *Chonetes compressa* is distinguished from all other papilionaceous *Chonetes* by its remarkably-flattened form; and it has, apparently, a very limited vertical range in the Carboniferous Limestone. I have compared specimens of *Ch. compressa* with the type-specimen of *Ch. papilionacea*; and, so far as the imperfect nature of the latter admits of a comparison, the following differences may be noted :—(1) The pedicle-valve of *Ch. papilionacea* is appreciably convex (this is inferred from the concavity of the brachial valve in the type-specimen), whereas that of *Ch. compressa* is almost completely flat. (2) *Ch. papilionacea* is a larger and more transverse shell. (3) Spine-apertures are stronger and more numerous on the ribs of *Ch. compressa*.

Without contending for the specific distinctiveness of *Ch. compressa*, I consider that, in a subsequent revision of the papilionaceous *Chonetes*, it must be recognized as a well-defined type, characteristic of a limited horizon, and that a distinguishing appellation is therefore desirable.

---

[1] Now preserved in the British Museum (Natural History), South Kensington.

[2] See ' Monogr. Brit. Foss. Brachiop.' (Palæont. Soc.) vol. ii (1858–63) p. 182 & pl. xlvi, figs. 3–5 *b*. Davidson states that figs. 3 & 4 of his plate represent the original specimen. But these figures depict a wonderfully-perfect shell, and can only be regarded as an imaginative restoration.

## EXPLANATION OF PLATE I.

### Avonian Corals and Brachiopods from the Midland Area.

[All the figured specimens are preserved in the Author's collection; and they are shown of the natural size, except where otherwise stated.]

Fig. 1. *Dibunophyllum derbiense*, sp. nov. (p. 75). Horizontal section. $D_2$ subzone; Monsal Dale (Derbyshire).

2. *Dibunophyllum matlockense*, sp. nov. (p. 74). Horizontal section. $D_2$ subzone; near Wensley (Derbyshire).

3. *Koninckophyllum proprium*, sp. nov. (p. 70). Horizontal section; × 1·36. $D_2$ subzone; near Wensley (Derbyshire).

4. *Clisiophyllum* aff. *M'Coyanum*, Thomson (p. 73). Horizontal section. $D_2$ subzone; Darleybridge (Derbyshire).

5. *Lonsdalia duplicata* (Mart.) (p. 72). Horizontal section. $D_2$ subzone; Monsal Dale (Derbyshire).

Figs. 6 a & 6 b. *Productus setosus*, Phil., var. *tissingtonensis*, nov. (p. 77). $D_3$ subzone; Tissington (Derbyshire).

Fig. 6 a = Convex valve; fig. 6 b = Another specimen: view of frontal portion of a convex valve, to show the nature of the ribbing. (Mesial fold imperfectly preserved); × 1·1.

Figs. 7 a & 7 b. *Chonetes compressa*, nom. nov. (p. 78). $D_2$ subzone, Wirksworth (Derbyshire).

Fig. 7 a = Pedicle-valve (imperfect); fig. 7 b = Another specimen, brachial valve.

## DISCUSSION.

Dr. WHEELTON HIND congratulated the Author on his detailed and accurate work. He felt most pleased that the Author's researches had completely vindicated the speaker's previous publications on the area in question and on North Wales. He had no adverse criticism to make, but would discuss the important bearing of details. As to North Wales, at the top of $D_2$ lithological structure varied considerably on the same horizon, and it was impossible to map by lithology. The cherts might replace any part of the series $D_2$, and were evidently not original depositions. The true cherts were chiefly found in the upper part of the *Dibunophyllum*-Zone, but occasionally some of the Pendleside Limestones were very cherty.

The very fossiliferous deposits of Park Hill, Wetton, etc., in the *Lonsdalia*-Zone were correctly referred to that horizon. The speaker had always regarded them as shell-banks, and to that extent original. All kinds of fossils, which must have inhabited different bathymetrical zones, with others which undoubtedly lived in the shell-bank, were jumbled up together without any definite stratification. In connexion with these beds, the speaker alluded to beds of rolled and water-worn shells at Castleton and other places outside the area now dealt with.

There could be no doubt that the succession in North Staffordshire was similar to that in North Wales, and that both areas belonged to the same province.

The pre-Carboniferous physiography of the area was an interesting question, for in Derbyshire the *Dibunophyllum*-Zone, the Pendleside

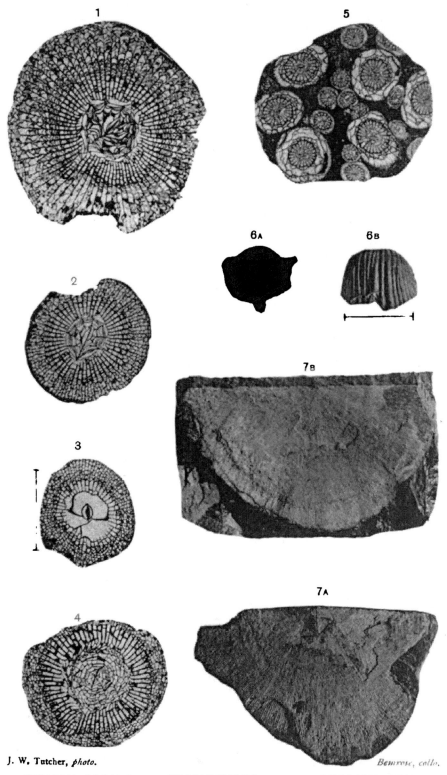

J. W. Tutcher, *photo.*

*Bemrose, collo.*

AVONIAN CORALS AND BRACHIOPODS FROM THE MIDLAND AREA.

Series, and the Millstone Grits were all at the maximum thickness, and thinned away eastwards, westwards, and southwards.

It was difficult to compare the Derbyshire and Bristol Carboniferous areas because, although in each there was a complete conformable Carboniferous succession, yet the question remained; what was happening in the South-Western Province?—where the succession was

Coal-Measures,
Millstone Grit = *Cyathaxonia*-Beds, *fide* Sibly,
D₂,

while the several thousand feet of detrital matter, represented by the Pendleside Series and Millstone Grits, were being laid down in the Derbyshire area ; the Coal-Measures of Bristol being, if anything, higher than the Lower Coal-Measures of Staffordshire.

Mr. C. B. WEDD congratulated the Author on the completion of another piece of careful Carboniferous zoning, and concurred with the results obtained, so far as they affected that part of the district with which he was familiar. It was satisfactory that the Author had been able to determine the relationship to the rest of the limestone of the puzzling brachiopod-beds of Park Hill and other places on the west side. The Author had referred to the lithological changes that took place between the west and east sides, particularly in the greater development of cherty limestone at the top on the west side. The matter needed further research in its relation to faunal distribution.

The speaker pointed out an apparently great thickening of the $D_2$ subzone in the north-west of the region, as compared with the south-east—where that subzone was only about 200 feet thick, as defined by the incoming of the *Cyathaxonia*-fauna above and by the horizon of the lower lava of Matlock below. Just above that lava the $D_2$ coral-fauna was usually abundant, while he had not found it lower.

The Author had mentioned two local unconformities at the junction of the limestone with the overlying shales. One of these at Darley Dale showed an anticlinal dome of limestone dissected by quarrying operations. If stripped of the shale above, the dome would have a knoll-like aspect. On the north and east sides these shales, nearly horizontal, overstepped the denuded edge of the cherty limestone (there normally about 50 feet thick) on to the white limestone below.

Mr. J. A. DOUGLAS commented on the extreme thickness of the *Dibunophyllum*-Zone in the Midland District, as being interesting in connexion with some recent work that he had been doing on the Carboniferous Limestone in the West of Ireland (Co. Clare). The general succession there was :—

|  |  | *Thickness in feet.* |
|---|---|---|
| Upper Limestone | | 1900 |
| Lower { unstratified | | 750 |
| { stratified | | 450 |
| Lower Limestone-Shales | | 150 |
| | Total | 3250 |

The top of $Z_1$ subzone was found at the top of the Lower Limestone-Shales, and Horizon $\gamma$ in the middle of the stratified Lower Limestone. There remained about 2750 feet to be accounted for by the three remaining zones. In the Rush sequence on the eastern coast of Ireland, the following thicknesses had been determined by Dr. Vaughan and Dr. Matley:

|  | Feet. |
| --- | --- |
| *Seminula*-Zone | 440 |
| *Syringothyris*-Zone | 870 |
|  | 1310 |

Assuming a somewhat similar succession in Co. Clare, the thickness of the *Dibunophyllum*-Zone would be about 1440 feet. This hypothetical calculation seemed to fit in with the observed faunal succession: the thickness of the limestone in North Clare was about 1500 feet, and appeared to include all three *Dibunophyllum*-subzones—from the top of the *Seminula* to the *Cyathaxonia*-subzone. The speaker also commented on the sudden reappearance of *Zaphrentis* in the uppermost beds, after dying out at the top of the *Zaphrentis*-Zone.

Prof. E. J. GARWOOD congratulated the Author most heartily on the accomplishment of a very successful piece of work. As the hour was very late, and there was another interesting paper to be read, he would only ask the Author one question. Did he consider the '*Cyathaxonia*-Beds' of his district to be the equivalent of any part of the typical Yoredale Series of the Pennine Chain, as the speaker had recently found *Cyathaxonia*-Beds above the '*Latissima*'-Bed in the typical Yoredale area?

The AUTHOR thanked the Fellows for the cordial reception given to his paper. He remarked on the interesting nature of Mr. Douglas's brief description of the Carboniferous Limestone in the West of Ireland. Replying to Prof. Garwood's question, he stated that he had no personal acquaintance with the Yoredale sequence: but the discovery in that sequence of *Cyathaxonia*-Beds above beds with a $D_2$ fauna clearly indicated the equivalence of some part of the Yoredale Series to the *Cyathaxonia*-subzone of the Midland area.

5. *On a* COLLECTION *of* FOSSIL PLANTS *from* SOUTH AFRICA.  By
ALBERT CHARLES SEWARD, M.A., F.R.S., F.L.S., F.G.S., Pro-
fessor of Botany in the University of Cambridge. (Read
November 6th, 1907.)

[PLATES II–VIII.]

CONTENTS.

|                                    | Page |
|------------------------------------|------|
| I. Introduction                    | 83   |
| II. Description of the Specimens   | 85   |
| III. Conclusion                    | 104  |
| IV. Bibliography                   | 105  |

## I. INTRODUCTION.

SINCE the publication of my account of the ' Fossil Floras of Cape
Colony' in the fourth volume of the 'Annals of the South African
Museum' (1903) additional records of some of the floras have been
obtained from several localities by members of the Geological
Survey of that Colony. It is this recently-acquired material,
forwarded to me for examination by the Director of the geological
staff, Mr. A. W. Rogers, which forms the subject of the present
communication. The majority of the specimens were collected
from the Molteno Beds and from the Burghersdorp Beds; a few
were obtained from the Uitenhage Series, a higher geological
horizon; and others from the Lower Karroo rocks. The Lower
Karroo plants are dealt with in a separate paper by Mr. Leslie and
myself on the Vereeniging flora [1]; the Uitenhage species are described elsewhere.[2] With the exception of *Schizoneura africana*,
a Permian species from the lowest beds of the Beaufort Series,
we are now concerned with the Molteno and Burghersdorp species
alone.

It is customary to divide the Karroo system of Cape Colony into
three sections [3]: the Lower Karroo, comprising, in ascending order,
the Dwyka Series and the Ecca Series; the Middle Karroo or
Beaufort Series; and the Upper Karroo or Stormberg Series. The
uppermost strata of the Beaufort Series have been named the
Burghersdorp Beds, from the typical development of the rocks
in the neighbourhood of Burghersdorp, a small town about 30 miles
south of the frontier of the Orange-River Colony, on the railway
which runs from East London to the Transvaal. The Molteno
Beds, so named from the town of Molteno, about 25 miles south
of Burghersdorp, are placed at the base of the Stormberg Series,
the sequence being, then, as follows :—

---

[1] Seward & Leslie (08). The numerals in parentheses after authors' names
refer to the dates in the Bibliography, p. 105.

[2] Seward (07*).

[3] Rogers (05) p. 147; Hatch & Corstophine (05) table facing p. 33.

| | |
|---|---|
| UPPER KARROO or STORMBERG SERIES. | Volcanic Beds. Cave Sandstones. Red Beds. Molteno Beds. |
| MIDDLE KARROO or BEAUFORT SERIES. | Burghersdorp Beds. |

In his account of the 'Geological Survey of the Divisions of Aliwal North, Herschel, Barkley East, and part of Wodehouse,' Mr. Du Toit writes [1] :—

'There is a marked lithological difference between the Burghersdorp and the Molteno Beds. Red and purple are the predominating tints of the softer rocks in the lower formation, and there are never any carbonaceous beds. Consequently it has been thought necessary to draw the dividing-line at the summit of these bright-coloured rocks and place them in the Beaufort Series. It must be admitted that to our present knowledge this boundary-line is not coincident with one and the same stratigraphical horizon throughout, as the colouring occasionally rises very close to that important geological bench-mark the 'Indwe Sandstone,' while at other places it is very much below it. . . . The age of the Burghersdorp Beds is proved by the fossils they contain. The presence of the labyrinthodonts and fishes indicates that the formation is homotaxial with the Keuper (Upper Trias) of Europe. The Burghersdorp Beds may also be considered to be equivalent to the Hawkesbury Series of New South Wales, which also contains labyrinthodont-remains and fishes of not only the same genera, but of closely allied species. The age of the Australian formation is now well established as being Upper Triassic. . . . The presence of lepidodendroid stems [2] in the Burghersdorp Beds is interesting as showing we have here surviving one of the typical Palæozoic types.'

This reference to *Lepidodendron*-stems is probably based upon specimens from Aliwal North, which, although presenting a superficial resemblance to such stems, are more likely to be gymnospermous, as pointed out in the description of a fossil for which the name *Strobilites laxus* is suggested.[3] Mr. Du Toit continues :—

'The evidence of the plants of the Molteno Beds points to their being of Rhætic age,[4] which thus confirms the view that the Burghersdorp Beds are Upper Triassic. The Molteno Beds may thus be the equivalent of the Wianamatta Series of New South Wales.'

For further information in regard to the stratigraphy of the rocks from which the plants were collected, reference should be made to the Annual Reports of the Geological Commission of the Cape of Good Hope, and more particularly to the accounts of surveys by Mr. Du Toit, in which mention is made of the several localities where the plant-yielding beds have been examined.[5] It would seem that the boundary between the Burghersdorp and the Molteno Beds is not always clearly defined : a comparison of the two floras is made in the concluding section of this paper (pp. 104–105), from which it will appear that certain species are common to both horizons.

Mr. Du Toit has drawn my attention to the occurrence of a zone of transition between the Molteno and the Burghersdorp Beds,

[1] A. L. Du Toit (05) pp. 81–82.      [2] See p. 100 of the present paper.
[3] See p. 101.      [4] Seward (03).      [5] A. L. Du Toit (05) & (06).

which was carefully searched for fossils in order to discover whether any evidence existed of a palæontological break between the two series. The species *Thinnfeldia sphenopteroides*, sp. nov., Cala River, *Tæniopteris Carruthersi*, Indwe R., and *Pterophyllum* sp., cf. *Pt. Tietzii*, Kraai-River Bridge, were obtained from this transition-zone within 30 or 40 feet of the line taken as the base of the Molteno Beds. It is noteworthy that two of these are common to the Molteno and to the Burghersdorp Beds.

Molteno Beds.—Omitting for the present the majority of the plants previously recorded from the Molteno Beds, the following are the species now described from this horizon :—

*Schizoneura Carrerei*, Zeill. Near Dordrecht.
*Schizoneura* sp. Basutoland.
*Thinnfeldia odontopteroides* (Morr.). Vaalbank; near Jamestown; Konings Kroon, Elliot.
*Thinnfeldia* sp. Maudesley, Lady Grey.
*Thinnfeldia sphenopteroides*, sp. nov. Konings Kroon, Elliot.

*Tæniopteris Carruthersi*, Ten. Woods. Konings Kroon, Elliot.
*Cladophlebis (Todites) Rœsserti* (Presl). Indwe River.
*Pterophyllum* sp. Konings Kroon, Elliot.
*Baiera moltenensis*, sp. nov. Near Dordrecht.

The following are the species described from the Burghersdorp Beds. Those that are marked with an asterisk appear to be identical with Molteno species :—

*Schizoneura* sp. Burghersdorp.
*Thinnfeldia sphenopteroides*, sp. nov. Cala River, 2 miles west of Cala.
*Tæniopteris Carruthersi*, Ten. Woods. Indwe River.
*Danæopsis Hughesi*, Feistm. Lady Frere.
*Odontopteris Browni*, sp. nov. Aliwal North.

*Strobilites laxus*, sp. nov. Orange River, opposite Aliwal North.
*Pterophyllum* sp., cf. *Pt. Tietzii*, Schenk. Kraai-River Bridge, Aliwal North.
*Stigmatodendron dubium*, sp. nov. Aliwal North.

## II. DESCRIPTION OF THE SPECIMENS.

### Group EQUISETALES.

#### Genus SCHIZONEURA.

Fossils referred to this genus have been collected from three localities: the Molteno Beds, 1 mile from Dordrecht; Basutoland; and Burghersdorp.

SCHIZONEURA CARREREI, Zeill.    (Pl. II, fig. 1.)

The Dordrecht specimen consists of portions of slender branches bearing numerous, long, filiform leaves; the axis is characterized by narrow and slightly-prominent ribs and indistinctly-marked nodal regions (Pl. II, fig. 1). There is no doubt as to the identity of the specimen represented in the figure with the type previously described from the Molteno Beds as *Sch. Krasseri*.[1] The leaves, some of which are at least 6 centimetres long and not more than 1 millimetre broad, correspond exactly to those borne on Prof. Zeiller's species from Tongking, which he originally described as *Phyllotheca indica* and afterwards, from the examination of better material, assigned to a new species *Sch. Carrerei*.[2] The opinion previously expressed as to the probable identity of the South African and Tongking plants receives support from the discovery of the leaf-bearing specimens, and it is therefore advisable to discard the name *Sch. Krasseri* in favour of *Sch. Carrerei*.

SCHIZONEURA sp. *a*.    (Pl. III, figs. 1 & 2.)

The specimen from the Burghersdorp Beds represented in Pl. III, fig. 1, is a cast of a partly-flattened stem 5 centimetres in diameter, showing part of a pith-cast with numerous internodal ribs; separated from it by 3 to 4 millimetres of rock we have an impression of the external surface of the plant. The surface is smooth on one part of the fossil, while on the other it is folded into ridges which probably do not represent original features. On the nodal line are two well-defined scars, and traces of more can be seen on the folded region.

Other examples from the Burghersdorp Beds of Burghersdorp consist of portions of pith-casts, with transverse grooves marking the nodal regions and branch-scars as circular depressions. The ridges are, for the most part, continuous from one internode to the next. Fig. 2 shows a cast from Burghersdorp, with an internode 7 centimetres long, characterized by very small and crowded ribs.

Some sandstone-casts from the Stormberg Beds of Basutoland, though less distinctly preserved, appear to be indistinguishable from the Burghersdorp specimens. In the absence of leaves it is impossible to say whether the two sets of casts are specifically identical with the Molteno fossils from Dordrecht (Pl. II, fig. 1); in the narrowness of the ribs there is a close agreement, but this in itself need not denote specific identity.

SCHIZONEURA sp. *β*.

A somewhat different type of cast from the Stormberg Beds of Basutoland is represented on a reduced scale (rather less than three-quarters of the natural size) in fig. 1 (p. 87). This specimen, if found in Palæozoic rocks in Europe, would doubtless be named *Calamites*. The middle internode has a length of 7 centimetres; the ribs vary a little in breadth, but are less numerous and broader than those of *Sch. Carrerei*. Circular depressions on one of the nodal lines indicate the position of branches. The internodal ridges and grooves are in some cases continuous from one internode to the next, but others exhibit a marked alternation; the continuity of the ribs is more clearly seen on the reverse side of the specimen. There is no indication of any infranodal canals or of

[1] Seward (03) p. 48 & pl. ix, figs. 5–6.
[2] Zeiller (02) p. 137 & pls. xxxvi–xxxviii; (82) p. 301 & pl. x, figs. 1–2.

leaf-scars; the absence of the latter may well be due to the nature of the material of which the fossil consists. At the tapered end some of the ridges tend to converge; below the narrowest region, where they are much less distinct, their course is very irregular, and they become oblique or almost horizontal. It is possible that the rapid narrowing of the cast is due to the decrease in diameter of the pith at the junction of two axes of the plant, as in the genus *Calamites*. In the absence of leaves we cannot speak with certainty as to the affinity of the fossil, but the presumption is in favour of the genus *Schizoneura*.

Fig. 1.—Schizoneura *sp.* β (*pith-cast, rather less than three-quarters of the natural size*).

As regards the comparison of these different examples of *Schizoneura* with species from other parts of the world: *Sch. Carrerei* has been fully described by Prof. Zeiller[1] and recorded from Tongking, China,[2] and South Africa. It is possible that a portion of a pith-cast figured by Schenk from Rhætic rocks of Persia[3] may be identical with this species.

The occurrence of long and narrow leaves in connection with some Rhætic specimens doubtfully identified by Prof. Nathorst[4] with *Sch. hoerensis* (His.) suggests the possibility of a close affinity between that species and the African plant. Casts from Jurassic strata

[1] Zeiller (02) p. 137 & pls. xxxvi–xxxviii.
[2] Krasser (00) p. 146 & pl. iii, figs. 1–3 *a*.
[3] Schenk (87) pl. viii, fig. 48.
[4] Nathorst (78) pp. 24–26 & pl. x, figs. 6–8.

of China[1] have recently been described as identical with the Scanian species. Another instance of the occurrence of a similar form of cast is afforded by a specimen from the island of Kotelny, figured by Prof. Nathorst[2] as *Schizoneura* sp., which he compares with a fossil figured by Mr. Newton & Dr. Teall from Franz-Josef Land as *Phyllotheca.*[3]

The sandstone-cast represented in Pl. III, fig. 1, bears a striking resemblance to Equisetaceous stems figured by several authors from the Bunter Beds of the Vosges[4] and by Heer from Switzerland[5] as *Calamites* or *Equisetum Mougeotii.* In the European species the regularity of the ribs is probably the result of the presence of strands of strengthening tissue in the stem; but in the Burghersdorp specimens (Pl. III, fig. 1) the ridges are confined to a part of the surface. Although there appear to be no essential differences between the European Triassic species and the African type, we are hardly justified in assuming specific identity. There is no reason to suppose that several species of the genus may not appear to be identical, if represented only by their pith-casts and impressions of a leafless cortex.

In the case of mere pith-casts, attempts at accurate determination must be even more futile. As examples of some of the many specimens bearing a resemblance to those from Burghersdorp, mention may be made of *Calamites Guembeli*[6] figured by Schenk from the Rhætic of Franconia (a species regarded by Prof. Nathorst[7] as identical with *Schizoneura hoerensis*), and of *Equisetites arenaceus* as figured by Schœnlein[8] from the Keuper of Germany.

The larger cast with broader ribs represented in text-fig. 1 (p. 87) may be compared with some of the specimens figured as *E. Mougeotii,*[9] and with a New Mexican fossil which Mr. Fontaine has named *E. Knowltoni.*[10] A more striking similarity is, however, presented by a tapered pith-cast figured by Mr. Etheridge, Jun.[11] from the Hawkesbury Sandstone of Port Jackson.

As regards the bearing of these comparisons on the question of geological correlation, *Schizoneura Carrerei* is a Rhætic species; but the other specimens to which I have not given a specific designation are of comparatively-little value as indices of age—they favour a reference of the rocks to a Rhætic or to a somewhat lower horizon.

The fossils from Basutoland, presented to the South African Museum by Dr. Long, were obtained from a locality beyond Mafeking

[1] Yokoyama (06) pp. 29–30 & pl. vii, fig. 10.
[2] Nathorst (07) p. 3 & pl. i, fig. 1.
[3] Newton & Teall (97) p. 504 & pl. xli, figs. 1–3.
[4] Schimper (74) pl. xii; Schimper & Mougeot (44) pl. xxix.
[5] Heer (76ᵃ) pl. xxvii, fig. 10.
[6] Schenk (67) pl. i, figs. 8–10.
[7] Nathorst (78) pp. 24, 25.
[8] Schœnlein & Schenk (65) pl. ii; Jæger (27) pl. iii.
[9] Schimper (74) pl. xii, fig. 4.
[10] Fontaine & Knowlton (90) p. 283 & pls. xxiii–xxiv.
[11] Etheridge (90) pl. xvii.

and from the Little Caledon River. The Stormberg Series is known to be represented in Basutoland, and these *Schizoneura*-casts may, therefore, be of Stormberg age.

## SCHIZONEURA AFRICANA, Feistm. (Permian.)

In an appendix to Bain's paper on the geology of Southern Africa, Sir Joseph Hooker[1] described and figured a fossil which was found by Bain in the Roggeveld (Fish River); no name was proposed for the specimen. As Mr. Arber[2] points out in his recent Catalogue, Feistmantel referred the Fish-River fossil with some hesitation to the genus *Schizoneura*, naming it *Sch. (?) africana*.

Fig. 2.—Schizoneura africana, *Feistmantel : torn leaves and section of stem, three-fifths of the natural size.*

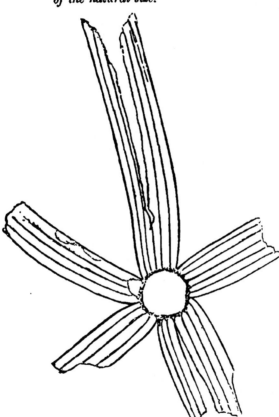

The specimen represented in fig. 2 was collected by Mr. Rogers from the lowest beds of the Beaufort Series (Bain's locality), assigned to a Permian horizon. There can be no doubt as to the identity of this and other specimens found by Rogers with the original specimen figured by Sir Joseph Hooker. The stem extends vertically through the rock, and on the exposed surface shown in the drawing portions of five leaves are seen attached to a node. The leaves consist of linear laminæ, with very distinct and rather prominent parallel veins, united to form a narrow collar in connexion with the stem.

Mr. A. W. Rogers calls my attention to the vertical position of the stems of this plant, which, as he points out, conveys the impression of stems preserved in their position of growth.

[1] Bain (52) p. 227 & pl. xxviii, fig. 1.
[2] Arber (05) p. 13.

The stem shown in the figure has a diameter of 1·4 centimetres ; the longest leaf measures 8 centimetres and is 1·4 cm. broad. A comparison of this specimen with the figures given by Feistmantel of *Sch. gondwanensis*[1] from the Talchir, Damuda, and Panchet Series of India leads one to suggest a possible identity ; the resemblance is very close, and there can be little doubt as to the relationship, if not identity, of the African and Indian plants.


## FILICALES.

Having regard to the recent demonstration of the impossibility of identifying ferns by the characters of sterile leaves or even by means of fertile specimens which do not exhibit reproductive organs in a good state of preservation, it is with considerable hesitation that such a genus as *Thinnfeldia* is included in the Filicales.


### Genus THINNFELDIA.[2]

Attention has elsewhere been called to the close resemblance between plants described under the names *Thinnfeldia, Ptilozamites, Ctenopteris, Cycadopteris, Lomatopteris* ; I have suggested that the use of different names has led to an exaggeration of slight differences which are in many cases of little importance.[3] Ettingshausen's genus *Thinnfeldia*, as represented by the type-species *Th. rhomboidalis* and by the southern type *Th. odontopteroides* (Morr.), is characterized by short and broad pinnules borne on long linear pinnæ as well as directly on the rachis of bipinnate fronds, and by the apparent dichotomy of the frond-axis (Pl. IV, fig. 1). The venation exhibits considerable variation : it is described as being like that of *Alethopteris*, but with a less-developed midrib ; or, if a median vein is not present, it is characterized by the secondary veins being given off from a common vascular branch from the pinna-axis.[4] Neither definition adequately describes the venation of *Thinnfeldia*-pinnules. In the segments of *Th. rhomboidalis* and of *Th. odontopteroides* there may be a distinct midrib, from which forked lateral branches arise at an acute angle ; but in pinnules of the latter species a midrib is frequently absent, and when this is the case the veins by no means always arise from one common vascular strand. In the pinnule represented in text-fig. 3 B (p. 91), some of the veins are clearly branches of the axis of the pinna, while the greater number are branches from a common strand. In the ultimate segment shown in text-fig. 3 A, the veins appear to be all independent and given off direct from the axis of the pinna. We may describe the pinnules of *Th. odontopteroides* (to deal with one species for the sake of clearness) as possessing a midrib which dies out towards the apex of the lamina, and gives off either simple or

[1] Feistmantel (79) pl. i, figs. 2 & 3.          [2] Ettingshausen (52) p. 2.
[3] Seward (03) pp. 51–52 ; (04) pp. 174–75 & figs. 28–29 (pl. xvii).
[4] Zeiller (00) p. 97 ; Potonié (99) p. 148.

forked secondary veins; or as possessing several simple or dichotomously branched veins, which are direct branches from the axis
of the pinna or rachis; or, finally, as exhibiting a combination of
these types, the veins being in part branches of one or more larger
veins and in part direct offshoots of the pinna-axis.    Text-
figures 3 A–3 D (below) illustrate these different forms of venation
in the pinnules of *Thinnfeldia.*

In some of the larger specimens of the genus another character
is exhibited : namely, the apparent dichotomy of the main axis of

Fig. 3.—*Pinnules of* Thinnfeldia odontopteroides *(A–D) and*
Ptilozamites *(E) showing venation.*

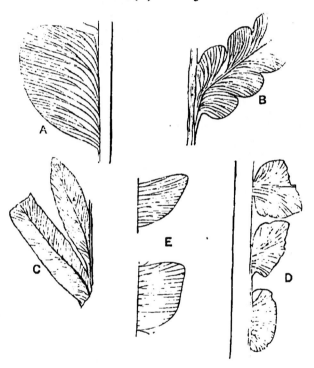

[A–D are South African specimens; E is after Nathorst.]

the frond; this is well shown in Feistmantel's figures of *Th. odontopteroides* [1] and in South African examples of the same species.

To turn to *Ctenopteris* and *Ptilozamites* : the former name,
originally suggested by Brongniart for the Liassic plant *Ct. cycadea,* [2]
is used in preference to the term *Ctenozamites,* proposed by Prof.
Nathorst, [3] on the ground of priority.   These generic names are applied

[1] Feistmantel (90) pls. xxiii–xxv, &c.
[2] Saporta (73) pp. 351, 352.        [3] Nathorst (78) p. 122.

to fronds either simple or branched, which in habit and in the
form of the ultimate segments agree very closely with *Thinnfeldia*.
Prof. Nathorst's species from the Rhætic of Scania and Prof. Zeiller's
specimens from Tongking may suffice as examples. It would seem
that the chief distinguishing feature between these fronds and those
of *Thinnfeldia* is in the venation. In *Ptilozamites* and *Ctenopteris*
the pinnules are without a midrib, and the simple or forked veins
are all direct branches from the axis of the pinna or rachis; this
type of venation is represented in pinnules of *Ptilozamites* reproduced
from Nathorst[1] in fig. 3 E (p. 91). We have seen that a pinnule of
*Thinnfeldia* may also exhibit the same form of venation (figs. 3 A
& 3 D); but, as a rule, the veins are found to curve downwards at
the base of the lamina before coming into contact with the axis of
the pinna (fig. 3 B). As our knowledge of the fructification[2] of the
genera that have been mentioned is very incomplete or almost *nil*,
we must rely on vegetative characters for distinguishing marks; and
it is necessary to decide how far these supply criteria for generic
distinctions. Granting that, in many cases, the venation of the
ultimate segments furnishes a means of separating *Thinnfeldia* from
*Ctenopteris* and *Ptilozamites*, it is more than doubtful whether these
differences, which are not constant, can be accepted as of generic
rank. Without attempting a revision of the various species referred
to the genera *Ptilozamites*, *Ctenopteris*, *Cycadopteris*, and *Thinnfeldia*,.
I would express the opinion that *Ctenopteris Sarrani* of Zeiller[3] is
not generically distinct from *Thinnfeldia odontopteroides* as figured
by Feistmantel and other authors from Australia and elsewhere.

THINNFELDIA ODONTOPTEROIDES (Morris). (Pl. IV, fig. 1 & Pl. V,
        fig. 1.)

The variable character of this species as regards the size and
shape of the segments and their venation, alluded to in my former
paper on African plants and pointed out by other writers,[4] renders the
task of delimiting species almost hopeless when we have to trust to
fragments of sterile pinnæ. Some of the examples of *Thinnfeldia*
included in the collection submitted to me are unquestionably
specifically identical with specimens already figured from South
Africa, while others (text-fig. 3 & Pl. V, fig. 1) are characterized
by broader leaflets and are clearly identical with the larger fronds
described by Feistmantel[5] from the Hawkesbury Series of New
South Wales. It is possible that more than one species is represented, but the occurrence of intermediate forms favours the use of
the designation *Th. odontopteroides* in a comprehensive sense.

I would, however, point out that it is not improbable that under
the designation *Th. odontopteroides* more than one specific type is
included. While recognizing this possibility, I do not at present

[1] Nathorst (78) pl. xii, figs. 1 *b* & 1 *c* (*Ptilozamites Heeri*, Nath.).
[2] Raciborski (94) p. 206 & pl. xx, figs. 1-2; Zeiller (00) p. 97.
[3] Zeiller (02) p. 53 & pls. vi-viii.
[4] Feistmantel (90) p. 104; Shirley (98) p. 21.    [5] Feistmantel (90) pl. xxiv.

consider the available data sufficient to enable us to draw a distinction between variations within one species and differences worthy of specific rank.

The piece of frond represented in Pl. IV, fig. 1 (from the Molteno Beds of Konings Kroon) has leaflets identical with those shown in fig. 8, pl. vii, of my former paper [1] ; but it exhibits an additional feature in the dichotomy of the frond-axis, a character which Potonié and other authors are no doubt correct in considering as primitive. Pl. V, fig. 1 illustrates an example of a leaf from Vaalbank, of which the rachis bears pinnæ with pinnules of the larger type characterized by numerous forked veins. Pinnules are borne also on the rachis. In another specimen from the same locality the segments are still larger, one of them (fig. 3 A, p. 91) having a length of 1·8 centimetres and a breadth of 1·5 cm.; this and other fragments bear a striking resemblance to Feistmantel's larger fronds from New South Wales. Several examples, such as that shown in text-figs. 3 B & 4, demonstrate the passage, from linear segments with a mid-rib giving off clusters of forked veins and with a lamina showing different degrees of lobing, to pinnæ with short and broad ultimate segments agreeing in all respects with those represented in Pl. V, fig. 1. The pinnule shown in fig. 3 C (p. 91) occurs on an axis which bears also segments identical with those represented in fig. 3 B, and thus forms a connecting-link between the types of frond illustrated in Pl. IV,

Fig. 4.—Thinnfeldia odontopteroides (*four-fifths of the natural size*).

---

[1] Seward (03) p. 55.

fig. 1 & Pl. V, fig. 1. The three pinnules attached to a piece of rachis shown in fig. 3 D (p. 91) serve as examples of a passage, from several slightly-divergent veins springing direct from the rachis, to a type of venation characterized by a midrib giving off forked secondary veins.

In his Tongking Flora, Prof. Zeiller figures some pieces of pinnæ which he names *Pecopteris (Bernoullia!)* sp.[1]; these bear so close a resemblance to entire or slightly-lobed segments of *Th. odontopteroides* like those figured in text-fig. 4 (p. 93), that one is inclined to suggest a specific identity. It is noticeable that, in the Swiss Keuper fern *Bernoullia helvetica*, as figured by Heer[2] and by Dr. Leuthardt,[3] the venation is distinct from that of *Thinnfeldia*. The smaller examples of *Th. odontopteroides* also agree very closely in habit with *Cycadopteris heterophylla*, Zig., as figured by Dr. Raciborski[4] from Poland and by De Zigno[5] from Jurassic rocks of Italy. The fossil described by Prof. Szajnocha as *Cardiopteris Zuberi*[6] from Rhætic rocks of Cacheuta in the Argentine Republic should in all probability be referred to the larger form of *Th. odontopteroides* or to Zeiller's Tongking species *Ctenopteris Sarrani*. A comparison may also be made with *Th. indica* var. *media*, figured by Mr. Shirley[7] from the Ipswich Beds of Queensland; and with *Th. odontopteroides* var. *normalis*[8] of the same author, which is probably identical with the larger form of the South African plant. Specimens which may be identical with *Th. odontopteroides* are recorded by Feistmantel[9] from more than one locality in India.

### Thinnfeldia sphenopteroides, sp. nov.   (Pl. IV, fig. 2 & Pl. V, fig. 2.)

The collection includes two specimens which are referred, with some hesitation, to *Thinnfeldia*; the larger of the two is from the Molteno Beds of Konings Kroon (Pl. V, fig. 2), and a second specimen (Pl. IV, fig. 2) was obtained from the Burghersdorp Beds, 2 miles west of Cala, on the Cala River. I am inclined to regard these specimens as specifically identical. The specimen represented in Pl. IV, fig. 2 has a fairly-broad rachis 6·5 centimetres long, giving off alternate pinnæ at a wide angle. The upper pinnæ bear entire pinnules which reach a length of 8 millimetres; faintly-preserved secondary veins are given off from a midrib at an acute angle. The lower pinnæ have acuminate segments with a serrate edge, the teeth forming in some cases distinct pinnules. This specimen occurs on the reverse side of the rock upon which the

[1] Zeiller (02) p. 34 & pl. i, figs. 14–16.
[2] Heer (76*) pl. xxxviii, figs. 1–6.
[3] Leuthardt (04) vol. xxxi & pls. xix–xx.
[4] Raciborski (94) pl. vi, fig. 28.
[5] Zigno (56) vol. i, p. 158 & pl. xviii; see also Saporta (73) pl. lix.
[6] Szajnocha (88) p. 233 & pl. ii, fig. 1.
[7] Shirley (98) pl. v, fig. 1.
[8] *Ibid.* pl. xi.
[9] Feistmantel (81) p. 85 & pl. xxiii A, figs. 7–9.

example of *Th. odontopteroides* represented in Pl. IV, fig. 1 is preserved. The Cala-River specimen (Pl. V, fig. 2) consists of part of a pinna 15 centimetres long, bearing obliquely-attached pinnules entire in the apical portion of the pinna, but for the most part lobed. The midrib is clearly defined, but the lateral veins are only faintly indicated in a few places.

As regards the affinity of the plant, there is a close resemblance in habit, which may amount to specific identity, with *Th. incisa* figured by Saporta [1] from the Lower Lias of France, and by Count H. zu Solms-Laubach [2] from the Rhætic of Chile. A dichotomously-branched piece of a frond, described by Feistmantel, from New South Wales, as *Gleichenia dubia*,[3] bears some resemblance to *Thinnfeldia sphenopteroides*.

On the other hand, it is possible that these fossils should be placed in the genus *Sphenopteris*, many species of which they resemble. The discovery of more complete examples may confirm this; but the general appearance of the pinnæ, with their stout axes, would seem to favour the choice of *Thinnfeldia*.

### Thinnfeldia sp. (Pl. II, figs. 2 & 3.)

The collection includes several pieces of pinnæ from the Molteno Beds of Maudesley, Lady Grey, which appear to be specifically distinct from the other specimens referred to *Thinnfeldia*; they are too small to justify the institution of a new name, and it is not clear whether they are more correctly named *Thinnfeldia* or *Pachypteris*.[4]

The example shown in Pl. II, fig. 2 consists of a winged axis, bearing entire oblique pinnules, in each of which there appear to be a few diverging veins.. Pl. II, fig. 3 represents a fragment in which the lobes are provided with dichotomously-branched veins arising as a single strand from the axis of the pinna. These fragments may all belong to one species; but the identification of terminal pieces of pinnæ must be attended with considerable risk of error.

### Genus DANÆOPSIS.

### Danæopsis Hughesi, Feistm. (Pl. VI & text-fig. 5, p. 96.)

The very imperfect impression from the Burghersdorp Beds of Lady Frere, 1500 feet below the Molteno Beds, represented in Pl. VI (natural size), consists of part of a rachis with portions of pinnæ, the longest of which measures 14 centimetres in length. The axis of each pinna forms the midrib of a broadly-linear segment attached to the rachis by the whole of the base. None of the segments are complete; the lamina, which reaches a breadth of 3·3 centimetres, is entire or slightly lobed. It is impossible to

[1] Saporta (73) pl. xlii.
[2] Solms-Laubach (99) pp 599–600 & pl. xiv, figs. 3–4.
[3] Feistmantel (90) p. 111 & pl. xxvi. fig. 3.
[4] Cf. *Dichopteris visianica*, Zigno (56) vol. i, pls. xii & xiii.

make any definite statement as to venation, but in one place there is an indication of crowded veins almost at right angles to the axis of a pinna.

A second example of what is regarded as the same type is shown as a diagrammatic sketch in text-fig. 5. This specimen is from the Burghersdorp Beds of Lady Frere; the main axis is 38·5 centimetres in length, and is characterized by an apparent dichotomy near the base. The pinnæ are less distinctly preserved than in the smaller example; one arm of the forked rachis bears a portion of a lamina, 5·5 centimetres broad and 12 cm. long; the midrib is clearly shown, but there are no signs of secondary veins. The thicker lines in the sketch indicate what are believed to be the actual outlines of the segments, as at *a* & *b*; in places the lamina appears to be lobed, but the brown iron-oxide stain representing the pinnæ is too blurred to enable one to make out the form with any degree of certainty. Portions of lamina on the rachis point to a decurrence of the segments, as in the impression shown in Pl. VI.

Fig. 5.—Danæopsis Hughesi, *Feistmantel: reduced diagram, showing the branching of the rachis.*

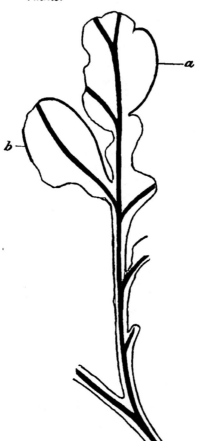

In spite of the unfavourable state of preservation of the two specimens, there can be little doubt as to their close agreement, if not specific identity, with Feistmantel's species from the Middle Gondwana rocks of India.[1] The resemblance as regards the form and size of the segments is complete, although it is impossible to say how far the venation-characters are in agreement; another common feature is the dichotomous branching of the rachis as shown in text-fig. 5, as in several of Feistmantel's illustrations of the Gondwana plant.[2] Feistmantel

[1] Feistmantel (82) p. 25, pls. iv-x & xviii-xix.
[2] Feistmantel, *op. cit.* pls. v, vi, & x.

has also figured a portion of a similar type of leaf as *Danæopsis
rajmahalensis*[1] from rocks referred to the Jurassic System; it
is, however, difficult to say how nearly allied to the older species
this very imperfect specimen from the Rajmahal Hills may be.
*D. Hughesi* has been recorded by Dr. Krasser[2] from China, and
from the Rhætic rocks of Tongking Prof. Zeiller figures the same
species.[3] The portions of pinnæ of which the latter author speaks
as *Tæniopteris* cf. *MacClellandi*[4] also exhibit a close resemblance to
the African fossil; but the type-specimens of this species, described
originally by Oldham & Morris[5] as *Stangerites MacClellandi*, are
certainly distinct from the specimens represented in Pl. VI & text-
fig. 5. The specimen described by Mr. Shirley as *Neuropteris
punctata*,[6] from the Ipswich Beds of Queensland, may well be
identical with *Danæopsis Hughesi*. Though perhaps not specifically
identical, there is a striking likeness between *D. Hughesi* and
*D. marantacea*, described by Dr. Leuthardt and by Heer[7] from the
Keuper of Basel, and recorded also from Stuttgart.[8] Fertile pinnæ
of the European type point to its affinity with the Marattiaceæ;
but no evidence is available as to the fructification of the southern
type.

## Genus ODONTOPTERIS.

ODONTOPTERIS BROWNI, sp. nov.   (Pl. VII.)

The specimen from the Burghersdorp Beds of Aliwal North,
represented in Pl. VII (three-quarters of the natural size), consists
of a portion of a frond 19 centimetres long; the rachis is indicated
by a shallow groove, 4 millimetres wide. The lamina of the
alternate pinnæ has the form of an irregularly-lobed expansion,
divided in places into distinct pinnules attached by broad bases
and provided with a midrib. The widest part of the left-hand
pinna is 3·7 centimetres broad. The rachis is flanked by a lobed
wing representing the decurrent bases of lateral branches. It is
not possible to make out the venation-characters.

It is among Permian species that we find the closest resemblance
to the species which I have named *Odontopteris Browni*, after
Mr. Alfred Brown, to whom the South African Museum is indebted
for this and several other interesting specimens from Aliwal North.
The frond described by Ad. Brongniart from the Permian of Russia
as *O. Fischeri*,[9] is also characterized by the inequality of the ultimate
segments; *O. obtusa* as figured by Weiss,[10] and *Neuropteris obliqua*,

[1] Feistmantel (77) pls. xxxviii & xlviii.
[2] Krasser (00) p. 145 & pl. ii, fig. 4.
[3] Zeiller (02) pl. ix, figs. 1 & 1 *a*.
[4] *Ibid.* pl. ix, figs. 3–5.
[5] Oldham & Morris (63) pp. 33–34 & pl. xxiii.
[6] Shirley (98) pl. xiv, fig. 2.
[7] Leuthardt (04) vol. xxxi, pl. xiii; Heer (76*) pl. xxiv, fig. 1.
[8] Schimper (74) pl. xxxvii; Saporta (73) pl. lxv.
[9] Brongniart, in Murchison's ' Russia ' (45) p. 7 & pl. A, fig. 4.
[10] Weiss (69) p. 36 & pls. ii–iii, vi.

Gœpp.,[1] are similar types of leaf.  I am not aware of any Triassic or Rhætic fossils that bear so close a resemblance to the African leaf as the Palæozoic species to which reference has been made.


### Genus CLADOPHLEBIS.

CLADOPHLEBIS (TODITES) RŒSSERTI (Presl).  (Pl. VIII.)

In the absence of fertile specimens it is better to adopt the non-committal term *Cladophlebis*, with the addition of *Todites*, as an indication of what I have little doubt is the true position of the species.

A specimen from the Molteno Beds on the Indwe River, represented in Pl. VIII, shows part of a broad rachis, 16 centimetres long, giving off linear pinnæ which must have reached a considerable length; the longest of the incomplete pinnæ is 13 centimetres long, and of comparatively-uniform breadth.  The pinnules are short and broad, in some cases slightly falcate; dichotomously-branched secondary veins spring at an acute angle from a midrib. In habit and in the venation of the ultimate segments the specimen recalls *Todites Williamsoni*[2] from Inferior-Oolite rocks, as also the Rhætic fern described by Schenk from Franconia as *Acrostichites Gœppertianus*,[3] and more recently by Prof. Zeiller under the name of *Cladophlebis (Todea) Rœsserti*[4]; the resemblance to the latter type appears close enough to warrant the use of this specific name. The African frond differs from the majority of specimens hitherto referred to this species in the somewhat smaller size of the pinnules, but this can hardly be regarded as a sufficient reason for the institution of a new name.  The leaves described by Dr. Hartz from Greenland as *Cladophlebis Rœsserti*, var. *grœnlandica*,[5] are characterized by pinnules of unusually-large size.  The Indwe fossil may be compared also with *Pecopteris Rütimeyeri*, Heer,[6] figured by Dr. Leuthardt from the Keuper of Basel; with *Lepidopteris stuttgartiensis* (Jæg.)[7] from the Keuper of Stuttgart; and with fronds figured by Mr. Fontaine from the Rhætic of Virginia.[8]


TÆNIOPTERIS CARRUTHERSI, Ten. Woods.

This species, previously described from the Molteno Beds,[9] is represented by portions of several leaves from the same beds at Konings Kroon, varying considerably in breadth, and characterized by dichoto-

---

[1] Gœppert (41) Lief. 5 & 6, pl. xi.
[2] Seward (00) pl. xv, figs. 1–3.
[3] Schenk (67) pls. v & vii.
[4] Zeiller (02) p. 38 & pls. ii–iii.
[5] Hartz (96) pp. 228–31 & pls. vii–x, xii.
[6] Leuthardt (04) vol. xxxi, pl. xv, figs. 1 & 2.
[7] Schimper (74) pl. xxxiv.
[8] Fontaine (83) pls. xi–xiv, xxvii.
[9] Seward (03) pp. 59–61; Feistmantel (89) pp. 65–66 & pl. ii, figs. 6–10 [sep. cop.].

mously-branched and simple veins given off at right angles to a prominent midrib. The example shown in fig. 6 has a broader lamina than any specimen so far figured from South Africa. Fragments of *Thinnfeldia* and *Ctenopteris* occur in association with the *Tæniopteris*-leaves.

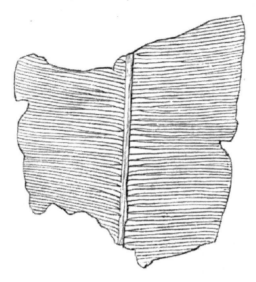

Fig. 6.—Tæniopteris Carruthersi, *Ten. Woods, natural size.*

A specimen from the Burghersdorp Beds of the Indwe River appears to be indistinguishable from the Molteno fragment.

*T. virgulata*[1] from Tongking and *T. immersa*[2] from Scania may be compared with the type from South Africa; also forms from India and elsewhere described as species of *Macrotæniopteris*.

## GINKGOALES.

### Genus BAIERA.

BAIERA MOLTENENSIS, sp. nov.   (Pl. II, fig. 4.)

In view of the variation observed in the form of the leaves of the recent species *Ginkgo biloba*, it is hopeless to attempt to discriminate, within narrow limits, between the numerous fossil examples of the genera *Ginkgo* and *Baiera*. The leaf represented in Pl. II, fig. 4 bears a close resemblance to leaves described from Jurassic and Rhætic rocks; but, as it differs from any of the specimens hitherto recorded from South Africa, it is convenient to make use of a new designation. A slender petiole terminates in a deltoid lamina, dissected into forked linear segments with numerous dichotomously-branched veins.

The only specimen in the collection (Pl. II, fig. 4) was obtained from the Molteno Beds, 2 miles north of Dordrecht (Cape Colony). In the form of the lamina it agrees with the Jurassic species *Baiera Phillipsi*,[3] but it is no doubt specifically distinct therefrom;

[1] Zeiller (02) pl. xiv.
[2] Nathorst (78) p. 87 & pl. xix, fig. 6.
[3] Seward (00) pl. ix, fig. 4.

it resembles also *B. tœniata*, figured by Schenk [1] from the Rhætic of Germany.

Among other species with which the Dordrecht specimen may be compared, the following may be named:—*Ginkgo sibirica*, a Jurassic species, of which the smaller forms were figured by Heer [2] from the Arctic regions, and by Mr. Fontaine [3] from the Jurassic flora of Oregon; *G. flabellata*, Heer, from the Jurassic of China [4]; *G. Schmidtiana*, Heer, n. f. *parvifolia*, described by Dr. Krasser, [5] also from the Jurassic of China; an Australian Jurassic species figured by Mr. Stirling [6] and by myself [7] as *Baiera australis*, M'Coy; also *B. Guilhaumati*, Zeill., [8] from the Rhætic of Tongking; and *Gingko Muensteriana*, Heer, recorded by Schenk [9] from the Rhætic of Persia.

## CONIFERALES (?).

### Genus STIGMATODENDRON.

STIGMATODENDRON DUBIUM, sp. nov.     (Pl. III, fig. 3.)

At first sight the concave mould from Aliwal North, reproduced rather less than half the natural size in Pl. III, fig. 3, suggests a comparison with *Stigmaria* or with a Lepidodendroid stem; it is this superficial resemblance which accounts for the statement that *Lepidodendron*-stems have been obtained in the Burghersdorp Beds of Aliwal North. The length of the specimen is 30 centimetres, and its greatest breadth 7 cm. The preservation is too imperfect to admit of a satisfactory diagnosis; the specimen probably represents a plant bearing spirally-disposed prominences, to which leaves were attached. In some places the rounded prominences show a central depression which gives them an appearance like that of the rootlet-scars of a *Stigmaria*; the lower part of the specimen, as shown in the photograph, is characterized by numerous slightly-elongated pits, which may mark the position of leaf-cushions. The contrast presented by the surface of the fossil at different parts is no doubt the result of different degrees of decortication.

The Carboniferous plant described by Mr. D. White from Missouri as *Omphalophloios cyclostigma* [10] presents some resemblance to the Aliwal-North specimen; but, so far as it is possible to found an opinion on so imperfect a specimen, I am inclined to regard the plant as more closely allied to a Gymnospermous than to a Lycopodiaceous genus. A comparison may be made with Eichwald's *Stigmatodendron Ledebourii* [11] from the Carboniferous of Russia; this

[1] Schenk (67) pl. v, figs. 1–4.
[2] Heer (77) pl. xi.
[3] Ward (05) pl. xxxiii, fig. 8.
[4] Yokoyama (06) pp. 27–28 & pl. vii, figs. 6-9.
[5] Krasser (05) pp. 604-605 & pl. ii, figs. 4–5.
[6] Stirling (00) pl. i, fig. 3.
[7] Seward (04) pl. xviii, figs. 36 & 37.
[8] Zeiller (02) pl. l, figs. 16–19.
[9] Schenk (87) pl. viii, fig. 44.
[10] White (98) pls. xx–xxiii.
[11] Eichwald (60) p. 208 & pl. xviii. fig. 5.

generic name is applied to stems with pith-casts of the *Tylodendron (Schizodendron)*-type, and surface-features not unlike those of the specimen shown in Pl. III, fig. 3. The occurrence of petrified wood in association with pith-casts like that figured by Eichwald demonstrates the Araucarian nature of some at least of these Palæozoic stems. The stem described by Mougeot [1] as *Araucarites valdajolensis*, and more recently by M. Fliche [2] from the Permian of the Vosges, also offers some resemblance to the African stem. It is not suggested that we have enough evidence before us to warrant the reference of the Aliwal-North fossil to the Araucarieæ; my point is that it is more likely to be the impression of a coniferous than of a lycopodiaceous stem.

A small piece of pith-cast from Burghersdorp presented to the South African Museum by Dr. Kannemeyer is of the *Tylodendron*-type, and may belong to a stem like that represented in Pl. III, fig. 3.

### Genus STROBILITES.[3]

STROBILITES LAXUS, sp. nov.    (Pl. V, fig. 3 & text-fig. 7, p. 102.)

The specimens here figured were obtained from Burghersdorp Beds, at a locality on the Orange River opposite Aliwal North, in the Orange-River Colony. Pl. V, fig. 3 (half the natural size) represents an impression of an axis 20 centimetres long; 1·3 cm. broad at the basal end, which is not the actual base of the axis; and tapering to a breadth of 4 mm. at the apex. Numerous appendages are seen in side-view, attached by a horizontal stalk 5 mm. broad and 1·5 cm. long, which bend upwards distally into a lamina characterized by a rounded upper edge and radially-disposed folds or ridges. It is possible that the distal lamina was prolonged somewhat below the termination of the pedicel; but, so far as can be seen, the spirally-disposed appendages consist of a horizontal stalk and a more or less semicircular free laminar termination which formed a protective covering to the strobilus. There is no indication of seeds; these were probably borne on the adaxial side of the distal end of each sporophyll. Spirally-arranged pits on the face of the axis mark the position of vascular strands which supplied the sporophyll, and a clearly-defined groove on some of the stalks (*a*, fig. 7, p. 102) indicates the course of an outgoing bundle. The specimen represented in Pl. V, fig. 3, shows on one side a small piece of an axis with a few sporophylls, like those in text-fig. 7; and on the other side (as shown in Pl. V, fig. 3) we have a view of the surface of the strobilus.

As regards the nature of this strobilus, it is probably Gymnospermous, and a comparison is at once suggested with modern Cycads and Conifers. A partly-dissected cone of a Cycad presents

---

[1] Mougeot (52) p. 27 & pl. iv.
[2] Fliche (03) pp. 130–32.
[3] This convenient designation is adopted in the sense in which it was used by Schimper & Mougeot in 1844.

a fairly-close resemblance to the fossil reproduced in fig. 7 in the form of the woody axis and in the arrangement and shape of the appendages. In the absence of seeds it is rash to carry the comparison further. Among fossil species the reproductive shoots of *Voltzia* bear a fairly-close resemblance to the Orange-River specimens: the bracts of *Voltzia brevifolia* figured by Brongniart [1] are similar in their corrugated surface to those shown in the figure. Similarly, *V. coburgensis* [2] from the Keuper of Stuttgart (although smaller) is characterized by similar bracts, as also *V. heterophylla* [3] as well as examples of the same genus figured by various authors from Triassic and Permian rocks. [4] A somewhat similar type is represented by Heer's genus *Leptostrobus* from the Jurassic of Siberia. [5] *Schützia anomala*, Gein., as figured by Gœppert [6] from Permian rocks, differs from *Strobilites laxus* in the form of the appendages; and Renault's *Cycadospadix milleryensis*, [7] though presenting a superficial likeness to the African strobilus, probably is generically distinct. Some detached bracts associated with pieces of vegetative twigs from Rhætic or Jurassic rocks of German East Africa, which Dr. Potonié [8] has described under the name *Voltziopsis*, may also be compared with the larger sporophylls shown in Pl. V, fig. 3.

Fig. 7.—Strobilites laxus, *sp. nov.: axis of strobilus with appendages, one-half of the natural size.*

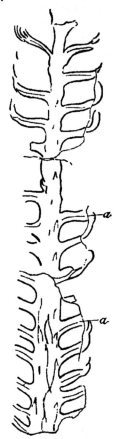

[1] Brongniart (28) pp. 447, 449 & pl. xvi.
[2] Schenk in Zittel (90) fig. 199, p. 290.
[3] Schimper (74) pl. lxxiv.
[4] Schimper & Mougeot (44) pls. vi-xv; Heer (76) pl. xxii; Schütze (01) pl. vii.
[5] Heer (77) pl. xiii, figs. 10-15.
[6] Gœppert (64) p. 161 & pls. xxiii-xxiv.
[7] Renault (93) pp. 329-31 & pl. lxxiii.
[8] Potonié (00) p. 504, fig. 29.

## CYCADOPHYTA.

### Genus PTEROPHYLLUM.

PTEROPHYLLUM sp., *cf.* PT. TIETZII, Schenk.　(Pl. II, fig. 5.)

The very incomplete specimen, from the Burghersdorp Beds at Kraai-River Bridge, represented in Pl. II, fig. 5 is similar to several species of the genus from Rhætic rocks in different regions, and it may be compared with some of the Jurassic species as well as with species of Triassic age. The axis, 9 centimetres in length, forms a fairly-prominent ridge, from which are given off at right angles linear segments of unequal breadth : the divisions of the lamina are characterized by numerous parallel veins, apparently not less than nineteen in a breadth of 5 millimetres of lamina. The longest segment reaches a length of 2·2 centimetres ; the greatest breadth at the base is 1·2 centimetres, and the narrowest segment is 6 millimetres broad. Owing to the absence of a perfect lamina, it is impossible to describe the form of the distal end. The great number of *Pterophyllum*-fronds in Triassic and Jurassic rocks differing but little one from the other in the relative abundance of the veins and in the form of the segments renders impossible the accurate determination of imperfect specimens. It is, however, interesting to find evidence of the existence in South Africa of this widely-spread genus. In view of the close resemblance of the Burghersdorp specimens to *Pterophyllum Tietzii*, first described by Schenk[1] from the Rhætic of Persia and afterwards recognized by Prof. Zeiller[2] in the Tongking flora, we may speak of them as *Pterophyllum* sp. cf. *Pt. Tietzii*. The similarity of the frond-fragment shown in Pl. II, fig. 5 to several other species of the genus detracts from the value of this member of the Burghersdorp flora as an index of geological age.

As examples of other forms of *Pterophyllum* resembling the African plant and in some cases probably identical with it, I may mention *Pt. longifolium* and *Pt. Jægeri*[3] of Brongniart, figured by Heer and Leuthardt from the Keuper of Switzerland : the Tongking species *Pt. inconstans* and *Pt. Portali*[4] ; *Pt. multilineatum* from the Ipswich Beds of Queensland and *Pt. yerongense* from the same locality[5] ; *Pt. æquale*, a species recorded by Prof. Nathorst from the Rhætic of Scania, as also by Schenk and Fontaine from the Jurassic of China and Oregon respectively[6] : specimens from the Rhætic of Honduras figured by Newberry[7] ; and a Greenland plant compared by Dr. Hartz with *Pt. inconstans*.[8] Similar, but not identical, specimens are figured from the Rajmahal Hills of India.[9]

[1] Schenk (87) p. 6 & pl. vi, figs. 27-29.　[2] Zeiller (02) p. 189 & pl. xlvii.
[3] Heer (76*) pls. xxx-xxxvi ; Leuthardt (03) vol. xxx, pls. v-vi & x.
[4] Zeiller (02) pp. 177, 186 & pls. xliii, xliv, xlvi.
[5] Shirley (96) pls. vii & vii *a* ; (98) pl. xxii.
[6] Nathorst (78) p. 67 & pl. xv, figs. 6-10 ; Schenk (83) pl. xlviii, fig. 7 ; Ward (05) pl. xx.
[7] Newberry (88) pl. viii.
[8] Hartz (96) pp. 235-36 & pl. xv, figs. 6, 8, 9.　[9] Oldham & Morris (63).

PTEROPHYLLUM sp.    (Pl. II, fig. 6.)

The specimen from the Molteno Beds of Konings Kroon, shown in
Pl. II, fig. 6, consists of a small piece of a frond 3·5 centimetres
long; the parallel-veined segments are continuous one with the other
at the base.   The inclination of the segments suggests proximity
to the apex of the leaf.   The veins, which are less numerous than
in the specimen represented in Pl. II, fig. 5, are in some cases
dichotomously branched near the rachis.

The fragment resembles *Nilssonia acuminata* figured by Schenk[1]
from Franconia, and *Pt. Richthofeni* described by the same author
from the Jurassic of China.[2]   *Ctenis Potockii*, Rac., from Jurassic
rocks in Poland[3] resembles the Molteno specimen, except in the
*Ctenis*-type of venation: *Pt. Portali*, Zeill., already compared with the
previous specimen, presents some resemblance to the fragment
shown in Pl. II, fig. 6.

### III. CONCLUSION.

The following list includes the Stormberg plants previously
described, together with the species dealt with in this paper :—

| | |
|---|---|
| *Schizoneura Carrerei*, Zeill. | *Tæniopteris Carruthersi*, Ten. Woods. |
| *Schizoneura* sp. | *Chiropteris cuneata* (Carr.). |
| *Thinnfeldia odontopteroides* (Morr.). | *Chiropteris Zeilleri*, Sew. |
| *Thinnfeldia rhomboidalis*, Ett. | *Baiera stormbergensis*, Sew. |
| *Thinnfeldia sphenopteroides*, sp. nov. | *Baiera Schenki*, Feistm. |
| *Thinnfeldia* sp. | *Baiera moltenensis*, sp. nov. |
| *Cladophlebis (Todites) Rœsserti* (Presl). | *Pterophyllum* sp. |
| | *Phœnicopsis (Desmiophyllum) elongata* (Morr.). |
| *Cladophlebis* sp., Feistm. | *Stenopteris elongata* (Carr.). |
| *Callipteridium stormbergense*, Sew. | |

The additional species afford further evidence in favour of
assigning the plant-beds of the Stormberg Series to a Rhætic
horizon.   It is noteworthy that no specimens of *Glossopteris* have
been obtained; this genus, which played so prominent a part in the
floras of the Lower and Middle Karroo Series, is represented in the
Rhætic flora of Tongking.

We have as yet discovered but a small number of types in the
Stormberg Beds; but, in its general facies, the flora shows a
striking similarity to Rhætic floras in other parts of the world.
The absence of any examples of *Clathropteris*, *Dictyophyllum*, and
*Camptopteris*—ferns which must have formed a conspicuous feature
in the Rhætic vegetation of Tongking and Europe—constitutes an
interesting peculiarity of the African flora.   The recent discovery
of a fragment of *Clathropteris* in beds of uncertain age in Egypt[4]
affords the only known evidence of the occurrence of this family of
ferns on the continent of Africa.

[1] Schenk (67) pl. xxxii, figs. 1–7 & pl. xxxiii, fig. 1.
[2] Schenk (83) p. 247 & pls. xlvii–xlviii.
[3] Raciborski (94) pl. xvii, figs. 2–5.
[4] Seward (07).

### The Burghersdorp Beds.

The list of Burghersdorp species is tabulated on p. 85. Omitting those species which are common to the Molteno Beds, the available evidence is not sufficient to justify a pronouncement as to geological horizon. The species *Thinnfeldia sphenopteroides* and *Tæniopteris Carruthersi*, common to both Burghersdorp and Molteno Beds, were obtained from the transition-zone referred to on p. 84. *Schizoneura* sp., *Odontopteris Browni*, *Strobilites laxus*, and *Stigmatodendron dubium* were collected from horizons 200 to 500 feet below the Molteno Beds. *Danæopsis Hughesi*, from Lady Frere, was found 1500 feet below the Molteno Beds, in rocks assigned by Mr. Du Toit to the Triassic Period.

*Danæopsis Hughesi* is recorded from the Rhætic of Tongking and China, and in India it is an abundant type in the Middle Gondwana Series.

*Odontopteris Browni* closely resembles Permian species referred to the same genus, and *Strobilites laxus* is compared especially with Triassic species of the genus *Voltzia*.

The inference is, that while possessing certain Rhætic types the flora, as a whole, points to a somewhat lower horizon. The similarity between Triassic, particularly Keuper, and Rhætic floras is, however, so close that it is unsafe to place too much trust in the evidence afforded by a few imperfect specimens. The Molteno and Burghersdorp floras are clearly marked off from the floras described by Prof. Zeiller from the neighbourhood of Johannesburg and by myself from Vereeniging; Prof. Zeiller's plants are assigned to the Beaufort Series, while those from Vereeniging are probably referable to the Ecca Series.

### IV. BIBLIOGRAPHY.

ARBER, E. A. N. (05). 'Catalogue of the Fossil Plants of the *Glossopteris*-Flora in the Department of Geology, Brit. Mus. (Nat. Hist.)' London, 1905.

BAIN, A. G. (52). 'On the Geology of Southern Africa' Trans. Geol. Soc. ser. 2, vol. vii (1845–56) p. 175.

BRONGNIART, A. (28). 'Essai d'une Flore du Grès Bigarré' Ann. Sci. Nat. vol. xv (1828) p. 435.

BRONGNIART, A. (45). *See* MURCHISON, R.

BUNBURY, Sir CHARLES J. F. (61). 'Notes on a Collection of Fossil Plants from Nágpur, Central India' Quart. Journ. Geol. Soc. vol. xvii (1861) p. 325.

DU TOIT, A. L. (05). 'Geological Survey of the Divisions of Aliwal North, Herschel, Barkly East, & Part of Wodehouse' Ninth Ann. Rep. Geol. Comm. Cape Colony for 1904 (1905) p. 73.

DU TOIT, A. L. (06). 'The Geological Survey of Glen Grey, & parts of Queenstown & Wodehouse, including the Indwe Area' Tenth Ann. Rep. Geol. Comm. Cape Colony for 1905 (1906) p. 97.

EICHWALD, E. D' (60). 'Lethæa Rossica' vol. i (1860) Stuttgart.

ETHERIDGE, R., Junr. (90). 'A Large *Equisetum* from the Hawkesbury Sandstone' Proc. Linn. Soc. N. S. Wales, ser. 2, vol. v (1890–91) p. 445.

ETTINGSHAUSEN, C. VON (52). 'Begründung einiger neuen oder nicht genaubekannten Arten der Lias- & Oolithflora' Abhandl. k.-k. Geol. Reichsanst. vol. i (1852) pt. iii, no. 3.

FEISTMANTEL, O. (77). 'Jurassic (Liassic) Flora of the Rajmahal Group in the Rajmahal Hills' Mem. Geol. Surv. India (Pal. Ind.) ser. 2, vol. i, pt. ii (1877).

FEISTMANTEL, O. (79). 'The Flora of the Talchir-Karharbari Beds' *Ibid.* ser. 2, vol. iii, pt. i (1881).

FEISTMANTEL, O. (81). 'The Flora of the Damuda & Panchet Divisions' *Ibid.* pt. iii (1881).

FEISTMANTEL, O. (82). 'The Fossil Flora of the South Rewah Gondwána Basin' *Ibid.* vol. iv, pt. i (1882).

FEISTMANTEL, O. (89). 'Uebersichtliche Darstellung der geologisch-palæontologischen Verhältnisse Süd-Afrikas' Abhandl. k. böhm. Gesellsch. Wissensch. ser. 7, vol. iii (1889).

FEISTMANTEL, O. (90). 'Geological & Palæontological Relations of the Coal & Plant-bearing Beds of Palæozoic & Mesozoic Age in Eastern Australia & Tasmania' Mem. Geol. Surv. N. S. Wales, Palæont. No. 3 (1890).

FLICHE, P. (03). 'Note sur des Bois silicifiés Permiens de la Vallée de Celles (Vosges)' Bull. Soc. Sci. Nancy, ser. 3, vol. iv (1903) p. 129.

FONTAINE, W. M. (83) 'Contributions to the Knowledge of the Older Mesozoic Flora of Virginia' U.S. Geol. Surv. Monogr. vi, 1883.

FONTAINE, W. M. (89). 'The Potomac or Younger Mesozoic Flora' U.S. Geol. Surv. Monogr. xv, 1889.

FONTAINE, W. M., & F. H. KNOWLTON (90). 'Notes on Triassic Plants from New Mexico' Proc. U.S. Nat. Mus. vol. xiii (1890–91) p. 281.

GŒPPERT, H. R. (41). 'Die Gattungen der fossilen Pflanzen' Bonn, 1841.

GŒPPERT, H. R. (50). 'Monographie der fossilen Coniferen' Natuurk. Verh. Hollandsch. Maatsch. Wetensch. te Haarlem, pt. vi (1850).

GŒPPERT, H. R. (64). 'Die fossile Flora der Permischen Formation' Palæontographica, vol. xii (1864–65).

HARTZ, N. (96). 'Planteforsteninger fra Cap Stewart i Östgrönland' Meddel. om Grönl. vol. xix (1896) p. 215.

HATCH, F. H., & G. S. CORSTORPHINE (05). 'The Geology of South Africa' London, 1905.

HEER, O. (76). 'Über Permische Pflanzen von Fünfkirchen in Ungarn' Mitth. Jahrb. k. Ung. Geol. Anst. vol. v (1876) pt. i.

HEER, O. (76*). 'Flora fossilis Helvetiæ' Zürich, 1876.

HEER, O. (77). 'Flora fossilis Arctica' vol. iv (1877).

HOOKER, Sir JOSEPH D. *See* BAIN, A. G.

JÆGER, G. F. (27). 'Über die Pflanzenversteinerungen welche in dem Bausandstein von Stuttgart vorkommen' Stuttgart, 1827.

KRASSER, F. (00). 'Die von W. A. Obrutshew in China & Central-Asien 1893–1894 gesammelten fossilen Pflanzen' Denkschr. k. Akad. Wissensch. Wien, vol. lxx (1900–01) p. 139.

KRASSER, F. (05). 'Fossile Pflanzen aus Transbaikalien, der Mongolei & Mandschurei' *Ibid.* vol. lxxviii (1905–06) p. 589.

LECTHARDT, F. (03) (04). 'Die Keuperflora von Neuewelt bei Basel' Abh. Schw. Palæont. Gesellsch. vol. xxx (1903) & vol. xxxi (1904).

MOUGEOT, A. (52). 'Essai d'une Flore du Nouveau Grès Rouge des Vosges' Ann. Soc. d'Émulat. des Vosges, vol. vii, pt. ii (1851).

MURCHISON, R., E. DE VERNEUIL, & Count A. KEYSERLING (45). 'Géologie de la Russie d'Europe' vol. ii (1845). London & Paris.

NATHORST, A. G. (78). 'Om Floran i Skånes kolförande Bildningar' Sver. Geol. Undersökn. Ser. C (1878–86).

NATHORST, A. G. (07). 'Über Trias- & Jurapflanzen von der Insel Kotelny' Mém. Acad. Imp. Sci. St. Pétersb. ser. 8, vol. xxi (1907) No. 2.

NEWBERRY, J. S. (88). 'Rhætic Plants from Honduras' Amer. Journ. Sci. ser. 3, vol. xxxvi (1888) p. 342.

NEWTON, E. T., & J. J. H. TEALL (97). 'Notes on a Collection of Rocks & Fossils from Franz-Josef Land, made by the Jackson-Harmsworth Expedition during 1894–96' Quart. Journ. Geol. Soc. vol. liii (1897) p. 477.

OLDHAM, T., & J. MORRIS (63). 'The Fossil Flora of the Rájmahál Series, Rájmahál Hills' Mem. Geol. Surv. India (Pal. Ind.) ser. 2, vol. i, pt. i (1863).

POTONIÉ, H. (99). 'Lehrbuch der Pflanzenpalæontologie' Berlin .1899.

POTONIÉ, H. (00). 'Fossile Pflanzen aus Deutsch & Portugiesisch-Ostafrika' Deutsch-Ostafrika, vol. vii (1900) p. 495.

RACIBORSKI, M. (94). 'Flora Kopalna' Krakowie, 1894.

RENAULT, B. (93). 'Bassin Houiller & Permien d'Autun & d'Épinac. Flore fossile—II^ème Partie' (Text, 1896; Atlas, 1893) Minist. Trav. Publ.—Études des Gîtes Minéraux.

ROGERS, A. W. (05). 'An Introduction to the Geology of Cape Colony' London, 1905.

SAPORTA, Comte G. DE (73).  'Les Plantes Jurassiques' in A. d'Orbigny's 'Pal.
    Franç.' ser. 2, Végét. vol. i (1873).
SCHENK, A. (67).  'Die fossile Flora der Grenzschichten des Keupers & Lias
    Frankens' Wiesbaden, 1865–67.
SCHENK, A. (83).  'Pflanzliche Versteinerungen' in Richthofen's 'China' vol. iv
    (1883) p. 245.
SCHENK, A. (87).  'Fossile Pflanzen aus der Albourskette gesammelt von E. Tietze'
    Biblioth. Bot. vol. ii (1887–89) pt. vi.
SCHIMPER, W. Ph. (74).  'Traité de Paléontologie Végétale' (Atlas) Paris, 1874.
SCHIMPER, W. Ph., & A. MOUGEOT (44).  'Monographie des Plantes fossiles du Grès
    Bigarré de la Chaine des Vosges' Leipzig, 1844.
SCHIMPER, W. Ph., & A. SCHENK (90).  Zittel's 'Handbuch der Palæontologie:
    II. Abth.—Palæophytologie' Munich & Leipzig, 1890.
SCHŒNLEIN, J. L., & A. SCHENK (65).  'Abbildungen von fossilen Pflanzen aus
    dem Keuper Frankens' Wiesbaden, 1865.
SCHUBTZE, E. (01).  'Beiträge zur Kenntniss der Triassischen Koniferen-Gattungen:
    Pagiophyllum, Voltzia, & Widdringtonites' Jahresheft Ver. Vat. Naturk.
    Württemberg, 1901, p. 240.
SEWARD, A. C. (00).  'Catalogue of the Mesozoic Plants in the Dept. of Geology,
    Brit. Mus.  The Jurassic Flora.  I.' London, 1900.
SEWARD, A. C. (03).  'Fossil Floras of Cape Colony' Ann. S. African Mus. vol. iv,
    pt. i (1903).
SEWARD, A. C. (04).  'On a Collection of Jurassic Plants from Victoria' Rec. Geol.
    Surv. Vict. vol. i, pt. iii (1904) p. 155.
SEWARD, A. C. (07).  'Fossil Plants from Egypt' Geol. Mag. dec. 5, vol. iv (1907)
    p. 253.
SEWARD, A. C. (07*).  'Fossil Plants from South Africa' Ibid. (1907) p. 481.
SHIRLEY, J. (96).  'Two new Species of Pterophyllum' Proc. Roy. Soc. Queensl.
    vol. xii (1896).
SHIRLEY, J. (98).  'Additions to the Fossil Flora of Queensland' Geol. Surv.
    Queensl. Bull. No. 7.  Brisbane, 1898.
SOLMS-LAUBACH, Graf H. zu (04).  'Die strukturbietenden Pflanzengesteine von
    Franz-Josefs-Land' K. Svensk. Vet.-Akad. Handl. n. s. vol. xxxvii (1903–04)
    No. 7.
SOLMS-LAUBACH, Graf H. zu, & G. STEINMANN (99).  'Das Auftreten & die Flora
    der Rhätischen Kohlenschichten von La Ternera (Chile)' Neues Jahrb.
    Beilageband xii (1899) p. 581.
STIRLING, J. (00).  'Notes on the Fossils of South Gippsland' Reports on the
    Victorian Coalfields, No. 7.  Melbourne, 1900.
SZAJNOCHA, L. (88).  'Über fossile Pflanzenreste aus Cacheuta in der Argentinischen
    Republik' Sitzb. k. Akad. Wissensch. Wien, vol. xcvii (1888–89) p. 219.
WARD, L. F., A. WANNER, F. H. KNOWLTON, & W. M. FONTAINE (00).  'Status of
    the Mesozoic Floras of the United States.  I. The Older Mesozoic' Twentieth
    Ann. Rep. U.S. Geol. Surv. (1898–99) 1900, p. 211.
WARD, L. F., F. H. KNOWLTON, & W. M. FONTAINE (05).  Id. II. U.S. Geol.
    Surv. Monogr. xlviii, 1905.
WEISS, C. E. (69).  'Fossile Flora der jüngsten Steinkohlenformation & des Roth-
    liegenden im Saar-Rhein-Gebiete' Bonn, 1869–72.
WHITE, D. (98).  'Omphalophloios, a New Lepidodendroid Type' Bull. Geol. Soc.
    Amer. vol. ix (1898) p. 329.
YOKOYAMA, M. (06).  'Mesozoic Plants from China' Journ. Coll. Sci. Imp. Univ.
    Tokyo, vol. xxi (1906) Art. 9.
ZEILLER, R. (82).  'Examen de la Flore fossile des Couches de Charbon du Tongking'
    Ann. des Mines, ser. 8, vol. ii (1882) p. 299.
ZEILLER, R. (00).  'Eléments de Paléobotanique' Paris, 1900.
ZEILLER, R. (02).  'Flore fossile des Gîtes de Charbon du Tonkin' Minist. Trav.
    Publ.—Études des Gîtes Minéraux: Col. Françaises, 1902–03.
ZIGNO, Baron A. DE (56–85).  'Flora fossilis formationis Oolithicæ' Vols. i & ii.
    Padua, 1856–85.

I would express my gratitude to the Assistant Secretary of the
Geological Society, for the care and attention which he has bestowed
on the verification and correction of references to literature.

## EXPLANATION OF PLATES II–VIII.

[All the figures are of the natural size, unless stated otherwise.]

I wish to thank my friend Mr. C. A. Barber for the drawings reproduced in Plate II and as text-figures 2, 5, & 7 (pp. 89, 96, & 102).

The specimens are preserved in the South African Museum, Cape Town.

### PLATE II.

Fig. 1. *Schizoneura Carrerei*, Zeill.: stem with leaves. (See p. 85.)
Figs. 2 & 3. *Thinnfeldia* sp.: portions of pinnæ. (See p. 95.)
Fig. 4. *Baiera moltenensis*, sp. nov. (See p. 99.)
    5. *Pterophyllum* sp. cf. *Pt. Tietzii*, Schenk. (See p. 103.)
    6. *Pterophyllum* sp. (See p. 104.)

### PLATE III.

Fig. 1. *Schizoneura* sp. *a*: pith-cast and cortical surface showing branch-scars. (See p. 86.)
    2. *Schizoneura* sp. *a*: pith-cast. (See p. 86.)
    3. *Stigmatodendron dubium*, sp. nov. Rather less than one-half of the natural size. (See p. 100.)

### PLATE IV.

Fig. 1. *Thinnfeldia odontopteroides* (Morr.): forked axis of a frond. (See p. 93.)
    2. *Thinnfeldia sphenopteroides*, sp. nov.: part of a frond, showing entire and lobed pinnules. (See p. 94.)

### PLATE V.

Fig. 1. *Thinnfeldia odontopteroides* (Morr.): pinnæ with a larger type of segment than that shown in text-figs. 3 *a*–3 *d* (p. 91); see also p. 93.
    2. *Thinnfeldia sphenopteroides*, sp. nov.: a single pinna. (See p. 95.)
    3. *Strobilites laxus*, sp. nov.: surface of strobilus. Half the natural size. (See p. 101.)

### PLATE VI.

*Danæopsis Hughesi*, Feistmantel. (See p. 95.)

### PLATE VII.

*Odontopteris Browni*, sp. nov. Three-quarters of the natural size. (See p. 97.)

### PLATE VIII.

*Cladophlebis (Todites) Rœsserti* (Presl). (See p. 98.)

[For the Discussion, see p. 125.]

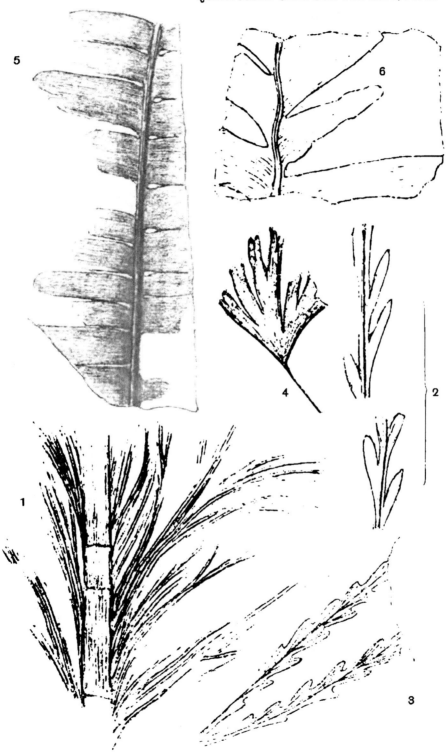

C. A. Barber, *del.*

*Bemrose, collo.*

SCHIZONEURA, PTEROPHYLLUM, ETC.

Bemrose, collo.

SCHIZONEURA AND STIGMATODENDRON.

2

1

*Bemrose, collo.*

**THINNFELDIA.**

2 1

3

THINNFELDIA AND STROBILITES.

D. Elliott, *photo.*

*Bemrose, collo.*

DANÆOPSIS HUGHESI, FEISTMANTEL.

Bemrose, collo.

ODONTOPTERIS BROWNI, SP. NOV.

Bemrose, colo.

CLADOPHLEBIS (TODITES) RŒSSERTI (PRESL).

6. PERMO-CARBONIFEROUS PLANTS *from* VEREENIGING (TRANSVAAL).
By ALBERT CHARLES SEWARD, M.A., F.R.S., F.L.S., F.G.S.,
Professor of Botany in the University of Cambridge, and
THOMAS NICHOLAS LESLIE, F.G.S.   (Read November 6th, 1907.)

[PLATES IX & X.]

CONTENTS.

                                                    Page
I. Introduction .......................................... 109
II. Description of the Specimens ........................ 113
III. Conclusion ......................................... 122
IV. Bibliography ....................................... 123

## I. INTRODUCTION.

THE township of Vereeniging, on the northern bank of the Vaal River, close to its junction with the Klip River, is situated on the southern boundary of the Transvaal Colony, rather more than 40 miles south of Johannesburg on the railway which runs to Bloemfontein and Naauw Port. Geologically, Vereeniging is important as the locality from which the greater number of Palæozoic South African plants have been obtained; the species hitherto described are frequently cited by authors—not always with the same conclusions—in reference to the geological age of the strata in this part of the Transvaal.

The large striated boulders weathered out of the surrounding matrix on the bank of the Vaal River afford a striking demonstration of the nature of the Glacial Conglomerate, the term advocated by Mr. E. T. Mellor[1] in preference to that of the Dwyka. We are not concerned with the precise method of formation of the conglomerate, but we are convinced that Sutherland was correct in his opinion, expressed more than 40 years ago, that the boulder-beds owe their origin to the action of ice, and this (we believe) is the view of those geologists who have had an opportunity of examining the evidence at first hand. The conglomerate, as shown in the accompanying section (fig. 1, p. 110), is succeeded by coal-seams, sandstones, and shales; it is mainly from the sandstones that the plants have been obtained. Most of the specimens were found in a sandstone-quarry a mile and a half from Vereeniging,[2] on the banks of the Klip River about 1 mile from its confluence with the Vaal; others were collected from a sandstone-bar which crosses the Vaal channel a mile and a half west of Vereeniging.

In 1897 Mr. D. Draper, who sent to one of us for description a few plants from a quarry 2 miles east of Vereeniging, contributed a paper in which he assigned a Triassic age to the coal-bearing

---

[1] Mellor (04) p. 21. The numerals in parentheses after authors' names refer to the dates of publication; see Bibliography, p. 123.
[2] Leslie (04) p. 85.

strata.[1] The evidence furnished by the plants clearly points, however, to a Permo-Carboniferous age. Geologists are now agreed in assigning the plant-beds to a sub-Triassic horizon; but there is some difference of opinion in regard to the choice between the Middle or the Lower Karroo System.

The Karroo System is much more completely represented in Cape Colony than in the Transvaal; in the former region it is classified as follows by Mr. A. W Rogers[2] in his book on the Geology of Cape Colony :—

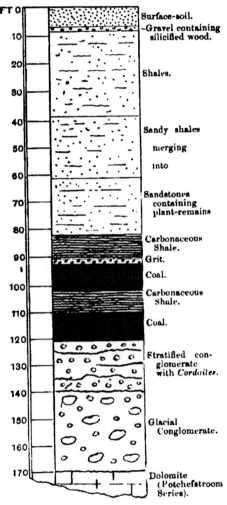

Fig. 1.—*General section at Vereeniging.* [*T. N. L.*]

FT 0

Surface-soil.
-Gravel containing silicified wood.

Shales.

Sandy shales

merging

into

Sandstones containing plant-remains

Carbonaceous Shale.

Grit.

Coal.

Carbonaceous Shale.

Coal.

Stratified conglomerate with *Cordaites*.

Glacial Conglomerate.

Dolomite (Potchefstroom Series).

Upper Karroo—Stormberg Series.
Middle Karroo— Beaufort Series.
Lower Karroo—Ecca Series. }
Dwyka Series. }

The Dwyka Conglomerate is thus separated from the Ecca Series as a distinct subdivision. By some authors, as in the 'Geology of South Africa,' by Drs. Hatch & Corstorphine,[3] the Ecca Series is spoken of as including the Dwyka Conglomerate with the associated sandstones and shales. Without expressing any opinion on the evidence for the separation of the Dwyka from the Ecca Series as afforded by the stratigraphy of Cape Colony, we shall refer to the Lower Karroo of the Transvaal as the Ecca Series. A reference to the numerous papers of recent years, which speak well for the present geological activity in South Africa, shows that opinion is divided as to the exact position of the Vereeniging beds. The coal-seams at Vereeniging are described by Dr. Hatch[4] as occurring in the lowest part of

[1] Draper (97).
[3] Hatch & Corstorphine (05) p. 197.
[2] Rogers (05) p. 147.
[4] Hatch (05) & (06).

the Ecca and interbedded with the Dwyka Series; they are separated from the underlying Potchefstroom Series by an unconformity.
The sandstone plant-bearing beds are thus classed by this author
as Lower Karroo, a view shared by Dr. Corstorphine,[1] who holds
that the Vereeniging beds are equivalent to the Lower Carboniferous in other parts of the world. This view has been expressed
also by Dr. Molengraaff[2] and by Mr. Dunn.[3]

On the other hand, Mr. Mellor (*loc. jam cit.*) thinks that the
Vereeniging beds should be classed with the Beaufort Series of
Cape Colony (Middle Karroo) rather than with the Ecca Series
(Lower Karroo). This author writes—

'The uncertainty attaching to the evidence of fossil plants could not be
better shown than by the somewhat remarkable fact that the supporters both
of the Ecca and of the Beaufort correlation claim that the palæontological
evidence is in their favour.' (*Op. cit.* p. 100.)

We admit the impossibility of using certain fossil plants as
determining evidence in deciding between a Lower and an Upper
Karroo horizon, but the fact that the palæobotanical records are
appealed to by supporters of different views does not necessarily
render such records valueless. It must be remembered that the
number of plant-species so far obtained from Vereeniging is small,
and allowance must also be made for the possibility of error in
dealing with a flora some members of which are common to both
divisions of the Karroo System. We admit the danger of dogma-
tizing on insufficient data, but we venture to dissent from the
opinion that the fossils favour the inclusion of the Vereeniging
strata in the Middle Karroo rather than in the Ecca Series. The
question of correlation of the Transvaal rocks with European
equivalents is dealt with later; it is, however, impossible to apply,
with any degree of confidence, the same nomenclature to the
divisions of the rocks of Gondwanaland as we find convenient in
the Northern Hemisphere.

Although the records of fossil plants from the continent of Africa
are unfortunately scanty, they point to one conclusion of great
interest: the species obtained from Cape Colony, the Transvaal,
Zululand, and Rhodesia are for the most part members of the
widely-spread flora of Permo-Carboniferous age which has left
remnants in India, South America, and Australia; while from the
coalfield of Tete on the Zambesi in Portuguese East Africa, in
latitude 16° S., several species have been described which point to
the existence in that region of the Stephanian flora of Europe—
the Upper Coal-Measures of British geologists. Representatives
of the following genera were recorded in 1883 by Prof. Zeiller[4]

---

[1] Corstorphine (04) pp. 174–75.
[2] Molengraaff (04); quoted by Mellor (06) p. 99.
[3] Dunn (98).
[4] Zeiller (83) pp. 594–95. For references to records of the *Glossopteris*-flora
in Africa, see Arber (05*) Bibliography, p. 227.

from the Tete coal-beds :—*Pecopteris*, *Callipteridium*, *Alethopteris*, *Annularia*, *Sphenophyllum*, *Cordaites*, and *Calamites*.

None of the Tete species have been proved to occur in the South African rocks, unless we make an exception in the case of *Cordaites borassifolius*, which bears a fairly close resemblance to *Nœggerathiopsis Hislopi*; we do not, however, think that the similarity amounts to specific identity. The genus *Sphenophyllum* has been recorded from Natal,[1] but the identification is based on a small fragment; this genus occurs in the *Glossopteris*-flora of India. We have referred with some hesitation one of the recently-discovered specimens from Vereeniging to *Callipteridium*, but the evidence is by no means satisfactory. Granting the occurrence of one or two of the Tete plants in more southern latitudes, the fact is clear that Prof. Zeiller's list of plants denotes a flora distinct from the *Glossopteris*-flora of Gondwanaland. Many years ago George Grey[2] described some northern plants from Cape Colony which have often been quoted as pointing to the existence of the European and North American facies in the Cape rocks; but, as one of us[3] has elsewhere pointed out, there is strong reason to believe that these species were recorded in error as South African fossils, and that they were imported into the country with European or American coal. So far, we have no grounds for asserting the existence of the *Glossopteris*-flora in Africa north of Rhodesia; on the other hand, it is clear that the European Upper Carboniferous flora extended as far south as the Zambesi, thus demonstrating the occurrence of two distinct floras in Africa towards the close of the Palæozoic Period.[4] It is important to bear in mind how few species have been recorded from South Africa; this is in all probability due, not merely to our ignorance through lack of material, but in part at least to the nature of the *Glossopteris*-flora, which, though rich in certain species, was poor in the number of its members—a fact probably associated with the glacial conditions of which abundant evidence exists. This is, at least, a familiar explanation which obviously suggests itself as a reasonable hypothesis. The small number and the imperfect state of preservation of the plants obtained from pre-Carboniferous rocks in South Africa[5] make it impossible to attempt to draw a comparison between the *Glossopteris*-flora and the flora which preceded it. The occurrence in Australia of older rocks with plant-remains tempts one to express the opinion that the *Glossopteris*-flora succeeded a flora comparable with the Lower Carboniferous or Devonian flora in the Northern Hemisphere. The fragmentary remains described from the Witteberg Series of Cape Colony are not inconsistent with this view.

We have long suspected that the distinction between the *Glossopteris*-flora and the Upper Carboniferous and Permian floras of the Northern Hemisphere has been exaggerated; although it is undoubtedly true that a striking difference exists, not only in the

[1] Arber (05*) p. 36.    [2] Grey (71).    [3] Seward (03) p. 88.
[4] Arber (05*) pp. xvii–xviii & map; Seward (03*) p. 833; Zeiller (97).
[5] Seward (03) p. 102; Schwarz (06).

greater paucity of species, but also in the extraordinary abundance of *Glossopteris*, and in the occurrence of *Gangamopteris* and other genera in the southern flora. The facts in regard to the existence of *Glossopteris* in Northern Europe in Permian times are too well known to need recapitulation, nor need we refer to the South American flora, which Prof. Zeiller[1] has shown to include northern as well as southern species. We are concerned primarily with the African Palæozoic plants south of the Zambesi, and we would call special attention to the fact that the discovery of *Lepidodendron* at Vereeniging adds another link between the northern and southern floras: in addition to *Lepidodendron*, we have *Sigillaria*, a fairly-common plant at Vereeniging; also *Bothrodendron*; and, as we think, the genus *Cordaites*. Future discoveries may increase the list of northern types, but it is unlikely that the South African was comparable in wealth of species with the European flora; it is, however, certain that there was more in common between the two botanical provinces than it has been customary to suppose. The question of the age of the Vereeniging rocks, as indicated by the plants, is briefly discussed in the concluding section of this paper (p. 122).

## II. DESCRIPTION OF THE SPECIMENS.

The following are the species so far obtained from the Vereeniging sandstones: those marked with an asterisk are recorded for the first time:—

*Schizoneura* sp.
*Glossopteris indica*, Schimper.
*\*Glossopteris angustifolia*, Brongniart, var. *tæniopteroides*, nov.
*Glossopteris angustifolia*, Brongniart.
*Glossopteris* sp. cf. *Gl. retifera*, Feistmantel.
*Gangamopteris cyclopteroides*, Feistmantel.
*\*Callipteridium* sp.?
*Neuropteridium validum*, Feistmantel.

*Bothrodendron Leslii*, Seward.
*\*Lepidodendron vereenigingense*, sp. nov.
*\*Lepidodendron Pedroanum* (Carruthers).
*Sigillaria Brardi*, Brongniart.
*Psygmophyllum Kidstoni*, Seward.
*Cordaites (Nœggerathiopsis) Hislopi* (Bunbury).
*Conites* sp.

## GLOSSOPTERIS ANGUSTIFOLIA, Brongn., var. TÆNIOPTEROIDES nov.
(Pl. IX, fig. 2; text-figs. 2 & 3, p. 114.)

The incomplete leaf shown in Pl. IX, fig. 2 (14 centimetres long, 1·8 cm. broad at the upper end and 1·1 cm. broad at the lower end, which is probably not far from the base of the lamina) appears to be identical with *Glossopteris angustifolia*, in the form of the frond and in the curvature of the secondary veins. A distinct midrib occupies the middle of the leaf, and increases in breadth towards the base of the specimen; numerous veins are given off at an acute angle, which are often forked near the point of origin and dichotomously branched near the edge of the lamina and in other

[1] Zeiller (95) p. 628.

places (text-figs. 2 & 3). With the exception of two or three lateral anastomoses, one of which is shown in text-fig. 3, there are no cross-connexions between adjacent veins. The chief difference between this specimen and the genus *Tæniopteris*, apart from the very rare anastomoses, consists in the greater inclination of the lateral veins to the midrib—a difference, perhaps, of no great importance. The fossil does not conform in its venation to normal

Figs. 2 & 3.—Glossopteris angustifolia, *var.* tæniopteroides, *nov. dichotomously-branched secondary veins showing one cross-connexion in fig. 3. (× 3½.)*

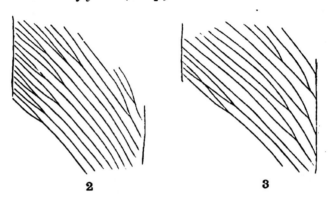

2                                    3

specimens of *Glossopteris*. A plant figured by Sir William Dawson, from New Brunswick, as *Megalopteris (Neuropteris) Dawsoni*, Hartt,[1] exhibits a close resemblance to the Vereeniging leaves; the venation is of the same type, except in the apparent absence of cross-connexions between the veins of the Canadian fossil. Dawson notes a close resemblance to *Glossopteris*, and adopts the sub-generic title *Megalopteris* in order to give point to his hesitation in describing the leaves as those of the genus *Neuropteris*; he describes the New Brunswick plant as pinnate, and a figure published by Andrews[2] shows the compound nature of the frond. Fontaine & White[3] record a second species from the Upper Carboniferous strata of Virginia, and their species—*M. sewellensis*—is mentioned by David White[4] from the Pottsville Series. A more recent record of a plant assigned to *Megalopteris* is by Mr. Arber[5] in his description of the fossil flora of the so-called 'Culm-Measures' of North-West Devon; a fragment of a leaf which he submitted to Mr. Kidston was compared by that author with Dawson's *Megalopteris*. The Devon fragment has a breadth of nearly 5 centimetres; the veins

[1] Dawson (71) p. 51 & pl. xvii, figs. 191–94.
[2] Reproduced by Prof. Zeiller (00) fig. 85, p. 111.
[3] Fontaine & White (80) p. 11.
[4] White (95) p. 315.
[5] Arber (05) p. 307 & pl. xx, fig. 16.

are highly inclined to a conspicuous midrib, and the general appearance recalls *Glossopteris* : Mr. Arber writes :—

'It appears to me that the nervation is only very occasionally anastomosed, and that the union between the lateral veins is more apparent than real.' (*Loc. cit.*)

As regards the geological age of the beds from which *Megalopteris* has been recorded, the so-called Devonian rocks of New Brunswick have been assigned by Mr. Kidston[1] to the Upper Carboniferous, and the Culm of Devon is now recognized as probably Middle Coal-Measures. The Vereeniging leaf may be compared also with a single pinnule of the Indian fern *Danæopsis Hughesi*[2] described by Feistmantel from the Damuda Series ; but we are persuaded that the two are not generically identical. The leaf represented in Pl. IX, fig. 2 is no doubt a simple frond, and not a pinnule of a compound leaf ; it therefore seems to us to exhibit a closer resemblance to *Lesleya* than to *Megalopteris*. This genus was instituted by Lesquereux,[3] for some *Glossopteris*-like leaves from Pennsylvania with a spathulate lamina and dichotomously-branched veins curving upwards from the midrib. The same type of leaf has been recorded also from the Commentry coal-field,[4] and more recently another species has been figured by Prof. Zeiller[5] from the Stephanian of France. It may fairly be argued that we should refer the Vereeniging specimens to *Tæniopteris*, but the venation is not such as one is accustomed to associate with that genus. We have decided to adopt the generic name *Glossopteris*, and to designate the specimens *Gl. angustifolia*, var. *tæniopteroides*. This decision is the result of a letter received from Prof. Zeiller, to whom we submitted a drawing and description of the specimens : our thanks are due to him for what we regard as a satisfactory solution of our difficulty. Certain examples of *Gl. indica* described by Prof. Zeiller[6] from India exhibit a case of variation in the degree of anastomosis between the veins analogous to that in the leaf shown in Pl. IX, fig. 2, and in text-figures 2 & 3 (p. 114), as compared with the usual venation of *Gl. angustifolia*. One of the leaves[7] of *Gl. indica* figured by Prof. Zeiller is characterized by secondary veins with few cross-connexions, and, as he points out, it suggests *Tæniopteris* rather than *Glossopteris* ; but the occurrence of transitional forms connecting this type with the normal leaves of this species leaves no doubt as to the correctness of the identification. A specimen figured by Messrs. Jack & Etheridge,[8] from Queensland, as *Tæniopteris* sp. ind., agreeing with the Vereeniging fossil in shape and in the absence of lateral anastomoses, may possibly afford another example

[1] On the age of the Canadian rocks, see Matthew (01) & White (02).
[2] Feistmantel (82) pls. iv-x.
[3] Lesquereux (79) pl. xxv & (80) p. 142.
[4] Renault & Zeiller (88) p. 285 & pl. xxiii, fig. 6.
[5] Zeiller (06) pp. 112–13 & pl. xxxii, figs. 7–7 *a*.
[6] Zeiller (02) pp. 8 *et seqq.*
[7] *Ibid.* p. 11 & pl. iii, fig. 3.
[8] Jack & Etheridge (92) pl. xvi, fig. 4.

of this variety of *Glossopteris angustifolia*. It is interesting to find so extreme a case of departure from the normal type of venation as that of the narrow leaves represented in our figures: it demonstrates the danger of placing too much trust in venation-characters in the identification of isolated specimens.

GLOSSOPTERIS ANGUSTIFOLIA, Brongniart.

This species has been previously recorded from Vereeniging under the name of *Gl. Browniana*, var. *angustifolia*. As the impressions

Figs. 4 & 5.—Glossopteris Browniana : *fig. 4=portion of leaf, natural size; fig. 5 = venation-reticulum (× 3½).*

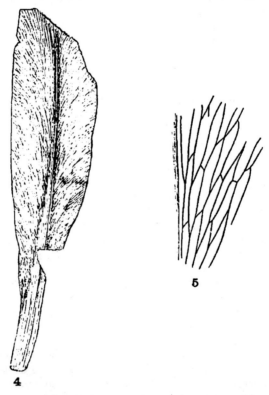

4                                                    5

on the sandstone are often very indistinctly preserved in regard to the venation, it is not improbable that some of the specimens should have been referred to the variety *tæniopteroides*; but, as the use of this term is rather a matter of convenience than an indication that we think the two kinds of leaf belonged to different plants, the precise form of the venation does not affect the question of the occurrence of Brongniart's species in the Vaal beds.

GLOSSOPTERIS INDICA, Schimper.

Large leaves of this species have been previously recorded from

Vereeniging. The veins are often faintly marked on the impressions on the rock, but in some cases the preservation is such as enables us to identify the species without hesitation.

### GLOSSOPTERIS BROWNIANA, Brongniart.  (Text-figs. 4 & 5, p. 116.)

In former papers on plants of the *Glossopteris*-flora the specific name *Browniana* has been used by one of us in a wider sense, as including *Gl. indica* and *Gl. angustifolia* : we now follow Prof. Zeiller in adopting the more restricted use of these specific terms. The fragment shown in fig. 4 consists of the basal portion of a frond, which appears to possess the venation-characters of *Gl. Browniana* as represented in Prof. Zeiller's drawings of the type-specimen.[1] A small piece of the lamina is enlarged in fig. 5 ; the veins are not preserved with sufficient clearness to render possible a larger camera-lucida drawing.

### GLOSSOPTERIS sp., cf. GL. RETIFERA, Feistmantel.  (Text-fig. 6.)

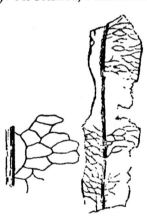

Fig. 6.—Glossopteris *sp.,* *cf.* Gl. retifera, *Feistmantel.*

Fig. 6 represents a fragment of a *Glossopteris*-frond distinguished from the other Vereeniging species by the greater size of the venation-reticulum; the larger meshes are 2·5 millimetres long and 1 mm. broad. *Glossopteris retifera*, Feistmantel,[2] from the Damuda Beds of India and from Cape Colony, Natal, the Orange-River Colony, and Zululand,[3] is characterized by large meshes like those of the Vereeniging fragment. There are also other species possessing a similar type of venation ; but, until more complete specimens are discovered, the solitary example recently found by one of us may be designated *Glossopteris* sp., cf. *Gl. retifera.*

### GANGAMOPTERIS CYCLOPTEROIDES, Feistmantel.  (Pl. X, fig. 3.)

The photograph, reproduced rather more than half the natural size in the figure, shows an imperfect specimen of a frond with the venation-characters more clearly preserved than in any examples previously recorded from this locality. The incomplete leaf is 20 centimetres long, with a maximum breadth of 7 cm. ; the lamina is spathulate, terminating in a blunt apex ; there is no prominent midrib as in *Glossopteris*, its place being taken by a few crowded

[1] Zeiller (96) p. 363, figs. 8–10.
[2] Arber (05*) p. 83.
[3] Etheridge (01) pl. xiii, fig. 7 ; also Seward (07) p. 69, pl. viii, figs. 8, 10 & pl. ix, figs. 5–6.

veins pursuing a vertical course and gradually passing obliquely upwards and outwards towards the upper end of the lamina. While bearing a resemblance to *Gangamopteris kashmirensis*, Sew.,[1] the specimen is, we believe, identical with Feistmantel's species from the Talchir and Karhabari Beds of India.[2]

CALLIPTERIDIUM sp.   (Pl. IX, fig. 3; & text-fig. 7.)

The faintly-marked impression (10 centimetres by 2·5 cm. in breadth) represented in Pl. IX, fig. 3 consists of an axis bearing alternately-placed obtuse and slightly-falcate pinnules attached by the whole of the base.   Each pinnule has a well-marked midrib (text-fig. 7); the secondary veins are almost completely obliterated, with the exception of a very few indistinct traces here and there, which show that they were curved and forked.   The more perfect pinnules have a length of 1·3 centimetres and a breadth of 5 millimetres. We are not aware of any fossil from the Lower Karroo of South Africa with which to compare this fragment. In habit the pinna is similar to that of *Clado-phlebis Roylei*, Arber[3]: the species originally described by Royle as *Pecopteris Lindleyana*, and afterwards from the Damuda Beds of India by Feistmantel as *Aletho-pteris Lindleyana*. We cannot hope to determine the very indistinct specimen with any degree of certainty, but we do not consider its resemblance to the Indian species sufficiently close to justify the use of the same name.   The species *Callipteridium gigas* (Gutbier), figured by Renault & Zeiller,[4] from Commentry, bears a close resemblance to the Vereeniging specimen; we must wait, however, for more evidence before suggesting specific identity with any known type.

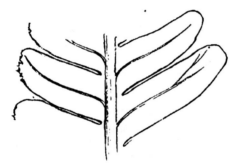

Fig. 7.—Callipteridium *sp.: pinnules much enlarged.*

SIGILLARIA BRARDI (Brongniart).[5]

Specimens of this species were described at length in a paper read before the Society in 1897.   Larger examples of the same form have since been found in the Vereeniging quarry; one of the largest that we have seen measures 30 by 50 centimetres.

[1] Seward (05) pp. 3–6 & pls. viii–ix.
[2] Feistmantel (79) pls. xi–xiv, &c.
[3] Arber (05*) p. 142.
[4] Renault & Zeiller (88) p. 199 & pl. xv.
[5] Seward (97) p. 326 & pls. xxii–xxiii.

LEPIDODENDRON VEREENIGINGENSE, sp. nov.   (Pl. X, figs. 1 & 2;
    and text-fig. 8.)

The fragment shown in Pl. X, fig. 2 (7·3 centimetres long)
represents a sandstone-cast exhibiting spirally-disposed leaf-cushions
approximately 1·8 centimetres in length.   It is probable that the
actual surface is not preserved, but the amount of decortication
must have been trifling: each leaf-cushion consists of a raised
upper portion, the leaf-scar region, characterized by a short groove
which we interpret as marking the position of the vascular bundle
and possibly also of the parichnos connected with the leaf.   The
converging ridges below the prominent leaf-scar indicate the
probable limits of the leaf-cushions, the form of which cannot be
made out in detail in the absence of more perfect specimens.

The impression represented in Pl. X, fig. 1 (18 centimetres by
3 cm.) is probably that of a stem very similar to, or perhaps identical with, that shown in fig. 2.   Spirally-disposed and somewhat
indistinct areas cover the surface of the fossil; their shape and size
suggest *Lepidodendron* leaf-cushions, and this comparison receives
support from the appearance presented by the upper part of some
of the areas (text-fig. 8), which shows traces of a median prominence and of two lateral depressions in the position of the leaf-
bundle and the two arms of the
parichnos.   A zone (Pl. X, fig. 1 A),
2 centimetres deep, is characterized by
crowded areas of much smaller size,
similar in shape to the leaf-scars of a
*Sigillaria*.   The most probable explanation of this interruption in the regular
sequence of elongated leaf-cushions is,
that it affords evidence of some zonal
variation in the nature of the scars,
such as we are familiar with in certain species of *Sigillaria*, but which
is uncommon in *Lepidodendron*.   An
example of zonal variation has been
figured by Dr. Potonié in *Lepidodendron
Volkmannianum*, Sternberg, from the
Culm of Magdeburg[1]; in that stem
the elongated cushions are succeeded
at intervals by narrow zones of shorter
cushions, similar to those on the
Vereeniging specimen.   Specimens described by Mr. Carruthers[2] as *Lepido-*

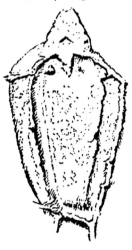

Fig. 8.—Lepidodendron
    vereenigingense: *leaf-
    cushion* ( × 4).

*dendron nothum*, Unger, from Queensland, also exhibit a similar
zonal variation in the size of the scars.

We are disposed to regard the fossils figured in Pl. X as

[1] Potonié (01) p. 115, fig. 71 & (05) pt. iii, p. 51.   See also Nathorst (94)
pl. viii, fig. 2.
[2] Carruthers (72) p. 353 & pl. xxvi.

examples in different states of preservation of the same species, for which we propose the name *Lepidodendron vereenigingense*. Feistmantel [1] has figured a very imperfect cast from the Lower Carboniferous of New South Wales, which he compares with *L. Volkmannianum*, but the specimen is too indistinct to determine. The preservation of the specimens shown in Pl. X, figs. 1 & 2, is not such as to permit of a critical determination; the leaf-cushions appear to be of the type of *L. aculeatum*,[2] but we do not think that the Vereeniging plant is specifically identical with that species.

LEPIDODENDRON PEDROANUM (Carruthers).    (Pl. IX, fig. 1.)

The sandstone-cast of a flattened stem (21·5 centimetres by 10 cm.), represented three-fifths of the natural size in the figure, appears to be distinct from *L. vereenigingense*. The leaf-cushions are shorter and relatively broader; the breadth is from 8 to 9 millimetres, the length approximately 1 cm.: a broadly-rounded arch forms the upper part of each cushion, and the sides taper rather rapidly towards the lower end. In some of the cushions it is possible to detect faint indications of the parichnos and leaf-trace scars, but the surface-features have been partly obliterated. A *Lepidodendron* of this type might be easily mistaken for *Sigillaria Brardi*, but in the example before us the characters are clearly those of a *Lepidodendron*. The form of the cushions agrees with that of certain European species of the genus: the agreement is, however, closer with *L. Pedroanum* (Carr.), a South American plant first described by Mr. Carruthers [3] and more recently figured by Prof. Zeiller.[4] A similar type of stem is figured by Prof. Nathorst from Bear Island as *Lepidodendron* cf. *Pedroanum*.[5] A less distinct specimen from Vereeniging, figured by one of us [6] in a former paper, as probably a species of *Sigillaria*, should, we think, be transferred to this species. Prof. Zeiller writes that a comparison of the plant represented in Pl. IX, fig. 1, with his Brazilian specimens leads him to confirm our opinion that the South African plant is specifically identical with *L. Pedroanum*.

CORDAITES HISLOPI (Bunbury).    (Text-figs. 9 & 10, p. 121.)

The species *Nœggerathiopsis Hislopi* has long been known from South Africa, but the specimens recently obtained from Vereeniging are less incomplete than those previously described. The examples shown in text-figs. 9 & 10 demonstrate the close resemblance to *Cordaites* more clearly than any specimens hitherto figured: that represented in fig. 10 is 84 centimetres long, and appears to be

[1] Feistmantel (90) pl. xi, fig. 1.
[2] We are indebted to Mr. Kidston, to whom we sent the photographs reproduced in Pl. X, for this comparison.
[3] Carruthers (69) p. 151 & pl. v.
[4] Zeiller (95) pl. viii, figs. 1-4.
[5] Nathorst (94) pl. xi, fig. 1.
[6] Seward (97) pl. xxiv, fig. 3.

complete; the lamina gradually broadens below the apex, reaching a maximum breadth about 23 centimetres from the tip; the narrow base is 2·8 centimetres wide.    Fig. 9 shows an even better specimen from the Museum of the Geological Society of South Africa at Johannesburg: it is 60 centimetres long; the apex is somewhat obtuse, and the narrow base is preserved intact.    The veins are not very clearly preserved; they are numerous, and in the broader part of the lamina slightly inclined towards the edge of the lamina.

Figs. 9 & 10.—Cordaites Hislopi *(fig. 9 is about ½, and fig. 10 is about ⅛ natural size).*

9        10

The genus *Nœggerathiopsis* is abundantly represented in India, New South Wales, South America, and other regions.[1]    The highest horizon from which it has been recorded is represented by the Rhætic of Tongking.[2]    The Tongking examples are smaller than those from South Africa, but in other respects they appear to be identical: in that region, as in others, the leaves occur in association with Gymnosperm-seeds.  Prof. Zeiller, while placing *Nœggerathiopsis* in the Cordaitales, prefers to preserve its generic identity on the grounds that (i) the fine longitudinal lines which occur between the veins of a *Cordaites*-leaf are not found in *Nœggerathiopsis*; and (ii) the stomata do not occur in regular lines as in *Cordaites*, but are scattered irregularly between the veins.[3]

The Vereeniging specimens do not enable us to pronounce an opinion on these characters, but they do not seem to us to constitute a serious objection to the use of a common generic name. The striking agreement between the leaves of *Nœggerathiopsis* and *Cordaites*, together with their frequent association with Gymnosperm-seeds, favours the adoption

[1] Arber (05*) p. 183.        [2] Zeiller (03) p. 149 & pl. xl.
[3] Zeiller (03) p. 153 ; see also Zeiller (02) p. 31.

of the generic name *Cordaites*. Another fact worthy of mention is the recent discovery at Vereeniging of stumps of trees with spreading roots, surrounded by a rock containing abundant leaves of *Nœggerathiopsis*: the roots are similar to those of *Cordaites* figured by Grand'Eury.[1] The Vereeniging leaves may be compared especially with *Cordaites palmæformis* (Gœppert) and *C. principalis* (Germar).[2]

CONITES sp.    (Text-fig. 11.)

A specimen from Vereeniging has already been described under this name[3]; another fragment of what is no doubt the same type is represented in the figure: it consists of crowded bodies re-

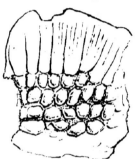

Fig. 11.—*Conites sp.* (× 3).

sembling cone-scales, with irregularly-polygonal bases barely 1 millimetre across, having flattened longitudinally-striated sides 1·5 mm. broad. The likeness to a piece of a small Araucarian cone, formerly noticed, is again suggested by this specimen, but the discovery of more satisfactory material may lead to an entirely-different conclusion. There is some resemblance between this fossil and one figured by Prof. Zeiller[4] from Carboniferous rocks in Asia Minor, under the name *Plinthiotheca anatolica*, but we do not regard the pair as more than superficially similar.

### III. CONCLUSION.

In endeavouring to determine the age of the Vereeniging beds from the evidence of the fossil plants, we must consider each record individually, and then adjust the balance of probabilities from the point of view of the flora as a whole.

*Schizoneura* sp.—We possess very incomplete data in regard to the type of Equisetaceous plant represented in the Vereeniging flora. The fossil described in 1897[5] as an Equisetaceous stem is much too imperfect to serve as an index of age; and, in the absence of well-preserved specimens, we cannot draw any conclusion from fragments belonging to a class of plants with so wide a range as the Equisetales.

[1] Mellor & Leslie (06) p. 127; Grand'Eury (90) pl. vi, figs. 14–16.
[2] Renault & Zeiller (88) p. 585 & pl. lxvi; Grand'Eury (77) p. 216 & pl. xxi, fig. 7.
[3] Seward (97) p. 331 & pl. xxii, fig. 2.
[4] Zeiller (99) p. 54 & pl. iv, fig. 18.
[5] Seward (97) p. 325 & pl. xxii, fig. 4 *b*.

*Glossopteris angustifolia.*—This species, which is characteristic of the Damuda of India and occurs in the Rhætic of Tongking, is perhaps more in accordance with a Middle than with a Lower Karroo horizon.

*Glossopteris Browniana.*—This species has also been recognized in the Rhætic flora of Tongking, and it is abundant in the Damuda Beds of India; it would seem to indicate the Beaufort rather than the Ecca Series.

*Glossopteris indica.*—This species is recorded from the Permian of Russia; it occurs in the Talchir-Karharbari, as well as in the Damuda Beds of India. It furnishes no decisive evidence as to a choice between the Beaufort and the Ecca Series.

*Gangomopteris cyclopteroides.*—This species, like the last, occurs in Russia, as also in the Talchir and Damuda Beds of India; it is, however, characteristic of the lower horizon.

*Lepidodendron Pedroanum.*—The Brazilian rocks from which this type is recorded are spoken of by Prof. Zeiller as representing the summit of the Carboniferous or the base of the Permian.

*Lepidodendron vereenigingense.*—We do not consider that the state of preservation of the material so far obtained justifies any definite expression of opinion as to geological age, but we regard the evidence as more favourable to an Upper Carboniferous than to a Permian horizon.

*Bothrodendron Leslii.*—The evidence afforded by *Bothrodendron* is not conclusive, but it points rather to the lower than to the higher Karroo horizon. The European species with which the African stems agree most closely are from the Lower Carboniferous and the Upper Devonian.

*Psygmophyllum Kidstoni.*—This genus ranges from the Lower Carboniferous to the Permian, and does not therefore afford decisive evidence.

On the whole, we are disposed to consider the Vereeniging flora as indicative of the Ecca rather than of the Beaufort Series.

## IV. BIBLIOGRAPHY.

ARBER, E. A. N. (05). 'The Fossil Flora of the Culm-Measures of North-West Devon, &c.' Phil. Trans. Roy. Soc. ser. B, vol. cxcvii (1905) p. 291.

ARBER, E. A. N. (05*). 'Catalogue of the Fossil Plants of the *Glossopteris*-Flora in the Department of Geology, Brit. Mus. (Nat. Hist.)' London, 1905.

CARRUTHERS, W. (69). 'On the Plant-Remains from the Brazilian Coal-Beds' Geol. Mag. vol. vi (1869) p. 151.

CARRUTHERS, W. (72). 'Notes on Fossil Plants from Queensland, Australia' Quart. Journ. Geol. Soc. vol. xxviii (1872) p. 350.

CORSTORPHINE, G. S. (03). 'Note on the Age of the Central South African Coal-field' Trans. Geol. Soc. S. Africa, vol. vi (1903–04) pt. ii, p. 16.

---

[1] Seward (03) p. 87.

CORSTORPHINE, G. S. (04). 'The History of Stratigraphical Investigation in South Africa' Rep. S. African Assoc. Adv. Sci. (Johannesburg Meeting) 1904, p. 145.

DAWSON, J. W. (71). 'The Fossil Plants of the Devonian & Upper Silurian Formations of Canada' Geol. Surv. Canada, 1871.

DRAPER, D. (97). 'Notes on the Occurrence of *Sigillaria, Glossopteris,* & other Plant-Remains in the Triassic Rocks of South Africa' Quart. Journ. Geol. Soc. vol. liii (1897) p. 310.

DUNN, E. J. (98). 'On Sub-Karoo Coal' Trans. Geol. Soc. S. Africa, vol. iv (1898–99) p. 115.

ETHERIDGE, J., Junr. (92). *See* JACK & ETHERIDGE.

ETHERIDGE, J., Junr. (01). 'Notes on Fossil Plants from the Saint-Lucia Bay Coalfield, Enselini River (Zululand)' First Rep. Geol. Surv. Natal & Zululand, 1901.

FEISTMANTEL, O. (79). 'The Flora of the Talchir-Karharbari Beds' Mem. Geol. Surv. India (Pal. Ind.) ser. 12, vol. iii, pt. i (1881).

FEISTMANTEL, O. (82). 'The Fossil Flora of the South Rewah-Gondwána Basin' *Ibid.* vol. iv, pt. i (1882).

FEISTMANTEL, O. (90). 'Geological & Palæontological Relations of the Coal & Plant-bearing Beds of Palæozoic & Mesozoic Age in Eastern Australia & Tasmania' Mem. Geol. Surv. N. S. Wales, Pal. No. 3 (1890).

FONTAINE, W. M., & I. C. WHITE (80). 'The Permian or Upper Carboniferous Flora of West Virginia & S.W. Pennsylvania' Second Geol. Surv. Penn. (1880).

GRAND'EURY, F. C. (77). 'Flore Carbonifère du Département de la Loire & du Centre de la France' Mém. Acad. Sci. Instit. France, vol. xxiv (1877).

GRAND'EURY, F. C. (90). 'Géologie & Paléontologie du Bassin Houiller du Gard' St. Étienne, 1890.

GREY, G. (71). 'Remarks on some Specimens from South Africa' Quart. Journ. Geol. Soc. vol. xxvii (1871) p. 49.

HATCH, F. H. (05). 'British Association Visit to Vereeniging.—A short Account of the Chief Points of Interest' Johannesburg, 1905.

HATCH, F. H. (06). [Presidential Address delivered to the Geological Society of S. Africa] Proc. Geol. Soc. S. Africa, 1906, p. xxi. [Accompanying vol. ix (1906–07) of Trans. Geol. Soc. S. A.]

HATCH, F. H., & G. S. CORSTORPHINE (05). 'The Geology of South Africa' London, 1905.

JACK, R. L., & J. ETHERIDGE, Junr. (92). 'The Geology & Palæontology of Queensland & New Guinea' Brisbane, 1892.

LESLIE, T. N. (04). 'The Fossil Flora of Vereeniging' Trans. Geol. Soc. S. Africa, vol. vi (1903–04) p. 82.

LESQUEREUX, L. (79) (80). 'Description of the Coal-Flora of the Carboniferous Formation in Pennsylvania' Second Geol. Surv. Penn. Text, 1880; Atlas, 1879.

MATTHEW, G. F. (01). 'A Backward Step in Palæobotany' Trans. Roy. Soc. Canada, ser. 2, vol. vii (1901) sect. iv, p. 113.

MELLOR, E. T. (04). 'On some Glaciated Land-Surfaces occurring in the District between Pretoria & Balmoral, &c.' Trans. Geol. Soc. S. Africa, vol. vii (1904–05) p. 18.

MELLOR, E. T. (06). 'The Position of the Transvaal Coal-Measures in the Karroo Sequence' Trans. Geol. Soc. S. Africa, vol. ix (1906–07) p. 97.

MELLOR, E. T., & T. N. LESLIE (06). 'On a Fossil Forest recently exposed in the Bed of the Vaal River at Vereeniging' Trans. Geol. Soc. S. Africa, vol. ix (1906–07) p. 125.

MOLENGRAAFF, G. A. F. (04). 'Geology of the Transvaal' Johannesburg, 1904. [We have not seen this work.]

NATHORST, A. G. (94). 'Zur Palæozoischen Flora der Arktischen Zone' K. Svensk. Vetensk.-Akad. Handl. vol. xxvi (1894) No. 4.

POTONIÉ, H. (01). 'Die Silur- & die Culm-Flora des Harzes & des Magdeburgischen' Abhandl. k. Preuss. Geol. Landesanst. n. s. Heft xxxvi (1901).

POTONIÉ, H. (05). 'Abbildungen & Beschreibungen fossiler Pflanzen-Reste der palæozoischen & mesozoischen Formationen' Abhandl. k. Preuss. Geol. Landesanst. (1905).

RENAULT, B., & R. ZEILLER (88). 'Études sur le Terrain Houiller de Commentry: Livre 2ᵐᵉ. Flore fossile' Bull. Soc. de l'Indust. Min. ser. 3, vol. ii (1888) & vol. iv (1890).

ROGERS, A. W. (05). 'An Introduction to the Geology of Cape Colony' London, 1905.

SCHWARZ, E. H. L. (06). 'South African Palæozoic Fossils' Rec. Albany Mus. vol. i (1906) p. 347.

SEWARD, A. C. (97). 'On the Association of *Sigillaria* & *Glossopteris* in South Africa' Quart. Journ. Geol. Soc. vol. liii (1897) p. 315.

SEWARD, A. C. (98). 'Notes on the Plant-Remains' [Appendix to a Paper by F. H. Hatch, on a Geological Survey of the Witwatersrand & other Districts in the Southern Transvaal] Quart. Journ. Geol. Soc. vol. liv (1898) p. 92.

SEWARD, A. C. (03). 'Fossil Floras of Cape Colony' Ann. S. A. Mus. vol. iv (1903) p. 1.

SEWARD, A. C. (03*). 'Floras of the Past: their Composition & Distribution' Address to Sect. K, Rep. Brit. Assoc. (Southport) 1903, p. 824.

SEWARD, A. C. (07). 'On a Collection of Permo-Carboniferous Plants from the St. Lucia (Somkele) Coalfield (Zululand) and from the Newcastle District (Natal)' Trans. Geol. Soc. S. Africa, vol. x (1907) p. 65.

SEWARD, A. C., & A. S. WOODWARD (05). 'Permo-Carboniferous Plants & Vertebrates from Kashmir' Mem. Geol. Surv. India (Pal. Ind.) vol. ii (n. s.) No. 2, 1905.

WHITE, D. (95). 'The Pottsville Series along New River (West Virginia)' Bull. Geol. Soc. Amer. vol. vi (1895) p. 305.

WHITE, D. (02). 'Stratigraphy *versus* Palæontology in Nova Scotia' Science, n. s. vol. xvi (1902) p. 232.

ZEILLER, R. (83). 'Note sur la Flore du Bassin Houiller de Tete (Région du Zambèze)' Ann. des Mines, ser. 8, vol. iv (1883) p. 594.

ZEILLER, R. (95). 'Note sur la Flore fossile des Gisements Houillers de Rio Grande do Sul' Bull. Soc. Géol. France, ser. 3, vol. xxiii (1895) p. 601.

ZEILLER, R. (96). 'Étude sur quelques Plantes fossiles, en particulier *Vertebraria* & *Glossopteris* des environs de Johannesburg (Transvaal)' Bull. Soc. Géol. France, ser. 3, vol. xxiv (1896) p. 349.

ZEILLER, R. (97). 'Les Provinces Botaniques de la Fin des Temps Primaires' Rev. Gén. Sci. p. 5 (Jan. 15th, 1897).

ZEILLER, R. (99). 'Étude sur la Flore fossile du Bassin Houiller d'Héraclée (Asie Mineure)' Mém. Soc. Géol. France, Paléontologie, Mém. No. 21.

ZEILLER, R. (00). 'Éléments de Paléobotanique' Paris, 1900.

ZEILLER, R. (02). 'Observations sur quelques Plantes fossiles des Lower Gondwanas' Mem. Geol. Surv. India (Pal. Ind.) vol. ii (n. s.) 1902.

ZEILLER, R. (03). 'Flore fossile des Gîtes de Charbon du Tonkin' Minist. Trav. Publ.—Études des Gîtes Minéraux: Col. Françaises, 1902-03.

ZEILLER, R. (06). 'Bassin Houiller & Permien de Blanzy et du Creusot—Fasc. ii, Flore Fossile' Minist. Trav. Publ.—Études des Gîtes Minéraux de la France, 1906.

## EXPLANATION OF PLATES IX & X.

[The specimens are preserved in the South African Museum, Cape Town.]

### PLATE IX.

Fig. 1. *Lepidodendron Pedroanum* (Carruthers); three-fifths of the natural size. (See p. 120.)

2. *Glossopteris angustifolia* var. *tæniopteroides*; natural size. (See p. 113.)

3. *Callipteridium* sp.; natural size. (See p. 118.)

### PLATE X.

Figs. 1 & 2. *Lepidodendron vereenigingense*, sp. nov.; natural size. (See p. 119.)

Fig. 3. *Gangamopteris cyclopteroides*, Feistmantel; about half the natural size. (See p. 117.)

## DISCUSSION (ON THE TWO FOREGOING PAPERS).

Dr. F. H. HATCH said that all the plant-remains that had been described at various times from Vereeniging were found in the sandstone-beds which immediately, and conformably, overlie the coal-seams at that locality. That they included so many species was due to the untiring industry of Mr. T. N. Leslie, who combined with the business of stone-quarrying an inexhaustible enthusiasm for geological pursuits.

He rejoiced that Prof. Seward confirmed the view that the Coal-Measures of Vereeniging belonged to the Ecca Series. This was the view that had been advocated by Dr. Corstorphine and himself in their 'Geology of South Africa.' The Transvaal Coal-Measures, including those of Vereeniging, had been originally considered by Dr. Molengraaff to be of Stormberg age; but later on he had come to the conclusion that they corresponded to the Beaufort Beds of the Cape, and that the Ecca Series was not represented at Vereeniging. This view had also been adopted by Mr. Kynaston and Mr. Mellor, of the Transvaal Geological Survey. It did not seem to be supported by the fossil evidence now laid before the Society. The speaker wished to ask Prof. Seward whether he considered all the Coal-Measures of the Transvaal to be of Ecca age, or whether it was his opinion that there had been two distinct cycles of coal-deposition—one in Beaufort times (Middelburg Coalfield), and one in the Ecca period (Vereeniging Coalfield).

Mr. R. D. OLDHAM said that the only remarks that he wished to offer on the very interesting paper on the Vereeniging plant-remains had reference to the concluding passages, in which the Authors seemed to minimize the distinction between the Upper Carboniferous and Permian flora of Europe and North America on the one hand, and that of India, South Africa, and Australia on the other. He himself did not think that the mere occurrence of a few specimens of some of the more typical northern forms in Africa, or the abolition of a few generic distinctions, should be allowed in any way to obscure the essential differences in the type of the two floras.

Prof. SEWARD, replying to the previous speaker, explained that, while agreeing with him as regarded the well-marked differences between the Northern and Southern floras of Permo-Carboniferous age, he wished to call attention to recent discoveries which tended to connect rather more closely the two botanical provinces. The question raised by Dr. Hatch as to the relative ages of the Middelburg and Vereeniging coal-seams could hardly be answered satisfactorily without further evidence. Some of the Lower Mesozoic plants dealt with by the Author in the first paper were contributed by Mr. Brown, of Aliwal North.

D. Elliott, *photo.*  Bemrose, *collo.*

LEPIDODENDRON, GLOSSOPTERIS, AND (?) CALLIPTERIDIUM.

LEPIDODENDRON, AND GANGAMOPTERIS.

7. On the STRUCTURE and RELATIONS of the LAURENTIAN SYSTEM in
EASTERN CANADA. By FRANK DAWSON ADAMS, D.Sc., F.R.S.,
F.G.S., Logan Professor of Geology in McGill University,
Montreal. (Communicated by permission of the Director of
the Geological Survey of Canada. Read November 6th,
1907.)

[PLATES XI–XIII.]

### CONTENTS.

|   |   | Page |
|---|---|---|
| I. | Introduction | 127 |
| II. | Structure of the Area | 130 |
| III. | The Invading Bathyliths | 130 |
| IV. | The Rocks of Sedimentary Origin | 136 |
| V. | The Amphibolites | 137 |
| VI. | The Gabbros and the Nepheline-Syenites | 139 |
| VII. | Contact-Phenomena about the Borders of the Granite-Bathyliths | 141 |
| VIII. | Distribution and Thickness of the Grenville Series | 142 |
| IX. | Relation of the Grenville Series to other Pre-Cambrian Series | 144 |
| X. | Summary | 145 |

## I. INTRODUCTION.

WHEN Sir William Logan, in the early years of the Geological
Survey of Canada, was gradually unravelling the stratigraphical
succession as displayed in the Dominion, he found that at the base
of the whole column lay the crystalline rocks of the Laurentian
Mountains. The name 'Laurentian Mountains' had been previously
given to that great stretch of iron-bound coast which lies along
the north of the Gulf of St. Lawrence and is not, properly
speaking, a mountain-range at all, but is merely the margin of a
great rock-plateau—the Laurentain peneplain—which forms a
portion of the northern protaxis of the North American continent.
Logan's studies in the Province of Quebec led him to believe that
the Laurentian System, as he termed it, consists of a series of
highly-crystalline limestones interstratified with quartzites and
gneisses, which in their turn overlie a great thickness of foliated
orthoclase-gneiss, the foliation of the latter being regarded by him
as the survival of an almost obliterated bedding.

He subsequently found in Eastern Ontario a series of rocks which
he considered in all probability to represent the Grenville Series in
a less altered state, and to this he gave the name of the 'Hastings
Series.' Later investigations showed that the anorthosite of the
Laurentian System is of intrusive origin ; but little further light was
thrown upon the relations of the underlying limestone-series (which
is now termed the Grenville Series) to the Lower or Fundamental
Gneiss. The relation of the Grenville and the Hastings Series also
remained uncertain.

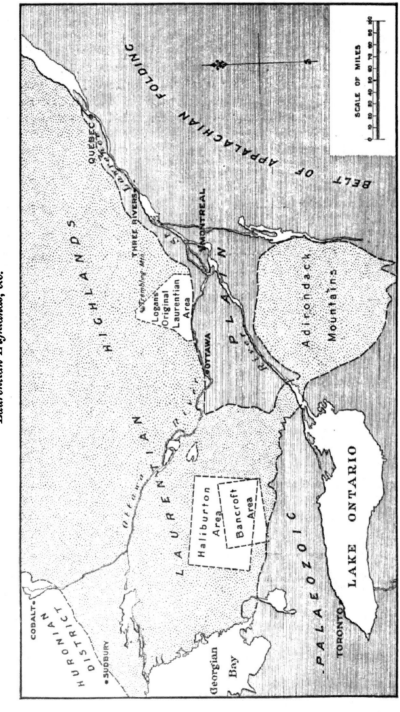

Fig. 1.—Sketch-map, showing the position of the Haliburton and Bancroft areas in relation to the Laurentian Highlands, etc.

The work of Prof. Lawson in the Lake-Superior region, which is from 800 to 1000 miles farther west on the margin of the Laurentian protaxis, has shown that in that region there are great bodies of orthoclase-gneiss which form the base of the geological column, and are, therefore, in position the equivalent of the Fundamental Gneiss of Logan. This gneiss, as Prof. Lawson has shown, cuts up through the oldest sedimentary series in that region, namely, the Keewatin, in the form of bathyliths. The stratigraphical succession in that western district, however, is entirely different from the succession in the eastern portion of Canada where Logan's original Laurentian area is situated. Neither the Grenville nor the Hastings Series occurs there. It became evident, therefore, that if a satisfactory knowledge of the character, structure, relations, and origin of Logan's Laurentian succession in Eastern Canada was to be obtained, this could only be secured by selecting some large area of these rocks and mapping it in much greater detail than had been previously attempted, the mapping being accompanied by a thorough petrographical study of the various rock-types that occur in the area, employing in this study all the varied resources of modern petrography. The most suitable area in the Dominion for this purpose was that embraced by Sheet 118 (Haliburton sheet), of the Ontario and Quebec series of geological maps which are being issued by the Geological Survey of Canada. This lies near the border of the Laurentian protaxis, north of Lake Ontario and east of Lake Huron.

The writer, in conjunction with Dr. A. E. Barlow, of the Geological Survey of Canada, was accordingly instructed by the late Dr. G. M. Dawson, then Director of the Geological Survey, to make a detailed study of this area, which was a virgin field, no geological examination of it having been previously undertaken.

As the mapping progressed, it seemed best to extend the work to the south-east, beyond the limits of the Haliburton sheet. Two maps were accordingly prepared, one, consisting of the Haliburton sheet, forming part of the regular series of geological maps above mentioned—this being prepared on the scale of 4 miles to the inch,—and the other embracing the south-eastern portion of this sheet together with the district lying to the south-east of it, which was designated as the Bancroft sheet. These together represent an area of 4200 square miles. This second map, embracing as it does an area of much greater complexity, and one which affords a key to the geology of the rest of the district, was prepared on the scale of 2 miles to the inch. It comprises an area of 1955 square miles. A copy of the Bancroft sheet (Pl. XIII) accompanies this paper. The sketch-map (fig. 1, p. 128) shows the respective position of these areas.

The field-work occupied a period of eight years, and it is proposed in the present paper to outline very briefly the chief results obtained : reserving the presentation of the detailed studies made upon the nepheline-syenites of the area with their associated corundum-deposits, the genetic relations of the amphibolites, and certain other points, for a series of papers by Dr. Barlow and myself which

will appear elsewhere, and reserving also the detailed description
of the area itself for a Report which will be published by the
Geological Survey of Canada during the present year (1908).

## II. STRUCTURE OF THE AREA.

A cursory inspection of the accompanying map (Pl. XIII) will
show that, geologically speaking, this Laurentian country is underlain
by a diversified series of stratified rocks (Grenville Series), among
which limestones preponderate, resting upon and invaded by an
enormous body of gneissic granite.

To the south-east the sedimentary series is largely developed,
and is comparatively free from igneous intrusions. Towards the
north-west, however, the granite, in ever-increasing amount, arches
up the sedimentary series and wells up through it, in places disintegrating it into a breccia composed of shreds and patches of the
invaded rock scattered through the invading granite, until eventually
connected areas of the sedimentary series disappear entirely and over
hundreds of square miles the granite and granite-gneiss alone are
seen, holding however, in almost every exposure, inclusions which
represent the last scattered remnants of the invaded rocks. The
type of structure presented by the invading granite is that of a
bathylith. In the present paper, the term bathylith is used in
the sense in which it was employed by Prof. Lawson in his
classic work on the Lake-of-the-Woods and Rainy-Lake districts of
Canada, to designate great lenticular or rounded bosses of granite
or granite-gneiss which are found arching up the overlying strata
through which they penetrate, disintegrating the latter, and
possessing a more or less distinct foliation, which is seen to conform
in general to the strike of the invaded rocks when these latter have
not been removed by denudation.

## III. THE INVADING BATHYLITHS.

The bathyliths of the area are well shown on the Bancroft sheet
and have a general trend in a direction about N. 30° E., which is
also the direction in which the area is folded. They are in some
cases isolated occurrences; in other cases they occur in linear series
so constituted, that it is evident that a very small amount of additional erosion, by removing the intervening cover, would convert the
series into a single long narrow bathylith.

Within the area of the bathyliths themselves the strike of the
foliation follows sweeping curves, which are usually closed and
centred about a certain spot in the area where the foliation becomes
so nearly horizontal that its course and even its existence, where
the surface is level, becomes difficult to recognize. From these
central areas of flat-lying gneiss, the dip of the gneiss (where it can
be determined) is usually found to be outward in all directions. The
bathyliths are, therefore, undoubtedly formed by an uprising of the

granite-magma from below, and these foci indicate the axis of greatest upward movement and that along which the granite-magma has been supplied most rapidly.

These centres are not, however, in all cases areas of more rapid uplift; but, on the contrary, the gneissic foliation in some cases dips inward in all directions towards the centre, thus marking them as places where the uprise of the magma was impeded, being there slower than in the adjacent portions of the district—that is to say, places where the overlying strata have sagged down into the granite-magma.

If this district presents the basement of a former mountain-range now planed down, the direction of this mountain-range was about N. 30° E., or in a general way parallel to the course of the valley of the St. Lawrence.

The movements in the granite to which reference has been made did not take place solely while the rock was in the form of an uncrystallized or glassy magma. They continued as the rock cooled and while it was filled with abundant products of crystallization, the movement being brought to a close only by the complete solidification of the rock. Evidence of protoclastic structure can therefore be seen throughout all the areas coloured as granite or granite-gneiss in the map, except in the case of a few small bodies of granite apparently of more recent age. This protoclastic structure is marked by the presence of more or less lenticular, broken fragments of large individuals of the felspar, in a fluidally-arranged mosaic of smaller allotriomorphic felspar-grains with quartz-strings and a few biotite-flakes. This fluidal arrangement, which constitutes the foliation of these rocks, is seen in every stage of development, there being an imperceptible gradation from the perfectly-massive forms occasionally seen, through the more or less gneissic varieties, to thinly-foliated gneisses. It is impossible to separate the several varieties. They constitute progressive developments of one and the same structure, and are different phases of one and the same rock-mass.

The granite-gneiss is undoubtedly of igneous origin, is very uniform in its mineralogical composition, and differs distinctly from the sedimentary gneisses or paragneisses of the area. It is medium to rather fine in grain, and composed almost entirely of quartz and felspar, the latter preponderating. Some biotite is present, but in very subordinate amount. The rock in the southern bathyliths occasionally contains a little hornblende. While the felspar is always reddish in colour, a large proportion of it is really an acid oligoclase. The rock would ordinarily be classed as an albite-granite or granite-gneiss, and, although the lime-soda felspar preponderates, should be so classed, since it resembles a granite in every respect.

Two analyses of typical specimens of this granite are tabulated on the following page :—

| | I. Per cent. | II. Per cent. |
|---|---|---|
| $SiO_2$ | 73·33 | 76·99 |
| $TiO_2$ | 0·17 | ... |
| $Al_2O_3$ | 13·55 | 12·45 |
| $Fe_2O_3$ | 0·58 | 1·03 |
| FeO | 1·53 | 0·49 |
| MnO | 0·04 | tr. |
| CaO | 1·66 | 0·98 |
| MgO | 0·45 | 0·21 |
| $K_2O$ | 3·12 | 4·29 |
| $Na_2O$ | 5·01 | 3·46 |
| $CO_2$ | ... | none. |
| $H_2O$ | 0·45 | 0·26 |
| Totals | 99·89 | 100·16 |

I = Gneiss, Township of Methuen, Lot 17, Range V (M. F. Connor, analyst).

II = Gneiss, Township of Livingstone, Lot 10, Range V (N. Norton-Evans, analyst).

No. I is seen under the microscope to consist of microcline and plagioclase, with small amounts of quartz and of an untwinned felspar, as well as a very subordinate amount of biotite and hornblende.

It is impossible in the case of this analysis to calculate the exact proportions of the iron-magnesia constituents which are present, on account of the fact that the exact composition of these minerals is not known. The 'norm,' however, is given below. By this is meant the calculation of the analysis into the form of certain standard minerals, showing the mineralogical composition of a rock into which such a magma might crystallize under slightly-different conditions.[1] The norm represents in this case very nearly the true percentage of the various minerals present, although diopside and hypersthene are calculated as present, which are represented by other combinations in the actual rock. It is as follows :—

| | |
|---|---|
| Orthoclase | 18·35 |
| Albite | 42·44 |
| Anorthite | 5·28 |
| Quartz | 27·72 |
| Diopside | 2·57 |
| Hypersthene | 1·92 |
| Magnetite | 0·93 |
| Ilmenite | 0·30 |
| Total | 99·51 |

In this rock the albite and anorthite shown in the analysis are combined, in the form of an acid plagioclase which is present in a

[1] See 'Quantitative Classification of Igneous Rocks' by Whitman Cross, J. P. Iddings, L. V. Pirsson, & H. S. Washington, University of Chicago Press, 1903, p. 147.

proportion far exceeding in amount that of the potash-felspar, a fact which is also shown by separations with Thoulet's solution. The rock takes its place in the Quantitative Classification as a lassenose.

No. II is seen under the microscope to be composed essentially of felspar and quartz, with a small amount of biotite. Untwinned felspars, apparently orthoclase and microcline, are present in large amount, and the proportion of felspar-grains showing the ordinary albite-twinning is small. A little iron-ore and a very few minute individuals of apatite and zircon complete the list of constituents present. A separation of the constituents of the rock by means of Thoulet's solution showed that the amount of oligoclase present was considerably greater than that of orthoclase and microcline taken together, a conclusion confirmed by the analysis. This, when calculated out, shows the rock to have the following percentage composition (mode):—

| | |
|---|---:|
| Orthoclase | 25·58 |
| Albite | 29·34 |
| Anorthite | 5·00 |
| Quartz | 37·68 |
| Biotite | 0·90 |
| Magnetite | 1·39 |
| Water | 0·26 |
| Total | 100·15 |

It will thus be seen that the amount of anorthite present is sufficient, when united with the albite, to give 34·34 per cent. of an acid oligoclase having the formula $Ab_6An$, thus bearing out the results obtained by the Thoulet separation. This combination, as compared with the orthoclase, is present in about the proportion of 3 to 2. This rock, in the Quantitative Classification, is a tehamose.

Throughout the granite-gneiss almost everywhere in the area dark inclusions are present. These are often very abundant, and consist of amphibolite or closely-allied rocks. Their presence in the Bancroft area has in the accompanying map (Pl. XIII) been emphasized at the expense of artistic effect by printing dark-green spots upon the granite wherever these amphibolite-inclusions are abundant. In some places, on account of their abundance and angular character, the granite presents the appearance of a breccia. These fragments, while usually more or less angular, have sometimes been softened and drawn out in the direction of the movement of the gneiss so as to impart to the rock a streaked or banded appearance (see fig. 2, p. 134). In other places, the inclusions have been so completely permeated by the granite-magma that they are utterly disintegrated. Every stage of passage from the sharply-angular inclusions to the final products of disintegration can be traced in many places, although in most cases the inclusions are well marked and sharply defined against the enclosing gneiss. At many points throughout the red

This shows what is usually the final stage in the destruction of the cover of the batholiths, the inclusions being here, however, much more abundant than usual.

granite-gneiss of the bathyliths, moreover, streaks of grey gneiss are found. It is estimated that, taking the granite-gneiss of the whole area examined, the amphibolite-inclusions represent about 10 per cent. of its volume and this grey gneiss another 10 per cent.

The origin of these amphibolite-inclusions and of the masses of grey gneiss is not only a question of much interest, but one of considerable importance to the true understanding of the geological processes which have been at work in this region.

As is well known, similar inclusions of dark basic rocks of the nature of amphibolite are found in very many occurrences of granite, especially those of Archæan age, in various other parts of the world, and they have been the subject of much investigation and widespread discussion. By many geologists they have been considered to be basic differentiation-products from the acid magma, while others have looked upon them as fragments of foreign rocks caught up by the granite.[1] In the region at present under discussion there are three ways in which it would be possible to consider them as having originated :—

(1) As the basic differentiation-products (ausscheidungen) from the granite-magma.

(2) As portions of the rock forming the walls or roof of the bathylith, which had fallen into the granite-magma and had partaken of its subsequent movements.

(3) As fragments of intrusive masses, dykes, stocks, etc., which, if the granite be supposed to represent the original subcrust in a softened or remelted condition, cut through this crust and were connected with basic effusives at the surface: these masses, having been torn to pieces by the subsequent movements of the softened granite, now appearing as scattered fragments.

A careful study of all parts of the area has failed to furnish any evidence that the first is the true explanation anywhere. There is positive proof that the second is the correct and only explanation of the inclusions in several parts of the area, and it is an explanation not opposed to the facts in any part of the area. The inclusions in some places, more especially in the great northern granite-gneiss areas, may have originated in part as set forth in the third explanation. The form of the inclusions sometimes suggests this ; but the movements in the granite have been so great, and the inclusions have been so torn to pieces, that it has been impossible to decide whether any of them have been derived from the source indicated under this head.

---

[1] C. H. Smyth, Jr., 'Report on the Crystalline Rocks of St. Lawrence County' N. Y. State Mus. 49th Ann. Rep. 1895, vol. ii (1898) p. 490. The black inclusions in the granite-gneisses of the Adirondacks are considered to be broken masses of an older rock caught up by the granite-gneiss when the latter was still in a molten condition. B. Frosterus. 'Bergbyggnaden i Sydöstra Finland' Bull. Comm. Geol. Finl. vol. ii, No. 13 (1902) p. 157, considers that the amphibolites, which are characteristic associates of the granite-gneiss of Southern Finland, are probably for the most part altered dyke-rocks. Some of them still show a gabbro-like structure.

## IV. THE ROCKS OF SEDIMENTARY ORIGIN.

### The Limestones.

The limestones in this Laurentian district are very thick, and underlie a large part of the area. In their more altered form they closely resemble those described by Logan in the areas examined by him; but to the south-east of the Bancroft sheet, where the invading granite is less abundant and the alteration of the invaded strata is correspondingly less pronounced, the limestones appear in less altered forms, and eventually pass into fine-grained greyish-blue varieties in which the bedding is perfectly preserved and concerning whose truly-sedimentary character there can be absolutely no doubt. It is impossible on the map to represent the gradual transition of the comparatively-unaltered blue limestone into the coarsely-crystalline white marble. This, however, takes place by the development in the former of little strings or irregular patches of coarsely-crystalline white calcite, usually following the bedding-planes. These become larger and more numerous on going north in the area towards the granite-intrusions, until eventually the whole is transformed into a great development of white marble. Here and there through this marble, where the bodies of the rock are very thick, small remnants of the original blue limestone can occasionally be found, as is indicated on the map, in the township of Monmouth.

Enormous bodies of nearly-pure limestone occur in many parts of the area; but elsewhere this limestone is impure, owing to the presence of grains of various silicates distributed through it, or to the presence of little bands of silicates representing impurities in the original limestones, which, under the influence of metamorphism, develop into gneisses and amphibolites of various kinds. Where these little gneiss-bands or amphibolite-bands become increasingly abundant, the limestone passes over into paragneiss or into some one of the varieties of amphibolite.

### The Quartzites.

Quartzite is not common in this area, the most extensive development being that which occurs as a band crossing the township of Monmouth. It is found interstratified with crystalline limestones and rusty-weathering gneisses of sedimentary origin.

There is every reason to believe that these quartzites represent, in most cases at least, altered sandy sediments.

### The Gneisses of Sedimentary Origin (Paragneisses).

These rocks differ distinctly in appearance from the foliated granite-gneisses already described as constituting the bathylithic intrusions. They are fine in grain, and show no protoclastic or cataclastic structure, the original material having been completely recrystallized. They have, therefore, an allotriomorphic structure, with a tendency of certain of the constituent minerals to elongate themselves in the direction of the original bedding. While quartz, felspar, and biotite are among the constituents present, the mica is usually more abundant than in the granite-gneisses; but, in addition to these, garnet, sillimanite, graphite, and pyrite are very frequently present, the last-named mineral giving rise to a prevailingly rusty colour on the weathered surface. These gneisses occur in the form of well-defined beds, and are usually found intimately associated with the limestones. They resemble in many respects the hornstones which are found in granite contact-zones, but are rather more coarsely crystalline than is usual in this class of rocks.

## V. THE AMPHIBOLITES.

Intimately associated with these sedimentary gneisses and the limestones on the one hand, and with the gabbros and diorites on the other, is another class of rocks which are grouped under the name of amphibolite. While many varieties of these rocks occur in the area, differing considerably one from the other in appearance, they have as common characteristics a dark colour and a basic composition. Quartz, which is one of the commonest constituents in the gneisses, is absent, or is present only in very small amount; while hornblende and felspar, the latter chiefly plagioclase, are the main constituents of the rock. Pyroxene or biotite often replaces the hornblende in part. A pale-green colour has been used in the Bancroft sheet to represent the amphibolites, which colour serves well to indicate the relation of certain varieties to the gabbro and diorite-intrusions of the area, represented by a deeper shade of green.

These rocks underlie large areas, as will be seen from the accompanying map (Pl. XIII). They also occur so intimately associated with certain developments of the limestones, in the form of interbedded layers, that these limestone-amphibolite occurrences have been mapped separately. In places, the sedimentary gneisses also fade away into occurrences of amphibolite when traced along the strike. Masses of amphibolite too, as has been mentioned, abound as inclusions throughout the granite of the bathyliths.

These amphibolites furthermore are not peculiar to this area, but occur abundantly everywhere in the Laurentian. They have always proved to be one of the chief difficulties in the way of a correct understanding of the geology of this system, seeing that it has been impossible to do more than indulge in conjectures concerning their origin. The same difficulty has been met with in the case of these and allied rocks occurring elsewhere, as, for instance, the trap-granulites of the Saxon Granulitgebirge or the amphibolites of the crystalline complex of certain portions of the Alps, the origin of which remained in doubt while that of the rocks wherewith they are associated had been definitely determined.

Two of the more common varieties of these amphibolites are represented by special designations on the map (Pl. XIII). One of these, which has been termed feather-amphibolite, always occurs in thin bands interstratified with limestone, and derives its name from the curious feather-like development displayed by large skeleton-crystals of hornblende or pyroxene which appear on the plane of stratification of the rock, to which they give a striking appearance when it is split along this direction (see Pl. XII). The other variety of amphibolite, which also frequently occurs as heavy bands in the limestones, is of a finely-granular character without very distinct foliation; and, on the weathered surface, it presents a uniformly, minutely-speckled appearance, owing to the intimate admixture of the minute grains of hornblende and felspar. On this account, during the prosecution of the field-work, this variety was designated as 'the pepper-and-salt amphibolite,' and in the legend of the Bancroft sheet it is designated as granular amphibolite.

Still other varieties differ from this granular amphibolite, in being somewhat coarser in grain or less regular in composition.

As the result of a very careful examination, it has been possible to prove conclusively that in this area the amphibolites have originated in three entirely different ways, the resulting rocks, although of such diverse origin, often being identical in appearance and composition. This remarkable convergence of type, whereby rocks of widely-different origin come to assume identity of character, explains the difficulty which has been experienced up to the present time in arriving at a satisfactory conclusion concerning their genetic relations.

(a) Some of these amphibolites result from the metamorphism and recrystallization of sediments. To this class belong the feather-amphibolites above described, which usually occur in thin bands alternating with crystalline limestone, and are evidently of like origin. They represent siliceous or dolomitic laminæ in the calcareous deposit. In many cases the bands of crystalline limestone become thinner and less abundant, and the composite rock passes gradually over into a body of pure feather-amphibolite. Whether the granular amphibolite, which is also found very frequently and over wide areas alternating with bands of limestone, is in some cases of similar origin, it has not been possible up to the present time to decide.

(b) Certain granular amphibolites represent altered igneous intrusions, for they are found in the form of dykes cutting across the stratified white crystalline limestone, on the shores of Jack's Lake in the township of Methuen. The limestones here dip at a low angle to the south, and are excellently exposed in the form of low cliffs about the side of the lake. The typical granular amphibolite can be seen rising above the surface of the water in the form of vertical dykes, cutting directly across the stratification of the limestone. These, which are 1 to 2 feet wide, can frequently be seen on reaching a certain bedding-plane to have been bent over in the direction of the bedding-plane which they follow and torn apart by movements in this plane, the limestone-strata having, during their upheaval, experienced somewhat extensive movements along their bedding-planes. The dykes, after having followed the bedding-planes for a certain distance, once more cut vertically across the latter and so reach the surface. Such dykes when seen on limited exposures of the bedded surface of the limestone, especially in contorted districts, would usually present the appearance of inter-stratified masses of amphibolite.

This amphibolite has the regular allotriomorphic structure of a completely recrystallized rock, and differs from any of the normal igneous rocks. Under the microscope it is identical with an amphibolite described by Dr. Teall, which was developed by the alteration of a diabase-dyke where crossed by a line of shearing. In the case of these Canadian dykes, however, the amphibolite is not confined to that portion which has been clearly subjected to movement, but forms the whole mass of the dyke.

(c) Amphibolites which are identical in physical character and in composition with those described under (b) are also produced by the metamorphic action exerted by the granite-bathyliths on the limestones through which they cut. This is a remarkable fact, and one which at first sight seems scarcely credible. It is, however, a change which has undoubtedly taken place on a large scale.

In addition to the amphibolites having originated in the three ways above mentioned, it is highly probable, judging from their character and mode of occurrence, that the amphibolite-bands associated with the large gabbro- and diorite-masses—as, for instance, that running in a north-easterly and south-westerly direction through the township of Wollaston, and that occurring in the south-eastern portion of the township of Cardiff, thence crossing Chandos into Anstruther—represent highly-altered basic volcanic ashes and lava-flows, connected with vents represented by the gabbro-stocks. The latter of these amphibolite-bands presents a great variation from place to place, in the character of the constituent rock. While in some places it is well banded, elsewhere it is streaked or presents an appearance strongly resembling flow-structure, with lighter-coloured lath-like forms highly suggestive of felspar-phenocrysts thickly scattered through it, while elsewhere the appearance suggests an original amygdaloidal structure. The rock, however, is so completely recrystallized, that a microscopic examination does not yield any conclusive evidence concerning its original character.

## VI. The Gabbros and the Nepheline-Syenites.

In addition to the amphibolites which are of igneous origin, there are several great intrusions of gabbro in the area. They are composed of a dark basic gabbro, containing a considerable amount of hornblende, which mineral, however, is often, and probably always, of secondary origin.

One of the most interesting and important groups of rocks in the
area is that consisting of the nepheline- and associated alkali-
syenites.  These rocks are, as a rule, light in colour and coarse in
grain, and generally show a more or less distinct foliation which
coincides in direction with that of the surrounding rocks.  The
rock in places displays a remarkable coarseness of grain, passing

Fig. 3.—*Limestone with lit-par-lit injections of granite, filled with grains of various
silicates, being in course of alteration into amphibolite.  Maxwell's Crossing,
Township of Glamorgan, Ontario (Canada).*

into nepheline-syenite-pegmatite, in which masses of nepheline a
yard in diameter may be found.  The rock, furthermore, in the
north-eastern portion of the area presents the phenomenon of a
magma supersaturated with alumina, from which the excess of
alumina has separated out in the form of crystals of corundum.
These corundum-bearing syenites have been made the basis of an
extensive industry, being worked for corundum on a large scale at

Craigmount, a few miles beyond the north-eastern limit of the Bancroft sheet.

The nepheline-syenite and its associated alkali-syenites represent a peripheral phase of the granite-intrusions. A description of these rocks, with a discussion of their mode of occurrence and genetic relations, will be found in the Transactions of the Royal Society of Canada for the year 1908.

### VII. CONTACT-PHENOMENA ABOUT THE BORDERS OF THE GRANITE-BATHYLITHS.

About the borders of the various areas of granite and granite-gneiss, contact-action is pronounced and often very striking. If the invaded rock be amphibolite, fragments torn from it are found scattered about in the gneiss, giving rise to inclusions presenting the various characters already described.

When the granite invades bodies of limestone, on the other hand, the phenomena resulting from the intrusion are more varied. The invading rock metamorphoses the limestone, and the products of alteration may be divided into three classes :—

(1) The alteration of the limestone into masses of granular green pyroxene-rock, usually containing scapolite, or into a rock consisting of a fine-grained aggregate of scales of a dark-brown mica.

(2) Intense alteration of the limestone along the immediate contact into a pyroxene-gneiss or amphibolite.

(3) In addition to these alteration-products, in certain cases the granite dissolves or digests the invaded rock, after having altered it in one or other of the manners above mentioned.

The alteration-products of the first class may be considered as due to the heated waters or vapours given off by the cooling magma, that is, to be of pneumatolytic origin ; while the alteration-products of the second class result from the more immediate action of the molten magma itself. The products of these two classes of alteration have much in common, however, and naturally pass one into the other.

The evidence of the alterations of the second class, whereby the limestone is converted into amphibolite, is briefly as follows :—The sedimentary series, consisting chiefly of limestones interstratified with amphibolites, the former making up about one-half of the volume of the whole, is invaded by the granite-bathyliths, torn to pieces, and scattered as fragments through the invading rock. These fragments are all composed of amphibolite, and none consisting of limestone can be found. The persistence of this phenomenon throughout the whole area suggests an alteration of limestone to amphibolite.

In certain places, especially about the border of the Glamorgan bathylith, where the line of contact is especially well-exposed for study, a gradual passage of the limestone into amphibolite can actually be observed, the former rock having gradually developed in it felspars, hornblende, and pyroxene in progressively-greater amount, until it eventually becomes an amphibolite (see fig. 3, p. 140).

A detailed description of this alteration, with a chemical and mineralogical study of the transitional rocks, will be found in the Report to which reference has already been made (p. 130).

Evidences of the alterations of the third class are less frequent and less striking. Nevertheless, in certain cases it appears to be practically certain that there has been a distinct solution of the invaded rocks by the granite. This, however, probably took place on a comparatively small scale.

An occurrence of this kind is found on the southern extension of Kasshabog Lake, in the township of Methuen. Here the banded amphibolite is invaded by the granite-gneiss, which has broken it into fragments and partly dissolved some of them, giving rise to a greyish, streaky-looking mass of irregular composition, much lighter in colour than the amphibolite and darker than the granite, being grey instead of reddish (see Pl. XI).

Other examples of the same phenomenon, but on a larger scale, may be seen at many places about the margin of the Anstruther bathylith. At the northern end of this occurrence, where the granite-gneiss of the bathylith runs up into the township of Monmouth, it is bounded on the north by an extension of what is known as the Catchecoma Gneiss. This is a basic rock, which resembles in appearance a light-coloured amphibolite. To the north of the Catchecoma Gneiss is a dark amphibolite, and then a band of limestone. The granite-gneiss, elsewhere red, becomes grey in colour and poor in quartz as this northern boundary is approached, and passes into the Catchecoma Gneiss, which is at first seen to hold a few tear-shaped inclusions of the amphibolite; these become increasingly numerous as the contact is approached where the amphibolite is reached, through which there run streaks of the invading rock. Evidently the amphibolite has been partly dissolved by the granite-magma, and the Catchecoma Gneiss here consists apparently of the granite-magma rendered basic by the solution of amphibolite.

## VIII. Distribution and Thickness of the Grenville Series.

In an area where the geological structure is so complicated, and where the strata have been invaded by such immense bodies of igneous material, it is difficult to determine the true succession and thickness of the sedimentary series. As will be seen, however, by consulting the accompanying map (Pl. XIII), the area is traversed by the Hastings road, which for a distance of 25·3 miles passes continuously across the limestones and amphibolites of the Grenville Series, and throughout this whole distance crosses these rocks nearly at right angles to their strike.

Furthermore, throughout the whole distance these strata dip in a southerly direction at high angles. Here and there, at long intervals and for a few yards, a reversed or northerly dip can be observed; but this is merely local, owing to a minor undulation in the strata, and has no stratigraphical significance. The angle of the dip naturally varies somewhat from place to place, but the average dip may be taken as 45°. This is a minimum estimate, the average dip along the whole section being in all probability somewhat higher. This gives a thickness to the Grenville Series along this line of section of 94,406 feet.

It is scarcely possible that the series attains so enormous a thickness, but it must be noted that along the whole length of this section a continuous alternation of beds of varying character is presented, and therefore it is not a foliation but a true bedding that is observed and measured. It is, furthermore, to be noted that although this series may have been repeated by isoclinal folding, there is no stratigraphical evidence that such is the case, and this folding has nowhere brought up the basement upon which the series was deposited—a fact which indicates again that the series, even if so folded, is extremely thick.

It may be safely stated that the Grenville Series presents by far the thickest development of pre-Cambrian limestone in North America, and that it presents at the same time one of the thickest series of pre-Cambrian sediments on that continent.

Not only has the Grenville Series a great thickness, but it has a great superficial extent. It is exposed more or less continuously over an area of 83,000 square miles in Eastern Canada and the State of New York. In areal extent, therefore, it can be compared in North America only with certain of the greatest developments of the Palæozoic limestones, as, for instance, the Knox Dolomites of the Southern Appalachians. In all probability, its original areal distribution was considerably greater than above stated, although this cannot be definitely determined on account of the great erosion to which the Laurentian protaxis has been subjected.

It may here be mentioned that the 'Hastings Series,' a designation given by Logan to certain rocks of the Madoc district, has proved, as Logan conjectured might be the case, to have no independent existence, but to be merely the less metamorphosed portion of the Grenville Series seen in the southern part of the Bancroft area. It is, however, practically certain that in this Madoc district the comparatively-unaltered rocks, which were designated by Logan as the Hastings Series, really consist of two unconformable series; and it is possible also that in the Grenville Series, as shown upon the Bancroft sheet, there may be two formations separated by an unconformity—as suggested by the occurrence of certain conglomerates, the position of which is shown upon the map (Pl. XIII). If, however, there are proved to be two formations within this area, these are identical in petrographical character, and are so intimately infolded and so highly metamorphosed that their respective distribution in the Bancroft area cannot now be determined.

### IX. RELATION OF THE GRENVILLE SERIES TO OTHER PRE-CAMBRIAN SERIES.

In the southern portion of the Laurentian Highlands to the west of the area occupied by the Grenville Series—that is, north of Lake Huron and in the district about Lake Superior, Rainy Lake, and Lake of the Woods—other pre-Cambrian series, differing essentially in petrographical character from the Grenville Series, are found. These are, enumerated in ascending order, the Keewatin, Huronian, and Keeweenawan Series. Up to the present time the Grenville Series has nowhere been found in contact with these; but it is hoped that the relation of these eastern and western pre-Cambrian developments may eventually be determined, in order that a correlation may be made between them. Until this has been done, however, their relations must remain a matter of mere conjecture. The two successions, then, are as follows:—

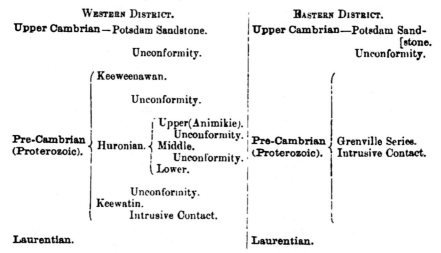

It will be noticed that here the term Laurentian is used in a somewhat different sense from that in which it was employed by Logan. In Logan's original classification of the Laurentian, this term—apart from the Upper Laurentian, which was proved to be composed essentially of anorthosite-intrusions—included two series differing in character, namely, the Lower Orthoclase-('Fundamental') Gneiss and the Grenville Series. Now that investigations have shown that these two series differ in origin (one being essentially a great development of very ancient sediments, and the other consisting of great bodies of igneous rock underlying and intruded through them), it becomes necessary to separate these two developments in drawing up a scheme of classification. As the lower gneisses forming what has been termed the 'Fundamental Gneiss' have an enormously-greater areal development than the overlying sedimentary series, constituting as they do a very large part of the whole northern protaxis, and forming the basis upon which the

Grenville Series rests, it has been proposed that the term Laurentian be restricted to this great development of igneous gneisses.[1]

The Grenville Series is thus separated from the Laurentian System, and the name is employed to designate the sedimentary series which overlies the lower gneisses and granites. The name Laurentian will, in addition to its geological use, continue to have a geographical or physiographical significance, as, for instance, in the term Laurentian Protaxis, which latter forms so striking a feature of the continent of North America, and is underlain chiefly by the gneisses of the Laurentian System.

In its petrographical character and in the display of the products of metamorphism which it presents, this great area on the southern border of the Canadian protaxis resembles in many respects certain classic localities of the 'Grundgebirge' on the Continent of Europe,[2] but in none of them, with the possible exception of the Scandinavian Peninsula, can the successive stages of the metamorphism be so clearly traced, or its final products be studied in such enormous development. The area is very instructive, as presenting a section of the deeper portions of the appareils granitiques, the 'roots of the mountains,' laid bare for study by the processes of denudation.

The Laurentian protaxis from early times has been relatively an area of progressive uplift; while that of the great plains to the south forms an area of progressive sinking, since upon it has been deposited in successive stages a series of great systems of sedimentary rocks.

Here, along the border of these two great geological units, the deep erosion reveals, it would seem, the mechanism of elevation, the granite-magma rising from the depths, and in all probability passing out from beneath the subsiding area to the south, lifting the old Laurentian Highlands as the liquid in the Bramah press lifts the ram when the piston sinks.

## X. SUMMARY.

(1) The Laurentian System of Sir William Logan in Eastern Canada consists of a very ancient series of sedimentary strata—largely limestones—invaded by enormous volumes of granite in the form of bathyliths, representing what Logan termed the Fundamental Gneiss

(2) This sedimentary series is one of the most important developments of pre-Cambrian rocks in North America, and

---

[1] 'Report of the Special International Committee on the Nomenclature of the Pre-Cambrian Rocks of the Lake-Superior Region' Journ. Geol. Chicago, vol. xiii (1905) p. 89; 'Report of a Special Committee on the Correlation of the Pre-Cambrian Rocks of the Adirondack Mountains, the "Original Laurentian Area" of Canada & Eastern Ontario' *ibid.* vol. xv (1907) p. 191.

[2] A. Sauer, 'Das alte Grundgebirge Deutschlands, &c.' Comptes Rendus, du IX^ème Congrès Géol. Internat. (Vienna) 1903, and other papers.

presents the greatest body of pre-Cambrian limestones on that continent.

(3) This great pre-Cambrian limestone series is best designated as the Grenville Series.

(4) The invading bathyliths of granite are of enormous extent. They possess a more or less distinct gneissic structure, due to the movement of the magma which developed a fluidal, and, in the later stages of intrusion, a protoclastic structure in the rock.

(5) The granite-gneiss of the bathyliths not only arched up the invaded strata into a series of domes, but 'stoped' out portions of the sides and lower surface of the arches, the fragments torn off from the walls and roof by the invading granite being found scattered throughout the mass of the invading rock. This 'stoping,'[1] however, probably developed only a small part of the space which the granite now occupies.

This structure is thus identical with that found by Prof. Lawson in the Keewatin area of the Lake-of-the-Woods district, west of Lake Superior, and by the present writer in the district north of the Island of Montreal. It is a structure which probably persists throughout the whole northern protaxis of the continent.[2]

6) The invading granite not only exerted a mechanical action upon the invaded strata, but also by its action upon these latter gave rise to a variety of metamorphic products, among which one of the most important is amphibolite produced by its action upon the limestone.

(7) The nepheline-syenite is a peripheral phase of the granite-intrusions, and is developed chiefly along the contact of the granite with the limestone. The nepheline-syenite magma frequently contained a large excess of alumina which, upon the cooling of the rock, separated out as corundum, giving rise to corundum-syenites which are extensively worked for this mineral.

(8) The invading bathyliths and allied intrusions of granite appear to occupy the greater part of the great northern protaxis of Canada, which has an area of approximately 2,000,000 square miles. It has therefore been considered advisable to restrict the name Laurentian to this great development of the Fundamental Gneiss, which, although intrusive into the Grenville Series, nevertheless underlies and supports it.

(9) The relation of the Grenville Series, forming the base of the geological column in Eastern Canada, to the Huronian

[1] See R. A. Daly, 'The Mechanics of Igneous Intrusion' Amer. Journ. Sci. ser. 4, vol. xv (1903) p. 269.
[2] F. D. Adams, 'On the Geology of a Portion of the Laurentian Area lying to the North of the Island of Montreal' Ann. Rep. Geol. Surv. Can. n. s. vol. viii (1896–97) part J.

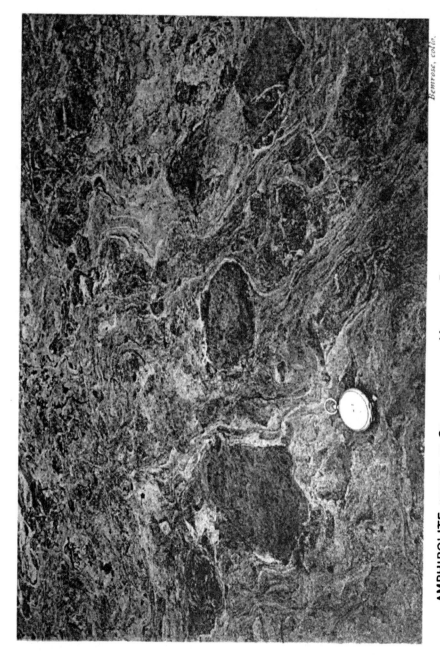

*Bemrose, colo.*

AMPHIBOLITE INVADED BY GRANITE OF THE METHUEN BATHYLITH AND PARTLY DISSOLVED BY IT.

benrose, collo.

'FEATHER-AMPHIBOLITE' (ALTERED SEDIMENT).

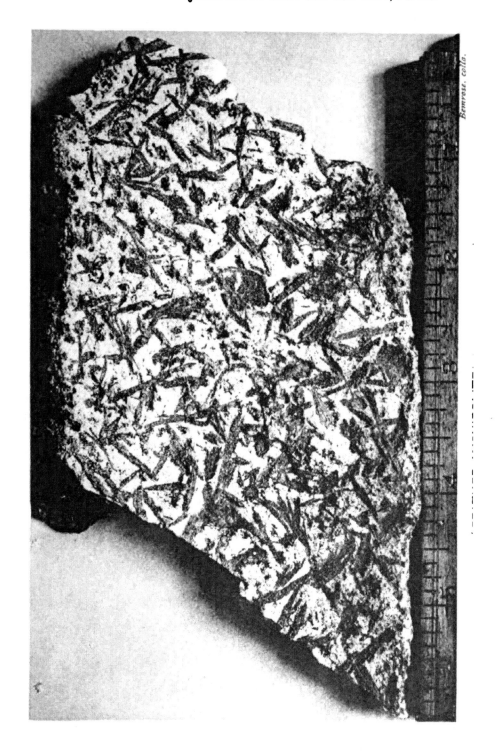

Bemrose, colla.

ectio

eol. Soc. Vol. LXIV, Pl. XIII.

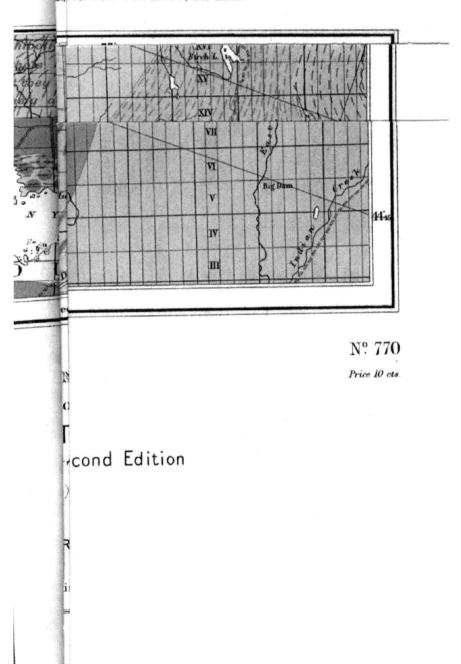

N°. 770

*Price 10 cts.*

cond Edition

and Keewatin Series, which are the oldest stratified rocks in the western part of the protaxis, has yet to be determined, the two not having so far been found in contact; nowhere, moreover, either east or west, has the original basement upon which the first sediments were laid down been discovered—these are everywhere torn to pieces by the granite-intrusions of the Laurentian.

## EXPLANATION OF PLATES XI–XIII.

### Plate XI.

Amphibolite invaded by granite of the Methuen bathylith and partly dissolved by it. Kasshabog Lake, Township of Methuen, Ontario (Canada).

### Plate XII.

'Feather-amphibolite' (altered sediment). Township of Wollaston, Ontario (Canada). The scale shown in the plate is in inches.

### Plate XIII.

Geological map of portions of Hastings, Haliburton, and Peterborough Counties (Ontario), on the scale of 2 miles to the inch (Bancroft sheet). Re-published by permission of the Geological Survey of Canada.

## Discussion.

The PRESIDENT alluded to the revolution of opinion regarding the origin of the Archæan gneisses since the publication of Lehmann's epoch-making work on the Saxon granulites. The old idea that the structure-planes of these gneisses represent the bedding of original sediments has been generally abandoned on both sides of the Atlantic; and the rocks in question are now recognized to be, for the most part, plutonic igneous masses which acquired these characteristic structures as the result of enormous pressure and movement and of more or less complete recrystallization under great earth-stresses. It was satisfactory to find this modern view, which had been long ago applied to the Laurentian gneiss of Canada, ably supported by the further evidence brought forward by the Author from his prolonged investigations. Until the memoir which he now laid before the Society was in print, it was hardly possible to appreciate how much it added to our previous knowledge of the subject. There was one portion of it to which the President called attention, as not unlikely to evoke criticism— the statement that amphibolites of identical type could result from three entirely-different sources. It was difficult to believe that the type should not present more or less distinctive variations in each case. But the wide experience and proved accomplishment of the Author (who had returned to Canada after the Centenary celebrations) entitled his conclusions to the most attentive consideration. The publication of the full paper, with all its detailed proofs, would be awaited with much interest. Meanwhile the Society welcomed this fresh contribution to our knowledge of the oldest rocks of a region which the labours of Logan and his associates had made classic ground in the history of Geology.

Dr. TEALL said that, in the absence of the Author, and with only a portion of the paper before them, anything of the nature of criticism would be out of place. It was evidently a most important communication. The results of the detailed mapping of a portion of the typical Laurentian area appeared to show that the relations of the granitoid gneisses to the surrounding rocks were similar to those of the more or less allied rocks of the Rainy-Lake region described by Prof. Lawson many years ago.

With regard to the formation of amphibolites in different ways, he could only say that he had not met with any evidence in support of the view that amphibolites having the same structure and composition could be formed from the alteration of both impure limestone and basic igneous rocks.

Mr. BARROW regarded the paper as of great importance, throwing a very suggestive light on problems that were met with in the Scottish Highlands. The oldest rocks of that region are sediments, together forming a huge aureole of thermometamorphism, and while they show their least altered aspect along the southern Highland border, they become increasingly metamorphosed towards the north-west, the alteration extending from near Stonehaven to Omagh in Ireland. In the centre of the aureole, where most highly crystalline, they are flooded with granitic material which has assumed a foliated structure. This gneiss, as in the Laurentian area, tends to occur in a laccolitic form, usually built up of a vast number of slightly-separated sills.

The speaker had been led to the conclusion that the Lewisian gneiss is essentially a sill-like or interlacing mass nearly horizontal, intruded into the Highland rocks, and that it occupies approximately a definite stratigraphical horizon defined by certain limestones and shales, just as the Laurentian gneiss was held by the Author to be an intrusive mass at the horizon of the Grenville Limestone.

8. CHRONOLOGY *of the* GLACIAL EPOCH *in* NORTH AMERICA.  By
Prof. GEORGE FREDERICK WRIGHT, F.G.S.A.  (Communicated
by Prof. E. J. GARWOOD, M.A., Sec.G.S.  Read January 8th,
1908.)

[Abstract.]

IN the case of Plum Creek, Lorain County (Ohio), the study of the
activity of the stream and of the amount of work which it has done
since a certain stage of the Glacial Epoch, has yielded important
results.  This stream began the erosion of its trough when the
temporary lake, held up in front of the ice, was maintained for a
considerable period at the level of its Fort-Wayne outlet; it has
never had anything more resistant than Till to act upon.  From
a given section, 5000 feet long, it has excavated 34,000,000 cubic
feet of Boulder-Clay, removing it from exposed banks 1600 feet long.
Twelve years' erosion of a 500-foot length of a part of the trough
of the stream under observation, and from banks 1000 feet long,
gives a rate of 8450 cubic feet per annum.  Therefore, the removal
of 34,000,000 cubic feet from the 5000-foot section would give a
period of 2505 years.  Considerations tending to lengthen the
estimate are the former forestation of the area and the increased
gradient in the artificial cut-off.  Those tending to shorten the
estimate are the present wider flood-plain, the time taken for
forests to grow, and the probably greater former water-flow.
The erosion of the Niagara Gorge began considerably later than
that of Plum Creek, and probably dates from midway between the
disappearance of the ice from Northern Ohio and from Quebec.  If
conditions have been uniform, the age of the Gorge would be 7000
years.  As the Niagara Limestone is thinner at the mouth of the
Gorge, and the Clinton Limestone has dipped out of sight at the
Whirlpool, there is nothing in the stratigraphy to indicate a slower
recession in the past than in the present.  Moreover, nearly one-
third of the erosion has been accomplished by two pre-Glacial
streams, one from the south and a smaller one from the north.
Therefore, the Author concludes with considerable confidence that
the Gorge is less than 10,000 years old, and that the ice of the
Glacial Epoch continued down to that time, to such an extent over
the lower St. Lawrence Valley and Central New York that it
obstructed the entire eastern drainage of the Great Lakes.
There is nothing which would lead to a longer estimate of the
time which has elapsed since the Kansan stage of the Glacial Epoch
than that approved by Prof. Calvin of Iowa, and agreed to by Prof.
Winchell.  These assume 8000 years as the limit for post-Glacial
time, and that a multiple of this by 20, amounting to 160,000,
would carry us back to Kansan time.  This, however, would still
leave as long a period still earlier, for the advance of the ice.  The
Author's impression is that the whole epoch may well have been
compassed within 200,000 years.

DISCUSSION.

The PRESIDENT remarked that to many geologists the chief interest of the Author's paper would lie in the evidence brought forward with regard to the value of geological time. As was well-known, the Niagara Gorge had often been used as a chronological measure, but with wide differences of opinion as to its significance. Modern investigation of the dynamics of denudation had tended to diminish the amount of time once demanded for various kinds and examples of erosion. There would, therefore, probably be a good deal of sympathy with the Author in his endeavour to minimize the length of the period required for the excavation of the Niagara Gorge. But the evidence adduced by him would require to be carefully weighed, together with that which had been brought forward by previous observers.

Mr. G. W. LAMPLUGH remarked that the Author's paper afforded one more illustration of the difficulties which were encountered, owing to the complexity and uncertainty of all the factors, when an attempt was made to find a measure in years for even this most recent period of geological time. Only a few months ago, Prof. J. W. W. Spencer had contributed a paper to the Society in which he deduced an age of 39,000 years for the Niagara Falls, from the same data which the Author interpreted as representing a period of less than 10,000 years. Evidently, geologists were still very far from attaining an estimate on which they could rest any confidence. Yet the problem held hope of solution, and every sincere effort to solve it deserved a hearing.

Dr. H. S. POOLE remarked that, being acquainted somewhat with glacial conditions on both coasts of Canada, he was impressed by the seeming freshness of the data. Two exposures especially suggested but a short intervening period. In the one case there was a perched granite-erratic, some 5 feet long, resting upon a shaft of Lower Cretaceous blue shale in the cove next to Nanoose on the eastern shore of Vancouver Island. The height of this shale-column (2 feet 4 inches) gave a measure of the erosion by the tides on soft argillaceous shale. The other case was in the river flowing out of Comox Lake higher up the same shore. The lake was at the foot of a glacier in a deep gorge of the mountain-range bounding the coal-field; and the accumulated morainic matter had choked the outlet and deflected the river to flow over a volcanic barrier along the foot of the range, and over a deposit of Till which the swirling waters of the river had so far but partly removed.

Prof. P. F. KENDALL joined the previous speakers in thanking the Author for his valuable communication. Opinion in this country was steadily trending in favour of a shorter post-Glacial chronology than that formerly admitted when British geologists were generally under the domination of Croll's astronomical explanation of the cause of the Ice-Age. It was satisfactory to find fresh confirmation of the newer views coming from America. There were two factors that might necessitate an extension of the Author's estimate of the rate of erosion of Plum Creek: the old oxbow that had been utilized for the construction of the reservoir was the expression of a tendency of the stream to meander, and this tendency still remained under the artificial condition now set up—with the result that the stream, instead of taking a straight course through the new channel, had swung from side to side and executed a larger amount of lateral erosion than it would have done in the old channel to which it had adjusted itself. Again, the deformation of the high-level lake-beach implied an uplift to the north that had increased the gradient of the southward-flowing streams.

The AUTHOR, in reply, said that direct evidence of the brevity of the continuance of the Matawan diversion from Niagara of the drainage of the Great-Lake Basin was adduced by Dr. Warren Upham from the warped upper shore-line of glacial Lake Agassiz. There the beach rises towards the north, until it is 400 feet above the latest beach. This differential elevation occurred during the period of the recession of the ice from the United States border to Hudson's Bay. From the smallness of the delta deposited by the Cheyenne and other rivers at the level of the upper beach, and from the limited accumulation of dunes at the southern end of Lake Agassiz, compared with that at the southern end of Lake Michigan, it was clear that Lake Agassiz continued only for 1000 or 2000 years, showing that the northerly elevation of 400 feet proceeded at a rate which would have closed the Matawa outlet after about that length of time. As the latitudes corresponded, this rate of elevation was altogether probable.

**9.** *On* ANTIGORITE *and the* VAL ANTIGORIO, *with* NOTES *on* OTHER
SERPENTINES CONTAINING THAT MINERAL.     By Prof. T. G.
BONNEY, Sc.D., LL.D., F.R.S., F.G.S.     (Read February 5th,
1908.)

CONTENTS.

|  |  | Page |
|---|---|---|
| I. The Original Specimen and the Val Antigorio | ......... | 152 |
| II. Other Antigorite-Serpentines | ............................ | 158 |
| III. Note on Bowenite | ........................................... | 169 |

I. THE ORIGINAL SPECIMEN AND THE VAL ANTIGORIO.

THE exact locality of the type-specimen of antigorite is apparently
unknown, as I found when preparing my portion of the paper by
Miss Raisin and myself on the minerals forming serpentine.[1]
E. Schweizer, who first described it,[2] states that the specimen
(5 inches long, 2 inches wide, and 2 inches thick) was in the
collection of D. F. Wiser of Zurich, who had bought it the year
before

'von einem mit Mineralien handelnden Bauer aus Oberwallis, nach dessen
Aussage diese Substanz in kleineren und grösseren, bisweilen einen Fuss
langen, dünnschiefrigen Platten im Antigoriothale bei Domo d'Ossola gefunden
werden soll';

and was unable to obtain any more precise information from the man.
It has been subsequently noticed,[3] among others, by Des Cloizeaux,

---

[1] Quart. Journ. Geol. Soc. vol. lxi (1905) p. 690.

[2] Pogg. Ann. vol. xlix (1840) p. 595. He says that it is 'wenig glänzend,'
semi-transparent in thin plates to transparent in the thinnest, with H=2·5
and S.G. = 2·622, and gives two analyses which he afterwards withdrew as
incorrect, the amount of water having been much underestimated.

[3] In the following works:— (1) Kenngott, 'Mitth. an Kenngott Uebers. Min.
Forsch.' 1856-57, p. 72, asserts that antigorite can be traced into ordinary
serpentine. (2) G. J. Brush, Amer. Journ. Sci. ser. 2, vol. xxiv (1857) p. 128,
gives a correct analysis, saying that it proves antigorite to be one of the slaty
varieties of serpentine. (3) A. Des Cloizeaux, 'Man. Min.' vol. i (1862) p. 110.
(4) Neumann, 'Elemente der Min.' 1877, p. 579, says that many include it
with serpentine. (5) Dr. E. Hussak, Tschermak's Min. & Petr. Mitth. n. s.
vol. v (1883) p. 65, refers antigorite to a pre-existing pyroxene, describing
and analysing specimens from Sprechenstein, etc. (6) Prof. A. Cathrein, Neues
Jahrb. vol. i (1887) p. 151, adds interesting particulars of Tyrol serpentines,
saying that those from augitic rock do not contain chromite or picotite, and
quotes Kišpatič as saying (Mitth. aus d. K. Ungar. Geol. Anst. vol. viii, 1886-90,
p. 198) that antigorite had come from a hornblende. (7) MM. A. Michel-Lévy &
A. Lacroix, 'Les Min. des Roches' (1888) p. 278, quote Prof. Rosenbusch as
attributing ordinary serpentine to the transformation of peridote and amphibole,
the leafy forms (bastite and antigorite) to the same pyroxenes, especially the
enstatite-family. (8) Prof. F. Zirkel, 'Lehrbuch der Petrogr.' 2nd ed. vol. iii
(1894) p. 384. (9) Prof. G. Tschermak, 'Lehrbuch der Min.' 5th ed. (1897)
p. 514. (10) Prof. H. Rosenbusch, 'Elem. der Gesteinlehre' (1898) p. 524.
(11) Prof. Carl Hintze, 'Min.' vol. ii (1897) p. 765, clearly connects antigorite
with pressure. (12) M. A. Michel-Lévy, Comptes Rendus, vol. cvi (1888)
p. 779, gives, with other minerals, antigorite du Valais, orthorhombic,
lengthening or flattening parallel to g¹, extinction with it 0°, optical sign — ve.
(13) The optical properties of antigorite from the 'Val d'Antigorio' are
mentioned also by Klein, Neues Jahrb. vol. ii (1895) p. 127.

Naumann, Hintze, Lévy & Lacroix, Tschermak, Brush, Rosenbusch, and Zirkel; the last adding to a full and precise description
an extensive bibliography.    But none of these authorities define
the locality more exactly : each, as is not unnatural, being content
with stating that the mineral came from the Val Antigorio, though
Dr. Hussak and one or two of the later writers have noted its occurrence in other places.  I failed, though some time was spent on
the search, to obtain any better information from books on Italian
geology,[1] or the maps in our Society's Library ; moreover, no
serpentine is recorded in the Val Antigorio on sheet xviii of the
Swiss Geological Survey-map.    That, however, hardly amounted to
proof of its non-occurrence, because, as this district is in Italy, the
map of it would probably be more or less of a compilation.

The completion of the Simplon tunnel has rendered the Val
Antigorio so much more accessible than formerly from the valley of
the Rhone, that I determined to end my stay in Switzerland last
summer by paying it a short visit.   I had once walked up it from
Domo d'Ossola on my way to the Val Bedretto by the San Giacomo
Pass, and had no recollection of serpentine,[2] but that was so long
ago as 1860, and before I paid any particular attention to rocks ;
though, as it happened, I had shortly before obtained my first
specimen of antigorite-serpentine in the neighbourhood of the
Viso, taking it then as a singular instance of 'a serpentine-schist.'
Again, in 1883, I had crossed from the Rhone Valley to the Tosa
Falls by the Gries Pass, returning by the Hohsand Pass and the
Binnenthal, without noting serpentine ; but this brought me only
into the Val Formazza, as the upper part of the Tosa Valley is
called, the name being changed without any geographical reason
into Val Antigorio at a little village called Passo.[3]  The latter title
is dropped and that of the Val d'Ossola assumed at the junction of
the Val di Vedro (down which runs the Simplon road and railway).[4]  On the same side, about 10 miles higher up, the Val Devero
comes down from the Geisspfad Pass (leading to Binn), and about
2 miles below the Val di Vedro, that is, a little above Domo
d'Ossola, the Val Bognanco descends, not from the watershed of the

---

[1] Dr. S. Traverso, 'Geologia dell' Ossola' Genoa, 1895, does not mention
antigorite or the occurrence of serpentine in the Val Antigorio, though giving
several localities in tributary valleys (including the Val Vigezzo) where that
rock and even peridotites occur.  Owing to a singular oversight, I did not
make acquaintance with this very full account of the geology of the area
drained by the Tosa and its tributaries till after my return, which I regret,
though it would not have much aided me in my special investigations.

[2] Serpentine is not mentioned by H. B. de Saussure (' Voyages dans les Alpes '
ch. ix), whose description of the scenery and rocks of the Val Antigorio is a
model of careful observation.

[3] The sketch-map (p. 154) may make the geographical details more intelligible.

[4] As might be expected, writers differ in the limits assigned to the Val
Antigorio.  H. B. de Saussure (' Voyages dans les Alpes ' 1796) places the
upper one at St. Michel, just below the entrance of the Val Devero ; W. S. King
(' Italian Valleys of the Pennine Alps ' 1858, p. 545) carries it a little higher,
to about Premia ; John Ball (' Central Alps ' 1873 edition, p. 250) puts it at
Foppiano, 2 miles above Passo.  I have followed Bædeker (' Guide to Switzerland ') as a trustworthy authority.

Pennine chain, but from a short spur which runs out eastward
from the Portjen Grat. On the eastern side, the Val Vigezzo and
perhaps the Isorno Valley are the only tributaries of any importance—the mouth of the former being almost opposite to that of
the Val Bognanco.

Under the circumstances, I thought that my best chance of running
the antigorite to ground was to go up the Val Antigorio from Domo
d'Ossola, keeping a sharp look-out for serpentine either as an erratic
or *in situ* ; and, if no sign of it appeared, to examine the pebbles
in the bed, both of the Tosa and of its tributaries, since these

*Sketch-map of the Val-Antigorio district.*

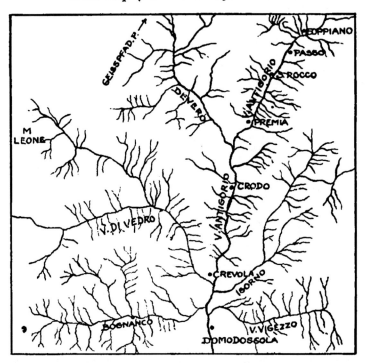

would show whether any important mass of that rock occurred
in the Val Formazza or in the other valleys. The test, though
obviously imperfect, is a fairly safe one, unless the outcrop be quite
small.

In applying it, I had the kind assistance of my friend, the Rev.
Edwin Hill, who about a fortnight before had joined me at Saas
Grund, and thus had become as familiar with antigorite-serpentines
as with those of the Lizard. A walk about Domo d'Ossola on the
evening of our arrival gave some hope of success, for among the
pebbles paving its streets serpentine of the Saasthal type is not
rare. Next morning we drove up the Tosa Valley to San Rocco,

distant between 17 and 18 miles from Domo d'Ossola. The road, on leaving this town, runs over a stony plain, where also the pebbles gave promise of serpentine, but these were left unexamined for the present; and, after passing the junction with the Simplon road at Crevola, we entered the beautiful Val Antigorio. Here and there the road skirts knolls of a variety of gneiss, now commonly called after the valley: its chief constituents are quartz, white felspar, and rather abundant biotite; its cliffs and its mode of weathering' suggest a granite, with a rather irregular jointing on a large scale, but the rock generally exhibits a fairly-definite cleavage-foliation, and is thus extensively quarried, as in De Saussure's time, to make posts, steps, or flags for roofing, fencing, and paving.[1] Gradually the sides of the valley become more craggy, and the alluvial plain by the Tosa narrows away on approaching the mouth of the Val Devero, the torrent from which rushes through a fine, though not very deep, gorge below Baceno, a townlet picturesquely perched on a headland between the two valleys. Beyond this, after passing through Premia, we enter the grander part of the Val Antigorio, with its magnificent crags, frequent waterfalls, and rich vegetation.[2]

At San Rocco,[3] about half a league below Passo, the bed of the valley (perhaps a quarter of a mile wide from cliff to cliff) is fairly level, and thus boulders and pebble-beds are not unfrequent by the riverside. Here we began our examination, walking up the road for about 3 miles, nearly to Rivasco, examining the outcrops of rock and the huge fallen masses, now abundant by its side, and making our way at intervals (six or seven times in all, including once just below San Rocco) to promising places by the river. We saw nothing from the road but Antigorio gneiss, and it formed the great majority of the pebbles and boulders, a few being pressure-modified diorites, and a still smaller number a greenish granitoid rock. Not one was serpentine, from which I infer this rock to be either absent from, or very rare in, the Tosa Valley above Premia.

We had now to ascertain the quarter from which the lower part of that valley had received pebbles of serpentine. Early next morning we left San Rocco, and after crossing the Devero torrent came to a spot at the foot of a slope by the roadside, where, on the previous day, I had noticed a few blocks of serpentine (the last

---

[1] That is to say, it is petrographically a gneiss, but is no doubt a pressure-modified granite. It is very fully described by Dr. S. Traverso in his 'Geologia dell' Ossola' 1895, pp. 59–69; also by Prof. H. Schardt, Archives des Sciences Physiques & Naturelles, ser. 3, vol. xxx (1893) p. 484.

[2] The band of white marble shown in the Swiss map near Premia was not visible by the roadside; but I found the rock next day both on heaps of road-metal and among the river-pebbles near Domo d'Ossola, nor was the Oberer gneiss with the micaceous variety containing unusually large garnets, of which I got specimens in 1860, at all well exposed (for a description see S. Traverso, op. cit. pp. 49–57). This gneiss differs considerably in aspect from the Antigorio gneiss, and reminded me of one variety common in the Saasthal.

[3] Here, it may be mentioned, the Albergo Vesci affords very fair accommodation.

visible).[1]   As at least a dozen were scattered over the few yards
from which the surface-soil had been partly removed, and two or
three of them were almost in contact, I infer that a fair number
must be concealed by the vegetation.   The blocks were angular or
subangular in form, varying in diameter up to about half-a-yard,
and the rock very closely resembled much of that in the Saasthal,
being of a fairly dark-green colour, slightly mottled with blacker
spots, so tough and hard that satisfactory specimens were difficult
to obtain.   It was but slightly schistose, developing under the
hammer an irregular jointing.   Under the microscope the rock is
found to consist of antigorite, a residual augite, and an iron-oxide.
The first needs little more than mention, as it resembles much of
that described in our paper of 1905: it is practically colourless and
non-pleochroic in a thin slice; it occurs in flakes, with hardly an
approach to orientation and rather variable in size, the largest
being about ·025 inch in length, but most of them not exceeding
the half of this.   The augite, forming about one-eighth of the
rock, occurs in irregular grains or granules, often with a slightly
' dusty' aspect, the former sometimes giving, for a space of about
a fiftieth of an inch, fairly uniform polarization-tints, sometimes
broken up, perhaps by pressure, into differently-coloured granules.
The mineral is in process of conversion into antigorite, for it
includes or is pierced by flakes of the latter, which bear no relation
to the cleavage-planes in the few cases where these can be detected.
The iron-oxide occurs in sporadic granules and irregularly-outlined
grains, occasionally pierced by small flakes of antigorite.   Examined
by reflected light they have a general resemblance to magnetite,
but the lustre seems to me not quite so bright as is usual; so
possibly they are chromite or ilmenite.

Evidently these blocks are relics of the glacier which formerly
descended the Val Devero—part of a scattered lateral moraine on
its right bank.   At the head of this valley the map records an
outcrop of serpentine, measuring about 2500 yards from east to
west, and 1500 yards from north to south, the apparent thickness of which is said to be 'several hundred feet'.[2]   This is
crossed by the Geisspfad Pass (8365 feet) from Binn to Baceno.
Some years ago my friend Mr. J. Eccles, F.G.S., kindly gave me
two specimens of this rock.   These consist mainly of an acicular
green hornblende embedded in talc.   But as the former mineral
indicates pressure-metamorphism,[3] and a schistose serpentine may
be altered into a talc-schist,[4] and as they were obtained near the
junction with gneiss on the Swiss side, they are probably abnormal;
for according to Dr. Preiswerk's account of the mass, to which I shall
again refer, the bulk of it, which on the Italian side breaks up into
separate sill-like intrusions, must often resemble the above-described

[1] The place was nearly opposite the actual junction of the Devero torrent
with the Tosa and at least 100 feet (I forgot to take a note) above it.
[2] John Ball, ' Central Alps ' p. 254 (ed. 1866).
[3] Quart. Journ. Geol. Soc. vol. xlix (1895) p. 94.
[4] Geol. Mag. dec. iii, vol. vii (1890) p. 540.

rock. But the number of the boulders shows that there must be other outcrops in the Val Devero : and Dr. S. Traverso [1] states that serpentine occurs, among other localities, on the Pizzo del Cervandone, where it is said to contain both unaltered olivine and asbestos.

We had next to determine whether any quantity of serpentine was received from the Val Bognanco and the Val di Vedro, the streams from which, at their junction with the Tosa, are only about three-quarters of a mile apart, and thus, as their fans are practically continuous, a boulder brought down even by the former might very well be reckoned as occurring in the Val Antigorio. After returning to Domo d'Ossola, we examined the stony plain deposited by the torrent from the Val Bognanco, the main channel of which must, I think, have formerly flowed to the south of its present position. Here water-worn fragments of serpentine were abundant : the larger (some 15 or 18 inches in diameter) more angular than the smaller, which were often flattened ellipsoids in shape; and the rock varying in structure from fairly massive to rather schistose. It was in fact indistinguishable from that so common in the upper part of the Saas Valley. Besides these, we found a few pebbles of a rock consisting of a fibrous green hornblende and rather saussuritic felspar, bearing some resemblance to one variety of the noted euphotide from the Allalin Glacier, and many of gneiss, which, however, generally was not of the 'Antigorio' type.

From this we went on to an extensive pebble-bed on the right bank of the Doveria torrent, and thus part of the fan from the Val di Vedro. Here serpentine was almost rare, and I saw only one pebble of the euphotide just mentioned, but the Antigorio gneiss was much more abundant, other varieties also occurring. The Swiss map shows two rather small outcrops of serpentine in the Val Bognanco,[2] and none in the Val di Vedro ; but I think that the facts stated above justify the conclusion that this rock must occupy a considerable area in the former, and may even have a few small outcrops in the latter valley ; though we must not forget that the Tosa, when in flood, might contribute some pebbles to the stony plain which is usually the 'dumping-ground' of the Doveria.

After this we crossed the Tosa above Domo d'Ossola, where it is divided into three or four channels, and examined the pebbles on an island very near its grass-grown eastern bank. This, under ordinary circumstances, must be out of range of the two above-named streams, but some stones might have come from the Val Devero, or have been brought by the tributary from the Val Vigezzo (which we were unable to visit). Here pebbles of serpentine were not very common, but of the usual types ; we also found some of a white or greyish marble, occasionally micaceous, representing that already mentioned ; a few of the hornblendic euphotide ; a fair amount of the Antigorio gneiss with some other varieties, and sundry

[1] 'Geologia dell' Ossola' 1895, pp. 169-71.
[2] Scale $\frac{1}{100,000}$. In Dr. Traverso's map (scale $\frac{1}{250,000}$) there are at least four, one being crossed by the torrent not far from the mouth of the valley.

crystalline rocks, including that called grüner schiefer by the Swiss geologists.  I have examined under the microscope a specimen of serpentine from the Val Bognanco, and another from the shoal near the left bank of the Tosa, which might possibly have come from the Val Devero, but more probably from the Val Vigezzo, selecting the one to represent a moderately schistose variety, and the other one of the most schistose.  The former rock is of a rather light greenish-grey colour, with small dark mottling.  Under the microscope it is seen to consist of matted antigorite, the flakes seldom, if ever, exceeding ·007 inch, and showing sometimes ' thorn-structure,' sometimes a slight parallelism.  The only trace of augite consists of ' cloudlets ' of minute granules, seeming, with ordinary light, like a dust, only a very few of which show a fairly bright-yellow tint with crossing nicols.  The iron-oxide is much as is described above.  The other specimen, rather conspicuously schistose, is of a greyish-green colour, slightly mottled with dark ; under the microscope it is seen to consist of antigorite, with a little residual augite in aggregated granules, which often have a more flaky aspect and lower polarization-tints than is usual (perhaps from incipient decomposition), and with magnetite, both obviously crushed.  The antigorite is small, seldom, if ever, exceeding ·004 inch, and shows a foliated structure, though not quite so conspicuously as I had expected.  Enough to say that these serpentines of the Tosa valley, in both megascopic and micro-scopic aspect, so closely resemble those with which I was already familiar in the Vispthal, that I could not distinguish them, if without labels.

We see then that antigorite-serpentine, probably derived from an augite-olivine rock, is abundant in the region west of the Tosa from Foppiano to Domo d'Ossola, and is found in the Val Vigezzo,[1] but its occurrence *in situ* in the Val Antigorio itself is very doubtful. Thus the original specimen may have been obtained, either from an erratic in the lower part of that valley, or from an actual outcrop in a tributary one (such as the Val Devero or the Val Bognanco), to which the name of the main valley has been rather inaccurately attached.  The proof of its absence from the Val Antigorio is obviously not complete, but could only be made so by long and laborious work, for which I have now neither the strength nor the inclination, and I am content to leave the task to members of the Italian Geological Survey.

## II. Other Antigorite-Serpentines.

Since the publication in November 1905 of the paper by Miss Raisin and myself, I have obtained some more information on antigorite. About a year ago, Dr. J. M. Bell, Director of the New Zealand

[1] Here, according to Dr. Traverso (' Geologia dell' Ossola ' 1895, pp. 166–169), peridotites also occur.

Geological Survey, kindly sent me a copy of its 'Bulletin,' which contained a description of some serpentines and other rocks (designated the Pounamu Formation), illustrated by unusually good and large figures of microscopic sections.[1] Two of these, entitled ' an altered olivine-rock ' and ' a serpentine-schist,' obviously consist of antigorite, although that name is not used; indeed it would be impossible to have a finer or more characteristic representation of the mineral than the former one affords.   Dr. Bell states that these rocks must originally have been peridotites and ' are generally massive, though sometimes fairly schistose,' the latter figure representing a variety from a region which has obviously undergone great pressure-metamorphism.   Our hopes of meeting during his recent visit to England were unfortunately frustrated, but I received just before completing this paper a box containing about a dozen fine specimens of dunite, serpentines, and allied rocks, which in accordance with his instructions had been sent to me from New Zealand.   Four of these, the most important for my present purpose, I had immediately sliced; but I trust before long to examine the remainder,[2] and tender my most hearty thanks to Dr. Bell and other members of the Survey for so valuable a gift.

Of those four, the dunite (from the Dun Mountains, Nelson) is a block, measuring nearly $7 \times 5 \times 3$ inches, of greenish-yellow colour, showing occasional blackish and dull-green specks, with a slight cleavage, rudely parallel with the broader surfaces. Under the microscope it is seen to consist chiefly of grains of olivine, very clearly exhibiting interrupted lines of crush, in which serpentinization is incipient; a few of the larger grains show a rather vaguely-defined oscillatory twinning, probably also a result of pressure. A little diopside is present in the slice, as also some rather rounded subtranslucent and deep-brown grains of chromite, or perhaps in some cases picotite. A handsome specimen of an ' actinolite-and-talc rock from a boulder, Clear Creek, Mikonui (Toaroha District),' has a general resemblance to the rock described above (p. 156) from the northern margin of the Geisspfad mass of serpentine; but the actinolites, many of which are rudely parallel, are more numerous

---

[1] New Zealand Geol. Surv. n. s. Bull. No. 1, ' Geology of the Hokitika Sheet, North Westland Quadrangle' by J. M. Bell & Colin Fraser, 1906. See Ch. viii (the plates are not numbered).   The figures appear, with brief descriptions of the slices (without, however, using the name antigorite), in Prof. Sollas's Memoir on the Rocks of Cape Colville Peninsula, New Zealand, vol. ii (1906) pp. 186–202.

[2] [Slices from these reached me immediately after this paper was read.   The following are most nearly connected with it :—(1) ' Ultrabasic rock, Dun Saddle' : a dark compact rock, with some rather small bastite, consisting of olivine, more or less serpentinized, bastite, sometimes much altered, (?) diallage (one grain), and picotite. (2) ' Serpentine, Dun Saddle' : a dark, rather uniform serpentine, which shows under the microscope a pale yellowish-green tint and the usual ' meshwork' serpentine, marked out by strings of magnetite-granules, with a slight parallelism.   There are some small grains of chromite and a few (rather larger) of a more steatitic aspect, possibly indicating the former presence of a pyroxene in very small quantities.   Two other interesting specimens are described below.]

and much larger, some being at least an inch long; while the talc, as becomes very plain on microscopic examination, is less abundant.[1]

That the other two specimens were antigorite-serpentines was obvious at a glance. One (boulder in Cross River, Mikonui, Whitcome Pass District), a somewhat flat flake, measuring fully 6 × 5 inches, and about an inch and a half thick, with a slight and rough cleavage oblique to the broader face, is a mottled rock—dark purplish-green, and lighter green, here and there irregularly streaked with a still paler green. Microscopic examination shows it to be composed of antigorite, with a fair amount of residual augite, perhaps a few flakelets of talc, and iron-oxide, with a little sulphide. The antigorite-flakes have a slightly tufted and occasionally somewhat acicular habit, attaining not seldom a length of about ·03 inch. There is a fair amount of residual augite, often 'stabbed' by the other mineral, which, so far as I can ascertain, is not related to the cleavage-planes of the augite, except that in a few cases, where the remnant is a very narrow wedge, this extinguishes at a rather small angle with its sides. The granules of iron-oxide are irregularly distributed and in one or two places, which are free from residual augite, they suggest the former presence of a 'mesh-work.' Of the occasional larger grains, one is distinctly translucent, and of a rich brown colour; others slightly so: thus chromite, or possibly picotite, must be present. The light-coloured streaks mentioned above, when examined with a lens, included a mineral with some resemblance to olivine; but, as a little of the powder showed under the microscope distinct, rather elongated, prisms with a low extinction-angle, it must be a variety of actinolite. The second specimen, from Griffin Range, Hokitika (Turiwate District), is a still larger slab, rather darker in colour, which retains on one side a portion of an external surface with a bright brown tint and a slightly 'corded' structure. A slice, cut perpendicular to, and in the direction of, the slight cleavage, proves to be wholly composed of antigorite and iron-oxide; the latter being apparently not very abundant or large in grain, but now and then pierced by the former, to which it locally imparts a rich sienna-brown stain. The antigorite-flakes are smaller, not more than one-third of the length of those in the other specimens, and generally narrower in proportion to their length. Some parts of the slice, where the smallness is rather marked, show an approach to 'thorn-structure'; others a distinctly tufted grouping, which occasionally is slightly cruciform

[1] A specimen labelled 'coarse peridotite (Dun Saddle, Nelson), probably with bronzite,' is crowded with close-cleaved specimens of the latter mineral, sometimes about an inch long or wide. Examination of it, when powdered, leads me to refer the bulk of it at any rate to diallage. [A slice, received since this paper was read, shows that a diallage is the dominant mineral, but there is some enstatite (probably bastite); and, I think, a few grains (sometimes poecilitic) of a brownish-yellow, slightly-fibrous. obviously much-altered mineral, probably representing a ferriferous member of this group (bronzite or perhaps hypersthene). A grain or two of olivine may be present, with some granules of iron-oxide. I should think it likely that the rock formed dykes or veins cutting the dunite.]

or almost spherulitic : the axes of the former showing some inclination (though it is not very marked) to parallelism with, and per-
pendicularity to, the direction of the slight cleavage.  I have noticed
this tendency to an acicular or dagger-like form occasionally in my
Alpine specimens; and if either of these two had been given to me
as coming from one of the regions mentioned above, I should not
have had any suspicions.  I may add that among the other interesting
specimens is a much slickensided piece of a dark-green serpentine,
closely resembling some of those from the Engadine, described
below.  It comes from Asbestus Creek, Mikonui (Toaroha District).
[Microscopic examination shows the resemblance to be as close as
possible.   The rock consists of serpentinized olivine with some
grains of chromite and a much altered, close-cleaved mineral,
probably once enstatite.  In parts it shows signs of fracture under
pressure, which has given rise to curving lines of more or less
fibrous serpentine, the fibres lying either along or oblique to their
direction.   Here and there an approach to a rather minute 'thorn-
structure' may be detected, but nowhere any thoroughly typical
antigorite.]

The Mineralogical Museum at Cambridge contains three specimens of antigorite - serpentine, about which Prof. Lewis and
Dr. A. Hutchinson have kindly supplied me with information.  Two
are in the Wiltshire Collection (presented in 1897), one purchased
from Foote, the other from Baldon ; both being labelled ' Zermatt,
Switzerland.'  I have little doubt that they were obtained near
the well-known tarn (about 9000 feet) at the base of the peak of the
Riffelhorn.[1]   The third specimen has been for many years in the
Museum, and its locality is not known ; but it is so like the others
that it might well be from the same place.

The result of my journey led me to re-examine the specimens in
the Mineral Collection at the British Museum (Natural History), and
to enquire more particularly into their history, and I gladly take this
opportunity of thanking Mr. L. J. Spencer for his kind assistance.
They are as follows :—(1) A pale-green slab measuring about 6 by
$4\frac{1}{2}$ inches, rather thin, but opaque, purchased from F. H. Hoseus,
mineral-dealer at Basel, in 1871 : his label gives Maderanerthal
(Switzerland), which is corrected in Mr. Fletcher's handwriting to
Zermatt.   It might very well have come from the base of the Riffelhorn or the neighbouring part of the Gorner Grat. (2) A flake, $2\frac{1}{2}$
by 2 inches, transparent green, without any black mottling ; one of
the Allan-Greg specimens received in 1860 without number, and
entered in an appendix by the late T. Davies to the catalogue of
that collection as : ' Antigorite, Antigorio Valley : this also much
resembles Riffelberg specimens. (3) A thin oval slab, $5\frac{1}{2}$ by nearly
$3\frac{3}{4}$ inches, polished on both sides, translucent in parts, rich green
mottled with dark : entered under date 1829 (Allan-Greg Collection)
as ' noble serpentine' without locality, to which T. Davies has

---

[1] See my paper, Geol. Mag. dec. iii, vol. vii (1890) p. 533.

added ' Antigorite, Antigorio Valley.' (4) A thin polished slice, resembling the last in translucency and colour ($2\frac{1}{2}$ by $2\frac{1}{4}$ inches), probably acquired before 1837: registered by T. Davies as 'Antigorite, Antigorio Valley.' (5) A box, with a lid, made of thin polished slabs cemented together, $3\frac{3}{4} \times 1\frac{3}{4} \times 1\frac{1}{2}$ inches; material similar to the last two: this specimen has the same history as No. 4. (6 & 7) Two paper-knives, mounted in wooden handles, material similar to that of other polished specimens; entered, under date 1831, as ' noble serpentine,' with the remark ' This substance occurs in boulders on the shore of the Island of Ischia near Naples.' As I have never landed on Ischia, I cannot say more than that it is one of the last places in which I should have expected to find serpentine of this type.

I regret to say that, when writing my note on the microscopic section made in 1905,[1] I supposed it to have been cut from No. 2, to which the megascopic description applies. But I now find that it represents No. 4, a small portion of which was ground down to the requisite thinness. A second study of this slice has made me less confident about the very few and very ill-preserved pyroxenes being enstatite. I was led to this conclusion by observing traces of a parallel cleavage (with straight extinction) in one or two grains, but have found in specimens from the Saasthal (sliced since those words were written) that occasionally the larger flakes of antigorite (formed from grains of diallagitic augite somewhat bigger than the rest) locally arrange themselves, side by side, so as to present, with their straight extinction, a rather close resemblance to a serpentinized enstatite.[2] In any case, whether these mottled rocks were originally saxonites, lherzolites, or augite–olivine peridotites, it is evidently uncertain from what localities they were obtained.

During our stay at Saas Grund last summer, we examined (as I had done on previous occasions) the boulders of serpentine which abound in the moraines of the Fee Glacier and on the bed of the main valley between that village and the Mattmark Inn.[3] Near the latter they are exceptionally numerous in two places: one, just at the lower end of the Mattmark See, where the path crosses a slope of broken rock, mostly a fissile antigorite-serpentine, which very probably formed part of the right moraine of the Allalin Glacier, when the ice extended across the river[4]; the other, a short distance above the inn, where the gigantic ' Blauenstein,'[5] with its two associates, one of

---

[1] Quart. Journ. Geol. Soc. vol. lxi, p. 700.

[2] The structure of one grain, I may add, rather resembles that of olivine, though the strings are not marked out by iron-oxide.

[3] See the paper by Miss Raisin and myself in this Journal, vol. lxi (1905) pp. 707–709.

[4] As it did in 1860.

[5] For a figure, see E. Whymper, ' A Guide to Zermatt & the Matterhorn' 7th ed. (1903) p. 189; J. de Charpentier (' Essai sur les Glaciers' 1841, p. 252) states that in 1821 old men were still alive, who had heard their fathers say that they had seen it ' sur le dos du glacier.' As the size has been variously stated, I may say that I measured it roughly in 1891, and found the length to be 58 feet, the breadth 50 feet, and estimated the height as about equal to the length.

which would elsewhere be considered very large, and a host of smaller blocks, represent a scattered moraine of the Schwarzenberg Glacier. In 1905, I described a slice from the least of the trio and this year managed to detach from the Blauenstein itself a loose fragment just big enough to furnish a slice. The rock consists of antigorite, with a fair amount of residual augite in granules suggestive of crushed grains, and some iron-oxide and sulphide. One portion of the slice shows rather distinctly a 'puckered' foliation. Thus the rock has undergone pressure, though it is not now at all fissile. I had neglected to carry away specimens of the Allalin moraine, but that defect was kindly remedied by my friends, Messrs. J. J. Lister, F.R.S., and R. H. Rastall, F.G.S., who brought me three good cabinet-specimens: one barely, another moderately, and a third very fissile, and slightly puckered. A slice from the second shows, as I was certain would be the case, that it is rich in antigorite, much of it small and with a foliated aspect. It also contains a little residual augite and some iron-oxide suggestive of crushing.

I again visited the great dyke of fissile serpentine [1] which cuts calc-mica-schist on the western flank of a mound on the Fee Alp, to which the figures 2136 metres (7081 feet) are attached. It is marked on sheet xxiii of the Swiss Geological-Survey map, but I think that the breadth is rather exaggerated.[2] Its junction with the calc-mica-schist was not well exposed on the more northern side, but on the southern it was clearer; and, notwithstanding much crushing and an oblique fault, it still remained unbroken for 2 or 3 feet, showing a good weld with a slightly wavy surface. The serpentine also completely overarched a mass of much contorted calc-mica-schist about a couple of yards wide and a little more in height,[3] the more northern side of which apparently exhibited a slight interlamination of serpentine and the schist, as if the former had thrust a tongue or two into the latter and both had been crushed out together. On the other side a little wedge of the schist was isolated in crushed serpentine: also a small patch of serpentine, measuring about 2 by 3 inches, still adhered to the face of the included mass of calc-mica-schist. I have no recollection of having seen the latter, either in 1891 or in 1901, and the notes then made differ in some details from what we saw last summer, so I think that the face of the cliff must have been changed in the interval by falls of rock. The serpentine again crops out, after being concealed beneath turf, scree, and moraine, on the steep rocky slope descending to the northernmost arm of the Fee Glacier. Here it is, if possible, yet more crushed, and the junctions are masked.

Another and much greater mass of serpentine occurs on the same 'buttress of an alp' at a considerably higher level. This is the Langefluh, a broad promontory of rock, about two-thirds of a mile in length, running almost north and south between the arms of the Fee Glacier, and rising ultimately to a height of 2875 metres

---

[1] The microscopic structure is described at p. 709 of vol. lxi of this Journal.
[2] In the face of the cliff it was perhaps more than 20 yards broad, but the section may be oblique.
[3] This statement is from memory; I forgot, at the time, to record the figures.

(9433 feet), with a precipitous eastern face, up which a narrow path leads obliquely from the Fee Alp.    The whole, so far as I could see,[1] is serpentine, rather fissile where first traversed, but afterwards generally massive.    This is of the usual rather dull-green colour, mottled with darker patches (the fissile specimens being of a paler tint, no doubt from incipient weathering), and the exposed surfaces are changed to a fawn-brown colour.    In fact, the blocks so abundant in the moraines of the Fee Glacier, specimens of which were described in 1905, represent either this mass or some part of the Allalinhorn (13,235 feet) of which it may be a spur.    The rock is considerably harder and tougher than the ordinary bastite-serpentine, and as the surface is everywhere rounded by ice-action, it is difficult to obtain well-shaped specimens.    I took samples:— (1) at the spot where I turned back (probably about 200 feet below the highest point); (2) from about half-way between this and the place where the path reaches the top of the cliff; and (3) from the fissile part, near its base.

The first (1) consists of the following minerals:—antigorite in rather irregularly matted flakes, seldom exceeding ·005 inch in diameter—those in one or two little patches being distinctly smaller than the rest.    A few minute granules giving bright polarization-tints may be residual augite, but occasionally bear some resemblance to talc.    One or two grains of fair size and irregular outline, of a very pale warm-brown tint, show a close parallel cleavage, ex-tinguishing parallel to it with crossed nicols and giving in other positions a dull but rich blue colour; flakes of antigorite sometimes pierce these grains, sometimes lie between their cleavage-surfaces. A mineral presenting a resemblance to this occurs in one of the Anglesey serpentines,[2] where I think that it represents a member of the enstatite-group.    The second (2) consists of a similar antigorite, but with some residual augite, pierced and often ' riddled ' by flakes of the other mineral, which, to judge from the polarization-tints, may have formed grains about 0·1 inch in diameter.    Granules of iron-oxide and sulphide are rather numerous, but irregularly distributed, being often apparently associated with the augite and probably showing signs of crushing.    The third, not the most fissile variety of (3), consists of antigorite and iron-oxide (hardly any sulphide) as above: both exhibiting a more definite foliation, and the latter occurring in more distinct layers, which suggest here and there the crushing-out of grains, and sometimes impart a brown stain to the neighbouring serpentine.    No residual augite is visible.

It is rather remarkable that none of the specimens prepared either for this or for our former paper contain any residual

[1] Want of time obliged me to turn back near the foot of the rocky mound at the upper end.

[2] That from near a quarry south of Cru-Glas, Quart. Journ. Geol. Soc. vol. xxxvii (1881) p. 45.

olivine.[1] In a few the matted antigorite is traversed by tiny strings of opacite resembling those in a serpentine formed from that mineral, or it occupies small spaces in one of the larger grains of pyroxene, suggestive of pœcilitic olivine; but that antigorite can be produced from olivine seems to be certain. Dr. F. Becke, in his valuable paper on 'Olivinfels & Antigorite-Serpentine' from the Stubachthal,[2] distinctly states that the unaltered rock consists of olivine and picotite, sometimes with a diopside. It shows signs of a cataclastic structure, and flakes of antigorite can be seen in the cracks of the grains of olivine, separating them into granules, but not forming so characteristic a meshwork as in the ordinary process of serpentinization, while in other parts of the mass the change to an antigorite-serpentine is complete. Dr. H. Preiswerk[3] also, in his concise and interesting account of the serpentine at the upper part of the Geisspfad Pass, says that the mass in its central portion is a dunite, though it contains diallage towards the periphery, where it occasionally becomes almost a diallagite. Antigorite is produced from both its minerals, but seems to come more directly from the pyroxenic constituent, and a little actinolite is a usual alteration-product.[4] Again, Dr. J. M. Bell in his reply, dated December 7th, 1907, to an enquiry about the specimens of antigorite-rock, forwarded to me from New Zealand, says:

'I feel confident that the parent rock was mainly olivine, with perhaps a little pyroxene, either orthorhombic or monoclinic. One gets apparently the transition of this rock into dunite.'

In No. 3 of the Bulletin ('The Geology of the Parapura Subdivision, Karamea, Nelson'), for which I am also indebted to him, serpentines and talc-schists (sills and perhaps dykes) are described (Ch. ix), which break through highly metamorphic strata and may possibly be of Haupiri (? Devonian) age. The former consist chiefly of antigorite, with minor quantities of talc, chromite, etc.; the latter, no doubt a further stage of alteration, due partly to pressure, pass

---

[1] Last autumn, a friend suggested to me that some clear sienna-brown grains, in a slice from a specimen obtained on an old moraine near the Findelen Glacier, were titanolivine. As his experience is large and that mineral has been obtained in this district, I have again examined not only that slice, but also the others with residual pyroxene. The form of the grains, however, is more suggestive of augite than of olivine; a rudely shaped prism may be tinted at one end, clear at the other; the pleochroism seems hardly strong enough for titanolivine, and the extinction in both coloured and uncoloured grains is oblique and like that of augite. Hence I think the former only a result of staining (see our paper of 1905, p. 706).

[2] Tschermak's Min. Petr. Mitth. n. s. vol. xiv (1894-95) p. 271.

[3] Eclog. Geol. Helvet. vol. vii (1901-1902) p. 123.

[4] R. von Drasche, Tschermak's Mineral. Mitth. p. 1, in Jahrb. K. K. Geol. Reichsanst. vol. xxi (1871), describes the formation of antigorite (without, however, using the name) from an olivine-rock. The Cogne serpentines (see Quart. Journ. Geol. Soc. vol. lix, 1903, pp. 58-60) on the whole favour the formation of antigorite from olivine.

into the former, and evidently are generally similar to some that I have described from the Alps.[1] Both, it is said,

'have apparently resulted from the alteration of some olivine-rock, most probably dunite, as judged by the presence of chromite in greater or lesser quantity' (p. 66).

Some, however, of my specimens, as described in 1905,[2] exhibit very clearly the direct production of antigorite from augite, and prove that the latter mineral must have been so abundant in the original rock as to make it an olivine-augite rock, like some of that in the Vosges, where the pyroxenic constituent occasionally dominates.[3] It must also have been very closely related to the hornblendic serpentines from the Lizard coast between Mullion and Lower Predanack,[4] besides the well-known one from the Rauenthal[5] (for hornblende and augite are practically isomorphous), and in all these the monoclinic constituent is occasionally more abundant than the olivine[6]; and that there was a like excess in some of these specimens of Alpine serpentines appears, from the abundance of the residual augite in the slices, to be very probable.

That this mineral is converted into antigorite more readily than olivine seems, however, fairly certain. When I saw, now several years ago, the bastite-serpentines in the Eastern Grisons and the Mont Genèvre district, I naturally took my specimens from the parts least affected by pressure, and thus had hardly any material for studying its effects. From this difficulty I was relieved by Miss Raisin, who very kindly halted on her way to Pontresina last September to examine the serpentines near the Julier road, and has provided me with an ample supply of specimens from the crushed parts of outcrops east of Tiefenkastell, the Val da Faller, and by the Silser See.[7] These are seen at a glance to be very different from the antigorite-serpentines. Pressure makes the latter fissile, converting them, when it has been very severe, into slabs or even slates, as already described, but it breaks up these bastite-serpentines into lenticular masses, more or less irregular in form. Their exterior is covered by a lustrous dark-green film, showing slickensides, but when the rock is broken across its character is comparatively normal, and flakes of bastite can sometimes be detected.

I have examined slices from seven of the most promising specimens. They come from an outcrop near the Silser See at the head

---

[1] Geol. Mag. dec. iii, vol. vii (1890) p. 533, & dec. iv, vol. iv (1897) p. 110.

[2] Quart. Journ. Geol. Soc. vol. lxi (1905) pp. 706–12; also several specimens collected since the reading of that paper.

[3] Op. cit. p. 697.

[4] This variety occurs at other localities on the peninsula. See this Journal, vol. lii (1896) p. 46.

[5] Geol. Mag. dec. iii, vol. iv (1887) pp. 67–69, & Miss C. A. Raisin, this Journal, vol. liii (1897) p. 246.

[6] It is also noteworthy that the hornblende-serpentine at the Lizard is distinctly harder to break and rougher to the touch than the ordinary bastite-serpentine.

[7] Described in my paper, Geol. Mag. dec. ii, vol. vii (1880) p. 538.

of the Inn Valley, and from three localities connected with the upper valley of the Oberhalbstein Rhine, namely, at Salux, in the Val da Faller, and from near the high-road south of Tiefenkastell.[1] Of two specimens from the first place, both exhibit serpentinized bastite and traces of olivine (in the characteristic meshwork) ; they contain here and there a rather fibrous variety of serpentine, often with a slightly tufted habit (? chrysotile or picrolite), which in one specimen assumes a more flaky character, and thus approaches antigorite.   In the Val da Faller the serpentine occurs in four masses, three dyke-like and the fourth more irregular in outline, having probably one outlying patch.   Of specimens from these, the first, in one case, shows the meshwork indicative of former olivine, altered bastite, and some augite, none of the serpentine having the antigoritic habit ; another specimen affords little evidence of the original minerals, and is becoming talcose, but the serpentine, when not of the usual habit, is at most fibrous.   The second mass shows serpentinized olivine and enstatite, the latter retaining traces of the usual cleavage, but almost inert to polarized light except at the edges, where it has some little resemblance to antigorite.   There are also some irregular grains of augite.   Fibrous serpentine is rather commoner than usual, but typical antigorite is not present. A specimen from the third mass retains traces of altered olivine, but though evidently much crushed, even to showing some ' crumpling,' it does not contain antigorite.   A flaky specimen (9 feet from the junction) of a probable outlier of the fourth mass, exhibits under the microscope a felted, somewhat foliated aggregate of a serpentinous mineral (rather minute), in which are small acicular prisms of a mineral with much the same refractive index, but higher polarization-tints and a rather large extinction-angle.   If the former represent antigorite, it is very abnormal.   A flattish, rather fissile flake, about as hard as the finger-nail, ' from N. of Salux,'[2] consists mainly of a rather minute and fibrous mineral, with grey polarization-tints, and a felted-foliated structure, which is probably nearer to steatite than true serpentine ; but an uncut specimen resembles a normal olivine-serpentine, and may retain traces of bastite.   Of three specimens from the mass near the village of Rofna (south of Tiefenkastell[3]) on the Julier road, one, though crushed and veined, retains some indications of altered olivine, has recognizable bastite, and is unusually rich in an iron-oxide (probably chromite) : another contains some altered bastite, locally darkened with granules of magnetite, and suggests the former presence of olivine, but is traversed by some rudely parallel veins, occupied by a fibrous serpentine (? picrolite) arranged at right angles to their general direction, which occasionally exhibit a slight approach to the mica-

[1] For further particulars, see Geol. Mag. *ut supra*.   I restrict, for the sake of brevity, the present notice of microscopic structures to those germane to the purpose of this paper.
[2] On the western slope of the Oberhalbstein valley, between Molins and Tiefenkastell.
[3] Geol. Mag. dec. ii, vol. vii (1880) p. 539.

168     PROF. T. G. BONNEY ON ANTIGORITE     [May 1908,

like habit of antigorite. The third consists of a mass of acicular
flakes with a general parallelism and slightly wavy structure, a few
of which have a higher refractive index than the rest. This
approaches nearer to the antigorite exhibited in very fissile specimens, but cannot be called a satisfactory example of that mineral.

Thus the evidence of these specimens of crushed bastite-serpentines from the Rhætian Alps seems at first sight unfavourable to
the very clear and precise statements of Becke and Proiswerk. We
may perhaps offer the following explanation of the discrepancy.
When a peridotite rich in olivine (for instance, dunite) is acted on
by pressure,[1] it becomes slightly slabby, and microscopic examination
shows that mineral to occur in grains, rather variable in size, with
some little approach to a parallel ordering ; in other words, the
rock shows signs of a crush-structure. Turning to the antigorite-
rocks of the Alps, we find that some of these exhibit, by means of
the residual augite, clear indications of having been more or less
crushed. The flakes of the antigorite in some cases are arranged
at right angles to the pressure, but in others they lie at all angles,
and are even 'matted' together. In the latter cases the development
of antigorite seems to have made the rock as a whole more solid ;
while in the former, as the fissility increases, the size of the flakes
diminishes.[2] I infer, then, from examination of the specimens in
my collection, that, in the case of many, an augite-peridotite was
first more or less crushed : next, the comminuted parts (most of the
olivine and some of the augite) were converted (still under some
pressure) into antigorite, which change often had the effect of making
the rock less fissile than it had been. By the renewal of severe
pressure, the layers of residual augite and of antigorite might be
folded, or, if the former mineral had disappeared, the mass might be
rendered very fissile, with diminution of the size of the constituents,
as we find in the most 'slaty' antigorite-serpentines. In other
words, owing to the comparative uniformity of the rock, pressure
acts upon it as on any other nearly homogeneous mass. and produces
a very conspicuous cleavage. In the latter case, then, the stages
are : (1) augite-olivine rock, (2) the same somewhat cleaved, (3) antigorite-rock, comparatively massive, and (4) antigorite-'slate' (consequence of renewed pressure). Thus many of the antigorite-rocks,
described in this paper, are, speaking in general terms, in the third
stage, while others are intermediate between it and the fourth,
which is completely reached by the most fissile specimens.

But a peridotite, whether with augite or enstatite, or with both
these minerals, which has been converted into a serpentine like
that in the Rhætian Alps, has in consequence become brittle ; hence,
under pressure, it forms a 'crush-breccia' with fragments of various
shapes, irregularly angular, as well as lenticular. These, if the

[1] I have examined specimens from New Zealand and from Norway.
[2] Gorner Grat, Fee Alp, Col de Vallante. etc. The same thing occurs
commonly in mica-schists, which may be so crushed as to be distinguished
with difficulty from ordinary phyllites.

pressure be continued, slide one over the other[1] and thus often elude much further crushing.[2] In the last extreme an antigorite-serpentine may perhaps be produced, but then it will be of the most 'slaty' type.

Thus these later observations confirm the opinion founded on work done before the summer of 1905, namely, that while antigorite apparently forms with greater facility from augite than from olivine, pressure is a most important factor in its production,[3] and this should come into play before the minerals have undergone much alteration. Enstatite, while forming a mineral rather of the antigorite-type, seems, if uncrushed, generally to retain some distinctive characteristic; so that I think we cannot, as has been suggested, place it nearly on the same level with augite as the parent of the mineral, named with dubious authority from the Val Antigorio.[4]

### III. NOTE ON BOWENITE.

The above-described studies led me to re-examine some miscellaneous slices of serpentine in my cabinets, among which was one of bowenite given to me by the late General McMahon, soon after writing his paper on that mineral—or rather rock—from Afghanistan.[5] The microscopic structure, as it differed much from that of the serpentines on which I was then occupied, had escaped my memory, but on looking at it recently, I was surprised at its resemblance to antigorite. Needless to say that my late friend's description is accurate, though perhaps in the specimen before me flakes are more numerous than fibres,[6] which, however, may be due to my being practised in identifying the former; also, though I occasionally see three directions of orientation for the flakes, only one seems to me definite enough to be suggestive of a cleavage. In other words, I note here and there a group of flakes—running up to about ·02 inch in length—lying parallel with and near one another—suggesting the former presence of a diallage or a bastite. At high (not always right) angles with these are occasional shorter flakes, or groups of such, parallel one with another, while some parts of the slice show 'thorn-structure' on a smaller scale, as described in our paper of 1905. Scattered about the field are a few needles or flakes with a higher refractive index than those forming the groundmass, though not yielding brighter polarization-tints.

---

[1] The surfaces are so completely slickensided that a new fracture must be made to show the rock.

[2] That is the reason why very fair specimens of the normal rock can often be obtained from the middle part of an Alpine mass, the outer crush-zones having acted like a 'packing' of shavings or sawdust to the rest.

[3] Quart. Journ. Geol. Soc. vol. lxi (1905) p. 714.

[4] Without marked pressure olivine changes into ordinary serpentine more readily than enstatite, and that than augite (perhaps also than hornblende). To produce antigorite pressure seems essential, and this apparently makes augite pass into that mineral more readily than into ordinary serpentine in the other case.

[5] Min. Mag. vol. ix (1890) p. 187.

[6] The flakes, however, not unfrequently are rather dagger-shaped.

Still, I think them indicative of actinolite or partly-altered residual pyroxene. As we find only very slight traces of any ferriferous constituent, I would suggest the possibility of the rock having originally consisted almost entirely of an augite akin to diopside (like some which occur in Canada) rather than, as my late friend suggested, an olivine-rock from which the iron has been leached out.

### DISCUSSION.

Dr. J. S. FLETT congratulated the Author on having traced the antigorite-serpentine of Val Antigorio to its source. These rocks were full of interest, though rare. Very few examples occurred in the British Isles : the speaker had met with some in Perthshire accompanying the great epidiorites that go with the Loch-Tay Limestone ; he had also seen specimens which were believed to come from Shetland, and were as perfect as any that the Author of the paper had exhibited on this occasion. In Unst and Fetlar, in the extreme north of Scotland, there were large masses of serpentine known to geologists through the descriptions of Hibbert, Heddle, Peach, and Horne. In Balta Sound and Haroldswick the Unst serpentine was intersected by many veins of pyroxenite. The whole complex had been sheared, and in these veins antigorite was developing from the pyroxene, which corroborated the Author's views as to the origin of this mineral.

Mr. J. ALLAN THOMSON instanced a case of pseudomorphism of olivine by an antigorite-like mineral in the hornblende-peridotite of Greystones. It differed from true antigorite in possessing a very faint pleochroism and higher birefringence. The Author had concluded in his former paper that these properties, which he had sometimes found in minerals accompanying antigorite, were accidental. They might, however, be explained on Prof. Tschermak's hypothesis of the composition of the orthochlorites as solid solutions of the antigorite- and amesite-molecules. Dr. Weinschenk considered iddingsite as a pleochroic antigorite.

The interesting point about the pseudomorph was that the antigorite-flakes lay parallel to the clinodomes of the olivine, which met at an angle of about 60°. The resulting 'gitter'-structure might easily be confused with the lattice-structure of serpentine derived from a non-aluminous amphibole. Dr. Weinschenk had described the same phenomena in the olivine of the Stubach serpentine, and considered the antigorite as an original mineral intergrown with olivine by 'piezocrystallization.'

The AUTHOR said that he was much interested to hear from Dr. Flett that antigorite-serpentines had been found in Shetland, and should look forward to reading the account of them. The replacement of olivine by antigorite, in the case described by Mr. Thomson, was remarkable ; but he thought that any definite relation between the flakes of the latter and the crystal-figure of the former mineral was very rare. He thanked the Fellows present for having listened so patiently to a statement which had taken more time than he had anticipated.

10. *On the* APPLICATION *of* QUANTITATIVE METHODS *to the* STUDY *of the* STRUCTURE *and* HISTORY *of* ROCKS.   By the late HENRY CLIFTON SORBY, LL.D., F.R.S., F.L.S., F.G.S. (Read January 8th, 1908.)

[PLATES XIV-XVIII.]

### CONTENTS.

| | | Page |
|---|---|---|
| I. | Introduction | 171 |
| II. | Final Velocities | 172 |
| III. | Angles of Rest of Sand and of Small Pebbles | 174 |
| IV. | The Effects of Currents | 176 |
| V. | Ripple-Drift | 181 |
| VI. | Varying Size of the Grains | 185 |
| VII. | Drift-Bedding | 186 |
| VIII. | Joints of Encrinites, etc. | 189 |
| IX. | Very Fine-Grained Deposits | 189 |
| X. | The Green Slates of Langdale | 196 |
| XI. | Washing-up, etc. of Clays | 199 |
| XII. | On the Interspaces between the Constituent Grains of Deposited Material | 200 |
| XIII. | Segregation | 203 |
| XIV. | Contraction of Rocks after Deposition | 214 |
| XV. | Concretions | 215 |
| XVI. | Spots in Welsh Slates | 220 |
| XVII. | Slip-Surfaces | 222 |
| XVIII. | Surfaces of Pressure-Solution | 224 |
| XIX. | Determination of the Pressure to which Rocks have been Subjected | 227 |

## I. INTRODUCTION.

IN the case of nearly all branches of science a great advance was made when accurate quantitative methods were used instead of merely qualitative. One great advantage of this is that it necessitates more accurate thought, points out what remains to be learned, and sometimes small residual quantities, which otherwise would escape attention, indicate important facts. Since it applies to nearly all branches of geology, it is necessarily a wide subject, but so connected together that it seems undesirable to divide it.

My object is to apply experimental physics to the study of rocks.

At least six different kinds of physical questions are involved, some of which have been sufficiently studied, but others require experiments which would be very difficult to carry out, and all that I can now do is to endeavour to deduce plausible results from what is known. In doing this, it may be necessary to assume cases sufficiently simple for calculation, which may but imperfectly correspond to natural conditions, so that the results may be only approximately correct. In some cases, facts seem to show that there are important properties connected with subsiding material

which cannot be explained in a satisfactory manner. Notwithstanding this, it appears desirable to do the best that I can with
the material at my disposal, hoping to lead others to do what I
intended to do, and correct such errors as are now unavoidable.

In order to clear the way for subsequent detail, I describe a few
general facts. To learn the final velocities of subsiding sediment
I made many experiments, and found it a most complex question,
requiring much more study. Coarse and somewhat fine sand-grains
subside and collect at once on the bottom in a fairly-settled condition, yet the interspaces between the grains may amount to half
the total bulk. Very fine-grained material, when more than 1 per
cent. of the water, behaves in a totally-different manner, and, as a
whole, somewhat like an imperfect liquid; and, in extreme cases,
even after standing for a year, it may contain 90 per cent. of
water. Very fine-grained sand possesses this latter property to a
slight extent.

## II. Final Velocities.

In the year 1859 I made many experiments, in order to learn the
laws regulating the subsidence of various solid substances in
water, more especially of sand and flakes of mica. Their size was
first carefully measured with a micrometer-microscope, and those
were selected which were of fairly-uniform diameter in all directions,
but only the smallest were adopted for the calculations. These
grains were carefully introduced separately in a wet condition into
a tall jar of water, and the number of seconds which they occupied
in subsiding a foot and a half was observed. In experimenting
with spheres, cubes, and thin plates of glass, as well as with grains
of sand and mica, it was found that the relation between the final
velocity and the diameter is of so complex a character that it
cannot be expressed in any simple manner, as though the result
depends on complex conditions. I therefore fall back on experiment, and deal only with such cases as are of geological interest;
but I may say that spheres, cubes, and plates of glass yield similar
results.

### Grains of Sand.

My best experiments were with grains varying from $\frac{2}{5}$ to
$\frac{1}{200}$ inch in diameter, which gave final velocities from about a foot
down to ·055 foot per second. For diameters varying from two-
fifths to a fifth of an inch, the final velocity was found to agree
well with the supposition that it varies as the square root of the
diameter. When the diameter is about a tenth of an inch this law
gives too large a result, but when it is about a fiftieth of an inch
this excess increases, and when the diameter is about a hundredth
of an inch the final velocity is only half what it would be if
the same law holds true for the small grains as for the large. In
fact, for grains measuring a hundredth of an inch in diameter and
somewhat less, the final velocity varies nearly as the diameter.
It seems to me probable that these facts may be explained by

supposing that an adherent film of water is dragged down with the grains, the relative effect of which would be greater as their diameter became less. The results are closely as if this film were about a thousandth of an inch thick. My data were, however, not sufficient to prove this, and yet they make it sufficiently probable to be adopted provisionally. It may thus be supposed that the thickness of the film may increase when the particles move more slowly through the water; and, if so, the final velocity must depend on very complex conditions, and in the case of extremely-small particles it may decrease more and more than the value of $d$. We may thus easily understand why the subsidence of extremely-minute separate particles is so very slow, even as slow as an inch per day. However, this is greatly influenced by the amount of suspended matter, for, when there is much, the granules collect together into small pellets, which subside far more rapidly than the separate smaller granules. These facts must be carefully borne in mind in studying very fine-grained rocks.

It may be well to give in tabular form the approximate final velocities in feet per second, deduced from many experiments for separate grains of sand of various sizes, it being understood that the results would vary to some extent with the shape of the grains.

### Table I.

| Shortest diameter | | | | | |
|---|---|---|---|---|---|
| Shortest diameter | $\frac{1}{5}$ | inch | ·910 foot | } | coarse sand. |
| ″ | ″ | $\frac{1}{10}$ ″ | ·680 ″ | | |
| ″ | ″ | $\frac{1}{20}$ ″ | ·430 ″ | } | medium sand. |
| ″ | ″ | $\frac{1}{100}$ ″ | ·106 ″ | | |
| ″ | ″ | $\frac{1}{200}$ ″ | ·052 ″ | } | very fine sand. |
| ″ | ″ | $\frac{1}{1000}$ ″ | ·010 ″ | | |

These velocities are of fundamental importance in many questions connected with stratified rocks.

### Flakes of Mica.

Flakes of mica of small size and varying thickness follow the same general laws as sand; but, when the thickness remains constant, and the area is greater, the final velocity increases with the area up to a certain value and then decreases. The value of this maximum velocity varies closely as the square root of the thickness. I have no observation of facts which would be explained by the above peculiarities; and the flakes of mica in stratified rocks are usually too small for their application. However, it follows from my experiments that thin flakes of mica of considerable area would subside much more slowly than grains of sand of small area; thus we can easily understand why, as is so common, mica and fine sand occur in separate layers.

### III. Angles of Rest of Sand and of Small Pebbles.

## Sand.

A knowledge of the angle of rest of different varieties of sand, under various conditions, is of great interest, since its sine is a simple measure of the friction which would otherwise be difficult to ascertain, and must have had a preponderating influence in connexion with the drifting forwards and deposition of the material of many rocks. It sums up the general effect of the density, size, and shape of the grains, the character of their surface, and the relative lubricating influence of the superficial layer of water.

I made many experiments in a glass trough, so that I could measure the angle of rest under different conditions. One very important point is that the angle at which moving sand stops and accumulates differs materially from that at which it gives way, after having become stationary; and this explains many important facts.

Experimenting with the coarse angular sand of the Millstone Grit, washed to get rid of the decomposed felspar, and sieved so that the grains varied in size from about ·03 to ·07 inch, and averaged about ·05, I found that the angle of rest in water was about 41° when coming to rest, but about 49° when giving way after being at rest. In the case of sand varying in size from ·005 to ·020 inch, and averaging about ·010, the angle when coming to rest was about 34°, and after being at rest it gave way at 36°. In the case of very fine-grained sand from Alum Bay, in which the grains varied from ·001 to ·005, and averaged about ·003 inch, the angles were respectively 30° and 33°. It is thus clear that, to a slight extent, the fine sands acted more as a liquid, the difference between the angles being 2° or 3° instead of 8°. When the above-mentioned coarse and fine sands were mixed in equal quantities, it was difficult to prevent separation, since the coarse grains ran down over the fine, and accumulated at a higher angle than the fine; but, by using great care to prevent this, I found that the angles were about 34° (or the same as for the fine sand named above) and 38°, or 2° more than when no coarse sand was present.

## Pebbles.

A rounded quartz-pebble measuring ·4 by ·25 inch easily ran down a slope of the coarse Millstone-Grit sand at 25°, and came to rest when it was at about 20°. It scarcely sank at all into the surface of the sand. In the case of the finer sand, the pebble just ran down at 20°, but did not sink much. When in water the very fine Alum-Bay sand is extremely soft and mobile, so that even a pebble measuring only ·2 by ·15 inch half sank into it, and would not run down the surface until the whole gave way. All these facts agree well with the supposition that the thin film of water adhering to the grain has more and more effect on the properties of the material in proportion as the particles are smaller. Thus, if the thickness be the same for 0·1 as for 0·001 inch in diameter, I calculate that the relative effect would be 450 times as great in the latter case. This must have a most important influence in modifying the deposition of coarse and fine-grained material; and it seems to me that all the facts that I have described are of fundamental importance in studying stratified rocks, and well deserve a much more complete investigation.

Thus, for example, the above-described facts show that the different amount of sinking of the small pebble causes the friction to be 57 per cent. more in the case of very fine sand than in that of coarse. On the contrary, a current of water would have much less power, since only half its surface would be exposed. It would thus be almost impossible for a small pebble to occur in fine sand, since a current much less than sufficient to drift along the pebble would wash away the sand; whereas, in the case of the coarse Millstone-Grit sand, the pebble would be washed along much more easily, and the sand washed away with much more difficulty, so that it is easy to understand why pebbles are so common in such rocks as the Millstone Grit, and absent in the finer-grained sandstones of the Coal-Measures. The common occurrence of, as it were, a bed of small pebbles at the lower part of many beds of drifted sand is also easily explained, since on arriving at the top of the slope at the angle of rest of the coarse sand, the great majority of the pebbles would roll down to the bottom and only a few stick higher up in the sand. In a similar manner, these facts would probably explain many other details of structure which have attracted little attention.

### Possible Explanation of the Angles of Rest of Different Sands.

As will be shown in the sequel, when sand is deposited and well shaken, the grains arrange themselves on an average so that the percentage of interspaces is the same as that deduced theoretically for such an arrangement as would give rise to depressions bounded by a mean slope of 30°, up which a grain would have to be raised to be carried away. If a general surface of such a kind were inclined at an angle of 30°, the above-mentioned small slope would be level: therefore the grain would not require any lifting, and the only force to be overcome to let it go free would be that required to start motion and overcome friction. Taking all the facts into consideration, it appears to me that the most probable supposition is that, when the slope is such that the grain slips off and slides down, the force of gravitation acting at that angle is just in excess of that which kept it in position, and that this force varies as the sine of the angle of the slope. Part of this is balanced by the conditions, and the rest by friction. If these suppositions are correct, it follows that the variation in the angle of rest for different kinds of sand

depends mainly on these latter retarding conditions. Assuming
that the sine of the angle of rest is a measure of all the forces just
balanced, we may calculate as follows. For grains of ·05 inch in
diameter the sine is ·755, and for ·01 it is ·588. Hence for each
·01 above ·01 the value of the sine increases about ·042. Sub-
tracting this from ·588 we get ·546, which is the sine of 33·6°, or
closely that of the angle of rest for grains ·003 in diameter. The
excess over 30° may be due to the force necessary to start movement,
or to the somewhat different arrangement of the surface-grains from
that assumed. These facts seem to show that the above-named
resistance is of little value where the grains are small, but increases
nearly as the diameter of larger grains. At all events, these suppositions explain the variations in the angle of rest sufficiently well
for the purposes of this paper.

## Relation between the Angle of Rest and the Velocity of a Current.

I trust that it will not be thought that I am making mountains
of molehills, when I discuss in detail the properties of grains of
sand; but it must be borne in mind that the very existence of some
mountains must have depended on the properties of their constituent
grains. As described above, the most probable angle of the slope
of the minute depressions on the surface of sand is about 30°, up
which a grain would have to be lifted before it would be washed
along by a current. In addition to this, there would be friction to
be overcome, so that the effective angle may be about 33°.

It seems to me, therefore, that these conditions are so closely the
same as in the case of the angle of rest, that the sine of this angle
may be looked upon provisionally as a measure of the resistance that
must be overcome by a current just able to drift along the sand. At
all events, this seems to give satisfactory results, when we compare
one variety of sand with another.

## IV. The Effects of Currents.

## Velocity of Current Able to Start or Maintain Drifting.

As in the case of the friction of one surface on another, there is
a difference between the current necessary to start the motion of
sand and that which is necessary to maintain it. This is well seen
in the case of the angle of rest—since the angle at which sand slips
down after having been at rest, and that at which moving sand is
brought to rest, differ materially. Very important results depend
on this property. We may, I think, provisionally calculate the
velocities of current required to start and maintain the drifting of
different varieties of sand from these angles, as measured in each
case. It is, however, important to bear in mind that drifting on a
rippled surface is not the same as on one without ripples.

## Conclusions to be drawn from the Change in the Angle of Rest in Various Rocks.

When material like sand or oolitic grains is drifted along the bottom to where the velocity of the current is so reduced by increased depth that the material can be no longer washed along, it falls down on a slope at the angle of rest. By this means a bed may have been formed several hundred yards long, and the angle of rest can easily be determined, allowance of course being made for the true dip of the strata. This sort of bedding should be carefully distinguished from irregular deposition, which may very properly be called false bedding. As it is formed by the drifting along of the material, I have always called it drift-bedding.

The value of the original angle of rest can usually be estimated from the nature of the deposit; but, in many cases, it has been subsequently much reduced by chemical or mechanical changes in the rock, and the alteration in the thickness of the bed can be learned by comparing the values of the tangents of the original angle of rest and of the present angle. In the case of irregular or thin drift-beds or drifted ripples, the original angle of rest may have been materially less than normal, because of the current sweeping down the slope, and thus it could not be relied on. There is also doubt regarding the original value when, as in some limestones, the rock has been so changed that the character of the material when deposited is imperfectly known. I much regret that I did not see the importance of these facts in years gone by, and did not measure the angle of rest in many cases suitable for these calculations; but fortunately I have sufficient data to show the kind of results that could be obtained by a more complete application of this method, now that all parts of the subject have been more developed.

### Freshwater Limestone, Binstead (Isle of Wight).

The angle of good drift-bedding was found to be as a mean about 24°; and, assuming that originally it was about 34°, the reduction in thickness has been from 100 to 66, or a contraction of 34 per cent., which to a large extent may have been due to the filling-up of original cavities by carbonate of lime derived from aragonite-shells in close proximity.

### Lower Greensand near Folkestone.

I measured several good cases, and found the mean angle of drift-bedding to be close on 20°, in sand which would originally have had an angle of about 34°. This would indicate a contraction of from 100 to 54, or of 46 per cent., which must to some extent be due to the filling-up of the interspaces, but also to removal of material by solution.

N 2

## Magnesian Limestone.

There is so much uncertainty respecting many important particulars connected with this rock, that I should say nothing about it if it were not in the hope that it may help to clear up the difficulties. One thing that seems fairly certain is, that in South Yorkshire, North Derbyshire, and Nottinghamshire, the rock was not deposited as it now is. In many places the material has been drifted along the bottom, but it is difficult or impossible to know what would be the original angle of rest or the amount of the interspaces.

Many years ago I made a considerable number of chemical analyses, and found that, as a general rule, the specimens contained an excess of carbonate of lime above that which is found in a true dolomite. I then concluded that in many, if not all, cases this excess was due to infiltrated calcite. Sometimes there appeared to be good evidence that the rock had been changed from a limestone after deposition, but in others that dolomite-mud had been deposited originally. In the county of Durham the excess of carbonate of lime in the Magnesian Limestone is great; and it seems to me that some of the exceptional concretionary structures seen there may have been due, in part, to the original deposit having been to some extent aragonite, afterwards segregated and crystallized as calcite.

As determined by the boiling-water method described farther on, the empty spaces in the rock in South Yorkshire vary from 9 to 29 per cent., and in one case were increased from 11 to 21 per cent. by the action of dilute acid, perhaps due partly to the removal of infiltrated calcite. On the whole, these values do not differ materially from those found in rocks of Oolitic age, and, like them, indicate no great pressure.

I have fairly-complete particulars of two cases near Conisborough. In one at Crookhill the angle of a drift-bed is now 18°. If originally the material were of moderate grain, the angle of rest would have been about 34°: this would indicate a contraction from 100 to 48. The cavities might have been originally about 48 per cent. and are now about 8 per cent., so that, as indicated by them, the contraction has been to about 56·5 of the original. This indicates a removal of 8 or 9 per cent. of solid matter. In a good case at Cadeby the angle is 20°, but the cavities amount to 27 per cent.: this indicates a contraction of 54 per cent., and the removal of 17 per cent. of solid material. Taking the mean of the four determinations, it should appear that the rock is now about 52·5 per cent. of its original thickness and that 13 per cent. has been removed; these, however, must be looked upon as only rough approximations, because the original character of the rock is unknown.

## Millstone Grit.

For some miles north and south on the west side of Sheffield, the Millstone Grit contains many excellent examples of characteristic drift-bedding. At one time, it was puzzling to find that the mean angle of the inclined beds in a quarry at Bell Hag, where the sand-grains measure on an average ·01 inch in diameter. is only about 25°, since the angle of rest for such sand is 34°. However, on further study it was found that this reduction in the angle agrees with what would be the effect of the alterations that have taken place in the rock. Pebbles of felspar are common, and on close examination it was seen that what was originally felspar-sand has been decomposed, and the resulting clay forced into the interspaces between the grains of quartz. In the case of such sand when recently deposited and not shaken, the interspaces amount to about 46 per cent., whereas they are now only 15 per cent., thus showing a contraction of 36 per cent. of the original volume. The tangent of the original angle is ·674, and therefore that of the altered rock should be 64 per cent. of this, which nearly agrees with the tangent of 25°, as seen in the rock. · Hence, both the change in the angle and that in the amount of interspaces agree in showing that the thickness of the rock is about two-thirds of the original. As indicated by the angle of rest, the average contraction for all the above-described rocks is from 100 to 59, which is a very considerable change.

## Drifting on a Horizontal Surface.

According to Du Buat ('Traité d'Hydraulique'), the velocity of a current near the bottom is about half the mean velocity of the whole depth. Possibly, however, that of the water in contact with the sand is still less. My experiments and observations showed that, in shallow water, the mean velocity of the current just able to wash up sand measuring about a hundredth of an inch in diameter is about ·4 foot per second. Before being moved, the surface would be very similar to that of sand inclined at the angle of rest, and it seems probable that, as in that case, the force necessary to lift the sand out of the depressions against gravity and overcome friction, so as to move it forward, must be nearly as the sine of the angle of rest, which in this case is ·59. The final velocity of such sand is ·106 foot per second, so that the calculated velocity of a current just able to move the sand would be $·59 \times ·106 = ·063$ feet per second, which is not quite a sixth of the observed mean velocity, or about a third of that near the bottom according to Du Buat. This lower velocity is, however, that in actual contact with the sand, which must certainly be considerably less than higher up. On the whole, considering all the circumstances, we may conclude provisionally that the velocity in contact with the sand is about a sixth of the mean velocity, although this might not be correct in the case of deep water.

## Effects of Current on Sand.

Fifty-nine years ago, when I was living at Woodbourne, a country-house on the east side of Sheffield, there was at the bottom of the small park a brook entirely under my control. In order to investigate a number of questions, I constructed a place for experiment with some self-registering appliances. I could easily regulate and measure the depth and velocity of the current within certain limits. By these experiments, and by observations made in a clear brook at Fulwood (near Sheffield), I came to the conclusion that, when the velocity of the current is about 6 inches per second, sand with grains about a hundredth of an inch in diameter is drifted along slowly, and a surface is produced, grained in the line of the current, but no ripple-marks are formed. When the velocity is somewhat greater than 6 inches per second, ripples are produced. When it is about 1 foot per second, these are well developed and advance about 3 inches per minute, by the sand being washed up on the exposed side and deposited on the other; which velocity may be looked upon provisionally as an average for undoubted drifted ripples. If the velocity attains 18 inches per second, the ripples are destroyed by the washing-away of the sand; but the surface may still show graining in the line of the current. Much depends, however, on whether sand is or is not being deposited from above; since, when it is, ripples are produced at a somewhat lower velocity and advance more quickly. These results applied to the case of water varying from 1 to 8 inches in depth, and might be very different in the case of much deeper water. I have long felt that such experiments ought to be conducted on a much larger scale, but have never had the opportunity in a suitable and convenient place. free from disturbance. In the present state of the subject it may be assumed that, in the case of moderately-fine sand, the well-developed ripple-drift, so common in certain rocks, indicates a current with a mean velocity of about 1 foot per second.

Assuming that the sines of the angles of rest are a fair measure of the friction which must be overcome to move the sand when at rest, and to continue the motion when drifting over the same sort of sand, and also that the effective action of a current of about 1 foot per second varies as the velocity, I calculate out the following table. It must, however, be looked upon as little more than a provisional illustration, since it is possible that many other factors should be taken into account. They are not velocities, but the relative forces needed to move the sand along the bottom, where the current would be much reduced by friction.

TABLE II.

| | Coarse sand. | | Fine sand. | | Very fine. | |
|---|---|---|---|---|---|---|
| Angles of rest ............... | 41° | 49° | 24° | 26° | 30° | 33° |
| Sines of angles.............. | ·65 | ·75 | ·56 | ·59 | ·50 | ·54 |

Assuming, for the sake of simplicity, that the effective action of a current on grains of sand of varying size but of similar shape varies directly as the exposed surface, and that the frictional resistance to be overcome varies directly as their weight, the velocity of a current just able to drift them along would be when these two quantities are equal; that is to say, roughly speaking, that the necessary motive power would vary directly as the size of the grains. Now, as already described, the mean velocity just able to drift grains a hundredth of an inch in diameter is a little under ·5 foot per second, or say ·4 foot.  Hence, in the case of Millstone-Grit sand measuring a twentieth of an inch in diameter, it would be about 2 feet per second; and for the very fine Alum-Bay sand $\frac{1}{300}$ inch in diameter, it would be ·13 foot.  Combining these results with those deduced from the angles of rest, we obtain the following :—

TABLE III.

| Size of grains ..................... | $\frac{1}{20}$ inch. | $\frac{1}{100}$ inch. | $\frac{1}{300}$ inch. |
|---|---|---|---|
| Mean current just able to drift ... | 2·00 feet. | 0·40 foot. | 0·13 foot. |
| Mean current just able to wash up | 2·24 feet. | 0·44 foot. | 0·17 foot. |

Though deduced from entirely different data, these results agree well with the fact that the weight of the grains varies as the cube of their diameter, and the surface exposed to the current varies as the square.

As shown later, the velocity at the very bottom just enough to drift the sand up the ripples is only ·09 foot, which agrees with the fact that a velocity of 12 inches washes up the sand vigorously; and, when the mean velocity is 18 inches and that at the bottom 3, the sand can scarcely maintain itself.  We thus have two important limits—one just sufficient to wash it along, and the other to wash it away, which had no upper limit.

V. RIPPLE-DRIFT.

Only that structure is considered which is produced by a current moving in one direction, as shown by the detailed characters.  This is a most interesting structure, since it enables us to ascertain with approximate accuracy, not only the direction of the current and its velocity in feet per second, but also the rate of deposition in fractions of an inch per minute.  This introduction of minutes and seconds into geology may probably surprise those who are accustomed to deal with long geological periods, but it must be remembered that my minutes and seconds can be verified by experiment, which cannot be done with their long periods.

The production of this structure (see Pls. XV & XVI) involves a number of variable conditions, namely, the depth and velocity of the current; the size, shape, and density of the drifted material; the length and height of the ripples, and the rate at which deposition is taking place from above; and it is necessary to enter somewhat fully into detail, in order to show the data from which conclusions may be drawn.

It is convenient, in the first place, to consider the case when no deposit is being formed from the superjacent water, material being merely drifted along the bottom. Also, for the sake of simplicity, we may assume that the sand consists of grains having an average diameter of about a hundredth of an inch, and that the length of the ripples is about $3\frac{1}{2}$ inches, which I find is a common size in many rocks. I shall also consider only their length and height, since the third dimension may be looked upon as uniform and as having no influence on the ratios under discussion.

By very carefully studying some excellent ripples on the shore at Ryde and Sandown, I found that, although their average length varied from 1·3 to 12 inches, their shape was almost identical, the exposed side being inclined at about 18° and the sheltered at about 30°. Hence, for ripples $3\frac{1}{2}$ inches long, the height would be ·72 inch, which corresponds to what is seen in older rocks. However, for a reason which I do not fully understand, some ripples $3\frac{1}{2}$ inches long are only about ·36 inch high, and the slopes are inclined at 9° and 19°. Those formed in my experiments at Woodbourne seem to have been of this character, and I found that with a current of about 1 foot per second they advanced 3 inches per minute. So far as I can judge, their length was about 4 inches, which would give a minute and a third as the time in which they would advance their own length, which I call their period. It seems very probable that this period would be nearly the same for ripples varying considerably in length, since the exposed surface from which the sand is washed up would vary directly as the length of the ripples, and we may, therefore, assume that the period of ripples $3\frac{1}{2}$ inches long would be 1·33 minute. The question then is, what would be the period for those that are ·72 inch high? The amount of material to be drifted forward in their period would be $\frac{·72}{·36}=2$, and there is no reason to believe that it would be drifted along more quickly. On the contrary, it would have to be washed up a slope of 18° instead of 9°; and, adding the angle of rest when such sand gives way for the effect of the small depression, the extra inclination is 54° instead of 45° and the extra force required $\frac{\text{sine } 54°}{\text{sine } 45°}=1·14$. Hence, probably the period for ripples ·72 inch high would be $1·33\times2\times1·14=3$ minutes; but this must be looked upon as merely an approximation, which needs confirmation by experiment on a larger scale. It must also be remembered that all my calculations refer to sand of medium coarseness, with grains about a hundredth of an inch in diameter. The tables given in this paper supply the data for calculating the results for coarser or finer sand.

## Ripple-Marks, etc.

My experiments at Woodbourne showed that when the velocity of the current was only about 0·1 foot per second no ripples were formed, even when sand was deposited from above. When the velocity was from a quarter to half a foot per second, ripples were produced when deposit took place, though not otherwise, but they did not advance. This appears, therefore, to be the condition necessary to produce such ripple-marks as are seen in some thinly-bedded rocks, which show almost or quite symmetrical ripple-forms, but little or no effect of drifting. When this does occur a true rippled surface is seldom visible; but, in a section perpendicular to the stratification, inclined laminæ are seen, and a surface of peculiar character is shown when the rock is broken parallel to the plane of bedding.

## Production of Ripples and their Relations.

As shown by my experiments and observations, when the mean velocity of a current decidedly exceeds 6 inches per second, ripples are formed; and when it is 1 foot per second they are well developed and advance about 3 inches per minute, by the washing-up of the exposed side and deposition on the sheltered side. The formation of these ripples makes a considerable change in the conditions, since the sand must be drifted up the slopes. Very careful observation of excellent ripple-marks on the shore at Ryde and Sandown showed that the angle of the slopes exposed to the current was very nearly 18° in the case of both long and shorter ripples. The surface would be very similar to that when a horizontal one is tilted up 18°, and the grains would have to be washed up this as well as over the small depressions between the grains, so that for calculation we have $18° + 36° = 54°$. The sine of this multiplied by the final velocity is $·85 \times ·106 = ·09$ foot per second, which multiplied by 6 gives ·54 for the same velocity, in close agreement with observation.

## Washing-away of Ripples.

I found that in shallow water ripples are washed away when the mean velocity of the current is 18 inches per second and upwards. This is when, at the very bottom, it is so strong as not to allow sand to remain at an angle of 18°. This result may not apply in the case of deep water. I found, however, that some sand may remain at the bottom with a current of 18 inches per second, grained in the line of motion, though not in the form of ripples. Hence, although the normal conditions for a horizontal grained surface are not much above 6 inches per second, cases may occur when the velocity is 18 inches, as may often be seen in clear brooks; but it would usually be easy to distinguish the two conditions by studying their relation to ripple-drift. Considering all the complex factors, it is satisfactory to find that the observations can be harmonized quantitatively by a few probable suppositions.

## Ripple-Drift with Deposition from Above.

The structure of ripple-drift shows that when deposit is formed from above, it is accumulated on the protected side of the ripple in thin layers at the angle of rest. That this deposition would reduce their period admits of no doubt, since the protected side would advance more rapidly. As the ripples move forward a portion is washed up from the exposed side, and an amount equal to that deposited from above is left, and covered up by the next ripple advancing from behind. It thus seems to follow that the amount drifted forward, independent of the deposition, is the same as when there is no deposit from above. The question is, what is the effect of the deposit on the rate at which this normal amount is washed along? Since the total to be removed would be greater, it is quite possible that it would have a retarding influence and lengthen the period of the ripple. At the same time, since, as I have shown, the velocity of the current some little distance from the bottom is considerably greater than on the actual surface of the sand, the subsidence of material would increase the velocity of the current at the bottom, and therefore shorten the period of the ripples. All these suppositions ought to be verified by experiment; but, in the meantime, it seems to me that we may assume provisionally that the above-mentioned two influences may so far compensate one another, that they may be neglected. I therefore calculate as follows :— The normal area of the section of a ripple perpendicular to the surface in the line of the current is $\frac{3 \cdot 5 \times \cdot 72}{2} = 1 \cdot 26$ inch. The area of the material deposited is $3 \cdot 5\,d$, when $d$ is the thickness of the deposit in inches. Then the period of the ripple would be

$$3 \times \frac{1 \cdot 26}{1 \cdot 26 + 3 \cdot 5\,d} = \frac{3}{1 + 2 \cdot 8\,d}.$$

These values, however, must be looked upon as only approximate, but yet most probably of the true order of magnitude, and sufficiently near the truth to warrant the conclusions described later.

The rate of deposition would be $\dfrac{d}{\text{period}}$.

## Length of Ripples.

The exact relation between the size of ripples and the conditions under which they are formed requires further study. If consideration were confined to those usually seen in rocks, it would appear most probable that their size depends to a great extent on the character of the sand. The smallest that I have seen are only about three-quarters of an inch long in a very fine-grained sandstone.

The usual size is 3 to 4 inches in medium sandstone. They are not well seen in the coarse-grained Millstone Grit, in which, however, they may be perhaps about a foot long. To judge from these facts alone, it would seem as though the length varied somewhat as the velocity of the current necessary to wash along the sand. The ripples seen on the sea-shore would in many cases agree with this supposition. The mean length at Ryde was 3·7 and at Sandown 6·9 inches. Now and then I have come across some which, so far, I am quite unable to understand. The most remarkable were at the northern end of the Menai Strait, where there was an extensive development of ripples some feet long. I was unable to learn the exact conditions under which they were formed, but still they make me think that other factors besides the size of the grains of sand may occasionally play a very important part. The current in the Menai is certainly strong, and the chief difficulty is, not to understand why the ripples are long, but why they are not washed away. It may be that the current along the bottom itself was not particularly strong, while that higher up was much greater, which determined the length of the ripples.


## VI. Varying Size of the Grains.

Another question of much importance in connexion with the structure of sandstones and some limestones is the relative size of the grains found mixed together. In some cases these are nearly all of the same size, but in others, between certain limits, they differ almost as much as possible. In many sandstones, although there is considerable uniformity, numerous smaller grains occur in the spaces between the larger. The exact cause of this occurrence deserves more study; but, as bearing on the question, I may refer to the fact that a good many small grains may exist among the coarse without producing any marked change in the angle of rest. Many years ago I paid much attention to the general question, and contrived a simple instrument for readily measuring the size of the grains; but it is only lately that the study of a different class of rocks in Herefordshire has thrown light on the true nature of the problem. Unfortunately, direct observations are difficult in the case of consolidated rocks.

Taking everything into consideration, the most important general conclusion appears to be that more or less perfect similarity in the size of the grains usually indicates a sorting of the material by a current at the very bottom of comparatively-shallow water; whereas great irregularity in the size indicates that the material was deposited from much deeper water, in which there was little current at the bottom, though a good deal of current higher up. This is, of course, one of the most important points in connexion with many rocks.

## Possible Connexion between the Structure of a Rock and the Depth of the Water.

If the final velocity ($f$) at which a grain of sand subsides in a deep current is the same as in clear still water, so that my experimental results can be utilized for calculations, it follows that the time taken to subside through a given depth ($d$) would be $\frac{d}{f}$ seconds. Also, if it were carried along by a current of V miles per hour for a distance of L miles the time taken would be $\frac{L}{V}$. If, then, we considered a case in which during the time a grain subsided from the top to the bottom, we should have $d = f \times \frac{L}{V}$. Since $f$ is known by experiment, the depth depends on two independent variables, the value of which can be roughly estimated, so as to see whether the result is in any way probable. Assuming then that the grain of sand is a hundredth of an inch in diameter, having a final velocity of ·11 foot per second, and that the distance to which it can be drifted is 10 miles, by a current of 4 miles per hour, we have for the depth ·11 × 9000 = 990 feet = 165 fathoms, which appears to me so unreasonably great as to indicate some flaw in the argument. Possibly, in subsiding in muddy water the bigger grains collect into pellets with the finer and with organic matter of little density, so that the rate of subsidence is much less than ·11 foot per second. Supposing that it were only a tenth of that, the depth calculated as above would be only 16½ fathoms, which is not unreasonable. On this principle we could explain how fairly-coarse sand could be carried for some miles and accumulate with fine-grained material which had subsided from a lower level, where the velocity of the current was less. Quantitative results are at present out of the question, but it seems extremely probable that the difference in the structure makes it possible to distinguish between deposits formed from deep water and those formed from shallow. It is even possible that further study would enable us to form some estimate of the actual depth.

The chief defect in some of the foregoing conclusions is that the influence of the depth of the water is so imperfectly known. This probably cannot alter materially the relation between the sand and the current, on the actual surface of the bottom, but might considerably modify the relation between this and the mean velocity and that of the upper surface, so that some of the velocities given may not be strictly correct.

## VII. DRIFT-BEDDING.

What I have always called drift-bedding is formed when sand is drifted along, if the water is of proper depth and the current sufficiently strong to carry it on, until it arrives where the depth is so much increased, and the current so greatly reduced, that it is

unable to wash sand any farther, the sand being therefore thrown
down at the angle of rest, forming a bed the thickness of which
corresponds to the increased depth. Numerous examples of this
structure, on a small scale, may be seen on sandy roads after
rain. The thickness of the bed ($t$) does not bear a constant
relation to the depth of the water, either before or after deposition. It may be abnormally small, when the reduction in the
velocity of the current merely causes the sand to be thrown down
at a less angle than the normal angle of rest, owing to the
current sweeping down the face of the slope, and causing the
stratula to be S-shaped, curved at the top and bottom. On the
contrary, the increase in depth may be indefinitely great, so as
to give rise to a thick bed at the true angle of rest, perhaps
modified at the bottom by a talus due to the giving way of the
deposit, caused by breaking waves or other disturbances. Between
these two extremes is what may be called a n o r m a l l y thick bed,
where the increase in depth and the diminution of the current are
just sufficient to allow of the sand accumulating at the true angle
of rest, in a bed the thickness of which bears a definite relation to
the depth of the water and the character of the sand, so that the
depth may be determined.

Judging from the Millstone Grit near Sheffield, when the thickness of the bed ($t$) and the angle of the stratula ($a$) are abnormally
small, $\dfrac{t}{\sin a} = \dfrac{t'}{\sin a'}$, and therefore in each case we may calculate
the value $t$. Considering the independent evidence of great variation
in depth, this yields reasonable conclusions, and assists in giving
the true value of $t$.

In studying particular rocks, allowance must be made for the
contraction which has occurred since deposition. What should be
learned in each case is the smallest thickness of the beds when the
angle of rest is just true. This may vary considerably in different
parts of the same rock, since the depth has often been reduced by
as much as 20 feet by one continuous drift, over a flat bottom of
considerable area, leaving the water so much more shallow. In
varying currents in shallow water, there is often much confusion
and much that may be called f a l s e b e d d i n g, from which little
can be learned by calculation.

Having then determined, in a more or less satisfactory manner,
the normal thickness in one or more particular cases, the question
remains, what was the actual depth of the water before and after
deposition? Experiments are wanted on a fairly-large scale, with
plenty of water under complete control, in order to ascertain the
general facts. In the absence of these, it is necessary to fall back
on what I learned in another manner. I found that sand of the
average diameter of a hundredth of an inch is drifted along with a
current of 1 foot per second, and, if it arrives where the depth is
twice as deep, so that the velocity is reduced to 6 inches per second,
it is thrown down and accumulated at the true angle of rest. Both
these limits are doubtless subject to variation, according to circum-

stances, but they may probably be looked upon as a fair average from which to determine approximately the depth : the result being that when the sand is drifted the depth is $t$, and when deposited $2t$. However, since the bottom past the slope would be somewhat protected by the slope, the possible depth in the two places may be $2t$ and $3t$. These depths seem small, but, so far as is known, they are of the right order of magnitude. In any case $d + t$ must be decidedly greater than $d$, which means that $d$ is not great compared with $t$, and may be small.

## Application to Particular Rocks.

I made many observations in the Great Oolite near Bath. In one good case near Box were two drift-beds, each about 15 feet thick, drifted from nearly opposite quarters. These were separated by a bed full of borings showing little evidence of current. In other places were beds only 1 to 3 feet thick. My data are imperfect, since I did not determine the angle of rest; but they indicate a depth varying from a few feet up to perhaps 20 or 30 feet, or more in places where there is no evidence of depth.

I have records of very many measurements in the Millstone Grit near Sheffield, and the general conclusion seems to be that the water was of extremely-variable depth, and generally shallow. Thus at Bell Hag the true angle of rest, as altered by consolidation, is 25°, and the rock is now 70 per cent. of its original volume. With this angle are beds 25° and 5 inches thick, 20° and 36 inches thick, and 17° and 15 inches thick, which can be explained approximately by supposing that in one part or another, before and after deposition and filling up, the depth varied from 12 to 18 feet down to 1 or 2 feet, with a general average of 6 to 10 feet.

## General Conclusion respecting Sandstones, etc.

The facts now described enable us to divide sandstones and analogous rocks in the following manner :—

1. Thinly- or thickly-bedded rock, without ripples or drift-bedding, and showing little or no graining of the surface in the line of the current. Good examples of this occur in the Old Red Sandstone of the Black Mountains, in the Llanthony valley. This could be explained by supposing that the water was at considerable depth, and the material mainly deposited from above, not drifted along the bottom, where the velocity of the current was much less than 6 inches per second.

2. Thinly-bedded rock, with well-marked graining of the surface in the line of the current, indicating a mean velocity varying up to about 6 inches per second, but showing few or no ripple-marks.

3. More or less thick masses of rock almost entirely made up of ripple-drift. This must have been when the velocity of the current was something like a foot per second, but varying with the character of the sand, which drifted it along the bottom accompanied by more or less rapid deposition from above; and, as the ripples advanced, more was deposited on the sheltered side than was washed up on the exposed side, so that the rate of deposition would be known if our knowledge of the advance of ripples were more complete. But,

so far as the facts are known, deposition at something like the rate of a quarter to half an inch per minute may be looked upon as a common average.

4. What I have called d r i f t - b e d d i n g in numerous published papers is when the sand is drifted along the bottom to a point where the depth is so much greater and the velocity of the current so reduced that it is thrown down at the angle of rest. The velocity of the current is indicated by the nature of the sand; and probably further experiments would enable us to learn the approximate depth, which probably was small, since an increase of a very few feet made so great a difference in the strength of the current. Excellent examples of this structure are common in many rocks, and the direction and character of the current are sometimes found to have been very uniform over a wide area.

Some examples of what has been called ' false - bedding ' are irregular accumulations from which no accurate conclusions can be deduced.

### VIII. JOINTS OF ENCRINITES, ETC.

Each plate and spine of echinoderm and each joint of encrinite is, as it were, a single crystal of calcite, having a complicated external and internal organic structure. The minute, twisting, hollow, internal spaces of big spines are full of air in dry specimens, expelled and replaced by water on boiling, and must be full of sea-water when the animal is alive. It is no doubt by this that the carbonate of lime is introduced when these joints, etc. become almost or quite solid on fossilization. The structure of the test of all species that I have examined, and of the joints of the living *Pentacrinus* is practically the same, so far as the cavities are concerned. In the case of a big spine of *Echinus*, I found that the hollow spaces amounted to 51 per cent. of the volume, and the specific gravity when dry was 1·32, and when full of water 1·83: hence, the excess of weight over water is less than one half of that of a solid shell of the same bulk. These facts fully explain the very special characters of fossilized echinoderms. They do not decay, but are filled with infiltrated calcite in crystalline continuity with the original, so that the structure is similar to that of a single crystal with the usual cleavage. The specific gravity being so small and their form so very favourable, joints of encrinites would be washed along by a current which would not move fragments of more solid shells and corals of similar size, the specific gravity of which is from 2·7 to 2·8. We can thus easily understand why they so often occur almost or quite free from other material. The same general principles would, to some extent, apply to foraminifera and small univalves. Separate valves of bivalve shells, on the contrary, easily turn over and lie with their convex side upwards, so as to offer much resistance to a current, and may thus be sorted by being left alone.

### IX. VERY FINE-GRAINED DEPOSITS.

The properties of extremely-minute particles of clay and chalk differ in some remarkable particulars from those of sand, as though a thin adherent film of water played a most important part, when they subside and afterwards become more or less consolidated.  Sand subsides quickly, and almost at once attains a state of comparative stability.  On the contrary, in the case of very finely-divided clay and chalk, although they may not take long to subside and leave the water almost clear, yet the accumulated deposit, after settling for a day, acts like an imperfect liquid, and contains no less than 86·5 per cent. of water in the case of clay, and 74·3 per cent. in that of chalk, so that the particles must be comparatively far from touching one another.  With such fine-grained material an extremely-thin layer of water would suffice.  Thus, for particles $\frac{1}{10,000}$ inch in diameter, a film $\frac{1}{25,000}$ inch thick would explain what occurs when no pressure is present, squeezed out thinner when under pressure. On keeping, the material slowly settled; but, even after a week, the amount of included water was still 79·8 per cent. in clay, and 68·1 per cent. in chalk.  After no further contraction in volume occurred, the amount of included water was 75·5 per cent. in clay, and 64·6 per cent. in chalk.  In one case, pipe-clay which had been kept for about a month until no further subsidence was visible, was kept for a whole year without further contraction, and was found still to contain about 75 per cent. of water.  In the case of some fine-grained mud from a depth of 2500 fathoms, collected by the *Challenger*, after it had stood until no further subsidence took place, the amount of included water was no less than 89 per cent.  This permanent state is reached most probably when the downward pressure of the particles is equal to the cohesion of the surface-film of water.  Hence, we may conclude that, since this pressure would increase with the thickness of the deposit lying above, the amount of included water would decrease as the depth became greater, a conclusion which agrees well with observed facts.

When actually dried, after having subsided as much as they would, both clay and chalk gave evidence of considerable contraction, and the volume of included air was in clay 37·9 per cent. and in chalk 41·4 per cent.  On water being again added without disturbing the material, this swelled up considerably, as though the water forced itself in energetically, and the final volume of water was in the clay increased to 62·9 per cent., and in the chalk to 57·2 per cent.  It was extremely interesting to observe the difference in the two materials, for the clay easily broke up into laminæ in the plane of subsidence, but the chalk did not.  The great contraction in thickness had developed a sort of imperfect cleavage in the clay, but not in the chalk—most likely because the clay contains many flat particles, and the chalk few.

## The Deposition, etc. of Fine-Grained Material.

Possibly many may think that the deposition and consolidation of fine-grained mud must be a very simple matter, and the results of little interest.  However, when carefully studied experimentally, it is soon found to be so complex a question, and the results dependent on so many variable conditions, that one might feel inclined to abandon the enquiry, were it not that so much of the history of our rocks appears to be written in this language.

The method employed in my experiments was to break up thoroughly in water some fine-grained yellow clay from my garden, due to the decomposition of a Coal-Measure shale, and, allowing the coarse matter to subside, to pour the finer into beakers of various sizes, with nearly perpendicular sides. After the contents of these had been well stirred up, the extent of the subsidence was carefully marked and measured at equal intervals, at first of a quarter of an hour, and later of one and two days.

The laws regulating the deposition and consolidation of clay in still water are very complex, and differ completely according to the relative amount of the solid material. When this is less than about 1 per cent., the particles remain separate, and appear to subside with a final velocity depending on their size and density. The result is that, in the earlier stages, the coarser grains collect at the bottom, and the supernatant water is not clear near the surface, but is increasingly muddy downwards. On further standing, finer and finer-grained mud reaches the bottom, and the water becomes less and less muddy. The upper part remains more or less turbid for a considerable time, since the final velocity of the finest grains is only about 1 inch per day. The result is that the subsided mud is moderately firm, but far from homogeneous, being possibly a sort of very fine sand at the bottom, and the finest possible clay at the top. This may be looked upon as a normal layer for one period of mud. On the contrary, if the amount of solid material is decidedly more than 1 per cent. of the volume, the grains collect together into small compound masses, which subside with a small velocity, quite unlike that of the larger or smaller constituent grains, forming an almost liquid mud, and leaving the supernatant water almost clear from the beginning. This mud slowly decreases in volume by forcing out the entangled water, but may remain in a semi-liquid state for a long time, which explains a number of interesting facts. The grains of varying size may thus be very little separated, and an almost homogeneous deposit formed, with a mere trace of division into layers; though, on final consolidation, it may show fissility analogous to imperfect slaty cleavage.

The following tables (IV & V, pp. 192 & 193) show the character and rate of deposition in the case of the less and the more muddy water during the first two hours and the first eight days. The intermediate state is best shown by an experiment in which the proportion of mud was larger, described later.

It will be seen from Table IV that, when the mud collects at the bottom as separate grains, it is at first in a somewhat loose condition and afterwards settles down; but, if the amount were considerable, it might remain for many weeks in a semi-fluid condition.

In an experiment in which the percentage-volume of the dry mud was 15½, semi-liquid mud continued to subside for about

o

six weeks, and then, although soft, was not liquid.  The water was
removed and the whole left several months to dry, when it greatly
contracted in volume ; but, though looking quite solid, it was found

TABLE IV.

| Depth of water 2·30 inches. | | 2·90 inches. | |
|---|---|---|---|
| _Hours._ | _Mud at bottom._ | _Clear water._ | _Liquid mud._ |
| ¼ ..................... | ·12 | ·05 | 2·85 |
| ½ ..................... | ·23 | ·14 | 2·76 |
| ¾ ..................... | ·35 | ·20 | 2·70 |
| 1 ..................... | ·40 | ·30 | 2·60 |
| 1¼ ..................... | ·35 | ·50 | 2·40 |
| 1½ ..................... | ·30 | ·60 | 2·30 |
| 1¾ ..................... | ·28 | ·70 | 2·20 |
| 2 ..................... | ·27 | ·80 | 2·10 |
| _Days._ | | _Days._ | |
| 1 ..................... | ·20 | 1 ............. | 1·33 |
| 2 ..................... | ·18 | 2 ............. | 1·08 |
| 3 ..................... | ·16 | 3 ............. | 1·02 |
| 4 ..................... | ·15 | 4 ............. | ·99 |
| 5 ..................... | ·14 | 5 ............. | ·94 |
| 6 ..................... | ·13 | 6 ............. | ·90 |
| 7 ..................... | ·12 | 7 ............. | ·88 |
| 8 ..................... | ·12 | 8 ............. | ·87 |
| Dry ..................... | ·03 | Dry ......... | ·16 |
| Solid ..................... | ·02 | Solid ...... | ·11 |

by the oil-method (described later) to contain only two-thirds of its
volume of solid material, the rest being invisible cavities.    Table V.
(p. 193) shows the amount of subsidence in hundredths of an
inch, smoothed down, for every two days until the volume became
permanent, and in the lower part the constant volume when wet
and when dry.

As shown in Table V, the successive differences prove that
the predominant influences vary greatly as subsidence goes on.
During the last few weeks the first differences are nearly equal,
as though the rate of subsidence were nearly uniform ; whereas
during the first few days, it is not until we arrive at the fourth
order of differences that they become nearly equal.    Towards
the end, when no further subsidence occurs, although there was
five times as much water as solid material, it is as though the
gravity of the minute particles were just balanced by the cohesion
of a film of water.    For about four weeks before this, the rate of
subsidence varied nearly as the amount of space through which the
rising water had to escape upwards, but in the first few days the
rate approaches the fourth power of the time, as in the case of
water passing through small pipes.    It will thus be seen that we
have to deal with a very complex subject.

TABLE V.

| Days. | Depth of clay. | | Differences. | | |
|---|---|---|---|---|---|
| 0 ................. | 186 | | | | |
|  |  | 40 | | | |
| 2 ................. | 146 | | 14 | | |
|  |  | 26 | | 4 | |
| 4 ................. | 120 | | 10 | | 1 |
|  |  | 16 | | 3 | |
| 6 ................. | 104 | | 7 | | 0 |
|  |  | 9 | | 3 | |
| 8 ................. | 95 | | 4 | | 1 |
|  |  | 5 | | 2 | |
| 10 ................. | 90 | | 2 | | 0 |
|  |  | 3 | | 2 | |
| 12 ................. | 87 | | 0 | | |
|  |  | 3 | | | |
| 14 ................. | 84 | | 1 | | |
|  |  | 2 | | | |
| 16 ................. | 82 | | 0 | | |
|  |  | 2 | | | |
| 18 ................. | 80 | | 0 | | |
|  |  | 2 | | | |
| 20 ................. | 78 | | | | |
|  |  | 2 | | | |
| 22 ................. | 76 | | | | |
|  |  | 2 | | | |
| 24 ................. | 74 | | | | |
|  |  | 2 | | | |
| 26 ................. | 72 | | | | |
|  |  | 2 | | | |
| 28 ................. | 70 | | | | |
|  |  | 2 | | | |
| 30 ................. | 68 | | | | |
|  |  | 2 | | | |
| 32 ................. | 66 | | | | |
|  |  | 2 | | | |
| 34 ................. | 64 | | | | |
|  |  | 1 | | | |
| 36 ................. | 63 | | | | |
|  |  | 1 | | | |
| 38 ................. | 62 | | | | |
|  |  | 1 | | | |
| 40 ................. | 61 | | | | |
|  |  | 1 | | | |
| 42 ................. | 60 | | | | |
|  |  | 0 | | | |
| 44 ................. | 60 | | | | |
|  |  | 0 | | | |
| 46 ................. | 60 | | | | |
| Dry ............. | 15 | | | | |
| Solid ............. | 10 | | | | |

To investigate fully what occurs under natural conditions would be a difficult undertaking, because some of the most important facts could be learned only in rough weather when it would be impossible to collect material. The result is that some of the most striking peculiarities of many of our rocks cannot be satisfactorily explained experimentally, or by appeal to what now takes place.

When dry hydrous pipe-clay was pressed together by hand it contained 43·4 per cent. of interspaces. On applying more pressure they amounted to 24·4 per cent., or closely as in the case of spheres arranged to occupy the least volume ; but on further pressure they were reduced to 21·4. These results were very different in the case of ignited pipe-clay, for even after great pressure the interspaces were 48 per cent. Hence it seems clear that when the clay is hydrous, the grains are sufficiently soft and mobile to yield and partly fill up the interspaces, which is an important fact to bear in mind in studying the structure of many rocks.

The change produced by varying amounts of water in clay is of much interest. When only 40 per cent. of the volume of water is present, hydrous pipe-clay breaks easily and is not plastic. With 45 per cent. it is just plastic and soft, and completely plastic with 50 per cent. It thus appears that complete plasticity depends on the presence of rather more water than is sufficient to fill the interspaces. When less than this, its action is probably that of suction, but when more, it acts as a lubricant. This must also be important in connexion with the consolidation of many natural rocks.

## The Effects of Currents.

Although the laws of the deposition of clays in still water had first to be learned, yet it seems quite certain that in many cases the results must have been greatly modified by gentle currents. Suitable experiments would require a considerable stream of clear water and special arrangements. However, judging from the rate of subsidence, the velocity of current necessary to produce decided effects must vary much according to the nature of the mud, and must be of some such order of magnitude as from 1 inch to 1 foot per hour for very fine mud, and 1 foot per minute for coarser.

It is easy to understand how irregularities in velocity can be produced. I have paid a good deal of attention to the movements of currents in tidal estuaries. The velocity varies much vertically, and although there is often a strong current in mid-stream, there is none (or else an eddy) towards the shore. Moreover, vortices are often formed with horizontal axes more or less perpendicular to the direction of the current, which on one side may bring up mud and carry it down the other. The result of all such actions would be to produce more or less variations in the suspended mud ; and, when the movement of the water becomes sufficiently slow, layers of different texture may be deposited. It would be extremely difficult to verify this by collecting mud from deep water and studying its microscopical structure; at present, therefore, it is necessary to make inferences from experiments. At the same time, the subject is so complex that unknown conditions may vitiate some of the conclusions.

So far as I can judge, a gentle current of varying velocity in muddy water would explain the structure of many rocks which have alternating layers of different character, some very fine-grained and others more sandy, the thickness of merely an inch having a complex history of deposition and microscopical denudation. However, at all events in the older rocks, cases are fairly common which seem to require much more rapid slight alterations in the current than seem likely to have affected the general mass of water. Since the bottom of a current is retarded by friction and moves more slowly than that higher up, it seems probable that eddies are formed causing the water at the bottom to move with sufficiently-varying velocity to modify the deposition, and to give rise to very thin laminæ. I am sorry that I have not been able to verify this experimentally; but the structure of the ripple-drift in the green slates of Langdale, described later (Pl. XV), seems to prove the existence of such pulsations, whatever may be the true cause. In the ripple-drift on the side where the material was thrown down on a slope, in what represents the 'ripple-period,' may be counted eighty layers of slightly-varying material; and, since the most probable length of this period is half a minute, they would indicate about 160 pulsations in a minute. Similar thin layers are seen in a part where the current was not sufficiently strong to produce ripples, but they are thicker, as though the pulsations were slower. Since the calculated period depends on so many factors, all subject to error, it would perhaps be best to assume that when the current is too slow to produce ripples or drift-sand, the pulsations were, roughly speaking, of about the magnitude of one per second, which would indicate that the thickness of a single layer was deposited in that time. This must be looked upon as only an approximation; but, at all events, it is an interesting and plausible conclusion, and agrees fairly well with the probable period of the pulsations which must accompany the bottom-ripples.

## Application to Particular Rocks.

Although I possess a fairly-large collection of thin sections of slate-rocks, yet the variations due to chemical and mechanical changes are so numerous that I have but few throwing light on this particular question. I have, however, some excellent examples. In one from the Skiddaw Slate of Portinscale there are darker and paler layers of different-sized grain, evidently due to water depositing different material; but these layers are divided into more or less well-marked laminæ, varying from ·002 to ·010 inch in thickness, and therefore, perhaps, indicating that the rate of

deposition varied from about 7 inches to 3 feet per hour. A second specimen from another locality indicates a rate of from 9 inches to 3 feet per hour. Different specimens of the slate-rocks near Moffat indicate deposition of from 12 to 18 inches per hour. Various specimens from near Bangor indicate from 9 to 18 inches per hour. On the whole, my specimens give from 7 inches to 3 feet, but the usual rate is from 9 to 18 inches per hour. These may seem quick rates, but of course they refer to periods of decided current bringing deposit, which may have been separated by long intervals without deposition, as in the case of the green slates described later.

I have made thin sections of fine-grained rocks which break up at once when wetted, by hardening them with Canada balsam; but, until quite recently, I never suspected that anything of special interest could be learned from sections of soft clays, and it is now quite out of my power to collect and prepare such material. Judging from my experiments, much could be learned respecting the conditions under which such rocks were formed. It would be a wide branch of study, and would necessitate microscopical work on a large scale. The examination of the rocks in a natural condition is enough to show that the structure of clays differs enormously, and indicates formation under very different conditions; but there is always some doubt as to their true structure, when not made into thin sections.

A puzzling question is the origin of thick beds of almost homogeneous fine grain, like the slates of Penrhyn and Llanberis, since they may have been formed in two different ways, either by a gentle and uniform current, continuously drifting very uniform material, or by the deposit of cohered mud from very tranquil water. It is, however, possible that the above-named slates may originally have had a thin laminar structure, which was obliterated when cleavage was developed. So far as can be judged from the rocks in a natural condition, a homogeneous structure is common in our later deposits, and seems to indicate drifting by a very gentle current to spots where there was scarcely any at all. As examples, I may name deposits in old lakes, much of the Gault and Specton Clay, and some Coal-Measure shales. The structure of much of the Boulder-Clay must be explained in a different manner. The Gault of Aylesford, the Kimmeridge Clay near Filey, and the Lias near Whitby, show laminar structure due to currents.

We thus see that the history of fine-grained rock is written in a well-defined special language, still imperfectly understood, for want of adequate experimental study, both in the field and microscopically.

## X. The Green Slates of Langdale. (Pls. XIV–XVI.)

Probably no better example could be found of the effects of currents acting for a short time, than specimens that I procured from the quarries in Langdale. These structures would probably have been overlooked, if the slates had not been wetted by a shower of rain ; but, in order to see them to perfection, the surface of the slate should be ground flat and smooth, and coated over with a thin layer of so-called ' negative ' varnish.

In my specimens the plane of cleavage on which the structures are seen is inclined at about 45° to the stratification, and in calculating out the results allowance has been made for this, and also for the change of dimensions when the cleavage was developed. The existence of this constitutes, however, a great advantage, since the rock has been compressed so as to be very nearly solid, the cavities amounting to only 0·5 per cent. ; whereas in analogous rocks from the Coal-Measures they amount to over 13 per cent. Moreover, the character of the rock is eminently favourable for exhibiting the structure, since the fine-grained material is a pale green, and the coarser a dark green. The microscopical structure shows clearly that practically the whole material is a volcanic ash ; and the structure in many cases is as though this had been deposited from above, with little or no drifting along the bottom or sorting by a current. In the following account of my specimens, I adopt for calculation, etc. the general conclusions already explained. Pl. XIV is a reproduction of a photograph of a case where the current was so gentle that only very fine-grained green material was deposited in just the same creamy semi-liquid condition as recently-deposited clay in which the amount of included water is about 80 per cent., so that it can be easily washed up by a gentle current. Then must have come a fresh volcanic disturbance and deposit of ashes, with a current moving from left to right, which broke up this semi-liquid material into what might be compared with breaking waves, some of which were permanently entangled in the ash, and others carried away. This not only shows the original character of the deposits, but also roughly the time that elapsed between the disturbances. Very fine-grained material does not remain in this semi-fluid condition for more than a few weeks ; and therefore we have permanent evidence that, in some cases, the volcanic disturbances were separated by only a short interval. Other specimens indicate much longer periods, the breaking-up in similar cases being comparatively small.

The next illustration (Pl. XV) is of a case where the current set in and soon increased to probably about 9 inches per second, being able to develop ripples, yet not strong enough to drift along any but the finer material. The rate of deposition can be learned from the central portion when the current was at its maximum. The ripples were about $3\frac{1}{2}$ inches long, of normal height, and the thickness of the tails of the drift, corrected for bedding and cleavage, is ·86 inch. Then, in accordance with what I have explained in connexion with ripple-drift, the period of the ripples would be $3·0 \times \frac{2·52}{2·52 \times 7 \times ·86} = ·49$ minute, in which time ·86 inch was deposited. This is equal to about $1\frac{3}{4}$ inches per minute of the rock in its present state, or to about 2¾ inches when deposited; but, since the current was probably less than 12 inches per second, the rate of deposition may be looked upon as about 2 inches per minute. This may seem rather a large amount, but the facts appear to justify the conclusion, which is not unreasonable in the case of a volcanic eruption. The current would seem to have set in somewhat suddenly, and to have continued for about 2 minutes, after which fine semi-liquid mud was deposited, somewhat broken up by a fresh eruption of ashes, which, judging from my experiments, probably took place in the course of a few weeks or months.

Another specimen is very different, and shows that the current suddenly increased from under 6 inches per second to 12 inches for a doubtful period, but probably for about 2 minutes, during which deposition took place at the rate of only ·10 inch per minute.

The third illustration (Pl. XVI) is of great interest. In the lower part is level bedded deposit, indicating a current too small to develop ripples. This gradually increased until it was strong enough to wash along the sandy ashes, and produce a thin bed of true ripple-drift, deposition taking place at the rate of ·4 inch per minute. The current then gradually decreased, and could no longer drift along the coarser part of the material, and the fine-grained semi-liquid clay was deposited, and was partly in this state when a fresh disturbance brought coarser ashes and broke up and entangled some of the creamy material.

The maximum angle at which stratula dip is of much interest, as indicating the character of the material when it was deposited. Making all the necessary corrections, and allowing for the compression from the condition of a newly-deposited rock to one almost solid, I find that the angle of rest of the material must have been closely the same as that for a fine-grained volcanic sand. Hence, although the slate is now of almost exactly the same hardness throughout, we have good physical evidence that one part was originally fine loose sand, and the other a semi-liquid clay.

All these results must be looked upon as only approximate, but they are as likely to err on one side of the truth as on the other. As will be seen, the rate of deposition varied greatly, but all my specimens agree in showing that currents set in more or less suddenly, and, after continuing for a few minutes, died out. It seems to me, therefore, much less likely that they were currents of the kind so common during the deposition of many rocks, than due to volcanic disturbances accompanying the throwing-out of the ashes of which the rock is composed. It is possible that further study in the quarry would show cases in which the current acted for a longer period. I describe only some of the specimens that I collected and prepared in a suitable manner. At all events, there seems, to be here good evidence of the rate of deposition, and indication of the intervals between different volcanic disturbances.

## Ripple-Drift in other Rocks.

The detailed study of ripple-drift in other rocks is far more difficult than in the Langdale Slates, because the colour of the material does not vary so much, and my collected specimens do not enable me to give such precise results. One, however, which is fairly characteristic of Coal-Measure sandstones, indicates a current of about 1 foot per second, and deposition at the rate of about two-thirds of an inch per minute, as the rock now is, or 1 inch per minute in its original condition. Beds of varying ripple-drift of considerable thickness are common, and they differ widely from the Langdale Slates just described. The careful study of the rocks *in situ* would probably yield interesting results, and furnish information respecting the exact nature of the currents. There certainly appears good evidence to show that deposition up to $1\frac{1}{4}$ inches per minute was common, but associated with possibly long intervals during which there was little deposition. It must also be borne in mind that there may have been currents of over 18 inches per second, which would wash up the sand and leave little or no evidence of their existence, if no coarse material existed in the district.

I possess a specimen from the Lower Coal-Measures at Ringinglow near Sheffield, which, like the Langdale Slates, shows a current of about 1 foot per second, acting for a short time, so as to produce ripples, and not merely graining of the surface (like in the rest of the rock), as if due to currents varying frequently up to somewhat less than 6 inches per second.

## XI. WASHING-UP, ETC. OF CLAYS.

The velocity of current needed to just wash up very fine-grained deposits must necessarily depend so much on the length of time that has elapsed since they were deposited and their state of consolidation, as well as on the effect of the associated small animals and plants, that in many cases all calculation is impossible. Judging from my experiments, recently-deposited fine clay, unmodified by minute organisms, would be washed up by a very gentle current, since its density differs so little from that of water; and we may safely conclude that it would not be permanently accumulated, except in more or less still water. On the contrary, I have dredged up fine-grained mud, made so tenacious by *Jassa pulchella* and other small organisms, that it was almost impossible to wash it out of the dredge. Banks of such mud would resist a much stronger current than one that would wash away sand, so that calculation from the size of the grains is out of the question. However, it is more important to consider the velocity of current that would allow of deposition; but, even then, very much would depend on the quantity held in suspension and on the extent to which the particles collected into compound groups. Assuming that no deposit would be formed when the current was stronger than the final velocity, it seems probable that for granules ·001 inch in diameter the velocity of the current could not be above ·01 foot per second, equal to about 36 feet per hour, and for those ·0001 inch in diameter about $3\frac{1}{2}$ feet per hour or less. At all events, for fine-grained clays these velocities are probably of the true order of magnitude, though possibly too great.

### XII. On the Interspaces between the Constituent Grains of Deposited Material.

A knowledge of the relative volume between the constituent grains of rocks, as originally deposited, or as modified by subsequent mechanical or chemical changes, throws much light on many interesting questions. In studying this subject the foundation is to a large extent mathematical; and, in order to facilitate calculation, it was desirable to assume that the grains are spheres of equal size, uniformly arranged in various ways, so as to occupy as much or as little space as possible or some intermediate amount. Possibly this problem has never before been treated from its geological side. For the sake of simplicity, I have made my calculations as though there were only eight spheres, but so treated the question that the results would be the same as if the numbers were so great that the effects of the outer surfaces could be neglected.

(1) The first case to consider is when four spheres are arranged as a square, and the other four placed directly over them, so that each sphere rests upon only one, and the bounding surface of the whole is a cube. The radius of each sphere is taken as unity, and therefore the length of each side of this cube is 4, and the volume 64. The united volume of the spheres themselves is then $\frac{4}{3}\pi \times 8 = 33.51$. Hence their relative volume is $\frac{33.51}{64} = 52.36$ per cent., and of the interspaces 47·64 per cent.

(2) The next case is when four spheres are arranged as a square, and the other four tilted over, so that each rests upon two, and the bounding surface is a parallelepiped, four sides of which are squares and the others parallelograms having angles of 60° and 120°, so that the height above the square base is $2\sqrt{3}$, and the volume $2\sqrt{3} \times 4 \times 4 = 55.42$, whereas that of the spheres alone is 33·51. Hence the relative volume is $\frac{33.51}{55.42} = 60.46$ per cent., and the relative volume of the interspaces is 39·54 per cent.

(3) The third case is when four spheres are arranged as a square, and the other four tilted over in the line of one diagonal, so that, if the number were indefinitely great, each would rest upon four. This would give a parallelepiped having a square base, and two edges inclined at 45° to the base, so that the height would be $2\sqrt{2}$, and the volume $2\sqrt{2} \times 4 \times 4 = 45.25$. Hence the relative volume would be $\frac{33.51}{45.25} = 74.05$ per cent., and that of the interspaces 25·95 per cent.

(4) The last case that we need consider is when the base itself
is not square, but the spheres so shifted that each one touches two,
and the base is a parallelogram, having angles of 60° and 120°; and
the other spheres are arranged as much as possible in the same
manner. It is, however, impossible to have each one resting upon
three when the number is indefinitely large, but there are alternate
rows with 1 on 3 and 3 on 3 cross ways. We thus get for the axes
of the bounding parallelepiped $2\sqrt{4-\sec^2 30°}$, $2\sqrt{3}$, and 4: so that
the volume is $2\sqrt{4-\sec^2 30°} \times 2\sqrt{3} \times 4 = 45\cdot25$, or exactly the
same as in the last case considered, and the relative amount of
interspaces 25·95 per cent. This is a very interesting result, since
it shows that, when occupying the least volume, the spheres could be
moved about considerably, without altering the volume. I may say
that, in order to test my calculations, I made very careful measured
drawings, and obtained practically the same results.

## Experiments with Spherical Shot.

My experiments were made in a glass bulb holding a known
weight of water, and the amount of interspaces was ascertained from
the weight of water between the grains, when full of water; and,
in other cases, from the weight of the material used, compared with
that of an equal volume, if it had been solid lead. When the
small shot was filled into the bulb without shaking, the volume of
the interspaces was 47·2 per cent., which thus agrees closely with
47·64 per cent., calculated for spheres occupying as much space as
they can when each touches six. When the glass bulb was turned
about and well shaken, so as to cause the shot to occupy as small a
space as it would, the interspaces were reduced to 40 per cent.
This agrees closely with 39·54, found by calculation in case No. 2,
for spheres arranged rectangularly in two directions, but one over
two in another. It is scarcely probable that such an arrangement
is brought about by shaking, but the above agreement is remarkable.

I then hammered the same shot, thus obtaining disks with a
diameter about three times their thickness. On filling these gently
into the bulb and afterwards well shaking them, the amount of
interspaces was found to be practically the same in both cases as
if they had been spheres. This is somewhat remarkable, but of
much interest in connexion with sand built up of grains of irregular
shape; for it shows that, if these are of fairly-uniform size, in the
long run they occupy nearly the same volume as if they were
spheres.

## Experiments with Quartz-Sand.

As might be expected, the results differ materially with sand of
different character. In the case of the somewhat coarse and
angular sand of the Millstone Grit, having grains on an average
·05 inch in diameter, when filled in variously, but not shaken, the

average volume of the interspaces was 49·4 per cent., and when well shaken 43·5 per cent. In the case of Calais sand, the grains of which had a mean diameter of about ·01 inch, the interspaces as above were respectively 45·8 and 38·7 per cent. The means of all my experiments with both kinds of sand were, for not shaken 47·0 per cent., and for well shaken 40·0, which agree remarkably well with 47·2 and 40·0 found in the case of shot. In no case with sand of fairly-uniform grains did shaking reduce the volume of the interspaces to anything like the theoretical minimum, namely 25·95 per cent. In the case of finely-powdered sand, having grains on an average $\frac{1}{300}$ inch in diameter, when filled in quickly the interspaces were 47 per cent., and when well shaken 34 : this much smaller amount being probably due to the greater relative range in the size of the grains.

## Sand with Grains of Extremely Variable Size.

Theoretically, the admixture of fine sand with coarse ought greatly to reduce the amount of the interspaces. For example, if the spaces between the coarse grains were filled with fine sand, the interspaces should be 40 per cent. of 40 per cent. : that is, only 16 per cent. ; but in no case have I obtained so low a result by experiment. Thus, on mixing the coarse Millstone-Grit sand with an equal volume of Calais sand, I found the interspaces, when filled in quickly, to amount to 38 per cent., and when well shaken, 32 per cent. When equal quantities of these two sands and of the powdered sand were mixed, the interspaces when shaken were further reduced to 28·9 per cent. This, however, is far greater than it would be theoretically, if arranged with intelligent design ; it might probably be the result, if the sands were exposed to pressure and vibration for an indefinitely-long period. The facts, nevertheless, clearly show that, as might have been expected, the proportion of interspaces in such sand as would be deposited from deep water, and not sorted by bottom-currents, would be much less than in well-washed sand. Hence, other things being equal, the amount of interspaces gives some indication of the relative depth of the water, which agrees well with many general facts. Calais sand mixed with half its weight of pipe-clay, when gently compressed contained 36·7 per cent. of interspaces, which was reduced to about 18 per cent. by a pressure roughly estimated at about equal to 60,000 feet of superimposed rock. In the case of clay alone it was only 14·6 per cent. We thus see that the effect of clay is great.

## Small Flakes of Mica.

When fine particles of mica were put into a brass tube, the amount of interspaces was about 74 per cent., and by moderate pressure this was reduced to 55 per cent. When the mica was well shaken before pressure the amount was about 57 per cent., and when afterwards compressed it was reduced to 52. These facts show clearly how very far small flakes are from arranging themselves in the smallest space, since, even when somewhat compressed, they occupy more than the maximum for spheres arranged rectangularly.

## XIII. SEGREGATION.

Before further considering the cavities in sedimentary rocks, it is desirable to point out the difference between two extreme forms of alteration subsequent to deposition. One, which may be called segregation from the outside, is when the cavities originally existing between the ultimate particles have been more or less completely filled, usually by carbonate of lime, introduced from without from contiguous water or deposits, the original grains being unchanged. The other may be called internal segregation, and is when original material migrates from one place to another, leaving empty spaces, and making other parts more or less completely solid. As examples of the former, I may cite some calcareous sandstones, and a case from St. Helena, where the original rounded grains of corallines and shells are quite unchanged, but the spaces between them filled with crystalline calcite; and as an example of the latter, a limestone from Binstead (Isle of Wight), where the original fragments of shell have been completely removed, leaving empty cavities, and the carbonate of lime has been transferred to the intermediate spaces. A combination of both these changes is seen in many limestones.

## Coral-Reef Limestones.

An analogous transfer from one part to another may result in irregular cavities, and in a far more solid intermediate material than the original deposit, conditions which are very characteristic of those coral-reef rocks that I have been able to examine. Through the kindness of the Trustees of the British Museum and Dr. A. Smith Woodward, I have been able to study carefully four specimens from various depths in the boring through the reef at Funafuti. In all of these there are empty spaces, in no way like casts of decayed bodies, but of the most irregular shape: when small, some may represent bubbles of gas, and when larger they are of such irregular shape as to defy description. Their surface is generally covered with small rounded protuberances. I cannot explain the facts better than by internal segregation, causing the material to collect into certain parts, so as to make them nearly solid, and to leave other parts void, for lack of matter to make all solid.

These cavities are so unevenly distributed as to make it useless to determine their amount from a small piece, but Dr. W. M. Hicks kindly ascertained the specific gravity of the whole of each specimen with the large balances at the Sheffield University, from

which I could calculate the amount of empty cavities completely
enclosed in the solid rock. Then, by careful measurement and
calculation, I was able to determine approximately the volume of
the cavities open to the outside. Combining these volumes with
those calculated from the specific gravity I obtained the following
results :—

### TABLE VI.

From   150 to   160 feet deep   18 per cent.
  „   643 to   646  „  „   32  „  „
  „   755 to   766  „  „   20  „  „
  „  1080 to  1090  „  „   29  „  „

Mean=about  25

It will thus be seen that, from the four specimens studied, no law
can be deduced connecting the empty spaces with the depth; but it
might be apparent, if all the specimens were studied in the same
manner. The mean value is, at all events, of the same order
of magnitude as would occur in deposits that were consolidated
by internal segregation without being first subjected to any considerable pressure, and it affords no certain evidence of material
segregation from the outside. The hardness and structure completely prove the great extent of the internal segregation.

The limestones from Bermuda and Bahama contain analogous
cavities; but their total volume seems much smaller, and some look
as if they were spaces originally occupied by bubbles. At all
events, both these and the Funafuti specimens differ in a marked
manner from nearly, if not quite, all the 500 thin sections of
British limestone in my collection.

## Determination of the Amount of Interspaces in Natural Rocks.

In studying the interspaces in rocks, two courses are open to us.
We may determine their volume in the rock as it now exists,
which may or may not have any connexion with its original
condition; or, by studying a thin microscopical section, we may
ascertain their relative volume in the early condition of the rock,
before it was materially changed by subsequent deposition or
solution of material. The former is much the most important
when looking upon the rock as a building-stone, but the latter,
when we wish to learn the history of its deposition.

To enter into full particulars would be almost equivalent to
writing a treatise on the microscopical structure of rocks; and
I shall therefore take it for granted that, in the cases here
considered, there is no practical difficulty in distinguishing between
the materials originally deposited and those subsequently introduced by infiltration. Having then selected a suitable portion
of a suitable specimen, a photograph or a careful *camera-lucida*
drawing is made on thin cardboard of uniform thickness, showing

the original constituent fragments and the interspaces. These are then accurately cut out with scissors and their weight determined separately, from which the percentage of the interspaces can be at once calculated. The volume of the very minute interspaces existing in the grains themselves cannot thus be determined, but is not needed for the purpose in hand. The method which I have adopted in determining the interspaces in the whole rock as it now exists, is to boil thoroughly a portion in water in a flask, and tightly cork it when full of hot steam, so that on cooling there is a partial vacuum. After remaining for a few days the fragment is taken out, the loose water removed, and the weight of the fragment full of water determined. If thought necessary, the process may be repeated, so as to make sure that there is no increase in weight. The fragment is then dried until its weight is constant. The specific gravity of the rock being known, the volume of the open spaces can then be easily calculated. Those completely closed may be neglected for the purpose in hand, though in all cases they may cause the determinations to be somewhat too small. There are cases in which these two methods give nearly the same result, but others in which they are absolutely different, on account of changes since deposition.

In order to clear the way for subsequent descriptions, it may be well to state a few general conclusions applicable to the case when the grains may be treated as if they were spheres. Deposited quickly and shaken very slightly, the interspaces may amount to nearly half the volume, but the grains are then in a state of unstable equilibrium. On shaking, a sort of equilibrium is established, when the tendency to settle into smaller volume and the resisting friction are nearly equal, in which case the interspaces amount to about 40 per cent. of the volume. Another much more stable equilibrium is when the grains, probably under greater pressure, have arranged themselves so as to occupy the smallest space without their shape being altered, namely, where the interspaces amount to about 26 per cent. Another final condition occurs rarely and partially in limestones that have been subjected to the intense pressure which produced slaty cleavage, when the original interspaces have been almost or entirely obliterated. It will thus be seen that the detailed study of sandstones and some allied rocks is a very special, wide, and complex subject, which is likely to lead to a new class of results.

## Application to Particular Rocks.

For some of the purposes of this paper limestones are by far the most suitable. Thin sections of coarse-grained sandstones are difficult to prepare, and teach so little that I have made very few. Considering how many thin sections of limestone I have made, very few are suitable for calculations, because the three axes of the original fragments are not sufficiently equal to enable us to treat them as spheres. In some cases, where the original deposit consisted of fragments of bivalve shells, more than one-half of the present solid rock must have been a subsequent chemical deposit from solution, brought in by percolating water. It is manifest that calculations in such cases are of little value. Deposits almost entirely composed of oolitic grains of nearly equal size are very suitable, and so are those composed of small joints of encrinites or fragments of shells or corals worn into fairly equi-axed grains of nearly equal size. Cases totally unfit for calculations are common, in which the grains are of very unequal size, and the spaces between the larger filled by smaller, as though not sorted by a bottom-current.

Sprudelstein, Carlsbad.—The amount of spaces between the almost spherical grains, as determined by the *camera-lucida* method, was found to be 44·3 per cent., which corresponds to what happens when deposited spheres are only slightly shaken. They must have been soon filled with infiltrated material in such a manner that all further settling was impossible.

Recent deposit, St. Helena.—What was given to me as such many years ago, is composed almost entirely of rounded grains of calcareous algæ, nearly all of one size. The amount of interspaces ascertained by the camera is 39·6 per cent. This corresponds very closely with 40 per cent. in the case of shot or sand well shaken. They are almost completely filled by infiltrated calcite, and probably this took place at an early period in the history of the rock, and its structure was thus made permanent. This specimen is extremely interesting, because the percentage of interspaces corresponds so closely with that observed in many older rocks, down to the Silurian.

Oolitic rocks.—It appears to me that a good deal remains to be learned respecting the exact conditions under which our Oolitic rocks were formed, since they differ so much from any deposits associated with recent coral-reefs that I have been able to examine, in which I have found only a very few oolitic grains of a kind rarely seen in British rocks. These generally appear to have been formed originally of calcite, a few of aragonite, and probably in certain districts of a mixture of the two. Over a considerable area in the Great Oolite, what was the original deposit is now a mere wreck. Properly to explain all these variations would require further researches of various kinds. For my present purpose, some of these rocks are of especial interest—because the oolitic grains can very fairly be looked upon as small spheres. In the first place, I will consider cases in which there has been little change since deposition.

Oolites of the Lincolnshire district, etc.—I have two excellent microscopical sections of a specimen given to me, and said to come from near Grantham (see Pl. XVII, fig. 1). The nearly spherical grains are quite hard, and the interspaces almost entirely empty, containing only a few small crystals of calcite. The volume of these interspaces, as determined by the *camera-lucida* method, was found to be 25·3 per cent., which, allowing for slight compression, corresponds remarkably well with 25·95, the theoretical minimum for spheres. It should appear therefore, that, although mere shaking will not cause grains of shot to arrange themselves in the least volume, pressure (and perhaps earthquake-shocks) acting through geological periods will produce this result; but of course not, if the interspaces had been filled by infiltrated calcite at an early part of the history of the rock.

I have examined some analogous rocks from the same part of England by the boiling-water method. The building-stone of Ketton was found to contain 29·7 per cent. of empty spaces, and another specimen from near Stamford 36·3 per cent. This latter was extremely soft when obtained in the quarry, and the grains themselves may not be solid. The excess over 26 per cent. may, therefore, not be due to the grains not having accommodated themselves to the least volume, but to the different manner in which the interspaces were determined, those in the grains themselves having no influence in the case of the Grantham specimen.

Portland oolite.—Determined by the *camera-lucida* method, the Portland building-stone was found to contain 23·6 per cent. of interspaces, only to a small extent filled with infiltrated calcite; but it can be seen that the grains have been to a slight extent pressed together, so as to explain why the interspaces are less than 26 per cent. When determined by the boiling-water method, those now empty were found to amount to 22 per cent., which smaller amount as thus determined is no doubt due to infiltrated calcite. It is, however, only particular portions of the Portland rocks that are at all suitable for the purpose in hand; for, in some, the oolitic grains have been changed since deposition in an unusual and remarkable manner, especially when near the Dirt-Bed.

Oolitic beds in the Carboniferous Limestone of Clifton, near Bristol.—In one excellent case the original interspaces must have amounted to 40 per cent., but these are now filled by infiltrated calcite. This agrees with the supposition that this infiltration occurred before the deposit was subjected to much pressure, though in another specimen belonging to my friend Mr. T. S. Cole, and photographed by him, the interspaces had been reduced to 32·6 per cent., or even less.

Oolitic bed in the Wenlock Limestone, near West Malvern.—Determined by the *camera-lucida* method, the original interspaces were found to have been 39·6 per cent.; and thus, like the above-described Carboniferous Limestone, they must have been filled by infiltrated calcite at an early period in the history of the rock. The mean of the two is 40·2, which is practically identical with what occurs in the case of shaken shot and sand, and in the recent rock from St. Helena. This seems to me a very interesting conclusion, since it shows that right down to the Silurian Period the infiltrated calcite was introduced while the rock was still what would now be called 'recent.' In other cases it must have been introduced when the rock was much older, or only partially up to the present time.

Modified oolites.—The freestones of Corsham (near Bath), Minchinhampton, and Cheltenham differ remarkably from those near Grantham and Ketton, inasmuch as the original oolitic grains are now mere residues, and the present solidity of the rock is due to the interspaces having been filled by infiltrated calcite. By the *camera-lucida* method, I found that in the Cheltenham rocks the interspaces originally amounted to 46 per cent., which does not materially differ from what is found in the Sprudelstein of Carlsbad (see p. 206). It seems to indicate a somewhat rapid deposition, and little disturbance before the grains were permanently fixed by the infiltration of calcite. As I pointed out in my address to the Geological Society in 1879,[1] there is good reason to believe that the grains in a few of our oolitic rocks were originally deposited as aragonite, but others as calcite; and that the former have since been changed, though not the latter (except in the case of the Portland rocks, as described above). It seems quite possible that some may originally have been a mixture of these two minerals, and that, in the same manner as in the case of some fossil-shells, the aragonite-portion has been removed and the calcite-portion left. At all events, this would explain why some parts of the oolitic grains have been removed, so as to give rise to their partly-decayed character. Much more experiment is needed to ascertain the exact conditions limiting the production of aragonite and calcite. Temperature certainly, but evidently other things also have great influence. So far, I have found very few oolitic grains in recent coral-reef rocks, and these seem to be aragonite. The conditions under which our characteristic oolitic rocks were formed appear to me to have involved shallow water, perhaps rather warm, and highly charged with carbonate of lime, which not only gave rise to the oolitic grains, but also crystallized out between them very soon after they were deposited. One specimen of the building-stone of Corsham gave, by the boiling-water method, 25·6 per cent. as the amount of cavities now existing; but the microscopical structure shows that this must have little to do with the original condition, although it may have some connexion with the amount of cavities when the oolitic grains were partly decomposed. I very much regret that I did not measure the angle of rest of the material, since a knowledge of the change in its value would probably have furnished valuable information. Judging from the facts at my disposal, the above-

---

[1] Quart. Journ. Geol. Sol. vol. xxxv (1879) Proc. p. 84.

described differences in the oolitic grains vary in different beds and in different localities, but seem to extend over a considerable area.

Limestones composed of fragments of calcareous organisms.—When made up of joints of encrinites or of fragments of shells or corals so nearly equi-axed that they may be treated as imperfect spheres, their study leads to much the same results as in the case of oolites. All my best specimens of Oolitic age belong to the Coralline Oolite. That shown in Pl. XVII, fig. 2 was found to have originally contained 43·3 per cent. of interspaces, and another from Oxford 43·1. Yet another from Filey contained 53·1 per cent., this larger amount being probably due to the fragments having too flat a shape to be strictly comparable with spheres. A Devonian limestone from Hope's Nose (near Torquay), composed of small joints of encrinites, gave 45·6 per cent. Leaving out the specimens from Filey, the other three give as a mean 44 per cent., or almost exactly the same as the Sprudelstein of Carlsbad. Everything therefore agrees with the supposition that the material was deposited rather quickly, and not much shaken or pressed before the interspaces were filled with infiltrated calcite. A specimen of the lower part of the Carboniferous Limestone near Bristol, mainly composed of fragments of encrinites, seems to have contained only 25 per cent. of interspaces, as though they were not filled up with calcite until after the material had been exposed to considerable pressure; and a specimen from the Wenlock Limestone of Easthope (Pl. XVIII, fig. 1) contained only 17·7 per cent., which seems to have been due to the still closer pressing-together of the angular and irregular fragments of shells, corals, and encrinites.

Taking, then, all these facts into consideration, the study of the interspaces seems to indicate that, as might have been expected, the effects of pressure are more marked in the older than in the newer rocks. It reaches, however, its maximum in some Devonian limestones associated with well-developed slaty cleavage. This is notably the case in a portion of a thin bed composed of joints of encrinites at Ilfracombe, in some parts of which nearly all traces of the original interspaces have been obliterated.

Magnesian Limestone.—The empty spaces seen with the microscope in some specimens, as in that of Bulwell (near Nottingham), are really places left empty when the crystals of dolomite were formed. In this they amount to 13·3 per cent.; but the whole history of the rock is too complex and difficult of understanding to make it desirable to do more than allude to it, as an example differing entirely from most others that I have described.

## Cavities determined by the Boiling-Water Method.

Although the percentage of cavities now existing in a rock may throw little light on its original formation, yet it is of great interest in connexion with the present condition of the rock. Many of my experiments were made with building-stone, in order, if possible, to obtain some clue to the cause of their variable durability; but I will mass them together, and give such results as are of geological interest.

Sandstones.—First of all, we may compare the sandstones of New Red, Carboniferous, and Old Red age, of which I have examined a fair number, but only from a few districts, so that my results cannot be looked upon as necessarily applying to every place. Those of New Red age were from Maer in Staffordshire, and Mansfield in Nottinghamshire. Leaving out a shaly bed, the mean for the different places near Maer is 25 per cent., which agrees closely with the minimum for spheres and for fairly-uniform grains of sand. The variation from 21·5 to 28·8 may be explained by variation in the grains and the presence of a small amount of infiltrated carbonate of lime. The very friable sandstone at Mansfield, in which the rock-houses were excavated, contains 33·5 per cent. of vacuities; which looks as though the grains had never completely accommodated themselves to the smallest volume. The very special and excellent building-stones contain on an average only 16·9 per cent. of vacuities, and thus approach closely to the building-stones from the Old Red of Herefordshire; like them, the greater solidity is due partly to infiltrated calcite, and partly to deposition in deeper water, with less sorting of the material by bottom-currents.

The sandstones of Carboniferous age were from South Yorkshire, Derbyshire, and the Forest of Dean. The vacuities vary from 8·7 to 14·8 per cent., the mean being 11·1. This small amount is sometimes due to the original cavities having been, to a considerable extent, filled up by decomposed felspar; but sometimes it may be ascribed to the feebleness of the bottom-current.

The Old Red specimens studied were building-stones from various quarries in Herefordshire; and, leaving out those containing an unusual amount of carbonate of lime, the vacuities vary from 16·1 to 21 per cent., the mean being 18·4. In those containing much carbonate of lime, some of which are building-stones of remarkable durability in pure country-air, the cavities have been to a large extent filled up, and the mean is only 6 per cent. This infiltration and the greater depth of water and less bottom-current, and also exposure to pressure for a longer time, will explain why, on an average, there is a marked difference between the sandstones of Old and those of New Red age.

The Gannister near Sheffield is, in some cases, an excellent example of the almost complete filling-up by infiltrated quartz of the interspaces in a deposit of very fine sand. When fractured surfaces are examined with a microscope, many small crystals may be seen. The boiling-water method shows that, in some specimens, free from the rootlets of *Stigmaria*, the empty cavities amount to less than 1 per cent., which is far below what occurs in recently-deposited sand of fine grain. It seems to me probable that slight deposition of quartz may play an important part in causing the grains to cohere, in many sandstones which are not disintegrated by long exposure to strong acids, and thus resist exposure to the weather remarkably long.

Limestones of Oolitic age.—I have made many determinations of the open interspaces by the hot-water method; but their present structure is due to so many complex conditions, that the results are of little value in connexion with my present purpose. In the case of building-stones, the maximum was 37 per cent. and the mean of the maximum values about 31. The minimum for the more solid was 13 per cent. and the average about 15. This is as though such limestones were more or less solidified by infiltrated calcite not long after deposition, and as though the process had not been carried out so completely as in the case of many older rocks.

Kentish Rag.—By the boiling-water method I found that, in its natural condition, this rock contains only about 3·5 per cent. of open interspaces; whereas the much-weathered rock contains 26·1 per cent., owing to the removal of soluble material, which left the rocks with about the same amount of interspaces as in the case of the most closely-packed fragments.

The cavities in many other rocks will be considered, when dealing with the pressure to which they have been subjected.

## Determination of the Cavities in Fine-Grained Rocks.

The physical characters of different fine-grained rocks vary so much that the fairly-accurate determination of the cavities is in some cases quite easy, but in others difficult. This is due to the combination of a number of curious relations between a certain class of rocks and water, which they seem to contain in four or five different conditions:—(1) The water is combined chemically, but lost on strong heating; (2) it is absorbed, somewhat like an occluded gas; (3) it is condensed from a damp atmosphere among the very minute particles, but not in such quantity as to fill the cavities; (4) when the rock is placed in water, the latter fills up the cavities; and (5) it may not only fill them, but interpenetrate the material with such force as to swell it to a considerable extent, or even break it up completely and cause it to occupy about twice and a third the volume of the solid material. One result of the absorption of water from a damp atmosphere is that it may be almost impossible to decide what ought to be looked upon as the correct weight. This is certainly not due to mere fine division, since very finely-powdered calcite does not increase in weight in an atmosphere saturated with water, whereas clays largely composed of decomposed felspar vary considerably in weight from day to day, according to the state of the weather, the amount varying up to at least 5½ per cent. Very much remains to be learned respecting the connexion of these facts with the history of the rocks; but they are evidently of fundamental importance, and in some way are connected with the age of the rocks. One striking fact is, that specimens of different geological periods may look almost alike, and yet differ enormously in their reaction with water.

Then, again, we have to consider the amount of soluble salts dissolved out by water, as shown by the loss of weight. The amount and the nature of these form a subject worthy of careful study. My results are but imperfect, because deduced from experiments made specially to learn other facts. So far as they go, they make it appear possible that in fine-grained shales there are to some extent the salts originally contained in the water from which the shales were deposited; this was slowly lost by evaporation, since the amount of salts is sometimes far greater than in the volume of sea-water that would fill the cavities. There is also in the specimens examined more salt in the shales deposited in sea-water than in corresponding rocks from the freshwater Coal-Measures.

When fine-grained rocks are treated with water, there is generally a certain amount of swelling, which may be so small as to be invisible, and there is no breaking-up; but sometimes the tumescence is so great and energetic, that the specimen quickly breaks up from a fairly-hard rock into a soft clay. In such cases, it is of course impossible to determine the amount of natural cavities by means of water, and almond-oil or benzol must be used. In this event allowance must be made for what may be dissolved by these liquids. When the rock does not break up, the volume of absorbed water may be considerable, and due almost entirely to swelling, the amount of oil or benzol absorbed being comparatively small. After being soaked with water, the specimen may, or may not, contract to its original volume. on drying. Then, again, after the specimen has been kept in water for several days, its weight when dried may be considerably less than it was, owing to the removal of soluble salts, which may amount to several per cent.

## The Structure of Fine-Grained Deposits.

The results of my experiments with clay and chalk explain the structure of many deposits of nearly all ages. It appears as though the comparatively-recent mud of our estuaries may remain for a very long time in a sort of semi-fluid condition. That in the wide mud-flat in the Deben, opposite Waldringfield, which may have been there for ages, is so soft that an oar can be pushed down into it for a good many feet with scarcely any resistance, the mud being in much the same condition as the clay in my experiments, which did not subside more on keeping. In other cases, the upper part is very soft; but the material becomes firmer at a lower level, where it may have existed for ages under some little pressure. The much older clays and shales agree with what would happen if more and more included water had been squeezed out by the pressure of superincumbent material; and their fissility is like that produced in my experiments, being due, not to any alternation of different materials in the plane of bedding, but to the necessary change in ultimate structure brought about by the great decrease in thickness. As shown by these experiments, the interspaces in clay which had settled so as to become somewhat stable amounted in extreme cases to no less than 86 per cent. of the volume, whereas in the fine-grained shales of the Coal-Measures they amount only to 13 per cent., which indicates a probable reduction to about a sixth of the original volume. Considering the nature of the material, this would be quite adequate to develop an imperfect cleavage in the plane of bedding, in accordance with the principles which I have described in my papers on slaty cleavage. The experiments also explain the change consequent on the weathering of the shale, which has become soft, and now contains 39·2 per cent. of interspaces; this corresponds to what happens when the dried clay swells up by water forcing itself into it, such an effect being no doubt increased in the shale by frost.

As bearing on the production of schistosity in shales and of cleavage in slates, I may mention an experiment that I made with what was given to me as 'Brodie's graphite.' This, when filled into a brass tube about 2 inches long, was loose and bulky, but could be compressed down to about a quarter of an inch by a tightly-fitting brass rod, when it was found to be fairly solid, and to possess a more perfect cleavage than any slate, in the plane perpendicular to the direction of compression.

Chalk.—My experiments with fine-grained chalk show that, when deposited so as to arrive at a kind of temporary stability, it is a sort of imperfect liquid; and this was probably the case with the natural deposit. The amount of interspaces might well have been more than 70 per cent. My impression is that, many years ago, I examined a soft chalk in which they were still about 50 per cent. Artificially deposited, very fine-grained chalk, when contracted by drying without any pressure, contains 41 per cent. of interspaces, or sensibly the same as shaken shot or sand. The clunch used for internal artistic work was found, by the boiling-water method, still to contain 34 per cent. The Chalk of the Yorkshire coast has been much hardened by infiltrated calcite, and contains only about 15 per cent. Probably, then, the reduction in thickness of natural chalk has been to about 45 per cent. of the original thickness, which is a much smaller reduction than in shales; and this, combined with the difference in the character of the material, will explain why, in the case of the natural rocks, and in my experiments, no fissility was developed approaching that of shales.

Cavities in slate-rocks.—The determination of the exact amount of cavities in rocks possessing cleavage is rendered difficult by a peculiarity which, in most cases, is of no importance. After boiling in water, there can be little doubt that, as a rule, nearly all the loss of weight on drying is due to liquid water which existed in the cavities. In the case of slate-rocks, which are so nearly solid, what otherwise would be small effects become of importance. Thus, in the case of the Penrhyn slate, after being boiled in water, and kept in the water until the weight was constant, the specimen on being dried in the atmosphere at the natural temperature indicated (by loss) the existence of about ·24 per cent. of interspaces; but, when it was dried at a very moderate heat near a fire, there was a further small loss, which, if due to liquid water which had been in cavities, would indicate that these amounted to nearly a half per cent. This should make a very considerable difference in the calculated pressure, discussed later (p. 227). It seems, however, improbable that liquid water would remain in the rocks when dried for several days in the air of a warm sitting-room, and more probable that the further loss in weight represents water occluded in, or loosely combined in some way with, the solid material. If so, the question arises whether part or even all of the water lost after boiling is not also thus combined, and does not represent cavities. On the whole, in the present state of the question, it is probably the best to adopt a mean result, and to conclude that the empty spaces in the Penrhyn slate amount to ·24 per cent.

### XIV. Contraction of Rocks after Deposition.

This may be very little, or as much as 90 per cent. of the original thickness, even when nothing has been removed chemically. In the case of sandstones and allied rocks, having at first about 46 per cent. of cavities, the contraction when the grains had accommodated themselves to the least volume would be about ·25 per cent., but much less if the sand consisted of grains of extremely-variable size. Much depends, however, on whether the cavities had or had not been filled with calcite at an early period; and a rock may now be almost quite solid, and yet may have contracted very little. Manifestly, then, we must rely on the evidence furnished by each particular case. As shown already, the best is that afforded by the change in the angle of rest of well-developed drift-bedding or ripple-drift. Information of a less reliable character may be furnished by concretions, as will be shown when dealing with them.

The contraction in the case of very fine-grained rocks may have been very much greater, since, even after standing for a year without further subsidence, such material may contain 90 per cent. of water; whereas consolidated older rocks of analogous character may have been made almost solid by the squeezing-out of this water—so that, in extreme cases, shales and slates may occupy only a ninth of the volume which they possessed when originally deposited. At all events, it is important to bear in mind that the thickness of many of our rocks may now be very much less than the original.

## XV. Concretions.

The accurate, detailed study of concretions is a promising enquiry, likely to yield interesting and unexpected results. Except in the case of the green spots in some slates, which I studied carefully many years ago, I have unfortunately made but few accurate measurements in the field ; and I must now rely on what can be learned from such specimens as are in my collection, which, however, include those of nearly all geological periods. It is desirable to divide them into those formed before they were finally deposited, and those formed in the rock after its deposition. The former division includes oolitic grains, pisolites, and a few analogous objects ; and the latter, more or less rounded bodies of very diverse character.

### Pisolites.

The mean ratios of the three principal axes of the examples in my collection of Oolitic age are 0·4, 1, and 1·33, no two being equal, and the shortest being unusually short. This is largely due to the flat nucleus. In a sandstone at Barlborough, near Sheffield, probably of Lower New-Red-Sandstone age, the ratios of the axes are 1, 1, and 1·41, and the well-developed grains are remarkably uniform in size. They are composed of fine sand held together by carbonate of lime, and their peculiar form was probably due to rolling along the bottom.

One very important fact connected with pisolites is that their flatter surfaces are often inclined at various angles to the stratification, as though deposited irregularly from a rather strong current. Concretions formed after deposition usually have their longer axes all nearly in the plane of stratification.

### Oolitic Grains.

These are often remarkably uniform in size in each part of the rocks, as though more or less sorted by a current of water.

### The Plane of Symmetry.

So far as I can judge from the specimens in my collection, the plane of symmetry of the rocks in three cases out of four coincides with the plane of stratification, but in one-fourth of the cases it is inclined at an angle varying from 5° to 10°. This is apparently in no way due to chance, being uniform in all the specimens from the same place. Those in my collection are not adequate to clear up all the difficulties, which would require extensive work in the field. The main question is whether the inclined plane of symmetry was produced at the time of deposition, or long after. If produced at the time, it seems to indicate that in that particular place the bottom was not quite horizontal, but inclined at a considerable angle, and that, although the layers of different quality lie in the plane of stratification, the unequi-axed particles were deposited as they fell horizontally. Subsequently the material settled in a perpendicular line, so that the unsymmetrical structure was increased. If these suppositions are allowable, all the facts seem explained. If the inclined plane of symmetry was produced long after deposition, it would indicate that the rock as a whole was somewhat compressed in a line perpendicular to this plane, so that it is analogous to one having a very imperfect slaty cleavage; but, considering all the circumstances, this seems extremely doubtful. Possibly, however, both explanations may be true in particular cases.

### Concretions formed *in situ* in Stratified Rocks.

Their actual size is of secondary importance, and may vary greatly. The most important consideration is the relative length of their axes, which may be called $a$, $b$, and $c$, $a$ being the shortest and $c$ the longest. This may depend, to a considerable extent, on the length of the axes of the original nucleus, which we may call $x$, $y$, and $z$. Round this the material of the concretion has been collected; and the thickness in different directions depends, to a great extent, on the structure of the rock. When this is the same in all directions in a particular plane, which we may call t h e p l a n e of s y m m e t r y, the thickness of the deposit may be called $T$; but perpendicular to this it may differ, and may be called $T'$, the water penetrating equally well in all directions along the plane of symmetry, though with greater difficulty perpendicular to it, probably because the flat particles of the rock lie mainly in the plane of symmetry. This is assuming that, when the nucleus is elongated, its thickness is constant. If this varies much, there may be a corresponding variation in the thickness of the deposit; in extreme cases, therefore, the concretion may taper off to a sharp point, or show other abnormalities. We may, then, generalize the axes as follows:—$x+2T'$, $y+2T$, $z+2T$. If, as in some cases, $x$, $y$, and $z$ are small or nearly equal, and $T$ and $T'$ are also equal, the concretion is a sphere. In many cases, however, though $x$, $y$, and $z$ are small or nearly equal, $T'$ is less than $T$, owing to the structure of the rock, and the result is that two axes are equal and the third less. In other cases $x$, $y$, and $z$, and perhaps also $T$ and $T'$, are unequal, and consequently all the axes differ. In a few cases, two axes are equal and the other much longer, owing to an elongated nucleus. Of course, the effect of the nucleus becomes relatively less as the concretion increases in size. In some cases, owing to variations in the nucleus, examples of several of the above-named groups are found in the same rock, but sometimes all belong to one of them.

It seems probable that, in most cases, the concretions were formed at an early period in the history of the rock, while the nucleus was still chemically active.

The relative length of the axis perpendicular to the plane of symmetry seems to have depended chiefly on the nature of the material in which the concretion was formed, and on the amount of contraction which had previously taken place. If the original deposit consisted of particles more or less completely symmetrical in all directions, a considerable amount of contraction would produce little or no effect, and the growth of the concretion would take place equally in all directions. This would explain why the concretions in the Magnesian Limestone are almost perfect spheres. In the case of those in fine-grained sandstone at Arborthorne (near Sheffield), the axis perpendicular to bedding is 90 per cent. of those in its plane. The thickness of sand quickly deposited is reduced to 89 per cent. when well shaken, or to about the relative length of the shorter axis in the Arborthorne concretions, and is exactly the same as the mean for them and the green spots in the Old Red Sandstone. The shortest axis in one from shale at Woodbourne is 49 per cent. of the mean of those in the plane of symmetry. When fine clay which has subsided for a day is allowed to subside for a year, the contraction is 54 per cent. of the original, and would have been close on 49, if the measurement had been taken earlier in the day, or if the clay had been subjected to the pressure of superincumbent deposit. The explanation that I would suggest is that, as may be seen with the microscope, many of the fine particles of clay are flat flakes, and these to a great extent subsiding as compound granules would originally be inclined at all angles to the horizon. Then, when the deposit contracted vertically, they would become less and less inclined, and the permeability for water would be increased in the plane of symmetry and decreased in a line perpendicular to it. In such a case, the relative length of the short axes of the concretion would indicate the approximate amount of contraction. This conclusion would, however, apply to a particular class of rock alone, and then only approximately.

## Special Examples.

The concretions in the Magnesian Limestone seen along the coast north of Sunderland vary much in size, but when not interfered with by others are almost true spheres, the axes being 100 : 100 : 100, and when they leave impressions upon one another these are almost perfect circles. In my best specimens no axis differs from the mean by more than a hundredth of an inch. The nuclei must, therefore, have been small, and the surrounding material of very uniform structure in all directions.

The concretions in a fine-grained sandstone at Arborthorne (near Sheffield) are a good example of those which have the axes in the plane of stratification nearly equal, and that perpendicular to it shorter. The means for the bigger specimens are 92 : 100 : 100, and for the smaller 87 : 100 : 103—thus showing the greater effect of the nucleus on the smaller, and in both cases the effect of the different structure of the rock in a direction perpendicular to the bedding.

A red sandstone used in Gloucester, which looks very like some of the Old Red Sandstone of the Black Mountains, contains very perfect green spots, varying in size from very small up to 1 inch or more in diameter, which can easily be measured to a hundredth of an inch. The material is of fine grain, the particles varying in size from a hundredth of an inch down to very small. It is very compact, and by the boiling-water method was found to contain only 7·2 per cent. of cavities. There is no indication of a bottom-current of as much as 6 inches per second ; and the whole structure is that of a deposit formed in fairly-deep water, the chief current being some distance from the bottom. In the plane of symmetry the ratios of the axes are 100 : 101, the variations from this being only a hundredth of an inch. Perpendicular to the plane of symmetry the axes are 88 : 100, or closely the same as in the concretions at Arborthorne. Unlike them, they cannot be obtained separate, and are merely the red colour discharged by the deoxidizing action of some nucleus. It is important to observe that the plane of symmetry in all my specimens is inclined at about 10° to the stratification, probably because the bottom was not horizontal.

A small concretion from the Coal-Measures at Woodbourne (near Sheffield) is an excellent illustration of the laws of formation. It is split open through the centre, showing the exact shape of the nucleus, which is very much like the seed of a plant. The dimensions of this are : perpendicular to the plane of symmetry ·2 inch, and in the plane ·33 and ·50. In this plane the deposit is on two sides ·55, and on the other two ·60 ; so that, including the nucleus, we have for the entire concretion $·33 + 2 \times 55 = 1·43$ and $·50 + 2 \times 60 = 1·70$. Hence there is not equality, but rather more deposit in the line of the long axis of the nucleus, probably due to a slight difference in structure in the direction of the gentle current, which caused the long axis of the nucleus to lie in that direction. Perpendicular to the plane of symmetry, we have for the shortest axis $·20 + 2 \times ·28 = ·76$; so that the three axes are ·76, 1·43, and 1·70. It is also important to notice that the plane of approximate symmetry is inclined to the stratification at an angle of 5° in the line of the longest axis of both nucleus and concretion, as though the bottom dipped in the line of current.

In the case of a concretion from the Coal-Measures at Broomfield (Sheffield), in a fine-grained sandstone, the plane of symmetry appeared to be inclined at about 20° to the stratification, which may be partly due to compression near a fault.

In driving a drift through the Lower Coal-Measures at Stannington (near Sheffield), some very large and perfect concretions were found in a sandy shale. One of these, over 7 inches in diameter, gives as the ratio of the axes 78 : 100 : 103. Besides this, I collected a considerable number of much smaller size, down to less than an inch in diameter. The variation in their shape is so great, that at first sight it might seem impossible to deduce from them any general conclusions. A few differ completely from the rest, being broad and flat, imperfectly consolidated, and break up in the plane of bedding. In my specimens the ratios of the axes are closely the same as 40 : 100 : 101. By far the greater number are, however, hard and solid, but vary in general shape, one tapering off to a point at both ends. Taking, as usual, the shortest axis in the plane of bedding as 100, the longest axis varies from 207 to 100 and the shortest from 94 to 55, the means of all my twenty specimens being 81 : 100 : 127. Those which are almost circular in the plane of bedding, and therefore have a nearly-symmetrical nucleus, give for the axes 79 : 100 : 101; which differ from those in the case of the large specimen by about a hundredth of an inch. Hence, at the time when the concretions were formed, the relative permeability of the rock in a line perpendicular to the stratification was about 79 per cent. of that in its plane. The prevailing greater length of one axis in the plane of bedding was probably due to the nucleus being more or less elongated, combined with a slight want of symmetry in the rock, due to current. I have entered into all these details, in order to show that the proper discussion of very unpromising material yields nevertheless extremely satisfactory and concordant results.

Fortunately, I possess a few specimens of coarse shale with included concretions. These show that the layers of the rock do not pass through the concretions, but curve round them, as if the shale had been compressed to about half its thickness since they were formed, unless they (to some extent) pushed it aside in growing. Of this there seems to be no good evidence, whereas experiment shows that there must have been a great vertical contraction in shales and clays. This is, however, a question which needs further investigations, differing from any that I have been able to carry out.

The following (Table VII) is a list of all the concretions which I have studied, with the ratios of their axes, the shortest axis in the plane of bedding being taken as 100 :—

### TABLE VII.

*All axes nearly equal.*

| | | | |
|---|---|---|---|
| 1. Magnesian Limestone, Sunderland | 100 | 100 | 100 |
| 2. Post-Glacial, Bridlington | 103 | 100 | 106 |

*Two axes nearly equal.*

| | | | |
|---|---|---|---|
| 3. In fine sand, Arborthorne | 90 | 100 | 101 |
| 4. Green spots, Old Red Sandstone | 88 | 100 | 101 |
| 5. Lower Coal-Measures, Stannington (small) | 79 | 100 | 101 |
| 6. Do. do. do. (large) | 78 | 100 | 103 |
| 7. Fish-nodule, Old Red Sandstone | 53 | 100 | 103 |
| 8. Imperfect, Stannington | 40 | 100 | 101 |

*Elongated nuclei.*

| | | | |
|---|---|---|---|
| 9. Post-Glacial, Bridlington | 100 | 100 | 222 |
| 10. Pyrites in Chalk | 100 | 100 | 444 |

*All axes unequal.*

| | | | |
|---|---|---|---|
| 11. Gault, Lidhurst | 88 | 100 | 153 |
| 12. Post-Glacial, Bridlington | 86 | 100 | 136 |
| 13. Lower Coal-Measures, Stannington | 81 | 100 | 127 |
| 14. Oxford Clay | 77 | 100 | 143 |
| 15. Coal-shale, Woodbourne | 54 | 100 | 190 |

Nos. 1, 3, 4, 5, 8, & 13 are means of a number of specimens, and the rest single good cases.

In the case of pyrites in chalk, it seems clear that this pushed aside the chalk and did not include it.    On the contrary, when concretions of carbonate of lime or iron were formed in sandstone, they appear to have filled up the interspaces between the grains, and did not displace them.    In some rocks, both kinds of action may have combined.

## XVI. Spots in Welsh Slates.

Many years ago I made nearly 200 measurements of these spots, determining the length of greatest and least axes to about a hundredth of an inch, excluding those manifestly much influenced by stratification.

At that time I little thought what interesting conclusions could be drawn from them, and my object was merely to ascertain the amount of compression to which the rock had been subjected when the cleavage was developed.    I even then saw that the original spots were not spheres, and endeavoured to make my observations so that the stratification was inclined at all angles to the cleavage, and the spots could be treated as spheres in making my calculations.    In some cases this was approximately correct, but not in others; and my results were not sufficiently accurate for the purpose now in hand. I devoted therefore some weeks to the discussion of the observations, my aim being to learn what was the condition of the material when first deposited; the period in its history when the spots were formed; their exact shape; the extent of the consolidation to which the rock had been exposed, before cleavage was developed; the amount of lateral compression caused by the elevation of the Welsh mountains; and the change in dimensions and structure of the rock, caused by the compression.    Since this may appear an impossible programme, it will be necessary to enter into much detail, in order to show how the facts enable us to learn all these particulars approximately.

In many cases, when measuring the axes of the spots, I also determined the direction of the stratification: but this could not always be done, and in some cases there is so much contortion that the conclusions are doubtful.    I invariably kept separate measurements made in the plane of cleavage and perpendicular to it.    They were made in a quarry at Bethesda, in one at the bottom of Nant Ffrancon, in the great Penrhyn quarry, and in sundry quarries near Llanberis.    The first step was to calculate the relative length of the longest axis, that of the shortest being taken as unity.    In some places, where the stratification was fairly uniform, this ratio did not differ materially in as many as 26 cases; but in others there was a wide difference, because of the stratification cutting the cleavage at various angles.    This was visible at once by marking the value of each measurement along a straight line.    It was then seen that, for certain calculations, the measurements in the quarry at Bethesda were extremely good, since the long axis of the spots seems to be inclined at all angles to the cleavage. Those in the quarry at Penrhyn in a plane perpendicular to the cleavage were also well distributed at all angles, but in the plane of cleavage were inclined on an average at $27°$ to the horizontal. In the quarries in Nant Ffrancon and at Llanberis, the data, being intermediate, are not good for calculation.

Although having much in common with concretions, the spots were due to the deoxidization of the peroxide of iron. They are really ellipsoids; but, since the calculations require the ratios of the axes in particular planes, we need not consider the third dimension.

In studying the rocks *in situ*, it was easy to see that the axis of the original spots was longest in the plane of stratification; and the question to be first considered is, what was the exact ratio of the axes? It was assumed, in the first place, that in the plane perpendicular to the cleavage, when the rock was compressed, the sectional area of the spot remained the same; so that, for example, if the axis in the line of the pressure was reduced to one-half, that at right-angles was increased to double. If then the longest axis of the spot was inclined at all angles to the cleavage, the maximum value of the ratio between the longest and the shortest axis must be when the stratification was nearly in the plane of cleavage, and the smallest ratio when it was nearly perpendicular to the cleavage. It can thus be easily shown that the ratio of the shortest axis of the original spot, compared with its longest, was the square root of the smallest ratio after cleavage was developed, divided by the largest. In the quarry at Bethesda, perpendicular to the cleavage, the smallest ratio is $1:4$ and the largest $1:10$. Hence we have $\sqrt{\frac{4}{10}} = \cdot632$, that is the axes of the original spots were $63:100:100$. In the quarry at Penrhyn the extreme ratios are $1:4\cdot78$ and $1:11\cdot96$, which give $\sqrt{\frac{4\cdot78}{11\cdot96}} = \cdot632$, or the same as Bethesda. However, the probability is, that in both cases the result is somewhat too large. Combining the measurements made at both quarries, and taking the means of the maxima and minima, we get $3\cdot66$ and $10\cdot37$; and therefore $\sqrt{\frac{3\cdot66}{10\cdot37}} = \cdot597$. Consequently, I conclude that the axes of the original spots were about $60:100:100$. In the quarry at Bethesda, in the plane of cleavage we get $\sqrt{\frac{1\cdot26}{3\cdot01}} = \cdot645$, whereas at Penrhyn we have $\sqrt{\frac{1\cdot21}{1\cdot86}} = \cdot836$. These last two results agree with what would be expected from the manner in which the axes of the original spots were inclined to the cleavage. At all events, it seems reasonable in further calculations to adopt the conclusion that, before cleavage was developed, the axes of the spots were about $60:100:100$.

The next thing to consider is, what change was produced by the compression of the rocks. For the quarry at Bethesda, the mean ratios of all my observations are, in the plane of cleavage $1:2\cdot01$, and perpendicular to the cleavage $1:7\cdot10$; and for the quarry at Penrhyn, $1:1\cdot60$ and $1:6\cdot99$. The great discrepancy between the results in the plane of cleavage is mainly due to the fact, that at

Bethesda the spots had their axes distributed at nearly all angles to the cleavage, but at Penrhyn at angles varying from 17° to 41°, the means of all my measurements being 27°. Calculating from this, and correcting accordingly, we obtain as the corrected ratio $1 \cdot 60 \times \frac{865}{648} = 1 \cdot 86$. The mean for both quarries would thus be $1:1 \cdot 94$ and $1:7$, and the length of the shortest axis $\frac{1 \cdot 94}{7 \cdot 04} = \cdot 275$. The length of that in the line of strike being taken as unity, we obtain the following results:—

Before cleavage was developed ......... $\cdot 600 \times 1 \cdot 00 \times 1 = \cdot 60$

After cleavage had been developed ... $\cdot 275 \times 1 \cdot 94 \times 1 = \cdot 53$

Hence, the reduction in volume due to pressure was from 60 to 53, or about 11 per cent. The most satisfactory explanation of this is that, before compression, the rocks contained about 11 per cent. of cavities, which were almost completely squeezed up, since the slate now contains only about ·24 per cent. This 11 per cent. must be looked upon as only approximate, since it depends on four quantities all subject to error. I consider, however, the result very satisfactory in showing that, before cleavage was developed, the rock was, if anything, rather more consolidated than the fine-grained beds of the Coal-Measures, an inference which agrees admirably with the microscopical structure described in other parts of this paper.

These various data seem to lead to the following conclusions:—

(1) The material when deposited was not exactly a clay, since the axes of the spots were originally 60:100:100, instead of more nearly 52:100:100.

(2) The spots were formed early in the history of the rock, before the deoxidizing power of some nucleus was lost.

(3) The rock was fairly hard and consolidated.

(4) It was subjected to enormous pressure, and so changed in dimensions in different directions that cleavage was developed.

(5) The facts appear to establish conclusively the mechanical origin of cleavage.

## XVII. SLIP-SURFACES.

On carefully examining some varieties of much-contorted mica-schist, it is very easy to see that, in many cases, there has been an irregular giving-way of the rock in a plane perpendicular to the pressure, and one bent portion has slipped over another, so as to give rise to a surface of partial or complete discontinuity. A similar structure can be seen with the microscope in thin sections of some imperfectly-cleaved slates; and that these slip-surfaces are, as it were, microscopic faults, often from a hundredth to a thousandth of an inch apart, is proved by the upthrow or downthrow of very thin beds, or by broken flakes of mica, the movement being a hundredth of an inch or much less.

As seen under the microscope, these slip-surfaces in section look like very thin black lines, on the whole perpendicular to the line

of pressure, as shown by small contortions of the bedding; yet
they are seldom straight, being, as it were, drawn by a shaking
hand. They are sometimes parallel for a short distance, but
usually unite with or branch into each other. Although small
in size, these slips are sometimes so numerous that, if those in a
square inch of surface were united end to end, they would extend
to a length of fully 50 feet; and, if the surfaces of those in a cubic
inch were united, they would give an area of 5 or 6 square feet.
It need not be wondered, then, that they play so important a part
in the structure of the rock; and they prove most conclusively
that, when it was compressed by the force which developed the
cleavage, the rock did not give way as a truly-plastic substance,
but to a large extent yielded as though fairly hard. These slip-
surfaces are in fact analogous to the slip-planes in metals described
by Prof. J. A. Ewing & Mr. W. Rosenhain.[1]

The detailed study of these slips in different rocks is very
instructive. I have examined carefully all my numerous thin
sections of rocks allied to slates, and find that in those without
cleavage comparatively-long slips are absent, and even short ones
occur only when there is a very sudden change in the nature of
the rock, as, for example, from fine sand to clay. Highly-cleaved
thickly-bedded slates, like those of Penrhyn, show very few, if any
long slips. On close examination, however, of a section perpendicular to the cleavage in the line of dip, vast numbers of those a
hundredth of an inch in length or less can be seen; but they
are not so much developed in the line of strike.

I have an excellent section of a purple slate from Birnam (near
Dunkeld), containing a band composed of a mixture of a green and
a colourless mineral, bent into contortions which show that there
has been great compression in a line perpendicular to the cleavage.
The above-mentioned minerals must have been formed before the
cleavage, since they are broken up in the most remarkable manner,
and the structure of the fine-grained purple slate near the junction
is very instructive. At the round ends of the contortions, where
the green band has protected the purple slate from compression, its
structure is almost exactly like that of an uncleaved rock; whereas
alongside the contortions, where there must have been great
differential movement, the purple slate looks like a complete mass
of slip-surfaces, which are only $\frac{1}{2000}$ or $\frac{1}{3000}$ inch apart. In passing
away into the purple slate the longer slips rapidly decrease in
number, and there are only slips of a hundredth of an inch or so in
length between the constituent particles of the rock. It will thus
be seen that there is good evidence to prove that, when the rock
was greatly altered in dimensions by pressure, it was so hard that
the crystalline mineral was broken up, and the purple part yielded
by slip-surfaces. These conclusions are well borne out by similar

[1] Phil. Trans. Roy. Soc. ser. A, vol. cxciii (1900) p. 353.

facts. In a considerable number of different localities I have met with fine-grained, spotted slate-rocks; and, on careful examination with the microscope, it was easy to see that the spots are small imperfectly-developed crystals of chiastolite, somewhat broken up and compressed, with their long axes in the plane of cleavage. The relation between these and the surrounding rock clearly shows that, when slaty cleavage was developed, the rock was nearly as hard as chiastolite, yielding little more to compression.

As already shown, the best slates of Penrhyn prove that, in the line of dip, portions of rock which before cleavage were 100 : 100 are now on an average 100 : 705. The small flakes of mica, or a mineral of similar character, which constitute so large a portion of the rock, may be assumed not to have changed their dimensions, and thus the entire yielding of the rock must have been due to the giving-way of the surrounding finer particles. There must consequently have been a great relative movement; and, assuming as a fair average that the flakes of mica form one half of the rock, the surrounding material must have been elongated along the line of dip from 1 to 1 to 1 to 14, whereas the flakes were not elongated at all. It is thus easy to understand why there is so vast a number of minute slip-surfaces perpendicular to the pressure among the ultimate constituent grains in the line of dip, and why such surfaces are much less developed in the line of strike, where little elongation could occur. A number of these facts were overlooked in my early papers, and they show that the compression of the rock would alter its structure much more than I suspected. The change in the position of the flakes would be twice as great as I calculated. Instead of half of them being as before cleavage spread over 90°, they would after compression be spread over only 8°; and this, combined with the numerous small slip-surfaces, easily explains the fissility of the rock.

Slate near Penrhyn, which has been much changed in appearance by a trap-dyke, still shows well-marked traces of the previously-existing slip-surfaces, so that the rock cannot have been softened by heat. In the mica-schist between Aberdeen and Stonehaven, with cleavage-foliation and therefore metamorphosed after compression, all traces of slip-surfaces have been obliterated.

## XVIII. SURFACES OF PRESSURE-SOLUTION.

In my Bakerian lecture to the Royal Society [1] I showed that pressure increases the solubility of the greater number of soluble salts. Also in my paper on the impressed limestone-pebbles of the Nagelfluh [2] in Switzerland, I showed that the impressions could not have been produced by simple mechanical action, since it is

[1] Proc. Roy. Soc. vol, xii (1863) p. 538.
[2] Neues Jahrb. 1863, p. 801.

only the carbonate of lime that has been removed by solution, and the whole of the insoluble material of the stone has been left, as carefully determined by suitable means.

An equally striking example of pressure-solution was described in my address to the Geological Society,[1] in which I showed that in a Devonian limestone at Ilfracombe the joints of encrinites have been partly dissolved where the pressure which produced the cleavage was at a maximum, and the dissolved calcite has crystallized out where the pressure was at a minimum. Until quite recently I did not recognize fully how important a part this action plays in many other cases.

What I propose to call **surfaces of pressure-solution** are often numerous and small; but some years ago I obtained from the Carboniferous Limestone of Stoney Middleton (Derbyshire) specimens in which they are unusually large. The normal characters are layers of dark, apparently bituminous, material extending over a considerable area, passing up and down like larger and smaller interlocking teeth. Sometimes one of these layers branches into two, which may again unite, and they cannot have been due to stratification. The most probable origin of the bitumen is that it is a residue of the solution of the limestone; and that solution of carbonate of lime has occurred is clearly proved, by the manner in which the layers pass into the shells of brachiopoda and into encrinites. This is shown by the accompanying text-figure. In the centre, not shaded, is a portion of a shell with well-preserved structure, and, as will be seen, the zigzag bituminous layer (shown black) passes quite through the centre, and partly on each side into two depressions filled with the limestone (shown shaded throughout). The laminar structure of the shell seems to have slightly influenced the direction of solution.

*Tooth-like structure penetrating, by removal, a fossil shell and the surrounding limestone, most probably by pressure-solution. (Magnified 4 diameters.)*

Taking all the facts into consideration, it seems as though both pressure and solution have acted, and in some cases their combination will explain the facts. However, when we come to examine the detail of

[1] Quart. Journ. Geol. Soc. vol. xxxv (1879) Proc. p. 89.

the Stoney-Middleton specimens, of which I have ten excellent microscopical sections of unusual size, it seems almost impossible to explain why the pressure should have been at a maximum along so complex and tooth-like a surface; and sometimes I feel tempted to conclude that a cause may have acted, about which we know little or nothing. The quantity of carbonate of lime dissolved and transferred to where the pressure was less must have been considerable, as shown in the figure by the amount of shell removed.

It is chiefly in those Devonian limestones in which slaty cleavage has been developed that surfaces of pressure-solution on a small scale are common, and play an important part in modifying the structure, since they have often conspired in altering the form of joints of encrinites and other organisms. In a few cases, however, notably in a specimen from Kingskerswell, the rock has been greatly changed as a whole, and joints of encrinites altered from about 1 : 1 to 1 : 4. There is also another interesting fact which for a long time puzzled me—that is, the alteration in crystalline calcite in which pressure has sometimes given rise to curved cleavage, or broken up the crystal into thin layers of twinning, similar to what can be produced by a knife, as shown by H. Baumhauer.[1]

## Oolites with Pressure-Solution.

The most remarkable specimen in my possession is one from the Carboniferous Limestone on the south side of the gorge at Clifton. As will be seen from Pl. XVIII, fig. 2, instead of the grains being well separated or merely touching one another, as in Grantham Oolite, they (as it were) interpenetrate to a considerable extent by surfaces of pressure-solution, and yet their structure is not materially disturbed. This interpenetration could not have occurred, if the interspaces had been filled by infiltrated calcite before the rock was subjected to great pressure. This seems to have acted in a line perpendicular to the stratification, for there is little or no interpenetration in the plane of bedding. In the part figured the interspaces amount to only 11 per cent., which is a great reduction from 26 per cent., and closely corresponds with the change of dimensions calculated from the shape of the oolitic grains, which is from 100 to 83. The production of this exceptional specimen may be explained by supposing that the interspaces remained unfilled until after the rock had been exposed to great pressure, and that the cavities were then filled by material possibly transferred by pressure-solution from the altered oolitic grains.

[1] Zeitschrift für Krystallographie, vol. iii (1879) p. 588.

In some places east of Sheffield similar surfaces of interlocking teeth, separated by a thin layer of earthy residue, are met with in the Magnesian Limestone, which well deserve further study, and might show that it is necessary in the case of dolomites to take into account other circumstances besides pressure and simple solution.

### XIX. DETERMINATION OF THE PRESSURE TO WHICH ROCKS HAVE BEEN SUBJECTED.

That the pressure brought to bear when mountains were elevated and slaty cleavage developed was very great will readily be admitted, since it causes fairly-hard rocks to yield as if more or less plastic. It appeared to me, however, unsatisfactory to remain content with merely calling it a great pressure, and not to attempt to form some estimate of its value in tons to the square inch, or the weight of so many feet of superincumbent rocks. I therefore attacked this problem, both by experiment and by the discussion of my observations made with different rocks.

My first experiments were made in strong brass tubes, ·6 inch in internal diameter, into which a solid brass rod fitted. Finely-powdered dry pipe-clay was used, since the presence of water would have greatly increased the difficulties. The tube was filled with this clay and it was compressed by hand with the brass rod, and so much added as to make the length of the column of clay 2 inches. Then gradually increasing pressure was applied, and the reduction of volume determined by measurement. The weight of water filling the tube up to 2 inches and that of the clay were known, and also the specific gravity of the solid material of the clay, from which it was easy to calculate the percentage of empty spaces, when variously compressed. Taking the solid volume of the clay as 100, that of the interspaces was, when pressed by hand, 76·7; when the brass rod was driven in by moderate blows of a 1 lb. hammer, it was 34 per cent.; and with hard blows, 21·4 per cent. This method, however, did not enable me to estimate properly the pressure. This was attempted by forcing in the rod by a screw, with a pressure estimated at not much short of 10 tons, or about 30 tons to the square inch, which is equal to the pressure of about 75,000 feet of superincumbent rock. In this case the amount of interspaces was 29·2 per cent. It is, however, probable that it would have been a good deal less, if the pressure had been continued for a long time. These experiments, therefore, merely show that, in some way or other, the interspaces vary inversely as the pressure.

The Table (VIII) on the following page is a list in descending order of all my determinations of the interspaces in clays, shales, and slates, adopting what seem to be the most probable results. The amounts are percentages of volume.

TABLE VIII.

| | | | | | |
|---|---|---|---|---|---|
| Clay from an old lake at Sewerby ... | 49·5 | | Gault, Aylesford ........................ | 28·1 | }24·0 |
| After Boulder-Clay, Bridlington ... | 33·9 }32·0 | | „ Folkestone ............... | 25·0 | |
| Alluvial clay, Orgreave .............. | 30·2 } | | „ „ bottom ......... | 18·9 | |
| New Red Marl, Leamington ........ | 34·4 }32·3 | | Speeton Clay, weathered .............. | 18·4 | }13·6 |
| „ „ „ „ ........ | 30·0 } | | „ „ unweathered ......... | 8·8 | |
| „ „ „ from a deep boring . | 10·0 | | Coal-Meas. nr. Nottingham, 510 ft. . | 13·4 | |
| „ „ „ „ „ „ . | 9·0 }7·5 | | „ „ 829 ft. . | 14·6 | }12·9 |
| „ „ „ „ „ „ . | 6·2 { | | „ „ 1190 ft. . | 10·7 | |
| „ „ „ „ „ „ . | 4·8 } | | „ Brightside ................ | 14·3 | }12·5 |
| Tertiary Clay, Watch Point ......... | 29·8 | | „ Darnall ..................... | 12·8 | |
| „ „ Whitecliff ............. | 28·4 }28·8 | | Wenlock Shale, Malvern, weathered. | 14·1 | }10·0 |
| „ „ Barton Cliff ......... | 28·3 } | | „ „ unweathered. | 5·8 | |
| Boulder-Clay, Bridlington ............ | 25·5 | | Slate, Mawnan (Cornwall) ........... | 5·9 | |
| „ „ „ ......... | 25·5 }24·8 | | Slates, etc., Moffat, black ............. | 5·2 } | |
| „ „ „ ......... | 23·4 } | | „ „ .............. | 3·8 } | |
| „ „ Balby (nr. Doncaster). | 24·1 }24·0 | | „ „ red ........... | 3·4 }3·6 | |
| „ „ „ . | 23·9 } | | „ „ green ......... | 2·1 } | |
| Kimmeridge Clay, Oxford ............ | 30·7 }24·8 | | Slate, Hele, Ilfracombe ............... | 3·5 }2·4 | |
| „ „ Filey ............... | 19·0 } | | „ „ .............. | 1·3 } | |
| Liassic clay, Bath ..................... | 27·7 | | Westmorland slate, black ........... | 0·55 } | |
| „ „ „ ..................... | 23·0 }24·4 | | „ „ Coniston ...... | 0·52 }0·49 | |
| „ „ Robin Hood's Bay ... | 22·5 } | | „ „ Langdale ...... | 0·40 } | |
| | | | Purple slate, Penrhyn ................. | 0·24 | |

A few remarks on these results may be apposite. The amount of invisible cavities in the apparently-solid deposit from an old lake at Sewerby is so unusual, that I thought I had made a mistake— until I found that a second experiment gave exactly the same result. The probable explanation is that the material is of abnormal character, and not comparable with clay. The percentage of cavities in the New Red Marl in some cases seems so abnormally great as to indicate the removal by weathering of some constituent, which is easily understood when we find that specimens from a considerable depth in a deep boring, given to me by Mr. J. A. Howe, contain so little of interspaces and also crystals of intercrystallized calcite, giving fractures of uniform reflection. The amount of cavities in a number of specimens of Boulder-Clay is so remarkably uniform, as to make me think that this deposit deserves further study. It is so much less than would agree with the small pressure of the material now lying over them, as to make me think that the clay has been somewhat compressed by the lateral pressure which forced it along, or by superincumbent ice, or by some other special cause not fully understood. The great variation in the Gault and Kimmeridge Clay is probably due to carbonate of lime. The much smaller amount in the Speeton Clay than in the Gault, as in the Yorkshire Chalk compared with that from many other localities, is certainly due to this cause. The Liassic clays were fairly satisfactory. Taking everything into consideration, the Coal-Measure shales give good results. The specimens of Wenlock Shale at my disposal were unsatisfactory, since one contains too much carbonate of lime, and the other is too much weathered. The variations in the slaty rocks of Mawnan, Moffat, and Hele are in some cases most certainly due to varying pressure connected with slaty cleavage. What is wanted is the careful study of more and better specimens, unaltered by infiltration, chemical action, or surface-weathering, collected so as to be specially suitable for this subject.

It will thus be seen that, in some cases, the results for different specimens agree sufficiently well, and therefore the mean may be relied upon as approximately correct. In other cases, there are great differences, sometimes certainly due to the presence of too much carbonate of lime, and sometimes to the specimens being too much swollen and weathered. Collecting together those cases which seem most trustworthy for calculation, we may compile the following list :—

TABLE IX.

| | | | |
|---|---|---|---|
| Alluvial clay, etc. | 32·0 | Coal-Measure shales | 13·2 |
| Tertiary clay | 28·8 | Slate-rocks, Moffat | 3·6 |
| Boulder-Clay | 24·4 | Slate-rocks, Hele | 2·4 |
| Liassic clay | 24·4 | Slates, Westmorland | 0·49 |
| Gault | 24·0 | Slate, Penrhyn | 0·24 |

It will thus be seen that there is a fairly-uniform decrease in the amount of cavities, in passing from clays which have been subjected to very little pressure, down to the oldest rocks; and a most marked decrease in those with well-developed slaty cleavage. The question then arises whether the compression is due to age or to pressure. Although quite prepared to believe that mere age may have some effect, when combined with pressure, yet taking all into consideration, and bearing in mind my experiments with clay, it seems to me more probable that the chief cause of the compression was the pressure of superincumbent rock, or of that which developed slaty cleavage.

Though it seems almost certain that the amount of interspaces varies in some way inversely as the pressure, their exact relation is unknown. Possibly it could be learned by experiments with a testing-machine, by means of which suitable pressures could be applied continuously for a long time. It seems, however, undesirable to delay the publication of this paper, and better to make use of the data now known. It is clear that the law must be of such a kind that the effect of a given increase in pressure is much greater on material which has been slightly compressed and contains a large amount of cavities, than on highly-compressed rocks. It is, of course, not the compression of the cavities, but the deformation of the solid particles involved in filling them up which is of prime importance; and this must be relatively greater and greater as their amount becomes smaller and smaller. This must have been brought about by the slow giving-way of minute grains during long geological periods, and not by the sudden fracture of large objects, as taken into account in studying the strength of materials for engineering purposes.

The percentage of cavities in fine-grained clays of great antiquity but never exposed to the pressure of more than a few feet of superincumbent material, is about 33 per cent.; and, after careful consideration, it seemed to me probable that the formula connecting cavities and pressure may be of the form:

$$\text{constant quantity} \times \frac{32 - \text{cav.}}{32 \times \text{cav.}}$$

In order to make the best use of the material at my disposal, I adopted the following plan to learn the value of the constant. The amount of cavities in clays of great antiquity, which have never been exposed to a pressure of more than a few feet of super-incumbent material, is about 32 per cent.; and I endeavoured to ascertain from known geological data the thickness of super-incumbent strata corresponding to a medium amount of cavities. The best cases at my disposal were from the Coal-Measures near Sheffield, and the calculated cavities in the Penrhyn slate before cleavage was developed. The former gave $13\frac{1}{2}$ per cent. of cavities for a medium thickness of 2500 feet, and the latter 11 per cent. for a thickness of about 3400 feet of rock, as now compressed, of specific gravity estimated at 2·85, which equals 3976 feet of rock of specific gravity $= 2\cdot50$. Combining these together, I obtained for $13\frac{1}{2}$ per cent. of cavities a pressure of 2700 feet of rock, instead of 2500, which would agree with the supposition that 200 feet of the uppermost part of the Coal-Measures has been lost by denudation. As a first attempt, I therefore worked on the supposition that for no pressure the cavities are 32 per cent., and for 2700 feet $13\frac{1}{2}$ per cent.

On the whole, it seems to me probable that the necessary force may vary as the ratio between the amount of solid material and that of the cavities, commencing at 32 per cent.; something like the strength of a beam of the same thickness with a long or a short span. From this it would follow that, when the cavities approach 32 per cent., a small pressure would produce considerable effect; whereas, when the percentage is small, a great increase in pressure would be necessary to produce much influence. On this supposition, the law connecting cavities and pressure would have the form

$$2700 \text{ feet} \times \frac{\dfrac{100 - \text{cav.}}{\text{cav.}} - \dfrac{100 - 32}{32}}{\dfrac{100 - 13\cdot5}{13\cdot5} - \dfrac{100 - 32}{32}}$$

So far as I can see, this agrees with all the facts of the case, and yet it must be looked upon as only a plausible approximation. Although this and the previous formula differ much, yet, strange to say, they yield so nearly the same results as to make me think that they may not be far wrong.

The Table (X) on the following page was calculated from the formula just given, and shows not only the ratio between the volume of the solid material and the cavities, but also the pressure in feet of rock of specific gravity 2·5, and that in tons per square inch.

TABLE X.

|  | $\dfrac{100-c}{c}$ | Feet of rock. | Tons per square inch. |
|---|---|---|---|
| Little pressure ...................... | 2·123 | 0 | 0 |
| Tertiary clays ...................... | 2·472 | 220 | 0·102 |
| Boulder-Clay ........................ | 3·032 | 573 | 0·265 |
| Liassic clays ........................ | 3·160 | 616 | 0·285 |
| Gault ................................ | 3·167 | 658 | 0·304 |
| Coal-Measure shales .............. | 6·407 | 2·700 | 1·250 |
| Penrhyn slate before cleavage ... | 8·091 | 3·807 | 1·764 |
| Slate, Mawnan ...................... | 15·949 | 8·715 | 4·040 |
| Moffat rocks ........................ | 26·777 | 15·550 | 7·200 |
| Hele, Ilfracombe .................. | 40·666 | 24·310 | 11·250 |
| Slates, Westmorland............... | 203·080 | 126·800 | 58·700 |
| Slate, Penrhyn ...................... | 416·700 | 261·500 | 121·000 |

Compared with clays, shales, and slates, limestones and sand-stones are unsatisfactory for the determination of pressure, since those of different ages vary so much in important particulars. Still, the mean results of a considerable number of specimens are never-theless of some interest. Thus the average amount of interspaces in fifty samples of Oolitic limestones is 32·2 per cent. of the solid material. In the Magnesian Limestone it is 19·2, and in the Carboniferous Limestone it is 11 per cent., whereas in the Carrara marble it is only 0·7 per cent. These numbers agree fairly well with the conclusions deduced from the clays.

In the case of sandstones my results are, for the cavities in the New Red Sandstone 66 per cent. of the solid material; for the sandstones of the lower part of the Coal-Measures and the Millstone Grit 25 per cent.; and for the Old Red Sandstone of Herefordshire 45 per cent. These results agree in a rough way with the others, but the differences in the depth of the water and in the mineral constitution make them valueless for calculating pressure.

---

In conclusion, I may say that a number of my numerical values must be looked upon as only approximate, though probably of the true order of magnitude. More accurate results would often require complicated experiments on a large scale, which could be carried out only in a specially-organized laboratory, or in a small clear river with artificial arrangements to control the current.

### EXPLANATION OF PLATES XIV-XVIII.

[Plates XIV-XVI are slightly-reduced photographic reproductions from the slates, and the other plates are reproduced from my own drawings.]

### PLATE XIV.

This shows the breaking-up of a fine-grained deposit soon after deposition, while still in a semi-liquid condition. (Green slate, Langdale.) See p. 197.

### PLATE XV.

This shows ripples with not much drifting forward, rapid deposition, and slight breaking-up of the fine-grained material, while still somewhat soft. (Green slate, Langdale.)  See p. 197.

### PLATE XVI.

In this is a thin layer of ripple-drift, over which is a fine-grained deposit, very little broken up by the current bringing the coarser material, as if partly consolidated.  (Green slate, Langdale.)  See p. 198.

### PLATE XVII.

Fig. 1. Oolite from Grantham, showing an amount of empty spaces nearly equal to the theoretical minimum. (Magnified 50 diameters.) See pp. 206-207.
   2. Coralline Oolite from Scarborough, in which the interspaces, some filled with calcite, are nearly of the same volume as when recently deposited with little shaking. (Magnified 50 diameters.) See p. 209.

### PLATE XVIII.

Fig. 1. Wenlock Limestone from Easthope, showing angular fragments much squeezed together. (Magnified 25 diameters.) See p. 209.
   2. Carboniferous Limestone from Bristol : an unusual example of oolitic grains considerably influenced by pressure-solution. (Magnified 50 diameters.) See p. 226.

## DISCUSSION.

The PRESIDENT observed that any paper coming from their veteran comrade, Dr. Sorby, could not fail to be full of suggestion and to be marked by that wealth of experimental detail and sagacious calculation for which all his scientific writings had been distinguished.  The present communication was the result of many years of experiment and reflection, although the Author was now confined to his room and unable longer to continue the prosecution of active research.  It was probably safe to say that, although only his own brief summary of results had been read to the meeting, the paper when published would be found to mark a new starting-point for the investigation of the origin, history, and chronology of rocks.  An interesting point of connexion could be noticed between the two papers communicated to the Society that evening. Dr. Wright, while lessening the length of the unit in the geological time-scale, still dealt with a period of several thousand years.  It would be remembered that Baron Gerard de Geer, as the President had recently announced, had discovered, among the marine deposits that followed the retreat of the ice-sheet in Sweden, a remarkable repetition of distinct layers which he interpreted as indicating the succession of seasons in a series of years.  And he was believed to have lately detected among the deposits of the inland Glacial lakes a similar series of apparently-seasonal deposits.  But Dr. Sorby, in the paper of which they had heard an abstract, thought himself in a position to speak confidently of the number of minutes which

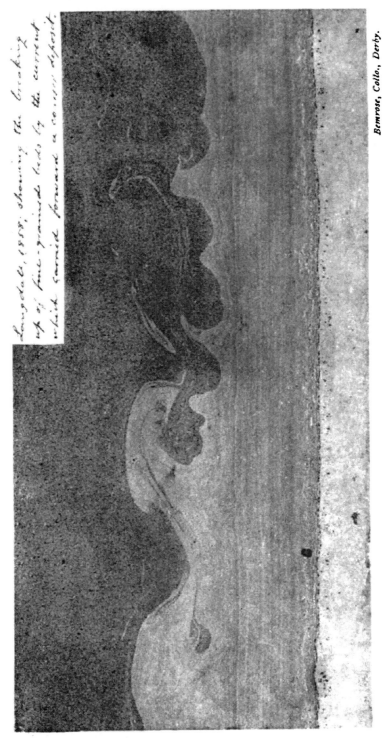

Bemrose, Collo., Derby.

GREEN SLATE, LANGDALE, SHEWING THE BREAKING-UP OF A SEMI-LIQUID DEPOSIT.

Bemrose, Collo., Derby.

GREEN SLATE, LANGDALE, SHEWING RIPPLE-DRIFT WITH GENTLE CURRENT AND RAPID DEPOSITION.

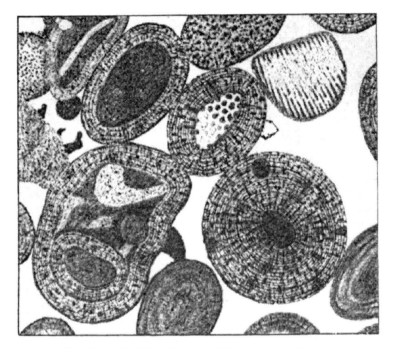

FIG. 1.—OOLITE, GRANTHAM, × 50 DIAMS.

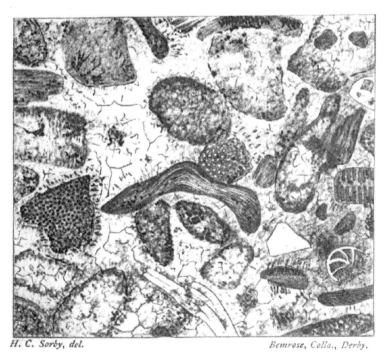

H. C. Sorby, del.                                        Bemrose, Collo., Derby.

FIG. 2.—CORALLINE OOLITE, SCARBOROUGH, × 50 DIAMS.

WENLOCK LIMESTONE, EASTHOPE, × 25 DIAMS.

*H. C. Sorby, del.*                *Bemrose, Collo., Derby.*

CARBONIFEROUS LIMESTONE, BRISTOL, × 50 DIAMS.

certain layers of sediment had taken for their deposition. The geological world would await with impatience the publication of his full paper, and the Society would meanwhile return to him its hearty thanks for having honoured it by communicating so important a memoir, and would express the earnest wish that he might still live to complete the preparation of other papers embodying the result of his long years of quiet work in experimental geological dynamics.

Prof. JUDD, while pointing out that it was impossible to discuss (and much less to criticize) the paper from the abstract, directed attention to its highly-suggestive character. Like all the work of the Author, its value consisted not only in the conclusions arrived at by him, but still more in the indication of new methods of observation, and novel lines of reasoning, which could not fail to have an important influence on the future development of geological science. He was sure that all present united in sympathy with the Author in his enforced absence from them; in admiration for the energy with which, despite all difficulties, he continued his researches; and in the hope that they would receive still further contributions to science from his hand.

Mr. E. A. MARTIN wished to call especial attention to the allowance made by the Author for contraction in some of the older rocks. Estimates had been made of the Earth's age, according to the number of feet of total thickness of existing strata; but no allowance had in such estimates been made, as a rule, for compression. An attempt in this direction was made in the 'Geological Magazine' for August 1907, but few would have anticipated that the older rocks must be allowed to have contracted to 20 per cent. of their original thickness, or even in the case of the Chalk to 45 per cent. The publication of the paper would be awaited with very great interest.

11. GLACIAL BEDS *of* CAMBRIAN AGE *in* SOUTH AUSTRALIA.   By
the Rev. WALTER HOWCHIN, F.G.S., Lecturer in Geology
and Palæontology in the University of Adelaide.   (Read
November 20th, 1907.)

[PLATES XIX–XXVI.]

CONTENTS.

|                                                      | Page |
| I. Introduction ...................................... | 234 |
| II. Geographical Extent ........................... | 234 |
| III. Geological Age of the Beds .................. | 236 |
| IV. Description of the Beds ...................... | 239 |
    (*a*) General Features.
    (*b*) The Erratics.
    (*c*) Glaciation.
    (*d*) Effects of Mechanical Strain.
| V. Illustrative Sections............................ | 248 |
    (*a*) Onkaparinga-River Section.
    (*b*) The Sturt-Valley Section.
    (*c*) Appila-Gorge Section.
    (*d*) Northern Areas: Sections.
| VI. General Considerations ...................... | 255 |
    (*a*) The Ice-Agent.
    (*b*) ? Interglacial Periods.


I. INTRODUCTION.

IN April 1901, the present writer read a 'Preliminary Note on the
Existence of Glacial Beds of Cambrian Age in South Australia,'
before the Royal Society of South Australia.[1]   Subsequent investigations have demonstrated the great extent of these beds, both
in thickness and in geographical prevalence, and have materially
strengthened the evidences of their glacial origin.   Publication of
these results was delayed until the stratigraphical relationships of
the beds in question had become better known.   Researches into
the geology of the Mount-Lofty and the Flinders Ranges were
undertaken for this purpose, with the result that the subject can
now be discussed upon definite data.[2]


II. GEOGRAPHICAL EXTENT.

The beds under review have their southernmost outcrop on
the Onkaparinga River, 20 miles south of Adelaide.   South of this

[1] Trans. Roy. Soc. S. Austral. vol. xxv, p. 10.
[2] Bibliographical references and other matters cognate to the subject will be
found in the following papers:—'The Geology of the Mount-Lofty Ranges,
Part I' Trans. Roy. Soc. S. Austral. vol. xxviii (1904) p. 253; and *ibid.*
Part II, vol. xxx (1906) p. 227.

position they become obscured by the Tertiary sandstones of McLaren Vale, and by a fault of some magnitude in which the higher beds of the Cambrian series are brought into juxtaposition with the lower beds at a divergent strike.

North of the Onkaparinga, the glacial beds are occasionally seen as inliers of the Tertiary sandstones and clays, until the River Sturt is reached, 7 miles south of Adelaide. Here the beds cross the stream obliquely, about 1 mile from the main South Road, and occupy both sides of the valley for a distance of nearly 2 miles up stream. The glacial beds in this locality are determined on their northern side by a dip-fault, which cuts them off.

From this point, northwards, the deep alluvial deposits of the Adelaide Plains obscure the older series of rocks, along the strike, for a distance of 50 miles. The glacial beds, with the associated members of the Cambrian series, reappear on the west side of Kapunda, and thence they occur (with slight interruptions from faulting) in parallel belts as far as the northern extremities of the Flinders Ranges.

Many of the more prominent heights and ranges of hills owe their elevation to the resistance which the glacial beds and the underlying quartzites offer to the agents of waste, as compared with the associated slates. Razorback and Mount Bryan, north of the Burra, each about 3000 feet high, consist mainly of glacial till. These beds also form the highest portions of the Petersburg Ranges, as well as Stuart's Lookout, the Depôt, Pekina Hill, Mount Remarkable, the Oladdie Hills, and other considerable elevations of the 'lower north' districts.

In the course of several visits to the Flinders Ranges the glacial outcrops were followed, along their strike, for 60 miles, through the country lying north-east of Leigh's Creek, and to the west and north-west of Lake Frome as far as the Daly and Stanley Mines. Mr. H. P. Woodward, in 1884 (when Assistant Government Geologist), traced them still farther in the same direction, to Billy Springs and Hamilton Creek, in the neighbourhood of Mount Babbage (nearly at the north-eastern extremity of the Flinders Ranges); and in these localities the included erratics were found to be of great size.

The till-beds, carrying glaciated erratics, occur also in the Willouran Ranges, on the west side of Hergott, 440 miles north of Adelaide, in 29° 50' lat. S. This is the northernmost point at which the beds have been found *in situ*, but erratics, similar to those which occur in the till-beds, are found scattered over the plains, or forming part of rearranged material, in the Lake-Eyre district, which may have been derived from the waste of the glacial beds along the margin of the basin.

The known extension of the beds, in a north-and-south direction, from the Onkaparinga River to the Willouran Ranges, equals 460 miles. The greatest width is found along a line ranging fr m Port Augusta, at the head of Spencer's Gulf (where the beds crop out in Mundallio Creek, on the western side of the Flinders Ranges);

Fig. 1.—*Diagrammatic section of the Lower Cambrian beds, from the River Torrens to Gulf St. Vincent.*
(Distance = about 15 miles.)

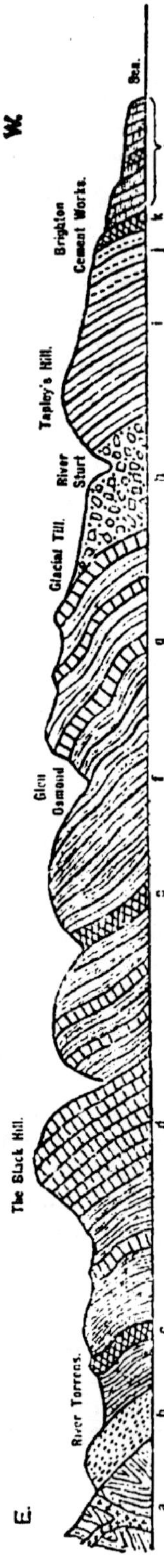

*a* = Pre-Cambrian.
*b* = Basal grits and conglomerates.
*c* = Lower (or River-Torrens) Limestone.

*d* = Thick quartzite.
*e* = 'Blue-Metal' Limestone.
*f* = Thick (or Glen-Osmond) Slate.

*g* = Glen-Osmond and Mitcham Quartzite.
*h* = Glacial Beds.
*i* = Tapley's-Hill Slates.

*j* = Impure siliceous limestones.
*k* = Brighton Limestone.
*l* = Purple slates, quartzites, etc.

and thence they are repeated in successive folds, in an easterly direction, to the Barrier Ranges of New South Wales, in which last-named locality Mr. D. Mawson, B.Sc., has recently noted their occurrence. This makes a width across the main line of strike of 250 miles.

### III. GEOLOGICAL AGE OF THE BEDS.

The discovery in 1879[1] of *Archæocyathinæ* and other organisms in the Palæozoic rocks of Yorke Peninsula, and, at later dates, of a similar fauna in the Flinders Ranges, and also at Sellick's Hill, in the southern portion of the Mount-Lofty Ranges, supplied important data for the determination of the geological age of a vast series of beds which form the central highlands of South Australia. While the occurrence of Cambrian fossils defined the geological horizons locally, it remained for many years a doubtful question as to how far the rocks of the Mount-Lofty and associated ranges, as a whole, could be referred to the same age. The prevailing impression for some time was that the Mount-Lofty Ranges, with their highly-metamorphosed rocks, were older than the Cambrian.

Recent investigations have demonstrated that the highlands extending from Cape Jervis in the south, to Lake Eyre and Lake Frome in the north, are included, for the main part, in one great geological series, the individual members of which are conformable to each other. The beds which carry characteristic Cambrian organic remains occur near the upper limits of the series.

[1] Otto Tepper, Trans. & Proc. Phil. Soc. Adelaide, 1878–79, p. 71; R. Etheridge, Jun., Trans. Roy. Soc. S. Austral. vol. xiii (1889–90) p. 10; R. Tate, *ibid.* vol. xv (1891–92) p. 183.

The order of succession in the beds is perfectly clear (see fig. 1, p. 236). In the Sturt River, near Adelaide, the glacial beds are seen to underlie the Tapley's-Hill Slates. The latter pass up into calcareous slates, which, near Brighton, become a very pure limestone, oolitic in structure, bluish in its lower portions and reddish in the upper. A buff-coloured, dolomitic limestone rests upon the latter, and is overlain by purple slates, thin quartzites, and limestones of the same colour, which form a coastal belt of rocks, half a mile wide. Passing under the sea, they reappear under similar lithological features (including *Archæocyathina*-Limestones), on the opposite side of Gulf St. Vincent.

The importance of the purple-slate division is not apparent from the section visible near Adelaide, as for the most part it is covered by the waters of the Gulf over a width of nearly 40 miles. In the Flinders Ranges these chocolate-coloured rocks have a great development, and comprise the whole of the mountain-ranges in a 50-mile section, occurring between Parachilna (on the Northern Railway-line) and the western side of Lake Frome. Between Parachilna Gorge and Wirrialpa (40 miles), the beds form a vast dome, Blinman occupying the centre of the curve, and the *Archæocyathina*-Limestones crop out at both extremities, exhibiting reversed dips.

While no distinct unconformity can be recognized in this series, a convenient division is established by regarding the Brighton Limestones as a dividing-line between the lower and the upper beds. Such a division is supported by geographical as well as by lithological considerations: the Mount-Lofty Ranges being typical of the former, and the Flinders Ranges of the latter; while a purple or chocolate coloration is characteristic of the beds above this line of division, but is not present in the beds below that line.

Although this very thick series includes numerous limestones, of greater or less development, it is only at two horizons that fossils have been definitely determined. The more important of the two is distinguished by *Archæocyathina*-marbles, which must have formed coral-reefs in the Cambrian seas fully 200 feet thick. The corals are thickly crowded together and beautifully preserved. In some localities they occur as chalcedonic pseudomorphs, which weather into relief. Mr. T. G. Taylor, B.Sc., of Sydney, is engaged on the elucidation of these forms for description.

The fauna of the *Archæocyathina*-marbles (as hitherto described[1]) comprises the following forms :—

| | |
|---|---|
| *Archæocyathinæ* (in great variety) of which the rock is mostly composed. | *Hyolithes communis*, Billings. |
| | *Hyolithes conularioides*, Tate. |
| *Stenotheca rugosa*, Hall. | *Dolichometopus Tatei*, H. Woodward. |
| *Ophileta subangulata*, Tate. | *Ptychoparia australis*, H. Woodward. |
| *Platyceras Etheridgei*, Tate. | *Ptychoparia Howchini*, Eth. fil. |
| *Ambonychia macroptera*, Tate. | *Olenellus (?) Pritchardi*, Tate. |
| *Orthisina compta*, Tate. | *Microdiscus subsagittatus*, Tate. |
| *Orthis (?) peculiaris*, Tate. | *Leperditia* sp. |
| *Salterella planoconvexa*, Tate. | *Hyalostelia*. |

---

[1] *Op. jam cit.* & 'A Further Cambrian Trilobite from Yorke Peninsula' R. Etheridge, Jun., Trans. Roy. Soc. S. Austral. vol. xxii (1897–98) p. 1.

The second fossiliferous horizon of the series occurs, from a rough estimate, at about 1000 feet above the *Archæocyathina*-Beds, in a pink or grey oolitic limestone in the Wirrialpa district. The fossils are mainly confined to a band a few inches thick; but, within these limits, the rock is in places almost entirely composed of the massed and broken shells of *Obolella* and other organisms, chiefly the former. Mr. Robert Etheridge, jun., of the Australian Museum, Sydney, has made the following determinations from this bed[1]:—

| | |
|---|---|
| *Olenellus* sp. | *Orthis (?) Tatei*, Eth. fil. |
| *Obolella wirrialpensis*, Eth. fil. | *Orthis (or Orthisina)* sp. |
| *Obolella wirrialpensis*, var. *calceoloides*, Eth. fil. | *Hyolithes communis*, Billings. |

That these limestones, with their typical Cambrian fossils, are superior in position to the glacial beds can be verified by numerous cross-sections. Near Adelaide an uninterrupted succession of outcrops (with a consistent westward dip), may be passed over in a distance of 3 miles, showing an ascending series from the glacial beds of the Sturt Valley to the purple slates and limestones of the coast near Brighton.

The purple slates increase in breadth as they pass southwards from this locality, and their continuity is broken by the fault-escarpment of the Willunga range of hills. These hills, on their coastal side, also consist of the purple-slate series; but the fault has brought the higher beds, including the *Archæocyathina*-Limestones, into close relationship with the lower slates and limestones. Similar instances, where the superior position of the purple slates to the glacial beds can be seen, occur between Mount Remarkable and the coast, and also in sections across the north-eastern portions of the Flinders Ranges.

Further evidence bearing on the geological age of the glacial deposits is obtained by an examination of the beds which occur below the glacial horizon (see fig. 1, p. 236). In this lower section of the series the lithological features are in strong contrast with those exhibited by the upper beds. There is an entire absence of the purple slates and fossiliferous limestones, the beds consisting chiefly of thick felspathic quartzites, clay-slates, and phyllites, which can be followed in a descending order of succession to the basal grits and conglomerates resting on a pre-Cambrian complex.[2]

The beds of glacial origin are separated from the base of the Cambrian series, by a less thickness of rock than that which intervenes between them and the limestones containing the Cambrian fauna near the upper limits of the Cambrian series.

[1] Trans. Roy. Soc. S. Austral. vol. xxix (1905) p. 246.
[2] For particulars of the lower members of the Cambrian series, see 'The Geology of the Mount-Lofty Ranges, Part II' Trans. Roy. Soc. S. Austral. vol. xxx (1906) p. 227.

## IV. DESCRIPTION OF THE BEDS.

### (a) General Features.

The beds which give evidence of glacial origin may be described as consisting mainly of a groundmass of unstratified, indurated mudstone, more or less gritty, and carrying angular, subangular, and rounded boulders (up to 11 feet in diameter), which are distributed confusedly through the mass. It is, in every respect, a characteristic till. The included stones sometimes occur in pockets or groups, but the rock never becomes a typical conglomerate. Coarse angular grits and quartzites often occur in the form of irregular deposits, mixed with the finer groundmass, and these may or may not carry boulders. In places the beds become highly siliceous and very close in the grain, probably owing to the introduction of silica-charged waters, which have given rise to much quartz-veining at some points. In a similar manner, in the neighbourhood of impure calcareous zones, calcite or quartz-calcite veins may occur. Where the till is in its normal condition, it generally exhibits numerous small cavities, from which the more perishable included rock-fragments have disappeared, leaving behind them external casts in the matrix.

In most sections there are more or less regularly-stratified beds or bands, which occur at various horizons in the till. These may be of quartzite, finely-laminated slate, or limestone. The last-named seldom exceed 2 or 3 feet in thickness, are often gritty, and contain angular stones. The slates, in their fine lamination, bear some resemblance to the overlying Tapley's-Hill Beds; but, while the latter usually maintain an exact parallelism of deposit, even to the minutest lines, the slates of the till exhibit transverse bedding to a remarkable extent. It is only by the presence of these regularly-bedded intercalated deposits, that the dip of the thick unstratified till can be judged.

The thickness of the glacial series has been proved up to 1500 feet. The interbedded members may divide the till proper into two or more divisions, yet in all cases the latter shows a preponderating thickness in the sections. The more remote northern outcrops have not been studied so fully as those in the south; but observations, so far as they have gone, seem to indicate that in the far north the boulder-clay has been interrupted by regularly-bedded deposits to a greater extent than is characteristic of the beds in the southern parts of the country.

When the till is of an earthy, or non-siliceous, nature, it frets away rapidly by weathering, and sometimes forms cavernous shelters in the faces of cliffs. Under such circumstances, with a friable and freshly-exfoliated surface, its resemblance to the Pleistocene Boulder-Clay of Europe is very striking.

## (b) The Erratics.

The occurrence of isolated and irregularly-distributed boulders is a constant feature in the exposures of the gritty mudstone, or till; but these stones vary in size, relative numbers, and to some extent in their petrological types, in different localities. A close-grained and very siliceous quartzite usually supplies the commonest variety. These quartzite-boulders are clearly distinguishable, even macroscopically, from the bedded quartzites which are sometimes present in the till, and also from the quartzites which occupy an inferior position to the glacial beds in the Cambrian series.[1]

A rough attempt has been made, in several localities, to estimate the relative numbers of the various kinds of stones occurring as erratics. The following are given as examples of this attempt at grouping, and in each case the various classes of stones are mentioned in the order of their frequency of occurrence.

(1) Petersburg Ranges, 160 miles north of Adelaide. —Quartzite, gneiss, dark porphyry, coarse-grained granite, schorlaceous quartz, pink porphyry, rocks from basic dykes, graphic granite, mica-schist, and siliceous limestone.

(2) Another locality in the Petersburg Ranges. — Light-coloured quartzites, fine-grained whitish granite, aplite, chloritic gneiss, mica-schist, gneissic granite, quartz-porphyry, coarse granite (with pink orthoclase), pegmatite, quartz-felsite, coarse white granite, and garnet-gneiss.

(3) Jamestown, 150 miles north-west of Adelaide.— Here the boulder-beds are decomposed, and form excellent soil for wheat-growing. The farmers have cleared their land of the larger boulders by harnessing horses to them, and dragging them to the fences. In some places the stones are too numerous and large for this method of clearance, and plots are left uncultivated. In one of these the following erratics were noted in their order of frequency :—Gneiss of various kinds, including some exhibiting augen-structure; white granite, with porphyritic crystals of orthoclase; quartzite, aplite, biotite-schist, muscovite-schist, dark porphyry, pegmatite, pink granite, and white marble. A quartz-porphyry erratic in this group measured 9 feet 6 inches in length; and a large quartzite-boulder near it exhibited a fine glacial polish, as also striæ.

(4) The Burra, 100 miles north of Adelaide. — The erratics in this locality are, as a rule, relatively smaller and fewer in number than usual. The following were the largest noted:— Quartzites, up to 12 inches; porphyritic rock, 15 inches; mica-schist, 2 feet; aplite, 2 feet 9 inches.

None of the boulders found in the till are of local origin. Some are of well-known types which are characteristic

[1] See W. G. Woolnough, 'Petrographical Notes on some South Australian Quartzites, Sandstones, & Related Rocks' Trans. Roy. Soc. S. Austral. vol. xxviii (1904) p. 207.

of the pre-Cambrian rocks of the country, while others cannot be identified as such. At the time when the glacial deposits were laid down, the pre-Cambrian floor, on the east side of the meridian of Gulf St. Vincent, was covered by several thousand feet of Cambrian sediments. The erratics of pre-Cambrian origin would probably, therefore, have travelled considerable distances before coming to rest on the morainic banks forming in the Cambrian Sea.

## (c) Glaciation.

Although the general features of the beds supplied a strong *prima-facie* probability that they represented an ancient till, their glacial origin was not affirmed until the discovery of ice-scratched boulders placed the question beyond doubt. This culminating evidence was obtained, in the first instance, at Petersburg (on the Northern Railway from Adelaide) in 1901, and was subsequently confirmed during a visit to the same place by Prof. T. W. E. David, F.R.S., Mr. E. F. Pittman, the Government Geologist of New South Wales, and myself. In association with those two experienced geologists, fifteen glaciated stones were obtained during a search of two hours.

The erratics are frequently facetted, as well as striated, under ice-action. The striæ vary in depth and direction on the same face, and are often as distinct and fresh-looking as those which occur on the stones of the Pleistocene Boulder-Clay. Under strong pressure and movement in their bed, some of the boulders exhibit evidences of abrasion; but this, as will be explained later, produces features altogether distinct from glacial striation and cannot well be confounded with it.

That these ice-marked stones are a general characteristic of the Cambrian till, is evident from their having been found in most localities whenever opportunity permitted a search for them. Some of the more interesting outcrops for their occurrence are the Petersburg Ranges, the Depôt Hill (near Black Rock, north of Petersburg), Pekina Hill (near Orroroo), Mount-Cone Range (east of Mount-Bryan Railway-station, where, in a single visit, thirteen excellent examples were found), Appila-Creek Gorge (near Laura), and the Daly and Stanley Mines (north-eastern parts of the Flinders Ranges). A very powerfully-striated boulder was obtained from the till, near the Burra; and another was obtained *in situ*, in the Willouran Ranges, near Hergott, at the northernmost position in which the Cambrian glacial beds have been determined.

Up to the present, eighty very definitely-glaciated boulders have been secured from various localities in the Cambrian till, besides the known occurrence of many other examples where the erratics were too large for removal. Illustrations of a few of these ice-marked stones are given in Pl. XIX & figs. 2–5 (pp. 242–45).

Fig. 2.—*Ice-scratched boulder from the Cambrian till, Black Rock, near Orroroo (South Australia).*

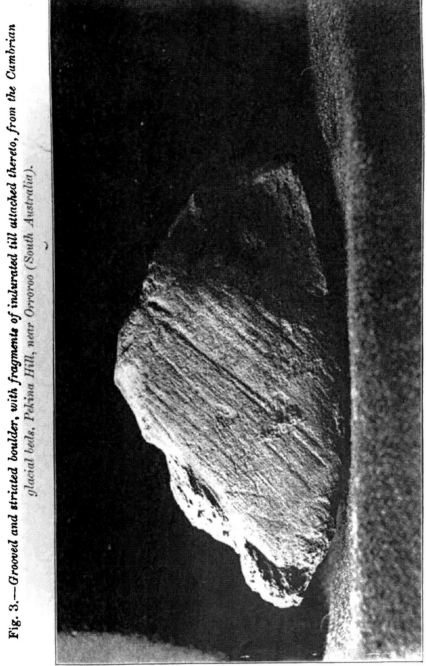

Fig. 3.—*Grooved and striated boulder, with fragments of indurated till attached thereto, from the Cambrian glacial beds, Pekina Hill, near Orroroo (South Australia).*

[The original specimen, No. 14,465, is preserved in the Collection of the Geological Society of London.]

Fig. 5.—*Ice-scratched boulder, in place, in the Cambrian till, Petersburg Ranges (South Australia).*

Fig. 6.—*Quartzite-boulder from the Cambrian till of Petersburg (South Australia), illustrating the form of striation produced by pressure exerted by mass-movement in the bed.*

## (d) Effects of Mechanical Strain.

In some localities, such as the Sturt Valley and the Petersburg Ranges, for example, the beds have been in the zone of great fold-movements and give evidences of strain. A rough kind of cleavage, at a high angle, has been developed, causing the rock to split up into coarse flaggy masses, which weather into serrated edges and often form bold cliff-faces. The coarseness and unevenness of the ground-mass prevent fine lamellar division on the cleavage, but the rock usually exfoliates in smaller or larger flakes along the planes of cleavage. The groundmass has by pressure become kneaded round the included stones; and, in the process of flaking off, these stones form a bulging centre to lenticular flakes, regulated in size according to the size of the included boulder.

The pressure that has induced cleavage in the bed has also shown its effects on the boulders. These, especially the boulders of elongated shape, have undergone a partial revolution in the bed, so as to take a position in which the longer axis has become parallel with the cleavage-planes. In this movement some of the stones have become slightly distorted, and many show the effect of friction in the form of pseudo-striation on exposed surfaces. In the case of angular fragments the edges are sometimes bevelled off, and marked by strong parallel striæ covering the entire face of abrasion. In other instances, these lines of scour diverge radially from a prominent part of the boulder, as though the latter had become scraped in consequence of a differential movement in the groundmass as compared with the boulder, which latter would offer greater resistance to movement. This pseudo-striation, owing to movement in the bed, differs from glacial striation in its uniform character and extent. The lines are of equal size and depth, are parallel one to the other over wide surfaces, and are often flanked by ridges (see fig. 6, p. 246); while the glacial striæ are generally individual or patchy in their occurrence, of varying intensity, and divergent in direction. By these distinctive features the two classes of striation can be easily differentiated.

Another mass-movement has also taken place (probably subsequent to that which induced the cleavage), in which mechanical strain operated along the planes of cleavage. This movement has exerted a drag on the boulders, and caused a great number of them to fracture across their short diameters and at right angles to the cleavage. These fractures are often very numerous, dividing the stone into laminæ, with gaping interspaces, which are sometimes filled with secondary minerals, such as quartz or calcite. Many are, however, free from deposit which might occur from the removal of soluble minerals that at one time occupied the cavities. Examples are not uncommon in which deposits of fibrous calcite have been partly removed in this way. Similar cross-fractures are seen in many of the fragments which make up the coarse grits of the glacial beds, especially when the stone is viewed on a joint-face.

Movements on a larger scale are sometimes indicated by the beds being scarred with quartz, as in the Sturt Valley, where at several places there is a local development of quartz in horizontal veins and lenticles, or in reclining folds, arising probably from some measure of thrust. In rare instances these quartz-veins pass into pegmatites. Passage-forms occur in which the felspathic elements are present only in sporadic crystals, and at one place (in the Sturt Valley) a true pegmatite attains, for a short distance, a thickness of at least a foot.

## V. ILLUSTRATIVE SECTIONS.

The beds of glacial origin are, as a rule, clearly defined in their stratigraphical limits, both at their upper and at their lower boundaries. At their upper limits an abrupt change takes place, from indurated boulder-clay to an overlying thick deposit of fine-grained slate (Tapley's-Hill Slate), which is sometimes calcareous and typically quite free from grit or sand. This bed exhibits very distinctive and persistent features as a banded or ' ribbon '-slate,[1] and differs locally, mainly, in being fissile by cleavage in the south, and fissile along bedding-planes in the northern districts. Underlying the till are fine-grained laminated quartzites (sometimes argillaceous), of wavy structure, passing down into a thick series of quartzites and slates which form the hilly ridges of the Mount-Lofty and other ranges, as in the Mitcham and Glen-Osmond Beds.

The following examples of cross-sections will illustrate the stratigraphical features of the glacial beds.

### (a) Onkaparinga-River Section.   (Fig. 7, p. 249.)

This locality is about 20 miles south of Adelaide. The river here has cut deeply into the Lower Cambrian strata, which exhibit an order of succession similar to that observed near Adelaide, as illustrated in fig. 1 (p. 236). The glacial beds are exposed in the river-valley, at a distance of 6 miles from the coast, in an outcrop of $1\frac{3}{4}$ miles, in one direction, and three-quarters of a mile in the other. On the north and west sides, the continuity of the beds is broken by faults; on the south, they pass under the Tapley's-Hill banded slates, which follow in superior position ; and on the east, they are determined by the outcrop of their base and the underlying (Mitcham) quartzites coming to the surface.

The river intersects the beds on the eastern side of the glacial area, and then, by taking a sudden curve to the west, flows for fully a mile along the strike of the beds, near their upper limits. In the latter case, several cliffs of the till rise almost perpendicularly to a height of about 250 feet (see fig. 7).

[1] See specimen No. 14,489, preserved in the Collection of the Geological Society of London.

Fig. 7.—*Sketch-section across the glacial beds of the Onkaparinga Valley.*
*(Length = about three-quarters of a mile.)*

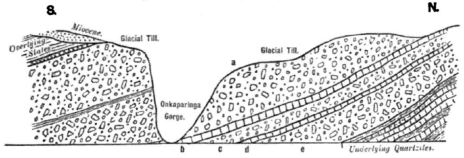

[For the explanation of *a, b, c,* etc., see the accompanying descriptive section.]

The following are the general features of the section :—

##### OVERLYING BEDS.

Miocene sands, sandstones, and gravels.
Banded slates of Cambrian age (Tapley's-Hill Beds), with 2 feet
    of impure limestone at their base.

##### GLACIAL.                                                    *Feet.*

*a* = Third, or upper, till-bed.—Very characteristic. A gritty mud-
    stone, with numerous erratics measuring up to 3 feet in diameter,
    the latter being chiefly granites, gneisses, and quartzites. At one
    horizon there is a slaty belt, which is calcareous in part, showing a
    dip S. 20° E., at 40°. Estimated thickness .............................    400
*b* = Quartzite.—Massive, but somewhat irregular in occurrence, and
    containing in one place a confused assemblage of pebbles. This hard
    rock occupies the bed of the stream (along the strike), for 200 yards,
    where it forms minor ridges and troughs, and weathers into large
    spheroidal masses. Thickness .............................................     14
*c* = Second, or middle, till-bed.—Carries erratics, but is somewhat
    more slaty in structure than the first and third tills. Thickness ...     50
*d* = Quartzite. Has a dip of 25°. Thickness .............................      8
*e* = First, or lowest, till-bed.—Lithology similar to that of the
    third, or thick till. Thickness ..........................................    120
                                                                        ———
                                                                          592

##### UNDERLYING BEDS.

Laminated, fine-grained quartzite of wavy structure. The laminæ
    vary in thickness from a sixteenth of an inch to 1 inch. The
    presence of strongly-marked cleavage in the till, and its complete
    absence in the underlying wavy quartzites, makes a conspicuous
    distinction between the two sets of beds. These beds present an
    exact lithological agreement with the highest members of the
    Mitcham Quartzites which underlie the till in the Adelaide district.

#### (*b*) The Sturt-Valley Section.

#### (Figs. 8, 9, pp. 250, 252 & Pls. XX–XXIII.)

The Sturt River is a small stream which rises near Mount Lofty
and finds its outlet in the estuary of the Patawalonga, a few miles
south of Adelaide. In Miocene times, a Cambrian peneplain,

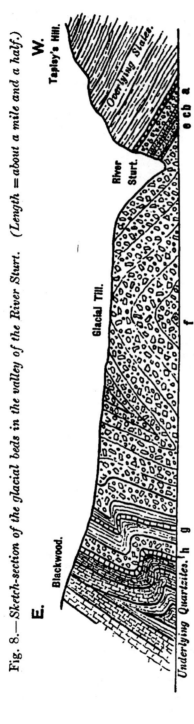

Fig. 8.—*Sketch-section of the glacial beds in the valley of the River Sturt.*    (*Length = about a mile and a half.*)

W.
Tapley's Hill.
Overlying Slate.
e cb a
River Sturt.
Glacial Till.
f
Blackwood.
g
Underlying Quartzites. h
E.

[For the explanation of *a*, *b*, *c*, etc., see the accompanying descriptive section, p. 251.]

skirting the Mount-Lofty ranges, became covered with freshwater and estuarine deposits, which are now at considerable elevations. About 7 miles south of Adelaide, a deep gorge of the Sturt River (Pl. XX) dissects this Miocene plateau, which is from 800 to 1000 feet above sea-level, and exposes the Lower Cambrian beds in excellent sections. The glacial series form the leading geological features of the Sturt Valley, and may here be conveniently studied with respect both to their upper and their lower limits, as well as their lithological characteristics. The high angle of cleavage in the beds, together with the undermining action of the stream, has exposed immense faces of rock, which afford striking sections of the till, rising in steep terraces for several hundred feet on each side of the valley.

The river cuts obliquely across the strike. The junction of the till with the overlying Tapley's-Hill Slates follows the south-western bank of the stream, on the western side of the outcrop; while the base of the glacial series is seen on the eastern side, in a strike nearly due north and south, and is intersected on that side by the Adelaide & Melbourne Railway. Railway-cuttings in the glacial beds occur, from a little east of the viaducts to the Metropolitan Brick-Works, near Blackwood, where the glacial clay (by excluding the bigger erratics and passing the remainder through a powerful mill) is utilized for brick-making.

The glacial outcrop, in this instance, measures 2 miles in its north-and-south direction and a mile and a half in width. Its northern extension is limited by a fault which throws the underlying beds across the normal strike ; and, on the south, the beds are obscured by overlying Miocene sandstones and gravels. In their upper limits, the glacial beds vary in dip from 35° to 50° south-westward ; but at their base a reversed fold has thrown the underlying laminated quartzites on to the till with a dip to E. 20° S., at 70°. (See Pl. XXVI.)

In an unstratified bed of great thickness, as is the case in this and other sections of the Cambrian till of South Australia, it is a difficult matter to estimate the thickness with accuracy, more especially as the strongly-marked cleavage obscures the folding to which the beds may have been subjected : therefore, in the following section of the Sturt-Valley beds, the figures in relation to the thick till must be taken as approximate only. (See fig. 8, p. 250.)

OVERLYING BEDS.

Tapley's-Hill laminated and banded slates, with about 4 feet of impure dolomitic limestone at their base, resting immediately upon characteristic till.

| GLACIAL. | Thickness in feet. |
|---|---|
| $a$=Highest till-bed, with numerous erratics ............................... | 45 |
| $b$=Grits and till, intimately mixed in irregular patches ............... | 12 |
| $c$=Black slaty till, calcareous in places and carrying a few erratics. | 14 |
| $d$=Blue limestone, on top of grits, very local in occurrence ......... | 2 |
| $e$=Strong grits, fine to coarse and in places including pockets of stones. They are somewhat irregular in occurrence, and develop prismatic jointing.................................................................. | 10 |
| $f$=Thick till, sometimes slaty and in places becoming a distinct grit ; but it is characteristically a gritty mudstone, with numerous erratics of foreign origin measuring up to 4½ feet in length. Cleavage-strike N. 15° E. to N. 20° E., at 60° to 70° easterly ......................... | (?) 600 |
| $g$=Yellow and buff decomposed kaolinized slates, without stones, and very fine-grained. They include a band of contorted quartzite, about 3 feet thick ............. ................................. | 72 |
| $h$=Bottom till, with erratics................. ........ ......................... | 40 |
| | 795 |

UNDERLYING BEDS.

Finely-laminated quartzites and arenaceous slates, sharply defined in junction with the overlying till ; dip E. 10° N. at 70°. Can be well seen in the bed of the Sturt River, and in railway-cuttings near the Metropolitan Brick-Works, where the fine lamination shows the minute and excessive contortion attendant on the reversed fold, in a very high degree.

The precipitous sides of the Sturt Gorge are unfavourable for the collection of glaciated stones ; but several very characteristic examples of glaciation have been secured in the pits of the Metropolitan Brick Company.

E. F. Pittman photogr.

## (c) Appila-Gorge Section.    (Figs. 4 & 10, pp. 244 & 254.)

The Appila Creek takes its rise at Tarcowie, and, after a course of
24 miles, finds its outlet by marshy flats into the Rocky River near
Laura, which is distant 86 miles by rail north of Adelaide.  About
5 miles from its source the creek turns abruptly westwards, cutting
a gorge through a low range of hills which have a north-and-south
direction.  The gorge is about half a mile long, and for about
three-fourths of this distance it is cut through glacial beds.  For the
greater part, the river cuts the beds within a few degrees of a true
cross-section ; and in the remainder of the distance a section across
the strike can be continued, by following a small tributary which
comes in at the angle of the stream.

The strata throughout are at a high angle of dip, for the most part
varying from 85° to 90° eastwards ; and they present, therefore,
very favourable conditions for calculating the thickness of the beds.

The boundaries of the glacial beds are strongly marked, both at
their lower and at their upper horizons.  Immediately below are
massive quartzites, which, from their superior hardness and nearly-
vertical position, weather into great rampart-like ridges.  These beds
are the equivalent of the Mitcham Quartzites, which occupy a similar
position in the section near Adelaide.  The upper boundary of the
glacial beds is marked by a sharp line of division, in which boulder-
clay with big erratics is covered by a homogeneous fissile slate or ·
shale : this is the equivalent of the Tapley's-Hill ribbon-slate, but
splits more readily along the bedding-planes than the latter does.

A rough measurement of the glacial series in this section gives a
total thickness of 1526 feet, which is split up into three sub-
sections :—(a) An upper till of 120 feet ; (b) an interbedded series
of slates to 656 feet ; and (c) a lower till of 750 feet.  The following
is a detailed description of the section (see fig. 10, p. 254):—

OVERLYING BEDS: Laminated and banded slates, dipping eastwards
at 80° to 90° (=Tapley's-Hill Slates).

GLACIAL.                                          *Thickness in feet.*

| | | |
|---|---|---:|
| $a=$ | Upper till, with numerous erratics, some glaciated ............... | 120 |
| $b=$ | Slates, with few or no erratics ......................................... | 480 |
| $c=$ | Quartzites and slates, alternating in beds about 3½ feet thick. | 18 |
| $d=$ | Slates, with wavy structure, which gradually become calcareous towards their base ...................................................... | 60 |
| $e=$ | Thin, impure, buff-coloured limestones (in bands from 1 to 9 inches thick), separated by partings ........................ | 18 |
| $f=$ | The above pass down into more definite limestones, which include an erratic of micaceous gneiss, 9 inches long ............... | 12 |
| $g=$ | Quartzite, including a slate-band of 6 inches .................... | 27 |
| $h=$ | {Slate ......... ............................... 13 feet} {Band of slate with small erratics  ...  1 foot} {Slate ................................................... 6 feet} ............ | 20 |
| $i=$ | Bluish limestone, in wavy bands about 1 inch thick ............ | 3 |
| $j=$ | Quartzite ................................................................ | 18 |
| $k=$ | Lower till, with numerous erratics, some glaciated ............... | 750 |

UNDERLYING BEDS: Massive quartzites, passing down into
siliceous slates and thin bands of quartzite.  Dip E. 20° S. at
80°. (=Mitcham Quartzites.)    **1526**

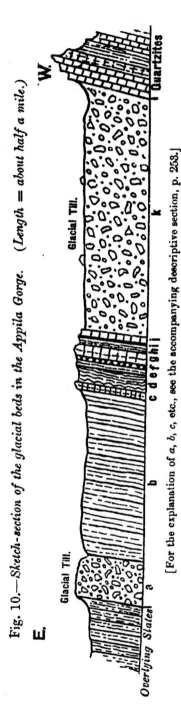

Fig. 10.—*Sketch-section of the glacial beds in the Appila Gorge.*    (*Length = about half a mile.*)

[For the explanation of *a*, *b*, *c*, etc., see the accompanying descriptive section, p. 253.]

On the upper slopes of the gorge the till has been considerably weathered and eroded, and the surface is covered with erratics. Among these a dark porphyry is a common form : one example of this type, on the south side of the stream, measures $7\frac{1}{2}$ feet in length. On the north side of the river a lenticular mass of brown grit (measuring 10 feet in greatest thickness) occurs in the lower till-bed about halfway up the hill. Several big granite-boulders of various kinds also occur on that side of the valley, near the junction with the underlying quartzites. In the course of three visits to this outcrop several good glaciated stones were obtained, and others were seen that were too large for removal.

(*d*) Northern Areas : Sections. (Figs. 2–6, 11, 12 & Pls. XIX, XXIV, XXV.)

Two geological sections are given in figs. 11 & 12 (pp. 256 & 257), which are typical of the northern portions of the Mount-Lofty Ranges and the southern and eastern Flinders Ranges.

Fig. 11 is a diagrammatic representation of the main outcrops, as they occur across the strike in a west-and-east direction from Port Germein, on Spencer's Gulf, to Mount Grainger, which is situated 7 miles north of Oodla-Wirra Railway-station (on the Petersburg & New-South-Wales Border Railway), covering a distance of 60 miles. In this section the glacial till makes eight distinct outcrops, in anticlinal and synclinal curves ; and in each case (in association with the underlying quartzites) forms prominent ridges. The more yielding banded slates of the Tapley's-Hill Series, which overlie the till, have weathered into the low-lying ground between the ridges. The highest member in the section is the equivalent of the Brighton Limestone, of the type-district, and is strongly developed in a synclinal trough between Pekina and Orroroo. The Mount-Grainger Gold-Mine is situated in the till-bed, the gold occurring with quartz-veins, and also clinging to the external surfaces of the boulders which are fed to the stampers for the recovery of the gold.

Fig. 12 (p. 257) is a geological section taken at right angles to that shown in fig. 11, following a south-and-north direction, from the Yunta Ranges in the south to Oopina in the north, covering a distance of 30 miles. This line of section crosses the Petersburg & New-South-Wales Border Railway at Yunta Railway-station. The section is nominally along the line of strike (which is indicated in the section at Teetulpa, and the Bushy-Peak Range); but the beds are in places strongly influenced by periclinal folding, which throws the strike into curves and creates a dip along the prevailing line of strike. The till appears in four distinct outcrops, and the associated beds are similar to those which occur in the same relation in fig. 11.

## VI. General Considerations.

### (a) The Ice-Agent.

The nature of the ice-agent which operated in laying down the vast accumulations of morainic material (represented by the Cambrian glacial beds) is of great interest, as bearing on the physical geography of these latitudes in early Cambrian times. The weight of evidence seems to be against the hypothesis of land-ice, of any great extent, existing within the area concerned. In no instance has the morainic material been seen resting unconformably upon a rock-surface of an earlier period. There is consequently no glaciated 'floor,' which might be expected to occur in the case of land-ice of considerable extent.

Again, while usually there is a strongly-marked lithological discordance at the junction of the till and the immediately-underlying bed, there is presumptive evidence that the morainic matter was laid down in an area of continuous sedimentation. The great Cambrian geosyncline was at that time a dominant factor in crust-movements, and would ensure an increasing marine area with a stratigraphical sequence of deposits; while the nature of the sedimentation would be profoundly influenced by the encroachments of the ice-borne material over the area. The suggestion made by Mr. H. P. Woodward, in 1884,[1] that this 'boulder-clay' had its origin from

---

[1] 'Report on the Mines, Hills, &c. of the Range to the East of Farina & Leigh's-Creek Railway-Station' Parliamentary Paper No. 40 (South Australia) Adelaide, 1884, p. 3.

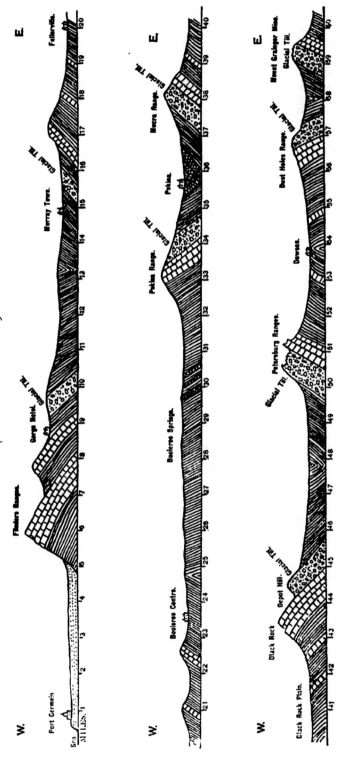

Fig. 11.—Diagrammatic section of the glacial beds in a west-and-east direction, from Port Germein to Mount Grainger
(Distance = 60 miles.)

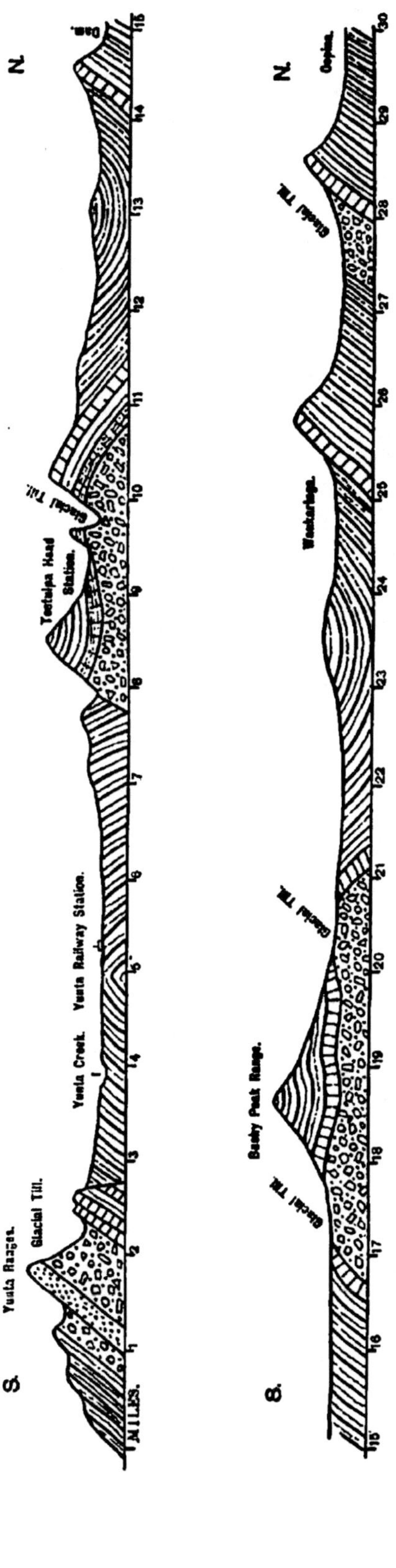

Fig. 12.—Diagrammatic section of the glacial beds in a south-and-north direction, from the Yunta Ranges to Oopina. (Distance = 30 miles.)

'floating ice,' appears to furnish the explanation which is most in accordance with the known facts.

That the morainic material forming the till-beds had its primary source in upland glaciers seems beyond doubt. The enormous amount of waste represented by the beds in question, as well as the great size of some of the erratics, demands a more powerful agent of transport than shore-ice; while the highly-glaciated condition of many of the boulders might be caused by subglacial movement and wear in the earlier part of their journey.

Many of the included stones in the till have evidently been water-worn prior to their transportation, and in some cases these stones show glacial striæ. This suggests that the watershed which produced the glaciers was not completely ice-bound in its drainage; but tributary streams probably carried their water-worn material down to the main valleys, where the glaciers would occur far below the limits of the permanent snow-line. Rounded stones, in this way, might become part of the ground-moraine, and having been caught up into the lower part of the ice-sheet, would be carried off when the glacier broke away and floated off as an iceberg. Shore-ice might also pick up

s 2

beach-pebbles, and impart striation to them by scraping the bottom before coming to rest.

It is difficult to determine the exact position of this old Cambrian ice-field. The pre-Cambrian highlands are only indicated, at the present time, by sunken reefs and low peneplains. The largest known area of pre-Cambrian rocks that comes within the range of probability for such an ice-field includes part of the continental shelf, together with the geological axes found in Yorke Peninsula, Kangaroo Island, and Eyre Peninsula.

Yorke Peninsula is an old pre-Cambrian ridge that remained above sea-level during most of the Cambrian Period, and was finally submerged only at so late a stage in the geosynclinal folding as to receive but a thin deposit of Cambrian material, and that limited to the later deposits. The only circumstance known, calculated to throw light on the direction of the ice-drift, is the discovery in the Petersburg Range of two erratics of graphic granite (one glaciated), that show identical features with a rock of the same character, *in situ*, in southern Yorke Peninsula, 122 miles from the spot where the erratics were found. This would indicate a drift from south-west to north-east, radiating from that part of the country where the greatest known exposure of pre-Cambrian rocks exists and around which the Cambrian beds thin out. Shore-ice would be quite equal to the transport of the two erratics just mentioned.

## (b) ? Interglacial Periods.

Attention has been directed to the possibility of the glacial conditions being arrested at certain stages by intercalated periods of higher temperature and a restricted distribution of morainic material. Some grounds for believing that such was the case is suggested by the interbedded slates and limestones, which are often completely, or approximately, free from coarse material, and exhibit bedding-planes of sedimentation. At present, however, the evidences for one or more distinct interglacial periods, that were general in their effects, cannot be regarded as conclusive. Where well-defined interglacial periods occur, we may expect that such periods will be indicated by zones which possess some stratigraphical resemblance over wide areas. This, however, does not appear to be the case, as the intercalated beds occur at various horizons in the till with a marked irregularity in different districts. Local causes may have led to a temporary variation of sediment in certain areas, at one time closing the avenues to floating ice, leaving them open almost exclusively to fluviatile sediment, and at other times reversing these conditions. Fuller data must be awaited before any definite conclusions can be reached as to the possible climatic alternations which may have occurred during the progress of the Cambrian Ice-Age in South Australia.

E. F. Pittman, photo.

Bemrose, Collo.

POLISHED AND ICE-SCRATCHED BOULDER FROM THE CAMBRIAN TILL OF PETERSBURG (SOUTH AUSTRALIA).

J. Greenlees, photo.                                              Bemrose, Collo.

GORGE OF THE RIVER STURT IN CAMBRIAN TILL.

E. F. Pittman, photo.

Bemrose, Collo.

VIEW OF CAMBRIAN TILL IN STURT-RIVER GORGE, ILLUSTRATING THE GENERAL
CHARACTERISTICS OF THE GLACIAL BEDS.

*J. Greenlees, photo.*                                       *Bemrose, Collo.*

VIEW OF CAMBRIAN TILL, STURT-RIVER GORGE, INCLUDING A BIG
SUBANGULAR BOULDER OF QUARTZITE WITH TRANSVERSE
FRACTURES.

Bemrose, Collo.

J. Greenlees, photo.

VIEW OF CAMBRIAN TILL, WATERFALL GULLY, BAROOTA, FLINDERS RANGES,
INCLUDING A BIG ANGULAR ERRATIC OF QUARTZITE (FRACTURED).

J. Greenlees, photo.

Bemrose, Collo.

SECTION IN BLACKWOOD RAILWAY-CUTTING, SHEWING THE BASE OF THE CAMBRIAN TILL WITH THE UNDERLYING LAMINATED QUARTZITES, AND THE INVERSION OF THE BEDS.

## EXPLANATION OF PLATES XIX-XXVI.

### PLATE XIX.

Polished and ice-scratched boulder from the Cambrian till of Petersburg (South Australia). Found and photographed by Mr. E. F. Pittman, Government Geologist of New South Wales.

### PLATE XX.

View in the gorge of the River Sturt, which has been cut in the Cambrian till.

### PLATE XXI.

View of the Cambrian till, in the Sturt-River gorge, illustrating the general characteristics of the glacial beds.

### PLATE XXII.

Another view of the glacial beds in the same river-valley.

### PLATE XXIII.

Another view of the same, showing a big subangular boulder of quartzite with transverse fractures.

### PLATE XXIV.

View of characteristic Cambrian till, in Waterfall Creek, Baroota (Flinders Ranges).

### PLATE XXV.

Another view of the till in Waterfall Creek, including a big angular erratic of quartzite (fractured).

### PLATE XXVI.

Section in Blackwood Railway-cutting, near Adelaide, showing the base of the Cambrian till with the underlying laminated quartzites (Mitcham Series), and the inversion of the beds.

[For the Discussion, see p. 260.]

12. *On a* FORMATION KNOWN *as* 'GLACIAL BEDS *of* CAMBRIAN AGE'
    *in* SOUTH AUSTRALIA.   By H. BASEDOW and J. D. ILIFFE.
    (Communicated by Dr. J. MALCOLM MACLAREN, F.G.S.   Read
    November 20th, 1907.)

[Abstract.]

SOME 8 miles south of Adelaide a typical exposure of the conglomerate is bounded on the east by a series of alternating quartzitic
and argillaceous bands of rock, comprising the central and western
portions of a fan-fold, partly cut off by a fault.   Further evidence of
stress in this margin is given in the fissility, pseudo-ripple-marks,
contortion and fracture, and obliteration of bedding in the quartzite-
bands, and in the pinching-out of them into lenticles and false
pebbles.   On the west side the conglomerate is bounded by the
'Tapley's-Hill Clay-Slates,' and there is evidence from the nature
of the junction-beds that the conglomerate itself is isoclinally folded.
In that portion of the conglomerate which is adjacent to its
confines, 'boulders' of quartzite are apparently disrupted portions
of quartzite-bands, since these are in alignment with the truncated
portions of bands still existing, and are of similar composition.
The Authors are not at present in a position to account for the
presence in the conglomerate of boulders of rocks foreign to the
beds that border the conglomerate, or of such as possess markings
comparable to glacial striæ, by their theory of differential earth-
movements ; but they consider that a boulder-bed subjected to lateral
pressure would probably lend itself to the production of 'false
pebbles,' through the disruption of intercalated hard bands within
itself or on its boundaries.

DISCUSSION (ON THE TWO FOREGOING PAPERS).

Dr. A. STRAHAN considered the first paper to be a lucid and convincing account of an extremely-interesting series of deposits.   The
association of schistose rocks and slates with beds of glacial origin
had led to the development of some unusual phenomena, but the
superinduced structures due to earth-movements on the one hand,
and the original characters due to the action of ice on the other
hand, appeared to him to have been well illustrated in the two
papers.   The puckering and the disruption of rock-bands into
separate blocks simulating boulders were familiar features in rocks
which had been subjected to great pressure.   There was this difference, however, between a 'crush-conglomerate' which had originated in this manner and the beds for which a glacial origin had
been claimed, in that the latter contained true boulders of foreign
material.   The peculiar characters of the glacial deposit had been
admirably illustrated in the first paper.   Such deposits, whether of

Pleistocene, Cambrian, or any other age, had a highly-characteristic appearance, due presumably to the haphazard assemblage of diverse materials.  At a distance all looked alike, and it was only on close examination that the hardening due to infiltration of silica, and other differences, became apparent.

Some glacial deposits of early age in the Varanger Fiord, described before the Society in 1897 (Quart. Journ. Geol. Soc. vol. liii, p. 137), rested on a glaciated platform of the quartzite with which the 'till' was interbedded.  The question had then been raised by the President how the sand could have been sufficiently indurated to retain striations so soon after its deposition.  Various explanations had been suggested, but none were wholly satisfactory.  He enquired whether a similar platform had been observed under the Australian 'till.'  It would be interesting also to know whether there was proof that the ice had descended to or below the sea-level of the period.

Dr. J. M. MACLAREN said that the notes which he had communicated might be considered a contribution toward the discussion of Mr. Howchin's paper.  They were apparently intended to prove no more than that certain rocks, claimed by Mr. Howchin as 'erratics' in glacial beds, were merely fragments faulted in from the adjacent quartzites.  While the Authors of the second paper had made out a fair case for their point, they had thrown no light on the origin of the beds as a whole.  All the Archæan and Cambrian conglomerates that he had seen were of the boulder-bed type, and he offered, as a general suggestion, a torrential origin for many of these, comparing them in point of view of matrix, of dispersion, character, and size of boulder, and of extent of deposit, with the great boulder-beds now being formed at the head of the Assam Valley, at the debouchments of the Lohit Brahmaputra, Dihon, and other Eastern Himalayan rivers.  Although these were fluviatile deposits, it was quite conceivable that striated pebbles might occur in them— pebbles that, in a single monsoon season and without loss of striæ, were transported from terminal moraines to the broad valley-plains at the mouths of the gorges.  With regard to the South Australian conglomerates under discussion, his knowledge of them was much too limited to permit the expression of any opinion as to their origin.

Mr. R. D. OLDHAM commented on the completeness of the evidence which the Author of the first paper had brought forward, and the masterly way in which it had been marshalled to show that the beds described by him presented a combination of characters which, so far as we knew, was only to be found, as a whole, in beds of glacial origin.  He did not think that this conclusion was seriously invalidated by the suggestion made by the Authors of the second paper regarding the possibility of a different origin of a part of the beds dealt with by Mr. Howchin.  He had, himself, been struck with the resemblance shown by the specimens and photographs to some ancient deposits of presumably-glacial origin with which he was acquainted, and more especially with the Blaini 'conglomerate' of the Outer Himalayas, which had undergone a very similar amount of disturbance to those described by Mr. Howchin. These deposits had been regarded as Permian, on the strength of the resemblance of the associated beds to some of those associated with the Upper Carboniferous of Kashmir; more recently, their assumed glacial origin had been used to correlate them with the glacial beds of Cambrian age in Australia, China, and elsewhere. As no fossils had been found, there was little to choose between these two guesses; but the fact that a glacial origin had been accepted as a satisfactory working hypothesis, by observers who had studied them in the field, might be accepted as presumptive evidence in favour of the correctness of Mr. Howchin's conclusions.

Mr. G. W. LAMPLUGH observed that the descriptions of the bouldery rocks contained in the first paper, and even the specimens and photographs exhibited in illustration of it, would apply, with very slight alteration, to some portions of the Dwyka 'tillite' (to use the term proposed by Prof. Penck) of South Africa. Similar beds of older date than the Dwyka had also been recently discovered in South Africa. No agency other than glaciation was known which was capable of producing rocks of this character. Their thickness, continuity, and sameness of composition, however, far exceeded that of any post-Tertiary glacial deposit known to the speaker, and seemed still to require explanation.

If rocks of this kind were dragged and distorted by earth-movement, it was very probable that some degree of disruption would occur at their junction with strata of different composition; and the Authors of the second paper appeared to have found some evidence for this. But the matter was of secondary consequence, and did not touch the essential characteristics of the rock. The problems raised by the presence of these ancient 'tillites' in the Southern hemisphere were of the highest importance to geologists, and all new information bearing on the subject would be eagerly welcomed.

Mr. A. W. ROGERS said that those specimens that showed the pebbles in the matrix were very like the Dwyka 'tillite' of Cape Colony, in places where that rock had been involved in mountain-folding; and Mr. Howchin's description of the Australian exposures would fit not only the Dwyka 'tillite', but that in the Table-Mountain Series also. The absence of a striated floor was characteristic of the three 'tillites' of different ages in Cape Colony, where they rested conformably upon older rocks. The repeatedly-jointed pebbles were also a very characteristic feature of the Cape 'tillites,' even where the rocks had not been folded.

Dr. A. P. YOUNG remarked that the bed of the Baltic, covered by the Scandinavian glaciers when they forced their way over on to the North German plain, would, in his opinion, if exposed give sections of Boulder-Clay comparable as regards thickness with those now described; and that the floor of the ground-moraine, formed mostly of contemporaneous deposits, would in general be free from scratches.

Mr. C. B. HORWOOD observed that, as he was familiar with the

Dwyka Series, in various parts of the Transvaal, Orange-River Colony, and Natal, he would like to endorse all Mr. Lamplugh's remarks with regard to the great and very remarkable similarity of the specimens exhibited, from South Australia, with specimens which might be obtained from the Dwyka Beds.

Mr. A. E. KITSON said that, from personal acquaintance with the Sturt-Valley section, he was satisfied as to its glacial origin. Although he believed that many of the striæ were the work of ice, he did not attach so much importance to them as to the general character of the beds. The great disparity in size and the difference in composition of the boulders, and especially the occurrence of boulders 8 to 10 feet in diameter, embedded in masses of what was originally mud, could not (he thought) be attributed to any other agency than ice. Undoubtedly the beds had suffered much crushing, and, although some of the blocks along the contact of the conglomerates and quartzites might be due to dynamic agency, that would not satisfactorily explain the occurrence of the big boulders that were found in the lower portion of the conglomerate.

Prof. GARWOOD commented on the striking resemblances, between the deposits shown in the photographs and Pleistocene and recent glacial deposits in different parts of the world, and on the typical glaciated appearance of many of the boulders exhibited on the table. He thought that perhaps too little value had been attached by some of the speakers to the evidence of glacial origin provided by the scratches which these boulders exhibited; many of these showed typical glacial grooves, some of which crossed each other at right angles. He did not think that these could have been impressed by crush-movement, which would tend to produce parallel striæ in any one zone.

In reply to Dr. Strahan he quoted a passage from Mr. Howchin's paper, in which that Author commented on the absence of any striated platform under the Australian ' tillite '.

13. *The* ORIGIN *of the* PILLOW-LAVA *near* PORT ISAAC *in* CORNWALL. By CLEMENT REID, F.R.S., F.L.S., F.G.S., and HENRY DEWEY, F.G.S. (Communicated by permission of the Director of H.M. Geological Survey. Read January 22nd, 1908.)

[PLATES XXVII & XXVIII.]

THE volcanic mass which we are about to describe occupies a definite horizon in the Upper Devonian, in the part of North Cornwall lying between Padstow and Bodmin Moor. We propose to confine our remarks to this limited area; for the point with which we deal is merely the mode of origin of this particular eruptive rock. Our views may, or may not, be applicable to other pillow-lavas; but the subject is so beset with difficulties, that we prefer to confine our attention to a limited region, where cliff-sections are exceptionally fine and inland quarries are also clear. We will not deal with the question of correlation, even with neighbouring areas.

## Previous Literature.

The volcanic rocks near Port Isaac were noticed by De la Beche in 1839.[1] He mentions the vesicular character of some of them, and suggests that they were contemporaneous with the slates in which they occur. He does not allude to their peculiar structure.

In 1848 Nicholas Whitley noticed and figured the peculiar concentric structure,

'as if it had rolled down a declivity and become partially cooled during its progress, and then consolidated into the rock which it now constitutes; in fact, much like the ends of bales of cloth piled one on another.'

He speaks of the centre of each circle being generally composed of a nodule of crystallized gypsum, and compares this structure with that of some of the Vesuvian lavas.[2]

The petrological characters of these rocks were described in 1878 by J. A. Phillips,[3] who gave an analysis of a specimen in which the amygdules were filled with calcite. Only a small portion of this calcite, however, can have belonged to the original rock, which was once highly vesicular, though now solid through the infilling of the amygdules.

In 1902 Mr. Howard Fox described 'Some Coast-Sections in the Parish of St. Minver.'[4] In this paper reference is made to the spheroidal structure which is very frequent throughout all this range of cliff, and one of the spheroids is figured.

[1] 'Report on the Geology of Cornwall, &c.' pp. 88–89.
[2] 'On the Remains of Ancient Volcanoes on the North Coast of Cornwall, in the Parish of St. Minver, &c.' 30th Ann. Rep. Roy. Inst. Cornwall, App. vi, p. 62 (1848–49).
[3] Quart. Journ. Geol. Soc. vol. xxxiv, p. 483.
[4] Trans. Roy. Geol. Soc. Cornwall, vol. xii, pt. viii, p. 670.

Pillow-lavas have been described from many parts of the world, and the isolation of the individual pillows has been commented on by various writers. Banded vesicular structure has also been referred to as occurring towards their periphery; more rarely it has been noticed as increasing towards the centre. The origin of the pillow-structure has been much discussed, but the general trend of opinion is in favour of the view that the lava-streams flowed into or under water. Pillow-lavas differ so greatly in different localities in various parts of the world, that it seems very doubtful whether all can have originated in the same way; they are also widely distributed in time. The pillows described in this paper are of a peculiar and apparently unusual type.

## Description of the Occurrence.

The area around Port Isaac has been mapped on the 6-inch scale by us for the Geological Survey during the past two seasons, with the result that the complicated outcrops of lava prove to belong almost entirely to a single sheet. This sheet is interstratified near the top of the grey slates which form the lower part of the Upper Devonian strata of this region. A little lava of similar character occurs at a somewhat higher stage, in purple and green slates; but our description will be confined to the more massive sheet, probably 200 feet or more thick, seen in the cliffs on each side of Port-Quin Bay, and in inland quarries in the parishes of St. Minver and St. Endellion.

The best places to study these lavas are the bold cliffs of Pentire and Kellan Head; for, though much of the cliff-face is inaccessible, plenty of good exposures can be found without dangerous climbing. Clear inland sections may be seen at various places, some of them being close to the high road. For instance, the Church-Hill Quarry, from which the road-metal is obtained, is just outside Port Isaac. The quarry by the roadside shows the pillows obscurely; but immediately above, though invisible from the road, is a much finer section in a newer quarry. Very fine exposures are also seen inland in a deep quarry a quarter of a mile north of Trelights, and in shallower pits just west of Trelights.

The cliff at Pentire shows a mass of pillow-lava to a height of 258 feet; the Kellan-Head section is about 200 feet high. In neither case, however, is it possible to say whether the total thickness may not be much greater, or whether, on the other hand, there may not be some duplication by overthrusting. We can be certain, however, that great masses are quite free from shear-planes. So far as we have been able to ascertain, this is the maximum visible development of the sheet, which would suggest that the vent must be sought for more to the north, and under the sea.

A series of photographs of the sections has been taken for the Geological Survey by Mr. T. C. Hall. The two photographs selected for reproduction show the characteristic features of the rock. The lava is highly vesicular, and, however thick the mass may be, it usually consists of an accumulation of detached pillows piled one upon another. The pillows seem to have rolled over and over, and to have settled down while still sufficiently soft to take impressions of the contiguous spheroids. They cannot, however, have been very fluid, for triangular spaces were commonly left where adjacent spheroids did not fit. These interstices and the vesicles were afterwards filled with nearly pure calcite, which in some places has been replaced by chert.

Not only were spheroidal pillows of lava piled up to make a single sheet, but in a few cases detached spheroids can be found isolated in the shales, a few inches, or even a few yards away from the main mass. It is unfortunate that, although the main mass may have completely resisted shearing (as is shown in the photographs, Pls. XXVII & XXVIII), yet there has been considerable movement at the top and bottom of the sheet. This usually makes the exact relation of the lava to the sediments somewhat difficult to trace out. We can only say that there seems occasionally to be a little alteration of the sedimentary strata, and also a small amount of disturbance and inclusion of sedimentary material (apparently mud, not slate) near the base of the lava. The greater number of the supposed inclusions have, however, a totally-different origin, for they are merely infiltrations of calcite.

The shearing at the junction of the lavas and sediments usually makes it difficult to determine whether detached pillows owe their isolation to this cause, or were detached from the main mass, at the time of their emission, while still hot. In some cases there seems no doubt that detached spheroids showing in section a perfectly-rounded outline, with no impression of other spheroids, are in their original position. The difficulty of photographing a cliff-face, only accessible by climbing, has made it impossible to obtain a satisfactory illustration of one of these occurrences.

As already mentioned, the main mass of lava seems to be of great thickness, and apparently it is the accumulation of a single out-burst, during which the rock flowed only a few miles. We have to explain, however, in what manner a sheet of this sort can be built up of completely-detached spheroids and be highly vesicular from top to bottom. The structure is quite unlike that of ropy lavas, or of any recent lavas of which we have heard. If individual spheroids be studied, we think that the clue may be obtained.

The pillows of which the mass is made up vary in size from about 1 to 8 feet in diameter, the majority measuring perhaps 2 or 3 feet; pillows having a diameter of less than a foot are rare. Each spheroid has definite boundaries; and, even where the surfaces are in close contact, they are separated by a thin skin from the adjacent spheroids. As already mentioned, though somewhat flattened and dented, the pillows were not soft enough to mould themselves to the underlying pillows at all points, and triangular and more or less rectangular spaces occur where the pillows do not meet.

The structure of the spheroids is shown in the numerous natural sections exposed upon joint-faces, and each is seen to consist of a series of alternating concentric bands of more or less amygdaloidal rock. The amygdules are smallest in the outermost layers, and decrease in number but increase in size towards the interior. The centre is often highly vesicular, with a large cavity from which the infilling calcite has been weathered out. Some of these central cavities occupy a large area of the section, measuring as much as 2 feet in diameter in a pillow 6 feet in diameter. In short, each pillow is a gigantic thick-walled bubble, blown out by the included steam and other gases, and showing the stretching of the walls in the concentric bands of drawn-out vesicles which occupy the outer part of its substance.

## Formation of the Pillows.

Though the inflation of the pillows seems so obvious in the field, we could not for a long time understand how it happened that this inflation took such a peculiar form. Why did not the whole sheet expand into a thick mass of vesicular pumice, instead of forming these characteristic spheroids?

While studying the lava, it struck us that the pillows were so spongy and full of cavities, that before the vesicles were infilled with calcite the pillows must have been very light. We therefore attempted to measure the cubic contents of rock and interspace in the larger pillows. This proved to be more difficult than we had anticipated. Photographs show numerous sections through spheroids; but unless the section happens to be taken exactly through the central cavity, we must underestimate the total bulk of the cavities. Tangential sections miss the central cavity, and may only pass through the outer and closer zones. Perhaps no one section that we have measured passes exactly through the centre of the mass, but we have selected two, one of which is figured (Pl. XXVIII), as representing fairly well the usual structure.

The obvious and simplest method of measuring the relation of vesicle to solid rock would seem at first sight to be by decalcification of a whole pillow, so as to remove the infilling of the vesicles, and allow a direct comparison of the weight before and after the calcite was removed. But apart from the practical difficulty of dealing with a mass containing 10 or more cubic feet, there was the obvious objection that some part of the carbonate must be a decomposition-product of the igneous rock, and to remove the whole would lead to underestimation of the original weight. Also, some of the vesicles are filled with silica, others with chlorite. We have, however, measured the approximate area of vesicle and rock in successive shells in the pillows, and have calculated the cubic contents of each in the different shells seen in the sections.

We do not pretend that the result is more than a rough approximation; but it is very curious. Taking the original specific gravity of a lava of this sort as about 2·7, cavities occupy nearly one-half of the mass, reducing the specific gravity of the whole pillow, in the two examples measured, respectively to 1·40 and 1·45.

The exceptionally-spongy character of this lava is very striking, and light was thrown on it from an unexpected quarter. Happening to look at an article in 'Science Progress' for October 1907, on 'Bread-making' by Mr. A. E. Humphries, the ex-President of the National Association of British & Irish Millers, we were struck by the statement as to the bread-making qualities of different flours. Chemical composition seemed to throw little light on this quality; it depends on the physical capacity of the dough for retaining the bubbles of gas set free by the yeast. Wheat-flour has this capacity, barley and rye-flours do not possess it; and wheat-flours vary considerably in this respect, though their chemical composition varies so little. Applying this experience to the lava, it would seem that this molten mass was not only full of steam, but was in a state to retain great part of the steam in the vesicles. We will not venture to say exactly why this particular lava will blow into bubbles, and another will not; but in this case we have a lava which, notwithstanding its great and probably sudden expansion, did not blow to pieces or lose most of its gas, but retained enough of its steam to swell up and form a sponge.

The lightness of the pillows above described does not much assist us, if the eruption were subaërial. The lava, however, occurs in the midst of purely-marine strata, and in all probability represents a submarine eruption, as Dr. Teall has suggested is the case with other pillow-lavas. When looked at from the point of view of submarine eruption, the highly-vesicular character of the rock assumes extreme importance. The space occupied by vesicles is so great as to form a very large percentage of the total cubic contents; and, when we take into account also the big central cavity, the question arises whether some of the pillows would not be so light as actually to float in sea-water, so long as the vesicles were filled with steam.

If some of the spheroids were so buoyant as to float, some of these more buoyant masses may be represented by the puzzling isolated pillows, which look so like bombs, but seem never to have been broken by a fall. Even in the main mass we have been unable definitely to find broken spheroids; the angular clinkers which occur in the quarry west of Trelights may be such, but the better sections in the cliff do not appear to show any.

Very little tuff is associated with this particular eruption, although some of the inland localities seem to show fragmental material partly replacing the sheet of lava towards its thin edge. Unfortunately, however, where the sheet becomes thin it has been sheared to pieces, and therefore we now feel convinced that certain fragmental rocks at first thought to be tuff are merely sheared lava. A good section showing this passage of vesicular lava into sheared fragmental rock, may be seen in the northern bank of the Camel, about a mile north-west of Wadebridge. The top and bottom of the thick sheet also commonly show fragmental rock resembling tuff.

Thus we appear to be dealing with a type of eruption comparable

Bemrose, collo.

T. C. Hall. photo.

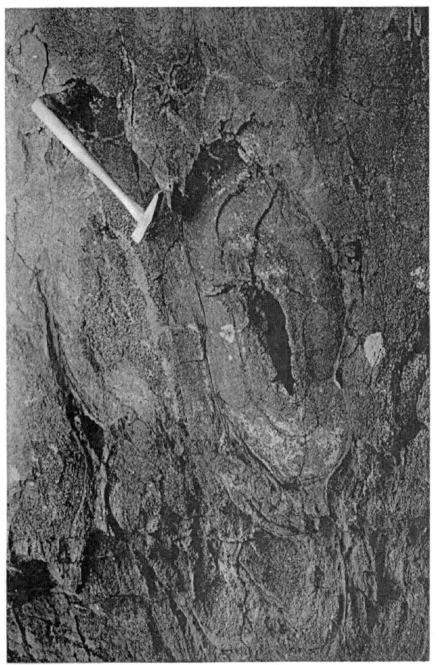

Reinware. collo.

T. C. Hall phot.

with that described by Dr. J. S. Flett & Dr. Tempest Anderson,[1] in the West Indies, except that, instead of being subaërial, it occurred at the bottom of the sea. The particles which gave off the steam were not small grains and pebbles, but were masses of 2 or 3 feet or more in length, and having nearly the same specific gravity as sea-water, they rolled as easily as the smaller particles in air. The whole sheet, though composed of large nearly-solid spheres, must have moved almost like a liquid. This reduction of weight caused by the buoyancy of the vesicles would be still further increased, if we allow for the jacketing of the spheroids for a time by a shell of escaping steam.

It seems, therefore, that the lava was in a true spheroidal state, each large drop ejected swelling up independently and forming a pillow more or less surrounded by escaping steam, so that the flowing mass on the sea-bed formed a mobile sheet of rolling spheres, seldom touching one another till they cooled. As soon as the steam condensed, however, water would be sucked into the vesicles, and the pillows would settle down.

### EXPLANATION OF PLATES XXVII & XXVIII.

#### PLATE XXVII.

Photograph of part of the cliff-face at Pentire, in St. Minver, showing several contiguous pillows in a thick mass of lava. In the centre is shown, between the pillows, a cavity afterwards filled with calcite. The pillows are partly moulded on each other, but have not been squeezed into narrow spaces. Most of the sections in this photograph are tangential, and do not intersect central cavities; but one pillow above, and another below, the hammer show this hollow, out of which the calcite has been weathered.

#### PLATE XXVIII.

This plate illustrates the internal structure of a single pillow from the same locality. The section probably is nearly central, and shows the central cavity surrounded by a spongy zone, outside which is seen banded, more or less vesicular rock.

### DISCUSSION.

The PRESIDENT remarked that all the examples of pillow-lavas with which he was acquainted were undoubtedly true lavas, and belonged to submarine eruptions. Some of them, however, must have been poured out in shallow water, as was particularly observable in the case of the Lower Carboniferous basalts of the Fife coast. These lavas were thin sheets, often not more than 15 or 20 feet in thickness, and they, as well as the associated tuffs, were intercalated among shallow-water deposits, such as cyprid-shales and limestones, coal-seams with fire-clays, thin sandstones and ironstones. Some of the basalts had caught up portions of the mud on the sea-bottom, but in others the muddy, sandy, or ashy sediment of the next deposit had fallen into the interspaces between the pillows.

[1] Phil. Trans. Roy. Soc. ser. A, vol. cc (1903) pp. 353–553.

Dr. FLETT remarked that he was under the disadvantage of not having seen the Authors' sections in the field, and there were some respects in which this pillow-lava differed to a certain extent from those with which he was acquainted. It was very highly vesicular and many of the pillows were hollow, and there were strong arguments in support of the hypotheses brought forward. In Anglesey and at Tayvallich hollow pillows occurred, but were few and might be due to weathering. At Saltash and Mullion Island they must be uncommon, for the speaker did not recollect having seen any. The hypothesis contained in the paper rested on facts which might well be believed to be of importance; but in our ignorance of what went on in submarine eruptions, it was difficult to say how far they could be held to account for the phenomena of pillow-formation. The theory propounded recalled to the speaker's memory the description of a submarine eruption off Pantelleria in 1891, when large bombs were projected and, after rolling on the surface of the water in clouds of steam, finally exploded with a loud noise. These hollow bombs presented some analogy to the hollow pillows of Port Isaac.

A study of several of the best-known pillow-lavas of Great Britain had led the speaker to the conclusion that these rocks belonged for the most part to a peculiar group—the 'spilites.' Pillow-formation occurred sometimes in basalts and other rocks, but the best examples were usually spilites. The peculiarities of this group were pointed out by Dr. Teall in describing the spilites of the Southern Uplands of Scotland, namely, that while they were essentially basic rocks, they were rich in oligoclase-felspars. Near Plymouth, some lavas of this type contained phenocrysts of albite. The rocks described by the Authors were of the same character.

Dr. TEALL said that he considered that the communication was an important contribution to our knowledge of pillow-structure. The facts, which were evidently well exposed, had been clearly described and admirably illustrated. When he and Mr. Fox wrote their paper on the rocks of Mullion Island, they were not able to give a satisfactory account of the origin of the structure. The pillows of Mullion Island appeared to agree in form and dimensions with those described by the Authors, but they were much less vesicular, and he did not think that any theory which postulated a low average specific gravity would apply to that case. That the pillows were individualized at the time of consolidation was certain; but he had no clear idea as to how they could be produced so uniformly through a great thickness of rock.

Mr. O. H. EVANS mentioned that the structure described in the paper was well developed in lavas, of probably Mesozoic age, in the Taltal coast-region of the Atacama Desert, in Chile. In the particular instance that he had in mind, the 'pillows' occurred at a height of 900 feet above the sea, in a stratum of fine tuff, between enormous accumulations of igneous agglomerate forming part of a great formation described by Darwin as of submarine volcanic origin. The speaker had noted them, at the time of observation, as being 'volcanic bombs, flattened by pressure ; the weathered examples break up into roughly-concentric rings. Many of them are highly vesicular in the middle, and filled with calcite and epidote. The rock is so greatly epidotized as to be green in colour.' On seeing the specimens and photographs now exhibited, and hearing the Authors' lucid description of the structure, he had little hesitation in concluding that the Chilian example belonged to the same class.

Dr. TEMPEST ANDERSON mentioned two instances of pillow-lava, at Aci Castello in Sicily and Cape Rezkjanos in Iceland, which were both on the sea-shore. A lava-stream which crossed Lake Myvatn, in Northern Iceland, and extended some miles down the valley below the lake, had on its surface a number of spiracles. Some of those in the lake had thrown up cinder-cones 200 or 300 feet high, the ejecting agent being steam furnished by the water in the lake and the mud in its floor. The smaller ones, chiefly on the lava-stream below the lake, where the action was less violent, had thrown out masses of lava comparable in size and shape to pillow-lava, which had formed small cones. As these had been built upon subaërially, there was no coating of mud to separate the masses. If the process had taken place wholly under water, the necessary mud might have been present, and the structure seen at Aci Castello might have been exactly reproduced.

Mr. G. BARROW drew attention to the similarity in mode of arrangement of the vesicles in these pillow-lavas and those in the broken-open slag-blocks of which the great Tees Breakwater was built. These blocks were obtained from the blast-furnaces, the slag running into small box-shaped iron trucks. In ordinary practice these trucks were emptied so soon as they were filled, and while the bulk of the slag was still molten ; but, when wanted for the break-water, some had to stand for several hours, until a sufficient number of truckfuls had been obtained to make up a train, which was then taken by an engine to the end of the breakwater. In this way, the whole of the slag in some of the trucks became completely solidified. When broken open the blocks proved to be vesicular throughout, the vesicles being arranged roughly parallel to the outer walls of the block, just as the vesicles were parallel to the outer wall of the pillows in the lavas ; and, further, the central part of the slag-blocks was the most coarsely vesicular—in fact, almost hollow. When broken up by the sea, fragments of this slag floated away, some drifting to various parts of the east coast of England, others even to the shores of Holland : they were supposed to be of volcanic origin, and a fair number were brought to the Jermyn-Street Museum, where their true origin was finally determined.

A point of special importance was the fact that, when the liquid slag flowed into the truck, no explosive gas was given off; the slag flowed very much like water. It was clear that, if gas was present at all, it was occluded. The speaker thought that these gases were set free, if not actually developed, only at the moment of solidification or crystallization. The slag-bubbles or vesicles were, on the whole, much larger than those of the pillow-lavas, suggesting that the latter were formed under considerably greater pressure. That the lavas were free to move was clear, and it seemed that the combination of freedom and pressure could be best obtained on the floor of a tolerably-deep sea, as the Authors suggested. The amount of occluded gas that could be present in a perfectly-solid rock had been shown by Mr. Harker in the Geological-Survey Memoir on Skye, in a case where freedom to move was far less and the pressure clearly much greater.

Mr. USSHER stated that the pillow-lavas of Devon and Cornwall were emitted during the later stages of the eruptions of the Ashprington Series, which in the Totnes area began during the lower stages of the Middle Devonian. Traced westwards, the Middle Devonian eruptions became less frequent and those in the Upper Devonian more important. Nowhere throughout their whole outcrop had he seen pillow-lavas of so great a thickness as those in the area described by the Authors. The pillow-lavas of the Plymouth area south of Saltash alluded to by Dr. Flett, although well-developed, were not very thick, and were accompanied by tuffs in which he had last Easter found a fragment of slate with *Styliola*, a fossil characterizing the lower grey beds of the Upper Devonian in the Plymouth and Padstow areas. South of Saltash, near Henn Point, several beds of chert were interbedded with the pillow-lavas, the intercalation forming a small triangular mass in the upper part of the low cliff. In the extension of these spilite-lavas, pillow-structure had very seldom been detected; but rocks of this character at or about the same horizon were found at intervals, from Newton Abbot westwards to the district described.

Mr. CLEMENT REID, replying for both Authors, thanked the Fellows for the reception of their paper. Dr. Flett had remarked on the slight resemblance between this eruption and that of Mont Pelé; the only resemblance that they suggested was in the steam-cushions on which in both cases the fragments rolled.

Pillow-lavas were usually associated with fine-grained marine strata, and with deposits such as radiolarian cherts which suggested some depth of water. Perhaps the varying types of pillow might be connected with the different depth of water into which lavas had been ejected, and the consequent variations of pressure and temperature in the boiling water surrounding them.

14. *The* ST. DAVID'S-HEAD 'ROCK-SERIES' (PEMBROKESHIRE).   By
JAMES VINCENT ELSDEN, B.Sc., F.G.S. (Read February 5th,
1908.)

[PLATES XXIX–XXXII—MICROSCOPE-SECTIONS.]

#### CONTENTS.

|                                                          | Page |
|----------------------------------------------------------|------|
| I. Introduction ........................................ | 273  |
| II. General Description ................................ | 273  |
| III. Characters of the Rock-Types ..................... | 277  |
|    (a) The Basic Type.                    |      |
|    (b) The Acid, that is, Quartz-bearing, Type. |  |
|    (c) The Intermediate Type.             |      |
|    (d) The Aplite-Veins.                  |      |
| IV. Petrographical Details ............................ | 285  |
| V. Relations of the Rock-Types ........................ | 290  |
| VI. Age of the Intrusions.............................. | 292  |
| VII. Summary and Conclusion ........................... | 292  |

### I. INTRODUCTION.

IN a former paper, communicated to this Society,[1] I gave a
general description of the St. David's-Head intrusions.  On that
occasion I expressed the opinion that this area would repay a more
detailed investigation, and I have since made a systematic examination of these rocks, both in the field and in the laboratory,
confining my attention to the two large parallel intrusions forming
the St. David's-Head and Carn-Llidi masses respectively.  With the
exception of the general account given in my former paper, these
rocks do not appear to have been previously described in any
detail.

Several distinct types of rock occur in these masses, and it is the
purpose of this paper to discuss their differences with the object of
examining the problem of their origin.  Briefly, the main point to
be determined is whether these are to be regarded as an igneous
complex, or whether they constitute a 'rock-series,' derived from a
common magma by some process of differentiation.

### II. GENERAL DESCRIPTION.

The two intrusions take the form of vertical sills intruded
between almost perpendicular shales of Arenig age.  They are
composed of at least four types of rock, which, although closely
allied, present marked mineralogical differences, often easily
distinguishable in the field.   There is a dark, basic variety,
typically seen in parts of Carn Llidi, Carn Llidi Bechan, Carn Hen,

---

[1] 'On the Igneous Rocks occurring between St. David's Head & Strumble
Head' Quart. Journ. Geol. Soc. vol. lxi (1905) p. 579.

Fig. 1.

Geological Sketch-map of the
St. DAVID'S HEAD AREA.

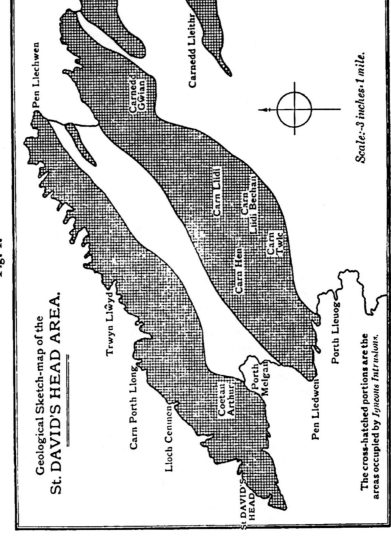

Pen Llechwen

Carnedd
Gwian

Carnedd Lleithr

Carn Llidi

Carn
Llidi Bechan

Carn Hen

Carn
Twlc

Trwyn Llŵyd

Carn Porth Llong

Lloch Cennen

Coetan
Arthur

Porth
Melgan

St DAVID'S
HEAD

Pen Lledwen

Porth Lleuog

Scale:-3 inches:1 mile.

The cross-hatched portions are the
areas occupied by Igneous Intrusions.

and occasionally at Pen Lledwen and in parts of the St. David's-Head mass. This melanocratic type is moderately coarse in grain. It stands in conspicuous contrast to a leucocratic variety, often much coarser in grain, with abundant felspar and more or less quartz. This latter type forms only occasional streaks in the Carn-Llidi mass, but in the St. David's-Head mass it occupies a far larger area and becomes the predominant variety. It is especially prominent in the strip adjoining the coast in a north-easterly direction from St. David's Head.

In addition to these apparently extreme varieties, a considerable bulk of the masses seems to be of an intermediate character, somewhat variable in colour and texture, but easily distinguishable in the field from either of the above-mentioned types. This forms the predominant rock in the Carn-Llidi mass, but in the St. David's-Head mass it is subordinate to the more acid type. Finally, there are some thin veins of a fine-grained rock looking like an aplite. These, however, do not seem to be very abundant.

The above-described types of rock might easily be looked upon as a normal result of differentiation *in situ*, as typically exemplified in the gabbro of Carrock Fell, and in many other cases where basic rocks exhibit a coarse-grained acidic core. A more detailed study in the field, however, scarcely supports this view. There is not only no border-segregation in the mass as a whole, but the acid type seems to have a somewhat capricious distribution, passing occasionally by very sudden transitions into the more basic varieties, among which it can sometimes be seen to lie in irregular bands, having a fairly-sharp line of demarcation. These acid streaks are not confined to the heart of the mass, but occasionally extend into the neighbourhood of the marginal contact-zones. In a general sense, however, they conform to the strike of the intrusions. The proportions in which the extreme types occur are locally very different, the more acid rock being far more abundant than the basic rock in the westernmost part of the Carn-Llidi mass, and in the eastern part of the St. David's-Head mass. The acid rock, in short, does not appear to represent merely the residual mother-liquor occupying the core of the intrusion.

It is desirable at this stage to examine the field-relations of these rocks in greater detail. The shales at the junctions of the intrusions are indurated, but no very extensive mineral alteration is apparent in hand-specimens. The igneous rock at the contact has a fine-grained sahlband, which can be followed for a distance of several feet into the mass. Microscopic examination shows that some assimilation of the country-rock has taken place. The character of the intrusion is considerably modified at the margins. The felspars, in small ragged laths, have an approximately-straight extinction. They are apparently more acid than those of the main mass of the rock, and appear to be oligoclase. Augite in small crystalline grains is abundant, and the iron-ores, which are but moderately developed, usually have the appearance of magnetite.

Enstatite, if it was ever present, is now represented by pale
irregular patches of chloritic matter.   There are also some partly-
digested fragments of country-rock and some quartz-xenocrysts.
The latter have corroded outlines, fringed with a shell of small
augite-crystals, precisely similar to those noticed by Mr. Harker in
the marginal part of the Skye gabbro (see Pl. XXX, fig. 1).   These
are evidently undigested remnants of the country-rock : they occur
in all my slides from the contact-zone.   A series of slides was
prepared from this zone beneath the south-eastern flank of Carn
Llidi, in order to ascertain, if possible, to what extent assimilation
had taken place.   Quartz-xenocrysts can thus be traced to a distance
of about 6 feet from the margin, beyond which distance rhombic
pyroxene begins to be well individualized, and, except in texture,
the rock mineralogically resembles that of the main mass.

An interesting point in connexion with these marginal rocks is
the occasional appearance of a delicate micropegmatite within 10
yards of the margin, where the grain of the rock is still fine, owing
to rapid cooling.   This occurrence of micropegmatite so near the
margin, its general distribution throughout the more acid portions
of these intrusions, and its absence from the aplite-veins, are
significant in connexion with theories respecting the origin of
granophyric structure.[1]

On the whole, the chief marginal modifications which these
intrusions exhibit seem to be the result of rapid cooling, combined
with a certain amount of assimilation of country-rock.

Structural modifications.—There are no true porphyritic
crystals in the marginal zones, from which it may be inferred that
the magma was intruded in a wholly liquid state.   In a general
sense the texture of the rock becomes coarser in proportion to the
distance from the cooling surfaces : but there are cases where coarse
and fine-grained rocks are in close juxtaposition.   The rocks vary
in texture from subophitic to granular, and are occasionally almost
pan-idiomorphic (see Pl. XXX, fig. 5).

A distinct banded structure is exhibited in parts of the St.
David's-Head mass.   This is particularly evident in the neighbourhood of the cromlech known as Coetan Arthur, north-west of
Porth Melgan.   The bands consist of thin alternate layers of
light and dark rock, often not more than an inch wide.   On
the weathered surface the light bands stand out in relief, and
contrast strongly with darker and more decomposed layers between
them.   The strike of the foliation is approximately parallel to that
of the intrusion.   Thin sections of the light and dark bands show
that they differ mainly in the relative proportions of their constituent minerals.   In the light bands felspars and quartz predominate, while in the dark bands pyroxenes are more abundant.
The distinction agrees generally with that displayed by the basic
and acid types of rock described above.   The minerals in the banded

[1] See R. H. Rastall, 'The Buttermere & Ennerdale Granophyre' Quart.
Journ. Geol. Soc. vol. lxii (1906) p. 270.

rock show no evidence of orientation, from which it is concluded that these bands consolidated after the motion, by which they were produced, had ceased. This was not the case in other parts of the mass, as, for example, along the coast between Carn Porth Llong and Trwyn Llwŷd. Here we find evidence that some amount of movement was in progress during crystallization, in some parts a marked flow-structure being seen (Pl. XXX, fig. 4), and in other cases the crystals themselves having been broken and disturbed. These evidences of movement have only been noticed in parts of the St. David's-Head mass. In the Carn-Llidi intrusion I found no appreciable signs of banding, flow-structure, or crystallization under dynamic stress.

The occurrence of banded structure has an important bearing upon the origin of the different rock-types. Banded gabbros have been described from many localities. They have been noted by Sir Archibald Geikie and by Mr. Harker in the Cuillin Hills (Skye),[1] by the latter in the Carrock-Fell gabbro,[2] and by numerous other observers in various parts of the world. The structure seems to be best explained by fluxion in a heterogeneous magma; and the conclusion is, therefore, drawn that, in that part of the St. David's-Head intrusion where this structure is exhibited, an acid[3] and a basic magma coexisted in parallel bands, which consolidated before diffusion had time to reduce them to a state of homogeneity.

In the Carn-Llidi mass, although there seems to be no definite banding, there are acid and basic streaks, forming irregular lenticles, roughly aligned in the general direction of the intrusion. In many parts more or less perfect mixture seems to have taken place, the extreme types being then scarcely recognizable.

It is possible that local variations in viscosity played the chief part in causing these differences. Viscosity is determined not only by temperature, but also by the composition of the magma, the presence of magmatic water, and other causes, all of which factors might vary locally. Extreme fluidity, aided by a high temperature or other causes, would tend to promote diffusion and homogeneity. This result seems to have been largely realized in the neighbourhood of Carn Twlc and Carnedd Gŵian, while at Pen Lledwen, and in parts of Carn Llidi and St. David's Head, schlieren are more in evidence, as if the magma here was in a more pasty condition.

### III. Characters of the Rock-Types.

In order to arrive at a more intimate knowledge of the different rock-types exhibited in this area, not only were thin slices prepared for microscopic examination, but a representative specimen of each

---

[1] 'The Tertiary Igneous Rocks of Skye' Mem. Geol. Surv. U. K. 1904, p. 91.

[2] Quart. Journ. Geol. Soc. vol. l (1894) p. 319.

[3] The term 'acid' is here used to denote rocks containing primary quartz. The silica-percentage is rarely high enough to entitle these rocks to a place in the acid group as generally understood.

of the types was selected for chemical analysis. I give below the results obtained, reserving for another section of this paper the discussion of the petrographical features in detail. In carrying out the chemical analyses the procedure advocated by Mr. W. F. Hillebrand was followed. The alkalies were determined by the Lawrence-Smith method, which, with proper care, is believed to give very trustworthy results. The combined water, in the presence of a considerable percentage of ferrous iron, could not be accurately determined by ignition; and either Penfield's method, or, in some cases, the method of direct absorption was accordingly followed. For the iron-estimations reduction by sulphuretted hydrogen and titration by permanganate was adopted; and titanium was estimated by the colour-method, with hydrogen-peroxide and standard titanium-solution.

### (a) The Basic Type.

Specimens of this type collected from Carn Hen, Pen Lledwen, Carn Llidi, Carnedd Gwian, Lloch Ceninen, and elsewhere in this area, show a close agreement in mineralogical character. The rocks consist of a basic plagioclase, rhombic and monoclinic pyroxene, ilmenite, some biotite, and a little apatite. The felspars give fairly-high extinctions measured from the albite twinning-planes, and appear to belong to the labradorite-species. Rhombic pyroxene showing marked pleochroism, but less ferriferous than hypersthene, is about equal in quantity to augite. The latter mineral is brown in colour, often shows strong basal striation, and very frequently is normally twinned. Biotite is present in all the specimens, but in relatively-small quantity. Ilmenite is but moderately abundant. In order of consolidation felspar seems invariably to have preceded the other minerals, penetrating both pyroxenes, and moulding both ilmenite and biotite.

The chemical composition of this rock was found to be as follows:—

|  | Per cent. | Molecular proportions. |
|---|---|---|
| $SiO_2$ | 49·67 | 828 |
| $TiO_2$ | 1·13 | 14 |
| $Al_2O_3$ | 12·46 | 121 |
| $Fe_2O_3$ | 1·77 | 11 |
| FeO | 8·71 | 121 |
| MnO | 0·09 | 1 |
| CaO | 9·57 | 171 |
| MgO | 10·50 | 262 |
| $Na_2O$ | 2·42 | 40 |
| $K_2O$ | 0·63 | 6 |
| $P_2O_5$ | 0·13 | 1 |
| $H_2O$ − | 0·37 |  |
| $H_2O$ + | 2·82 |  |
| $CO_2$ | trace | Specific gravity = 2·96 |
| Total | 100·27 |  |

Calculating the mineralogical composition of this rock from the molecular proportions, the following approximate result is obtained, omitting water :—

| | | |
|---|---|---|
| Albite | 20·9 | } = 40·9 Labradorite. |
| Anorthite | 20·0 | |
| Bronzite | 22·5 | |
| Augite | 22·2 | |
| Biotite | 6·5 | |
| Ilmenite and magnetite | 4·1 | |
| Apatite | 0·3 | |
| Total | 96·5 | |

That this is a thoroughly-basic rock is evident. Although no olivine was recognized in any of the specimens, the invariable presence of biotite in this type and its absence from all other types is significant, and seems to suggest that at a certain concentration the orthosilicate-molecule may, in combination with potash and alumina, form biotite in place of olivine.

This rock is interesting, as being of a type not very common in the British Isles, where distinctly-basic rocks of the gabbro-class, with prominent rhombic pyroxene, have not often been noted. The analysis shows considerable resemblance to certain rocks from the United States and elsewhere, described as norites, analyses of some of which are tabulated below :—

| | I. | II. | III. |
|---|---|---|---|
| $SiO_2$ | 49·67 | 48·23 | 49·28 |
| $TiO_2$ | 1·13 | 1·00 | 0·87 |
| $Al_2O_3$ | 12·46 | 18·26 | 15·76 |
| $Fe_2O_3$ | 1·77 | 1·26 | 1·86 |
| FeO | 8·71 | 6·10 | 8·94 |
| MnO | 0·09 | ... | 0·20 |
| CaO | 9·57 | 9·39 | 10·51 |
| MgO | 10·50 | 10·84 | 8·21 |
| $Na_2O$ | 2·42 | 1·34 | 2·58 |
| $K_2O$ | 0·63 | 0·73 | 0·76 |
| $P_2O_5$ | 0·13 | 0·07 | 0·11 |
| $H_2O-$ | 0·37 | 0·26 | 0·47 |
| $H_2O+$ | 2·82 | 2·00 | 1·10 |
| $CO_2$ | trace | 0·43 | 0·36 |
| Totals | 100·27 | 99·91 | 99·01 |

I. Biotite-norite, St. David's Head (Pembrokeshire). Analysis by A. V. Elsden.
II. Bronzite-norite, Crystal Falls (Michigan). Analysis by G. Steiger, Journ. Geol. Chicago, vol. vi (1898) p. 382.
III. Hornblende-norite, Prospect Hill, Litchfield (Conn.). Analysis by W. F. Hillebrand, Bull. U.S. Geol. Surv. No. 228 (1904) p. 43.

In my former paper I called this rock a 'biotite-norite,' and, in spite of the vague signification which the term norite has acquired, it seems the most convenient name to adopt in this case. In both chemical and mineral constitution this rock differs essentially from the normal gabbros and diabases. The analysis shows

a high magnesia-percentage as compared with both the Carrock-
Fell gabbro and the Whin-Sill diabase, both of which are enstatite-
bearing rocks, and the rock is apparently higher in magnesia than
the Skye gabbros examined by Mr. Harker.

An interesting feature also of this rock is, that by reversing the
alkalies a typical absarokite-magma would result.

Illustrations of this type are shown in Pl. XXIX, figs. 1 & 2.

## (b) The Acid Type.

The leucocratic variety, as mentioned above (p. 275), is most
abundant in the St. David's-Head mass, although streaks and
irregular patches occur in the Carn-Llidi mass. For chemical
analysis a sample was selected from near Trwyn Llŵyd. The
following is its percentage-composition :—

|  | Per cent. | Molecular proportions. |
|---|---|---|
| $SiO_2$ | 52·31 | 872 |
| $TiO_2$ | 1·45 | 17 |
| $Al_2O_3$ | 17·38 | 169 |
| $Fe_2O_3$ | 2·99 | 18 |
| $FeO$ | 5·21 | 72 |
| $MnO$ | 0·22 | 3 |
| $CaO$ | 9·95 | 177 |
| $MgO$ | 3·76 | 94 |
| $Na_2O$ | 3·96 | 64 |
| $K_2O$ | 0·75 | 8 |
| $P_2O_5$ | 0·20 | 1 |
| $H_2O-$ | 0·30 | |
| $H_2O+$ | 2·05 | |
| $CO_2$ | trace | |
| $Cl$ | 0·02 | |
| | 100·55 | Specific gravity = 2·87 |
| Less O=Cl | ·01 | |
| Total | 100·54 | |

The theoretical mineralogical composition calculated from these
figures is as follows :—

| Quartz | 2·1 | |
|---|---|---|
| Orthoclase | 4·4 | |
| Albite | 33·5 | } = 60·4 Plagioclase. |
| Anorthite | 26·9 | |
| Augite and hornblende | 17·5 | |
| Bronzite | 6·1 | |
| Magnetite and ilmenite | 6·6 | |
| Apatite | 0·4 | |
| Total | 97·5 | |

This type differs from the basic type of Carn Hen in its greater
acidity and distinctly-higher proportion of salic minerals. Free
quartz is present, and the potash indicates some orthoclase. Micropegmatite is fairly abundant. The felspars belong to rather acid
varieties of plagioclase, although, when considered together, they

scarcely reach the composition of andesine. Some zoning of the felspars may generally be noticed in the neighbourhood of quartz-areas, the inner zones being apparently more basic than the later separations. There is no biotite, but some hornblende occurs as an accessory constituent. The proportion of apatite is generally somewhat greater than is indicated in the particular sample selected for analysis.

This rock appears to be a typical enstatite-bearing quartz-gabbro. It is often very coarse in grain. The proportion of rhombic to monoclinic pyroxene varies greatly in different specimens, as also does the quantity of free silica, which is rather less than the average in the specimen analysed. It is probable that the greater viscosity of this type facilitated clotting. There is evidence, also, as mentioned above (p. 277), that some movement was going on in parts of the magma during solidification. These causes alone would account for considerable local differences in composition.

Illustrations of this type are shown in Pl. XXIX, fig. 5 & Pl. XXX, fig. 3.

### (c) The Intermediate Type.

Excluding the aplite-veins, the above-described rocks seem to form respectively the basic and acid extremes of the main mass of these intrusions. A considerable proportion of the rock, however, has intermediate characters, and differs from the basic type, on the one hand, by the presence of a little more silica and the absence of biotite; and from the acid rocks, on the other, by the scarcity of hornblende and quartz, although a little of the latter mineral (probably in some cases of secondary origin) is sometimes visible. Apatite, although more conspicuous than in the basic type, is less abundant than in the acid varieties. There seems to be, also, a gradual passage from this intermediate variety into each of the extreme types, making it somewhat difficult to select a typical example for analysis. The specimen taken for this purpose is a rather compact, fine-grained rock from the eastern flank of Carn Llidi, about 10 yards from the margin.

The following is the result:—

|  | Per cent. | Molecular proportions. |
|---|---|---|
| $SiO_2$ | 50·55 | 842 |
| $TiO_2$ | 1·58 | 19 |
| $Al_2O_3$ | 15·00 | 144 |
| $Fe_2O_3$ | 2·54 | 15 |
| FeO | 7·90 | 109 |
| CaO | 7·85 | 140 |
| MgO | 6·25 | 156 |
| $Na_2O$ | 3·53 | 56 |
| $K_2O$ | 1·10 | 11 |
| $P_2O_5$ | n. d. | |
| $H_2O-$ | 0·55 | |
| $H_2O+$ | 3·14 | Specific gravity = 2·92 |
| Total | 99·99 | |

Calculating from these figures, the following mineralogical composition is obtained :—

| | | |
|---|---|---|
| Orthoclase | 6·11 | |
| Albite | 29·34 | } =50·74 Plagioclase. |
| Anorthite | 21·40 | |
| Augite | 13·92 | |
| Bronzite | 18·54 | |
| Ilmenite and magnetite | 6·36 | |
| Total | 95·67 | |

It is evident from the foregoing percentages that the plagioclase is of a more basic type than that occurring in the previously-described rock. There is also a larger proportion of potash, a result which would scarcely be expected. Micropegmatite is rarely exhibited.

The resemblance between this analysis and that of a specimen of the Whin Sill, described by Dr. Teall,[1] is very striking. The two are tabulated together below for comparison :—

| | Specimen from Carn Llidi. | Whin Sill (Roman Station). |
|---|---|---|
| $SiO_2$ | 50·55 | 50·71 |
| $TiO_2$ | 1·58 | 1·92 |
| $Al_2O_3$ | 15·00 | 14·78 |
| $Fe_2O_3$ | 2·54 | 3·52 |
| FeO | 7·90 | 8·95 |
| MnO | n. d. | 0·31 |
| CaO | 7·85 | 8·21 |
| MgO | 6·25 | 5·90 |
| $Na_2O$ | 3·53 | 2·76 |
| $K_2O$ | 1·10 | 1·39 |
| $H_2O-$ | 0·55 | 1·78 |
| $H_2O+$ | 3·14 | — |
| Totals | 99·99 | 100·23 |
| Specific gravity = | 2·92 | 2·94 |

There is also a very marked similarity between the petrographical characters of these rocks, although the felspar of the St. David's-Head specimen seems to be rather more basic than the andesine of the Whin Sill. It is still more striking that the above-named specimen of the Whin-Sill rock contains bronzite, whereas the Cauldron-Snout variety, of slightly-different composition, has only the monoclinic variety of pyroxene. The presence of the rhombic variety seems here, as at St. David's Head, to have been mainly determined by the relative proportions of lime and magnesia, as suggested by Prof. J. H. L. Vogt.

Illustrations of this type are shown in Pl. XXIX, figs. 3 & 4.

[1] See Quart. Journ. Geol. Soc. vol. xl (1884) p. 654.

## (d) The Aplite-Veins.

There are also some fine-grained veins which penetrate the acid type of the main rock. These are very thin, and by no means common. The specimen selected for analysis occurs near the northern margin of the Carn-Llidi mass, not far from Pen Lledwen. Under the microscope it is seen to consist mainly of felspar and quartz, with some disseminated iron-oxide, but without any ferromagnesian minerals. The felspars have square-shaped idiomorphic outlines and are usually rather turbid, but occasionally they show plagioclase-striation. The quartz is interstitial, and no micropegmatite is visible. The junction with the coarser gabbro seems to be well-defined in hand-specimens, but under the microscope it is less definite, the aplite passing gradually into the intersertal material of the coarser rock. It is evidently, therefore, of contemporaneous origin. These aplite-veins have not been noticed in the more basic portions of the mass, but may nevertheless occur.

A chemical analysis of this rock gave the following result :—

|  | Per cent. | Molecular proportions. |
|---|---|---|
| $SiO_2$ | 71·18 | 1186 |
| $TiO_2$ | 0·48 | 144 |
| $Al_2O_3$ | 14·89 | 6 |
| $Fe_2O_3$ | 2·11 | 13 |
| FeO | 1·21 | 16 |
| CaO | 0·82 | 14 |
| MgO | 0·14 | 3 |
| $Na_2O$ | 6·85 | 112 |
| $K_2O$ | 1·70 | 18 |
| $H_2O-$ | 0·24 | |
| $H_2O+$ | 0 64 | |
| Total | 100·26 | |

Specific gravity = 2·62

The above composition admits of the following mineral proportions :—

| | |
|---|---|
| Quartz | 22·68 |
| Orthoclase | 10·01 |
| Albite | 58·69 |
| Anorthite | 3·90 |
| Magnetite and ilmenite | 3·22 |
| Total | 98·50 |

In apportioning the molecules there is a small excess of alumina, ferric oxide, and magnesia, which is probably accounted for by the presence of hydrated decomposition-products of the felspar, by which the free silica would of course be proportionately reduced. The rock is evidently a soda-aplite (see Pl. XXIX, fig. 6). Since no free orthoclase can be detected microscopically, this mineral is possibly included in the albite-crystals, either in solid solution or in perthitic intergrowth. Analyses of albite-crystals often show a certain percentage both of potash and of lime.[1]

Soda-aplites of somewhat analogous composition have been described by Dr. J. D. Falconer in rocks from the Bathgate and Linlithgow Hills.[2] Our specimen is also not unlike Mr. Spurr's tonalite-aplite or yukonite, from the Yukon River.[3] Percentage analyses of these and other soda-aplites are tabulated below, for comparison :—

|  | I. | II. | III. | IV. | V. |
|---|---|---|---|---|---|
| $SiO_2$ ......... | 71·18 | 71·26 | 74·79 | 77·00 | 74·21 |
| $TiO_2$ ......... | 0·48 | 0·28 | 0·17 | 0·07 | 0·30 |
| $Al_2O_3$ ........ | 14·89 | 11·87 | 12·59 | 13·60 | 14·47 |
| $Fe_2O_3$ ........ | 2·11 | 0·10 } | 1·19 | 0·41 | 0·35 |
| FeO ......... | 1·21 | 2·12 } |  | ... | 0·50 |
| CaO ......... | 0·82 | 2·88 | 3·58 | 0·70 | 1·71 |
| MgO ......... | 0·14 | 1·08 | 0·31 | 0·00 | 0·28 |
| $Na_2O$ ......... | 6·85 | 6·73 | 5·10 | 5·78 | 7·62 |
| $K_2O$ ......... | 1·70 | 0·05 | 0·21 | 1·50 | 0·10 |
| $P_2O_5$ ......... | n. d. | 0·10 | trace | trace | 0·07 |
| $H_2O-$ ...... | 0·24 | 0·62 | 0·09 | 0·23 | 0·15 |
| $H_2O+$ ...... | 0·64 | 2·71 | 1·03 | 0·48 | 0·23 |
| Totals ... | 100·26 | 99·80 | 99·06 | 99·77 | 99·99 |

I. Soda-aplite, St. David's Head (Pembrokeshire). Analysis by A. V. Elsden.

II. Segregation-vein, Kettlestoun Quarry. Described by J. D. Falconer, Trans. Roy. Soc. Edin. vol. xlv, pt. i (1906) p. 147.

III. Tonalite-aplite (yukonite). Analysis by H. N. Stokes, Bull. U.S. Geol. Surv. No. 228 (1904) p. 270.

IV. Aplite (alsbachite), Fallou Hill, Enfield (Mass.). Analysis by G. Steiger, ibid. p. 40.

V. Soda-granulite, Mariposa (California). Analysis by W. F. Hillebrand, ibid. p. 240.

As bearing upon the origin of the aplite-veins of St. David's Head, it is important to note that these do not resemble in composition the intersertal portion of the main mass. In addition to the aplite-veins there are also some conspicuous veins of quartzite, often showing great regularity and running in parallel bands in the coarser gabbros. These sometimes reach a foot in width: they must be regarded as secondary, in the present state of our knowledge.

I have now shown that in the St. David's-Head intrusions several types of rock, chemically and mineralogically distinct, are represented. These results may be summarized in the following tabular view :—

[1] See Bull. U.S. Geol. Surv. No. 228 (1904) 'Analyses of Rocks from the Laboratory of the U.S. Geol. Surv. 1880 to 1903' by F. W. Clarke, pp. 24, 41.
[2] Trans. Roy. Soc. Edin. vol. xlv, pt. i (1906) p. 147.
[3] Bull. U.S. Geol. Surv. No. 168 (1900) p. 229.

| • | Plagioclase. | Rhombic Pyroxene. | Monoclinic Pyroxene. | Iron-Ores. | Biotite. | Hornblende. | Apatite. | Quartz. | Orthoclase. |
|---|---|---|---|---|---|---|---|---|---|
| Basic ...... | — | — | — | — | — | | — | | |
| Medium ... | — | — | — | — | | — | — | — | |
| Acid ...... | — | — | — | — | | — | — | — | — |
| Aplite...... | — | | | — | | | — | — | |

## IV. PETROGRAPHICAL DETAILS.

I propose now to call attention to some features of petrographical interest shown in these rocks.

Felspars.—Beginning with the felspars, these are usually rather unsatisfactory for optical study, being generally somewhat turbid, perhaps owing to the fact that outcrop-specimens only can be examined. Where satisfactory extinctions can be measured, these point to the presence of labradorite in the most basic types; but the proportion of the albite-molecule increases in the more acid varieties, so that all gradations from labradorite through andesine to oligoclase in the zone of assimilation, and nearly pure albite in the aplite-veins, can be traced. The chemical analyses tend to confirm this; but, as the felspars of the more acid types are sometimes zoned by a species of lower refractive index than quartz, it is clear that even in the same rock they are not always of uniform composition. Orthoclase may be assumed to be a constituent of the micropegmatite, which often characteristically frames the felspars in the acid types. The alteration of the felspars presents some noteworthy features. In most cases the alteration-product is granular and opaque. Generally epidote is rare, but occasionally this mineral becomes conspicuous, as along the northern margin of the St. David's-Head mass, where veins of epidosite occur. One of the most interesting changes in the felspar, occasionally exhibited, is the development of a mineral giving rather square-shaped sections and rectangular cleavages, which seems to form in company with quartz from the breaking-down of large felspar-crystals. This mineral has not yet been identified with certainty. In my former paper, where I was relying upon indifferent material, its straight extinction, refractive index, cleavages, and birefringence led me to think that this mineral might be one of the scapolite-

group. With the more favourable specimens now available this
conclusion has proved to have been wrong, for the mineral is biaxial.
Dr. J. S. Flett has very kindly compared my specimens with still
more favourable examples found by him in another locality.
Although many of the physical characters point to prehnite, a
chemical analysis will probably be necessary before a definite
determination can be made (see Pl. XXX, fig. 6).

*Pyroxenes.*—Next to the felspars the pyroxenes are the most
abundantly represented, and their characters are remarkably uniform
wherever they occur. They are absent from the aplite-veins.
Rhombic pyroxene is usually present, sometimes in the form of a
ferriferous enstatite, with the pleochroism of bronzite; but in many
cases it is represented by bastite-pseudomorphs (see Pl. XXXI,
fig. 2). It also seems to be occasionally changed to a fibrous transparent pseudomorph of high birefringence, apparently one of the
amphiboles. A few sphene-granules are sometimes enclosed in the
rhombic pyroxenes. Enstatite generally crystallized later than the
felspars, by which it is often penetrated. Generally it clearly
preceded the monoclinic pyroxene; occasionally it, as certainly,
followed that mineral, and encloses it (see Pl. XXX, fig. 2); while
often the two forms are crystallographically intergrown, as was
also observed by Dr. Teall in the Whin-Sill rock.[1] Here and there
are twins, one component of which is bronzite and the other augite
(see Pl. XXXII, figs. 1, 2, 3, & 5). In this case the plane of composition appears to be the orthopinacoid of the latter. The variable
sequence of crystallization, and the frequent intergrowths with
augite seem to lend support to the views of Prof. Vogt, who has
shown that upon theoretical grounds, and on the assumption that
the crystallization-curves of the ferriferous rhombic and monoclinic
pyroxenes belong to Roozeboom's Type V, the sequence of these
minerals should be dependent upon the relative proportions of lime
and magnesia present in the magma.[2] In this case the simultaneous
separation of these minerals, as shown by intergrowths and compound twins, might represent the eutectic composition. The
monoclinic pyroxene is pale-brown in thin section. Usually it is
remarkably free from alteration, showing no uralite-fringes, and
possessing the birefringence of a perfectly-fresh ferriferous augite, the
maximum value of $\gamma-\alpha$ being about 0·022, as tested by Dr. Michel
Lévy's colour-diagram. The maximum extinction-angle is about 40°.
No pleochroism has been detected. The most characteristic
inclusions are numerous rounded fragments of a paler pyroxene,
generally altered to greenish pseudomorphs. These seem often to
be optically oriented parallel to the *c* axis of the crystal: to these
I shall refer again. There are at least two distinct varieties of
augite, distinguished by the presence or absence of a well-marked

[1] Quart. Journ. Geol. Soc. vol. xl (1884) p. 649.
[2] 'Silicatschmelzlösungen' pt. i (1903) p. 129 & *ibid.* pt. ii (1904) p. 109
(Vidensk. Selsk. Skrifter Christiania).

striation parallel to the basal plane, often called the sahlite-striation. Very rarely there seem to be imperfect indications of diallagic striation, in the form of a pinacoidal parting. The striated and unstriated types are generally both present. The striated structure can also be detected, although to a less extent, in the more ophitic types (see Pl. XXXI, figs. 5 & 6). In this respect these rocks differ from those described by Mr. Harker from Skye.[1] I have not been able to find here any corroboration of his suggestion that this structure may possibly be connected with the depth at which consolidation took place; for it is by no means confined to the heart of the intrusions. There is here good material for studying the structure in all its forms; and the conclusion seems to be necessary that, although the schillerization, by which this structure is rendered conspicuous, is a secondary feature, the structure itself is primary. That a certain amount of schillerization is necessary to develop the structure seems to be indicated by its frequent patchy occurrence in the same crystal. Occasionally it is only exhibited along the course of minute cracks and irregular fissures, where incipient alteration might be expected to take place. That the structure is not entirely secondary seems to be indicated by the occasional occurrence of striated and unstriated augite intergrown together, in which case the unstriated augite usually fringes the striated form, and is, therefore, of later growth (see Pl. XXXI, fig. 6). Examples also occur in which twinned crystals, instead of exhibiting the normal herring-bone structure, show the basal striation only upon one component. In other cases, an unstriated augite-crystal includes a corroded fragment of the striated kind. There appears, also, to be some relation between the occurrence of striated structure and the development of enstatite. Thus crystallographic intergrowths of augite and enstatite are common, but I have not observed enstatite intergrown with a striated augite. This conclusion, however, has only the support of negative evidence.

Dr. Teall, in his description of this structure in the augite of the Whin Sill, has suggested the possibility of its representing an ultra-microscopic crystallographic intergrowth of rhombic and monoclinic pyroxene, analogous to the perthitic structure of some felspars. This view is to some extent supported by the observations of Dr. A. Osann[2] and Dr. A. H. Phillips,[3] who conclude that it is due to primary polysynthetic twinning. A similar origin has been advocated by Prof. W. Wahl,[4] who detected, in specimens of diabase from Föglö (Åland), examples of augite in which the striæ, instead of continuing from edge to edge of the crystal, terminate sharply in places against the prismatic cleavage. I have noticed many such cases in the rocks now under discussion. I have also found examples such as Prof. Wahl describes, in which a

[1] 'The Tertiary Igneous Rocks of Skye' Mem. Geol. Surv. U.K. 1904, p. 110.
[2] Neues Jahrb. vol. i (1884) p. 45.
[3] Amer. Journ. Sci. ser. 4, vol. viii (1899) p. 267.
[4] 'Die Enstatitaugite' Tschermak's Min. & Petr. Mitth. n. s. vol. xxvi (1907) pp. 21, 26.

polysynthetic lamellation appears to be indicated by a different extinction-angle in alternate lamellæ.

All the foregoing observations seem to lend support to the perthitic theory. Increased interest attaches to this view in the light of the recent synthesis, by Messrs. E. T. Allen, F. E. Wright, & J. K. Clement, of a monoclinic form of magnesium-metasilicate.[1] According to them this substance is tetramorphic, the stable form being the monoclinic magnesia-pyroxene, into which all the other forms pass at temperatures above 1150° C., the change being monotropic. Enstatite was only produced at lower temperatures. Under certain conditions an orthorhombic magnesia-amphibole was formed, with a transition-point at about 400° C., when it passed into monoclinic amphibole. As MM. Fouqué and Michel-Lévy have discovered the presence of monoclinic magnesia-pyroxene in meteorites, the question arises whether this substance may not also exist in igneous rocks. Analyses by Dr. Teall,[2] and by A. V. Merian,[3] seem to show that the enstatite-molecule is present in these striated pyroxenes; and it is, therefore, not unlikely that the basal striation referred to above may be due to a minute parallel intergrowth of monoclinic magnesia-pyroxene and augite. We may carry this theory still further: Dr. Teall detected in the Whin-Sill rock a pale pyroxene of earlier formation than the augite, and similar observations have been made elsewhere.[4] I have noted this occurrence in many diabases, and in the St. David's-Head rocks the numerous circular inclusions in many of the augites seem to be of a similar nature. It is possible that all these are the monoclinic form of magnesia-pyroxene.

Iron-Ores.—The iron-ores are distributed with fair uniformity through all the types, and are never abundant. In no case has any tendency to marginal concentration been noticed. In the most basic variety they are even less conspicuous than in the more acid rocks. They occur mostly in the form of titaniferous magnetite or ilmenite, and are usually more or less altered to leucoxene. In order of separation this mineral is by no means confined to the earliest phase, but is more often moulded upon the felspars, with very irregular outlines, though occasionally exhibiting rhombohedral forms. Very commonly it forms long strips bordering other crystals, or patches partially enveloping the felspars. Pyrites in small quantity is present in a few instances.

Biotite.—Biotite is confined to the most basic types of rock, and is therefore more commonly found in the Carn-Llidi intrusion. It is always a primary constituent, is never very abundant, and invariably separated later than the felspars, upon which it is

[1] Amer. Journ. Sci. ser. 4, vol. xxii (1906) pp. 385-438. See also J. W. Judd, Quart. Journ. Geol. Soc. vol. xlii (1886) p. 65 (footnote).
[2] Ibid. vol. xl (1884) p. 649.
[3] Neues Jahrb. Beilage-Band iii (1885) p. 289.
[4] W. Wahl, op. cit. passim.

moulded (see Pl. XXIX, fig. 2). It is of a rich red-brown, with normal pleochroism, and is sometimes bleached by iron-separation. The occurrence of this mineral seems to have been strictly determined by the composition of the magma. No inclusions have been noticed in it.

Hornblende.—Hornblende, like biotite, is but sparingly represented, and, with rare exceptions, occurs only in the more acid varieties. At Carnedd Lleithr it becomes abundant, and the rock passes into the class of enstatite-diorites. It separated, in most cases, later than the pyroxenes, and occurs both in separate crystals and as an outgrowth upon augite. It is brown in colour, and seems to be always a primary constituent. Secondary hornblende (as an alteration-product of augite) is very rare in these rocks, and uralite is practically absent in all the slices. Some transparent fibrous alteration-products after enstatite may possibly be rhombic magnesia-amphibole, allied to the kupfferite described by Messrs. Allen, Wright, & Clement,[1] as the extinction is parallel to the elongation of the fibres. This point, however, requires further investigation.

Apatite.—The distribution of apatite in these rocks presents some features of interest. This mineral is not very conspicuous in the basic varieties, but becomes rather a prominent constituent of the acid types, in which it often forms crystals of considerable size. As chlorine was found in the analysis of this type, the mineral may possibly be in the form of chlor-apatite. It is noteworthy that Mr. Harker observed a similar distribution of chlor-apatite in the Skye gabbros, where it was only found in the more acid varieties.[2]

In the St. David's-Head rocks this peculiarity of distribution is also reflected in the separate slices, where the microscope shows it to be largely concentrated in the quartz-areas, and to a smaller degree in the felspars; it is rarely found in the pyroxenes. I put this curious fact to a rough quantitative test. Thus in sixteen rock-slices it was found that the number of apatite-crystals recognizable amounted to 1142, of which 824 were enclosed in quartz, 259 in felspar, 26 in pyroxenes, and 33 in other minerals. Considering the fact that quartz rarely forms more than 5 per cent. of the rock, it appears remarkable that so large a proportion of the apatite should be concentrated in the mineral which was the last to consolidate. Apatite-inclusions can be so readily recognized in the pyroxenes that they could scarcely escape detection. It is difficult to account for this curious fact, but two explanations seem possible. Either the separation of apatite was delayed by the presence of some substance which increased its solubility; or it was formed, as usual, in the early stages of consolidation, but was rejected by the

[1] Amer. Journ. Sci. ser. 4, vol. xxii (1906) p. 406.
[2] 'Tertiary Igneous Rocks of Skye' Mem. Geol. Surv. U. K. 1904 p. 113

pyroxenes owing to some peculiarity of surface-tension, leading to capillary repulsion instead of attraction. We may, in such a case, imagine, in the early stages of consolidation of the magma, a scattered dust of the minerals of first separation, in this case apatite, and a kind of selective inclusion of these in the subsequently-formed crystals. There are reasons for believing that this selective action does in fact take place in certain cases. An objection to this view, however, is that in the rocks of other localities the pyroxenes often do contain apatite-crystals in fair abundance.[1] In my opinion, the greater preponderance of apatite in the more acid rocks in the St. David's-Head area seems to point to the conclusion that the bulk of the phosphoric acid was originally contained in the acid portion of the magma.

## V. RELATIONS OF THE ROCK-TYPES.

Whatever view we may take of the differentiation-process which has resulted in the various types of rock described in the foregoing pages, it is clear that these suggest a typical rock-series, primarily derived from a common magma. It will be convenient here to illustrate graphically the chemical relations of the different types. For this purpose we may use the method of Prof. Iddings,[2] plotting the silica-percentages along an abscissa, and the other oxides along ordinates erected at the successive points thus obtained. For the sake of space a part only of the complete diagram is shown (fig. 2, p. 291). It is evident, from an examination of this figure, that the curves thus obtained deviate in some cases from even an approximate linearity. We have, of course, to remember that many things may occur during the consolidation of a magma to interfere with a linear result.[3] Thus, owing to convection-currents, magmatic flow, and other causes, crystals do not necessarily remain in the positions in which they consolidated. This must be particularly true in the early stages of crystallization. It is only by making an extensive series of analyses, and by averaging the results, that these factors can be even partly eliminated. Analyses of isolated samples of rock can only be expected to give a rough approximation to the composition of the magmas from which they originated. It is probably for this reason that we find the lime-curve following a somewhat erratic course instead of conforming, as might have been expected, to those of magnesia and iron. Neither the curve for titanium nor that for potash suggests differentiation of the Carrock-Fell type, and in view of the fact that the soda-lime felspars were almost invariably among the first minerals to separate, it is difficult to explain, upon the theory of differentiation *in situ*, the large proportion of soda in the aplite-veins. The whole of the facts,

[1] See J. D. Falconer, Trans. Roy. Soc. Edin. vol. xlv (1906) p. 141.

[2] 'The Origin of Igneous Rocks' Bull. Phil. Soc. Washington, vol. xii (1892-94) pp. 89-214.

[3] Upon this point see A. Harker, 'On Igneous-Rock Series & Mixed Igneous Rocks' Journ. Geol. Chicago, vol. viii (1900) p. 389.

indeed, seem to be opposed to the theory of differentiation *in situ.*
Acid streaks form a characteristic feature in many basic intrusions,
as, for example, the coarse pegmatoid veins at Penmaenmawr, the
core of the Whin-Sill intrusion, the coarse veins in the Rowley-
Rag mass, etc.   In all these cases, however, there is a deficiency in
the acid veins of the minerals of early separation.   This is not the
case in the rocks now under consideration.   When we consider the
distribution of the felspars, the titaniferous iron-ores, and other
facts connected with the sequence of crystallization of these rocks,
it is impossible to look upon the quartz-bearing rocks of this series

Fig. 2.—*Diagram illustrating the chemical relations of the various
types of the St. David's-Head 'rock-series.'*

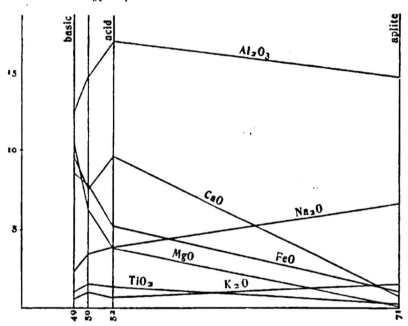

as the acid residuum or mother-liquor of a partly-consolidated
magma.   Perhaps the greatest difficulty in accepting this view,
however, is the mode of occurrence of these different types as seen
in the field.   In many places these are found to pass one into
the other by quite sudden transitions; and in the banded rocks we
have evidence that two magmas coexisted side by side, in streaky
lines drawn out by flow during their injection.

   I am driven, therefore, to the conclusion that this is a case
of intrusion of a mixed magma from a magma-basin in
which a partial gravity-differentiation had already
taken place.   The different degrees of re-admixture, which
subsequently occurred, were possibly determined, to a great extent,
by local variations in viscosity.

The range of specific gravities of these rock-types accords well with the hypothesis of a differentiated magma-basin.  This is shown by the following table :—

|  | Specific gravity. |
| --- | --- |
| Aplite | 2·62 |
| Quartz-enstatite-diorite | 2·87 |
| Enstatite-diabase | 2·92 |
| Biotite-norite | 2·96 |

The extreme basic phase of this series would be a pyroxenite, which might be expected to occur in connexion with these intrusions. Although none of my specimens can be referred to this type, it is approximately represented by the dark streaks in the banded varieties.

## VI. Age of the Intrusions.

It remains to consider whether any conclusions can be drawn as to the age of these intrusions.  In connexion with this point it is significant that, although the Arenig strata have been sharply folded, the igneous masses show no sign of movement since their consolidation.  In the field there is a conspicuous absence of shear-planes and other signs of fracture.  Under the microscope the constituent minerals are remarkably free from any of the usual evidences of dynamic metamorphism.  I take this to be an indication that no profound earth-movements have affected this region since the consolidation of the injected rocks.  The key, therefore, to the age of these intrusions seems to lie in the period of the last great disturbance which completed the tilting of the Cambrian and Ordovician rocks of Pembrokeshire, and compressed them against the pre-Cambrian ridge of St. David's, to the axis of which their strike is approximately parallel.  Now, the Llanrian lavas, lying a few miles farther north, are of Llandeilo and Bala age, and these rocks have been affected by this compression.  The St. David's-Head intrusions are, therefore, evidently younger than the Bala period, and may have been injected during the post-Bala disturbances.  At the same time, the possibility that they may be of post-Carboniferous, or even of still later age, cannot be altogether excluded.

## VII. Summary and Conclusion.

I will now briefly recapitulate the conclusions suggested by the preceding investigation :—

(1) The St. David's-Head and Carn-Llidi intrusions are of complex composition, ranging from a basic biotite-norite to an acid quartz-enstatite-diorite, and finally soda-aplite.  Throughout all the types, except the aplite-veins, there is a high magnesia-percentage.

(2) The extreme types sometimes pass sharply one into the other, at other times are mixed in various proportions.

(3) They do not represent a composite intrusion, but simultaneous intrusions of an imperfectly-mixed magma.

(4) There is no evidence of differentiation *in situ*, the facts suggesting a common origin from a differentiated magma-basin.

(5) The aplite-veins may represent the most acid phase of this differentiated magma.

(6) Petrographically the rocks are of considerable interest, as exhibiting types not very commonly occurring in the British Isles. They also afford unusual facilities for the study of both rhombic and monoclinic pyroxenes, and appear to throw light upon the origin of the sahlite-striation in the latter.

(7) The probable age of the intrusions is not greater than that of the earth-movements which folded the Arenig strata in this district.

(8) The observations recorded in the foregoing pages seem to point to the conclusion that acid streaks and cores in basic igneous rocks may not always be due to differentiation *in situ*.

In conclusion, I desire to express my obligation to my son, Mr. A. V. Elsden, B.Sc., F.I.C., for invaluable assistance in carrying out the chemical work connected with this paper.

## EXPLANATION OF PLATES XXIX–XXXII.

[All the figures are taken with a 1-inch objective, ordinary light.]

### PLATE XXIX.

Fig. 1. Bi tite-norite, Carn Llidi, showing rhombic and monoclinic pyroxene, plagioclase and iron-ore. Rhombic pyroxene occupies the centre of the field, and is mottled owing to alteration. ($\times$ 15 diameters.) See p. 279.

2. The same, showing biotite in the centre of the field, and in the lower right-hand corner. ($\times$ 20 diameters.) See p. 288.

3. Bronzite-diorite, Carn Llidi, showing a large bronzite-crystal on the right-hand margin, and augite developed into hornblende in the lower left-hand corner. The remainder of the field is occupied with augite, plagioclase, and opaque iron-ore. ($\times$ 20 diameters.) See p. 282.

4. Diabase, Carn Llidi, showing augite, plagioclase, and opaque iron-ore. The augites show basal striation, with patchy schillerization. ($\times$ 15 diameters.) See p. 282

5. Quartz-diabase, St. David's Head, showing a large augite-crystal in the lower right-hand corner, with a fringe of hornblende on the left margin. A large plagioclase-crystal occupies the top left portion, and there is some interstitial micropegmatite. ($\times$ 20 diameters.) See p. 281.

6. Soda-aplite, Pen Lledwen, showing albite, quartz, and a little iron-ore. ($\times$ 15 diameters.) See p. 283.

### PLATE XXX.

Fig. 1. Quartz-xenocryst, with augite-fringe, from the marginal zone. ($\times$ 20 diameters.) See p. 276.

2. Marginal zone a little farther in than fig. 1, showing the development of enstatite towards the left centre. ($\times$ 15 diameters.) See p. 276.

3. Granophyric variety, St. David's Head, showing zoned felspar, fringed by micropegmatite. ($\times$ 20 diameters.) See p. 285.

Fig. 4. Rock from Trwyn Llŵyd, showing fluxion-structure. Crystals of
    rhombic and monoclinic pyroxene, plagioclase, and opaque iron-ore
    are elongated in the direction of flow. (× 20 diameters) See
    p. 277.

5. Rock from Porth Melgan, showing idiomorphic pyroxenes. (× 20
    diameters.) See p. 276.

6. Specimen from the central ridge of the St. David's-Head mass, showing
    felspar-alteration. Near the right-hand margin a plagioclase-crystal is
    seen, partly replaced by quartz and a mineral presumed to be prehnite.
    (× 20 diameters.) See p. 285.

## PLATE XXXI.

Fig. 1. Large rhombic pyroxene, typically developed in the basic varieties.
    The specimen is from Carn Llidi. (× 15 diameters.) See p. 286.

2. A similar crystal, enclosing felspars. (× 15 diameters.) See p. 286.

3. Intermediate type, showing rhombic and monoclinic pyroxene, and
    plagioclase. The order of crystallization is here plainly revealed.
    The large augite-crystal on the right exhibits basal striation. (× 15
    diameters.) See p. 286.

4. A large crystal of rhombic pyroxene occupies the bottom of the field,
    plagioclase the centre, and monoclinic pyroxenes, with basal striation,
    the top. (× 15 diameters.) See p. 287.

5. On the left a large crystal of augite, with basal striation, shows partial
    schillerization. The remainder of the field is occupied by plagioclase,
    and chloritic alteration-products. (× 15 diameters.) See p. 287.

6. The greater part of the field is occupied by a large crystal of augite
    with basal striation, optically intergrown at the bottom with an
    unstriated augite-crystal. (× 15 diameters.) See p. 287.

## PLATE XXXII.

Fig. 1. The upper margin of the slice shows an interlocked twin-crystal of
    rhombic and monoclinic pyroxene, the composition-plane being the
    orthopinacoid of the latter. The section is cut approximately
    parallel to the clinopinacoid, the augite extinguishing at about 35°
    to the twinning-plane. (× 10 diameters.) See p. 286.

2. At the bottom of the field is a twin-crystal, consisting of rhombic and
    monoclinic pyroxene. The remainder of the field is made up of
    rhombic and monoclinic pyroxene, plagioclase, and quartz. (× 15
    diameters.) See p. 286.

3. In the top left-hand corner is a twin of rhombic and monoclinic
    pyroxene cut transversely. The rest of the field contains plagioclase,
    augite developed into enstatite, and opaque iron-ore. (× 20
    diameters.) See p. 286.

4. This shows parallel development of rhombic and monoclinic pyroxene,
    in the upper portion of the field. (× 15 diameters.) See p. 286.

5. This shows three twins of rhombic and monoclinic pyroxene, all cut
    transversely to the c axis. (× 15 diameters.) See p. 286.

6. Section illustrating reversed order of crystallization, pyroxene preceding
    felspar. (× 20 diameters.) See p. 286.

## DISCUSSION.

Dr. J. S. FLETT said that this paper was of the greatest interest
to him, as he had had occasion to investigate two sets of rocks
which had many points in common with those described. By
whatever names they might be called—quartz-norites, quartz-
gabbros, hypersthene-diabases, quartz-diabases, sahlite-diabases,
quartz-dolerites, etc.—they all consisted of rhombic pyroxene,

QUART. JOURN. GEOL. SOC. VOL. LXIV, PL. XXIX.

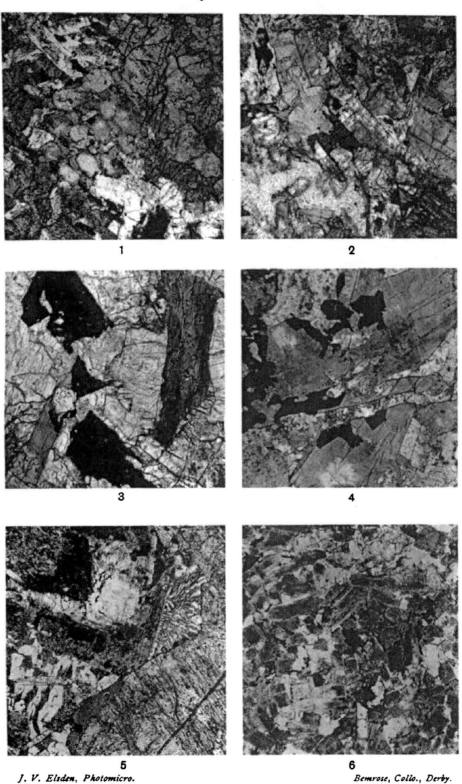

J. V. Elsden, Photomicro.

Bemrose, Collo., Derby.

IGNEOUS ROCKS OF ST. DAVID'S HEAD.

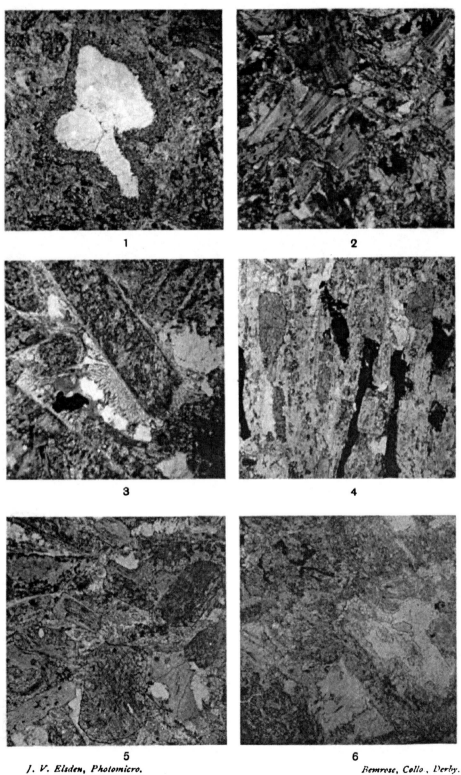

1

2

3

4

5

6

*J. V. Elsden, Photomicro.*                                        *Bemrose, Collo , Derby.*

IGNEOUS ROCKS OF ST. DAVID'S HEAD.

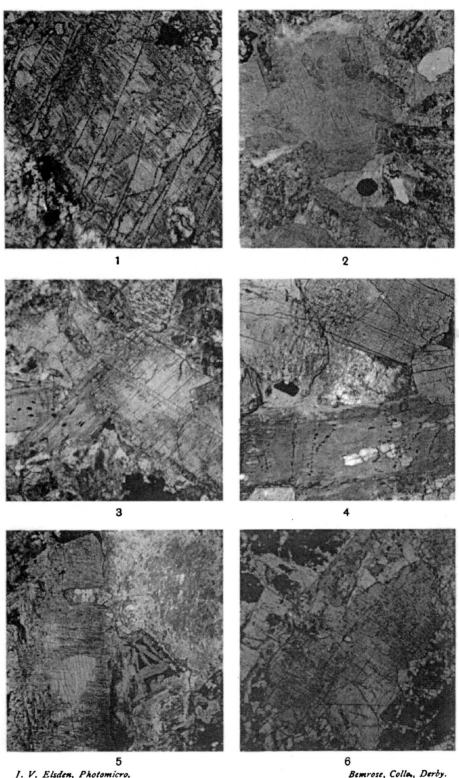

J. V. Elsden, Photomicro.

Bemrose, Colla, Derby.

IGNEOUS ROCKS OF ST. DAVID'S HEAD.

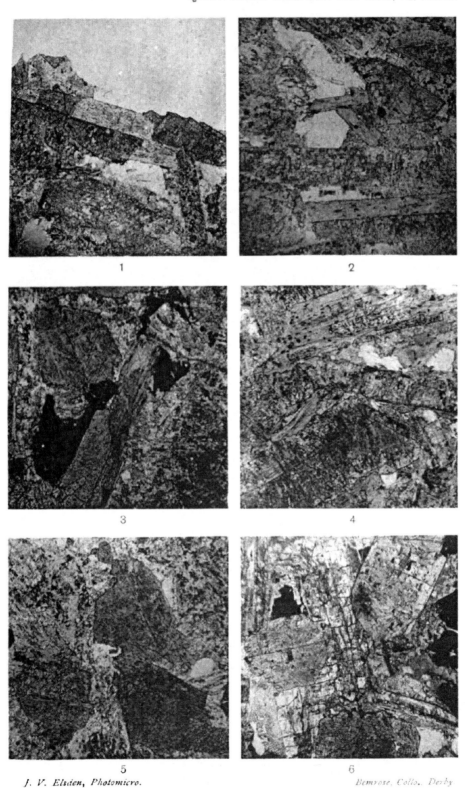

1     2

3     4

5     6

*J. V. Elsden, Photomicro.*        *Bemrose, Collo., Derby*

**IGNEOUS ROCKS OF ST. DAVID'S HEAD.**

two varieties of augite, plagioclase-felspar, quartz, and micropeg-matite; they had arisen at three different epochs from three distinct British magmas. They occurred in the Ordovician of Wales, in the late Carboniferous of Scotland and the North of England (Whin Sill), and as Tertiary intrusions in Arran, Argyllshire, and other parts of the West of Scotland. Many of the features of the Welsh rocks which the Author had described were repeated in the most curious fashion in the Scottish quartz-diabase sills. The older augite of these rocks was a very interesting mineral; it had the pleochroism and many of the characters of hypersthene, but was monoclinic with an extinction-angle of about 40°. Dr. Wahl had recently published an investigation of this mineral (sahlite, magnesium-diopside, enstatite-augite), showing that it had often a very small axial angle and exhibited great variations in this respect. In the Scottish rocks the speaker's experience was that the axial angle of the older augite was smaller than that of the second augite, but often not much less. Recently, however, on examining sections of the Whin Sill from Belford (Northumberland), he had observed that the sahlite, which was very abundant in that rock, was often uniaxial, an example of a mineral of monoclinic symmetry, optically uniaxial, and with its single optic axis making an angle of 40° with its principal crystallo-graphic axis.

Mr. J. ALLAN THOMSON mentioned, as a confirmation of the hypo-thesis that the previous speaker had put forward, the demonstration by Prof. Vogt that enstatite and diopside formed a discontinuous series of mixed crystals. This could be more easily understood if the enstatite entering into the diopside-molecule were monoclinic. Prof. Vogt had placed the enstatite-diopside series in Type IV of Roozeboom's types of mixed crystals, one of his arguments being that enstatite was never posterior to diopside in crystallization. They had seen, however, in the Author's figures a plate of enstatite pœcilitically enclosing augite.

Dr. F. H. HATCH enquired as to the nature of the felspars, whether they were anorthoclase or albite.

Mr. E. B. BAILEY remarked that the Scottish Permo-Carboniferous quartz-dolerites showed an exactly similar association of basic, intermediate, and 'acid' types, the dark and light patches frequently occurring side by side, without any evidence of flow-structure, indicating differentiation in situ. The principle involved appeared to be the immiscibility of the extreme products at a temperature slightly above the consolidation-point of the rock. The speaker drew attention to the analyses of the three types, by Mr. G. S. Blake, quoted by Dr. Falconer in his excellent paper on the petrology of the Bathgate Hills, which furnished a very perfect example of 'straight-line' variation, thus strengthening the Author's conclusions.

Mr. H. H. THOMAS observed, with reference to the age of the St. David's-Head rocks, that they were clearly intrusive into Arenig sediments. In West Pembrokeshire there were several horizons in the Ordovician System marked by volcanic activity, but it seemed improbable that that of the St. David's-Head rocks corresponded with any of them. The Author had observed that the complex had suffered no movement since its consolidation, and in view of the extensive post-Carboniferous disturbances which had affected the district to the south-east the speaker considered that the intrusion most likely took place in post-Carboniferous time.

The AUTHOR, in reply, thanked Dr. Flett for his interesting remarks on the recurrence of eruptions of similar types of rock in different geological periods, and he was glad to have his support with regard to the nomenclature of the rocks, and other points mentioned in the paper. As to the relative order of crystallization of enstatite and augite, alluded to by Mr. Allan Thomson, the view of Prof. Vogt, that the separation of augite before enstatite was impossible on theoretical grounds, referred particularly to iron-free enstatite, and not to the ferriferous varieties described in the paper. In reply to Dr. Hatch, he said that the felspars in the aplite-veins appeared to be solely albite. With respect to Mr. Bailey's reference to non-consolute magmas, this theory certainly had support from recent discoveries in physical chemistry, but the evidence in the St. David's-Head intrusions scarcely warranted the assumption of a separation of the magma into two or more non-consolute magmas *in situ*. Mr. Thomas referred to the possible age of the intrusions, upon which the Author's evidence was admittedly obscure, the only clear point being the complete absence of any sign of earth-movements since the consolidation of the rocks in question. In conclusion, the Author thanked the Fellows for their kind reception of his paper.

15. *The* Two Earth-Movements *of* Colonsay.  By William Bourke
    Wright, B.A., F.G.S.  (Communicated by permission of the
    Director of H.M. Geological Survey.  Read February 19th,
    1908.)

[Plates XXXIII & XXXIV.]

The field-work which forms the basis of the present communication
was carried out by Mr. E. B. Bailey and the Author in the summer
of 1907, in the course of the geological survey of the island of
Colonsay.  The systems of folding displayed here and in the sister
isle of Oronsay were found to possess features of more than usual
interest, and special attention was given to the subject as far as
the rapid nature of the work permitted.  The investigation was
facilitated by the rocky character of the islands, the surface of
which is but little obscured by superficial deposits.  A fairly continuous series of observations was thus rendered possible, and
although a thorough understanding of the subject was by no means
arrived at, yet certain facts came to light which may possibly have
an important bearing on the orogenic history of the Highlands.
For clearness and convenience of reference the subject will be
discussed under the following heads :—

    I. The Stratigraphy and Chief Tectonic Features of the Islands.
    II. The Igneous Rocks.
    III. The Two Earth-Movements.
    IV. The Relation of the Earth-Movements to the Lamprophyres.
    V. The Relation of the Earth-Movements to the Plutonic Masses.
    VI. The Varied Age of the Lamprophyres.
    VII. The Nature of the Second Cleavage.

### I. The Stratigraphy and Chief Tectonic Features of the Islands.

The sedimentary rocks of supposed Lower Torridon age which
form the greater part of Colonsay and Oronsay consist of an alternating series of grits, flags, and mudstones, with a well marked bed
of sandy limestone near the top.  A description of the various
members of this series is not essential to the present discussion, but
a general idea of the relation of the beds may be obtained from fig. 1
(p. 298).  The Colonsay Limestone, which, with the beds above and
below it, constitutes an easily recognizable horizon, occurs on the
eastern coast of the island, dipping out to sea at a low angle.  If a
traverse be made in a westerly or southerly direction across the
islands from this outcrop, successively lower beds are passed over,
all dipping east or north-east at gentle angles ; and on finally
reaching the extreme outlying parts of Oronsay and Ardskinish,
there is still no indication of any base to this enormously thick
series of sediments.  Throughout this whole traverse one has
passed continuously from higher to lower beds, and there has been

Fig. 1.—*Sketch-map of the stratigraphy of Colonsay and Oronsay,
to show the structure.*   (Scale: 2 miles = 1 inch.)

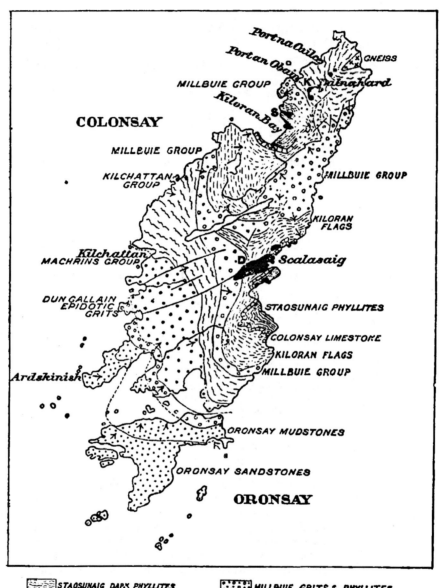

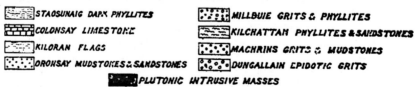

STAOSUNAIG DARK PHYLLITES          MILLBUIE GRITS & PHYLLITES
COLONSAY LIMESTONE                 KILCHATTAN PHYLLITES & SANDSTONES
KILORAN FLAGS                      MACHRINS GRITS & MUDSTONES
ORONSAY MUDSTONES & SANDSTONES     DUNGALLAIN EPIDOTIC GRITS
PLUTONIC INTRUSIVE MASSES

K-Kentallenite   S-Syenite   D-Diorite   ↘-Dip of Strata

[The rock-groups, though in some cases constant, exhibit in others great lateral
  variation.  The dips shown in the map have been selected to illustrate the
  main structure.  There is much minor complication due to folding.]

no repetition of any importance. In the northern part of Colonsay the relations are slightly more complex. The outcrop of the limestone mentioned above skirts the east coast of the island for some distance, and then passes out to sea north of Scalasaig. A traverse made thence to Kiloran Bay passes at first over successively lower beds dipping south-eastwards, and then the dip is reversed and the same series is repeated in ascending order until the limestone is once more reached. The anticline thus crossed has a north-easterly trend and brings to the surface along its axis the rocks of the Kiloran and Millbuie Groups which underlie the limestone. From the manner in which the limestone circles round Kiloran Bay, it is clear that the latter here occupies the centre of a synclinal basin. Finally the north end of the island has an anticlinal structure and a mass of gneiss, presumably of Lewisian age, occupies the centre of the fold which has a north-east trend. It has proved impossible to determine whether this is part of the old irregular floor on which the Torridon sediments have been laid down, or whether its relations to these sediments is due to thrusting.

It will thus be seen that the structure is, broadly speaking, not at all complex. Over the greater part of the islands, we find a single conformable sequence of sediments dipping east and north-east at gentle angles, and in the extreme north the upper portion of the same series forming a marked synclinal basin flanked by two anticlines.

## II. THE IGNEOUS ROCKS.

The igneous intrusions of Colonsay and Oronsay are best described under three heads : —

    (a) Three main plutonic masses and several smaller ones.
    (b) An extensive series of lamprophyre dykes and sheets.
    (c) A number of Tertiary dykes of basalt.

(a).—Of the plutonic masses, that with which we are most concerned in the present paper lies on the northern side of Kiloran Bay. It is in its central portions a hornblende-syenite, but exhibits towards its margins a basic phase, which is perhaps best described under the name of hornblendite. It is intruded in the centre of a remarkable siliceous breccia, the material of which it has caught up and incorporated in its mass. The breccia contains, besides fragments of the neighbouring Torridonian sediments, both angular blocks and well rounded waterworn boulders of pebbly quartzite. There is not space for entering here into a discussion of the rather difficult question of its origin. It will be sufficient to say that there are two possibilities with regard to it. It may be of the nature of a plutonic breccia formed during the intrusion of the syenite, the waterworn boulders being derived from some conglomeratic bed lying below; or it may be a subaërial breccia formed in a fissure or pipe, into which the waterworn boulders and other material dropped from above. It must be admitted that the latter supposition is by far the more probable. One would expect an intrusion-breccia to have, in places at least, an igneous matrix, and the matrix of this breccia is always siliceous and never igneous. One might also expect to find attached to boulders derived from a conglomerate some fragments of the matrix in which they were embedded, and none of the numerous boulders seen in the magnificent exposures of this rock in the scars in Kiloran Bay show the slightest trace of any such matrix. Whatever be the origin of this peculiar breccia, it has, as will appear later, an important bearing on the subject-matter of the present paper.

The so-called 'Scalasaig Granite' is the largest mass of igneous rock in the island. It is a diorite, but exhibits certain characters indicating an affinity to the Balnahard kentallenite mentioned below. In some respects, however, it is not unlike the Kiloran syenite, which it resembles in being associated at its margins with immense masses of breccia.

The Balnahard mass is a typical kentallenite, reproducing very faithfully several of the various phases of this rock described by Mr. Kynaston from Glen Orchy.

The smaller plutonic masses are four in number, and are all syenitic in character. One occurs in Laimaolean, one in Pigs' Paradise, and two to the north of Balnahard. Of these last two one has a small amount of breccia at its margin.

(*b*).—The 'lamprophyre' dykes and sheets are both numerous and of widely different ages. The great majority of them are so decomposed as to render determination impossible. Many effervesce freely with acid.[1] A few of the more recent, however, are comparatively fresh, and these, while varying in character from place to place, may all be described as vogesites. Lamprophyres of all ages are abundant in the northern half of the island, but are wanting in the extreme south of Colonsay and in Oronsay.

(*c*).—Basalt dykes of Tertiary age are fairly common in the southern half of the islands, but become rare and are finally wanting towards the north. They have the usual north-west and south-east trend. Two dykes of monchiquite having a similar trend, and probably of much the same age, have also been found.

## III. The Two Earth-Movements.

Perhaps one of the most noticeable features of the Torridon sediments of these islands is the presence of a well marked cleavage. It is of course best developed in the more pelitic beds, being a true close cleavage of the slaty type, produced by parallel arrangement of the mineral particles of which the rock is composed. Owing to its obvious similarity to the slaty cleavage of other districts, there

---

[1] While there is a considerable presumption that all these dykes are lamprophyres, yet many are in so advanced a state of alteration as to make it impossible to say so positively.

can be no doubt that it was produced, during a period of movement, in the planes normal to the greatest pressure. In the northern part of Colonsay it preserves a remarkable parallelism to the bedding, but may be seen here and there to cross it on the crest of an isoclinal fold, having been produced at the same time as this fold and along its axial plane. In the south of the islands we find what appears to be the same cleavage crossing the bedding over large areas without the accompaniment of any such folding. In its production, the arrangement of the pre-existing clastic micas in planes perpendicular to the greatest stress has probably gone hand in hand with the development of secondary seri-citic mica along these planes. This growth of secondary minerals in a definite series of planes, however close these planes may be, is an incipient type of folia-tion. We shall, how-ever, in future refer to it as the first cleavage.

Fig. 2.—*Diagram illustrating by shading the general increase in the intensity of the second movement from west to east, the curved lines being lines of approximately equal movement. Zone 1 is unshaded, Zones 2, 3, and 4 are shown with increasing degrees of shading.*

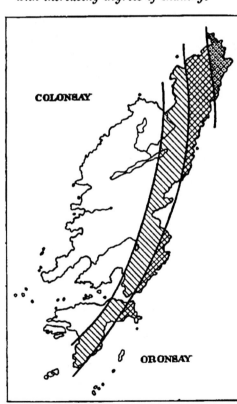

On the western side of the islands the first cleavage presents plane or only slightly wavy faces, but eastwards it becomes progressively more folded and crinkled, and on the eastern coast has been subjected to intense puckering. At the same time a new cleavage is developed, which, slight at first, becomes towards the eastern coast fairly well marked, and in the extreme north - east entirely dominates the minor features in the structure of the country. This relation is ex-pressed in fig. 2, in which zones of increasing intensity of both folding and cleavage are shown by different degrees of shading. In Zone 1 the effect is trivial, amounting only to a slight waviness of the laminæ of the first cleavage in the more pelitic beds. In Zone 2 a pronounced puckering of these laminæ is observable, but little or no cleavage yet accompanies it. In Zone 3 the puckering becomes acute and the accompanying cleavage well marked, and as Zone 4 is approached its planes become so close as almost completely to destroy any facility of splitting along the first cleavage.

The relation of the second cleavage to a corresponding system of folds is, as might be expected, far more obvious than in the case of the first cleavage. It preserves, at least in the softer beds, a strict general parallelism with the axial planes of these folds, and undoubtedly owes its origin to the same compressive forces which produced them. We have, in the two cleavages of the islands and in the folding accompanying them, the record of two periods of stress, and consequent movement, of which one is clearly later than the other. How much later remains to be determined.

Fig. 3.—*Section about 2 feet long on the coast north of Port na Cuilce (Colonsay), showing a small lamprophyre sill* (L) *and quartz-veins* (Q) *in phyllite.*

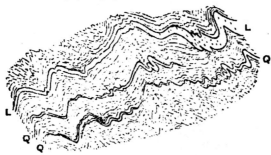

[The quartz-veins lie along the planes of the first cleavage, and the lamprophyre sill has also been intruded along the same set of planes. Both the quartz-veins and the lamprophyre have been folded and cleaved by the second movement.]

The analogy with the sequence of events described by Mr. C. T. Clough [1] in the Cowal district of Argyll is remarkable. In both instances there is a primary 'foliation' of the rocks, and in both the planes of this foliation are affected by folding and cleavage due to secondary movement. Mr. Clough held that these two movements were distinct, because the planes of secondary cleavage cut not only those of the first cleavage, but also the quartz-veins formed along the latter. Where actual cleavage has not been developed, the effect of the later movement can still be recognized in the folding and crinkling of both the early cleavage and the accompanying quartz-veins. An exactly similar relation occurs in Colonsay. Quartz-veins clearly formed along the first cleavage have been folded and even cleaved during the second movement (see fig. 3). Still, good as is this evidence, it is, perhaps, not quite convincing. We have had the good fortune in Colonsay to come upon better.

[1] 'The Geology of Cowal' Mem. Geol. Surv. Scotl. 1897, chapt. ii.

## IV. THE RELATION OF THE EARTH-MOVEMENTS
## TO THE LAMPROPHYRES.

A large number of the lamprophyre dykes so abundant in Colonsay are obviously intruded along the first cleavage, and as obviously folded and cleaved by the secondary movement. These run in a general way parallel to the strike of the first cleavage, dip with it, and occasionally cut across it in such a manner as to leave no doubt that they are subsequent to it. Moreover, marginal relations such as that shown in fig. 5 (below) are not uncommon, and are quite inconsistent with the idea that the primary cleavage could be subsequent to the dykes. The relations of the secondary cleavage are quite as clear. Again and again this cleavage can be traced from the adjoining schists right into the body of the lamprophyre, and repeatedly we find the lamprophyre affected by the folds

Fig. 4.—*Section on the shore south-east of Eilean Dubh, and north of Port na Cuilce (Colonsay), showing a lamprophyre sill (A) in the phyllite intruded along the primary cleavage and folded and cleaved by the secondary movement.*

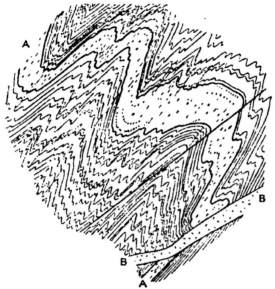

[A small dyke (B) of later age than the secondary movement is seen at the bottom of the section. Scale: 2 feet=approximately 1 inch.]

Fig. 5.—*Margin of lamprophyre in phyllite, on the coast north of Kiloran Bay, showing its relation to the first cleavage, which stops short at the edge of the sill, and does not penetrate it.*

which contort the planes of primary cleavage along which it lies. Moreover, the distribution of cleaved lamprophyre dykes and sheets throughout the islands is one of remarkable significance. Their number increases rapidly as we pass from the area of slight to that of intense secondary movement. Thus in Zone 1 (fig. 2, p. 301) we scarcely ever see a lamprophyre showing even incipient cleavage. In Zone 2 they are to be found, but are neither strikingly cleaved nor abundant. In Zone 3 even the larger and more massive dykes have suffered, and the smaller ones are often remarkably folded and cleaved. In Zone 4 they are reduced to a schistose state, and do not strike one at first glance as markedly different from the adjoining phyllites.

It will, perhaps, be conceded that we have in the intrusion of this series of dykes a fair indication of a very considerable lapse of time between the two movements. It has been found possible, however, to go even further than this.

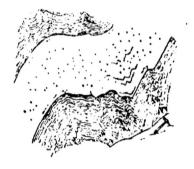

Fig. 6.—*Lamprophyre dyke on the shore north of Port an Obain, northern end of Colonsay, intruded along the cleavage of the primary movement, and involved in the folding of the secondary movement.*

## V. The Relation of the Earth-Movements to the Plutonic Masses.

A careful examination of the syenite to the north of Kiloran Bay has thrown considerable light on the question. The remarkable breccia occurring along the margins of the plutonic mass, and referred to above, contains abundant fragments of the adjoining Torridon sediments, exhibiting clearly the primary cleavage and lying at all angles to one another. They plainly had this cleavage impressed upon them before their inclusion in the breccia, which must therefore have been formed at a period subsequent to the first movement. The syenite, which contains caught-up fragments of the breccia, cannot be earlier than it; and it is, therefore, quite safe to conclude that both syenite and breccia are distinctly later than the first movement.

Evidence of the relation of the syenite and breccia to the secondary movement is also forthcoming. They are traversed by several dykes which have been affected by this movement. The most remarkable of these is to be seen cutting the syenite on Eilean Easdale. It is about $3\frac{1}{2}$ feet wide and has a general trend about N. 10° E., but takes a decided double bend about the middle of its course. A band about a foot wide on the east side of the dyke is rather fine-grained, but the rest is coarser. There are, besides, very

fine-grained chilled margins in contact with the syenite. The
secondary cleavage in the dyke is very conspicuous in the coarse-
grained portion, and is also well shown by the elongation of the
black spots in the chilled margin. It is throughout vertical, or dips
at very high angles. Its distinctness from flow-structure is very
obvious, since it may be seen crossing the banding of the dyke at
a very consider-
able angle. At
the southern end
it strikes, in the
fine-grained por-
tion N. 20° W.,
and in the coarse-
grained W. 20°
N.; a little north
of the bend it is
W. 15° N., far-
ther north N.
30° W., N. 40°
W., and W. 25°
N. to N.W. In
the adjoining
syenite of Eilean
Easdale there
are marked lines
of crushing and
shearing, accom-
panied by a rude
mineral arrange-
ment with a
trend W. 40° N.
The great scar
of breccia and
syenite which
forms the land-

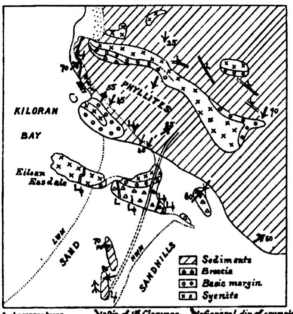

Fig. 7.—*Sketch-map of the Kiloran syenite intrusion.*
*(Scale : 6 inches = 1 mile.)*

L - *Lamprophyre.*    ↘ - *Dip of 1ˢᵗ Cleavage.*   ↘ - *General dip of crumpled*
L₁ - *Cleaved Lamprophyre.*   ↗ - - *Axial Planes of 1ˢᵗ Cleavage.*
↘ - *Dip of Strata.*    2ⁿᵈ *Folding.*    ↘ - *Pitching anticline in bedding.*

ward continuation of Eilean Easdale is crossed by five lamprophyre
dykes. Three of these, which are of small breadth, from 6 to 8 inches,
show the secondary cleavage in a very marked way. Another,
which is very massive and about 4 feet broad, shows no cleavage
where it cuts the breccia and syenite, but its obvious continuation
can be seen to the south, in the schists, and there it shows a distinct
though not powerful cleavage. As the syenite is thus cleaved, and
is traversed by cleaved lamprophyres, and as the direction of this
cleavage corresponds fairly well with that produced in the adjoining
schists by the secondary movement, it is pretty clear that it must
be prior in age to the secondary movement. As an obvious further
test, we went carefully over the fragments of schist exposed in the
breccia, with the object of ascertaining if any had been affected
by the secondary folding and cleavage before being included in it.

x 2

We found altogether only two or three pieces of rock which showed the primary cleavage affected by secondary crinkling, and these occurred under such relations that it was probable that the crinkling was impressed on them while in the breccia. They all lay transverse to the direction of the secondary cleavage, and we found no crinkled fragments in which the primary cleavage lay parallel to this direction.

It is important to note that the lamprophyre dykes which traverse the syenite are chilled against it. The syenite must clearly have been cool before their intrusion.

We may therefore draw the conclusion that, between the first and second movements in the schists, there elapsed sufficient time for—

    (1) the intrusion of a fair-sized plutonic mass;
    (2) the cooling of the same; and
    (3) the intrusion of an extensive series of lamprophyre dykes.

The other plutonic masses of the island are all later than the first movement, but their relation to the second is not quite so obvious as in the case of the Kiloran syenite. The diorite of Scalasaig is traversed by a lamprophyre dyke showing distinct cleavage, and is therefore presumably of inter-movement age. An attempt to determine microscopically the time-relation of the crinkling to the hornfelsing of this mass and of the Balnahard kentallenite, has not, up to the present, been crowned with success. The occurrence of similar types of the two last-mentioned masses lends support to the idea that they belong to the same suite of intrusions.

## VI. The Varied Age of the Lamprophyres.

A very large proportion of the lamprophyres were intruded in the period between the two movements. Many of them were, as we have seen, later than the syenite; some of them were certainly earlier, for blocks of decomposed lamprophyre have been obtained from the breccia.

There occur also in Colonsay a certain number of vogesite dykes and sills, which are clearly later than the second movement. These have generally, but not exclusively, an east and west trend, and are in their manner of intrusion much more independent of the structure of the rocks than their predecessors. Two such dykes cross the northern end of the island in an approximately east and west direction, dipping southwards at a considerable angle. On the coast, about a quarter of a mile north of Port na Cuilce, the relation of one of these to the secondary folding is well seen (fig. 8, p. 307). It cuts across and truncates the folds of the secondary system in such a manner as to leave no doubt that it is subsequent to them. East of Port na Cuilce the other is very well exposed, having a thickness of 20 to 40 feet. It is very heterogeneous in character, and is charged with numerous fragments of vein-quartz. A few pieces of phyllite, showing the crinkling produced in the cleavage by the secondary movement, can be seen enclosed in the dyke here and there. The crinkling could not in this case have been produced after the fragment had been incorporated in the dyke, for the numerous structural lines close by in the dyke show no such puckering. Petrographically this dyke is a vogesite, but it contains in the eastern part of its course considerably more biotite than in the western.

Fig. 8.—*Margin of an east and west vogesite dyke north of Port na Cuilce truncating the folds produced by the second movement in the first cleavage.*

[Scale = about one third of the natural size.]

An east and west dyke probably of this age can be seen in Port an Obain, cutting a slightly cleaved dyke having a north and south trend parallel to the primary cleavage. The later of these two dykes is a vogesite; the earlier, like all the other cleaved lamprophyres, is far too decomposed for identification.

A 7-foot vogesite-dyke of irregular east and west trend, occurring on the shore west of Kilchattan, is, judging from its remarkable freshness, probably of this age; and the 15-foot vogesite sill, which runs in a north-easterly and northerly direction across the hills north of Kilchattan, and dips in a westerly direction contrary to the cleavage and bedding, is, with some others in different parts of the island, to be referred to this period.

### VII. The Nature of the Second Cleavage.

The secondary cleavage in Colonsay is always, at least in the softer beds, strictly parallel to the axial plane in the corresponding folds, and has therefore been undoubtedly produced in the plane normal to the direction of greatest compression. Emphasis is laid on this very obvious fact, because the cleavage is not a slaty cleavage, but a true strain-slip cleavage. The investigations of many eminent geologists, from Sharpe and Haughton down to Heim, Harker, and Van Hise, have proved beyond a doubt that slaty cleavage has in all cases been produced in the normal plane. No such confident general assertion can be made with regard to strain-slip cleavage, which, on account of its analogy to thrusting, has been supposed by some to have probably been produced parallel to the planes of easiest shearing. Indeed, it is not at all improbable that structures arising in different ways may be at present grouped under the term ' strain-slip,' which is generally understood to be equivalent to the ' ausweichungsclivage ' of Heim.[1]

[1] 'Mechanismus der Gebirgsbildung' Basel, 1878, vol. ii, p. 54.

In the present case we are dealing with what may be called
'alternating strain-slip,' by which it is meant to imply that the
shearing motion along the various planes of gliding has not been
everywhere in the same direction.    On two adjacent gliding-planes
the motions may be equal and opposite, and thus compensate one
another; or on several successive planes the shear may be continuously in the same direction, and then continuously back again
on the next succeeding ones.    This structure is illustrated in figs.
1 & 2, Pl. XXXIV.

It is exactly analogous to cases figured by Prof. Heim[1] and Mr.
Harker.[2]  Owing to the compensating action of the alternation, there
may be on a large scale no differential movement in the direction of the
strain-slip cleavage plane.    This is one step towards the explanation
of the production of the latter in the normal plane.    There is a
difficulty, pointed out by Mr. Harker, in supposing any gliding or
faulting motion whatsoever strictly perpendicular to the direction
of greatest pressure, since there is no component of shear in this
direction.    Such motion would certainly seem to be theoretically
impossible in a rock made up of laminæ of absolutely uniform
strength.    The phyllites in which this structure is produced in
Colonsay are, however, far from uniform.    In the cases shown in
Pl. XXXIV strong quartzose bands traverse the phyllites parallel
to the first or slaty cleavage, and are buckled into folds of which the
axial planes are parallel to the second cleavage.    We may presume
that each lamina will give rise under compression to folds whose
amplitudes are a direct function of its strength.    As the movement
progresses, the considerable displacement of the crest and trough of
the folds in the stronger laminæ will draw and thrust to one side
the adjacent phyllite, and adjustment will take place most easily by
shearing along the limbs of the much smaller folds produced in the
mica-laminæ of the phyllite.

The folding and subsequent strain-slip would seem therefore to
be the result of stresses acting on a decidedly heterogeneous rock,
in which the weaker laminæ became folded on a smaller scale, and
then adjusted themselves by fold-faults to the form of the stronger
laminæ.    Prof. Heim long ago showed how this structure arose in
pelitic bands intercalated between stronger beds of dolomite or grit,
the successive strain-slip bands being moved over one another along
planes parallel to the axial planes of folding in such a manner as to
adjust themselves to the form of the stronger beds :—

'Die Mikrofaltenverwerfungen sind jedoch nicht an der umgebogenen Stelle
am stärksten ausgebildet, sie erlangen ihren Höhepunkt an beiden Schenkeln
zu der Seite der Umbiegungsstelle, während an der letzteren mehr nur wellen-
förmiger Schichtenverlauf vorkommt. Zu beiden Seiten gegen die Schenkel
hin beherrschen die Verwerfungslinien das Bild. Die Reste der Schichtung

[1] *Op. cit.* Atlas, pl. xv.
[2] 'Report on Slaty Cleavage & Allied Rock-Structures' Rep. Brit. Assoc.
(Aberdeen) 1885, pp. 838, 840.

zwischen denselben sind nur bei starker Vergrösserung noch ganz sicher in ihrem S-förmig gekrümmten Verlauf zu erkennen, und liegen symmetrisch auf beiden Seiten der Mittellinie der ganzen Umbiegung. Die Verwerfungslinien zeigen nach beiden Schenkeln hin die Tendenz, dieser Mittellinie parallel sich zu stellen, und schneiden deshalb die Biegungsschenkel unter schiefem Winkel, sie lassen sich mit scharfer Loupe auf frischem Bruche als Rutschspiegel erkennen. Diese Faltenverwerfungslinien sind Flächen starker Differential-bewegungen, welchen entlang durch Verschiebungen das plastische Material von den Mittelschenkeln, wo es gequetscht wurde, gegen die Umbiegungsstellen auswich, und dort hinströmend sich anhäufte.'[1]

It is worth remarking that similar strain-slip can be observed in connexion with the slaty cleavage of the first movement, the gliding-planes being coincident with the cleavage. Mr. Clough[2] has figured a case of this associated with the analogous slaty cleavage of Cowal.

An interesting result was obtained by mapping the planes of secondary cleavage, or, where these were not well enough developed to be readily observable, the axial planes of secondary folding. The result is shown in fig. 9 (p. 310). The curved lines indicate the strike of the planes, and their dip is shown by the arrows. The constancy of the strike and dip in some areas contrasts with their irregularity in others, where the condition of affairs cannot be adequately expressed on a small scale map. The remarkable variation in the direction of the stresses still awaits explanation.

In suitable situations in various parts of Colonsay a third system of crinkling is developed, with axes having a general east and west trend. This has the appearance of being later than the second movement just described, but it is difficult to produce any definite evidence on this point. The puckerings are usually so small and feeble that they are difficult to trace, except under exceedingly favourable circumstances, and next to impossible to pick out from the folds of the second movement, except where they cross these latter at a considerable angle. Planes of easy fracture resulting from sporadic zigzag displacement, the ' knickungsebenen ' or buckling-planes of Brögger,[3] are found here and there, having the general direction of the planes of the third movement.

With the exception of a comparison with the district of Cowal, no discussion of analogous results of movement in other districts has been attempted. Thus, for example, no reference is made to the work of Mr. Lamplugh in the Isle of Man, where the rocks have been affected by successive movements separated by periods of intrusion. It is felt that such discussion would be futile, unless grounds for exact correlation could be brought forward.

---

[1] 'Mechanismus der Gebirgsbildung' vol. ii (1878) pp. 52–53.
[2] 'The Geology of Cowal' Mem. Geol. Surv. Scotl. 1897, p. 12 (fig. 3).
[3] W. C. Brögger, 'Die Silurischen Etagen 2 & 3 im Kristianiagebiet & auf Eker' Kristiania, 1882. Also figured and described by Mr. Harker, Rep. Brit. Assoc. (Aberdeen) 1885, p. 839.

Fig. 9.—*Sketch-map showing the strike and dip of the axial planes of the secondary folds and of the strain-slip cleavage in Colonsay and Oronsay, on the scale of 2 miles to an inch.*

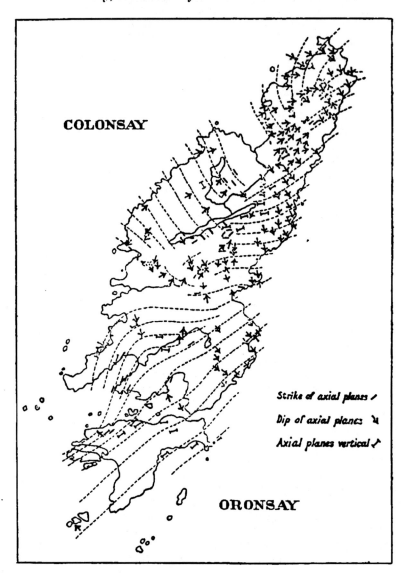

[The broken lines indicate the strike, and the arrows indicate the direction of dip of the axial planes. The dip is in general steep, especially in the areas of constant strike; but, where the strike is irregular, the dip is sometimes very low.]

R. Lunn, Photo.

QUART. JOURN. GEOL. SOC. VOL. LXIV, PL. XXXIV.

FIG. 1. × 18 DIAMS.

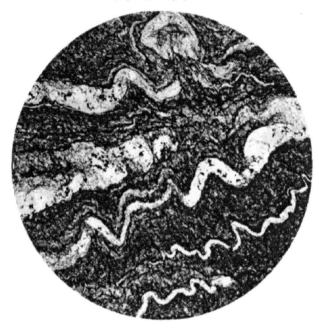

FIG. 2. × 18 DIAMS.

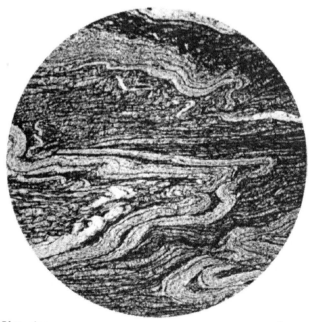

*T. C. Hall, Photomicro.*

*Bemrose, Collo., Derby.*

PHYLLITES FROM COLONSAY.

## EXPLANATION OF PLATES XXXIII & XXXIV.

### PLATE XXXIII.

Horizontal surface of rock on the coast south of Cnoc Corr, at the north-eastern end of Colonsay, showing sandy phyllite with the second cleavage running in straight lines from left to right across the picture, and crossing the bedding. Traces of the first cleavage are recognizable in microscopic section, but its relation to the bedding is not obvious.

### PLATE XXXIV.

[The slides are preserved in the collection of the Geological Survey.]

Fig. 1. Phyllite (slide 13524) on the shore near Cnoc Corr, in the north-eastern end of Colonsay (Zone 4, fig. 2, p. 301), showing the first cleavage crossing the figure from left to right, with quartz-veins segregated along it. The second cleavage, an alternating slip-cleavage, is seen crossing the first almost at right angles, in a direction parallel to the axial planes of the folding by which both the quartz-veins and the first cleavage have been affected. (×18 diams.)

    2. Phyllite (slide 13527 B) on the shore south of Eilean Dubh. The first or slaty cleavage is parallel to the folded bedding and quartz-veins, and the strain-slip cleavage, as before, coincides with the axial planes of the folds. (×18 diams.)

## DISCUSSION.

Dr. TEALL said that two movements were strikingly evident in many parts of the Southern Highlands, but he did not think it safe to infer that the two movements in one locality were necessarily contemporaneous with the two movements in another locality. The Author had conclusively shown that in Colonsay the two dominant movements were separated by an intrusion of igneous rocks, and this represented an important step in advance.

Dr. FLETT said that the Author had been fortunate in working in a district where the structures produced by the first movement had not been obliterated by the second movement. In the speaker's experience, it was exceptional to find the effects of two periods of pressure so well characterized and so well preserved. The plutonic rocks described from Colonsay by the Author (syenites, diorites, and kentallenites) had the stamp of the newer granite-series of the Scottish Highlands. These intrusions had been proved to be early Devonian, or perhaps in part late Silurian. The age of the first movement was not quite clear, but it might possibly be an earlier stage of the same process of folding. In that case, Colonsay furnished an instance of two epochs of earth-pressure, separated by a period during which pressure was relieved and igneous dykes were injected. Similar phenomena were very well shown in the Lizard district of Cornwall.

Mr. LAMPLUGH said that, as the last speaker had referred to a possible relation between the Colonsay movements and those in the South-West of England, it might be worth recalling that a sequence of movements had likewise been detected in an intermediate area—the Isle of Man—where, again, the dyke-rocks seemed to have been injected in the intervals between separate movements or separate phases of a great epoch of movement.

The PRESIDENT remarked on the importance of the definite ascertainment of distinct periods of earth-movement in the tectonic construction of the crystalline rocks of the Scottish Highlands. He was personally conversant with the grounds on which a Torridonian age had been assigned to certain rocks on the west coast of Scotland. But it was only an hypothesis, highly probable, though not yet, so far as he knew, proved to be true. The Author had spoken of the Colonsay rocks as Torridonian, without further comment; and the President asked whether any more definite indication of their age had been ascertained than was available when the ground in Islay, Iona, and the west of Mull was examined. With regard to the age of the later earth-movements in the Highlands, to which Dr. Flett had alluded, it had long been recognized that some of them were not older than the early part of the Old-Red-Sandstone Period. The President had even connected them with superficial changes giving rise to the basins in which a large part of the Lower Old Red Sandstone was accumulated.

The AUTHOR, in reply to the President's enquiry regarding the presumption as to the Torridonian age of the sediments, referred to the correlation made by Dr. Peach in the recently issued memoir on the Geology of Islay, and stated that the comparison of Colonsay with the Rhinns of Islay, made recently by Mr. Bailey and himself, had tended to confirm that correlation in so far as it placed the sedimentary rocks of both districts in the same great group. With regard to a possible correlation with the Diabeg Group of Skye, the Author could not speak from his own experience, but he had had the advantage of the opinion of Mr. Clough, who originally mapped the latter district, and, after seeing the Colonsay succession, considered that the similarity of types in the two areas was sufficient to justify the assumption that they were dealing with a portion of the same general sequence. The relation to the gneiss in the northern end of Colonsay was not sufficiently clear to be regarded as evidence of the Torridonian age of the sediments.

The Author had refrained from making any correlation with the folding in other districts, feeling that such generalization was premature in the present state of our knowledge. Mr. Clough had suggested the possibility of a movement in the district of Cowal prior to that which produced the foliation of the Dunoon phyllites. If an analogous movement had occurred in Colonsay, its results had been most effectually cloaked by the later movements. The term lamprophyre had certainly been used in a very wide sense in the paper. The advanced decomposition of the dykes and sills intruded before the second movement, was in favour of the idea that they belonged to the lamprophyre group. Those later than the second movement were typical vogesites. The Author referred again to his indebtedness to Mr. Bailey for help and advice, both in the field and in the writing of the paper.

16. *A* Note *on the* PETROLOGY *and* PHYSIOGRAPHY *of* WESTERN LIBERIA (WEST COAST *of* AFRICA).  By JOHN PARKINSON, M.A., F.G.S. (Read March 18th, 1908.)

[PLATE XXXV—MAP.]

### I. PETROLOGY.

BY the kind permission of Sir Harry Johnston, G.C.M.G., I am enabled to make the following brief contribution to the geology of part of Western Liberia.   The district described lies to the north and north-east of Monrovia, in Montserrado county, and includes the lower part of the basin of the St. Paul or Ding River.   These notes are the result of a seven months' journey in the Republic.

Taking the southern part first, it should be noted that garnet-schists and various gneisses, for the most part greatly decomposed, are exposed in the neighbourhood of Whiteplains and along the Caresburg Road.   In typical specimens of the former collected near Whiteplains, garnets are abundant, much cracked and very irregular in outline.   Flakes of biotite are common, quartz is occasionally plentiful; and the felspar is, at least partly, an acid plagioclase.   Phenocrysts are rare.   Kyanite-schists are probably associated with these rocks, for the distinguishing mineral is common in the gravels of the streams, but it has not yet been traced to the parent rock.

These garnet-biotite-granulites or schists form a well-marked group, probably distinct from the commoner gneisses with which they are associated.   In the latter the occurrence of a monoclinic, and possibly also of a rhombic, pleochroic pyroxene is worthy of note.   Quartz is common, and occurs typically in elongated lenticles.

The Whiteplains garnetiferous rocks may be correlated with others petrographically similar, found between Suen and Arthington on the western bank of the St. Paul, and with garnet-graphite-gneisses and tremolite-schists at the last-named settlement.

Northwards as far as Marakorri, westwards to Takwema and eastwards to Sanoyei, no similar rocks were found.

The Arthington rocks are associated to the south, between that settlement and Millsburg, with granitic orthogneisses and with foliated hornblende-schists.   The last-named are common throughout the district described.

I am indebted to Mr. F. T. Byrde, Assoc.R.S.M., for the opportunity of examining some rock-specimens collected near Grand Basa, and to the north of that port.   They are comparable with the rocks of Arthington and Whiteplains.

From the neighbourhood of Basa itself comes a fine-grained biotite-garnet-gneiss, from near Dieh's Town a chlorite-schist, and from Mount Findly a garnet-hornblende-quartz rock. Closely related to the last is a specimen collected between the Koi Falls and Stanley Wharf; the hornblende is replaced by hypersthene. To the north-west a magnetite-hypersthene-rock is found associated with acid gneisses and hornblende-schists in the neighbourhood of Mount Barclay, and a related rock occurs near Gwela and Bornde to the north of that hill.

In the northern part of the district various types of biotite-gneiss and hornblende-schist form the Po Range; which is, with its subsidiary ridges, the watershed between the Lofa and St. Paul Rivers. The variation will be shown by the following types collected *in situ* from the bed of a single stream, itself of no great dimensions. They are a massive hornblende-gneiss, a streaky semi-porphyritic gneiss with laminæ rich in hornblende, a hornblende-gneiss of finer grain than either of the above, a biotite-gneiss, and a rock indistinguishable in a hand-specimen from a granite.

The rocks from other parts of the Range visited by me do not greatly differ from these, although some biotite-gneisses from the western slopes are rather coarser in grain, and contain phenocrysts of a pink orthoclase. It is noteworthy that gneissose veins may be seen clearly transgressing the foliation of the hornblende-schists, and are thus shown to be on the whole later in date.

A prevalent east-and-west foliation (magnetic) distinguishes the rocks north of the Arthington-Whiteplains area, and is apparently correlated with lithological variations.

The probable igneous origin of many of these gneisses and associated rocks is suggested by an exposure at Von on the St. Paul River, where a coarse quartz-felspar vein of pegmatoidal habit cuts clearly across the foliation of the biotite-gneiss, but is apparently an integral part of the complex.

Among the various members of this complex, however, certain rocks were found which have the appearance of sediments: thus, on the banks of a stream some 3 miles north of Bomboma, hæmatite-schists occur; they consist of quartz and hæmatite, usually in alternating laminæ. Unfortunately, time did not allow of the relations of these rocks to the surrounding gneisses being ascertained; but Mr. Byrde tells me that he has found similar rocks to the north of the Basa country, and it is possible that we have in them part of the schist-series of Arthington and Whiteplains.

The remainder of the district, and this is by far the greater part, consists of acid gneisses in which biotite is usually the sole ferromagnesian mineral, and microcline is common. These rocks are often slabby in habit, the quartz having a marked tendency to form streaks and lenticles. Garnets are of rare occurrence. Later granites and pegmatites are absent, but a specimen which is practically a pegmatite has been forwarded by Mr. Byrde from the Basa country.

Of the dyke-rocks five specimens have been sliced for examination.  Of these, two were collected by Mr. Byrde, and are from the lighthouse-rock at Grand Basa, and from Hartford on the St. John River; the others are from Sûlwangei, Burrorje, and Horpa Town.  Although varying in grain, these rocks are singularly constant in petrological characters; they are ophitic dolerites consisting of transparent laths of bytownite or labradorite, a rather reddish augite, and ilmenite.  In the example from Grand Basa there is a little interstitial micropegmatite, and in that from Horpa are some pseudomorphs apparently of olivine.

The numerous dykes met with to the north of Kaka, in the Po Range, between Bellaparamu and Gambrebu, in the neighbourhood of Zow Town, and on the St. Paul River above Punga, do not differ sufficiently the one from the other or from those above mentioned to merit a more detailed examination.

## Conclusions.

In conclusion I would suggest:—

(a) That we have indications in the southern part of the district, namely, Arthington, Whiteplains, Caresburg, and Basa, of a series of garnetiferous gneisses, tremolite-schists, kyanite-schists or gneisses, garnet-graphite-gneisses, etc., associated with others of granitic type.

These latter are apparently free from microcline, and contain a pleochroic pyroxene.

(b) That these rocks are replaced on the north, that is, around Takwema, Marakorri, Sanoyei, and Kaka, by biotite-gneisses and hornblende-schists, which have an approximate and singularly constant (magnetic) east-and-west foliation-strike.  Microcline is common.

(c) That these old crystalline rocks are cut by an extensive series of basalts and ophitic dolerites, resembling so closely the post-Cretaceous dykes of Southern Nigeria that it is difficult to avoid the conclusion that they are of the same age.

## II. Physiography.

The principal features of the physiography of Liberia, as above limited, are the low-lying character of the country, the very gradual rise northwards from the shore-level to at least the latitude of Marakorri (about 7° 13′ lat. N.), and in relation to these the mature character of the Lofa, St. Paul, Mahé, Burror, and Junk Rivers.  The fall of the St. Paul is about 10 feet per mile (aneroid determinations) over that part of its course which I visited, that is, from Millsburg (tidal) to Burukai, a distance of nearly 70 miles, along which waterfalls (as distinct from rapids) are rare.

The tributary and main streams approximate at least in grade;

but in one observed instance, where the Tuma falls into the St. Paul, the remnants of a hanging valley can be seen.

Alluvial flats raised above flood-level are conspicuous in many river-valleys.

A line trending about 280° true, and passing a little to the south of Boporo, near Horpa, and a town a short distance to the north of Degbe, approximates to the southern limit of the hill-country, and is not far removed from the coast-line in direction, about 300° true.

Flat-topped ridges and isolated hills, trending parallel to the foliation of the gneiss, are characteristic of the country around Sanoyei and Boporo.

The hill-ranges near the former town, rising from the well-marked peneplain on the south, are very clearly seen from the country to the north of Kaka; and at Boporo the successive ridges forming the outlying spurs of the Po Range are to me very suggestive of successive terraces of marine denudation.

A submergence of 700 feet would cover the southern part of Western Liberia with water almost as far north as 6° 50' lat. N. Throughout there is a striking absence of late deposits in the form of old gravels and sands.

## EXPLANATION OF PLATE XXXV.

Sketch-map of part of Western Liberia, on the scale of 16 miles to the inch.
(From surveys executed by Mr. S. M. Owen, A.R.S.M., and others.)

## DISCUSSION.

The PRESIDENT commented on the value of the communication as to the nature, and more especially the strike, of this geologically little-known region. Further details in respect to the hæmatite-schists would be welcome; they seemed to suggest the Dharwar Series.

Dr. J. W. EVANS referred to the fact that the Po and Boporo hill-ranges were parallel to the strike of the crystalline rocks, and enquired whether there was any evidence of such a variation in the nature of the latter as would account for these features by differences in the rate of erosion. He remarked on the comparative rarity of hanging valleys at low altitudes in the tropics, where glacial conditions could not have affected the character of the erosion. While admitting that the hanging valleys of the west coast of tropical Africa might be accounted for by the rejuvenation of the main streams due to the rise of the land relatively to the sea, he thought that they might be the result of local variations in the rainfall at a time when (as was not improbably the case) this region was less well watered than at present.

M. M. ALLORGE enquired whether the Author had found any traces of the former extension of the Cretaceous sandstones in the areas traversed by him.

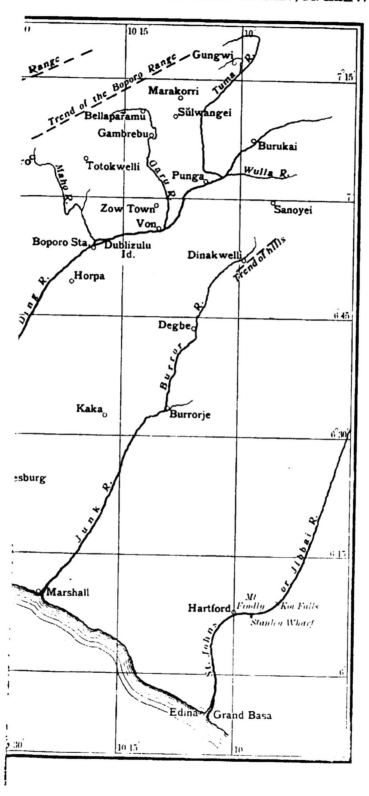

The AUTHOR, after thanking the Fellows for their kind reception of his paper, said, in reply to the President, that without additional knowledge on his part of the Dharwar Beds of India, and also of the hæmatite-schists of Liberia, he could not venture on a parallel between them.   Answering Dr. Evans's question as to the origin of the valley between the Po and Boporo ranges, he said that when in Liberia he concluded that the valleys were due to selective erosion, but that he had not been able satisfactorily to determine the existence of softer rocks along them.   The hanging valleys, he thought, were probably due to rejuvenation, rather than to variation in rainfall; but until the ground near the sources of the St. Paul had been investigated, no certain conclusion could be reached.   No Cretaceous beds had been discovered by him in Western Liberia, although he thought it possible that such might be found on the eastern frontier and on the north-western border of the Republic; but of such an occurrence no satisfactory evidence was available.

17. NOTES *on the* RIVER WEY.   By HENRY BURY, M.A., F.L.S.,
F.G.S.   (Read February 19th, 1908.)

[PLATES XXXVI & XXXVII—MAPS.]

### CONTENTS.

|  |  | Page |
|---|---|---|
| I. | Introduction | 318 |
| II. | The Relation of the Wey to the Blackwater | 319 |
| III. | The Palæolithic Gravels of Farnham | 323 |
| IV. | The Alton District | 327 |

## I. INTRODUCTION.

THAT part of the River Wey which lies within the Wealden area
may for convenience be divided into six sections ; but it is almost
entirely with the last three that the present paper is concerned.
(See Pl. XXXVI.)

Section I is a consequent river, cutting through the Chalk at
Guildford, and is marked on Pl. XXXVI as ' River Wey (Consequent).'   It is the only portion of the Wey that rises in the Weald
Clay, its upper waters being mainly derived from a subsequent river
running nearly parallel to the Lower Greensand escarpment.

Section II is a subsequent stream flowing in from the east,
parallel with the Chalk escarpment, and joining Section I at
Shalford.   It is described in Topley's ' Geology of the Weald' as
the Tillingbourne.

Section III is another subsequent river joining Section I from
the west at Broadford.   Between Godalming and Broadford its
course is north-easterly, but from Tilford to Godalming its general
direction is easterly, parallel to the Hog's Back, which lies about
3 miles to the north.   This branch, which may for convenience be
called the Godalming River, receives several tributaries from
the south, some from Hindhead, others from the Lower Greensand
ridge between Hindhead and Hascombe.   The latter form notches
in that ridge, and seem to have been reduced in length by the
retreat of the Lower Greensand escarpment before branches of the
River Arun.   Some unimportant obsequent streams drain the
Lower Greensand area to the north, between this river and the
Hog's Back (Chalk escarpment).

Section IV, or the Tilford River, is now a continuation
westwards of Section III, although it will be shown to have had a
separate origin.   It also is roughly parallel to the Chalk escarpment, which here has a nearly due north-easterly course.   About
5 miles south-west of Tilford the river forks : the smaller branch
continues the line of the main river westwards, rising as an
obsequent stream at the foot of the Chalk escarpment at Selbourne.
It receives two obsequent tributaries from the north, one of which,
opposite Bentley, I shall have occasion to refer to later as the

**Blacknest Stream.** The more important branch of Section IV, only a portion of which is shown in Pl. XXXVI, rises in a deep valley in the Lower Greensand between Blackdown and Hindhead (from both of which it receives contributions), and flows at first nearly due west to Liphook: there it turns north-westwards, and, after being joined by a stream (marked as 'Deadwater' on the Ordnance-Survey map) which receives the drainage of Woolmer Pond, and of a large flat area to the west of Hindhead, it turns north-eastwards to join the main trunk of Section IV not far from Headley. It will be referred to later on as the **Headley Stream.**

**Section V** is a short obsequent stream joining Section VI to Section III at Tilford, which is thus the meeting-place of three sections (III, IV, and V). For convenience it may be called the **Waverley River**, from the Abbey founded on its banks; but there is no need to describe it here.

**Section VI** is another longitudinal river, parallel to Section IV, but running close to the base of the Chalk escarpment. It follows a very straight course from Alton to a mile east of Farnham, where it joins Section V almost at right angles; but its continuations above Alton are too complex to be described here. Both this and Section IV are marked in the maps as the River Wey; but for the sake of clearness they will be referred to in this paper as the Farnham and Tilford Rivers respectively.

## II. The Relation of the Wey to the Blackwater.
### (Map, p. 320.)

The former extension southwards of the River Blackwater is recognized by Prof. W. M. Davis,[1] but all that he says is that 'the Wey has recently taken off the head of the Blackwater.' An attempt will here be made to show some of the details of the process by which this result was brought about, though unfortunately, owing to the softness of the strata, but few definite traces of earlier stages can now be found. The Farnham River, where it curves round into the Waverley Valley, is just 200 feet above O.D. This curve is bounded on the north by a steep bank 50 to 70 feet high, and when we have surmounted this, we find ourselves, after traversing a space of almost level ground, slowly descending into the Blackwater Valley. The total width of the gap in the Chalk escarpment, which thus forms a col between the two rivers, is, at the 300-foot level, about 2 miles, but almost in the centre of the gap a mound of Chalk rises to 295 feet, and thus divides it into two valleys (east and west), each about 50 feet deep, and nearly a mile in width. It is the western of these two valleys which lies opposite the bend of the Farnham River (see Map, p. 320). A small stream, coming down from Hungry Hill in an easterly direction, runs to the bottom of this valley, and then, about opposite the Chalk mound, turns abruptly southwards, and descends through a short ravine

---

[1] Geogr. Journ. vol. v (1895) p. 146.

*Map showing the relation of the Wey to the Blackwater.*

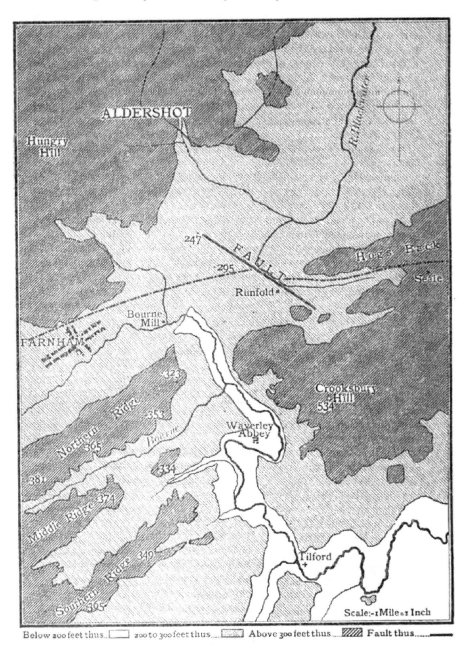

Below 200 feet thus ☐   200 to 300 feet thus ☐   Above 300 feet thus ☐   Fault thus ▨

[The heavy broken line marks the lower edge of the Chalk.]

to the Farnham River at Bourne Mill. About a mile to the north of this stream, and roughly parallel to it, another brook descends from Hungry Hill, and forms the present head of the Blackwater; it continues on an east-south-easterly course till it comes opposite the end of the Hog's Back, and then turns sharply northwards.

The valley to the east of the above-mentioned Chalk mound deserves especial attention. A subsequent valley runs down past Seale at the foot of the Hog's Back, and at present only produces a mere trickle of water; but there is a suggestion that it may once have extended nearly to Puttenham, before being beheaded by an obsequent tributary of the Godalming River. At first sight it looks as if this tiny stream flowed to the south of the Chalk mound to join the Farnham River, but more careful observation reveals the fact that it turns northwards near Runfold and flows out over the Chalk to join the Blackwater. This very interesting fact—that a stream does still flow out from the Wealden to the Tertiary area at this point—was, I find, noted by George Long in 1839,[1] but was afterwards entirely overlooked. Topley,[2] indeed, asserts that there is no stream flowing through this pass, although the alluvium deposited by it is marked on the Geological-Survey map.

It has long been known that pebbles derived from the Hythe Beds of the Lower Greensand, which must have come at least as far as from Hindhead, are to be found in the gravels to the north of the Chalk in this region. They occur very sparingly in the ' Southern Drift'[3] to the north of Farnham, 600 feet above O.D.; much more frequently in the lower, and probably later gravels bounding the Blackwater Valley (Fox Hills, Chobham Ridges, Hartford-Bridge Flats, etc.)[4]; and in moderate quantities in gravels lying on the Chalk itself in the gap already described (Water Lane, see 6-inch Ordnance-Survey map). All this showed to earlier writers that there must have been some Wealden river flowing northwards in this region; but, until the principles of river-capture had been fully expounded by many writers on both sides of the Atlantic, its connection with the recent river-system could not be clearly understood. With our present knowledge, we may safely assume that at no very distant date there was a consequent river coming down from Hindhead and flowing through this gap, after being joined by the Tilford and Farnham Rivers on the west, and the Seale stream on the east. But it is a curious fact that this consequent river is hard to identify among the many streams from Hindhead, and it is possible that during the present cycle of erosion it never attained to any great size[5]; while many of the Lower Greensand pebbles were doubtless supplied by the other streams which are now collected by the subsequent Tilford River. It is doubtful whether there was ever a stream of importance

[1] Proc. Geol. Soc. vol. iii (1838–42) p. 101.
[2] ' Geology of the Weald ' Mem. Geol. Surv. 1875, p. 279.
[3] J. Prestwich, Quart. Journ. Geol. Soc. vol. xlvi (1890) p. 161.
[4] H. W. Monckton, *ibid.* vol. xlviii (1892) pp. 29 *et seqq.*
[5] The Darent is another Wealden river which has no well-marked consequent head.

joining this consequent river from the east; certainly the bulk of
the Godalming River must be regarded as a subsequent outgrowth
from the Guildford Wey.  The next stage of evolution seems to
have been the capture of the consequent river and the Tilford
stream by the Godalming River at, or near, Tilford.  I can find no
direct evidence of this, and nothing to show how much the level of
the river at Tilford was lowered by this capture; but it is perhaps
significant that, while flints are found in fair numbers in the
gravels on both sides of the Tilford River, they are almost entirely
absent in the Godalming Valley, except at a very slight elevation
above the present river-bed.

The Waverley Valley would at this stage be left practically dry,
but the Farnham and Seale Rivers would still continue to join the
Blackwater.  Previous to this the whole gap in the Chalk between
Hungry Hill and the Hog's Back formed one wide valley, but now
the mass of water was so far diminished that the Seale and
Farnham Rivers got separated, and proceeded to carve out each its
separate valley, leaving the existing Chalk mound between them.
If this be a correct interpretation of the facts, this mound may be
taken (with due allowance for recent denudation) as a measure of
the level of the river-bed at the time when the consequent river
was diverted; and we shall see other reasons later on [1] for thinking
that this is the case.  We may further infer that the erosion of
the Blackwater Valley since that time has been extremely slow,
for the tiny Seale stream has been able to carve out a comparatively
wide valley.

The final change by which the present river-system was established was doubtless the outgrowth of an obsequent stream from
Tilford, along the line of the old consequent valley (Waverley
Valley) until it met the Farnham River; then the latter turned
aside from the Blackwater, and rapidly lowered its bed some 50 feet
to accommodate itself to the level of the Godalming River.  Herein
lies the interest of a gravel-capped terrace which runs along the
south side of the Farnham Valley, from its junction with the
Waverley Valley to a point some 3 miles farther west.  It stands
about 50 feet above the present river-bed, and thus corresponds
closely in level with the watershed now dividing the Wey from the
Blackwater.  It is, in fact, a remnant of the old river-bottom, and
affords a useful example of the formation of a terrace by river-
capture, without any help from local or general elevation; while
the steepness of the bank below is an indication that the changes
which gave rise to it were both rapid and recent.[2]

The entrance to the Waverley Valley presents a striking contrast
with the Farnham Valley, out of which it leads, being much narrower
and steeper; and indeed it exhibits just the features which we
might expect to result from the diversion of a longitudinal river into
a small obsequent valley.  The latter does not follow exactly the
line of the old consequent valley, but has shifted more to the east.
This is shown, not only by the steepness of the left bank all the way

[1] § III, p. 326.
[2] Other proofs of this are to be found all the way up the valley.

to Tilford, but also by a remnant of the old obsequent river-bed, still traceable on the right bank from Tilford up to about the mouth of the Bourne, and exhibiting, as we might expect, a steeper gradient than the present river.    Traces, too, of the old consequent river are to be found on this side, but they will be discussed in § III.

Two points in connection with the old river-bed between the Wey and the Blackwater must be dealt with briefly before we leave the subject.

(1) It has already been mentioned that Lower Greensand fragments are less common in the gravels lying in this pass ('Water Lane,' etc.) than in the older gravels on the Fox Hills.  The explanation of this is simple : the latter (nearly 400 feet above Ordnance-datum) received their supply direct from Hindhead by way of the consequent river ; but the gravels of Water Lane (about 250 feet) were laid down long after the capture of the consequent river, and their Hythe-Bed pebbles therefore were only derived at second hand from the older gravels bordering the Farnham Valley.

(2) In the preliminary description of this region it was seen that a stretch of nearly level ground separated the Blackwater from the edge of the steep bank which bounds the Farnham Valley on each side of Bourne Mill.  It might be expected from its origin that most of this old river-bed would drain towards the Blackwater ; but such is not the case.  The actual turning-point, so far as I can ascertain, is at a spot to the east of Weybourne House, marked 247 feet on the 6-inch Ordnance-Survey map, about 1500 yards from the Farnham River, and half that distance from the Blackwater.  It happens that this point is close to, if not on, the line of fault, as mapped by the officers of the Geological Survey ; and it is, therefore, just possible that some slight earth-movement has taken place here in recent times.  Perhaps, however, it is more probable that this is a case of 'aggradiug'—the Blackwater, which comes down from Hungry Hill almost at right angles to the plain, having deposited so much sediment as to dam back the drainage of the marshy land to the south.  In either case a very small alteration of level would be sufficient to give rise to the present conditions.

### III. The Palæolithic Gravels of Farnham.

The high ground between the Tilford and Farnham Rivers, from the Blacknest Valley (opposite Bentley) in the west to the Waverley Valley in the east, is readily divided, as the map shows (Pl. XXXVI) into a western or Alice-Holt area and three parallel ridges ; but there are good grounds for believing that these ridges have been only recently separated, and that the whole must be regarded as the dissected remnant of an old plateau of river-origin.  Only one small patch in the north-western corner of Alice Holt rises above the 400-foot contour, but almost the whole of the ground shown on the map as being above 300 is, in fact, more than 350 feet above Ordnance-datum.  The plateau shows, especially along the northern

ridge, a general slope to the north-east; but there are indications
also of a less regular slope towards the south-east, as the following
measurements, taken along lines at right angles to the Farnham
Valley, will show :—

|  |  | *Feet.* |
|---|---|---|
| 1. North-western corner of Alice Holt | ......................... | 400 |
|  | 1 mile south-east of this ....................... | 393 |
|  | ¾ mile farther south-east ...................... | 361 |
| 2. Clay Hill (Wrecclesham) ...................... | | 388 |
|  | Base of southern ridge (Rowledge)............ | 367 |
| 3. Northern ridge (a little east of ' Highlands').............. | | 370 [1] |
|  | Eastern end of middle ridge ................. | 374 |
|  | Southern ridge (corresponding part) ............. | 349 |

The actual heights would, of course, be altered by removing the
drift which is present at all these points, but the relative levels
would scarcely be affected.

The northern edge of the plateau corresponds approximately with
the axis of the flexure which gives rise to the Peasemarsh inlier
(near Guildford), and is here dying away, not being traceable
farther west than Bentley [2]: and this flexure gives rise not only to a
westerly dip, which brings the Lower Greensand to the surface
about half way along the northern ridge, but also to a slight
southerly dip, in consequence of which this outcrop of the Lower
Greensand is pushed farther eastwards on the southern ridge than
on the northern, although, as we have seen, the former is somewhat
the lower. With the exception of these eastern ends of the ridges,
the whole plateau consists of Gault.

Patches of drift (mostly gravel) occur on all the higher parts of
the plateau, especially along the northern ridge, where its greatest
depth is given by Lasham [3] as 40 feet, and by Monckton & Mangles [4]
as 25 feet: it would be interesting to know the exact spots at
which these very great depths occurred, but I do not think that
they can have been on the crest of the ridge, where the thickness
rarely exceeds 10 feet. It is from this northern ridge that the
most perfect of the well-known Palæolithic implements of Farnham
have been obtained; many, it is true, occur in the gravel-beds
slightly lower down, on the southern slope of the Farnham Valley,
but these are almost invariably waterworn,[5] and are probably
derived from the plateau. The drift of the middle and southern
ridges is usually much less thick, and varies greatly in character,
being sometimes mainly sand; but where gravel occurs it is very
similar in character to that of the northern ridge, except that it
contains a far larger percentage of chert and other Lower Greensand
pebbles. Monckton & Mangles, whose careful account of the
Farnham gravels should be consulted, describe as a river-gravel a
bed (marked D on their diagram), which lies apparently at the base

[1] This is approximate only: the rest are from the Ordnance Map. The last
of the series (349 feet) probably does not belong to the plateau proper: see
p. 326.
[2] 'Geology of the Weald' Mem. Geol. Surv. 1875, p. 229.
[3] Coll. Surrey Archæol. Soc. vol. xi, p. 27.
[4] Proc. Geol Assoc. vol. xiii (1893-94) p. 77.      [5] *Ibid.* p. 78.

of the middle ridge ; and I have no hesitation in ascribing a similar origin to the gravels of Rowledge and the southern ridge.

The patches of drift scattered over Alice Holt I have had no opportunity of studying in section, but from examination of the surface-material I should judge their composition to be very similar to that of the Rowledge gravels—certainly Lower Greensand pebbles are present in greater quantity than on the northern ridge.

In ascribing all these drift-beds to one river, which also planed down the underlying Gault and Lower Greensand, I am running counter to the teaching of the maps of the Geological Survey, on which only the gravel of the northern ridge is described as 'River-Gravel,' while all the other beds are classed as 'Gravel and Sand of uncertain age and origin.' I do not know the grounds for this distinction, but perhaps the following passage from Topley's 'Geology of the Weald' (p. 196) throws some light upon it :

'Flints are scattered about over the high land of Farnham, Frensham, and Thursley Commons,[1] and over Alder Holt; but these are probably the remains of the Chalk which once covered the lower beds and are not a deposited gravel.'

This, of course, was written before Monckton's & Mangles's recognition of some of the beds as of fluviatile origin ; but, quite apart from that, it should have been obvious that mere disintegration of the Chalk and Upper Greensand could not plane down the lower strata to one level, and that this planing is conclusive in favour of river-action.

But, although the formation of this plateau by a river admits of no doubt, yet it is not at once obvious what the course of that river was. At the present day we find the Farnham River immediately on the north, and the Tilford River on the south, with no vestige in either case of a former watershed which would enable us to identify our plateau-river with either. It is true that the gravel of the northern ridge is continued for a short distance down the slope of the Farnham Valley, while on the southern ridge the drift hardly extends to the edge: but that, of course, is not conclusive, and on the other hand the tendency, already noted, of the whole plateau to slope south-eastwards might be held to point to the Tilford stream as the modern representative of the plateau-river. The key to the problem lies, I think, in the junction with the old consequent river which we have already traced : for, while it is easy to understand how this junction might shift downstream (that is, northwards) it hardly seems possible for the Tilford River, if it formerly joined in as far north as the plateau extends, to have shifted its point of junction upstream to Tilford. We have already seen reason to believe that the consequent river was not beheaded till a lower level than the plateau had been reached ; and I will now add some further evidence pointing in the same direction.

Each of the three ridges of the plateau, after maintaining for a considerable distance the plateau-level (of which 350 feet may be

[1] Farnham Common embraces the eastern ends of the three ridges ; Alder Holt is the name erroneously substituted for Alice Holt on the old Ordnance-Survey map.

considered the lowest point), drops with some suddenness to a lower platform, half a mile or more in extent, before its final plunge into the Waverley Valley. The relation of this platform, which is still well over the 300-foot level, and is covered with gravel, can best be studied at the end of the northern ridge, on which the following gradients are found :—

1. From Alice Holt (400 feet) to Greenhill (353 feet, about a mile south-east of Farnham) from 1 in 650 to 1 in 250. Average for 3½ miles = 1 in 413.
2. From Greenhill to the edge of the Waverley Valley (about 320 feet), 1 in 90.
3. Slope of Waverley Valley = 1 in 12.

It is, I think, a reasonable assumption that this lower platform is a remnant of the left bank of the consequent valley as it was just before it was beheaded. How much farther east it extended and how much lower than 320 feet it fell, there is no direct evidence to show, since the old bed of the river, together with the whole of its right bank, has been destroyed in the formation of the obsequent Waverley Valley. Taken, however, in connection with the Chalk mound (295 feet) in the pass a mile farther north, it justifies, I think, my assumption that the latter represents approximately the level of the river at the time when it was beheaded. Further evidence may perhaps be derived from the character of the gravel of this lower platform on the northern ridge, but at present only a superficial examination is possible, and that is seldom satisfactory: so far I have found but few Hythe-Bed pebbles in it: but it is curious that these pebbles, which are scarce along most of this ridge, suddenly become common at Greenhill. In view of this irregularity in their distribution, it would probably be unwise to draw conclusions from the presence or absence of these Hythe-Bed fragments on the various portions of the plateau; but a few general remarks may be useful. Many of them are distinctly angular, and although they must have come originally from Hindhead,[1] may have reached their present position only from an older drift; but the bulk of them probably came direct at the time when the plateau was formed. How many streams were concerned with this supply, it is impossible now to say, but probably the principal source was the Headley River; and to this I attribute the formation of the south-western portion of Alice Holt, which, as the map (Pl. XXXVI) shows, is out of the line of the river coming from the Alton Valley and forming the rest of the plateau. This connection of the Headley with the Farnham River appears to have been maintained, after the plateau was abandoned, along the line of the Blacknest Stream, which cuts a gap in the line of hills almost 100 feet deep, and only 50 feet above the bed of the Farnham River. No doubt this Headley stream was finally captured by the Tilford River (which must until then have been but small), though I know of nothing to show exactly at what stage this took place.

[1] R. A. C. Godwin-Austen (Quart. Journ. Geol. Soc. vol. iv, 1848, p. 260) attributes the 'cherty sandstone' so common on the southern ridges to the Upper Greensand; but I have failed to match it among local specimens of that age, and believe that almost the whole of it comes from the Hythe Beds.

In conclusion, it is worthy of remark that the Alice-Holt plateau, on which the drift must have accumulated under rather peculiar conditions, stands quite alone in the western area of the Weald. The only other extensive sheet of high-level gravel is on Hungry Hill, 250 feet above this plateau; but it belongs to a far earlier period (Southern Drift), and contains no traces of Palæolithic man. If, as is possible, this Southern Drift marks the close of the first cycle of erosion [1] (and it can scarcely be earlier), then more than half the denudation of the second cycle had taken place before the Palæolithic gravels were deposited; but, on the other hand, all the adjustments which we have followed, from the capture of the consequent river to the diversion of the Farnham River, are of decidedly later date than those implements.

## IV. THE ALTON DISTRICT. (Pl. XXXVII.)

The Farnham branch of the Wey (Section VI) runs a very straight course between Alton and its turning into the Waverley Valley—a distance of about 10 miles,—but passes over several different strata. Roughly speaking, the lowest third of its course is in Lower Greensand; the middle third in Gault; and the upper third in Upper Greensand and Chalk. But, although the main valley is continued up to Alton, what is generally regarded as the head of this branch of the river comes in from the south nearly a mile below that town, not far from the village of Wilsham, and is marked in the 6-inch Ordnance-Survey map as the Caker Stream (see Pl. XXXVII). Following it up towards its source we first pass through a narrow gorge in the Chalk, and almost immediately find ourselves in a broad and flat valley, which seems at first sight to stretch all the way to Selbourne (8 miles); but the southern end of it, though separated by no very well-marked watershed, drains into the Oakhanger Stream (Section IV). On the east side of this valley the Upper Greensand rises, with a gentle dip-slope, to about 500 feet above Ordnance-datum; while on the west is a range of Chalk hills, rising to about the same height, but interrupted by frequent valleys, and presenting extensive surfaces of nearly-level ground. The Caker Stream runs, for the most part, at the junction of the two strata; while the Chalk, however, contributes but little to it, several streams join it from the Greensand slopes, and it is to these that Topley alludes when he writes [2]:—

'The streams which feed the Wey itself' [that is, the Farnham branch] 'take their rise often in the Upper Greensand itself, and flow over the Chalk to the north and north-west. The drainage of this north-eastern' [north-western is meant] 'corner of the Weald is exceedingly curious and unlike that of any other parts of the district.'

But, before attempting an explanation of this very interesting fact, we must first face the larger problem (not directly referred to by Topley) of how so great an extent of Chalk ever came to drain into the Wealden area. Elsewhere the only contributions of the Chalk

[1] See W. M. Davis, Geogr. Journ. vol. v (1895) p. 135.
[2] 'Geology of the Weald' Mem. Geol. Surv. 1875, p. 196.

to the Wealden drainage take the form of isolated obsequent
streams, seldom more than 2 or 3 miles in length; but here, in
the Alton district, we find an extremely-complicated system of
Chalk valleys, which spread over something like 50 square miles
of country, all uniting together at, or close to, Alton, and discharging
their waters into the Wealden area about 2 miles north-east of
that town.

The most important line of drainage in this Chalk area is a
valley which comes in from the south, past the villages of East
Tisted, Faringdon, and Chawton, and which may conveniently be
referred to as the Tisted Valley. From Privett Station, which
is nearly its southernmost point, to Alton, it is about 7 miles
long; and it is everywhere wide and open, and receives numerous
lateral tributaries. Of these, the longest ($4\frac{1}{2}$ miles) has rather
an unusual direction, rising in Medstead Hill, and running about
south-eastwards to join the main valley near East Tisted. A little
farther north are two valleys coming in from the south-east, which
deserve notice, not so much on account of their length (2 to $2\frac{1}{2}$ miles),
as because they reach the Chalk escarpment, and (one of them
dividing into two) form three deep notches in it. The upper
portions of these valleys, near the escarpment, are exceedingly wide
and flat, with a very gentle gradient towards the Tisted Valley;
and it is, I think, impossible to avoid the conclusion that they
were already well established before the escarpment reached its
present position. Opposite each of the notches, which are 150 feet
in depth, is an obsequent tributary of the River Rother.

Another important valley which also joins the main valley at
Alton comes from Lasham Hill, about $4\frac{1}{2}$ miles from that town,
and has in the main a south-easterly course, but turns sharply
eastwards at its lower end. It may be conveniently referred to as
the Lasham Valley, and its approximate parallelism to the
Medstead branch of the Tisted Valley should be noted. Not far
from Lasham Station it is joined almost at right angles by a valley
which starts on the north side of Medstead Hill, and runs a course
about 3 miles long rather to the east of north.

Besides these two important valleys there is a third, also joining
in at Alton, which is worthy of mention rather for its position than
for its size. It starts at the 'Golden Pot' Inn, $2\frac{1}{2}$ miles north of
Alton, and runs due south, with all the characters of an ordinary
obsequent valley; but it is interesting because it lies right in the
line of the Tisted Valley, and has at its head a distinct, though not
very deep notch, in the line of Chalk hills; while on the north side
of this notch is a tributary of the River Whitewater. It is further
to be noted that this valley lies exactly at the point at which there
is a change in direction of the ridge of Chalk hills which here
forms the watershed between the river-system under consideration
(Wey) and the more direct tributaries of the Thames—the Whitewater, Lyde, and Loddon. On its east side this ridge runs north-
eastwards, parallel with the Farnham Valley; while on the west it
runs north-westwards, in the direction of Kingsclere, and parallel
with the Lasham Valley.

It will be seen that the valley-system in the Chalk round Alton is complex, and presents several features by no means easy to understand. The district is known to present a number of subsidiary folds,[1] and when these are worked out in detail they will probably throw light on the river-system ; at present, however, they are not, so far as I can gather, sufficiently well known to be of much assistance. But although we are unable to follow all the steps in the evolution of this system, we may perhaps allow ourselves some speculation as to its most salient feature—the connection with the Wealden area. It will, I think, be evident from the foregoing description, and it is still more obvious on the ground itself, that this valley-system was established at a very early period, when the Chalk spread much farther to the east than at present, and that its connection with the Wealden area is clearly secondary ; but where, then, did it discharge its waters before this connection was made? The first suggestion that presents itself, as a possible working hypothesis, is that the Tisted Stream is the remnant of an old consequent river, which joined the Whitewater by way of the Golden Pot, and was afterwards captured by the Farnham River, which we will regard for the present as a subsequent river belonging to the Wealden area. It will be worth while to examine in some detail the various propositions involved in this hypothesis.

(1) Is the Tisted Stream the remnant of a consequent river?—The main water-parting in the western area of the Weald is formed by the Petersfield anticline. In it one of the western branches of the Wey (Deadwater) rises not far from Liphook, while it is easy to trace its connection with those branches of the Rother which join that river at Iping and Selham. The westernmost branch of the Rother, it is true, appears to be an exception, since it reaches almost as far north as Selbourne; but I do not believe that this represents its primitive position. The way in which it follows the soft beds of the Lower Greensand round the curved end of the Wealden dome suggests strongly that its presence north of the anticline is due to a modern encroachment, assisted possibly by the beds having been already levelled by the river to which Woolmer Pond belongs. Anyone who visits the district will see that it is still encroaching, and that it is likely at no very distant date to capture Woolmer Pond itself.

This view is borne out by a study of the Chalk district immediately to the west of Petersfield ; for here we find the Meon River rising in the anticline and flowing southwards, while our Tisted Valley starts from a point only a little to the north of this line. It is therefore very unlikely that there should be, in so narrow an area, separate lines of water-parting for this branch of the Rother and the rivers on either side of it.

Farther west again, although the Petersfield anticline is still traceable, it is no longer dominant ; and the Rivers Itchen, Test, and Avon, in a gradually lengthening series, take their origin in

[1] 'The Cretaceous Rocks of Britain—The Upper Chalk of England' Mem. Geol. Surv. vol. iii (1904) p. 183.

the anticline which gives rise to the Kingsclere, Shalbourne, and
Pewsey inliers. It will be seen, therefore, that the area drained by
the Tisted Stream corresponds to that of the Meon River, and that
the two together occupy an intermediate position between the rivers
of the Weald, rising in the Petersfield anticline, and the rivers of
the Hampshire Uplands, rising in the Kingsclere anticline; and
there can be no question that, if the Tisted Stream flowed at
the present day past the Golden Pot, and into the Whitewater,
we should unhesitatingly ascribe to it a consequent origin.[1]

(2) Is there any evidence of a former connection with
the Whitewater?—The alignment of the Tisted and Golden-Pot
Valleys with a tributary of the Whitewater is suggestive, but of
course not conclusive: it may be due to chance, or to something in
the folding of the Chalk at this point; for, as we have seen, the
Golden-Pot Valley marks a change in the line of hills. Given
the alignment, the notch in the hills would follow as a matter
of course, and as there is no gravel in this notch, or in the valleys
immediately north and south of it, it cannot be said that there is
any clear evidence of a former connection. We may even argue
against it, that it is unlikely that a river which had a fairly-straight
run to the Thames would be captured by one (the Blackwater)
which pursues a very devious route; but this is not an insuperable
difficulty, for although we know nothing of the causes which have
led the Blackwater to assume its present course, it is hardly likely
that that course is primitive. Lower Greensand fragments are
found in the region drained by the Whitewater,[2] and it is tempting
to suppose that they were brought here by the Tisted Stream; but
so far I have found none in the Tisted Valley, nor any evidence
that it was connected with the Wealden Beds.

(3) Did the Farnham River originate as a subsequent
river in the Wealden area?—It is well known that an anticline runs past Farnham, as far west as Bentley; and we have seen
evidence on pp. 323–26 that the river ran along and even south of
this line at no distant date, though it now lies slightly farther
north. We can easily understand how such a longitudinal anticline might give rise to a subsequent river, and therefore, if the
eastern end of the Farnham River, which runs through Gault and
Lower Greensand, stood alone, we should be in no doubt as to its
origin; but it is its western end which makes us pause. That
a Wealden river should eat its way back through a mile of Upper
Greensand (a highly resistant rock in this region) and 2 miles of
Chalk is not indeed impossible, though certainly improbable; but
that it should accomplish this feat without leaving any traces of

[1] It might have been expected that the consequent rivers in the west of the
Weald would not run north and south, but would radiate from the end of
the Wealden dome. If, however, there is any trace of this radiation within the
Wealden area, there is none outside, and our Tisted Valley is parallel with
the Whitewater and Loddon on the north, and the Meon, Itchen, Test, and
Avon on the south.
[2] H. W. Monckton, 'On the Gravels south of the Thames from Guildford
to Newbury' Quart. Journ. Geol. Soc. vol. xlviii (1892) p. 37.

recent origin—without any narrowing of its valley or steepening of its sides—is well-nigh incredible. Yet that section of the valley which lies between Alton and Cuckoo's Corner (the junction of Chalk and Upper Greensand) shows a bottom as wide and almost as flat as at Farnham itself; and indeed from one watershed to another it is actually much wider than at that town, some 8 miles lower down. There is plenty of evidence in the neighbourhood to show that the Lower Chalk is comparatively non-resistant, and is readily levelled down when exposed; but, if the valley is an outgrowth from the Weald, how did such a width of these strata become exposed? And, even if we assume (without any justification) that all the Chalk is soft in this region, we are still in difficulties with the Upper Greensand, which is, beyond all doubt, a highly-resistant rock. The only explanation that I can find which will meet all these facts is, that a broad valley must have been already formed here in the Chalk (and perhaps Eocene Beds) and have been already connected with the Blackwater near Farnham, before the Wealden strata of this region were uncovered. An examination, however imperfect, of the history of the denudation of the Weald will show us that this conclusion is not so improbable as it may at first sight appear.

It is generally agreed that the Weald, after passing through a first cycle of denudation was reduced almost to a plain. This used to be referred to as a plain of marine denudation, but perhaps at the present time Prof. W. M. Davis's view would receive more support—that it was a peneplain due to fluviatile erosion. But, although this belief in a plain has long existed, no satisfactory attempt has, so far as I know, been made to show at what horizons we may seek at the present day for remnants of it. I am far from possessing enough knowledge to attempt such a reconstruction, and in what follows I am merely seeking to ascertain the lowest points that may have been reached by parts of that plain, so as to get some idea of the extension of the Chalk at the close of the first cycle of erosion. In the western portion of the Weald, with which alone I am concerned at present, the highest point is Blackdown Hill (918 feet) immediately south of Hindhead; but nothing as high as this is found in either the North or the South Downs. Therefore we may probably infer that the upheaval which ushered in the present cycle of denudation was of a differential character, affecting the central axis more than the sides, and perhaps also raising the southern slopes more than the northern, since we find several points in the South Downs rising above 800 feet (including Butser Hill, 889 feet), while in the North Downs we find only two hills west of Dorking which rise above the 700-foot level—White Down (712 feet), near Dorking, and Holybourne Down (728 feet), close to Alton. If, then, we wish to ascribe any lower points to the plain, we must, on the marine theory, postulate some longitudinal irregularities in the upheaval, as well as the above-mentioned transverse one. But it is less necessary to do this if we adopt the fluviatile hypothesis, since a peneplain allows of the existence of hills of moderate height above the general base-level of denudation.

In this way it may be possible to regard the Southern Drift on the hills above Farnham (Beacon Hill, Cæsar's Camp, and Hungry Hill, 615 feet at the highest point) as part of the original peneplain. In suggesting this I must not, however, be understood to express any opinion as to the origin of these beds : I am only, as I said before, seeking for the lowest point of the peneplain, and no one is likely to look for it lower than this Southern Drift.   Now at this horizon the Upper Greensand would certainly be exposed along the crest of the anticline opposite Farnham, perhaps as far west as the village of Wrecclesham ; but I do not think that the Gault would be uncovered except in the actual bed of the consequent river (Waverley Valley) ; and, as the Upper Greensand is here almost as resistant as the Chalk itself, there cannot at that time have been much of a subsequent river of Wealden origin at this point.   South of the anticline, too, the Chalk would extend to within 2 or 3 miles of Hindhead, while to the west of Wrecclesham it would be continuous with the Hampshire Uplands.   All this vast area of Chalk must have had its own lines of drainage ; and, although these perhaps were mainly transverse (consequent), yet the wonder is, not that the Farnham River should have originated in this area, but that other longitudinal rivers in the Weald should not show traces of a similar origin.   Perhaps when they are more carefully examined they will be found to do so.

All this, though it does not directly affect the question of whether the Tisted Valley was ever continuous with the Whitewater, renders that hypothesis much less necessary.   While the Farnham Valley was held to be of Wealden origin, an earlier outlet for the Tisted Valley had to be found somewhere ; but now it seems possible that the connection of the two valleys may date back nearly, if not quite, to the time of the plain, or beginning of the present cycle of denudation.   The present height of the Golden-Pot pass is 584 feet above Ordnance-datum ; and, allowing for recent reduction, which, with a valley on each side it must have undergone, we arrive at a level not far short of that of the Southern Drift, which I have here assumed (but without any fixed convictions on the subject) to belong to the first cycle of denudation. As to what extension these valleys may have had before that time, it is perhaps hardly profitable to speculate.[1]

A word may be added here concerning the comparative inconspicuousness of the Chalk escarpment along the Farnham Valley, noted by Drew[2] and apparently connected by him with the lowness of the dip ; this ought, however, to produce precisely the opposite result.   I believe it is partly due to the hardness of the Lower Greensand, which masks the Chalk slopes from many points of view by forming an imperfect escarpment of its own ; and, in part also, it may indicate that these Chalk slopes are not in their origin an escarpment at all, but rather the sides of an open Chalk valley, such as may be found at the present day all over the Hampshire Uplands.

[1] The great development of lateral valleys in the Tisted, as compared with the Farnham, Valley should be noted, but does not necessarily imply a difference in age.

[2] Quoted by W. Whitaker, ' Geology of the London Basin ' Mem. Geol. Surv. vol. iv (1875) p. 358.

The Caker Stream.—It will be remembered that the Caker Stream flows for some distance at the junction of the Chalk and the Upper Greensand. These junction-beds are sandy,[1] and there is abundant evidence all along the foot of the western Downs that they constitute a line of special weakness. The Lower Chalk also, as we have seen, is non-resistant, and here, as elsewhere, forms large areas of nearly level ground. The Malm Rock (Upper Greensand), on the other hand, is very hard, and has been but little removed from the hills to the east of this valley.

There is hardly any room for doubt that the present conditions have been brought about by the simple removal of the Chalk from part of a river-system originally established in the Chalk alone, and that this result has been greatly facilitated by the presence of the weak junction-beds; but the details of the original valley-system are rather obscure. The wall of Chalk separating this valley from the nearly parallel Tisted Valley is broken through in three places by wide and flat passes, and the drainage in all three gaps is mainly towards the Tisted Valley. If the original drainage had been along the present line of the Caker Stream, by a valley comparable to, though smaller than, the Tisted Valley, we should certainly expect tributaries from this western side, as well as those which, as we have already seen, flow in from the Greensand. The comparative absence of these, coupled with the size and apparent age of the three branches of the Tisted Valley, leads me to think that the latter indicate the original lines of drainage, which the Caker Stream, being the first to reach the soft junction-beds, has succeeded in capturing one after the other.

It is, however, unnecessary to enter into further discussion of this point, because the conclusion of main interest to us is the same in any case—namely, that we have here another example of the conversion of a Chalk valley into a Wealden one. In the Farnham Valley it is the lower end which has changed its character; here, by an odd combination of circumstances, it is the upper end of the stream which has entered the Wealden Beds; but the time is perhaps not so very far distant when the rest of the Chalk will be removed between Wilsham and Cuckoo's Corner, and then this stream will be difficult to distinguish throughout its course from one of purely Wealden origin.

### EXPLANATION OF PLATES XXXVI & XXXVII.

#### PLATE XXXVI.

Map on the scale of 2 miles to the inch, showing the six sections of the River Wey which lie within the Wealden area. The upper part of the River Wey (consequent) and the branch of the Headley Stream which comes down from Haslemere are not included.

#### PLATE XXXVII.

Map of the Alton district, on the scale of 2 miles to the inch. The courses of the principal valleys are marked by dotted lines, and the heavy broken line marks approximately the lower outline of the Chalk.

---

[1] 'The Cretaceous Rocks of Britain' Mem. Geol. Surv. vol. i (1900) p. 113 & vol. ii (1903) p. 60.

DISCUSSION.

Dr. R. D. ROBERTS said that some months ago the Author had shown him the rough draft of the paper with illustrative maps, and had taken him over a part of the ground. He had been greatly interested, and had formed the opinion that the Author was doing a very admirable piece of work. He much regretted the absence of the Author, whom he had hoped to hear in person laying before the Society the results of his observations. It was difficult to follow the paper without the maps, and quite impossible to discuss it in any effective way. He felt sure, however, that when the paper was printed with the illustrative maps, the Fellows would find it to be a most interesting and valuable contribution to the study of the development of river-systems.

Prof. WATTS stated that the Author had expressed his regret that his absence, caused by illness, had prevented him from reading the paper, and presenting a proper series of illustrations on the screen. He regarded the paper as a very careful piece of work, and thought that it ought to be published as an example of the researches carried out by the Author in his district.

Mr. G. W. YOUNG joined with previous speakers in deploring the absence of the Author and of maps to illustrate the paper. He thought that there could be little doubt that the upper waters of the Wey did, at one time, form part of the Blackwater system. In a paper read before the Geologists' Association last year, now passing through the press, he (the speaker) had already suggested that their capture by the Wey was caused by local earth-movements. His view was that the Hog's-Back movement did not take place until long after the general elevation of the Wealden anticline, and after the principal river-systems of that district had been established. Then a sharp movement took place in the extreme north-western corner, which bisected the Blackwater system and diverted the head-waters of that stream into the Wey system. Near Farnham there was evidence of shearing and of both dip and strike-faulting, the latter in one place showing a throw of probably not less than 200 feet—for the zone of *Terebratulina gracilis*, the uppermost zone of the Middle Chalk, could be seen abutting against the base of the Lower Chalk. He welcomed the appearance of the paper as a contribution to the elucidation of a very interesting, but hitherto somewhat neglected problem.

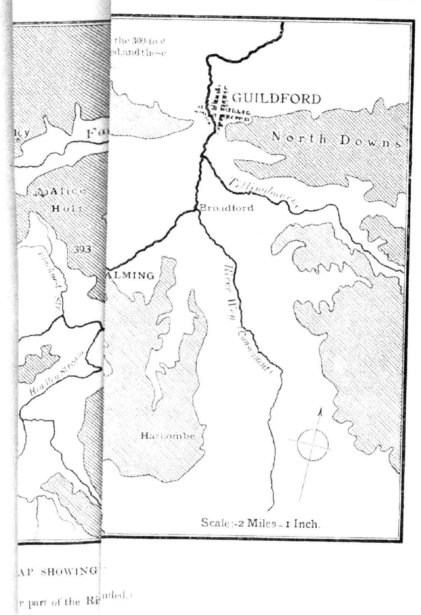

the 300-fo t
d, and those

GUILDFORD

North Downs

Fa

Tillingbourne

Alice
Holt

Broadford

393

ALMING

River Wey Conequent

Heath Stream

Hascombe

Scale :-2 Miles _ 1 Inch.

AP SHOWING

r part of the Ri      inded.

18. SOLUTION-VALLEYS *in the* GLYME AREA (OXFORDSHIRE).    By the
Rev. E. C. SPICER, M.A., F.G.S.    (Read May 6th, 1908.)

[PLATES XXXVIII & XXXIX.]

IN the plateau composed of Great Oolite rocks between the
Evenlode and the Cherwell there is a series of remarkable valleys
of similar character running in various directions.    The area to be
briefly considered is triangular : the base is formed by the strike-
valley of the Upper Swere running north-eastwards, and by its
continuation from the Great Rollright water-parting running
south-westwards.    The Dorn and the Glyme define an inner triangle
in this area (see map, p. 336).

It will be seen that the streams run in many different directions.
Reference to a contoured map will show that there are innumerable
valleys connected with and opening into the numerous streams
draining the area, and that their trend varies.    In the main,
however, they are either strike-valleys or dip-valleys, though in the
field their trend is not so evident.    The valleys always begin
suddenly upon the plateau, and descend with steep sides along
winding courses into the nearest evident stream.    The upper part
of each valley is always dry.    The cross-valleys are usually dry
throughout.    There are no terraces in the valleys, and there is no
drift upon the plateau, nor any alluvium in the streams.    The
general appearance of the plateau-valleys is not of erosion but
subsidence, as if an enormous snake had left a cast upon a yielding
surface.

Taking any part of the area, such as that where Grimm's Brook
enters the Glyme west of Wootton on the right bank (Pl. XXXVIII,
fig. 2), it will be seen that the plateau consists of ordinary weathered
limestone-rock, and that the brook-valley enters the river-valley at
right angles, making no impression whatever upon the opposite
bank, but sinking into the stream surrounded by a broad marsh.
Higher up the brook-valley are many cross-valleys which enter the
brook-valley from each side, and these cross-valleys have other
valleys entering them also in a similar manner.    The mouth of a
cross-valley entering the brook-valley is seen in Pl. XXXVIII,
fig. 3.    A well-used farm-road runs down this valley, which simply
merges into the left bank of the brook-valley shown in fig. 2 without making any further impression upon it.    All the valleys above
the brook-valley are usually dry, but the general contour of the dry
valleys and the brook-valley is similar.    There are no terraces.
The ground sinks from the plateau in symmetrical and equal
slopes.    There is no more evidence of mechanical disturbance at
the mouth of any valley than there is at the source.    The entering
valley has no effect whatever upon the course of the main valley
into which it simply sinks.

Sketch-map of the Wootton region, on the approximate
scale of 2 miles to the inch.

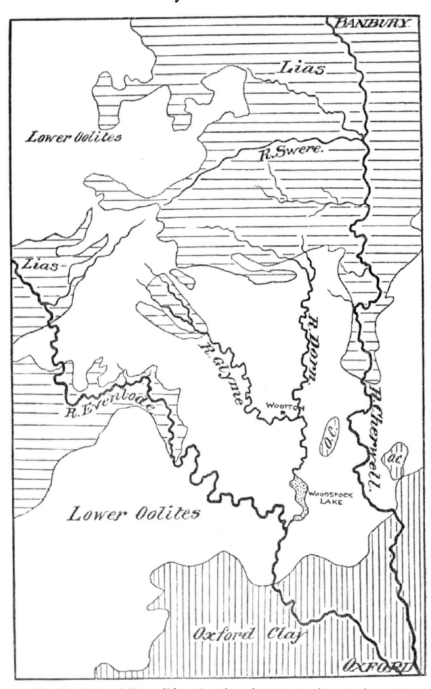

BANBURY.

Lias

Lower Oolites

R. Swere.

Lias

R. Glyne

R. Dorn

R. Cherwell

R. Evenlode

Wootton

O.C.

O.C.

Woodstock
LAKE

Lower Oolites

Oxford Clay

OXFORD

[The Evenlode and Cherwell have been brought nearer to the central area, in
order to show their trend-relations.]

In some cases a bar runs across the valley, and this bar is
occasionally tunnelled by a stone drain to prevent accumulation of
water during floods, which leave, after subsidence, a coating of lime-
carbonate sediment upon the herbage and thus render it useless.
The presence of such a bar would be impossible if the valley were
due to erosion. The emergence of water in the valleys is determined by some of the numerous bands of clay in the Great Oolite.
If no impervious band crosses the valley, the valley is dry throughout, and the water eventually emerges in the form of soakage, or
else in a marked stream frequently beginning (as in a valley near
Enstone) in a bubbling spring.

As these cross-valleys are followed upwards, they gradually
become narrower and shallower, and merge as gently into the
plateau above as they do into the main valleys below. Whether
short or long, they have the same character: they are the same in
whatever direction they trend. As they are followed downwards,
the change in their character is simply determined by their development into stream-valleys. The valley-floor along which the stream
runs becomes flattened, and the stream gradually meanders over it
as the valley widens. But the narrowest stream-valley with a
level floor has the same characters as the broad Evenlode. There
is a complete gradation.

On following the Glyme downwards to its junction with the Dorn
at Wootton, the valley is seen to widen almost insensibly. The
banks retreat continuously farther from the stream, and the level
valley-floor becomes gradually broader. The amount of water also
increases little by little as more and more cross-valleys are passed.
The Glyme at its junction with the Dorn at Wootton meanders
over its level floor without any regard to the curving banks of the
wide valley that contains it (Pl. XXXIX, fig. 1). The junction
of the two streams is curious. Upon the map the Glyme seems to
enter the Dorn Valley, but it simply resumes a direction which it
has farther up-stream; and the Dorn, a younger river apparently,
flows into the Glyme at a point up-stream, at right angles and
opposite to a bank upon which it has made no impression whatever
(see the arrow in fig. 1, Pl. XXXIX), as it certainly would have done
if the Dorn Valley had been produced by a body of water sufficiently strong to erode a channel of this magnitude by overground
mechanical action. But the Dorn Valley containing a small and
strong stream subsides into the developed Glyme Valley, in the
same way as any dry valley enters another, making no more
impression at its entrance. The united streams then flow through
Blenheim-Park Lake and meander out into the clay-plain to join
the Evenlode. The length of the Glyme from its source to Wootton
is about 8 miles, and in that distance it falls 400 feet. It rises
near Chipping Norton, and simply begins upon a wide plateau
beyond which the valley at the base of the triangle first mentioned
runs deeply at right angles to it.

Here, then, is a stream, originating upon a plateau, with no gap
at its head, that sinks quietly downwards and in a few miles

reproduces all the characteristic features of the Evenlode, its high banks curving sharply round above a flat-bottomed valley upon which a small stream meanders like a 'misfit' (see Pl. XXXIX, fig. 1).

The spectre of erosion which appears to haunt almost every valley upon the earth's surface must, I think, be banished from the Great Oolite plateau. The valleys under consideration have no single confirmatory mark of erosion. They swing to and fro, but that is all. The existing plateau-slopes are not steep enough to give sufficient erosive force to water, and there is not enough existing water for the purpose if they were. In most of the valleys there is no water at all. A deeply-eroded valley ends in an alluvial fan, or in a cone of aggraded material, but these valleys show no sign of ever having had such terminations: there are no gravel-deposits, no gravel-terraces; they melt into the main valley and disappear.

There is also no sign of the past existence of any surrounding heights sufficiently great to have produced streams strong enough to carve out the valleys by mechanical erosion. The whole region appears to have been never anything but a gently-tilted plateau.

The number and the varied direction of the valleys and their absolute similarity taken together are also strongly against any theory of mechanical erosion, for what conditions could be imagined that could produce similar results in various directions crowded together upon the same area? This type of valley, moreover, is entirely confined to the limestone. The clay-valleys in the Oxford area are wide and shallow, whether Oxfordian, Kimeridgian, or Selbornian. The only valleys at all similar are those very short ones (as upon Shotover and Cumnor) where sand and clay rest upon Corallian limestone, or plateau-gravels upon Portland Rock.

The idea that I venture to suggest occurred when noticing in the Dorn Valley the course of a small waterway about 20 yards long entering the stream almost at its level. This stream runs out of a small hill for a few months only in every year. A small c i r q u e rises above the head of it, eating back into the hill. The sides of the very short valley advancing towards the stream are steep like those of the surrounding valleys. An underground waterwheel some distance above it is thickly coated with stalactite. The water contains, therefore, a considerable amount of carbonate of lime in solution. The connexion of the c i r q u e with the short valley suggested that the limestone-rock was being removed in solution, and that upon its removal the insoluble material sank down nearly to the issuing water-level in such wise as to form a flat floor.

On climbing the bank and walking down-stream, a shallow, winding, dry valley was seen stretching across the ploughed corn-land and meandering into the distance upwards while sinking downwards towards the Dorn. It occurred to me that, if underground solution were the cause of the c i r q u e, it might be the cause of the longer valley, but stronger water-action must be looked for. The valley was followed down to the Dorn with a certain amount of anxious interest, and it was a pleasure to find an issuing permanent stream emerging at the Dorn stream-level in the very mouth of the dry entering valley. The issuing stream is called 'Puffit's Well,' and is near Holly Bank, a short distance from Wootton. Standing near this dry valley one looks up the Dorn, which is seen meandering across a level floor like the level floor of the little cirque-stream; the contours of the Dorn Valley are seen to reproduce the contours of the dry valley wandering through the corn-fields. The imagination travels to the Evenlode with characters similar to those of the Dorn, but on a larger scale; and the spectre of mechanical erosion vanishes from the limestone-plateau.

A great many valleys do not show the issuing stream, yet many have marshy ground where they join the main river-valley, and this marshy ground is very interesting.

A landowner upon the Dorn bank desired to make a fish-pond, and excavated a wide tank some 3 feet deep in the valley-floor near the stalactite-covered waterwheel, but said that when filled all the water leaked away through 'worm-holes.' It is irregular behaviour for a worm to burrow over 3 feet deep, and, moreover, the excavated earth was said to be full of small bones. On going to see these 'small bones' I found them to be long broken pipes of carbonate of lime with hollow centres (hence the 'worm-holes'), and concretionary rings around the hollows. These underground stalactites had grown round roots which had afterwards decayed, and they formed a considerable amount of the soil to a depth of 4 feet at least, at the opening flat of an issuing valley. Here, then, was a possible explanation of the gradual infilling of the valley-floor, since it appeared that these stalactites formed an underground scaffolding for fresh rainwash humus to lodge upon. I have seen the valley-floor of the Glyme completely covered with water that did not drain away for six months; and in some of the curves of the Glyme, which are really soakage-bowls, a good deal of marsh-water occasionally lies in corners because it is supplied from underground sources and can but slowly soak away (Pl. XXXIX, figs. 1 & 2).

When, after flooding, the water finally soaks away, the herbage is thickly coated with white powder, quite destroying the pasture; and it was this fact which caused a farmer to carry the Grimm's-Valley water underground for nearly half a mile along a fertile bottom of pasture-land.

The valleys, therefore, seem to be slowly filled with precipitates which become mixed with mud and spread across the 'flood-plain,' on a level expanse along which the stream slowly meanders from side to side. Local evidence is thus not wanting to show that a very considerable amount of carbonate of lime is removed in solution, even more than is accounted for by the analysis of water from the issuing springs, since they deposit much before issuing.

A stalactite was recently removed, from the roof of the Grand-Junction Canal tunnel passing through the limestone near Blisworth, which was 10 feet long and more than a foot in diameter. This had formed at one point in 100 years.

The mean amount of dissolved material carried down by the Thames is 1502 tons daily, or 548,230 tons annually.[1] If only 800 tons of this whole amount removed be taken as consisting of carbonate of lime, it is estimated that 140 tons of this material alone are removed yearly from each square mile; while, if the whole amount of 1500 tons daily be reckoned, the amount removed is over 260 tons annually per square mile, which represents 3900 cubic feet annually, or 390,000 cubic feet per century from every square mile.[2] This material is not removed broadly and equally over the area, but by streams issuing at definite spots in connexion with valleys in every case, where accordingly the resultant surface-modification is localized.

There are roughly 450 feet of permeable strata in the Great and Inferior Oolite, above 540 feet of impervious Fuller's Earth and Lias. An investigation of the Cotteswold rocks recorded by Mr. Wethered in Quart. Journ. Geol. Soc. vol. xlvii (1891) p. 559 et seqq., shows that there is less than 1 per cent. of insoluble matter in the purest beds, and over 67 per cent. in the argillaceous beds. This insoluble residue is chiefly quartz; then come felspars, zircon, rutile, and tourmaline. At Leckhampton, for example, there is 94 per cent. of carbonate of lime alone in the Great Oolite rock. It seems a most remarkable circumstance that so many people have performed these striking laboratory-experiments with their consequent calculations; and yet when they have seen the deeply-indented valleys peculiar to the limestone and Chalk-regions have always, inevitably and universally, with, so far as I can discover, no single exception, considered them as the results of surface-erosion, or else have confined themselves to digging gratefully fossils out of their sides. An early writer[3] invokes mechanical action, in various forms, to account for Chalk-valleys ending in pot-holes: breakers on the shore, torrential rivers, the inundation of earthquake-waves, swirls of torrent-water, and so forth; and, although Prestwich immediately corrects him by referring them to solution, and on p. 223 of the same volume of the Quarterly Journal gives some remarkable solution-results, he, in a most extraordinary way, just misses their application to valley-formation. Thence it is a far cry to the latest memoir of the Geological Survey, in which the Evenlode Valley is still regarded as the result of a denudation-scour.

The base-level of erosion in impervious rock is reached when a river is graded, but the slowest and clearest meandering stream fed from pervious soluble rocks is still a degrading agent of extra-

[1] J. Prestwich, Quart. Journ. Geol. Soc. vol. xxviii (1872) p. lxvii, &c.
[2] See Sir Archibald Geikie's 'Text-Book of Geology' 3rd ed. (1893) pp. 378-79.
[3] J. Trimmer, Quart. Journ. Geol. Soc. vol. x (1854) p. 238.

ordinary power, and the base-level of solution will not be reached until all the chalk and limestone have disappeared.

One further striking piece of evidence of the removal of material underground is found in the gaping fissures often noticed in the quarries on the plateau around the Evenlode watershed, near Stow-in-the-Wold and Moreton-in-the-Marsh, where the limestone-bands appear to be stretched and shattered in a manner that has often been commented upon, but never, so far, explained. This disintegration of the limestone is seen in a less degree in the area under consideration.

Further evidence of local disintegration is given in the recently-issued Memoir of the Geological Survey accompanying the Oxford Sheet (1908), where on p. 107 it is stated that

'the two principal consequent rivers of the district [that is, the Evenlode and the Cherwell] have eroded their channels along downfolds of the strata.'

The evidence supporting this is quoted thus:—

'In the case of the Evenlode the Great Oolite strata incline slightly upwards from the river on the Combe side and on the Long Hanborough side.'

Without questioning the probability of simple downfolds trending in two such remarkably different directions along an elsewhere almost uniform dip-slope, it may be said that this sudden sag at the edge of the valleys, which is easily seen at Enslow Bridge (and appeared, when I observed it, to be no more than a slight down-turning of the straight edges of the strata above the river-valley), illustrates the way in which superincumbent strata sag when support is locally removed by underground solution. The view of the memoir in question appears to be that the Evenlode cut 'the winding gorge west of Hanborough,' and is 'a perfect example of erosion by a meandering river' (p. 112). On the other hand, the suggestion intended to be conveyed by this paper is that an Evenlode Mississippi is unnecessary. Something brought Triassic pebbles into the Evenlode; but, since the morphology of that river is accurately represented in the Glyme area, which is absolutely free from any drift, it is suggested that the drift used the Evenlode Valley precisely as a waggon uses a road.

The main valleys in this region are approximately dip-and-strike valleys, but the term 'joint-valleys' may perhaps be applied to them. Percolating water will reach a master-joint or a series of master-joints, and dissolve out a winding course underground. The water from the neighbouring joints will gradually tend to leak into the master-joint line, and thus a winding area of weakness will be established which tends continually to widen. The ground above this weakened line will slowly subside, and at length the weakened material will be entirely removed, exposing the stream. The young stream will flow—as it does—in a valley with the contour of a dry valley; but, as the banks gradually dissolve away farther from the main stream, the widened valley-floor will become choked by solution-débris mingled with fine flood-sediment. This will form a level flood-plain from bank to bank, over which the stream will wander helplessly, except when it is merged in a broad area of shallow water stretching from bank to bank when the rocks on each side are saturated with water that oozes quietly out into the main valley and deposits more material upon the level floor.

Valleys of a similar character are found (as at Stonesfield, and above Box near Bath) in all the Great Oolite region, and a gradation is suggested to the Mendip, Yorkshire, and Derbyshire valleys with their underground streams and huge unroofed valleys similar in origin to that of Cheddar.

It may be asked why, if these Great Oolite valleys are solution-valleys, the same theory does not apply to the valleys of the Chalk? The answer is that it does, and it is hoped to show later that the solution-theory may be applied in a still more striking way to the Chalk-valleys.

The adoption of any violent mechanical hypothesis, such as a Welsh Thames, or an Oxford-Lake gorge, or glacial scour, or the rush of marine currents, or the march of an ice-cap, will become unnecessary, if the long-continued action of an efficient agent proceeding quietly is found sufficient to account for the facts. The meandering Thames above Oxford fed by water from the limestone-plateau may lose the interest of a legendary past, but will be studied with increased interest in the present as the rational result of the causes that I have ventured to indicate, and therefore as a river still in vigorous solvent activity, and not in a moribund condition of senile mechanical decay.

### EXPLANATION OF PLATES XXXVIII & XXXIX.

#### PLATE XXXVIII.

Fig. 1. Head of dry valley near Stonesfield: Evenlode Valley in the distance. The plateau (here covered with drift) sinks suddenly into several winding valleys similar to that which is represented. All these valleys merge into the Evenlode Valley, thus widening its banks locally, and largely producing its winding curves. The Evenlode flows under the tree-covered ridge on the right of the picture, on the side nearest the observer.

2. Brook-valley (with trees) entering the Glyme Valley. The plateau, quite free from drift, sinks in a manner similar to that seen in fig. 1, into dry valleys entering the brook-valley (with trees), which in its turn similarly enters the stream-valley of the Glyme, surrounded by marshy ground, at the right of the picture. The Glyme Valley runs lengthwise across the picture.

3. Mouth of developed dry valley, with characteristic cross-contours, entering the left bank of a brook-valley near Grimm's Dyke. The observer is looking up the valley.

#### PLATE XXXIX.

Fig. 1. The Dorn Valley is seen emerging on the left just beyond the soakage-bowl. The Dorn stream enters the Glyme near the arrow, but makes no impression upon the straight spur on the right. The Glyme-Dorn then turns round this spur, and flows down the valley to the right towards Woodstock, along a valley similarly flattened by solution-débris.

2. The same area flooded with quiet water covering the stream-meanders. This flooded condition sometimes lasts for several months when the rocks are saturated.

Quart. Journ. Geol. Soc. Vol. LXIV, Pl. XXXVIII.

FIG. 1. HEAD OF DRY VALLEY NEAR STONESFIELD.
EVENLODE VALLEY IN THE DISTANCE.

FIG. 2. BROOK VALLEY (WITH TREES ENTERING GLYME VALLEY.

FIG. 3. MOUTH OF DRY VALLEY ENTERING BROOK VALLEY,
NEAR GRIMMS DYKE

E. C. Spicer, Photo.                                    Swan Electric Engraving Co. Ltd

Quart. Journ. Geol. Soc. Vol. LXIV, Pl. XXXIX.

FIG 1.   THE GLYME, WITH SOAKAGE-BOWL AT THE
DORN JUNCTION, WOOTTON.

THE DORN ENTERS AT THE LAST CURVE IN THE PICTURE AGAINST THE
SLOPING SPUR ON THE RIGHT.

FIG. 2.   THE GLYME VALLEY FLOODED.   (WOOTTON)

R. C. Spicer, Photo.                    Swan Electric Engraving Co. Ltd.

DISCUSSION.

M. M. ALLORGE, who stated that he had been over a part of the ground with the Author, commented on the very few traces of mechanical erosion visible over the Great Oolite plateau, on the number of dry valleys, and especially on the occurrence of reversed grades in the thalwegs of some, which he attributed to chemical solution. They reminded him of the Carboniferous-Limestone regions and the cul-de-sac valleys or kesselthäler of the Karst in Istria, where underground solution was undoubtedly the controlling factor of the topography. He thought that the features in the district described could only be adequately portrayed by a model, owing to the thin character of the limestone and the climatic conditions. He considered that solution had acted by a gradual melting-down of the limestone, not by unroofing subterranean channels. He thought that one of the most interesting results of the Author's investigations was the explanation suggested for the 'misfit rivers' of the district.

Mr. E. A. MARTIN welcomed the paper. He thought that it contained a partial solution of the question of the origin of the Rubble-Drift and dry Chalk-valleys, which had been attributed by Mr. Clement Reid to other causes. The speaker had for a long time doubted the efficacy of Mr. Reid's theory of a frozen soil, and thought that in 'solution-valleys' there was possibly a better explanation. He did not, however, wish to attribute too much to the solution-theory. Wherever there was running water, there must, of course, have been a certain amount of erosion; but the two together, solution and erosion, went hand-in-hand to excavate the Chalk-valleys.

Mr. H. B. WOODWARD dissented from the Author's explanation of the Glyme valleys. The Great Oolite contained bands of marl or clay, especially in the lower portions; springs were given out at different horizons; and there were no signs of dislocation in the quarries to indicate subsidence. Moreover, there was much evidence of mechanical erosion in the clay brought down by the streams, notably in the lake in Glympton Park, the mud from which was being dredged when he visited the area. All the facts tended to show that the valleys were eroded by ordinary chemical and mechanical processes.

Mr. G. W. YOUNG was glad to hear that the Author considered that the dry valleys of the Chalk were also due to solution, as it supported the views advocated by the speaker in a paper read before the Geologists' Association some three years previously. He felt that, if the Author's view was correct in regard to these Jurassic rocks, there was a still stronger case in regard to the Chalk, where the plateau was protected by an impervious capping of clay, so that the dissolving action of the rainfall was confined to the unprotected valley-areas, which were thus gradually eaten deeper and deeper.

Mr. W. BALDWIN congratulated the Author upon the interest of his paper, and readily accepted the theory of solution-valleys in the Mountain Limestone, where caverns had been unroofed. He had examined the valley near Box Hill, in Surrey, one of those mentioned

by the previous speaker, and was of opinion that that, too, had been
formed largely by chemical action in a similar manner to many of the
Derbyshire dales.    He felt, however, that the action was a combined
one, namely, chemico-mechanical.    Although he was unfamiliar
with the Glyme area, the slides exhibited appeared to him to show
none of the characteristic features of the chemico-mechanical
valleys of the Chalk or the Carboniferous Limestone.    If the
Author's views were correct, then the valleys to which he had
referred had been considerably modified by subaërial erosion.

Mr. G. BARROW, while admiring the Author's enthusiasm, thought
that he was inclined to push the solution-theory of the origin of
the valleys under discussion a little too far.    At no great distance
to the north-east, the Great Western Railway cuttings showed that
nearly all the lime had been dissolved out of most of the calcareous
sandstone, which formed the bulk of the lowest portion of the Lower
Oolite.    This dissolution had taken place evenly, without any reference to special lines of drainage, such as small valleys or hollows.
Once a valley had been formed, in rocks capable of solution, the composition of the latter did undoubtedly facilitate the widening and
deepening of the valley by solution.

Prof. GARWOOD expressed his great interest in the subject dealt
with by the Author.    He asked whether the even-graded valleys,
shown in the photographs, were typical of these 'solution'-valleys.
He would have expected to find surface-depressions occupied, at all
events in flood-time, by water due to unequal depression of the
surface.    In districts where he had studied the effects of solution
in the Alps, this was always a characteristic feature.

The PRESIDENT thought that the Author had entered upon a very
promising field of investigation, and agreed with him in attributing
a very important rôle to subterranean solution, an agency which
seemed to have played a great part in the formation of the dry
valleys of the Chilterns.    The absence of any features resembling
d o l i n a was certainly a difficulty, but in an advanced stage of
erosion these might disappear or pass into hollows resembling
c i r q u e s.

The AUTHOR briefly replied, saying that the characteristic limestone valley-contours immediately ceased, and were replaced by
a level floor cut by a narrow stream-gorge, when the Lias was
reached in descending the Charlbury and other valleys: but such
confirmatory marks of erosion were never observed in any limestone-
valley.    He hoped to deal with the region much more fully and
in greater detail at a later period, as suggested by the President.
The evidence presented in the field left, however, no conclusion
possible but that lowering action in the dry valleys was entirely
underground and due to solution.

19. On *METRIORHYNCHUS BRACHYRHYNCHUS* (DESLONG.) *from the* OXFORD CLAY *near* PETERBOROUGH. By E. THURLOW LEEDS, B.A. (Communicated by Dr. HENRY WOODWARD, F.R.S., F.G.S. Read March 4th, 1908.)

[PLATES XL & XLI.]

THIS species of *Metriorhynchus* was first described by E. Eudes-Deslongchamps in 1868 in his ' Notes Paléontologiques,' [1] and was based on an imperfect skull obtained from Oxfordian strata in the department of Calvados (Lower Normandy). He was led to distinguish it from other species of *Metriorhynchus* on account of the shortness of the snout ('museau' is the word which he employed, under which term he included every thing in front of the orbits), the principal feature determining the species being found in these bones. In his table of Metriorhynchidæ (*op. cit.* p. 294) he defines it as follows :—

'Museau très court, pointe des os nasaux atteignant et même dépassant la suture des os intermaxillaires.'

He mentions one other mutilated skull found near Poitiers, and now in the Museum at Paris. Besides this, Prof. Bigot, of the University of Caen, to whom I owe my best thanks for photographs of the type-specimen and for much valuable information, tells me that there is in the Muséum de la Faculté des Sciences at Caen a very mutilated skull with part of the vertebral column, and another fragment of a skull, which may probably be referred to *Metriorhynchus brachyrhynchus.*

Apart from these, I can learn of no other specimens. The species is not mentioned in the ' Catalogue of Fossil Reptilia in the British Museum ' (Lydekker, 1885) nor in ' British Fossil Vertebrata' (Smith Woodward & Sherborn, 1890). Prof. E. Fraas, in his monograph on the Thalattosuchia, [2] among which he includes the Metriorhynchidæ, compares it with *Dacosaurus* and *Geosaurus*, and in his table of Thalattosuchia (p. 67) he finds a parallel to it in the Portlandian *Geosaurus giganteus*, which (he says) possesses all the important features given in Deslongchamps's diagnosis of *M. brachyrhynchus.* Dr. W. E. Schmidt [3] classifies *M. brachyrhynchus* in the same group as *M. Jækeli*, the name which he gives to a skull of *M. superciliosus* from the neighbourhood of Peterborough, while he places *M. superciliosus* and *M. Blainvillei* in another group. Dr. G. von Arthaber [4] is undoubtedly correct in condemning this classifi-

---

[1] Where not otherwise noted, all references to Deslongchamps are to his ' Notes Paléontologiques,' pp. 333–43 *passim* & pl. xxiii.

[2] ' Die Meer-Crocodilier (Thalattosuchia) des oberen Jura, &c.' Palæontographica, vol. xlix (1902–03) p. 1.

[3] Zeitschr. Deutsch. Geol. Gesellsch. vol. lvi (1904) Monatsber. p. 100.

[4] ' Beiträge zur Kenntniss der Organisation & der Anpassungserscheinungen des Genus *Metriorhynchus*' Beiträge z. Pal. & Geol. Œsterr.-Ungarns, vol. xix (1906) p. 293.

cation as faulty, and in restoring the genus to its original position in Deslongchamps's table.

The type-specimen, according to Deslongchamps, was found in the zone of *Ammonites cordatus*, that is, English Upper Oxfordian. Prof. Bigot writes to me that it came from Callovian strata (Continental division). He remarks :—

'Il ne peut y avoir de doute à cet égard: on ne sait pas exactement dans quel lit des carrières du Mesnil de Bavent; mais les exploitations d'argile de cette région sont dans les couches à *Reineckia anceps, Kepplerites Gowerianus* et *Proplanulites Kœnigi* .....'

The above-mentioned ammonites are characteristic of Lower Oxfordian strata in England.

Two skulls of *Metriorhynchus*, of a species previously unknown to him, have recently been obtained by my father, Mr. A. N. Leeds, F.G.S., from the Saurian zone of the Lower Oxford Clay, in the neighbourhood of Dogsthorpe, Peterborough. Unfortunately, no other parts of the skeleton were found with them, even the mandibles being missing. The skulls were discovered (curiously enough) at different levels, about the same time, but undoubtedly belong to the same species. After careful examination and comparison of the two skulls with the description and figure of the type-specimen published in the 'Notes Paléontologiques,' and with photographs of it kindly sent to me by Prof. Bigot, I have come to the conclusion that they are to be identified with *M. brachyrhynchus*. As I believe that this is the first recorded occurrence of this species in English strata, and as the skulls help to throw additional light on the cranial osteology of *M. brachyrhynchus*, especially in the parts which are wanting in the type-specimen, I propose to give some account of them, in the hope that it may amplify Deslongchamps's lucid description.

The skulls are exceedingly massive throughout, all the bones being thick and strong; in this respect they compare very favourably with the slender, slightly-built cranium of *M. superciliosus*. They are neither of them quite perfect, but most fortunately the one supplements the other, although both are perfect in one of the most interesting parts, namely, the frontal region, and the part from the nasals to the præmaxillæ. The first skull, to which I shall refer as No. 164 (Leeds Catalogue), lacks the anterior portion of one præmaxilla and some parts of the back of the skull. In the second skull, No. 165 (Leeds Catalogue), the anterior portion of the præmaxillæ is entirely absent, also the articular portion of one quadrate; but, on the other hand, the posterior part of the palatines is very well preserved, taking into account the crushing which all skulls from the Oxford Clay of the Peterborough district undergo, and the postfrontals laterally viewed have almost preserved their natural contour.

| Measurements in millimetres. | No. 164. | No. 165. |
|---|---|---|
| Length of skull ...................................... | 700 | about 680 |
| Length of præmaxilla ................................ | 155 | about 155 |
| Distance, præmaxillæ to nasals ...................... | 15 | 0 |
| Length of nasals (median line) ..................... | 200 | 220 |
| Length of frontal.................................... | 200 | 185 |
| Length of præfrontal ................................ | 115 | 117 |
| Length of parietal ridge to occipital condyle ...... | 130 | 120 |
| Breadth across quadrates ..... ................... | 245 | 224 |
| Breadth across postfrontals ........................ | 300 | 270 |
| Breadth across frontal (at orbits) .. .............. | 105 | 115 |
| Breadth across præfrontals ......................... | 223 | 216 |
| Breadth across nasals (at point of præfrontals) ... | 165 | 160 |
| Breadth across maxillæ (at point of nasals)........ | 85 | 85 |
| Breadth across præmaxillæ ......................... | 70 | — |
| Length of nasals (to point between præfrontal and frontal) ..................................... | 245 | 230 |
| Length of palatine ................................. | 260 | 265 |
| Breadth of præfrontal............................... | — | 80 |

One measurement in Deslongchamps's description requires some explanation. In his diagnosis of the species, he tabulates various measurements which, if added together, give as the length of the skull about 700 millimetres, which is the length of the larger Eyebury specimen. On p. 337 (*op. jam cit.*) he says:—

'La longueur totale de cette tête, depuis le condyle de l'occipital jusqu'à la troncature antérieure du museau, est de 59 centimètres et de 62 environ, si on y ajoute la région intermaxillaire qui est absente.'

In the type-specimen the præmaxillæ are imperfect, only 40 mm. of the total length being preserved. Dr. von Huene, of Tübingen University, who was in England lately and subsequently visited Caen, very kindly measured this portion for me. This, with the other measurements given, makes up the total length of 590 mm. On p. 333, Deslongchamps estimates the total length of the præmaxillæ to have been 150 mm., so that the missing portion was 110 mm. long, making the total length of the skull 700, not 620 millimetres, which is apparently a miscalculation.

I shall employ throughout *M. superciliosus* for purposes of comparison, as it is the best-known species of *Metriorhynchus*.

The first of the two skulls is one of the longest skulls of *Metriorhynchus* found in the Peterborough district, while both considerably exceed *M. superciliosus* in width. The proportion of the breadth (taken across the præfrontals) to the length is, in this case, roughly speaking 1 : 3·2, while in *M. superciliosus* it is 1 : 4·5. Considering that a large skull of the latter species measures 670 mm. in length, this may be said to constitute a very great difference between them, apart from other variations. Despite the length of the skull of *M. brachyrhynchus*, the great breadth across the præfrontals and postfrontals gives at first sight an impression of shortness, as both skulls present in a remarkable degree the feature upon which Deslongchamps founded his species. In No. 164 there is only an interval of 15 mm. between the posterior end of the præmaxillæ and the anterior point of the nasals, while in No. 165 even this interval is wanting; and it is indeed a question whether the point of the nasals does not pass beyond the præmaxillæ, although a slight displacement of the bones through crushing precludes any definite assertion.

The skull widens without interruption from the præmaxillæ to the postfrontals, the greatest width being attained at the posterior edge of the orbits, from which point it again decreases in width, though only by the amount of 50 mm. measured across the widest point of the quadrates. There is entirely lacking the long, uniformly-wide portion of the maxillæ, which is to be seen in *Metriorhynchus superciliosus*. In this respect *M. brachyrhynchus* is more comparable with *M. Moreli*, which, as Deslongchamps points out, increases in width in the same manner.

The præmaxillæ are stoutly-made bones, 155 mm. long, Deslongchamps's estimate being about correct, and 70 mm. broad at their greatest width. So far as can be judged from the one complete præmaxilla, they were more swollen than those of *M. superciliosus*; and certainly the constriction behind the 3rd tooth, in which the 4th tooth of the mandible fitted, is much more marked than in the latter species. Again, the suture at its junction with the maxilla is different. In *M. superciliosus* it runs in a gentle uninterrupted curve from the alveolar border to the posterior point of the præmaxilla on the median line; whereas in *M. brachyrhynchus* it runs at first at a little more than a right-angle towards the middle for a distance of about 45 mm., from which point it turns backwards at a sharp angle, so that the posterior end of the præmaxilla, instead of being practically triangular, consists merely of a narrow point. As in other species of *Metriorhynchus*, there are only three teeth in the præmaxilla.

Maxilla.—As is of necessity the case, this is the species of *Metriorhynchus* in which the maxilla shares the least in the formation of the median dorsal line, for in No. 165 it is entirely excluded by the nasals, and in No. 164 for all but a distance of 15 mm. The anterior end of the maxilla is stunted in agreement with the form of the præmaxillary suture, as is clearly shown in Deslongchamps's figure (pl. xxiii, 1c).

The teeth in the maxilla are 18 in number, making the dentary formula for the upper jaws 42, which is the number stated by Deslongchamps. The alveoli are much larger than in *M. superciliosus*, and are divided one from the other by wider interalveolar ridges.

Dr. G. von Arthaber [1] doubts the correctness of the dentary formula

---

[1] Beitr. zur Paläont. & Geol. Œsterr.-Ungarns, &c. vol. xix (1906) p. 293.

given by Deslongchamps, as he supposes all the Metriorhynchidæ to have had between 50 and 56 teeth in the upper jaws, and ascribes the error to the imperfection of the skull; but a reference to Deslongchamps's figure will show that, considering the size of the alveoli, it would be impossible to add more than two or three teeth to the maxilla, and the skulls in the Eyebury Collection bear out fully the undoubted correctness of his estimate. Only a few imperfect teeth are preserved; they do not differ noticeably from those of *M. superciliosus*.

**Nasals.**—Considering the great distance by which the nasals encroach on the median line, it is surprising to find that they agree in length along that line with two skulls of *M. superciliosus*, in which there is an interval of 60 and 70 millimetres between the nasals and the præmaxillæ; but they are, of course, much longer along their exterior border as they widen out more rapidly, attaining a width of 160 mm., and more at the point of the præfrontals. They are almost smooth anteriorly, but are marked with slight grooves in the median ramus of their posterior end, the portion outside the præfrontals being sculptured with long sharp ridges.

**Frontal region.**—The frontal bone is greatly developed in this species, exceeding that of *M. superciliosus* by some 35 to 50 mm. in length and 10 to 25 mm. in breadth, taken across the narrow part of the orbits. In No. 164 the frontal is 200 mm. long and 105 mm. wide, in No. 165 it is 185 mm. long and 115 mm. wide: while a skull of *M. superciliosus* of average length (655 mm.) shows a length of 150 and a width of 94 mm. It is the great development of the frontal and præfrontals that helps to impart so massive an appearance to the skull.

The præfrontals are enormous, being 115 mm. long and 80 mm. broad, as compared with 90 and 55 mm. respectively in *M. superciliosus*. The deflex processes of the bones on their inner surface are also very robust. Deslongchamps writes concerning the præfrontals (*op. jam cit.* pp. 337–38):—

'dans le genre Métriorhynque, c'est l'espèce où ce frontal antérieur occupe le plus d'espace dans le contour de l'orbite.'

The suture of the frontal and præfrontal commences at the centre of the interior border of the orbit, and the posterior border of the præfrontal from that point to its exterior corner measures some 70 mm. in length; for, instead of the curved exterior border which we find in *M. superciliosus*, this border in *M. brachyrhynchus* is practically at right angles to the exterior margin of the skull.

It has just been stated that the suture of the frontal and præfrontal commences at the centre of the interior border of the orbit. Not only is this the case, but it forms almost a continuous line with the curve of the postfrontal right up the point of the frontal, except for a slight deviation, where the posterior point of the nasal separates the præfrontal from the point of the frontal.

Deslongchamps in his figure (pl. xxiii) makes this suture commence more anteriorly on the interior border of the orbit. As this seemed to be almost the only difference that I could find between Deslongchamps's specimen and those at present under consideration, I asked Dr. von Huene to investigate this point for me, and I am deeply indebted to him for the trouble that he has taken. He wrote to me that the suture commenced at the centre of the orbit. This has now been further confirmed by an interesting letter which I have received from Prof. Bigot. He writes with regard to the photographs that he sent :—

'Les traits noirs marquent les sutures des os telles qu'elles ont été tracées par Deslongchamps, mais M. von Huene a du vous dire que les frontaux antérieurs ne sont pas exactement limités en arrière sur la figure de Deslongchamps, qui a pris une cassure pour une suture. J'ai fait la correction à l'encre sur l'épreuve.'

On the photograph Prof. Bigot has drawn the suture commencing at the same place as in the two skulls before me, the result being that it traces, with but unimportant variations, the course which I have described above. I say 'unimportant variations,' as I have found in examining numerous skulls of *M. superciliosus* that variations are always to be found in the line of this suture, the sutures of the two præfrontals in the same skull even sometimes differing slightly, with one exception, namely :—that the point of commencement of the suture on the orbit is always the same within a distance of 2 or 3 millimetres ; that is to say, that, while in *Metriorhynchus brachyrhynchus* the suture starts at the centre of the orbit, in *M. superciliosus* it commences at, or very close to, a line drawn across the anterior border of the orbits.

In consequence of the correction made above, Deslongchamps's description of the frontal (*op. cit.* p. 334) no longer holds good :—

'triangulaire en avant, quadrilatère en arrière, grâce à deux angles rentrants que déterminent, sur les côtés, le développement inusité des frontaux antérieurs.'

A reference to that author's figure (pl. xxiii) will elucidate this description. In reality, the frontal is triangular in form throughout. Another result of this correction is that the portion of the border of the orbit occupied by the frontal is reduced. Deslongchamps gives it as 50 mm., whereas the distance from its junction with the postfrontal to the suture of the præfrontal is between 30 and 40 millimetres in the specimens now described.

Deslongchamps states that the præfrontals are 60 centimetres wide, and are less developed in width than those of *M. superciliosus* and *M. hastifer*, being more similar to those of *M. Blainvillei* and *M. Moreli*. In the type-specimen the præfrontals are imperfect, and it is evident that Deslongchamps bases his estimate of their width on a restoration such as appears in his figure. This restoration is made to correspond with that of the temporal orbits, which are too narrow. The true breadth of the præfrontals is 80 mm., while in *M. superciliosus* 60 mm. appears to be an extreme width, the usual width being about 55 mm. Deslongchamps gives no measurements of this bone in his description of the last-named species, so that I am unable to compare them with his measurements of *Metriorhynchus brachyrhynchus*.

The sculpture of the frontal region in No. 165 coincides exactly with Deslongchamps's description. The frontal is comparatively smooth, with numerous irregular but superficial pittings radiating from the centre, while the præfrontals are covered with strongly-marked sculpture of the same nature. In No. 164 this sculpture is greatly intensified, the indentations on the frontal being almost grooves.

The postfrontal is an exceedingly massive and powerfully-developed bone, widening from its junction with the frontal as far as the anterior and exterior corner of the temporal fossæ, at which point it attains a width of 50 millimetres, compared with 30 mm. in *M. superciliosus*. The bone forms a distinct angle, instead of the slight angle little more than a curve in the same bone of *M. superciliosus*, thus corresponding to the opposite angle in the præfrontal. The orbit, owing to the great development of the posterior border of the præfrontal with its straight edge and the anterior border of the postfrontal, does not show the sinuous curve which is seen in *M. superciliosus*, but has an angular appearance, the two bones mentioned above lying at an angle of 50° one to the other, the angle itself being rounded off by the free edge of the frontal.

The skull attains its greatest width just behind the posterior corner of the orbits. In No. 164 the width amounts to 300 millimetres, in No. 165 to 270; but, as the bones of the temporal region in the former have suffered considerably from crushing, the latter measurement approximates more nearly to the original width of the skull.

The parieto-frontal crest is 35 mm. broad at the anterior border of the temporal fossæ, decreasing slowly in width towards the parietal region; at the suture of the frontal and parietals it measures 20 mm. across, from which point it tapers rapidly to some 5 mm. in width at a distance of 25 mm. from the back of the parietal ridge; after that it widens again very quickly, until it attains a width of 30 mm. at its posterior edge. In skull No. 164 crushing has altered the shape. The crest is 150 mm. long. The bones of the back of the skull possess in the same marked degree the massiveness which is so noticeable a feature of the whole skull; especially remarkable in this respect are the quadrates, which measure in width at their articulating surface 60 mm. In *M. superciliosus*, 45 mm. is the approximate width for full-sized skulls, and the bones are far less substantial.

I come now to that which is, in some respects, the most interesting portion of the skull, namely, the palatines, pterygoids, and vomers. They are preserved in both skulls more or less, but those of No. 165 are in better condition. In skulls of *Metriorhynchus*

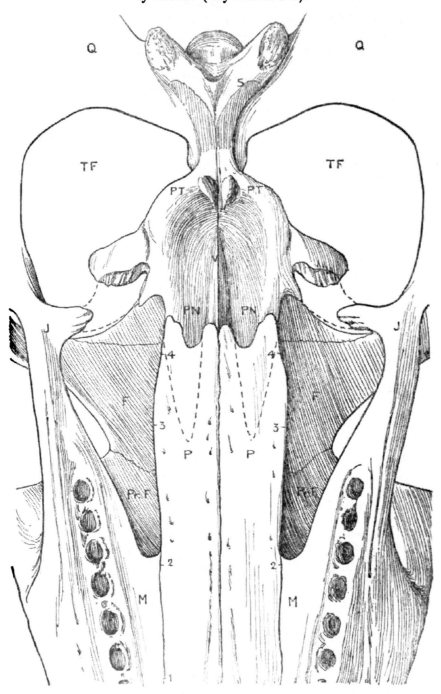

Fig. 1.—*Restoration of the hinder portion of the palatal aspect of No. 165 (half natural size).*

EXPLANATION OF FIG. 1 (p. 352).

Q = Quadrate.
S = Sphenoid.
TF = Temporal fossa.
J = Jugal.
PT = Pterygoid.
V = 'Vomerine element.'

PN = Posterior nares.
P = Palatine.
M = Maxilla.
F = Frontal.
PrF = Præfrontal.

Dotted lines on palatines = Anterior extent of pterygoids.
Shaded portion of pterygoids = Probable restoration posteriorly.

[The maxillæ are represented slightly crushed inwards, as in No. 165, in order to include the jugals in the figure.]

*superciliosus* obtained in the Peterborough district, these bones are very rarely found in sufficiently-good preservation to allow of their being restored in their entirety, partly on account of their thinness. It is to the general massiveness of the skulls of *M. brachyrhynchus* here described that we owe the possibility, in the present instance, of reconstructing these bones out of the numerous fragments in which they were excavated.

The palatines present the same truncated suture at their junction with the maxillæ, the two long gutters, and the vaulted central portion without any marked keel, which Deslongchamps noted. Posteriorly they widen and flatten out, until at a distance of 215 millimetres from their anterior end they bifurcate, the outer rami being the longer by about 15 mm., the intervening notches limiting anteriorly the exits of the posterior nares. The palatines have a sutural junction with the maxillæ laterally of about 115 mm. Their total length is 265 mm.

In consequence of the bifurcation of the palatines posteriorly, the opening of the posterior nares anteriorly is also bifurcate. Deslongchamps figures it, in the case of other Metriorhynchidæ, as pointed anteriorly; but in *M. brachyrhynchus*, at any rate, this is not the case, as the palatines are united in the median line throughout their length. However, as the median rami of the palatines are somewhat slender, it is possible that they may not have been preserved in Deslongchamps's specimens. *M. superciliosus*, as found near Peterborough, shows the same disposition of the posterior palatine border as *Metriorhynchus brachyrhynchus*.

In skull No. 165 the greater part of the palatines has been left detached from the rest of the skull, to admit of examination of the inner aspect, which is very well preserved. It shows the vomers in position, forming with the palatines the nasal canals. Anteriorly the canals occupy the whole width of the two bones (fig. 2, 1, p. 354), having an outer wall and a median ridge with a curved intervening surface. Very soon, however, the canals commence to converge towards the inner half of the bones. At the point of convergence the outer walls rise and become more massive where the deflex processes of the præfrontals meet them to support the frontal region (fig. 2, 2). In recent skulls which I have examined, these processes meet the palate at the junction of the palatines and pterygoids, and the vomers are situated forward of this point. In *Metriorhynchus* they appear to have been in contact with the

2 A 2

Fig. 2.—*Sections of the nasal canals taken at the points marked on the palatines in fig. 1 (p. 352) as numbered. (Natural size.)*

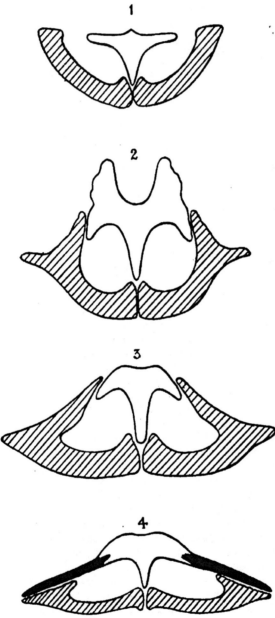

[The vomerine element is left blank; the palatines are shaded; and the pterygoids are shown black.]

palatines and vomers only, and the greater part of the latter lies posteriorly. Behind this junction with the præfrontals the exterior half of the palatines becomes flatter, and the outer walls thinner, overlapping the vomers (fig. 2, 3 & 4) until at 80 millimetres from their posterior end they diverge towards the outer posterior rami into which they merge.

Vomers.—So far I have referred to these bones in the plural, as in all reptiles they are paired; but in the present instance I have great hesitation in stating such to be the case, as I can find no trace of a suture throughout the whole length of the bony portion which constitutes the vomerine element. I have also examined the same portion in several specimens of *M. superciliosus* in the Eyebury collection, one of which is probably a fairly-young individual, and the same peculiar absence of any trace of a suture is to be noticed. It is, of course, highly probable that there were two bones, and that they were fused together perhaps at a comparatively early stage in the animal's growth; but there remains still an interesting question as to whether the vomers were not represented by a single bone in the Metriorhynchidæ. I can find no description of the vomers in any work dealing with this genus. It is to be hoped that further discoveries and investigation may settle the point.

In order to simplify description, I propose to treat the vomerine element as one bone, for all practical purposes T-shaped in section. Towards its anterior end, though imperfect in the specimens here described, it was probably coextensive with the palatines. It divides the nares from that point to their posterior outlets. Anteriorly the nares were enclosed by the maxillæ, as in the modern Gharials. The perpendicular of the T is wedge-shaped, its point interlaced between the median walls of the palatines, while the horizontal arms extend to meet the outer walls of the palatines. The upper surface of these arms is grooved. This groove, shallow at first, deepens a little farther backwards, with high ridges on either side against which the outer walls of the palatines lie; it dies out gradually antero-posteriorly, the outer arms of the bone curving downwards and underlying the outer walls of the palatines. At the point where the outer walls of the palatines diverge, the 'vomerine bone' begins to taper away to a point some 25 mm. behind the palatines. The divergence of the outer walls thus leaves a gradually-widening open canal in the palatines, which however was covered in by the anterior end of the pterygoid. The outer walls of the palatines present a striated surface which lay in conjunction with a similar one in the pterygoids, while the pterygoids were evidently united to the 'vomerine bone' as far as the posterior end of the latter. The 'vomerine bone' thus formed a ridge dividing the roof of the posterior nares. By the courtesy of Dr. A. Smith Woodward, Keeper of the Geological Department in the British Museum (Natural History), I have been enabled to examine various specimens in the National Collection. In an almost complete skull of *Pelagosaurus typus* (Bronn), Catal. No. 32599, which is figured and described by Deslongchamps,[1] there is a marked ridge noticeable in the roof of the posterior nares. Deslongchamps considers that it marks the line of division between the two pterygoids anteriorly, as he remarks is the case in the other Teleosaurians. It is a question, however, whether this ridge does not form part of the vomers, as in the instance of *Metriorhynchus*.

Among the specimens of *Steneosaurus* in the British Museum, I cannot find one that shows this part of the palate clearly enough to say whether such is the case also in other species of the Teleosaurian Crocodiles, although in one specimen the bones as preserved render it more than probable. Deslongchamps makes no mention of the vomers; and, except in the case of *Pelagosaurus*, he does not figure any such ridge.

---

[1] E. Eudes-Deslongchamps, 'Le Jura Normand' pt. i (1877) p. 26.

The pterygoids are slightly crushed out of their original position, and, owing to fracture, their relations with the basis cranii are obscure. Posteriorly the pterygoids united, and show a tuberosity on each side of their median line. Anterior to this they curved upwards and outwards, to form the roof of the posterior nares; they are then separated by the point of the vomerine, as I have already remarked. At their exterior border the pterygoids, which posteriorly have a thickened edge, widen out rapidly to form the lateral ramus that joined the transverse bone: this bone is unfortunately missing. Anterior to the main lateral ramus is a second and more slender one, after which the bone forms a curve and runs forward almost to a point, becoming very thin. The lateral ramus had a slight upward curve to form the transpalatine arcade; its posterior border is thick, its outer edge thin, while the anterior border presents a roughened surface right into the notch, between it and the second ramus, with which surface the transverse bone had sutural connexion. On the exterior surface of the pterygoids there is a marked depression, into which the outer ramus of the palatines fitted.

To sum up, we find in the Eyebury specimens the characteristics determining Deslongchamps's species, although the præfrontals, which are in keeping with the general massive development of the skull, are wider than he supposed; and we are able to reconstruct with almost absolute certainty the region of the posterior nares, showing the bifurcated opening with the vomerine element running back almost to the sphenoid—a feature which I think future research and discoveries will prove to be common to all the Metriorhynchidæ.

In conclusion, I wish to express my gratitude to Dr. C. W. Andrews, F.R.S., for much kind assistance rendered to me while working at the British Museum (Natural History), and also to acknowledge several valuable suggestions made by him.

### EXPLANATION OF PLATES XL & XLI.

[The figures are about one-sixth of the natural size.]

#### PLATE XL.

Upper aspect of skulls of *Metriorhynchus brachyrhynchus* (Desl.), Nos. 164 & 165 (Leeds Catal.).

#### PLATE XLI.

Palatal aspect of the same.

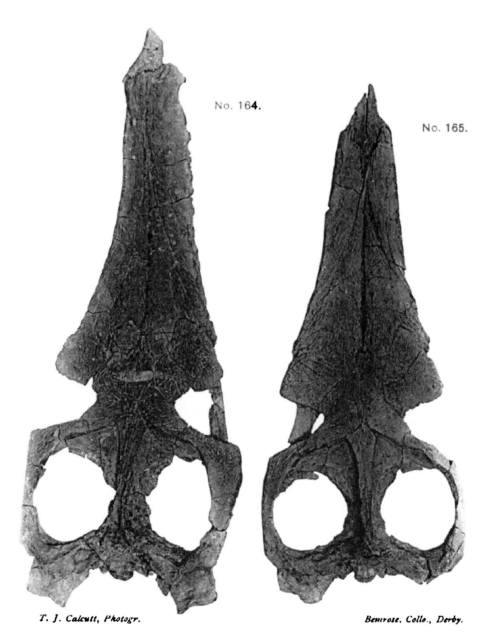

No. 164.

No. 165.

T. J. Calcutt, Photogr.

Bemrose, Collo., Derby.

**Upper aspect of skulls of** *Metriorhynchus brachyrhynchus* **(Desl.),**
**Nos. 164 & 165 [Leeds Catal.].**

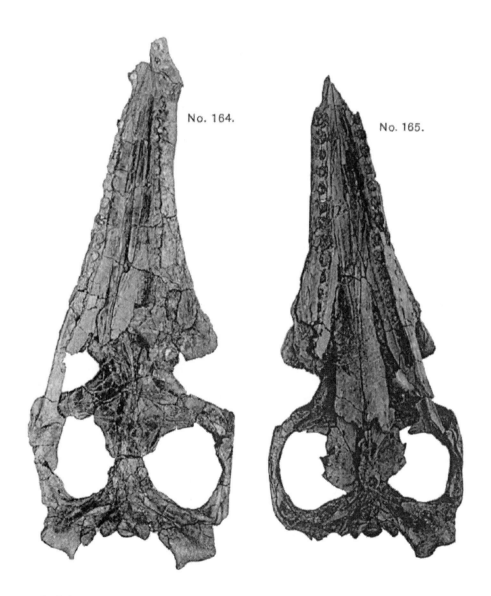

No. 164.

No. 165.

T. J. Calcutt, Photogr.

Bemrose, Collo., Derby.

**Palatal aspect of skulls of *Metriorhynchus brachyrhynchus* (Desl.), Nos. 164 & 165 [Leeds Catal.].**

## DISCUSSION.

Dr. HENRY WOODWARD complimented the Author upon the clearness and excellence of his description of *Metriorhynchus brachyrhynchus*, and referred to the excellent work performed by his father, Mr. Alfred N. Leeds, F.G.S., and his uncle also, in discovering and preserving the reptilian remains from the Oxford Clay of Peterborough. Having had the advantage of his father's training, the Author ought to surpass him in his future scientific work, by reason of his increased opportunities.

Dr. A. SMITH WOODWARD directed attention to a skull of *Metriorhynchus* which had been obtained by Dr. F. Ameghino from a Jurassic formation in Neuquen (Patagonia). As in the Oxford Clay at Peterborough, this Teleosaurian was associated with the ganoid fish, *Hypsocormus*, of which the speaker also exhibited specimens received from Dr. Ameghino.

Dr. C. W. ANDREWS congratulated the Author on having taken up the description of some of the magnificent material in his father's collection. He referred to the great interest of the account of the structure of the nasal passage and internal nasal opening; a description which was only possible with specimens in which the different elements could be taken apart and their relations to one another examined—a condition that was fulfilled in the case of many of the reptilian skulls collected by Mr. A. N. Leeds from the Oxford Clay of Peterborough.

The PRESIDENT thought it a matter for congratulation when an Author so ably maintained the family-tradition. In a work so full of careful detail it was difficult to single out particular points, but the observations on the posterior nares were especially interesting. That a closely-allied form both of this reptile and its companion-fish occurred in South America afforded a welcome confirmation of the zonal correlation founded on the invertebrata.

The AUTHOR briefly expressed his thanks for the reception accorded to his paper.

20. *On some* FOSSIL FISHES *discovered by* Prof. ENNES DE SOUZA *in the* CRETACEOUS FORMATION *at* ILHÉOS (STATE *of* BAHIA), BRAZIL. By ARTHUR SMITH WOODWARD, LL.D,, F.R.S., F.L.S., V.P.G.S. (Read May 20th, 1908.)

[PLATES XLII & XLIII.]

THE .precise extent of the Lower Cretaceous formation on the coast of Bahia (Brazil) still remains undetermined. Last year, Mr. Joseph Mawson gave to the Society an account of the deposits referable to it in the neighbourhood of Bahia itself[1]; through Dr. Orville A. Derby, Prof. Ennes de Souza, of Rio de Janeiro, has now submitted to me some fossil fish-remains from Ilhéos, which prove that it extends at least to that point, 130 miles south of the area previously described. The specimens represent three new species, but two of them are closely related to those from Bahia, and the third appears to belong to a typically Cretaceous form of Clupeoid fish which has not hitherto been found in America. Prof. de Souza has generously presented these fossils to the British Museum (Natural History), where they form an interesting supplement to Mr. Mawson's collection. They are preserved in bituminous shale like that in which most of the fossil fishes occur near Bahia.

MAWSONIA MINOR, sp. nov. (Pl. XLII, figs. 1–3.)

A Cœlacanth is represented by the remains of the greater part of a skeleton of a fish about 60 centimetres long, by part of a cranium, and also by a few bones of a smaller head. The ridged ornament on some of the external bones shows that the species belongs to the genus *Mawsonia*, which is only known from Bahia.[2]

The head of the type-specimen is so much crushed, that it is only of interest as showing the characteristic rugose ornament on part of the cranial roof and on one of the gular plates. Some of the tubercular teeth on the inner bones are also seen. The right operculum, exposed from within but partly flaked away at the postero-inferior màrgin, is characteristically Cœlacanth, and its greatest depth slightly exceeds its greatest width. As well shown by the smaller specimen (Pl. XLII, fig. 3), the outer face of this bone is ornamented with coarse radiating ridges, which are partly reticulate near the point of suspension and are finely striated near the posterior and inferior border. As shown by an impression on the same specimen, the angular bone (Pl. XLII, fig. 2) rises into a rounded coronoid eminence, and its outer face is covered with an ornament of radiating ridges.

The remains of the trunk and fins are scattered in the type-

---

[1] Quart. Journ. Geol. Soc. vol. lxiii (1907) pp. 128-31.
[2] *Ibid.* pp. 134-37 & pls. vii-viii.

specimen, and the dorsal fins are replaced nearly in the natural position in Pl. XLII, fig. 1. The neural and hæmal arches of the axial skeleton immediately in advance of the tail are remarkably long and slender, with a gentle curvature. From sixteen to eighteen vertebral segments, with stout arches and appended axonosts, support the principal part of the caudal fin; and there are remains of a few terminal slender rays which may indicate the presence of a supplemental caudal fin. The anterior dorsal fin ($d^1$) comprises eight stout rays, of which the right and left halves are loosely apposed and sometimes slightly displaced in the fossil. These rays, which are quite smooth and show no traces of denticles, are all undivided in their basal two-thirds, but finely articulated distally; and they gradually decrease in size backwards, so that the hindmost is only half as long as the foremost ray. The fin is directly supported by the usual thin plate of bone, the proximal end of which is lacking in the fossil. The posterior dorsal fin ($d^2$) is crushed and distorted, but is evidently somewhat smaller than the anterior dorsal, with much more slender and more extensively articulated rays. Its laminar support, as usual, is forked below, with the stouter limb inclined forwards. The anal fin ($a$), which displays its lobate character, resembles the posterior dorsal, but is somewhat smaller. It comprises about twenty rays, which are closely articulated for more than half of their length. The rays of the principal caudal fin are very stout and pressed close together, but they cannot easily be counted, because their right and left halves are loose and partly displaced. Their total number is about 16. These rays are quite smooth, without any trace of denticles; they are all closely articulated distally for less than half of their length. There are no remains of scales, but various fragments of smooth plates are probably referable to the air-bladder.

The small fish now described differs specifically from *Mawsonia gigas* in the rounded shape of the coronoid process of the angular bone, and in the finely-striated ornament of the operculum; so that it may be named *Mawsonia minor*. Its chief interest, however, depends on the fact that it exhibits for the first time several of the characters of the trunk and fins of the genus to which it belongs. It is now clear that *Mawsonia* differs from all known Jurassic and Cretaceous Cœlacanths in lacking denticles on the fins. It is also probable that the fish was scaleless, for the condition of the type-specimen is such that at least some of the ridges or denticles of the scales should have been preserved if they had been originally present.

### Lepidotus Souzai, sp. nov. (Pl. XLIII, figs. 1 & 2.)

A new species of *Lepidotus* is represented by part of a head (Pl. XLIII, fig. 1), and by the crushed and partly-scattered remains of a nearly complete fish, which cannot have measured less than a metre in length. It is a short and stout species, probably much like the Wealden *L. Mantelli* in proportions, and is remarkable for the very prominent ornamentation of its external bones and scales.

Except the narrow preoperculum, the external bones, so far as preserved, are coarsely ornamented with tubercles of enamel on the highest points of thick, beaded ridges. The supratemporals (*s.t.*) are evidently subdivided into a series of irregular plates, and the outer element is deeply cleft behind, where the slime-canal leaves it. The postorbital cheek-plates are also subdivided irregularly. The operculum (*op.*), which is about two-thirds as broad as deep, has an especially conspicuous ornament, the tubercles being arranged on ridges radiating from the point of suspension. No traces of ring-vertebræ are observable, although there are remains of calcified vertebral arches.

The scales are very deeply overlapping, and exhibit the forward production of the two anterior angles, which is characteristic of the genus *Lepidotus*. They are not excessively thickened, while their peg-and-socket articulation is feeble. The exposed portion of the principal flank-scales immediately behind the pectoral arch (Pl. XLIII, fig. 1) is somewhat deeper than broad, and covered with thick enamel, which is impressed with six to eight radiating furrows. The broad ridges between these furrows often bear large tubercles. The scales farther back on the trunk are still more strongly tuberculated, and even those on the caudal pedicle are not quite smooth. On most of these scales, in fact, the tubercles predominate and obscure the original ridges, while the enamel is confined to small patches of irregular shape on the summits. This condition is especially well seen on some of the broad scales near the ventral border (Pl. XLIII, fig. 2) just in front of the anal fin.

Portions of all the fins can be seen, and correspond in position and characters with those of the typical *Lepidotus*. All the rays are especially stout, with close articulations distally: they are about 12 in number in the anal fin, which exhibits the usual very large fulcra anteriorly.

The well-marked new species of which Prof. Ennes de Souza has discovered the parts now described, may be appropriately named in his honour, *Lepidotus Souzai*. It is distinguished from all known species by the remarkable tuberculation of the scales.

SCOMBROCLUPEA SCUTATA, sp. nov.   (Pl. XLIII, figs. 3 & 4.)

A small Clupeoid fish, about 12 centimetres long, is represented by two specimens, the type (fig. 3) especially displaying the head and paired fins, the other (fig. 4) showing some additional features of the trunk. It seems to have been a slender species with a relatively-large head, the maximum depth of the trunk being contained probably five times, the length of the head with opercular apparatus about three times, in the total length of the fish.

The head exhibits a typically Clupeoid mouth, with the mandibular articulation beneath the hinder part of the eye, and the bones of both jaws ornamented by longitudinal wrinkles. A large supramaxilla is conspicuous above the arched maxilla. The dentary bone rises rapidly to bound a small gape, and there are no traces of teeth. A deep groove for a slime-canal traverses the lower border

Quart. Journ. Geol. Soc. Vol. LXIV, Pl. XLII.

MAWSONIA.

G. M. Woodward del. et lith.

West, Newman imp.

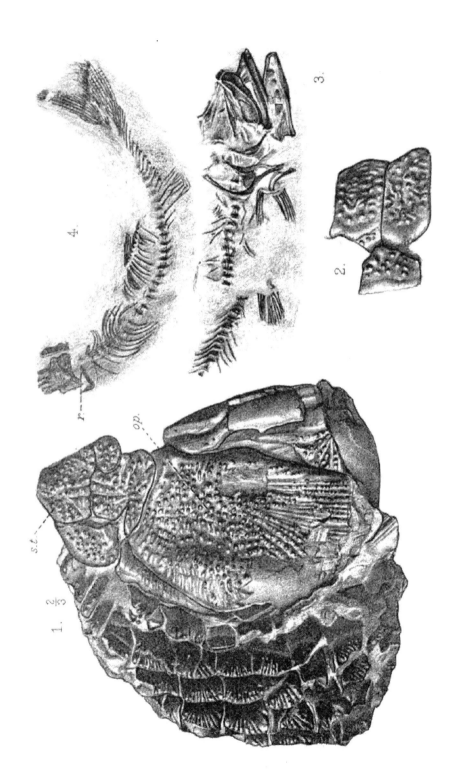

of the mandible. The opercular apparatus is narrow, and there is space for an expanded preoperculum, of which part can be seen.

The vertebræ are about 40 in number, half referable to the caudal region. The centra are much-constricted cylinders, scarcely longer than deep, and slightly strengthened by a few longitudinal ridges. The ribs are long and stout, each impressed with a longitudinal groove. The separate neural spines immediately behind the head are expanded into narrow laminæ. A few inter-muscular bones are seen in the abdominal region.

In all the fins except the caudal the rays are slender, with a long undivided basal portion. In each pectoral fin eight rays can be counted. The pelvic fins are opposed to the dorsal, and in the type-specimen they appear to be not much smaller than the pectorals. The dorsal fin in the second specimen is observed to comprise twelve rays. Its foremost support is expanded into a large wing, and the following six supports are also more or less winged. The anal fin in the same specimen arises at least as near to the pelvic fins as to the caudal. It is quite small and short, with only nine supports ; extending along the long interval behind it there is, however, a spaced series of seven thick, shining scales, which are of uncertain shape but have the appearance of ridge-scales accidentally displaced upwards. Although not connected with any fin-supports or fin-rays, they suggest the thickened ventral ridge-scales associated with the anal finlets in *Scombroclupea*. The caudal fin is forked, and its relatively stout rays are articulated nearly to the base.

Scales are not preserved in the type, but traces of thin cycloid scales are seen on the tail of the second specimen. One very large ventral ridge-scale (Pl. XLIII, fig. 4, *r*) is also observable in the front part of the abdominal region in the latter specimen, its hinder prominence (turned forwards in the fossil) being sharply pointed.

The fish thus described is obviously a Clupeoid, not differing much from *Clupea* itself; and its most striking peculiarity is the spaced row of small thickened scales between the anal and the caudal fins. These scales, as already mentioned, suggest the anal finlets of the European Cretaceous *Scombroclupea* ; and, if they do not actually mark the points of attachment of such finlets, they seem to represent the little thickened scales which accompany them in the genus just mentioned. I therefore name this new Brazilian fish *Scombroclupea scutata*. It is distinguished from the two definitely-known species [1] not only by its anal ridge-scales, but also by the number of the rays in its fins.

There is fragmentary evidence of at least one other ganoid fish in Prof. Ennes de Souza's collection, but the specimens described in the foregoing pages are all that admit of satisfactory determination. These are enough to prove that the shales at Ilhéos belong to the same Lower Cretaceous Series as those in the neighbourhood of Bahia itself; and they indicate the same mingling of typically

---

[1] 'Catal. Foss. Fishes Brit. Mus.' pt. iv (1901) pp. 135–38.

Jurassic and typically Cretaceous forms of fishes. *Lepidotus Souzai*, as shown by the subdivision of its supratemporals and cheek-plates, belongs to the Upper Jurassic and Wealden section of the genus which it represents; while the strong tuberculations on its scales suggest that it is one of the latest representatives of its race. The Cœlacanth *Mawsonia* might be either Jurassic or Cretaceous, but has hitherto been met with only in Bahia. The Clupeoid *Scombroclupea* occurs most abundantly in the Upper Cretaceous (Turonian) of the Lebanon, but is also found just above the Neocomian in Istria and Dalmatia, perhaps also in the Neocomian of Switzerland.

## EXPLANATION OF PLATES XLII & XLIII.

### PLATE XLII.

Fig. 1. *Mawsonia minor*, sp. nov.; tail and anal fin, with the two dorsal fins displaced backwards, one-half of the natural size. *a*=anal fin; *c*=caudal fin; *d¹*, *d²*=anterior and posterior dorsal fins. [Brit. Mus., No. P. 10567.]

2. The same; greater part of the right angular bone of the mandible, outer aspect, natural size. [Brit. Mus., No. P. 10569.]

3. The same; left operculum, outer aspect, natural size. [Same specimen.]

### PLATE XLIII.

Fig. 1. *Lepidotus Souzai*, sp. nov.; opercular apparatus, anterior scales, etc., right side, two-thirds of the natural size. *op.*=operculum; *s.t.*=supratemporals. [Brit. Mus., No. P. 10601.]

2. The same; ventral scales, natural size. [Brit. Mus., No. P. 10566.]

3. *Scombroclupea scutata*, sp. nov.; type-specimen, lacking tail, natural size. [Brit. Mus., No. P. 10570.]

4. The same; imperfect skeleton, natural size. *r.*=ventral ridge-scale, displaced. [Brit. Mus., No. P. 10571.]

## DISCUSSION.

The PRESIDENT commented on the value of the communication both to geology and to palæontology. It was fortunate when outlines so complete as those exhibited by the Author could be reconstructed from such fragmentary material as he had at his disposal.

Mr. E. T. NEWTON congratulated the Author on the acquisition of material which enabled him so satisfactorily to confirm the Lower Cretaceous (or Wealden) age of the strata in the neighbourhood of Bahia and for a long distance to the south of that town. He also complimented the Author on the interesting and lucid manner in which he had put before the meeting the osteological details of the fossil fishes, by which their near alliance with Wealden forms in other parts of the world was clearly shown.

21. *The* GEOLOGICAL STRUCTURE *of the* ST. DAVID'S AREA (PEMBROKE-SHIRE). By JOHN FREDERICK NORMAN GREEN, B.A., F.G.S. (Read April 15th, 1908.)

[PLATE XLIV—MAP.]

CONTENTS.

| | Page |
|---|---|
| I. Introduction | 363 |
| II. The Cambrian | 364 |
| III. The Pebidian | 366 |
| IV. The St. David's Granophyre | 373 |
| V. Extent and Boundaries of the Dimetian | 373 |
| VI. Quartz-Porphyry Dykes | 374 |
| VII. Relation of the Cambrian to the Granophyre and the Volcanic Series | 375 |
| VIII. Summary | 381 |

## I. INTRODUCTION.

THERE is probably no district in Wales with regard to the geology of which such serious divergencies of opinion exist as the neighbourhood of St. David's. The only rocks upon which authorities are in any way agreed are the sedimentary Lower Cambrian deposits, which form the geological datum-line for the area; and differences exist even here, as to whether they include contemporaneous tuffs, and as to the composition of the basal conglomerate and sandstone. With regard to the age of the various acid and basic tuffs, the basic igneous rocks, the quartz-porphyries, and the granitoid rock of St. David's, relatively to the Cambrian and *inter se,* entire disagreement exists throughout.

The interpretations of the sequence fall, however, into two main groups, associated respectively with the names of Dr. Hicks and Sir Archibald Geikie. The former is, on the whole, supported by Prof. Bonney, Prof. McKenny Hughes, and the late J. F. Blake, who were all well acquainted with the district; and the conclusions arrived at by Sir Archibald Geikie and Dr. B. N. Peach have been confirmed after careful examination by Prof. C. Lloyd Morgan.

The problem may be simplified by eliminating one point of disagreement. The late Dr. Hicks considered that the tuffs, sheets, and dykes could be divided into two unconformable series, termed by him A r v o n i a n (earlier) and P e b i d i a n. No other observer has confirmed this hypothesis, and, in order to avoid prolixity, it is proposed not to make any special reference to it. Eliminating, then, this point, the two conflicting views may be summarized as follows :—

(1) GEIKIE and LLOYD MORGAN. The tuffs form the base of, are conformably overlain by, and pass up into the Cambrian rocks. The St. David's granite, with associated quartz-porphyries, is intrusive in and later than both tuffs and Cambrian; the junctions exposed between them are intrusive, at least in most cases.

(2) HICKS.  The tuffs (Pebidian) are unconformably overlain by Cambrian deposits, which are largely composed of their detritus.  The St. David's granitoid rock is both pre-Cambrian and pre-Pebidian, the exposed junctions with the tuffs and Cambrian being all faulted.  The quartz-porphyries are not connected with the granitoid rock.

The literature of the subject, up to 1883, has been fully summarized by Sir Archibald Geikie in his paper in vol. xxxix of this Journal (pp. 262–66).  Of those which have appeared since, the most important are Dr. Hicks's defence in vol. xl (1884) p. 507, and the paper with a map of rock-exposures by Prof. Lloyd Morgan in vol. xlvi (1890) p. 241.

A study of these papers led to the conclusion that the only hope of definitely settling the problem lay in the preparation of a detailed map of the district; and the work was begun by laying down the outcrops of the Cambrian rocks, as accurately as possible, on the 6-inch maps.  These outcrops were found to be much faulted, and the faults thus indicated could be followed into the adjacent tuffs, which latter, after allowing for the discontinuity caused by these faults, were successfully resolved into a series of marked constancy when traced from one part of the district to the other.

The faults are so numerous in and near the cliffs that the coast-section fails to afford complete guidance to the complex structure of the area, which could not have been unravelled if the inland exposures were not very numerous.  Some difficulties in mapping are caused by the local presence of Boulder-Clay, but the only large continuous mass of it occurs in a band, running east and west, to the north of the city, and thus lies outside the critical area.

Thanks to Dr. Hicks the Cambrian succession is well known, and the following short account may be given, as providing the most trustworthy basis and the datum-line for other rocks.

## II. THE CAMBRIAN.

The Cambrian in the St. David's area is represented by (a) the Caerfai or *Olenellus*-Beds; (b) The Solva or Lower Paradoxidian; (c) The Menevian, or Upper Paradoxidian; and (d) The *Lingula*- or *Olenus*-Beds.

### (a) The Caerfai Beds.

(1) Basal Conglomerate.—This has been described in detail by several observers, particularly by Sir Archibald Geikie & Dr. Peach[1] and by Dr. Hicks.[2]  It is variable in texture, but always very coarse at or near the base, where, in addition to rolled quartz and quartzite-pebbles, there are usually boulders of the neighbouring Pebidian.  The pebbles and grit are set in a sparse matrix, which is highly micaceous.  The conglomerate causes a marked feature

[1] Quart. Journ. Geol. Soc. vol. xxxix (1883) p. 288.
[2] Rep. Brit. Assoc. 1890 (Leeds) pp. 803–804.

when underlying pasturage or paths, and is consequently easy to trace and to map with exactness, where not obscured by drift.

The finest exposure is that in the Caerbwdy Valley, where it attains a thickness of 70 feet: usually it is about 40 feet thick. Normal junctions with the Pebidian are shown east and west of St. Non's Bay, at Maen Bachau, and at Whitesand Bay. The conglomerate has been most assiduously searched by investigators for fragments of the Pebidian and Dimetian. Subangular pebbles comparable with the former are common, but no undoubted coherent fragment of the latter has been found.

(2) Green Sandstone.—A fine-grained, well-bedded rock, weathering ochreous where moist. In the specimens that I have examined, the grains are of uniform size, measuring about ·1 to ·2 millimetre in diameter, and principally quartz. Felspar is fairly plentiful, and there are also grains of felsite, palagonite, clastic biotite, ilmenite, and ferruginous spherulites.

The matrix is plentiful, mainly of chlorite associated with minute particles of various minerals, such as epidote, and, where crushed, sericite. With such a composition the rock might be expected to be sensitive to thermal metamorphism.

The usual thickness of the Green Sandstone is from 400 to 500 feet, but near Porth-Clais it thins considerably, down to between 150 and 200 feet. Some of the diminution may be owing to compression, as it is more squeezed in this district than elsewhere.

(3) Red fossiliferous Shales, with *Lingulella primæva*, etc.—These beds are usually not more than 50 feet thick, and have been put with the next group in the maps.

(4) Purple Sandstone.—This is usually about 900 feet thick, and near the top becomes a coarse grit, with small granitoid pebbles that have been compared to the Dimetian.[1]

### (b) The Solva Beds.

The Lower Solva Beds consist of 150 feet of yellow grits and flags; the Middle and Upper Solva of 1500 feet of grey or greenish flags and sandstones, with a purple band about one-third way up the series.

### (c) The Menevian.

This division consists of about 600 feet of black shale.

The foregoing succession is substantially that recorded by the late Dr. Hicks.

The detailed mapping of these Cambrian rocks reveals a system of faults, most of which have their general direction either from north-north-east to south-south-west or from east to west. These

---

[1] T. G. Bonney, Quart. Journ. Geol. Soc. vol. xlii (1886) p. 358.

faults, the position of which can be determined with great accuracy owing to the marked lithological differences among the Cambrian rocks, cut up the volcanic group into a series of blocks, or areas within which faulting does not occur, unless the possibility of pre-Cambrian faulting be taken into consideration. No evidence has, however, been found that any fault exists which does not cut the Cambrian rocks when traced up to their boundary.

The order of sequence of the beds in each block has been noted, and the portions of the succession thus obtained have been pieced together into a series that has yielded consistent results over the whole district.

The entire succession, so far as known, has a visible thickness of over 3000 feet on the west side of the St. David's granite, where the whole of the sequence is seen. On the east the upper half only occurs, but seems thicker than the corresponding portion on the west. The real base is nowhere seen.

### III. The Pebidian.

From the highest to the lowest known beds, the Pebidian series consists essentially of submarine rhyolitic and trachytic tuffs. A certain amount of intermediate material (augite-andesite) occurs in the lower half, which is distinctly more basic, and, speaking broadly, coarser than the upper half. In the eastern area, the later rhyolitic phase is ushered in by a great acid conglomerate. The fragments in this conglomerate and elsewhere are, except when very small, well rolled, and are associated (except in the bands of finest grain) with a variable amount of quartz-grains which seem in all cases to have been derived from igneous rocks, and occasionally, though rarely, show unabraded crystal-forms. Broken felspars, both orthoclase and acid plagioclases, are found plentifully throughout the series. Lenticles of pink or green shale occur at several horizons. Contemporaneous lavas appear to be totally absent. The rocks that have been described as lavas are, as will be shown later, all post-Cambrian intrusions.

The Pebidian rocks fall readily into fourteen or fifteen constant subdivisions, which group themselves naturally into four series (A, B, C, D), to which it seems convenient to give local names from the locality where each is typically developed and can be best studied. Their sequence is tabulated in the index accompanying the map (Pl. XLIV), with the letters which I have attached to the various bands. Assistance in mapping is also afforded by a quartz-felspar-porphyry sill which maintains a constant horizon.

### (A) The Penrhiw Series.

The lowest or Penrhiw Series is named from the fine exposures in the neighbourhood of Penrhiw Vicarage, north of St. David's. It consists of alternations of red and green tuffs, becoming progressively more felspathic and gritty towards the top.

The lowest bed shown in the district (A 1) is composed of purple-red and grass-green hälleflintas,[1] occasionally with coarser bands. It is well developed at both ends of the bridge north of the cathedral, and at the point west of Porthlisky. It undoubtedly exists, as shown by the numerous blocks in the soil, east of Carn Poeth, but it is not there seen *in situ*.

In microscopic section the absence of felspars such as are found in the later silicified rocks of D 4 and F 2 is noticeable. The rock consists of sericite and quartz, with grains of chlorite and opaque matter and occasional epidote. Quartz largely predominates, forming a fine-textured aggregate.

The next subdivision (A 2) is best exposed at the fine sections in the western cliff of Porthlisky; and again in the quarries of Penrhiw, north of the cathedral. The identity of the beds at these two localities, fully 2 miles apart, is singularly striking. The sub-division consists throughout of alternations of red and green gritty tuffs. The lower bands are fine-grained and sheared, the upper part is coarser. The red tuffs are often somewhat basic, and weather in a rusty manner. A distinctive characteristic is the presence of bluish fragments which weather white. In microscopic section, these fragments are seen to be bits of devitrified glass crowded with globulites (?). The outline of the fragments is a suc-cession of little concavities, but it is not clear whether these are due to original gas-bubbles or to the weathering-out of a perlitic structure. A certain number of true vesicles filled with siliceous matter undoubtedly occur, but they do not seem sufficiently numerous to account for the peculiar outline of the fragments. The matrix of the red tuff is ferruginous, and includes felspars and decomposition-products.

In the green tuffs felspars are more plentiful, and the matrix is nearly isotropic, apparently consisting chiefly of scales of a pale chlorite. The included fragments are mostly olive-green flakes of a felsite much like that of the red tuffs, but containing a consider-able amount of chlorite. Fragments of vesicular trachyte resembling that presently to be described in connexion with B 2 (p. 369) occasionally occur.

A noticeable point in the felsite-fragments of both red and green tuffs, is the occurrence in the devitrified ground-mass of elongated areas with ragged margins, which extinguish straight. This peculiarity in structure may be due to an original trachytic com-position. The green tuffs are progressively more felspathic and gritty towards the top, passing gradually into the next subdivision.

(A 3)—Wherever the bed just described is seen, it is overlain by a felspathic grit (A 3), which is one of the most useful horizons in the Pebidian. In the extreme south-west of the district, near

---

[1] I use the term hälleflinta as indicating a homogeneous silicified rock with conchoidal fracture, and porcellanite as indicating a similar rock but with splintery fracture.

Ramsey Sound, it covers a wide area and is coarser than elsewhere. In hand-specimens, the rock is white or pale green, and contains scattered, subangular, pink or purple fragments ; these sometimes weather out, leaving ferruginous hollows.    Under the microscope, the rock is seen to consist essentially of grains of quartz and decayed felspar, set in a dusty epidotic matrix, with strings of chlorite and occasional fragments of felsite.    The characteristic purple fragments are apparently hornblende-trachyte containing numerous vesicles.    The ground-mass consists of small felspar-laths, extinguishing straight, showing marked fluidal arrangement, mingled with a great number of minute ferruginous grains to which the colour of these fragments is due.    The vesicles are filled with some mineral, tending to form radial aggregates, which may be a zeolite.    A few of the phenocrysts are orthoclase, but the majority are ferruginous pseudomorphs after hornblende, which in some cases contain corrosion-channels.    The nature of the ground-mass of the tuff, in which these purple fragments are embedded, shows clearly that the ferruginous infiltration or replacement occurred before deposition in the tuff.

Not more than 150 feet of A 1 appears to be shown, and the remainder of the Penrhiw Series is about 800 feet thick, most of which is formed of A 2.

Schistose sill.—Above A 3 there occurs almost invariably a foliated quartz-felspar-porphyry sill, to be described later.

## (B)  The Treginnis Series.

The tuffs of the second or B series cover a large area to the west of St. David's, and are specially well shown on the farm of Treginnis-uchaf.    The series is distinguished from all others by its basic character and by the occurrence of scattered fragments, fairly well rolled, varying from 2 to 20 centimetres in diameter, of red rock, described as a quartz-andesite,[1] which seems, however, to be a rhyolite.

The lowest bed of the series (B 1) is a gritty tuff composed of dull-red fragments in a green base.    There is considerable variation in the nature of these fragments, the most abundant being a red, vesicular, glassy trachyte, very similar to that which will be presently described, but with much ferruginous matter.    Less abundant are fragments of red glass with augite- and plagioclase-phenocrysts, a red rhyolite, and a rock apparently identical with the hornblende-trachyte of A 3.    The thickness of B 1 is very variable, from a mere passage-bed a few yards thick at Penyfoel to at least 150 feet near Rhoson.    It passes gradually into B 2, and has not always been separated from it on the map (Pl. XLIV).

[1] C. Lloyd Morgan, 'The Pebidian Volcanic Series of St. David's' Quart. Journ. Geol. Soc. vol. xlvi (1890) p. 258.    The exposures marked on his map as diabase-tuff with quartz-andesite belong to this series.

(B 2)—The dominant component of the Treginnis Series (B 2) is a slightly gritty rock, of more basic composition than any other member of the Pebidian. It is at least 500 feet thick, and possibly much thicker in some places; but this horizon is usually so folded, and also distorted by basic intrusions, that an exact estimate is difficult.

The commonest phase of this subdivision has a characteristic mottled appearance, consisting of dark-green pebbles in a scanty red matrix, thus giving the effect of a red network on a green ground. This red matrix is highly ferruginous, and mostly opaque under the microscope; but it contains quartz-grains, small chips of lava, and patches of chlorite. The green pebbles consist of highly-vesicular glassy trachyte, the cells of which are filled with epidote and chlorite, a common arrangement being a lining of epidote surrounding chlorite. Numerous orthoclase-laths occur, commonly measuring from ·02 to ·03 millimetre in diameter. They are more or less epidotized, and show marked fluidal arrangement. The vesicles may be so numerous that the rock is almost pumiceous. This mottled type, which weathers in a rusty ferruginous way, covers fully five-sixths of the area occupied by B 2. The matrix, however, may increase in quantity and vary considerably in colour. The most important variation is that which occurs plentifully in the extreme south-west of the district, near Penmaenmelyn and Porth Henllys, in which the matrix makes up at least half of the rock and is dark green in colour. It can be seen in several places, notably on the promontory east of Pen-dal-aderyn, to pass into the common type. This green matrix is a little paler than the red in thin section, otherwise showing no difference by transmitted light; but the trachyte-fragments in the only specimen examined are full of ortho-clase-phenocrysts, which I have not found numerous elsewhere. Another variety, with a copious pale-green or pinkish-green matrix, may be seen near Trefeithan.

Most of the specimens of B 2 contain fragments of a rock composed of abundant augite-phenocrysts set in a hyalopilitic ground-mass of decayed felspars (andesine), augite, iron-ore, and various products of alteration; and also fragments of a rhyolite with perfect quartz-bipyramids. Both of these lava-fragments contain veins and occasional vesicles filled (before denudation) with—in the augite-andesite, chlorite—and in the rhyolite, calcite.

The filling of these veins before deposition in B 2 shows that the andesite and rhyolite were already somewhat altered; but the trachyte-fragments, on the other hand, were still comparatively fresh: for their marginal vesicles have been filled with the ferruginous matrix of the enclosing tuff, showing that they were still empty at the time of deposition. Some vesicles have been partly filled by ferruginous matter, and subsequently lined with epidote.

The big scattered pebbles of red rock which characterize the Treginnis Series show under the microscope a dusty devitrified glass with strong flow, numerous phenocrysts of orthoclase and plagioclase, and small quartz-bipyramids—apparently a rhyolitic structure. The lava has picked up little bits of a trachyte.

2 B 2

In the Pebidian rocks so far described the ground-mass is largely chloritic even when iron (red)-stained. The higher beds now to be described have a different type of ground-mass, but the change is not abrupt, being rather of the nature of a passage.

### (C) The Caerbwdy Series.

These higher beds cover nearly all the volcanic area east of St. David's. Their junction with the underlying Treginnis Series is clear only in a strip of country, barely 600 yards wide, running east and west through Treginnis-isaf, south-west of St. David's, in which a nearly complete Pebidian succession has been preserved.

The Caerbwdy Series is always felspathic, and has a characteristic bluish-green coloration, often mixed with white. The texture in hand-specimens changes greatly from one horizon to another, varying from a coarse conglomerate to a hälleflinta; under the microscope the matrix presents a characteristic appearance throughout the series. It consists of a clear mosaic of quartz, the minute components of which range commonly from ·01 to ·10 millimetre in diameter; but it varies in texture from point to point, coarser and finer patches and ramifications being irregularly intermingled. Chlorite is always intimately intermixed with this ground-mass, and when plentiful aggregates into irregular patches. The mineral is pale in thin sections, fibrous, and of low birefringence. Granular epidote occurs in nests and strings. Embedded in this matrix, throughout the series, are scattered broken crystals of orthoclase and oligoclase, measuring from ·2 to ·8 millimetre in length.

This matrix is clearly the result of the alteration of a fine-grained acid ash, and in a few cases small concave fragments may be recognized in ordinary light; but they are indistinguishable between crossed nicols, owing to the silicification which the rock has undergone. This series attains a thickness of at least 1500 feet, and can be studied most easily in the magnificent section along the Caerbwdy Valley, about a mile east of the city. The lowest portion of the series (C 1) forms a passage from the basic Treginnis to the acid Caerbwdy rocks. It is only exposed east of Treginnis-isaf, the lower part having a greenish matrix, with red and green enclosures, the upper part being felspathic, green and white. It has not been separated from C 2 on the map (Pl. XLIV).

The next division (C 2) has been termed by previous observers the Clegyr Agglomerate, but should rather be classed as a conglomerate. It is highly felspathic and variable in texture, with bands of porcellanite. The normal white and bluish-green matrix contains patches (often an inch in diameter) of the black or greenish-black chlorite, previously referred to. In this are embedded rolled pebbles of hälleflinta and quartz-porphyry of all sizes, sometimes exceeding 30 centimetres in diameter.

Above the Clegyr Conglomerate comes a finer-grained rock (C 3) composed of the same materials. No definite line can be drawn between the two, but the change is sufficiently rapid for field-mapping. The included bits of hälleflinta and patches of chlorite do not as a rule measure more than 4 or 5 millimetres in diameter. It is well exposed in the Caerbwdy Valley and on Carn Gwil Geli, north of Treginnis-isaf. The rock becomes finer at the top, where it passes into bedded blue hälleflinta (C 4).

The finest section of C 4 is again in the Caerbwdy Valley, where it has been quarried and is at least 90 feet thick. It is here an evenly-stratified, blue, bluish-green, or green rock with bands of yellow, minutely-porous stone, all breaking with a conchoidal fracture. The blue and green stone is translucent in thin splinters, and often looks like bottle-glass. Thin bands occur of coarser felspathic rock. Microscopically the rock is of the usual Caerbwdy type, but with little chlorite and only rare felspar-crystals. This bed can be easily traced, on account both of its lithological characters and of the clearness of the exposures, and consequently is an important clue in working out the details of the structure. From the Caerbwdy Valley it can be followed north-eastwards up to the main road, and south-westwards to the cliffs of St. Non's Bay, of which it forms a considerable part. West of St. David's it is again exposed 150 yards west of Treginnis-isaf and on Carn Fach, both localities being within 200 yards of the cliffs of Ramsey Sound.

Above the hälleflinta just described comes a thick group of felspathic and porcellanitic rocks (C 5), much like C 3 in general appearance, but often distinguishable by the absence of the fragments of green hälleflinta usually seen in the lower division. The most typical rock has a peculiar 'pepper-and-salt' appearance, due to the presence of multitudes of greenish-black specks set in a pale felspathic ground. The specks are shown by the microscope to be patches of chlorite or epidote, in a ground-mass of normal Caerbwdy type. Here and there a few bands occur in which quartz-grains (of igneous origin) are sufficiently numerous to give a gritty aspect to the rock.

### (D) The Ramsey-Sound Series.

This series is characterized by the presence of a considerable amount of sericite due to shearing, and by the comparative rarity of fragments of lava or older tuffs. The rocks are usually rather soft and thoroughly schistose.

The lowest division (D 1) is a sheared blue (occasionally yellowish-white) rock, sometimes exhibiting grains of quartz and felspar, but otherwise without recognizable fragments. Often the shearing has taken place along irregular surfaces, breaking the rock up into rugose lenticles; but more frequently, especially in the northern part of the area, it is finely fissile, indeed almost papery. Thin sections show that it is closely allied to the Caerbwdy Series, and is indeed but a slight modification of the same material, the only important difference being the presence in some specimens of pyrites.

Owing to the readiness with which it decomposes, good natural exposures are not common, but an excellent section may be seen in the banks of the Alan River, three-quarters of a mile north of St. David's. The total thickness, where measurable, is about 200 feet.

The next division (D 2) consists mainly of schistose rocks, built up of red and green lenticles containing small 'eyes' of variable composition. These eyes are commonly composed of felspar or quartz, but occasionally of felsite, altered trachyte, or magnetite. The lenticles in which they are set consist essentially of chlorite and sericite in minute scales. Interbanded with the above is always a fissile pale-green or yellow rock, flecked with olive-green. A good exposure occurs near Carn-arwig, in the cliffs of Ramsey Sound, where the thickness is about 300 feet: a little farther north the gradual passage to the underlying beds is clearly exposed. The section of these beds at Porthlisky has been described and referred to by various authors, notably Sir Archibald Geikie, who recognized their identity with the rocks of Ramsey Sound; but the amount of shearing here is quite exceptional, and consequently they do not afford good material for the study of the original characters of the rock.

This division is overlain by purple or yellow porcellanites (D 3), sometimes containing quartz-grains. They seem to be about 120 feet thick at Porthlisky, but are so torn out by shearing that no trustworthy measurement can be made. Slides of these rocks from Carn-arwig and the city of St. David's resemble those of the Caerbwdy Series; the broken felspars, however, undoubtedly include andesine, not recognized in the latter.

The highest tuffs shown in the district (D 4) form the north-eastern cliffs of Porthlisky. They consist of soft, pulverulent, schistose rocks of various pale colours, with a tendency to silicification in strings and patches. They differ markedly from any other part of the Pebidian, and are seen only at this locality.

In view of the great age of the Pebidian, the preservation of the original characters of many of the fragments in the tuffs is remarkable; thus the orthoclase-trachyte fragments in the Treginnis Series are almost as fresh as some of the Tertiary trachytes in Skye, described by Mr. Harker. The red rhyolite from the same series shows good flow-structures and unaltered felspar-phenocrysts; while occasional fragments of augite-andesite are less altered than the post-Cambrian intrusions described later, the felspar-laths being easily determinable. The chief alteration of the tuffs consists in the silicification of the matrix of the acid members, which is so marked that it seems to have been taken as evidence of thermometamorphism due to quartz-porphyries.

## IV. The St. David's Granophyre.

Immediately south of St. David's occurs the disputed granitoid rock, termed by Dr. Hicks 'Dimetian.' Its true nature as an igneous rock was demonstrated by Sir Archibald Geikie in 1883; and, as it has been frequently described, no more need be said with regard to its petrographical characters than that it is of variable texture, highly siliceous and coarsely granophyric, consisting of quartz, orthoclase, oligoclase, a little microcline, chlorite (probably after biotite), and ferruginous matter, with nests of epidote. It weathers in a fissile manner, and decays, where there is moisture, to a characteristic yellow colour. The quartz has a dirty appearance, owing to numerous inclusions, often specially developed along planes of cleavage.

The granophyre frequently shows signs of crushing, and is traversed by bands in which the rock is greatly shattered.

## V. Extent and Boundaries of the Dimetian.

According to Dr. Hicks, the Dimetian was of pre-Pebidian age and all its boundaries lines of faulting; the view taken by Sir Archibald Geikie was that the rock was a granite of post-Cambrian age and its boundaries, in the main, intrusive junctions.

Although many geologists have visited and written about the district, there is no really accurate map of the area covered by this rock; and the next step found necessary in this investigation was to lay down, as well as the ground would admit, its exact boundaries. At the extreme north-east of the mass a rock was found having a general resemblance to the ordinary Dimetian, but of a more porphyritic nature, the quartzes in particular being bi-pyramidal. A section shows its ground-mass to be granophyric, with a markedly finer structure than anything seen in the normal Dimetian, the other constituents being however identical. It seemed probable that this was only a marginal modification, and this view is supported by the fact that the same rock has been met with again in clear ground at the edge of the mass in several places, especially near Rock House on the north side and near Castell on the north-west side.

But it is on the west side that the most important evidence has been obtained, where a hitherto unobserved extension of the Dimetian of some size has been met with. Commencing about Rhoscribed Farm, a mile south-west of St. David's, this extension can be fairly well traced for a distance of 1100 yards westwards from the main outcrop as hitherto known. It forms a somewhat narrow belt about 300 yards wide, bounded on the north and south by faults, both of which can be seen cutting the Cambrian rocks in the cliff-face of Ramsey Sound. When traced towards the cliffs it was seen to undergo a change in character, and at the western part of the outcrop, about Treginnis-uchaf, is obviously identical with the foliated porphyritic sill already mentioned as occurring at a constant horizon in the Pebidian (p. 368). It is most important to note that the actual western edge of this prolongation is in contact with, and presumably passes under (for there is no sign of a fault), the member (B 1) of the Pebidian which forms the roof of this sill. As the exact position of the remaining boundaries of the Dimetian is not a matter of serious dispute, and the discussion of their nature and meaning with reference to the Cambrian is dealt with later (p. 377), it will be convenient now to give some further details of the sill, in view of its importance as bearing on the relation of the Dimetian to the Pebidian.

The sill has been traced for a considerable distance, and its out-crop is shown on the map (Pl. XLIV); clear evidence of its intrusive character is seen near Porth Henllys, where it breaks up and interdigitates with the beds of its roof (B 1). In thin section the intrusion always shows a parallel structure, and at times a banded structure, the matrix of the strips varying in texture from cryptocrystalline to a fairly coarse mosaic. In this are set porphyritic crystals of quartz, orthoclase, and oligoclase; the quartz, which is abundant, occasionally shows corrosion-channels, but is never rounded like the crystals seen in the quartz-porphyry dykes described below. The ortho-clase at times shows graphic intergrowth. The quartz-crystals are often broken, the larger being cracked and the different portions sometimes actually separated, but never dragged out. Numerous small jaggedly-triangular pieces of quartz also occur, especially when the rock is finer-grained; these appear to be the débris of larger crystals. A variable amount of sericitic mica is present in the ground-mass, suggesting a slight amount of cataclastic structure; but in some specimens the amount is so small, that the foliation of the rock is probably in the main protoclastic and to some extent connected with its viscous nature before consolidation.

The general petrological resemblance to the marginal modification of the granophyre, and the fact that this modification appears to pass into a rock identical with the sill and at the same horizon, suggest that the latter is simply the tapering edge of a laccolitic intrusion of which the St. David's rock (Dimetian) is the core. If the views here put forward are justified, the granophyre must be intrusive in the Pebidian.[1]

## VI. QUARTZ-PORPHYRY DYKES.

In the St. David's area, in addition to the granophyre, there are a number of acid dykes (quartz-porphyries), described by Dr. Hicks as in the main of Arvonian age and therefore entirely unconnected with the Dimetian: the view taken by Sir Archibald Geikie was that they are not only connected with, but in some cases apophyses, or outward prolongations of the margins, of the granophyre. The term Arvonian has been dropped by general consent; but, although these dykes are probably a later phase of the granophyric

[1] The rock here described as a sill was included by Dr. Hicks in his Pebidian; a description of it was given by Thomas Davies, Quart. Journ. Geol. Soc. vol. xl (1884) p. 552, nos. 32 & 33.

magma, and thus of the same general age, no evidence has been found to suggest that any are apophyses of the latter.

It is not disputed that some of them cut the granophyre, but it has been contended that near Rock House, south of the city, the granophyre passes gradually into a material identical with that of the dykes. In the field close to (north of) Rock House there are two rocks present : one the marginal modification of the granophyre, the other a typical quartz-porphyry. The exposures are not clear enough to justify the positive statement that the porphyry cuts the marginal modification; but the former can be followed well within the main granophyre without in any way losing its identity. Outside the granophyre, near St. David's Cathedral, the quartz-porphyries are more abundant, but never lose their distinctive character; if they were the prolongation of the margins of the granophyre, they should have an unbroken course towards its edge. This, however, is not the case, for any connexion is severed at the surface by an outcrop of the Pebidian, exposed specially well at and about the Deanery. The view that these quartz-porphyries are separate from the granophyre seems to be confirmed by an examination of the ground-mass, which is microgranitic; while the finer phases sometimes approach the micropœcilitic structure, and this structure is maintained even when they occur well within the granophyre, as at Rock House. Spherulitic modifications have been described by various authors, but they do not afford any additional evidence against the view that the granophyre and the dykes are approximately contemporaneous.

So far, then, it has been shown that the granophyre is almost certainly intrusive in the Pebidian; and that the dykes are so is obvious, on the north side of St. David's Cathedral as well as in other localities. The relation of all these rocks to the Cambrian now remains to be considered.

VII. RELATION OF THE CAMBRIAN TO THE GRANOPHYRE
AND THE VOLCANIC SERIES.

There are two diametrically opposite views as to the relation of the Cambrian to Dr. Hicks's Pebidian and Dimetian : his view was that there was a great break in time marked by a violent unconformity; whereas Sir Archibald Geikie's view is (1) that there is no break of structural importance between the Cambrian and the Pebidian; and (2) that the Dimetian is an intrusion in the Cambrian. As two types of relationship are involved in the latter interpretation, it will be convenient to discuss each separately, beginning with the first.

Nature of the Junction between the Cambrian
and the Pebidian.

In mapping the ground, it has been found that the base of the Cambrian, in this particular area, cannot be proved to rest upon any member of the two lower series of the Pebidian. At the easternmost point of the district which has been mapped in detail, near Vachelich and Llandruidion, it is in contact with the lowest division (D1) of the Ramsey-Sound Series; and, from the breadth of outcrop of the latter, it must be near the top. Tracing the conglomerate westwards to the Caerbwdy Valley, it is seen resting upon the basal bands of the Ramsey-Sound Series, and so small is the thickness of these beds here that the staining described on p. 377 has extended through them to the underlying Caerbwdy Series (C5). At the arch in St. Non's Bay, which has been repeatedly described,[1] the conglomerate lies at some depth below the top of the Caerbwdy Series, as, allowing for a neighbouring dyke of quartz-porphyry, not more than 140 feet of its uppermost division (C5) appears to be present. Passing to the west of the Bay, the base of the Cambrian is clearly transgressive, as at the Stacks of the bathing-place, although it still reposes on C5, there is now only 40 feet of this division present. In the little Bay, south-south-west of St. Non's Chapel, only 15 feet of the division intervenes between the easily recognized hälleflinta (C4) and the base of the Cambrian. After passing this point, the junction is a faulted one and continues so for some distance.

It is thus seen that, between the Caerbwdy Valley and the western part of St. Non's Bay, the Cambrian has transgressed over fully 400 feet of the Pebidian.

On crossing the granophyre to the Porthlisky area, a patch of Cambrian hitherto unrecorded is seen to occur a little inland from the cliff; but, as its exact relations to the tuffs are not known, and the Pebidian rocks are greatly deformed, it does not afford trustworthy evidence of transgression. Nevertheless, if the view (also Sir Archibald Geikie's) that these schistose rocks are identical with those of Ramsey Sound be correct, the base of the Cambrian must be at least 1000 feet higher in the Pebidian than at St. Non's Bay.

The Cambrian conglomerate is not seen again, until the cliffs of Ramsey Sound are reached; but in the southern outcrops no normal junction occurs. As, however, it is now clear that the highest series is undoubtedly represented here, the argument just put forward holds good in this case, for we have at least 900 feet more Pebidian present below the Cambrian than at the western end of St. Non's Bay without reaching the base of the Cambrian. A normal junction does actually occur at the arch in Maen Bachau, the horizon in the Pebidian being probably the upper part (D3) of the Ramsey-Sound Series; but the outcrop is so narrow, and the rock so deeply stained, that its identification is difficult. The only other normal junction exposed is a mile and a half farther north, at Whitesand Bay, where the conglomerate rests upon D2, about the middle of the Ramsey-Sound Series, an horizon that is certainly at least 600 feet above that of St. Non's Bay.

From the evidence just given it may be fairly claimed that an unconformity between the Cambrian and the Pebidian has been established.

[1] See Quart. Journ. Geol. Soc. vol. xlvi (1890) pp. 244 *et seqq.*

## Staining by the Conglomerate.

Where the junction with the Pebidian is exposed, the rock immediately underlying the conglomerate, to a depth of from 10 to 20 feet, has always a peculiar red coloration, not observed in the Pebidian at any other point of the district. As this colour always decreases in intensity, in rocks of similar composition, farther from the base of the conglomerate, it is clearly due to staining. Whether this is produced by water percolating through the Cambrian, or by exposure during erosion, seems an open question; but, beyond any doubt, it has no connexion with a stratigraphical horizon. This staining is of considerable antiquity, for it is certainly older than the oldest faulting.

## Relation of the Cambrian to the Granophyre.

The detailed examination of the boundaries of the granophyre shows that most of the margins that can be traced with reasonable certainty are faults, which are shown in the accompanying map (Pl. XLIV). It is a point of the highest importance that these faults are in most cases the prolongation of faults clearly proved in the adjacent Cambrian. The facts regarding the faults themselves may be summarized as follows:—

(1) Along the southern margin of the main mass, the boundary is a reversed fault that crosses St. Non's Bay and dies out eastwards in a minor overfold. This is clearly one of the oldest faults in the district, for it is shifted 120 yards northwards by a later fault.

(2) For a considerable part of its outcrop the granophyre is bounded by faults that belong to a series, trending north-north-east and south-south-west, forming a feature and an integral part of the present structure of the district. One of these faults bounds the eastern side of the southerly prolongation of the granophyre, and is seen in the cliff-face at Ogof Llesugn, where it brings the Middle Solva Beds against the basal conglomerate. A branch-fault comes off here, and this fact has been noted by the late J. F. Blake, who accurately described and mapped this critical section. He showed that the outcrop of conglomerate seen here is at no point in contact with the granophyre, but is involved in a series of interlacing injections of basic igneous rock.[1] Basic intrusions of this type along lines of fault are a feature of the entire district.

(3) The western portion of the northern end of the granophyre is bounded by a great fault with a general west-north-west and east-south-east direction, the outcrop of which is again shown on the map (Pl. XLIV) cutting the Cambrian, both east and west of the city. The existence of this fault near the city was clearly grasped by Dr. Hicks, who failed, however, to trace its further course.

Owing to the exceptionally clear nature of the exposures in the Porth-clais area, all previous writers have focussed attention on the evidence seen there. One side claims all the junctions as essentially faults, the other as essentially intrusive. The maps given here show that these junctions are for the most part prolongations of faults proved by detailed mapping to cut the Cambrian; and thus Hicks's contention is, in this area, substantially correct. In order to make

[1] Quart. Journ. Geol. Soc. vol. xl (1884) pp. 299 *et seqq.*

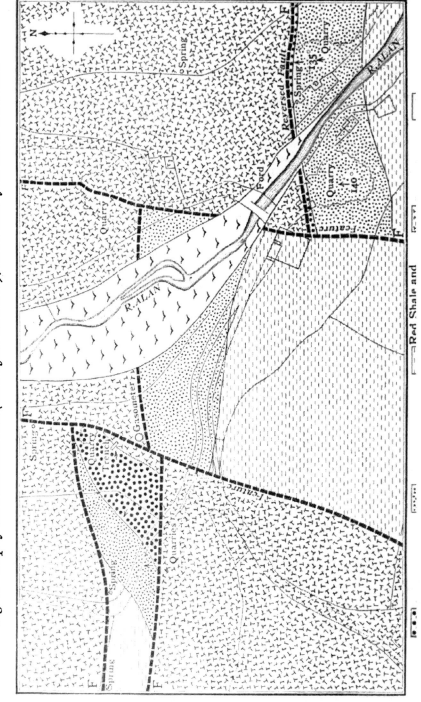

Fig. 1.—*Map of the Porth-clais area (basic dykes not shown), on the scale of 25 inches to the mile.*

sure of this point, this special area has been mapped out on the scale of 25 inches to a mile (fig. 1, p. 378). It was this detailed mapping that led to the discovery of the only known normal junction of the Cambrian and the granophyre, and the fact that this existed would probably have never been known but for the recent establishment of the Gas-works. Before these were erected, there was a farm-service road leading from the high road to a quarry in the conglomerate. This road formerly kept clear of the bank flanking the Alan in which the quarry occurs. In this bank-face, quite at the foot of the hill, fragments of the conglomerate only occurred, and it was a natural inference that this rock continued to the foot of the bank. When the Gas-works were built, the road had to be shifted closer to the bank, and, in so doing, the fault already mentioned as shifting the Cambrian at Ogof Llesugn was cut open, showing that the granophyre occurred on both sides of it.

It was thus obvious that there must be in the bank-face, on the west side of this fault, the original junction of the granophyre and the Cambrian conglomerate. Mr. G. Barrow, when on a visit to me, drew my attention to the supreme importance of this fact, and suggested a further visit with the object of cutting this junction open. This has since been done, and the section laid open exposes the Cambrian conglomerate resting upon the eroded surface of the granophyre. The position of the small opening made is shown on the 25-inch map, and has also been photographed; it has been left open for verification by subsequent observers.

The basal band of the Cambrian here is so like the decomposing Dimetian, that in a first opening made it was actually taken for it, and it was only distinguished by some very small pebbles of the characteristic pink quartzite which occurs in much larger pebbles higher up in the conglomerate. The actual junction is found in a second opening: the only means of distinguishing the two rocks at first was the presence of these minute pink pebbles, and it was not until the opening was enlarged that the junctions were defined.

It is clear that the basal band of the conglomerate is the finest débris of the granophyre, and however we may account for the fineness of this base of the conglomerate, it is accompanied by an equivalent diminution in size of the scattered pink quartzite-pebbles. There is no trace of faulting, or of any marginal modification of the granophyre, and no sign of thermal action is seen in the Cambrian when actually touching the igneous rock. The latter, on the contrary, shows clear signs of decay previous to the deposition of the Cambrian Conglomerate.

## Basic Intrusions.

The basic igneous rocks of the district have been classified by previous observers into two distinct series—(a) intrusive dykes, and (b) contemporaneous sheets or lavas. It is universally agreed that the former are post-Cambrian; but the latter have been held to be substantially contemporaneous with the Pebidian, and in view of what has gone before would therefore be pre-Cambrian. Evidence, however, has been obtained tending to prove that the latter are also post-Cambrian, and further, that they simply represent different modes of occurrence of the same material.

The rocks here described are striking features of the scenery west of St. David's, where they project like sea-stacks above the general rough platform-level of this part of the district. The material composing the stacks is of much finer texture than that of the more conspicuous masses near the north coast recently described by Mr. J. V. Elsden; in addition, they are locally vesicular, and these features have presumably led to their being described as lavas.

The small patch forming the stack nearest St. David's (Clegyr-foia) seems to be intrusive, but its age must clearly go with that of the more important mass on the west. The extent and mode of occurrence of the latter are shown on the map (Pl. XLIV); it is nearly 2 miles long, and, as its trend is roughly parallel to the strike of the Pebidian, it gives at first sight the impression of a sill or lava. Its true nature can be determined by examining its margins. Its junction with the Pebidian is very irregular, and is best exposed on and about Rhoson Crags. Here the continuity of the mass is broken by a long narrow strip, partly enveloped, of Pebidian, seen on the northern and eastern flanks of the crag, the junction being approximately parallel to the stratification of the tuffs; but on the south the margin makes a right-angled bend, and is seen on the bare rock-face to cut across the bedding for a distance of some 15 yards. It is thus clearly intrusive in the Pebidian.

As the mass is traced from north to south it is soon seen that, where the path of a fault known to cut the bedded rocks is crossed, no trace of the fault occurs in the basic igneous rock, raising at once a suspicion that it is even later than the post-Cambrian faulting. All doubt of the post-Cambrian age is dispelled by an examination of the coast-section at Carn-arwig. The cliffs here, for about a quarter of a mile, are exclusively composed of the same basic material, except at one locality; here the basal Cambrian conglomerate also occurs, as several (at least six) more or less lenticular masses completely enveloped in the igneous rock, which must thus be post-Cambrian. Three of these masses are shown in the accompanying photograph (fig. 2, p. 381), kindly taken, after considerable trouble, by Mr. John Barrow.

If the coast-section near the main mass of basic rock is examined, the fault-planes and ramifying cracks are often seen to be filled with basic material substantially identical in structure and composition with portions at least of the mass inland. These would seem to be films given off from the margin of the mass, and this view is strengthened by the fact that, although these small intrusions are very numerous in the district, they have not been met with piercing the larger masses.

Thus the field-relations do not support the view that these basic rocks are lavas, as has formerly been supposed; neither does the

mode of occurrence of the vesicles, when they are carefully
examined. They are not characteristic of the edges of the basic
masses; indeed, they rarely, if ever, occur near the margins, but rather

Fig. 2.—*Cambrian conglomerate involved in a basic intrusion ;
west of Carn-arwig, Ramsey Sound.*

J. Barrow photogr.

[B=Basic intrusion ; C=Conglomerate.]

some way within the intrusion. The best illustration of the latter
point occurs at Carn Howell, where small vesicles, usually about
3 millimetres in diameter, are very abundant, but at a distance
of at least 100 yards from the margin.


### VIII. SUMMARY.

The conclusions arrived at may be briefly summarized as
follows :—

(1) The Pebidian consists of a bedded series of tuffs, composed of
detrital volcanic matter deposited under water. Although
some of the material may have been blown directly into its
present position, the bulk has been washed down from a
land-surface.

(2) This has resulted in the formation of singularly persistent
bands of deposition, capable of being traced for considerable
distances and mapped out on the ground, the structure of
which has thus been determined.

(3) The process of mapping has shown clearly that there is a strongly marked unconformity between the Pebidian and the overlying Cambrian.

(4) The St. David's granophyre (Dimetian) is probably a laccolite, terminating along one edge at least in a sill-like prolongation clearly intrusive in the Pebidian. The post-Pebidian age of the whole is thus established.

(5) The actually observed junctions of the granophyre and the Cambrian are all faults—except in one case, where, on being cut open, the conglomerate is seen resting upon the eroded surface of the Dimetian. No trace of contact-action has been seen anywhere at the junction of these two rocks. The pre-Cambrian age of the granophyre is thus clear.

(6) No basic lavas have been met with in this area, those forming the 'stacks' being clearly of an intrusive nature and of post-Cambrian, if not of post-faulting, age.

The pre-Cambrian age of Dr. Hicks's Pebidian being so clearly proved, it seems only just that the name should be revived, if not indeed extended to other areas, as he suggested. The contemporaneity of the series with similar rocks of pre-Cambrian age in other areas cannot be claimed as definitely established; but, if any general name is applied to these rocks, such as those of Charnwood and the Uriconian, Dr. Hicks's term should have priority.

The friends at St. David's who have shown me kindness are too numerous to mention; but I must name Mr. H. P. Jackson, Master of the Secondary School, and Mr. William Davies, of Rhoscribed Farm, who kindly granted permission to dig a trench on his land and afforded us much useful information. Above all, I owe to Mr. George Barrow, not only the original suggestion that I should attack this complex area, but constant assistance and advice which alone made the production of this paper possible.

## EXPLANATION OF PLATE XLIV.

Geological map of the St. David's area, on the scale of 3 inches to the mile.

## DISCUSSION.

The CHAIRMAN (Dr. TEALL) referred to the keen controversy that had taken place in that room about a quarter of a century ago on the subject of the St. David's rocks, and remarked that the Author's very careful work tended to show that both the combatants were right and both were wrong.

Mr. BARROW drew attention to the gradual advances in our knowledge marked by the present paper. When Hicks began work at St. David's, the geologists of his day often took the faint foliation of such rocks as the Dimetian for the last trace of bedding in an intensely-altered sediment; and, holding this view, they

**GEOLOGICAL MAP**

OF THE

**ST. DAVID'S AREA,**

**PEMBROKESHIRE.** ·

Scale:—

3 Inches = 1 Mile.

N

naturally took the Dimetian for the oldest rock in the district. The view was strengthened by the fact, that until within the last two years every known junction with the Dimetian was a fault. Taking the view that it was a post-Cambrian intrusion, Sir Archibald Geikie looked for 'contact-action,' and thought that he had found it in the intensely-hardened aspect of some of the rocks. This hardening, however, was now known to be due to silicification, and was often best seen far away from the margin of the Dimetian. A wholly new interpretation had been given by the Author to the mode of occurrence of the fine-grained, more or less basic rocks that rose like stacks out of the platform south-west of St. David's. They contrasted so strongly in texture with the intrusions of St. David's Head that they were first naturally considered as approximately-contemporaneous sills in the Pebidian; the Author, however, had now conclusively shown that they were not only post-Cambrian, but later than the faulting.

Mr. J. V. ELSDEN said that, although he had seen many of the sections described by the Author, he was not in a position to discuss the main questions involved, as his own work had lain farther north. With regard to the basic intrusions, however, he had expected to find rocks of the St. David's-Head type in the St. David's complex, and had searched for them somewhat perfunctorily and without success. It was, therefore, with considerable interest that he recognized this type among the Author's specimens. The Author's observation that these basic intrusions were not affected by the post-Cambrian faulting was interesting, as tending to support the view at which the speaker had arrived with regard to the age of the St. David's Head intrusions, which might prove to represent a comparatively-late episode in the history of that area. He congratulated the Author upon the results of his careful and detailed investigations, which seemed so equally to divide the honours between previous workers.

Prof. W. W. WATTS referred to the importance, as illustrated by this paper, of detailed mapping of difficult areas. All the junctions of the 'Dimetian' with the surrounding rocks in this area were faults, except the one referred to by the Author, in which, as in other known cases, by the departure of the fault from the older rocks, a mere trace of newer rocks had been found in unconformable contact with the granophyre.

The AUTHOR desired to say that he was most grateful for the kind compliments paid to his work by the Chairman and others who had taken part in the discussion. Boulders of the rocks described by Mr. Elsden, which differed greatly from the characteristic basic intrusives of the district, were very common, but they undoubtedly also occurred *in situ*, the specimens shown being from a deep well.

22. *The* HIGH-LEVEL PLATFORMS *of* BODMIN MOOR *and their*
    RELATION *to the* DEPOSITS *of* STREAM-TIN *and* WOLFRAM. By
    GEORGE BARROW, F.G.S. (Communicated by permission of the
    Director of H.M. Geological Survey. Read March 4th, 1908.)

[PLATES XLV & XLVI.]

IN the south-west of Cornwall the ancient marine platform, of
Pliocene age, rises to a height of 430 feet above the sea, and its
upper limit is a steep slope, often a bluff. In the same area the
uplift of this platform has led to the deepening and cutting-back
of the larger valleys, giving rise to a steepening of slopes in the
lower part of the banks. This feature becomes less marked as
the valleys are ascended, and in the case of the River Camel it
disappears altogether at a distance of 22 miles from the sea.
Above this point the river-banks and also the ground above them,
now much over 430 feet high, retain in the main the same angle of
slope as that which they had in Pliocene times, though of course
they have been lowered to some extent by denudation.

The retention of the characters of the older scenery is naturally
most marked in the still higher grounds about the watershed of the
River Camel, part of which includes Davidstow Moor. This moor
also forms the gathering-ground of the Inney (a tributary of the
Tamar); and, if the watershed be crossed and the valley of this river
descended, the features just noted will be met with in reverse
order, as that area is approached within which the denudation of
post-Pliocene times has produced its most characteristic effects.


## The Upper Platform.

Of the older topography thus partly destroyed by post-Pliocene
denudation, the most striking feature in the higher part of the
area is presented by two well-marked high-level platforms, one
at 750 feet above the sea, and the other may be called the
1000-foot platform, although it is really a little below this
altitude. The latter was first recognized on Davidstow Moor,
where, considering its antiquity, it is remarkably well preserved;
but traces of it are to be seen on the surrounding high lands in
all directions. That it must once have covered a very large area
is evident, and it may possibly have its counterpart in Britanny.

On entering the higher ground, formed by the granite, near
Davidstow Moor, it is at once obvious that all the higher Tòrs
once stood out as islands. This character is well shown in the
ground above Trebartha Hall, some miles away in the south-eastern
part of the area; and, when a favourable point of view can be
selected, traces of the platform are to be seen over much of the
eastern half of the granite-area.

## The Middle Platform.

The remains of the 750-foot platform are met with nearer the sea, although still far up the valleys. This platform was first recognized about Camelford, stretching from the granite-margin westwards to the foot of Delabole Hill and sharply defined over much of the area.

Farther south, outside the western margin of the granite, denudation has removed most of the platform, but it is again seen within the granite-area about St. Breward, stretching for many miles in a south-south-easterly direction. It clearly owes its preservation to the superior hardness of the granite.

On the northern and eastern side of the granite the 750-foot platform is only encountered at a considerable distance seaward of the edge of the 1000-foot platform; but it is well marked about Bowithick, where a large alluvial flat lies practically on it, at the foot of the main slope formed by the edge of the granite. If the granite-margin be followed south-eastwards, further traces of the platform are met with in places, and they are specially well preserved where the rock in which the platform was cut consists of epidiorite, a rock which, when fresh, has exceptional powers of resisting denudation. Close to Trewint another extensive flat marsh lies practically upon this platform, occurring likewise at the foot of a great rising feature formed by the granite-margin; but farther south this feature commences below the 750-foot contour, and all traces of the platform, here founded on killas, have been lost. Above Trebartha Hall, this contour is seen to enter the granite itself, well up this sharp slope, and here also a large alluvial flat again indicates the position of the old platform.

A strange phenomenon connected with both platforms is the occurrence of extensive gently-sloping marshes at their higher margin. Examples have already been given in the case of the lower platforms, and the great Crowdy Marsh is a fine illustration of one occurring on the upper platform. But they are not confined to the higher platforms, for Mr. D. A. MacAlister and I found them even better developed at the edge of the 430-foot or Pliocene platform (Conce and Red Moors, south of Bodmin).

## Association of the Platforms with Superficial Deposits.

An economic interest attaches to the 750-foot platform, as the superficial deposits that bear tin, above this level, differ markedly at times from those below it. It is evident that, when the sea stood at the present 750-foot contour, there must have been already much granite-detritus on the higher slopes, and this locally contained tin-ore in abundance. But below this level there would appear to have been little or none, for the country had either not assumed the lower features which it at present possesses, or else the tin-bearing deposit was swept off during emergence. Thus there is

a far greater amount of decomposed material, capable of supplying
stream-tin, above this critical level, than below it; because above
this level we find the results of decomposition occurring both before
and after the 750-foot platform was cut, while below it the results
of the later decomposition alone are found.

### Association with Stream-Tin.

The great extent of the stream-works in the higher parts of
Bodmin Moor must be attributed to this cause.  In strips of
varying width they cover mile after mile of country, and the
industry for 1600 years has been carried on in situations that have
no parallel farther south in this district or at lower levels.  The
decomposition-products of the granite are to be seen wherever they
could find lodgment, and in many cases they contained much tin-
ore.  The most interesting occurrences are those met with on the
cols of watersheds, in hollows between two larger hills, a situation
in which, farther south, we should not expect to find either
decomposition-products or wash in any considerable quantity.  And
yet, in one instance, a thickness of no less than 40 feet has been
proved (see Pl. XLVI); and the antiquity of the deposit is so great
that every trace of felspar-crystals has vanished, leaving a yellow
clay in which even the quartz-crystals have fallen to pieces.

Similar material in similar positions has been met with all over
the higher part of the granite of Bodmin Moor, and is especially
abundant in the more northerly portion, where it has often been
found to contain a considerable amount of stream-tin.  The fact
that these older products of decomposition of the granite (wash or
head) are preserved only at high altitudes and at a considerable
distance inland from the coast, suggests at once a probable
explanation of their preservation, namely: that these soft deposits
must have been either frozen, or buried under a small snow-field
that accumulated during a part of the Glacial Epoch, when the
country farther south was subject to violent floods and that farther
north was more or less covered by an ice-sheet.  The material
itself is, of course, in parts of the same age as the 'head' of the coast,
generally held to have been formed during colder conditions, and
actually has a distinct Glacial deposit associated with its upper part
in the Scilly Isles.  The large district, much of it at least 1000 feet
above sea-level, on the southern edge of which these loosely-coherent
deposits have been somehow protected from denudation, is to this
day the coldest part of Cornwall; so it would of necessity have been
colder than the coast-area, in which signs of a colder climate are so
clear.  Indeed, actual evidence of the snow-field exists in the radial
distribution of the great boulders of granite from Roughtor and
similar high crags, suggesting that the rocks slid down snow-slopes,
an explanation tentatively offered by Mr. Clement Reid.

Whatever explanation is finally adopted to account for the
preservation of the old wash on the hill-slopes, this material is
fundamentally different from the normal valley-deposits, in which

the bulk of the old stream-works are situated. These ore-bearing deposits have evidently been submitted to the action of running water, which has swept the 'head' or wash just described into the valleys, washed away the finer and lighter components, and concentrated a more or less rounded gravel, amid which the tin-ore has been dropped on account of its higher specific gravity, although the size of its component grains is small. Generally speaking, it is mainly in such assorted wash that stream-tin work has been carried on at lower altitudes and farther south. But the old wash of the higher levels (the unassorted wash or 'head') retains most of the fine-grained material; the tin-ore in it is less concentrated, and it forms a lower-grade deposit, of which a larger quantity must be turned over to obtain a return equal to that of the low-level assorted wash.

'Unassorted wash' has been worked in many places on the hill-sides, and it is a source of surprise that the stream-workers should have been able to pick out the richer deposits despite their isolated position. The work in such cases progressed up hill, and was usually stopped at a point where one or more veins were discovered, too small generally to pay for working to any depth, although the soft decomposed portion close to the surface was generally extracted; these veins have been responsible for the local enrichment of the wash in their immediate neighbourhood.

Curiously enough, the very cause that led to the abandonment of the workings several years ago has now brought about its revival. For, together with the tin-ore derived from the veins, there was associated another mineral, wolfram, which could then only be separated from the tin by hand-picking, a process which became impracticable when the wolfram-fragments fell below a certain size. At the present time the wolfram, formerly a costly nuisance, is more valuable than the tin itself, being used in the manufacture of high-speed steel and armour-plates, and separation from the tin-ore can now be easily effected by the electromagnet. The history of this local wolfram-working, which marks the survival of streaming, is so curious that it is worth recording.

### The Buttern-Hill Wolfram-Deposit.

When the great marsh of Bowithick, south of Davidstow Moor, was turned over for tin many years ago, the streamers encountered a large amount of wolfram; and at the foot of Buttern Hill it was so abundant that work was stopped altogether. The wolfram was in such big pieces, that much of it was picked out by hand and thrown on one side in little heaps. These heaps of glistening mineral attracted the attention of a lad, who, thinking them valuable, hid some, and took specimens to the smelting-works, where he found that they were worthless. Many years afterwards, when the mineral had become valuable, he was reminded of his store by the enquiries after wolfram, and ascertaining that it was the

Fig. 1.—*Wolfram-deposit in high-level wash, Butlern Hill, north-west of Altarnun, Cornwall.* *(Stream-workings.)*

T. C. Hall photogr.

mineral that he had hidden, disclosed the hiding-place. This led to the reopening of the works at the point at which they had formerly been abandoned, but now search was made for the very mineral that had led to their stoppage.

### Nature of the Deposit.   (Fig. 1, p. 388.)

The wolfram-bearing deposit has been traced from the edge of the marsh, where it is part of the alluvial deposits, to a considerable distance up the hill-slope, where it forms part of the local 'head' or 'unassorted wash,' lying in a shallow hollow or broad groove pointing straight up the hill. The deposit is about 6 feet thick in the centre of the hollow, thinning away towards the margins, but with no appreciable diminution in the size of the constituents. The latter consist of small irregular fragments of granite and vein-quartz, associated with a considerable amount of finer material and many bigger fragments, some of which are a foot long. There is no sign of rounding in the fragments, nor of any bedding in the deposit, which is a perfect example of 'unassorted wash.' Through this the wolfram is disseminated in fairly-large pieces, one having been found, attached to some vein-quartz, as big as the top of a man's head.[1] Work has been carried on here for some time, and has proved continuously renumerative.

Above the unassorted wash is the usual cover of very fine recent wash, that everywhere rests upon the coarser material where these deposits are undisturbed; it varies in thickness here from 1 to 2 feet. Close to the foot of the hill the peat comes on, at first split up by seams of the finer material, but becoming solid at the edge of the marsh, which it once entirely covered. Resting directly upon the old wash are a number of isolated blocks of granite, often of considerable size; these are older than the finer deposit by which they are surrounded, although owing to their size they project above the surface and thus appear at first newer. These blocks are believed to have slid down frozen slopes, and as there seemed to be few signs of denting of the surface of the underlying wash, it seems reasonable to suppose that the latter was frozen; it is to this freezing that its escape from being denuded and swept into the marsh below is almost certainly due.

### Local Enrichment of the Wash.

From what has been said before, we should expect some vein or veins to occur close by, to account for the enrichment of this local wash; and this has proved to be the case, the small pits of the old workers being still clearly visible. They are scattered, and suggest that, as in the adjacent wash, no tin, but wolfram alone was present—a most unusual phenomenon.

[1] Presented by Mr. Harwood, one of the partners, to the Museum of Practical Geology in Jermyn Street, London.

## Summary.

The facts regarding this strange and absolutely unique deposit of wolfram may be summed up as follows:—

(1) It occurs above the 750-foot platform, and thus contains the whole of the materials of a very old and long-continued decomposition.

(2) It was probably protected from being washed away during periods of sudden floods, by being frozen, or snow-covered.

(3) A vein or veins occur close by, and the decomposition-products from these have been carried down into the adjacent hollow and thus have locally enriched the unassorted wash.

## Method of working the Deposit.

The working of this deposit is greatly facilitated by the steady rise of the granite-floor or 'shelf' upon which it rests. This rise is sufficient, not only to prevent all chance of waterlogging by the accumulation of débris in rear of the work, but also to admit of the building of a series of low walls or dams with the larger fragments of the débris. These walls, being built across the groove or hollow from which the wolfram-deposit has already been extracted, form a kind of settling-pond into which the extremely-muddy water, resulting from the washing of the 'unassorted head,' is directed. On reaching the wall the flow of the mud is at once arrested, the coarser sand-grains are immediately deposited, and the water which passes through the wall contains only the finest mud. But the sand, being deposited well above the wall, itself in turn acts as a still more efficient filter, so that in a short time the dirty water is actually filtered by sinking through this deposit of sand before reaching the wall at all, whereby complaints from riparian owners lower down are largely avoided. It will be seen at once that a fair slope is necessary to permit of the utilization of such a device. When this temporary settling-pond has been filled with sand and mud to the brim, it is of no further use, and another wall is built immediately above. The first settling-pond at the end of the operation has become a step in the hill-side; and, as the work proceeds, a series of these steps is built up, which are clearly shown in the photograph (Pl. XLV) taken by Mr. Hall.

As there is no water locally available, a good supply has been obtained from the head of an adjacent small stream, being brought round the end of Buttern Hill in a trench or leat; this terminates at the edge of the deposit far above the starting-point of the works, and thus much labour has been saved in wheeling the dug material to the washing-point.

The water from the leat is turned into a short wood-lined trough, terminating in a small waterfall with a drop of about 2 feet, a bar being placed at the lip of the fall, above the water, to regulate the flow. By raising or lowering this, more or less water passes under. The height of the fall, too, varies somewhat with the grain of the material treated; if the ore and associated earth is fine, the height is smaller, and conversely. Below the fall is a wooden trough, through which the mud flows away and on the floor of which the finer ore settles; the finer the ore is, the longer is this trough and the lower is its slope. The whole arrangement about the waterfall is called the tie or tye, and here the tieman or tyeman stands, who treats the deposit as it is brought in wheel-barrows by the diggers and thrown under the waterfall. Armed with a pronged fork, or (in common parlance) a potato-digger, the tyeman forks over the earth and its contents, thus assisting in washing away the finer mud and sand and picking out the larger fragments that will not pass the prongs. These fragments are picked over by another man, who separates big pieces of wolfram, or vein-quartz and wolfram, the rest being thrown aside. (See fig. 2, p. 392.)

After a number of barrow-loads have been turned over under the fall, a heap accumulates, composed of coarse fragments and sand associated with all but the most finely-divided wolfram. This is taken out, and later handed to the vanner, who vans it in small quantities at a time with a broad, slightly-concave shovel, which he dips repeatedly in a large tub of water. The cleanness and rapidity with which an expert does this is perhaps the most fascinating part of the whole process. As a certain amount of vein-quartz adheres to some of the larger pieces of wolfram, the ore from beneath the tye is crushed in a hand-mill and re-vanned, when it is ready for market. The finer ore that settles in the long wooden trough below the fall is also vanned, but needs no later treatment.

Except for the original cost of making the leat, the working expenses here are reduced to a minimum; the conditions are ideal, and the work has been steadily remunerative.

The success of this first venture encouraged a second start on the edge of the Marsh, at the point of emergence of the stream that feeds the leat already described. It was known that the ground had already been turned over for tin : but much wolfram had been left, and it was hoped that this would compensate for the small amount of tin left. As a result much more tin has been found than had been anticipated, together with much wolfram. But, while the conditions in the first case were almost ideal, the conditions in the second were the reverse. As much the same conditions must be met with in all the tin-bearing marshes on Bodmin High Moor, it seems advisable to give a brief description of their common features and of the work formerly carried on in them, and later to see what light the new work at Kenton Marsh throws on the question of re-starting stream-work on some of the other marshes.

Kenton Marsh is only one of a great number of nearly flat-based hollows, having a singularly small fall, that form a marked feature in the scenery of the Bodmin High-Moor granite. Before the advent of the stream-tinners, these hollows were entirely covered

Fig. 2.—*Stream-tin workings in Benton Marsh, north-west of Luxen Hill (Cornwall).*

with a sheet of peat, varying in thickness from 1 to as much as 15 feet, and in rare cases even more. Below the peat is the recent wash, a very fine deposit carrying no tin and also variable in thickness; this is always greatest where large streams flow through the marsh, and it is never thick where the stream is small. Below this is the tin-bearing gravelly deposit, formed during the cold period, when all the finest material was swept entirely away, leaving the tin somewhat concentrated in what is really the assorted wash swept down from the hill-sides. In working this deposit, it was found that in all cases the richest part lay in a distinct channel below the general level of the shelf or granite-floor on which the rest of the deposit lay; in this channel the gravel was thickest, and the tin most concentrated, but in many cases its course differs markedly from that of the stream at present flowing through these marshes. These old channels were steadily followed up by the streamers, who also worked the less rich gravel on either side as far as possible, or until it no longer paid to do so. It is generally supposed that most of the patches left in the lateral gravels were not worked because they were too poor, but it is most probable that the true cause in many cases is that they were waterlogged.

This waterlogging is due to the great change in climatic conditions: during the cold period the rush of water was great enough to prevent the deposition of any material above the basal gravel; but, as the rainfall greatly decreased, this was no longer the case and a process of infilling of these flats then followed. It began with the deposition of the recent very fine wash and culminated with the thick peat-growth. More than this, the base of the more recent stream was steadily raised, and now always stands some feet (at times many feet) above the base of the hollow or channel in which the stream-tin is most abundant.

Thus, unless they resorted to pumping, which they often did, it was impossible to start work within the marsh itself; the surrounding water-level was considerably above the work, and it was consequently necessary to start some way down the stream below the marsh, where the fall was greater. In many cases an artificial channel had to be made, to carry off the water of the main stream; but this difficulty was avoided when the old channel was a considerable distance from the existing higher channel.

The system of working was and is distinctly primitive, the field of operations covering only a small area at a time, which tends to a short-sighted policy in matters that may be of great consequence in the future. This was specially shown in the disposal of the refuse of the washings from the tie or tye, which was in most cases dumped down in heaps behind the working-face and tended to obstruct the escape of the water from the tye, so that the working-face of the deposit became waterlogged.

There seems good reason to believe that by this process many patches became waterlogged, and owing to this the streamers locally resorted to pumping to win the tin of the deeper channels. On the margins of the latter numerous patches of gravel have been left unworked, but whether these are sufficiently rich to pay with more modern methods is the problem that awaits solution.

In the deeper channels there was more gravel, and so the refuse-heaps were higher, and often stand out above the level of the peat at the present day ; they are often too small to be distinguished from a distance, but they are identified by the fact that bushes will and do grow on them, but will not grow on the peat.    Thus the presence or the position of the older channel can still often be traced by these heaps and the bushes growing on them.   In many cases the heaps were only as high as the peat, and no trace of them can be seen even close at hand ; but the bushes will still grow on these, and mark the position of a thicker gravel-deposit in a moss at the present time.

We may now return to the consideration of Kenton Marsh, and see what information can be gleaned from that ground.   Before the re-starting of the works the marsh was covered by a fairly-smooth sheet of peat, and at first its surface suggests that it has not been disturbed.    But an expert soon detects the sagging at the sides due to the washing-away of part of the deposits during streaming ; the hollow is masked, not actually hidden, by the recent peat-growth. In the centre of the marsh is a solitary bush with a green moss-patch in front ; the bush is growing on a tip of gravel, and the green patch marks a hole choked with a growth of soft moss, a death-trap to any one getting into it.   Towards the southern end of the marsh is a short line of bushes, showing that the deeper channel was followed here ; but the first bush suggests a solitary trial in waterlogged ground.   The general opinion, founded on the presence of these bushes, was that the whole marsh had been worked for tin, but it has proved wrong.

## The Recent Workings at Kenton Marsh.

On opening up the edge of the marsh, a mass of peat-fragments, rough gravel, and soft dirt, the refuse left by the previous workers, was met with ; evidently, the ground here had been turned over before.    It was at once seen that resort had been had to the old habit of throwing, or dumping, behind the face the refuse of the washings, for the bed of the stream, flowing from the marsh, has been blocked almost to the level of the floor or shelf of granite, an obvious impediment to start with.    Then the whole of the mass described had to be washed instead of the basal part only, involving the treatment of a large amount of barren material.   Further, the granite-floor or shelf seems to be more or less kaolinized, and becomes ' quick ' if much trampled on.   This floor, however, is uneven, and the inequality has resulted in the preservation of a number of small pockets of tin and wolfram.   Despite all draw-backs, the results were so encouraging that the marsh was tested to see how much of it had been streamed.   A trench through the peat starting from the opposite side showed that a large portion was untouched, the peat being of considerable thickness and undisturbed. Samples from the dirt below gave fairly favourable results on the whole, and there seems to be a reasonable prospect of success here in the future workings, if waterlogging is avoided. In view of the sheet of peat to be removed in the centre of the marsh, it certainly seems as if some far more efficient agent would be required than shovels and wheelbarrows for removing the overburden.

Further trials have been made on the hill-side near Fowey Well, where the old streamers had already turned over the narrow band of assorted or concentrated material. The material at the margin of the latter, on being tested, gave fairly good results; while the part already worked proved still to contain a considerable amount of tin. But a new method is being tried here; a small reservoir has been made as far up the hill as possible, and the water brought down in canvas-pipes, thus delivering a powerful jet against the loose deposits. The washed material passes over a wooden trough as before, and the ore collects on this, owing to its greater weight. It is too soon yet to express any opinion as to the results of the new departure.

From the foregoing observations it would seem reasonable to believe that in the higher parts of the Bodmin-Moor Granite there is still a considerable amount of tin left in the unassorted wash, bordering the true gravels, but the ore is more disseminated than in the latter. Even in these, however, there appears to be still left more than was expected; and moreover there are patches left unworked here and there, owing to waterlogging. The most important point, however, in connexion with the restarting of the stream-work is the sudden rise in the value of wolfram; practically the whole of this has been left, and much of the tin associated with it. A number of localities have been ascertained where this material is fairly abundant, and further enquiries will be made in the ensuing season; the knowledge is mainly confined to the old streamers, who are not very willing to impart it, as it obviously has a pecuniary value.

### The Connexion between the 750-foot Platform and a China-Clay Working.

The detailed survey of the Bodmin-Moor Granite has shown that all the more extensive marshes, through which only small streams flow, have a floor of kaolinized granite. This material, however, is valuable only if it leaves a soapy film without a trace of grit, when rubbed with the fingers. A very large amount of good china-clay does occur in these marshes, but there is a great impediment to its being worked. This impediment lies in the superficial deposits, previously described as having been recently thickened.

These consist of peat, silt, and gravel, and form the overburden that has to be removed before the clay can be worked. But it has already been pointed out that this clay (the 'shelf' of the stream-workers) is below the present water-level of the surrounding marsh, and the difficulty is to keep this marsh-water out of the pit; it is essential to do so, as the water is peat-stained in wet weather, and would render the clay of little value. So flat are these marshes in cross-section, and so small is their fall in the direction of the water-flow, that it would require a big drain nearly half a mile long to obtain a fall sufficient to keep the water out without pumping.

But in one case this difficulty does not occur; this is at Stannon Marsh, which lies above the 750-foot contour, and has sloping sides instead of a flat waterlogged base. This departure from the type-form is again connected with the 750-foot platform. At the time of its formation a bay-like hollow was formed in the lower part of the valley in which the marsh lies; and, on emergence from the sea, this was left as a flat-based valley. Water falling on the adjacent slopes would accumulate at the edges of the valley and tend to set up two distinct streams. This clearly occurred, and the two can still be traced; the northernmost carried most water and was the more deeply cut in its upper part, but both united before reaching the Camel.

Later on came the great post-Pliocene uplift, followed by a rapid cutting-back and deepening of the bed of the Camel and its tributaries. One of these, separated from the northernmost of the two streams just described by quite a low divide, has succeeded in breaching this divide and capturing the northern stream.

The united streams have continued the cutting-back process, until they have undermined the base and locally obliterated the southern-most of the two valleys formed in the early stages of denudation of the bay of the 750-foot platform. The process, however, is so recent that the stream flowing through the china-clay area is still bordered by sloping banks, and does not yet lie in a flat-based marsh: such a marsh will be developed in due course, as in the case of all the other streams traversing china-clay, but at present the cycle is incomplete. On the sloping bank left by incomplete denudation, the clay-pit of Stannon Marsh is situated, and the great trouble with peat-stained surface-water is avoided.

It may be worth while here to note a curious observation made by Dr. Tempest Anderson in St. Vincent (West Indies). The great outburst of ashes that took place recently levelled the base of a river-valley so as to make it flat in cross-section, and exactly the same result has been produced as in the case here quoted in connexion with the bay of the 750-foot platform; namely, two streams have been set up, one at each margin of the choked and partly-levelled valley.

T. C. Hall, Photo.

Bemrose, Collo . Derby.

WOLFRAM-DEPOSIT, BUTTERN HILL.

Distant view showing the series of step-walls devised to arrest the mud from the 'streaming' or washing-out of the wolfram.

T. C. Hall, Photo.

Bemrose, Collo., Derby.

**OLD STREAM-WORKINGS IN HIGH-LEVEL WASH.**

In the hollow on the watershed of the Fowey and the Penpont Water, south of Buttern Hill.

EXPLANATION OF PLATES XLV & XLVI.

PLATE XLV.

Wolfram-deposit, Buttern Hill (Cornwall). Distant view, showing the series of step-walls devised to arrest the mud from the 'streaming' or washing-out of the wolfram.

PLATE XLVI.

Old stream-workings in high-level wash, in the hollow on the watershed of the Fowey and the Penpont Water, south of Buttern Hill.

DISCUSSION.

Mr. CLEMENT REID remarked that the absence of disturbance in these high plateaux suggested that they were probably of later date than any of the great earth-movements of the South of England, which extended down to Oligocene times. They were clearly more ancient than the 430-foot plateaux of proved Older Pliocene date. This left only the Miocene; and to this unexplored period he suggested that the high plateaux of Bodmin Moor might belong. It was possible, however, that in the hard rocks of Cornwall comparatively little movement had taken place, and that the plateaux might be of earlier date; unfortunately, up till now no deposits found on them had given any clue to their age.

Mr. H. DEWEY congratulated the Author, with whom he had traversed much of the area described. In mapping contiguous areas, precisely similar features had been observed, especially between Davidstow Moor and the coast near Tintagel. In this district several flat-topped ridges could be seen, 1000 feet above O.D., separated one from the other by recent valleys. They thus constituted remnants of the ancient tableland. The speaker referred to the preservation in fair condition of an old bluff, the base of which was 920 feet above the sea; from this height the slope of the ground suddenly and rapidly increased until the height of 960 feet or thereabouts was reached, when the plateau-feature succeeded. This cliff-line was best seen on the main road between Boscastle and Delabole, near Condolden Barrow. On approaching the barrow from the south, a sudden rise in the road and fields was seen; and from several points of view this bluff had the appearance of a huge bank crossing the fields. When the road-gradients were drawn to scale, the change of inclination, though well seen, was not so striking as it appeared in the field. On first seeing this feature, the speaker attributed it to a band of harder rock; but, after the area had been mapped, the feature was seen to cut across rocks of varying degrees of hardness and different litho-logical characters. Although this was rather slender evidence, he considered the cliff suggestive of a periodical pause in the elevation of the land from the sea; such a cause was not, however, the only one to which the feature might be assigned. He welcomed the paper as an important contribution to the study of the evolution of Cornish scenery.

Mr. E. E. L. DIXON, after remarking on the interest which the platform rising to the 430-foot level possessed from its extensive development, not only in Cornwall and Devon, but also in South Wales, Ireland, and Britanny, proceeded to ask whether the evidence at present available justified the conclusion that it was a plain of marine denudation of the Pliocene Sea. In extent it was very different from the notches upon which rested the raised beaches around our coasts—in fact, it was approached only by the coast-platform of Norway recently described by Dr. Nansen, who regarded it as formed by a combination of marine and atmospheric erosion during a period of oscillating sea-level. The platform, which he described as being 'as much as 40 miles or even more' broad, was so much dissected by channels that waves could attack upstanding rocks at a distance from its edge; but no such channels existed over wide areas of the Cornish plain. Moreover, the Norwegian coast was fully exposed to the Atlantic, whereas parts of the Cornish plains, such as Goss Moor, formed bottle-necked gulfs almost enclosed by rising ground, where consequently wave-action would be reduced to a minimum.

The speaker quoted Mr. Reid's conclusion that the sea which deposited the Pliocene beds of Cornwall probably cut a notch at about the 430-foot level, but considered that the plain upon which some of the beds rested need not also have been eroded by the Pliocene sea. He had noticed in the Pyrenees how the super-position of marine beds on a platform of older rocks might lead to wrong conclusions as to the formation of the latter, for he had found that whereas, near Gavarnie, such a platform eroded in crystalline rocks had been overlain by Hippurite-Limestone, and had been consequently referred to as a plain of marine denudation worn down by the Cretaceous sea, at a short distance on the other side of the frontier it had been immediately overlain by a thin group of red Permo-Triassic beds, succeeded in turn and with apparent conformity by the Hippurite-Limestone. It was obvious that the platform had been eroded long prior to the Cretaceous submergence; and also presumably—since the Permo-Trias had rested in part on a denuded Hercynian granite-boss, and the great interval between the intrusion of the one and the deposition of the other had been a period of continental conditions—that the platform was an old desert-plain.

However, the speaker felt, not only that the Author had done great service in drawing attention to the remarkable Cornish plains, but also that in any case his observations would provide a valuable step towards the solution of a difficult problem.

Prof. W. W. WATTS remarked that a very valuable part of the paper was that which referred to the history of the Glacial Epoch in a practically unglaciated area. But the point of greatest interest to him was that it was clear from the paper that the successful mining of tin and wolfram, and even china-clay, in this area was the outcome of conditions not explicable by simple geological principles, but requiring advanced geological research to explain them. These deposits were apparently produced by a type of denudation ancient and now extinct; they were preserved in consequence of past climatal changes; and the conditions which permitted of their successful working were only to be understood as the outcome of advanced physiographic research.

M. M. ALLORGE remarked that there was a striking parallelism between the past geological history of Cornwall and that of Northern Britanny. Taking into account the morphological features of the two areas, he thought that there was some evidence that the lower platform, a little above 300 feet,—if not actually a sea-beach caused by marine abrasion,—had at least been temporarily covered by the Pliocene Sea, and sprinkled with marine sands at that period. With regard to the two higher platforms, he saw no positive evidence of marine encroachment during Tertiary time—there being no traces of old sea-cliffs and no remains of shore-conglomerates. It was therefore simpler to attribute the formation of the upper platforms to slow subaërial levelling and to the backward working of ruissellements during the Tertiary. Such a view would avoid the necessity of the intervention of a complicated series of oscillations of the sea-level. A single vertical oscillation of some 300 feet would in this case have taken place since the Pliocene Epoch, and could be accounted for by simple posthumous movements along the Armorican lines of weakness.

In regard to Glacial action, he had been struck by the very slight evidence for it in Cornwall and its great importance, on the other hand, in South Wales, where its strong influence was traced in the features of the scenery. He would like to know whether the Author could suggest any explanation of the difference of morphology of two districts otherwise so closely related. He welcomed the appearance of the paper, as an interesting contribution to the elucidation of the morphological features of South-Western Britain.

Mr. G. W. YOUNG thought that the Author's suggestion, that the preservation of the beds of non-coherent wolfram-containing detritus was due to the former existence of a snowfield, presented considerable difficulties. If their preservation was due to that cause alone, had not sufficient time elapsed since the passing-away of those Glacial conditions to allow of their removal by denudation? As the deposits in question had already been turned over and rearranged by man in his search for tin, could any reliance be placed on their present appearance? With regard to the theory that the large masses had slid down to their present position over frozen surfaces, he thought that the ordinary gravitational creep of such masses from higher to lower ground would be a sufficient cause.

Dr. A. STRAHAN remarked that the ore-deposits described by the Author corresponded in their character and origin with certain accumulations of galena which had been worked with much profit in North Wales. The ore there occurred as loose lumps distributed along the outcrops of lodes, and was known to the miners as 'gravel-ore' or 'round ore.' There was a suggestion in Cornwall of Glacial conditions having supervened after the distribution of the ore-deposits;

but in North Wales it was a fact that all the Glacial deposits were superimposed upon the 'gravel-ore.' These deposits were in some cases upwards of 200 feet thick, and the ore had been got by tunnelling along the surface of the underlying rock. The amount of material derived from the lodes by subaërial waste in post-Glacial times was quite insignificant in comparison with the 'gravel-ore,' a fact which confirmed the Author's view that the Cornish material was of considerable antiquity.

The PRESIDENT commented on the great interest of the paper, which showed signs of an interaction between scientific research and the renewed prosperity of the mining industry. The notion that plains of erosion were commonly formed by rain and rivers seemed to rest on an assumption that conditions remained unchanged for an indefinitely-long interval; but, apart from this, the Author seemed to have given direct evidence of the marine origin of the plains which he had described. The supposed frozen state of the ground during the Glacial episode might be more readily admitted if illustrated by existing instances.

The AUTHOR, in reply, stated that he was not yet satisfied as to the marine origin of the 1000-foot platform, but the 750-foot platform seemed clearly to be part of a plain of marine denudation. It occurred at apparently the same level on both sides of the granite-mass, with a watershed of killas between the two occurrences. Further, the great rising feature formed by the junction of the granite and killas, so conspicuous in many parts of Cornwall, was completely lost where it crossed the 750-foot platform. In place of being in a steep hill-face, it actually occurred well out on the flat ground (the platform) at the foot of the latter.

23. *On the* SUBDIVISIONS *of the* CHALK *of* TRIMINGHAM (NORFOLK).[1] By REGINALD MARR BRYDONE, F.G.S. (Read January 22nd, 1908.)

[PLATES XLVII & XLVIII—MAPS.]

THE Chalk in question is seen on the sea-shore when freed from shingle and sands by favourable tides, and portions of it rise as bluffs in the more recent deposits of the cliffs, being exposed from time to time as these beds in their turn are denuded away. This Chalk, by the evidence of its fossil contents, is younger than the Chalk of the *mucronata*-zone, which is the highest member of the White Chalk exposed elsewhere in England. This *mucronata*-Chalk dips generally eastwards, and, although exposed between Weybourne and Cromer, disappears just east of the latter place and is seen no more. The Chalk described in this paper lies on the top of *mucronata*-Chalk, and is correlated by its fossil-contents with the Chalk of Rügen. It is, therefore, in normal succession to the *mucronata*-Chalk, and represents the highest beds of the Cretaceous System existing in this country. It has not been found in any other part of the British Islands.

The literature on it is scanty, and for present purposes it will be useful to call attention to Mr. Clement Reid's 'Geology of the Country around Cromer' Mem. Geol. Surv. 1882; to the present writer's 'Stratigraphy & Fauna of the Trimingham Chalk,' 8vo, London (Dulau) 1900, and Geol. Mag. 1906, which gives a complete fauna of these beds and of the *mucronata*-Chalk between Weybourne and Cromer; also to Mr. A. J. Jukes-Browne's 'Upper Chalk of England,' vol. iii of the 'Cretaceous Rocks of Britain' Mem. Geol. Surv. 1904.

In a paper on the Chalk of Trimingham as a whole, published in the Geological Magazine for 1906, I indicated that several subdivisions of that Chalk could be made on lithological and palæontological grounds. The object of the present communication is to lay before the Society a sketch-map showing the geographical distribution of these subdivisions, with a brief account of their distinguishing features.

The main outlines of the map and nearly all the details have been laid down from observations made with a finely-divided compass and a tape-measure during the last thirteen months. For these practically absolute accuracy may be claimed. But, in many instances, details, and along the half-tide level on each of the three large blocks the main outlines, could only be supplied from observations made during the previous five years with a small compass and the distances paced. But the possible error in the position of any point, or in the course of the various lines of flints, can hardly ever be more than 10 feet in any direction. Even now it will be seen that there are a few areas where nothing is laid down positively, though Chalk must

[1] Edited for the Geological Society by C. Davies Sherborn, F.G.S., at the request of the Council and by consent of the Author.

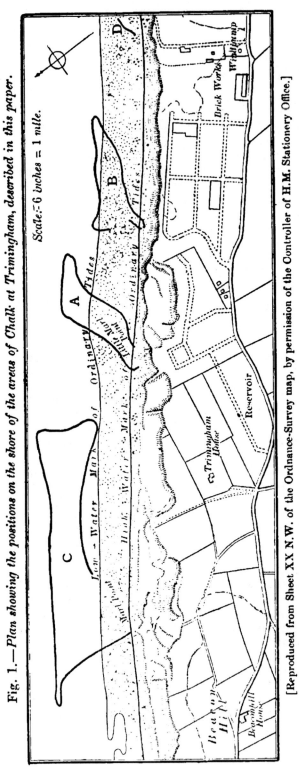

Fig. 1.—*Plan showing the positions on the shore of the areas of Chalk at Trimingham, described in this paper.*

Scale:- 6 inches = 1 mile.

[Reproduced from Sheet XX N.W. of the Ordnance-Survey map, by permission of the Controller of H.M. Stationery Office.]

occur there; and although I believe that in most cases I actually saw that Chalk during the six or seven years during which I studied this locality without realizing the possibility of mapping it, there is certainly a fair amount of Chalk in the northernmost block which has never been seen by me and the nature of which cannot be predicted. Wherever in such cases I consider that the nature of the Chalk can be predicted with great probability, I have indicated my views by broken lines of colour. The whole of the Chalk exposed on the foreshore comes under four heads, namely: Grey Chalk, White Chalk containing *Ostrea lunata*, White Chalk not containing *O. lunata*, and Sponge-Beds (very largely yellow); and I have coloured these respectively brown, blue, red, and yellow. Where any particular set of beds, not the only one of its general type, has appeared to occur more than once, I have indicated this by another letter. I have also tried to give some idea of the great variation of dip by using $\downarrow$ for dips estimated not to exceed 20°, $\updownarrow$ for those estimated to exceed 50°, and $\updownarrow$ for intermediate dips.

In describing the three great blocks in which the Chalk now occurs, it will be convenient to take first that (A) which terminates in the South Bluff—the only bluff now existing, as the much discussed North Bluff finally disappeared in February 1907, except for a small outlier of Grey Chalk which still remains. This block forms an east-and-west anticline. The lowest beds exposed in it are four beds of White Chalk appearing in a narrow oval close to the bluff, which are marked (a) on my map (Pl. XLVII). The line of flint (b) which separates the upper two of these beds is readily recognizable by the great size of the individual flints of which it is formed, these being far larger than the flints in any other line of flint seen at Trimingham. Fossils are fairly abundant in these beds; they have been carefully collected; and, although the total area exposed is relatively small, I have found the following significant forms:—

| | |
|---|---|
| *Porosphæra globularis*, very common. | *Serpula canteriata* (four-angled |
| *Porosphæra nuciformis*, rare. | variety), very rare. |
| *Echinoconus Orbignyanus* \*, rare. | *Terebratula sex-radiata*, common. |
| *Pentacrinus Agassizi* \*. | *Terebratulina Gisei* \*, very rare. |
| *Pentacrinus Bronni* \*. | *Terebratulina gracilis* \*, rare. |
| *Pentacrinus* sp. nov. | |

The forms marked with an asterisk are apparently confined to the Trimingham Chalk: they occur throughout it, and may be taken as the characteristic fauna of a zone comprising all the Chalk exposed at Trimingham. They are all quite rare in these beds. Small *Echinoconi* are abundant, but the great majority appear to be *E. abbreviatus*. This fact strongly suggests that these beds are very near the base of the zone, and this is confirmed by the single specimen recorded as *Pentacrinus* sp. nov. This is identical with the *Pentacrinus* abundant in the Overstrand erratics, which contain none of the peculiar Trimingham forms and must therefore be referred to the zone of *Belemnitella mucronata*. The near approach of these beds to the latter zone is also suggested by the occurrence of *Terebratula sex-radiata* and the abundance of *Porosphæra globularis*. It will doubtless surprise those who are familiar with the whole of our Senonian Chalk to find *Porosphæra* invested with significance, but the behaviour of the genus is remarkable. In the Senonian, and especially in the two upper zones, the regular forms *P. arrecta*, *P. globularis*, *P. nuciformis*, *P. galeata*, Stolley[1] [= *P. patelliformis*, Hinde, a name which must give place to that assigned by Dr. Stolley, whose description and figure are quite recognizable], and *P. pileolus* are widely and freely distributed, while irregular forms are rare. In the Trimingham Chalk irregular forms are abundant; while, of the regular forms, I have never found *P. arrecta* or *P. galeata*, I have but one specimen of *P. pileolus*, horizon uncertain, and *P. nuciformis* only occurs in a few very poorly characterized specimens in the beds under consideration and

---

[1] Mitth. Min. Inst. Univ. Kiel, vol. i, pt. iv (1892) p. 276 & pl. ix, fig. 8.

the two sets of beds immediately succeeding. *P. globularis* is very abundant in these lower beds, quite scarce in the three succeeding sets of beds, and has hardly ever been found by me in any of the other beds, in which it must be exceedingly rare. The thickness of the beds (*a*) exposed is probably about 8 feet.

The beds next above those just described are those designated by me as 'Sponge-Beds' (*c*). They are about 12 feet thick, strongly yellow in colour, and more or less hardened, sometimes so much so that a knife makes practically no impression, with the natural result that they always present a rugged surface on the foreshore. I have taken as their upward limit a greasy-looking and clayey bed, which for the last year or so has thrown out a fairly persistent spring of fresh water at the foot of the Bluff. Below the half-tide level only about half the thickness of the beds is cut through along the crown of the anticline, which is there much flatter than it is near the Bluff. As a result of this flattening, the two uppermost flint-beds, which both consist of long slender flints with pitted surfaces, occupy a considerable area on the foreshore and form an easily recognizable feature. *Thecidium vermiculare* appears in these beds. The four-angled variety of *Serpula canteriata* appears to be entirely confined to them and to the preceding and succeeding sets. A *Nautilus* which has been found in them is thought by Mr. G. C. Crick to be probably *N. Bellerophon*, a Danian form.

The next set of beds (*d*), about 9 feet thick, consist of White Chalk without *O. lunata*. Until quite recently they had never been well exposed for study, but a very fair idea of their fossil-contents has now been obtained. *Terebratula sex-radiata* and the four-angled variety of *Serpula canteriata* have both been found to persist in the lower part, while *Porosphæra globularis* is not infrequent. Up to this point large specimens of *Rhynchonella plicatilis* have been fairly abundant, but the species now becomes scarce and small.

The next set of beds, with *Ostrea lunata*, is the highest of this sequence yet known (*e*). It is a curious fact that nowhere in the foreshore has any trace been found of the highest line of flint seen in the Bluff, although the one next below it is frequently preserved. This top line of flint is very thick and solid. The strong line of flints seen, the second from the top in the Bluff, is the highest that is regularly preserved on the foreshore, and it forms a well-marked feature wherever it occurs. The double line of flints in yellowed chalk, which forms the base of this set of beds, is even more valuable in tracing them on the foreshore, for *Ostrea lunata* is so relatively scarce in the lowest bed of this set that it would often (but for this well-marked line of flints) be impossible to fix the boundary between this and the preceding set of beds without prolonged search. In collecting from below upwards, *Terebratula sex-radiata*, *Porosphæra nuciformis*, and the four-angled variety of *Serpula canteriata* apparently disappear for good before we reach the *lunata*-Chalk; and *Porosphæra globularis* disappears long before the top is reached. *Ostrea lunata* and *Crania spinulosa* here make their appearance, and *Thecidium vermiculare* becomes fairly common. These beds are at least 20 feet thick, and the total thickness of Chalk exposed in the block is estimated as at least 50 feet.

The next block (B) to the south is almost entirely, perhaps entirely, composed of the same or of some of the same beds as Block A, and like that area forms an anticlinal ridge running more or less from east to west (see Pl. XLVII). The only part of it which deserves any comment, or which may represent beds not already described, is the spur which runs up to the cliff-line (*f*). This spur is cut off from the main mass by a fault filled with clay (*g*). It consists of an anticlinal ridge formed by a very thick pseudotabular band (*h*) of flint, with *O.-lunata* Chalk immediately above and below it. This 'pseudotabular' band is as continuous as any ordinary tabular flint-band; but it is undoubtedly interbedded, and presents an extremely rugged surface, being apparently formed by the consolidation of the lower part only of a close-set line of flints of the ordinary type. As this ridge rises westward, that is, slantwise up the beach, at a lower angle than that of the beach, Chalk is preserved at the western end above the pseudotabular flint; while farther down the beach to the south the pseudotabular flint and the Chalk below it have been cut through to some depth, but without another line of flints being reached. Quite recently, on the exposure in the lower part of the ridge of a considerable part of the surface of the pseudotabular band, Pliocene beds (*i*) full of well-preserved marine shells were found in the interstices of the pseudotabular band and cropping out between it and the Glacial clay. These beds are dealt with in an appendix (p. 411). This ridge was traced in patchy exposures up to the foot of the cliff, and appeared to continue into the base thereof. There is nothing by which this pseudotabular band can be identified with any line of flints elsewhere exposed, but I strongly suspect that it is identical with the highest line of flints visible in the South Bluff (Block A). The seaward edge of this block (B) and the south side of the pseudotabular ridge are the only two instances known to me at Trimingham of the surface of the Chalk dipping gently under the clay.

The small strip of Chalk still farther south appears as a line (D) on the plan (fig. 1, p. 402). It was described by me in Geol. Mag. 1906, p. 78.

We now come to the northernmost block (C), the largest and by far the most important (Pl. XLVIII). Here only a relatively small space at the northern end is occupied by beds (*d' e'*) which may be identical with any previously described; but the correspondence in detail down to the nature of the flint-band forming the boundary between the Chalks with and without *O. lunata* is so exact that the identity is practically beyond doubt. The boundary of this area, so far as it has yet been traced, is a fault; and no guidance can be obtained as to the relative ages of the Chalk of the first two blocks (A, B) and the Chalk which forms the greater part of the block (C) now to be described. The beds in this block which are new to us are all disposed more or less in an anticlinal ridge running, as in the case of the other areas, east and west. From the lowest tide-level for a considerable way up the beach, the beds run with perfect regularity from one end of the block to the other, unbroken by any faults. In the centre of the anticline there is a considerable thickness of White Chalk (*k*) with *O. lunata*. This chalk covers a large area in the northern part of the block and reappears at the southern end in a small oval inlier. This is evidently a continuation of the main ridge; but, as some *O.-lunata* Chalk also occurs a little beachwards in more broken chalk where its extent cannot be mapped, it looks as if the anticline were flattening out and splitting up in this direction. Outside this *O.-lunata* Chalk comes Chalk (*l*), only distinguishable from it by the total absence of *O. lunata*, and outside that again more White Chalk (*m*) with *O. lunata*. I have not noticed anything else that is especially remarkable about the fossil-contents of these beds. Outside them comes finally Grey Chalk (*n*), which appears to be the highest of this sequence exposed. This Grey Chalk is readily distinguished from the other Grey Chalk of the block by the abundance in it of small *Ostrea vesicularis* and the absence from it of *Ostrea canaliculata*, *O. sulcata* (= *inæquicostata*, S. Woodward), and *Terebratula obesa*. It contains all the special Trimingham forms, except *Ostrea lunata* and probably *Crania spinulosa* and *Thecidium vermiculare*; and in it were found my only two specimens of *Trigonosemus pulchellus* and four of my five specimens of *Trigonosemus elegans*.

Only a small thickness of the *Ostrea-lunata* Chalk (*k*) in the centre of the anticline would apparently have been exposed if the beds had remained unbroken, but a fault (*o*) has thrown up to foreshore level the whole thickness of this Chalk and a considerable thickness of Grey Chalk (*p*) underlying it. The westerly extension of this Grey Chalk and of the lower beds of the central *O.-lunata* Chalk is covered by permanent sand; but, as they correspond in the minutest details with the mass of Grey Chalk overlain by Chalk with *O. lunata*, which is seen on the same line of strike immediately to the east of the North Bluff, they have been considered identical. This Grey Chalk (*p*) contains (though not in abundance) *Ostrea canaliculata*, *O. sulcata*, and *Terebratula obesa* (none of which have yet been found in any but Grey Chalk at Trimingham, and must be exceedingly rare in the White Chalk there if they occur at all). It also probably contains all the special Trimingham forms, except *O. lunata*, *Thecidium vermiculare*, and *Trigonosemus pulchellus*. One specimen of *Trigonosemus elegans* has been found in it. Its included flints are often of the smoke-coloured, soft, and poorly silicified type described from the Grey Chalk on the North Bluff in the Geological Magazine (1906, p. 74). These beds (*k, l, m, n,* and *p*) alone play any real part in forming the block, and their thicknesses may be estimated as follows :—

|  |  | *Feet* |
|---|---|---|
| *p* = Lower Grey beds | ..................... | 12 |
| *k* = Lower *Ostrea-lunata* beds | ............... | 20 |
| *l* = White Chalk without *O. lunata* | ......... | 8 |
| *m* = Upper *O.-lunata* beds | .................... | 10 |
| *n* = Upper Grey beds (at least) | .............. | 25 |
|  |  | 75 |

Only so much of them has been mapped as has been actually accessible, and this gives a maximum length of unbroken Chalk of about 700 yards. More Chalk has always been visible seawards; and at lowest tides rough ridges, apparently continuous with the block, are seen extending out at sea from its southern end for at least another 250 yards.

I have now dealt with the general structure of this block, but there are several small areas requiring special notice. The first and most important is the neck of Chalk leading to the much discussed North Bluff. This neck puzzled me extremely for a long time, for in small exposures there was practically nothing to suggest the existence of the fault (*v*) shown running through the neck. There is no seam of grit, clay, or crushed chalk marking the fault, and the strike and the character of the Chalk are practically the same on both sides. It was only an exceptionally clean and extensive exposure which gave me the clue—by showing that the dips on the two sides of the fault were opposed, though the strikes were so nearly identical. The Bluff in recent years has been wholly formed of the beds (*k'*) on the south side of this fault, and fortunately some of the beds which appeared in the Bluff can still be traced continuously down the neck and round to the south-east into a large mass of Chalk with a gentle northerly dip, which is obviously natural and not the result of inversion. Now, the section presented by the North Bluff

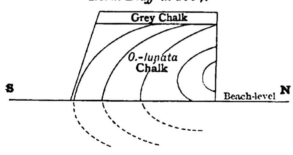

Fig. 2.—*Section presented by the North Bluff in 1904.*

was (roughly speaking) a section of the upper part of a fold lying on its side, as shown in the accompanying figure; and Mr. Clement Reid assumed, and in 1906 I adopted the assumption, that the upper part of this fold had had its original dip reversed, while the lower part had been inverted. It is, however, now clear that the lower part of the fold still retains its original dip, and that it is the upper part which has been inverted. Therefore the inverting force must have acted from the south, and not from the north as previously supposed. Thus we get this force entirely distinct from that which caused the main anticlinal folds and must have acted from the north, as these folds are always steepest on the south side. It is possible t^ the very curious S-shaped bend in the edge of the Grey Cha)' to the east and the bending of a few of the nearest beds are another effect of the inverting force.

It may be advisable here to recall that the invertin' Cretaceous age, as the Bluff showed that on a de' the inverted beds there had been deposited Grey '

Cretaceous fauna of great abundance, and indistinguishable by any physical or palæontological character from the lower Grey Chalk already dealt with or from an area of Grey Chalk to be dealt with later. The boundary between this Grey Chalk in the Bluff and the *Ostrea-lunata* Chalk beneath it, was marked in some places by a seam of grit swelling out into a bed of grit with pebbles of flint and chalk, but was marked in other places only by the sharp change in colour and fossil-contents. The probability suggested in the Geological Magazine (1906, p. 74, etc.) that the flints of this Grey Chalk were in definite beds has been shown by further and better exposures to be a fact, the large and perfectly silicified flints forming a band at the base, and the smaller, carious, and imperfectly silicified flints forming bands higher up.

The next small area (*t*) requiring special notice is the Grey Chalk already mentioned which occurs about 80 yards north-east of the North Bluff. A cursory glance shows that it cannot be in conformable sequence with the adjoining *O. lunata*-Chalk, and the question arises as to whether the boundary-line is a fault or an unconformity. Such parts of the boundary-line as I have been able to examine lend no support to the fault-theory, and afford but a feeble presumption in favour of an unconformity. Fortunately the surface of the Grey Chalk is deeply furrowed, and several of these furrows have cut down to *Ostrea-lunata* Chalk, in one case with what appeared to be a grit-seam at the boundary. I have, therefore, no hesitation in saying that these beds are lying unconformably on the *O.-lunata* Chalk, in which case they must be newer than any beds exposed in the regular sequence in this block. These grey beds correspond closely with the lower grey beds of this block, but even more closely with the Grey Chalk on the North Bluff, seeing that in both the characteristic fossils *Ostrea canaliculata*, *O. sulcata*, and *Terebratula obesa* are very abundant (especially *O. canaliculata*), and that they lie unconformably on different parts of the same set of *O.-lunata* beds. They are, therefore, considered as probably identical.

A third special area (*r*) is that of Grey Chalk and *Ostrea-lunata* Chalk to seaward of it which appears near the southern end of the block. This area is low-lying and therefore very rarely cleared of sand, but it appears possible that the Grey Chalk is identical with the 'upper grey beds' of opposite dip seen close by on the south. Probably there is another fault dividing them from the *O.-lunata* Chalk, but no certain identification of either the Grey Chalk or the *O.-lunata* Chalk is possible.

There are also two small exposures of hardened Grey Chalk (*s*) at the southern extremity of the block, and these undoubtedly formed part of the same bed. They are identical in fossil-contents with the neighbouring 'upper grey beds'; but no stratigraphical evidence concerning their relationship has been obtained, as they appear to be isolated by clay.

As some stress has been recently laid in argument on the relative positions of the Chalk and the Boulder-Clay, it seems desirable to point out how little evidence in favour of any particular hypothesis can be drawn from these relations. Whatever the cause of the occurrence of Chalk at Trimingham, it is hardly open to dispute that at no remote period the cliffs reached to the present low-tide level, and all the Chalk that we now see was wholly enveloped in clay. Any clay that is now found overlying Chalk may be equally well a remnant of this envelope, or a more recent overcreep from the great masses on the foreshore squeezed out by the weight of the cliffs behind : in neither case does it afford any argument as to the erratic or other condition of the Chalk. In the same way, the clay which separates the blocks of chalk may quite as likely be occupying the bottom of depressions—possibly synclinal folds—in the surface of a continental mass of Chalk, as be held to be a deep bed of Glacial clay with erratics of Chalk embedded in it.

I should like to take this opportunity of elaborating an argument which I stated too briefly in the Geological Magazine. This is the argument from the boring for the Mundesley Waterworks.[1] In this boring the top of Chalk *in situ* was found at 89 feet below the surface. The point at which the boring was made is not more than 80 feet above Ordnance-datum (which is roughly the half-tide level), so that the top of the Chalk at the Waterworks was just about at low-tide level. We have, therefore, at distances from a body of Chalk undoubtedly *in situ* varying from 1 to $2\frac{1}{2}$ miles, Chalk appearing at the same level in several huge masses which, even if detached, must extend downwards to a considerable depth, and rising to a maximum of about 40 feet above low-tide level. Even standing entirely by itself, this fact would seem to set up a *prima-facie* presumption that the masses in question are themselves *in situ*, and when a number of other considerations point to the same conclusion the presumption becomes very strong. Prof. Bonney has suggested an hypothesis (Geol. Mag. 1905, p. 397 etc.) that the Trimingham Chalk consists of erratics brought by floating ice; but, quite apart from any other considerations, the mechanical difficulties involved in the quarrying-out of any one of the three principal blocks, and the formation and retention under water during formation of the enormous volume of ice which would be required to float off the smallest of these blocks, seem absolutely prohibitive to the theory of transport by ground-ice, and there is at present no evidence in the British Isles of the existence in Glacial times at any point but Trimingham of a cliff of *Ostrea-lunata* Chalk from which such supposed erratics could be gathered by glacier-ice.

Some idea of the mass of Chalk which may have existed here in quite recent times, may be gathered by applying the measurement of the Bluffs given by Lyell [2] to show how much Chalk has been destroyed even since his day. Lyell states that the North Bluff was 105 yards long. As the maximum width of the neck leading

---

[1] Geol. Mag. 1906, p. 125; A. J. Jukes-Browne, 'The Upper Chalk of England,' vol. iii of the 'Cretaceous Rocks of Britain' Mem. Geol. Surv. U. K. (1904) p. 263.

[2] Phil. Mag. ser. 3, vol. xvi (1840) pp. 357 *et seqq.*

to the North Bluff is about 40 yards, it is clear that the face of Lyell's bluff was farther seaward than the point at which the neck starts, that is to say at least, and possibly much more than, 40 yards seawards of the present high-water level. As his figure of the Bluff indicates that it was at least 25 feet high, we have a mass of Chalk of the same superficial area as the neck leading to the North Bluff and 25 feet in depth removed in about 70 years; so that there is hardly any limit to be set to the amount of Chalk which may have existed above present levels to seawards in Glacial times and have since been destroyed. If, as is likely, the Bluffs in Lyell's day stood about equally distant from high-water level, the above calculation makes it fairly probable that the southernmost bluff of Lyell's day—which disappeared long ago—stood along the landward edge of some part of the block (B) above described, and not on any part of the ridge with the pseudotabular flint, which otherwise would seem the natural position to assign to it.

There is one more point to be considered, that is, the name to be attached to the zone created for the Trimingham Chalk if, as appears to be the case, it is inevitable that a zone should be created. Mr. Jukes-Browne[1] has suggested that the zone should be called 'zone of *Ostrea lunata*,' as characterized by the association of *Ostrea lunata, Pecten serratus, Echinoconus abbreviatus, Trochosmilia cornucopiæ, Thecidium vermiculare, Terebratulina Gisei,* and *T. gracilis.* Now, *Pecten serratus, Echinoconus abbreviatus,* and *Trochosmilia cornucopiæ* are all well-known and abundant fossils in the zone of *Belemnitella mucronata* in Norfolk, and are therefore of no use in separating the Trimingham Chalk from the zone of *B. mucronata.* I have shown that *Ostrea lunata* does not occur at all in more than half of the total thickness of Chalk exposed; while *Thecidium vermiculare* only occurs freely at one or two horizons in the *O.-lunata* Chalk, is very rare indeed in any White Chalk without *O. lunata,* and probably does not occur at all in any Grey Chalk. I have, therefore, objected to the adoption of Mr. Jukes-Browne's zone, because it is by its very definition inapplicable to the greater part of the Chalk which it is intended to cover, and such an objection would appear to be necessarily fatal. Hence the zone of Chalk at Trimingham, lying above the zone of *Belemnitella mucronata,* now divided and defined by me for the first time, requires a name.

The net result of this paper is to make it possible, for the first time, to form some idea of the extent and nature of the Chalk of Trimingham, which has been practically ignored by everyone who has discussed the Bluffs, except Mr. Clement Reid and Mr. Jukes-Browne.

I still adhere without reservation to the view expounded in the Geological Magazine (1906, pp. 124, 125), that these enormous masses of Chalk can only be *in situ* and must have once formed part of a large continuous mass; and that, as the various existing

---

[1] 'The Upper Chalk of England,' vol. iii of the 'Cretaceous Rocks of Britain' Mem. Geol. Surv. U. K. (1904) p. 12.

B

*...ore at Trimingham, Norfolk.*
*14 Feet = 1 Inch.*

blocks are most bulky at low water and least bulky at high water, the bulk of this large continuous mass must have lain to seawards rather than to landwards of the present coast-line. Moreover, it is quite possible that we have here preserved the last remnants of a land-area that was once in connexion with continental Europe.

### APPENDIX.

The Pliocene beds which, as above stated (p. 405), were found directly overlying the Cretaceous, consisted of a coarse dark sand about 9 inches thick, lying on and filling up the inequalities in the surface of a horizontal and practically continuous bed of flint, and succeeded by a bed of dark clay about a foot thick, which was in its turn succeeded by Glacial Clay with horizontal simulated bedding. The sand contained a great abundance of somewhat corroded shells, mainly in drifted masses, and the clay a quantity of *Tellinæ* with a few other shells, all in excellent preservation. The sand also contained in great quantity rolled lumps of a grey clay.

The Glacial Clay must have reached its present position very gently, for a channel in it disclosed a large and delicate, but quite uninjured shell, which rested upon and had its edges embedded in the Pliocene clay, while the greater part of it projected into the Glacial Clay.

Mr. Clement Reid has examined the specimens, and has kindly allowed me to quote the following remarks from his letter giving the result of his examination :—

'I have looked through your specimens, and find that they undoubtedly belong to the Weybourne Crag. The species are the same as those found at Cromer, but the assemblage suggests water a fathom or two deeper, and at the same time slightly more estuarine. *Littorina* and *Balanus*, which form so large a proportion of the shells at Cromer, are missing; but so too are the open-sea species which belong to the depth suggested by the rest of the shells. There is nothing to indicate the proximity of any Pliocene deposit other than the Weybourne Crag.

'The following species are represented :—

| | |
|---|---|
| *Astarte borealis.* | *Tellina obliqua.* |
| *Astarte compressa.* | *Tellina prætenuis.* |
| *Cardium edule.* | *Saxicava rugosa.* |
| *Cyprina islandica.* | *Buccinum undatum.* |
| *Mactra ovalis.* | *Natica catena* (?) |
| *Mya truncata.* | *Natica islandica.* |
| *Nucula Cobboldiæ.* | *Purpura lapillus.* |
| *Tellina balthica.* | *Littorina* (one small fragment).' |

The bivalves were all common, the univalves all very scarce. The specimens of *Mya truncata* almost invariably retained both valves, and were found in the position of life.

### EXPLANATION OF PLATES XLVII & XLVIII.
#### PLATE XLVII.
Plan of Blocks A & B of the Chalk exposed on the shore at Trimingham, on the scale of 144 feet to the inch.

#### PLATE XLVIII.
Plan of Block C, on the same scale.

DISCUSSION.

Mr. CLEMENT REID spoke of the great value of this palæontological work, but hoped that Mr. Brydone would reconsider his use of the term 'zone of *Terebratulina gracilis*.' It was true that the original *T. gracilis* was a British specimen probably from Trimingham, and that the old 'zone of *T. gracilis*' (in the Middle Chalk) did not contain that species. Still, to transfer the name to a totally-different part of the Chalk would lead to great confusion. He doubted the occurrence of the strong unconformity depicted in the middle of the Chalk, and showed a photograph of the same mass, taken in 1893 by Dr. Strahan. In this photograph the thin sandy bed (taken by Mr. Brydone as the base of his Grey Chalk) was seen to be folded with the other beds, and not to rest unconformably upon them. The speaker still considered that the disturbance was glacial: the upper beds of the Chalk being contorted without being completely detached.

The Rev. EDWIN HILL highly esteemed such careful records, and regretted that the Author's views could not be presented more satisfactorily that evening. Chalk was exposed elsewhere, both at beach-level and higher: he would wish to have heard what these exposures were. This 'bluff' he thought a displaced mass: the faults described would result from displacement.

The AUTHOR, in reply to Mr. Clement Reid, stated that his chief object in discussing the zonal name of the Trimingham Chalk was to show that the 'zone of *Ostrea lunata*,' proposed by Mr. Jukes-Browne, was associated with a definition which did not wholly apply to the Trimingham Chalk alone, and part of which only applied to less than half of the minimum thickness. So long as an accurate definition was adopted, it was immaterial which of the fossils restricted to Trimingham was adopted as name-fossil. He also pointed out that a proper deduction to be drawn from the fact that the Grey Chalk was clearly unconformable in the North Bluff at a point where the junction was in easy reach, but had appeared to Mr. Reid to be conformable at a point where the junction was higher up and less accessible, was that at the latter point the eroded surface of the White Chalk happened to run parallel to the flint-lines.

In reply to Mr. Hill, he pointed out that erratics were common in the neighbourhood of Cromer, but were in general highly shattered, and were apparently composed of normal *B.-mucronata* Chalk, differing thus *in toto* from the Trimingham Chalk. Also that 'Trimingham Bluffs' had long been an accepted name for the three bluffs described by Lyell, two of which were the 'North Bluff' and 'South Bluff' dealt with in the paper, and no other bluffs had ever been heard of by the Author in the area mapped.

24. *The* CARBONIFEROUS ROCKS *at* LOUGHSHINNY (COUNTY DUBLIN).
By CHARLES ALFRED MATLEY, D.Sc., F.G.S. *With an* ACCOUNT
*of the* FAUNAL SUCCESSION *and* CORRELATION. By ARTHUR
VAUGHAN, B.A., D.Sc., F.G.S. (Read March 18th, 1908.)

[PLATES XLIX & L—FOSSILS.]

### CONTENTS.

|  | Page |
|---|---|
| I. Introduction | 413 |
| II. Description of the Rocks | 415 |
| (A) Brook's End to Loughshinny Bay (*Cyathaxonia*-Beds). | |
| (B) Loughshinny Bay to Limekiln Cove (*Posidonomya*-Limestones and Loughshinny Black Shales). | |
| (C) *Dibunophyllum*-Limestones, north of Limekiln Cove. | |
| (D) Lane Conglomerate, with its Under- and Overlying Lime- stones. | |
| III. Sequence of Deposits in the Loughshinny Area | 433 |
| IV. Conditions of Deposition in the Rush-Loughshinny Area | 434 |
| V. Summary and Conclusion | 436 |
| VI. Faunal Succession and Correlation | 436 |
| VII. Notes on the Species figured in the Plates, and on some other Important Forms | 454 |

## I. INTRODUCTION.  [C. A. M.]

LOUGHSHINNY, a tiny fishing-village on the coast of County
Dublin, about midway between the larger villages of Rush and
Skerries, is well known to Dublin geologists for the fine exposures
of contorted strata exhibited in the neighbouring cliffs. These
exposures form part of an extensive coast-section of Carboniferous
rocks which may be followed, with a few interruptions, for about
5 miles from Rush on the south to Skerries on the north.

A description of the rocks in the southern portion of this coast-
section, from Rush as far north as a small cove called Brook's End,
was given by us in 1905,[1] together with an account of the faunal
succession and correlation of the beds. The present paper continues the description northward from Brook's End, and is intended
to be read in conjunction with our previous paper. The references
given to former literature and maps in that paper apply equally
to the ground now to be described.

Before, however, describing in some detail the rocks around
Loughshinny, it seems desirable to recapitulate very briefly the
sequence of the rocks in the Rush portion of the coast-section. At
Rush the lowest beds are a thick mass of dark slates (Rush Slates),
with intercalated limestone-bands; they pass up into the Rush
Conglomerates, and the latter into a calcareous group (Supra-
Conglomerate Limestones and Carlyan Limestones). The ascending
succession is as a whole from south to north, and the beds mentioned

---

[1] Quart. Journ. Geol. Soc. vol. lxii (1906) pp. 275–322.

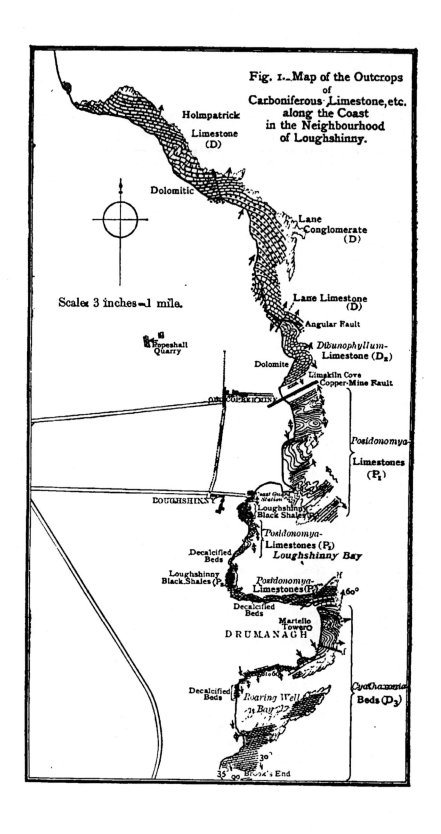

Fig. 1.—Map of the Outcrops
of
Carboniferous Limestone, etc.
along the Coast
in the Neighbourhood
of Loughshinny.

Holmpatrick
Limestone
(D)

Dolomitic

Lane
Conglomerate
(D)

Scale 3 inches=1 mile.

Lane Limestone
(D)

Angular Fault

Popeshall
Quarry

Dibunophyllum-
Limestone (D₂)

Dolomite

Limekiln Cove
Copper-Mine Fault

OLD COPPER MINE

Posidonomya-
Limestones
(P₁)

Coast Guard
Station

LOUGHSHINNY

Loughshinny
Black Shales (P₂)

Posidonomya-
Limestones (P₁)
Loughshinny Bay

Decalcified
Beds

Loughshinny
Black Shales (P₂)

Posidonomya-
Limestones (P₁)

60°

Decalcified
Beds

Martello
Tower

DRUMANAGH

Cyathaxonia
Beds (D₃)

Decalcified
Beds

Roaring Well
Bay

30°

35° 90° Brook's End

appeared, from the palæontological evidence available at the time, to range from the *Zaphrentis-* to the Lower *Seminula-*Zones. Fresh information set out in the present paper has, however, rendered this correlation doubtful, and the possibility that the conglomerates are of *Dibunophyllum-*age is now recognized by Dr. Vaughan. To the north of the Carlyan Limestones occurs an isolated outcrop of limestone (Kate-Rocks Limestones of possibly Upper *Seminula-*age); and, still farther north, a group of richly-fossiliferous cherty and earthy flaggy limestones with shales is assigned to a subdivision (*Cyathaxonia-*subzone) of the *Dibunophyllum-*Zone, and is correlated with the top of the Avonian of the Western Midlands of England. About 200 feet of the *Cyathaxonia-*Beds were recognized in the area then described.

## II. DESCRIPTION OF THE ROCKS.
### [C. A. M.]

### (A) From Brook's End to Loughshinny Bay. (*Cyathaxonia-*Beds). (Fig. 2.)

At Brook's End the *Cyathaxonia-*Beds, striking 10° north of east, are arranged in an asymmetrical syncline, those on the south side of the cove being vertical or nearly so,[1] while on the north the dip is at an angle of 30° to 35° in a southerly direction. The axis of the syncline is poorly exposed, but shows some minor contortions along it near high-water mark.

The *Cyathaxonia-*Beds hereabouts consist of two divisions:—

(*a*) A lower set of thinly-bedded impure limestones, with abundant small lenticular nodules imparting to the beds an 'augen'-appearance; they are interstratified with thicker bands of purer non-nodular limestones (see fig. 10, p. 291, *op. jam cit.*).

(*b*) An upper set of impure limestones, more thickly-bedded than the 'augen'-set, and much less frequently exhibiting the 'augen'-like character of the lower beds.

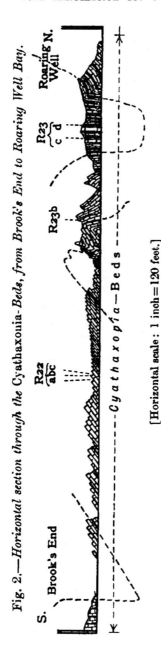

*Fig. 2.—Horizontal section through the Cyathaxonia-Beds, from Brook's End to Roaring Well Bay.*

[Horizontal scale : 1 inch = 120 feet.]

---

[1] Quart. Journ. Geol. Soc. vol. lxii (1906) fig. 10 & p. 293.

Both sets contain numerous seams of chert and partings of black shale.

The beds of the higher set can be followed from Brook's End

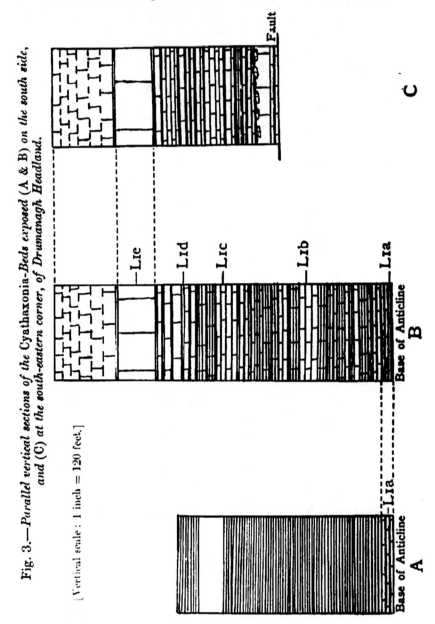

Fig. 3.—*Parallel vertical sections of the Cyathaxonia-Beds exposed (A & B) on the south side, and (C) at the south-eastern corner, of Drumanagh Headland.*

[Vertical scale : 1 inch = 120 feet.]

downward through a thickness of 100 feet or more until, towards Roaring Well Bay, those of the lower set are reached. The dip which hitherto has been steady now changes, and the beds turn

over sharply to the north, are closely folded, and are somewhat contorted. The beds have clearly undergone considerable
compression. The nodules in them are squeezed into lenticles
arranged obliquely to the bedding, the angle of dip is crossed by a
system of close joints which approaches a rough cleavage, and the
chert-seams are occasionally puckered. But for the presence of
the dark seams of chert, the bedding would occasionally be quite
obscured by the jointing. Some of the beds are vertical and con-
ceal a synclinal fold (see fig. 2, p. 415).[1]

Fossils are abundant in many layers of the beds just described, and the assemblage is much the same as that found in
the *Cyathaxonia*-Beds nearer Rush, with which the strata have
already been identified, both on lithological and on stratigraphical
grounds.

In the next bay to the north, Roaring Well Bay, the exposures
are interrupted for a space by the sand of the shore and the Glacial
Drift of the cliffs; but, on the north side of the bay, formed by the
cliffs of the south side of Drumanagh Headland, beds of *Cyathaxonia*-horizon dip southwards at about 50°. They have been
measured as closely as circumstances admit, and it is found, by
tracing the beds downward step by step from the seaweed-covered
rocks fringing the shore to the lowest-exposed bed of an anticline
which forms a conspicuous feature at the north-western corner of
Roaring Well Bay, that about 260 feet of this calcareous group is
exposed (figs. 3 B & 4). The majority of the beds consist of well-
bedded limestones; some are pure, but the greater number are

Fig. 4.—*Section in the cliff at the north-western corner of Roaring
Well Bay, showing the decalcification of the* Cyathaxonia-*Beds.*

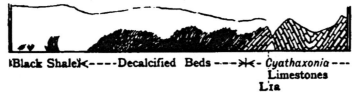

[Horizontal scale: 1 inch = 120 feet.]

nodular, very earthy, argillaceous, or cherty, and they are intercalated with shales. Some of the limestone-beds are thick, and,
especially in the higher zones, approach a massive character, one
such stratum being 30 feet thick.

Taking the lowest bed of the anticline mentioned above as a
datum-horizon and noting the upward succession towards the south

[1] The notation R 22 a, L 1 b, L 8 c, etc., shown in the vertical and horizontal
sections, refers to the horizons from which fossils have been obtained, as
catalogued in the faunal lists. A similar notation was employed in the Rush
paper. It should also be mentioned that the Glacial Drift, etc. has been disregarded in preparing the horizontal sections.

as revealed in the cliff along the western shore of the bay, it will
be found that only 10 feet of calcareous rock is exposed, and that
there the beds pass up into brightly-coloured shales and cherts that

Fig. 5.—*Decalcified* Cyathaxonia-*Beds in the cliff, Roaring Well Bay.*

have a decomposed appearance (fig. 5). The sequence (fig. 3 A,
p. 416, & fig. 4, p. 417) is as follows, in descending order :—

    (iii) Black shale, poorly exposed at the base of cliffs of Drift, and sepa-
          rated from (ii) by Drift.                    About 15 or 20 feet visible.
    (ii) Shales of various colours, usually weathering brown, with numerous
          bright-red shale-bands and layers of chert. The beds have a
          weathered aspect, some of them are contorted, and some cleavage is
          traceable in the lowest zones. They pass down into (i).
                                                  120 feet seen.
    (i) Limestones with red shale-partings, the highest bed being discon-
         tinuous and showing the effects of solution.
                          10 feet to the centre of the anticline.

The stratigraphy clearly shows that the 120 feet of shaly and
cherty material (ii) and possibly also the black shales (iii) are
remanié-beds resulting from the decalcification of cherty and
argillaceous limestones, shales, etc. as seen near by on the opposite
side of the anticline. The phenomenon is of the same character as,
but on rather a larger scale than, that described in the *Cyathaxonia-*
Beds near the Bathing-Place north of Rush.[1] The unexpected

---

[1] Quart. Journ. Geol. Soc. vol. lxii (1906) p. 293. [In addition to the
examples of decalcification there given, reference should also be made to the
numerous instances in North Wales of the perishing and solution of Carboniferous Limestones at the outcrop, described in the 'Geology of Flint, Mold, &
Ruthin' Mem. Geol. Surv. 1890, to which Dr. A. Strahan has been good
enough to draw my attention.—*C. A. M., July 7th, 1908.*]

appearance of these shales is mentioned in the Geological-Survey Memoir,[1] where it is noted that the ends of some of the limestone-beds seem to abut against them; but the opinion there held that the shales are the Upper Shales (that is, the *Posidonomya*-bearing Black Shales of Loughshinny) introduced by faulting seems quite untenable, except possibly as regards the small exposure of black shale referred to as (iii) above. The only faults that occur between the decomposed shales and the limestones are of insignificant throw, and altogether inadequate to account for the apparent disappearance of 250 feet of rock.

It is very possible that the highest 50 feet of weed-covered limestones, from which no fossils have been collected, may belong to the *Posidonomya*-Limestone beds that are seen on the north side of the Drumanagh headland; but the remaining 210 feet exposed on the south side of this headland are proved from the stratigraphy, and from the apparent absence of beds containing *Posidonomya Becheri*, to belong to that part of the *Cyathaxonia*-subzone which comes immediately below the *Posidonomya*-Limestones.

The prominent headland of Drumanagh projects between Roaring Well Bay on the south and Loughshinny Bay on the north, and is formed of an anticlinal mass of the highest beds of the Irish Carboniferous-Limestone formation. The rocks on the south side of the headland have just been described, and, if the coast along the eastern shore be now followed, a massive bed of limestone is first seen at the south-eastern corner; while, about 50 feet lower in the sequence, occurs another semi-massive brecciated and cherty limestone in about two beds, measuring together some 8 feet in thickness (see fig. 6, p. 420, and C of fig. 3, p. 416). This mass has a hummocky upper surface, due to many rounded inclusions of limestone, which range up to 3 feet in length. The centre of the anticline is now reached and is seen to be faulted, the fault-plane being filled with breccia cemented by calcite; but there does not seem to be any serious displacement of the beds.

The beds on the northern slopes of the anticline are well exposed along the shore. They dip at first seawards, that is, in an easterly direction; but the undulating strike soon veers to the west, and the dip becomes a northerly one. The beds have much the same lithological character as those exposed on the southern limb of the anticline. Three massive limestones occur in the sequence here. The lowest is 10 feet thick; the thickness of the second is much greater, but is difficult to determine, as from the lie of the fossils the limestone seems to have undergone some folding; the highest massive bed varies from 25 to 30 feet in thickness, is cracked all over, and is brecciiform towards the base. The top of this highest massive bed may conveniently be taken as the top of the normal *Cyathaxonia*-Beds, since the overlying beds, though yielding the same general fauna, are found to contain in addition at numerous horizons examples of *Posidonomya*, especially

[1] Expl. Sheets 102 & 112, Mem. Geol. Surv. Irel. 2nd ed. (1875) p. 64.

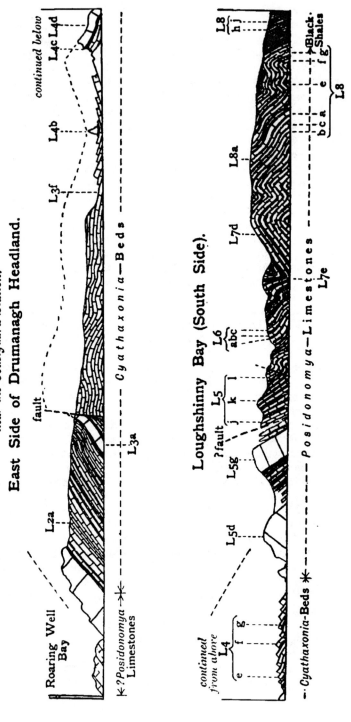

Fig. 8.—Horizontal section, from the south side of Drumanagh Headland to Loughshinny Village, near the Coastguard Station.

East Side of Drumanagh Headland.

Loughshinny Bay (South Side).

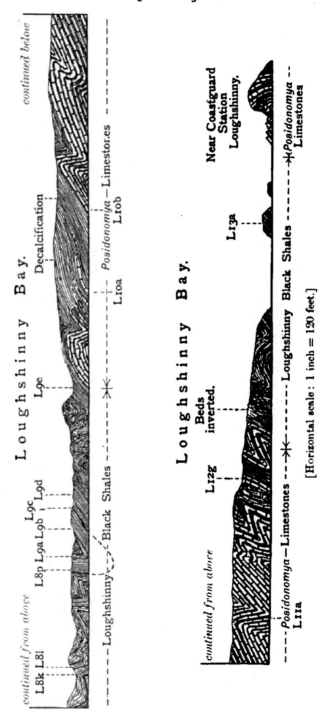

Loughshinny Bay.

*continued below*

Decalcification

L8k L8l   L8p L9aL9b L9c L9d   L9e   *Posidonomya*—Limestores
L10a   L10b

- - - - Loughshinny - - >< Black Shales - - - - - - >< - - - - - - - - - -

Loughshinny Bay.

Near Coastguard
Station
Loughshinny.

*continued from above*

Beds
inverted.

L12g   L13a

*Posidonomya*—Limestones - - - >< - - - Loughshinny Black Shales - - - - >< *Posidonomya*—
L11a                                                                          Limestones

[Horizontal scale : 1 inch = 120 feet.]

Fig. 7.—*Vertical section of the beds exposed between the fault on the east side of Drumanagh Headland and Loughshinny Bay.*

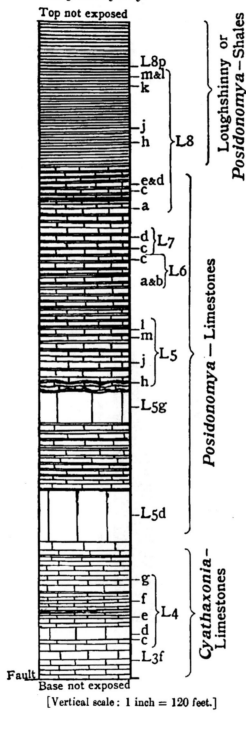

Top not exposed

L8p
m&l
k

j
h
} L8   Loughshinny or *Posidonomya*—Shales

e&d
c
a

d } L7
c }
c } L6
a&b }

l
m
j } L5
h

L5g

L5d

*Posidonomya*—Limestones

g
f
e } L4
d
c
L3f

*Cyathaxonia*—Limestones

Fault
Base not exposed

[Vertical scale : 1 inch = 120 feet.]

of *P. Becheri.* Hence they may be separated from the *Cyathaxonia*-Beds and distinguished by the term *Posidonomya*-Limestones.[1]

As the base of the *Cyathaxonia*-Beds has not been recognized in any of the sections along this coast, the complete thickness of that subzone in this region cannot be stated. We have seen that at least 210 feet of these beds occur on the south side of Drumanagh, at which locality the lowest beds exposed near Brook's End appear to be absent, and the total thickness of the exposures in this area cannot be less than 250 feet.

## (B) Loughshinny Bay to Limekiln Cove. (*Posidonomya*-Limestones and Loughshinny Black Shales.)

The northern side of Drumanagh forms the southern shore of Loughshinny Bay, and along it the beds above the highest massive limestone just mentioned are to be seen, thrown into numerous anticlines and synclines with, however, on the whole, an ascending succession to the

[1] On palæontological grounds, Dr. Vaughan would include in the *Posidonomya*-Limestone group the two uppermost of the massive limestones with their intervening strata, thus adding about 100 feet to their thickness. This view has been adopted in the succession of strata tabulated on p. 434 and in fig. 7.

north, until they pass (fig. 8, below) under the still higher group of Black Shales without limestones which form the cliffs of part of Loughshinny Bay.

The *Posidonomya*-Limestones are lithologically much of the same character as the *Cyathaxonia*-Beds below, but contain a larger proportion of black shales and dark argillaceous limestones. There are no massive limestones in this group; many beds of limestone, however, some grey, some dark, occur up to 4 feet in thickness, as well as numerous seams of chert. *Posidonomya Becheri* abounds in many layers, usually in dark calcareous shale or black shaly limestone, and *Posidoniella lævis* has also been recognized. About

Fig. 8.—*South-western corner of Loughshinny Bay : junction of the* Posidonomya-*Limestones with the Loughshinny Black Shales.*

9 feet below the top bed of these limestones two sandy ripple-marked surfaces occur. The strike of the ripple-marks approaches a north-westerly direction, and indicates that the trend of the old shore-line at this spot in Carboniferous times lay in that direction. The thickness of this limestone-group, ascertained by actual measurement of the individual beds, is 160 feet.[1] Some 30 feet may perhaps have to be added to this amount, as it is possible that a fault cuts off the westerly extension of the highest massive limestone of the *Cyathaxonia*-Beds and effects a displacement to this extent.

---

[1] Excluding the 100 feet referred to in the footnote on the preceding page.

The Loughshinny Black Shales now follow above the *Posidonomya*-Limestones. They consist of black shale with bands of soft black mudstone and many seams of chert, usually thin but occasionally as much as 2 feet thick. Plant-remains are not uncommon in some of the layers, while the thick cherty beds are locally rich in casts of brachiopods and lamellibranchs. Lamellibranchs (*Posidonomya Becheri, P. membranacea, Posidoniella lævis*) and cephalopods (*Thrincoceras, Glyphioceras spirale*) are found in some of the shales. (For faunal lists, see p. 446. The absence of *Pterinopecten papyraceus* should be noted, as this form occurs abundantly with *Posidonomya Becheri* in other parts of the Dublin district.)

The principal exposure of these shales is in the south-western portion of Loughshinny Bay, where they occur as a much contorted syncline between anticlines of the *Posidonomya*-Limestones. If these contorted beds are measured from their base on the south, the highest exposed bed proves to be about 105 to 110 feet above that base. They reappear again farther north in Loughshinny Bay, close to the village.

The *Posidonomya*-Limestones [1] that intervene between these two exposures of shale rise up into a succession of folds that are beautifully exhibited in the cliffs. At first somewhat symmetrically arranged like those on the south side of the bay, they rapidly become more intensely folded as they are followed northwards until they finally are somewhat overfolded (fig. 10, p. 425). One of the anticlines (fig. 9, p. 425) shows a normal fold in its lower beds, and passes into an overfold in the beds exposed higher in the cliff. At the point where the Black Shales reappear the dip is reversed; but the beds soon recover themselves, and have an angle of dip smaller than the normal.

Some further instances of decalcification may be observed on the shores of Loughshinny Bay, both north and south of the main synclinal mass of the Black Shales. On the southern shore a recess in the cliff shows an interesting stage in the solution of the *Posidonomya*-Limestones, as the limestone-bands may there be traced as layers of ochre lying among a mass of black shale and bands of chert. Among the ochre may be found lumps of little-altered limestone. Again, to the north of the main syncline of the Black Shales similar phenomena are exhibited, conspicuous limestone-beds of the *Posidonomya*-Limestone group frequently terminating among the more argillaceous rocks with which they are interbedded, at times disappearing almost completely, at other times being more or less replaced by ochreous matter.

The calcareous shales in these localities are also decalcified into ordinary argillaceous shale, and they then closely resemble the beds of the Black-Shale group. Indeed, there are indications that the Black-Shale group is itself in somewhat a decalcified condition, and that it once contained calcareous shale and cherty limestone. This view is suggested (*a*) by the fact that the fossils in the chert-bands

[1] Some of the strata here exhibit false bedding.

Fig. 9.—*Loughshinny Bay : fold in the* Posidonomya-*Limestones showing the passage from a normal anticline into an overfold.*

Fig. 10.—*Folded* Posidonomya-*Limestones, Loughshinny.*

are mostly represented by casts, and (*b*) by the difficulty in fixing
the true base of the Black Shales, the apparent base in localities
quite close to each other appearing to vary in horizon. Thus, the
highest bed of the main syncline of the Black Shales is, as stated
above, about 105 or 110 feet above the calcareous beds to the
south; whereas, if measured from the calcareous beds of the anticline on the north, the thickness seems to be considerably less,
and the *Posidonomya*-Limestone beds of that anticline appear to
pass laterally into beds indistinguishable from the lower Black-
Shale beds.

Another interesting feature of the *Posidonomya*-Limestones of
Loughshinny Bay is found in the phacoidal calcite-veins exposed
in some abundance on the bedding-planes of the folded limestones.
These phacoids, of all sizes up to some 3 inches in length, are
usually grouped side by side in linear series, in such a way that
the long axes of adjacent phacoids are subparallel and transverse
to the line joining their centres (see fig. 11). Such a linear series

Fig. 11.—'*Augen*'-*like cracks filled with calcite, in the* Posidonomya-
*Limestones, Loughshinny Bay.*

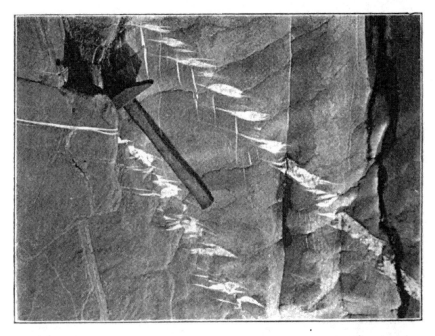

is often continued into a crack in the rock usually filled with calcite,
on the edges of which are frequently exhibited a number of broken
phacoids. The ends of the phacoids often tail out into the surrounding rock as delicate hair-like threads, which are very well
displayed owing to the contrast of colour between the black shaly

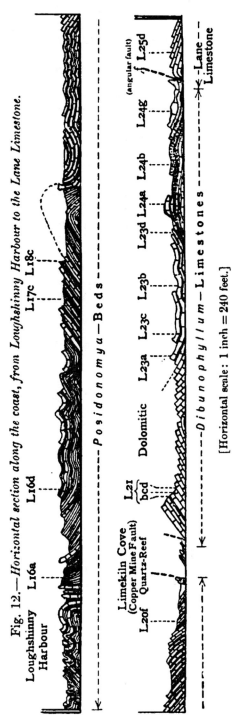

Fig. 12.—*Horizontal section along the coast, from Loughshinny Harbour to the Lane Limestone.*

[Horizontal scale: 1 inch = 240 feet.]

bedding-planes of the limestone-bands and the whiteness of the calcite. Phacoidal or 'augen'-structure in rocks is usually the result of compression. These structures, however, have been produced by tensile and torsional stresses that have opened out these 'augen'-cracks in the rocks, especially on the anticlines, during the folding of the beds, the cavities being subsequently filled up with calcite.

The Loughshinny Black Shales and the underlying *Posidonomya*-Limestones in the cliffs at Loughshinny strike across a sandy shore towards Loughshinny Harbour, where there is a good exposure of folded limestones associated with laminated argillaceous and calcareous shaly beds possessing much the same character as the *Posidonomya*-Limestones at which they strike. Fossils are, however, much less abundant at Loughshinny Harbour, and I did not meet with any of the bands of *Posidonomya Becheri* which are characteristic of the beds opposite. There may, then, be some justification for the fault which is situated at this spot on the Geological-Survey map, but for which I could see no stratigraphical evidence. At the harbour (fig. 12) the beds are folded into numerous steep anticlines and synclines, the dips being sometimes reversed. Higher beds come in to the north, the angles of dip become lower, and the beds roll over in a series of shallow folds for a distance of 500 yards. Marine fossils are abundant in certain limestone-beds in this series, and include a *Cyathaxonia*-fauna. The black calcareous shales associated with them contain plant-remains (*Calamites, Lepidodendron Rhodeanum,* etc.), lamellibranchs (*Posidonomya Becheri* and *Posidoniella lævis*), and *Nomismoceras.* The beds appear to belong to some portion of the *Posidonomya*-Limestones with perhaps some of the beds of the Loughshinny Black Shales.

These beds are cut off from the rocks farther north at a small nameless cove (called in this paper Limekiln Cove, from the substantial limekiln built at the head of it) by one or more faults, along the inland course of which copper-ore was mined many years ago. The Geological-Survey Memoir gives all the information concerning these mines that could be obtained by G. V. Du Noyer in 1849, from which it appears that there were three sub-parallel lodes, 50 feet apart, with a strike 30° north of east and a hade to the south.[1]   Below high-water mark I found that a reef of quartz, in places 10 to 14 feet wide, runs out to sea in the direction mentioned; and, as it contains some traces of copper, it apparently represents one of the lodes mentioned, probably the southernmost and principal lode.

## (C) *Dibunophyllum*-Limestones, north of Limekiln Cove.

The beds on the north side of Limekiln Cove are disposed in a well-marked dome, with dips ranging up to 35°. The lowest 40 feet of the beds exposed consist of light-brown dolomite, above which comes, on the south side of the anticline, 60 feet of limestone, in beds up to 5 feet thick. A quartz-pebble may be found occasionally in some of the upper beds, and nodules and seams of chert also occur. Shale-bands are quite rare, and the beds are quite distinct lithologically from those that are found to the south of the quartz-reef fault. Numerous quartz-veins and cavities lined with quartz-crystals occur in these limestones, in the neighbourhood of Limekiln Cove. The bedding is very regular.

The beds above the dolomite on the north side of the anticline are more shaly than those on the south side, and they also contain several beds of fine conglomerate, pebbly limestone, and pebbly shale; the inclusions consist of quartz-pebbles and fragments of Silurian rocks. The limestones here are also less regularly bedded than those on the south side of the anticline, being ordinarily lenticular in form, and they were certainly laid down in shallower water than those to the south. This fact, together with the abundance of detritus in the beds here, points to the proximity of land in a northerly direction. A massive limestone lies above the conglomeratic beds, and is itself in part conglomeratic. It contains numerous brachiopods similar to those recorded from the Curkeen-

---

[1] Expl. Sheets 102 & 112, Mem. Geol. Surv. Irel. 2nd ed. (1875) p. 70.

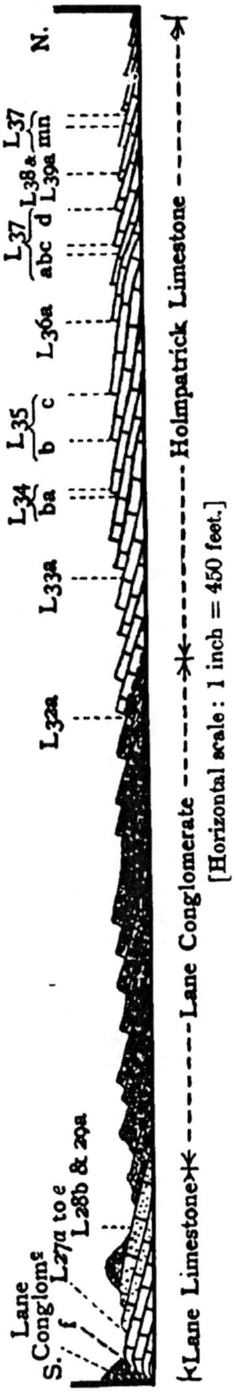

Fig. 13.—Horizontal section, north of the angular fault, along the coast in the townlands of Lane and Holmpatrick.

[Horizontal scale: 1 inch = 450 feet.]

Hill Limestone.[1] From the beds of this group *Dibunophyllum*, *Clisiophyllum*, *Lithostrotion irregulare*, and 'Petalaxis' have been obtained : hence it is clear that the beds lie somewhere in the *Dibuno-phyllum*-Zone. The upward development of this interesting conglomeratic episode is unfortunately interrupted by the fault that brings in the Lane and Holmpatrick beds.

## (D) The Lane Conglomerate, with its Under- and Overlying Limestones.

The remainder of the coast-section is of quite simple geological structure, the beds dipping with gentle undulations at low angles to the north-east and north. They are separated from the *Dibuno-phyllum*-Beds just described by an angular fault, the importance of which will be discussed presently.

The sequence of the beds north of the fault is as follows, in descending order (see fig. 13) :—

(c) Holmpatrick Limestone. Light-grey limestone, dolomitized in parts. Top not seen. About 180 feet exposed.

(b) Lane Conglomerate. Very coarse conglomerate. 200 feet thick.

(a) Lane Limestones. Limestones, frequently pebbly. Base not exposed. About 60 feet seen.

The beds are named from the townlands in which the exposures occur.

The Lane Limestones, for the most part evenly-bedded but sometimes tending to a lenticular arrangement, dip seawards at an angle of about 15° and pass up into the Lane Conglomerate. Some of the limestones contain an abundance of tiny white quartz-pebbles, while others are filled with round lumps of limestone which appear to be of detrital rather than of concretionary origin. Small Zaphrentid and Densiphyllid corals are abundant in these beds, also *Chonetes* cf. *comoides*, *Euomphalus*, etc.

The Lane Conglomerate is a very

[1] Quart. Journ. Geol. Soc. vol. lxii (1906) pp. 299 & 304.

coarse deposit, formed of subangular and rounded pieces of the Silurian rocks of the district. It extends along the shore, dipping at low angles, for about a quarter of a mile. Its thickness is estimated by the Geological Survey at about 200 feet,[1] and, judging from the dip of the beds and the extent of the ground which they cover, this estimate appears to be substantially correct.

This deposit succeeds the pebble-bearing limestones rather abruptly, and in its lowest beds large, boulder-like, rounded masses of Carboniferous Limestone are abundant, the matrix being also of limestone; but, so soon as the lowest beds are passed the remainder of the Conglomerate is found to be a great mass of almost uniform coarseness (fig. 14). The included blocks are of the same character

Fig. 14.—*Lane Conglomerate.*

as those found in the Rush Conglomerates, and range up to the same maximum size. Many are more than 2 feet in diameter, one measured $33 \times 22 \times 15$ inches, another $42 \times 30$ inches. The great majority of the inclusions have clearly had their origin in the Silurian rocks of the neighbourhood; pieces of a red pebbly sandstone occasionally present may, however, have been derived from the Old Red Sandstone.

---

[1] Expl. Sheets 102 & 112, Mem. Geol. Surv. Irel. 2nd ed. (1875) p. 65. The thickness, 80 feet, given in fig. 19 of that Memoir (p. 62), appears to be merely a clerical error; possibly 180 feet was intended.

The deposit differs from the Rush Conglomerates in several important respects :—

| RUSH CONGLOMERATE-GROUP. | LANE CONGLOMERATE. |
|---|---|
| (i) The bands of conglomerate are interstratified with shales and sandy flags. | The conglomerate retains its coarseness practically throughout ; the only interstratification of finer material observed in it was one inconstant bed of pebbly sandstone. |
| (ii) The matrix of the conglomerate-bands is usually a limestone. | Except at the base of the deposit, the conglomerate is wholly made up of detrital material. |
| (iii) Fossils are not uncommon at several horizons. | Fossils are apparently absent. |
| (iv) Conglomeratic conditions graduate both into the Rush Slates below and into the Limestones above. | The conglomerate begins rather abruptly, though there are pebbles in the underlying limestone that herald its incoming, and it ceases quite abruptly. |
| (v) Thickness = 500 feet. | Thickness = 200 feet. |

The beds both below and above the conglomerate also differ considerably in each area, those in the Rush area containing much more muddy detritus than those in the Lane and Holmpatrick Beds. The lithological characters do not, therefore, support strongly any correlation of the beds of the two areas.

The Holmpatrick Limestone succeeds the Lane Conglomerate abruptly ; the lower part of the first bed of the limestone is filled with large Silurian fragments, but above that bed no conglomeratic horizons occur. Except that some small quartz-pebbles may be found in the lowest [1] beds of the limestone, the next 180 feet is a clear-water deposit remarkably free from land-borne detritus, there being no shale-partings between the limestone-beds. The beds have a low dip, usually to the north, and form a rocky shore in the townland of Holmpatrick. They are, as a rule, good light-grey limestones ; but many of the beds, especially the lower, are more or less strongly dolomitized here and there. They are characterized by *Diphyphyllum subibicinum* and *Campophyllum Murchisoni*, which are abundantly present at numerous levels ; and at occasional horizons they are rich in brachiopods, particularly *Schizophoria resupinata*. About 180 feet of limestone is exposed before the beds disappear beneath the sands of Skerries Bay, where the coast-section of Carboniferous rocks terminates. The next exposures to the north, about a mile and a quarter away, are of Silurian slates and grits ; while north-east of the Holmpatrick Limestone, and only 750 yards from it, are the Silurian rocks of Shenick's Island, made up of grey and green grits, slates, and andesites, etc.: these Silurian rocks are of precisely the same kind

[1] One of the limestone-beds just above the conglomerate is obscurely oolitic. It is the only oolitic bed observed in the whole of the coast-section from Rush to Skerries.

as those forming the great bulk of the inclusions in the Lane and Rush Conglomerates.[1]

It will be convenient now to discuss the stratigraphical relationship of the Lane Limestones to the *Dibunophyllum*-Limestones, against which they are thrown by the angular fault already mentioned (p. 429). The fault-line has a sharp bend of 110° in its course; it runs from high-water mark seawards, at first in a north-easterly direction, but before reaching low-water mark it bends round sharply in an easterly direction across the seaweed-covered rocks. A second fault splitting off this eastern branch in a south-easterly direction brings in a mass of Lane Conglomerate, which thus lies between Lane Limestone on the north and *Dibunophyllum*-Limestones on the south. A continuation of the north-easterly branch in its original direction produces a fault of small throw, effecting a slight displacement in the Lane Limestone. Still another fault strikes off the main fault; it skirts the low cliff of Drift just above high-water mark, and, running in a north-north-westerly direction, throws down the Lane Conglomerate on the west against the underlying Lane Limestone.

From the curvature of the beds along the eastern branch of the main fault, it seems probable that the downthrow of the beds is to the south. North of the fault there is a continuous sequence of about 440 feet of beds, none of which correspond with the *Dibunophyllum*-Limestones immediately south of this fault, except perhaps the dolomitic limestones forming the core of the anticline. If, as supposed, the downthrow is to the south, then the fault has a throw of at least 500 feet. Apart from the stratigraphical evidence, the importance of the fault-line is shown by the marked difference in the fauna of the beds on the opposite side of the fault. The beds on the south contain *Dibunophyllum Muirheadi* in some abundance, and an assemblage of brachiopods corresponding precisely with those obtained from the Curkeen-Hill Limestone (see p. 437); while on the north side of the fault these forms are replaced by *Zaphrentis*, *Densiphyllum*, and *Chonetes* cf. *comoides*, none of which are found on the south side.

The question of the horizon of these beds is discussed in the Geological-Survey Memoir,[2] and although all the beds north of the Copper-Mine Fault are designated 'Lower Limestone' on the 1-inch map (Sheet 112) in accordance with the views of G. V. Du Noyer, J. Beete Jukes expressed the opinion that

' it is more reasonable to suppose that there is no true Lower Limestone anywhere north of Rush, but that all the beds belong to the upper part of the series, or the part not very far below the Coal-Measures, whatever may be their lithological characters.'

---

[1] At the southern end of Shenick's Island is a coarse conglomerate lying unconformably upon the grits and andesites, etc. It differs in appearance from the Lane Conglomerate, only in the fact that its matrix is reddish in colour. In the Geological-Survey Memoir and the Survey 1-inch map this deposit is regarded as the supposed base of the Old Red Sandstone; but it differs markedly in aspect from the Old Red Conglomerates exposed close to the railway near Donabate. In my opinion it is more probably a local beach-rock of Carboniferous age, and on, or not far from, the horizon of the Lane Conglomerate.          [2] Expl. Sheets 102 & 112, 2nd ed. (1875) pp. 65–66.

He also argues that the Rush and Lane Conglomerates are contemporaneous, on the ground that the fact of a

'conglomerate of Silurian pebbles occurring in the Carboniferous Limestone would seem to be stronger lithological evidence in favour of the beds wherever those conglomerates occur, being on the same geological horizon, than any mere differences in the colour or texture of the limestone associated with them could be against it.'

In the absence of direct stratigraphical evidence, the settlement of these two points—that is to say, the age of these beds and the contemporaneity of the two conglomerates—must be left to palæontological methods. As regards the former, Dr. Vaughan considers, from an examination of the fauna of the Lane and Holmpatrick Limestones, that both limestones lie in the *Dibunophyllum*-Zone, but below the *Cyathaxonia*-Beds. Stratigraphical reasons already given seem also to place them in a part of the zone below that occupied by the *Dibunophyllum*-Limestones of the coast immediately north of the Copper-Mine Fault. As regards the second point, Dr. Vaughan, having reviewed the evidence on which he previously fixed the horizon of the Rush Conglomerate, is now satisfied (see p. 442) that that Conglomerate may possibly belong to the *Dibunophyllum* - Zone. The palæontological evidence supports therefore, to some extent, Jukes's view of the correlation of the two conglomerates. It is not, however, necessary to regard these two deposits as being precisely of the same horizon. The Rush Conglomerate-Group, with its intercalations of fine-grained material and its much greater thickness, would probably require a longer period for its deposition than the Lane Conglomerate; and, moreover, the physical conditions under which the Carboniferous deposits of the Dublin district were laid down were such as to make the local occurrence of conglomeratic conditions at various horizons not unlikely.

### III. SEQUENCE OF DEPOSITS IN THE LOUGHSHINNY AREA.
### [C. A. M.]

An attempt may now be made to piece together the sequence of the rocks occurring in the Loughshinny area.

The highest beds are certainly the Loughshinny Black Shales. They are underlain by the *Posidonomya*-Limestones, and these by the *Cyathaxonia*-Beds of Upper *Dibunophyllum*-age. The *Dibuno-phyllum*-Limestones (of the age, apparently, of the Curkeen-Hill Limestone) must be placed below the *Cyathaxonia*-Beds; and at seemingly a still lower level in the *Dibunophyllum*-Zone must be placed the Holmpatrick Limestone, with its underlying Lane Conglomerate and Lane Limestone. The beds may, therefore, be tabulated as follows, the palæontological zones being determined by Dr. Vaughan:—

| Stratigraphical Zones. | Thickness exposed, in feet. | Palæontological Zones. | Correlated Beds in the Rush Area. |
|---|---|---|---|
| Loughshinny Black Shales (top not exposed). | 110 | Upper *Posidonomya*-Zone (P$_2$). | Not represented. |
| *Posidonomya* - Limestone Group. | 260 | Lower *Posidonomya*-Zone (P$_1$). | Not represented. |
| *Cyathaxonia*-Beds (base not seen). | 200 | *Cyathaxonia*-Subzone (locally divisible into | *Cyathaxonia*-Beds of the Bathing-Place (north of Rush) and Giant's Hill. |
| (Gap) | (Gap) | (Rush paper) D$_{3b}$ D$_{3a}$ (Loughshinny paper) but overlapping). | |
| *Dibunophyllum* - Lime - stones. | 100 | Upper *Dibunophyllum*-Zone (D$_2$). | Curkeen-Hill Lime- stone. |
| (Gap) | (Gap) | | |
| Holmpatrick Limestone ... | 180 | ? D (of unknown position). | ? Carlyan Limestone. |
| Lane Conglomerate ......... | 200 | | ? Rush Conglomerate- Group. |
| Lane Limestones ............ | 60 | | ? Rush Slates (top part only). |
| Total thickness of deposits exposed in the Lough- shinny coast-section ... | 1110 | | |

## IV. Conditions of Deposition in the Rush-Loughshinny Area. [C. A. M.]

From the description given in this and in our former paper of the lithological character of the Carboniferous deposits laid down in the Rush and Loughshinny areas, it will be clear that this region was close to an old shore-line of the Carboniferous Lime-stone sea. The actual position of that coast-line would of course vary from time to time with the rise or fall of the land, but it appears to have been situated almost parallel to and a short distance seaward of the present coast-line between Rush and Skerries, and then to have veered from Skerries westwards. Some overlapping of deposits against the old sea-margin would take place during periods of subsidence, while at times of elevation recently-formed limestone would be exposed to the action of the waves and be broken into those rounded masses that are found embedded in the strata at various horizons in the series. All the deposits are of marine origin, and for the most part they were formed in shallow water; there was, in all probability, considerable lateral variation in the character of the deposits.

The oldest beds—the Rush Slates—were laid down probably at or near the mouth of a river that drained a region of dark Ordovician or Silurian slates. The contributions of mud, at first almost continuous, became more intermittent in Rush-Conglomerate and Carlyan-Limestone times, although even then they were made in considerable quantity. This mud seems to have been carried only a short distance to the north, if the correlation of these deposits with the Lane and Holmpatrick beds is correct, as very little argillaceous material is found in these latter beds.

The Lane and Rush Conglomerates must both have been formed quite close to the shore : although the overlap on to the shore itself is not exposed, except perhaps at Shenick's Island. While at Lane strong currents prevailed continuously, as shown by the thick continuous mass of very coarse conglomerate, there were at Rush many and considerable fluctuations in the force of the marine currents, indicated by the numerous intercalations of finer pebbly and sandy layers and fine laminated shales among the coarser conglomerate-beds.

The *Dibunophyllum*-Limestones north of the Copper-Mine Fault represent apparently a continuance of the clear-water conditions of the Holmpatrick Limestone. The dolomitic character of the lowest beds may be original, and indicate a shallow-water phase. The upper beds are, for the most part, well-stratified clear-water limestones on the south ; but, as already stated on p. 428, they pass laterally, northwards, into irregular lenticular limestones with intercalated bands of black shale and fine conglomerate. These facts suggest strongly that the land lay in close proximity to the north or north-east. The Popeshall Limestone, about one-third of a mile to the west, and the Curkeen-Hill Limestone, about a mile to the west, both of which, as shown by their fossils, are approximately of the same horizon as the *Dibunophyllum*-Limestones of the coast, are clear-water limestones without any shaly partings.[1] Whether they represent a deeper-water phase of the beds on the coast, or belong to a slightly higher or slightly lower horizon than the latter, cannot at present be stated. They may bridge over the gap between the Holmpatrick and the *Dibunophyllum*-Limestones.

The *Cyathaxonia*-Beds, *Posidonomya*-Limestones, and the Lough-shinny Black Shales form a continuous sequence in which the gradual cessation of normal Carboniferous-Limestone conditions by the slow shallowing of the water and the increasing invasion of muddy sediment is clearly indicated. Ripple-marks and, occasionally, false bedding in the beds just below the shales, as well as the numerous remains of land-plants found in these upper beds, together with the almost complete disappearance of calcareous deposits in the highest exposed part of the series, show that a new phase in the history of Carboniferous physical conditions had at length set in.

[1] The section at Curkeen Hill shows about 120 feet of good continuous limestone. [A short search in the disused limestone-quarry at Popeshall resulted in the discovery of the following species :—*Productus aculeatus*, Mart. (?), *Schizophoria resupinata*, Mart. (common), *Spirifer striatus*, mut., *Martinia glabra*, Mart. (Dav.) (common), *Athyris* cf. *glabristria* (Curkeen-Hill form) (abundant), *Athyris* cf. *expansa*, Phill. (Dav.), *Pugnax acuminata*, Mart., and *Rhynchonella* (?) *reflexa*, de Kon.—*C. A. M., July 7th, 1908*.]

## V. SUMMARY AND CONCLUSION.  [C. A. M.]

The following is a summary of the most important points dealt with in the foregoing pages.

(1) About 1100 feet of Carboniferous rocks are exposed in the neighbourhood of Loughshinny. They consist mainly of limestones, but they include a thick mass of coarse conglomerate (Lane Conglomerate) and many intercalated beds of shale and chert. The highest beds are the Loughshinny Black Shales, with seams of chert. The rocks have been much folded, and to some extent are faulted.

(2) The lowest beds belong to some part of the *Dibunophyllum*-Zone, while the higher range through *Cyathaxonia*-Beds into *Posidonomya*-Limestones and *Posidonomya*-Shales of Pendleside age.

(3) The Lane Conglomerate may be on or near the horizon of the Rush Conglomerate, as it is now admitted that the latter may be of *Dibunophyllum*-age.

(4) Local decalcification has caused the more or less complete disappearance of some of the *Cyathaxonia*- and *Posidonomya*-Limestones.

In conclusion, I wish to express my best thanks to Dr. Vaughan for his willing help in again undertaking the examination and description of the fossils, the results of which are set out in the following pages; also to Dr. Wheelton Hind for examining the lamellibranchs, gasteropods, etc., to Mr. R. G. Carruthers for help in regard to some of the corals, and to Dr. R. Kidston, F.R.S., for examining the plant-remains.

## VI. FAUNAL SUCCESSION AND CORRELATION.  [A. V.]

[* denotes a form figured in the text or in the Plates which accompany this paper.]

### (1) Fauna of the *Dibunophyllum*-Limestones; (L 23, L 24, and L 21).

In ascending order :—

```
{ (x) includes L 23 a, b, d and L 24 a.
{ (y)    „      L 23 c, L 24 b, and L 21 d.
{ (z)    „      L 24 g and L 21 c, b.
```

### (i) Corals:

(x)...... *Syringopora* cf. *ramulosa*, Goldf., Ed. & H.
(y)......\*Densiphylloid *Zaphrentis*, sp. nov.
(x & y)...... *Cyathophyllum Murchisoni*, Ed. & H.   Common.
(x & y)...... *Lithostrotion* aff.[1] *cyathophylloides*, Vaughan.
(x)...... *Petalaxis Portlocki*, Ed. & H.
(x & y)......\**Carcinophyllum curkeenense*, sp. nov.
(x & y)......\**Clisiophyllum* cf. *curkeenense*, Vaughan.
(y & z)......\**Dibunophyllum* aff. *Muirheadi*, Thoms. & Nich.
(x)......\**Dibunophyllum* aff. *Muirheadi*, var.[2] or sp. nov.

---

[1] Convergent on *Koninckophyllum* θ, Vaughan.
[2] Convergent on *Clisiophyllum curkeenense*, Vaughan.

(ii) Brachiopods:

(x, z)...... *Productus* aff. *antiquatus*, Sow.
(x, z)...... *Productus concinno-longispinus.*
(z)...... *Productus sulcatus*, Sow.
(x, y)...... *Productus* aff. *giganteus* (Mart.).[1]
(z)......  ...... and var. near *Pr. edelburgensis*, Phill.
(x)...... *Productus aculeatus* (Mart.).
(z)......  ...... and var. near *Pr. Youngianus*, Dav.
(z)...... *Productus plicatilis*, Sow.
(z)...... *Leptæna* cf. *distorta* (Sow.).
(x, z)...... *Schizophoria resupinata* (Mart.).
(x, y, z)...... *Spirifer* aff. *bisulcatus*, Sow.
(y, z)...... *Spirifer* aff. *striatus* (Mart.)[2] and varieties.   Abundant.
(z)...... *Reticularia lineata* (Mart.).
(x, y, z)...... *Reticularia lineata* (Dav.).[3]   Common.
(z)...... *Martinia glabra* (Mart.) & (Dav.), and circular variety.
(z)...... *Dielasma* near *ficus*, M'Coy.

### Equivalence to the Curkeen Limestone.

The abundance of striate Spirifers in identical varieties, the close resemblance of the brachiopod-faunas, and the occurrence in both limestones of *Clisiophyllum curkeenense* and a Koninckophylloid *Lithostrotion*, suggest the equivalence of the *Dibunophyllum* and Curkeen Limestones.   The Curkeen fauna is, however, abnormal in the rarity of *Dibunophylla*, and in the great abundance of brachiopods; and in these characters it approximates to a 'Knoll'-phase. The facts are satisfactorily accounted for by regarding the Curkeen Limestone as a contemporaneous phasal development of the *Dibunophyllum*-Limestones.

### Correlation with the Lower Part of $D_2$ in the South-Western Province.

The remarks made on p. 304 of the Rush paper, Quart. Journ. Geol. Soc. vol. lxii (1906), apply generally to the fauna of the *Dibunophyllum*-Limestones.

The absence of highly-developed Clisiophyllids and the general similarity of the coral-assemblage to that of $D_1$ in the South-Western Province strike the eye in the field.   The brachiopods, however, suggest a higher horizon:—Compare the occurrence of *Productus longispinus*, the abundance of *Reticularia lineata* (Dav.), and the presence of *Martinia glabra*.   On the other hand, the form of *Productus giganteus* lacks the latissimoid habit and old-age marks so characteristic of $D_2$ specimens, while *Pr. longispinus* is rare and *Pr. margaritaceus* has not been found.   [It is very important to recognize that we are, as yet, unacquainted with any strong development of

---

[1] Resembling the form common in $D_1$ of the South-Western Province—not Martin's form.
[2] Not Martin's form—see note on genus in Quart. Journ. Geol. Soc. vol. lxii (1906) p. 310.
[3] *Non* (Mart.)—form small and globose; dental plates usually concealed.

brachiopod-beds in $D_1$, and that consequently our knowledge of the $D_1$ brachiopod-fauna is very incomplete.]

The fauna of the *Dibunophyllum*-Limestones may, therefore, be assigned to early $D_2$.

### (2) The Lane Limestone, Lane Conglomerate, and Holmpatrick Limestone.

#### (*a*) Fauna of the Lane Limestone (L 25 to L 29).

In ascending order :—

$\begin{cases} (x) \text{ includes L 25 } d \text{ and L 27 } a, b, c. \\ (y) \quad\quad,, \quad\quad \text{L 27 } d, e, \text{ L 28 } b, \text{ and L 29 } a. \end{cases}$

#### (i) Corals:

$(x, y)$...... *Zaphrentis Omaliusi*, var. *densa*, Carruthers. $\Big\}$ Very abundant.
$(x)$......\**Zaphrentis Omaliusi*, var. *ambigua*, Carruthers.
$(y)$...... Densiphylloid *Zaphrentis*, sp. nov.
$(y)$...... Campophyllid. Rare, and at the top only.

#### (ii) Brachiopods:

$(y)$...... *Productus humerosus*, Sow. A single, poor specimen, found loose.
$(y)$...... *Chonetes* cf. *comoides* (J. Sow.). Abundant, and of large size.
$(x, y)$...... *Schizophoria resupinata* (Mart.).

The abundance of *Zaphrentis Omaliusi* in the variants *densa* and *ambigua* is a character common to the Lane Limestone, the Rush Slates, and the *Zaphrentis*-Beds of the Colne area.

The incoming of a Campophyllid at the top of the Lane Limestone and the persistence of a small *Zaphrentis* into the basal beds of the Holmpatrick Limestone indicate that the two Limestones, although separated by the thick Lane Conglomerate, are faunally continuous, and that the estimation of level may be deduced from their joint fauna.

#### (*b*) The Lane Conglomerate is unfossiliferous.

#### (*c*) Fauna of the Holmpatrick Limestone.

In ascending order :—

(w) includes L 32 *a* and L 33 *a*.
(x)    ,,    L 34 *b*, *a*, and L 35 *b*.
(y)    ,,    L 35 *c* and L 36 *a*.
(z)    ,,    L 37 *a*, *b*, *c*, *d*, L 38 *b*, L 39 *a*, and L 37 *m*, *n*.

#### (i) Corals:

$(w, z)$...... *Syringopora* cf. *ramulosa* (Goldf.), Ed. & H. and vars. Common.
$(x)$...... *Michelinia* cf. *tenuisepta* (Phill.). Common.
$(z)$...... *Michelinia megastoma* (Phill.). Rare.
$(y)$...... *Zaphrentis* cf. *Enniskilleni*, Ed. & H. (Densiphylloid variant.)
$(x, z)$...... *Campophyllum Murchisoni*, Ed. & H., and variants.
$(z)$......\**Diphyphyllum subibicinum* (M'Coy). Abundant.
$(y)$......\*Clisiophyllid (a new genus).

(ii) Brachiopods:

    (x)...... *Productus concinno-longispinus.*
    (z)...... *Productus corrugato-hemisphericus.*
    (z)...... Giganteid *Productus.*
  (w, x)...... *Productus* cf. *rugatus,* Phill.
    (x).. ... *Productus aculeatus* (Mart.).
(w, x, y, z)...... Papilionaceous *Chonetes.*
  (x, y)...... *Schizophoria resupinata* (Mart.).   Abundant.
    (x)...... *Spirifer* cf. *planicosta* (M'Coy) } and allied forms.
  (x, y)...... *Spirifer* aff. *bisulcatus,* Sow. }
    (x)...... *Martinia glabra* (Mart.) & (Dav.).

### Suggested Correlation of the Lane and Holmpatrick Limestones with some part of D in the South-Western Province.

It is extremely unfortunate that this series cannot be horizoned stratigraphically, seeing that the fauna is in many respects a peculiar one.

If the above identification of the brachiopods from imperfect and scanty material is correct, the following facts suggest that the level of these beds cannot be lower than D of the South-Western Province:—

> Planicostate Spirifers are common only at the top of the Limestone-Massif in the Western Midland Area, North Wales, etc.
>
> *Productus humerosus* is common in a D fauna, both at Caldon Low (Western Midlands) and near Breedon (Leicester).
>
> *Productus longispinus* and *Martinia glabra* are characteristic $D_2$ species.

Although the coral-species are numerous in individuals, the number of species is small and the genera are those least adapted to the attainment of precision in horizon.

*Diphyphyllum subibicinum* has no representatives in the South-Western Province below $D_1$, at which level the typical *Campophyllum Murchisoni* is also met with for the first time. In the Ingleborough area, however, it occurs in the basal conglomerate $(S_1)$ and it is not uncommon in C–S of Arnside.

> *Michelinia* cf. *tenuisepta* differs from the typical form of the species in its wider tubes, and is known from D of several localities. The new genus of Clisiophyllid is represented in Dr. Matley's collection by a single unsatisfactory specimen, which agrees with one that I have obtained at the top of the Midland Massif near Wetton, and with another from R 18 c (*Cyathaxonia*-Beds) of the Rush sequence. The rarity of specimens and their close similarity to early forms from γ detract from their value as evidence of horizon.
>
> The new species of Densiphylloid *Zaphrentis* recorded from the *Dibunophyllum*-Limestone [1] appears to be identical with a specimen from the Lane Limestone.

The *Zaphrentes* of the Lane Limestone are identical with those of the Rush Slates, and agree better with the (?) D forms of the Colne area than with the Tournaisian *Zaphrentes* of the South-Western Province. *Z. Omaliusi,* var. *ambigua,* the striking variant which is common to the Rush Slates, the Lane Limestone, and

---

[1] And occurring in the Lower Limestone of Scotland (*fide* R. G. Carruthers).

Horrocksford Quarry (Colne), is as yet not certainly known below $D_1$, at which level a single specimen was found by Mr. E. E. L. Dixon in the Gower peninsula; it occurs rarely in P (see under L 18 c) associated with *Posidonomya*.

The evidence seems to warrant the suggested horizon, but does not throw any light on the relative positions in D of the Lane and *Dibunophyllum*-Limestones.

## (3) The Rush Slates, Rush Conglomerate, and Carlyan Limestone.

[Emendations of, and additions to, the faunal lists published in the Rush paper.[1]]

(a) **Rush Slates** (*loc. cit.*).

> For *Zaphrentis* cf. *Phillipsi*, substitute
> *Zaphrentis Omaliusi*, var. *densa*, Carruthers[2] and
> *Zaphrentis Omaliusi*, var. *ambigua*, Carruthers.

(b) **Rush Conglomerate** (*megastoma*-beds) (*op. cit.* p. 296).

R 10 j and R 11 a......    For Carcinophylloid Clisiophyllid, substitute
                          *Clisiophyllum* cf. *oblongum*, Thoms.

R 12 b  .................    For *Michelinia*, mut. towards *Beaumontia*, read
                          *Michelinia tenuisepta* (Phill.).

(c) **Carlyan Limestone** (*op. cit.* p. 297).

R 14 a ......    Add to list:—
> *Syringopora* cf. *reticulata*, Goldf.
> *Lithostrotion cyathophylloides.*    Common.
> *\*Lithostrotion*-like Clisiophyllid.
> *Productus* cf. *concinnus*, Sow.

The fresh material from the Carlyan Limestone suggests that it is, as stratigraphically indicated, a continuation of the *megastoma*-series.

Re-examination of the correlation suggested in the Rush paper (p. 300), namely:—

Rush Slates—$Z_2$; *megastoma*-beds and Carlyan Limestone—C to $S_1$.

This correlation depended upon the similar succession of similar coral-faunas, as set out in the following table:—

---

[1] 'The Carboniferous Rocks at Rush (County Dublin)' Quart. Journ. Geol. Soc. vol. lxii (1906) p. 295.
[2] 'A Revision of some Carboniferous Corals' Geol. Mag. dec. 5, vol. v (1908) p. 28.

|  | $Z_2$. | $C-S_1$. |
|---|---|---|
| IN THE SOUTH-WESTERN PROVINCE. | Abundance of *Z. Omaliusi*.[1] <hr> Absence of (1), (2), (3), (4). | Entrance and abundance of ⎰ (1) *Michelinia* cf. *megastoma*. <br> (2) Cyathophyllids. <br> (3) *Lithostrotion*. <br> Entrance (and rarity) of (4) Clisiophyllids of *Lithostrotion*-type. |
| AT RUSH. | Abundance of *Z. Omaliusi*, var. *densa* and *Z. Omaliusi*, var. *ambigua*. <hr> Absence of (*a*), (*b*), (*c*) (notwithstanding the great thickness of the series). | (*a*) *Michelinia megastoma* (common). <br> (*b*) *Lithostrotion cyathophylloides* (abundant). <br> (*c*) Clisiophyllids of *Lithostrotion*-type (rare). |
|  | Rush Slates (*Zaphrentis*-Beds). | Rush Conglomerate (*Michelinia* cf. *megastoma*-Beds). |

The following newly-discovered facts throw considerable doubt upon the foregoing correlation :—

(*a*) *Zaphrentes*, identical with those of the Rush Slates, occur in equal abundance near Colne and in the Lane Limestone, and in both cases the horizon is probably D. The similar forms which abound in $Z_2$ exhibit obvious differences.[1]

Nevertheless, *Z. Omaliusi*, var. *densa* is the prevalent *Zaphrentis* in C, and *Z. Omaliusi*, var. *ambigua* occurs in $D_1$ (no *Zaphrentes* being yet known from the S beds of the South-Western Province).

(*b*) A specimen of *Michelinia tenuisepta*, found loose near the top of the Rush Conglomerate (near R 12 *b*), is identical with the form common in the *Cyathaxonia*-Beds here assigned to $D_{3b}$, and is not known from the $C-S_1$ level.

(*c*) *Clisiophyllum* cf. *oblongum* bears a much closer resemblance to the highly-developed Clisiophyllids of D than to the *Lithostrotion*-like Clisiophyllids of $S_1$.

(*d*) *Michelinia megastoma* (Phill.) is probably a D species; the megastomatids of $C-S_1$, both in the South-Western Province and at Arnside, belong rather to *M. grandis*, M‘Coy.

(*e*) The new *Productus*—*Productus* cf. *fimbriatus*, Rush paper, pl. xxx, fig. 6—from the top of the *megastoma*-beds, occurs commonly in P (L 5).

On the other hand :—

(*a*) The dominant coral of the *megastoma*-beds and of the Carlyan Limestone—*Lithostrotion cyathophylloides*—is markedly more Cyathophylloid than *Lithostrotion* cf. *affine* of the DP phase,

---

[1] See Quart. Journ. Geol. Soc. vol. lxii (1906) p. 314.

and approaches nearest to a form rare in CS$_1$ of the South-Western Province and of Ravenstonedale.[1]

(*b*) The *Lithostrotion*-like Clisiophyllids of the *megastoma*-beds and of the Carlyan Limestone agree more closely with S$_1$ forms from the South-Western Province, the Ingleborough area,[1] and Arnside than with any D form yet known.

In fact, the Carlyan fauna suggests S$_1$ and not D; the material, however, is scanty and poor.

Reviewing the whole evidence:—The broad resemblance to a Z$_2$–C–S$_1$ sequence is not confirmed by identity of detail. On the other hand, the evidence for a D horizon is far from conclusive, and the failure to find an unquestionably Viséan form in the whole thickness of the *Zaphrentis*-Slates is without parallel in fossiliferous D beds. The final solution of the question of level must await fresh evidence.

## Faunal Comparison of the Rush and Lane Conglomerates.

Resemblances:—

An identical *Zaphrentis*-facies precedes each.
*Michelinia* succeeds *Zaphrentis* as a common fossil.

Differences:—

The Rush Conglomerate is fossiliferous; the Lane Conglomerate barren.

*Michelinia megastoma* is common in the Rush, but rare above the Lane, Conglomerate. In the case of *Michelinia* cf. *tenuisepta* the reverse is true.

*Campophyllum* aff. *Murchisoni* and *Diphyphyllum sub-ibicinum* abound above the Lane, and are absent from the Rush, Conglomerate.

*Lithostrotion cyathophylloides* abounds in the Rush, no *Lithostrotion* is met with above or below the Lane, Conglomerate.

*Chonetes* cf. *comoides* abounds at the top of the Lane Limestone, but is absent from the Rush Slates: papilionaceous *Chonetes* are, however, common in the Carlyan Limestone.

We can, therefore, deduce no closer approximation of age than is expressed within the range and abundance of the Rush-Lane *Zaphrentes*, and this broad interval would allow of considerable difference of horizon.

The abundance of small *Zaphrentes* usually accompanies such shallow-water deposits as are liable, by no great physiographical change, to pass into conglomerates or dolomites, and *Michelinia* often survives the actual change.

(In no small measure, the broad similarity of the Z$_2$–C fauna of the South-Western Province to that of the Rush Slates and Con-

[1] From material collected by Mr. Cosmo Johns.

glomerate is due to the fact that the sequence of physiographical conditions was identical in the two areas. For example, just as *Michelinia* occurs in the conglomerate of Rush, so the same genus is one of the very few corals that occur in the Mid-Avonian dolomite of the Bristol area.)

### (4) The *Cyathaxonia*- and *Posidonomya*-Beds—$D_3$ and P.

(R 17, R 21, and R 18 of the Rush paper ; and R 22, R 23, L 3 $f$,
and L 4 to L 9 of the present paper.)

Locally, this series may be usefully subdivided into the following ascending sequence :—

$D_3$. Subzone of *Cyathaxonia rushiana*.
- $D_{3a}$. *Zaphrentis* aff. *Enniskilleni.* (Clisiophyllids common.)
- $D_{3b}$. *Michelinia tenuisepta.* (Clisiophyllids rare.)

D P. A phase characterized by a Cyathophylloid *Lithostrotion.*

P. Zone of *Posidonomya Becheri* and *Martinia ovaliglabra*, sp. nov.
- L$^r$ & Mid.P.
  - Michelinoid *Favosites.*
  - *Productus striatus.*
  - *Nomismoceras rotiforme.*
- Up$^r$ P.
  - *Glyphioceras spirale.*

### (4 a) Fauna of $D_{3a}$ (R 17, R 21, and R 18 of the Rush paper).

(See faunal résumé, *op. cit.* p. 301.)

The fauna closely resembles that of the *Dibunophyllum* and Curkeen Beds ($D_2$).

The following fossils do not pass up (locally) into higher beds.

Corals :
Clisiophyllids of several types.
Caninoid and simple Koninckophylloid *Campophylla.*
*Lithostrotion* of the *L.-Martini* type.

Brachiopods :
The typical forms of *Productus corrugatus* and *Pr. hemisphericus.*
*Spirifer striatus* and varieties.
The typical forms of *Athyris glabristria.*
*Leptæna analoga* and varieties.

*Zaphrentis* aff. *Enniskilleni* is rare, but links this division with the $D_{2-3}$ beds of the Gower peninsula.
*Cyathaxonia rushiana* links $D_{3a}$ with $D_{3b}$, and passes on, in a narrow mutation, into P.
*Densiphyllum rushianum* and *Syringothyris subconica* also pass up.

## (4 b)  Fauna of $D_{3b}$ (R 22 and R 23).

In ascending order :—

> (x) includes   R 23 b.
>
> (y) includes $\begin{cases} \text{R 22 } c \text{ and R 23 } c. \\ \text{R 22 } b \text{ and R 23 } d. \\ \text{R 22 } a. \end{cases}$

### (i) Corals :

(x)...... *Cladochonus.*
(y)...... *Syringopora* cf. *ramulosa* (Goldf.), Ed. & H.
(x, y) .....\**Michelinia tenuisepta* (Phill.) (typical form).
(x)...... Densiphylloid *Zaphrentis* (including *Z. Omaliusi*, var. *densa*, Carruthers).
(x, y)......\**Zaphrentis Omaliusi*, var. *ambigua*, mut. σ nov.
(x)...... *Densiphyllum rushianum*, sp. nov.
(x, y)...... *Pseudamplexus* spp.
(x, y)......\**Cyathaxonia rushiana*, Vaughan.  Common.
(x)...... *Cyathophyllum Murchisoni*, Ed. & H.
(x, y)...... Diphyphylloid *Lithostrotion.*

### (ii) Brachiopods :

(x, y)...... *Productus* cf. *concinnus*, Sow.
(y)...... *Productus margaritaceus* (Phill.)?
(x)...... *Syringothyris subconica* (Mart.).

$D_{3b}$ is distinguished from $D_{3a}$ by the paucity of brachiopods, by the absence (or rarity) of Clisiophyllids, and by the occurrence of a narrow-tubed *Michelinia* [1]; the two series are linked by *Cyathaxonia rushiana* which persists, in a mutation, into P.

The rapid extinction of the Clisiophyllids marks the top of the Avonian in all areas; the paucity of brachiopods and the prevalence of *Michelinia* are phenomena dependent on bathymetric conditions.

The closer general resemblance of the $D_{3a}$ fauna to that of $D_2$ suggests that $D_{3b}$ is, on the whole, higher than $D_{3a}$; the two divisions ($D_{3a}$, $D_{3b}$) are, however, so closely linked that overlapping is probable.

The absence of a typical high-$D_2$ fauna suggests that at least the lower part of $D_3$ is a phasal equivalent of $D_2$—as is also probably the case in Gower.

## (4 c)  Fauna of the DP Phase (L 3 ƒ and L 4).

### (i) Corals :

> *Syringopora* cf. *ramulosa* (Goldf.), Ed. & H.
> Densiphyllids including
>    *Zaphrentis Omaliusi*, var. *densa*, Carruthers.  ($=$ Lane form.)
>    Densiphylloid *Zaphrentis*, sp. nov.  ($=$ form from L 21 d and Lane.)

---

[1] The *Michelinia* of $D_{3b}$ is intermediate between the wider-tubed form of $D_2$ and the Michelinoid *Favosites* of P.

*Amplexi-Zaphrentis.*[1]
*Cyathaxonia* (rare).
*Lithostrotion* cf. *affine* (Fleming), Ed. & H.   Abundant.

### (ii) Brachiopods:

Latissimoid *Producti.*   Common at one or two levels.
*Productus spinulosus,* Sow.
*Productus,* sp. nov.   (Rush paper, pl. **xxx**, fig. 6.)

The abundance of a Cyathophylloid *Lithostrotion* and the
occurrence of Densiphylloid *Zaphrentes* of the Rush type and of the
same *Productus,* sp. nov., give to this series the faunal aspect of the
*megastoma*-beds, and demonstrate that, at a high level in D, it is
possible to meet with a fauna dominated by a Cyathophylloid *Lithostrotion* and yielding no convincing evidence of its high horizon.

In the present instance, however, the phase was of short
endurance both in time and in space: for, south of Drumanagh Head
(L$_1$ and L$_2$), beds of the same approximate age contain the same
*Lithostrotion* (abundantly) associated with fossils characteristic of
the horizon.   The horizon of this phase is definitely fixed stratigraphically by the continuity of the sequence upwards into the
P beds.

### (4 *d*)  Fauna of the P Zone (L 5 *d* to L 9).

In ascending order [2] :—

Lower  P = (x) includes L 5 *d, g, h, j, k, m.*
Middle P = (y)     „     L 5 *l,* L 6 *a, b, c,* L 7 *c, d,* L 8 *a, b, d, k, l, m, n.*
Upper  P = (z)     „     L 8 *p* and L 9 *a, b, c, d, e.*

### (i) Corals:

(x)......\**Michelinia tenuisepta,* var. *favositoides* nov.
(x)......\**Zaphrentis Enniskilleni,* Ed. & H.
(x, y)...... Densiphyllids including forms near :
           { Densiphylloid *Zaphrentis,* sp. nov.
(y)...... { A species common at Bradbourne.
           { A species common at Dunbar.
(y)...... *Cyathophyllum Murchisoni,* Ed. & H.
(x, y)...... *Lithostrotion* aff. *irregulare.* (Phill.), Ed. & H.
(y)......\**Koninckophyllum* cf. *interruptum,* Thoms. & Nich.
(x)......\**Lonsdaloid Carcinophyllum.*

---

[1] This descriptive generic term has the same connotation as *Caninia,*
Michelin (in its original sense), as has been recently demonstrated by
Mr. R. G. Carruthers, Geol. Mag. dec. 5, vol. v (1908) p. 158.   It is here
retained, in order to maintain unison with the Rush paper.
[2] In the map (fig. 1, p. 414) and in the synoptical table (p. 434) Lower and
Middle P are included together in P[1], and Upper P is equivalent to P[2].

### (ii) Brachiopods:

(x, y)... *Productus antiquatus*, Sow.
(x, y)... *Productus concinnus*, Sow., and varieties including
(z)... ... form convergent on *Marginifera*.
(x, y)... *Productus sulcatus*, Sow.
(x, y, z)... *Productus longispinus*, Sow., and varieties.
(y, z)... *Productus* aff. *scabriculus* (Mart.).
(x)... *Productus punctato-fimbriatus*.
(x)... *Productus* cf. *rugatus*, Phill.
(x)... *Productus spinulosus*, Sow.
(x, y)... *Productus*, sp. nov. (Rush paper, *loc. supra cit.*)
(y)... *Productus corrugato-hemisphericus* (fine-ribbed).
(x, y)... *Productus margaritaceus*, Phill.
(x, y)... *Productus aculeatus* (Mart.) and *Pr. Youngianus*, Dav.
(x, y)...*Productus striatus* (Fischer), Dav.
(x)...*Productus proboscideus*, de Verneuil, de Kon.
(x, y)... *Productus giganteus* (Mart.).
(y)... *Productus* aff. *latissimus*, J. Sow.
(x)... *Productus* cf. *mesolobus*, Phill.

(x, y, z)... Orthotetids including
(z)... { *Derbya* cf. *senilis* (Phill.). *Derbya grandis*, Waagen.
(x, y, z)... *Schizophoria resupinata* (Mart.), including gigantic
*...and spinous vars.
(x, y, z)... *Spirifer* aff. *bisulcatus*, Sow., including
(x)...*...form convergent on *Sp. integricosta*, Phill.
(y)...*Spirifer* cf. *convolutus*, Phill.
(y)... *Spirifer* cf. *attenuatus*, Sow.
(x)... *Martinia glabra* (Mart.) and
*...a mutation common in (z).
(x, y)... *Martinia ovalis* (Phill.).
(x, z)...*Martinia ovaliglabra*, n. sp.
(x, y, z)...*Reticularia lineata* (Mart.) & (Dav.): (globular and transverse forms).
(x, z)...*Spiriferina insculpta*, Phill. (large form).
(x)...*Athyris* cf. *planosulcata* (Phill.), Dav. (cf. Dav. pl. li, fig. 12).
(z)...*Actinoconchus* sp.
(z)... *Camarophoria* cf. *crumena* (Mart.), Dav.
(x)... *Pugnax pleurodon* (Phill.) & (Dav.).
(x)... *Dielasma* sp. (lentiform species).

### (iii) Lamellibranchs:

(y)...... *Posidonomya Becheri* (Sow.). Abundant. First record at L 5 *l*; last at L 8 *l*.
(y, z)...... *Posidonomya membranacea* (M'Coy). Abundant in z. First record at L 8 *h*.
(x, y, z)...... *Posidoniella lævis* (Brown). From L 5 *h* to end.
(z)...... *Aviculopecten dissimilis* (Phill.). Abundant in L 8 *p* and L 9 *c*.

### (iv) Cephalopods:

(y)...... *Glyphioceras* cf. *crenistria* (Phill.).
(z)...... *Glyphioceras spirale* (Phill.). Common at L 9 *c*.

## Distribution of the most important P-Fossils within the Limits of the Zone.

*Michelinia favositoides* and Lonsdaloid *Carcinophyllum* occur only in the lower and middle parts (see repetition in L 18 *c*, L 20 *f*).
*Productus striatus* attains its maximum in the lower and middle

parts. *Productus proboscideus* occurs only at one level, at the base (L 5 *d*).

*Posidonomya* abounds in the middle and upper parts (*P. Becheri* being the first species to enter).

*Glyphioceras spirale* occurs only in the upper part.

These facts have probably local value; the brachiopod-fauna is, however, so essentially similar throughout, that the subdivisions are very indistinctly differentiated.

On the other hand, the P-fauna is markedly distinct from that of the Curkeen and *Dibunophyllum*-Limestones (Lower $D_2$):—

(1) Many of the best-known and most abundant Viséan gentes have dropped out, at least in their typical forms.

> Examples:
>
> *Productus corrugatus, Productus hemisphericus, Athyris glabristria, Leptæna analoga, Syringothyris laminosa.*

(2) Other gentes show degeneration or excessive specialization.

> Examples:
>
> Michelinoid *Favosites*, Lonsdaloid *Carcinophyllum, Koninckophyllum* cf. *interruptum, Athyris* cf. *planosulcata, Martinia glabra,* mut., *Derbya grandis, Spiriferina insculpta,* mut.

(3) Others again indicate instability by the rapid production of several strongly-marked and differentiated variants.

> Examples:
>
> *Schizophoria resupinata* in its gigantic and spinous varieties.
> *Martinia glabra* in its great variety of form and in its convergence with *Martinia ovalis.*
> *Spirifer* aff. *bisulcatus* in convergence with several cognate species and in highly ornamented varieties.

(4) Certain genera which reach their acme in post-Avonian time become abundant for the first time.

> *Camarophoria, Derbya.*

### Occurrence of the most important P-Forms in other Areas.

(In most cases a single outside locality is cited; the instances could, however, be multiplied many-fold.)

(i) Corals:

*Michelinia tenuisepta,* var. *favositoides,* the ultimate stage of *M. tenuisepta,* is common in $D_1$ at Bradbourne (Derbyshire).

Densiphyllids:—One type is common at Bradbourne, another at Dunbar.

Dendroid Lithostrotions are rare and consist, almost entirely, of narrow forms, as is universally the case near the top of the Avonian.

Lonsdaloid *Carcinophyllum* has been found by Dr. Wheelton Hind at Poolvash (Isle of Man) in the 'Knoll' Limestones.

(ii) Brachiopods:

*Productus striatus*, a protean species marking an old-age stage in the gens of *Pr. corrugatus*, is common in the Cracoe 'Knolls.'

*Productus proboscideus*, an old-age variant of the gens of *Pr. undatus*, has been found by Dr. Wheelton Hind at Park Hill and Castleton, in the highest beds of the Midland Massif.

*Chonetes Buchiana* is identical with the high-D form of Dunbar and Fife, and a nearly-allied form occurs at the top of the Midland Massif.

*Derbya grandis* is abundant in the Millstone Grit of Pateley Bridge.

*Schizophoria resupinata* :—The giant form occurs at Astbury (Staffs.); the spinous variant is abundant at Congleton Edge (Staffs.) in beds of P-age.

*Spirifer* aff. *bisulcatus*:—This gens splits up into several highly-specialized variants, which can be matched from all British areas at the same horizon.

*Martinia glabra* :—The small form is extremely abundant at Castleton.

*Martinia ovaliglabra* occurs, in a larger form, in $D_3$ of North Wales, and beautiful specimens have been sent to me for identification by Dr. Wheelton Hind and Mr. J. T. Stobbs.

*Athyris* cf. *planosulcata* :—The form figured in this paper is known from several localities at the top of the Midland Massif.

*Camarophoria* cf. *crumena* is common at the same level at Pateley Bridge.

(iii) Lamellibranchs:

Dr. Hind has recorded the presence of *Posidonomya Becheri* at the top of the Midland Massif at Castleton : it occurs also at the base of the Yoredales in Wensleydale (*fide* Dr. Hind and Mr. Cosmo Johns). Its occurrence in the Pendleside Group is co-extensive with the development of that group.

## Comparison of the Lower Part of P with the Highest Level (the 'Knoll' Level) in the Limestone-Massif of the North-Western Midlands.

A faunal comparison of the highest beds of the Limestone-Massif at Park Hill and Castleton with P of the Loughshinny sequence reveals so many points of resemblance—extending to the community of peculiar, and therefore presumably short-lived, variants, such as *Productus proboscideus*—as to suggest probable identity of horizon.

If this be so, the *Cyathaxonia*-Beds ($D_{3a}$, $D_{3b}$) of the Irish sequence are represented by massive limestone in the 'Knoll' areas of the North-Western Midlands.

The fact[1] that the *Posidonomya*-maximum succeeds the Limestone Massif at these points almost immediately (as it does the basal P-beds of Loughshinny), without the intervention of a thick series of cherty, thinly-bedded limestones, is in agreement with this suggestion.   We should further expect that whenever, in the North-Western Midlands, *Cyathaxonia*-Beds are well developed (as, for example, in the Worslow sequence) the underlying limestone should contain a lower $D_2$ fauna : this remains to be demonstrated.

### Comparison with the Lower Limestones of Fife.

Material collected by Dr. Matley reveals the practical identity of the brachiopod-fauna both in species and in variants, and this resemblance extends in large measure to the Densiphyllids and Zaphrentids.   On the other hand, Clisiophyllids are rare at Loughshinny and extremely abundant in Scotland, where they exhibit that remarkable wealth of variation which heralds rapid extinction. (The Scottish development can be closely paralleled by the Aberdo and Hendre Limestones of North Wales.)[2]

### (5)  Repetitions of Sequence.

#### (5 a)  Fauna of the Beds South of Drumanagh Head (L 1, L 2, and L 3).

**(i) Corals:**

*Cladochonus.*
*Syringopora* cf. *ramulosa* (Goldf.). Ed. & H.
*Syringopora* cf. *geniculata*, Phill. (very narrow form).
*Michelinia tenuisepta*, var. *favositoides* nov.
*Densiphyllum* cf. *charlestonense*, Thomson.
*Amplexi-Zaphrentis* (cf. *Zaphrentis Enniskilleni*, Ed. & H.).

*Cyathaxonia rushiana*, Vaughan.
*Cyathophyllum Murchisoni*, Ed. & H. (abundant).
*Lithostrotion* cf. *affine* (Flem.), Ed. & H. (abundant).
*Lithostrotion irregulare* (Phill.), Ed. & H.
*Lithostrotion junceum* (Flem.), Ed. & H.

**(ii) Brachiopods:**

Giganteid *Productus.*
*Spirifer* aff. *bisulcatus*, Sow.

*Spirifer attenuatus*, Sow.

The level of these beds is clearly D P, and probably below the first occurrence of *Posidonomya*.

*Lithostrotion* cf. *affine* indicates L 4, the Michelinoid *Favosites* links with the basal beds of P, and *Cyathaxonia rushiana* suggests the persistence of that species into early P time.

[1] In 'The Palæontological Succession of the Carboniferous Rocks in the South of the Isle of Man' (Proc. Yorks. Geol. Soc. vol. xvi, pt. ii, 1907, p. 137) Dr. Wheelton Hind suggests the probable equivalence of the 'Knoll' level at Poolvash with $D_2$, and draws attention to the attenuation of the cherty thinly-stratified *Cyathaxonia*-Beds in the 'Knoll' areas of the North-Western Midlands.

[2] See W. Hind & J. T. Stobbs, Geol. Mag. dec. 5, vol. iii (1906) pp. 397, 398.

(5 *b*) Fauna of the *Posidonomya*-Beds North of Loughshinny Harbour (L 16 to L 30).

(i) Corals:

*Cladochonus.*
*Michelinia tenuisepta*, var. *favositoides*
 nov.
*Zaphrentis Omaliusi*, var. *ambigua*,
 Carruthers.
Zaphrentid which occurs in the Mill-
 stone Grit of Scotland (*fide* R. G.
 Carruthers) (cf. *Z. Omaliusi*, var.
 *densa*, Carr., and cf. Densiphylloid
 *Zaphrentis*, sp. nov., of the *Dibuno-
 phyllum*-Limestone).

*Zaphrentis* aff. *Enniskilleni*, Ed. & H.
*Amplexi-Zaphrentis.*
*Pseudamplexus.*
*Cyathaxonia rushiana*, Vaughan.
Lonsdaloid *Carcinophyllum.*

(ii) Brachiopods:

*Productus antiquatus*, Sow.
Members of the series *Productus
 concinno-longispinus* (including *Pr.
 lobatus*, Sow.).
*Productus scabriculus* (Mart.), Dav.
*Productus punctatus* (Mart.), Dav.

*Schizophoria    resupinata*    (Mart.)
 (spinous var.).
*Spirifer bisulcatus*, Sow. (variety exhibiting bilateral asymmetry).
*Martinia (?).*

(iii) Lamellibranchs:

*Posidonomya Becheri* (Sow.).

(?) *Posidoniella lævis* (Brown).

(iv) Cephalopod:

(L 17 *c*) *Nomismoceras rotiforme* (Phill.).

(v) Plants:

*Lepidodendron Rhodeanum*, Sternberg, and longitudinally-striate plant-
stems.

*Posidonomya* is not uncommon, and links the beds with P; the
Michelinoid *Favosites* and Lonsdaloid *Carcinophyllum* suggest a
low level in that zone, as does *Nomismoceras rotiforme*. The persistence of *Cyathaxonia rushiana* into P is clearly demonstrated:
the form is, however, distinct.

(5 *c*) Repetition of the *Posidonomya*-Beds at Loughshinny Harbour (L 10 to L 13).

In ascending order ................... $\begin{cases} \text{x includes L 10 } b, \text{ L 10 } a \\ \qquad\qquad\quad \text{L 11 } a \\ \text{y includes L 12 } g \\ \qquad\qquad\quad \text{L 13 } a \end{cases}$

(i) Corals:

(**x, y**)................
and (L 5 *d*, 5 *m*, 6 *c*)
(**y**) ...................

$\begin{cases} \textit{Lithostrotion} \text{ aff. } \textit{irregulare} \text{ (Phill.), Ed. & H.} \\ \textit{Diphyphyllum} \text{ cf. } \textit{gracile}, \text{M'Coy.} \end{cases}$
*Lithostrotion Portlocki* (Bronn), Ed. & H.
 (old-age variant).

(y) ..................... 'Calophyllum,' sp. (old-age characters).
    Compare Thoms. & Nich., Ann. & Mag. Nat. Hist.
    ser. 4, vol. xvii (1876) pl. vi, figs. 6 & 6 a.

(y) .....................
and (DP, L 6 c) } Cyathophyllum Murchisoni, Ed. & H.

y) ..................... Koninckophyllum sp. (old-age variant).
    Compare K. interruptum, Thoms. & Nich.

(x) ..................... Clisiophyllum cf. oblongum, Thoms.

## (ii) Brachiopods:

(x, y) .................. Productus antiquatus, Sow., Pr. concinnus, Sow., Pr. longi-
    spinus, Sow., and a transverse, sulcate variant of
    Pr. semireticulatus (Mart.) (common in L 10 b).

(x, y) ..................
and (L 4, L 6) Latissimoid Producti, including typical Pr. latissimus,
    J. Sow. (common in L 12 g).

(x) ......................
and (L 5 m, L 7) Aculeate Producti, including Pr. spinulosus, Sow., Pr.
    Youngianus, Dav., and Productus, sp. nov.

(x, y) .............. Productus elegans, M'Coy, and a strongly spinous variety
    of Pr. punctatus (Mart.).

(y) ................... Productus scabriculus (Mart.), Dav.

(x) ................. Chonetes Buchiana, de Kon. (typical form).

(x) .................... Orthotetid (exaggerated ribbing).

(y) .................... Spirifer aff. bisulcatus, Sow.

(x) .................... Spirifer cf. planicosta, M'Coy.

(y) and (L 6 c) ..... Spirifer convolutus, Phill.

(x, y) ................. Martinia glabra (Mart.), Dav. and M. near ovalis (Phill.).

(x) .................... Reticularia lineata (Dav.).

(y) and
    (L 5 k, L 5 m) ... } Athyris cf. planosulcata (Phill.), Dav.

(y) and
    (L 8 p, L 9 c) ... } Camarophoria crumena (Mart.), Dav. (equivalent to Dav.,
    pl. xxv, fig. 4a).

## (iii) Lamellibranchs:

(L 10 b, 13 a) and
    (L 5 h onwards)... } Posidoniella lœvis (Brown).

(L 11 a) and
    (L 5 l to L 8 l) ... } Posidonomya Becheri (Sow.) (abundant).

(L 13 a) and
    (L 8 h onwards)... } Posidonomya membranacea (M'Coy).

## (iv) Cephalopods:

(L 13 a) and (L 9 e)...Glyphioceras spirale (Phill.).

The position of these beds is definitely fixed by stratigraphy and
with equal precision by palæontology, as shown in the above list
by the indices of the levels in the main sequence at which the
same fossils occur.

## (6) The Association of an Avonian Fauna with *Posidonomya Becheri.*

From the foregoing lists of fossils from the *Posidonomya*-Beds
(namely, the main sequence L 5 to L 9, and the repetitions L 16 to
L 20 and L 10 to L 13), it is clear that, at Loughshinny, characteristic Avonian fossils (as, for example, *Cyathophyllum Murchisoni,*

*Lithostrotion irregulare, Productus giganteus, Pr. latissimus*) occur in common association with *Posidonomya Becheri* throughout its maximum.

Elsewhere this fact has seldom been observed, owing to the more complete establishment of *Posidonomya*-conditions.

## [The Inter-Relation of the Uppermost Avonian and the Lower Pendleside.

It has been my anxious desire in this paper to recognize to the full the large amount of excellent work which Dr. Wheelton Hind has done since the publication of the paper by himself and Mr. J. A. Howe on the ' Pendleside Group' (Quart. Journ. Geol. Soc. vol. lvii, 1901, p. 347), in further elucidation of that important contribution. With this object in view, I have attempted to commence the P zone at Loughshinny with the lowest level included by him in the Pendleside Series.

In the report of the Committee on ' Life-Zones in the British Carboniferous Rocks' (Rep. Brit. Assoc. York meeting, 1906, p. 311), Dr. Hind sets out the following subdivisions of the Pendleside Series :—

|  |  |  | Equivalent horizons at Loughshinny. |
|---|---|---|---|
| | Zone of *Gastrioceras Listeri* | Lower Coal-Measures. Millstone Grit. | |
| | Zone of *Glyphioceras bilingue*. | | |
| | Zone of *Glyphioceras spirale* Zone of *Glyphioceras reticulatum* | } *Glyphioceras diadema*. | [= Up$^r$ P.] |
| *Cyathaxonia*-Beds. | Zone of *Posidonomya Becheri* ...*Nomismoceras rotiforme*. | | [= Mid. P.] |
| | Zone of *Prolecanites compressus*. D$_2$. | | [= L$^r$ P.] |

The lower portion of this table expresses the essential facts of the sequence at Loughshinny.

The lowest zonal index—*Prolecanites compressus*—has not been found, but the fauna of Lower P agrees with that which Dr. Hind states to be associated with that index in the Western Midland area (*op. cit.*). Middle P is a strong maximum of *Posidonomya Becheri*, and *Nomismoceras rotiforme* has been recognized by Dr. Hind in our material from that division. *Glyphioceras spirale* immediately succeeds, and characterizes Upper P.

Hence, in the P zone at Loughshinny, we have a typical Pendleside sequence and the inception of the Upper Carboniferous molluscan fauna of the British Isles. This is reason enough for changing our standard zonal indices at this point, from those marking moderate depth to those indicating shallow water.

At Loughshinny, however, a *Cyathaxonia*-fauna is intercalated in the *Posidonomya*-maximum and persists up to the zone of *Glyphioceras spirale*. This fauna is in perfect continuity with that of the *Cyathaxonia*-Beds below (D$_{3a}$, D$_{3b}$) and contains a large number of typical Avonian forms. We must, therefore, recognize that the Lower Pendleside and the Uppermost Avonian are the expressions of contemporaneous faunas.—*May 30th, 1908.*]

The important task of determining the lamellibranchs recorded in § VI and the Appendix has been undertaken by Dr. Wheelton Hind; to him also we owe the identification of the gasteropods and cephalopods.

The notes on plants are by Dr. Robert Kidston, F.R.S.

Mr. R. G. Carruthers, of H.M. Geological Survey, has rendered very valuable assistance in the determination of the Zaphrentids in accordance with his recent research, and has identified a large number of the specimens in this group.

Dr. Ivor Thomas, of H.M. Geological Survey, has kindly assisted in references to the literature.

I have great pleasure in recording my personal indebtedness to the British Association for two grants which have enabled me to defray the expenses of coral-slicing and photography. Mr. J. W. Tutcher has spared no trouble in the large amount of photography which accurate study of coral-slices demands, and I embrace this opportunity of acknowledging his invaluable help.

### APPENDIX TO § VI.

The following lists contain fossils not included in § VI, either because, at present, they are of no value for zonal correlation, or because the identification is uncertain. The indication of level is that employed in § VI.

*Dibunophyllum*-Limestone:

(y)...*Zaphrentis Omaliusi*, var. *densa*, Carruthers (?).
(z)...*Productus scabriculus* (Mart.), Dav. (?).
(x, z)...*Productus striatus* (Fischer), Dav. (?).
(z)...Orthotetid.

(z)...*Athyris* cf. *glabristria* (Phill.).
(z)...*Pugnax acuminata* (Mart.)?
(z)...*Pugnax pleurodon* (Phill.), (Dav.).
(z)...(*Rhynchonella*) *reflexa*, de Kon. (?).

Lane Limestone:

(y)...*Syringopora* cf. *reticulata* (Goldf.), Nich.
(y)...*Leptæna analoga* (Phill.).
(x, y)...Orthotetid.
(x)...*Rhipidomella* sp.

(y) { *Entalis ornata*.
      *Euomphalus deliquus*.
      *Bellerophon tenuifascia*. }

Holmpatrick Limestone:

(w)...Zaphrentid and Caninid.
(y)...*Lithostrotion*-like Clisiophyllid.
(x)...*Productus corrugato-striatus*.
(x)...*Leptæna analoga* (Phill.), var. (cf. *L. distorta* (J. Sow.)).

(w, x)...Orthotetid.
(x)..*Rhipidomella* sp.
(x)...*Athyris* cf. *glabristria* (Phill.).
(w)...*Conocardium rostratum*.
(w)...*Conocardium decussatum*.

Rush Conglomerate (Quart. Journ. Geol. Soc. vol. lxii, 1906, p. 296):

(R 10 m)...For *Clisiophyllum* aff. *curkeenense*, Vaughan, read *Lithostrotion*-like Clisiophyllid.

Curkeen Limestone (*op. cit.* p. 299):

For *Cyathaxonia contorta* Vaughan, read (?) *Carcinophyllum* (p. 464).

*Cyathaxonia*-Beds :

### D$_{3b}$

(y)...*Amplexi-Zaphrentis.*
(y)...(?) ' *Cyathaxonia* ' *costata*,
    M'Coy.
(y)...*Lithostrotion* sp.

(y)...Orthid.
(y)...Glabrous Spiriferid.
(x)...Athyrid.
(x)...Phillipsid.

### DP

(L 4 e)...*Productus corrugato-striatus.* |     *Schizophoria (?).*

### *Posidonomya*-Zone (P) :

(y)...*Syringopora* cf. *ramulosa*
    (Goldf.), Ed. & H.
(x)...*Michelinia tenuisepta* (Phill.)?
(y)...Cyathophylloid variant of
    *Lithostrotion Martini*, Ed.
    & H.
(x)...*Fistulipora minor*, M'Coy.
(x)...*Productus longispinus*, Sow.
    var.(cf.*Pr.sinuatus*,deKon.).
(x)...*Productus punctatus* (Mart.),
    Dav.—small form.
(x, y)...*Chonetes* sp.—small papilion-
    aceous form.

(x)...*Spirifer* cf. *striatus* (Mart.),
    Dav.(?).
(x)...*Spiriferina* cf. *biplicata*,
    Dav.
(y)...(?) *Cyrtina* cf. *carbonaria*,
    (M'Coy).
(x)...*Aviculopecten plicatus.*
(x)...*Aviculopecten clathratus.*
(x)...cf. *Capulus angustus.*
(z)...*Metoptoma pileus* (Phill.).
(y)...(?) *Stroboceras sulcatum.*
(y)...*Thrincoceras.*

(L8 *l*)...Longitudinally - striate plant-stems and other plant-remains (the
    surface of certain beds is covered with narrow curved filamentous
    markings—? plants).

### Repetition of P (L 10 to L 13) :

(y)...*Michelinia* sp. (thick-walled).
(y)...Densiphylloid *Zaphrentis*—a
    large form; cf. *Z. Enniskil-
    leni*, Ed. & H.
(y)...*Amplexi-Zaphrentis.*

(y)...*Fistulipora* cf. *incrustans*,
    Nich. & Foord.
(x, y)...*Schizophoria resupinata*
    (Mart.), Dav.
(y)...*Rhipidomella (?).*
(x)...Phillipsid.

### VII. NOTES ON THE SPECIES FIGURED IN THE PLATES, AND ON SOME OTHER IMPORTANT FORMS. [A. V.]

In accordance with the main purpose for which I undertook the study of Dr. Matley's material, the species figured and described in this section have been selected entirely on account of their value (1) in zoning the Rush-Skerries sequence itself, and (2) in correlating the various rock-groups of this sequence with those of other areas. Facts of purely palæontological interest have been reserved for future exposition.

Frequent reference is made in this section to the following works :—

JOHN PHILLIPS: ' Illustrations of the Geology of Yorkshire ' pt. ii.   London, 1836.

FREDERICK M'COY: ' British Palæozoic Fossils ' 1851–55.

ALPHONSE MILNE-EDWARDS & JULES HAIME: ' Monogr. Brit. Foss. Corals pt. iii (1852) Palæont. Soc.

THOMAS DAVIDSON: 'Monogr. Brit. Foss. Brachiop.' vol. ii (1858–63) Palæont. Soc. (Referred to under the abbreviation—'Davidson.')

JAMES THOMSON & H. ALLEYNE NICHOLSON: 'Generic Types of Palæozoic Corals' Ann. & Mag. Nat. Hist. ser. 4, vol. xvi (1875) pp. 305, 424; vol. xvii (1876) pp. 60, 123, 290, 451; & vol. xviii (1876) p. 68.

JAMES THOMSON: 'Corals of the Carboniferous System of Scotland' Proc. Phil. Soc. Glasgow, vol. xiv (1882–83) p. 296.

C. A. MATLEY & A. VAUGHAN: 'Carboniferous Rocks at Rush' Quart. Journ. Geol. Soc. vol. lxii (1906) p. 275 (referred to under the abbreviation 'Rush paper').

R. G. CARRUTHERS: 'Revision of some Carboniferous Corals' Geol. Mag. dec. 5, vol. v (1908) pp. 20, 63, & 158.

## I. CORALS.

### Michelinia.

MICHELINIA MEGASTOMA (Phillips).

*Calamopora (?) megastoma*, Phillips, 'Geol. Yorkshire' pt. ii, p. 201 & pl. ii, fig. 29.
*Michelinia megastoma*, Edwards & Haime 'Monogr. Brit. Foss. Cor.' pt. iii, p. 156 & pl. xliv, fig. 3 a.

Calices large (exceeding 1 centimetre in diameter) and not very numerous. Epitheca without 'rootlets,' and revealing the form of the enclosed corallites. Corallum flattened and expanded. Walls thickened, and lined with closely-packed vesicles.

The holotype is preserved in the Gilbertson Collection, British Museum (Natural History), and, judging by the locality ('Bolland'), came from Viséan beds.

Differences.—*Michelinia grandis*, M'Coy, ' Brit. Palæoz. Foss.' p. 81, pl. iii c, fig. 1, differs in its tall corallum and in the fact that the walls are not specially thickened.

(It now appears probable that the commonest Megastomatid from C–S₁ of the South-Western Province agrees with *M. grandis*, M'Coy, rather than with Phillips's species.)

Occurrence.—*Michelinia megastoma* is common in the Rush Conglomerate and rare in the Holmpatrick Limestone. The *Michelinia* from the Derbyhaven Limestone of the Isle of Man appears to be identical.

MICHELINIA TENUISEPTA (Phillips). (Fig. 15, p. 456.)

*Calamopora (?) tenuisepta*, Phillips, *op. cit.* p. 201 & pl. ii, fig. 30.
Non *Michelinia tenuisepta*, Edwards & Haime, *op. cit.* p. 155 & pl. xliv, fig. 1.
Non *Michelinia tenuisepta*, de Koninck, ' Nouvelles Recherches sur les Anim. Foss. du Terrain Carb. de la Belgique' (1872) p. 133 & pl. xiii, figs. 2–2 a.

Holotype lost (originally in the Gilbertson Collection).

The following characters can be deduced from Phillips's description and figure :—Corallum conically expanded; corallites long and narrow. Calices numerous and unequal (the average width is less than 5 millimetres).

Specimens from D$_3$ of the Rush-Skerries sequence and from D$_3$ of Bradbourne (Derbyshire) exhibit the following characters :— Corallites narrow, with very thin walls. Calices very numerous and unequal (average width = 4·5 millimetres).

Fig. 15.—Michelinia tenuisepta (*Phillips*): *enlarged view of calices* (× 2), *from the* Cyathaxonia-*Beds* (D$_{3b}$) *of Rush*, R 22.

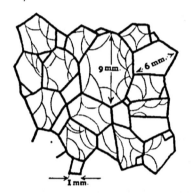

The internal structure consists mainly of flat tabulæ which, in the narrow portions of the tubes, stretch completely across ; concurrently with increase of diameter, a lining of loose vesicles makes its appearance at the wall.

The striking characters are the thin walls and the interposition of small calices.

Occurrence.—This species is very abundant in D$_{3b}$, and a specimen from the *megastoma*-Beds is indistinguishable. The Holmpatrick form seems also to agree in all essential points, but has only been examined in the field. The species is very abundant at Bradbourne, and occurs rarely in D$_{2-3}$ of Gower.

MICHELINIA TENUISEPTA, var. FAVOSITOIDES, nov.    (Pl. XLIX, fig. 11.)

This form is homœomorphic with *Favosites*, but differs in the following points :—(1) The majority of the tabulæ, although stretching completely across, are seldom continuously horizontal : (2) The tabulæ are frequently replaced by broad vesicles ; (3) The mural pores are large and scattered.

On the other hand, the relationship of the form to *M. tenuisepta* is obvious, the differences being entirely dependent on the narrowness of the corallites.

Occurrence.—This variety is common in, and characteristic of, the lower part of P ; it immediately succeeds the maximum of the typical form of *Michelinia tenuisepta*. It is equally abundant in D$_3$ at Bradbourne (Derbyshire).

### Zaphrentis and Densiphyllum.

ZAPHRENTIS ENNISKILLENI, Ed. & H.    (Pl. XLIX, fig. 13.)

Z. *Enniskilleni*, Edwards & Haime 'Monogr. Brit. Foss. Cor.' pt. iii, p. 170 & pl. xxxiv, fig. 1.

Prox. Z. *Enniskilleni* & Z. *patula*,[1] Thomson & Nicholson, Ann. & Mag. Nat. Hist. ser. 4, vol. xvi (1875) p. 428 & pl. xii, figs. 5–6.

[1] Non *Caninia patula*, Mich.

The holotype [1] is preserved in the Geological Society's Collection (R. 5460).

In this specimen, a deep fossula extends to the centre, where it forms a narrow chasm; near the wall it apparently expands rapidly. Eight septa compose each lateral group; the counter-series consists of nineteen regularly-spaced septa, of which the central one is more strongly pronounced. The lateral breaks are conspicuous and de-pendent.

*Z. Enniskilleni*, Thoms. & Nich. differs (1) in the closer approximation and more regular spacing of the septa; (2) in the narrowness of the fossula throughout its length.

Enniskillenids from the Dublin sequence.—The figured specimen from the lower part of P is the only example of the typical species; it is remarkable for the strong contraction of the inner portion of the fossula.

*Zaphrentis* aff. *Enniskilleni* from the *Cyathaxonia*-Beds ('Rush paper' p. 315 & pl. xxix, fig. 2) differs in its smaller size, the expanded inner portion of the fossula, and in the shortening of the counter-septa (*v. i.*).

Enniskillenids from other areas.—The form figured by Thomson & Nicholson (*v. s.*) is common in the Lower Limestones of Scotland.·

The Derbyhaven Limestone of the Isle of Man contains in abundance a *Zaphrentis*, which appears to agree in external characters with the type of *Z. Enniskilleni*. Horizontal sections exhibit considerable looseness of septal grouping and a widely-gaping fossula, constricted in its inner portion, but to a far less extent than is the case in the specimen figured here.[2]

*Z.* aff. *Enniskilleni* is common in $D_{2-3}$ of Gower [3]; it agrees essentially with the species from $D_3$ of Rush, but exhibits a higher degree of specialization in the greater prominence of the counter-septum, and in the deviation of the counter-septa from a radial direction.

ZAPHRENTIS OMALIUSI, var. AMBIGUA, Carruthers.    (Pl. XLIX, figs. 6 *a* & 6 *b*.).

*Z.* cf. *Phillipsi*, var. (1), 'Rush paper' p. 314.
*Z. Omaliusi*, var. *ambigua*, Carruthers, Geol. Mag. dec. 5, vol. v (1908) p. 28, pl. iv, figs. 5 & 6.
(The figured specimens were identified by Mr. Carruthers.)

Fig. 6 *a* exhibits well the bifossulate character of this variety, and

[1] The Council of the Geological Society very kindly granted permission for the cutting of the specimen; but, being doubtful of success, I shirked the responsibility.

[2] The foregoing remarks are founded on the study of specimens collected by Dr. Wheelton Hind.

[3] This form will be fully described in a forthcoming paper on the Gower sequence by Mr. E. E. L. Dixon and myself.

also the quadrantal arrangement of the septa into four stalked groups—a striking feature of certain sections.

Fig. 6 *b* is less distinctly fossulate and approaches *Z. Omaliusi* var. *densa*, Carruthers, *op. cit.* p. 29, pl. iv, figs. 7 & 8.

*Z. Omaliusi*, var. *ambigua* and var. *densa* are the commonest corals in the Rush Slates and in the Lane Limestone; they also occur rarely in the lower part of P. Their occurrence in other areas has been described in § VI (pp. 440, 441).

A Densiphylloid form of the *Zaphrentis-Omaliusi* group occurs in the Lane Limestone, and ranges into the Lower P-beds.

The adult is strongly Densiphylloid, and bears considerable resemblance to the new species of Densiphylloid *Zaphrentis* described below. In the adult the septa are straight and very closely approximated, and the fossula is very inconspicuous.

Young stages exhibit the typical plan of *Z. Omaliusi*, although the greater number of septa is very noticeable.

Mr. Carruthers identified a specimen of this form as :—

'Cf. *Z. Omaliusi*, var. *densa* (occurs in the Millstone Grit of Garnkirk).'

ZAPHRENTIS OMALIUSI, var. AMBIGUA, mut σ. (Pl. XLIX, fig. 8.)

(?) *Amplexus* (*Cyathopsis*) *cornu-bovis*, Thoms. & Nich. *op. cit.* vol. xvii (1876) p. 65 & pl. vii, fig. 6 [1]; non Michelin sp.

Compare *Z. Omaliusi*, var. *ambigua*, Carruthers, *op. cit.* p. 28 & pl. iv, fig. 6.

This coral appears to be an example of phylogenetic old-age, evident in :—

(1) Its narrow, twisted form; (2) The root-like excrescences and coarse annulation of the epitheca; (3) The thin, irregular, and crumpled septa; and (4) The strongly pronounced intermediates.

Horizontal sections show great irregularity and variation of septal plan. The one here figured illustrates the similarity of phylogenetic old-age with ontogenetic old-age (as exhibited in Mr. Carruthers's figure (*loc. supra cit.*) of an old individual of the typical group).

Most sections exhibit both counter and cardinal fossulæ, the former being the more conspicuous.

The septa are spidery and, as a rule, continuously concave to the cardinal fossula; the counter-septa are closely packed and remarkably crinkled. Usually, the inner ends of the septa are fused together at the centre, and in the calyx they produce a sharp crest.

This mutation has only been found in $D_{3b}$, where it is not uncommon; the specimen figured by Thomson & Nicholson was found in the Lower Limestones of Scotland.

[1] The figure of '*Amplexus cornu-bovis*' suggests a section of this species in which the continuity of the septa has been destroyed; I have obtained a similar section from the figured specimen.

A new species of Densiphylloid ZAPHRENTIS. (Pl. XLIX, fig. 2.)

Compare *Zaphrentis* sp. (?), Thoms. *op. cit.* pl. vi, fig. 19, and *Densiphyllum charlestonense*, Thoms. *op. cit.* pl. vi, fig. 21.

The adult species is characterized by its straight, closely-approximate septa, the thickened ends of which are fused together into a dense central mass. The intermediates are short, but conspicuous. The cardinal septum is shorter than the rest.

The fossula is inconspicuous, and, being bounded by two straight septa, is constricted as in the D mutation of *Z. Delanouei*, referred to by Mr. R. G. Carruthers.[1]   Alar breaks can be made out without difficulty.

The tabular intersections are almost completely circular.

At an earlier stage the section appears to agree with *Zaphrentis* sp., Thoms. The young stage shows a parallel-sided fossula and de-pendent alars as in *Z. Delanouei*. Hence this species is probably a Densiphylloid derivative from the *Z.-Delanouei* gens.

Differences from similar forms.—(1) *Densiphyllum rushianum*. Our species has straighter and more numerous septa, distinct lateral breaks and intermediates, and a wall of normal thickness.

(2) *Zaphrentis Delanouei*, constricted mutation, Carruthers (*loc. cit.*), has the same type of fossula, but differs in the smaller number of septa, the suppression of intermediates, and in the much closer approach to *Z. Delanouei* observable in young sections. ·

(3) *Densiphyllum charlestonense*, Thoms. Our species appears to differ in its prominent intermediates and in the central massing of the septal ends. [Mr. Carruthers (*op. cit.* pp. 27 & 30) considers *D. charlestonense* to be closely comparable with *Z. Omaliusi* var. *densa*.]

The typical form occurs only in the *Dibunophyllum*-Limestone. A similar (probably identical[2]) form is found commonly in the Lower Limestones of Scotland and in $D_{2-3}$ of Gower.

DENSIPHYLLUM RUSHIANUM, sp. nov.

*Densiphyllum*, Vaughan, 'Rush paper' p. 318 & pl. xxix, fig. 6.

Sufficient material being now to hand, this species can be definitely named.

Form elongate, cylindro-conical, laterally compressed, usually but slightly cornute. Wall very thick; epitheca smooth, unconstricted.

Horizontal section.—The most striking characters are (1) the very thick wall; (2) the regularity of the septa and the absence of alar breaks; and (3) the constriction of the inner end of the fossula.

The septa are well spaced, and thickened at their attachment to

[1] Geol. Mag. dec. 5, vol. v (1908) pp. 65-66.
[2] *Fide* R. G. Carruthers.

the wall as well as at the centre, where they are fused together; in the cardinal region they are usually concave to the fossula (although occasionally straight or very slightly convex).

The constriction of the fossula is similar to that seen in the D mutation of *Zaphrentis Delanouei* mentioned above, and the fossula apparently lies in all cases on the concave side.

Both theca and epitheca are abnormally thick, and intermediates are buried in the theca.

The early stage exhibits a parallel-sided fossula and distinct alar breaks; the curvature of the septa in the cardinal region is slightly concave to the fossula.

Although the general resemblance of the adult coral is certainly to the gens of *Z. Delanouei*, the early stage does not strengthen the evidence.

A variant from P shows a remarkable thickening of the septa, which brings them nearly into contact; in other respects it agrees with the typical form.

*D. rushianum* is common in both $D_{3a}$ and $D_{3b}$, and the typical form persists into P (L 18 c). The variant occurs in the Middle *Posidonomya*-Beds (L 7).

Other Densiphyllids.

(*a*) The constricted D mutation of *Z. Delanouei* mentioned by Mr. R. G. Carruthers, *op. cit.* p. 65.

A specimen has been identified by Mr. Carruthers from P. The mutation is, according to him, abundant in the Lower Limestone of Scotland.

(*b*) A new species of *Densiphyllum*, abundant at Bradbourne (Derbyshire), occurs in P.

A specimen has been discovered by Mr. Carruthers in the shales above the Massif near Colne.

### Cyathaxonia.

Cyathaxonia rushiana, Vaughan.    (Pl. XLIX, fig. 9.)

'Rush paper' p. 316 & pl. xxix, figs. 3, 3 *a*, & 3 *b*.

The additional figure included in the present paper illustrates a character of the septa which is not always obvious.

The horizontal section shows a series of spine-like projections on the sides of the septa, indicating the presence of interseptal dissepiments either originally incomplete or subsequently, in great part, destroyed.

Further study of the species suggests that the projection of an axial columella is merely due to the unequal resistance offered by the several concentric shells of which the solid central cylinder is built up, the middle shells being more easily removed.

This species is common throughout the *Cyathaxonia*-Beds ($D_{3a}$ and $D_{3b}$) and extends into P.

## Diphyphyllum.

DIPHYPHYLLUM SUBIBICINUM (M'Coy).    (Pl. XLIX, fig. 7.)

*Caninia subibicina*, M'Coy, 'Brit. Palæoz. Foss.' p. 89 & pl. iii I, fig. 35.

Form elongate and cylindrical.    Tabulæ broad and flat, without columella.    Fossula very shallow and inconspicuous.

The septa and the external vesicular area are *Lithostrotion*-like; the major septa fall considerably short of the centre, the minor septa project inwards beyond the ring of vesicles, and all the septa are of the same thickness.

This species is essentially a large *Lithostrotion* without a columella, and is therefore a good example of the genus *Diphyphyllum*.

Differences. — *Cyathophyllum giganteum* (Mich.), Thoms. & Nich. *op. cit.* vol. xvii, pl. vi, fig. 1, differs in the feeble development of the minor septa and in the more advanced (Clisiophylloid) character of the vesicles.

*D. subibicinum* is abundant in the Holmpatrick Limestone, where it is associated with *Campophyllum Murchisoni*, Ed. & H.

In the South-Western Province it occurs commonly in $D_1$ with the same associate.    Mr. Cosmo Johns, F.G.S., has sent me a few specimens from the Basal Conglomerate of Ingleboro' ($S_1$), and this is the earliest record of the species.    Dr. Wheelton Hind has collected it from the Derbyhaven Limestone (Isle of Man).    M'Coy's figured specimen came from Kendal, and is almost certainly from $C-S_1$.[1]

## Koninckophyllum.

KONINCKOPHYLLUM sp.    (Pl. XLIX, fig. 14.)

Cf. *Koninckophyllum interruptum*, Thoms. & Nich. *op. cit.* vol. xvii, p. 303, pl. xii, fig. 3 (a species characterized by its discontinuous columella).

There are two specimens in Dr. Matley's collection, both of which probably belong to the same species.

The fragment from L 7 shows no columella, whereas the figured specimen from L 12 *g* exhibits this character clearly.    Both specimens are from approximately the same level in P.

The densely-packed vesicles distinguish the later and typical *Koninckophylla* from the earlier and more *Lithostrotion*-like forms typified by *Koninckophyllum* θ, Vaughan.    The partial disappearance of the columella indicates a further stage in evolution.

In the South-Western Province, highly-developed *Koninckophylla* do not appear before $D_2$, and all the species are continuously columellate.

A similar form occurs at Astbury (Staffs.) in the volcanic beds, which are referred by Dr. Wheelton Hind to the P level.    The specimens figured by Thomson & Nicholson were obtained from the Lower Limestones of Scotland.

---

[1] The *Michelinia-megastoma* Bed of Prof. E. J. Garwood, Geol. Mag. dec. 5, vol. iv (1907) p. 70.

## Lithostrotion.

LITHOSTROTION cf. AFFINE (Martin), Ed. & H.    (Pl. XLIX, fig. 10.)

Compare *Lithostrotion affine* (Martin), as figured by Edwards & Haime in 'Monogr. Brit. Foss. Cor.' pl. xxxix, fig. 2 ; and compare also *Lithostrotion cyathophylloides*, Vaughan, figured in the 'Rush paper' pl. xxx, figs. 1 & 1 a.

The spacing of the major septa agrees with *Lithostrotion affine* ; their continuation to the columella with *L. cyathophylloides*.

The corallites are very often in close union—a character unknown in the coral of the *megastoma*-beds. Again, the calyx is sharp-rimmed, whereas *L. cyathophylloides* has its calicular wall as broad as in a *Cyathophyllum*.

Occurrence.—This species is abundant at the top of the *Cyathaxonia*-Beds, where it characterizes a peculiar faunal phase.

The same form occurs in the *Cyathaxonia*-Beds of the Western Midlands.


Diphyphylloid variant of LITHOSTROTION IRREGULARE from P (L 10 *b*).

Cf. *Diphyphyllum gracile*, M'Coy.

The tabulæ are convex and smooth, the columella being usually wanting. (The central cylinder is commonly found detached, and suggests an *Orthoceras*.)

This form is common in $D_2$ of the Avon section.


### *Lithostrotion*-like Clisiophyllids.

The general characters of this large group are :—

(1) A dense axial nucleus confined to the middle of the central area, and enclosing a prominent columellar plate.
    In the calyx the whole nucleus is usually cemented into a solid, smooth-sided, strongly-projecting axial spike. Pl. XLIX, fig. 3, is a section of a young example of this group (probably *Clisiophyllum curkeenense*), cut immediately above the floor of the calyx in order to show this character.

(2) A narrow external vesicular ring.

(3) Major and minor septa strongly developed within the vesicular ring, and extending without appreciable thinning to the wall.

The group can be divided into two sections :—

I. Corals with a short and stout columella, from which short radiating lamellæ project and become rapidly merged in the loose and irregularly-reticulated intersections of the broad central area.

*Clisiophyllum curkeenense*, Vaughan ('Rush paper' p. 320 & pl. xxx, fig. 2), in which the medial and external areas are very strongly differentiated, is the most highly-specialized member of this group.

II. Corals in which the axial mass is bisected by a long columellar plate, and forms a densely-reticulate oval nucleus within the broadly-reticulate central area.

(*a*) The Clisiophyllid characteristic of the basal beds of Ingleton (S₁ ; see Cosmo Johns, Geol. Mag. dec. 5, vol. iii, 1906, p. 322) has a broadly and regularly-reticulated central area enclosing a very finely-reticulated oval nucleus, which is bisected by the thick columellar plate. The septa are stout, well spaced, and continuous to the wall. Minor septa are regularly developed after the *Lithostrotion*-plan, and are only slightly less prominent.

(*b*) The Cyathophylloid Clisiophyllids from S₁ of the Frome district (Mendips) figured by Dr. T. F. Sibly [1] exhibit a strongly-differentiated axial nucleus, but the septation is markedly Cyathophylloid.

(*c*) The Clisiophyllid from the Carlyan Rocks (Pl. XLIX, fig. 1) has an axial nucleus almost identical with that of Dr. Sibly's fig. 5 *b*, while the septation agrees with that of the Ingleton species. Hence the affinities of the Carlyan coral are strongly with forms from CS₁. A species from D₂₋₃ of Thorpe Cloud (Derbyshire) has a similar axial mass, but the septal plan is as highly developed as in the D₂ *Koninckophylla*.

## Dibunophyllum.

DIBUNOPHYLLUM aff. MUIRHEADI, Thoms. & Nich. (Pl. XLIX, figs. 4 *a* & 4 *b*.)

Compare Thoms. & Nich. *op. cit.* vol. xvii (1876) p. 459 & pl. xxv, fig. 4.

This species belongs to the same section as *Dibunophyllum θ*, Vaughan, but is more highly developed. Simple forms intermediate between it and *Dibunophyllum θ* are commonly associated with the latter in D₁ of the Ingleton area,[2] and highly-developed variants characterize D₂ of the same province[3]: it is common in the Lower Limestone of Fife.[4]

Fig. 4 *b* differs in the markedly-differentiated external ring and in the firmly-drawn characters of the central area; in the first-mentioned peculiarity this species shows convergence with *Clisiophyllum curkeenense*.

Both species are common in the *Dibunophyllum*-Limestone (Lower D₂).

[1] Quart. Journ. Geol. Soc. vol. lxii (1906) pl. xxxi, figs. 5 *a* & 5 *b*.
[2] From material collected by Mr. Cosmo Johns.
[3] From material collected by Prof. E. J. Garwood.
[4] From material collected by Dr. C. A. Matley.

## Carcinophyllum.

CARCINOPHYLLUM CURKEENENSE, sp. nov.    (Pl. XLIX, fig. 5.)

Form cylindro-conical, with smooth epitheca.

Horizontal section.—The central area is circular and sharply delimited; it is composed of a thick irregular diametral columella, from which ten or twelve thick, irregular, and knotted lamellæ radiate and fill up almost the whole of the area. The medial area is radiated by thirty (at a diameter of 15 millimetres) short and stout major septa; the minor septa do not project into this area. The external area is a dense thick ring, formed by the perfect approximation of the major and minor septa, which are of equal thickness and in complete contact. There is some indication of a narrow peripheral ring of loose structure.

This species presents structural characters intermediate between those of forms from Lower S and Upper D. In Lower S of the Mendips and Tenby a closely-similar form occurs, which differs in the distinct separation of the septa in the external ring. In $D_3$ of Cracoe a similar form was collected, in which thin prolongations of the minor septa into the medial area were conspicuously shown.

The figured specimen is from the *Dibunophyllum*-Limestone ($D_2$), and certain ill-defined corals from the Curkeen Limestone probably belong to this species.


Lonsdaloid CARCINOPHYLLUM.    (Pl. XLIX, fig. 12.)

This degenerate form is probably an old-age derivative from the preceding species.

The regularity of the external ring is broken down, and this area is now composed of the knobbed and bulbous bases of the septa. The peripheral area is enlarged, and occupied by irregularly anastomosing offshoots of the septal series.

Specimens are not uncommon in the lower part of P.

Dr. Wheelton Hind has collected the same form from the 'Knoll' level of Poolvash (Isle of Man).


### A New Genus of Clisiophyllid.[1]    (Fig. 16, p. 465.)

I have only seen three incomplete specimens of this interesting coral:—one from the top of the Limestone-massif at Wetton (Derbyshire); the second from the *Cyathaxonia*-Beds of Rush (R 18 *c*, 'Rush paper' p. 299—there described as an 'Aulophylloid

---

[1] In the original definition of *Clisiophyllum* (Dana in 'Narr. U.S. Explor. Exped.' 1838–42, vol. vii, Zoophytes, p. 355 & pp. 361, 362) the following characters are clearly suggested as diagnostic:—(1) vaulted tabulæ; (2) no columella; and (3) an external ring of radiated vesicles. Our new genus agrees with *Clisiophyllum*, Dana, in characters (1) and (2), but differs markedly in the absence of (3). The present-day conception of *Clisiophyllum* as a columellate coral is apparently unwarranted.

*Clisiophyllum*' on account of its septation); and the third from the Holmpatrick Limestone.

The central cylinder is entirely built up of a great number of strongly and uniformly-arched tabulæ, fitting one over the other, and bound together by thin radiating lamellæ. (This cylinder is easily separable from the septal tube which surrounds it.)

Fig. 16.—*A new genus of Clisiophyllid: diagram constructed from a specimen found in D₂₋₃ at Welton (Derbyshire). (Magnified 2½ diameters.)*

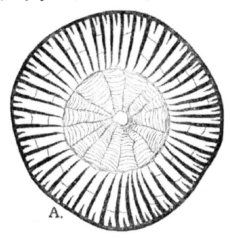

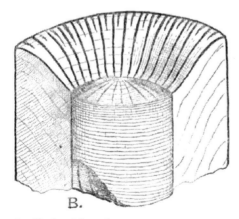

A=Horizontal section.
B=Solid specimen dissected and restored, showing the central cylinder.

The central area of a horizontal section consequently exhibits a series of very close concentric intersections radiated by thin flexuous lamellæ. A small area at the very centre is usually entirely free from structures of either kind (except when the section is tangential to one of the tabulæ).

The major septa are thick, equal and close-set, and the septal ring is practically unbroken at any point. Interseptal vesicles are very scarce, and consequently the septa have nearly smooth sides. There is no external vesicular ring, but the septa are firmly attached to the wall. Minor septa are conspicuously developed, but project a very short distance inwards from the wall.

The earliest Clisiophyllids are simple examples of this type, agreeing in the regular ring of septa firmly attached to the wall, in the absence of a differentiated external area, and in the structure of the central cylinder. The later forms are, however, more highly developed.

## II. BRACHIOPODS.

[Note.—'Davidson' signifies Davidson, 'Monogr. Brit. Foss. Brach.' vol. ii (1858-63) Palæont. Soc.]

### Productids.

### Productus.

PRODUCTUS PROBOSCIDEUS, de Verneuil.   (Pl. L, fig. 1.)

Davidson, pl. xxxiii, figs. 1-4, & Suppl. vol. iv (1874-82) pl. xxxvi, fig. 13.

This species occurs only near the top of the *Dibunophyllum*-Zone. Davidson records it from Settle and Drogheda.   Dr. Wheelton Hind has collected a few specimens from Park Hill and Castleton. The specimen here figured was collected by Dr. Matley from Lower P (L 5 *d*), where the species is apparently not uncommon.

The general type of ribbing and wrinkling immediately recalls *Productus undatus*, and the following facts throw light on the line of evolution which has resulted in the remarkable form under discussion :—

(1) In $S_1$ and Lower $S_2$ of the South-Western Province, a transversely-wrinkled variant from the stock of *Productus corrugato-hemisphericus* is common (see Proc. Bristol Nat. Soc. vol. x, 1903, pp. 131-34 & pl. ii, fig. 4).

(2) Mr. J. T. Stobbs has sent me a large number of specimens of typical *Productus undatus* from Redesdale (Northumberland), where the species occurs abundantly ; many of these approach very close to the specimens from the South-Western Province mentioned above.

The associated corals indicate $D_1$.[1]

(3) Specimens of *Productus undatus* from immediately below the Hardraw Limestone of the Yoredale Province ($D_2$), sent to me by Mr. Cosmo Johns, exhibit great variability and elongation of form.

Piecing together these several facts, the history of *Productus proboscideus* is probably much as follows :—The ancestral stock of *Pr. corrugato-hemisphericus* emitted in early S-time a continuously-wrinkled variant, the characters of which became more and more firmly impressed until, in late S and early D-time, *Pr. undatus* reached its maximum stability and abundance.   In late D-time the gens became moribund, and its characters therefore unstable, resulting in rapid variation and great irregularity.

PRODUCTUS STRIATUS (Fischer).   (Pl. L, fig. 2.)

Compare Davidson, pl. xxxiv, figs. 1 & 3.

This species is abundant in Lower and Middle P of the Rush-

---

[1] Prof. Barrois informs me that *Productus undatus* characterizes beds in the Belgian sequence which are probably referable to S or $D_1$.

Skerries sequence, and characterizes the same level in the Midland and Northern areas.

The figure shows the common form of the Irish specimens.

*Productus striatus* obviously belongs to the group of *Pr. corrugatus*, with which it agrees in the type of ribbing and in the rapidity with which it narrows towards the beak.

PRODUCTUS, sp. nov.

*Productus* cf. *fimbriatus*, 'Rush paper' p. 308 & pl. xxx, fig. 6.

Specimens of this form are not uncommon in Lower and Middle P, but are too fragmentary to permit a complete definition of the species.

The pedicle-valve has the form of *Productus fimbriatus*. The ornament consists of concentric bands, practically smooth between the erect pustules.

The brachial valve is deeply grooved concentrically, and the intermediate ridges bear scattered crenulations, more numerous at the cardinal angles. The interior of the brachial valve has often a puzzling resemblance to a pedicle-valve of *Productus rugatus* (see Davidson, pl. xli, fig. 6).

## SPIRIFERIDS.

### Spirifer.

SPIRIFER BISULCATUS, var.: cf. *Sp. integricosta*. (Pl. L, figs. 3 *a* & 3 *b*.)

The number of variants from the typical form of *Sp. bisulcatus*, J. Sow., is, in $D_3$, very large and doubtless dependent, to a considerable extent, upon the great variation of conditions which marked that phase.

The variant here figured has a transverse form, few strong simple ribs separated by deep furrows, and a prominent truncated mesial fold divided by two grooves near its margin. The area is broad between the beaks.

The peculiarity of this variant lies mainly in its shape: the left-hand side being usually rounded, and the right-hand side square, with a consequent shortening of the area on the left-hand side.

The resemblance to *Sp. integricosta* is merely apparent, and is limited to the division of the fold and the shortening of the hinge-line.

This variant occurs in Lower P somewhat plentifully; it is interesting to note that, at precisely the same level in Nidderdale, near Pateley Bridge, a form of *Spirifer bisulcatus*, having the same ribbing and fold, occurs, in which the cardinal angles are produced, unequally on the two sides, into long spines.

SPIRIFER cf. CONVOLUTUS, Phill.   (Pl. L, fig. 4.)

The figured fragment of a brachial valve differs in several points from Phillips's type (re-figured in Davidson, pl. v, figs. 9--11).

The fold is deeply grooved along the middle, and is strongly truncated; the flank-ribbing is suppressed, and entirely absent from the greater part of the left flank; although the early growth-lines indicate sharply-acuminate cardinal angles, the angle increases rapidly with age. The fine laminose foliation at the growth-lines is beautifully shown, and is strikingly Athyroid.

This remarkable shell was collected by Dr. Matley from the *Posidonomya*-Beds of L 6 *c*.

## Spiriferina

SPIRIFERINA INSCULPTA (Phillips).   (Pl. L, fig. 9.)

Compare Davidson, pl. vii, figs. 52–55.

The figured fragment is a cast of the brachial valve, and is interesting as the highest record of the species—Upper *Posidonomya*-Beds. The large size and exaggerated ornament are shown in the figure.

## Martinia.

MARTINIA GLABRA, mut. P.   (Pl. L, fig. 8.)

The form agrees with that of *M. glabra*, var. *decora* (Phill.), Davidson. The sharp radiating ridges seen on the cast are characteristic of the genus.[1]

The lozenge-shaped mesial platform, seen on the cast of the pedicle-valve, indicates a deep muscular depression inside the valve, and has only been observed in this late variant. The latest members of many brachiopod gentes exhibit a precisely similar emphasis of the muscular scars; as, for example, *Daviesiella comoides*, *Schizophoria resupinata*, etc.

This mutation occurs only in the Upper P Beds, where it is abundant at two levels (L 8 *p* & L 9 *c*).

MARTINIA OVALIGLABRA, sp. nov.   (Pl. L, fig. 5.)

Pedicle-valve as in *Martinia glabra*. Hinge-line long, but less than the width of the shell.

The brachial valve has a broad gentle mesial swelling, within which the mesial fold is scarcely differentiated.

The cardinal region is free from radial ornament; the flanks and fold are divided into broad low radial ribs by a small number of radial creases. The fold is very inconspicuously divided into three, and there are four or five stronger ribs on each flank in the young specimen figured.

Both valves are beautifully ornamented with close-set, fine, concentric growth-lines.

---

[1] The occurrence of a similar character in *Athyris glabristria* and *A. plano-sulcata* suggests that this feature is mainly dependent on form.

This species agrees with *Martinia ovalis* in the plan of ribbing, but differs markedly in form and length of hinge-line.

Towards the end of Avonian time, the gens of *Martinia glabra* gave birth to a large number of variants, most of which are smooth and differ only in form, although this difference is often strongly marked.

*Martinia ovalis* and the species here described are ribbed deviations from the same gens, exhibiting reversion towards the earliest-known *Martinia*, namely *M.* cf. *linguifera*, of which a very few examples have been found in $Z_2$ and $\gamma$ of the South-Western Province.

*Martinia ovaliglabra* ranges, in the Rush-Skerries sequence, through the beds containing *Posidonomya*, and is an important zonal fossil.

Mr. J. T. Stobbs has collected some beautiful examples from the highest Avonian of the North Wales area.

### Reticularia.

RETICULARIA LINEATA (Mart.).

 = *Reticularia imbricata* (Sow.) & (Phill.).
 = *Spirifera lineata* var. *reticulata*, Davidson (*pars*), pl. xiii, figs. 11 & 12.

The dental plates are sub-parallel and conspicuous; the ornament consists of broad imbricating bands bearing broad rib-like spines. Specimens are met with, somewhat rarely, in the *Dibunophyllum*-Limestone and in Lower P.

RETICULARIA LINEATA (Dav.).

 = *Spirifera lineata*, Davidson (*pars*), pl. xiii, figs. 5, 8, & 10.

Small globose form with suppressed ornament. Dental plates markedly divergent, and therefore approximate to the inner wall of the umbonal region; subsequent shell-deposit frequently includes and conceals them within the thickened wall.

Specimens are common in the *Dibunophyllum*-Limestone and in Lower P; extremely abundant at the ' Knoll' level in the Western Midlands and Yorkshire; and not uncommon in $D_2$ of the South-Western Province.

### ATHYRIDS.

#### Athyris (*Actinoconchus?*).

ATHYRIS cf. PLANOSULCATA (Phillips).   (Pl. L, fig. 6.)

 = *Athyris planosulcata*, Davidson, pl. li, fig. 12.

This form appears to be a variant from *Athyris expansa* (Phillips); it is characterized by the circular outline and by the strong development of radial ridges on the cast. Specimens are not uncommon in Lower P.

From an examination of the specimens in the Gilbertson Collection (British Museum), upon which Phillips founded his two species *expansa* and *planosulcata*, I am inclined to differ somewhat from Davidson's interpretation, which is excellently illustrated in Dav. pl. xvi. Figs. 4, 4 *a*, & 4 *b* there appear to be typical examples of *Athyris expansa* (see Phillips, ' Geol. Yorkshire,' pt. ii, pl. x, fig. 18).

The type of *Athyris planosulcata* is obviously a slightly abnormal variety; but, having priority of position both in Phillips's text and plate, it must absorb *A. expansa*. I agree, therefore, with Davidson in the matter of the forms which he refers to *A. planosulcata* in pl. xvi; but I consider that, in including fig. 4, he has rejected Phillips's species *A. expansa*.

Figs. 17 & 18, pl. xvi, and fig. 4, pl. xvii, exhibit such peculiarity of form and radial striation as to deserve specific separation. They characterize the ' Knoll ' level of the Midlands, Yorkshire, etc., and are doubtless extreme variants of *A. planosulcata*.

## ACTINOCONCHUS (?). (Pl. L, fig. 10.)

This species is common in the chert-beds of the upper part of P.

In shape and in its thick expansions it agrees with *Actinoconchus paradoxus*, M'Coy, and the pedicle-valve has the same small pointed beak.

The peculiarity, illustrated in the figure of a cast of the brachial valve, lies in the elongated pit which indicates a thick septal projection. This character [1] and the absence of the strong radial ridges appear to separate this form from *Athyris planosulcata*.

## ORTHIDS.

### Schizophoria.

#### Spinous variant of SCHIZOPHORIA RESUPINATA (Martin). (Pl. L, fig. 7.)

This variant is common in P, but specimens are fragmentary.

The surface is covered with short spines, and growth-halts are strongly marked. The area in the pedicle-valve is often very large and *Syringothyris*-like, and when this is the case the beak is usually curved to one side. The muscular scars are very deeply impressed.

Study of a fine series collected by Dr. Wheelton Hind from P of Congleton Edge has demonstrated how instable are the characters of this gens at the top of the Avonian.

[1] Hall & Clarke ('Handbook of the Brachiopoda' Geol. Surv. N.Y. 13th Ann. Rep. 1893–94, p. 780) give the presence of a median septum in the pedicle-valve as a character of the genus *Actinoconchus*, but cite no authority for the statement.

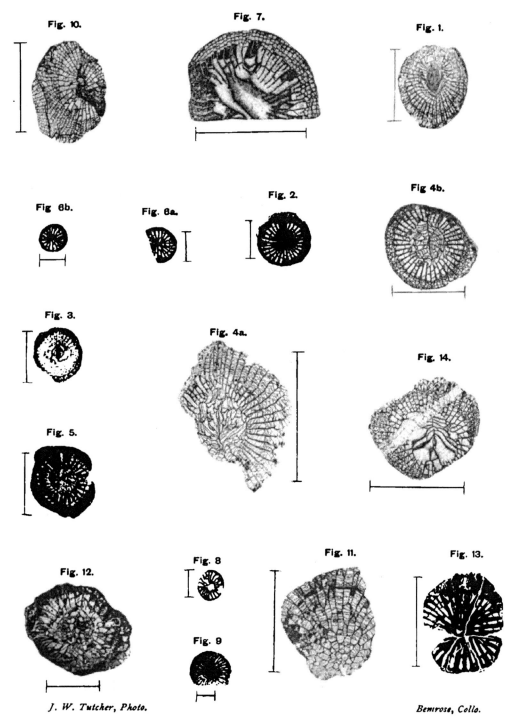

Fig. 10.

Fig. 7.

Fig. 1.

Fig 6b.

Fig. 6a.

Fig. 2.

Fig 4b.

Fig. 3.

Fig. 4a.

Fig. 14.

Fig. 5.

Fig. 12.

Fig. 8

Fig. 11.

Fig. 13.

Fig. 9

*J. W. Tutcher, Photo.*

*Bemrose, Collo.*

AVONIAN CORALS FROM THE RUSH-SKERRIES SECTION
(COUNTY DUBLIN).

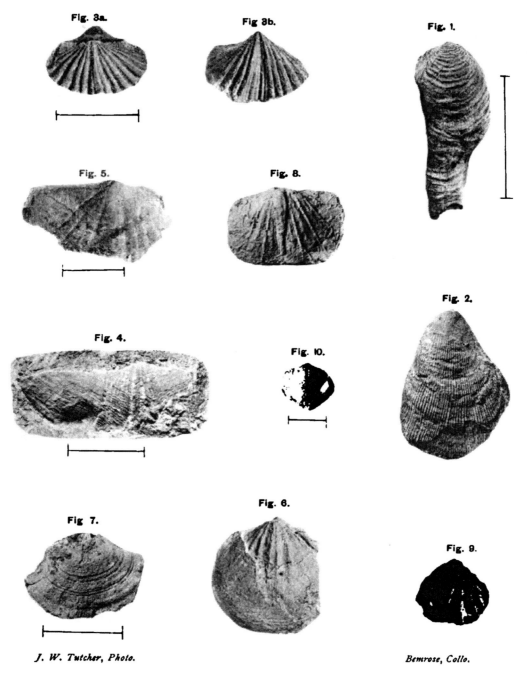

J. W. Tutcher, Photo.

Bemrose, Collo.

BRACHIOPODS FROM LOUGHSHINNY (COUNTY DUBLIN).
Associated with *Posidonomya Becheri.*

## EXPLANATION OF PLATES XLIX & L.

### PLATE XLIX.

AVONIAN CORALS from the Rush-Skerries Section (County Dublin).

Fig. 1. *Lithostrotion*-like Clisiophyllid (p. 463).   Horizontal section ;  × 1·25. Carlyan Rocks (top of the *megastoma*-beds).

2. Densiphylloid *Zaphrentis*, sp. nov. (p. 459).   Horizontal section ;  × 1·4. L 21 *d*, *Dibunophyllum*-Limestone.

3. *Lithostrotion*-like Clisiophyllid (cf. *Clisiophyllum curkeenense*, Vaughan) (p. 462).   Horizontal section ;  × 1·1.   Showing the structure of the axial spike.   Near L 24 *b*, *Dibunophyllum*-Limestone.

Figs. 4 *a* & 4 *b*. *Dibunophyllum* aff. *Muirheadi*, Thoms. & Nich. (p. 463). Horizontal sections ;  × 1·2.   *Dibunophyllum*-Limestone.
   Fig. 4 *a* represents the typical species. L 21 *b*; and fig. 4 *b* represents a form convergent on *Clisiophyllum curkeenense*, Vaughan. L 23 *a*.

Fig. 5. *Carcinophyllum curkeenense*, sp. nov. (p. 464).   Horizontal section ;  × 1·25.  L 23 *a*, *Dibunophyllum*-Limestone.

Figs. 6 *a* & 6 *b*. *Zaphrentis Omaliusi*, var. *ambigua*, Carruthers (p. 457).   Horizontal sections ;  × 1·25.  L 27, Lane Limestone.
   Fig. 6 *a* represents the typical variety; and fig. 6 *b* represents a form comparable with var. *densa*, Carruthers.

Fig. 7. *Diphyphyllum subibicinum* (M'Coy) (p. 461).   Horizontal section ;  × 1·2.  L 39 *a*, Holmpatrick Limestone.

8. *Zaphrentis Omaliusi*, var. *ambigua*, mut. σ nov. (p. 458).   Horizontal section ;  × 1·25.  R 23 *b*, *Cyathaxonia*-Beds.

9. *Cyathaxonia rushiana*, Vaughan (p. 460).   Horizontal section ;  × 2. R 23 *b*, *Cyathaxonia*-Beds.

10. *Lithostrotion* cf. *affine* (Flem.), Ed. & H. (p. 462).   Horizontal section ;  × 1·2.  L 4 *e*, D-P Phase.

11. *Michelinia tenuisepta*, var. *favositoides* nov. (p. 456).   Vertical section ;  × 1·2.  L 20 *f*, *Posidonomya*-Beds.

12. Lonsdaloid *Carcinophyllum* (p. 464).   Horizontal section ;  × 2.  L 18 *c*, *Posidonomya*-Beds.

13. *Zaphrentis Enniskilleni*, Ed. & H. (p. 457).   Horizontal section ;  × 1·2.  L 5 *j*, *Posidonomya*-Beds.

14. *Koninckophyllum* sp. (cf. *K. interruptum*, Thoms. & Nich.) (p. 461). Horizontal section ;  × 1·2.  L 12 *g*, *Posidonomya*-Beds.

### PLATE L.

BRACHIOPODS from Loughshinny (County Dublin).

Fig. 1. *Productus (Proboscidella) proboscideus*, de Verneuil (p. 466).   Pedicle-valve ;  × 1·5.  L 5 *d*, Lower *Posidonomya*-Beds.

2. *Productus striatus* (Fischer) (p. 467).   Pedicle-valve ; natural size. L 5 *j*, Lower *Posidonomya*-Beds.

Figs. 3 *a* & 3 *b*. *Spirifer bisulcatus*, var. (cf. *Sp. integricosta*, Phillips) (p. 467). L 5 *d*, Lower *Posidonomya*-Beds.
   Fig. 3 *a* represents the brachial valve ;  × 1·25.   Fig. 3 *b* represents the pedicle-valve ; natural size.

Fig. 4. *Spirifer* cf. *convolutus*, Phillips (p. 468).   Brachial valve ;  × 2·33. L 6 *c*, Middle *Posidonomya*-Beds. (Much enlarged, to show ornament.)

5. *Martinia ovaliglabra*, sp. nov. (p. 468).   Fragment of brachial valve ;  × 2.  L 5 *m*, Lower *Posidonomya*-Beds. (Much enlarged, in order to show ornament.)

6. *Athyris* cf. *planosulcata* (Phillips) (p. 469).   Brachial valve ; natural size. L 5 *k*, Lower *Posidonomya*-Beds. (Compare Dav. pl. li, fig. 12.)

7. *Schizophora resupinata* (Martin), spinous var.  L 7 *c*, Middle *Posidonomya*-Beds.  Fragment enlarged to 1·5, in order to show ornament.

Fig. 8. *Martinia glabra* (Martin), old-age mutation (p. 468).  Pedicle-valve; natural size.  L 8 *p*, Upper *Posidonomya*-Beds.

9. *Spiriferina insculpta* (Phillips), large form (p. 468); natural size.  Fragment of impression, to show ornament.  L 8 *p*, Upper *Posidonomya*-Beds.

10. *Actinoconchus (?)* sp. (p. 470).  Brachial valve;  × 1·2.  L 8 *p*, Upper *Posidonomya*-Beds.

### DISCUSSION.

Dr. WHEELTON HIND most heartily congratulated the Authors on the final result of their work on the Rush sequence.  He felt that he was in entire agreement with their results.  He was much interested in the identification of an upper and a lower *Posidonomya*-Zone.  When writing the description of *Posidonomya Becheri* for the monograph on British Carboniferous Lamellibranchs, he had with some temerity figured specimens from the limestone of Castleton, in which *Productus striatus* and *Pr. proboscideus* were associated with it, and the species was known to occur in the shales connected with the Hardraw-Scar Limestone of Wensleydale.  The Upper *Posidonomya*-Beds were the most important, because in them the zone-fossil was associated with a new fauna, characterized by various goniatites and *Pterinopecten papyraceus*.  The sequence at Rush was homotaxial with that of the Carboniferous rocks in the Midland area and in the Isle of Man.

With regard to *Productus humerosus*, this fossil occurred in the uppermost beds of the *Dibunophyllum*-Zone at Swinden Moor in Yorkshire, where it was associated with Zaphrentids of a high *Dibunophyllum*-facies.  The distribution of *Michelinia* was of interest: a *megastoma*-like form was very common in the Isle of Man with a *Dibunophyllum*-fauna, and it was also found at the base of the Arnside Series.  *Michelinia tenuisepta* was very common in the *Cyathaxonia*-Beds of Bradbourne (Derbyshire).  Zaphrentid corals were a marked feature in the Upper *Dibunophyllum*-Zone of Derbyshire, Yorkshire, and the Isle of Man.  Therefore the speaker thought that the later correlation of Dr. Vaughan was the more probable.

The speaker remembered with great pleasure having been taken over the section by Dr. Matley some few years ago, before the publication of Dr. Vaughan's enlightening work, and having recognized that, at any rate, the *Posidonomya*-Beds gave an important horizon for correlation with other areas.

Mr. E. E. L. DIXON, in congratulating the Authors on an important piece of work, observed that the sequence at the top of the Avonian at Rush was of great interest, and he only regretted that it had not been carried out before the recent work in Flintshire, as it would have shown that the difference between some of the conclusions as regarded the correlation arrived at in that district, and those of previous observers, was not so great as the previous speaker had supposed.

Mr. G. W. LAMPLUGH complimented the Authors on the excellence of their work upon this important and difficult section.  Their results had simplified the interpretation of the succession and would have far-reaching consequences, as it was here, if anywhere, that the structure of the Carboniferous basin of this part of Ireland could be unravelled.    He enquired what method had been employed in measuring the thickness of the Rush and Lane Conglomerates, as the amount stated was greater than he should have anticipated in intra-formational conglomerates of this type.    While acknowledging his inability to criticize the palæontological data, he remarked on the change now proposed in the Authors' previous classification of the lower beds of the Rush sequence, and he asked whether the new results were in any way dependent upon stratigraphical considerations.    He enquired also in what respect the fauna of the Lane Limestone differed from that of the Holmpatrick Limestone, as this might be a case in which the stratigrapher would have to rely entirely upon the palæontologist.

Mr. COSMO JOHNS remarked that he had noticed recently a tendency to regard the Avon section as something not exactly normal.    This was because in other areas that had been described the rocks were laid down under rather different conditions.    For that reason, he regretted the unavoidable delay in communicating the results of his investigations in North-West Yorkshire, where he had found a Viséan facies identical with that of the South-Western Province.    For example, on Ingleborough he had mapped faunal lines which could be matched assemblage for assemblage with those of the Viséan of the South-West.    The normal $S_1$ was followed by $S_2$ with its scanty fauna; $D_1$ came in with its characteristic assemblage at the base, and was succeeded by $D_2$.    The base of $D_2$ lay below the top of the Great Scar Limestone, and thus the whole of the Yoredale Series of Phillips was included in the upper part of $D_2$, while the Main or Upper Scar Limestone had a fauna that corresponded with the top of $D_2$ in the South-Western Province. In both areas, the Millstone Grit immediately succeeded.    If, now, two such well-known areas, so far apart and so extensive, were identical, he would urge that they should be regarded as the normal Viséan sequence.    If that were granted, then he would ask the Authors which of their stratigraphical zones they would correlate with the top of $D_2$ in, say, the Avon section.    There could be no question as to the great value of the results achieved by the Authors, in having worked out in such detail the faunal sequence and stratigraphy of so very difficult an area.

Mr. J. A. DOUGLAS gave a very brief comparison of the Upper Limestone succession on the western coast of Ireland with that of the Rush-Skerries sequence.    The district of Burren in North Clare was perhaps the finest example of a limestone-country in the British Isles.    The country was practically devoid of vegetation and drift, and was built up of huge jointed limestone-terraces which had often almost an artificial appearance.    The beds dipped very slightly at an angle of 1° or 2° southwards.    The thickness of the Upper Limestone from sea-level to the overlying shales was about 1500 feet, and the succession varied but slightly in lithological characters.    The bulk of the limestone was of a pale-grey colour and finely crystalline in texture, often conspicuously crinoidal, and containing an abundance of chert, especially towards the summit. The conditions of deposition must have been very uniform, and there were no traces of local upheaval, as in the Lane and Rush Conglomerates. At the base—that was, at sea-level—the fossils pointed to late *Seminula*-age; and consequently the overlying series must represent some or all of the higher zones. Among the most characteristic fossils he might mention *Dibunophyllum Muirheadi*, *Carcinophyllum*, Clisiophyllid *Lithostrotion*, *Cyathophyllum Murchisonæ*, giant Productids, and *Lithostrotion* of *Martini-*, *junceum-*, and *irregulare*-types. No Zaphrentids had been recorded until near the top of the succession, where they took the place of the Clisiophyllids, the only brachiopod recorded being *Productus scabriculus*. *Cyathaxonia* had not yet been found; consequently, the exact horizon of these top beds must still remain undecided.

The PRESIDENT welcomed this fresh advance in our knowledge of the zonal succession of the Carboniferous Limestone. The occurrence of unexpected difficulties was usually a favourable symptom in the progress of investigation; and that, despite a general concordance between the results of workers in other regions, there was no lack of difficulties on this occasion was a matter for congratulation. No doubt Dr. Vaughan would know how to meet them. He agreed with Dr. Matley in regarding the nodular character of the limestone as a phenomenon in which pressure had played no part.

Dr. VAUGHAN thanked the President, and all those who had spoken, for their kind remarks, and for the lenient manner in which they had accepted a change of view in regard to the possible horizon of the Rush Conglomerate, demanded by the progress of faunal research. In reply to Mr. Lamplugh, he did not think that the determination of horizon was unduly influenced by knowledge of the stratigraphy, seeing that palæontology was only called in where stratigraphy was at fault. On account of the lateness of the hour, he hoped that those who had raised interesting questions with regard to the sequence in other areas would excuse an immediate reply.

Dr. MATLEY, in reply to an enquiry made by Dr. Hind, described the nature and source of the pebbles in the Rush and Lane Conglomerates, and stated, in response to a question from the President, that he had not observed any fragments of Lambay Porphyry.

With regard to Mr. Lamplugh's remarks, the thickness of the Rush Conglomerate-Group (500 feet) certainly was approximately correct; that of the Lane Conglomerate (200 feet) was arrived at on the assumption that these beds were laid down horizontally, an assumption that seemed to be justified by the fact that the dip of the conglomerates corresponded fairly well with that of the under- and overlying limestones. Both on stratigraphical and on palæontological grounds it seemed quite impossible that the Holmpatrick Limestone could be the same formation as the Lane Limestone repeated by folding. In conclusion, he thanked the Fellows for their kind reception of the paper.

25. *The* HORNBLENDIC ROCKS *of* GLENDALOUGH *and* GREYSTONES (COUNTY WICKLOW). BY JAMES ALLAN THOMSON, B.A., B.Sc., F.G.S. (Read June 17th, 1908.)

### CONTENTS.

|  | Page |
| --- | --- |
| I. Introduction | 475 |
| II. The Hornblendic Rocks of Glendalough | 476 |
| III. The ' Quartz-Mica Diorite ' Series | 485 |
| IV. The Contact-Phenomena of the Amphibolite | 491 |
| V. The Hornblendic Rocks of Greystones | 492 |

## I. INTRODUCTION.

THE two occurrences of hornblende-rocks of which this paper treats have been briefly described before, that of Glendalough under the name of amphibolite by Prof. Sollas,[1] that of Greystones as hornblende-picrite by Prof. Watts.[2] Both these authors felt that there were points of interest about these rocks which required fuller working-out; and when, at Prof. Sollas's suggestion, I commenced the study of the amphibolite, Prof. Watts kindly offered to delay the publication of an interesting communication which he had in hand on the picrite, so as to allow me to give a complete description of both rocks. In recording my thanks I have also to mention Prof. Cole, Mr. Seymour, and Dr. Flett, to whom I am indebted for facilities to examine sections in the Geological-Survey collections and for many fruitful suggestions.

Both these rocks are intrusive into Ordovician strata in the east of County Wicklow. This area has been described in detail in the Geological-Survey Memoir,[3] its igneous rocks are well known from the descriptions by Prof. Watts,[4] and its geological history has been discussed by Prof. Sollas.[5] The outstanding feature is, that into a thick mass of arenaceous and argillaceous sediments and inter-calated volcanic rocks of Cambrian and Ordovician age, there was intruded in laccolitic form an immense mass of granite. The intrusion of the Leinster Granite seems to be connected with the Caledonian system of folding: for its outcrop runs in a north-east to south-west direction for some 30 miles, from Killiney to New Ross. At a distance from the granite the Ordovician sediments have been ' contorted, plicated, overthrust, and cleaved into slates ' by the pressure of the folding; but in its neighbourhood there is

---

[1] ' On the Transformation of an Amphibolite into Quartz-Mica-Diorite' Rep. Brit. Assoc. 1893 (Nottingham) p. 765.

[2] *Ibid.* p. 767.

[3] J. B. Jukes & G. V. du Noyer, Explanations to accompany Sheets 121 & 130, Mem. Geol. Surv. Irel. 1869.

[4] A. McHenry & W. W. Watts, 'Guide to the Collections of Rocks & Fossils belonging to the Geological Survey of Ireland ' Dublin, 1895.

[5] ' The Geology of Dublin & its Neighbourhood ' Proc. Geol. Assoc. vol. xiii (1893–95) p. 91.

2 K

superimposed on this dynamic effect an intense contact-meta-morphism.  The altered rocks crop out for a distance of 2 miles from the granite, although below the surface the distance of the latter may be really much less.  The contact-zone consists of genuine mica-schists, while, near the granite, andalusite, garnet, and other minerals make their appearance.

After this uplift of the land by the early Caledonian folding, there appears to have been a land-surface until Carboniferous times. In the beach-deposits and conglomerates of this period are found angular and rounded fragments of the Leinster Granite, 'a proof of the exposure at this time of the granite from beneath its cover.' Following the deposition of the Carboniferous came the great earth-pressures of the Armorican folding, and Prof. Sollas believes that their effect may be traced in a cross-wrinkling of the Ordovician schists at Glendalough.  No other period of deposition or of mountain-building has left any important mark on the area here described, if we except the Glacial Epoch, to which in all proba-bility is due the greater part of the profound erosion that granite and schists have suffered and the deposition of widespread erratic material.

## II. The Hornblendic Rocks of Glendalough.

These form a small boss on the south side of Camaderry, a ridge that separates the Vale and Lake of Glendalough from the Valley of Glendassan.  The Vale of Glendalough has the characteristic U-shape that is associated with glacial and fluvioglacial erosion, and its sides are formed of cliffs of granite and schists, with large screes on the north side.  The amphibolite lies about half a mile east of the boundary between granite and schists, and almost touches the cliffs, but no trace of it can be found on the cliff-face.  That it is an intrusive igneous rock is amply proved by the zone of contact-alteration which it has induced in the surrounding sedimentaries.

From the great amount of shearing which the original rock has undergone in comparison with the granite, and from the fact that its hardened contact-zone has withstood the foliating action of the earth-pressures, there is no doubt that it is older than the granite. The relations of the two rocks are analogous to those of the intrusions of the Scottish Highlands, the amphibolite being com-parable with the pre-foliation intrusive rocks, and the granite with the newer granites.

The interest of the hornblendic rock lies in 'the remarkable change in character and composition which it undergoes on passing from the eastern to the western boundary.'  It passes from an 'amphibolite' to a 'quartz-mica-diorite.'  Prof. Sollas attributes this change to the metasomatic action of quartz-veins which traverse the schists in its neighbourhood.

A detailed microscopic examination has revealed a wonderful heterogeneity in so small a boss.  Five types of rock may be distinguished, forming two series:—hornblende-peridotite with passages to an amphibolite, a zoisite-amphibolite, an actinolite-rock, and the 'quartz-mica-diorite' series. All these rocks weather to immense rounded boulders which can seldom be in place. A few distant though strong joint-planes cross the more massive rock, but yield no evidence of shearing on their faces. Exact mapping is frustrated by the gradual passages between the different rocks, and by the jumbling of the boulders. The actinolite-rock is restricted to the boundary, and this is exposed only on the north-east and east sides. The 'diorite' is confined to the south-western corner of the boss, and the zoisite-amphibolite is found most abundantly between it and the amphibolite on the north. Each of these types will now be described in detail.

### (1) The Hornblende-Peridotite (fig. 1).

In hand-specimens, this rock is seen to consist almost entirely of large crystals of a greenish hornblende, on the cleavage-surfaces of which small, rounded, dull patches are apparent—the typical lustre-mottling of hornblende-peridotites. The crystals of hornblende

Fig. 1.—*Hornblende-peridotite from Glendalough, showing pœcilitic structure in hornblende (shaded) with tremolite-rims (unshaded).*

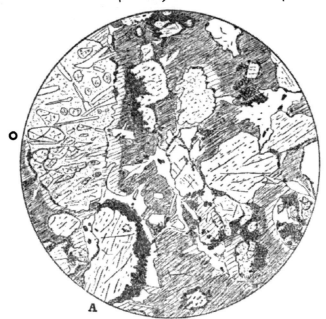

[O=Olivine ; A=Augite. The augite is surrounded by a resorption-margin of magnetite, and the olivine is largely converted into chlorite (colourless) spotted with magnetite. The magnification is 30 diameters.]

attain an inch and a half in their greatest diameter. Occasionally small scattered scales of mica appear on the cleavage-planes of the hornblende. The specific gravity is 3·04.

2 K 2

In sections the minerals that present themselves are apatite, magnetite, pyrite, olivine, augite, amphiboles of various colours, chlorite, and calcite. The augite and olivine are included poecilitically in large plates of hornblende.

Apatite is a very rare constituent, and is generally semi-opaque with fine inclusions.

The olivine has often the appearance of being remarkably fresh, but has really been destroyed in part. It has a slight reddish-brown hue and a higher relief than is usual, both these characters being due to a very fine schiller-structure. Examination under high powers reveals the presence of numerous, small, opaque inclusions arranged in parallel rows. The crystals sometimes show a tendency to idiomorphism, and the rows of inclusions are then parallel to the elongation. Where the crystal-form has been destroyed, the extinction parallel to the rows shows that they are arranged in a pinacoidal plane of the crystal. The olivine is penetrated by the usual cracks. It never shows any phenomena of serpentinization along the borders or cracks, but the latter are penetrated by fibres of chlorite. At the junctions of the cracks there are often rounded blotches of pyrite.

The augite is a colourless variety, with little trace of schiller-structure. The crystals are of small size, and are often twinned on (100). They are rarely idiomorphic. Generally they are included in hornblende, and are then, as a rule, bordered by a zone of magnetite-dust of variable thickness. The relations are suggestive of magmatic resorption of the augite, with formation of hornblende.

Several varieties of amphibole may be distinguished by colour, even within the same crystal; but a green hornblende is predominant. It forms large plates, seldom with regular boundaries, although small cross-sections of clearly-cut prisms are found. It is not markedly pleochroic in green and yellowish tones:—X pale yellow to colourless, Y yellow-green, Z bluish-green. The bi-refringence is fairly strong. The varieties in colour diverge in two directions, to a brownish hornblende and to a colourless tremolite.

The tremolite is often outgrown on the green hornblende in crystallographic continuity, the boundary sometimes appearing to correspond with crystallographic faces. The tremolite, as usual, shows higher interference-colours. There is, in addition, a considerable amount of tremolite occurring independently—for the most part in the form of plates, which resolve themselves under crossed nicols into irregular fibrous aggregates.

The brown hornblende is generally found in large plates, which show a transition to green. The pleochroism is: X brown, Y yellow-brown, Z brown with a lilac tinge. It is a common brown hornblende and not basaltic hornblende.[1] It seems probable

---

[1] Dr. Weinschenk ('Die Gesteinsbildenden Mineralien' Freiburg i. B., 1901, p. 105) distinguishes between common brown hornblende with little or no titanic acid and extinctions up to 18°, and basaltic hornblende with titanic acid up to 5 per cent. and extinctions up to 10°.

that the brown variety is original, and the green an alteration-product of the former.

A peculiar structure resembling coarse schillerization is common in the brown hornblende. It consists of blotches or fine rows of iron-ores crossing the cleavage-traces obliquely. Similar structures are found in the hornblende-peridotites of Molenick (East Cornwall) and of Penarfynydd (Anglesey).[1] It seems certainly in the former case to result from the magmatic resorption of the augite and its replacement by the hornblende, and may be ascribed to the same process here.

Chlorite-minerals occur in two habits. In the first their form in large plates with ragged edges suggests that of a mica, and an occasional increase of the birefringence strengthens the probability that the chlorite is replacing this mineral. The other is associated with olivine, which it penetrates in small laths, and represents with tremolite an alteration of that mineral. This chlorite is less pleochroic, but more birefringent than the other.

Mr. H. E. Clarke, B.A., of Jesus College, Oxford, has kindly analysed this rock with the following result:—

|  | I. | II. | III. | Mean. |
|---|---|---|---|---|
| $SiO_2$ ...........| 43·39 | 43·32 | 43·52 | 43·41 |
| $Al_2O_3$ ...........| 9·09 | ... | 9·12 | 9·10 |
| $Fe_2O_3$ ...........| 9·31 | ... | 9·46 | 9·38 |
| $FeO$ ..............| 7·25 | 7·26 | 7·24 | 7·25 |
| $MgO$ ..............| 16·80 | ... | 16·43 | 16·62 |
| $CaO$ ..............| 9·22 | 9·30 | 9·55 | 9·36 |
| $Na_2O$ ...........| 0·04 | ... | ... | 0·04 |
| $H_2O +$ .........| 3·45 | ... | ... | 3·45 |
| $H_2O -$ .........| 0·14 | ... | ... | 0·14 |
| $S$ ................| 0·56 | ... | ... | 0·56 |
| $CO_2$ ............| 0·09 | ... | ... | 0·09 |
| Totals ... | 99·34 | | | 99·40 |

Traces of oxides of titanium, chromium, manganese, and nickel, also of potash and fluorine, were noted. Phosphorus-pentoxide, zirconia, and chlorine were looked for, and found to be absent.

Between this type of rock, a somewhat sheared but still recognizable hornblende-peridotite, and the reconstituted amphibolite to be described later, there is every stage, the most interesting being an augite-amphibolite still retaining the evidence of pœcilitic structure (fig. 2, p. 480). It contains large plates of brown hornblende passing locally into the green, and crowded with small rounded patches consisting of tremolite grown in optical continuity with the enclosing plate. That these patches mostly represent olivine may be seen by tracing all the intermediate stages. Often confused rounded aggregates of chlorite, spotted with magnetite and pyrite, show a less complete alteration of the olivine, of which unaltered kernels may be observed. These aggregates are usually

[1] J. J. H. Teall, 'British Petrography' 1888, p. 97.

enclosed in green hornblende, with a small intervening zone of tremolite. Occasionally, instead of this massive replacement of olivine, that mineral is replaced by a tangled aggregate of extremely fine tremolite-needles (pilite of Prof. Becke). Talc, if present, occurs in extremely small quantity.

In some of these intermediate types, while there is no longer any unaltered olivine to be seen, augite is abundant and mica appears. It is feebly pleochroic, with strong birefringence and a low axial angle. Its resemblance to that in the Schriesheim rock and that in scheelite is very great. It forms plates which take their shapes

Fig. 2.—*Amphibolite from Glendalough, retaining the pœcilitic structure of tremolite within brown hornblende. (Magnified 30 diameters.)*

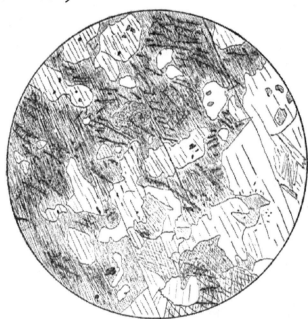

from the small hornblende-prisms around, and seems therefore to be of later formation and probably secondary. The plates are frequently penetrated by flakes of tremolite, and with them is associated occasionally a honey-coloured epidote in rounded granules. The mica is clearly in course of alteration to the chlorite above described (p. 479).

## (2) The Amphibolite (fig. 3, p. 481).

This type differs from the foregoing, in that the larger hornblende-crystals are separated one from the other by a finer-grained material of a lighter green, which is still formed mainly of hornblende but in smaller crystals. Specific gravity = 3·04.

In thin sections scarcely any trace of the pœcilitic structure is to be seen. The rock consists almost entirely of amphiboles, with a little apatite, clinozoisite, sphene, magnetite, and pyrite.

A prism of apatite was found in only one section. The sphene occurs abundantly, most often within crystals of feebly-coloured hornblende, in small isolated grains of more or less characteristic shape. Rarely it is moulded on the magnetite, which is present in small quantity. Pyrite is very plentiful, and is also confined almost entirely to the colourless amphibole.

The amphiboles exhibit less variety than in the previously-described types. They are mostly pale green to colourless, and

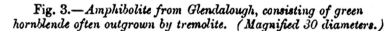

Fig. 3.—*Amphibolite from Glendalough, consisting of green hornblende often outgrown by tremolite. (Magnified 30 diameters.)*

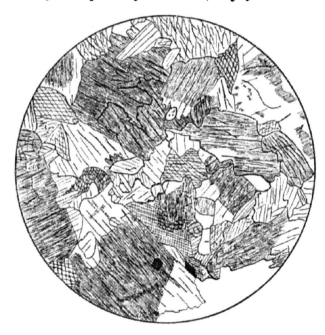

occasionally form a colourless border to a pleochroic green hornblende. The brown hornblende fails almost entirely, and the deeper green varieties occur only as remnants within the paler varieties. The larger crystals have, as a rule, good crystalline boundaries; the smaller ones form flakes penetrating aggregates of clinozoisite. Pleochroic halos round small colourless inclusions occur in the green hornblende. Often the interior of the larger plates is occupied by a ragged aggregate of twinned clinochlore.

In this series, then, we see a hornblende-peridotite containing augite and olivine pass by the alteration of these into a rock consisting almost entirely of hornblende, the hornblendefels of the

Germans. An analogous case of the derivation of an amphibolite from an olivinfels has been described by Dr. E. Dathe,[1] and furnishes Prof. Rosenbusch with his argument for the frequent derivation of hornblendcfels from peridotites.[2]

At Glendalough a further change has taken place, whereby sphene and pyrite separate out, and appear to deprive the hornblende of its pigment, so that it passes from a green or brown hornblende into a pale actinolite.

Most of the hornblende existing in the amphibolite and a good deal in the other types is clearly secondary, and from its idiomorphic forms would be called 'recrystallized' (fig. 3, p. 481). For such cases Prof. F. Becke has proposed the term idioblastic.[3] He points out that, in the formation of the crystalline schists, the relative idiomorphism is not to be considered as denoting the order in which they have formed, since in the secondary formation of minerals in a rock undergoing metamorphic reconstitution the resulting minerals differ in their power of crystal-growth. He specially instances the case of albite in the tonalite-gneiss of the Zillerthal,[4] which in the struggle for space is allotriomorphic towards the hornblende, but idiomorphic towards calcite and chlorite. The use of Prof. Becke's term seems conducive to clearness of description.

## (3) The Actinolite-Rock (fig. 4, p. 483).

In this type the hornblende, instead of being massive, is split up into numerous divergent fibres, often clustered together into tufts and radiating groups. There are no signs of schistosity. The rocks are in general light-coloured, and can often be seen to bear pale minerals of the epidote-group in druses. In places the rock carries a large proportion of chalcopyrite, and it is evident that it has been affected by the veins which traverse the adjacent schists. The specific gravity is 3·04.

In sections the rock is seen to consist almost entirely of actinolitic hornblende, with a small amount of zoisite, sphene, and sulphides. A single crystal of apatite was found.

The amphiboles vary in different specimens from a colourless tremolite to a pale actinolite. In types allied to the amphibolite the actinolite-fibres are grouped in parallel clusters, and seem then to represent original plates of hornblende. In the extreme types the parallel clusters are subordinate to the radial and sheaf-like bundles. Fine inclusions of sulphides are scattered throughout the

---

[1] ['Ueber Olivinfels von Habendorf bei Langenbielau in Schlesien'] Zeitschr. Deutsch. Geol. Gesellsch. vol. xxxviii (1886) p. 913.

[2] 'Elemente der Gesteinslehre' 2nd ed. (1901) p. 525.

[3] 'Ueber Mineralbestand & Struktur der kristallinischen Schiefer' C.R. IXème Congrès Géol. Internat. Vienna, 1903 (1904) p. 553.

[4] ['Vortrag über die krystallinen Schiefer der Alpen'] Tscherm. Min. & Petr. Mittheil. n. s. vol. xxi (1902) p. 356.

actinolite, and grains of sphene occur within the larger flakes
(fig. 4).

A pale-brown mica occurs sparingly, in small flakes inserted
between the actinolite-fibres or within the larger ones.    The
minerals of the epidote-group consist, for the most part, of granular
clinozoisite collected in irregular patches which are penetrated by
needles of actinolite.    But there is also a coloured mineral of

Fig. 4.—*Actinolite-rock from Glendalough, showing actinolite,
sphene, pyrite, and zoisite.   (Magnified 30 diameters.)*

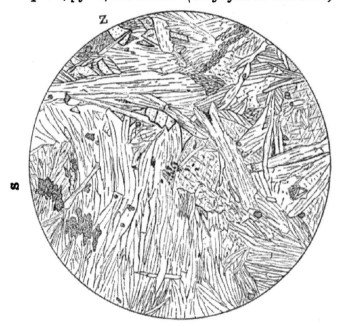

[Z=Zoisite ;   S=Sphene.]

rectangular form, exhibiting pleochroism from deep to pale brown,
with lateral outgrowths of clinozoisite, properties characteristic of
a l l a n i t e.   It has produced a pleochroic halo in the surrounding
actinolite.    Small halos round indeterminable grains are believed
to have the same origin.

### (4) The Zoisite-Amphibolite.

These rocks contain pœcilitic crystals of hornblende, enclosed in
a granular matrix which is white with zoisite.    Sulphides are
abundant.    The specific gravity is 3·00.

Within the amphibolite runs a vein, about an inch wide, of a
water-clear clinozoisite and a dull felspar.    The clinozoisite forms
stout prisms with square section, and well-defined crystal-faces
moulded by the felspar ($\frac{1}{8}$ inch diam. $\times$ $\frac{1}{2}$ inch).    Often the vein is

drusy, and minute crystals point into the cavities.  Sections of the
vein give good facilities for studying the microscopic characters of
clinozoisite (fig. 5).  It stands out clearly from the somewhat turbid
felspar, by reason of its higher refractive power.  The elongation is
parallel to the *b*-axis, as in epidote.  Most longitudinal sections
show numerous strongly-marked cleavages [parallel to C(001)], but
these are seldom very close.  They are crossed by strong but
irregular cracks like those in olivine.  Cross-sections parallel to
B (010) also show the cleavages, and when the crystal is twinned

Fig. 5.—*Clinozoisite-vein in amphibolite from Glendalough, showing
clinozoisite, hornblende, and sphene.  (Magnified 30 diameters.)*

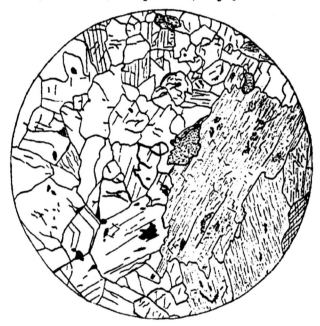

parallel to A (100), as frequently occurs, the cleavage-lines meet at
an oblique angle on the twinning-plane ($2\beta = 129°$ nearly), affording
a clear demonstration of the monoclinic nature of the mineral.
Longitudinal sections without cleavage-traces also occur, and these
must be parallel to C (001), and show twin lamellæ.  The birefringence is variable even in the same section, but the abnormal prussian-
blue tints of clinozoisite predominate over the yellows of iron-poor
epidote.  There is frequently a gradual passage between the two.
A zonal structure is often well marked, the clinozoisite occupying
the centre and the epidote the margins; but there is no constancy
in this order, and the mineral composition often varies in patches
not zonally distributed.

The felspar of the vein agrees in specific gravity and refractive
indices with albite.  A few actinolite-needles penetrate it.  The
vein has thus the character of a coarse saussurite.

The zoisite-amphibolite differs from the rocks already described, only by the greater proportion of the zoisite-minerals. Of these there are two. Besides separating off a colourless monoclinic zoisite from orthorhombic zoisite on the one hand, and from coloured or strongly birefringent epidote on the other, Dr. Weinschenk distinguishes two varieties of orthorhombic zoisite, according to the position of the plane of the optic axes. Zoisite $a$ gives anomalous blue interference-colours, zoisite $\beta$ normal pale-grey of the first order. The latter variety occurs somewhat plentifully in some sections with the clinozoisite. It has a superficial resemblance to apatite, from which it may be easily distinguished by the absence of cross-fracture, as well as by its biaxial character. Clear untwinned felspar, probably albite, is associated with it. These minerals are not restricted to aggregates lying between the hornblende-crystals, but also occur scattered throughout the poecilitic plates.

The hornblende is of the same general character as in the other rocks. It is mostly of the bleached type, full of separated sphene, and with only occasional remnants of green or brown. The idioblastic structure is not so well developed. Mica is more abundant than in any of the previous types, and is of the same pale colour. It forms jagged plates within the hornblende, and very often is elongated across the length of the latter.

The abundance of zoisite seems to point to a former content of felspar in this rock. The scarcity of albite and the absence of muscovite, which generally accompany zoisite in saussurite, further show that the felspar must have been very basic. The rock may have been a picrite.

### III. The 'Quartz-Mica-Diorite' Series.

This series of more acid rocks occurs in the south-western corner of the boss, as big boulders similar in size and shape to those of the other rocks. At one place, a vein was found penetrating the amphibolite. In appearance the rocks are much whiter, due to the presence of quartz and felspars. In the 'bladed type,' the hornblende is elongated into long greenish prisms, on the cleavage-faces of which a profusion of scales of a pale-brown mica may be seen.[1] A few boulders of a whiter colour, due to a larger proportion of quartz and felspar, contain hornblende with a more actinolitic habit and greener colour, and in addition numerous dodecahedra of a pale-red garnet. The specific gravities are variable, with a mean of 2·95. The geological relationships of these differences could not be made out.

These rocks are abnormal, both in mineral composition and in structure, and are conceived to be mixed rocks formed by the

[1] Prof. G. A. J. Cole ('On the Growth of Crystals in the Contact-Zone of Granite & Amphibolite' Proc. Roy. Irish Acad. vol. xxv, 1905, sect. B, p. 117) agrees with Prof. Sollas in attributing this rock to the action of acid veins on the amphibolite, and points out the stimulus given to recrystallization by the conditions of the interaction.

absorption of the amphibolite-series by an acid magma. The presence of acid veins in the adjoining schists was difficult to verify owing to the number of granite-erratics, and to the dense covering of fern, but Prof. Sollas has described their occurrence.

In section, the minerals identified are pyrite, ilmenite, garnet, apatite, sphene, clinozoisite, epidote, allanite, hornblende, mica, labradorite, and quartz. Of these the brown hornblende, clinozoisite, epidote, and in part the sphene, are xenocrysts: the other minerals being due to the absorption of basic material in the acid magma.

The key to the sequence of events is given by the apatite. This mineral occurs rarely in the peridotite and its variants, but is extraordinarily developed in some specimens of the rock under consideration. It can safely be assumed to belong to the intrusive magma, and proves that the intruding veins were not mere quartz-veins, but at least pneumatolytic apophyses of a plutonic magma, if not dykes of granitic material itself. The apatite occurs in long, often very slender prisms, occasionally in stouter and unusually large individuals. The cross-fracture is well-developed, and by movements along these planes the crystals are often bent and broken. It is enclosed most generally in the felspars, or in the quartz-felspar mosaic, but is also found within the garnet, the mica, and the radiating tufts of actinolite. It thus appears that the re-crystallization of the hornblende into actinolite, and the formation of mica and garnet are subsequent to the consolidation of the apatite.

Ilmenite is an occasional constituent in skeletal growths, generally within the actinolite. Sphene is much more abundant, with varying habit. Small granules are moulded on ilmenite and occasionally on clinozoisite. Larger independent crystals are often acicular, and occasionally have a habit resembling apatite. The sphene occurs in greatest abundance within actinolite and mica, or in their neighbourhood. It is occasionally developed in parallel needles, lying in the directions of cleavage of the mica-plates, but extending beyond their boundaries (fig. 8, p. 489).

The minerals of the epidote-group are colourless for the most part, and consist then of clinozoisite, with occasional yellow interference-colours denoting the passage to iron-poor epidote. They form large well-cleaved prisms, often penetrated by actinolite, and moulded by quartz. Such an association of well-crystallized zoisite and water-clear basic felspars is quite abnormal in an igneous rock (fig. 6, p. 487). Besides the bigger crystals, these minerals occur in a kind of graphic structure with felspar. Groups of small angular crystals are enclosed poecilitically in a large plate of labradorite. Each group in itself has a prismatic or somewhat rounded outline, and the individuals of the group are all in optical continuity. It is difficult to imagine a graphic intergrowth of zoisite or epidote and felspar. It seems rather probable that the larger prisms of these minerals have been attacked by the magma, but not totally dissolved, and the remaining skeletons included in the growing felspar-crystal. A similar inclusion of a partly-destroyed xenocryst is observed within the actinolite.

Besides these colourless minerals of the epidote-group, a brown allanite occurs in small quantity, with the usual outgrowth of clinozoisite. It has determined a pleochroic halo in the surrounding actinolite. Most of the pleochroic halos are found, however, round minute colourless grains which sometimes resemble apatite. These are mostly clinozoisite, but occasionally a core of allanite may be detected.

Fig. 6.—*The 'mixed rock,' Glendalough ; clinozoisite and actinolite lying in a matrix of quartz and felspar. (Magnified 30 diameters.)*

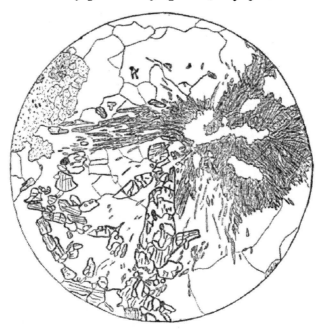

The garnet shows thoroughly idiomorphic outlines, and includes apatite, clinozoisite, biotite, and actinolite. The last two may, however, have penetrated along its cracks. There is no evidence to show that its presence is due to absorption of the schists, as Prof. Cole has suggested.[1]

The hornblende presents generally an actinolitic habit, and is green in colour. Even the large-bladed types are resolved in sections into numerous parallel fibres, while a sheaf-like splitting at the ends is universal. Elegant radial clusters of actinolite are common, and isolated fibres are found in the felspar, quartz, and garnet. An important exception to this habit occurs in a few large plates, which consist outside of fibrous actinolite as usual, but contain in their centre irregular remnants of brown hornblende with the peculiar striations already described. It is the same as

[1] Proc. Roy. Irish Acad. vol. xxv (1905) sect. B, p. 119.

that occurring in the peridotite, and proves incontestably that the brown hornblende is a xenocryst (fig. 7).

Fig. 7.—*The 'mixed rock,' Glendalough, showing xenocrysts of brown hornblende within actinolite, sphene, iron-ores, felspar (clear), mica, and chlorite (right-hand lower portion of the figure). (Magnified 30 diameters.)*

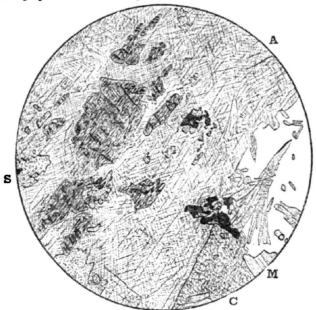

[S = Sphene ; A = Actinolite ; M = Mica ; C = Chlorite.]

A pale biotite, almost absent in some specimens, is extremely abundant in others. It shows pleochroism from brown to colourless, and a very low axial angle. Pleochroic halos are not so abundant as in the actinolite, but seem to be determined by the same mineral. The mica is never idiomorphic in habit, but consists of small allotriomorphic plates apparently moulded on hornblende, apatite, sphene, clinozoisite, quartz, felspar, and garnet. Its relation to the hornblende, included within the largest plates, and always most abundant around the actinolite-fans, bears out Prof. Sollas's suggestion that it has been derived from this mineral by the action of the intruding magma. A similar origin for the mica of hornblende-rocks has been described by many authors.

Although the mica is apparently moulded on quartz and felspar, it may not be posterior to these minerals, but may have been itself partly resorbed before their solidification. Skeletons of acicular sphene occur within many of the micas and extend beyond their margins, but are bounded beyond the mica-crystals by parallel planes on which the felspars have been moulded (fig. 8, p. 489). This suggests that the mica once had a greater extension. There is, however, no border of iron-oxide to bear witness to a magmatic resorption.

In the types poor in quartz, the felspars form large plates, with coarse albite-twinning and very well-developed pericline-twinning. A zonary structure is rare. Where quartz is abundant a clear mosaic of smaller grains occurs, but often large plates of felspar

Fig. 8.—*The 'mixed rock,' Glendalough : corroded crystals of biotite (penetrated by acicular sphene), actinolite, and apatite lie in a matrix of felspars.   (Magnified 30 diameters.)*

are bordered with a graphic intergrowth. The regularity of this is disturbed by the crushing that the rock has undergone. All the felspars have refractive indices higher than quartz, and the extinction-angles show that the chief species is labradorite.

I made the following percentage analysis of one of the most acid types :—

| | | |
|---|---|---|
| $SiO_2$ | .......................... | 59·78 |
| $TiO_2$ | | |
| $P_2O_5$ | ..................... | 16·43 |
| $Al_2O_3$ | | |
| $Fe_2O_3$ | .......................... | 0·92 |
| FeO | .......................... | 6·84 |
| MgO | .......................... | 2·94 |
| CaO | .......................... | 9·15 |
| $K_2O$ | .......................... | 2 36 |
| $Na_2O$ | .......................... | 1·44 |
| $H_2O+$ | ..................... | 0·93 |
| $H_2O-$ | ..................... | 0·12 |
| | Total ............ | 100·91 |

The high percentage of lime shows that the absorbed material came from the zoisite-amphibolite rather than from the peridotite. The abnormality of the composition, compared with that of a normal igneous rock having the same silica-percentage, consists in the high value for lime and the low value in alkalies. Such an abnormality is, as Mr. Harker has pointed out, to be expected in a mixed igneous rock.[1] His other conclusion, however, that mixed rocks are of nearly the same age, since absorption only goes on when the earlier-formed rock is still hot, does not seem to be borne out in this case. The occurrence of zoisite-xenocrysts shows that the picrite was altered to a rock resembling a crystalline schist in composition, before absorption took place.

The mixed igneous rocks which have attracted the most general attention are those of Skye and Carlingford, where in each case a granophyre has invaded a gabbro of nearly the same age. But, since the majority of basic igneous rocks are represented by amphibolites in the crystalline schists, and since the latter were formed in the deeper levels of the crust where invasions of granite are abundant, one would expect that rocks formed by the admixture of amphibolite and granite would be the commoner group. A search through the literature of the subject shows that they are common. Dr. C. Callaway has described the absorption of dark diorite by granite in the Malverns.[2]    Prof. G. A. J. Cole has described many cases of interaction of granite and amphibolite in Donegal, giving rise to rocks which he has compared with quartz-diorites and hornblende-granites.[3]    Tourmaline-bearing amphibolites are found in the Tyrol[4] and in the Italian Alps.[5]    Hornblende-granulites are formed on the invasion of eclogite-amphibolites by granulites in the Aiguilles Rouges.[6]    Somewhat similar phenomena are described by Prof. L. Duparc & Dr. F. Pearce from the Urals[7]; and in Finland Dr. Sederholm has described absorption of many varieties of crystalline schists on a large scale.[8]    These few examples serve to show the widespread nature of the phenomena, and permit us to recognize among mixed rocks a distinctive group formed by the absorption of amphibolites by granitic magmas.

---

[1] 'Igneous Rock-Series & Mixed Igneous Rocks' Journ. Geol. Chicago, vol. viii (1900) p. 389.

[2] Quart. Journ. Geol. Soc. vol. xlv (1889) p. 496.

[3] Proc. Roy. Irish Acad. vol xxv (1905) sect. B, pp. 119 et seqq.

[4] B. Lindemann, 'Petrographische Studien in der Umgebung von Sterzing in Tirol' Neues Jahrb. Beilage-Band xxii (1906) p. 536.

[5] W. Salomon, 'Ueber Alter, Lagerungsform & Entstehungsart der periadriatischen granitisch-körnigen Massen' Tscherm. Min. & Petr. Mittheil. n. s. vol. xvii (1897) p. 274.

[6] E. Joukowsky, 'Su les Éclogites des Aiguilles Rouges' Arch. des Sc. Phys. & Nat. Genève, vol. xiv (1902) pp. 151-71 & 261-81.

[7] 'Recherches géologiques & pétrographiques sur l'Oural du Nord' Mém. Soc. Phys. & Hist. Nat. Genève, vol. xxiv (1905) p. 484.

[8] 'Ueber eine archäische Sedimentformation im südwestlichen Finland' Bull. Comm. Géol. Finlande, no. 6 (1899).

### IV. THE CONTACT-PHENOMENA OF THE AMPHIBOLITE.

The Ordovician sediments into which the peridotite was intruded can be studied for a few feet only on the north-eastern side of the boss and for a few yards on the eastern side. Beyond these limits the ground is lower and covered with turf and fern, and it seems probable that the rocks are softer. When the ground can be studied again at a distance, it consists of silvery phyllites and mica-schists, with occasional lenticles of quartz-schist, the metamorphism of which is ascribed by Prof. Sollas to the contact-action of the Leinster Granite.

The contact-rocks along the north-eastern margin of the boss present a peculiar gnarled appearance. No lines of bedding can be traced for more than a few inches without interruption. There are in general three kinds of bands, which probably correspond to differences in deposition. These are bands of granular quartz, dense brown bands which prove to consist of minute garnets, and layers which are characterized by the predominance of stout plates of biotite set at right angles to the bedding. The interruptions consist in part of anastomosing veins of quartz, garnet, or biotite; and in part of a sudden loss of the banded character, and its replacement by a confused aggregate of coarse and fine patches of the same minerals. The junction of these rocks with the actinolite-rock is sharp.

In sections, biotite, muscovite, magnetite, chlorite, garnets, quartz, and occasionally felspar, may be recognized.

The biotite forms the largest crystals. Longitudinal and basal sections possess highly irregular outlines (fig. 9, p. 492). It encloses garnet, muscovite, magnetite, and occasionally quartz, and is moulded ophitically on these minerals. Pleochroic halos are abundant, many of them round zircon.

The biotite is partly altered into a pale chlorite, which contains, besides the above-mentioned inclusions of the biotite, large blotches of magnetite. The alteration proceeds along the cleavage in an exceedingly-regular manner, so that the biotite seems to be intergrown with chlorite. The halos are preserved in the chlorite, retaining their greater pleochroism and a higher birefringence than the surrounding mineral.

The muscovite is in much smaller individuals than the biotite, generally in rectangular sections, frequently twinned, and grouped in varying ways. In some layers the muscovite forms a felted mass, almost to the exclusion of quartz and garnet.

The crystals of garnet are often so small, that they may lie wholly within the surfaces of a thin section; and their perfect idiomorphism may be seen by focussing. They seem to be free from all inclusions but iron-ores.

The quartz is rarely so fine-grained that the crystal-boundaries cannot be recognized. They are generally polygonal or circular, and never show the interlocking of a dynamically-formed schist.

The contact-rocks on the eastern side of the boss are more regular in appearance than those just described. The banding by the garnets is quite parallel and continuous. The mineral composition is, however, the same. In one rock an acid plagioclase was found in addition: it possesses highly-irregular boundaries, and is full of inclusions.

Fig. 9.—*Biotite-muscovite-garnet hornfels at the contact with peridotite, Glendalough, showing biotite (in process of alteration into chlorite), garnet, and magnetite, in a ground-mass of quartz and muscovite. (Magnified 30 diameters.)*

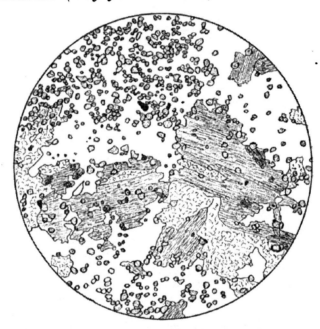

These rocks can best be described as **hornfels**. The contact-phenomena round the amphibolite do not greatly differ from those round the granite, except that the welding of the rocks has been more complete in the amphibolite-aureole. Round the granite andalusite is very abundant, but this is due probably to original differences of composition in the sediments. Tourmaline is also found.

### V. The Hornblendic Rocks of Greystones.

Prof. Watts described in 1893 a dyke of hornblende-peridotite traversing the Ordovician rocks on the coast at Greystones. My material was collected from two parallel dykes, a few hundred yards south of the breakwater. Mr. Seymour informs me that he knows of a third in the harbour. It seems probable that it was from this that the sections in the Geological-Survey collection were made.

The two dykes that I examined lie practically in the bedding-planes of the Ordovician rocks, which strike E. 30° N. to W. 30° S. and dip about 70° northwards. The dykes are each about 20 feet thick, and are separated by 30 feet of sedimentary deposits. They have suffered considerably from crushing, are phacoidal on the margins, and show asbestos on the joint-planes. The sea has been able to erode the centres of the dykes, so that they cause small indentations of the coast.

The appearance of the rocks is very different from that of the Glendalough series, although they seem to have had a similar history. The lustre-mottling is not exhibited on so large a scale, and the colour is much greener. There is a similar impregnation with sulphides. In both dykes there is present a reddish rock, with felspar and a bladed type of hornblende. Veins of this rock may be found traversing the normal peridotite.

Microscopic examination shows that a transformation from peridotite to amphibolite has gone on, as at Glendalough, but with a greater development of talc.

The sections of least-altered peridotite (Survey-slide, No. 658) show pseudomorphs of idiomorphic olivine enclosed in pœcilitic plates of brownish-green and green hornblende. The olivine seems to have predominated over the hornblende. No traces of augite are seen, although a few colourless patches within the hornblende may represent it. Mica is very rarely present within the hornblende, and apatite occurs only in small quantity.

The pseudomorphs after olivine preserve in many cases the characteristic form of the original crystals, and are traversed by strings of magnetite and pyrite along the irregular cracks of the olivine. Set perpendicularly to these cracks is the usual zone of serpentine. Complete serpentinization is not, however, the rule. The interior is usually filled with tremolite, which gives so many sections with straight extinction and parallel cleavages that it was at first mistaken for iddingsite. It has sometimes a regular disposition with regard to the olivine. Besides the pseudomorphs retaining the olivine-shapes, there are irregular areas of the section which consist of a finely-granular serpentinous aggregate crowded with small, idioblastic, green hornblende-crystals, and occasionally penetrated by fibres of chlorite and tremolite. Talc in fine flakes and calcite in irregular grains lie scattered through the aggregates.

The next stage might be termed a talc-amphibolite. The former presence of olivine can only be detected by the occurrence of colourless patches of tremolite within the hornblende, and by the abundance of talc. Serpentine is rare, but chlorite becomes more abundant. The hornblende is frequently outgrown by tremolite. Sphene occurs sparingly, and zoisite has been detected in only one slide.

In the sheared rock from the walls of the dykes, the large plates of hornblende are broken up to small ragged pieces, often with wavy fibrous outgrowths of tremolite. The green hornblende is partly replaced by tremolite and ores. There is a little sphene. The pœcilitic structure has entirely disappeared. Talc is practically absent, but there is a great development of chlorite, in which small elliptical grains of quartz are abundant. There is no well-marked parallel structure, but the fibres of tremolite are often bent, and the chlorite winds among the amphiboles like the ground-mass of an augen-gneiss. Undulose extinctions are common in most of the minerals.

The felspathic rocks found within both dykes are composed chiefly of a pale-green hornblende, an acid plagioclase, and a greenish-yellow epidote. The hornblende is often in the form of elongated idiomorphic crystals, showing in cross-sections the *b*-pinacoid (010) besides the prisms. Twinning parallel to (010) is common. The frequent occurrence of tremolite-patches within the hornblende seems, however, to relate it to that of the amphibolite. The force exerted by growing crystals, which has formed the subject of experimental investigations by Messrs. G. F. Becker & A. L. Day,[1] is often exemplified in these rocks by the manner in which calcite and chlorite have forced apart the hornblende along its cleavages. Granular epidote is very abundant, and occasionally the mineral is developed in radiating aggregates. Apatite is more abundant than in the peridotite, and forms fine needles resembling sillimanite in habit.

All these minerals lie in a mosaic of felspar and quartz. The felspar is twinned on the albite-law, and seems to be mostly oligoclase. Quartz is seldom abundant, and forms local graphic intergrowths with the felspar.

The relation of this felspathic rock to the peridotite cannot be gleaned from the evidence so clearly as at Glendalough. That it is also an intrusive acid vein which has partly absorbed the peridotite is possible, and is suggested by the tremolite-patches within the green hornblende. The rocks differ from the mixed rocks of Glendalough in the absence of mica, garnet, zoisite, and sphene, in the abundance of epidote, and in the more acid nature of the felspar.

Peridotites occur as common differentiation-products with much more acid rocks in Scotland. It is possible that the intrusive vein was thus related to the Greystones peridotite.

## DISCUSSION.

The PRESIDENT commented on the importance of the results obtained by the Author, which seemed to afford conclusive proof of the transformation of a highly-basic rock by the introduction of granitic material. Observations in the field had left some doubt in his own mind as to the precise nature of the intrusive veins in this

[1] 'The Linear Force of Growing Crystals' Proc. Wash. Acad. Sci. vol. vii (1905) p. 283.

case, although he had expressly mentioned the presence of potash-felspar as one of their constituents.    It was satisfactory to find that this point had been definitely decided.    It was to be hoped that the facts now recorded might prove to have some bearing on the formation of many quartz-hornblende schists.

Prof. W. W. WATTS stated that he had studied one of the rocks described, under the direction of the President, and the other as an officer of the Geological Survey.    The most important point that he had discovered in connexion with the Greystones rock was the alteration of the olivine.    At first olivine passes into serpentine, then into tremolite, and lastly the tremolites grow at the expense of the containing hornblende, until they become idiomorphic, the original outlines of the olivine having been entirely destroyed.

Mr. A. GIBB MAITLAND drew attention to the resemblance between the geology of the district and certain of the mining features of Western Australia.

The AUTHOR thanked the Fellows for their patient hearing of a somewhat technical subject, and for the compliments paid to his work.    The only phenomenon that he had remarked comparable to that described by Prof. Watts was the idioblastic development of hornblende.    With regard to the possibility of economic deposits, he referred to the impregnation of sulphides seen in the rocks of both areas, and in similar rocks in Donegal described by Prof. Cole.    He welcomed the President's suggestion of a ' shelter-spot,' especially as it did not invalidate the argument for the age of the amphibolite.    Mr. Seymour had described one on the west of the Leinster Granite.    His experience of quartz-hornblende-schists was too small for him to offer an opinion as to the President's suggestions.

26. *On the* OCCURRENCE *of* FOOTPRINTS *in the* LOWER SANDSTONES *of
the* EXETER DISTRICT. By ARTHUR WILLIAM CLAYDEN, M.A.,
F.G.S., Principal of the Royal Albert Memorial University
College, Exeter. (Read June 17th, 1908.)

[PLATE LI.]

I HAVE long felt, for reasons which need not be detailed here, that
the Red Rock Series of the Exeter district was mainly of subaërial
origin, the breccias and associated sands having accumulated on a
strip of country bounded on the west by high hills carved out of
the folded Culm, while a large sheet of water lay to the east.
The frequent indications of aqueous deposit would be due to
variations in the level of the water such that it occasionally over-
spread much of the littoral region, and rearranged and levelled the
subaërial accumulations.

Such a district seems to be exactly suited for the preservation of
the footprints of any animals which might descend from the hills
to wander over the low-lying sandy shores. I have, therefore,
repeatedly searched the surfaces of blocks freshly fallen from the
cliffs near Exmouth, where the 'Lower Marls with occasional
Sandstones' reach the coast, and every other section that I could
find in which the natural surfaces were laid bare.

Sun-cracks on the surfaces of thin lenticular seams of marl are
often to be found, as well as other signs of the supposed conditions.
The upper part of some of the sandstones weathers out in a curious
way, leaving an irregular network of concretionary structures,
strongly suggestive of a matted network of underground stems,
such as those of the sand *Carex* or the recent Equisetaceæ. But
nothing of undoubtedly organic origin has been found.

Away from the coast suitable exposures are rare. Roadside
cuttings and sand-pits do not show the bedding-surfaces, and the
sand is generally much too loose to give impressions.

Hard sandstone has been uncovered close to Exeter in one of the
large brickfields, but its surface appears to be smooth. With this
exception, the brecciated marls in which these pits are excavated
are full of a confused mass of volcanic débris in so advanced
a state of decomposition that it is most unlikely that organic
remains would be preserved.

The sandstones classed as 'Lower Sandstones' in the Geological
Survey-map have always seemed to promise best, especially where
they abut upon the Culm, but suitable exposures are very rare.
Some of the beds afford excellent building-material which has been
used occasionally, but the quarries have been long abandoned and
are now greatly overgrown.

Three of these old quarries are in the sandstone-district between
the Culm promontory of Stoke Hill and the Culm inlier of Asholyst
Forest. All parts of the sand are thus but a short distance from

the hills, among the rocks of which any contemporary animals would be most likely to find congenial lurking-places.

Two of the quarries lie close together, about half a mile north-east of the village of Broadclyst, and it is probably the more northern of these of which Dr. Shapter records as yielding some specimens of ripple-marked stones, tracings of annelids, 'the claw-like footmarks of two species of small crustaceans and obscure impressions of other objects (*Posidonia*).' [1] This last suggestion opened up a possibility that the mantle of sandstone might have been penetrated, and some of the underlying Culm have been reached at a spot where basement Culm happened to come up. I have therefore examined the quarry and rubbish, but failed to find a single fragment of Culm-rock of any kind. Whatever the 'claw-like footmarks' may have been, they must have belonged to the 'Lower Sandstones.'

The third quarry in this district lies nearer to Stoke Hill, about a third of a mile east-north-east of Poltimore Church. It is mentioned in the Geological-Survey Memoir [2] as follows:—

'At about a quarter of a mile east of Poltimore a large quarry, said to have been worked to a depth of 100 feet from the surface, exposed evenly-laminated brown and blackish rock-sand on brown and reddish sandstone in layers averaging 2 inches thick in the upper 4 feet, 3 to 7 inches in the next 5 feet, and below that attaining to a foot in thickness. A workman stated that the bottom beds were thick, and had been used in the construction of bridges over the London and South-Western Railway, as the rock hardens on exposure. The upper beds are used for hedging, etc. The surfaces of the laminæ in the brown and blackish rock are stained red. The dip appeared to be N. 40° W. at an angle of 17°. Unless the planes are due to false bedding on a large scale, it appears probable that the high dip is due to the proximity of a fault.'

This quarry has been recently reopened by a firm of stone-masons, Messrs. Collard & Sons, of Exeter, who are raising excellent stone in some quantity.

Having heard that work had been recommenced, and bearing in mind Dr. Shapter's record for a spot only a mile away, as well as the general suitability of the place for the preservation of organic traces, it was arranged that the quarry should be visited on May the 9th by our College Field-Club. On reaching the excavation, it was seen that the method of working is conceived on correct principles. The stone is lifted in large slabs, stratum after stratum, so that considerable areas of the original surfaces are laid bare.

No traces, however, even of ripple-marks could be detected on the extensive surfaces exposed in the quarry, and the workmen reported in answer to enquiries that they had never seen any marks upon the stone. But the smooth curving surfaces were so strongly suggestive of accumulation on a gently shelving shore (some of the dip being probably original), that I felt it impossible to be satisfied without further search, and turned to examine a large quantity of stone which stood stacked not far away, awaiting removal. In a few minutes I was rewarded by finding a slab with undoubted

[1] 'The Climate of the South of Devon' 2nd ed. (1862) p. 87.
[2] 'The Geology of the Country around Exeter' 1902, p. 28.

footprints of an Amphibian or Reptilian type, and after I had shown this to the members of the Club, two more pairs of prints, of a similar character, were found by one of the students.

A few days later I made a more careful search than had been possible on the former occasion, and found numerous less perfect marks apparently due to a larger animal, and a track consisting of 30 pairs of footprints crossing a large slab.

As these sandstones are locally the base of the whole New Red Series, and are closely related to the volcanic rocks and breccias usually classed as Permian, the occurrence of organic records among them assumes a greater interest than would have been the case if they had been well up in the Trias. They are certainly far below the beds in which Dr. Johnston-Lavis found his *Labyrin-thodon*[1] and those in which Mr. Whitaker discovered a jaw of *Hyperodapedon*.[2]

It seems best, therefore, to announce the fact at once, without waiting to accumulate more material.

Five specimens have been secured, and three of them, A, B, & C, may well have been made by the same individual. Specimen A shows detached prints, some parts of the track having been obliterated. They are sufficient to prove that the animal had three large toes and one small one, and was therefore not very different from the creature which made the more perfect tracks to be described later on. The tracks agreed in size with two other prints, B & C, which do not show sufficient detail to tell much about the creature that made them. In both cases the sand was evidently loose, and rather too dry to give a good impression; and in more than one print it is possible to see plainly where the sand broke loose at the side of the hole, and flowed into it as the animal lifted its foot. In both specimens the fore and hind feet seem to have been of much the same size, and to have sunk almost equally deeply into the sand. They agree also in a peculiar way: the prints of the right feet are much deeper than those of the left. One of the limbs of the left side, apparently the fore limb, appears to have been carried in such a way that it only touched the ground once, and then quite gently, although the slabs show several places where it should have been impressed. The one gentle touch happens to have left faint indications of four toes, and is the only print in which they are preserved at all. The length of the stride varies from a maximum of 30 to a minimum of 22 centimetres.

The other two slabs, D & E, show prints which, as the measurements suggest, must have been made by smaller and different individuals. The first found was D, which shows five or six pairs of footmarks, two of which are on its extreme edge.

The animal was digitigrade, neither manus nor pes showing any sign of a foot-pad. The length of stride is 12 centimetres; and, measuring from the centre of each print to the median line, the distance is in all cases about 3 cm. The prints of the manus,

[1] Quart. Journ. Geol. Soc. vol. xxxii (1876) p. 274.
[2] *Ibid.* vol. xxv (1869) p. 152.

which fall slightly in front of those of the pes, are comparatively
faint, each digit being represented by a small round dot, as if only
the tips of the digits had touched the ground, and then quite
lightly. The pes, on the contrary, has sunk deeply in, and the
marks of each toe are elongated ovals—somewhat sharper in front.
Evidently the centre of gravity of the animal must have been
situated in the pelvic region.

Both limbs had four digits, the one farthest from the median line
being smaller than the other three. If this may be regarded as
the fifth digit, then 4 was the longest, 3 slightly shorter, and
2 again slightly shorter. Some of the prints only show the marks
of the three longest digits.

Although there is so much difference in the weight carried by
them, the manus seems to have been of much the same size as
the pes.

There is no trace on any of the slabs of a tail having dragged
upon the sand; but it is difficult to understand how the centre of
gravity can have been so far back, unless the head and fore part
of the body had been counterpoised by some such appendage.

The longest and much the most perfect track is that which I
have called E. This runs along the length of a large stone which
Messrs. Collard & Sons most readily cut from a much larger slab.
The track (which is a cast) is about 1·5 metres long, and contains
thirty pairs of prints, many of which are quite sharply defined.

The animal had all the characters of the last described, except
that the digits 5 and 2 were nearly equal, and that the creature
was somewhat smaller. Its full stride was 9 centimetres, and the
centres of manus and pes were only 2 cm. out of the median line.

The print of the manus generally falls about 1 cm. in front of
that of the pes, but the spacing is irregular, and towards the end
of the track the animal evidently paused for a moment, as if
hesitating. There is no indication of the small digit having diverged
from the others, but 4, 3, and 2 do diverge slightly inwards towards
the median line.

The track shows that, as the animal walked, it sometimes threw
nearly all its weight on the right limbs, sometimes on the left.
This cannot be an illusion due to partial obliteration, nor can it be
due to variations in the texture of the sand, because the prints are
uniformly sharp. In two cases the left manus has only left a slight
mark of the two longest toes, and in one case it has made no mark
at all. The corresponding marks of the right limbs are particularly
deep. Possibly the centre of gravity may have swayed from side to
side with the movements of the head or tail.

In no case is there anything to suggest either claws, a sole to
the foot, or a fifth digit. The prints do not resemble any of those
figured in the reports of the British Association Committee now at
work on the Flora and Fauna of the Trias, nor any others at once
accessible. They are least unlike the toe-marks of some animals
which are classed as Cheirotheroid, but differ from them in the
absence of a divergent digit, the absence of anything like the palm

of the hand or sole of the foot, and the fact that the feet were not brought into the median line in the act of walking. They suggest rather a primitive form of short-bodied animal, which was beginning to rely upon three toes of the hind limb to do most of the work of locomotion.

The rock is a red sandstone which hardens on exposure, two tests giving 1·81 and 1·93 tons per inch as the crushing strength. It is mainly composed of grains of quartz, some of which are very perfectly rounded. An analysis communicated to me by Messrs. Collard & Sons shows 72·27 per cent. of silica, 8·62 per cent. of lime, 4·94 per cent. of magnesia, and 12 per cent. of carbon-dioxide and moisture.

The surfaces are sometimes slightly ripple-marked, and the large slab which carries E is traversed by a series of dark curving lines, which look like lines of fine dark dust washed up as the water gently overflowed a thin stratum of wind-blown dust by which the footprints had been covered and fixed.

As work proceeds the quarry will be carefully watched, and if the stone meets with a sufficient demand to justify extensive operations, there is every reason to hope that numerous traces of animal-life may be procured.

The lessees are fully alive to the scientific interest of such remains, and have given every facility, for which I must express my thanks to them, as well as for presenting all the specimens to our local Museum.

## EXPLANATION OF PLATE LI.

This represents about two-thirds of the entire slab E. The light should come from the top of the page. The 'length of stride' is the distance between two successive prints of the same foot.

## DISCUSSION.

The PRESIDENT welcomed this addition to our knowledge of the Red Rocks of Devon, and trusted that the identification of the fossil footprints might assist in the correlation of the deposits in which they occurred.

Mr. WHITAKER suggested that there seemed to be a general con-sensus of opinion, that the beds among which these footprints occurred were possibly of Permian age.

The AUTHOR replied that the beds in which the prints occurred were considerably below the Budleigh-Salterton Bed, being separated therefrom by some hundreds of feet of sands and marls. He had not referred to Hitchcock's work on the Connecticut footprints, having been so far unable to make anything like a thorough search for records of similar remains. He believed that the chief reason for assigning the beds to Permian time was the fact of their close relation to the Exeter lavas, and a reluctance to suppose that volcanic activity persisted into the Trias. In conclusion, he thanked the Fellows for their reception of the paper.

27. *The* BASIC INTRUSION *of* BARTESTREE, *near* HEREFORD. By Prof. SIDNEY HUGH REYNOLDS, M.A., F.G.S. (Read June 17th, 1908.)

[PLATE LII—MICROSCOPE-SECTIONS.]

CONTENTS.

|                                                    | Page |
|----------------------------------------------------|------|
| I. Introduction, and Field-Relations               | 501  |
| II. The Altered Rocks                              | 501  |
| III. General Relations of the Intrusive Rocks      | 503  |
| IV. Description of the Intrusive Rocks             | 503  |
| V. Conclusion                                      | 510  |

## I. INTRODUCTION, AND FIELD-RELATIONS.

THE field-relations of the basic intrusion of Lowe's-Hill Quarry near Bartestree were fully described by Murchison,[1] but, although the dyke has been several times mentioned by later geologists[2] no detailed account has yet been given of its structure. The dyke is of considerable interest, both from its own character and from the alteration to which it gives rise in the Old Red Sandstone. It has a thickness of about 35 feet, and strikes in an east-north-easterly direction through the Old Red marls and sandstones which here lie almost horizontally. As represented in the 1-inch Geological-Survey map, the dyke has a length of about half a mile, striking across the road which leads southwestwards from Bartestree, and extending from about the middle of Tidnor Wood on the south-west to near Bartestree Convent on the north-east. At present, however, the only exposures are at Lowe's-Hill Quarry and for a short space immediately to the south-west. No trace of trap could be found west of the road; and, although fairly abundant débris occurs in Tidnor Wood, it appears to be derived entirely from Old-Red-Sandstone rocks.

The Lowe's-Hill rock, though not now worked, has formerly been largely quarried; and a long cutting has resulted, the sides of which are formed by Old Red sandstone and marl, while the trap is exposed at the end.

## II. THE ALTERED ROCKS.

(a) North of the trap.—On the northern side of the cutting, an undulating line, fairly easily followed up the face of the cliff, marks the edge of the intrusion. Against this strikes the Old Red, consisting of alternating bands of sandstone and shale, both

[1] 'Silurian System' 1839, pp. 185–86.
[2] J. Phillips, Mem. Geol. Surv. vol. ii, pt. i (1848) p. 180; H. E. Strickland, Quart. Journ. Geol. Soc. vol. viii (1852) p. 384; R. Dixon, Trans. Woolhope Nat. Field-Club, 1867 (1868) p. 180; & J. D. La Touche, *ibid.* 1891 (1892) pp. 166–68.

considerably metamorphosed. At a distance of a few feet, however, from the edge of the intrusion, a fault passes obliquely up the quarry-face and is marked by a band of breccia. The presence of this fault does not interrupt the progressive metamorphism of the Old Red, this probably indicating that it is of earlier date than the intrusion. The fault-plane apparently forms the northern face of the quarry for some 40 yards, but the exposures are very bad here, the rocks being much obscured by talus and brambles. At the end of this ill-exposed portion the northern face of the quarry has been cut back some 10 feet from the fault-line, exposing a section of Old Red marl and sandstone, the lower beds of the marl being thrown into slight undulations. The rock seen at this portion of the quarry-face (which, owing to the cutting-back, lies at a distance of some 18 feet from the edge of the dyke) is unaltered, except that the prevalent red colour of the marl is more than usually mottled with yellow. A few feet nearer the dyke, however, the marls begin to show signs of alteration; the red coloration disappears; and the rock becomes at first in places pale yellow, but in the main hard and purplish-grey with yellow spots and patches, the appearance of which was suggestive of dolomite. They proved, however, on chemical examination to be of not very definite mineralogical composition, consisting mainly of silicate of alumina and carbonate of lime, with only a subordinate quantity of carbonate of magnesia.[1] Were it not for its softness, a hand-specimen of the prevalent grey rock might, as was noticed by Murchison, at first sight be taken for an igneous rock. Microscopical examination of the altered marls showed small grains of quartz and flakes of mica with much iron-staining, but did not disclose any facts of importance. The sandstone does not commence to show signs of alteration at so great a distance from the dyke as does the marl; but, as the line of contact with the trap is approached, the sandstone and marl are strongly metamorphosed, the marl becoming very hard and splintery, while the sandstone loses its red colour and is rendered very hard and grey. Microscopical examination of this altered sandstone shows some interesting contact-phenomena (Pl. LII, fig. 6), the quartz-grains being corroded and the felspars recrystallized. Mr. Harker informs me that he is familiar with this type of metamorphism in the Torridon Sandstone of Rum, and has described it in the Geological-Survey memoir on the ' Geology of the Small Isles of Inverness-shire '[2] now in the press.[3]

(b) South of the trap.—On the southern side of the quarry, where a thickness of about 12 feet of altered rock is exposed, the contact-phenomena differ somewhat from those on the northern side, as the sandstone is far less in evidence than the marl. The latter rock, however shows alteration into a hard grey material

---

[1] I am indebted to my colleague, Mr. O. C. M. Davis, B.Sc., for this information.

[2] P. 13.

[3] Published subsequently to the reading of this paper.

with pale spots and patches, which partly consist of epidote and, as was noted by Murchison, have a superficial resemblance to amygdules. The alteration is strongly marked, right up to the edge of the cutting at the south-western end near the trap; but farther north-eastwards, where the cutting widens somewhat, unaltered red sandstone is exposed.

Phillips (*loc. jam cit.*) noticed the occurrence of rude columnar jointing in the sedimentary rocks adjacent to the dyke—the columns being arranged at right angles to the margin of the trap, and extending for a distance of several feet. This is scarcely noticeable at the present time.

### III. General Relations of the Intrusive Rocks.

As regards the nature of the intrusion, the earlier writers refer to the rock as a greenstone; Murchison states that it is composed of hornblende, olivine, and felspar. The Rev. J. D. La Touche, who gives a full account of its field-relations, describes it as a greenstone or diorite. A microscopical examination, however, shows that the rock is clearly basic. It is not, however, a simple uniform intrusion, but is composed of several allied though differing types of dolerite and basalt. A comparatively slight examination soon shows that, while the main part of the dyke is a compact fine-grained basalt, doleritic material prevails near the southern margin and to a less extent near the northern.[1] There is often some difficulty in distinguishing between the two rock-types in the field, especially as the basalt when weathered tends to resemble the dolerite; and a more detailed examination, while confirming the fact that the central part of the dyke is predominantly basaltic and the marginal part predominantly doleritic, made it clear that the two rock-types are intimately intermingled, patches of basalt occurring in the predominantly-doleritic portion and *vice versa*.

### IV. Description of the Intrusive Rocks.

Owing to the very considerable amount of variation in the character of the rock in different parts of the intrusion, a somewhat detailed description will be necessary.

### (A) The Dolerites.

Two distinct types may be recognized:—

(1) Along the southern margin of the intrusion a rather fine-grained dark yellowish-green doleritic rock, having the low specific gravity of 2·65 and containing 45·45 per cent. of silica, prevails. Excellent junction-specimens with the Old Red Sandstone are readily obtainable from a thin layer of dolerite which covers the Old Red forming the southern wall of the quarry nearest the trap.

---

[1] The Rev. J. D. La Touche (Trans. Woolhope Nat. F.-C. 1891, p. 167) says that the central part is more coarsely crystalline than the marginal part.

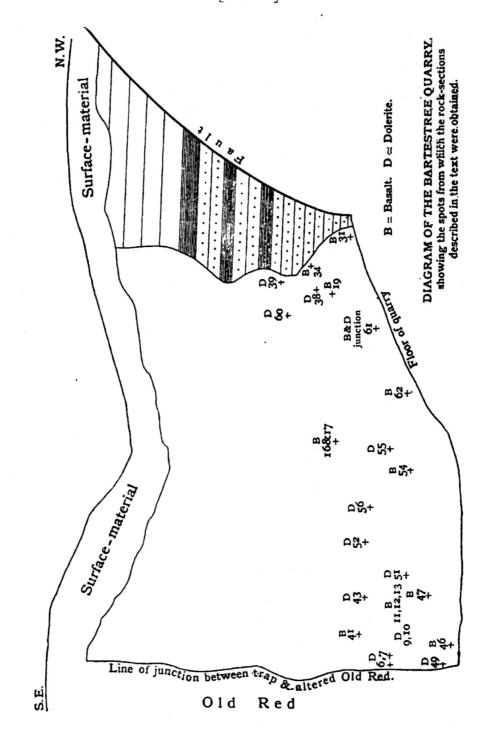

DIAGRAM OF THE BARTESTREE QUARRY.
showing the spots from which the rock-sections described in the text were obtained.

B = Basalt.  D = Dolerite.

Two sections of this rock were examined. The first (6),[1] passing through the actual junction with the Old Red, consists mainly of fair-sized labradorite-crystals and augite completely altered into a yellow, apparently serpentinous mineral, which wraps round and encloses the felspars. No olivine occurs. Magnetite and leuco-xenized ilmenite are both abundant, the latter occurring in small irregular patches, the former in rather long crystals. The last quarter-inch of the section in immediate contact with the Old Red contains a fair amount of calcite in irregular patches, and a little quartz which was no doubt picked up from the Old Red; the felspars too are larger, fresher, and more abundant than in other parts of the section. A section (7) taken 3 inches from the junction with the Old Red, while agreeing with that just described in consisting mainly of labradorite and serpentinized augite, differs in the following respects:—there is no ilmenite, and the abundant magnetite occurs chiefly in irregular grains instead of elongated crystals; needles of apatite are plentiful; and pseudomorphs in carbonate after olivine are abundant: these are of no great size, about ·5 millimetre being the maximum diameter. A third section (49), taken from close to the junction with the Old Red near the floor of the quarry, shows further differences. No olivine, either fresh or altered, occurs, a little biotite is present, small apatite-needles are very abundant, and the iron-ore is chiefly ilmenite. In addition to the presence, as in the two previous slides, of patches of ser-pentinized augite, this mineral occurs abundantly in small, fresh, brightly-polarizing grains, and forms also a few relatively-large twinned crystals.

(2) The prevalent type of doleritic rock is, however, a coarser-grained dark-green rock, occurring principally near the southern margin of the dyke, but also at various points near the centre and the northern margin. It is a heavy rock, specimens from near the southern margin giving a specific gravity of 2·84 to 2·88 and a silica-percentage of 43·03. In sections from two neighbouring spots (9 and 10) near the southern margin, olivine in a completely serpen-tinized state, but sometimes showing good crystal-outlines, is one of the most abundant minerals. These crystals are of considerable size, sections sometimes showing a length of 1½ mm. The augite is all very fresh and polarizes brilliantly, being partly 'granulitic,' partly in fair-sized non-ophitic crystals which do not show any sign of pleochroism. The augite and olivine are by far the most abundant minerals, the olivine in one section forming at least one-third of the bulk of the rock. Small augite-granules polarizing with the greatest brilliance are gathered together into nests, and in one case form a band 2 to 3 millimetres broad stretching across the section. Fairly fresh labradorite is plentiful, but does not play so important a part as in the doleritic rocks previously described. Magnetite is

[1] The spots from which the sections indicated by the numerals in parentheses were obtained are shown in the accompanying diagram of the quarry-face (p. 504).

abundant, but ilmenite is not present. Plentiful apatite-needles penetrate all the other constituents. The most interesting fact about the rock is, however, the occurrence of analcime, the presence of which was first recognized by Mr. Harker. This mineral has already been described in British dolerites from the following localities :—Titterstone Clee [1]; Car Craig [2] and Gullane Hill,[3] in the Edinburgh district; Spalefield [4] near Anstruther; Bathgate [5] in Linlithgowshire, and Kidlaw in Haddingtonshire; Dippin [6] (Arran); and Hendre Quarry, Berwyns.[7]

In the Bartestree rocks the analcime is usually fresh, but sometimes converted into some other zeolite in bundles of fibres. It forms patches, frequently with a length of about half a millimetre; while in the Gullane-Hill rock they measure as much as 3 mm. in diameter, and are not very much smaller in the rock from Claughland Point (Arran). These patches fill up the gaps between the felspar-laths, and their relations to the other constituents closely resemble those in the Dippin rock figured by Mr. Harker,[3] and that from Spalefield described by Dr. Flett.

There is nothing in the Bartestree dolerite to suggest the former presence of nepheline, and the general freshness of the felspars and the absence of varieties rich in soda make it improbable that the analcime is due to the alteration of felspar, as is suggested by Mr. Young in the case of the Gullane-Hill rock. It seems probable, then, that the analcime is of primary origin, as is maintained by Mr. Harker with regard to the Dippin rock. Owing to the presence of analcime, this rock may be grouped with the teschenites.

Sections showed the occurrence of doleritic rocks at a number of points (see diagram, p. 504) farther towards the centre and the northern margin of the dyke. Thus rocks from the spots 43, 51, & 52 are of the same general type as that just described, the serpentinized olivine being extremely abundant. Analcime is especially plentiful at 51 (Pl. LII, fig. 1) and 52. A rock from the spot numbered 56, still farther towards the centre of the dyke, and an identical rock from 60, near the northern margin, are also well-marked dolerites but of a rather different type: the serpentinized olivine, which shows good crystal-outlines, is not so abundant as in the rocks just described, and analcime does not occur. Augite, both

[1] S. Allport, Quart. Journ. Geol. Soc. vol. xxx (1874) p. 550.
[2] J. J. H. Teall, 'British Petrography' 1888, p. 191 & pl. xxii, fig. 1.
[3] J. Young. Trans. Edin. Geol. Soc. vol. viii (1903–1905) pp. 326–35.
[4] J. S. Flett, Mem. Geol. Surv. Scot. Appendix to 'The Geology of Eastern Fife' 1902, pp. 392–93.
[5] 'Summary of Progress of the Geological Survey for 1905' 1906, pp. 74 & 75.
[6] A. Harker, in Mem. Geol. Surv. Scot. 'Geology of Northern Arran, &c.' 1903, pp. 112–14.
[7] T. H. Cope & J. Lomas, Rep. Brit. Assoc. (Southport) 1903, pp. 664–65.
I am greatly indebted to Dr. Flett for drawing my attention to some of the foregoing references.
[3] 'Petrology for Students' 4th ed. (1908) p. 147.

granulitic and in large idiomorphic crystals, is abundant. The rock at the spot numbered 55 (Pl. LII, fig. 2) is similar but rather finer-grained, showing some approach to the structure of a basalt. The felspar and augite (which is almost entirely 'granulitic') are very fresh; and the olivine, which is very abundant and evenly distributed, is completely serpentinized. A few well-terminated and slightly ophitic augite-crystals occur.

As the northern margin of the intrusion is approached, a doleritic type very rich in olivine is again met with, as at (38). At (39) a beautiful type occurs, in which fresh augite forms about half the bulk of the rock: this is one of the coarsest types met with, the plagioclase-phenocrysts, which have a maximum extinction-angle of 35°, reaching a length of 2 millimetres. At the base of the quarry near the northern margin, where the boundary of the dyke dips in below the altered Old Red, is a green type of dolerite (34) rich in ilmenite. In all these sections, the felspar is in laths showing twinning on the Carlsbad and albite-types, with maximum extinction-angles of about 35 to 40°: it is probably a basic labradorite.

### (B) The Basalts.

By far the largest portion of the dyke is formed by a fine-grained basaltic rock which shows but little variation in a hand-specimen, being a black, compact, usually fresh basalt of uniform grain, with small felspars and dark augites figuring prominently in it.

A series of sections was examined, taken at intervals across the whole thickness of the basalt, and showed the rock to be very uniform in character except for the presence or absence of olivine.

Four sections, two (11) from the actual junction with the principal southern mass of dolerite, and the others (12 & 13) from a distance of 2 and 3 inches respectively from the junction, all agree as to the character of the ground-mass, which consists of little plagioclase-needles associated with augite and magnetite-grains, both minerals occurring in great abundance. All these sections also agree in the character of the felspars, which form laths having an average length of ·5 to ·75 millimetre, and giving extinction-angles that suggest labradorite of a less basic type than in the dolerite. The augite, however, varies considerably in the different slides. In sections 11 (Pl. LII, fig. 4) and 12 the augite is almost entirely in the form of fair-sized crystals with irregular, sometimes indistinct, and often corroded margins, and presenting a peculiar speckled appearance owing to the separation of magnetite. Some of the augite, however, occurs in fresh, idiomorphic, well-cleaved crystals with no separation of magnetite. This type of augite is the only one represented in section 13. The sections (11 & 12) cut from the marginal 2 inches of the basalt are quite devoid of olivine; section 13, however, contains abundant olivine, some of it serpentinized, some of it wholly or partly replaced by a fibrous, noticeably-pleochroic, and brilliantly-polarizing mineral, which appears to agree closely with a mineral observed under

similar conditions by Dr. Flett in the case of the Spalefield rock,[1] and
with the pseudomorphs described and figured by Dr. H. H. Arnold-
Bemrose[2] from Potluck (north-west of Tideswell). Dr. Arnold-
Bemrose, who kindly examined one of my slides, agrees that the
resemblance to the Potluck pseudomorphs is very close, and
considers that the replacing substance is a mica-like mineral.

The rock at (46), from near the junction of the dolerite and basalt
at the southern border, exhibits an interesting intermingling of the
two rock-types, as, while mainly basaltic, it shows many included
patches of doleritic material, passing with irregular ill-defined
boundaries into the basalt. Mr. Harker suggests a comparison
with the 'glomero-porphyritic structure' of Prof. Judd.[3] The same
feature is shown in the rock at the spot numbered 62. The rock
from (46) differs from all the others, in the fact that the abundant
olivine is in the main perfectly fresh (Pl. LII, fig. 3). The rock
at (41) contains no olivine, and the augite shows separation of
magnetite as in (11).

At the spot numbered 47, a beautiful rock-type of medium
coarseness occurs. Abundant serpentinized olivine, showing good
crystal-outlines, is present; and the augite, although forming a few
phenocrysts, is mainly in the form of small and very fresh grains
filling the interstices between the felspars.

Sections from the spots (54) and (16) near the middle of the
dyke and from (17)—a point near (16), although its precise position
was not recorded, agree in the fact that the augite, which is very
abundant, shows as a rule corrosion of its borders and much
separation of magnetite; but, while at (54) and (17) no olivine is
present, at (16) it is abundant.

At a spot very close to (17) a rock occurs, having a specific gravity
of only 2·69, and is to be grouped rather with the augite-andesites
than with the basalts.

A section from (61), a point approaching the northern border,
shows an undulating line of junction between two sharply-defined
rock-types, basaltic and doleritic. The felspar-laths of the basalt
tend to accumulate along the line of junction with the dolerite and
to be arranged with their long axes parallel to the edge. The
character of the junction makes it clear, not only that the basalt
was a later intrusion than the dolerite, but that the dolerite was
completely consolidated before the intrusion of the basalt. An
interesting section comes from (19), a point at a distance of 6 feet
from the northern edge of the dyke. It consists in the main of
basalt, showing the usual augite with corroded borders and separation
of magnetite; but the basalt includes patches of dolerite and also a
number of glassy patches which are dark, nearly isotropic, and
imperfectly variolitic.

The occurrence of basaltic as well as doleritic material in the
immediate neighbourhood of the northern margin is shown by the
presence of a fine-grained basalt devoid of olivine at the points (31)

[1] Appendix to 'The Geology of Eastern Fife' Mem. Geol. Surv. Scot. 1902, p. 392.
[2] Quart. Journ. Geol. Soc. vol. l (1894) p. 613 & pl. xxiv, fig. 3.
[3] Ibid. vol. xlii (1886) p. 71.

and (34), where, as seen in the diagram (p. 504), the dyke passes in below the Old Red. The rock from (31) resembles that from (61) in showing sharply-defined junctions between doleritic and basaltic material (Pl. LII, fig. 5), many small patches of dolerite being enclosed in the basalt.

The following silica-percentages and specific gravities, some of which have been already referred to in the foregoing account, were determined in the chemical laboratory at University College, Bristol, by Mr. J. H. Sturgess:—

| Position in quarry-face. | Character of rock. | Sp. gr. | Silica-percentage. |
|---|---|---|---|
| 6 | Dolerite, greenish variety from near the southern margin | 2·65 | 45·45 |
| 9 | Olivine-analcime-dolerite (teschenite) | 2·84 | — |
| 10 | Olivine-analcime-dolerite (teschenite) | 2·88 | 43·03 |
| 11 | Basalt | 2·93 | — |
| 54 | Basalt | 2·84 | 45·60 |
| 17 | Basalt | 2·93 | 48·26 |

The characters of the various rock-types which have now been described may be summarized as follows:—

Dolerites.—The prevailing type is a heavy olivine-analcime-dolerite or teschenite, formed of olivine generally serpentinized, labradorite, fresh non-pleochroic and non-ophitic augite, iron-ores, analcime, and apatite. But the rocks of the prevalent type may vary as regards the amount of olivine, the relative abundance of the granulitic and well-crystallized types of augite, the nature of the iron-ore, and the presence or absence of analcime.

Near the southern margin is a lighter, somewhat green, finer-grained type generally free from olivine (which, if present, is represented by pseudomorphs in carbonate), and further containing labradorite, augite sometimes fresh (but as a rule altered into a yellow, probably serpentinous mineral), apatite, and occasionally a little biotite.

Basalts.—The prevailing type has a fine-grained ground-mass, formed of felspar-needles with augite- and magnetite-grains, and includes phenocrysts of felspar (of a less basic type than in the dolerite), and of augite, the latter being very generally corroded and marked by the separation of magnetite.

Many of the basalts, however, contain olivine, either fresh or serpentinized.

Small areas of glass are frequent in the basalt, and in one case relatively-large imperfectly-variolitic areas were met with. Small areas of doleritic material are frequently included in the basalt, the boundaries between the two rocks being in some cases sharply defined, in other cases ill-defined.

2 M 2

## V. Conclusion.

The rocks just described, though showing a large amount of variation, are all closely related; and the facts seem most readily explicable on the view that, in the Bartestree dyke, we have evidence of three successive injections of basic material. First, in all probability, came the green dolerite without fresh or serpentinized olivine, chiefly seen near the southern margin. Then followed the darker, coarser teschenite, which (judging from the sharply-defined junctions) was completely solidified before the intrusion of the basalt. This latter rock formed the central and major portion of the dyke, enclosing here and there patches of the teschenite, and further sending veins into the marginal portion. The basalt-magma brought up with it numbers of small ill-defined patches of coarser material, and here and there portions of the magma solidified in a glassy condition.

As regards the date of the intrusion, all that can be learnt from field-evidence is that it is later than the Old Red Sandstone. The strong resemblance of the dolerite to many of the other Midland dolerites, and especially to the Clee-Hill rock, suggests that it belongs to the same series, in which case it would not be earlier than very late Carboniferous.

Prof. Watts[1] remarks on the very close resemblance between some of the Midland dolerites and some of those of Scotland and the North of England, and suggests that the former group, like the latter, may really be of Tertiary age. The presence of analcime affords no indication as to whether the rocks are of Carboniferous or of Tertiary age, this mineral having been met with in British doleritic rocks of both these periods. In the non-pleochroic and almost entirely non-ophitic character of the augite, the Bartestree rock approaches more closely to the Carboniferous than to the Tertiary dolerites.

I wish to acknowledge my great indebtedness to Mr. Alfred Harker, F.R.S., both for help in examining my sections, and for the loan of sections of other analcime-bearing rocks.

### EXPLANATION OF PLATE LII.

[The numerals in parentheses refer to the diagram, p. 504.]

Fig. 1. Teschenite (51), near the southern margin of the dyke: × about 25.
  The large, roughly-triangular, clear patch in the left half of the figure is analcime. The dark patch in the right-hand top corner consists partly of serpentinized olivine, partly of magnetite. The remainder of the section is occupied by labradorite-laths, apatite-needles, and augite-grains. (See p. 506.)

 2. Olivine-dolerite (55), near the middle of the dyke: × about 25.
  This shows several completely-serpentinized olivines, with numerous labradorite-laths and augite-grains, the latter being best seen near the base of the figure. (See p. 507.)

---

[1] Proc. Geol. Assoc. vol. xv (1898–99) pp. 399–400, & *ibid.* vol. xix (1905–1906) pp. 178–80.

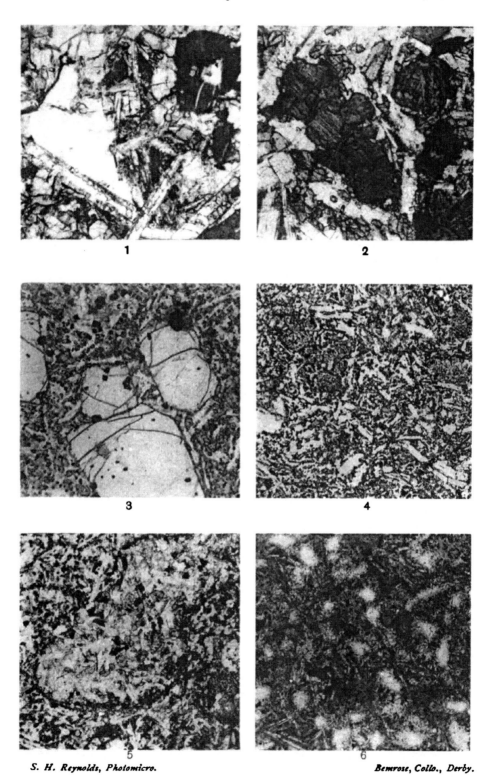

S. H. Reynolds, Photomicro.

Bemrose, Collo., Derby.

IGNEOUS AND ALTERED ROCKS FROM BARTESTREE.

Fig. 3. Olivine-basalt (46), near the base of the southern margin of the
dyke: × about 25.

    The whole or parts of three well-formed and very fresh olivine-
crystals are seen. Grains of magnetite and of very fresh augite with
felspar-laths make up the rest of the section. (See p. 508.)

    4. Basalt (11), near the southern margin of the dyke: × about 15.

    No olivine is present in this section, and the augite-crystals, which
are not very clearly seen in the photograph, are characterized by the
corrosion of their borders, and by the separation of magnetite, giving
them a speckled appearance. (See p. 507.)

    5. Basalt with doleritic patches (31), near the base of the northern
margin of the dyke: × about 15.

    An irregularly-rounded patch of dolerite is seen enclosed in the
basalt, much magnetite and augite being aggregated along the line
of junction. (See p. 509.)

    6. Altered Old Red Sandstone, close to the northern margin of the
dyke: × about 25. (See p. 502.)

    The clear areas are patches of quartz with corroded borders.
Numerous needles of recrystallized felspar are also visible.

## DISCUSSION.

The PRESIDENT thought that the explanation offered by the Author
was correct; it was applicable to all the composite dykes that
had come under his own observation.

Dr. HATCH congratulated the Author on having so well described
an excellent example of a multiple dyke. Judging by the thin
sections thrown on the screen, he thought that the micro-structure
of the Bartestree rocks was comparable to that of some of the
well-known types of Carboniferous dolerite occurring in the
Midland Valley of Scotland. He asked the Author what was
the distinction that he made between 'dolerite' and 'basalt' in
the present case. He (the speaker) deprecated the application of
the terms 'basalt' and 'andesite,' which should be reserved for
basic and intermediate lava-types, to rocks of undoubted hypabyssal
character (such as those of Bartestree), of which the proper
equivalent designations were dolerite and porphyrite respectively.

Mr. J. V. ELSDEN said that he had been particularly interested in
the Author's conclusion that the analcime recognized in some parts
of this dyke was of primary origin. Most of the admitted occurrences of primary analcime had been in connexion with rocks
consolidated under considerable pressure. As some of the Author's
specimens contained glassy patches, he would like to ask whether
the analcime might not be altered glass.

The AUTHOR said, in reply to Dr. Hatch, that he had used the
term 'dolerite' to denote a relatively coarse-grained rock, and
the term 'basalt' to denote one of relatively fine grain. In reply
to Mr. Elsden, he stated that the analcime was found in the freshest
of the doleritic rocks; and, in reply to a question asked by the
President, that ilmenite was present in certain parts of the dyke.

28. *On the* FOSSILIFEROUS SILURIAN ROCKS *of the* SOUTHERN HALF *of the* TORTWORTH INLIER. By FREDERICK RICHARD COWPER REED, M.A., F.G.S., and Prof. SIDNEY HUGH REYNOLDS, M.A., F.G.S. (Read June 3rd, 1908.)

CONTENTS.

| | Page |
|---|---|
| I. Introduction | 512 |
| II. Description of the Exposures | 513 |
| (1) The Llandovery Beds | 513 |
| (a) The Charfield-Green Area. | |
| (b) The Avening-Green, Damery, Ironmill-Wood, and Tortworth Areas. | |
| (c) The Daniel's-Wood Area. | |
| (d) The Middlemill and Woodford Areas. | |
| (e) The Eastwood-Park Area. | |
| (2) The Wenlock and (?) Ludlow Beds | 522 |
| (A) The Western Area. | |
| (a) The Horseshoe-Farm Area. | |
| (b) The Whitfield and Falfield Areas. | |
| (c) The Daniel's-Wood and Tortworth Areas. | |
| (d) The Stone and Woodford Areas. | |
| (B) The Charfield-Green Area. | |
| III. General Succession of the Silurian Rocks | 534 |
| IV. Mutual Relations of the Rocks, and Earth-Movements affecting them | 535 |
| V. General Remarks on the Fossils | 535 |
| VI. Summary and Conclusions | 537 |
| VII. Lists of Fossils | 538 |

## I. INTRODUCTION.

IN the Quarterly Journal of the Geological Society for 1901 (vol. lvii, pp. 267-84 & pls. x-xi) is a paper by one of us, in collaboration with Prof. C. Lloyd Morgan, dealing with the igneous rocks and the associated sedimentary deposits of the Tortworth Inlier. The present communication may be regarded as, to some extent, supplementary to the above. Full references to the earlier work on the district having been given in the paper just mentioned, they will not be repeated here.

The field-work has been carried out by one of us (S. H. R.); the identification of the fossils, involving the re-examination of the various public and private collections, by the other (F. R. C. R.).

The expense of the work, which has involved the digging of a number of trenches and the opening-up of a series of old quarries, has been lightened latterly by means of a grant from the British Association for the Advancement of Science. We are much indebted to the landlords, the Earl of Ducie, Earl Fitzhardinge, and Sir George Jenkinson, Bart., for their kindness in facilitating these excavations. We desire also to thank Mr. J. Harle, Lord Ducie's agent, and Mr. J. Peter, Lord Fitzhardinge's agent, for help and information.

## II. DESCRIPTION OF THE EXPOSURES.

### (1) The Llandovery Beds.

The Llandovery rocks crop out along an area generally from 1 to 2 miles wide, which follows the general trend of the Carboniferous Limestone rim of the Bristol Coalfield, and stretches in a north-westerly direction from Charfield Green to the neighbourhood of Woodford and Middlemill, and then, after an interval occupied

Fig. 1.—*Geological map of the Tortworth Inlier and the immediate neighbourhood.*

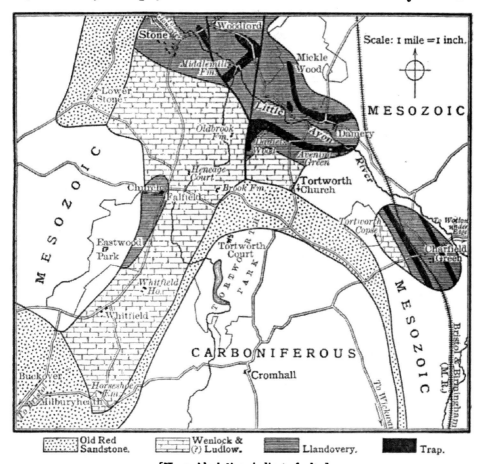

[Heavy black lines indicate faults.]

by Wenlock rocks, from Falfield to a point in Eastwood Park south-east of the House. The continuity of the outcrop to the north of Charfield Green is broken for a space by the overlap of the Trias, and the exposures in the south-western part of the area are exceptionally poor and scanty. The best exposures occur in the northern and eastern portions; and it is only in them that the contemporaneous igneous rocks, which add a special interest to the Tortworth Llandovery series, are met with.

For purposes of description, the regions where Llandovery rocks are found may be classified as follows;—

    (a) The Charfield-Green Area.
    (b) The Avening-Green, Damery, Ironmill-Wood, and Tortworth Areas.
    (c) The Daniel's-Wood Area.
    (d) The Middlemill and Woodford Areas.
    (e) The Eastwood-Park Area.

### (a) The Charfield-Green Area.

This patch of Silurian rocks, which has a maximum length of about a mile and a width of about half a mile, is surrounded on all sides by Keuper. In the Geological-Survey map it is shown as consisting (apart from the two trap-bands) entirely of Llandovery rocks, but the north-western part really consists of Wenlock strata.

In the paper already mentioned, the exposures immediately associated with the trap are described. The following additional exposures of Llandovery rocks may be enumerated:—

    (1) By a little pond, a short distance north-west of Pool Farm.
    (2) An old, greatly overgrown quarry, 150 yards east-north-east of Charfield Station. Inspection of Buckland & Conybeare's map shows this to be probably Long's Quarry, from which certain fossils in the Jermyn-Street collection were obtained. Weaver mentions the occurrence of strontium-sulphate in Long's Quarry.
    (3) In the bed of the small stream which, flowing in a north-easterly direction, joins the Little Avon near Ebury Hill. The lower trap-band is well exposed, both in the stream and in the field to the south, and overlying the trap is red micaceous sandstone.

The above-mentioned exposures are all east of the Midland Railway. West of the line, Llandovery sandstone dipping from 30° to 35° west-south-westwards occurs in the bed of a little stream, about midway between Vine Cottage and Hillhouse Farm; and a short distance farther north, at Fowler's-Court Farm, there is a considerable exposure of Llandovery rocks dipping at 10° W. 15° S.

At all these localities the Llandovery dips in a westerly or south-westerly direction, and possesses the same lithological character as in the better-exposed region in the neighbourhood of Damery. The prevalent fossils are—*Cœlospira hemispherica, Atrypa reticularis, Chonetes striatella* var., *Phacops Weaveri,* and *Encrinurus punctatus.*[1]

All the exposures as yet described are in rocks underlying the upper trap-band; but, in the previous communication already mentioned, an account is given on pp. 270 & 271 of a small section in Cullimore's Quarry, Charfield Green, where fossiliferous calcareous ash occurs overlying the upper trap-band. Recent cutting-

---

[1] The authors of names of fossils being cited in the general table appended to this paper (pp. 538-43), it has been thought unnecessary to repeat them throughout the paper.

back of the hedge has exposed a considerably larger and better
section of ashy limestone and other material occupying a hollow in
the trap (see fig. 2, below).    The section is as follows :—

| | Thickness in | feet | inches |
|---|---|---|---|
| (5) Surface-soil ................................................................ | | — | — |
| (4) Limestone, sometimes nearly pure, sometimes full of minute ashy particles, occasionally with bigger lapilli of vesicular basalt.  Crowded with fossils, chiefly brachiopods ................................................ | | 1 | 0 |
| (3) Band of compact grit, containing *Stricklandinia lirata* and *Spirifer plicatellus* var. *radiatus* ........................ | | 0 | 1 to 3 |
| (2) Band of gritty limestone, when unweathered containing in places much finely-divided ashy material, but as a rule considerably decalcified.  Crowded with fossils, chiefly corals ................................................ | | 1 | 0 |
| (1) Compact fine-grained material, resembling baked shale and resting on the trap ...................................... | | 0 | 1 to 3 |

Fig. 2.—*View of part of Cullimore's Quarry, Charfield Green.*

[Scale : 1 inch=rather less than 1 foot.]

A = Patch of trap surrounded by sedimentary material.
B = Patch of sedimentary material enclosed in the trap.

The section above described appears to be the same as that
recorded by Weaver,[1] and illustrated by his pl. xxxix, fig. 2.    The
two fossiliferous bands seem to be those which he says are

'composed of sandstone, slate-clay, carbonate of lime, oxide of iron, and trap-
like matter, intermixed . . . .'

He mentions the occurrence of numerous corals, bivalves, and a
trilobite in these bands.    He represents, however, the strata as

---

[1] Trans. Geol. Soc. ser. 2, vol. i, pt. ii (1824) p. 334.

partly interbedded with the trap, which is not in accordance with our observations.

Weaver draws special attention to the band of compact material ('grey hornstone') forming Band 1 in the foregoing section, and discusses the question as to whether it owes its hard character to alteration by the heat of the trap.

This section has yielded a large series of fossils, in addition to those mentioned on p. 271 of the previous paper; and the presence of *Stricklandinia lirata*, *Phacops Weaveri*, *Strophomena compressa*, *Streptelasma elongatum*, and *Heliolites parasitica*, although not affording conclusive evidence, indicates a Llandovery rather than a Wenlock age.

The following are the additional species met with [1]:—

| | |
|---|---|
| *Favosites gothlandica.*** | *Strophomena compressa.** |
| *Favosites Forbesi.* | *Strophomena* cf. *antiquata.* |
| *Favosites aspera.* | *Strophomena corrugatella* var. |
| *Favosites Hisingeri.* | *Atrypina Barrandei.* [2] |
| *Alveolites* sp. | *Atrypa reticularis.*** |
| *Heliolites Murchisoni.* | *Orthis calligramma*, var.** |
| *Heliolites parasitica.* | *Orthis elegantula.* |
| *Hallia mitrata (?).* | *Orthis rustica.* |
| *Cyathophyllum* sp. | *Triplecia insularis.* [2] |
| *Streptelasma elongatum.* | *Stricklandinia lirata.** |
| Monticuliporoid (indet.). | *Plectambonites transversalis.* |
| *Favositella (?)* sp. | *Horiostoma globosum* var. *sculptum.* |
| A new Bryozoan. [2] | *Horiostoma discors (?).* |
| *Fenestella* sp. | *Euomphalus* sp. |
| *Meristina tumida.* | *Cornulites serpularius.* |
| *Spirifer elevatus.* | *Lichas* sp. |
| *Spirifer crispus* var. | *Cheirurus bimucronatus.* |
| *Strophomena funiculata (?).* | *Phacops Weaveri.* |

Lord Ducie's collection contains *Modiolopsis mytilimeris* and *Grammysia* sp., in greenish-grey sandstone unlike any rock now exposed.

At the time of publication of the previous paper in the Quarterly Journal no fossils had been found in the bed of grey sandstone, which is described (p. 271) as interbedded with shale above the calcareous ash at Cullimore's Quarry; from this we have now, however, obtained *Atrypa reticularis*, *Cœlospira hemispherica*, *Streptis monilifera (?)*, *Rhynchonella serrata*,[2] and *Alveolites* sp.[2]

### (b) The Avening-Green, Damery, Ironmill-Wood, and Tortworth Areas.

These, the most fossiliferous localities for Silurian rocks in the district, are situated on a bed of sandy limestone or calcareous sandstone having a thickness of about 500 feet, and lying between

[1] The sign * in our fossil-lists indicates that the species is abundant; and ** that it is very abundant.

[2] Found by Mr. F. J. Richards.

the upper and the lower trap-bands.    The principal fossiliferous
localities are :—

    (*a*) By the stream at Avening Green;
    (*b*) The small quarry and road-cutting south of Damery Bridge. At
        both Avening Green and Damery the sections have been recently
        opened up ;
    (*c*) Ironmill Wood ; and
    (*d*) By the stream 25 yards north of Crockley's Farm.  Nothing is now
        exposed in place, but many fossils may be obtained from débris at
        either of these two last-named localities.

Lists of fossils from Avening Green and Damery are given in
the previous paper already mentioned, and a large number of
additional species has been obtained (see list appended to this
paper, p. 538).

The commonest fossils are those mentioned on p. 514 as prevalent
in the Charfield-Green area, with (in addition) *Tentaculites anglicus*,
*Orthis elegantula*, *Rhynchonella serrata*, *Stricklandinia lirata*,
*Leptæna rhomboidalis*, *Strophomena compressa*, *Spirifer crispus*,
and *Horiostoma globosum*.  The only graptolite from the Tortworth
district with which we are acquainted is a well-preserved *Monograptus priodon* from Damery, in the Museum of Practical Geology,
Jermyn Street, London.

The rocks mentioned above lie below the trap of Avening Green
and Crockley's Farm, and there is no visible evidence as to the
nature of the rock overlying the trap in the area to the west of
Avening Green.  Several trenches were dug, with the view of
clearing up this point: two of these were to the south of the
Tortworth footpath, about 200 yards south-west of Avening
Green.  These were taken to a depth of 4½ feet (the southern) and
3½ feet (the northern) without entering the rock *in situ*; but the
abundance and uniformity in character of the blocks of micaceous
flaggy sandstone met with showed that this might be safely taken
as the rock occurring here.  The presence of *Stricklandinia lirata*
with *Horiostoma globosum* and *Phacops Downingiæ* (?) shows that
the deposit is of Llandovery age.  Two other trenches at points
about 350 yards north-north-east of Tortworth Church were in
Keuper marl, but in one case red Silurian grit was reached below
the marl.

There are now no exposures of Llandovery rock at Tortworth
itself; but Lord Ducie's collection contains *Strophomena compressa*
from 'near Tortworth Church,' and some of the older collections,
such as Lord Ducie's and that in Jermyn Street, contain a good
many fossils labelled 'Tortworth.'  It is probable, however, that in
some cases the label is intended to bear a general reference to the
district as a whole.

### (*c*) The Daniel's-Wood [1] Area.

The only exposures in this region are in the bed of the little
stream traversing the southern part of the wood.  In the previous

---

[1] This is referred to as 'Priests Hill' in the maps by Sanders and the
Geological Survey.

Fig. 3.—*Geological sketch-map of the neighbourhood of Daniel's Wood and Middlemill.*

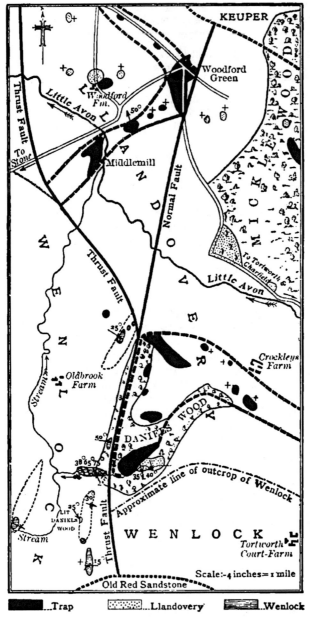

Scale:—4 inches = 1 mile

▇▇▇...Trap   ⠿...Llandovery   ▭...Wenlock

[Probable lines of outcrop are indicated by broken lines. The sign + indicates that the deposit is not visible at the surface, but was proved by trenching.]

paper a list of fossils is given (p. 274), obtained from blocks in the bed of this stream, but the Llandovery had not been met with in place, the exposures being very bad and formerly almost inaccessible owing to the dense tangle of brambles cumbering the bed of the stream. Lord Ducie, however, most kindly had the vegetation cleared away, and the section can now be adequately examined. It includes both Wenlock and Llandovery strata as well as trap, and is described in some detail in the sequel. We may here, however, mention that the Llandovery, which weathers into a stiff clay with bands of grit and decalcified sandy limestone, proves to dip in a south-easterly direction and to overlie the trap regularly. Though so different lithologically, it is therefore on the horizon of the calcareous ash of Charfield Green. Mr. J. Harle informs us that the two fields between Daniel's Wood and the bend of the road southeast of Crockley's Farm are formed chiefly of stiff clay, so that it is clear that, as one would expect, the Daniel's-Wood Llandovery extends farther eastwards. The only fossils, in addition to those mentioned in the previous list, that we have found, are :—*Palæocyclus præacutus*, which occurs in scores on certain slabs, *Strophomena arenacea*, and *Cyclonema coralli*. The *Favosites* mentioned in the previous list is (we believe) *Favosites Hisingeri*.

The Museum of Practical Geology (Jermyn Street) contains the following fossils preserved in yellow sandstone, and labelled 'west of Crockley's Farm' :—

| | |
|---|---|
| *Palæocyclus præacutus.* | *Leptæna rhomboidalis.* |
| *Cœlospira hemispherica.* | *Orthis elegantula.* |
| *Stricklandinia lirata.* | *Tentaculites anglicus.* |

These probably came from Daniel's Wood.

### (d) The Middlemill and Woodford Areas.

Several exposures of red micaceous sandstone occur in the neighbourhood of Woodford Farm, but we found no fossils in them.

Through the kindness of Lord Fitzhardinge, we have been able to open up the exposure of highly-fossiliferous Llandovery at the old Horsley or Middlemill Quarry. The fossils, chiefly corals, had previously been obtained in somewhat soft, brown, sandy, greatly-weathered rock, but the cutting-back of the face of the quarry showed that this material was really a pink sandy limestone in a decalcified state.[1] The rocks dip at 50° north-north-westwards, and the section is as follows :—

| | Thickness in | feet | inches |
|---|---|---|---|
| (4) Surface-material, crowded with blocks of highly-vesicular trap | | — | — |
| (3) Pink sandy limestone, in the main completely decalcified, crowded with large fossils and with scattered lapilli ... | | 2 | 9 |
| (2) More compact, pink, less gritty and less decalcified limestone, devoid of large fossils | | 0 | 9 |
| (1) Trap chiefly vesicular, but more compact near the top... | | — | — |
| Thickness of the sedimentary series | | 3 | 6 |

We are able to add the following fossils, nearly all derived from Band 3 in the above section, to the list given on p. 278 of the previous paper :—

| | |
|---|---|
| *Cyathophyllum* sp. | *Anastrophia deflexa.* |
| *Alveolites* sp. | *Atrypa reticularis.* |
| *Cœnites labrosus.* | *Rhynchonella decemplicata.* |
| *Heliolites parasitica.* | *Rhynchonella borealis.* |
| *Heliolites interstincta.* | *Cœlospira hemispherica.* |
| *Favosites aspera.* | *Strophomena compressa.* |
| *Favosites Hisingeri.* | *Horiostoma globosum.* |
| Monticuliporoid. | *Cyrtoceras* sp. |
| Stromatoporoid. | *Orthoceras annulatum.* |

---

[1] This deposit is no doubt the one to which Weaver (Trans. Geol. Soc. ser. 2, vol. i, pt. ii, 1824, p. 331) refers as having been found by the Rev. Dr. Cooke.

The commonest fossils are *Stricklandinia lirata* and *Favosites gothlandica*, the latter occurring in such large and continuous masses as to form practically a small reef.

Although nothing is seen resting upon the ashy limestone, there is an exposure (in the western part of the quarry) of shales with grit-bands dipping at 40° to 50° north-westwards, the strike being such as to bring the strata directly over the ashy limestone; and that they rest on it is further shown by the fact that, although not seen in place, many blocks of ashy limestone occur on the quarry-floor just below the shale-and-grit exposure, and excavation would no doubt expose the rock *in situ*.  Some of the grit-bands are crowded with *Favosites Hisingeri*, while *Palæocyclus præacutus* and *Atrypa reticularis* are common as well; *Cœlospira hemispherica, Strophomena compressa, Favosites Forbesi (?)*, and *Lindstræmia bina* were also found.  The abundance of *Favosites Hisingeri* and *Palæocyclus præacutus* strongly recalls the type of Llandovery which overlies the upper trap-band at Daniel's Wood and the same deposit at Eastwood; while the resemblance, both lithological and faunistic, between the ashy limestones at Middlemill and Charfield Green becomes more apparent, the more the deposits are studied and the fossils are collected.  The great abundance of *Favosites gothlandica* at each locality is most characteristic, while *Stricklandinia lirata* and *Heliolites parasitica* are common at both places.  These considerations lead irresistibly to the conclusion that the two deposits are on the same horizon, and that consequently the Middlemill trap is not, as was formerly supposed, a continuation of the lower trap-band as seen at Damery and Micklewood, but is the upper trap-band brought in a second time by faulting or folding.  In support of this view is the fact that two trenches dug in the field to the south-east of the pond at Woodford Green, and directly in the run of the trap (supposing that it, as was formerly believed, extended across from Micklewood to Woodford Green), proved to be in Llandovery sandstone.

A further point supporting the view that the Middlemill, Woodford, and Woodford-Green trap-masses belong to the upper band, lies in the fact that quartz-xenocrysts are common at these localities as they are in the upper trap-band at Daniel's Wood and near Fowler's-Court Farm, Charfield, while they have not been noted in any rocks undoubtedly belonging to the lower trap-band.

Llandovery sandstone is exposed on the banks immediately south-west of Middlemill Quarry, where it probably dips under the trap. The following fossils were found here:—

| | |
|---|---|
| *Lindstræmia bina.* | *Stricklandinia lens.* |
| *Lindstræmia subduplicata,* var. *crenulata.* | *Stricklandinia lirata.* |
| *Triplecia insularis (?).* | *Rhynchonella serrata.* |
| *Strophomena arenacea.* | *Rhynchonella* sp. |
| *Orthis elegantula.* | *Phacops* sp. |
| | *Encrinurus punctatus.* |

This assemblage is quite comparable with that found in the strata between the two trap-bands at Damery.  No exposures were discovered in the fields to the south-west of Middlemill between the stream and the Gloucester road; but Llandovery débris may be found at several points, and at one spot a quarter of a mile south of Middlemill Farm contained *Lindstrœmia* sp., *Atrypa reticularis*, and *Rhynchonella Davidsoni*. The Llandovery rocks form a rather strongly-marked terrace (corresponding to the 50-foot contour-line), overlooking the Little Avon from Middlemill past Stone for a distance of at least half a mile. South of the Gloucester road they have not been found *in situ*, although at one point, about 250 yards west-south-west of Heathermead, an old overgrown working yielded blocks containing *Lindstrœmia* sp. and *Stricklandinia lirata*. To the north of the road there is a section in the bed of a streamlet, some 150 yards north-west of 'The Elms.' About 8 feet of hard red unfossiliferous sandstone, with bands of sandy limestone crowded with brachiopods, is here seen dipping south-westwards at 25°. We found at this place *Atrypa reticularis*, *Stricklandinia* sp., and *Lindstrœmia bina*. Abundant débris thrown out in deepening a ditch at 'The Elms' contained *Cœlospira hemispherica*, *Stricklandinia lirata (?)*, and *Orthis polygramma (?)*. There is an overgrown working in similar material, in a little copse farther north, and much débris is scattered about.

The most fossiliferous locality in this part of the area is at Woodford Hill, on the right bank of the stream, where the rock forms a terrace comparable to that overlooking the stream on the left. There is a small quarry at a point about 300 yards due west of Matford Farm, and between this point and the old trap-quarry by the high road big blocks of very fossiliferous calcareous sandstone occur in abundance. We found here the following fossils:—

| | |
|---|---|
| *Horiostoma globosum.* | *Stricklandinia lirata.* |
| *Trochonema* sp. | *Orthis elegantula.* |
| *Spirifer* sp. | *Orthis reversa (?).* |
| *Atrypa reticularis.* | *Lindstrœmia subduplicata,* |
| *Meristina* sp. | var. *crenulata.* |
| *Stricklandinia lens.* | |

Llandovery rocks were formerly exposed north of the trap, in the road opposite the Fox Inn. Nothing is now to be seen *in situ*, but from débris found among the bushes we obtained *Strophomena* sp., *Orthis* sp., *Lindstrœmia* sp., and *Favosites Forbesi*.

All these exposures to the east of the stream are in rocks which apparently underlie the trap-band (upper), and are therefore on the same horizon as those of Damery and Avening Green.

The Sedgwick Museum contains a number of fossils from Woodford and Woodford Green. Many of these were doubtless derived from the now completely-overgrown road-section near the Fox Inn. The only other exposure with which we have met in this region is at an old quarry, about half a mile north-west of Woodford. With the help of Mr. E. Peter of Berkeley, this has been identified as Ponting's Quarry, shown in Buckland & Conybeare's map. The rock here is a red, somewhat calcareous sandstone, with bands of hard white grit and shaly partings. Crinoid stem-joints and *Rhynchonella decemplicata*, Sow., are very abundant; and we also found *Encrinurus punctatus, Orthoceras (?)* sp., *Ctenodonta* sp., and *Favosites* sp. The presence of *Rhynchonella decemplicata*, which, according to Davidson, is restricted to the Llandovery, induces us to refer this exposure to that horizon.

### (e) The Eastwood-Park Area.

The southernmost spot where there is indubitable evidence of the presence of Llandovery rocks is at a little copse in Eastwood Park, about 150 yards west-south-west of the 14th milestone from Bristol. Here, in débris of calcareous sandstone of the usual type, the following fossils were found :—*Palæocyclus præacutus, Leptæna rhomboidalis, Orthis elegantula (?), Strophomena compressa*; and, the rock being exposed by trenching, the following additional species were found :—*Favosites Forbesi (?), Atrypa reticularis*, and *Rhynchonella serrata(?)*. This deposit closely resembles that of Daniel's Wood, both lithologically and faunistically, especially in the great abundance of *Palæocyclus præacutus*. Red sandstone with *Phacops* sp. and obscure brachiopods was observed to be associated with the highly-fossiliferous calcareous sandstone, but the mutual relations of the two deposits were not clear.

There are several old quarries in Eastwood Park, but all are now very much overgrown or full of water. One of these, lying about 200 yards south-south-west of the post-office at Falfield, provided the stone from which Falfield Church was built. It is in the main a reddish sandstone, but sometimes becomes calcareous, sometimes argillaceous and fissile. Lord Ducie's collection contains a number of fossils from Eastwood, some in a hard red calcareous sandstone, others in a whitish sandstone (see lists, pp. 538, 540). Those in the reddish matrix were probably derived from the quarry referred to above.

The following fossils were obtained from red sandstone-material brought to the surface in digging graves in Falfield Churchyard :—*Cœlospira hemispherica, Atrypa reticularis*, and *Favosites* sp.

### (2) The Wenlock and (?) Ludlow Beds.

In the Geological-Survey map on the 1-inch scale the Wenlock Beds are shown forming a band with an average width of about half a mile, stretching in a north-north-easterly direction from Brinkmarsh Farm and Whitfield on the south to Cinderford Bridge,[1] a point about half a mile south of Middlemill, on the north. Here they are shown cut off by an east-and-west fault; they are also shown as shifted by an east-and-west fault at about the middle of their outcrop, a point immediately south of Falfield Mill. They are indicated as bounded on the east by a strip of Ludlow rocks, narrow in the main but widening to the south in the neighbourhood of Horseshoe Farm. As regards their western boundary,—

---

[1] Neither Cinderford Bridge, nor the roads which in the Geological-Survey map are seen approaching it, are now in existence.

from Cinderford Bridge as far south as Falfield they are shown as resting on the Llandovery; while, from near Falfield to Whitfield, they are represented as overlapped on the west by the Trias. They are represented as including two very regular bands of limestone, one immediately below the Ludlow and a second at about the middle of the Wenlock Series. No Wenlock Beds are shown on the eastern side of the horseshoe margin of the Bristol Coalfield, or between the Old Red and the Llandovery west of Tortworth Church.

In William Sanders's map the limestone is not represented as forming two regular bands, but as a good deal broken up.

Our mapping is in disagreement with that of the Geological Survey in the following respects :—

(1) We find an area of Wenlock rocks in the south-eastern part of the region in the neighbourhood of Charfield Green, where the Survey-map shows only Llandovery beds.[1]

(2) We find an area of Wenlock, and probably Ludlow, intervening between the Old Red and the Llandovery south of Daniel's Wood.

(3) We find the Wenlock of Falfield separated from the Trias of Eastwood by a narrow band of Llandovery.

(4) Although a few fossils which suggest Ludlow affinities have been met with at various spots, we have obtained no clear evidence of the presence of rocks of this horizon, except in the region to the south of Daniel's Wood, and even here the normal Ludlow fauna of Herefordshire and Shropshire is not met with.

(5) In the Geological-Survey map a large area of Llandovery is shown between Lower Stone and Falfield. The exposures here are very scanty, but such as we have been able to obtain indicate that this area is occupied by Wenlock rocks.

(6) In the Geological-Survey map the Wenlock Limestone is shown forming two very regular bands. While the lower limestone-band runs with regularity, we do not find this to be the case with the upper. Thus, while at the southern end of the outcrop at Whitfield there are clearly two regular bands as shown in the Survey-map, farther north near Gambril Lane there are no present indications of limestone-bands; while yet farther north, in the area west and south-west of Daniel's Wood, there are three parallel bands, although perhaps this may be due to faulting or folding.

For purposes of description, the Wenlock Beds may be divided into those of

(A) The Western Area, including the districts of Horseshoe Farm, Whitfield and Falfield, Daniel's Wood and Tortworth, Stone and Woodford; and

(B) The Eastern or Charfield-Green Area.

### (A) The Western Area.

This is by far the larger and more important of the two, and extends from the neighbourhood of Horseshoe Farm, near Milbury Heath on the south, to the neighbourhood of Middlemill on the north, a distance of rather over 3 miles (fig. 1, p. 513).

Throughout the area exposures are very bad, and no quarrying

---

[1] This was noted by Prof. C. Lloyd Morgan, Brit. Assoc. (Bristol) 1898, Excursion Handbook (Tortworth) No. 17, p. 11.

is now carried on. The limestone-bands are, however, generally easily traceable, either by the ridges to which they give rise or by means of old quarries.

(*a*) The Horseshoe-Farm area.—The only spot in the southernmost part of the area where exposures occur is in the neighbourhood of Horseshoe Farm. This lies within the large area shown on the Geological-Survey map as Ludlow, and close to the outcrop of the Old Red Sandstone. Horseshoe Farm, too, is interesting as being the only spot in the Tortworth Inlier (with the exception of Purton Passage) where Murchison recognized Ludlow rocks. He describes them as follows :—

'A few beds there [that is, at Horseshoe Farm] contain some of the fossils, particularly *Cypricardia* [= *Orthonota*] *amygdalina*, and pass conformably into the overlying Old Red Sandstone, and downwards into beds with *Asaphus* [= *Phacops*] *caudatus*, etc.' ('Silurian System' 1839, p. 455.)

Partly with the view of clearing up the point as to the occurrence of Ludlow rocks at this locality, Lord Ducie some two years ago had a well sunk in the field to the north of Horseshoe Farm. The material passed through consisted, in the main, of a variable series of greenish sandy and marly beds with a little limestone. The only fossils found were crinoid-stems and a few indeterminable brachiopods. In the lane, however, south-east of the farm there is a good exposure of a variable series of fissile red and yellow sandstones, sometimes micaceous, sometimes calcareous, alternating with bands of hard grit. From these we obtained a considerable suite of fossils (see list, pp. 541–43, which, however, also includes fossils from Lord Ducie's collection), and although the presence of *Chonetes striatella*, *Orbiculoidea rugata*, *Aviculopecten Danbyi*, and probably *Cucullella antiqua*, suggests Ludlow beds, the general facies is Wenlock. The strata lie almost horizontally, dipping at an angle of less than 10° south-eastwards, this low dip explaining the great increase in the width of the Wenlock outcrop.

The Jermyn-Street Museum contains two specimens of *Phacops Weaveri* from Horseshoe Farm, which were figured by Salter.[1] These are entered as of Ludlow age, and occurring on the same block are examples of *Rhynchonella nucula*. Salter describes the trilobites as representing a 'larger form of the species' (*Ph. Weaveri*); and, with regard to the age of the beds, he says that 'it is possible there is a boss of May Hill Sandstone at this place.' But the reference of these two specimens to the same species as the typical May-Hill *Phacops Weaveri* may well be questioned.[2] The matrix, too, in which the fossils are preserved is unlike anything with which we have met at Horseshoe Farm, and resembles the Wenlock Limestone of the district.

---

[1] 'Monogr. Brit. Trilob.' (Palæont. Soc.) 1864, p. 58 & pl. iii, figs. 2–3.
[2] The specimens have recently been minutely re-examined by one of us (F. R. C. R.), and their specific distinction from the May-Hill form is regarded as indubitable

In the field to the south of the southern end of Cromhall Lane there is a large swallet, and some bushy depressions which probably mark others. These are on the line of strike of two thin limestone-bands, which are shown in Sanders's map in the fields east of Brinkmarsh Lane near Highwood. No trace is now to be seen of these bands, but the presence of the swallet is suggestive of their existence.

(*b*) The Whitfield and Falfield areas.—We pass now to the description of the main Wenlock outcrop. The lower of the two limestone-bands is decidedly the better exposed and the more fossiliferous.

Commencing at the southern end, it is first seen in the old Brinkmarsh Quarry at Whitfield, to the west of Brinkmarsh Lane; and at another old quarry near Rifle Cottage, to the east of the lane. It is in these two quarries, and especially in the western one, that the great majority of the Wenlock fossils labelled ' Whitfield ' in the older collections have been found.

Weaver[1] describes in detail the section at Brinkmarsh Quarry, but for many years it has been so much overgrown that little could be seen. Recently, however, part of the southern side of the quarry was opened up, and the following section was obtained :—

|  | *Thickness in feet* | *inches.* |
|---|---|---|
| (8) Red clay crowded with fossils, especially *Hallia mitrata* and *Orthis basalis* | 1 | 6 |
| (7) Celestine-band | 0 | 1 |
| (6) Earthy limestone | 1 | 0 |
| (5) Celestine-band | 0 | 1½ |
| (4) Thinly-bedded sandy limestone, with grit-bands and shaly partings | 3 | 0 |
| (3) Lenticular band of celestine (maximum thickness) | 0 | 3 |
| (2) Thinly-bedded sandstone and shale | 0 | 4 |
| (1) Thickly-bedded sandy limestone, with some more gritty bands | 4 | 0 |
|  | 10 | 3½ |

At a point about 40 yards east of this section another part of the quarry-face was cleared, and yielded the following section :—

|  | *Thickness in feet* | *inches.* |
|---|---|---|
| (3) Rubbly limestone | 2 | 0 |
| (2) Red clay, with a little rubbly limestone; the lower beds are crowded with *Hallia mitrata* and *Orthis basalis* | 10 | 0 |
| (1) Sandy limestone | 1 | 6 |
|  | 13 | 6 |

Band 8 in the previous section is clearly the lower part of Band 2 in this section.

[1] Trans. Geol. Soc. ser. 2, vol. i, pt. ii (1824) p. 337; Weaver's description is quoted in the Geological-Survey Memoir on the East Somerset & Bristol Coalfields, 1876, p. 11.

At the western end of the quarry there is a continuous exposure of Band 1, massive limestone, somewhat sandy on the whole. A thickness of not less than 15 feet is seen here. The same rock is seen in places along the northern face of the quarry, where it is in the main very much overgrown. The total thickness of massive limestone in this quarry is probably not less than 25 feet. The dip varies in amount and direction in different parts of the quarry, but on the whole is 20° or less in a south-westerly direction.

The occurrence of three well-marked bands of celestine is interesting. The presence of the mineral in this quarry was originally noted by Weaver[1] and subsequently mentioned by Murchison ('Silurian System' 1839, p. 455).

A somewhat similar section is exposed in the eastern or Rifle-Cottage quarry. The main section at the end of the quarry is as follows :—

|  | Thickness in feet | inches. |
|---|---|---|
| Thinly-bedded rubbly limestone and shale, with numerous fossils ............ about | 4 | 0 |
| Compact, rather thickly-bedded and somewhat sandy limestone ; as a rule unfossiliferous, but with fossiliferous bands ............ | 15 | 0 |
|  | 19 | 0 |

Part of the foregoing section is also exposed on the southern side of the approach to the quarry, where clay with rubbly limestone and some fissile flags are seen resting upon more massive limestone of a somewhat sandy character.

For a list of the fossils from the Wenlock quarries at Whitfield, see pp. 541–43.

Limestone-débris was met with at several points along the strike of the lower limestone-band near Whitfield, and a fairly well-marked ridge indicating its outcrop extends for some distance to the north of Whitfield House. Then, however, for a distance of half a mile there is little evidence of the presence of limestone, the most abundant material thrown up by ploughing or occurring as débris in the fields being red sandstone.[2]

About 250 yards south of the old windmill at Falfield the limestone begins again, and forms a prominent feature extending as far as Falfield water-mill, and rising to a height of some 50 feet above the stream which bounds it on the east. There is an old quarry in red sandy limestone at the southern end of this ridge, and in the neighbourhood of Falfield windmill considerable exposures of limestone are seen dipping eastwards at 45°.

Murchison (loc. supra cit.) describes the following section as occurring here. At the top :—

[1] Trans. Geol. Soc. ser. 2, vol. i, pt. ii (1824) p. 337.
[2] Mr. J. Harle informs us, however, that agricultural operations have proved the occurrence of the limestone-band here.

(4) 'Rubbly red, sandy, calcareous beds.

(3) Thin, irregularly bedded, almost lenticular masses of purple and grey limestone, passing down into ash-coloured shale, with very thin courses of greyish-blue limestone, the shale being loaded with many of the corals and encrinites peculiar to the Wenlock Limestone....

(2) Purple and grey strong-bedded limestone, 20 to 30 feet thick, highly charged with encrinites, and the beds separated by courses of red shale.

(1) Red and green schistose beds, passing down into hard purple sand-stone and grit.'

It is now very difficult to obtain fossils here; but the locality is a well-known one, and in former times numerous fossils were to be found.

North of Falfield water-mill the limestone-band continues to be well marked, and bears several small disused pits. Sandy limestone dipping at 40° S. 30° E. is exposed at the southern end of Heneage Court, and here we found

| | |
|---|---|
| *Favositella interpunctata.* | *Naticopsis* sp. |
| *Atrypa reticularis.* | *Phacops caudatus.* |
| *Rhynchonella diodonta.* | *Calymene Blumenbachi.* |

The band can be followed right through Skeay's Grove, and is well exposed at the northern end, where shaly partings separate beds of limestone about 15 inches thick. *Cyathophyllum (?)* was found, but fossils (with the exception of indeterminable crinoids) were scarce. The rock dips eastwards at 22°. Weaver[1] gives details of a section about 25 feet thick at Skeay's Grove.

A ridge marked by a series of small overgrown pits shows the extension of the limestone for over 300 yards to the north of Skeay's Grove; but then it dies out, and there is no evidence of its occurrence north of Oldbrook Farm.

The upper or eastern limestone-band is neither so well marked nor so continuous as the western. Commencing at the southern end, the first trace is at a point south of Little Whitfield Farm, where numerous blocks of red limestone are strewn over the fields. Thence it stretches to Brinkmarsh Farm, whence a prominent ridge extends in a north-north-easterly direction for about a quarter of a mile. Blocks of limestone from Brinkmarsh Farm were found to contain *Orthis elegantula*, *Atrypa reticularis*, and *Leptæna rhomboidalis* in some abundance.

Mr. Hudson, of Brinkmarsh Farm, has recently sunk a series of shallow pits in search of celestine, along the southern margin of the large field to the north of the farm. From the westernmost hole lying nearly due north of the farm, shale and red and green grit were obtained, together with a good deal of celestine in blocks, one measuring $18 \times 8 \times 6$ inches. The second hole showed the same material, with celestine in smaller quantities; a third and fourth farther east, and lying respectively north and south of the hedge, were in highly-fossiliferous thinly-bedded Wenlock

---

[1] Trans. Geol. Soc. ser. 2, vol. i, pt. ii (1824) p. 336, quoted in Mem. Geol. Surv. 'East Somerset & Bristol Coalfields' 1876, p. 10.

Limestone, overlain by red and green flaggy sandstones. The fossils recorded in the list on pp. 541–43, as coming from the upper limestone-band at Whitfield, were found here.

From the end of the Brinkmarsh-Farm ridge as far as a point west of Tortworth-Court gas-works, a distance of about a mile, no surface-indication can be found of the existence of the upper limestone-band; but Mr. Harle informs us that it has been proved by agricultural operations to extend for some distance to the north-north-east of Whitfield farm. Near the gas-works exposures are again met with, and at one point which appears to correspond with the position of Barber's Quarry in Buckland & Conybeare's map, the limestone dips eastwards at 50°. Sanders's map shows an area of limestone at Brook Farm, but no trace can now be found of its presence. The Sedgwick Museum contains a small series of fossils from Barber's Quarry.

A small ridge of limestone, with poor exposures from which we obtained no fossils, lies close to the right bank of the stream north-east of Falfield water-mill.

(c) The Daniel's-Wood and Tortworth areas.—As has been already mentioned, the region west and south-west of Daniel's Wood shows three parallel limestone-ridges—the third being possibly a repetition of the second by faulting or folding. The westernmost, that of Heneage Court and Skeay's Grove, has been already described; the second, which commences by the stream a quarter of a mile due north of Brook Farm, shows two distinct lithological types—a flaggy micaceous sandstone, and underlying it a peculiar, highly-fossiliferous, coarsely-crystalline limestone with many little mud-pans, occasional grit-pebbles, abundant fragments of horny brachiopods, and a considerable number of other fossils.[1]

Little Daniel's Wood, near the right bank of the stream, stands on the third of these parallel ridges. About the middle of its western margin are poor exposures of sandy crinoidal limestone dipping at 25° in a south-easterly direction. We found a considerable number of fossils here, and others in crinoidal limestone and in calcareous sandstone which is poorly exposed at the southern end of the wood (see list, pp. 541–43).

There is also an exposure of limestone near the north-eastern corner of the wood, where the dip is 30° E. 20° S.; here we found *Calymene Blumenbachi*.

Through the kindness of the Earl of Ducie a series of trenches was dug on the slope of the hill south of Little Daniel's Wood. The positions of these are shown in the plan (fig. 4, p. 529).

No. 1—the southernmost, entered Old Red Sandstone at a depth of a foot, and was carried to a depth of nearly 5 feet without reaching any other material.

---

[1] [Since the reading of our paper, the cutting of additional sections has proved the presence of ashy particles in this deposit; it becomes therefore comparable with that at Cullimore's Quarry, and may be of the same (that is, Llandovery) age.]

No. 2 entered red and green calcareous sandstone or sandy limestone, with bands of compact rubbly limestone, at the depth of about 6 feet. The overlying material consisted of clay, with blocks of the same rocks as those that lower down were found *in situ.* No fossils were met with, except obscure crinoids and brachiopods. The rock closely resembles deposits of undoubtedly Wenlock age in various parts of the area. At the spot marked **X** in the accompanying plan (fig. 4) a slight scarp occurs, and at this point a cutting was made, which (though it disclosed nothing *in situ*) brought to light large numbers of blocks of Wenlock Limestone. The presence of Wenlock strata here and at trench No. 2 is in harmony with the westerly dip of the Ludlow at trench No. 3.

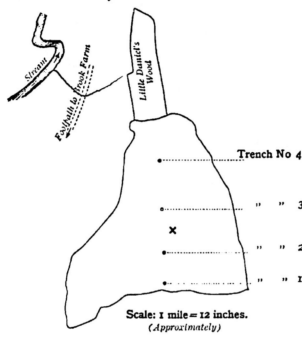

Fig. 4.—*Plan of trenches dug on the hill-slope south of Little Daniel's Wood.*

Trench No 4

„    „   3

„    „   2

„    „   1

Scale: 1 mile = 12 inches.
(*Approximately*)

[The irregular line enclosing the area on which the trenches were dug marks the boundary of a field.]

No. 3, at the depth of about a foot, entered red calcareous sandstone with limestone-bands dipping 15° westwards, that is, in a direction the reverse of that of the prevalent dip of the Wenlock throughout all the region on the west and south. The calcareous sandstone is full of lamellibranchs—*Pterinæa retroflexa,* Wahl., *Modiolopsis* cf. *Nilssoni,* His., *Modiolopsis* sp., *Orthonota* cf. *amygdalina,* Sow., *Orthonota* cf. *decipiens,* M'Coy, *Anodontopsis* cf. *securiformis,* M'Coy; and contains also *Nucleospira pisum,* Sow., *Orthis elegantula, Rhynchonella nucula,* Sow., *Chonetes striatella* (?) Dalm., *Cornulites serpularius,* Schloth., and *Favosites* sp. The thin limestone-bands contain many crinoid-stems. This assemblage of fossils, although not that typical of the Ludlow of Herefordshire and Shropshire, is rather of a Ludlow than of a Wenlock character, and indicates that Murchison was justified in his

opinion that a thin representative of the Ludlow Series
occurs in the Tortworth area.

No. 4 was carried to a depth of 4 feet in superficial material,
and in clay with bits of sandy limestone containing crinoids
and obscure brachiopods.

Material similar to that occurring in trench No. 3, and especially
red calcareous sandstone full of lamellibranchs, is thrown up by
the plough in large quantities in the fields between Tortworth
Farm and Daniel's Wood; and there can be no doubt that this
area, which is shown on the Geological-Survey map as Llandovery,
is mainly occupied by post-Llandovery strata. We found *Cornulites
serpularius* and abundant examples of *Pterinæa retroflexa* and
crinoid-stems in the blocks of red calcareous sandstone mentioned
above; and Lord Ducie's collection contains *Cornulites serpularius*,
*Ctenodonta* sp., *Modiolopsis* sp., *Pterinæa* sp., and *Pt. orbicularis*,
labelled 'Tortworth' and occurring in a similar rock.

All the Wenlock exposures hitherto described (except those in
the Whitfield Quarries where the outcrop swings round to the
west) dip in an easterly or south-easterly direction at a not very
high angle, and their outcrop follows more or less regularly that of
the Old Red Sandstone. The little stream, however, which flowing
through Daniel's Wood joins the main stream about 300 yards
south of Oldbrook Farm, shows Wenlock strata the dip of which
is in an altogether different direction, being in the main north-
westerly and often at a very high angle. These high and
discordant dips are readily explicable, as due to the reversed fault
which we believe runs along the western side of Daniel's Wood
and brings the trap over the Wenlock.

The strata occurring in the bed of the little stream were described
in the former paper (to which we have several times referred)
and an illustrative section was there given.[1] The greater facilities
for observation now available show that this section is incorrect, and
that the Llandovery of Daniel's Wood overlies, not underlies, the
trap—the stream for part of its course flowing not far from the
junction between the two, and exposing now the Llandovery, now
the trap.

As has already been stated, the Wenlock strata are seen in
the stream-bed some little distance west of the wood, dipping
north-westwards at 30°; farther east the dip rapidly increases,
until at the edge of the wood it is 75°, and just within the wood
the beds are vertical. Vertical strata continue for the next
25 yards or so, and at one point the rocks are slightly inverted
so as to dip east-south-eastwards at a very high angle. Then, for
some 15 yards the stream follows the strike, the beds retaining
their vertical position. We found a few fossils of possibly Wenlock
type—*Orthonota* sp., crinoid-stems, and *Rhynchonella nucula*—at
this point. Then for some 40 yards there are no exposures, which
is unfortunate as we cross here the line of the fault, the next
exposure being of trap. Other trap-exposures occur for a distance

---

[1] Quart. Journ. Geol. Soc. vol. lvii (1901) p. 273, fig. 1.

of some 70 yards or so, at first in the bed of the stream, but farther east at points near the right bank. At several spots still farther east are small and poor exposures of Llandovery rocks (shale or stiff clay, with grit-bands and decalcified sandy limestone full of fossils) dipping at 35° to 40° south-eastwards, the dip being such as to bring the beds over the trap. One of these is at a point about 15 yards west of the foot-bridge. No exposures are to be seen east of the foot-bridge. A list of fossils from the Wenlock strata of the stream-bed west of Daniel's Wood is given on p. 273 of the previous communication, and to it we can now add:—

| | |
|---|---|
| Aulopora serpens. | Rhynchonella Lewisi. |
| Tentaculites sp. | Rhynchonella nucula. |
| Lichas sp. | Pentamerus (?) rotundus. |
| Phacops sp. | Chonetes striatella. |
| Spirifer plicatellus. | Orthonota sp. |
| Orthis elegantula. | Horiostoma sp. |

Two other exposures of Wenlock Limestone occur along the western side of Daniel's Wood. The one near the middle of its western border, and just within the limits of the wood, shows about 10 feet of somewhat sandy and unfossiliferous limestone dipping eastwards at 50°. The other is a rather more considerable exposure, forming a slight scarp parallel to the north-western edge of the wood. The dip here is 25° east-south-eastwards, and the rock consists of red limestone and mottled red and purple sandstone. Here we found Calymene Blumenbachi, Atrypa reticularis, Favosites Forbesi, and Rhynchonella Davidsoni (?).

Another small exposure, in the ditch a few yards to the north, contained Calymene Blumenbachi and Rhynchonella sp. An old overgrown depression north of the hedge probably marks a further extension of this band of limestone.

(d) The Stone and Woodford areas.—In the area west of the Gloucester road, between Stone and Falfield, Llandovery rocks are shown in the Geological-Survey map, but the few scattered exposures now visible are all probably in Wenlock rocks. The few dips obtainable are in various directions. Two of these exposures occur in the lanes west of Falfield Farm; a short distance to the east of the stream is a good exposure of red crystalline limestone and red sandstone containing Alveolites sp., Hallia sp., Atrypa reticularis, crinoid-stems, and a big Euomphalus. The dip of the beds was not ascertainable. West of the stream, however, is another exposure dipping at 35° to 40° south-eastwards. Here we obtained Strophomena euglypha, Trematospira Salteri (?), Spirifer sp., and Phacops caudatus.

At the turn of the stream, about 150 yards north of this exposure, hard red and mottled crystalline limestone is exposed in the stream-bed and dips at 25° north-westwards. Atrypa reticularis and Rhynchonella sp. were the only fossils met with at this point.

Some 300 yards farther north by west, red sandy limestone practically in situ yielded Phacops caudatus, Strophomena compressa, and Atrypa reticularis.

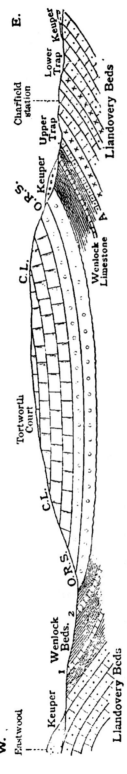

Fig. 5.—*Section from Eastwood to Charfield Green.* (*Scale : 2 inches = 1 mile.*)

[1 & 2 = Respectively the upper and the lower limestone-bands in the Wenlock ; A = Ash ; C.L. = Carboniferous Limestone ;
O.R.S. = Old Red Sandstone.]

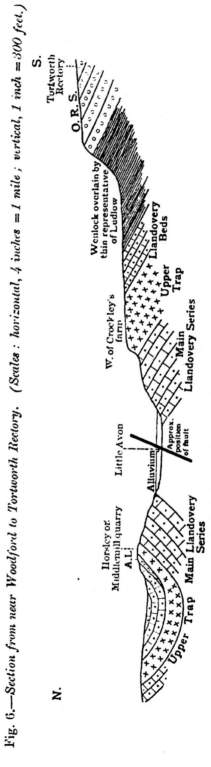

Fig. 6.—*Section from near Woodford to Tortworth Rectory.* (*Scales : horizontal, 4 inches = 1 mile ; vertical, 1 inch = 300 feet.*)

[A.L. = Ashy limestone ; O.R.S. = Old Red Sandstone.]

Another small exposure occurs at a cottage west of the high road, and about 150 yards south of Catherine Villa. Here, in a highly-crinoidal red rock (clearly a decalcified sandy limestone), we found *Strophomena compressa* and numerous crinoidal remains. No further exposures were found between this point and Stone Bridge. There, however, the small road-cutting by the farm shows compact unfossiliferous limestone, and much débris of similar material occurs in the neighbouring fields. No dip was obtainable at this point. About 200 yards east of the farm the following little section occurs :—

| | Thickness in feet | inches. |
|---|---|---|
| (7) Red, fissile. calcareous sandstone passing down into | } 3 | 0 |
| (6) Thinly-bedded ferruginous limestone, passing into | | |
| (5) Dark sandy limestone, coarser above than below ... | 1 | 3 |
| (4) Ferruginous and calcareous grit, with many bryozoa. | 0 | 6 |
| (3) Coarsely-crystalline gritty limestone, full of fragmentary fossils | 1 | 0 |
| (2) Hard, thinly-bedded, reddish, sandy limestone, with many crinoids | 1 | 0 |
| (1) Very fissile, thinly-bedded, calcareous sandstone, full of crinoids, passing down into shale with a band of limestone 2 inches thick at the base ...... | 5 | 3 |
| | 12 | 0 |

In Band 1 of the foregoing section we obtained *Stropheodonta filosa* (?), *Scenidium Lewisi* (?), *Orthis elegantula*, and *Phacops Stokesi* or *Downingiæ*. *Strophomena compressa* and *Stenopora fibrosa* occurred in Band 2.

Mr. W. D. Lang kindly examined the bryozoa, but unfortunately they were not identifiable.

### (B) The Charfield-Green Area.

A band of Wenlock Limestone can be traced along the western border of the Silurian area close to the Triassic outcrop, and is marked by small quarries long overgrown. It is seen in the hedge-bank about 100 yards south of Poolfield Farm, and a short distance to the north-west it occurs at a little old overgrown quarry, part of which was cut back so as to show 4½ feet of mottled pink and yellowish, somewhat rubbly limestone, with marly partings, dipping south-westwards at 27°. Below this limestone, shale crowded with *Cœnites juniperinus* was exposed a few years ago.

Numerous fossils were obtained from blocks of limestone used in building an old wall near Poolfield Farm, the material having very probably been derived from this or from a neighbouring quarry.

About 150 yards north of Poolfield Farm a thickness of 21 inches of mottled pink and yellowish, somewhat rubbly limestone with marly partings is seen resting on about 2 feet of red and green flaggy sandstone, the dip being 25° west-north-westwards.

To the west of this area lies Tortworth Great Copse, which mainly stands upon Trias. The eastern border is, however, probably formed of Silurian rocks, as Lord Ducie has crinoid-stems in a green sandstone-matrix, and *Bellerophon dilatatus, Modiolopsis mytilimeris, Pterinæa* sp., *Rhynchonella* sp., and a fish-spine (?) in a white limestone-matrix from this locality. If the fossil last mentioned is really a fish-spine, it probably points to the presence of Ludlow rocks.

We have been unable to find any sign of exposures in the eastern part of the copse.

### III. General Succession of the Silurian Rocks.

Although the general succession may be fairly easily ascertained, it is impossible in many cases to give any approximation to the thickness of the several bands.

The following is the succession :—

Old Red Sandstone. *Feet.*

Ludlow Series.
Fossils found in a trench to the south of Little Daniel's Wood are of Ludlow character, and the presence of these rocks is possibly indicated by fossils from Horseshoe Farm and Tortworth Great Copse. But the typical Ludlow fauna of Herefordshire and Shropshire has not been met with, and the series is clearly much attenuated.

Wenlock Series.
5. Fissile red and yellow sandstones with gritty and calcareous bands, seen at Horseshoe Hill and south of Little Daniel's Wood ; thickness doubtful.

4. Upper limestone-band variable in character, seen at Whitfield, near Brook Farm, and at Little Daniel's Wood ; thickness perhaps ............................... 25.

3. Variable non-calcareous beds showing no permanent exposures ; thickness at Falfield, according to Phillips, about .............................................. 500

2. Highly-fossiliferous red clay or shale with rubbly limestone and celestine-bands, seen at the Whitfield quarries ........................................... about 12 (seen)

1. Lower limestone-band—a thickly-bedded, somewhat sandy limestone, seen at the Whitfield quarries and at Charfield Green ; thickness about ................. 30

[Thickness of the Wenlock Series = perhaps about 625 feet.]

Llandovery Series.
6. Grit overlying the ashy limestone of Middlemill, and shales with grit and highly-fossiliferous calcareous sandstone of Daniel's Wood and Eastwood ; thickness not ascertainable.

5. Highly-fossiliferous ashy limestone of Charfield Green and Middlemill ; thickness at Charfield Green about 2¼ feet, at Middlemill ................................. 3½

4. Upper trap-band seen at Charfield Green, Avening Green, Daniel's Wood, Middlemill, and Woodford Green ; thickness at Charfield Green about .............. 60

3. Sandy limestone and calcareous sandstone and grit, as a rule crowded with fossils ; thickness both at Charfield Green and at Damery about ......................... 500

2. Lower trap-band seen at Charfield Green, Damery, and Mickle Wood ; thickness at Damery about ......... 185

1. Micaceous sandstone with *Lingula Symondsi* seen in Damery quarry ; base not exposed.

Phillips gives 1200 feet as an estimate of the thickness of the Llandovery Series at Charfield Green. We should estimate the total thickness of the Llandovery Series (including the trap-bands) at about 800 to 850 feet. The total visible thickness of the Silurian System in the Tortworth Inlier may be taken at about 1500 feet.

## IV. MUTUAL RELATIONS OF THE ROCKS, AND EARTH-MOVEMENTS AFFECTING THEM.

The Tortworth Silurian rocks are affected by the post-Carboniferous flexures which produced the Bristol Coal-Basin, and the outcrop of the beds in the main regularly follows the horseshoe-shaped outcrop of the Old Red Sandstone. This is particularly the case in the Charfield-Green neighbourhood, where all the rocks dip regularly in a south-westerly or south-south-westerly direction, and in the region between Falfield and Whitfield, where the dip is in an easterly or east-south-easterly direction.

South of Whitfield the outcrop of the Silurian—still in conformity with that of the Old Red—swings round to the west.

In the neighbourhood of Daniel's Wood and Middlemill, this regularity is lost, and the geological structure becomes difficult to understand. The two bands of trap and associated Llandovery, which were approximately parallel one to the other and at an uniform distance apart in the Charfield-Green and in the Damery-Avening Green regions, now diverge : the lower band striking in an almost northerly direction through Mickle Wood until it is probably overlapped by the Trias, while the higher band swings round southwards and is brought by the thrust-fault running along the western side of Daniel's Wood over the Wenlock Series. This fault is probably to be prolonged past Middlemill to Woodford.

The occurrence of the upper trap-band and overlying strata at Middlemill is probably due to a second fault which shifted them northwards from Daniel's Wood, the strata being further folded into a syncline.

The remarkable narrowness of the Old-Red-Sandstone outcrop from Tortworth to Horseshoe Farm suggests the prolongation of the fault along the western side of Daniel's Wood still farther southwards, so as to cut out the lower beds of the Old Red. We are, however, of opinion that the variability in the thickness of the Old Red Sandstone and the probable absence of the greater part, or even locally of the whole, of the Ludlow Series, are to be attributed to upheaval and erosion of the area in late Silurian and early Devonian times.[1] This would be in conformity with what apparently took place in South Wales [2] and in the Mendips.[3]

## V. GENERAL REMARKS ON THE FOSSILS (by F. R. C. R.).

## Llandovery.

The separation of Lower and Upper Llandovery horizons in this area is not very obvious from the palæontological evidence. The distribution of the brachiopoda is generally a guide, and the relative

[1] Prof. Lloyd Morgan makes practically the same suggestion in the Excursion-Handbook, No. 17, Brit. Assoc. (Bristol) 1898, p. 12. Phillips also clearly recognized that there was a non-sequence between the Tortworth Silurian and the Old Red. His words (Mem. Geol. Surv. vol. ii. pt. i, 1848, p. 197) are :— 'We can admit here only the upper part of the Old Red Series ; the lower part is entirely deficient ... we have ... a case of real unconformity of area between the Old Red and the Silurian strata, without local disturbance of the dips.'

[2] 'Summary of Progress of the Geological Survey for 1901' (1902) pp. 38-40.

[3] Quart. Journ. Geol. Soc. vol. lxiii (1907) p. 234.

abundance of certain species has been frequently considered an indication of the age of the beds; but the sporadic occurrence of many in this area, coupled with the local prevalence of certain forms and the rarity of others, suggests that differences of environment exercised the predominant influence. For example, the typical Upper Llandovery *Pentamerus oblongus* is very rare, although in places a real May-Hill assemblage of fossils is present, including such species as *Palæocyclus præacutus, Strophomena compressa, Cœlospira hemispherica,* etc. The curiously-irregular local distribution of the brachiopoda in the Llandovery was long ago noticed by Murchison. The negative evidence furnished by the scarcity or absence of such forms as *Meristella crassa* and *M. angustifrons* may be of more than usual value, owing to the very large number of fossils examined and the variety of the localities from which they have been obtained.

If *Cœlospira hemispherica* is truly restricted to the Upper Llandovery, as Murchison believed, we have to acknowledge that its practically-ubiquitous presence forbids us from regarding any of the fossiliferous Llandovery beds as belonging to the Lower division.

With regard to certain less widely-distributed species, there is a form which appears to be a variety of *Chonetes striatella*: it occurs at Damery Bridge and elsewhere. We are accustomed to regard this species as typically a Ludlow one, but Murchison mentioned it from May Hill.

In the case of the long-ranging *Rhynchonella nucula,* it is quite possible that we may be dealing with examples of homœomorphy, although, in the absence of knowledge of the internal characters of specimens from different horizons, we cannot affirm that such is the case.

Regarding the Llandovery fauna of this area as a whole, we must admit that, despite certain local peculiarities and especially deficiencies, it has the stamp of the Upper division. The occasional presence of Wenlock forms suggests in places transitional beds.

### Wenlock.

In the case of the Wenlock fauna, we note the comparative rarity of trilobites and of recognizable genera of crinoids; the abundance of *Hallia mitrata*; the presence of certain locally-peculiar brachiopods (such as *Strophomena Waltoni*); the abundance of certain others elsewhere rare (as, for example, *Rhynchonella Davidsoni* and *Orthis basalis*); and the absence of a host of species, especially among the corals, crinoids, and brachiopods, which usually are prominent.

The occurrence of *Strophomena compressa* at several localities amidst a fauna with a Wenlock facies extends the known vertical range of this species, for Davidson does not record it above the Upper Llandovery.

The whole facies of the Wenlock fauna in this area is somewhat peculiar, and the rich and varied assemblage of organisms which we are wont to associate with the typical Wenlock development is wanting. But, from the succession and from the lithological characters of the beds, it may be inferred that the shallower or more muddy water was an important factor in determining the features of the local marine fauna.

## Ludlow.

The question of the occurrence of true Ludlow Beds has been discussed in the foregoing pages from field-evidence and from stratigraphical considerations. The palæontological evidence is slight, but suggestive. The strongest and most direct indications come from the calcareous sandstone full of lamellibranchs in one of the trenches south of Little Daniel's Wood. Here the whole faunistic stamp is undoubtedly higher than that of the Wenlock, and all the lamellibranchs are Ludlow forms, though some range down. The other fossils support this conclusion.

The presence of *Aviculopecten Danbyi* in sandy beds near Horseshoe Farm is strong evidence of the presence of Ludlow deposits, for this species is typically an Upper Ludlow one, and apparently has not been found below that horizon. However, only the one specimen of it in Lord Ducie's collection has come under our notice, and the fossils with which it is associated in the same locality include several which are not known from so high an horizon—*Rhynchotreta cuneata, Rhynchospira Baylei, Orthothetes pecten, Strophonella funiculata, Orthis rustica, Triplecia Salteri, Scenidium Lewisi*, none of these being recorded above the Wenlock. It is possible that all the fossils from this locality are not from precisely the same stratigraphical horizon, and the different lithological characters of the rocks in which they occur point the same way.

## General.

No new species have been detected among the collections of Silurian fossils from the Tortworth area; but, in many cases, the material has been too imperfect to permit of more than the determination of the genus. It is also obvious that the British Wenlock species of corals require revision, and there is much work to be done on the lamellibranchs as well.

### VI. Summary and Conclusions.

(1) Certain corrections are made in the mapping, Wenlock beds for example being shown to occur in the Stone and Tortworth areas, and Llandovery in that of Eastwood.

(2) Previous statements as to the thinness and imperfect development of the Ludlow rocks and as to the probable exposure of the district to erosion in Ludlow and Lower Old-Red-Sandstone times are confirmed.

(3) The igneous episode is shown to have been confined to the Llandovery.

(4) The number of recorded fossils has been largely augmented.

We cannot conclude without expressing our very great indebtedness to the Earl of Ducie, who has taken much interest in our work and has assisted it in every possible way. We wish also to express our most sincere thanks to Prof. C. Lloyd Morgan, F.R.S., and to Dr. A. Vaughan for help and suggestions.

## VII. Lists of Fossils.

### (i) List of Fossils from the Llandovery Beds.

| [The sign ? indicates that the identification is doubtful.] | Charfield | | | | | Daniel's Wood and Tortworth | | | Damery, Iron-mill Wood, & Crockley's Farm. | | | | Avening Green. | | | Middlemill and Woodford. | | | | Eastwood. | |
|---|---|---|---|---|---|---|---|---|---|---|---|---|---|---|---|---|---|---|---|---|---|
| | Our Collection. | Bristol Museum. | Sedgwick Museum. | Lord Ducie's Coll. | Jermyn Street. | Our Collection. | Lord Ducie's Coll. | Jermyn Street. | Our Collection. | Bristol Museum. | Lord Ducie's Coll. | Jermyn Street. | Our Collection. | Lord Ducie's Coll. | Jermyn Street. | Our Collection. | Bristol Museum. | Sedgwick Museum. | Jermyn Street. | Our Collection. | Lord Ducie's Coll. |
| Vioa prisca | | | | | | V | | | | | | | V | | | | | | | | |
| Monograptus priodon, Bronn | | | | | | | | V | | | | | | | | | | | | | |
| Palæocyclus præacutus, Lonsd. | | | | | | V | | V | V | | | | V | V | | | | | | V | V |
| Palæocyclus sp. | V | | | | | | | | | | | | | | | | | | | | |
| Lindstræmia bina, Lonsd. | | | | | | V | | | V | V | | | | V | | V | | | | | |
| Lindstræmia subduplicata, M'Coy | V | V | | | | V | | | V | | | | | | | V | | | | | |
| Lindstræmia subduplicata var. crenulata, M'Coy | | | | | | | | | V | V | | | | | | V | | | | | |
| Lindstræmia uniserialis, M'Coy | | | | | | | | | V | V | | | | | | | | V | | | |
| Streptelasma elongatum, Phill. | V | | | | | | | | V | | | | V | V | | | | | | | |
| Streptelasma sp. | | | | | | | | | | | | | | | | | | V | | | |
| Hallia mitrata (?) His. | V | | | | | | | | | | | | | | | | | | | | |
| Cyathophyllum sp. | | | | | | | | | | | | | | | | V | | | | | |
| Favosites aspera, D'Orb. | V | | | | | | | | | | | | | | | V | | | | | |
| Favosites Bowerbanki, M.-Edw. | V | | | | | | | | | | | | | | | V | | | | | |
| Favosites Forbesi, M.-Edw. | V | | | | | V | | | V V | | | V | ? | | | V | | | | ? | |
| Favosites gothlandica, Fougt. | | | | | | V | | | | | | | | | | V | | | | | |
| Favosites Hisingeri, M.-Edw. | | | | | | V | | | | | | | | | | V | | | | | |
| Favosites sp. | | | | | | V | | | | | | | | | | | | | | | V |
| Favositella sp. | V | | | | | | | | | | | | | | | V | | | | | |
| Alveolites sp. | V | | | | | | | | | | | | | | | V | | | | | |
| Cænites juniperinus, Eichw. | | | | | | | | | V | | | | | | | V | | | | | |
| Cænites labrosus, M.-Edw. | V | | | | | V | | | | | | | | | | V | | | | | |
| Aulopora serpens, Linn. | | | | | | V | | | | | | | | | | V | | | | | |
| Monticuliporoid | V | | | | | | | | V | | | | | V | | V | | | | | |
| Heliolites interstinctus, Linn. | | | | | | | | | | | | | | | | V | | | | | |
| Heliolites Murchisoni, M.-Edw. | V | | | | | | | | | | | | | | | V | | | | | |
| Heliolites parasitica, Nich. & Eth. | V | | | | | | | | | | | | | | | V | | | | | |
| Stromatoporoid | | | | | | | | | | | | | | | | V | | | | | |
| Ptilodictya lanceolata, Goldf. | | | | | | | | | | | | | V | | | | | | | | |
| Ptilodictya sp. | | | | | | | | | V | | | | | | | | | | | | |
| Fenestella sp. | V | | | | | | | | | | | | | | | | | | | | |
| ? New bryozoan | V | | | | | | | | | | | | | | | | | | | | |
| Cornulites serpularius, Schloth. | V | | | | | ? | V | | | | | | | ? | | | | | | | V |
| Tentaculites anglicus, Salt. | V | | V | | | | | | V | | V V | V | | | | | ? | | | | V |
| Periechocrinus sp. | | | | | | | | | | | | | | V | V | | | | V | | |
| Crinoidal fragments | V | | | | | V | V | | V | | | | V | | | | | | | V | V |
| Lingula Symondsi, Salt. | | | | | | | | | | | | | | | | | | | | | |
| Lingula sp. | | | | | | | | | V | | | | | | | | | | | | |
| Eichwaldia Capewelli, Dav. | | | | | | | | | | | V | | | | | | | | | | |
| Strophonella euglypha, His. | ? | | | | | | | | | | V | | | | | | | | | | |

| List of Fossils from the Llandovery Beds (continued). | Charfield. | | | | | Daniel's Wood and Tortworth. | | | Damery, Iron-mill Wood, & Crookley's Farm. | | | | Avening Green. | | | Middlemill and Woodford. | | | | Eastwood. | |
|---|---|---|---|---|---|---|---|---|---|---|---|---|---|---|---|---|---|---|---|---|---|
| | Our Collection. | Bristol Museum. | Sedgwick Museum. | Lord Ducie's Coll. | Jermyn Street. | Our Collection. | Lord Ducie's Coll. | Jermyn Street. | Our Collection. | Bristol Museum. | Lord Ducie's Coll. | Jermyn Street. | Our Collection. | Lord Ducie's Coll. | Jermyn Street. | Our Collection. | Bristol Museum. | Sedgwick Museum. | Jermyn Street. | Our Collection. | Lord Ducie's Coll. |
| *Leptæna rhomboidalis*, Wilck. | V | | | V | V | V | | | V | | | V | V | V | | V | | | | V | V |
| *Plectambonites transversalis*, Wahl. | V | | | | | | | | V | | | | | | | | | | | | |
| *Strophomena* cf. *antiquata*, Sow. | V | | | | | | | | | | | | | | | | | | | | |
| *Strophomena arenacea*, Salt. | V | | | V | | V | | | ? | | V | | | | | V | | | | | |
| *Strophomena compressa*, Sow. | V | | V | | | V | | | V | V | | V | V | | | V | | | | V | ? |
| *Strophomena corrugatella* var., Dav. | V | | | | | | | | | | | | | | | | | | | | |
| *Strophonella funiculata*, M'Coy | V | | V | | | | | | | | | | | | | | | | | | |
| *Triplecia insularis*, Eichw. | V | | | | | | | | | | | | ? | | | | | | | | |
| *Streptis* (?) *monilifera*, M'Coy | V | | | | | | | | | | | | | | | | | | | | |
| *Chonetes striatella* var., Dalm. | V | V | | | | | | | V | V | | | V | | | | | | | | |
| *Orthis calligramma*, Dalm. | V | | | | | | | | V | | | | | | | | | | | | |
| *Orthis elegantula*, Dalm. | V | | | | | V | V | V | V | V | | V | V | | | V | | | | | V |
| *Orthis hybrida* (?) Sow. | | | | | | | | | V | | | | | | | | | | | | |
| *Orthis polygramma*, Sow. | V | | | | | | | | | | V | | V | | | | | | | | |
| *Orthis reversa*, Salt. | | | | V | | | | | | | | | V | | | | | | | | |
| *Orthis reversa* var. *mullockensis*, Dav. | V | | | | | | | | | V | | | V | | | | | | | | |
| *Orthis rustica*, Sow. | | | | | | | | | | | | | V | | | | | | | | |
| *Scenidium Lewisi* (?) Dav. | | | | | | | | | V | | | | | | | | | | | | |
| *Anastrophia deflexa*, Sow. | | | | | | | | | | | | | V | | | | | | | | |
| *Stricklandinia lens*, Sow. | | | | | | | | | | | V | | V | | | | | | | | V |
| *Stricklandinia lirata*, Sow. | V | | | | | V | | | V | | V | V | V | | | V | | | | | |
| *Pentamerus oblongus*, Sow. | V | | | | | V | | | | V | | | | | | | V | V | | | |
| *Pentamerus undatus* (?) Sow. | | | | | | | | | V | | | | | | | | | | | | |
| *Pentamerus* sp. | | | | | | V | | | | | | | | | | | | | | | |
| *Rhynchonella Davidsoni*, M'Coy | | | | | | | | | | | | | | V | | | | | | | |
| *Rhynchonella borealis* (?) Schloth. | | | | | | | | | | | | | V | | | | | | | | |
| *Rhynchonella decemplicata*, Sow. | | | | | | | | | | | | | V | | | | | | | | |
| *Rhynchonella nucula*, Sow. | V | | | | | V | | | V | | V | V | V | | | | | | | | |
| *Rhynchonella serrata*, M'Coy | V | | | | | | V | | | | V | V | V | | | | | | | | ? |
| *Rhynchonella Weaveri*, Salt. | | | | | | | | V | | | | | | | | | | | | | |
| *Rhynchonella Wilsoni*, Sow. | | | | | | V | | | | | | V | | | | | | | | | |
| *Atrypina Barrandei*, Dav. | V | | | | | | | | | | | | | | | | | | | | |
| *Atrypa imbricata*, Sow. | | | | | | | | | | | | | V | | | | | | | | |
| *Atrypa reticularis*, Linn. | V | V | V | | V | V | | V | V | V | V | V | V | | | V | | | V | V | V |
| *Spirifer crispus*, His. | V | | | | | V | | V | V | V | V | | | | | | | | | | |
| *Spirifer elevatus*, Dalm. | V | | V | | | V | | | V | | | V | | | | | | | | | |
| *Spirifer plicatellus* var. *globosus*, Salt. | V | | | | | | | | | | | | | | | | | | | | |
| *Spirifer plicatellus* var. *radiatus*, Sow. | V | | | | | | | | | | | | | | | V | | | | | |
| *Spirifer* sp. | | | | | | | | | V | | | | V | | | | | | | | |
| *Cyrtia exporrecta*, Wahl. | | | | | | | | | V | | | V | | | | | | | | | |
| *Rhynchospira Baylei*, Dav. | V | | | | | | | | V | | | | | | | | | | | | |
| *Cœlospira hemispherica*, Sow. | V | V | V | | V | V | V | V | V | V | V | | V | | | V | | V | | V | V |
| *Meristina tumida*, Dalm. | V | | | | | | | | | | | | | | | | | | | | |
| *Meristella angustifrons*, M'Coy | | | | | | V | | | V | | | | | | | | | | | | |
| *Meristella* sp. | | | | | | | | | | | | | V | | | | | | | | |

| List of Fossils from the Llandovery Beds (continued). | Charfield | | | | | Daniel's Wood and Tortworth | | | Damery, Iron-mill Wood, & Crockley's Farm | | | | Avening Green | | | Middlemill and Woodford | | | | Eastwood | |
|---|---|---|---|---|---|---|---|---|---|---|---|---|---|---|---|---|---|---|---|---|---|
| | Our Collection. | Bristol Museum. | Sedgwick Museum. | Lord Ducie's Coll. | Jermyn Street. | Our Collection. | Lord Ducie's Coll. | Jermyn Street. | Our Collection. | Bristol Museum. | Lord Ducie's Coll. | Jermyn Street. | Our Collection. | Lord Ducie's Coll. | Jermyn Street. | Our Collection. | Bristol Museum. | Sedgwick Museum. | Jermyn Street. | Our Collection. | Lord Ducie's Coll. |
| Pterinæa retroflexa, Wahl. | | | | | | | | | V | | | | | | | | | | | | |
| Pterinæa sp. | | V | | | | V | | | | | | | | | | | | | V | | |
| Ctenodonta sp. | | | | | | V | | | | | | | | | | | | | | | |
| Grammysia sp. | | | V | | | | | | | | | | | | | | | | | | |
| Modiolopsis mytilimeris, Conrad | | | V | | | | | | | | | | | | | | | | | | |
| Modiolopsis sp. | | | | | | V | | | V | | | | | | | | | | | | V |
| Goniophora cymbæformis, Sow. | V | | | | | | | V | | V | | | | | | | | | | | |
| Orthonota sp. | | | | | | V | | | | V | | | | | | | | | | | |
| Pleurotomaria sp. | V | | | | | V | | | V | | | | V | | | | | | | | |
| Murchisonia sp. | | | | | | | | | | V | | | | | | | | | | | |
| Euomphalus sp. | V | | | | | | | | | | | | | | | | | | | | |
| Cyclonema cf. delicatulum, Lindst. | | | | | | | | | | V | | | | | | | | | | | |
| Cyclonema corallii, Sow. | | | V | | | V | | | | | | | V | | | | | | | | |
| Trochonema sp. | | | | | | | | | | | | | | | | V | | | | | |
| Loxonema sinuosum, Salt. | | | | | | | | | | V | | | | | | | | | | | |
| Loxonema sp. | | | | | | | | | | V | V | | | | | | | | | | |
| Holopella obsoleta, Sow. | | | V | | | | V | | | | V | | | | | | | | | | V |
| Holopella tenuicincta, M'Coy | | | | | | | | | | | V | | | | | | | | | | |
| Holopella sp. | V | | | | | | | | | | | | | | | | | | | | |
| Holopea sp. | | | | | | | | | V | | | | | | | | | | | | |
| Horiostoma globosum = sculptum, Sow. | V | | | | | V | | | V | | V | | V | | | | | | | | |
| Horiostoma discors (?) Sow. | V | | | | | | | | | | | | | | | | | | | | |
| Platyceras sp. | | | | | | | | | V | | | | | | | | | | | | |
| Bellerophon trilobatus, Sow. | | | | | | | | | V | | | | | | | | | | | | |
| Bellerophon sp. | | | | | | | | | V | | | | | | | | | | | | |
| Pterotheca avirostris, Salt. MS. | | | | | | | | | | | | | V | | | | | | | | |
| Orthoceras annulatum, Sow. | | | | | | | | | | | | | | | | | | | | | |
| Actinoceras Blakei, Foord | | | | | | | | | | | | | V | | | | | | | | V |
| Actinoceras subconicum, Salt. MS. | | | V | | | | | | | | V | | | | | | | | | | |
| Cyrtoceras sp. | V | | | | | | | | | | | | | | | V | | | | | |
| Trochoceras sp. | | | V | | | | | | | | | | | | | | | | | | |
| Gomphoceras sp. | | | V | | | | | | | | | | | | | | | | | | |
| Proetus sp. | | | | | | | | | | | V | | | | | | | | | | |
| Lichas sp. | V | | | | | V | | | | | | | | | | | | | | | |
| Calymene Blumenbachi, Brong. | | | | | | V | | | V | | | | | | | | | | | | |
| Calymene sp. | | | | | | | | | | | | | V | | | | | | | | |
| Encrinurus punctatus, Brünn. | V | | V | | | V | | | V | | V | | V | V | | V | V | V | | | |
| Encrinurus sp. | | | | | | V | | | | | | | | | | | | | | | |
| Cheirurus bimucronatus, Murch. | V | | | | | V | | | | | | | | | | | | | | | |
| Cheirurus sp. | | | | | | | | V | V | | | | | | | | | | | | |
| Phacops caudatus, Brünn. | | | | | | | | | | | | | | V | | | | | | | |
| Phacops Downingiæ, Murch. | | | | | | | | | V | | | | | | | | | | | | |
| Phacops elegans, Sars & Bock | | | | | | | | | V | | | | | | | | | | | | |
| Phacops Weaveri, Salt. | V | | V | V | V | | V | V | V | V | | V | | ? | | | | | | | V |
| Phacops sp. | | | | | | | | | V | | | | | ? | | | | V | | | V |
| Beyrichia sp. | | | | | | | | | V | | | | | | | | | | | | V |
| Primitia sp. | | | | | | | | | V | | | | | | | | | | | | |

### (ii) List of Fossils from the Wenlock Beds.

**V** = from the lower limestone-band; **+** = from the upper limestone-band or overlying beds; **0** indicates that the exact horizon, whether from the upper or from the lower band, is uncertain; **?** indicates that the identification is doubtful.

| | Whitfield. | Horseshoe Farm. | Falfield District. | Daniel's-Wood District. | Stone and Woodford. | Obarfield. |
|---|---|---|---|---|---|---|
| Cyathophyllum trochiforme, M'Coy | V | | | | | |
| Cyathophyllum articulatum, Wahl. | V | ... | V | | | |
| Cyathophyllum angustum, Lonsd. | V | | | | | |
| Cyathophyllum sp. | V | ... | V | + | | |
| Hallia mitrata, His. | V | ... | V | | | |
| Hallia sp. | ... | ... | | + | | |
| Zaphrentis sp. | V | | | | | |
| Favosites aspera, D'Orb. | | | | | | |
| Favosites cristata, Blum. | ... | ... | | + | | |
| Favosites Forbesi, M.-Edw. | V | ... | + | + | | |
| Favosites gothlandica, Fougt. | ... | ... | | + | | |
| Favosites Hisingeri, M.-Edw. | V | ... | V+ | | | |
| Favositella interpunctata, Nich. & Foord | ... | | V | | | |
| Alveolites repens, Fougt. | ... | ... | V | + | | |
| Alveolites sp. | V | ... | ... | + | 0 | |
| Cœnites intertextus, Eichw. | V | ... | V | | | |
| Cœnites juniperinus, Eichw. | V | ... | V | ... | ... | 0 |
| Aulopora serpens, Linn. | ... | ... | | + | | |
| Syringopora bifurcata, Lonsd. | V | | | | | |
| Syringopora sp. | V | | | | | |
| Thecia swinderenana, Goldf. | V | ... | + | | | |
| Monticuliporoid | V+ | + | + | + | 0 | |
| Monotrypa crenulata, Nich. | V | ... | V | + | | |
| Stenopora fibrosa, Goldf. | V | ... | ... | ... | 0 | |
| Propora tubulata, Lonsd. | V | | | | | |
| Tentaculites anglicus, Salt. | ... | + | ... | ? | | |
| Cornulites serpularius, Schloth. | V | ... | V | | | |
| Cornulites sp. | ... | ... | | + | ... | 0 |
| Periechocrinus moniliformis, Mill. | ... | ... | ... | + | | |
| Crinoidal stem-joints | V+ | + | V+ | + | 0 | 0 |
| Fistulipora sp. | V | | | | | |
| Fenestella sp. | V | | | | | |
| Ptilodictya scalpellum, Lonsd. | V | | | | | |
| Lingula sp. | ... | ... | ... | + | | |
| [Orbiculoidea rugata, Sow.] | ? | + | + | | | |
| Orbiculoidea sp. | V | ... | ... | + | | |
| Crania striata (?) Sow. | V | | | | | |
| Stropheodonta filosa, Sow. | V | ... | ... | ? | ? | |
| Leptæna rhomboidalis, Wilck. | V+ | + | V | + | | |
| Plectambonites transversalis, Wahl. | ... | ... | ... | + | | |
| Plectambonites (?) Fletcheri, Dav. | ... | ... | ... | + | | |

| LIST OF FOSSILS FROM THE WENLOCK BEDS (continued). | Whitfield. | Horseshoe Farm. | Falfield District. | Daniel's-Wood District. | Stone and Woodford. | Charfield. |
|---|---|---|---|---|---|---|
| *Strophonella funiculata*, M'Coy | V | + | ... | + | | |
| *Strophomena euglypha*, His. | ... | + | ... | ++ | | |
| *Strophomena compressa*, Sow. | + | ... | ... | ++ | 0 | 0 |
| *Strophomena Waltoni*, Dav. | V | ... | V | | | |
| *Orthothetes pecten*, Linn. | V | + | ... | + | | |
| [*Chonetes striatella*, Dalm.] | ... | + | ... | ... | 0 | |
| *Chonetes* sp. | + | | | | | |
| *Orthis basalis*, Dalm. | V | ... | + | | | |
| *Orthis biloba*, Linn. | | | | + | | |
| *Orthis elegantula*, Dalm. | V+ | + | V | + | 0 | 0 |
| *Orthis rustica*, Sow. | | + | | | | |
| *Scenidium Lewisi*, Dav. | ... | + | ? | ... | ? | |
| *Anastrophia deflexa*, Sow. | ... | ? | | | | |
| *Pentamerus galeatus*, Dalm. | V | + | | | | |
| *Pentamerus rotundus*, Sow. | | | ... | + | | |
| *Rhynchotreta cuneata*, Dalm. | + | + | V | | | |
| *Rhynchonella borealis*, Schloth. | V+ | | | | | |
| *Rhynchonella Davidsoni*, M'Coy | V | ... | + | ? | | |
| *Rhynchonella diodonta*, Dalm. | V+ | ... | V+ | + | | |
| *Rhynchonella Lewisi*, Dav. | | | | ++ | | |
| *Rhynchonella nucula*, Sow. | V+ | ... | ... | + | ... | 0 |
| *Rhynchonella Stricklandi*, Sow. | + | + | | | | |
| *Rhynchonella Wilsoni*, Sow. | + | | | | | |
| *Atrypa reticularis*, Linn. | V+ | + | V | ... | 0 | 0 |
| *Atrypa imbricata*, Sow. | V | | | | | |
| *Glassia læviuscula*, Sow. | V | | | | | |
| *Spirifer crispus*, His. | V | ? | ... | + | | |
| *Spirifer elevatus*, Dalm. | V+ | ... | ... | ++ | | |
| *Spirifer plicatellus*, Linn. | ... | + | V | + | | |
| *Spirifer sulcatus*, His. | ... | + | | | | |
| *Rhynchospira Baylei*, Dav. | ... | + | | | | |
| *Rhynchospira Bouchardi*, Dav. | V | | | | | |
| *Trematospira Salteri*, Dav. | V | + | ... | ... | 0 | |
| *Whitfieldella didyma*, Dalm. | V | ... | V | + | | |
| *Meristina tumida*, Dalm. | ... | + | ... | | | |
| *Meristella* sp. | V | ... | ... | + | | |
| | | | | | | |
| *Pterinæa exasperata*, Goldf. | V | | | | | |
| *Pterinæa lineata*, Goldf. | V | | | | | |
| [*Pterinæa lineatula*, D'Orb. | ... | + | | | | |
| *Pterinæa planulata*, Conrad | + | | | | | |
| *Pterinæa retroflexa*, Wahl. | ... | + | ... | + | ... | 0 |
| *Aviculopecten Danbyi*, M'Coy | ... | + | | | | |
| *Ctenodonta anglica*, D'Orb. | ... | ... | ... | + | | |
| *Cucullella antiqua*, Sow.] | ... | + | | | | |
| *Grammysia cingulata*, His. | V | ... | V | | | |
| *Modiolopsis mytilimeris*, Conrad | ... | ... | ... | ... | ... | 0 |
| *Modiolopsis* sp. | ... | + | ... | ... | 0 | |
| *Goniophora* sp. | V | | | | | |
| *Orthonota* sp. | ... | + | ... | + | | |
| | | | | | | |
| *Naticopsis* sp. | ... | ... | V | | | |
| *Holopella* sp. | V | | | | | |
| *Holopea* sp. | V | | | | | |

| LIST OF FOSSILS FROM THE WENLOCK BEDS (continued). | Whitfield. | Horseshoe Farm. | Falfield District. | Daniel's-Wood District. | Stone and Woodford. | Charfield. |
|---|---|---|---|---|---|---|
| Horiostoma globosum = sculptum, Sow. | V | ... | + | | | |
| Horiostoma discors, Sow. | V | | | | | |
| Platyceras cornubicum, His. | V | ... | V | | | |
| Platyceras oppressum, His. | V | | | | | |
| Platyceras sp. | + | ... | ... | + | | |
| Bellerophon dilatatus, Sow. | ... | ... | ... | ... | ... | 0 |
| Bellerophon sp. | + | ... | ... | + | | |
| Orthoceras sp. | ... | ... | ... | + | | |
| Gomphoceras æquale, Salt. | V | | | | | |
| Illænus sp. | V | ... | ... | ... | ... | 0 |
| Proetus sp. | ... | ... | V | | | |
| Lichas sp. | V | ... | ... | + | | |
| Calymene Blumenbachi, Brongn. | V+ | ... | V | + | | |
| Encrinurus punctatus, Brünn. | + | + | | | | |
| Homalonotus sp. | V | ... | ... | ... | ... | 0 |
| Phacops caudatus, Brünn. | V+ | + | V | ... | 0 | |
| Phacops Downingiæ, Murch. | V+ | + | ... | ... | ? | |
| Phacops Weaveri, Salt. | ... | + | | | | |
| Phacops sp. | ... | ... | ... | + | ... | 0 |
| Beyrichia Klœdeni, M'Coy | ... | ... | ... | + | | |
| Beyrichia sp. | V | ... | ... | + | ... | 0 |
| Primitia sp. | ... | ... | ... | + | ... | 0 |

## DISCUSSION.

The PRESIDENT remarked that, when he first visited Tortworth some thirty years ago, he was chiefly impressed with the unpromising nature of the exposures, a feeling that was deepened when he recently paid a visit to the district under the guidance of Prof. Reynolds. The Authors were all the more to be congratulated on their successful mapping, which could only have been accomplished by much patience and perseverance. The trend-line of the district ran north and south, in the Malvernian direction, and the meridional direction again set in farther north in the Pennine chain. Thus, although the movements which had affected the area were Hercynian, the direction was perpendicular to the Armorican. The cause of this anomaly still remained obscure ; it might have lain in the influence of the coast-line of ' St. George's Island,' or it might have been of a more general nature. He enquired whether the Authors were prepared to throw any light on this question. There was no unconformity between the Old Red Sandstone and the Ludlow at Rhymney, near Cardiff.

Mr. HUDLESTON admitted that he had never seen the Tortworth Inlier, but was much interested in what had just fallen from the

President.   He had himself pointed out in his presidential address to Section C of the British Association at Bristol, ten years ago, that, in the great post-Carboniferous uprise of that region, the change from the east-and-west or Armorican axial line, to the north-and-south or Pennine axial line, takes place in the Vale of Berkeley.   It was for local geologists to describe the details of these movements, and, if possible, to ascertain the cause.

The Fellows were much indebted to the Authors for the fresh information now afforded; and it might be gathered that, on the whole, the Wenlock and Ludlow rocks were much less fossiliferous at Tortworth than in areas farther afield.   The presence of celestine clearly pointed to infiltration from above, and it might be that such action had tended to produce alteration in the beds, especially in those of a calcareous nature, which had acted unfavourably as regards the preservation of fossils.

Dr. C. G. CULLIS remarked upon the interesting discovery by the Authors of masses of celestine in beds of Silurian age; but he believed that such masses were not themselves of that age.   Much evidence, indeed, pointed to their being of secondary origin.   The mineral had never been recorded from Silurian beds of any other part of the country; it was confined to this particular locality— a locality in which it also occurred in the Carboniferous Limestone, the Millstone Grit, and the Keuper Marl.   If it were claimed to be of Silurian age in the Silurian beds, it could equally be claimed to be of Carboniferous age in the Carboniferous Limestone and Millstone Grit, and of Triassic age in the Keuper Marl; and it seemed very improbable that the peculiar conditions necessary for the deposition of strontium-sulphate persisted continuously, or even intermittently, in the region from Silurian until Triassic times.   The celestine was most abundant in the Keuper Marl, which rested horizontally upon the upturned edges of the underlying Palæozoic rocks, and in this formation there was collateral evidence that the conditions during deposition were precisely those suitable for the precipitation of this and other sulphates.   The occurrence of the mineral in various underlying formations could be simply explained by the downward percolation along joints and bedding-planes of waters containing small quantities of sulphate in solution, and the substitution of this for calcareous carbonate under favourable conditions.

With regard to the vertical and slightly-overturned structure of the Silurian strata described by the Authors, he referred to the fact that a precisely-similar structure was to be traced northwards across the Severn through the various Silurian exposures, as far at least as the remote end of the Malverns.   In the latter region it had always seemed to him that the disturbance might have been caused by the crushing of the older Palæozoic rocks against a stationary buttress or 'knob' formed by the pre-Cambrian massif.   That massif had a similar north-and-south alignment to that of the upturned or overturned Silurian beds of the Malverns, May Hill, Newnham, and Tortworth inliers; and he suggested, as a tentative explanation, that the extreme disturbance along this line might be an expression of the prolongation, beneath the surface, of such a buttress in a southerly direction.

He also congratulated the Authors upon having made a valuable addition to our knowledge of the Palæozoic geology of this part of England.

Prof. REYNOLDS briefly replied, saying, in answer to Dr. Cullis, that the Authors were fully prepared to accept his suggestion with regard to the derivation of the celestine.

Mr. REED commented on the absence of any palæontological evidence of the occurrence of Lower Llandovery beds. The Upper Llandovery of the district was characterized by the presence of certain species peculiar to the locality or rare elsewhere (as, for example, *Phacops Weaveri, Cœlospira hemispherica*, etc.), and the non-occurrence or rarity of some typical forms, such as *Pentamerus oblongus*. A certain admixture of Wenlock species was probably connected with the calcareous nature of some of the beds. The Wenlock Series accordingly showed no such hard-and-fast line of division palæontologically from the Llandovery as usual. The rarity of recognizable crinoids and massive corals, the want of variety in the trilobites, and the occurrence of certain local peculiar species (such as *Orthis basalis*) were noticeable features. The Ludlow formation was undoubtedly present in the area, as proved by the discovery of *Aviculopecten Danbyi, Anodontopsis securiformis*, etc., but fossils were scarce in it.

29. *The* BALA *and* LLANDOVERY ROCKS *of* GLYN CEIRIOG (NORTH
WALES). By Dr. THEODORE GROOM, M.A., F.G.S., and PHILIP
LAKE, M.A., F.G.S. (Read May 20th, 1908.)

[PLATE LIII—MAP.]

### CONTENTS.

|  | Page |
|---|---|
| I. Introduction | 546 |
| II. Literature | 547 |
| III. Section in the Glyn Valley | 551 |
| IV. Detailed Description of the Subdivisions | 555 |
| V. Structure of the Area | 580 |
| VI. Comparison with other Areas | 589 |

## I. INTRODUCTION.

IT was in continuation of the work which we had begun at Corwen
that in 1892 we paid our first visit to Glyn Ceiriog.[1] At Corwen
we had been unable to detect any decisive proof of unconformity at
the base of the Corwen Grit; but in the Bala Beds below we did not
find the characteristic fossils of the Sholeshook Limestone or of
other Upper Bala deposits, and were therefore led to believe that
the highest beds of the Bala Series were absent, and that there was
probably an unconformity which was too slight to be visible in so
small an area.

The section at Glyn Ceiriog encouraged the hope that higher
Bala Beds might there be found, and it seemed, moreover, to afford
excellent opportunities for the examination of the whole Bala Series.
To judge from the map of the Geological Survey, or from a cursory
inspection of the ground, it would be difficult to imagine a locality
more favourably situated for the purpose. The valley of the Ceiriog
appears to cut through the whole of the Bala Series, from the lowest
ash-band up to the Glyn Grit; and, owing to the steepness of its
banks, the rocks are admirably exposed, while most of the beds are
fossiliferous almost to excess.

It was not long, however, before we found unexpected difficulties.
The same succession, or rather the upper portion of it, should
appear in the nearly parallel valleys of Tyn-y-twmpath and Nantyr;
but when we examined those valleys we found beds that were
quite unlike any in the Ceiriog Valley, and yet it seemed improbable
that the character of the deposits and of their fossil contents should
change completely in so short a distance. It was not until we
had paid several further visits to the district that we found the
explanation.

Although the section in the Ceiriog Valley appears complete, both
on the map and in the field, this appearance is really deceptive.
The valley is crossed by a long fault that runs nearly parallel to
the strike of the beds and dips at nearly the same angle as the beds

[1] This village is often locally called Glyn.

themselves, and thereby a considerable portion of the succession is cut out. Such a fault is not easy to detect; but we have now traced it from east to west for a distance of 5 miles, and there is evidence that it extends considerably farther westwards.

Owing to the difficulty of detecting faults of this nature, it is quite possible that there may be others that we have overlooked; but, if so, their effect appears to be unimportant, and (excepting for the fault already noticed) the succession in the Glyn Valley seems to be unbroken.

We have failed to discover any evidence of unconformity between the supposed Corwen Grit and the Bala Beds below; and the fossils obtained from the grit (which is here often calcareous) agree very closely with those from the uppermost Bala Beds of the district. The most important palæontological break occurs, not at the base, but at the top of the grit, between the latter and the Llandovery Slates above. The grit itself must, therefore, belong to the Bala Series. Since, however, there are certain palæontological differences between the beds immediately below the grit at Corwen and those immediately below the grit at Glyn, it is possible that the Glyn Grit may not be the precise equivalent of the Corwen Grit. On this point we prefer, for the present, to suspend our judgment, and to confine ourselves to the statement that the grit at Glyn belongs definitely to the Bala Series and not to the Llandovery.

## II. LITERATURE.

1841. J. E. BOWMAN. 'Notice of Upper Silurian Rocks in the Vale of Llangollen, North Wales; & of a Contiguous Eruption of Trap & Compact Felspar' Trans. Manchester Geol. Soc. vol. i, pp. 194–211, & 2 sections (on pl. vi).

1843. ADAM SEDGWICK. 'On the Older Palæozoic (Protozoic) Rocks of North Wales' Proc. Geol. Soc. vol. iv, pp. 251–68, with map & sections. See also Quart. Journ. Geol. Soc. vol. i (1845) pp. 5–22.

1846. DANIEL SHARPE. 'Contributions to the Geology of North Wales' Quart. Journ. Geol. Soc. vol. ii, pp. 283–316, & pls. xii (map)–xiii.

1850. Geological Survey, Quarter-sheet 74 SE. Re-issued, with alterations, in 1855.

1859. D. C. DAVIES. 'The Geology of Glyn Ceiriog' Oswestry & Welshpool Nat. Field-Club & Arch. Soc., Report of Meetings 1857–64 (1865) pp. 32–36.

1864. D. C. DAVIES. 'On the Bala Limestone & its Associated Beds in North Wales' Proc. Liverpool Geol. Soc., Session 5, pp. 21–30, with one section.

1865. D. C. DAVIES. 'List of Fossils described from the Bala Limestone & its Associated Beds of North Wales' Proc. Liverpool Geol. Soc., Session 6, pp. 30–34.

1865. D. C. DAVIES. 'A Walk over the "Ash-Bed" & "Bala Limestones" near Oswestry' Geol. Mag. vol. ii, pp. 343–47, with one section.

1866. A. C. RAMSAY. 'The Geology of North Wales' Mem. Geol. Surv. vol. iii.

1867. J. W. SALTER. 'Bala & Hirnant Limestone' (Letter) Geol. Mag. vol. iv, pp. 233–34.

1867. D. C. DAVIES. 'Bala & Hirnant Limestones at Mynydd Fron Frys in Glyn Ceiriog' (Letter) Geol. Mag. vol. iv, pp. 283–84.

1872. D. C. DAVIES. 'On the Overlapping of several Geological Formations on the North Wales Border' Proc. Geol. Assoc. vol. ii (1873) pp. 299–308, with map & sections.

1879. R. ETHERIDGE. 'On the Occurrence of the Genus *Ramipora* (Toula) in the Caradoc Beds of the Neighbourhood of Corwen' Geol. Mag. dec. 2, vol. vi, pp. 241-44 & pl. vi.

1885. THOMAS RUDDY. 'List of Caradoc or Bala Fossils found in the Neighbourhood of Bala, Corwen, & Glyn Ceiriog' Proc. Chester Soc. Nat. Sci. pt. iii, pp. 113-24.

1885. G. W. SHRUBSOLE. 'Note on *Glauconome disticha*, from the Bala Beds of Glyn Ceiriog' Proc. Chester Soc. Nat. Sci. no. 3, pp. 98-100.

1893. P. LAKE & T. T. GROOM. 'The Llandovery & Associated Rocks of the Neighbourhood of Corwen' Quart. Journ. Geol. Soc. vol. xlix, pp. 426-39, with map & sections.

1893. T. H. WALLER. 'Note on a Rock from Glyn Ceiriog' Midland Naturalist, vol. xvi, pp. 201-204.

1894. T. McKENNY HUGHES. 'Observations on the Silurian Rocks of North Wales' (paper read in 1886) Proc. Chester Soc. Nat. Sci. no. 4 (1894) pp. 141-60, with two sections.

1897. JOHAN KIÆR. 'Faunistische Uebersicht der Etage 5 des norwegischen Silursystem' Videnskabsselskabets Skrifter: I. Mathematisk-naturv. Klasse, 1897, No. 3. (Kristiania.)

1904. T. H. COPE & J. LOMAS. 'On the Igneous Rocks of the Berwyns' Rep. Brit. Assoc. 1903 (Southport) pp. 664-65.

1904. THOMAS H. COPE. 'Types of Rock-Flow in the Ceiriog Valley & their Analogies with River-Structure' Proc. Liverpool Geol. Soc. vol. ix, pt. 4, pp. 303-31.

The earliest account of the geology of the district with which we are acquainted, is to be found in Bowman's paper on the Silurian rocks of the Vale of Llangollen. That author is concerned chiefly with the Silurian beds; but he also describes in some detail the igneous rocks of the Ceiriog, and comes to the conclusion that they are intrusive. He seems to consider the crag which overlooks Pandy ('Pen y Graig' of his paper) as a neck through which the igneous rocks have been poured.

But by far the most important of the earlier references to the district are those in Sedgwick's paper on the older Palæozoic rocks of North Wales. Unfortunately the published abstract is somewhat brief, and the sections, three of which pass through this region, are on a scale too small to show the details of the succession. Both the abstract and the sections were prepared by Warburton from the original manuscript, and Sedgwick states that they do not fairly represent his views, and that he himself cannot understand the sections.[1] It is clear, however, that in this neighbourhood he recognized three main subdivisions in the rocks which are coloured as Bala on the Geological-Survey map, namely: (1) a lower group formed by the beds south of Pont-y-Meibion; (2) a middle group full of fossils, and containing several bands of contemporaneous volcanic rock; and (3) an upper group, including the two well-known limestones, which are placed by Sedgwick high above the Bala Limestone. The third group

'passes upwards into pale-coloured earthy slates and these seem to pass, without a break, into the overlying Denbigh flagstone.' (Quart. Journ. Geol. Soc. vol. i, 1845, p. 14.)

Subsequently he came to the conclusion that the upper series is not

[1] Preface to Salter's 'Catalogue of the Collection of Cambrian & Silurian Fossils contained in the Geological Museum of the University of Cambridge' 1873, p. xxvii.

far from the horizon of the Bala Limestone, and that the passage upwards into the Denbigh Flags is apparent rather than real.

Daniel Sharpe, in his 'Contributions to the Geology of North Wales,' gives some details concerning this district, and his map shows several intrusive masses in the neighbourhood of the Ceiriog. In his notes he expresses his indebtedness to a manuscript map by Bowman for this portion of North Wales.

The Geological-Survey map of the district was published in 1850, and again, with alterations and additions, in 1855. It seems to have been largely the work of Jukes, and extracts from his notes will be found in the chapter on the Berwyn Hills in Ramsay's memoir on the Geology of North Wales. Three bands of ash are traced upon the map, and two bands of limestone, the lower of which is considered to be on the horizon of the Bala Limestone. The Tarannons are represented as unconformable on the beds below. The boundary drawn upon the map is nearly correct; the simulation of unconformity is, however, due to faulting, which affects not only the Tarannon and Wenlock Beds, but also the beds below.

On the Geological-Survey map no Llandovery beds are recognized in the district, and the Tarannon Shales are represented as resting directly on the Bala Series. In a letter to the 'Geological Magazine' in 1867, Salter suggests that the upper limestone of Mynydd Fron Frys may be the equivalent of the Hirnant Limestone, and that the northern end of the hill probably consists of Llandovery rocks. He also says that the hill of Pentre and the slopes above Tal-y-garth are almost certainly Llandovery. In a subsequent letter, D. C. Davies states that he had already arrived at the same conclusion.

The fullest account of the local succession which has yet appeared is to be found in a series of papers by D. C. Davies, and despite certain errors in interpretation, which detract from the value of his work, his account is so near to the apparent truth that it will be well to give his results in some detail.

Of his several papers we may take that of 1872 (published in 1873) as representing his final conclusions. In the second section accompanying this paper (Proc. Geol. Assoc. vol. ii, p. 303)—a section from Pont-y-Meibion to Pont Dolwern—he recognizes the following subdivisions, in descending order :—

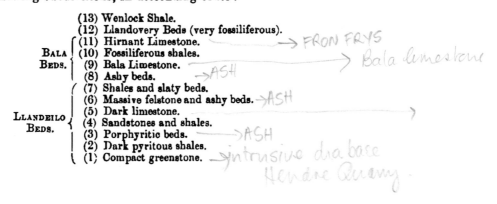

|  |  |
|---|---|
|  | (13) Wenlock Shale. |
|  | (12) Llandovery Beds (very fossiliferous). |
| BALA BEDS. | (11) Hirnant Limestone. |
|  | (10) Fossiliferous shales. |
|  | (9) Bala Limestone. |
|  | (8) Ashy beds. |
| LLANDEILO BEDS. | (7) Shales and slaty beds. |
|  | (6) Massive felstone and ashy beds. |
|  | (5) Dark limestone. |
|  | (4) Sandstones and shales. |
|  | (3) Porphyritic beds. |
|  | (2) Dark pyritous shales. |
|  | (1) Compact greenstone. |

The compact greenstone (No. 1 of the foregoing succession) is the intrusive diabase worked in the Ceiriog Granite Company's quarry immediately south of the area covered by our map. Nos. 3, 6, & 8 are apparently the three ash-bands of the Geological Survey; No. 9 is the limestone of Dolhir and Cefngoed, which is correlated by the Survey, as well as by Davies, with the Bala Limestone; and No. 11 is the upper limestone marked upon the Geological-Survey map. Concerning the lowest band of limestone, No. 5, there appears to be some confusion. In Davies's earlier section along the same line he places this limestone above the second ash (No. 6 of his section), and states that it is met with near some old mines in the neighbourhood of Hafod-y-gareg on the Teirw. These old mines still exist, and fossils occur in the beds near by, but we have found no limestone there. The beds above the second ash are, however, often calcareous; and in Nant Blaen-y-cwm[1] there is a small outcrop of definite limestone, at or about this horizon. We have never found any limestone below the second ash, and our observations therefore agree with Davies's first section rather than with his last. It may be observed that Sedgwick shows a third band of limestone, besides the two in the upper group, and in his Section VIII places it in the bed of the Teirw; but the smallness of the scale employed makes it difficult to identify the several bands of 'porphyry.'

As for Davies's classification into Llandeilo and Bala, it will appear subsequently that (in the line of his section) there is indeed a considerable palæontological break at the base of the Dolhir Limestone (No. 9 of his section), and that the fossils above are very different from the fossils below. Nevertheless, both must be referred to the Bala Series, as that group is generally understood, and of the presence of Llandeilo Beds above the lowest ash there is no evidence.

According to Davies, there is an unconformity at the base of the Llandovery Beds and towards the west they overlap the Hirnant Limestone and the beds below, until they lie almost on the Bala Limestone itself. It may be observed, however, that in his map Davies includes in the Llandovery a large area near Moel Ferna which is certainly occupied by Bala Beds; and even in his line of section the hill of Pentre, the beds of which he calls 'Llandovery,' is in reality formed almost entirely of Bala rocks. We shall show that his identification of the beds close to Glyn as Llandovery is correct, but we cannot accept his boundary elsewhere.

Moreover, in the map accompanying Davies's paper the Tarannons are restricted to a very short and narrow strip of ground by Moel Ferna, and are overlapped on both sides by the Wenlock Beds, while east of Dol-y-Wern the overlap increases until the Wenlock lies directly on the Bala Series. It is difficult to understand on what grounds Davies based his boundaries near Moel

---

[1] Nant Blaen-y-cwm is the direct continuation, west of the limits of our map (Pl. LIII), of the valley of the Teirw. The name Teirw is, in this part, applied to a tributary stream that comes in from the north.

Ferna, but towards the east it is clear that he was deceived by the fault that runs from Dol-y-Wern towards the south-south-east.

Since the appearance of Davies's paper but little has been written on the area in question. Mr. Thomas Ruddy gave a list of fossils from Cefn-goed, Nant Iorwerth, and Pont Hafod-y-gynfawr; Prof. Hughes has published a list of fossils from the supposed Corwen Grit of the latter locality, and we ourselves have added several species to this list. Mr. T. H. Waller has described a specimen from the 'China-ash bed' near Pont-y-Meibion, and concludes that it is a volcanic ash. This is the lowest ash of the Geological Survey.

The last paper to which it will be neccessary to refer was communicated by Messrs. Cope & Lomas to the British Association in 1903. In it they maintain that the 'greenstone' of Hendre, south of Pandy, and the three ash-bands shown on the Geological-Survey map are all intrusive. With regard to the greenstone there has never been any question, and there is little doubt that the Coed-y-glyn rock, which Messrs. Cope & Lomas identify as the 'Little Ash' of Jukes, is also intrusive. But in the case of the other bands we find no evidence of intrusion, and we agree with the majority of previous observers that they consist chiefly of ashes and tuffs. As will be shown in the sequel, the rock of the Coed-y-glyn quarries is not the 'Little Ash' of Jukes.

### III. SECTION IN THE GLYN VALLEY.

Despite the long strike-fault mentioned in the introduction, by far the most perfect section in the district is exposed in the valley of the Ceiriog between Glyn and Pandy; and, in order to make the general succession clear, it will be convenient to begin with a brief description of this section, supplementing it by a short account of the upper beds, which are not shown in the valley itself, but appear on the hillside in the immediate neighbourhood. We shall then take each of the subdivisions in turn and describe it in detail, tracing its distribution throughout the area of our map.

Cwm-Clwyd Ash.—So far as we have seen, the dark slates and sandstones that lie below the lowest band of ash are, in this neighbourhood, almost completely unfossiliferous; and, as they hardly come within the area with which we are concerned, we shall leave them out of consideration, and begin with the lowest ash-band itself, which may be termed the 'Cwm-Clwyd Ash.'

This is formed of some 250 feet of volcanic rocks, which are very distinctly bedded and include ashes and tuffs of various degrees of coarseness. The whole series is finely exposed in the cliffs at the entrance to the lateral valley known as Cwm Clwyd.

Teirw Beds.—The ash is succeeded by a band of slate, followed by a great mass of sandstones with intercalated beds of slate. Some of the sandstones are very compact, but more generally they are coarse and contain a large amount of volcanic material and many fragments of slate. They are finely exposed in the quarries that have recently been opened on the right bank of the Ceiriog immediately above Pandy, and may also be seen in the old Teirw-Hill quarry, in the corner between the Teirw and the Ceiriog.

The sandstone is followed by some 500 or 600 feet of slaty beds with occasional siliceous bands. They appear at intervals in the wood on the right bank of the Ceiriog, and also on the lower slopes of Craig-y-Pandy.

Craig-y-Pandy Ash.—Upon these slaty beds rests the second ash of the Geological Survey. It forms the fine crag known as Craig-y-Pandy, and has been quarried from time to time both on Craig-y-Pandy itself and also in the 'China-clay Quarry'[1] on the right bank of the river. The relations of this band to the beds above and below are sometimes very complex, but, as we shall show subsequently, the greater part, if not the whole, consists of tuffs and ashes, as the officers of the Geological Survey and most other observers have supposed.

Bryn Beds.—Immediately overlying the Craig-y-Pandy Ash is a series of slates and sandstones, the base of which is seen at the northern edge of the China-clay Quarry. About 60 or 70 feet above the ash is a sheet of intrusive rock which is extensively worked in Coed-y-glyn Quarry. The sheet appears to be very irregular and discontinuous, but may be traced at intervals for a considerable distance. It has apparently been

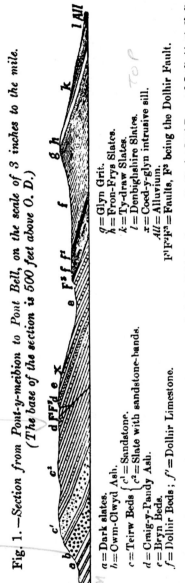

Fig. 1.—Section from Pont-y-meibion to Pont Bell, on the scale of 3 inches to the mile. (The base of the section is 500 feet above O. D.)

a = Dark slates.
b = Cwm-Clwyd Ash.
c = Teirw Beds { c¹ = Sandstone.
                { c² = Slate with sandstone-bands.
d = Craig-y-Pandy Ash.
e = Bryn Beds.
f = Dolhir Beds ; f′ = Dolhir Limestone.

g = Glyn Grit.
h = Fron-Frys Slates.
k = Ty-draw Slates.
l = Denbighshire Slates.
x = Coed-y-glyn intrusive sill.
All = Alluvium.
F¹F²F³ = Faults, F³ being the Dolhir Fault.

---

[1] 'Pandy Quarry' of the 6-inch Ordnance-Survey map.

almost universally mistaken for the 'Little Ash' of Jukes, but the 'Little Ash' lies at a higher level and is truly an ash.

Above this intrusive sheet lie some 400 feet of slates with beds of sandstone, which are sometimes very calcareous and contain numerous fossils. The 'Little Ash' itself is exposed at Pen-y-graig, where it is marked on the 1-inch map of the Geological Survey, but it is not visible at any other point in the valley, and does not appear in the line of the section.

The Dolhir Fault.—A long strike-fault now cuts off the top of these beds, slanting down the western side of the valley from Pen-y-graig to Dolhir, and up the eastern side, along the foot of a line of low cliffs, towards Pant. Its strike is east and west, and its dip is northwards at 20°.

Dolhir Beds.—The fault is followed by beds which differ completely in character and in fossils from those below. Immediately above the fault they consist of soft shivery slates with nodules of limestone. A little higher the nodules become more abundant, until they form a band consisting almost entirely of limestone, which has been quarried by the roadside above Dolhir and also on the opposite bank below Plas Einion. The limestone is followed by some 600 feet of slaty beds which continue nearly to the grit above. They again become calcareous as we approach the limestone at the base of the grit, and there appears to be no very definite line of demarcation between the two series.

Glyn Grit and Limestone.—The Dolhir Beds are overlain, apparently with perfect conformity, by a band which has usually been taken as the equivalent of the Corwen Grit. On the right bank of the Ceiriog the band begins with a crystalline limestone, which is well exposed in two small quarries on the top of Mynydd Fron Frys. In the upper part of the limestone thin siliceous bands begin to appear, and these gradually become increasingly abundant until they form a thick bed of platy sandstone, which may be traced almost uninterruptedly for 3 miles.

On the west side of the valley the limestone has not yet been detected, but the grit is of very considerable thickness and covers a large part of the hill-slope on the southern side of Nant Llafar.

As we are now by no means certain that either the limestone or the grit is the equivalent of the Corwen Grit, we propose for the present to speak of this band as the Glyn Grit, leaving its relations to the Corwen Grit for future study.

Fron-Frys Slates.—The grit is followed in Nant Llafar and on the slopes of Mynydd Fron Frys by grey slates with thin siliceous bands, very similar in character to the grey slates that we have described in the neighbourhood of Corwen. At Corwen, however, they seem to be almost unfossiliferous, while near Glyn

Ceiriog fossils are very abundant in some places. The fossils are distinctly Llandovery forms, and differ considerably from those of the beds below.

**Ty-draw Slates.**—On both sides of the Ceiriog the Fron-Frys Slates are succeeded by a considerable thickness of pale greenish slates, resembling the Tarannon Shales of other areas. They are visible at many points, and have been extensively quarried on the northern slope of Mynydd Fron Frys.

**Denbighshire Slates.**—The green slates are followed, apparently with perfect conformity, by the dark slates that form the lower portion of the Wenlock Series in this district. The relations of the two are not very well shown in the valley itself; but at Cefn-isaf the green slates are interbedded in their upper part with black bands very similar in character to the Denbighshire Slates, and the boundary appears to be very vague and indistinct. The Denbighshire Slates themselves are well exposed in the Glyn quarries and also elsewhere in this neighbourhood, but we do not propose to deal with them at length in this communication.

This completes the succession, so far as it is exposed in the valley of the Ceiriog between Pandy and Glyn Ceiriog, and excepting at the Dolhir Fault the sequence is apparently unbroken. This fault, however, cuts out the base of the Dolhir Beds and the top of the Bryn Series, and in the valley itself it is by no means clear how much of the succession may be missing. Fortunately, the fault runs somewhat obliquely to the strike, and consequently higher beds of the Bryn Series are exposed towards the east, while the beds below the Dolhir Series are exposed towards the west. The latter are dark graptolitic slates, entirely distinct from both the Bryn and the Dolhir Series; we therefore group them separately, and the whole succession, so far as it is exposed in the area of our map, is as follows :—

|  |  |  |
|---|---|---|
|  | Denbighshire Slates.................. | WENLOCK. |
|  | Ty-draw Slates ..................... | } TARANNON & |
|  | Fron-Frys Slates..................... | } LLANDOVERY. |
| Glyn-Valley Series. | { Glyn Grit and Limestone ......... | |
|  | { Dolhir Beds.......................... | |
|  | Graptolitic Slates ................. | |
|  | Break. | } BALA. |
| Pandy Series. | ( Pen-y-graig Ash ..................... | |
|  | Bryn Beds ........................... | |
|  | < Craig-y-Pandy Ash ............ .. | |
|  | Teirw Beds ........................... | |
|  | ( Cwm-Clwyd Ash...... ............. ) | |

## IV. DETAILED DESCRIPTION OF THE SUBDIVISIONS.

(1) **Cwm-Clwyd Ash.**—On the 1-inch Geological-Survey map this is marked as a continuous belt extending across the whole of the district. It is, indeed, exposed, west of our area, in the upper part of the Ceiriog; but between that point and the valley of the Ceiriog at Pandy it is scarcely ever visible, presumably on account of the covering of peat and heather that conceals the underlying rocks. The westernmost point in our map (Pl. LIII) at which it actually appears at the surface is in the woods of Erw-gerrig. Even here the exposures are very poor, and it is not until we cross to the east side of the Ceiriog that the band can be studied to advantage. It forms a series of fine crags near Cwm Clwyd, where the bedding is well displayed, some of the beds being very compact and others of medium grain. A remarkable nodular rock which occurs here presents a somewhat deceptive resemblance to an amygdaloidal lava, but under the microscope the material of the apparent nodules is seen to be similar to that of the matrix in which they lie.[1]

From Cwm Clwyd the band may be traced towards Spring Hill. For a considerable distance it lies at the top of Springhill Wood and in the fields above, gradually sinking down into the wood towards the east. About 450 yards west of the farm it is dislocated by a small fault. Beyond this it lies just within the northern margin of the wood, which it leaves to cross the stream immediately south of Spring Hill. Here it is very thin, compared with its great development at Cwm Clwyd, and is underlain by slate with sandstone-bands and overlain by sandstone. Beyond the stream it can be traced for some distance by the line of blocks on the hillside, but after 700 or 800 yards even these disappear beneath the heather, and there is no satisfactory evidence of the course that it takes. Our boundary is, therefore, drawn on the assumption that there has been no great change in the strike.

Near Llechrhydau the ash again comes into sight, at first as a small patch about 150 yards south-west of the farm, and again in full strength at Llechrhydau itself. At this point there has evidently been a very considerable amount of disturbance, and the exact relations of the beds are not very clear. The ash forms a broad band running nearly due south from the farm, and appears to lie conformably upon the sandstone and slates to the west of it, but to be separated from the beds on the east by a fault. About 300 yards south of the farm the ash is thrown into a small anticline faulted on one side, which is well exposed on the western bank of the stream.

A little farther south, the band crosses the Morda, and forms a line of picturesque crags along the crest of its eastern bank, where the character of the beds is well displayed. The greater part of the band consists of platy beds of fine or medium grain, but there are two or three beds of very coarse tuff containing more or less rounded

---

[1] See T. H. Waller, ' Midland Naturalist ' vol. xvi (1803) p. 201.

fragments, many of which are volcanic: among these are well-banded rhyolites. The very coarse tuffs are naturally variable in thickness and local in occurrence, but everywhere the band is distinctly stratified. The accompanying section (fig. 2) shows the succession in the southernmost crag.

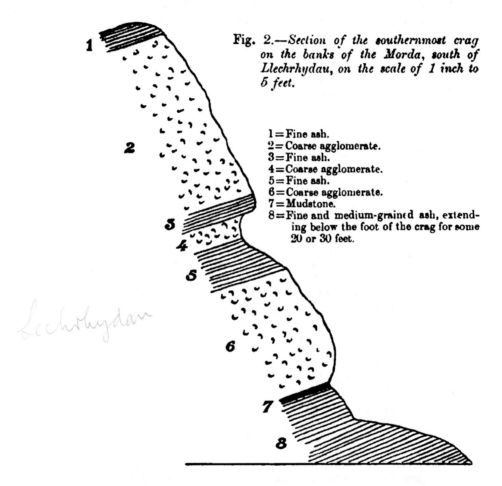

Fig. 2.—*Section of the southernmost crag on the banks of the Morda, south of Llechrhydau, on the scale of 1 inch to 5 feet.*

1 = Fine ash.
2 = Coarse agglomerate.
3 = Fine ash.
4 = Coarse agglomerate.
5 = Fine ash.
6 = Coarse agglomerate.
7 = Mudstone.
8 = Fine and medium-grained ash, extending below the foot of the crag for some 20 or 30 feet.

The ash now leaves the line of the Morda, and enters the wood of Cefn-coch. It is well shown in the stream that runs along the north-western boundary of that wood; but in the wood itself its course is indicated merely by loose blocks, and farther east the only actual exposure is in the little valley south of 'The Springs.' The outcrop of the band, as indicated on our map (Pl. LIII), is inferred from the distribution of the ash-blocks and the contour of the ground.

Nowhere in the course of this band have we seen any evidence of intrusion; and the regular stratification, the frequent alternations of fine and coarse beds, and the occasional inclusion of thin seams of interbedded slate, make it certain that the band as a whole is contemporaneous with the beds among which it lies. We have found no trace of the intense metamorphism of the overlying and underlying beds to which Messrs. Cope & Lomas refer.

(2) Teirw Beds.—The beds between the Cwm-Clwyd Ash and the Craig-y-Pandy Ash may be divided roughly into (i) a lower division, consisting chiefly of sandstones and grits with subordinate slates; and (ii) an upper division, consisting chiefly of slates with subordinate sandstone-bands.

The lower division is well exposed in the valley of the Teirw, especially upon the southern bank of the stream; in Teirw-Hill

Fig. 3.—*Slate-fragments in the grits of the Teirw Beds, at the quarries on the right bank of the Ceiriog at Pandy.*

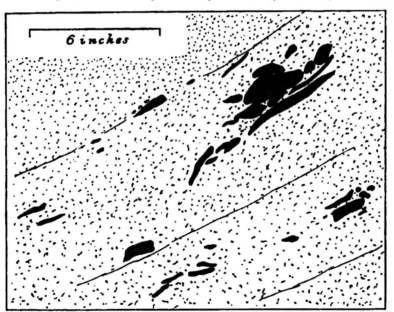

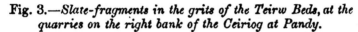

[The oblique lines show the direction of the bedding.]

Quarry; and in the new quarries opened on the right bank of the Ceiriog near Pandy. At Cwm Clwyd the sandstones do not lie directly on the ash, but are separated by some 50 or 60 feet of slate. Many of the beds are very coarse and contain volcanic fragments, while others are fine and compact. False bedding is occasionally well shown. The coarser beds are remarkable for the number of flattened fragments of slate that they contain (see fig. 3). Some of these are rounded or disc-like in shape, while

2 P 2

others are more irregular, and they are of all sizes up to at least 6 inches across. In the quarries on the right bank of the Ceiriog, the fragments of slate show a distinct tendency to lie obliquely to the bedding, the inclination being downwards from south to north, apparently indicating that the current in which they were deposited flowed from north to south. In the upper portion of the gritty series numerous fossils have been found, and among the chief localities may be mentioned the northern end of the quarries on the right bank of the Ceiriog at Pandy ; the old tramway-cutting along the southern bank of the Teirw ; and some small openings farther up this stream. Elsewhere in the area represented on the map (Pl. LIII) there are no very good exposures of these beds. Near Spring Hill, as has already been mentioned, the ash is overlain immediately by sandstone ; while at Llechrhydau the beds that immediately overlie the ash seem to have been cut out by a fault. The sandstones have been extensively quarried near Pandy for paving-stones, road-metal, and concrete.

The beds that rest upon these sandstones and grits are fairly exposed in the woods of Craig-y-gelli and Craig-y-Pandy, and also, less perfectly, on the right bank of the Ceiriog below Pandy. They consist chiefly of slates, with more or less numerous bands of sandstone. The sandstone-bands vary in thickness, from an inch or less up to about 4 feet.

The Teirw Beds are characterized especially by the abundance of gasteropods and lamellibranchs. Many of these pass up into the succeeding groups, but *Bellerophon nodosus, Cyclonema crebristria, Euomphalus corndensis (?)*, and *Modiolopsis M'Coyi* are, so far as our observations go, confined to this series. *Lingula tenuigranulata* and *Asaphus Powisi* are also characteristic, and do not occur in the beds above ; *L. tenuigranulata*, however, is rare or difficult to find. It may be remarked here that the greater number of these characteristic forms occur only in the sandy and ashy beds at the base of the series.

Fossils are sometimes abundant in layers so rich in volcanic material as to deserve the name of ash. Thus, in an old roadside quarry east-south-east of Llechrhydau, thin layers of ash are crowded with complete specimens of *Plectambonites sericea* and other fossils.

On the following page (559) is the list of the fossils that we have identified from the Teirw Beds.

(3) Craig-y-Pandy Ash.—In the area of our map (Pl. LIII) the westernmost exposure of this ash occurs in the neighbourhood of Ty'n-y-pistyll. From the farmyard it runs down into the Teirw, and then slants gently up the northern bank of the stream towards the east. Owing to a small fault, it terminates abruptly in a prominent crag, which rises through the wood about 400 yards below Ty-du ; but it reappears a little farther north in the rugged eminence near Ty-isaf. Here again it is displaced by another fault,

LIST OF FOSSILS FROM THE TEIRW BEDS.

| Found also in beds above. | In this and the following lists those species that are common or fairly common are indicated by the letter (c). These may be either locally abundant, or widely distributed in smaller numbers. | | Found also in beds above. |
|---|---|---|---|
| × | *Monticulipora fibrosa,* Goldf. (c). | *Ctenodonta* cf. *regularis,* Portl. | |
| | | *Ctenodonta varicosa,* Salt. (c)...... | × |
| ? | *Ortonia* sp. (c). | *Cucullella* (?) sp. | |
| | | *Modiolopsis* cf. *platyphyllus,* Salt | |
| × | *Lingula ovata,* M'Coy. | *Modiolopsis M'Coyi,* Salt. (= *M.* | |
| | *Lingula tenuigranulata,* M'Coy. | *modiolaris,* Conr. of M'Coy.) | |
| × | *Orthis calligramma,* Dalm. (c). | *Pterinæa* (?) sp. | |
| × | *Orthis elegantula,* Dalm. | | |
| | *Orthis vespertilio,* Sow. (c). | *Orthoceras politum,* M'Coy ...... | × |
| × | *Orthis retrorsistria,* M'Coy (c). | | |
| | *Pholidops* cf. *implicata,* Sow. | *Asaphus Powisi,* Murch. (c). | |
| × | *Plectambonites sericea,* Sow. (c). | *Calymene Caractaci* (?) Salt. .. .... | × |
| × | *Rafinesquina deltoidea,* Conrad. | *Calymene senaria* (Conrad) | |
| × | *Rafinesquina expansa,* Sow. (c). | Salter (a) ..................... | × |
| | | *Homalonotus* sp. | |
| × | *Bellerophon bilobatus,* Sow. | *Illænus Bowmanni,* Salt. ...... ... | × |
| | *Bellerophon nodosus,* Salt. | *Trinucleus concentricus,* Eaton (c). | × |
| | *Cyclonema crebristria,* M'Coy. | | |
| | *Euomphalus corndensis* (?) Sow. | *Tetradella complicata,* Salt. (c) ... | × |
| × | *Murchisonia gyrogonia,* M'Coy (c). | | |
| | *Pleurotomaria* (?) sp. | | |

and reappears below in the banks and bed of the river. For some 500 yards above Pont Hafod-y-gareg it occurs on both sides of the stream, and is greatly sheared in the neighbourhood of a fault that runs nearly along the line of the stream. The fault is visible a little east of the bridge, in a small tunnel that has been driven into the side of the hill.

At the bridge the band of ash crosses the river, and thence forms the rocky crest of the northern bank of the valley as far as Cráig-y-Pandy. Along this rugged crest the thickness of the band appears to vary considerably; but, as the strike of the beds above is sometimes oblique to the outcrop of the ash, it seems probable that, in places at least, a fault may run along the upper margin of the ash, and to this may possibly be due the apparent variation in thickness. The relations of the ash to the beds below are also extremely complex. Sometimes extensive masses of slate occur in the lower part of the ash, and sometimes great masses of ash occur in the upper part of the slates. These masses are not lenticular in shape, but often present square and abrupt terminations; and they have evidently not been deposited contemporaneously with the beds among which they lie.

One of the most remarkable cases of this kind is to be seen just

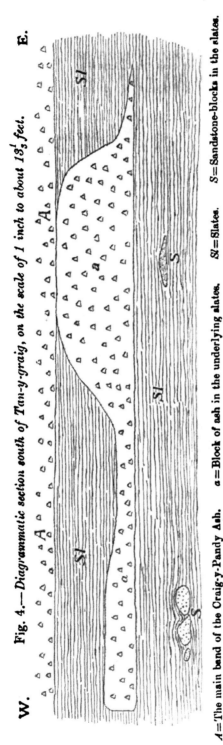

W.

E.

Fig. 4.—*Diagrammatic section south of Tan-y-graig, on the scale of 1 inch to about $18\frac{1}{3}$ feet.*

$A$ = The main band of the Craig-y-Pandy Ash.

$a$ = Block of ash in the underlying slates.

$Sl$ = Slates.

$S$ = Sandstone-blocks in the slates.

below the rocky crest due north of Tan-y-graig (see fig. 4). Here a mass of ash, about 81 feet long and of variable thickness, lies in the slates some little distance below the main ash-band. At its western end it terminates somewhat abruptly, but at its eastern end it tails out gradually. Where it attains its maximum thickness it seems to be in actual contact with the main ash-band above. Owing, however, to the difficulty of examination at this point, we cannot be certain that it is not separated by a narrow band of slate. At the western extremity of the mass a favourably-placed crag shows a transverse section of the band, and there is here a complex interpenetration of ash and slate curiously suggestive of an intrusive junction; but it suggests that the slate has been squeezed into the ash, rather than that the ash has been intruded into the slate (see fig. 5, p. 561).

Moreover, in this neighbourhood the relations of the slates to the interbedded sandstone-bands are very similar. A few feet below the mass of ash just described, several blocks and short bands of sandstone lie within the slates. They are not lenticular in shape, but often terminate in abruptly-squared or rounded ends; and in many cases they are evidently portions of bands that were once continuous. These bands have since been broken up, and the slate has been squeezed between the separated blocks.

From Craig-y-Pandy the ash descends the side of the valley and crosses the river, to reappear in the large quarry known as the 'China-clay Quarry' (Pandy Quarry of the 6-inch Ordnance-Survey map). Thence it forms a line of crags leading up the hill to the quarry at Cae Deicws, near which there is again a considerable amount of faulting and crushing.

Fig. 5.—*Sketch of the western end of the ash-block shown in fig. 4 (p. 560), looking eastwards.*

A = Ash.   Sl = Slate.

[In order to distinguish the ash from the slate, the fragments in the ash are shown very much bigger proportionately than they really are.]

From Cae Deicws the band may be traced by means of blocks to Nant Iorwerth, where it forms the bed of the stream for a considerable distance. From here eastwards to Ty-nant Wood there are no exposures; but where the Ty-nant stream leaves the moorland and enters the wood, the ash appears again. A small fault runs along the stream for some little distance, and displaces the ash to the north; but this fault appears to be of minor importance. Another fault crosses the stream lower down, about 100 yards south of Ty-nant, and repeats a small portion of the ash. Farther east the band of ash is generally concealed; but a line of blocks near the wood of Ty'n-y-rhyd appears to indicate its outcrop, and leads us to the great Cae-mawr Fault, which runs from N. 5° W. to S. 5° E. On the eastern side of this fault the ash is thrown about a mile to the south, and reappears in an isolated crag some 600 yards

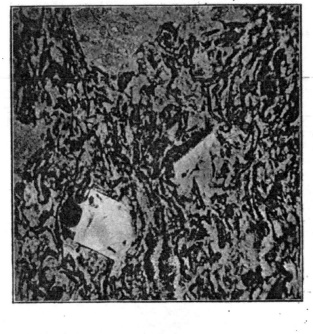

[The compact variety ; from the quarry on Craig-y-Pandy.]

7.

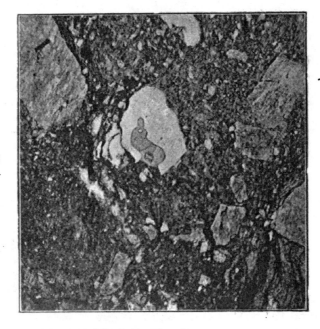

[The more usual, coarsely clastic variety ; from the scarp above the China-clay Quarry.]

6.

Figs. 6 & 7.—*Microscopic sections of the Craig-y-Pandy Ash.* (*Magnified about 21 diameters.*)

[ 563 ]

Fig. 8.—Columnar jointing in the Craig-y-Pandy Ash at Cae Deicws.

Cae Deicws

south-east of Llechrhydau.    Beyond this crag we know of no further exposures.

Throughout its course, the band consists mainly of a distinctly-clastic rock (see fig. 6, p. 562), which has very generally been greatly sheared so as to assume a schistose appearance, the foliation being oblique to the band.    It is usually full of included fragments of various sizes, and these weather out and give to the rock a characteristically rough and rugged surface.    Among the fragments we have found pieces of slate and rhyolite.

At some places, however, the appearance of the rock is entirely altered, and it becomes a compact felstone,[1] with included crystals of quartz and felspar.    This is the case, as already noted, in the crag which overlooks Pandy, in the China-clay Quarry, and in the quarry at Cae Deicws.    Between these points the ash is perfectly normal.

Wherever the felstone occurs the band is greatly thickened, and forms a kind of boss which seems to rise up into the beds above. At one time we were disposed to believe that the felstone was intrusive; but microscopic sections show that it is really a fine rhyolitic tuff, consisting of comminuted pumice and exhibiting the characteristic 'bogen-structure' (see fig. 7, p. 562.)

At Cae Deicws the felstone is very white and contains crystals of chalybite, which are apparently of secondary origin.    It shows well-developed columnar jointing (see fig. 8, p. 563), the columns at the eastern corner of the quarry becoming curved, apparently owing to the presence of a small fault.    In this quarry there is often a perfectly sharp line between the felstone and the more usual schistose ashes, but this seems to be due to the fact that the boundary between the two at this point is a fault.

In the China-clay Quarry there is a fine section of nearly the whole of the band.    The actual base is cut off by a fault, but the lowest beds that appear are ashy and schistose.    In the middle of the quarry the rock is a compact felstone, sometimes white, with big crystals of chalybite, and sometimes blue; while the upper portion of the band is again distinctly clastic, consisting of a tuff with large fragments.    The uppermost layers of this tuff contain broken brachiopod-shells (fig. 9, p. 565).    There is a perfect transition from the compact felstone of the middle of the quarry to the coarser tuff on both sides, and no line can be drawn between them.    Towards its margin the felstone includes fragments of slate and rhyolite, while towards the interior of the mass these fragments gradually become increasingly difficult to distinguish.

At Craig-y-Pandy a line of disturbance passes along the back of the crag, and is clearly shown in the small quarry that has been opened there.    On the northern side of the disturbance the rock is of the usual ashy character; but on the southern side, in the boss which forms the crag, it is mostly a compact felstone.    Towards the base, however, schistose and ashy beds again appear, and no

---

[1] We employ the term felstone as a field-name for a rock similar in appearance to a quartz-porphyry, but not necessarily intrusive.

sharp boundary-line can be drawn.   A peculiar feature here, which is also visible to some extent in Cae-Deicws Quarry, is that the felstone is sometimes banded.   Near the fault the banding is approximately parallel to the plane of the disturbance; but in some cases the banding is nearly parallel to the jointing of the rock, and

Fig. 9.—*Section at the top of the Craig-y-Pandy Ash, in the China-clay Quarry.   (Scale: 1 inch = 4 feet.)*

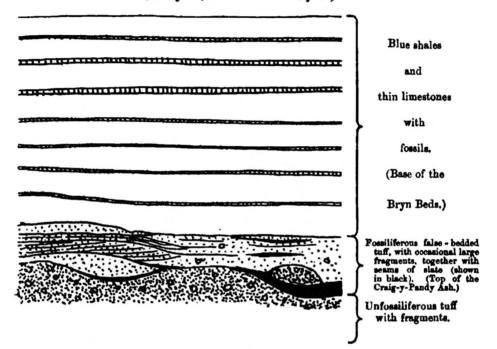

Blue shales

and

thin limestones

with

fossils.

(Base of the

Bryn Beds.)

Fossiliferous false-bedded tuff, with occasional large fragments, together with seams of slate (shown in black).   (Top of the Craig-y-Pandy Ash.)

Unfossiliferous tuff with fragments.

occasional blocks show an appearance very similar to that of the Moughton Whetstones.   The bands differ one from the other in no respect but colour, and are evidently of secondary origin.   At Craig-y-Pandy there is also a rudimentary attempt at the columnar jointing which is so well displayed at Cae Deicws.

The felstone has been extensively quarried, both at Pandy Quarry and at Cae Deicws, for the manufacture of china-clay and for setts.

(4) Bryn Beds.—Leaving out of consideration for the present the intrusive sheet worked in Coed-y-glyn Quarry, and seen at intervals throughout the district, the beds above the Craig-y-Pandy Ash and below the fault consist mainly of sandstones and shales, both of which are sometimes calcareous.   Immediately above the ash at the China-clay Quarry itself, they are especially characterized by a great abundance of *Rafinesquina ungula*, while the beds somewhat higher in the series are distinguished by the number

of fine and well-developed specimens of *Orthis elegantula* that occur in them; still higher the most characteristic fossils are trilobites.

In the western portion of our map (Pl. LIII) the thickness of this series is apparently very small, and there can be little doubt that the upper beds are cut out by the Dolhir Fault. Similarly, in the little stream about 250 yards east of Ty-isaf the lower beds only of the series seem to be present.

From this point eastwards the width of the band increases—an increase which seems to be due, not merely to changes in the slope of the ground and of the dip of the beds, but also to the appearance of higher and higher beds of the series, until in the Glyn Valley a thickness of some 500 feet is attained.

From the Glyn Valley eastwards these beds can easily be traced with frequent exposures to the streams of Nant Iorwerth and Ty-nant, a little to the east of which they end against the Cae-mawr Fault. On the other side of this fault they are to be seen in the valley of Craignant, but elsewhere exposures are very poor.

In general, as has already been stated, the series consists of sandstones and shales with calcareous bands. Fossils are very abundant in places, and among the commonest and most characteristic forms are *Tetradella complicata, Phacops apiculatus, Trinucleus concentricus,* and *Orthis elegantula*; but none of these are confined to this horizon. *Tetradella complicata* and *Trinucleus concentricus* are not found in the beds above, but they occur in the Teirw Beds; *Phacops apiculatus* ranges upwards into the Dolhir Beds, while *Orthis elegantula* extends from the Bryn Beds upwards into the Fron-Frys Slates. But outside the Bryn Beds the specimens of *Orthis elegantula* are always small and few in number; and so marked is the difference in size, that in this district a single well-developed specimen of the species is almost sufficient to prove that the rock in which it occurs belongs to the Bryn Beds. *Orthis turgida, Rafinesquina ungula,* and *Triplesia spiriferoides* are also characteristic.

At one or two points the character of the beds and of the fossils is distinctly peculiar, gasteropods and lamellibranchs being particularly abundant. The most remarkable of these exposures occurs in a small quarry, opposite the cottage called Bryn in Nant Iorwerth. This quarry is cut in a thick mass of sandstone, from which we have obtained the following fossils:—

*Monticulipora fibrosa*, Goldf.
*Monticulipora lens*, M'Coy.
*Ortonia* sp.
*Orthis elegantula*, Dalm.
*Plectambonites sericea*, Sow.
*Strophomena* sp.
*Ctenodonta varicosa*, Salt.
*Ctenodonta* cf. *transversa*, Portl.
*Modiolopsis postlineata*, M'Coy.
*Modiolopsis* cf. *securiformis*, Portl.

*Orthonota prora* (?) Salt.
*Orthonota* cf. *rigida*, Sow.
*Bellerophon bilobatus*, Sow.
*Raphistoma æquale*, Salt.
*Orthoceras politum*, M'Coy.
*Tetradella complicata*, Salt.
*Asaphus* sp.
*Homalonotus bisulcatus*, Salt.
*Phacops apiculatus*, Salt.

A somewhat similar series of fossils, also in a sandstone-band, occurs in an old trial-working above, and due east of, the China-clay Quarry :—

| | |
|---|---|
| Leptæna rhomboidalis, Wilck. | Murchisonia cf. turrita, Portl. |
| Orthis calligramma, Dalm. | Raphistoma æquale, Salt. |
| Orthis elegantula, Dalm. | Tentaculites anglicus, Salt. |
| Orthis testudinaria, Dalm. | Orthoceras politum, M'Coy. |
| Plectambonites sericea, Sow. | Tetradella complicata, Salt. |
| Ctenodonta varicosa, Salt. | Calymene senaria (Conrad) Salt. |
| Cucullella cf. planulata, Conr. | Phacops apiculatus, Salt. |
| Bellerophon bilobatus (?) Sow. | Trinucleus sp. |
| Murchisonia gyrogonia, M'Coy. | |

Finally, a band of sandstone presenting much the same characters crosses the Oswestry Road about 450 yards north of the sharp bend at Ty-nant. The exposure is too poor to allow of much collecting, and the only fossils that we obtained were :—

| | |
|---|---|
| Orthis elegantula, Dalm. | Raphistoma æquale (?) Salt. |
| Lingula ovata (?) M'Coy. | Tetradella complicata, Salt. |
| Platyschisma (?) sp. | Homalonotus sp. |

The following is a complete list of the fossils that we have identified from the Bryn Beds :—

| Found also in beds below. | | Found also in beds above. |
|:---:|---|:---:|
| × | Monticulipora fibrosa, Goldf. (c) ............ ............. | × |
| | Monticulipora lens, M'Coy ............................. | × |
| | Ptilodictya acuta, Hall ............. ............. | × |
| | Tentaculites anglicus, Salt. (c) ........................ | × |
| ? | Ortonia sp. | |
| | | |
| | Leptæna rhomboidalis, Wilck. ........................ | × |
| × | Lingula ovata, M'Coy. | × |
| × | Orthis calligramma, Dalm. ............................. | × |
| × | Orthis elegantula, Dalm. (c) ........................... | × |
| | Orthis porcata, M'Coy ........................... | × |
| | Orthis testudinaria, Dalm. ...... ........................ | × |
| | Orthis turgida, M'Coy. (c). | |
| | Platystrophia biforata, Schl. (c) ...... ............ | × |
| × | Plectambonites sericea, Sow. (c) ........................ | × |
| | Rhynchonella decemplicata, Dav. | |
| × | Rafinesquina expansa, Sow. ........................ | × |
| | Rafinesquina ungula, M'Coy (c). | |
| | Rafinesquina deltoidea, var. undata, M'Coy. | |
| | Rafinesquina deltoidea, var. simulans, M'Coy. | |
| | Strophomena antiquata, Sow. (c) ........................ | × |
| | Triplesia spiriferoides, M'Coy (c). | |
| | | |
| × | Bellerophon bilobatus, Sow. | |
| | Euomphalus prænuntius (?) Phil. ..................... | × |
| | Holopea concinna, M'Coy ........................ | × |
| × | Murchisonia gyrogonia, M'Coy. | |

| Found also in beds below. | LIST OF FOSSILS FROM THE BRYN BEDS (*continued*). | Found also in beds above. |
|---|---|---|
| | *Murchisonia* cf. *turrita*, Portl. | |
| | *Platyschisma* (?) sp. | |
| | *Raphistoma æquale*, Salt. (c). | |
| × | *Ctenodonta varicosa*, Salt. (c). | |
| | *Ctenodonta* cf. *transversa*, Portl. | |
| | *Cucullella* cf. *planulata*, Conr. | |
| | *Modiolopsis postlineata*, M'Coy. | |
| | *Modiolopsis pyrus*, Salt. (c). | |
| | *Modiolopsis* cf. *securiformis*, Portl. | |
| | *Orthonota prora* (?) Salt. | |
| | *Orthonota* cf. *rigida*, Sow. | |
| × | *Orthoceras politum*, M'Coy. | |
| | *Acidaspis* sp. | |
| | *Asaphus* sp. | |
| × | *Calymene senaria* (Conrad) Salt. ................ | × |
| | *Chasmops conicophthalma* (Bœck) Salt. .............. | × |
| | *Chasmops macroura*, Sjög. ......... .............. | × |
| | *Homalonotus bisulcatus* Salt. (c). | |
| | *Homalonotus rudis*, Salt. | |
| | *Lichas laxatus*, M'Coy ....... ........... ........... | × |
| | *Phacops apiculatus*, Salt. (c) ......................... | × |
| | *Phacops truncatocaudatus*, Portl. | |
| × | *Trinucleus concentricus*, Eaton (c). | |
| × | *Tetradella complicata*, Salt. (c). | |

(4 *a*) Coed-y-glyn Sill.—Near the base of the series just described, and generally separated from the Craig-y-Pandy Ash by a very small thickness of beds, there is an irregular intrusive sheet of rock which has commonly been mistaken for the 'Little Ash' of the Geological Survey, and is worked for road-metal in Coed-y-glyn Quarry. Although it runs nearly at the same horizon throughout its course, it is extremely variable in thickness and sporadic in its occurrence, or at least in its exposures. Its upper and lower surfaces, as seen in Coed-y-glyn Quarry, are both very irregular, and it seems to be distinctly intrusive.

The westernmost exposure of this rock in our map is near Ty'n-y-pistyll, whence the outcrop runs nearly parallel to the Craig-y-Pandy Ash, and is separated from it by a very small space; indeed, it is not impossible that the two rocks are here in actual contact, for no intervening beds are visible. The band cannot be traced so uninterruptedly as the Craig-y-Pandy Ash, and there is reason to believe that it is not actually continuous throughout; but it may be seen again at a little distance from the Craig-y-Pandy Ash, at several points near Hafod-y-gareg. It is not again visible until we reach the immediate neighbourhood of the Glyn Valley, where it is well shown in Coed-y-glyn Quarry. On the other side of the valley it is exposed only in a small trial-working some distance above the China-clay Quarry; here it is stated to have thinned out as working proceeded. Farther east, the only point at which it has been definitely identified is in Ty-nant Wood, close to the cottage.

By far the best exposure is that exhibited in the quarry at Coed-y-glyn. The rock is compact and generally blue in colour, at least in its central portions. Towards the top and the bottom it is often vesicular. Both the lower and the upper surfaces are very irregular, and the slates close by are sometimes indurated, so that the sheet seems to be distinctly intrusive. It is probable, however, that some of the irregularity is due rather to earth-movements than to the intrusive nature of the rock, for the beds at its base are much disturbed; but, how far these movements may be the effect of the intrusion, we are unable to say. The rock in places shows columnar jointing.

(5) **Pen-y-graig Ash.**—The intrusive sheet that has just been described is the rock which has commonly been taken for the 'Little Ash' of Jukes, and it is possible that the Geological Survey itself has sometimes mapped it as such. But a glance at the Survey-map will show that the line of the 'Little Ash' in the Glyn Valley is drawn, not through Coed-y-glyn Quarry, but considerably higher in the series, through the farm of Pen-y-graig. Here there is a true ash-bed, of which, however, only a very small portion exists at the surface, the rest being cut out by the strike-fault. This Pen-y-graig Ash is much more like the 'Little Ash,' as this is seen at Llandrillo and elsewhere. A small outcrop of similar rock, not more than 4 or 5 feet thick, is exposed in the quarry at Bryn, lying immediately above the sandstone mentioned on p. 566. Finally, in the valley of Craignant a band of similar ash, not more than 2 or 3 feet thick, may be traced at intervals running nearly along the line of the stream in the upper part of the valley, where it overlies a sandstone-bed. It is, however, by no means certain that all these exposures belong to the same band, and the great distance of the Craignant ash from the nearest outcrop of the Craig-y-Pandy band suggests that the former belongs to a much higher horizon.

(6) **Graptolitic Slates.**—Over the greater part of the area shown upon the map, the strike-fault that cuts off the top of the Pandy Beds is followed directly by the Dolhir Series, as in the Ceiriog Valley (fig. 1, p. 552). In the west of the area, however, the Dolhir Beds are underlain by dark graptolitic slates, the graptolites in which are unfortunately very badly preserved. Owing to the fact that the Dolhir Fault cuts obliquely across the strike, the greatest thickness of these slates is to be seen in Nant Tyn-y-twmpath in the extreme west of our map (Pl. LIII),

where they underlie beds containing a typical Dolhir fauna. Graptolites are abundant, but are too imperfectly preserved to be identified. Similar slates, occupying a similar position, are exposed in the stream by Ty'n-y-celyn. They are again seen in the small gully which lies about 250 yards north-east of Ty-isaf, and in the side of the footpath close to this gully we obtained *Dicellograptus elegans, Climacograptus*,[1] a few small brachiopods, and the thorax and tail of a small *Ampyx* or *Trinucleus*.

Similar dark slates with imperfect graptolites extend, below the true Dolhir Beds, for some little distance to the east of this last-mentioned locality; but they have entirely disappeared before we reach the valley of the Ceiriog.

In Nant Tyn-y-twmpath the graptolitic slates are underlain by pale slates containing a very peculiar fauna. These slates are distinct, both lithologically and palæontologically, from any other rocks in the area, and they evidently belong to a part of the succession that is elsewhere cut out by the Dolhir Fault. Until we have more closely examined the country which lies on the west, we hesitate to elevate them into a separate group, and content ourselves for the present with tabulating the list of fossils obtained from them :—

| | |
|---|---|
| *Leptæna rhomboidalis*, Wilck. | *Rafinesquina expansa*, Sow. |
| *Orthis Actoniæ (!)* Sow. | *Triplesia spiriferoides (!)* M'Coy. |
| *Orthis elegantula (!)* Dalm. | *Echinosphærites arachnoidea*, Forbes. |
| *Plectambonites sericea (!)* Sow. | |

Also several other forms that we have failed to identify.

(7) **Dolhir Beds.** — In Nant Tyn-y-twmpath and in the Ty'n-y-celyn stream the Graptolitic Slates are succeeded by the Dolhir Beds, which cover a broad strip of country extending eastwards as far as Pentre-cilgwyn, where they end against the great Cae-mawr Fault. On the other side of this they are nearly cut out by the Dolhir Fault.

Immediately above the black graptolitic beds the Dolhir Series consists of slates which are fragile and shivery in texture. They contain numerous fossils, and are well shown in the streams already mentioned; on the ridge north of Gelli; and on the ridge that runs from Aber-chwil to Plas Einion. Similar beds form the lowest portion of the series that is visible in the valley of the Ceiriog; and there they are accompanied by a band of limestone (30 feet or so thick), which has been quarried above Dolhir and also on the other side of the valley east of Plas Einion. West of the Ceiriog Valley this limestone is nowhere actually visible, but eastward it occurs at Cefngoed, where a small quarry has been opened in it; it is also seen in the road at Bedwlwyn.

The beds above the limestone consist chiefly of firmer slates; but towards the top, in the Ceiriog Valley, they become full of calcareous

---

[1] We are indebted to Miss G. L. Elles, D.Sc., for identifying these and our other specimens of graptolites.

nodules and appear to pass gradually into the limestone at the base of the Glyn Grit.

The fauna of the Dolhir Beds is by far the richest in the district, both in the number of species and in the number of individuals. So abundant indeed are the fossils, that scarcely a blow of the hammer fails to reveal some trace of organic life. A few of the species are found in the beds below, and some pass up into the Glyn Grit; but the greater number are confined to the Dolhir Beds themselves.

On examining the list of species from the district (pp. 572–73), it will be observed that the corals, crinoids, and cystoids are almost entirely confined to this horizon. A few of these pass upwards into the Glyn Grit, and one or two have been found in the Fron-Frys Slates; but none occur in the beds below the Dolhir Group (excepting in Nant Tyn-y-twmpath, where *Echinosphærites arachnoidea* has been found). Polyzoa also are very much more abundant in these beds than in any others, and the genera *Ptilodictya*, *Phyllopora*, and *Ramipora* are practically confined to this series. A considerable number of brachiopods have been found only in the Dolhir Group; while, among the trilobites, *Cybele*, *Cheirurus*, *Remopleurides*, and *Trinucleus seticornis* have not been found in the district, excepting in these beds.

(8) Glyn Grit.—The bed or series of beds that has hitherto been supposed to represent the Corwen Grit is not so uniform in character as the Corwen Grit of Corwen, and towards its base it is sometimes very calcareous, so much so indeed as to form a definite limestone. This limestone, however, is not constant, and west of the Ceiriog it seems to be represented by a soft, brown or chocolate-coloured sandstone, which is very much decayed and extremely fossiliferous. The limestone itself is best seen in the two small quarries on the top of Mynydd Fron Frys. It has also been worked on the side of the hill south of Hafod-y-gynfawr, but the quarry is now overgrown.

At the quarries on the top of Mynydd Fron Frys the limestone is overlain by a platy sandstone, and near the junction the two are interbedded with each other. Elsewhere the grit generally consists of an irregular, platy, and fairly compact sandstone. But, towards Tomen-y-meirw,[1] it is sometimes very coarse and contains fragments of slate.

Commencing at Tomen-y-meirw, the sandstone strikes nearly due eastwards to a fault which throws it to the south. It is again exposed in a small quarry by the roadside. Another fault, which may be seen in the quarry itself, throws it again to the south into the wood of Cefn-coch. It traverses this wood from west to eastl and runs thence to Pant-y-graig, where it forms a line of smal, cliffs in which many fossils may be found. The Aber-chwil Fault cuts it off at the eastern end of this cliff, and farther east it forms

[1] Tomen-y-meirw is a tumulus lying just on the northern border of our map (Pl. LIII), about 400 yards west of Nant Tyn-y-twmpath.

| Found in beds below. | LIST OF FOSSILS FROM THE DOLHIR BEDS. | Found in Glyn Grit. | Found in Fron-Frys Slates. |
|---|---|---|---|
| | *Aulacophyllum mitratum*, His. | | |
| | *Favosites aspera*, D'Orb. ........................ | × | |
| | *Favosites gothlandica*, Lam. | | |
| | *Halysites catenularia*, Linn. (c) ................ | × | |
| | *Heliolites inordinata (?)* Lonsd. | | |
| | *Heliolites interstincta*, Linn. (c). | | |
| | *Heliolites megastoma*, M'Coy (c) ................ | × | |
| | *Lindstrœmia subduplicata*, M'Coy (c) ............ | × | ? |
| | *Lindstrœmia subduplicata var. crenulata*, M'Coy (c) | × | |
| | *Lyopora favosa*, M'Coy. | | |
| | *Petraia elongata*, Phil. ........................ | × | |
| | *Petraia uniserialis*, M'Coy. | | |
| | *Propora tubulata*, Lonsd. (c) ................... | × | |
| | *Streptelasma æquisulcatum*, M'Coy. | | |
| | *Streptelasma craigense*, M'Coy. | | |
| | *Syringophyllum organum*, Linn. | | |
| | | | |
| | *Caryocystites Davisi*, M'Coy. | | |
| | *Caryocystites Litchi*, Forbes. | | |
| | *Echinosphærites arachnoidea*, Forbes. | | |
| | *Echinosphærites balthica*, Eichw. | | |
| | *Hemicosmites oblongus*, Pand. | | |
| | *Hemicosmites rugatus*, Forbes (c). | | |
| | *Hemicosmites squamosus*, Forbes. | | |
| | *Sphæronites (?)* sp. | | |
| | | | |
| | *Glyptocrinus basalis*, M'Coy ................... | × | |
| | | | |
| | *Palæaster obtusus*, Forbes. | | |
| | | | |
| × | *Monticulipora fibrosa*, Goldf. (c) ............. | × | × |
| × | *Monticulipora lens*, M'Coy (c). ............... | × | |
| | *Monticulipora* sp. | | |
| × | *Phyllopora Hisingeri*, M'Coy (c). | | |
| | *Ptilodictya acuta*, Hall (c). .................. | ? | |
| | *Ptilodictya costellata*, M'Coy (c). | | |
| | *Ptilodictya dichotoma*, Portl. (c). | × | |
| | *Ptilodictya explanata*, M'Coy (c) ............. | × | |
| | *Ptilodictya fucoides*, M'Coy. | | |
| | *Ptilodictya* sp. | | |
| | *Ramipora Hochstetteri*, Toula var. *carinata*, R. Eth. (c) .................................... | × | |
| | *Cornulites serpularius (?)* Schloth. | | |
| × | *Tentaculites anglicus*, Salt. | | |
| | | | |
| | *Clitambonites ascendens*, Pand. ............... | × | |
| | *Crania* sp. | | |
| | *Discina oblongata*, Portl. | | |
| | *Discina perrugata*, M'Coy. | | |
| | *Leptæna quinquecostata*, M'Coy (c) ........... | ... | × |
| × | *Leptæna rhomboidalis*, Wilck. (c) ............ | × | × |
| | *Lingula brevis*, Portl. | | |
| | *Obolella (?)* sp. | | |
| | *Orthis Actoniæ*, Sow. (c). ..................... | × | × |
| | *Orthis biloba*, Linn. .......................... | × | × |
| × | *Orthis calligramma*, Dalm. (c) ................ | × | × |
| | *Orthis confinis*, Salt. | | |

| Found in beds below. | LIST OF FOSSILS FROM THE DOLHIR BEDS (continued.) | Found in Glyn Grit. | Found in Fron-Frys Slates. |
|---|---|---|---|
| | *Orthis crispa*, M'Coy (c) ... | ? | × |
| | *Orthis elegantula*, Dalm. (c) ... | × | × |
| | *Orthis flabellulum*, Sow. | | |
| | *Orthis hirnantensis*, M'Coy | ... | ? |
| | *Orthis Lapworthi* (?) Dav. | | |
| | *Orthis parva*, Pander | × | |
| | *Orthis patera* (?) Salt. | | |
| | *Orthis Philipi*. Dav. | | |
| × | *Orthis porcata*, M'Coy (c) | × | × |
| × | *Orthis retrorsistria*, M'Coy. | | |
| | *Orthis* cf. *sagittifera*, M'Coy. | | |
| × | *Orthis testudinaria*, Dalm. | | |
| × | *Platystrophia biforata*, Schl. (c) | × | |
| × | *Plectambonites sericea*, Sow. (c) | × | ? |
| | *Plectambonites* sp. (c) | × | |
| | *Rafinesquina corrugatella*, Dav. | | |
| × | *Rafinesquina deltoidea*, Conr. | | |
| × | *Rafinesquina expansa*, Sow. (c) | ... | ? |
| | *Rafinesquina* cf. *shallockensis*, Dav. | | |
| × | *Strophomena antiquata*, Sow. (c). | | |
| | *Strophonella* cf. *euglypha*, His. | | |
| | *Triplesia* cf. *insularis*, Eichw. (c) | ... | × |
| | *Triplesia* cf. *spiriferoides*, M'Coy (c). | | |
| × | *Euomphalus prænuntius* (?) Phil. | | |
| | *Euomphalus* sp. | | |
| | *Holopea carinata*, Forbes. | | |
| × | *Holopea concinna*, M'Coy (c). | | |
| | *Lophospira* sp. | | |
| | *Trochonema lyratum*, M'Coy (c). | | |
| | *Cyrtoceras* cf. *sonax*, Salt. | | |
| | *Orthoceras velatum*, Blake. | | |
| | *Trochoceras cornu-arietis*, Portl. | | |
| | *Acidaspis dalecarlica*, Törnq. | | |
| ? | *Calymene Caractaci*, Salt. | | |
| × | *Calymene senaria* (Conrad) Salt. | | |
| × | *Chasmops conicophthalma* (Boeck) Salt. | | |
| × | *Chasmops macroura*, Sjög. | | |
| | *Cheirurus juvenis*, Salt. (c). | | |
| | *Cheirurus octolobatus*, M'Coy (c). | | |
| | *Cybele verrucosa*, Dalm. (c). | | |
| | *Dalmanites* sp. ... | × | |
| | *Encrinurus multisegmentatus*, Portl. (?). | | |
| | *Homalonotus* (?) sp. | | |
| × | *Illænus Bowmanni*, Salt. | | |
| | *Illænus Davisi*, Salt. | | |
| | *Illænus* cf. *Murchisoni*, Salt. | | |
| | *Phacops alifrons*, Salt. | | |
| × | *Phacops apiculatus*, Salt. (c). | | |
| | *Remopleurides* cf. *longicostatus*, Portl. | | |
| | *Stygina* sp. | | |
| | *Trinucleus seticornis*, His. | | |
| | *Trinucleus bucculentus*, Ang. | | |
| | *Primitia strangulata*, Salt. (c). | | |

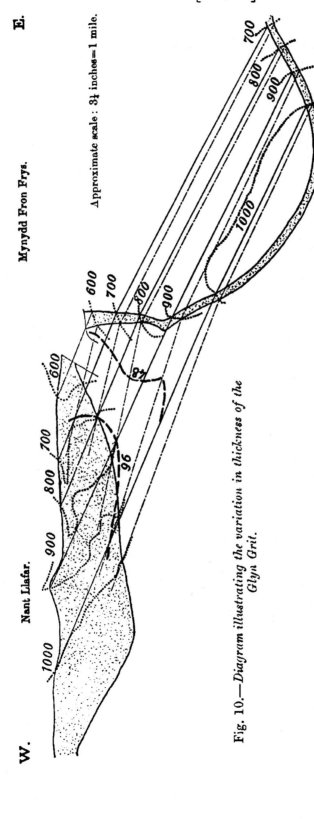

E.

Mynydd Fron Frys.

Approximate scale : 3¼ inches = 1 mile.

W.

Nant Llafar.

Fig. 10.—*Diagram illustrating the variation in thickness of the Glyn Grit.*

a large part of the northern slope of the hill south of Nant Llafar. Fossils are very abundant in a decayed band that occurs by the side of the road about 300 or 400 yards east of Pant-y-graig.

East of Plas Lleucu the grit forms not only the slope of the hill, but also the bed of the stream itself, and extends for a short distance up its northern bank. It is very well exposed at the end of the heaps of débris from the slate-quarries, and at other points in the stream and in the tramway - cutting. Fossils are fairly abundant throughout.

At the embouchure of Nant Llafar the grit crosses the valley of the Ceiriog by Pont Hafod - y - gynfawr. It may be seen in the road close to the bridge and in the wood behind the house, whence it passes up the side of the hill to the small quarries already mentioned. From these it curves down to the farm of Fron Frys, beyond which point it is lost in the drift and alluvium that cover the lower slopes of the hill; but a single block of limestone in the wood near Dol-y-wern appears to be nearly, if not quite, *in situ*.

Near Dol-y-wern, the Cae-mawr Fault crosses the valley and throws all the beds to the south; and the only place to the east of this fault where we have discovered the grit actually in place is Gwernydd-gymmal, where it is visible in the farmyard. Exposures in this part of the district are very poor; but the occurrence of occasional outcrops of the Fron-Frys Slates enables us to insert the line of the grit with some degree of accuracy.

The Glyn Grit is variable in thickness, and towards Nant Llafar, where it may attain a thickness of 150 or 160 feet, the rapidity of the variation becomes remarkable. In the accompanying diagram (fig. 10, p. 574) the dotted areas represent the outcrops of the grit on Mynydd Fron Frys and on the slopes of Nant Llafar, the two areas being separated by the alluvium of the Ceiriog. By joining the points where the upper edge of the grit crosses the contour-lines of 1000 feet, 900 feet, etc., we obtain approximate contour-lines of the upper surface of the grit, shown in the diagram as thin continuous lines. Contour-lines of the base of the grit may be obtained in a similar fashion, and these are shown in the diagram as thin broken lines.

It will be observed that the contour-lines of the upper surface are nearly straight and separated by approximately equal intervals, indicating that this surface is almost a plane. On Mynydd Fron Frys the contour-lines of the base are nearly parallel to those of the top and all but equidistant, showing that here the thickness is nearly uniform; but towards Nant Llafar they diverge rapidly. At any point where the contour-line 1000 of the upper surface crosses the contour-line 900 of the lower surface, it is evident that the top of the grit is 100 feet above the base. Assuming that the dip is 16°, the actual thickness of the grit at such a point will be approximately 96 feet. In this way are obtained the heavy broken lines marked 96 and 48, along which the thickness of the grit is 96 feet and 48 feet respectively.

An unconformity, either at the base or at the top of the grit, would explain the variation. The fauna of the grit is similar to that of the Dolhir Beds, and there appears to be a passage from the one to the other. The fauna of the Fron-Frys Slates is very different, and it is probable, therefore, that if there is any unconformity it is at the top of the grit; but it is not visible in any single section. In order, if possible, to determine the relations of the Glyn Grit and the Fron-Frys Slates, we made an excavation at the boundary in Nant Llafar, with the result shown in fig. 11 (p. 576). There is no visible sign of any interruption in deposition.

About 500 yards west of the Glyn-Valley Hotel there is a distinct break in the heart of the grit, and the beds above the break have the appearance of resting unconformably on the beds below. But we can detect no difference, either lithological or palæontological, between the beds on the two sides of this apparent uncon-

formity, and the break appears to be purely local.  It may be due
to irregularities of deposition, such as commonly occur in sandy
beds; or it may possibly be the result of a strike-fault of low dip.

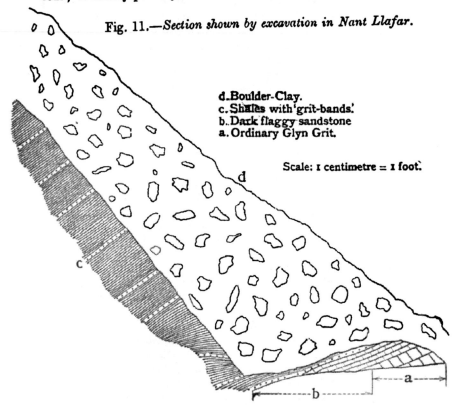

Fig. 11.—*Section shown by excavation in Nant Llafar.*

d. Boulder-Clay.
c. Shales with grit-bands.
b. Dark flaggy sandstone
a. Ordinary Glyn Grit.

Scale: 1 centimetre = 1 foot.

The fauna of the Glyn Grit and Limestone is very similar to that
of the Dolhir Series, although not quite so rich.  In the small pits
on Mynydd Fron Frys, where there is a limestone below and grits
above, corals are the predominant fossils.   In the roadside above
Plas Lleucu, and at Pant-y-graig, where soft chocolate-coloured beds
are intercalated among the grits, gasteropods are abundant.  But
few of the species are confined to this horizon, and by far the
greater number occur also in the beds below.

At Corwen, the fact that the Corwen Grit is overlain with
apparent conformity by beds that contain graptolites of Lower
Birkhill age, led us to conclude that the grit also is Llandovery,
although in that district we found no fossils in it.  At Glyn we have
not found the graptolitic shales; but fossils are by no means rare in
the grit.  These fossils, however, do not differ from those of the
Dolhir Beds below, and on the other hand are quite distinct from
those of the Fron-Frys Slates above.  Moreover, the upper part of
the Dolhir Beds is sandy, and contains calcareous nodules; and it
is sometimes very difficult to draw a precise line between the two
series.  We therefore include the Glyn Grit with the Dolhir Beds

in the Bala Series, and draw the line between the Ordovician and the Silurian at the top, not at the base, of the grit. At Corwen, however, there is a much more definite boundary between the Bala Beds and the Corwen Grit, and it is possible that the Glyn Grit and the Corwen Grit do not precisely correspond.

| Found in beds below. | LIST OF FOSSILS FROM THE GLYN GRIT AND LIMESTONE. | Found in beds above. |
|---|---|---|
| × | *Favosites aspera*, D'Orb. | |
| × | *Halysites catenularia*, Linn. | |
| × | *Heliolites megastoma*, M'Coy (c). | |
| × | *Lindstræmia subduplicata*, M'Coy | ? |
| × | *Lindstræmia subduplicata* var. *crenulata*, M'Coy. | |
| × | *Petraia elongata*, Phil. (c) | ? |
| | *Propora tubulata* (?) Lonsd. | |
| × | *Streptelasma equisulcatum*, M'Coy. | |
| | | |
| | *Glyptocrinus basalis*, M'Coy. | |
| | | |
| × | *Monticulipora fibrosa*, Goldf. (c) | × |
| × | *Monticulipora lens*, M'Coy. | |
| × | *Ptilodictya acuta* (?) Hall. | |
| × | *Ptilodictya dichotoma*, Portl. | |
| × | *Ptilodictya explanata*, M'Coy. | |
| × | *Ramipora Hochstetteri*, Toula var. *carinata*, R. Eth. (c). | |
| | | |
| | *Athyris* (?) sp. | |
| × | *Clitambonites ascendens*, Pander. | |
| | *Leptella* (?) cf. *llandeiloensis*, Dav. | × |
| × | *Leptæna rhomboidalis*, Wilck. (c) | × |
| × | *Lingula ovata*, M'Coy | × |
| | *Meristina* (?) cf. *nitida*, Hall. | |
| | *Meristina* (?) cf. *angustifrons*, M'Coy. | |
| × | *Orthis Actoniæ*, Sow. | × |
| × | *Orthis biloba* (?) Linn. | × |
| × | *Orthis calligramma*, Dalm. (c) | × |
| | *Orthis* cf. *confinis*, Salt. | |
| × | *Orthis crispa* (?) M'Coy | × |
| × | *Orthis elegantula*, Dalm. | × |
| × | *Orthis parva*, Pand. (c). | |
| × | *Orthis porcata*, M'Coy. | |
| × | *Platystrophia biforata*, Schl. | × |
| × | *Plectambonites sericea*, Sow. (c) | ? |
| × | *Plectambonites* sp. (c). | |
| | *Rhynchonella* cf. *Lewisi*, Dav. | |
| | | |
| | *Modiolopsis* (?) sp. | |
| | | |
| | *Bellerophon expansus* (?) Sow. | |
| | *Holopella tenuicincta*, M'Coy. | |
| | *Murchisonia* (?) cf. *pulchra*, M'Coy. | |
| | *Pleurotomaria* (?) sp. | |
| | *Platyschisma* cf. *helicites*, Sow. | |
| | *Trochonema triporcatum* (?) M'Coy. | |
| | | |
| | *Calymene* sp. | |
| × | *Encrinurus multisegmentatus*, Portl. | |
| | *Phacops Robertsi*, Reed. | |

(9) **Fron-Frys Slates.**—Wherever the beds immediately above the Glyn Grit are exposed, they consist of grey slates with thin arenaceous bands, and are similar in character to those that we have already described at Corwen. Occasionally they contain darker bands, but nowhere in this district have we discovered any graptolites such as are found at Corwen. As at Corwen, the slates show peculiar dark ramifications which easily distinguish them from any other beds with which we are acquainted. On the western side of Fron Frys they are some 50 feet thick.

These slates may be traced, following the Corwen Grit on its north side, wherever the latter is to be seen. The best exposures are perhaps in the stream at Tomen-y-meirw; on the northern slopes of Cefn-coch; in the valley of Nant Llafar; and on the hill of Fron Frys. In the eastern part of the map (Pl. LIII) they are also visible at one or two places.

There is a large quarry in these beds, close to the road near Hafod-y-gynfawr, in which the rock is considerably darker than is usual elsewhere; but this is probably due to the freshness of the exposed surfaces. No fossils were obtained in this quarry.

At Corwen we found very few fossils in these beds, with the exception of the graptolites in the black bands. But on Mynydd Fron Frys and Cefn-coch fossils are fairly abundant, and show clearly that the slates belong to the Llandovery Series. Brachiopods are the most abundant forms, and the most characteristic are *Pentamerus undatus* and several species of *Meristina*. Among the corals may be mentioned *Nidulites favus*.

| Found in beds below. | LIST OF FOSSILS FROM THE FRON-FRYS SLATES. | | Found in beds below. |
|---|---|---|---|
| × | *Lindstrœmia subduplicata (?)* M'Coy. | *Orthis Actoniæ*, Sow. .............. | × |
| | | *Orthis biloba*, Linn. ............. | × |
| × | *Petraia elongata (?)* Phil. | *Orthis calligramma*, Dalm. (c) ... | × |
| × | *Monticulipora fibrosa*, Goldf. (c). | *Orthis crispa*, M'Coy.............. | × |
| | | *Orthis elegantula*, Dalm. (c) ...... | × |
| | *Nidulites favus*, Salt. (c). | *Orthis hirnantensis (?)* M'Coy ... | × |
| | | *Orthis plicata*, Sow. | |
| | *Atrypa marginalis*, Dalm. (c). | *Orthis porcata*, M'Coy ........... | × |
| × | *Leptella (?)* cf. *llandeiloensis*, Dav. | *Pentamerus undatus*, Sow. (c). | |
| | | *Platystrophia biforata*, Schl. ...... | × |
| × | *Leptæna quinquecostata*, M'Coy (c). | *Plectambonites sericea (?)* Sow. ... | × |
| | | *Rafinesquina expansa (?)* Sow. ... | × |
| × | *Leptæna rhomboidalis*, Wilck. | *Triplesia* cf. *insularis*, Eichw. ... | × |
| | *Meristina (?)* cf. *crassa*, Sow. | | |
| | *Meristina (?)* cf. *furcata*, Sow. | *Acidaspis* sp. | |
| | *Meristina (?)* sp. (c). | *Encrinurus punctatus*, Brongn. | |
| | *Meristina (?)* sp. | *Illænus* sp. | |

(10) Ty-draw Slates.—The Fron-Frys Slates are followed by homogeneous pale-green slates, free from grit-bands, very similar in character to the Tarannon Shales of other areas. They are well exposed at Tomen-y-meirw; on the northern slopes of Cefn-coch; in Nant Llafar; on Mynydd Fron Frys; and along the old road from Glyn to Oswestry in the neighbourhood of Plas-on and Pwll-hir. On Mynydd Fron Frys they are about 90 feet thick, and have been extensively quarried.

There does not seem to be any unconformity between them and the Fron-Frys Slates below; but a fairly definite line can be drawn between the two, although near the boundary it is not always easy to say whether the rock belongs to the one series or to the other.

Wherever the junction between the Ty-draw Slates and the Denbighshire Series is well exposed, the two appear to be interbedded. This is particularly well shown in the stream which flows past Tomen-y-meirw. Towards the top of the Ty-draw Beds bands of dark slate are interbedded, and at the base of the Denbighshire Series bands of pale-green slate are included. Similar relations are visible at the junction near the farm of Cefn-isaf, but here the beds are not quite so well exposed. It is, therefore, impossible to draw an absolutely sharp line between the two series.

In general, the Ty-draw Slates appear to be quite unfossiliferous. In a dark band, however, in the midst of the series close to the farm of Cae-mawr, we found a somewhat badly-preserved graptolite which Miss Elles has kindly identified for us as *Monograptus Marri*, a species belonging to the Tarannon Series.

(11) The Denbighshire Series.—The Denbighshire Series covers a very large area in the Glyn Valley and the neighbouring district; and, although we do not propose in the present communication to deal with these beds in detail, it is necessary, in order to complete the account of the structure of the district, to describe their distribution.

In the whole of the western portion of our map (Pl. LIII) they lie immediately to the north of the Ty-draw Slates, and are particularly well exposed near Tomen-y-meirw and in the slate-quarries in Nant Llafar, as also at Glyn Ceiriog itself.

To the east of Glyn, where the valley of the Ceiriog assumes an easterly direction, they occupy the whole of the northern side of the valley. But, excepting for a small patch which extends across the river towards the cemetery, they do not occur south of the Ceiriog until we reach Dol-y-wern. Near that village, however, owing to the Cae-mawr Fault, which has already been mentioned, they cross the river and extend past Penllwyn to the quarry of Nant Gwryd-uchaf. They have not, however, been found on the south side of the little valley in which Plas-on lies.

## V. Structure of the Area.

At first sight, the structure of the area seems to be one of extreme simplicity. Throughout almost the whole of the district there is a nearly uniform dip from south to north, and the beds follow one another in regular order without any visible break. Only in the eastern portion of the region is there any appearance of interruption in the normal succession, and the Tarannon Shales and the overlying Wenlock Beds are represented by the Geological-Survey map as sweeping unconformably over the upper portion of the beds below. But exposures here are very poor, and a closer examination shows that this apparent overlap is due to faulting.

Nor is much complication introduced by the existence of a series of transverse faults, which for the most part run from north-north-west to south-south-east, and have their downthrow on the eastern side. The only effect of these faults is that all the beds are thrown back towards the south in a series of steps.

### Strike-Faults.

An examination of the beds in detail proves, however, that this apparent simplicity of sequence is broken by the existence of at least one strike-fault which lies nearly in the plane of the bedding, and consequently has hitherto escaped detection. As this fault is unquestionably the greatest disturbing factor in an otherwise normal succession, we shall begin by describing the evidence that proves its existence.

Careful collecting of fossils soon shows that the Bala Beds of the Ceiriog Valley may be divided into an upper and a lower series, distinguished one from the other by their faunas. In the upper beds we find, for example, *Ramipora Hochstetteri*, *Phyllopora Hisingeri*, *Ptilodictya*, *Trinucleus seticornis*, *Cybele verrucosa*, *Encrinurus*, and *Cheirurus*. None of these are to be seen in the lower beds, where, on the other hand, we find *Tetradella complicata*, *Trinucleus concentricus*, *Asaphus Powisi*, etc., which do not occur in the upper beds. *Orthis elegantula* is also especially characteristic of the lower beds; for, although it is found in the upper beds, the specimens there are always small and few in number.

The boundary between the two series is perfectly sharp, and can be traced with ease for a considerable distance, as shown upon the map (Pl. LIII). Near the farm of Dolhir it will be seen that, in crossing the valley, the boundary forms a V, indicating that the surface of separation between the upper and the lower series dips towards the north, at an angle of about 20°.

So far, there is nothing to show that the two series are not superposed in normal succession, although the abruptness of the palæontological change is somewhat against this view.

Near Dolhir, however, the boundary lies at the foot of a line of low cliffs which runs up from the farm towards the limestone-quarry above; and an examination of the rocks in these cliffs shows that, although the boundary is nearly parallel to the bedding of the upper series, it is not precisely coincident, but dips at a somewhat steeper angle, so that in passing down the boundary-plane we pass into continuously lower beds.

The beds of the lower series, on the other hand, dip at a slightly steeper angle than the boundary, so that the plane of separation is related to the beds themselves somewhat in the fashion shown in fig. 12. Such a plane cannot be a plane of normal deposition. It

Fig. 12.

might, indeed, be a plane of unconformity with accompanying overlap; but in that case the beds above would necessarily be marginal deposits, and of this we see no evidence.

Whatever the surface of separation may be, it can easily be traced from Nant Iorwerth to the neighbourhood of Hafod-y-gareg; and its outcrop shows clearly that, for a considerable distance, it is nearly a true plane.

The hypothesis of unconformity being almost excluded by the character of the beds, we conclude that this surface of separation is a fault of low dip; and the question now arises whether the motion of the upper beds relatively to the lower has been up or down this plane — whether, in fact, the fault is a thrust-plane or what Dr. J. E. Marr has called a lag-fault.

Fig. 13.

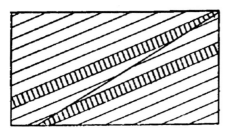

It is often assumed that a thrust-plane necessarily brings lower beds upon the top of higher, and that a fault that brings higher beds upon the top of lower must be of a different nature. But this is not necessarily the case; the effect of a thrust-plane is determined by the relative dips of the thrust-plane and of the beds themselves.

Fig. 14.

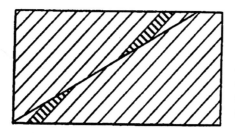

If both beds and fault dip in the same direction, then, provided that the dip of the beds is lower than that of the fault, an overthrust will bring older beds upon the top of newer (fig. 13). But if, on the other hand, the dip of the beds is steeper than that of the fault, then an overthrust will bring newer beds upon the top of older (fig. 14, p. 581). It is impossible, therefore, from the mere fact that the Dolhir Fault brings higher on to lower beds, to infer that it is necessarily a lag-fault.

In the section, fig. 1 (p. 552), it will be observed that the beds above the fault dip at a lower angle than the fault itself, while the beds below dip at a higher angle. This, as will be seen by reference to fig. 15, is what may happen if the fault affects the margin

Fig. 15.

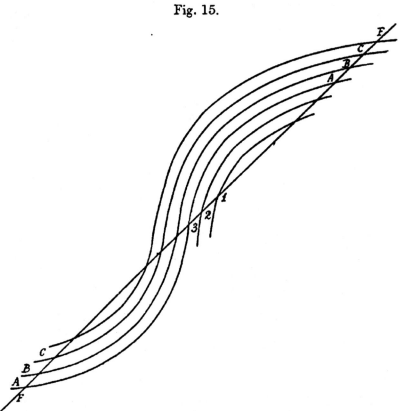

either of an anticline or of a syncline; and the Dolhir Fault lies on the southern margin of the Llangollen Basin, and also on the northern margin of the Berwyn Anticline. The diagram shows that either an upward or a downward movement, if of the proper extent, would bring the higher beds A, B, C (dipping at a low angle) upon the top of the lower beds 1, 2, 3 (dipping at a high angle). In such a case as this, it is clear that the anticline and syncline were formed before the fault.

The relations of the beds, therefore, tell us nothing of the direction of movement; and the only evidence that we can find is that the component beds of the Dolhir Limestone sometimes bend upwards as they approach the line of the fault. This would seem to indicate that the direction of movement of the rocks above the fault was downwards; but we cannot consider this evidence conclusive, especially in view of the fact that the upward bend is rarely seen.

Besides this great strike-fault, there appear to be a number of others of similar character which are, however, of considerably less importance and cannot be traced for any great distance. The evidence is most conspicuous in the neighbourhood of the second ash-band, where the folding of the hard ash along with the softer slates appears to have been accompanied by a considerable amount of shearing and fracturing, and the boundary of the ash is frequently a faulted one. This is particularly well shown at Cae Deicws and Craig-y-Pandy.

Near the China-clay Quarry the ash forms a line of crags which runs up the side of the valley towards Cae Deicws. But, near the top of the bank, a tongue of ash may be seen, separated from the main line of crags by slates and sandstones, and apparently at a lower stratigraphical horizon. This tongue, which does not extend very far, we take to be a portion of the ash repeated by a fault of rather low dip. In the quarry at Cae Deicws the effect of the disturbance is clearly seen, and one of the subsidiary faults appears to cause the curving of the columns shown on the right of fig. 8 (p. 563). On the opposite side of the valley, in the small quarry at Craig-y-Pandy, there is a very distinct line of crushing and slipping, presumably due to the same disturbance; and the fact that the beds immediately north of the ash do not strike parallel to the band indicates a faulted boundary.

At the southern margin of the China-clay Quarry there is a small fault; and on the north-eastern side of this the ash is greatly thickened, as if it had been crushed against the plane of movement.

Further signs of crushing, along the northern boundary of the same ash-band, are visible near Hafod-y-gareg, and the fault itself may be seen in an old trial-working about 100 yards east of the bridge.

It is clear, therefore, that there has been a very considerable amount of disturbance at the junction of the ash-band with the slates above and below, and the boundary is often faulted. Wherever this faulting is conspicuous, the ash is thickened and appears to have been partly converted into the peculiar compact rock resembling a quartz-porphyry, which has already been described (p. 564).

As will be shown in the account of the Cae-mawr Fault, there is probably a thrust-plane at the foot of the isolated crag of ash east of Llechrhydau.

Several faults, probably of small importance, are visible along the Glyn-Valley Railway, where this cuts through the Bryn Beds a short distance below the Dolhir Fault. They dip at from 55° to 60° northwards.

The remaining faults, so far as we are aware, are nearly vertical planes, and (with the exception of the Cae-mawr Fault) appear to be of the normal type.    There are two principal series :—the one set running nearly due north and south, or, in the western portion of the map, north-north-west and south-south-east ; and the other set running approximately from west-north-west to east-south-east.

## The North-and-South Series of Faults.

In the western part of the map there are two long faults running from north-north-west to south-south-east, both of which have their downthrow on the east.    The most conspicuous of these runs from near Tomen-y-meirw to Ty-isaf, and is very easily detected because it throws both the Glyn Grit and the ash-band some 200 yards to the south on its eastern side.    It crosses Nant Tyn-y-twmpath a little north of the road from Glyndyfrdwy to Glyn Ceiriog.    The absence of the higher zones of the Pen-y-glog Slates noted by Miss Elles[1] is probably due to this fault. Near the northern margin of our map (Pl. LIII) it is met by a fault running nearly due north and south, and likewise having a down-throw on the eastern side.

The second of the north-north-west to south-south-east faults extends from the uppermost of the Glyn slate-quarries through Aber-chwil, and probably into the valley of Cwm Clwyd.    At one time it was distinctly visible in the slate-quarry, where it brought the green slates on the west into contact with the Denbighshire Series on the east ; but the exposure is now concealed by a fall of drift and soil.    The effect of the fault on the Glyn Grit and on the Craig-y-Pandy Ash is small, although the greater part of its course is marked by a very distinct depression.

South of the ash-band its course is not very clearly shown ; but in the old Teirw-Hill Quarry close to Pandy there is a fault that lies approximately in the same line.    Near the ash-band the fault is met by a second fault, which runs from north to south, and has its downthrow on the western side.

Near Llechrhydau a group of three faults, which run nearly due north and south, will be seen on the map (Pl. LIII).    The westernmost of these is clearly shown in the stream west of the farm, where it brings slates on the west into contact with ash upon the east, the direction of the fault being N. 12° W.    Owing to the covering of drift and heather, it is impossible to be quite certain whether these slates are above or below the lowest ash-band.

The next of the series of faults passes immediately to the east of the farm, and an old trial-working appears to have been driven along it for some distance at the north-eastern corner of the farm-yard.    It is also seen a little farther north, where its face has been exposed for a short distance by the action of the weather, and its direction is N. 8° W.    The fault here hades steeply to the west.

[1] Quart. Journ. Geol. Soc. vol. lvi (1900) p. 398.

South of the farm the fault appears to curve somewhat eastwards, and then to resume a more southerly course.

But by far the most remarkable and the most important of this group of faults is the one that we have termed the Cae-mawr Fault. Trending in a direction a little west of north, it runs in nearly a straight line from near Llechrhydau past the farm of Cae-mawr to Dol-y-wern, and is probably continued northwards past Llangollen to the base of the Eglwyseg Crags. Despite its extent and importance it is the most elusive of the series, and has escaped the notice both of D. C. Davies and of the officers of the Geological Survey. The latter represent it as an unconformity at the base of the Tarannons, and the former as an unconformity at the base of the Wenlock; but the strike of the beds does not curve round in the way that such an explanation requires.

The exposures in this part of the district are very poor; but, in Ty-nant Wood, the Bryn Beds are well shown striking nearly due east; and the same beds are visible in place about 450 yards south by west of Cae-mawr, close to the line of the fault. East of the fault the Ty-draw Slates are exposed at intervals along the Oswestry Road, and the Fron-Frys Slates upon the hillside above, the strike being approximately from east to west, directly against the fault.

The continuation of the fault northwards can be traced in the hill north of Dol-y-wern. At Ty'n-y-celyn Brongyll the slates immediately on its western side contain graptolites belonging to the *Monograptus-riccartonensis* Zone of the Wenlock Series; while 350 yards to the east, Ludlow Beds with *Monograptus vulgaris* occur on the roadside below Bron-heulog. The Wenlock and the Ludlow Beds here strike towards each other, and a fault of some magnitude must therefore lie between the two exposures.

South of Cae-mawr Wood the southerly extension of the fault is concealed for more than a mile by the drift that hides the whole of the solid geology of this portion of the area. But, about 600 yards south-east of Llechrhydau, an isolated crag of ash stands high above the soil-covered slope. It has been mapped by the Geological Survey as a portion of the lowest ash-band; if this be correct, however, the band must for a short distance be of enormously greater thickness than it is anywhere else in the neighbourhood. We believe that this crag is the continuation of the Craig-y-Pandy Ash (which it resembles lithologically) thrown southwards by the Cae-mawr Fault.

It is, however, clear that the fault does not extend farther southwards; or, if it does, its throw is very greatly reduced: for the lowest ash-band runs right across its course, with not more than a slight dislocation in the line of the fault.

The striking feature of this fault is the remarkable apparent variation of its throw. Everywhere the beds upon its eastern side are newer than those with which they are in contact on the west; but if the movement has been vertically downwards, then the amount of the vertical throw increases rapidly towards the south as far as the crag already mentioned, beyond which the throw is suddenly reduced to a few feet. Even if we should be mistaken in identifying this crag as a part of the Craig-y-Pandy Ash, the difficulty remains. Although the newest beds lie on the eastern side of the fault, it is impossible, as the accompanying section (fig. 16) will show, to explain the relation of the beds upon the hypothesis that there has been any downward movement on its eastern side. The figure shows the Glyn Grit, the Dolhir thrust and other faults, the Craig-y-Pandy Ash and the Cwm-Clwyd Ash as they appear upon the two faces of the fault, the beds and faults upon the eastern face being indicated by thick lines and heavy shading, and the beds and faults upon the western face by thin lines and light shading. It will be observed that, on the western face, the Dolhir thrust (*tt*) and the top of the Glyn Grit (*gg*), if produced, meet at the point *o*. A vertically downward displacement of about 1380 feet on the east side would bring the Dolhir thrust into the position *T*, which it actually occupies; but it would at the same time bring the Glyn Grit nearly to the same point, whereas it really crops out at *G*, about 700 yards to the north. No simple vertical displacement can bring the lines *tt* and *gg* at the same time into the positions *TT* and *GG* respectively; and, since the distance from *T* to *G* is greater than that from *t* to *g*, it is clear that whatever vertical component the movement may have had must have been upwards on the eastern side of the fault.

Fig. 16.—*Section along the Cue-mawr Fault, showing the disposition of the beds upon the two faces.*

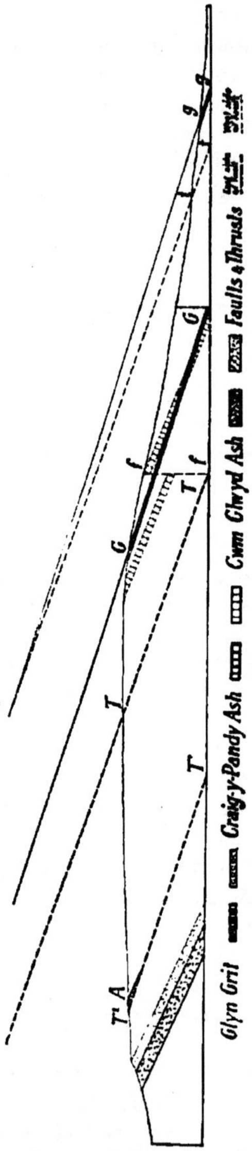

[Scale: 2 inches = 1 mile; base of section, 500 feet above O.D.]

Glyn Grit    Craig-y-Pandy Ash    Cwm Clwyd Ash    Faults & Thrusts

In order to determine the actual direction of the movement, all that is necessary is to produce the lines *GG* and *TT* to meet in a point *O* corresponding to the point *o* on the western side of the fault. A displacement of the beds parallel to themselves that would bring the point *o* to the position *O* will account for all the facts observed. The point *O* lies too far away to be shown upon the figure; but, considering the beds on the west of the fault to be fixed in position, it may be calculated that the movement upon the eastern side had a vertical component of 4690 feet upwards, a horizontal component of 14,830 feet southwards, and an inclination upwards and southwards of 17° 32'. Such a movement would bring the Craig-y-Pandy Ash to a point 140 yards north of the actual outcrop A, which is as near as the degree of accuracy obtainable in such observations can lead us to expect.

It will be seen in the section that the Cwm-Clwyd Ash is but little affected by this fault, and the movement must therefore have taken place upon a surface between the Cwm-Clwyd Ash and the Craig-y-Pandy Ash A. We have accordingly placed another thrust-plane T' T', inclined at an angle of 17° 32', at the base of the Craig-y-Pandy Ash A, where we had long suspected the existence of a fault.[1]

It should be observed that, in the foregoing calculation, we have taken no account of the small fault f. This was formed after the Cae-mawr Fault, and we have assumed that it was the block north of this fault that remained fixed, while the block on the south of it sank. If, on the other hand, it is the block on the south of f that retains its original position (relatively to the eastern side of the fault), the vertical component of the displacement along the Cae-mawr Fault must have been somewhat greater, and the angle of inclination slightly steeper; but the difference involved is very small.

Finally, it may be remarked that, owing to the very oblique angle at which the lines tt and gg meet, a slight error in observation will considerably affect the position of the points o and O; but the angle that the line oO makes with the horizontal will not be greatly affected. Therefore, although our results may not be mathematically exact, we think that there can be little doubt that the movement along the eastern face of the Cae-mawr Fault was upwards and southwards at a low angle approximating to $17\frac{1}{2}°$. On no other hypothesis is it possible to explain the relations of the beds on the two sides of the fault, as shown in the figure.

Owing to the almost complete absence of exposures farther east, it is impossible to determine with precision the faulting in that part of the district. The lowest ash-band is well exposed in the stream on the western margin of Cefn-coch Wood; but its course within the wood and towards the farm called the Springs can only be determined by the abundance of ash-blocks and the contour of the surface. The ash, however, is again exposed in situ at the head of the little valley about 250 yards south of the Springs. We conclude, then, as shown on the map (Pl. LIII), that there are two faults running about 10° west of north.

[1] We cannot altogether exclude the possibility that the isolated crag may be a faulted block of the Cwm-Clwyd Ash. In that case, the thrust T' T' must lie farther north, and must be accompanied by subsidiary thrusts and faults, forming a complex which the poorness of the exposures does not permit us to unravel. But the total effect of the complex must be equivalent to that of the single thrust shown in our section (fig. 16, p. 586).

Of the easternmost of these two faults there appears to be further evidence in the valley of Craignant, where the dips of the beds on the two sides of the fault are very different, and where, moreover, we have traced the narrow ash-band shown up to the western side of the fault but not beyond.

### The West-North-West and East-South-East Series of Faults.

The long fault belonging to this series in the western portion of our map is most clearly seen far away to the west in the neighbourhood of Corwen; but its effects are visible, at intervals, along its whole course. In our map (Pl. LIII) it cuts off the prominent hill of ash near Ty-isaf. Its continuation south-east of Hafod-y-gareg is concealed, and in the map we have represented it as ending against one of the other series of faults in the valley of the Ceiriog; but it probably continues beyond this.

Another fault belonging to this series extends from Nant Iorwerth to Ty-nant. At the former locality it terminates the strongly-marked grit-band near Bryn; at the latter it repeats the Craig-y-Pandy Ash and the Coed-y-glyn intrusive sill. Its downthrow is therefore to the south. An interesting point, in connexion with this fault, is that it seems to end against the Dolhir strike-fault already described.

The remaining faults of this series are, to some extent, hypothetical. That there is a fault along the valley of the Ceiriog between Glyn and Dol-y-wern is clear, for otherwise the Ty-draw Slates would extend across the stream and appear upon the northern bank, where we actually find Wenlock Beds. Whether, however, this fault extends eastwards of the Cae-mawr Fault is at present uncertain, but the valley of Cilnant lies in the same line.

The fault drawn through the valley of Nant in the eastern part of the map is necessary to explain the relations of the Carboniferous Limestone on the north and the grey slates of Pwll-hir and the grit of Gwernydd-gymmal on the south. Moreover, in the lower part of the valley the whole of the northern bank appears to be made up of Wenlock Beds, and the whole of the southern bank of pale slates. Exposures, indeed, are rare, so that certainty is not attainable; but the soil of the northern bank is full of fragments of Wenlock Slate, the soil of the southern bank is equally full of fragments of the pale slates, and there is very little intermixture.

The dislocation of the Cwm-Clwyd Ash near Spring Hill, and of the Glyn Grit near Gwernydd-gymmal, seems to be due to a long fault which runs from W. 9° S. to E. 9° N., and appears to affect the Carboniferous rocks also. The exposures between these two localities are, however, so poor that it is scarcely possible to prove that the dislocations are due to a single fault.

## VI. COMPARISON WITH OTHER AREAS.

It requires but a brief inspection of the list of fossils from the Dolhir Beds to show that the fauna resembles that of the upper portion of the Bala Series in Pembrokeshire and in the Lake District. When, however, we compare the lower beds of these districts, the similarity diminishes or even disappears. In the Llandovery Series also the differences are so great, that no direct comparison with the rocks of those areas is possible; and it is to the shelly facies of the Llandovery, as developed on the Welsh Border, that we must look for the representatives of the Fron-Frys Slates of Glyn Ceiriog.

In the following pages, accordingly, we compare the Bala Beds with those of Pembrokeshire and of the Lake District, and the Llandovery Beds with those of Llandovery and other areas.

In South Wales[1] the Bala Series is divided by Dr. Marr and the late T. Roberts into the following subdivisions, in descending order :—

> *Trinucleus-seticornis* Beds.
> Slade Beds.
> Redhill Stage.
> Sholeshook-Limestone Stage.
> Robeston-Wathen Limestone.
> *Dicranograptus*-Shales (in part).

The *Dicranograptus*-Shales are considered by these authors to represent generally the Glenkiln Group and the lower part of the Hartfell Group of the Moffat area, and this is also the view that seems to be taken by later observers. The boundary between the Llandeilo and Bala Series therefore lies somewhere in the *Dicranograptus*-Shales; but its precise position has not yet been determined, nor has it been shown to what horizon the shales extend in an upward direction.

As these shales contain few fossils excepting graptolites, no direct comparison is possible with any part of the Glyn succession. Messrs. Cantrill & Thomas have, indeed, found one or two bands of limestone in the *Dicranograptus*-Shales, and from these a few trilobites, brachiopods, and other fossils have been obtained; but the number of species is small, and they do not afford a very satisfactory basis for comparison. The presence of *Trinucleus concentricus* var. *favus* suggests that these calcareous bands belong to the Llandeilo Series.

The precise position of the Robeston-Wathen Limestone is also somewhat doubtful. It unquestionably belongs to the Bala Series; but its relations to the Sholeshook Limestone appear to be obscure, for where the one is present the other is almost invariably absent.

---

[1] Marr & Roberts, Quart. Journ. Geol. Soc. vol. xli (1885) pp. 476–90; D. C. Evans, *ibid.* vol. lxii (1906) pp. 597–642; and T. C. Cantrill & H. H. Thomas, 'Geology of the South Wales Coalfield, pt. vii: The Country around Ammanford' (Sheet 230) Mem. Geol. Surv. 1907, pp. 8–36.

Marr & Roberts placed the Robeston-Wathen Limestone in the Middle Bala and the Sholeshook Limestone in the Upper Bala, but they expressed themselves with some reserve. In the presence of *Halysites, Heliolites*, and other corals, the Robeston-Wathen Limestone resembles the Dolhir Beds ; but it differs in the absence or rarity of cystideans and polyzoa, and of *Cybele, Cheirurus juvenis, Trinucleus seticornis*, and other trilobites. It contains, however, none of the characteristic fossils of the Pandy Beds ; and in the Glyn-Ceiriog district it must be represented, either by a part of the Dolhir Series, or by a part of the succession that is cut out by the Dolhir Fault. In either case, it is clear that the Robeston-Wathen Limestone belongs to a higher horizon than the Pandy Series.

Whatever uncertainty may exist as to the correlation of the *Dicranograptus*-Shales and the Robeston-Wathen Limestone, there can be no doubt that the succeeding beds are approximately the equivalents of the Dolhir Series. In both we have the same abundance of corals, cystideans, and polyzoa; in both *Cybele verrucosa, Trinucleus seticornis, Cheirurus juvenis, Ch. octolobatus*, and *Remopleurides* are characteristic among the trilobites. The most important difference is the absence in the Dolhir Beds of *Phillipsinella parabola* and *Staurocephalus*, both of which are common in the Sholeshook Limestone.

The Redhill and Slade Beds do not differ essentially in fauna from the Sholeshook Limestone, although they seem to be less fossiliferous and to contain fewer species of trilobites. The limestone passes upwards into the Redhill stage, and no sharp line can be drawn between the latter and the Slade Beds. The three divisions appear to form a single natural group, and that group is characterized by a fauna similar to that of the Dolhir Series.

Since in South Wales the base of the Bala Series lies in the *Dicranograptus*-Shales, and in North Wales below the Pandy Beds, and since the Robeston-Wathen Limestone of South Wales belongs to a higher horizon than the Pandy Beds of North Wales, we are forced to conclude either that the Pandy Beds are represented by the upper part of the *Dicranograptus*-Shales, or that in South Wales they are altogether absent. In the latter case there must be a break in the succession below the Robeston-Wathen Limestone. Until, however, we know to what horizon the *Dicranograptus*-Shales extend there can be no certainty on this point.

The Bala or Coniston-Limestone Series of the Lake District was divided by Dr. Marr in 1892[1] into the following groups, in descending order :—

    III *b*.  Ashgill Shales.
    III *a*.  *Staurocephalus*-Limestone.
    II.   Sleddale Group.
    I.   Roman-Fell Group.

At that time he included the Keisley Limestone in the Sleddale

---

[1] Geol. Mag. dec. 3, vol. ix (1892) pp. 97–110.

Group; but he now,[1] like Mr. F. R. C. Reed, places it in Group III, and accordingly some alteration is necessary in the list of fossils given in his former paper. He also places the *Phyllopora*-Beds of Backside Beck above the true Ashgill Shales, but includes them in the same group, which he calls the Ashgillian.

Turning to the lowest or Roman-Fell Group, it will be found that it consists of ashes, ashy shales, and nodular limestones, the latter often composed almost exclusively of the tests of *Beyrichia*. The list of fossils is short; but it includes *Lingula tenuigranulata* and *Bellerophon bilobatus*, the former of which occurs in the Teirw Beds and the latter in both the Teirw and the Bryn Beds. *Trematis corona*, another characteristic fossil of the Roman-Fell Group, has not yet been found at Glyn Ceiriog. The remaining species do not appear to be especially characteristic; the palæontological evidence is therefore not very complete: but, so far as it goes, it points to the approximate equivalence of the Roman-Fell Group with the Teirw Beds.

Of the fossils in Dr. Marr's list from the Sleddale Group some eighteen have been found in the Bryn Beds. Among the more important forms that are common to the two we may mention *Tentaculites anglicus*, *Tetradella complicata*, *Lichas laxatus*, *Chasmops conicophthalma*,[2] *Trinucleus concentricus*, *Lingula ovata*, *Platystrophia biforata*, *Rafinesquina deltoidea*, *R. expansa*, and *Triplesia spiriferoides*. On the other hand, Dr. Marr's list (with the Keisley-Limestone fossils omitted) includes *Cybele verrucosa*, *Encrinurus*, *Remopleurides*, and *Trinucleus seticornis*, which in the Glyn district we should look upon as characteristic of the Dolhir Beds. On the whole, however, the fauna of the Sleddale Group is much nearer to that of the Bryn Series than to the fauna of any other group in the Glyn district: and the fact that the top of the Bryn Series is cut out by the Dolhir Fault may explain some of the discrepancies. Further, as Dr. Marr informs us, it is possible that some of the fossils recorded as from the Sleddale group, but not collected by himself, may in reality belong to the Ashgillian.

The Ashgillian Series of the Lake District is undoubtedly represented by the Dolhir Series of Glyn, although it is possible that neither the base nor the summit of the two exactly coincide. There is the same abundance of cystideans in the calcareous beds, and of polyzoa, including *Phyllopora Hisingeri*, in some of the more shaly deposits. The absence of *Staurocephalus* and *Phillipsinella parabola* at Glyn Ceiriog, and their presence both in South Wales and in the Lake District, is somewhat remarkable. But over the greater part of the Glyn area the base of the Dolhir Series, like the top of the Pandy Group, is cut out by the Dolhir Fault and the actual *Staurocephalus*-Limestone may be missing. We may conclude, therefore, that the Dolhir Beds belong to the Ashgillian Series; but that, in all probability, the whole of that series is not visible at Glyn Ceiriog.

[1] Geol. Mag. dec. 5, vol. iv (1907) pp. 59–69.
[2] *Phacops brevispina* of Dr. Marr's list. The species described by Salter as *Ph. conicophthalma* was supposed by Schmidt to be identical with his *Ph. brevispina*; but Salter's type shows the bases of long genal spines.

It has already been noted that the Glyn Grit is merely a sandy and calcareous facies of the upper part of the Dolhir Beds; and the general results of our comparison of the Bala Series of these areas may, therefore, be summarized in the following table. As the faunas of the various subdivisions of the Ashgillian Series are still very imperfectly known, no attempt is made in this table to correlate these subdivisions :—

| | South Wales. | Glyn Ceiriog. | Lake District. |
|---|---|---|---|
| ASHGILLIAN. | Slade Beds.<br>Redhill Beds.<br>Sholeshook Limestone.<br>Robeston-Wathen Limestone. | Glyn Grit.<br>Dolhir Beds. | *Phyllopora*-Beds.<br>Ashgill Shales.<br>*Staurocephalus*-Limestone. |
| CARADOCIAN. | — Gap ? —<br><br>*Dicranograptus*-Shales. | Graptolitic Slates.<br>— Gap. —<br>Bryn Beds.<br>Teirw Beds. | <br><br>Sleddale Beds.<br>Roman-Fell Group. |

The Fron-Frys Slates differ so much from those of the Lake District, and so little is known of the corresponding beds in South Wales, that direct comparison with those areas is impossible. Instead of graptolites they contain brachiopods and corals, and thus belong to the shelly facies of the Llandovery which prevails on the eastern borders of Wales. They are, however, continuous and lithologically identical with the Grey Slates of Corwen, in which we found graptolitic bands containing graptolites of the *Monograptus-gregarius* Zone. This is the uppermost zone of the Lower Birkhill Shales of Moffat, and it is therefore with the Lower Birkhill that the Grey Slates of Corwen and the Fron-Frys Slates of Glyn Ceiriog must be correlated. At Glyn we have found no graptolites, but the slates contain *Pentamerus undatus*, *Meristina (?)* cf. *crassa*, several other species of *Meristina*, and *Nidulites javus*. It is clear therefore that they belong to the Llandovery of the original Silurian area, and probably to the lower division of that series. It is interesting to note that, while the shelly facies of the Llandovery is found at Glyn, graptolitic bands have already made an appearance at Corwen, which lies only 8 miles away to the west. Farther west graptolites become still more abundant in the corresponding beds.

With the exception of the Tarannon graptolite *Monograptus Marri*, no fossils have yet been found at Glyn Ceiriog between the Fron-Frys Slates and the Wenlock Beds; but the former appear to pass without a break into the pale-coloured Ty-draw Slates, and these in turn to graduate upwards into the slates of the Wenlock Series. It seems, therefore, that the Ty-draw Slates must represent both the Upper

Llandovery and the Tarannon Shales; but it should be remembered that in such homogeneous unfossiliferous slates, showing little or no trace of bedding, it would be difficult to detect any break in the succession.

We do not propose to attempt any correlation of the British deposits with those of other countries; but reference may here be made to an important paper by Dr. Kiær [1] on the Norwegian Stage 5. This corresponds with the upper portion of the Bala Series, and it is divided by him into (5a) the uppermost *Chasmops*-Beds, and (5b) the *Meristella-crassa* Beds. The latter are followed by the Silurian, beginning with the zone of *Pentamerus undatus*.

In discussing the correlation of the Norwegian deposits, Dr. Kiær points out that the fossils which we formerly recorded from the Glyn Grit are almost all Bala forms; and, as we identified the Glyn Grit with the Corwen Grit, he places the boundary between the Ordovician and the Silurian above the Corwen Grit instead of below it. As we have already stated, the more detailed examination of the Glyn area has led us independently to the same conclusion, so far as the Glyn Grit is concerned; but we are not certain that the Glyn and Corwen Grits are identical.

The *Meristella-crassa* Zone does not appear to be present in the Glyn-Ceiriog District; but it is clear that the Fron-Frys Slates represent the *Pentamerus-undatus* Zone, which Dr. Kiær takes as the base of the Silurian System.

### EXPLANATION OF PLATE LIII.

Geological map of the country around Glyn Ceiriog, on the scale of 3 inches to the mile.

### DISCUSSION.

The PRESIDENT expressed his sense of the importance of detailed work, such as that so successfully accomplished by the Authors, in well-selected areas. The Authors were to be congratulated on their choice of an area, for it was one which had called forth the enthusiasm of Sedgwick, who, in a letter to Phillips, written in 1843, spoke of it as full ' of the most beautiful geology he had ever seen in his hammering life.' The Authors' views seemed to be in harmony with those expressed by Sedgwick at that time, since he also had regarded the black slates at the village of Ceiriog as the base of the system (Upper Silurian), and had divided the Cambrian (Sedgwick) into five zones.

The SECRETARY read the following extracts from a letter received from Mr. J. LOMAS:

' I wish to congratulate the Authors on their attempt to reduce the Glyn rocks to their proper succession. No better district could have been selected to serve as a type of the peripheral series of the Berwyn dome.

' The Authors evidently incline to the opinion that the igneous bands in the

[1] 'Faunistische Uebersicht der Etage 5 des norwegischen Silursystems' Videnskabsselskabets Skrifter, I. Math.-nat. Klasse, 1897, No. 3. (Kristiania.)

Pandy Series are contemporaneous ashes; but, so far as I can see, no evidence is brought forward except their fragmental condition. In the Craig-y-Pandy "Ash," included angular fragments of slate and limestone are common in the sheared upper margin. The overlying slates and limestones are also sheared, and it is highly probable that the limestone-fragments were introduced from the adjacent beds.

'The central portion of the "Ash" is compact, and shows beautiful columnar structure, both at Cae Deicws and Craig-y-Pandy. Hitherto, I have favoured the idea that the igneous bands might be intrusive, and were injected into the slates along planes of shearing when the rocks were folded. As a working hypothesis it has been useful, but I have long recognized that no definite results can be obtained without careful and detailed mapping of the sedimentaries.

'I am jointly responsible for the statement referred to by the Authors, that the slates in contact with the igneous bands show signs of thermometamorphism. It is true that they are usually of a harder and more compact nature near the margins; but, speaking for myself, I claim nothing more, and certainly do not compare the alteration with that which has produced spotted slates in connexion with the Hendre intrusion.'

Mr. O. T. JONES said that he wished to congratulate the Authors on their excellent account of a very interesting and difficult area. As compared with the sequence in South Wales, the Dolhir Beds could be matched exactly with the Redhill and Slade subdivision and the Sholeshook Limestone. Below that all correspondence between the districts ceased, for whereas in the South Welsh area the Lower Bala Beds contained graptolites almost exclusively and brachiopods were rare, in the area described in this paper the reverse was the case. It was certainly difficult to correlate the shelly beds and ashes of the Ceiriog district with the black graptolitic shales of South Wales, which were devoid of ashy material.

With regard to the Dolhir Fault, although the Authors had demonstrated that a certain amount of movement had taken place along that line, yet it was a curious fact that a break of a similar kind occurred at nearly the same level in South Wales—where it could be definitely proved to be an unconformity, with overlap of the Upper Bala upon the Lower Bala and Llandeilo Series. Nowhere along the line was anything of the nature of a beach-deposit found. The relation of the Llandovery to the Upper Bala was always a difficult question. The Glyn Grit corresponded in position with the Llandovery basal grit and conglomerate of South Wales, which was liable to precisely the same variation in thickness. The Lower Llandovery always showed close faunal affinities with the Upper Bala Series, but the speaker thought that more stress should be laid upon the incoming of new forms than upon the survival of older forms in delimiting the two groups.

He was glad to find that *Pentamerus undatus* occupied a relatively high position in the Llandovery of North Wales, as in South Wales.

Dr. H. J. JOHNSTON-LAVIS enquired as to the definition of the following terms used by the Authors:—'fine tuff,' 'coarse ash.' It seemed to him that the word 'ash' ought to be completely deleted from geological language.

Dr. STRAHAN, in reference to an explanation given of the structure of a part of the region, mentioned that he had had experience of a fault the downthrow of which was always on the same side; it traversed strata all dipping in the same direction, but along it, nevertheless, the outcrops were shifted neither in the same direction nor for an equal distance. The structure, at first sight, seemed impossible; but an explanation was found in the fact that the dip varied from 50° to 15° along the fault, and in the supposition that the movement of the fault was not vertical, but in a direction that lay between those inclinations. The varying effect upon the outcrops necessarily followed, as might be made apparent by drawing a section of curving beds, and sliding over it a tracing of the drawing, in the direction in which the fault was supposed to have moved.

Dr. GROOM said, in reply to Mr. Lomas's communication, that the Pandy Ashes were hardly such as could have been derived from the brecciation of igneous rocks, more particularly from intrusive masses. In places true bedding, and even false bedding, was clear; and the most compact rocks in the heart of the Craig-y-Pandy Ash showed typical 'bogen'-structure.

Mr. LAKE said that, in comparing the fauna of the Bryn Beds with that of the Sleddale Group, the Authors had removed, so far as was possible, from Dr. Marr's list the species that occurred only in the Keisley Limestone. Yet, even then, the Sleddale Group appeared to contain forms that belonged to a higher horizon than the Bryn Beds. As, however, the top of the Bryn Beds was cut out by the Dolhir Fault, this difference was partly explained. The Authors had considered the remarkable fact that a break occurred at the base of the Ashgillian Series in South Wales, as well as in the Glyn Valley. Nevertheless, they were convinced that in the latter area the break was due, in part at least, to a fault.

30. *On the* STRATIGRAPHY *and* STRUCTURE *of the* TARNTHAL MASS (TYROL).   By ALFRED PRENTICE YOUNG, Ph.D., F.G.S.   (Read May 6th, 1908.)

THE Tarnthaler Köpfe are an isolated mountain-mass in the north of the Tuxer Alps.   The appended sketch-map (fig. 1), together

Fig. 1.—*Sketch-map of the Tarnthaler Köpfe.*

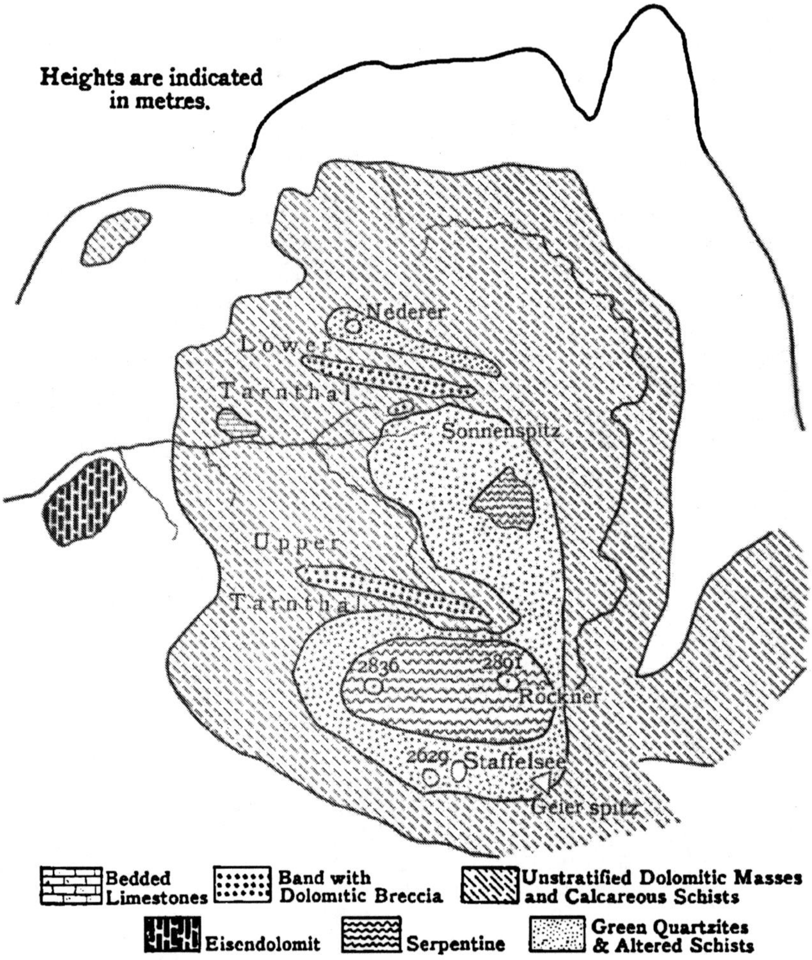

[Scale: $\frac{1}{37500}$, or 2·666 centimetres = 1 kilometre.]

with the sections (figs. 2 & 3) copied from Pichler and Rothpletz, affords a general idea of the geographical distribution of the rocks of which the mass is composed and the vertical section of their arrangement in the mountain-mass itself.

The stratigraphy of the mass has been very differently interpreted by various investigators. Their views will be found in the papers noticed below.

Fig. 2.—*Section taken from that published by A. Pichler in Zeitschrift des Ferdinandeums, ser. 3, pt. viii (1859) Profil xxviii.*

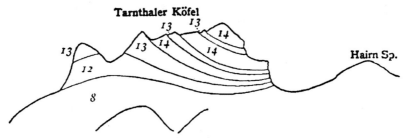

| | |
|---|---|
| 8 = Thonglimmerschiefer (mica-schists). | 13 = Bunte Schiefer (mottled slates). |
| 12 = Kalk & kalkschiefer des Lias (Liassic limestones and calc-schists). | 14 = Ophicalcite and serpentine. |

Adolf Pichler [1] in 1859 supposed the sequence of strata to be normal throughout, the capping mass of serpentine being treated as a sedimentary rock. He enumerates the following fossils, found in a grey limestone in place :—*Belemnites, Pentacrinus, Gervillia inflata, Lithodendron, Rhynchonella.* The whole mass of dolomite, with the calcareous schists above it, is shown in his section as Lias, in which formation the author includes the Rhætic.

Fig. 3.—*Section taken from fig. 51, p. 149, in Prof. Rothpletz's 'Querschnitt durch die Ost-Alpen' Stuttgart, 1894.*

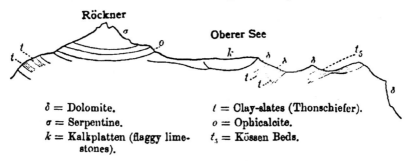

| | |
|---|---|
| δ = Dolomite. | t = Clay-slates (Thonschiefer). |
| σ = Serpentine. | o = Ophicalcite. |
| k = Kalkplatten (flaggy limestones). | $t_5$ = Kössen Beds. |

In 1894 Prof. A. Rothpletz [2] announced a further discovery of Rhætic fossils in this locality—*Terebratula gregaria, Modiola*

[1] 'Beiträge zur Geognosie Tirols' Zeitschr. des Ferdinandeums, ser. 3, pt. viii, pp. i–viii, 1–232, with map & 20 sections.
[2] 'Ein geologischer Querschnitt durch die Ost-Alpen' p. 75.

*minuta*, and several others. The igneous character of the serpentine is recognized; but otherwise the descriptions and sections seem to assume a normal and continuous succession of beds, from the Triassic dolomite below to the youngest 'Kalk-thon' and Wetzschiefer above.

In the same year Dr. F. E. Suess[1] published the results of his own studies in this region. The serpentine and quartzite-schists are held to be older than the calcareous schists and dolomites, and it is supposed that they were brought into their present position by a thrust or long fold with a push towards the north; the beds below the thrust-plane are held to be in normal sequence.

In 1903 appeared Prof. Termier's[2] paper on the structure of the Eastern Alps. The author accounts for the presence of these rocks by means of one or more recumbent folds (nappes), the roots (racines) of which are to be sought in the region of the Zillerthal Alps.

In 1905 appeared Prof. Frech's[3] work on the structure of the Central Alps of Tyrol. He adopts the explanation of the structure of the Tarnthal mass already given by Dr. Suess.

## DESCRIPTION OF THE ROCKS OF THE TARNTHAL MASS.

The whole of the lower ground of this district, over a wide area to the west and south of the mountain, is occupied by calcareous schists, the 'Brenner Schiefer.' These rocks reach up to the floor of the great cirque, at a level of 2100 metres above the sea on the western slope of the Tarnthal mass. From this point a continuous section is exposed up to the summit of the 'Nederer,' marked 2758 m. on the 'Generalstabskarte.'

The series commences with a massive dolomite, usually identified with the 'Hauptdolomit.' This rock shows no bedding-planes; it covers the slope for the next 330 metres (1082 feet).

Above this rock, and resting upon the dolomite at the level of 2480 metres, is the bedded limestone, the probable source of a fossil which I found on the slopes below, apparently of Liassic age. These cliffs must also include the site of the Rhætic fossils discovered by Prof. Rothpletz. The beds dip north-eastwards at an angle of about 20°. The softer bands of the rock appear to have been affected by shearing; the fossils also present evidences of distortion and faulting; but the more massive bands cannot have been very much disturbed. The thickness of these inclined beds is estimated at 15 or 20 metres (50 to 65 feet).

[1] 'Das Gebiet der Triasfalten im Nordosten der Brennerlinie' Jahrb. d. k. k. Geol. Reichsanst. vol. xliv, p. 589.

[2] 'Les Nappes des Alpes Orientales & la Synthèse des Alpes' Bull. Soc. Géol. France, ser. 4, vol. iii (1903) p. 711.

[3] 'Ueber den Gebirgsbau der Tiroler Zentralalpen' Wissensch. Ergänzungshefte zur Zeitschr. des D. u. Ö. Alpenvereins, vol. ii, pt. i.

Between these limestones and the conspicuously-foliated calcareous schists above them is a tolerably well-marked line of division,
which is probably of significance as regards the interpretation of
the tectonic relations.    In passing from the bedded limestones to

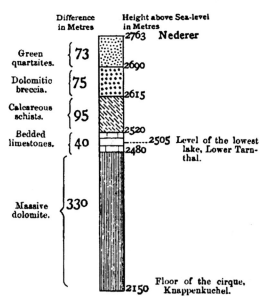

Fig. 4.—*Section from Knappenkuchel to the Nederer summit.*

the calcareous schists
there is no marked
change of dip; and
some thin bands of
solid limestone ap-
pearing at intervals
in the schists may be
taken to show that
the plane of bedding
here coincides ap-
proximately with that
of foliation.

Still higher up the
steep slope, on the
right bank of the
Lower Tarnthal, is a
very irregular band
of massive dolomitic
rock, freely traversed
by quartz-veins and
containing masses
of closely-cemented
breccia, the 'dolo-
mitic breccia.' In
this zone the effects
of shearing and crushing are displayed at their highest.    Softer bands
of the rock have taken on a platy structure simulating bedding, and
are seen winding through and round the harder masses in directions
which bear no relation to the dip of the schists.    Otherwise the
rock has shown itself to be singularly tenacious, and to have resisted
the shearing forces by which it has been kneaded into the more pliant
schists.    The breccia is quite undistorted; in the arrangement of
the fragments no one direction is predominant.[1]    Some fragments
seem to show the original bedding of the rock from which they are
derived.

The schists are continued above the dolomitic breccia; they become
richer in micas—bands and lenticles of green schist appear among
the grey.    At about 2700 metres without sensible break the rocks
begin to take on the characters of the crystalline schists.    These
include the green 'Tarnthaler Quarzit-Schiefer,' the 'Wetzstein-
und Dachstein-Schiefer,' which occupy the summit-ridges of the
Nederer and the Sonnenspitz.    The green rocks are dense quartzites
of exceedingly fine grain like that of a chert or hornstone.    By
the addition of abundant minute plates of chlorite in parallel

[1] Dr. F. E. Suess, however, notes distortion in the fragments of a similar
breccia at the Hippold Joch.

arrangement, and of tourmaline, they approach in character the so-called 'older phyllites,' from which they are distinguished by their finer grain. The induration and the fine puckering of some calcareous rocks associated with this group are no doubt due to contact-alteration by the neighbouring igneous rocks.

Dark red quartzitic rocks are found in several places, along with the green schists.

The green quartzitic rocks often exhibit sharp little folds marked by thin mineral bands, which may indicate the original bedding-planes. A strong southerly dip, due to foliation, predominates over the whole of the Upper Tarnthal between the Sonnenspitz and Röckner ridges.

The Nederer section terminates with the quartzitic schists. No actual occurrence of serpentine has as yet been observed on this ridge, but the relation of the serpentine to the schists is well shown in the neighbouring Upper Tarnthal and on the Röckner ridge.

Between the altered schists and the serpentine are seen some remarkable forms of 'ophicalcite.' Masses of calcareous schist, several feet in thickness, have been injected along the foliation-planes with the basic magma now represented by serpentine. Thin bands and lenticles of serpentine alternating with the schist impart to the rock a parallel structure, which gives the appearance of true bedding and suggests a relation of conformity with the schists below. These are, no doubt, some of the occurrences that led Pichler to include ophicalcite and serpentine in a conformable succession of sedimentary rocks.

But at Matrei and Pfons, where the rock-series resembles that of the Tarnthal, the ophicalcite is not in a form such as to suggest the explanation here given of its origin. The parallel structure is absent or imperfectly developed, and the calcite often appears in veins. The mode of formation of these mixtures of serpentine and calcareous rock is evidently subject to variation.

The general dip of the schists under the serpentine-mass of the Röckner led Prof. Rothpletz to the conclusion that the serpentine was in the form of a sill resting upon the syncline of schists. But the intrusive masses are very irregular in shape. This is well seen in the case of the small serpentine-mass in the Upper Tarnthal, on the southern slope of the Sonnenspitz ridge.

In view of the more recent hypotheses of Alpine structure, which assume a translation from a distance of some or all of the rocks composing this mass, it seems important to distinguish between characters impressed on the rocks in their original site (here called œcogenous characters) and those which may have been acquired during the movement (apœcous characters).

### Superimposed or Apœcous Characters of Rocks of the Middle Zone.

The distortion and partial foliation of the bedded limestones just above the dolomite may have been imposed during a movement of translation, but it does not appear that the fossils here are more deformed than those from the Lias of Southern Tyrol, where there is no question about the rocks being in their original site. But the conspicuous mechanical shearing of the calcareous rocks just above the bedded limestones, as also the strong folding and crushing in the region of the dolomite-breccia, may and probably has been acquired during movement.

## Original or Œcogenous Characters of Rocks of the Upper Zone.

The topmost layer of quartzite and other altered schists and the serpentine bear many characters which must have been acquired before any movement of translation began.

The parallel arrangement of the minute plates of chlorite in the quartzitic rocks (which also contain tourmaline) is a feature that must have been acquired at deep levels, under conditions similar to those determining the structure of the older crystalline phyllites.

The tourmaline is in the form of single, undistorted, minute rods, bounded by faces of the prism and often showing a terminal pyramid—characters which prove it to be the most recent addition to the minerals composing the quartzitic rock.

The close vicinity of rocks, presently to be described, which have been modified by contact with the serpentine, suggests that the tourmaline may be a contact-mineral. The serpentine, however, does not contain tourmaline. If not a contact-mineral, the tourmaline must be older than the serpentine-intrusion. In either case the tourmaline, the youngest product, was formed before the rock-mass left its original site.

## Serpentine.

The association of green schists with serpentine in several distinct occurrences (Mieselkopf, Matrei) has been noted by previous observers, as well as the occurrence of talc and magnesian minerals in the schists adjoining the serpentine.[1]

The igneous intrusion appears to have commenced at a time when the rocks were still under the influence of causes producing foliation. Recrystallization under stress is indicated by the formation of talc in the schists, by the presence of sheafy amphibole in parts of the serpentine-mass near the contacts.

That violent movements were in progress during the period of activity covered by the serpentine-intrusion is shown by the mode of injection of the serpentine in the ophicalcite, and by the numerous detached masses of altered calcareous rock found embedded in the serpentine at all levels up to the summits of the Röckner and the Little Röckner. Among these torn-off fragments

---

[1] See J. Blaas, ' Ueber Serpentin & Schiefer aus dem Brennergebiete ' Nova Acta Leop.-Carol. Akad. der Naturforscher, vol. lxiv (1894) no. 1.

are some which show the ophicalcitic structure, and thus bear witness to the ingress and complete consolidation of a portion of the serpentine-magma at a date prior to a final stage of the eruption in which the fragments were detached and carried off.

## Last Stage of the Intrusion.

The final accession of fluid magmas is represented by a core of serpentine which has crystallized by slow cooling in a state of rest, unsolicited by forces of shearing or stress. This is proved by the abundant remains of large pyroxene-crystals showing no direction in their arrangement, and by numerous pseudomorphs in bastite after pyroxene in composite crystalline growths which evidently still retain their original forms.

In the younger parts of the rock an occasional slight strain in the pyroxenes and some instances of cataclastic structure are the only indication of the survival of forces, which were at the last too attenuated to impose schistose structure on the rock.

The rock must have consolidated nearly in its present form while still in communication with the main magmatic reservoir, and before the commencement of the journey from the original to the present site.

The original igneous rock has been affected chemically, notably by serpentinization on an extensive scale. Some of the changes may possibly have taken effect during translation, but the change of form has been unimportant. The ophicalcite obviously acquired its banded structure on the original site, and has been translated without perceptible deformation. The same is true of the masses of indurated contact-schist.

It appears to me to be evident that the whole mass of serpentine, ophicalcite, and indurated schist still hangs together with the original relative positions of its parts, and that in the course of translation it has undergone no deformation and no interruption of continuity, beyond that due to minor faults and fractures.

## Summary of Conclusions.

As respects the general structure of the Tarnthal mass, my reading of it is as follows :—

The rock-series of the mass may be divided into three parts :—

(1) A lower section consisting of (1 a) principal dolomite (Rhætic) and (1 b) Liassic limestone, the upper beds being the youngest. This lowest portion is in normal position, and is scarcely disturbed.

(2) A middle section consisting of (2 a) calcareous schists, (2 b) a band of massive dolomite and dolomitic breccia, and (2 c) calcareous schists with green bands. This section shows marks of violent distortion and crushing.

(3) An upper section, consisting of more or less altered quartzite-schists, with calcareous schists, ophicalcite, and serpentine. This section retains most of its original character and form, and has undergone little mechanical disturbance since it left its ' root.'

This is summarized in the following synopsis :—

Zone 3 { Serpentine. / Ophicalcite. / Turnthal Quartzites, etc.

Zone 2 { Calcareous schists with green bands. / Dolomitic breccia. / Calcareous schists.

Zone 1 { Liassic limestone. / Principal dolomite (Rhætic).

The explanation of the structure now suggested is as follows :— The distinct line of division between the bedded limestones and the calcareous schists—that is, between Zones 1 & 2—marks approximately the lower limb of a long fold, the dolomitic breccia being thus a repetition in a highly attenuated form of the principal dolomite below.

As regards the relations between Zones 2 & 3, the interpretation is not so clear; the absence of any line of demarcation between these two series of rocks, which have been affected in different degrees by dynamic activity, gives rise to some difficulty. But the hypotheses that present themselves are :—

(a) The collective mass 2 & 3 is in inverted sequence, the serpentine and green schists belonging to an older series normally and immediately below the dolomite—the dolomitic breccia belonging to the lower limb of a fold, the upper limb of which is marked by an air-line above the serpentine.

Or (b) The dolomitic breccia represents the whole of the principal dolomite in a flattened fold, the nappe. The serpentine and quartzites have been brought into their present position by a long overthrust, the traineau écraseur of Prof. Termier. The relation of 1 and 2 in this case is one of enforced conformity, instances of which are known elsewhere.

31. Notes *on the* Geology of Burma. By Leonard V. Dalton,
B.Sc. (Communicated by Dr. A. Smith Woodward, F.R.S.,
F.L.S., V.P.G.S.  Read April 15th, 1908.)

[Plates LIV–LVII—Fossils.]

It is the object of this paper to present the results of geological
expeditions in the Irawadi valley carried out by my uncle Mr. W.
H. Dalton, F.G.S., and myself in the season of 1904–1905, and by
myself alone in 1905–1906, and to correlate these observations with
those made by previous writers, thus summarizing our present
knowledge of the geology of Burma generally and of the Tertiary
System of that country in particular.    To this end it is divided into
the following sections :—

|  | Page |
|---|---|
| I. Historical | 604 |
| II. Original Observations | 607 |
| III. General and Stratigraphical | 617 |
| IV. Palæontology | 622 |
| V. Recapitulation | 641 |

## I. Historical.

Dr. Fritz Nœtling in 1895[1] reviewed the work done on the geology
of Burma before that date, pointing out the remarkably-accurate
hypothetical arrangement of the rocks of Burma made by Buckland
in 1828,[2] and the absence of subdivision of the Tertiary System
previous to W. Theobald's paper on Lower Burma in 1873.[3]   In this
summary the 'Axial Group' of Theobald is referred to as certainly
not of Triassic age—a statement controverted by later examination
of the fossils of the Arakan Yoma and other parts of Lower Burma—
although found true in the sense that the group is a complex one
(as we now know), and neither Triassic nor Cretaceous alone, but
assignable to both of these.    While Dr. Nœtling's paper thus
reviews the greater number of the works published on the geology
of Burma, and in particular those relating to the Tertiary of the
better-known regions of the Irawadi basin, there are certain other
papers to which it is necessary to refer here, as they deal with
the outlying districts.   Of these the earliest is that of E. J. Jones
on the coals of the Chindwin Valley,[4] wherein he describes the

---

[1] Rec. Geol. Surv. India, vol. xxviii, p. 59.
[2] Trans. Geol. Soc. ser. 2, vol. ii, pt. iii, p. 377.  The fossils collected by
J. Crawfurd near Singu and Yenangyat on the Irawadi, referred to by
Buckland, are in the Museum of the Geological Society, and apparently include
several of the forms named many years later by Dr. Nœtling.  They are of
especial interest, as being the first fossils from Burma to reach this country.
[3] 'On the Geology of Pegu' Mem. Geol. Surv. India, vol x, p. 189.
[4] 'Notes on Upper Burma' Rec. Geol. Surv. India, vol. xx (1887) p. 170.

lithological character of the rocks of that district, but wrongly assigns a Cretaceous age to the Miocene coals of the Upper Chindwin, on the ground of the occurrence in them of fossil resin. In the same paper the Tertiary coals and lignite of the region south of Mandalay and in the Shan Hills west of Yamethin are described; while Dr. Nœtling's report of 1891[1] points out the interesting fact that Miocene coal is found only in the north-east-to-south-west valleys of the Shan Plateau, which tableland is formed of Palæozoic and metamorphic rocks. Lastly, the same author in his papers of 1893[2] and 1894[3] indicates the presence of Miocene rocks in the far north (amber-mines) and near Wuntho.

Passing to the review of work subsequent to the 1895 summary, we have the late G. E. Grimes's paper on the geology of the Yenangyat oilfield, and of Gwegyo and other localities in the Myingyan district.[4] Dr. Nœtling's description of the Miocene fossils of Burma was published in 1901[5], and has become a classic in Burmese geology. In 1906, Mr. G. H. Tipper, in a preliminary note on the Trias of Lower Burma,[6] refers to specimens of *Halobia Lommeli*, Wissm., found in Theobald's collections, which were labelled as coming from the Karenni, pointing to the occurrence of Triassic rocks in the east of Lower Burma. He here notes that the Trias of the Arakan Yoma is of less extent than was indicated by Theobald in 1873. In the following year the same writer published a further note[7] showing the complexity of the Axial Group, which he divides into (1) Upper Axials, including *Cardita*-Beds [Cretaceous], *Halobia*-Limestones [Trias], and shales, sandstones, and grits [Trias?]; and (2) Lower Axials, consisting of [unfossiliferous] flaggy shales and sandstones.

In 1906, Mr. R. D. Oldham also published a paper on the explosion-craters of the Lower Chindwin district, west of Monywa,[8] these being identical with the volcanic hills referred to by Jones in 1887[9] as an extension of the line of vulcanism running north and south through Narkondam and 'Paopadaung.' In 1906 also, Mr. E. H. Pascoe published accounts[10] of the stratigraphy of a Miocene area east-north-east of Kabat in lat. 21° 4' N., long. 95° 20' 30" E., and of that of Gwegyo, with a later note[11] in the following year on some fossiliferous lenticular marine limestones exposed in the Yenangyoung Miocene area in the 'Yenangyoung Stage,' the fossils found here prior to this time being chiefly derived from the lower division or 'Promeian' of Dr. Nœtling.

[1] 'Report on the Coalfields in the Northern Shan States' Rec. Geol. Surv. India, vol. xxiv, p. 99.
[2] 'On the Occurrence of Burmite, &c.' Ibid. vol. xxvi, pt. i, p. 31.
[3] 'Note on the Geology of Wuntho' Ibid. vol. xxvii, pt. iv, p. 115.
[4] Mem. Geol. Surv. India, vol. xxviii, pt. i (1898) p. 30.
[5] Palæontologia Indica (Mem. Geol. Surv. India) n. s. vol. i, no. 3.
[6] Rec. Geol. Surv. India, vol. xxxiv, p. 134.
[7] Ibid. vol. xxxv (1907) p. 119.
[8] Ibid. vol. xxxiv, p. 137.
[9] Ibid. vol. xx, pp. 176–77.
[10] Ibid. vol. xxxiv, p. 242.
[11] Ibid. vol. xxxv (1907) p. 120.

By the last-named author, the Tertiary rocks of Burma were classified as under:—

| Series. | Subdivision. | | Thickness in feet. |
|---|---|---|---|
| IRAWADI SERIES. | { Upper Irawadi Series. } <br> { Lower Irawadi Series. } | | 20,000 |
| ARAKAN SERIES. | Pegu Division. | { Yenangyoung Stage. } <br> { Prome Stage. } | 5,500 |
| | Bassein Division. | | 1,200 |
| | Chin Division. | | 10,000 + |

### (1) Arakan Series.

*a*) Chin Division.—This approximately corresponds with the "Axial Series' of Theobald, though to what extent is not exactly known. In any case, it is certain that portions of it are, as we have seen, Triassic and Cretaceous, while it may be, as suggested by Dr. Nœtling, that it includes no Tertiary rocks. In view of the supposed occurrence of *Halobia Lommeli* north-east of Rangoon, it is justifiable to presume that the Chin Division is represented there also, though not recorded by any observer.

(*b*) Bassein Division.—A series of impure fossiliferous limestones, blue marls, and brown or grey sandstones, with *Nummulites*, etc., and at the top a band (more than 10 feet thick) of highly-fossiliferous red nummulitic limestone. Regarded as Eocene.

(*c*) Pegu Division.—Divided by Dr. Nœtling into two subdivisions, Promeian and Yenangyoungian, the former (and lower) being distinguished by its blue clays and grey sandstones from the upper, where olive is the predominant colour. Correlated with the Miocene of Europe.

Very few fossils are known from the Promeian, and these only from one bed near Yenangyoung, although numerous species have been collected from the Yenangyoungian, indicating two facies, one brackish, the other marine.

### (2) Irawadi Series.

The subdivision of this series suggested by Dr. Nœtling is only preliminary, no extensive examination having been yet carried out. The group is considered by that author to be of Pliocene age and equivalent to the Siwaliks of India, which it much resembles.

(*a*) Lower Irawadi Series.—Yellow friable sandstones, with bones and much fossil wood.

(*b*) Upper Irawadi Series.—Sandstones similar to those of the lower division, with no bones and less fossil wood.

It is extremely doubtful whether the thickness of this series is as great as that suggested, but there are no data available for correcting the earlier estimate.

It is evident that some modification of the foregoing classification is desirable, in view of the later evidence brought forward
as to the ages of the lower members of the succession ; these changes
may be more fitly suggested in § III, when considering the general
results of the study of the various sections now to be described.

The additional information contained in the sequel relates to the
Pegu and Bassein divisions of the Arakan Series, new localities of
the former having been visited, while numerous fossils from the
latter are for the first time described.

## II. ORIGINAL OBSERVATIONS.

### (a) Thayetmyo District.   (Map, fig. 1, below.)

Some 8 miles west-north-west of Thayetmyo lies the village of
Padoukbin : near this locality the Burmah Oil Company are working
the petroleum of the lower part of the Pegu Division, the rocks of

Fig. 1.—*Sketch-map of the Padoukbin district.*

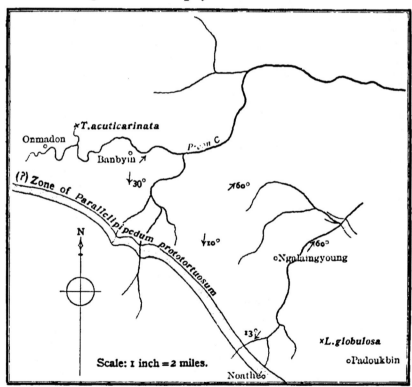

which are here bent into an anticlinal arch striking approximately
north-west and south-east, the dips on the north-eastern flank
being as a rule higher than those on the south-western, which are

less than 10° near the crest.   At Padoukbin village marls crop out ;
these pass north-westwards under petroliferous sandstone, and this
again under a hard fossiliferous sandstone, which extends along the
crest to a point some 2¾ miles from Padoukbin, north-westwards,
where the marls again crop out.   From this place the crest steadily
rises towards the nummulitic-limestone hills indicated by Theobald
as some 10 miles distant, the dips converging to the south-east,
and bringing in successively-lower horizons.

Two fossiliferous horizons were met with, cropping out below the
oil-sand of the Padoukbin native wells, and therefore in Dr. Nœtling's
' Prome Stage.'   The lower of these is found on the Yenanine choung
(choung = stream), a northern tributary of the Pwon choung,
about a mile west of Banbyin village, where a sandstone some
30 feet thick saturated with petroleum was found to contain *Turritella acuticarinata*, Dunk. and *Voluta (?) birmanica*, sp. nov.   About
100 feet above this, on the Pwon choung half a mile from Banbyin,
was found a thin sandstone in the marls, containing *Balanus tintinnabulum*, Linn.   This appears to correspond approximately with
an horizon in the marls about half a mile north-west of Padoukbin,
whence was collected *Lucina globulosa*, Desh. and a Venerid form
somewhat resembling the recent *Chione marmorata*, Lamk., with
casts of *Natica*, etc.   Some 150 feet above these horizons occurs
the fossiliferous sandstone already mentioned, the fossils from
which are unfortunately too poorly preserved for accurate determination, although from one locality a mile and a half north-west of
Padoukbin a species of *Conus*, and from the same sandstone half a
mile south of Banbyin a poorly-preserved *Ceratotrochus* (possibly
*C. Alcockianus*), were obtained.   This horizon, from its position
relative to the petroliferous sands, probably corresponds to the zone
of *Cytherea erycina*, Fav.[1]; and the shales immediately above this
horizon furnished, near the Padoukbin oil-workings, *Distorsio
cancellinus*, Roissy, with a cast possibly referable to *Calliostoma
Blanfordi*, Nœtl., and fragments of a small *Terebra* and a *Natica*.
*C. Blanfordi* and *Terebra Smithi*, Mart., occur in the zone of
*Cancellaria Martiniana* at Minbu,[2] but the evidence is too slender
for identification of the horizon.   On the Ngalaing choung, a
mile north-west by north of this spot, and half a mile east of
Ngalaingyoung village, a soft greenish sandstone in the clays
contained a fragment of a tooth, possibly referable to *Carcharias
gangeticus*, M. & H., also found in the zone above mentioned.   The
remaining fossils come from three different localities, but all apparently belong to the same palæontological horizon.   About three
quarters of a mile south-east of the outcrop of the supposed zone
of *Cytherea erycina*, south of Banbyin, a greenish sandstone was
found containing a poorly-preserved species of *Arca*.   From
road-metal from the quarry at Noathé, which is on the strike of
this bed, the following fossils were obtained :—*Dosinia protojuvenilis*, Nœtl., *Mactra protoreevesii (?)* Nœtl., and *Corbula socialis*,

---

[1] F. Nœtling, Palæontologia Indica (Mem. Geol. Surv. India) vol. i, no. 3
(1901) pp. 7, 10.        [2] *Ibid.* pp. 27, 28.

Mart., with a doubtful specimen of *Conus protofurvus*, Nœtl.; while, from a corresponding position on the north side of the axis, in a similar sandstone were obtained :—*Arca Burnesi*, Nœtl., var. *media*, *Conus scalaris*, Mart., and a fragment of a large *Arca* like *A. yawensis*, Nœtl. The assemblage of fossils and the lithological character of the matrix point to the identity of this horizon with that of *Parallelipipedum prototortuosum*, Nœtl., at Kama.[1] The dip of the strata passed over between Banbyin and Peikadin, the locality of the *Arca*, varied from 10° to over 45°, so that the thickness of clays between the two zones works out at not less than 1700 feet, in place of the 500 feet referred to by Dr. Nœtling as probably under the mark.[2]

### (*b*) Thayetmyo and Minbu Districts.
### (Map, fig. 2, p. 610.)

Proceeding south-westwards from Minhla for some 11 miles, one descends continuously in the Miocene Series, the dips varying from 7° to 30°, and from north to north-east. In the Tangaing choung, near Tangaing village (long. 94° 58′ E., lat. 19° 56′ N.), a coarse, grey, shelly sandstone was met with, dipping 30° to N. 45° E., and containing poorly-preserved fossils, including a fragment of *Ostrea* and *Arca Burnesi*, this species being found previously only in the zone of *Parallelipipedum prototortuosum* at Kama. In the Yezan choung, which flows from Toungu to join the Tangaing choung about 1 mile above (that is, north of) the village of that name, the north-easterly dip becomes accentuated, changing westwards to inversion and beyond to vertical and high easterly dips (60°+). In this stream, about 1 mile north of Toungu, near the inversion just mentioned, a bluish shelly and sandy marl, with bands of greenish calcareous sandstone, yielded the following fossils :—

| | |
|---|---|
| *Ceratotrochus Alcockianus*, Nœtl. | *Jouannetia protocumingi*, sp. nov. |
| *Paracyathus cœruleus*, Dunc. | *Discohelix minuta*, Nœtl. |
| *Eupsammia regalis*, Alcock. | *Solarium* sp. |
| *Actinacis Nœtlingi*, sp. nov. | *Sigaretus javanus*, Mart. |
| *Pecten irravadicus*, Nœtl. | *Cyprœa Everwijni* (?) Mart. |

Also numerous poorly-preserved specimens of a *Trochosmilia* (?), casts and poorly-preserved specimens of *Dione protophilippinarum* (?) Nœtl., *Tellina Hilli* (?) Nœtl., *Solarium maximum* (?) Phil., *Torinia Buddha* (?) Nœtl., and *Turritella*, *Oliva*, *Fusus* (?), *Natica*, *Voluta* (?), *Conus*, etc., the corals being particularly abundant. This assemblage appears to combine the faunas of the zones of *Paracyathus cœruleus* at Yenangyat, and *Cancellaria Martiniana* at Minbu,[3] while containing several forms new to Burma.

East of Toungu (8 miles south-west of Minhla) the dips remain high to the east, but south of it change to high angles west-south

---

[1] F. Nœtling, Palæontologia Indica (Mem. Geol. Surv. India) vol. i, no. 3 (1901) pp. 23, 24.
[2] *Ibid.* p. 22.     [3] *Ibid.* pp. 27-28, 35-36.

[ 610 ]

Fig. 2.—*Sketch-map illustrating Expedition B.*

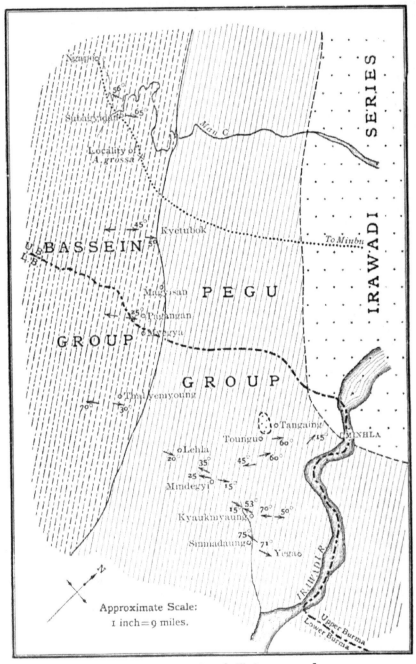

[*For* 'Thalyemyoung' *read* 'Thabyemyoung.]

westwards and south-westwards on the road leading to Kyaukmyaung village (long. 95° E., lat. 19° 50′ N.). Near the latter is the axis of an unsymmetrical syncline with dips of 15° eastwards and 53° westwards; the latter increases eastwards to 80° in about 100 yards, and half a mile down stream to vertical with slight inversion, these features being well seen in section in the Padi choung. The watershed of the Laungtahletaung range of hills, between Kyaukmyaung and Yega (long. 95° 5′ E., lat. 19° 51′ N.), coincides with the axis of an anticline succeeding the syncline just described, also seen in section in the Padi choung near Sinmadaung village, where the dip eastwards is 71° at the bottom of the section, and the crest is approximately horizontal, with a sharp turn-over to 75° on the west. East of this anticline the beds plunge under the Irawadi. No fossils were collected from these localities, where a uniform series of blue marls and grey sandstones were seen; but, on recrossing the Kyaukmyaung syncline, the Miocenes are found continuously exposed, dipping at angles of 25° and upwards to N. 20° E. South-west of, and close to, the village of Mindegyi (long. 94° 58′ E., lat. 19° 48′ N.), in a grey sandstone dipping 15° to N. 30° E., were obtained specimens of *Sigaretus* sp. and *Terebra* sp., Nœtl.(?), the latter being previously found only in the zone of *Paracyathus cœruleus* at Yenangyat.

West of the village, the dips change again to westerly at an angle of about 25°; and near the axis of this anticline, some 2 miles south of Mindegyi, the following species were found in the blue shales:—*Cantharus Martinianus*, Nœtl. sp. ( = *Cancellaria Martiniana*), and *Nucula Alcocki*, Nœtl., indicating an horizon equivalent to the zone of *Cancellaria Martiniana* at Minbu.

About a mile and a half west of Mindegyi, a grey calcareous conglomerate yielded poorly-preserved specimens of *Ceratotrochus Alcockianus (?)* Nœtl., *Turritella* sp. 2, and *Conus avaensis (?)* Nœtl.

Proceeding westwards for some 4 miles, the village of Lehla is reached: it lies in a syncline, dips being recorded a mile and a half east of the village of 34½° due west, and west of it, 19° and upwards to north-east. Finally, on the Minhla-Thayetmyo road at mile-post 54 from Thayetmyo, some 3 miles west of Lehla, a fine conglomerate containing shells, including a small *Pecten* and *Cassis (?)*, was found, this horizon being apparently below any known fossiliferous zone in the 'Promeian': for, as will be seen from the following observations, the Eocene boundary is at no great distance, and there is apparently little or no unconformity here between the older and the newer Tertiaries.

West of the last-named point, the exposures seen gave dips of 20° to 25° north-eastwards, and near Thabyemyoung (long. 94° 48′ E., lat. 19° 47′ N.) specimens were collected of *Ostrea yomaensis*, sp. nov. The surrounding shales include lenticular sandstones and, locally, veins of mineral resin and coal. The easterly dips continue for some 3 miles west of Thabyemyoung; and then, after an increase in angle through 35° and 50° to 69°, the beds turn over to south-west at angles of 69° and more, the crest of this anticline being marked by hot springs and mud-volcanos.

From near the crest in this locality an impure ferruginous limestone was obtained, full of shells of *Turritella* sp. 3.

Dips of 20° to 30° in a north-easterly direction were found north-north-west of Thabyemyoung; and 2 miles west-south-west of Myegya (long. 94° 45′ E., lat.19° 53′ N.), south of the Upper Burma boundary, a calcareous sandstone was found with *Venus granosa*, J. de C. Sow., and *Tellina (?)*.

Across the boundary, in the Minbu district, the same north-eastward dipping beds yielded the following species of fossils near the village of Magyisan (long. 94° 42′ E., lat. 19° 57′ N.) :—

(*a*) 1 mile south-east of Magyisan, light-blue clay with :

*Operculina Hardiei (?)* D'A. & H.  
*Paracyathus* sp.  
*Corbula harpa*, D'A. & H.

*Dolium* sp.  
*Pleurotoma Stoppanii (?)* Desh.

(*b*) 1 mile south of Magyisan :

*Ampullina grossa*, var. *oblonga*, Desh.

(*c*) Yengadin choung, 2 miles south by east from Magyisan :

*Nummulites* sp.  
*Arca manensis*, sp. nov.  
*Ampullina spherica (?)* Desh.  
*Natica* sp., cf. *N. obscura*, J. de C. Sow.

*Cerithium* sp. (cf. *Vicarya Verneuili*, D'Arch.).  
*Conus* sp.  
And fragments of a very large *Cerithium*.

Some 4½ miles north-west of Magyisan, near the village of Kyetubok, in the choung of that name, a bed of very shelly impure nummulitic limestone was found, dipping 60° to N. 60° E.—the rocks above this limestone for some distance having the same strike and dip, but containing no nummulites. There is no doubt that this limestone, here about 25 feet thick, is identical with that described by Theobald as marking the top of the Eocene in Lower Burma. The fossils determined from this bed were :—

*Nummulites Beaumonti (?)* D'A. & H.  
*Glycimeris* sp.  
*Thracia* sp.

*Cardium ambiguum*, J. de C. Sow.  
*Ficula Theobaldi*, Nœtl.  
*Oliva* sp.

Descending in the series westwards, I met with two fossiliferous horizons: one being a thin white limestone, made up of small globular bodies of Hydrozoan affinities and of various foraminifera, including *Operculina canalifera*, D'Arch., half a mile north-west of Kyetubok; and the other, at a lower point in the series in the Kyetubok choung, yielded a worn specimen of *Ampullina ponderosa*, Desh. After striking the Minbu-Ngape road north-west of the last-named localities, blocks of arenaceous limestone were found full of *Ampullina grossa*, Desh., var. *oblonga*. These come apparently from an horizon near that already cited as yielding this species south of Magyisan.

Still farther north-westwards, in the Man choung near Subagyidan (long. 94° 35′ E., lat. 20° 4′ N.), the north-easterly dips (20° to 35°) increase to 65° and 90°, and then turn over to W. 30° S. at 56°. On the crest of this anticline (evidently the same fold as that described south-west of Thabyemyoung) occurs a ferruginous clay, with beds of grey calcareous sandstone, yielding :—

| | |
|---|---|
| *Operculina canalifera*, D'Arch. | *Voluta pernodosa*, sp. nov. |
| *Ampullina grossa*, Desh., var. *spherica*. | *Fusus* sp. |
| | *Turritella* sp. 3 (?). |

East of the Man choung, and therefore at a higher horizon, near the same locality, were collected: *Voluta D'Archiaci*, sp. nov., *Cassidaria* sp., with poorly-preserved specimens of *Turritella (?)* and *Voluta (?)* and fragments of a large *Cerithium*, like that found near Magyisan. Finally, at a horizon some 50 feet higher, occur *Alectryonia Newtoni*, sp. nov., and *Cardium ambiguum*, J. de C. Sow., with fragments of *Ostrea*.

A pebble of grey calcareous sandstone was also picked up in the Man choung, at a point some 2 miles north of Subagyidan, containing *Operculina canalifera*, D'Arch., presumably from the horizon already noticed on the axis near the village referred to.

### (c) Magwe and Myingyan Districts.

No fossils were collected from the localities visited in these two districts, but sundry points of stratigraphical importance were observed in the Yenangyoung anticline and northwards. The Miocene rocks cropping out in the Khodoung oil-field extend as far south as the Sadaing Myouk choung, the mouth of which is some 4 miles south of the town of Yenangyoung; and at this point, where the Pliocene commences to occupy the crest of the fold, a section was seen showing clearly the amount of unconformity that exists here between the Miocene and the Pliocene. It does not appear that much, if any, denudation of the earlier beds took place, except along the very crest of the anticlinal fold. An inlier of Miocene was also observed near the village of Tatkan (long. 90° 54′ E., lat. 20° 37½′ N.), where again a slight unconformity was observed, insignificant bands of ferruginous conglomerate immediately above the base of the Pliocene apparently marking the place of the thicker bed seen round the Yenangyoung inlier, already described by Dr. Nœtling.

### (d) Minbu and Pakokku Districts.
### (Partly illustrated by the map, fig. 3, p. 614.)

A journey in a semicircle towards the Arakan Yoma and back to the Irawadi at Yenangyat yielded some interesting data. Leaving the bank of the Irawadi opposite Salé, the road follows the course of the Myenu choung, which here flows over Pliocene beds. These

at first dip very gently away from the river at about 4°, then a
synclinal trough is crossed, with a corresponding gentle dip on the
west side, which continues until Kanzanma, on the Seikpyu-Sawmyo
road, is passed, when the dip increases to 11°; and shortly afterwards the Pliocene gives place to Miocene, though, as one ascends
into the hills, patches of Pliocene are continually met with, lying
across the upturned edges of the Miocene. The rocks of the latter

Fig. 3.—*Sketch-map illustrating Expedition D.*

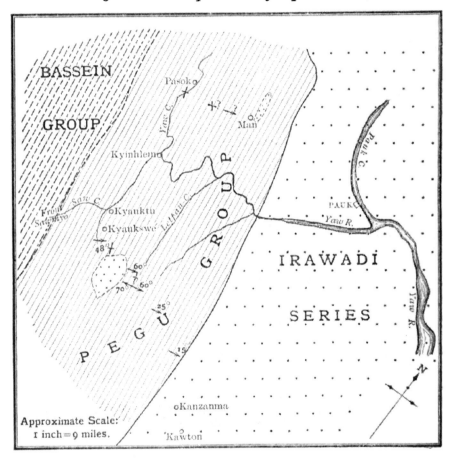

consist chiefly of shales in the upper portion; but subordinate sandstones occur, and, after the first 3000 feet or so, the sandstones and
shales alternate. At about the 25th mile from Sawmyo, the dips
increase from a comparatively low angle (10° to 25°) to 59°, 60°,
and even vertical, the whole series being very much disturbed and
crushed, so that it is not easy to determine the thickness of beds
passed over. At the head of the Letpan choung, between the 23rd

and 24th mile-posts, the crushing of beds containing much carbonaceous matter (and frequently coal) appears to have given rise to
natural-gas springs and other indications of volatile bituminous
matter, although this may be derived from bituminous beds like
those found in the Miocene of other parts of Burma. The Letpan
choung marks the axis of an unimportant anticline, the flanks of
which dip steeply away one from the other, the beds in many
places being vertical. Along the stream northwards, away from
the road, the dips are less steep; and, from near the crest, the
following fossils were obtained from the shales and from a bed of
sandstone interstratified with them :—

| | |
|---|---|
| *Paracyathus cœruleus*, Dunc. | *Natica (Globularia) gibberosa*, Grat. |
| *Arca* sp. | *Cypræa elegans*, Defr. |
| *Cardita protovariegata*, Nœtl. | *Busycon canaliculatum* (Linn.). |
| *Tellina* sp. | *Conus avaensis*, Nœtl. |

Also a species (apparently) of *Glycimeris*, akin to that found in
the Eocene (p. 612); and a *Cassis* poorly preserved, but similar in
size and shape to a form assigned by Dr. K. Martin to *C. cornuta*,
Linn., and found in the Miocene of Java. Only three of these
species have hitherto been described from Burma, and of these two
occur in the zone [1] of *Meiocardia metavulgaris*, Nœtl., at Singu, so
that the horizon may be equivalent.

From an unknown locality, some 3 or 4 miles down stream from
the foregoing, were brought specimens of *Batissa kodoungensis*,
Nœtl., which supply fuller knowledge of the species, only known
to Dr. Nœtling by fragments from Yenangyoung. The choung
here flows along the strike of the beds.

Passing from these localities by Kyaukswé (long. 94° 15′ E., lat.
21° 10′ N.) and Kyinhlein (94° 15′ E., 21° 15′ N.), the latter at
the junction of the Saw and Yaw rivers, to Pasok (94° 14′ E.,
21° 20′ N.), further evidence was obtained of great disturbance in
the Miocene strata of this region; this was especially noticed on
the right bank of the Yaw below Pasok, while near Kyinhlein
plant-remains were found in the shales and sandstones of the same
series.

Crossing the Yaw, the Miocene deposits, apparently now horizontal, were traversed to the village of Man (long. 94° 19′ E.,
lat. 21° 20′ N.); beyond this Pliocene was again met with, followed
in a range of low hills by Miocene, the latter having yielded near
Man village *Paracyathus cœruleus*, Dunc., *Cerithium (?)* sp., with
two species of *Conus* and a lamellibranch probably belonging to the
Veneridæ.

A rapid traverse across the Pliocene valley of the Yaw brings
us to the Yenangyat anticline already described by Grimes and
others. On this fold, at a point near the crest some 10 miles north
of Yenangyat, was obtained *Melongena pseudobucephala* (Nœtl.);

---

[1] F. Nœtling, Palæontologia Indica (Mem. Geol. Surv. India) vol. i, no. 3
(1901) p. 32.

and a mile and a half north of Lanywa, which is 9 miles south of Yenangyat, *Cassidea acanthina*, sp. nov., also *Natica obscura*, Sow., possibly from the zone of *Paracyathus cœruleus*. A mile farther south, *Turritella* sp. 1 and a large *Natica* occur in coarse shelly sandstone at a slightly-higher horizon.

### (e) Pakokku and Lower Chindwin Districts.

In the northern districts, as has already been noted, the Miocene deposits appear to be, for the most part, unfossiliferous, so that the observations made under this head are mainly of a stratigraphical nature. The country north of Pakokku, for about 25 miles, consists of approximately-level ground with but few elevations, the whole rising gently from the river northwards. These plains consist of the characteristic soft yellow or white Pliocene sands, with patches of red alluvial gravel; pieces of fossil wood are also of frequent occurrence. North of Myaing, some 25 miles from Pakokku, a range of hills covered with a low scrub rises from the plain with a north-north-westerly strike; the Pliocene sands dip at high angles away from the hills on the west, and are underlain by a coarse conglomerate forming the western slope of the range, the dip of this being about 30°. The pebbles are of large size, ranging up to 6 inches or more in length, and the whole aspect of the rock is unlike those above it, the matrix being darker in colour, and possessing in every way rather a Miocene than a Pliocene aspect. Leaving this range on the west side, the high dips are found to prevail in the Pliocene for half a mile across the strike, after which no exposure was seen until 2 miles away from the range when the dip had decreased to 15°, and at about 1 mile west of Taungzon village (long. 94° 43′ E., lat. 21° 40′ N.) rocks of the same series were found dipping 10° north-eastwards; while a mile and a half west of Taungzon, Miocene shales were found to succeed the Pliocene (though the boundary was not seen) with relatively low easterly dips, becoming violently contorted to the west for a short distance near the crest of an anticline of the Miocene, which has low dips again westwards. The Miocene sandstones of this locality are, like those of Yenangyat, inclined to be conglomeratic, although the pebbles are not so large as those seen near Myaing.

Returning to the Myaing range, the same high dips are met with some 4 miles north of Myaing, and the eastern dips (for the range is anticlinal in structure) are even steeper, the characteristic Pliocene being noticed, apparently horizontal, at a mile east of the range; while some 8 miles north of Myaing the same fold had dips of 43° on the west and 55° on the east side. At the last-named point, the limit of the 'dry zone' of Burma is reached, this approximately coinciding with the boundary between the Pakokku and Lower Chindwin districts; and here, as elsewhere in the jungle-regions of Burma, it is possible to distinguish at once by the vegetation whether one is on Pliocene or on Miocene rocks. Teak and bamboo are the rule on the latter, eng-daing forest with stunted bamboos on the former.   From the boundary of the Chindwin division northwards as far as Kabaing (long. 94° 43′ E., lat. 22° 13′ N.) Pliocene continues ; no dips were observed, except a possible 5° westwards half a mile south-west of Kabaing ; but, since in a range of hills running northwards from near Nyaungbinle (94° 42′ E., 22° 20′ N.) Miocene rocks crop out with anticlinal structure, the fold probably extends southwards in a less marked degree in the overlying Pliocene.   From Nyaungbinle, the Mahu Daung, as this range is called, extends towards Mingin on the Chindwin River, and shows a series of blue shales and grey conglomeratic sandstones under the Pliocene—bent into an unsymmetrical arch, the eastern flank of which dips at about 70° to 90° and the western at 15° to 50°.   The pebbles in the sandstones are fairly large and irregularly distributed in the grey sandstone-matrix, this character persisting up to the lower limit of the Pliocene.   Some thin beds of purple marls occur in the Miocene of this district near the top.

### III. GENERAL AND STRATIGRAPHICAL.

In the foregoing pages a series of observations have been recorded relating to the Tertiary of Burma, of which those regarding the Eocene rocks are confined to one district, whereas the Miocene has been studied at several points in the Irawadi Valley.

In the hitherto unstudied Bassein Stage, several fossiliferous horizons have been noted, and it seems possible to correlate the various sections and to determine certain palæontological zones in a tentative way.   The lowest horizons are those yielding *Turritella* sp. 3 near the anticlinal crest south-west of Thabyem-young, and various fossils (including *Operculina canalifera*) with a cast of *Turritella*, possibly the same species, on the crest in the Man-choung near Subagyidan.   From general considerations, these two may be assumed to be the same and termed 'the *Turritella*-Zone.' We have also another fossil occurring in considerable quantity, in a bed found at two points about 10 miles distant along the strike, namely *Ampullina grossa*, var. *oblonga*, and in both cases about 6000 feet above the assumed *Turritella*-Zone.   This, therefore, appears to be a sufficiently well-defined horizon to be termed 'the Zone of *Ampullina grossa*.'   In addition to these, what are perhaps better-marked zones exist, but they are at present observed only at one locality in each case : namely, the nummulitic limestone at the top of the Bassein Group, with *Nummulites Beaumonti* (?) in large numbers, and the thin band of white limestone largely made up of small globular hydrozoa, probably not less than 100 feet below the former.

At an horizon approximately corresponding to the last, and probably below rather than above it, in blue clays, *Corbula harpa* occurs in considerable numbers, so that this may be termed the zone of that fossil.   Hence, we have the following general section

of the Bassein Group in the west of the Minbu and Thayetmyo
districts, in ascending order :—

(1) *Turritella*-Zone. A ferruginous calcareous sandstone or impure limestone, thickness unknown, with numerous fossils, often full of shells
of *Turritella* (see p. 612).

(2) A thick series of shales and sandstones (with petroleum in some of the
sandstones, and carbonaceous material), with fossils at Subagyidan
up to about 50 feet above the top of (1) (see p. 613), *Venus granosa*
2 miles west of Myegya, about 4000 feet above (1) (p. 612). *Ostrea
yomaensis* at an horizon above this (p. 611), and sandstone with
*Ampullina spherica*, etc., close to the top (p. 612) ......... 6000 feet.

(3) Zone of *Ampullina grossa*. A grey impure limestone or highly-
calcareous sandstone with large shells of this species (p. 612).........
                                   Thickness unknown, but variable.

(4) Shales and sandstones, the latter often bituminous. *Ampullina
ponderosa* occurs near the top of these (p. 612) ........... 2000 feet.

(5) Zone of *Corbula harpa*, in blue clays found near Magyisan (p. 612).
                                   Thickness (?).

(6) Zone of Hydrozoa (p. 612) ........................................ 6 inches.

(7) Shales and sandstones ............................................. 100 feet(?).

(8) Zone of *Nummulites Beaumonti* (?), red, impure, very shelly limestone
(p. 612) ....................................................... 25 feet.

Giving a total thickness of 8125 feet or more.

The thicknesses tabulated above are all the least possible, so that
we must either assume that the 1200 feet estimated by Theobald
increases very greatly northwards, or that the upper 7000 feet or so
of the so-called ' Chin Shales ' of Dr. Nœtling are here fossiliferous,
and must be included in the Bassein Division of the Eocene, which
seems the more probable solution, since this group has never been
properly studied.   This leaves 3000 feet, according to Dr. Nœtling,
for the Chin Division, the age of which is not known ; but part of
it probably belongs to Theobald's ' Axial Series,' of the subdivision
of which something has already been said.   It is suggested, therefore, that, to accord with our later knowledge, the name of the
Chin Division be dropped, leaving only the Bassein and Pegu
Divisions for the Arakan Series, the former with a much increased
thickness ; and constituting as the Axial Series all those rocks
below the (as yet) unseen base of the Bassein Stage.

Passing now to the new data regarding the Pegu Stage, there
is no need to review in detail the stratigraphical relations of the
various fossils found in the upper portion ; but the relations of
the fossiliferous horizons of the lower beds may be conveniently
considered here.   In the Thayetmyo district the following horizons
were observed below the zone of *Cytherea erycina* (see p. 608) :—

(1) 150 feet below, sandstones and shales with *Lucina globulosa*, Desh.
and *Balanus tintinnabulum*, Linn.

(2) 250 feet below, sandstone with *Turritella acuticarinata*, Dunk., and
*Voluta* (?) *birmanica*, sp. nov.

As *Lucina globulosa* has not hitherto been found in Burma, it is
perhaps permissible to name the second bed the zone of that fossil ;
while the lowest fossiliferous horizon of this locality seems, from the

number of specimens of *Turritella acuticarinata* found therein, to
be fitly called the zone of that fossil.   An objection to this nomenclature is found, in that Dr. Nœtling's hypothetical zone of *T. acuticarinata* is at the top of the Pegu Stage in Lower Burma.  Since,
however, the fossil *Turritella* reported as occurring in the upper
portions of the series may equally well, according to Dr. Nœtling,[1]
be *T. simplex*, and since *T. acuticarinata* is more nearly allied to the
Eocene species, *T. fasciata*, Lamk., it seems possible that the higher
zone should be that of *T. simplex*; while this, 250 feet below the
horizon of *Cytherea erycina*, should be the zone of *T. acuticarinata*.[2]

The small *Pecten* and other fossils, mentioned on p. 611, indicate
a yet lower fossiliferous horizon near the bottom of the Miocene;
but the exact position of this is not known.

The division has been studied at several new localities, which
have yielded interesting data.  Thus, it is of interest to find what
appears to be the zone of *Paracyathus cœruleus* near Toungu (south-
west of Minhla), and at a similar horizon south-west of this, the
characteristic fossil of the zone of *Cancellaria Martiniana*, the first-
named occurring at Yenangyat, the second at Minbu, while here
the two horizons approximately correspond : one locality yielding
fossils found previously in either, but not both, of the zones.   It
is convenient to note here that it would seem that the form described
by Dr. Nœtling as *Cancellaria Martiniana* must be referred to
the genus *Cantharus*, and consequently the zone now becomes
that of *Cantharus Martinianus*.   It is noticeable that near Toungu,
where beds at approximately the horizon of the zone of *Parallelipipedum prototortuosum* are dipping eastwards at high angles,
Pliocene sands form the upper portion of the neighbouring hills, thus
indicating a considerable unconformity in this part of the country
between the two series.   The occurrence here of a fossil peculiar
to the zone of *P. prototortuosum*, previously only found at Kama to
the southward, is of interest.

A second new section of the Miocene now described is that
visited in the Yaw Basin, towards Sawmyo, where the occurrence
of an horizon corresponding to the zone of *Meiocardia metavulgaris*,
previously known at Singu, and of *Batissa kodoungensis* some miles
north of it along the strike, hitherto known only from one horizon
south of Yenangyoung, has already been mentioned (p. 615).

Finally, the conglomeratic nature of the Miocene rocks of the
Lower Chindwin and other northern localities, with their inclusion
of plant-remains, presents a feature pointing to the derivation
of their material from no great distance to the northward, and
indicates the existence of a Miocene estuary in this
district corresponding to that of the Irawadi of to-
day, although far to the north of it.

These investigations may also throw some light on the two

[1] Palæont. Indica (Mem. Geol. Surv. India) n. s. vol. i, no. 3 (1901) p. 26.
[2] [Data with which I have recently become acquainted seem to indicate that
*T. acuticarinata* occurs in abundance at more than one horizon in the series.]

questions of the subdivision and the thickness of the Pegu Group, which have by no means been thoroughly threshed out. The subdivision proposed by Dr. Nœtling, into Yenangyoungian and Promeian, was based upon the appearance of certain beds in a deep ravine in the centre of the Yenangyoung dome, and upon the assumption, from inadequate study of the lower beds of the group in Lower Burma, that they were unfossiliferous. As to the first of these, a purely lithological distinction, it is observed: (1) that the beds near the crest of the anticline at Yenangyoung, and in particular the clays, are noticeably blue in deep ravines at any point in this inlier; (2) that where continuous sections are exposed, as in the Yaw-Valley region, in jungle-country (as distinguished from the dry zone, with its facilities for weathering and oxidation), the whole series is equally blue in colour, and the olive tints described as characterising the Yenangyoungian are absent. Moreover, when Dr. Nœtling saw such a section of the Miocene in the Chindwin district, where the country is covered by forest, he noticed the absence of the olive tints, and attributed it to the absence of the Yenangyoungian: whereas, after passing from the known Yenangyoungian localities in the south of the Pakokku district, in the dry zone, to those of the Chindwin, through intermediate country less thickly covered with jungle, one is conscious only of a gradual change from olive in the more exposed regions to blue in the forest-covered districts on the north in corresponding beds; while the Upper Miocene of the Thayetmyo region shows the blue colour also, though to a less extent, as much in the topmost beds of the Miocene as in those immediately above the Eocene boundary. As to the second, fossiliferous horizons, as we have seen, do occur in Theobald's 'Sitsyahn Shales,' where these are exposed in the Thayetmyo district, and while no fossils have been found in wells drilled by the Burmah Oil Company in this series in the north, it needs but a very little knowledge of the system of drilling adopted in these oil-fields to enable us to realize how fortuitous it is that fossils, except perhaps from beds full of them, will be brought to the surface in anything like recognizable condition.

We see, therefore, that, in the first place, the olive tints of the Upper Miocene Beds in the exposed regions of the 'dry zone' appear to be due to weathering, as they are absent in the least exposed portions of these beds there, and absent also in the forest-clad regions elsewhere; in the second place, the lower parts of the Miocene in Lower Burma have been shown to contain fossils, and there is no legitimate ground for the assumption that the unexposed parts in Upper Burma are completely unfossiliferous. This throws us back, therefore, on the Pegu Stage as the only valid division; and from our present knowledge of the series there seems to be no ground for any further subdivision, since the character of the rocks is the same throughout. Some subdivision is perhaps desirable and possible; but it seems to be better to have none, rather than that based on an erroneous interpretation of the evidence. The series requires much fuller and more detailed study than has yet been given to it, before any sounder basis can be suggested.

As to the thickness of the rocks included in the Pegu Stage, we have data here to supplement the calculations published by Dr. Nœtling in 1901.[1] First, there is the traverse of the shales or clays intervening between the zones of *Cytherea erycina* and *Parallelipipedum prototortuosum*, where these are exposed west of Thayetmyo, which gives evidence of a thickness of not less than 1700 feet, bringing up the thickness of the beds between the zone of *Cytherea erycina* and the top of the Pegu Group to 3200 feet, assuming the thickness of the beds between the 'Kama Clay' and the top of the Miocene as 1000 feet. Secondly, there is the traverse of the lower portion of the Pegu Group in the north-west of the Thayetmyo district, where, assuming the fossils found near the crest of the Mindegyi anticline to represent an horizon approximately equivalent to the zone of *Cytherea erycina* (and the zone of *Cantharus Martinianus* must be considered as such), we obtain a thickness of not less than 4500 feet for the beds between the nummulitic limestone at the top of the Eocene and the zone of *Cytherea erycina*, or a total thickness for the Pegu Stage of about 7500 feet. This is under, rather than above, the actual amount where the series is fully developed, although the varying unconformity of Miocene to Pliocene prevents anything like accurate determination.

The Irawadi Series needs further detailed examination before more than general views can be expressed with regard to it. The similarity of the deposits to those of the Siwalik Beds of India leaves little doubt that they are at least approximately contemporaneous with them, and therefore, according to the view adopted by the majority of authors, of Pliocene age. This opinion, it may be said, entirely accords with the great contrast observed between the characters of the sediments of the Arakan and the Irawadi Series, with the unconformity of one to the other, and with the homogeneity of the thick mass of incompact sands that constitute the highest-seen Tertiary beds of Burma.

We arrive, then, at the following revised arrangement of the rocks of the west of Burma, which is, as far as possible, in accordance with the latest knowledge :—

| | | | *Thickness in feet.* | *Age.* |
|---|---|---|---|---|
| IRAWADI SERIES | | | 20,000 (?) | Pliocene (?) |
| ARAKAN SERIES | Pegu Group | | 7,500 | Miocene. |
| | Bassein Group | | 8,000 | Eocene. |
| AXIAL SERIES | Upper. | *Cardita*-Beds | (?) | Cretaceous. |
| | | *Halobia*-Limestones | (?) | Triassic. |
| | | Shales, schists, and grits. | (?) | (?) |
| | Lower. | Flaggy shales and schists. | (?) | (?) |

---

[1] Palæontologia Indica (Mem. Geol. Surv. India) n. s. vol. i, no. 3, p. 26.

## IV. PALÆONTOLOGY.[1]

### Description of the Miocene Fossils.

### CŒLENTERATA—Anthozoa.

#### CERATOTROCHUS ALCOCKIANUS, Nœtling.

1901. *Ceratotrochus Alcockianus*, Nœtling, Pal. Ind. n. s. vol. i, no. 3, p. 101 &
pl. i, fig. 1.

Localities.—Thayetmyo district: a mile and a half west of
Mindegyi ; 1 mile north of Toungu ; three-quarters of a mile south
of Banbyin.

#### PARACYATHUS CÆRULEUS, Duncan.

1886–89. *Paracyathus cæruleus*, Duncan, Journ. Linn. Soc. (Zool.) vol. xxi, p. 5
& pl. i, figs. 10–11.
1895. *Paracyathus cæruleus*, Nœtling, Mem. Geol. Surv. Ind. vol. xxvii, pt. i, p. 6
& pl. i, figs. 1–2.
1901. *Paracyathus cæruleus*, Nœtling, Pal. Ind. n. s. vol. i, no. 3, p. 102 & pl. i,
figs. 5–6.

Localities.—1 mile north of Toungu (Thayetmyo district) ;
Letpan choung, 10 miles east of Sawmyo (Pakokku district) ; near
Man village, 16 miles west of Pauk (Pakokku district).

#### EUPSAMMIA REGALIS, Alcock.

1893. *Eupsammia regalis*, Alcock, Journ. Asiat. Soc. Beng. vol. lxii, pt. ii, p. 144
& pl. v, figs. 8–8 a.
1895. *Eupsammia regalis*, Nœtling, Mem. Geol. Surv. Ind. vol. xxvii, pt. i, p. 6 &
pl. i, figs. 3–3 a.
1901. *Eupsammia regalis*, Nœtling, Pal. Ind. n. s. vol. i, no. 3, p. 103 & pl. i,
figs. 7–7 a.

Locality.—1 mile north of Toungu (Thayetmyo district).

#### ACTINACIS NŒTLINGI, sp. nov.   (Pl. LIV, fig. 1.)

Description. — Corallum branching ; diameter of branches
ranging from 4 to 25 millimetres. Cœnenchyma abundant, granu-
lated. Corallites small, projecting from the surface of the cœnenchyma. Diameter of calices = 3·5 mm. Septa of nearly uniform
proportions, well developed, compact, and somewhat crowded in
three cycles. Pali in front of all the septa round the columella.

Remarks.—Of the European Tertiary species, *A. Rollei*, Reuss,[2]
from the Oligocene of Styria and Italy, appears to offer the greatest
resemblance in calicular characters and structure of the cœnenchyma,
but this is a massive form ; in the dendroid species, *A. conferta*,
Reuss,[3] and *A. delicata*, Reuss,[4] from the Oligocene of the Southern
Alps, the calices differ considerably, having fewer septa, not
crowded, while in *A. conferta* the granules of the cœnenchyma are
very regularly arranged, radiating from the corallites.

Locality.—1 mile north of Toungu (Thayetmyo district).

[1] I wish here to acknowledge my indebtedness to Mr. R. Bullen Newton,
F.G.S., of the British Museum (Natural History), for the great amount of
assistance and advice received from that gentleman in the final reconstruction
and arrangement of this section for publication.
[2] Denkschr. k Akad. Wissensch. Wien, vol. xxiii (1864) p. 27 & pl. viii, fig. 6.
[3] *Ibid.* vol. xxviii (1868) p. 161 & pl. xii, fig. 5.
[4] *Ibid.* vol. xxix (1869) p. 249 & pl. xxv, fig. 5.

## MOLLUSCA—Lamellibranchiata.

### Family NUCULIDÆ.

NUCULA ALCOCKI, Nœtling.

1895. *Nucula Alcocki*, Nœtling, Mem. Geol. Surv. Ind. vol. xxvii, pt. i, p. 8 &
　　pl. i, figs. 5–7.
1901. *Nucula Alcocki*, Nœtling, Pal. Ind. n. s. vol. i, no. 3, p. 156 & pl. viii,
　　figs. 3–5.

Description.—Shell trigonal, inequilateral, transversely elongate, somewhat depressed. Umbo pointed, low, posterior. Margin crenulate.

The surface exhibits numerous fine radiating striæ, each of which corresponds to marginal crenulations, crossed by a few irregularly-placed growth-lines. Escutcheon large, concave, marked off by a rounded keel. Lunule long, narrow, well defined.

Remarks.—The specimen under observation agrees with Dr. Nœtling's description, except that he interprets the radial striæ on the surface as a secondary ornamentation, a view not borne out by the present example. The specimens figured by him appear to be casts only, and the supposed ornamentation of the escutcheon and lunule is probably the result of weathering of the area above the denticles, as in the case of our specimen. *Nucula placentina*, Lamarck,[1] from the Miocene and Pliocene of Europe, and *N. similis*, J. Sowerby,[2] from the London Clay, appear to be relatives of this form.

Locality.—2 miles south of Mindegyi (Thayetmyo district).

### Family ARCIDÆ.

ARCA BURNESI, D'Archiac & Haime.

1853. *Arca Burnesi*, D'Archiac & Haime, 'Description des Animaux Fossiles du
　　Groupe Nummulitique de l'Inde' p. 264 & pl. xxii, figs. 5 *a*–5 *d*.
1901. *Arca (Anomalocardia) Burnesi*, Nœtling, Pal. Ind. n. s. vol. i, no. 3, p. 131
　　& pl. v, figs. 6–9.

Localities.—Thayetmyo district: 2 miles east of Toungu; a mile and a half east-north-east of Ngalaingyoung.

ARCA METABISTRIGATA, Nœtling.

1901. *Arca metabistrigata*, Nœtling, Pal. Ind. n. s. vol. i, no. 3, p. 139 & pl. vi,
　　fig. 13.

Locality.—Near Prome, on the eastern bank of the Irawadi.

### Family PECTINIDÆ.

PECTEN IRRAVADICUS, Nœtling.

1895. *Pecten* cf. *Favrei*, Nœtling, Mem. Geol. Surv. Ind. vol. xxvii, pt. i, p. 7.
1901. *Pecten irravadicus*, Nœtling, Pal. Ind. n. s. vol. i, no. 3, p. 121 & pl. iv,
　　figs. 7–8.

Locality.—A mile north of Toungu (Thayetmyo district).

[1] F. Sacco, 'Molluschi Terziarii del Piemonte, &c.' pt. xxvi (1898) p. 46 &
pl. x, figs. 35–40.
[2] 'Mineral Conchology' vol. ii (1828) p. 207 & pl. cxcii, figs. 3, 4, & 10.

Family CYRENIDÆ.

BATISSA KODOUNGENSIS, Nœtling.    (Pl. LVI, figs. 1 & 2.)

1901. *Cyrena (Batissa) kodoungensis*, Nœtling, Pal. Ind. n. s. vol. i, no. 3, p. 183 & pl. xi, fig. 1.

Description.—The shell is large and orbicular.  Anterior margin round and short, passing gradually into the curved ventral margin, which is straight posteriorly and is met by the posterior margin at a right angle, the corner of which is rounded.  The posterior margin is straight, and passes over a rounded obtuse angle into the curved cardinal margin.

Beaks thick, incurved, prosogyrous; ligament strong; hinge powerful.  Three cardinals in each valve—the anterior shortest, inclined backwards, the others inclined forwards.  The middle one is the strongest in the left valve, the posterior being very long but thin; in the right, the posterior cardinal is longest and thickest.  Two fairly short anterior laterals in the right valve; posterior laterals at some distance from the cardinals, not perfectly known; corresponding sockets in the left valve.

The shell is very thick, covered with coarse irregular growth-striations.

DIMENSIONS IN MILLIMETRES (TWO SPECIMENS).

| Length. | Height. | Thickness. |
|---|---|---|
| 100 | 96 | 60 (?) |
| 90 | 80 | 50 |

Remarks.—Though from a distant locality and of greater size, these specimens, which are of brackish or freshwater origin, seem to belong to the same species as the fragments from Yenangyoung described by Dr. Nœtling, which were apparently collected from the same spot as those brought to England by J. Crawfurd in 1828, and referred to by Buckland as ' *Cyrena*.'[1]  The shells come from an horizon, according to Dr. Nœtling, high up in the Pegu Group; but, from my own observations, I should say that the bed containing them may perhaps be more properly included in the Irawadi Series.  The present specimens were brought to me by natives, and their horizon is not definitely known (see p. 615).  The size is much greater than that of *Batissa Crawfurdi*, Nœtling, from the Yenangyoung locality, and the species differ in important points.  The living *B. insignis*, Deshayes,[2] from the Philippines, appears to be a near relative, although the size of this is apparently not so great, nor is the shell so robust; but the hinge and the shape of the shell are very similar.  *B. producta*, Deshayes (*loc. cit.*), from the same locality, is more rounded posteriorly, but otherwise much resembles this species.

Locality.—Letpan choung, 10 miles east of Sawmyo (Pakokku district).

[1] Trans. Geol. Soc. ser. 2, vol. ii (1828) pt. iii, p. 386.
[2] Proc. Zool. Soc. 1854, p. 13.

## Family ASTARTIDÆ.

**CARDITA PROTOVARIEGATA, Nœtling. (Pl. LIV, fig. 8.)**

1901. *Cardita (Mytilicardia) protovariegata*, Nœtling, Pal. Ind. n. s. vol. i, no. 3, p. 164 & pl. viii, fig. 14, pl. ix, figs. 1–4.

Remarks.—This species appears to be very closely allied to *C. tjidamarensis*, Martin,[1] also doubtfully known from Burma; but in Dr. Nœtling's figure of the latter, the umbo appears to be more rounded than in the specimens under observation. On the other hand, it seems probable that the supposed weak development of the posterior ribs, referred to by that author as characteristic of *Cardita protovariegata*, is the result of weathering.

Locality.—Letpan choung, 10 miles east of Sawmyo (Pakokku district).

## Family LUCINIDÆ.

**LUCINA GLOBULOSA, Deshayes. (Pl. LV, fig. 1.)**

1830. *Lucina globulosa*, Deshayes, 'Histoire Naturelle des Vers' (Encyclopédie Méthodique) vol. ii, p. 373.
1865. *Lucina globulosa*, M. Hœrnes, 'Foss. Moll. Tert. Beck. Wien' Abhandl. k.-k. geol. Reichsanst. vol. iv, p. 223 & pl. xxxii, fig. 5.
1901. *Lucina globulosa*, Sacco, 'Molluschi Terziarii del Piemonte, &c.' pt. xxix, p. 67 & pl. xv, figs. 31–33, pl. xvi, fig. 1.

Description.—A large, inflated, orbicular right valve, with delicate concentric sculpture and prosogyrous beaks. Hinge not well preserved.

Remarks.—Though the anterior part of the shell is only preserved as a cast, there are indications of a deeply-excavated lunule, as in Sacco's variety *perlunulata*, found in greatest abundance in the Helvetian of Europe. The species is characteristic of the Helvetian and Tortonian stages of the European Miocene, and has been found in France, Italy, the Vienna Basin, Central Egypt, etc. (*Lucina pomum*, Desmoulins, is synonymous, according to Sacco.)

Locality.—Half a mile north-west of Padoukbin (Thayetmyo district).

## Family VENERIDÆ.

**DOSINIA PROTOJUVENILIS, Nœtling.**

1901. *Dosinia protojuvenilis*, Nœtling, Pal. Ind. n. s. vol. i, no. 3, p. 213 & pl. xiv. figs. 1–2.

Locality.—Noathé (Thayetmyo district).

## Family TELLINIDÆ.

**TELLINA sp.**

Description.—A much-crushed, slightly-elongate, oval bivalve, with fine concentric striations and indications of a faint posterior keel, probably belongs to this genus, and appears to be an undescribed species.

[1] 'Die Tertiärschichten auf Java' 1879–80, p. 112 & pl. xviii, fig. 1.

Remarks.—The specimen suggests a resemblance to *T. inflata*, Chemnitz (specimens preserved in the British Museum), living at Port Curtis, which has a faintly-marked posterior keel, fine concentric striations, and very faint, hardly-perceptible radial striæ; these radial striæ may also have been present on the fossil specimen.

Locality.—Letpan choung, 10 miles east of Sawmyo (Pakokku district).

### Family MACTRIDÆ.

MACTRA PROTOREEVESII (?) Nœtling.

1901. *Mactra protoreevesii*, Nœtling, Pal. Ind. n. s. vol. i, no. 3, p. 236 & pl. xvi, figs. 1-2.

Remark.—A cast only, with the chalky shell partly preserved.

Locality.—Noathé (Thayetmyo district).

### Family MYIDÆ.

CORBULA SOCIALIS, Martin.

1879–80. *Corbula socialis*, Martin, ' Tertiärschichten auf Java ' p. 92 & pl. xv, fig. 10.
1901. *Corbula socialis*, Nœtling, Pal. Ind. n. s. vol. i, no. 3, p. 239 & pl. xvi, figs. 3-5.

Locality.—Noathé (Thayetmyo district).

### Family PHOLADIDÆ.

JOUANNETIA PROTOCUMINGI, sp. nov.    (Pl. LIV, fig. 7.)

Description.—Small ovoid shells burrowing in yellowish sandy clay, valves gaping. Shell smooth behind, sculptured in front. Metaplax developed behind the beaks, which are inconspicuous. The sculptured portion of the valve is divided by a groove passing forward from the beak to the antero-ventral angle; on either side are divergent close-set striæ, curving backwards from the apex at the central groove in the direction of the hinge-margin.

Remarks. — This species is exactly similar to *Jouannetia Cumingi*, Sowerby, junr. (as labelled in Brit. Mus. collections), living in the Philippines and Port Jackson, except that it is smaller and has finer sculpture; it may perhaps be identical with *J. semicaudata*, Desmoulins,[1] from the Helvetian and Placentian of Piedmont and other European localities.

Locality.—A mile north of Toungu (Thayetmyo district).

### Gasteropoda.

### Family SOLARIIDÆ.

SOLARIUM sp.

Apparently this does not belong to any of the species described by Nœtling, but it is too poorly preserved for further determination.

Locality.—A mile north of Toungu (Thayetmyo district).

[1] F. Sacco, ' Molluschi Terziarii del Piemonte, &c.' pt. xxix (1901) p. 54.

## Family NATICIDÆ.

### SIGARETUS JAVANUS, Martin.

1879-80. *Sigaretus javanus*, Martin, 'Tertiärschichten auf Java' p. 80 & pl. xiii, fig. 9.

Description.—Shell small, wider than high, composed of four whorls. Spire low, depressed, body-whorl very much larger than the preceding. The ornamentation consists of numerous very fine revolving keels of unequal strength, one or more fine ribs being intercalated between two stronger ones, all crossed by irregularly placed growth-striations, giving the shell a somewhat cancellated appearance. Aperture and operculum not observed.

Remarks.—This species is very similar to, though smaller than, *Sigaretus neritoideus*, Linné.[1]

Locality.—A mile north of Toungu (Thayetmyo district).

### SIGARETUS sp.

A fragmentary specimen, showing fine spiral ribs, appears to be referable to this genus.

Remarks.—In view of the association of this species with *Terebra* sp. (*q. v.*), it seems possible that it is part of *Sigaretus neritoideus*, Linné, already found by Dr. Nœtling at a corresponding horizon (see above).

Locality. — South-west of Mindegyi village (Thayetmyo district).

### NATICA OBSCURA, J. de C. Sowerby.

1840. *Natica obscura*, J. de C. Sowerby, Trans. Geol. Soc. ser. 2, vol. v, pt. ii, p. 328 & pl. xxvi, fig. 2.
1901. *Natica obscura*, Nœtling, Pal. Ind. n. s. vol. i, no. 3, p. 284 & pl. xix, figs. 2-3.

Remarks.—Specimen determined by reference to the original figure, with which it agrees very well, although it does not appear to correspond with that of Dr. Nœtling.

Localities.—A mile and a half north of Lanywa (Pakokku district); a mile north of Toungu (Thayetmyo district).

### NATICA (GLOBULARIA) GIBBEROSA, Grateloup. (Pl. LVII, figs. 2 & 3.)

1828. *Natica gibberosa*, Grateloup, 'Tableau (Prodrome) des Coquilles Fossiles Tertiaires de Dax' no. 135 (Bull. Soc. Linn. Bordeaux, vol. ii, p. 151).
1840. *Natica gibberosa*, Grateloup, 'Conchyliologie Fossile des Terrains Tertiaires du Bassin de l'Adour' pl. ix, figs. 1-2.
1891, 1904. *Globularia gibberosa*, Sacco, 'Molluschi Terziarii del Piemonte, &c.' pt. ix, p. 1 & pl. i, figs. 1-5; pt. xxx, pl. xxiii, fig. 11.

Description.—A single specimen is under observation, and shows a big, fairly-robust shell, not less than 45 millimetres in height, having a large globose body-whorl, covered with more or less regular longitudinal striæ. Spire not complete, but short; umbilicus nearly closed by the callous inner lip.

Remarks.—This species, of which several varieties are known,

---

[1] Nœtling, Pal. Ind. n. s. vol. i, no. 3 (1901) p. 286 & pl. xix, figs. 6-7.

is found abundantly in the Tongrian of Dax, Piedmont, etc., but appears to have left no descendants in the present fauna of the Indian Ocean.

Locality.—Letpan choung, 10 miles east of Sawmyo (Pakokku district).

## Family TURRITELLIDÆ.

### TURRITELLA ACUTICARINATA, Dunker. (Pl. LVII, fig. 9.)

1847. *Turritella acuticarinata*, Dunker, Palæontographica, vol. i, pt. iii, p. 132 & pl. xviii, fig. 10.
1864. *Turritella acuticingulata*, Jenkins, Quart. Journ. Geol. Soc. vol. xx, p. 58 & pl. vii, fig. 1.
1879-80. *Turritella acuticarinata*, Martin, 'Die Tertiärschichten auf Java' p. 69 & pl. xii, figs. 3-4.
1901. *Turritella acuticarinata*, Nœtling, Pal. Ind. n. s. vol. i, no. 3, p. 274 & pl. xviii, figs. 5-7.

Locality. — Yenanine choung, near Banbyin (Thayetmyo district).

### TURRITELLA sp. 1.

A large species with rounded whorls, which were apparently smooth ; the specimen does not allow of accurate determination.

Locality.—Half a mile north of Lanywa (Pakokku district).

### TURRITELLA sp. 2.

A smaller species than the last, with angular whorls.

Locality.—A mile and a half west of Mindegyi (Thayetmyo district).

## Family CERITHIIDÆ.

### CERITHIUM sp. (?).

An imperfectly-preserved shell appears to belong to this genus and has prominent tuberculate ribs, but no further determination is possible.

Locality.—Near Man, 16 miles west of Pauk (Pakokku district).

## Family CYPRÆIDÆ.

### CYPRÆA EVERWIJNI (?) Martin. (Pl. LVII, figs. 5 & 6.)

1883-87. *Cypræa Everwijni*, Martin, Samml. Geol. Reichs-Mus. Leiden, ser. 1, vol. iii, p. 140 & pl. vii, fig. 140.

Description.—The shell is smooth, small, ventricose, pyriform ; aperture not central, expanded at the extremities. Outer lip crenulate, the inner being about double the breadth of the outer ; spire partly visible.

Remarks.—The specimen under observation is not very well preserved, but the shape and general characters are readily distinguishable, and would identify it with *C. Granti*, D'Archiac & Haime,[1] were it not for the partly-visible spire and crenulate lips.

Locality.—A mile north of Toungu (Thayetmyo district).

Nœtling, Pal. Ind. n. s. vol. i, no. 3 (1901) p. 290 & pl. xix, fig. 12.

CYPRÆA (CYPRÆDIA) ELEGANS, Defrance.    (Pl. LVII, figs. 7 & 8.)

1826. *Cypræa elegans*, Defrance, Dict. Sci. Nat. vol. xliii, p. 39.
1906. *Cyprædia elegans*, Oppenheim, Palæontographica, vol. xxx, pt. iii, p. 303.
1903. *Cypræa (Cyprædia) elegans*, Cossmann, 'Essais de Paléoconchologie Comparée' livr. v, p. 169 & pl. ix, fig. 8.

Description.—Shell ventricose, pyriform, covered with strong spiral ribs and finer longitudinal striations, giving to the shell a cancellated appearance. Aperture not central, narrow, curved; inner lip more than twice the width of the outer.

Remarks.—Dr. Cossmann takes *C. elegans*, Defrance, as the type of the subgenus *Cyprædia* (Swainson, 1840), to which the present specimen is accordingly referred. The species is known from the Lutetian of the Paris Basin (Cossmann, etc.), while it has been determined from beds of the same age in Italy, Austria, Asia Minor, and Egypt.

Locality.—Letpan choung, 10 miles east of Sawmyo (Pakokku district).

### Family CASSIDIDÆ.

CASSIDEA ACANTHINA, sp. nov.    (Pl. LVII, fig. 1.)

Description.—Shell very large and robust, spinose, not less than 100 millimetres high, composed of five whorls, the spire low, conical; body-whorl much expanded, flattening posteriorly towards the suture. The ornamentation consists of abundant revolving striæ of unequal strength crossed by abundant curved growth-striæ, coarse and fine intermingled, as in the case of the spiral striæ. Spines irregular; inner lip callous, reflected; outer lip not known, but apparently thickened and reflected.

Remarks.—According to Dr. Cossmann,[1] *Cassidea*, Bruguière, 1789, should be substituted for *Cassis*, Lamarck, 1799, hence its adoption here. *Cassidea mammillaris* (Grateloup),[2] from the Tongrian of the Adour Basin and the Tongrian and Helvetian of Piedmont, appears to be related to this form, which may possibly be identical with *C. postmammillaris*, Sacco, from the Tortonian of Piedmont.[3] *Cassidea tuberosa* (Linné),[4] a recent form from Brazil, etc., and reported from Japan and the Philippines, appears to be a relative.

Locality.—A mile and a half north of Lanywa (Pakokku district).

### Family TRITONIDÆ.

DISTORSIO CANCELLINUS (Roissy).    (Pl. LV, fig. 4.)

1805. *Murex cancellinus*, Roissy, 'Histoire Naturelle des Mollusques' vol. vi, p. 58.
1899. *Persona reticulata*, Martin, Samml. Geol. Reichs-Mus. Leiden, n. s. vol. i, p. 145 & pl. xxiii, fig. 336.

Description.—A single specimen only is under observation;

[1] 'Essais de Paléoconchologie Comparée' livr. v (1903) p. 123 & pl. v, fig. 10.
[2] 'Conchyliologie Fossile des Terrains Tertiaires du Bassin de l'Adour' 1840, pl. xxxiv, figs. 4 & 19.
[3] For these forms, see F. Sacco, 'Molluschi Terziarii del Piemonte, &c.' pt. vii (1890) pp. 11-17 & pl. i, figs. 3-11.
[4] 'Syst. Nat.' 12th ed. vol. i (1766) p. 1198; & Bruguière, 'Hist. Nat. des Vers' (Encycl. Méth.) vol. i (1792) p. 436 & pl. ccccvi, fig. 1, pl. ccccvii, fig. 2.

but the characters are so peculiar and strongly marked, that there is no difficulty in identification, when the fossil is compared with the living shells from Ceylon and the Philippines.

The spire consists of four or five whorls, all cancellated, the surface being divided into squares, and much distorted, especially the penultimate whorl, which, as well as the body-whorl (though in a less degree), has a vertical furrow at the commencement of the distortion: in the body-whorl this furrow is stronger, and is placed on the left side of and above the aperture, which is canaliculate.

Remarks.—Following G. W. Tryon,[1] *Distorsio*, Bolten, 1798, is adopted for this genus in place of *Distortrix*, Link, 1807, and *Persona*, Montfort, 1810. According to Dr. Cossmann, a species allied to *Distorsio cancellinus* is found in the recent deposits of Martinique;[2] and it is on the authority of the same author that the fragmentary form from the recent beds of Java, referred by Dr. K. Martin to *Persona reticulata*, Linné, is regarded as a synonym.

Locality.—Shales above the zone of *Cytherea erycina*, at Padoukbin.

## Family BUCCINIDÆ.

### CANTHARUS MARTINIANUS (Nœtling). (Pl. LV, figs. 6 & 7.)

1895. *Nassa Cautleyi*, Nœtling, Mem. Geol. Surv. Ind. vol. xxvii, pt. i, p. 32 & pl. vii, figs. 2–4.
1901. *Cancellaria Martiniana*, Nœtling, Pal. Ind. n. s. vol. i, no. 3, p. 332 & pl. xxii, figs. 13 a–13 c.

Description.—Shell elongate-oval; wide canaliculate aperture. Spire not completely seen, but apparently of about equal length with the aperture; body-whorl with transverse folds and weak spiral ribs, especially on the anterior part. Aperture with much thickened and crenulate outer lip; anterior and short posterior canals, columella with weak transverse plaits.

Remarks.—The characters of the specimen under examination are identical with those of *Cancellaria Martiniana*, Nœtling, from the base of the 'Yenangyoungian' near Minbu, except for the posterior canal and slightly-stronger transverse folds: the first of these characters easily escapes observation, and the difference of the second is too slight to be of importance. Dr. Nœtling refers to varices which may be observed on the whorls of this species, but none are shown in his figures, nor are any such to be seen on the present specimen.

The absence of these varices and the presence of a posterior canal would agree perfectly with Tryon's diagnosis of *Cantharus*, Bolten,[3] to which our specimen is accordingly referred. Of the forms of the same genus, *C. polygonus* (Lamarck),[4] from the Calcaire

[1] 'Structural & Systematic Conchology' Philadelphia, vol. ii (1883) p. 124.
[2] 'Essais de Paléoconchologie Comparée' livr. v (1903) p. 105.
[3] Tryon, 'Structural & Systematic Conchology' Philadelphia, vol. ii (1883) p. 143.
[4] 'Mémoire sur les Fossiles des Environs de Paris' Ann. Mus. Hist. Nat. Paris, vol. ii (1803) p. 319 & sep. cop. p. 58.

Grossier of the Paris Basin, agrees closely in shape and general characters, but it is larger and has more rounded ribs than *C. Martinianus.*

Locality.—2 miles south of Mindegyi (Thayetmyo district).


## Family FUSIDÆ.

### MELONGENA PSEUDOBUCEPHALA (Nœtling).

1901. *Pyrula pseudobucephala,* Nœtling, Pal. Ind. n. s. vol. i, no. 3, p. 318 & pl. xxi, figs. 5–6.

Remarks.—The reasons for adopting *Melongena,* Schumacher, in place of *Pyrula* for the group of shells which includes *Melongena bucephala,* Lamarck, and hence *M. pseudobucephala* (Nœtling) also, are fully discussed by Tryon,[1] and that author's nomenclature is here adopted.

Locality.—10 miles north of Yenangyat (Pakokku district).


### BUSYCON CANALICULATUM (Linn.).  (Pl. LV, fig. 2.)

1766. *Murex canaliculatus,* Linn. 'Syst. Nat.' 12th ed. vol. i, p. 1222.

Description.—The shell is ill-preserved, but the height of the part remaining is not less than 60 millimetres, and therefore the whole must have attained a considerable size. It is robust and pyriform, with an elongate canal, composed of a turretted spire and a large body-whorl.

Spire of five (or six) angular whorls with deeply-canaliculate sutures; ornamented with two stout revolving keels, from the posterior of which the surface slopes steeply upwards, while from the anterior keel it descends almost vertically to the suture. The body-whorl is large, angular posteriorly, rounded and possessing a long canal anteriorly; the inner lip is somewhat callous; it is curved in section.

Remarks.—*Busycon,* Bolten, 1798, is here adopted in place of the later name *Fulgur,* Montfort, since the species quoted by the first author[2] are all included by Tryon[3] in the genus *Fulgur.* A comparison with the recent species (in the British Museum) leaves no doubt of the identity with it of this shell; while, so far as can be judged from the figure, the *Sycum (?) canaliculatum* (Bellardi),[4] from the Tongrian of Liguria, may be an allied form, since its characters are rather those of *Busycon* than of *Sycum.*

Locality.—Letpan choung, 10 miles east of Sawmyo (Pakokku district).

[1] 'Structural & Systematic Conchology' Philadelphia, vol. ii (1883) pp. 134–35.
[2] 'Museum Boltenianum' Hamburg, 1798, p. 149.
[3] 'Structural & Systematic Conchology' Philadelphia, vol. ii (1883) p. 138.
[4] 'Molluschi Terziarii del Piemonte, &c.' vol. i (1873) p. 155 & pl. x, fig. 6; and Cossmann, 'Essais de Paléoconchologie Comparée' livr. iv (1901) p. 81.

## Family VOLUTIDÆ.

VOLUTA (?) BIRMANICA, sp. nov.    (Pl. LVII, fig. 10.)

*Description.*—Shell coniform, height not less than 32 millimetres; depressed conical spire, of which the apex may have been mucronate as in *Imbricaria*; aperture narrow. Columella straight, with spiral plications, of which the anterior are the stronger; outer lip thickened.

*Remarks.*—The smooth character of the shell renders it in appearance very like a *Conus*, but it is readily distinguished by the columellar plaits. Its true generic position must be regarded as doubtful. In this connexion the suggested relationship[1] of *Gosavia* to *Conus* and to *Imbricaria* is interesting, as this species also possesses characteristics belonging to both genera.

*Locality.* — Yenanine choung, near Banbyin (Thayetmyo district).

## Family TEREBRIDÆ.

TEREBRA sp.

(?) 1901. *Terebrum* sp., Nœtling, Pal. Ind. n. s. vol. i, no. 3, p. 340 & pl. xxii, fig. 19.

*Description.*—Shell small, turretted; apical angle small. Whorls ornamented with transverse ribs, curved on the lower part; but in a narrow band below the suture, separated from the main portion of the whorl by a faintly-marked furrow, the ribs are straight.

*Remark.*—This species appears to be identical with Dr. Nœtling's *Terebrum* sp., from the zone of *Paracyathus cœruleus* at Yenangyat.

*Locality.*—South-west of Mindegyi (Thayetmyo district).

## Family CONIDÆ.

CONUS SCALARIS, Martin.

1879–80. *Conus scalaris*, Martin, 'Tertiärschichten auf Java' p. 12 & pl. ii, fig. 4.

*Description.*—The shell (a cast) consists of eight whorls with deeply-canaliculate sutures, and a large acuminate body-whorl. The earlier six whorls form a steeply-inclined cone, but the last two descend more gently. Ornamentation not observed.

*Remark.*—The peculiar step-like form of the spire of this species readily distinguishes it.

*Locality.*—A mile and a half east-north-east of Ngalaingyoung (Thayetmyo district).

CONUS AVAENSIS, Nœtling.

1901. *Conus avaensis*, Nœtling, Pal. Ind. n. s. vol. i, no. 3, p. 362 & pl. xxiii, figs. 15–16.

*Localities.*—Letpan choung, 10 miles east of Sawmyo (Pakokku district); and (?) a mile and a half west of Mindegyi (Thayetmyo district).

[1] F. Stoliczka, Sitzungsberichte d. k. Akad. Wissensch. Wien, vol. lii (1865–66) pt. i, p. 179; and Palæontologia Indica 'Cretaceous Fauna of Southern India' vol. ii (1868) p. 73.

## ARTHROPODA—Crustacea.

### BALANUS TINTINNABULUM (Linné).

1758. *Lepas tintinnabulum*, Linn. 'Syst. Nat.' 10th ed. p. 668.
1853. *Balanus sublævis*, D'Archiac & Haime, 'Description des Animaux Fossiles du Groupe Nummulitique de l'Inde' p. 341 & pl. xxiv, fig. 15.
1879-80. *Balanus tintinnabulum*, Martin, 'Die Tertiärschichten auf Java' p. 131 & pl. xxiii, figs. 3-4.
1887. *Balanus tintinnabulum*, Martin, Samml. Geol. Reichs-Mus. Leiden, ser. 1, vol. iii, p. 40 & pl. iii, fig. 36.
1901. *Balanus tintinnabulum*, Nœtling, Pal. Ind. n. s. vol. i, no. 3, p. 368 & pl. xxiv, figs. 1-2.

Remarks.—The synonymy here given is that adopted by Dr. Nœtling, which it is of interest to include, as it indicates that this well-distributed recent species occurs also in the Miocene deposits of India, Java, and Burma.

Locality.—A quarter of a mile west of Banbyin (Thayetmyo district).

## Description of the Eocene Fossils.

### PROTOZOA—Foraminifera.

### OPERCULINA CANALIFERA, D'Archiac.

1850. *Operculina canalifera*, D'Archiac, 'Histoire des Progrès de la Géologie' vol. iii, p. 245.
1853. *Operculina canalifera*, D'Archiac & Haime, 'Description des Animaux Fossiles du Groupe Nummulitique de l'Inde' p. 182 & pl. xii, fig. 1; also p. 346 & pl. xxxv, fig. 5, pl. xxxvi, figs. 15-16.

The relative thickness and the rugose aspect of the young individuals serve to confirm the reference of the specimens to this form.

Localities.—Minbu district: Man choung, near Subagyidan; and near Kyetubok.

### OPERCULINA HARDIEI, D'Archiac & Haime.

1853. *Operculina Hardiei*, D'Archiac & Haime, 'Description des Animaux Fossiles du Groupe Nummulitique de l'Inde' p. 346 & pl. xxxv, fig. 6.

The thinness of this form, its highly-curved septa, rapidly-expanding whorls, small central chamber, and constantly small size seem to identify it with the above species from the Hala range of North-Western India.

Locality.—A mile south-east of Magyisan (Minbu district).

### NUMMULITES BEAUMONTI (?) D'Archiac & Haime.

1853. *Nummulites Beaumonti*, D'Archiac & Haime, *op. cit.* p. 133 & pl. viii, figs. 1-3.

Description.—Test lenticular, varying in thickness; numerous fine curved lines on the surface, radiating from the centre to the circumference. A transverse section shows an ellipse, more or less pointed at the ends of the longer axis; chambers large.

Locality.—East of Kyetubok (Minbu district).

NUMMULITES sp.

A small lenticular single individual, in conglomeratic sandstone with quartz-pebbles. Resembles the young of *N. Beaumonti*.

Locality.—2 miles south by east of Magyisan (Minbu district).

## CŒLENTERATA—Anthozoa.

PARACYATHUS sp.

A small simple coral, with expanding base and numerous septa, appears to belong to this genus.

Locality.—A mile south-east of Magyisan (Minbu district).

### Hydrozoa.

Small globular bodies (2 to 5 millimetres in diameter), making up the greater part of a thin bed of limestone, at first sight resembling foraminifera. On microscopical examination, they reveal a structure which seems to unite them with the Hydrozoa, and indicates a possible relationship to the genus *Parkeria*, Carpenter, from the Cambridge Greensand. Further research is required before a completer identification can be attempted, and for the above opinion the author is indebted to Mr. R. Bullen Newton, F.G.S.

Remark. — The rock yielding these organisms contains also various small foraminifera, including *Operculina canalifera* (?).

Locality.—Half a mile north-west of Kyetubok (Minbu district).

### MOLLUSCA—Lamellibranchiata.

#### Family ARCIDÆ.

ARCA MANENSIS, sp. nov.   (Pl. LIV, figs. 5 & 6.)

Description.—Shell small, arciform, inflated; umbo prosogyrous, situated in the anterior third of the length; cardinal margin straight, making an obtuse angle with the posterior margin, which passes under a rounded right angle into the slightly-curved ventral margin, and this passes gradually into the anterior margin.

The ornamentation consists of numerous fine radial ribs, coarser in the posterior region (which is separated by a rounded indistinct keel from the anterior portion); these are crossed by numerous fine concentric ribs, producing granules on the ventral portion, but imperceptible in the dorsal region.

Dimensions in millimetres.—Left valve, length =16·5; height =9·5; thickness =4·5.

Remarks.—*Arca textiliosa*, Deshayes, from the Bartonian of Paris,[1] has somewhat similar ornamentation, and the shell appears to be shorter in proportion to the height, and less inflated, than

[1] 'Description des Animaux sans Vertèbres découverts dans le Bassin de Paris' vol. i (1860) p. 881 & pl. lxvi, figs. 12-14.

in *A. manensis*. *Arca articulata*, Deshayes,[1] from the Lutetian, is
less regular in shape, while *A. Boutillieri*, Cossmann,[2] from the
same horizon, is smaller, and has coarser ornamentation, but otherwise is very similar to the present form.

Locality.—2 miles south by east of Magyisan (Minbu district).

GLYCIMERIS sp.

Description.—Shell rounded, inflated, almost symmetrical,
valves closed, margins dentate. Ornamentation unknown. Hinge-
surface flat, teeth not observed.

Locality.—Near Kyetubok (Minbu district).

### Family OSTREIDÆ.

OSTREA YOMAENSIS, sp. nov.   (Pl. LIV, figs. 2 & 3.)

Description.—Shell thick, irregularly inflated. Left valve
with irregular, concentric, foliaceous and radial sculpture: deformed
towards the beaks, with a marked depression anteriorly and a large
cartilage-groove and scar of attachment. Right valve smaller,
with fairly-fine concentric scaly sculpture only; somewhat depressed anteriorly.

Dimensions in millimetres.—Right valve: length =51,
height =74; left valve: length =58, height =100.

Remarks.—This species appears to be very much akin to
*Ostrea Raincourti*, Deshayes,[3] from the Paris Eocene, which, however, has no anterior depression: on the other hand, the latter
may not be a permanent character, especially in view of the fact
that a worn specimen of *Ostrea* from the same neighbourhood,
probably *O. yomaensis*, has no such mark.

Locality.—Near Thabyemyoung (Thayetmyo district).

ALECTRYONIA NEWTONI,[4] sp. nov.   (Pl. LIV, fig. 4.)

Description.—Left valve only. Thick, showing the scar of
attachment and grasping processes. Strong radial folds and wavy,
concentric, lamellar sculpture. Margin undulating. Cartilage-
groove short, truncate, turned in the dorsal direction, and bounded
by fairly well-marked ridges.

Dimensions in millimetres.—Left valve, length = 31;
height =43.

[1] 'Description des Animaux sans Vertèbres découverts dans le Bassin de
Paris' vol. i (1860) p. 882 & pl. lxx, figs. 7–9.
[2] 'Iconographie complète des Coquilles Fossiles de l'Éocène des Environs de
Paris' 1904, pl. xxxvi, fig. 110–19.
[3] 'Description des Animaux sans Vertèbres découverts dans le Bassin de
Paris' vol. ii (1860) p. 103 & pl. lxxxiii, figs. 10–11; and Cossmann & Pissarro,
'Iconographie complète des Coquilles Fossiles de l'Éocène des Environs de
Paris' 1904, pl. xlii, fig. 135–10.
[4] Dedicated to Mr. R. Bullen Newton, F.G.S.

Q. J. G. S. No. 256.                          2 σ

Remarks.—Only one left valve was collected, but from the figure of *A. Clot-Beyi* (Bellardi),[1] that form, found in the Mokattam Beds of Egypt (Middle Eocene), appears to be related.

Locality.—North-east of Subagyidan (Minbu district).

Family ANATINIDÆ.

THRACIA sp.

An oval inequilateral cast, with one marked posterior plication, and some indications of a second, curving anteriorly from the umbo, appears to be referable to this genus.

Locality.—Near Kyetubok (Minbu district).

Family CARDIIDÆ.

CARDIUM AMBIGUUM, J. de C. Sowerby.

1840. *Cardium ambiguum*, J. de C. Sowerby, Trans. Geol. Soc. ser. 2, vol. v, pt. ii, p. 328 & pl. xxiv, fig. 2.

Description.—Shell of moderate ·size, oval, inflated, inequilateral. Beaks pointed, prosogyrous. Hinge-margin angular, making an obtuse angle with the posterior margin, which passes under a rounded right angle into the crenulate ventral margin, and this again into the anterior margin under a rounded obtuse angle: the angle between the anterior and cardinal margin being also obtuse. The ornamentation consists of fairly-strong radial ribs, which are rounded and separated by interstices of about equal width.

Localities.—Minbu district: near Kyetubok; and north-east of Subagyidan.

Family VENERIDÆ.

VENUS GRANOSA, J. de C. Sowerby.

1840. *Venus granosa*, J. de C. Sowerby, Trans. Geol. Soc. ser. 2, vol. v, pt. ii, p. 327 & pl. xxv, fig. 7.
1901. *Venus granosa*, Nœtling, Pal. Ind. n. s. vol. i, no. 3, p. 197 & pl. xii, fig. 7.

Description.—Shell obovate, inflated, almost orbicular, with numerous concentric laminæ, some thin, but thicker ones forming fairly-regular concentric ribs, crossed by numerous radial striations, raising small granules towards the margin.

Remarks.—This species, as will be seen from the synonymy, is known both from the Eocene of North-Western India and from the Miocene of Burma.

Locality.—2 miles west-south-west of Myegya (Thayetmyo district).

[1] Mem. R. Acc. Sci. Torino, ser. 2, vol. xv (1854-55) p. 195 & pl. iii, figs. 4-5.

## Family MYIDÆ.

### CORBULA HARPA, D'Archiac & Haime.

1853. *Corbula harpa*, D'Archiac & Haime, 'Description des Animaux Fossiles du Groupe Nummulitique de l'Inde' p. 236 & pl. xvi, figs. 8–9.

Description.—Shell small, trigonal, inequivalve, somewhat inequilateral. Right valve larger, anteriorly truncate, with indented lunule, extended and gaping behind. Marked posterior keel, extending from the incurved slightly-prosogyrous beaks to the postero-ventral corner. Surface with numerous thick rounded ribs, very regularly placed, and separated by deep interstices of about the same width. Left valve smaller; posterior keel less marked; and without the regular ribs, the only ornamentation consisting of growth-lines.

Locality.—A mile south-east of Magyisan (Minbu district).

## Gasteropoda.

### Family NATICIDÆ.

#### NATICA sp.

A fragmentary specimen of a small species, with whorls flattened posteriorly as in *Natica obscura*, J. de C. Sowerby,[1] already described from the Miocene of Burma[2]; it may possibly be identical with that form.

Locality.—2 miles south by east of Magyisan (Minbu district).

#### NATICA (AMPULLINA) SPHERICA (?) Deshayes.

1829. *Natica spherica*, Deshayes, 'Description des Coquilles Fossiles des Environs de Paris' vol. ii, p. 176 & pl. xx, figs. 14–15.

Description.—Shell of moderate size, globose, with a prominent spire and large body-whorl. Spire of five rounded whorls, suture slightly canaliculate. The body-whorl is somewhat angular, though not noticeably so, and smooth save for transverse striations which are stronger towards the aperture. Inner lip callous and reflected.

Remarks.—There is an unusually-extensive callosity in the specimen, which covers the whole of the columella; but in other respects it very closely resembles the French species.

Locality.—Yengadin choung, 2 miles south by east of Magyisan (Minbu district).

#### NATICA (AMPULLINA) GROSSA, Deshayes.  (Pl. LVI, figs. 3 & 4.)

1866. *Natica grossa*, Deshayes, 'Description des Animaux sans Vertèbres découverts dans le Bassin de Paris' vol. iii, p. 65 & pl. lxx, figs. 24–26.

Description.—Shell large, robust, oval. Spire elevated, of five whorls, each slightly angular from posterior flattening; body-

[1] Trans. Geol. Soc. ser. 2, vol. v, pt. ii (1840) p. 328 & pl. xxvi, fig. 2.
[2] F. Nœtling, Pal. Ind. n. s. vol. i, no. 3 (1901) p. 284 & pl. xix, figs. 2–3.

whorl large, broadly rounded, smooth except for transverse striations near the aperture.  Inner lip callous and reflected.

Dimensions in millimetres. — Maximum height = 80 ; maximum width = 66.

Localities.—Var. *oblonga*, Desh., a mile south of Magyisan (Minbu district) and mile-post 31, Minbu-Ngapé Road ; var. *spherica*, Desh., near Subagyidan.

## Natica (Ampullina) ponderosa, Deshayes.

1829. *Ampullaria ponderosa*, Deshayes, 'Description des Coquilles Fossiles des Environs de Paris' vol. ii, p. 140 & pl. xvii, figs. 13–14.
1866. *Natica ponderosa*, Deshayes, 'Description des Animaux sans Vertèbres découverts dans le Bassin de Paris' vol. iii, p. 72.

Description.—Shell very robust, of moderately-large size (full height = about 48 millimetres), with a depressed conical spire and large body-whorl.  Spire of four or five whorls : the earlier rounded, the penultimate slightly angular from posterior flattening.  Aperture elongate, inner lip apparently not expanded.  Shell smooth, or covered with fine transverse striations.

Remarks.—The specimen is waterworn, and therefore its characters are imperfectly known; but the ponderous shell and slightly-elongate aperture afford marked characteristics for identification.

Locality.—West of Kyetubok (Minbu district).

### Family Turritellidæ.

## Turritella sp. 3.

Description.—A fairly-large species, elongate, regularly conical ; the earlier whorls are somewhat flattened, the later rounded. Marked ornamentation, consisting of three to eight spiral tuberculate ribs, with others intercalated between them ; smooth or nearly so on the earlier whorls, tuberculate and stronger anteriorly.  Two twinned ribs are situated in the shallow suture-canal on the later whorls, being single on the earlier whorls.

Remarks.—The specimens are too imperfectly preserved for accurate determination ; but the basal whorl is somewhat similar in its characters to that of *T. sulcifera*, Deshayes[1]; the latter, however, has not such prominent tuberculate ribs as in the present form.

Localities.—South-west of Thabyemyoung (Thayetmyo district); and (?) near Subagyidan (Minbu district).

### Family Cerithiidæ.

## Cerithium (?) sp.  (Pl. LIV, fig. 9.)

Description.—Shell poorly preserved and fragmentary, turretted, with a row of large tubercles along the suture, and a very faintly-

[1] 'Description des Coquilles Fossiles des Environs de Paris' vol. ii (1829 p. 278 & pl. xxxv, figs. 5–6, pl. xxxvi. figs. 3–4, pl. xxxvii. figs. 19–20.

marked row of smaller granules on the whorls. Aperture not observed.

Remark.—Although not in good condition, it seems probable that this is a relative of *Vicarya Verneuili*, D'Archiac,[1] from the Hala Range of North-Western India.

Locality.—2 miles south by east of Magyisan (Minbu district).


## Family CASSIDIDÆ.

CASSIDARIA sp.

A small species, too imperfectly preserved for further determination.

Locality.—North-east of Subagyidan (Minbu district).


## Family DOLIIDÆ.

DOLIUM sp. (Pl. LV, fig. 3.)

Description.—Shell pyriform, with a fairly-high spire of five whorls, and a large body-whorl. The ornamentation consists of numerous revolving flat ribs, fairly close together, the principal one equidistant—with an occasional faint intermediate riblet, such as may be observed in Menke's *D. costatum* from the Pacific, occurring also in the Miocene of Java (for the description, etc. of which see Dr. K. Martin).[2]

Locality.—A mile south-east of Magyisan (Minbu district).

FICULA THEOBALDI, Nœtling.

1901. *Ficula Theobaldi*, Nœtling, Pal. Ind. n. s. vol. i, no. 3, p. 298 & pl. xix, figs. 20–21.

Remarks.—There appears to be a relationship between *Ficula pannus*, Deshayes,[3] from the Paris Eocene, and this species, already described from the Miocene of Burma by Dr. Nœtling.


## Family FUSIDÆ.

FUSUS sp.

Shell turretted, elongate, of five whorls, separated by marked sutures, the earlier showing longitudinal plications, less clear on the later whorls. Body-whorl large, about two-thirds of the total height, with a narrow, elongate, straight canal. All the whorls are somewhat angular posteriorly, and covered with fine spiral

'Description des Animaux Fossiles du Groupe Nummulitique de l'Inde' (1853) p. 298 & pl. xxviii, fig. 4.
[2] 'Die Tertiärschichten auf Java' 1879–80, p. 40 & pl. vii, figs. 9–10.
'Description des Animaux sans Vertèbres découverts dans le Bassin de Paris' vol. iii (1866) p. 432 & pl. lxxxiii, figs. 1–4.

striations on the lower half, the upper part above the posterior angle being smooth.

Remarks.—*Fusus uniplicatus*, Lamarck,[1] from the Paris Eocene, is very similar in shape and characters to this form.

Locality.—Man choung, near Subagyidan (Minbu district).

### Family VOLUTIDÆ.

VOLUTA PERNODOSA, sp. nov.   (Pl. LVII, fig. 4.)

Description.—Shell with a large anteriorly-acuminate body-whorl and a fairly-prominent spire; large transverse varicose ribs and fine spiral striations. Aperture elongate, outer lip rather thin, plaits of columella and canal not observed.

Remarks.—This form appears to be a near relative of *Voluta nodosa*, J. de C. Sowerby,[2] from the English Eocene deposits, but the transverse ribs are stronger than in that form, and the spiral striæ more marked than in *V. Barrandii*, Deshayes,[3] from the 'sables moyens' of Paris.

Locality.—Man choung, near Subagyidan (Minbu district).

VOLUTA D'ARCHIACI, sp. nov.   (Pl. LV, fig. 5.)

1853. *Voluta* indet., D'Archiac & Haime, 'Description des Animaux Fossiles du Groupe Nummulitique de l'Inde' p. 327 & pl. xxxii, fig. 6.

Description.—Shell small, spire conical and mucronate, body-whorl large. The spire consists of five or more whorls with transverse plications, giving rise to a line of granules along the suture and at the posterior angle of the whorls; the last is clearly seen on the body-whorl, of which the ornamentation is reticulate, owing to the presence of spiral ribs of almost equal strength with the transverse plications. Aperture narrow, columella plicate; but neither of these features is well seen. The width = 14 millimetres.

Remarks.—This species appears to be identical with that of which Vicomte d'Archiac found fragments in the yellow limestone of the Hala Range, India, and is clearly allied to *Voluta ambigua* (Solander),[4] an Upper Eocene species from Barton in Hampshire; but the differences seem to warrant a separate specific name.

Locality.—North-east of Subagyidan (Minbu district).

### Family OLIVIDÆ.

OLIVA sp.

Shell oliviform, of small size, smooth, with a large body-whorl and a short prominent spire. Outer lip expanded beyond the penultimate whorl.

Locality.—Near Kyetubok (Minbu district).

[1] 'Mémoires sur les Fossiles des Environs de Paris' Ann. Mus. Hist. Nat. vol. ii (1803) p. 385, & sep. cop. p. 61, pl. iv, fig. 3 (? 1805).
[2] 'Mineral Conchology' vol. iv (1823) p. 135 & pl. cccxcix, fig. 2.
[3] 'Description des Animaux sans Vertèbres découverts dans le Bassin de Paris' vol. iii (1866) p. 587 & pl. cii, figs. 1-2.
[4] In G. Brander's 'Fossilia Hantonensia' London, 1766, p. 32 & pl. v, fig.6.

## Family PLEUROTOMIDÆ.

### PLEUROTOMA STOPPANII (?) Deshayes.

1866. *Pleurotoma Stoppanii*, Deshayes, ' Description des Animaux sans Vertèbres découverts dans le Bassin de Paris' vol. iii, p. 882 & pl. xcix, figs. 23–24.

Description.—Shell fusiform; spire of about equal length with the body-whorl; canal not observed. Aperture not preserved, but evidently elongate. The spire consists of seven whorls, slightly angular posteriorly, the angle apparently corresponding to the slit in the outer lip. The ornamentation consists of revolving ribs, faint on the earlier whorls. Body-whorl large, with numerous spiral ribs, not all of equal strength, posteriorly angular, anteriorly with canal, broken in the author's specimen.

Remarks.—The true *Pleurotoma Stoppanii*, Deshayes (= *Pl. laticlavia*, Beyrich, according to Dr. A. von Kœnen [1]), is found in the Oligocene of Europe. The horizon of the present form is near the top of the Bassein Group.

Locality.—A mile south-east of Magyisan (Minbu district).

## Family CONIDÆ.

### CONUS sp.

A fairly-robust species, with faint transverse striæ and a short spire. Specimen much crushed.

Locality.—2 miles south by east of Magyisan (Minbu district).

The Eocene species are all new to Burma, with the exception of *Ficula Theobaldi*, Nœtling, known from the Miocene (Pegu Group): the only hitherto described Bassein species being *Velates Schmideliana* (Chemnitz),[2] a Middle Eocene form, not found in any of the localities now visited.

## V. RECAPITULATION.

The following appear to be the most important of the new facts brought forward:—

(1) The presence of marine fossils in the lower part of the Pegu Stage, and in particular of the European Miocene (Helvetian-Tortonian) species, *Lucina globulosa*, Deshayes.

(2) The conjunction of northern and southern Burmese Miocene zones (as determined by Dr. Nœtling, Pal. Ind. n. s. vol. i, no. 3, 1901, p. 27) in the northern part of the Thayetmyo district.

(3) The identity of some of the Miocene species from the Letpan choung with European Eocene or Oligocene forms.

(4) The conglomeratic character of the Pegu Group in the Pakokku and Lower Chindwin districts.

(5) The invalidity of the subdivision of the Pegu Group into Promeian and Yenangyoungian.

---

1 Palæontographica, vol. xvi, pt. ii (1867) p. 88.
2 F. Nœtling, Rec. Geol. Surv. Ind. vol. xxvii (1894) p. 103 & pl. ii, figs. 1-2.

(6) The increased thickness of the Pegu Group revealed by study of completer sections than those previously known.

(7) The strongly-marked unconformity of the Irawadi Series to the Pegu Group as one recedes from the Irawadi, and the comparative conformity in the less disturbed regions.

It is suggested, as a point for further investigation, that there appears to be a possibility of a small development of a coralline facies in the Burmese Miocene (as in that of Java and India), indicated by the fauna of the locality near Toungu (Thayetmyo district), where a bed full of corals, including two genera new to Burma, contains also two species of mollusks previously known only from Java, and one new to science.

Finally, the history of the Tertiary Era in Burma, as we now know it, appears to have been much as follows:—In Eocene times, a shallow sea seems to have extended from the base of the Shan Plateau across the present site of the Arakan Yoma into India, gradually deepening westwards, this being slowly filled up by detritus of various kinds, until at the close of the period the conditions led to the deposition of a thin bed of limestone over at least the eastern area, after which some disturbance took place in the west of Burma, as well as in the rest of Eurasia, whereby a low ridge was formed along the line of the present Arakan Yoma, constituting an imperfect barrier, higher and more effective in the north than in the south. Thus, in Miocene times, a shallow sea extended over the present Irawadi Valley, which received the detritus of large rivers from the north and east. Deposits of terrestrial vegetation were laid down near the land, giving rise to coal-seams, while the sediments above and below were conglomeratic in their nature. At the same time that terrestrial organic materials were being thus carried down, including bones of land-animals, a marine and littoral fauna and flora existed in the south, and in the more open portions to the north, giving rise by their decay to petroleum-deposits. At length, the whole region became estuarine, owing to the filling-up of the basin and to a movement which greatly increased the height of the 'Arakan Yoma,' raising it above the sea, and led to the production of anticlinal islands or shallows in the sea to the east, while probably giving rise to the Pegu Yoma. The result of this upheaval was the denudation of the islands of partly-consolidated material, the erosion being greatest in the most prominent: so that when, in the Pliocene(?) Period, a thick series of estuarine and fluviatile deposits was laid down over these, a considerable overlap resulted, the Irawadi Series being quite conformable in places to the Miocene below, and elsewhere resting across its upturned edges. Finally, the whole region again became subject to a general elevation, whereby the Irawadi Series was laid bare to denudation, and the earlier anticlinal folds accentuated, resulting in the present conformation of the land—the Miocene being once more revealed as inliers in the mass of the Irawadi Beds, marking the position of the islands in the earlier estuary.

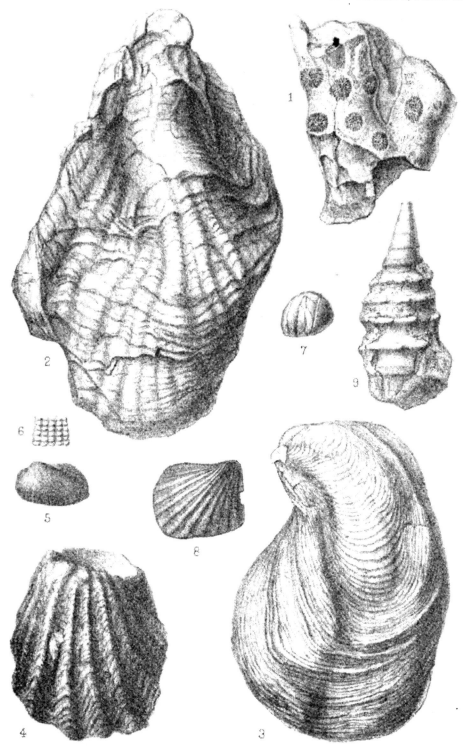

P. Highley del et lith.

West, Newman imp.

TERTIARY FOSSILS FROM BURMA

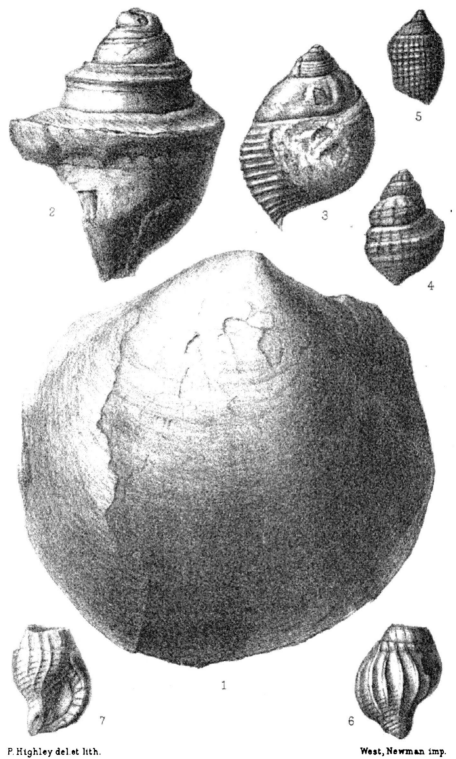

P. Highley del. et lith.

West, Newman imp.

TERTIARY FOSSILS FROM BURMA.

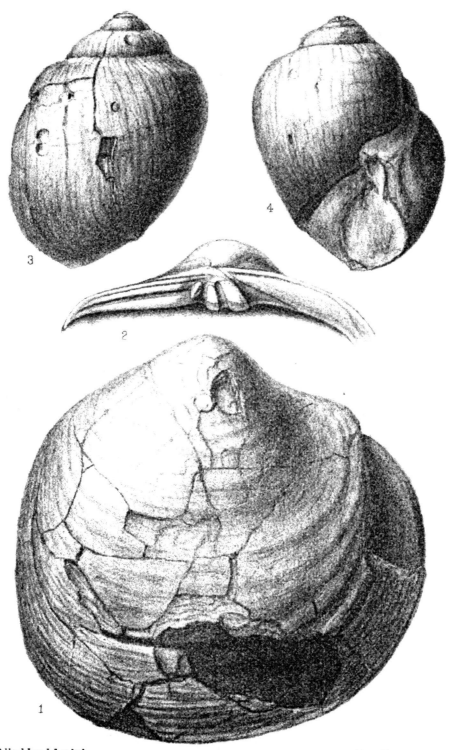

P. Highley del. et lith.

West, Newman imp.

TERTIARY FOSSILS FROM BURMA.

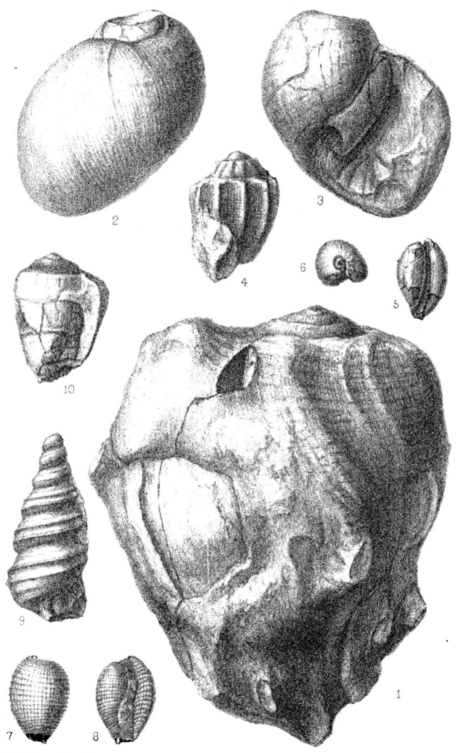

P. Highley del. et lith.

West, Newman imp.

TERTIARY FOSSILS FROM BURMA.

## EXPLANATION OF PLATES LIV-LVII.

[All figures are of the natural size, except where otherwise stated.]

### PLATE LIV.

Fig. 1. *Actinacis Nœtlingi*, sp. nov. (P. 622.)
2. *Ostrea yomaensis*, sp. nov. Left valve. (P. 635.)
3. Do. do. Right valve.
4. *Alectryonia Newtoni*, sp. nov. Left valve. (P. 635.)
Figs. 5 & 6. *Arca manensis*, sp. nov. Left valve. Ornamentation enlarged. (P. 634.)
Fig. 7. *Jouannetia protocumingi*, sp. nov. Left valve. (P. 626.)
8. *Cardita protovariegata*, Nœtling. Right valve. (P. 625.)
9. *Cerithium (?)* sp. (Pp. 638-39.)

### PLATE LV.

Fig. 1. *Lucina globulosa*, Deshayes. Right valve. (P. 625.)
2. *Busycon canaliculatum* (Linné). (P. 631.)
3. *Dolium* sp. (P. 639.)
4. *Distorsio cancellinus* (Roissy). (Pp. 629-30.)
5. *Voluta D'Archiaci*, sp. nov. (P. 640.)
6. *Cantharus Martinianus* (Nœtling). Back view, × 2. (Pp. 630-31.)
7. Do. do. Front view, × 2.

### PLATE LVI.

Fig. 1. *Batissa kodoungensis*, Nœtling. Right valve. (P. 624.)
2. Do. do. Do. do. dentition.
3. *Natica (Ampullina) grossa*, var. *oblonga*, Deshayes. Back view. (Pp. 637-38.)
4. Do. do. do. Front view.

### PLATE LVII.

Fig. 1. *Cassidea acanthina*, sp. nov. (P. 629.)
2. *Natica (Globularia) gibberosa*, Grateloup. Back view. (Pp. 627-28.)
3. Do. do. Front view.
4. *Voluta pernodosa*, sp. nov. (P. 640.)
5. *Cypræa Everwijni (?)* Martin. Front view. (P. 628.)
6. Do. do. Apical view.
7. *Cypræa (Cyprædia) elegans*, Defrance. Back view. (P. 629.)
8. Do. do. Front view.
9. *Turritella acuticarinata*, Dunker. (P. 628.)
10. *Voluta (?) birmanica*, sp. nov. (P. 632.)

### DISCUSSION.

The CHAIRMAN (Dr. J. J. H. TEALL) asked for the evidence on which the Pliocene rocks had been estimated at 20,000 feet.

Mr. R. BULLEN NEWTON congratulated the Author on the interest of his paper. He thought, however, that some additional information, in connexion with the Author's tabulated horizons, might be acceptable. The Irawadi Series, with its terrestrial and fluviatile vertebrate fauna, described by Buckland and Clift in 1828, from material collected by John Crawfurd, had recognized affinities with that found in the Siwalik-Hill formation of India, as well as with that yielded by the Pikermi deposits of Greece. All these beds were frequently alluded to as of Pliocene age, whereas in reality they were of Upper Miocene age, and belonged to the Pontian stage of those rocks (see A. de Lapparent's 'Traité de Géologie' 5th ed. 1906, pp. 1630 & 1632).   The fact that the Author had been able to determine a European Miocene shell, *Lucina globulosa*, in the lower or marine part of the Pegu Group, was evidence in favour of recognizing those beds as belonging to the Helvetian-Tortonian portion of the Miocene System, since the above-mentioned shell was characteristic of that horizon.   The Bassein Group, according to Dr. Nœtling, contained, among other mollusca, *Velates Schmide-liana*, one of the most typical shells of the Lutetian or Middle Eocene Period, which was found in Europe, Egypt, India, etc., and never occurred at a later stage of the Eocene, although Dr. Nœtling regarded it as favouring the Upper or Bartonian division of that system.   In India this gastropod occurred in the Khirthar Group of Sind.

The AUTHOR thanked the Fellows present for the way in which they had received his paper, and stated, in regard to the thickness of the Irawadi Series, that he had only quoted Dr. Nœtling's figures, which seemed to him to be very excessive.   In conclusion, he expressed the hope that his paper would prove effective in re-introducing the subject to British geologists, and in stimulating interest in its problems.

# GENERAL INDEX

TO

## THE QUARTERLY JOURNAL

AND

## PROCEEDINGS OF THE GEOLOGICAL SOCIETY.

Aber-chwil Fault (Glyn Ceiriog), 571, 584.

Aci Castello (Sicily), pillow-lavas of, 271.

*Actinacis Nætlingi*, sp. nov., 622 & pl. liv.

*Actinoconchus* (?), 470 & pl. l.

'Actinolite talc-rock' fr. New Zealand, 159–60.

Actinolitic rocks of Glendalough, 482–83 fig., 487 *et seqq.* & figs.

ADAMS, F. D., on the Structure & Relations of the Laurentian System in Eastern Canada, 127–47 figs. & pls. xi–xiii.

ADDISON, P. L., obituary of, lxix.

Africa (South), fossil plants from, 83–126 & pls. ii–x; *see also* Cape Colony, &c.

Agassiz, Glacial Lake, 151.

Alan R. (Pembrokeshire), 372–79.

Albite-granite of E. Canada, 130–35 fig. & chem. anals., 140 fig., 141–42 & pl. xi, 146.

*Alectryonia Newtoni*, sp. nov., 635–36, & pl. liv.

Allanite in Glendalough rocks, 483, 487.

ALLEN, H. A., [motion seconded by] cxxvii.

ALLENDALE, LORD, obituary of, lxvi–lxvii.

ALLORGE, M. M., [on Cornish & Breton platforms], 399.

Alsop-en-le-Dale & Tissington Ry. (Derbyshire), sects. descr., 59–61 fig.

Altarnun, *see* Buttern Hill.

Alternating strain-slip defined, 308.

Alton district (Hants), former & present physiography of, 327–33 & pl. xxxvii (map).

America (North), chronology of Glacial Epoch in, 149–51.

Amphibolite, inclusions of, in E. Canadian granite-gneiss, 133–35 fig.; amphibolites assoc. w. Grenville Series, 137–39 & pl. xii; limestones altered into do., 136, 140 fig., 141–42; amphibolite invaded by granite, 142 & pl. xi; amphibolite of Glendalough, 480–82 fig.; contact phenomena of do., 491–92 fig.; *see also* Hornblendic rocks.

Analcime in Bartestree dolerite, 506 & pl. lii (microscop. sect.), 511.

Analyses, chemical, of granite-gneiss, 132; of norites, 278, 279; of enstatite-quartz-gabbro, 280; of diabase, &c., 281–82; of soda-aplites, &c., 283–84; of hornblende-peridotite, 479; of Glendalough 'mixed rock,' 489; of Exeter sandstone, 500.

ANDERSON, T., [on pillow-lavas], 271.

ANDREWS, C. W., 356.

Angles of rest of certain solids in water, 174–76; conclusions to be drawn from change in, 177.

Annual General Meeting, ix–xlix.

Antigorio, Valle (& antigorite), 152–58 & map.

Antigorite-serpentines, &c., 152–70 & map.

'Anvil-stone' (palæolithic) fr. Ruscombe, v.

Apatite in St. David's-Head 'rock-series,' 289–90; in Glendalough rocks, 478, 481, 482, 486.

Aplite (soda-) of St. David's Head, 283-84 w. chem. anal. & pl. xxix (microscop. sects.).

Apœcous = superimposed characters of rocks, 600.

Appila Gorge (S. Australia), erratics in Cambrian till of, 241, 244 fig.; sect. descr. & fig., 253-54.

Arakan Series (Burma), 606, 607, 621.

*Arca Burnesi*, 623.

—— *manensis*, sp. nov., 634-35 & pl. liv.

—— *metabistrigata*, 623.

*Archæocyathina* - Limestones in S. Australia, 236, 237 w. list of foss.

Arenig Series of St. David's Head, intrusions in, 273, 292.

Armenia, geol. map presented, ii.

ARNOLD-BEMROSE, H. H., 63, 69.

Arvonian (non-existent), 363, 374.

Ash, *see* Glyn Ceiriog & Tortworth.

Ashford (Derbyshire), *Cyathaxonia*-subzone at, 58.

Ashgillian Series compared w. Dolhir Series, 591.

Assets, statement of, xlii.

*Athyris* cf. *planosulcata*, 469-70 & pl. l.

Auditors elected, v.

'Augen'-like cracks, *see* Phacoidal.

Augite in Glendalough rocks, 478.

Augite-amphibolite of Glendalough, 479-80.

Augite-andesite (Pebidian), 366.

Aureole of thermometamorphism in Scottish Highlands, 148.

Australia, South. *See* South Australia.

Austria, Geol. Surv. Maps presented, viii.

Avening Green (Gloucest.), Llandovery rocks of, 516-17.

Avonian (Upper) of Midland area, faunal success. in, 34-82 figs. & pl. i (foss.); *see also* Loughshinny.

Awards of medals & funds, xliii-xlix.

'Axial Series,' 621; *see also* Chin Division.

*Baiera moltenensis*, sp. nov., 99-100 & pl. ii.

Bala & Llandovery rocks of Glyn Ceiriog, 546-95 figs. & pl. liii (map).

Balance-Sheet for 1907, xxxviii-xxxix.

*Balanus tintinnabulum*, 633.

BALTZER, A., elected For. Corresp., iv.

Banded structure in St. David's-Head intrusions, 276-77.

BARBER, C. A., 108.

BARLOW, A. E., 129.

BARLOW-JAMESON fund, list of awards, xxxv.

BARON, Rev. R., obituary of, lxiv.

Baroota, *see* Waterfall Creek.

BARROW, G., 379, 382; the High-Level Platforms of Bodmin Moor & their Relation to the Deposits of Stream-Tin & Wolfram, 384-97 figs. & pls. xlv-xlvi, 400; [on thermometamorphic aureole, &c. in Scottish Highlands], 148; [on pillow-lavas], 271-72; [on geol. struct. of St. David's area], 382-83.

BARROW, J., 380.

Bartestree (Herefordshire), basic intrusion of, 501-11 fig. & pl. lii (microscop. sects.).

Basalts of Bartestree, 507-509 & pl. lii (microscop. sects.).

Basalt-dykes, Tertiary, in Colonsay, 300.

BASEDOW, H. (& G. D. Iliffe), on a Formation known as 'Glacial Beds of Cambrian Age' in South Australia, 260.

Basic intrusive rocks of St. David's area, 379-81; of Bartestree, 501-11 fig. & pl. lii (microscop. sects.); *see also* Dolerites, &c.

Bassein Division (Arakan Series), 606, 607 et seqq., 617-18, 621.

Bathylith, definition of term, 130; bathyliths invading Grenville Series in E. Canada, 130-35 fig., 140 fig., 141-42 & pl. xi, 146.

*Batissa kodoungensis*, 624 & pl. lvi.

BAUERMAN, H. [exhibits bottle-glass showg. viscid flow-structure], v.

Beaufort Series, *see* Burghersdorp Beds.

*Beaumontia* aff. *Egertoni*, 70.

Bedfordshire (& Herts.), palæolithic implements from, 1-7 figs.

*Belemnitella-mucronata* Zone at Trimingham, &c., 401, 403, 410, 412.

Belgium, Geol. Surv. maps presented, vii.

BELL, J. M., 158, 165.

BERTRAND, MARCEL, obituary of, l-liv.

Bibliography of S. African palæobotany, 105-107, 123-25; of antigorite, 152; of *Metriorhynchus*, 345; of Bala & Llandovery rocks of Glyn Ceiriog, 547-51; of the Tarnthaler Köpfe, 597-98; of Burmese geology, 604-606.

BIGSBY medallists, list of, xxxiv.

Binstead (I. of W.), freshwater limest., contraction in, 177.

Biotite' in Glendalough rocks, 488, 489 fig., 491, 492 fig.; biotite-norite, of Carn Llidi, 278-80 w. chem. anal. & pl. xxix (microscop.-sects.),

288–89; biotite-gneisses in W. Liberia, 313, 314.

Black Rock, *see* Orroroo.

Black Shales, *see* Loughshinny.

Blackwater R. (Surrey), relation of R. Wey to, 319–23 w. map.

Blackwood railway-cutting (S. Australia), Cambrian till, &c. in, 250–51 & pl. xxvi.

Blow Downs (Beds.), palæolith found on, 1.

Bodmin Moor (Cornwall), high-level platforms of, & their relat. to wolfram & stream-tin deposits, 384–400 figs. & pls. xlv–xlvi.

Bognanco, Valle (Italy), serpentine of, 157.

BONNEY, T. G., on Antigorite & the Val Antigorio, with Notes on other Serpentines containing that mineral, 152–70 & map.

Boulder-Clay in Hitchin district, 8 *et seqq.*; *see also* Drift, Glacial, *&c.*

Bowenite. 169–70.

Bowithick Marsh (Cornwall), 387.

'Brachiopod - beds' (*Lonsdalia* - subzone), 47 *et seqq.*

Brachiopodan homœomorphy: '*Spirifer glaber*,' 27–33.

*Brachythyris*, generic definition of, 30.

Bradbourne (Derbyshire), *Cyathaxonia*-subzone at, 61.

Bradwell Dale (Derbyshire), *Lonsdalia*-subzone in, 54.

Breccia, dolomitic, of Tarnthal mass, 599, 603.

Brinkmarsh Quarry (Whitfield), 525; Brinkmarsh Farm, 527–28.

British geology in Geol. Soc. publications, lxxv–xcvi.

Bronzite-diorite (& diabase) of Carn Llidi, 281–82 w. chem. anal. & pl. xxix (microscop. sects.).

Brook's End (Co. Dublin), sect. to Loughshinny Bay, descr. & fig., 415–22.

BROWN, ALFRED, 97, 126.

BRYDONE, R. M., on the Subdivisions of the Chalk of Trimingham (Norfolk), 401–11 figs. & pls. xlvii–xlviii (maps), 412.

Bryn Beds in Glyn-Ceiriog Valley, 552–53; detailed descr. of do., 565–68 w. lists of foss.

BUCKMAN, S. S., Brachiopod Homœomorphy: '*Spirifer glaber*,' 27–33.

Burghersdorp Beds, 83–84; fossil plants from, 85 *et seqq.*, 105.

Burma, geology of, 604–44 w. maps & pls. liv–lvii (foss.).

Burra, The (S. Australia), erratics in Cambrian till, 240.

BURY, H., Notes on the River Wey, 318–33 w. map & pls. xxxvi–xxxvii (maps).

*Busycon canaliculatum*, 631 & pl. lv.

Buttern Hill (Cornwall), stream-tin & wolfram deposits at & near, 386 *et seqq.* figs. & pls. xlv–xlvi.

Buxton (Derbyshire), sect. along Midland Ry. betw. Longstone and, descr., 37–42, 53.

Cae Deicws (Glyn Ceiriog), 561, 564, 565; columnar jointing in Craig-y-Pandy Ash at, 563 fig., 564.

Cae-mawr Fault (Glyn Ceiriog), 561, 566, 585–87 fig.

Caerbwdy Series (Pebidian), 370–71.

Caerfai Beds in St. David's area, 364–65.

Calcite-veins, phacoidal, in *Posidonomya*-Limestones, 426 fig., 427.

Caldon Low (Derbyshire), probable horiz. of *Productus-humerosus* Beds. of, 44.

*Callipteridium* sp., 118 fig. & pl. ix.

Cambrian (& Silurian) geology in Geol. Soc. publications, lxxvii–lxxix; Cambr. glacial beds in S. Australia, 234–63 figs. & pls. xix–xxvi; Cambr. of St. David's area, 364–66; relat. of do. to granophyre & volc. series, 375–81 figs.

Canada, Geol. Surv. maps presented, viii; (E.), struct. & relats. of Laurent. System in, 127–48 figs. & pls. xi–xiii.

*Cantharus Martinianus*, 630–31 & pl. lv.

Cape Colony, Geol. Surv. maps presented, ii, cxxxii; Rhætic plants from, 84 *et seqq.*

Caradocian, correlat. of, 592.

Carbonate of lime, natural solution of, in limestone-areas, 339–40, 343–44.

Carboniferous geology in Geol. Soc. publications, lxxxi–lxxxiv; Carb. rocks of Loughshinny, 413–74 figs. & pls. xlix–l (foss.).

Carboniferous Limestone of Midland area, faunal success. in, 34–82 figs. & pl. i (foss.); interspaces in Carb. L. oolite of Clifton, 207 & pl. xviii; surfaces of pressure-solution in C. L. of Stoney Middleton, 225–26 fig.; *see also* Loughshinny, *&c.*

*Carcinophyllum curkeenense*, sp. nov., 464 & pl. xlix.

—— (Lonsdaloid), 462 & pl. xlix.

*Cardita protovariegata*, 625 & pl. liv.

*Cardium ambiguum*, 636.

Carlyan Limestone, additions to fauna of, 440–42.

Carn-arwig (Pembrokeshire), 372; Cambr. conglom. involved in basic intrusion at, 380–81 fig.

Carn Llidi (Pembrokeshire), 273 *et seqq.*; biotite-norite of, 278–80 w. chem. anal., 288–89 & pl. xxix (microscop. sects.); bronzite-diorite & diabase of, 281–82 & pl. xxix (microscop. sects.); *see also* St. David's Head.

CARRUTHERS, R. G., 436, 453.

*Cassidaria* sp. (Eocene), 639.

*Cassidea acanthina*, sp. nov., 629 & pl. lvii.

Catalogue of Library, x, xiii.

Catchecoma Gneiss (E. Canada), 142.

Ceiriog, *see* Glyn.

Celestine in Silurian exposures of Tortworth, 525 *et seqq.*, 544, 545.

Centenary Conversazione, ii; Centenary Record, x; centenary review of published work of Geol. Soc., lxix–cxxi.

*Ceratotrochus Alcockianus*, 622.

*Cerithium (?)* sp. (Miocene), 628.

—— (?) sp. (Eocene), 638–39 & pl. liv.

ČERNÝŠEV, F., elected For. Corresp., v.

Chalk, contraction of, after deposition, 213; Chalk of Trimingham, subdivisions of, 401–12 figs. & pls. xlvii–xlviii (maps); *see also* Cretaceous.

Charfield-Green district (Gloucest.), Llandovery rocks of, 514–16 fig.; Wenlock Limest., &c. of, 533; sect. fr. C. G. to Eastwood, 532.

Cheirotheroid (?) footprints in Lower Sandstones of Exeter district, 496–500 & pl. li.

Chemical analyses, *see* Analyses; chem. relats. of rock-types in St. David's-Head 'rock-series,' 290–92 fig.

Chert, development of, in Carb. Limest. of Midland area, 56–57.

China-clay in Bodmin-Moor area, 395–96.

'China-clay Quarry,' *see* Pandy & Craig-y-Pandy.

Chin Division (Arakan Series), 606; non-existent (?), 618.

Chindwin (Lr.) & Pakokku districts (Burma), Tertiary rocks of, 616–17.

Chlorite-minerals in Glendalough rocks, 479, 491.

*Chonetes compressa*, nom. nov., 78–79 fig. & pl. i,

—— *crassistria* & cf. *crassistria*, 78.

—— cf. *hardrensis*, 78.

*Choristites*, generic definition of, 30.

Chronology of Glacial Epoch in N. America, 149–51.

Cinderford Bridge (Gloucest.), non-existent, 522.

*Cladophlebis (Todites) Rœsserti*, 98 & pl. viii.

Clare Co. (Ireland), Carb. Limest. of, 81–82.

CLARKE, H. E., 479.

Clays, washing-up, &c. of, 199; *see also* Fine-grained, &c.

CLAYDEN, A. W., on the Occurrence of Footprints in the Lower Sandstones of the Exeter District, 496–500 & pl. li.

Cleavages (two) in Colonsay rocks, 300 *et seqq.* figs.; nature of second cleavage *ibid.*, 307–10 w. map & pls. xxxiii–xxxiv.

Clegyr Agglomerate (Pebidian), 370.

Clinozoisite in Glendalough rocks, 483–84 fig., 486, 487 fig.

*Clisiophyllida, Lithostrotion*-like, 462–63; new genus of Cl., 464–65 fig.

*Clisiophyllum* aff. *M'Coyanum*, 73–74 & pl. i.

Coal-pebble fr. Nanaimo, iii.

Coed-y-glyn Sill (Glyn Ceiriog), 568–69.

COLE, T. S., 207.

COLLARD & SONS, 497, 499, 500.

Colonsay (Hebrides), earth-movements of, 297–312 figs. & pls. xxxiii–xxxiv.

Columnar jointing in Craig-y-Pandy Ash, 563 fig., 564; in Coed-y-glyn Sill, 569.

Comox Lake (B.C.), 150.

Concretions, 215–20.

Coniston-Limestone Series compared w. Bala Series of Glyn Ceiriog, 590–91, 592.

*Conites* sp., 122 fig.

Contact-phenomena around the Methuen bathylith (E. Canada), 141–42 & fig. on p. 140 w. pl. xi; do. of Glendalough amphibolite, 491–92; of Bartestree intrusion, 501–503.

Contraction of rocks after deposition, 177 *et seqq.*, 214; *see also* Interspaces.

*Conus avaensis*, 632.

—— *scalaris*, 632.

—— sp. (Eocene), 641.

Copper-mine, abandoned, on shore of Co. Dublin, 428.

Coral-reef limestones, proportion of cavities in, 203–204.

Coralline Oolite, interspaces in, 209 & pl. xvii (microscop. sect.).

*Corbula harpa*, 637.

—— *socialis*, 626.

*Cordaites Hislopi*, 120–22 figs.

Corundum-bearing syenites in E. Canada, 140–41.

Corwen Grit, its relat. to Bala Series & Glyn Grit, 547, 553, 571, 576–77, 578.

Council, report of, ix–xi; Council & Officers elected, xxiv–xxv.

Craig-y-Pandy Ash in Glyn-Ceiriog Valley, 552; detailed descr. of do., 558–65 figs.

Crake-Low cutting (Derbyshire), 59.

Cressbrook Tunnel (Derbyshire), 39, 41.

Cretaceous (Lr.) fishes fr. Ilhéos, 358–62 & pls. xlii–xliii; *see also* Chalk, &c.

Crockley's Farm (Gloucest.), 519.

CROSTHWAITE, P.M., [exhibits specim. fr. E. Yorks.], v.

Cullimore's Quarry (Tortworth), view of part of, 515.

CULLIS, C. G., [on Silur. rocks of Tortworth Inlier], 544–45.

Ourkeen - Hill Limestone, 428–29; = *Dibunophyllum*-Limestones, 433, 435, 437, 453.

Currents, effects of, on subsidence of solids in water, 176–81, 194 *et seqq.*; *see also* Drift-bedding, Ripple-drift, &c.

Cwm-Clwyd Ash in Glyn-Ceiriog Valley, 551; detailed descr. of do., 555–57 fig.

*Cyathaxonia rushiana*, 460 & pl. xlix; subzone of, in Midland area, 36 *et seqq.*, 50–53, 57–63; do. compared w. that of S.W. Province, 66; & compared w. that of Rush sequence, 68; in Loughshinny area, 415–22 figs., 433 *et seqq.*; fauna of do., 443–44, 454.

*Cyathophyllum regium*, 70.

*Cypræa (Cypræedia) elegans*, 629 & pl. lvii.

—— *Everwijni (?)*, 628 & pl. lvii.

DALTON, L. V., Notes on the Geology of Burma, 604–43 w. maps & pls. liv–lvii (foss.).

DALTON, W. H., 604.

Damery (Gloucest.), Llandovery rocks of, 516–17.

*Danæopsis Hughesi*, 95–97 fig. & pl. vi.

Danian (?) at Trimingham, 401 *et seqq.*, 410–11.

DANIEL-PIDGEON Fund, list of awards, xxxv; awarded to J. A. Douglas, cxxix.

Daniel's Wood (Gloucest.), Llandovery rocks of, 517–19 w. map; Wenlock Beds of, 528–31 fig.

Davidstow Moor (Cornwall), 384, 387, 397.

DAVIS, W., 382.

Decalcification of *Cyathaxonia*-Beds, &c., 417–18 fig., 424, 436.

Denbighshire Slates in Glyn-Ceiriog Valley, 554; detailed descr. of do., 579.

Densiphyllids (Loughshinny Carb. rocks), 460.

*Densiphyllum rushianum*, sp. nov., 459–60.

Derbyshire (N.), faunal success. in Carb.-Limest. of N. Staffs. and, 34–82 figs. & pl. i (foss.).

Devero, Valle (Italy), antigorite-serpentines from, 155–57.

Devonian geology in Geol. Soc. publications, lxxx–lxxxi; Devonian limestones, surfaces of pressure-solution in, 225, 226.

DEWEY, H., [on Bodmin - Moor plateaux], 397; (& C. Reid), the Origin of the Pillow-Lava near Port Isaac in Cornwall, 264–69 & pls. xxvii–xxviii.

Diabase (& bronzite-diorite) of Carn Llidi, 281–82 w. chem. anal. & pl. xxix (microscop. sects.).

*Dibunophyllum*-Limestones of Loughshinny area, 428–29, 433 *et seqq.*; fauna of do., 436–38, 453.

—— *derbiense*, sp. nov., 75 & pl. i.

—— *matlockense*, sp. nov., 74–75 & pl. i.

—— aff. *Muirheadi*, 463 & pl. xlix.

—— θ, subzone of, in Midland area, 36 *et seqq.*, 42–44; do. compared w. that of S.W. Province, 64.

Differentiated magma-basin, origin of St. David's-Head rock-series from, 292, 293.

Dimetian, extent & boundaries of, in St. David's area, 373–74.

Diorite of Scalasaig, 300.

*Diphyphyllum subibicinum*, 461 & pl. xlix.

*Distorsio cancellinus*, 629–30 & pl. lv.

DIXON, E. E. L. [on Cornish plateaux, &c.], 398.

Dogsthorpe, *see* Peterborough.

Dolerites of Bartestree, 503–507 & pl. lii (microscop. sects.), 509.

Dolhir Beds in Glyn-Ceiriog Valley, 553; detailed descr. of do., 570–71; lists of foss. from do., 572–73; Dolhir Fault, 553.

*Dolium* sp. (Eocene), 639 & pl. lv.

Dolomite in *Dibunophyllum*-Limestones, 428; dolomites of Tarnthal mass, 598 *et seqq.*

Donors to Library, lists of, xiv–xx.

Dorn Valley (Oxon.), 337 *et seqq.* & pl. xxxix.

*Dosinia protojuvenilis*, 625.

DOUGLAS, J. A., award fr. Daniel-Pidgeon Fund to, cxxix; [on Carb.-Limest. of W. coast of Ireland], 81–82, 473–74.

Dove Dale (Derbyshire), 55.

Drift, deep channel of, at Hitchin, 8–26 w. map & sects.; *see also* Glacial, *&c.*

Drift-bedding (in water-currents), 186–89; definition of, 177.

Drumanagh Headland (Co. Dublin), 419 *et seqq.*

DUCIE, Earl of, 512, 537.

Dunite fr. New Zealand, 159.

Dunstable (Beds.), palæoliths found near, 1, 2.

Dwyka Conglomerate, 109–10.

Dyke-rocks in W. Liberia, 315; *see also* Lamprophyres, *&c.*

Dye's Farm (Herts.), well-sect. descr., 13.

Earth-movements of Colonsay, 297–312 figs. & pls. xxxiii–xxxiv; do. affectg. Silur. rocks of Tortworth area, 535, 543.

Easthope (Shropshire), Wenlock Limest. from, 209 & pl. xviii.

Eastwood Park (Gloucest.), Llandovery rocks of, 522; sect. fr. Eastwood to Charfield Green, 532.

Ecca Series, 83, 110, 111; foss. plants fr. Vereeniging assigned to, 123.

ECCLES, J., 156.

Echinoderms, remains of, easily washed along by water-currents, 189.

Eilean Easdale, *see* Kiloran Bay.

Election of Auditors, v; of Council & Officers, xxiv–xxv; of Fellows, i, ii, iii, iv, v, vii, cxxvi, cxxvii, cxxix, cxxxi; of Foreign Members, i, iv; of For. Corresp., iv, v, cxxix.

Ellingham's Pit, *see* Leverstock Green.

ELSDEN, A. V., 293.

ELSDEN, J. V., the St. David's-Head 'Rock-Series' (Pembrokeshire), 273–94 figs. & pls. xxix–xxxii (microscop. sects.); [on geol. struct. of St. David's area], 383; [on primary analcime], 511.

Elton (Derbyshire), sect. descr., 54–55.

Engadine (Switzerland), serpentines from, 166–68.

Enstatite-quartz-gabbro of St. David's Head, 280–81 w. chem. anal. & pls. xxix–xxx (microscop. sects.).

Eocene of Burma, 606, 607 *et seqq.*, 611–12, 617–18, 621, 642.

Erratics in Cambrian till of S. Australia, 240–41 & figs. on pp. 242–46 & pl. xix.

Erw-gerrig (Glyn Ceiriog), 555.

Estimates for 1908, xxxvi–xxxvii.

*Eupsammia regalis*, 622.

EVANS, Sir JOHN, Some Recent Discoveries of Palæolithic Implements, 1–5 figs.; [resolution of Council on decease of], cxxxi.

EVANS, O. H., [on pillow-lavas of Taltal district], 270–71.

Evenlode valley (Oxon.), 335, 338 *et seqq.* & pl. xxxviii.

Exeter district (Devon), footprints in Lower Sandstones of, 496–500 & pl. li.

Falfield & Whitfield (Gloucest.), Wenlock Beds of, 525–28.

False bedding, restricted definition, 177, 187.

Farnham (Surrey), palæolithic gravels of, 323–27 & pl. xxxvi (map).

Faulting in St. David's area, 364 365–66, 377, 382, 383; in Glyn-Ceiriog area, 546–47, 580–88 figs.

Feather-amphibolites, 138 & pl. xii.

Fellows elected, i, ii, iii, iv, v, vii, cxxvi, cxxvii, cxxix, cxxxi; names read out, cxxxi, cxxxii; number of, ix, xxi; obituaries of, lix–lxix.

Felspars in St. David's-Head 'rock-series,' 285–86 & pl. xxx (microscop. sect.); in Glendalough 'mixed rock,' 489.

Felspathic rocks of Greystones, 494.

Felstone, restricted use of term, 564.

FFOOKS, E. A., [exhibits specims. fr. Mintern Magna], v.

*Ficula Theobaldi*, 639.

Financial report, xxxvi–xlii.

Fine-grained material, conditions of deposition, &c., 189–96; structure of, 212–14; *see also* Langdale Slates.

FITZHARDINGE, Earl, 512.

FLETT, J. S., [on Scottish antigorite-serpentines], 170; [on pillow-lavas], 270; [on quartz-norites, &c. of Britain], 294-95; [on earth-movements of Colonsay], 311.

Flinders Ranges (S. Australia), 234 *et seqq.*

Fluviatile origin of high-level deposits in Herts., &c, controverted, 5 *et seqq.*

Fluxion-structure in Trwyn-Llwyd rock, 277 & pl. xxx (microscop. sect.).

Footprints in Lower Sandstones of Exeter district, 496-500 & pl. li.

Foreign Correspondents elected, iv, v, cxxix; list of, xxvii.

Foreign geology in Geol. Soc. publications, xcvi-civ.

Foreign Members elected, i, iv; list of, xxvi.

Frant (Sussex), flint-implements from, cxxix.

Fron-Frys Slates in Glyn-Ceiriog Valley, 553-54; detailed descr. of do., 578 w. list of foss.

'Fundamental Gneiss' of E. Canada, 127, 129, 145, 146.

*Fusella.* generic definition of, 29.

*Fusus,* sp. (Eocene), 639-40.

Gabbros of E. Canada, 139.

Gaddesden Row (Herts), palæoliths found at, 3 & fig. on p. 2.

*Gangamopteris cyclopteroides,* 117-18 & pl. x.

Garnet in Glendalough rocks, 487, 491.

Garnet-schists (& gneisses), in W. Liberia, 313-14.

GARWOOD, E. J., x; [exhibits Carb. brachiopods], iv; [receives Lyell fund for T. F. Sibly], xlix; [on *Cyatharonia* - Beds in Yoredale area], 82; [communicates G. F. Wright's paper], 149.

GEER, Baron G. J. DE, elected For. Corresp., iv.

GEIKIE, Sir ARCHIBALD, on the Published Work of the Geological Society of London during the First Century of the Society's Existence, lxix-cxxv; elected Foreign Secretary, xxv; [addresses to medallists & recipients of awards], xliii *et seqq.*; [obituaries of deceased Fellows, &c.], l-lxix; [on earth-movements in Colonsay, &c.], 312.

Geological Society, published work of, during 1st century of existence, lxix-cxxv.

Geological-Survey maps presented, ii, v, vi, viii, cxxviii.

Glacial Conglomerate (Dwyka), 109-10; Glacial geology in Geol. Soc. publications, lxxxix-xcvi; Glac. Epoch in N. America, chronology of, 149-51; Glac. Cambrian beds in S. Australia, 234-63 figs. & pls. xix-xxvi; Glac. conditions in Cornish area, 386, 389, 390, 398 *et seqq.*

Glendalough (Wicklow), hornblendic rocks of Greystones and, 475-95 figs.

*Glossopteris angustifolia,* 116.
—— var. *tæniopteroides,* nov., 113-16 figs. & pl. ix.
—— *Browniana,* 117, & figs. on p. 116.
—— *indica,* 116-17.

*Glycimeris* sp., 635.

Glyme area (Oxon.), solution-valleys in, 335-44 w. map & pls. xxxviii-xxxix.

Glyn Ceiriog (N. Wales), Bala & Llandovery rocks of, 546-95 figs. & pl. liii (map).

Glyn Grit & Limestone (Glyn Ceiriog), 553; detailed descr. of do., 571-77 figs. & list of foss.

Gneisses, sedimentary, of E. Canada, 136-37; gneisses, &c. of W. Liberia, 313-14; *see also* 'Fundamental Gneiss,' Granite-gneiss, &c.

Grains of water-deposited material, varying size of, 185-86; interspaces betw. grains of such material, 200-203; *see also* Fine-grained.

Grainger Mt. (S. Australia), sect. to Port Germein, descr. & fig. 254-55, 256.

Grange (Borrowdale), specims. from, exhibited, cxxxii.

Granite & granite-gneiss of E. Canada, 130-35 fig. & chem. anals., 140 fig., 141-42 & pl. xi, 146; granite-gneisses of W. Liberia, 313.

Granitic magmas absorbing amphibolites, 490.

Granophyre of St. David's, 373; relat. of Cambrian to do., 377-79 w. map.

Grantham (Lincs.), Oolitic limest. from, 206-207 & pl. xvii.

Graptolitic Slates (Glyn Ceiriog), 569-70.

Gratton Dale (Derbyshire), sect. descr., 54-55.

'Gravel-ore' (galena), 399-400.

Great Oolite, solution-valleys in, 335-44 w. map & pls. xxxviii-xxxix.

GREEN, J. F. N., the Geological Structure of the St. David's Area (Pembrokeshire), 363–82 figs. & pl. xliv (map), 383.

Greensand (Lr.), contraction in, 177.

Grenville Series (Laurentian), 127, 129, 130, 136–37, 142–43; its relat. to other pre-Cambrian series, 144–45.

Greystones (Wicklow), hornblendic rocks of Glendalough and, 475–95 figs.

GRIESBACH, C. L., obituary of, lxiii.

GRIFFITH, NORTON, [presents maps of Semipalatinsk Territory], ii.

Grimm's Dyke (Oxon.), 335 & pl. xxxviii.

GROOM, T. (& P. Lake), the Bala & Llandovery Rocks of Glyn Ceiriog (North Wales), 546–93 figs. & pl. liii (map).

GROTH, P. VON, Wollaston medal awarded to, xliii–xliv.

Hæmatite-schists in W. Liberia, 314, 316, 317.

Hafod-y-gynfawr (Glyn Ceiriog), 578.

HALL, T. C., 265, 390.

Hälleflinta, definition of, 367.

Hanging valleys in W. Liberia, 316, 317.

HARKER, A., 410.

HARLE, J., 512, 518, 528.

HARRINGTON, B. J., obituary of, lxiv–lxv.

HARRISON, B., 5 et seqq.

Hastings Series (Laurentian), 127, 129, 143.

HATCH, F. H., [on Vereeniging coal-measures, &c.], 125–26; [on Bartestree intrusion], 511.

'Head' or wash of Bodmin-Moor area, 386 et seqq.

HECTOR, Sir JAMES, obituary of, lxi–lxii.

Hemel Hempstead, see Leverstock Green.

HERRIES, R. S., x.

Hertfordshire (& Beds.), palæolithic implements from, 1–7 figs.; see also Hitchin, &c.

High-level platforms of Bodmin Moor, & their relat. to stream-tin & wolfram-deposits, 384–400 figs. & pls. xlv–xlvi.

Highway-Close Barn railway-cutting (Derbyshire), 59.

HILL, Rev. E., 154; [on Trimingham Chalk], 412.

HILL, W., on a Deep Channel of Drift at Hitchin (Hertfordshire), 8–24 w. map & sects.

HIND, W., 69, 436, 453; [on Carb. Limest. &c. of Midland area] 80–81; [on do. of Rush sequence, &c.], 472.

'History of the Geological Society,' x.

Hitchin (Herts.), deep channel of Drift at, 8–26 w. map & sects.

Hiz Valley (Herts.), 12–13, 15 et seqq. w. sect.

HOBSON, B., lxvi.

Holmpatrick Limestone, 429, 431–32, 433, 434; fauna of do., 438–40, 453.

Holwell Bury (Herts.), boring at, 19.

Homœomorphy, brachiopodan ('Spirifer glaber'), 27–33.

Horizontal surface, drifting on, 179.

Hornblende in St. Davids-Head 'rock-series,' 289.

Hornblende-schists of W. Liberia, 313, 314.

Hornblendic rocks of Glendalough & Greystones, 475–95 figs.; see also Amphibolite.

Hornblendite of Kiloran Bay, 299–300.

Hornfels of Glendalough, 492 fig.

Horseshoe Farm (Tortworth), Wenlock & Ludlow Beds of, 524–25.

Horsley Quarry, see Middlemill.

HOWCHIN, Rev. W., Glacial Beds of Cambrian Age in South Australia, 234–59 figs. & pls. xix–xxvi.

HOWLEY, J. P., [presents geol. map of Newfoundland], ii.

HUDLESTON, W. H., [on Silur. rocks of Tortworth Inlier], 543–44.

HUDSON, —, 527.

HUGHES, T. W. H., obituary of, lxiii–lxiv.

Hungary, Geol. Surv. maps presented, iv, v.

Huronian, equivalents in E. Canada, 144.

Huttonian doctrines in Geol. Soc. publications, lxxii–lxxiv.

Hypersthene-magnetite rock in W. Liberia, 314.

Hypsocormus fr. Neuquen, cxxvi.

Ice-agency producing Cambrian till of S. Australia, 255–58; see also Drift, Glacial, &c.

Ickleford (Herts.), boring at, 18.

Idioblastic, definition of term, 482.

Ightham (Kent), implements found near, 5 et seqq.

Ilhéos (Brazil), Cretaceous fishes from, 358–62 & pls. xlii–xliii.

ILIFFE, J. D. (& H. Basedow), on a Formation known as 'Glacial Beds of Cambrian Age' in South Australia, 260.

Ilmenite in Glendalough rocks, 486.

Implements, palæolithic, fr. Beds. & Herts., 1–7 figs.; do. fr. Frant, cxxix.

Interglacial (?) periods in Cambrian of S. Australia, 258.

Interspaces in sedimentary rocks, 200–203, 205 et seqq.; determination of amount of, 204–205.

Intrusive rocks, basic, in St. David's area, 379–81; do. of Bartestree, 501–11 fig. & pl. lii (microscop. sects.); see also Lamprophyres, &c.

Ippollitts–Langley valley (Herts.), 13–14 w. sect.

Irawadi Series (Burma), 606, 621, 642, 644.

Ireland, Geol. Surv. maps presented, v.

Ironmill Wood (Gloucest.), Llandovery rocks of, 516–17.

Iron-ores in St. David's Head 'rock-series,' 288.

ISSEL, A., elected For. Member, iv.


JACKSON, H. P., 382.

JACKSON, W., 13.

Jamestown (S. Australia), erratics in Cambrian till near, 240.

Japan, Geol. Surv. maps presented, v.

JENKINSON, Sir GEORGE, 512.

Jet, glaciated, fr. E. Yorks., v.

JOHNS, C., [on Carb. Limest. succession], 473.

JOHNSTON-LAVIS, H. J., [exhibits cartoons of Vesuvius], cxxxi.

'Joint-valleys' defined, 341.

JONES, O. T., [motion seconded by], cxxxviii; [on Bala & Llandovery of Glyn Ceiriog], 594.

Jouannetia protocumingi, sp. nov., 626 & pl. liv.

Jurassic fossils fr. Neuquen, cxxxvi; see also Great Oolite, Liassic, &c.


Kaolin, see China-clay.

Karroo System, subdivision of, 83–84, 110–11.

Kasshabog Lake (Ont.), amphibolite invaded by granite-gneiss, 142 & pl. xi.

Keewatin Series, 129, 144, 147.

Keeweenawan Series. 144.

Kellan Head (Cornwall), pillow-lavas of, 265.

KENNETH, —, 19.

Kentallenites of Colonsay, 300.

Kentish Rag, interspaces in, 211.

Kenton Marsh (Cornwall), stream-tin workings on, 391–95 fig.

KIDSTON, R., 436, 453.

Kiloran Bay (Colonsay), limestone, &c. of, 299; hornblendite of, 299–300; margin of lamprophyre in phyllite on coast N. of, 303 fig.; syenite-intrusion of, 304–306 w. map.

KLEIN, J. F. C., obituary of, lviii–lix.

Koninckophyllum proprium, sp. nov., 70–71 & pl. i.

—— spp., 71–72, 461 & pl. xlix.

Kyanite-schists in W. Liberia, 313.

Kyetubok (Burma), 612.


LAKE, P. (& T. Groom), the Bala & Llandovery Rocks of Glyn Ceiriog (North Wales), 546–93 figs. & pl. liii (map).

Lake District, Coniston–Limestone Series, &c. compared w. Bala Series of Glyn Ceiriog, 590–91, 592.

LAMPLUGH, G., lxviii; [receives Lyell medal for R. D. Oldham], xlvi; [on Rush sequence, &c.], 472–73.

Lamprophyres of Colonsay, 300 et seqq., 304 et seqq.; relat. of earth-movements to do., 303–304 figs.; varied age of do., 306–307 fig.

Lane Conglomerate & Limestones. 429–33 figs., 434 et seqq.; fauna of do., 438–40, 453.

LANG, W. D., 533.

Langdale Slates, exemplifying condits. of deposit. of fine-grained material, 196–98 & pls. xiv–xvi.

Langley-Ippollitts Valley (Herts.), 13–14 w. sect.

LAPPARENT, A. DE, [resolution of Council on decease of], cxxxi.

LAPWORTH, C., 69.

Lassenose of E. Canada, 132–33.

LA TOUCHE, T. H. D., lxii, lxiv.

Laurentian, use of term, 144–45; Laur. System in E. Canada, struct. & relats. of, 127–48 figs. & pls. xi–xiii.

Lavas (pillow-) nr. Port Isaac, origin of, 264–72 & pls. xxvii–xxviii.

LAW, R., obituary of, lxviii.

'Leat' = flume or lade, 390.

LEEDS, A. N., 346, 357.

LEEDS, E. T., on *Metriorhynchus brachyrhynchus* (Deslong.) from the Oxford Clay near Peterborough, 345–56 figs. & pls. xl–xli.

Leinster Granite, 475, 476.

*Lepidodendron Pedroanum*, 120 & pl. ix.

—— *vereenigingense*, sp. nov., 119–20 fig. & pl. x.

*Lepidotus Souzai*, sp. nov., 359–60 & pl. xliii.

LESLIE, T. N. (& A. C. Seward), Permo-Carboniferous Plants from Vereeniging (Transvaal), 109–25 figs. & pls. ix–x.

Letpan Choung (Burma), 614–15.

Leucoxene in St. David's-Head 'rock-series,' 288.

Leverstock Green (Herts.), palæoliths found at, 3 & fig. on p. 4.

Lewisian Gneiss (?) of Colonsay, 299.

Liassic limestone of the Tarntbaler Köpfe, 598, 601 *et seqq.*

Liberia (W.), W. Africa, petrology & physiography of, 313–17 & pl. xxxv (map).

Library, progress of card-catalogue, xiii; lists of donors to, xiv–xx; Library & Museum Committee, report of, xi–xiii.

Lime, carbonate of, *see* Carbonate.

Limekiln Cove (Co. Dublin), sect. to Loughshinny Bay, descr. & fig., 422–28; *Dibunophyllum*-Limestones N. of, 428–29.

Limestones, metamorphosed, of Grenville Series, 136, 140 fig., 141–42; contraction in limest., 177; interspaces in do., 206 *et seqq.* & pls. xvii–xviii; surfaces of pressure-solution in do., 224–26 fig.; *see also* Carboniferous Limestone, &c.

LISTER, J. J., 163.

*Lithostrotion* cf. *affine*, 462 & pl. xlix.

—— *irregulare* (Diphyphylloid variant), 462.

—— -like Clisiophyllids, 462–63.

'Lit-par-lit' injections of granite into limestone, 140 fig.

Litton Tunnel (Derbyshire), sect. to Miller's-Dale Limeworks, 40.

Llandovery rocks of Tortworth Inlier, 513–22 figs., 534; remarks on foss. from do., 535–36; list of foss. from do., 538–40; (& Bala) rocks of Glyn Ceiriog, 546–95 figs. & pl. liii (map).

Llechrhydau (Glyn Ceiriog), 555, 564, 583, 584 *et seqq.*; sect. on banks of Morda S. of, 556.

Lofty (Mt.) Ranges (S. Australia), 234 *et seqq.*

LOMAS, J., [on Bala & Llandovery of Glyn Ceiriog], 593–94.

Longstone (Derbyshire), sect. along Midland Ry. betw. Buxton and, descr., 37–42, 53, 57–58.

*Lonsdalia duplicata*, 72–73 & pl. i.

—— *floriformis*, subzone of, in Midland area, 36 *et seqq.*, 44–50, 53–57; do. compared w. that of S.W. Province, 65–66.

—— *rugosa*, 73.

Loughshinny (Co. Dublin), Carb. rocks of, 413–74 figs. & pls. xlix–l (fossils).

LUCAS, TINDAL, 16.

*Lucina globulosa*, 625 & pl. lv.

Ludlow (?) & Wenlock Beds of Tortworth Inlier, 522–34 figs.; remarks on foss. from do., 436–37; list of foss. from do., 541–43.

LYELL medallists, list of, xxxi; L. geological fund, list of awards from, xxxiii.

MACALISTER, D. A., 385.

MACLAREN, J. M., [communicates paper by H. Basedow & J. D. Iliffe], 260; [moves resolution for poll of non-resident Fellows], cxxxi.

*Mactra protorecresii*, 626.

Magnesia, high percentage of, in St. David's-Head 'rock-series,' 292.

Magnesian Limestone, contraction in, since deposition, 178; inter-spaces in, 209; concretions in, 217, 219.

Magnetite-hypersthene rocks in W. Liberia, 314.

Magwe (& Myingyan) districts (Burma), Tertiary of, 613.

Magyisan (Burma), 612.

MAITLAND, A. GIBB, [seconds resolution for poll of non-resident Fellows], cxxxi.

Manifold Valley (Staffs.), *Lonsdalia*-subzone in, 56.

Manor Farm, *see* Wetton.

Map of the Hitchin valley, 9; map showg. outcrop of Carb. Limest. in Midland area, 35; map showg. posit. of Haliburton & Bancroft areas in relat. to Laurentian Highlands, &c., 128; (Canad. Geol. Surv.) map of portions of Hastings, Haliburton, & Peterborough Counties (Ont.), pl. xiii; map of the Val-Antigorio district, 154; map of the St. David's-Head area, 274; map showg. stratigraphy of Colonsay

& Oronsay, 298; do. illustratg. increase in intensity of second earth-movement in those islands, 301; map of Kiloran syenite-intrusion, 305; map showg. strike & dip of axial planes of secondary folds & of strain-slip cleavage in Colonsay & Oronsay, 310; map of part of W. Liberia, pl. xxxv; map showg. relation of Wey R. to Blackwater R., 320; map showg. the six sections of Wey R. that lie within Wealden area, pl. xxxvi; map of Alton district (Hants), pl. xxxvii; of the Wootton region (Oxon.), 336; of the Porth-clais area (Pembrokeshire), 378; of the St. David's area, pl. xliv; of the Trimingham Chalk, 402 & pls. xlvii–xlviii; of outcrops of Carb. Limest., &c. along the coast nr. Loughshinny, 414; of Tortworth Inlier & immediate neighbourhood, 513; of neighbourhood of Daniel's Wood & Middlemill, 518; of country around Glyn Ceiriog, pl. liii; of the Tarnthaler Köpfe, 596; of the Padoukbin & other districts in Burma, 607, 610, 614.

Maps presented, ii, iv, v, vi, vii, viii, cxxviii, cxxxii.

MARTIN, E. A., [motion proposed by], cxxvii; [exhibits flint-implemts. fr. Frant], cxxix.

*Martinia*, generic definition of, 30–31 et seqq.
—— *glabra*, mut. P, 468 & pl. l.
—— *ovaliglabra*, sp. nov., 468–69 & pl. l.

*Martiniopsis*, 32.

MATLEY, C. A., the Carboniferous Rocks at Loughshinny (County Dublin), 413–36 figs., 474.

Matlock district (Derbyshire), *Lonsdalia*-subzone, &c. in, 55; *Cyathaxonia*-subzone in, 58.

*Mawsonia minor*, sp. nov., 358–59 & pl. xlii.

*Melongena pseudobucephala*, 631.

Menevian shale (St. David's area), 365.

Mesozoic geology in Geol. Soc. publications, lxxxv–lxxxviii.

Methuen district (Ont.), granite-gneiss invading amphibolite, 142 & pl. xi.

*Metriorhynchus brachyrhynchus* fr. Oxford Clay nr. Peterborough, 345–57 figs. & pls. xl–xli.

Mica, final velocity of subsidence of flakes in water, 173; tendency of

flakes not to arrange themselves in smallest space, 203; see also Biotite, &c.

*Michelinia glomerata*, 69.
—— *megastoma*, 455.
—— *tenuisepta*, 455–56 fig.; var. *favositoides* nov., 456 & pl. xlix.

Middlemill & Woodford (Gloucest.), Llandovery rocks of, 519–22.

Middleton Dale (Derbyshire), *Lonsdalia*-subzone in, 54.

Midland area (N. Derbs. & N. Staffs.), faunal success. in Carb. Limest. of, 34–82 figs. & pl. i (foss.).

Miller's-Dale Limeworks(Derbyshire), sect. to Litton Tunnel, 40; Miller's Dale, faunal facies of *Lonsdalia*-subzone in, 48.

Millstone Grit, contraction in, since deposition, 179.

Minbu (& Thayetmyo) districts (Burma), Tertiary rocks of, 609–13 w. map; M. & Pakokku districts, do., 613–16 w. map.

Mindegyi (Burma), 611.

Miocene of Burma, 606, 607 et seqq., 613 et seqq., 618–21, 641–42.

Mitcham Quartzites (S. Australia), 248, 249 et seqq., 253.

Mojsisovics, J. A. E. von, obituary of, liv–lviii.

Molteno Beds, 83–84; fossil plants from, 85 et seqq.

Monsal Dale (Derbyshire), faunal facies of *Lonsdalia*-subzone in, 48.

MORGAN, C. LLOYD, 537.

Mullion I. (Cornwall), pillow-lavas of, 270.

MURCHISON medallists, list of, xxx; M. geological fund, list of awards from, xxxi.

Muscovite in Glendalough rocks, 491.

Museum, annual report on, xiii.

Myingyan (& Magwe) districts (Burma), Tertiary of, 613.

Myvatn, Lake (Iceland), pillow-lavas near, 271.


Names of Fellows read out, cxxxi, cxxxii.

Nanaimo (B.C.), coal-pebble from, iii.

Nanoose (B.C.), 150.

Nant Iorwerth (Glyn Ceiriog), 566, 581, 588.

Nant Llafar (Glyn Ceiriog), 553, 574, 579; sect. in, 576.

Nant Tyn-y-Twmpath (Glyn Ceiriog), 569, 570, 571, 584.

*Natica obscura*, 627.
—— sp. (Eocene), 637.

*Natica (Ampullina) grossa*, var. *oblonga*, 637–38 & pl. lvi.
—— (——) *ponderosa*, 638.
—— (——) *spherica (?)*, 637 & pl. lvi.
—— (*Globularia*) *gibberosa*, 627–28 & pl. lvii.
Nepheline - syenites of E. Canada, 140–41, 146.
Neptunism in Geol. Soc. publications, lxxi–lxxiv.
Neuquen (N. Patagonia), Jurassic foss. exhibited, cxxvi.
Newfoundland, geol. map presented, ii.
New Rand Goldfield (O.R.C.), map presented, v.
New Zealand, antigorite-serpentines, &c. from, 159–61, 165–66.
NEWTON, R. B., 622; [on Tertiary of Burma], 643–44.
Newton-Grange cutting (Derbyshire), sect. descr. & fig., 59–61.
Ngalaingyoung (Burma), 608.
Niagara Gorge (N. America), as a chronological measure, 149, 150.
Noathé (Burma), 608–609.
Norite, biotitic, of St. David's Head, 278–80 w. chem. anal. & pl. xxix (microscop. sects.).
*Nucula Alcocki*, 623.
Number of Fellows, &c., ix, xxi.
*Nummulites Beaumonti (?)*, 633.
—— sp. (Eocene of Burma), 634.

Obituaries of deceased Fellows, &c., l–lxix.
*Obolella*-beds in Cambrian of S. Australia, 238.
*Odontopteris Browni*, sp. nov., 97–98 & pl. vii.
Œcogenous (=original) characters of rocks, 601.
Ogof-Llesugn (Pembrokeshire), 377.
Old Mill, *see* Youlgreave.
Old Red Sandstone, altered, of Bartestree, 502 & pl. lii (microscop. sects.); O.R.S. of Tortworth area, 535.
OLDHAM, R. D., Lyell medal awarded to, xlvi–xlvii.
*Olenellus*-Beds, *see* Caerfai.
*Oliva* sp. (Eocene), 640.
Olivine, antigorite produced from, 165 *et seqq.*; antigoritic pseudomorphism of, 170; olivine in Glendalough rocks, 478.
Olivine-basalts & olivine-dolerites of Bartestree, 505–507, 507–509 & pl. lii (microscop. sects.).
Onkaparinga R. (S. Australia), sect. descr. & fig., 248–49.

Oolitic rocks, interspaces in, 206–209 & pls. xvii–xviii; ool. limest. in Lane-Conglomerate group, 437.
Oopina (S. Australia), sect. to Yunta Ranges, descr. & fig., 255, 257.
*Operculina canalifera*, 633.
—— *Hardiei*, 633.
Ophicalcite of Tarnthal mass, 600, 603.
Ordovician rocks of Glendalough, &c., 475, 491, 492; *see also* Glyn Ceiriog.
Oronsay (Hebrides), *see* Colonsay.
Orrorov (S. Australia), erratics in Cambrian till near, 241 & figs. on pp. 242–43.
*Ostrea lunata* (Trimingham Chalk), 402, 404 *et seqq.*, 410.
—— *yomaensis*, sp. nov., 635 & pl. liv.
OSWALD, F., [presents geol. map of Armenia], ii.
OWEN, S. M., 316.
Oxford Clay, *Metriorhynchus brachyrhynchus* from, 345–57 figs. & pls. xl–xli.

Pakokku (& Minbu) districts (Burma), Tertiary rocks of, 613–16 w. map; P. & Lr. Chindwin districts, do., 616–17.
Palæolithic implements fr. Beds. & Herts., 1–7 figs.; palæolithic gravels of Farnham, 323–27 & pl. xxxvi (map).
Palæontology in Geol. Soc. publications, cxi–cxiv.
Palæozoic geology in Geol. Soc. publications, lxxvii–lxxxv; *see also* Carboniferous, Silurian, &c.
Pandy (Glyn Ceiriog), slate-fragments in Teirw Grits at, 557 fig., 558; ash in 'China-clay Quarry,' 561.
Pandy Series, 554.
*Paracyathus cæruleus*, 622.
—— sp., 634.
Paradoxidian, *see* Menevian, Solva.
Paragneisses of Grenville Series, 136–37.
*Parallelipipedum prototortuosum*, zone of (?), 608–609, 619.
PARKINSON, J., a Note on the Petrology & Physiography of Western Liberia (West Coast of Africa), 313–16 & pl. xxxv (map), 317.
Pebbles, angles of rest of small (in water), 174–75.
Pebidian (St. David's area), 366–72; nature of junction w. Cambrian *ibid.*, 375–76.
*Pecten irravadicus*, 623.

Pegu Division (Arakan Series), 606, 607 et seqq., 618–21, 641.
Pekina Hill, see Orroroo.
Pen Lledwen (Pembrokeshire), soda-aplite of, 283–84 w. chem. anal. & pl. xxix (microscop. sects.).
Pendleside Series, local unconformity (in Midland area) between Carb. Limest. and, 63–64, & fig. on p. 62; inter-relat. of Lr. P. & uppermost Avonian, 402.
Penrhiw Series (Pebidian), 366–68.
*Pentacrinus* sp. nov (Trimingham Chalk), 403.
Pentire (Cornwall), origin of pillow-lava near, 264–72 & pls. xxvii–xxviii.
Pentreath (Anglesey), specms. of weathering from, cxxix.
Pen-y-graig Ash (Glyn Ceiriog), 569.
'Pepper-and-salt' amphibolite, 138.
Peridotite, hornblendic, of Glendalough, 477–80, figs. & chem. anals.; do. of Greystones, 492–94.
Permian geology in Geol. Soc. publications, lxxxiv–lxxxv; Perm. (?) sandstones of Exeter district, footprints in, 496–500 & pl. li.
Permo-Carboniferous plants fr. Vereeniging, 109–26 figs. & pls. ix–x.
PETER, E., 521.
PETER, J., 512.
Peterborough (Northants), *Metriorhynchus brachyrhynchus* fr. Oxford Clay near, 345–57 figs. & pls. xl–xli.
Petersburg Ranges (S. Australia), erratics in Cambrian till, 240, 245–46 figs. & pl. xix.
Petrography in Geol. Soc. publications, civ–cxi.
Petrology of W. Liberia, 313–15.
Phacoidal calcite in *Posidonomya*-Limestones, 426 fig., 427.
Phyllites showg. effects of alternating strain-slip, 308, 311 & pl. xxxiv (microscop. sects.).
Physiography in Geol. Soc. publications, cxiv–cxxi; physiogr. of W. Liberia, 315–16; of Wey R.-basin, 318–34 w. map & pls. xxxvi–xxxvii (maps).
Picrite, hornblendic, of Greystones, 475.
PIDGEON, see Daniel-Pidgeon Fund.
Pilite (acicular tremolite), 480.
Pillow-lava nr. Port Isaac, origin of, 264–72 & pls. xxvii–xxviii.
Pisolites, general characters of, 215.
Plant-remains fr. S. Africa, 83–126 figs. & pls. ii–x.
Platforms, see Bodmin Moor.

*Pleurotoma Stoppanii* (?), 641.
Pliocene marine platform of S.W. Cornwall, 384 et seqq.; Plioc. strata at Trimingham, 405, 411; Plioc. of Burma, 606, 613–14, 615–17, 621, 642 et seqq.
Plum Creek (Ohio), as a chronological measure, 149 et seqq.
Pont-y-meibion (Glyn Ceiriog), sect. to Pont Bell, 552.
POOLE, H. S., [exhibits coal-pebble fr. Nanaimo], iii; [on chronology of Glacial Epoch in Brit. Columbia], 150.
Porcellanite, definition of, 367.
*Porosphæra*, its distrib. in Chalk, 403–404.
Port Germein (S. Australia), sect. to Mt. Grainger, descr. & fig. 254–55, 256.
Port Isaac (Cornwall), origin of pillow-lava near, 264–72 & pls. xxvii–xxviii.
Port-na-Cuilce, see Colonsay.
Porthclais (Pembrokeshire), 365, 377–79 w. map.
Porthlisky (Pembrokeshire), 367, 372.
Porthmelgan (Pembrokeshire), idiomorphic pyroxenes in sill at, 276 & pl. xxx (microscop. sect.).
Portland Oolite, interspaces in, 207.
Portugal, hypsometric map presented, ii.
*Posidonomya*-Limestones in Loughshinny area, 422–28 figs., 433 et seqq.; fauna of do., 444–49, 450–52, 454.
Post-Bala age of St. David's-Head 'rock-series,' 292.
Post-Cretaceous intrusions in W. Liberia, 315.
POSTLETHWAITE, J., [exhibits specims. fr. Borrowdale], cxxxii.
POWER, E., obituary of, lxviii.
Pre-Cambrian geology in Geol. Soc. publications, lxxv–lxxvii; see also Proterozoic, &c.
Prehnite (?) in St. David's-Head rocks, 285–86 & pl. xxx (microscop. sect.).
Pressure to which rocks have been subjected, determination of, 227–31; pressure-solution, surfaces of, 224–26 fig. & pl. xviii.
PRESTWICH medallists, list of, xxxiv.
Priests' Hill, see Daniel's Wood.
*Productus concinnus*, 76.
—— *humerosus* Beds of Caldon Low, 44.
—— *longispinus*, gens of, 76–77.
—— *proboscideus*, 466 & pl. l.

*Productus setosus*, var. *tissingtonensis*
nov., 77 & pl. i.
—— *striatus*, 466-67 & pl. l.
—— sp. nov., 467.
Prome Stage (Arakan Series), 606,
641.
Protaxis, Laurentian, 145.
Proterozoic of Canada, 144 ; *see also*
Grenville Series.
*Pterophyllum* sp. cf. *Tietzii*, 103 &
pl. ii.
—— sp., 104 & pl. ii.
*Ptilozamites* contrasted w. *Thinnfeldia*,
90-92 fig.
Pyrites in Glendalough rocks, 481,
483 fig.
Pyroxenes in St. David's-Head ' rock-
series,' 286-88 & pls. xxx-xxxii
(microscop. sects.).

Quantitative methods applied to the
study of the structure & history of
rocks, 171-233 fig. & pls. xiv-
xviii.
Quartz-gabbro, enstatite-bearing, of
St. David's Head, 280-81 w. chem.
anal. & pls. xxix-xxx (microscop.
sects.).
' Quartz-mica-diorite ' series of Glendalough, 485-96 figs.
Quartz-porphyry dykes, in St. David's
area, 374-75.
Quartzites of Grenville Series, 136 ;
in Cambrian of S. Australia, 238,
248 *et seqq.*
Quartzitic rocks of the Tarnthal mass,
599-600, 603.

RAISIN, Miss C. A., 166.
Ramsey-Sound Series (Pebidian), 371-
72.
RANSOM, THEODORE, 16 *et seqq.*
RASTALL, R. H., 163.
REED, F. R. C. (& S. H. Reynolds),
on the Fossiliferous Silurian Rocks
of the Southern Half of the Tortworth Inlier, 512-43 figs.
REID, C., [on Bodmin-Moor plateaux],
397 ; [on fossiliferous Pliocene
beds at Trimingham], 411 ; [on
*Terebratulina gracilis* Zone], 412 ; (&
H. Dewey), the Origin of the Pillow-
Lava near Port Isaac in Cornwall,
264-69 & pls. xxvii-xxviii, 272.
Rest, angles of, of certain solids in
water, 174-76 ; conclusions to be
drawn from change in, 177.
*Reticularia*, generic definition of, 31.
—— *lineata*, 469.
REYNOLDS, S. H., the Basic Intrusion
of Bartestree, near Hereford, 501-

11 fig. & pl. lii (microscop. sects.) ;
(& F. R. C. Reed), on the Fossiliferous Silurian Rocks of the Southern Half of the Tortworth Inlier,
512-43 figs.
Rhætian Alps, crushed bastite-serpentines from, 167-68.
Rhætic age of Stormberg plant-beds,
104 ; do. of Tarnthal dolomite, 598,
602, 603.
Rhyolitic tuffs (Pebidian), 366 *et seqq.*
RICHARDS, F. J., 516.
Ripple-drift, 181-85 & pls. xv-xvi,
199.
Roaring Well Bay (Co. Dublin), sect.
to Brook's End descr. & fig., 415-19.
Rocks, application of quantitative
methods to study of structure &
history of, 171-233 fig. & pls. xiv-
xviii.
ROGERS, A. W., 89 ; [exhibits specims.
fr. ' glacial ' beds in Griquatown
Series], iii.
' Round ore,' *see* Gravel-ore.
ROUTH, E. J., obituary of, lxv.
RUDLER, F. W., [receives Wollaston
Medal for P. von Groth], xliii.
Rush-Loughshinny area (Co. Dublin),
condits. of deposition in, 434-35.
Rush Conglomerates contrasted w.
Lane Conglomerate, 431, 432-33,
442-43 ; R. C., &c., additions to
fauna of, 440-42.

Saasthal (Valais), serpentines of, 162-
64.
Sahlite-striation, *see* Striation.
St. David's (Pembrokeshire), geol.
struct. of area, 363-83 figs. & pl.
xliv (map).
St. David's Head (Pembrokeshire),
' rock-series ' of, 273-96 figs. &
pls. xxix-xxxii (microscop. sects.).
St. Non's Bay (Pembrokeshire), 376,
377.
St. Vincent Gulf (S. Australia), sect.
to Torrens R., 236.
SALTER, A. E., elected Auditor. v.
Sand, final velocities of subsidence in
water, 172-73 ; angles of rest of,
174, 175-76 ; effects of currents on,
180-81 ; interspaces betw. grains
of, 202 ; *see also* Drift-bedding,
Ripple-drift, &c.
Sandstones, interspaces in, 210-11 ;
concretions in, 217-18, 219 ; *see
also* Sand.
SAWYER, A. R., [presents map of New
Rand Goldfield], v.
Scalasnig (Colonsay), limestone, &c. of,
299 ; diorite of, 300.

SCHARDT, H., elected For. Corresp., cxxix.

Schillerization in pyroxenes of St. David's-Head ' rock-series,' 287 & pl. xxxi (microscop. sect.).

*Schizoneura africana*, 89–90 fig.

—— *Carrerei*, 85–86 & pl. ii.

—— sp. *a*, 86 & pl. iii.

—— sp. *β*, 86–87 fig.

*Schizophoria resupinata*, 470 & pl. l.

*Scombroclupea scutata*, sp. nov., 360–61 & pl. xliii.

Scotland, antigorite - serpentines in, 170.

Scottish Highlands, thermometamorphic aureole in, 148.

Segregation, effects of, in sedimentary deposits, 203–14.

Semipalatinsk Territory (Siberia), mining maps presented, ii.

Sericite abundant in Ramsey-Sound Series, 371.

Serpentine of Tarnthal mass, 601–602, 603; serpentines containing antigorite, 152–70 & map.

SEWARD, A. C., Murchison Medal awarded to, xliv–xlvi; on a Collection of Fossil Plants from South Africa, 83–108 & pls. ii–viii; (& T. N. Leslie), Permo-Carboniferous Plants from Vereeniging (Transvaal), 109–25 & pls. ix–x.

SHERBORN, C. D., x, xiii; [edits R. M. Brydone's paper], 401.

SHILCOCK, J., 13.

SHRUBSOLE, W. H., [motion seconded by], cxxvii.

SIBLY, T. F., the Faunal Succession in the Carboniferous Limestone (Upper Avonian) of the Midland Area (North Derbyshire & North Staffordshire), 34–80 figs. & pl. i (foss.); award fr. Lyell fund to, xlix.

*Sigaretus javanus*, 627.

—— sp. (Miocene), 627.

*Sigillaria Brardi*, 118.

Silurian (& Cambrian) geology in Geol. Soc. publications, lxxvii–lxxix: Silur. rocks of S. half of Tortworth Inlier, 512–45 figs.; *see also* Glyn Ceiriog.

SKEAT, Miss E. G., award fr. Murchison fund to, xlviii.

Skeay's Grove (Gloucest.), 527.

Slates, interspaces in, 213–14; origin of spots in, 220–222; *see also* Langdale slates.

Slip-surfaces, 222–24.

SMITH, WORTHINGTON G., 1, 3, 5.

Soda-aplite of St. David's Head, 283–84 w. chem. anal. & pl. xxix (microscop. sects.).

*Solarium* sp. (Miocene), 626.

SOLLAS, W. J., 475; elected President, xxv; [on Glendalough rocks, &c.], 494–95; [on Silur. rocks of Tortworth Inlier], 543; [on Bala & Llandovery of Glen Ceiriog], 593.

Solution-valleys in the Glyme area, 335–44 w. map & pls. xxxviii–xxxix; *see also* Pressure-solution.

Solva Beds (St. David's area), 365.

SORBY, H. C., [Council's resolution on decease of], cxxvii; on the Application of Quantitative Methods to the Study of the Structure & History of Rocks, 171–232 fig. & pls. xiv–xviii.

South Australia, Glacial beds of Cambrian age in, 234–63 figs. & pls. xix–xxvi.

SOUZA, ENNES DE, 358.

Special General Meetings, cxxvii–cxxviii, cxxxi, cxxxii.

Sphene in Glendalough rocks, 481, 483 fig.

SPICER, Rev. E. C., Solution-Valleys in the Glyme Area (Oxfordshire), 335–42 w. map & pls. xxxviii–xxxix, 344.

Spilites, 270.

*Spirifer*, generic definition of, 29.

—— *bisulcatus*, var., 467 & pl. l.

—— cf. *convolutus*, 468 & pl. l.

' *Spirifer glaber*,' 27–33.

*Spiriferina insculpta*, 468 & pl. l.

'Sponge-Beds' (Trimingham Chalk), 404.

Sprudelstein (Karlsbad), interspaces in, 206.

*Squamularia*, 33.

Staffordshire (N.), faunal success. in Carb. Limest. of N. Derbyshire and, 34–82 figs. & pl. i (foss.).

Staining of rocks nr. Cambro-Pebidian junction, 377.

Stannon Marsh (Cornwall), 396.

Stevenage & Hitchin Gap (Herts.), 10–11 w. sect.; materials filling same, 19–21.

*Stigmatodendron dubium*, 100–101 & pl. iii.

STIRRUP, M., obituary of, lxv–lxvi.

Stoke Hill (Devon), footprints in sandstones at, 497.

Stone & Woodford (Tortworth), Wenlock Beds, &c. of, 531–33.

Stoney Middleton (Derbyshire), surfaces of pressure-solution in Carb. Limest. of, 225–26 fig.

'Stoping' action of granite-bathyliths, 146.

Stormberg Series, 83-84; fossil plants from, 85 et seqq., 104.

STRACHEY, Sir RICHARD, obituary of, lix-lxi.

STRAHAN, A. [on N. Welsh gravel-ore], 399-400.

Strain-slip cleavage in Colonsay rocks, 308 et seqq.

Stream-tin (& wolfram-) deposits of Bodmin Moor, 384-400 figs. & pls. xlv-xlvi.

Striation (simulating glacial striation) prod. by mechanical strain, 247-48 & fig. on p. 246; striat. in pyroxenes of St. David's Head 'rock-series,' 287-88 & pl. xxxi (microscop. sects.), 293; see also Glacial.

Strike-faults in Glyn-Ceiriog area, 580-84 figs.

Strobilites laxus, sp. nov., 101-102 fig. & pl. v.

STURGESS, J. H., 509.

Sturt Valley (S. Australia), sect. fig. & descr., 249-51 fig.; Cambrian till in, 252 fig. & pls. xx-xxiii.

Subagyidan (Burma), 613.

Subsidence of solids in water, final velocities of, 172-73.

Sweden, Geol. Surv. maps presented, iv.

Syenites of E. Canada, 140-41, 146; syenite-intrusion of Kiloran Bay (Colonsay), 304-306 w. map.

Symmetry, plane of, in sedimentary rocks, 215-16.


Tæniopteris Carruthersi, 98-99 fig.

Talc-amphibolite of Greystones, 493-94.

Taltal district (Chile), pillow-lavas of, 270-71.

Tan-y-graig (Glyn Ceiriog), ash involved w. slates at, 559-61 figs.

Tapley's-Hill Slates (S. Australia), 237 et seqq., 248 et seqq.

Tarannon Shales, equivalents in Glyn-Ceiriog district, 554.

Tarnthal mass (Tyrol), stratigraphy & structure of, 596-603 figs.

TEALL, J. J. H., [on pillow-lavas], 270.

Tehamose of E. Canada, 133.

Teirw Beds in Glyn-Ceiriog Valley, 551-52; detailed descr. of do., 557-58 fig.; list of foss. from, 559.

Tellina sp. (Miocene), 625-26.

Terebra sp. (Miocene), 632.

Terebratulina gracilis, zone of, 412.

Tertiary geology in Geol. Soc. publications, lxxxviii-lxxxix; Tert. dykes in Colonsay, &c., 300; see also Eocene, &c.

Teschenite, see Dolerites.

Thabyemyoung (Burma), 611-12.

Thayetmyo (& Minbu) districts (Burma), Tertiary rocks of, 607-13 w. maps, 618-19.

Thermometamorphism, aureole of, in Scottish Highlands, 148; see also Contact-phenomena, &c.

Thinnfeldia contrasted w. Ptilozamites, &c., 90-92 fig.

—— odontopteroides, 92-94 fig. & pls. iv-v.

—— sphenopteroides, sp. nov., 94-95 & pls. iv-v.

—— sp., 95 & pl. ii.

THOMAS, H. H., award fr. Wollaston fund to, xlvii-xlviii.

THOMAS, I., 453.

THOMSON, J. A., the Hornblendic Rocks of Glendalough & Greystones (County Wicklow), 475-94 figs.; [on antigoritic pseudomorphism of olivine], 170.

Thracia sp. (Eocene), 636.

TIDDEMAN, R. H., elected Auditor, v.

Tie or tye (stream-tin washing), 391.

TIETZE, E. E. A., elected For. Member, i.

Till, Cambrian, in S. Australia, 234-63 figs. & pls. xix-xxvi.

'Tillites' of S. Africa, &c., compared w. Cambrian till of S. Australia, 262.

Tin, see Stream-tin.

Tissington railway-cutting (Derbyshire), sect. descr., 59.

Toadstones, Upper & Lower (Derbyshire), 38 et seqq.

Tomen-y-meirw (Glyn Ceiriog), 571, 578, 579, 584.

Torrens R. (S. Australia), sect. to Gulf St. Vincent, 236.

Torridonian (Lr.), of Colonsay & Oronsay, 297-99 w. map, 312; cleavage in, 300 et seqq.

Tortworth Inlier (Gloucest.), fossiliferous Silurian rocks of S. half of, 512-45 figs.

Tosa Valley (Italy), antigorite-serpentines, &c. of, 154 et seqq.

Toungu (Burma), 609.

Trachytic tuffs (Pebidian), 366 et seqq.

Transvaal Colony (S. Afr.), Geol. Surv. maps presented, vi; see also Vereeniging.

Trap, see Intrusive; also Bartestree, Tortworth.

TREACHER, LL. [exhibits 'anvil-stone' fr. Ruscombe], v.

Treginnis Series (Pebidian), 368-70.

Tremolite in Glendalough rocks, 478, 480, 481 figs.

*Trigonotreta*, generic definition of, 30.

Trimingham (Norfolk), subdivisions of Chalk of, 401-12 figs. & pls. xlvii-xlviii (maps).

Trust-funds, statement of, xl-xli; objects, &c. of, cxxi-cxxii.

Trwyn Llŵyd (Pembrokeshire), enstatite-quartz-gabbro of, 280-81 w. chem. anal. & pls. xxix-xxx (microscop. sects.); fluxion-structure in rock from, 277 & pl. xxx (microscop. sect.).

Tuffs (Pebidian), 366 *et seqq.*

Tungsten, *see* Wolfram.

*Turritella acuticarinata*, 628 & pl. lvii.

—— spp. 1 & 2 (Miocene), 628.

—— sp. 3 (Eocene), 638.

TUTCHER, J. W., 69, 453.

Twinning in pyroxenes of St. David's Head 'rock-series', 286, 287-88 & pls. xxxi-xxxii (microscop. sects.).

Ty-draw Slates in Glyn-Ceiriog Valley, 554; detailed descr. of do., 579.

Tye or tie (stream-tin washing), 391.

'Ultrabasic rock' fr. New Zealand, 159.

Unconformity, local, betw. Carb. Limest. & Pendleside Series, 63-64, & fig. on p. 62; unconformity, suggested, in pre-Cambrian of E. Canada, 143.

United States, Geol. Surv. maps presented, vi.

USSHER, W. A. E., [on pillow-lavas of Devon & Cornwall], 272.

Valleys formed by solution in the Glyme area, 335-44 w. map & pls. xxxviii-xxxix.

VAUGHAN, A., 537; [Faunal Succession & Correlation of the Carboniferous Rocks at Loughshinny], 436-72 figs. & pls. xlix-l, 474.

Vedro, Val di (Italy), gneiss, &c. of, 157.

Velocities (final) of subsidence of solids in water, 172-73; veloc. of current, relats. betw. angles of rest and, 176; veloc. of current able to start or maintain drifting, 176.

*Venus granosa*, 636.

Vereeniging (Transvaal), Permo-Car- boniferous plants from, 109-26 figs. & pls. ix-x.

Vesuvius, Mt., cartoons representg. stages of growth of, cxxxi.

Vigezzo, Valle (Italy), serpentine of, 157, 158.

*Voluta* (?) *birmanica*, sp. nov., 632 & pl. lvii.

—— *d'Archiaci*, sp. nov., 640 & pl. lv.

—— *pernodosa*, sp. nov., 640 & pl. lvii.

Wales (N.), faunal success. in Carb. Limest. compared w. that of Midland area, 66-67; (S.), Bala Series compared w. that of Glyn Ceiriog, 589-90, 592.

WALKER, J. F., obituary of, lxvii-lxviii.

Warslow (Staffs.), Carb. Limest. at, 61.

Wash or 'head' of Bodmin-Moor area, 386 *et seqq.*

Waterfall Creek (S. Australia), Cambrian till in, pls. xxiv & xxv.

Waterhouses (Staffs.), faunal facies of *Lonsdalia*-subzone at, 48; lithological character of do., 56; *Cyathaxonia*-subzone at, 61.

WATTS, W. W., lxviii, 475; [on struct. of St. David's area], 383; [on Glacial conditions in Cornwall], 398-99; [on Greystones picrite], 495.

Weathering, specims. of, fr. Pentreath, cxxix.

WEDD, C. B., 51, 55. 63, 69; [on Carb. Limest. of Midland area], 81.

Well-sections at Hitchin, &c., descr., 13 *et seqq.*

Wenlock (& ? Ludlow) Beds of Tortworth Inlier, 522-34 figs.: remarks on foss. from do., 536-37; list of foss. from do., 541-43; W. Limestone, oolitic beds in, 207-208; interspaces in W. L. of Easthope, 209 & pl. xviii.

Wernerian doctrines in Geol. Soc. publications, lxxi-lxxiv.

Wetton (Staffs.), Pendleside Series, &c. near, 61-63.

Wey, R. (Surrey), notes on, 318-34 w. map & pls. xxxvi-xxxvii (maps).

Whipsnade Heath (Beds.), palæolith found at, 2.

WHITE, H. J. O., award fr. Lyell Fund to, xlviii-xlix.

Whitfield & Falfield (Gloucest.), Wenlock Beds of, 525-28.

Wilbury Hill (Herts.), 9, 11; gravels of, 21.

Wirksworth (Derbyshire), *Lonsdalia-*subzone, &c. at, 55.

Wolfram (& stream-tin) deposits of Bodmin Moor, 384-400 figs. & pls. xlv-xlvi.

WOLLASTON medallists, list of, xxviii; W. Donation Fund, list of awards from, xxix.

Women, admission to Geol. Soc. of, cxxvii-cxxviii, cxxx, cxxxi, cxxxii.

Woodford & Middlemill (Gloucest.), Llandovery rocks of, 519-22; W. & Stone, Wenlock Beds, &c. of, 531-33; sect. fr. near Woodford to Tortworth Rectory, 532.

WOODHEAD, J. H., [exhibits specims. of weathering fr. Pentreath], cxxix.

WOODWARD, A. S., on some Fossil Fishes discovered by Prof. Ennes de Souza in the Cretaceous Formation of Ilhéos (State of Bahia), Brazil, 358-62 & pls. xlii-xliii; [exhibits Jurassic fossils fr. Neuquen], cxxvi; [motion proposed by], cxxviii.

WOODWARD, HENRY, [communicates E. T. Leeds's paper], 345.

WOODWARD, H. B., v, x, lxii, lxvii; [motion proposed by], cxxviii.

Wootton (Oxon.), solution-valleys in neighbourhood of, 335 *et seqq.* w. map on p. 336.

WRIGHT, G. F., Chronology of the Glacial Epoch in North America, 149, 151.

WRIGHT, W. B., the Two Earth-Movements of Colonsay, 297-311 figs. & pls. xxxiii-xxxiv, 312.

WYNNE, A. B., obituary of, lxii.


Yaw R. (Burma), 615, 619, 620.

Yenangyat anticline (Burma), 615-16.

Yenangyoung Stage (Arakan Series), 606, 620, 641.

Yengadin Choung (Burma), 612.

Youlgreave (Derbyshire), unconformity betw. Carb. Limest. & Pendleside Series near, 63-64, & fig. on p. 62.

YOUNG, A. P., on the Stratigraphy & Structure of the Tarntbal Mass (Tyrol), 596-603 figs.

YOUNG, G. W., [on Glacial conditions, &c. in Cornwall], 399.

Yunta Ranges (S. Australia), sect. to Oopina, descr. & fig., 255, 257.


*Zaphrentis* (Densiphylloid), sp. nov., 459 & pl. xlix.

—— *Enniskilleni*, 456-57 & pl. xlix.

—— *Omaliusi*, var. *ambigua*, 457-58 & pl. xlix; do. mut. *σ*, 458 & pl. xlix.

ZEILLER, R., 115, 120.

Zoisite in Glendalough rocks, 482 *et seqq.*; zoisite-amphibolite of Glendalough, 483-85 fig.

END OF VOL. LXIV.

**Vol. LXIV.**     NOVEMBER, 1908.     **No. 256.**
PART 4.

THE

# QUARTERLY JOURNAL

OF THE

# GEOLOGICAL SOCIETY.

EDITED BY

## THE ASSISTANT-SECRETARY.

[With Seven Plates, illustrating Papers by Principal A. W.
Clayden, Prof. S. H. Reynolds, Dr. T. T. Groom & Mr. P.
Lake, and Mr. L. V. Dalton.]

LONDON :

LONGMANS, GREEN, AND CO.

PARIS:—CHARLES KLINCKSIECK, 11 RUE DE LILLE.

SOLD ALSO AT THE APARTMENTS OF THE SOCIETY.

*Price Five Shillings.*

[Issued December 22nd, 1908.]

# LIST OF THE OFFICERS AND COUNCIL OF THE
# GEOLOGICAL SOCIETY OF LONDON.

Elected February 21st, 1908.

## President.

Prof. William Johnson Sollas, Ll.D., Sc.D., F.R.S.

## Vice-Presidents.

Frederick William Rudler, I.S.O.

Aubrey Strahan, Sc.D., F.R.S.

J. J. Harris Teall, M.A., D.Sc., F.R.S.

Arthur Smith Woodward, LL.D., F.R.S.

## Secretaries.

Prof. William Whitehead Watts, Sc.D., M.Sc., F.R.S.

Prof. Edmund Johnston Garwood, M.A.

## Foreign Secretary.

Sir Archibald Geikie, K.C.B., D.C.L., LL.D., Sc.D., Pres.R.S.

## Treasurer.

Horace Woollaston Monckton, Treas.L.S.

## COUNCIL.

Prof. Samuel Herbert Cox, F.C.S., A.R.S.M.

Prof. Edmund Johnston Garwood, M.A.

Sir Archibald Geikie, K.C.B., D.C.L., LL.D., Sc.D., Pres.R.S.

Alfred Harker, M.A., F.R.S.

Wilfrid H. Hudleston, M.A., F.R.S., F.L.S.

Finlay Lorimer Kitchin, M.A., Ph.D.

George William Lamplugh, F.R.S.

Richard Lydekker, B.A., F.R.S.

Principal Henry Alexander Miers, M.A., F.R.S.

Horace Woollaston Monckton, Treas.L.S.

Richard Dixon Oldham.

Prof. Sidney Hugh Reynolds, M.A.

Frederick William Rudler, I.S.O.

Prof. William Johnson Sollas, LL.D., Sc.D., F.R.S.

Leonard James Spencer, M.A.

Aubrey Strahan, Sc.D., F.R.S.

Charles Fox Strangways.

J. J. Harris Teall, M.A., D.Sc., F.R.S.

Richard Hill Tiddeman, M.A.

Prof. William Whitehead Watts, Sc.D., M.Sc., F.R.S.

Henry Woods, M.A.

Arthur Smith Woodward, LL.D., F.R.S., F.L.S.

George William Young.

## Assistant-Secretary, Clerk, Librarian, and Curator.

L. L. Belinfante, M.Sc.

## Assistants in Office, Library, and Museum.

W. Rupert Jones.     Clyde H. Black.

A. S. H. Dutneall.

## STANDING PUBLICATION COMMITTEE.

Prof. W. J. Sollas, *President.*

Prof. W. W. Watts. }

Prof. E. J. Garwood. } *Secretaries.*

Prof. S. H. Cox.

Sir Archibald Geikie.

Dr. F. L. Kitchin.

Mr. G. W. Lamplugh.

Mr. R. Lydekker.

Principal H. A. Miers.

Mr. H. W. Monckton.

Mr. L. J. Spencer.

Dr. A. Strahan.

Dr. J. J. H. Teall.

Mr. H. Woods.

Dr. A. S. Woodward.

## EVENING MEETINGS OF THE GEOLOGICAL SOCIETY
### TO BE HELD AT BURLINGTON HOUSE.

SESSION 1908–1909.

1909.

| | | |
|---|---|---|
| Wednesday, January | ................. | 13*—27* |
| ,, | February (*Anniversary* Friday, Feb. 19th) . | 10*—24* |
| ,, | March.................. | 10*—24 |
| ,, | April .................... | 7*—28 |
| ,, | May ............ ...... | 12* —26 |
| ,, | June ................. ...... | 16* |

[*Business will commence at Eight o'Clock precisely each Evening.*]

The dates marked with an asterisk are those on which the Council will meet.

# ADMISSION AND PRIVILEGES

## OF

# FELLOWS OF THE GEOLOGICAL SOCIETY OF LONDON.

EVERY Candidate for admission as a Fellow must be proposed by three or more Fellows, who must sign a Certificate in his favour. The Proposer whose name stands first upon the Certificate must have a personal knowledge of the Candidate.

Fellows on election pay an Admission-Fee of Six Guineas. The Annual Contribution paid by Fellows is Two Guineas, due on the 1st of January in every year, and payable in advance; but Fellows elected in November or December pay no Contribution for the current year. The Annual Contribution may, at any time, be compounded for by a payment of Thirty-Five Pounds.

The Fellows are entitled to receive gratuitously all the volumes or parts of volumes of the Quarterly Journal of the Society that may be published after their election, so long as their Annual Contributions are paid; and they may purchase any of the publications of the Society at a reduction of 25 per cent. under the selling-prices.

The Library is open daily to the Fellows between the hours of 10 and 5 (except during the fortnight commencing on the first Monday in September; see also next page), and on Meeting-Days until 8 P.M. Under certain restrictions, Fellows are allowed to borrow books from the Library.

---

## Publications to be had of the Geological Society, Burlington House.

**QUARTERLY JOURNAL.** (Vols. III to LXIV, inclusive.)

Price to Fellows, 13s. 6d. each (Vols. XV, XXIII, XXX, and XXXIV to LXIV, 16s. 6d.), in cloth.

**GENERAL INDEX TO THE FIRST FIFTY VOLUMES OF THE QUARTERLY JOURNAL** (1845-1894). Part I (A-La). Part II (La-Z). Price 5s. each. To Fellows 3s. 9d. each. [Postage 3d.]

**GEOLOGICAL LITERATURE** added to the Geological Society's Library during the years ended December 31st, 1894-1907. Price 2s. each. To Fellows, 1s. 6d. each. [Postage 2½d.]

**LIST OF THE TYPE- AND FIGURED SPECIMENS RECOGNIZED BY C. D. SHERBORN IN THE COLLECTION OF THE GEOLOGICAL SOCIETY**, verified and arranged, with additions, by the Rev. J. F. BLAKE. 1902. Price 3s. 6d. (bound in cloth); 3s. 0d. (in paper wrappers). To Fellows, 2s. 6d. and 2s. 0d. [Postage 3d.]

**HUTTON'S 'THEORY OF THE EARTH,'** Vol. III., edited by Sir ARCHIBALD GEIKIE, D.C.L., F.R.S. Price 3s. 6d. To Fellows, 2s. [Postage 4d.]

**THE GEOLOGY OF NEW ZEALAND.** Translated by Dr. C. F. FISCHER, from the works of MM. HOCHSTETTER & PETERMANN. With an Atlas of Six Maps.

Fellows may purchase One Copy of this book at 2s.; Additional Copies will be charged 4s. [Postage 5d.]

**THE HISTORY OF THE GEOLOGICAL SOCIETY OF LONDON,** by H. B. WOODWARD. F.R.S. Price 7s. 6d. To Fellows, 6s. [Postage 6d.]

# CONTENTS.

## PAPERS READ.

Page

25. Mr. Thomson on the Hornblendic Rocks of Glendalough and Greystones... 475

26. Principal Clayden on Footprints in the Lower Sandstones of the Exeter District. (Plate LI) ............................................................ 496

27. Prof. Reynolds on the Basic Intrusion of Bartestree. (Plate LII) ......... 501

28. Mr. Reed & Prof. Reynolds on the Fossiliferous Silurian Rocks of the Southern Half of the Tortworth Inlier ............................................ 512

29. Dr. Groom & Mr. Lake on the Bala and Llandovery Rocks of Glyn Ceiriog. (Plate LIII) ....................................................................... 546

30. Dr. Young on the Stratigraphy and Structure of the Tarnthal Mass ......... 596

31. Mr. Dalton on the Geology of Burma. (Plates LIV–LVII) .. ............... 604

TITLEPAGE, CONTENTS, AND INDEX TO VOL. LXIV.

[No. 257 of the Quarterly Journal will be published next February.]

[The Editor of the Quarterly Journal is directed to make it known to the Public that the Authors alone are responsible for the facts and opinions contained in their respective Papers.]

*₊* The Council request that all communications intended for publication by the Society shall be clearly and legibly written on one side of the paper only, with proper references, and in all respects in fit condition for being at once placed in the Printer's hands. Unless this is done, it will be in the discretion of the Officers to return the communication to the Author for revision.

The Library and Museum at the Apartments of the Society are open every Weekday from Ten o'clock until Five, except during the fortnight commencing on the first Monday in September, when the Library is closed for the purpose of cleaning; the Library is also closed on Saturdays at One P.M. during the months of August and September. It is open until Eight P.M. on the Days of Meeting for the loan of books, and from Eight P.M. until the close of each Meeting for conversational purposes only.

CPSIA information can be obtained at www.ICGtesting.com
Printed in the USA
LVOW091520170512

282187LV00006B/35/P